Poetry
Criticism

Guide to Gale Literary Criticism Series

For criticism on	Consult these Gale series
Authors now living or who died after December 31, 1999	*CONTEMPORARY LITERARY CRITICISM (CLC)*
Authors who died between 1900 and 1999	*TWENTIETH-CENTURY LITERARY CRITICISM (TCLC)*
Authors who died between 1800 and 1899	*NINETEENTH-CENTURY LITERATURE CRITICISM (NCLC)*
Authors who died between 1400 and 1799	*LITERATURE CRITICISM FROM 1400 TO 1800 (LC)* *SHAKESPEAREAN CRITICISM (SC)*
Authors who died before 1400	*CLASSICAL AND MEDIEVAL LITERATURE CRITICISM (CMLC)*
Authors of books for children and young adults	*CHILDREN'S LITERATURE REVIEW (CLR)*
Dramatists	*DRAMA CRITICISM (DC)*
Poets	*POETRY CRITICISM (PC)*
Short story writers	*SHORT STORY CRITICISM (SSC)*
Literary topics and movements	*HARLEM RENAISSANCE: A GALE CRITICAL COMPANION (HR)* *THE BEAT GENERATION: A GALE CRITICAL COMPANION (BG)*
Asian American writers of the last two hundred years	*ASIAN AMERICAN LITERATURE (AAL)*
Black writers of the past two hundred years	*BLACK LITERATURE CRITICISM (BLC)* *BLACK LITERATURE CRITICISM SUPPLEMENT (BLCS)*
Hispanic writers of the late nineteenth and twentieth centuries	*HISPANIC LITERATURE CRITICISM (HLC)* *HISPANIC LITERATURE CRITICISM SUPPLEMENT (HLCS)*
Native North American writers and orators of the eighteenth, nineteenth, and twentieth centuries	*NATIVE NORTH AMERICAN LITERATURE (NNAL)*
Major authors from the Renaissance to the present	*WORLD LITERATURE CRITICISM, 1500 TO THE PRESENT (WLC)* *WORLD LITERATURE CRITICISM SUPPLEMENT (WLCS)*

ISSN 1052-4851

Poetry Criticism

*Excerpts from Criticism of the Works
of the Most Significant and Widely
Studied Poets of World Literature*

Volume 56

Janet Witalec
Project Editor

GALE®

THOMSON
────────✦────────™
GALE

Detroit • New York • San Diego • San Francisco • Cleveland • New Haven, Conn. • Waterville, Maine • London • Munich

Poetry Criticism, Vol. 56

Project Editor
Janet Witalec

Editorial
Jenny Cromie, Kathy D. Darrow, Lemma Shomali, Timothy J. Sisler, Carol Ullmann

Data Capture
Francis Monroe, Gwen Tucker

Indexing Services
Synapse, the Knowledge Link Corporation

Rights and Acquisition Management
Denise Buckley, Lori Hines, Ann Taylor

Imaging and Multimedia
Dean Dauphinais, Leitha Etheridge-Sims, Lezlie Light, Dan Newell

Composition and Electronic Capture
Kathy Sauer

Manufacturing
Rhonda Williams

LIBRARY OF CONGRESS CATALOG CARD NUMBER 91-118494

ISBN 0-7876-7454-0
ISSN 1052-4851

Printed in the United States of America
10 9 8 7 6 5 4 3 2 1

Contents

Preface vii

Acknowledgments ix

Literary Criticism Series Advisory Board xi

v

Preface

*P*oetry Criticism *(PC)* presents significant criticism of the world's greatest poets and provides supplementary biographical and bibliographical material to guide the interested reader to a greater understanding of the genre and its creators. Although major poets and literary movements are covered in such Gale Literary Criticism series as *Contemporary Literary Criticism (CLC), Twentieth-Century Literary Criticism (TCLC), Nineteenth-Century Literature Criticism (NCLC), Literature Criticism from 1400 to 1800 (LC),* and *Classical and Medieval Literature Criticism (CMLC), PC* offers more focused attention on poetry than is possible in the broader, survey-oriented entries on writers in these Thomson Gale series. Students, teachers, librarians, and researchers will find that the generous excerpts and supplementary material provided by *PC* supply them with the vital information needed to write a term paper on poetic technique, to examine a poet's most prominent themes, or to lead a poetry discussion group.

Scope of the Series

PC is designed to serve as an introduction to major poets of all eras and nationalities. Since these authors have inspired a great deal of relevant critical material, *PC* is necessarily selective, and the editors have chosen the most important published criticism to aid readers and students in their research. Each author entry presents a historical survey of the critical response to that author's work. The length of an entry is intended to reflect the amount of critical attention the author has received from critics writing in English and from foreign critics in translation. Every attempt has been made to identify and include the most significant essays on each author's work. In order to provide these important critical pieces, the editors sometimes reprint essays that have appeared elsewhere in Thomson Gale's Literary Criticism Series. Such duplication, however, never exceeds twenty percent of a *PC* volume.

Organization of the Book

Each *PC* entry consists of the following elements:

- The **Author Heading** cites the name under which the author most commonly wrote, followed by birth and death dates. Also located here are any name variations under which an author wrote, including transliterated forms for authors whose native languages use nonroman alphabets. If the author wrote consistently under a pseudonym, the pseudonym will be listed in the author heading and the author's actual name given in parenthesis on the first line of the biographical and critical introduction. Uncertain birth or death dates are indicated by question marks. Single-work entries are preceded by the title of the work and its date of publication.

- The **Introduction** contains background information that introduces the reader to the author and the critical debates surrounding his or her work.

- A **Portrait of the Author** is included when available.

- The list of **Principal Works** is ordered chronologically by date of first publication and lists the most important works by the author. The first section comprises poetry collections and book-length poems. The second section gives information on other major works by the author. For foreign authors, the editors have provided original foreign-language publication information and have selected what are considered the best and most complete English-language editions of their works.

- Reprinted **Criticism** is arranged chronologically in each entry to provide a useful perspective on changes in critical evaluation over time. All individual titles of poems and poetry collections by the author featured in the entry are printed in boldface type. The critic's name and the date of composition or publication of the critical work are given at the beginning of each piece of criticism. Unsigned criticism is preceded by the title of the source in which it appeared. Footnotes are reprinted at the end of each essay or excerpt. In the case of excerpted criticism, only those footnotes that pertain to the excerpted texts are included.

- Critical essays are prefaced by brief **Annotations** explicating each piece.

- A complete **Bibliographical Citation** of the original essay or book precedes each piece of criticism.

- An annotated bibliography of **Further Reading** appears at the end of each entry and suggests resources for additional study. In some cases, significant essays for which the editors could not obtain reprint rights are included here. Boxed material following the further reading list provides references to other biographical and critical sources on the author in series published by Thomson Gale.

Cumulative Indexes

A **Cumulative Author Index** lists all of the authors that appear in a wide variety of reference sources published by Thomson Gale, including *PC*. A complete list of these sources is found facing the first page of the Author Index. The index also includes birth and death dates and cross references between pseudonyms and actual names.

A **Cumulative Nationality Index** lists all authors featured in *PC* by nationality, followed by the number of the *PC* volume in which their entry appears.

A **Cumulative Title Index** lists in alphabetical order all individual poems, book-length poems, and collection titles contained in the *PC* series. Titles of poetry collections and separately published poems are printed in italics, while titles of individual poems are printed in roman type with quotation marks. Each title is followed by the author's last name and corresponding volume and page numbers where commentary on the work is located. English-language translations of original foreign-language titles are cross-referenced to the foreign titles so that all references to discussion of a work are combined in one listing.

Citing *Poetry Criticism*

When writing papers, students who quote directly from any volume in the Literary Criticism Series may use the following general format to footnote reprinted criticism. The first example pertains to material drawn from periodicals, the second to material reprinted from books.

Sylvia Kasey Marks, "A Brief Glance at George Eliot's *The Spanish Gypsy*," *Victorian Poetry* 20, no. 2 (Summer 1983), 184-90; reprinted in *Poetry Criticism*, vol. 20, ed. Ellen McGeagh (Detroit: The Gale Group), 128-31.

Linden Peach, "Man, Nature and Wordsworth: American Versions," *British Influence on the Birth of American Literature*, (Macmillan Press Ltd., 1982), 29-57; reprinted in *Poetry Criticism*, vol. 20, ed. Ellen McGeagh (Detroit: The Gale Group), 37-40.

Suggestions are Welcome

Readers who wish to suggest new features, topics, or authors to appear in future volumes, or who have other suggestions or comments are cordially invited to call, write, or fax the Project Editor:

Project Editor, Literary Criticism Series
Thomson Gale
27500 Drake Road
Farmington Hills, MI 48331-3535
1-800-347-4253 (GALE)
Fax: 248-699-8054

Acknowledgments

The editors wish to thank the copyright holders of the criticism included in this volume and the permissions managers of many book and magazine publishing companies for assisting us in securing reproduction rights. We are also grateful to the staffs of the Detroit Public Library, the Library of Congress, the University of Detroit Mercy Library, Wayne State University Purdy/Kresge Library Complex, and the University of Michigan Libraries for making their resources available to us. Following is a list of the copyright holders who have granted us permission to reproduce material in this volume of *PC*. Every effort has been made to trace copyright, but if omissions have been made, please let us know.

Thomson Gale Literature Product Advisory Board

Edward Kamau Brathwaite
1930-

Contemporary Barbadian poet, playwright, literary critic, and scholar.

The following entry presents criticism of Brathwaite's poetry from 1968 through 2001.

INTRODUCTION

Brathwaite is one of the Caribbean's most honored writers. He is known chiefly for *The Arrivants* (1973), a trilogy of poetry volumes in which a uniquely Caribbean identity is set forth, incorporating ties to Africa and the lasting effects of slavery. Born in Barbados, Brathwaite has long been compared to another famous Caribbean poet, the Nobel Prize-winning Derek Walcott. Brathwaite was strongly influenced by the works of T. S. Eliot but his penchant for jazz, rhythmic experimentation, and his love of Caribbean vernacular are the most evident features of his poetry. His emphasis on the oral tradition in poetry has led him to produce several sound recordings. Holding positions at universities in the West Indies, England, and the United States, Brathwaite has had a distinguished academic career during which he has written and edited several highly respected works of criticism, essays, and scholarly histories of the Caribbean.

BIOGRAPHICAL INFORMATION

Brathwaite was born on May 11, 1930, in Bridgetown, the capital of Barbados. He attended the island's elite Harrison College, where he started a school newspaper to which he contributed essays about jazz. While at Harrison he also began publishing stories in *Bim,* an influential literary journal published in Barbados in which his writings would continue to appear for many years. In 1949 Brathwaite was awarded the Barbados Island Scholarship to Cambridge, where he studied history and English. He graduated with honors in 1953. After taking an additional year to earn a teaching certificate, in 1955 he joined the British colonial service and was posted on the Gold Coast, where he lived until 1962. While on the Gold Coast—which became Ghana during his time there—he held several civil service posts that put him into regular contact with the everyday people of West Africa, an experience that inspired his

poetry and informed much of his scholarly work. During his journeys to England and Africa, many of his poems and stories were broadcast on the BBC's *Caribbean Voices.*

On one visit home he met Doris Welcome, and in 1960 they were married. In 1962 Brathwaite left Ghana with his wife and infant son to take a position with the University of the West Indies. His return to the West Indies made him aware of many continuities between the cultures of rural Africa and the contemporary Caribbean. He began exploring these links in poems and chronicling them in scholarly writings. In 1965 he went to England to study at the University of Sussex, and in 1968 he was awarded a Ph.D. in history for research on slave and Creole culture in the Caribbean. As he embarked on his scholarly work, he also began to publish the poetry volumes eventually collected as *The Arrivants.* Published individually between 1967 and 1969, the three volumes of the *The Arrivants* garnered Brathwaite tremendous attention and praise. Brathwaite began taking guest appointments at prestigious universities such as Harvard and Yale while receiving honors such as Guggenheim and Fulbright fellowships, and, in 1994, the Neustadt International Prize for Literature. Whereas Brathwaite's first trilogy celebrated what he termed "nation language," his second trilogy of poems, written in the 1970s, presents fragments of speech, society, and culture that reflect the folk culture brought to the West Indies by the African slaves. It was also in the 1970s that Brathwaite began publishing under the name Kamau, given to him in Ghana.

Since the 1980s Brathwaite has been engaged in a project to bring to light the cultural, linguistic, and historical links between Africa and the Caribbean. The mid- and late 1980s proved a very difficult time for Brathwaite, as his wife died in 1986 and in 1988 Hurricane Gilbert destroyed his home and buried almost all his papers in mud. Two years later he was robbed and beaten in Jamaica. These traumas contributed to his decision to leave the West Indies in 1991 and take his current position at New York University.

MAJOR WORKS

Brathwaite's poetry has been a continued examination and celebration of the cultural and linguistic continuities between Africa and the Caribbean. *Rights of Passage* (1967), *Masks* (1968) and *Islands* (1969), which were published in 1973 as *The Arrivants,* remain Brathwaite's most lauded and discussed works. The poems move from Africa and the myths of the Ashanti empire to the Caribbean. John Povey interprets them as descriptions of a search for identity by both Brathwaite individually and the peoples of the Caribbean collectively. The Jamaican poet and critic Mervyn Morris sees *The Arrivants* as "a major document of African reconnection" that "draws attention to Caribbean continuities out of Africa." *Other Exiles* (1975), which includes poems written from 1950 to the collection's release in 1975, is more personal and introspective than Brathwaite's "national language" poetry. In the 1970s and 1980s Brathwaite published *Mother Poem* (1977), *Sun Poem* (1982) and *X/Self* (1987), all of which comprise an unnamed trilogy that seeks to reveal the fragmentary, historical links between Africa and the Caribbean. More disjointed and reliant on puns and wordplay, these poems reveal Brathwaite's debt to jazz masters such as Charlie Parker and John Coltrane. His most recent works have become more abstract, as is his *The Zea Mexican Diary* (1993), written in response to the death of his wife.

CRITICAL RECEPTION

Early in his career, Brathwaite was repeatedly compared with another famous Caribbean poet, Derek Walcott. Patrica Ismond concludes that Walcott is the better craftsman, a type of "poet's poet," but she praises Brathwaite for taking on the role of representative figure for the people of the West Indies, and for representing "their collective destiny." Indeed, most criticism of Brathwaite focuses on themes such as the continuities between Africa and the Caribbean or Brathwaite's cyclical theory of history and culture. Many critics do close readings of Brathwaite's poems to unearth the shards of African culture Brathwaite includes in his works. Simon Gikandi and others conclude that "oral languages take revenge against institutionalized poetic forms," and Norman Weinstein traces the influence of jazz in Brathwaite's work. Nana Wilson-Tagoe describes Brathwaite's poetry as a "mode of apprehension, in which the writer seeks community and image through a drama of consciousness." The vast majority of Brathwaite's critics celebrate his poetry for its rhythms and evocations of the African past in the Caribbean present.

PRINCIPAL WORKS

Poetry

Rights of Passage 1967

Masks 1968

Islands 1969

The Arrivants 1973

Other Exiles 1975

Days and Nights 1975

Black and Blues 1976

Mother Poem 1977

Soweto 1979

Word Making Man: A Poem for Nicolas Guillen 1979

Sun Poem 1982

Third World Poems 1983

Jah Music 1986

X/Self 1987

Shar 1990

Middle Passages 1992

Trenchtown Rock 1993

The Zea Mexican Diary 1993

Barabajan Poems, 1942-1992 1994

Words Need Love Too 2000

Ancestors 2001

Other Major Works

Odale's Choice (play) 1967

Folk Culture of the Slaves in Jamaica (history) 1970
   revised edition, 1981

CRITICISM

Jean D'Costa (essay date September 1968)

SOURCE: D'Costa, Jean. "Poetry Review." *Jamaica Journal* 2, no. 3 (September 1968): 24-8.

[*In the following essay, the author compares Brathwaite to Virgil and focuses on themes of exile.*]

It is significant that before Brathwaite the poet comes Brathwaite the historian. Only a historian could create so intimately and fully the world of *Rights of Passage* and *Masks.* This world is one we know well: that of the negro in the western hemisphere. But while others like Cesaire and Baldwin have treated this world fragment by fragment, Edward Brathwaite attempts a synthesis of a splintered, shattered area of experience, and manages to bind together in a single poetic vision both Louisiana and Brixton, the Golden Stool of the Asante and the slums of Harlem. In *Rights of Passage* we are shown the panorama in time and space of the exile and wanderings of the negro. In *Masks,* which completes our understanding of *Rights . . . ,* we are shown the world from which the transported slave came: a world which he now regards with some romanticism, some indifference, and much ignorance. Both books consist of lyric poems which develop a central theme, each poem an essential link in the argument of the whole. Such is the forcefulness of Brathwaite's vision in these thematic poems, that one is quite unable to set either book aside without reading to the end. This is not to say that the writing is all equally good, but that one is compelled to go with the poet through a series of interpretations and visions, and to pass judgement on the whole.

Rights of Passage introduces us first of all to the African homeland in the days before the slave trade. Brathwaite invokes a setting and a mood with Virgilian sharpness:

> Drum skin whip
> lash, master sun's
> cutting edge of
> heat, taut

> surfaces of things
> I sing
> I shout
> I groan
> I dream
> about

> Dust glass grit
> the pebbles of the desert:

In tracing the path of the exiled negro through time and space, Brathwaite is doing the same as Virgil in the *Aeneid.* Like Virgil, he evokes deep race memories, associations with a culture long past, yet still active in the present. The homeland which is recalled here is no sentimentalised paradise, nor is it a clear-cut, well-documented thing. Cruelty, death, betrayal are all known. Hardship is familiar. What is suggested is a mood, an echo of a life of which the conscious memories are lost, and only the subliminal remain:

> Grant, God,
> a clear release from thieves,
> from robbers and from those that
> plot and poison while they dip
> into our dish.
>   Flame,
> that red idol, is our power's
> founder: flames fashion wood; with
> powder, iron. Long iron
> runs to swords,
> to spears, to burnished points
> that stall the wild, the eyes, the
> whinneyings.
> Flame is our god, our last defence,
> our peril.
> Flame burns the village down.

A variety of symbols work upon the two underlying themes: death and regeneration. In all stages of *Rights,* these balancing symbols recur. In a sense they make the agony of transportation and deprivation more acute, for returning life is a sore trial to a broken and diseased organism:

> for our blood, mixed
> soon with their passion in sport

> in indifference, in anger,
> will create new soils, new souls, new
> ancestors; will flow like this tide
> fixed

> to the star by which this ship floats
> to new worlds, new waters, new
> harbours, the pride of our ancestors
> mixed

> with the wind and the water
> the flesh and the flies, the whips . . .

The death and rebirth of natural forms parallels and emphasises man's subjection to the same forces: "So many seeds / the cotton breeds / so many seeds / our fathers need." This constant balancing of positive and negative poles gives both passion and a kind of honesty to the mythical world of *Rights*. Assonance, alliteration, and the unexpected internal rhyme point the movement of feeling and argument.

In the section **'New World A-Comin' '** the psychology of exile and enslavement is explored. There is a neat suggestion of the incompatibility of the cultures of slave and slaver in the lines

> . . . we journeyed
> to this place
> to this meeting
> this shock
> and shame
> in the soiled
> silence.

The moral problem implied here will haunt us through the whole book. Tom, a symbolic figure introduced later in this section, becomes the focus of the problem, and the centre of conflict in which the forces of death and regeneration meet. The nostalgia for the lost homeland is transformed into a new nostalgia for a new land which can never replace the other, and yet gains a hold on the exile that cannot be denied. The emotional crisis of the homeless is stated in a manner which stresses the nature of the amputation:

> for we who have achieved nothing
> work
> who have not built
> dream
> who have forgotten all
> dance
> and dare to remember
>
> the paths we shall never remember
> again: Atumpan talking and the
> harvest branches, all the tribes of
> Ashanti dreaming the dream of
> Tutu, Anokye, and the Golden
> Stool, built in Heaven for our
> nation by the work of
> lightning and the brilliant adze:
> and now nothing
>
> nothing
> nothing
>
> so let me sing
> nothing
> now

From here we move on to the changed attitude of later generations, Tom's children born in the land of captivity, knowing no other. The hope expressed for them by him "hoping my children's eyes / will learn / not green alone / not Africa alone / not dark alone / not fear / alone . . .", this evaporates in the compromises of a new era. The slave and slaver are now face to face,

each inevitably corrupting the other, neither able to understand nor escape from the consequences of the situation:

> Boss man lacks pride:
> so hides his
> fear of fear and darkness
> in the whip.
>
> Boss man lacks pride:
> I am his hide
>
> of darkness. Bide
> the black times, Lord, hide
> my heart from the lips
> that spit . . .

This is the bitter statement of slavery at its height. It is presumably what Wilberforce and Lincoln fought against, though it is doubtful that they could have had much real insight into the nightmare they opposed. The humiliation and degradation are stated through the persona of Tom, no longer the floundering, founding father, but the enigmatic witness of corruption:

> They laugh and the white
> man laughs: each
> wishing for mercy, each
> fearful of mercy, teach-
> ing their children to hate
> their skin to its bitter root in the
> bone.

In these passages there are echoes of the spirituals, and of the Biblical language that is so much a part of the English-based negro creoles. At its best the language is evocative of that stage of negro culture which is being rapidly swallowed up by late twentieth century values. Sometimes the mood is jarred by a weakening of the language, or a lowering of intensity. Occasionally a note of banality creeps in:

> 'But to hell with this, nuncle!
> You fussy black Uncle
> Tom, hat in your hand!

The pressure builds up again as we follow the wanderings of the Negro in the days after emancipation. These are the days of migration to Panama, Cuba, New York and the northern industrial cities of the United States. Their pathos and futility are captured in the lines

> . . . In my small hired
> room, stretched out upon the New
> York Herald Tribune, pages
> damp from dirty lots, from locked
> out parks, from gutters; dark, tired,
> deaf, cold, too old to care to catch
> alight the quick match of your pity,
> I died alone, without the benefit of
> fire.

Now the exile is an infinitely complex thing, embracing journeys to any country or state that seems to offer security. No place is home, and everywhere varieties of sorrow and sickness show themselves. The later generations of our century, our grandfathers and fathers, adapt in various ways. Negro art becomes fashionable; negroes are acknowledged great sportsmen and great musicians (jazz only). A multitude of neuroses develop, and beneath all is the restless homelessness expressed in the poem **'Journeys'**.

The many cultures of the West Indian islands, of the Deep South and the northern urban ghettoes are explored in the latter poems. Here, bound together by a common theme of bewilderment and frustration, are the people of the shanty towns of Kingston, Port of Spain, and Harlem. Social alienation produces its hallucinatory compensations; and the Rasta

> . . . beard full of lichens
> brain full of lice
> watched the mice
> come up through the floor-
> boards of his down-
> town, shanty-town kitchen,
> and smiled. Blessed are the poor
> in health, he mumbled,
> that they should inherit
> this wealth. Blessed are the meek
> hearted, he grumbled,
> for theirs is this stealth.

The Rasta passage rings true as a sample of the linguistic and mental processes of that group. Some of the other passages in different dialects are less successful. This may partly be the result of poetic composition in an unfamiliar dialect, and the use of poetic transformations which do not match the vernacular on which they are based. The last poem in Part II is full of these minor linguistic weaknesses, which yet do not interfere significantly with our grasp of the spiritual and social dislocation they express.

Irony and satire, the weapons of contemporary negro society, are explored as Brathwaite looks at the life of the calypsonian, the Brixton migrant, the bank clerk on the make, the Black Muslim, and the small shopkeeper. The poem in Barbadian dialect attempts something akin to the satire and humour of Louise Bennett. Still the themes of regeneration and death, of despair and hope, persist, though submerged. It is this balance of opposites which keeps **Rights of Passage** above the level of raw propaganda, and denies the reader any easy sentimental escape. In **'Postlude Home'** is a statement of the climax of the journeys, the confusion, the fear, the bitterness, and bewilderment which marked the last three centuries:

> For we
> who have cre-
>
> ated nothing,
> must exist

> on nothing;
> cannot see
>
> the soil:
> good
>
> earth, God's
> earth, with-
>
> out that fixed
> locked mem-
>
> ory of love-
> less toil

Now the beginning of it all it just an echo

> I is find meself
> wonderin' if
>
> Tawia Tutu Anokye or
> Tom could'a ever
>
> have live
> such a life.

The epilogue does more than recall the beginning of the cycle of history. It closes with a statement which draws together the contraries that have been expressed throughout, and makes of them both a promise and a threat, a beginning and an end. The final couplet of the book reads

> There is no
> turning back.

There is that inevitability of development in **Rights of Passage** which all successful art must have. One is carried along in spite of one's self, and in the end one can look back on a journey of the mind, which has transformed and illuminated the commonplace and the known. There is no easy label for this kind of poetry. If such a writer could emerge to unite in a single vision the disasters and divisions of the Vietnamese people or the confusions and conflicts of the people of Red China, then one might feel that the disunity of the past was ending, if not that of the future. Brathwaite's ability to see the many journeys of the last three centuries as a related whole more is than the freakish vision of one man. Poets seize upon what is real, but latent and formless in their times, and give these things voice and brightness. Myth-makers, they bring before the conscious mind dreams and notions that have been shaping in the subconscious of generations. They cannot create richly without that gestative past in which countless men and women have lived, and felt, and done what is now memory and tradition, and the substance of myth.

The spirit of **Rights of Passage** is carried over into **Masks,** as the prefatory quotation suggests:

"Only the fool points at his origins
with his left hand."   Akan Proverb.

We are plunged at once into a celebration of West
African culture, as it is lived and felt from within by
those native to that area. Instead of the symbols of
exile, fire, disease, springing vegetation and dry sand,
there are the many musical instruments and their paral-
lels in nature. The animism of West African culture is
boldly expressed:

> There is a quick
> stick grows in the for-
> est, blossoms twice year-
> ly without leaves;
> bare white branches
> crack like light-
> ening in the harm-
> attan.
>
> But no harm
> comes to those who live near-
> by. This tree, the
> elders say, will never
> die.

There is a sense of the unity and interrelatedness of all
things, a linking of the quick and the dead, which can-
not be satisfactorily expressed by the term animism.
West African cultures have shown in a variety of forms
this sense of the interdependence of things. In **"The
Gong-gong"** it is not a philosophy, but a living reality:

> God is dumb
> until the drum
> speaks.
>
> The drum
> is dumb
> until the gong-gong leads
>
> it. Man made,
> the gong-gong's
> iron eyes
>
> of music
> walk us through the humble
> dead to meet
>
> the dumb
> blind drum
> where Odomankoma speaks.

As in *Rights* . . . the spirit of each generation, each
group was evoked by varieties of language and dialect,
so the richness and variety of the life set out in *Masks*
is made real by a telling use of West African languages
and names. Brathwaite has a sensitive ear for the
rhythms and melodies of language, and his use of terms
from the Akan dialects is elegant and exciting:

> Odomankoma 'Kyerema says
> Odomankoma 'Kyerema says

> The Great Drummer of Odomankoma says
>
> The Great Drummer of Odomankoma says
>
> that he has come from sleep
> that he has come from sleep
> and is rising
> and is rising
>
> like akoko the cock
> like akoko the cock who clucks
> who crows in the morning
> who crows in the morning

There is much more to the music of these exotic terms
than one might at first expect. As we are taken, poem
by poem, into the depths of West African life, we find
that the language creates an insight into past and
present, showing the limitations of the Western negro
returned 'home', and the blend of strangeness and
familiarity in his experience.

It is the strangeness that strikes one first. The land has
forgotten the exiles, has lived on past their going with
other thoughts. The series **'Pathfinders'** brings to us
the vastness and variety of the life of West Africa. The
exiled negro seems a small thing in the endless reaches
of forest and desert, river and lake. In it all there is the
muted theme of the smallness and greatness of man,
building, destroying, breeding, dying, planting, and
reaping. **'Chad'** sets out in cold, clear terms the enigma
of existence:

> This sacred lake
> is the soul
> of the world;
>
> winds whirl
> born in the soul
> of this dark water's world.
>
> This lake
> moulds
> the wars of the world;
>
> no peace in this world
> till the soul
> knows this dark water's
>
> world.

In this world strife and disorder have a prominent place,
and the butterflies of decay and rebirth appear to em-
phasise the basic oneness of this world with all others.
The bitterness of *Rights* . . . is absent, and in its place
instead is a futility all the more pernicious as it has no
overt focus:

> . . . the gold returns
> to dust, the walls
>
> we raised return again

to dust; and what sharp winds,
teeth'd with the desert's sand,
rise in the sun's day

brilliance where our mosques
mock ignorance, mock pride,
burn in the crackled blaze of time,
return again to whispers, dust.

The Arab element in West African culture appears, a feature alien and exotic to the non-native. **'Volta'** sums up the alienness, the vastness and the little-known tragedies of West African history:

For miles the land was bare and dry
for miles clear sky

and rock; three days we travelled,
dreaming; heavy tongues dumb,
soles and our ankles numb,
foreheads shocked with heat.
The land was empty and the

rainless arch of nothing stretching
stretched straight on.

The writing in *Masks* has little of the vernacular intimacy of *Rights of Passage.* This is inevitable, for the experience of *Masks* is that of the observer, not that of the member of the group. In the section **'Limits'** we traverse the length and breadth of West Africa, and are made to sense the qualities of space and change which make it what it is. This is essentially an examination from without, and it is also an experiment on many levels. In **'Volta'** quoted above, the tension and labour of this part of West African life are made real in the rhythms and assonances of the writing. The strong musical rhythms of the opening poems express the values and joys of a culture alien to us. The experiment brings us into the heart of things, and shows how close and yet remote that heart is. There is the danger here that the very alienness of the culture threatens the verse with obscurity, yet the forcefulness of the imagery, the symbols of water, river, journey, labour, forest, field and family sustain the flow of argument.

Real tension comes in **'The Return'.** This is Asante country, from which oral tradition claims that most of the West Indian negroes came. This is the classic sentimental journey, the search for another self who preceded the present self. But the mirror is blank, and no familiar face looks back from its surface:

I tossed my net
but the net caught
no fish

I dipped a wish
but the well
was dry

Beware
Beware
Beware

Oddly enough, the writing loses something of its pungency and certainty in this section. But even so the urgency of the theme dominates even the weakest passages, and the hypnotic quality of the verse expresses the feeling of unreality, of failure, of bewilderment:

I travelled to a distant town
I could not find my mother
I could not find my father
I could not hear the drum

Whose ancestor am I?

This is the turning point of *Masks.* The true search is now over, and from this we must move on to looking at the homeland as it now is, in itself, in its own right, a thing completely apart from the returning stranger. The poem 'Masks' tells the real sorrow of that world, a sorrow which the stranger shares because he is of the family of man:

Your tree
has been split
by a white axe
of lightning;
the wise
are di-
vided, the
eyes
of our elders
are dead.

Estrangement, exile, division are man's lot: the section ends with a statement of the universality of oblivion and loss.

The last two sections of *Masks* are **'Crossing the River'** and **'Arrival'.** Like Bunyan's Pilgrim, the exile has looked at his world, and at his imagined home, and must face both himself and his true environment. The rhythms of invocation and dance are very marked in the last two sections. The writing takes on a ritual quality, as it strives to express the hope of reconcilliation and healing. The image of water the cleanser, the healer, the life force, expresses the nature of this final stage of the search. Water in Asante culture has many symbolic values, and the word 'nsuo' is the base form for terms such as milk, blood, fish, and river. The poem **'Sunsum'** (spiritual blood, literally *su nsum*) sums up the meaning of the return to West Africa: "Welcome your brother now / my trapped curled tongue / still cries". But the hard truth is that there can be no answer to the plea for welcome, and whatever hope there is must exist in spite of the unalterable facts of alienation and oblivion:

The years remain
silent: the dust learns nothing

with listening;

. . . . .

the termites' dark teeth, three

hundred years working,
have patiently ruined my art.

Death, loss and despair are the themes of **'Sunsum'**
and **'Tano',** and we are made to feel even more acutely
than in *Rights of Passage* what is the real meaning of
homelessness, of rootlessness and isolation from family.
In **'The Awakening'** only the basic forces of life remain
to offer hope of help: the earth, the light of day, and
those spiritual energies symbolised in the Divine Drum-
mer. As in *Rights of Passage* there "was no turning
back", so in *Masks* the essential power of man to be
himself, to find himself, is stated as a duty, sacred and
inevitable:

> so slowly slowly
> ever so slowly
>
> I will rise
> and stand on my feet
>
> slowly slowly
> ever so slowly
>
> I will rise
> and stand on my feet.
>
> Like akoko the cock
> like akoko the cock
>
> who cries
> in the early dawn
>
> akoko bon'opa
> akoko tua bon
>
> I am learning
> let me succeed
>
> I am learning
> let me succeed. . . .

Patricia Ismond (essay date September-December 1971)

SOURCE: Ismond, Patricia. "Walcott Versus Brath-
waite." *Caribbean Quarterly* 17, nos. 3-4 (September-
December 1971): 54-71.

[*In the following essay, Ismond revisits and reconsiders
a once-common comparison between Brathwaite and
Derek Walcott. She finds Walcott by far the better crafts-
man.*]

Since Edward Lucie-Smith's pronouncement that the
West Indies must choose between Walcott and Brath-
waite, there has arisen something of a controversy about
these two figures. There is a sense in which this kind of
quarrel was inevitable in the present atmosphere of
liberation, and one of the first things that needs to be
established is that it is not an irrelevant question within
this context. Some attempt has been made to resolve
the issue by pointing out that it is futile to attempt a
comparison when the two are obviously doing such
widely different things. Those who take this position
have not, as far as I can gather, tried to examine the
differences if only to prove their point. Others think
that the whole thing falls into place when we see them
as complementary rather than opposed. This is the view
that Rohlehr expresses in his essay on *Islands,* entitled
"The Poet as Historian."[1] Here again no one has really
ventured to show in what ways they are complementary.
There remains, as a result, a great deal of indeterminacy
surrounding this matter, and it has tended to give rise to
a Brathwaite faction versus a Walcott. It is obvious that
behind this state of affairs is an issue that needs to be
faced. Either, on the one hand, there are deficiencies in
the poets concerned that makes this an authentic cleav-
age. Or, on the other hand, there are limitations in the
attitudes of the audience that get in the way of a proper
appreciation. There are accordingly, ghosts that need to
be laid, and the effort to come to terms with these is-
sues becomes necessary.

The cliche attitudes towards these two poets must be
taken as starting points, because behind every cliche at-
titude is a hard core of significance which must be the
true target of any such argument. Brathwaite is hailed
as the poet of the people, dealing with the historical and
social themes that define the West Indian dilemma. Wal-
cott is a little more difficult to place—appears at times
to pay passing attention to these matters, but more
consistently he seems to be a type of poet's poet, the
kind of luxury we can ill afford, and which remains Eu-
rocentric. The European literary postures he continues
to assume are evidence enough of this. These are the
stock attitudes, and it is quite clear that Walcott does
get the worse of the deal. Those who, recognising some
undeniable strength and relevance in his work, have
risen to his defence, have not really dealt adequately
with the essential Walcott. Mervyn Morris, for example,
in trying to show that Walcott is indeed concerned with
the problems of his environment, cites only those poems
which deal overtly with the themes of the colonial and
middle-passage experience.[2] In bringing these two poets
together, therefore, it would be dishonest not to recog-
nise at once that it is Walcott above all that needs to be
vindicated. At the same time, the true nature of Brath-
waite's achievement has been somehow blurred by the
very excesses of the enthusiasm with which he has been
hailed. Walcott, as a craftsman, towers far above Brath-
waite, but I think this is a matter that can be temporarily
put aside in a consideration of the content of their works
and the type of sensibility that emerges in each case. It
seems to me, moreover, that our best appreciation of

each does gain from looking at them vis-a-vis each other in this way. It seems, also that this kind of investigation, properly conducted, will shed some light on the multiple aspects of the West Indian malaise.

Brathwaite sets out, in his trilogy, to recreate the historical experience of the Black race in the New World, and to express the various aspects of their condition as a dispossessed people. Walcott is primarily the artist—a man for whom, as an individual, art is a means of exploring and seeking a hold on reality. This general outline of their purposes of course merely skims the surface, but it is noticeable that Walcott's purpose is the more vague and insubstantial at this point. To state these basic purposes in this way, however, is a necessary introduction into the argument. It immediately raises the question of Brathwaite as a public poet versus Walcott as a private poet. In the essay already alluded to, Rohlehr dismisses this approach as false and misleading. "Each of these poets is in his different way at once 'public' and 'private.'" he says.[3] The distinction remains valid however. When one regards Brathwaite as a 'public' poet, it is not at all to underestimate his capacity for a deep personal involvement in the psychic and spiritual disturbances he presents. The point is that Brathwaite has undertaken to present certain aspects of the experience of a group, suffers in his own person for them as a representative, and always in relation to his vision of their collective destiny. The epic endeavour behind the trilogy demands the heightened awareness and sensitivity without which the poem could not begin to be written. There is not the sense of Brathwaite as an isolated figure—which is pervasive in Walcott's poetry—for this very reason: that his is a representative posture.

The essential nature of Walcott's 'personal' endeavour, on the other hand, is not so readily discernible. It is something which emerges only when we watch the patterns unfold from the whole corpus. We are aware, first of all, of the variety of scenes and situations he moves through, and the unflagging tone of seriousness which he brings to bear upon all of them in turn. He dwells upon the domestic and provincial scenes of the islands and the peculiar nature of the 'tragic twist' within the confines of their own experience ("Tales of the Islands," *In a Green Night*). He withdraws into the world of the private symbol to examine the psychic disturbances of an almost existential condition ("The Swamp," *The Castaway*); he enters into the agonized fantasies of the old fiddlers at Parang to show how doomed these are to disillusionment ("Metamorphoses," *The Gulf*). Directing all these, however, are spiritual and moral energies that seem ever to be seeking to fulfill themselves (in *Green Night*) he aspires towards 'the mind that enspheres all circumstance'; in *The Castaway* towards conditioning himself to the fact of 'domesticity, drained of desire'; in *The Gulf,* towards an apprehension of the

awe which life's 'plainess' evokes. In working through to these there is a certain expansiveness and elasticity in Walcott's world that results in the variety already indicated. It is a feature that conveys the impression of a man responding to the chance encounter, almost extempore, and there is a quality of the unusual and unexpected in most of the events and situations that feature in his world. If Walcott is conscious of one abiding motivation in his search for a hold on reality—which is by definition essentially vague—it is the important part his art must play in affording him this realisation. The keynote is struck in the "Prelude" when he suddenly rises out of the curious dearth in which both he and his island lie prostrate:

> I go, of course, through all the isolated acts,
> . . . . .
> Until from all I turn to think how
> In the middle of the journey through my life
> O how I came upon you, my
> Reluctant leopard of the slow eyes.

It is this sense of a personal salvation that directs Walcott, and makes his a private enterprise sharply distinct from Brathwaite's. It is one of the sources of all the major differences between them and provides a significant point of departure for a comparison of the two.

The central value of Brathwaite's collective enterprise is succinctly stated in Jean D'Costa's review article, "The Poetry of Edward Brathwaite":

> . . . while others like Cesaire and Baldwin have treated this world (the New World negro's) fragment by fragment, Edward Brathwaite attempts a synthesis of a splintered, shattered area of experience, and manages to bind it together in a single poetic vision . . .[4]

Behind this effort his main objective remains, as he puts it in the concluding lines of *Islands,* to make out of the rhythms of these fragments 'something torn, and new'. The rhythms are accordingly chosen to convey the qualities of suffering and the type of sensibility that unites the Black race. To mention a few at random: the plaintive blues of the Southern negro; the frenzied jazz of his urban brother; the powerful pulsations of limbo therapy; the resonances of the dark mystery of African religious ritual. For Brathwaite the enaction of these rhythms is finally aimed at one thing; to set in vibration an awareness that is predominantly black; to liberate a way of thinking and feeling that is essentially new in so far as it is devoid of all the strains and elements of the Western myth. His donee, if one may put it this way, is the theme of the dispossession of the black man and the spiritual torpor resultant on it. But his aesthetic motivation, the creation of a Black Word separate and distinct from the Western Word, is what predominates. The concluding lines of the trilogy already cited point to this, and his preoccupation with resisting Western tradition is made explicit time and again in his poems. Now he considers our total alienation from the Western Word, the sentiments and visions of the 'masters.'

> So the stars
> remain my master's
> property . . .
>
>   . . . . .
>
> . . . we have no name
> to call us home, no turbulence
> to bring us soft -
> ly past these bars to miracle, to god,
> to unexpected lover.
>
>   (**"Homecoming,"** *Islands*)

and again:

> it is not enough to be free
> of the whips, principalities and powers
> where is your kingdom of the Word?
>
>   (**"Negus,"** *Islands*)

At other times he examines its pernicious effects, as he watches Christianity, as mythical expression of the Western tradition, reclaim Tizzic from the outlet the carnival ritual seemed to offer:

> Behind the masks, grave
>
> Lenten sorrows waited: Ash-
> Wednesday, ashes, darkness, death.
>
> After the *bambalula bambulai*
> he was a slave again.
>
>   (**"Tizzic,"** *Islands*)

This sort of attitude obviously belongs somewhere in the same ethos of liberation as Cesaire's vision, but an important distinction emerges from a comparison of the two. The latter sustains an impassioned dynamic of protest that derives from an original moral outrage at the unparalleled insult to the Negro race, and it is this one purpose that informs and discovers its own rhetoric. Brathwaite takes the suffering of the negro as a given subject, and is mainly concerned with sounding the varying strains that will create a language, a way of thinking and feeling peculiar to the experience. This makes Brathwaite's a predominantly aesthetic undertaking, by contrast with Cesaire's direct gesture of assertion and protest. Finally, Brathwaite's most serious opposition is aimed at the Western Word, and his craft works carefully at expunging it from black modes of feeling and expression.

Which is precisely the point at which the division between himself and Walcott begins. Walcott, aware of the growing resistance towards what is called his fascination with the Western tradition, has been stung recently into what seems a rather reactionary remark. In an article entitled "Meanings", he states rather squarely:

Yet I feel absolutely no shame in having endured the colonial experience. There was no obvious humiliation in it. . . . It was cruel but it created our literature.[5]

It would be terribly simplistic to conclude from this that Walcott is rejecting the past, our turbulent history, as having no bearing upon our present predicament. The statement has to be taken in context. Walcott has been examining the dual elements of the African and Western traditions in the West Indian experience, and how the two might unite to produce a peculiarly West Indian drama. For him the one has bequeathed an exuberance which must be subjected to the discipline of the classical tradition introduced by the other. The particular emphasis that needs to be noted here, however, is his readiness to acknowledge the relevance of both these traditions in the West Indian experience. It is no helpless submission to a fascination with Western myth that makes him continue to work within its medium. He is quite conscious of his relationship to it, as he fashions it to cater to his indigenous needs and experience. He refers to this relationship in "Exile" (*The Gulf*) as his 'indenture to her Word.' His essential approach is expressed in "Crusoe's Journal":

> into good Fridays who recite His praise,
>   parroting our master's
> style and voice, we make his language ours,
>   converted cannibals
> we learn with him to eat the flesh of Christ.

This awareness of his indenture to the Word of the Western tradition—its concept of man in relation to creation, its peculiar apprehension of man's spiritual destiny—amounts to almost an obsession with Walcott. Yet one needs to be careful in trying to grasp the true nature of his position here. There is in Walcott an active scepticism that reflects a generic condition of spiritual dispossession, the spirit of which is captured in "The Castaway" (*The Castaway*). It turns, of necessity, on a criticism of the Western myth, its betrayals and failures for believer and convert alike. To recognise this however, is to grasp as well that his resistance of it involves an immersion in its qualities of awareness. This two-fold aspect of his involvement is brought out in a passage like the following, permeated with fragmentary allusions to the gospels and the crucified Christ:

> Godlike, annihilating godhead, art
> And self, I abandon
> Dead metaphors . . .
>
>   . . . . .
> That green wine bottle's gospel choked with sand,
> Labelled, a wrecked ship
> Clenched seawood nailed and white as a man's hand.
>
>   ("The Castaway," *The Castaway*)

Thus, the 'green wine bottle' has associations with the symbol of 'new wine bottles' of the gospel, except that here, contrary to the promise of its greenness, it is choked with sand—symbolizing spiritual putrefaction. Similarly, behind the references to 'clenched seawood nailed' and 'man's hand' hovers the image of the crucifixion that has become perverted and menacing. Walcott is very much immersed in the Western spiritual atmosphere. While Brathwaite rejects it as an imposture and imposition on the grounds of its being alien to the sensibility of the Black people, Walcott consciously faces it to resist the perplexities and confusions with which it is fraught. For him, to maintain this sceptical awareness is to work out, through modes of apprehension bequeathed by Western influence, his own sense of humanity and 'God's loneliness.' This question of acceptance of the Word is perhaps the fundamental issue between the two poets. To appreciate its full significance one needs to look closely at this aspect of their work.

The peculiar anguish of dispossession from which Brathwaite starts sends him in quest of some sort of spiritual baptism. The basic scheme of the trilogy follows the three stages given in M. Arnold Van Gennep's book entitled *Les Rites de Passage*. In this latter, which may well have provided Brathwaite with his title for the first part of the trilogy, the French anthropologist sees all primitive ceremonies as a passage through three states: first, the effort to withdraw from a profane world that revolves round one's awareness of it; second, a withdrawal during which experience moves on a sacred plane; and third, a reinstatement into the ordinary world.[6] *Masks* represents that second stage of withdrawal into a sacred world, and it is symbolic of Brathwaite's quest for some kind of initiation into the mysteries of the heart of darkness. Jean D'Costa rightly draws attention to the tentative nature of this movement in the poetry,[7] where he seems, at his best, to be hovering on the brink of two worlds, one dead, the other powerless to be born. The former seems to prevail, so that despite the birth-pangs aroused by the powerful pulsations of the drum ritual, he returns to this sense of negation:

> But my spade's hope,
> shattering stone,
> receives dumbness back
>
> for its echo.
> Beginnings end here
> In this ghetto.

> **("Sunsum," *Masks*)**

At other times he reaches very close to a discovery of the possibilities of suffering and renewal in the intensities of African religious ritual. This is enacted in the section **"Eating the Dead"** (*Islands*), a mode of communion with the supernatural that belongs in the African metaphysic and its concept of evil:

> It seems
> a long way now from fat, the shaking bone, the
>   laughter. But I

> can show
> you what it means to eat
> your god, drink his explosions of power
>
> and from the slow sinking mud of your plunder, grow.

Behind the multiple aspects of his presentation of Black reality, Brathwaite is indeed burrowing his way into the depths of a spiritual consciousness and a language of belief. This search for gods runs parallel with his desire for discovering a new Word. It is a search that revolves round an African twilight of the gods, and hovers between the condition of limbo and inferno in the ways already suggested. It is also in passages like these that he acquires the greatest strength, as he moves beyond the 'surfaces of things.'

Walcott's experience of spiritual conflict also moves between similar levels of limbo and inferno, arising from a generic strife between the will to believe and the glaring conditions of a reality that mock this desire. His efforts to gain access to these levels of consciousness involve energies just as violent self-immolating. In a poem like "Dogstar" (*The Castaway*) this is very much the principle at work. The intense heat of his own tropical setting seems to join forces with the elemental energies of the raging Dogstar, as Walcott becomes aware of the destructive dynamic at the heart of things. It opens for him the prospect of hell, and the eternal menace of death. Out of the inensities of this inferno glow images of a corresponding heaven, and he is tossed between this double vision in such a way as to be left utterly confused:

> Shovelled in like sticks to feed earth's raging oven,
> consumed like heretics in this poem's pride,
> these clouds, their white smoke, make and unmake
>   heaven.

Walcott starts from a contemplation different from the initiation rites in which Brathwaite is engaged, but what seems most important to both is the near-overwhelming strain of the spiritual effort. In each it draws upon the same dynamic of holy rage and awe. The main point here, however, is that Walcott enacts this drama within the mythical symbols of Christianity, not as an orthodox system, but for the traditional power of its images of heaven and hell, of *paridiso* versus *inferno*. To stress this point is to draw attention to an aspect of poetry in general that is much overlooked in the present clamour for 'literature engagee'. Every poet reverts now and then into the most private recesses of 'pure' poetry. To begin to deal with mysterious rites or a confrontation with death readily lends itself to the visionary frontiers of such 'pure poetry'. Thus, when Walcott in his retreats into the visionary draws upon the Christian symbols of heaven and hell, he is following much the same artistic course as Brathwaite is in seeking inspiration in the symbols of African traditional religion. Conversely, given the nature of visionary exploration, Brathwaite is no more engaged in creating a Word that communicates more powerfully to us by virtue of its being African. The ceremony of **"Eating the Dead,"** as Brathwaite presents it, explores a mystique that arouses a response in us because the emotive drives point to the quality of the spiritual crises, despite our unfamiliarity with its modes and ritual. The Christian symbols feature in the same way in Walcott's spiritual overtures. Any rejection of his poetry on this score comes finally from a failure to understand the ultimate processes of poetry, and on a blind concept of what protest truly involves. It is not the mere gesture of supplanting in poetry one set of symbols *qua* symbols, by another that makes for an act of self-assertion. That aspect of Brathwaite's poetry which proposes this sort of thing—and it is very much present—is claiming much more for itself than it is really doing. Yet, one needs to proceed cautiously and draw the distinction between this attempt at installment of an African concept of reality and his effort to distill the sense of a people broken in spirit, that movement in his work which has more to do with protest. It strikes a characteristic note in a passage like this, describing the pathos of Tom's failure:

> poised
> in that fatal attitude
>
> that would have smashed
> the world, or made it, he
> let the hammer
>
> down; made
> nothing, un-
> made nothing;
>
> his bright
> hopes down
> his own
>
> bright future
> dumb,
> his one
>
> heroic flare
> and failure
> done.

("Anvil," Islands)

There remains, I think, at the heart of his aesthetic a basic irresolution between these two movements, or rather, a confounding of the one with the other. On the one hand his desire to rehabilitate an African pantheon and mythology as the medium for suffering. On the other, his aim to capture the peculiar anguish of Black oppression. They are not the same thing, though the fragmentary technique of the trilogy helps to create the illusion of an orchestration of these two intentions. It is on this second level rather than on the first that Brathwaite shows a meaningful involvement. Against this

can be measured the peculiar quality of involvement that emerges from Walcott's orientation towards reality. The most authentic differences between them arise from here, and the wider implication of Walcott's immersion in the Western tradition emerges as something far more positive and less of an anachronism than it is made out to be. It takes its place, within the specific terms of poetry, in the complex directions of the struggle for liberation.

In a seminar on West Indian poetry, Brathwaite considers Walcott a humanist and points out the limitations of this approach. The humanist poet, Brathwaite thinks "is often speaking away from that society rather than speaking in towards it."[8] Brathwaite concedes that the humanist poet draws his inspiration from the society, but what is implied in the quotation given above is that all such inspiration is sophisticated away from any relevance. A humanist Walcott certainly continues to be, and the tradition of humanism in which he tries to find his bearings derive again from the Western orientation. That is to say, Walcott's awareness of man in search of fulfillment and man the victim of adversity follows the patterns evolved in the Western Imagination. Western philosophy, going as far back as Plato, conceives of man as a creature endowed with the capacity for Truth and Beauty through which he can attain transcendence over the dark forces that threaten to undermine his humanity. African wisdom follows another angle of approach. Arising out of the exigencies of the African experience, it sends the African Imagination in search of a more precipitate contact with Evil. The spiritual energies are engaged in a direct placating of Evil that involves an absorption in its darker mysteries— something of what Conrad perceives in his *Heart of Darkness.* Brathwaite captures the essence of this philosophy in the following lines, hinting at the significance of the fetish for the African:

> symbol sickness fetish for our sickness.
> For man eats god, eats life, eats world, eats wicked-
> ness.
> This we now know, this we digest and hold;
> this gives us bone and sinews, saliva grease and sweat;

("Adowa," Masks)

In the Western imagination the thrust is upwards; in the African downwards.

The above explications aims at drawing the distinction between the two, in order to recognise more clearly *how* Walcott is involved in the Western tradition of humanity. It is important to understand how, working within this broad perspective Walcott evolves a humanism that relates to the West Indian conditions. Anyone who fails to come to grips with this aspect of his sensibility, will in their attempt to find him "relevant", be glossing over a significant part of his achievement.

To illustrate this point one need only to take a look at the group of poems entitled "A Tropical Bestiary" (*The Castaway*) These represent the essential Walcott just as strongly as "Tales of the Islands" (*Green Night*). In the former however, he is directly engaged in orienting himself to reality on a philosophical level. He starts from a recognition that his attempts to achieve transcendent vision remain ineffectual, and strives towards the resilience that will accept this as a *fait accompli* of human limitations. With the poetic concentration that such an external image affords him, he sees the reality enacted in the fate of the Ibis that "fades from her fire";

> Pointing no moral but the fact
> Of flesh that has lost pleasure in the act
> Of domesticity, drained of desire.
>
>   ("Ibis")

The painful pulsations of desire still linger, though, in the human psyche:

> Pulse of the sea in the locked heaving side.
>
>   ("Octopus")

When Walcott passes from this reflective level into the human scene, the perspective is still the same. This is true of a poem like "Hawk" (*The Gulf*). He enters into the spirit of the folk festivity as the old fiddlers play at Parang. The agonised strains of their 'tension lines' expresses their yearning for some keen spur to drive them to their dreams, and they look back nostalgically to the powerful purpose that spurred on the violent Caribs, for example. The presiding genius of the hawk is involved, symbol of strife and torture, but, abruptly, the sharp dissonance of the hawk of their actual surroundings brings them back to earth and the futility that mocks such sentiments:

> Slaves yearn for their master's talons,
> the spur and the cold, gold eyes,
> for the whips, whistling like wires,
> time for our turn, gabilan!
> But this hawk above Rampanalgas
> rasps the sea with raw cries.
> Hawks have no music.

These are the reaches of Walcott's humanism and they are inspired by the kind of destitution he sees about him. In following these movements between desire and negation, he does not point directly to its sources in social or historical deprivation—but the sense of defeat concentrated in his treatment does recreate the world of these old rum-guzzlers in their rustic setting, caught within the confines of their vegetable life, cheerless and hopeless but for their drunken visions and the occasional rhythms of the old parang. That Walcott approaches them through these modes of apprehension does not refine away the concreteness of their world and its specific conditions. It does not thin into 'irrelevance.'

This consideration of Walcott's humanism is a necessary preliminary if we are to weigh it against Brathwaite's mission of protest. The questions then become: How does Walcott's humanistic approach serve the West Indian dilemma as compared to Brathwaite's kind of protest. How do these peculiar positions reveal their respective types of involvement in their environment—always bearing in mind a comment of Dennis Scott's, that neither of them is offering us a programme for social reform.[9] And since every diagnosis of a malaise hints at possibilities of renewal and relief, however indirectly, how do their visions of West Indian hope and renewal compare. These are among the questions that must arise in a comparison of the two.

The essential tone of Brathwaite's protest is captured in one of his most-quoted passages. It is one in which he rises to a rare flash of original imagery:

> and we float, high up over the sighs of the city,
> like fish in a gold water world.
>
> we float round and round
> in the bright bubbled bowl
> without hope of the hook,
> of the fisherman's tugging-in root.

Brathwaite's vision of the destitution of the Black people rests on this final diagnosis of their plight; they are a people doubly benighted in a lost world, and the hopelessness of this condition is perhaps his most insistent theme. The circumstances behind this plight have their origin in our history of displacement and subjugation. It is the historical consciousness, quite obviously, that provides him with his viewpoint, and leads him to penetrate the sinister aspects of our unnatural encounter with Europe. He traces the interrelations between the material, psychological and spiritual effects in such portraits as that of the Rasta man. The lingering presence of Babylon, a legacy of the colonial system that fixed the relations between colour and prosperity, has relegated the Rasta man to the absurd dimensions of his world. The sources of the oppression that prompt his ironic hallucinations are shown to be indeed sinister:

> Brother Man the Rasta
> man, hair full of lichens
> head hot as ice
>
> watched the mice
> walk into his poor
> hole, reached for his peace
> and the pipe of his ganja
> and smiled how the mice
> eyes. . . .
> . . . like rhinestone
> and suddenly startled like
> diamond.

These are matters of fundamental concern in West Indian reality, and Brathwaite implies that our very alertness to these injustices will engender a positive condition of restlessness. In this lies the greatest possibilities of assertion and realisation. Gerald Moore grasps this condition of restlessness as Brathwaite's main positive:

> Only by embracing this restlessness can the negro conceive it as a forward movement . . . The search is what defines the race giving it purpose and momentum.[10]

In the article already cited Rohlehr witnesses a prophetic fulfilment of this vision. As he watches the protest marches in Trinidad, Brathwaite's insight into the continued tribal wanderings of the Black race strikes home:

> Right now it is drought in Trinidad, and those young men with fixed faces looking blankly into an unimaginable future and marching are fulfilling a deep tribal dream.[11]

In this kind of criticism there is a hint of 'mythologizing'—there is a point at which, on its own terms, this becomes archetypal and is no longer peculiar to the African tribal experience. Be that as it may, Brathwaite's restlessness aims at feeling its way out of the trappings of such oppression. The conflicts and confrontations that set it in motion are directly associated with the historical aftermath.

Walcott's approach does not bring him to quite this kind of diagnosis. That he brings a certain type of diagnosis to bear upon various aspects of his society cannot be denied. But the humanistic angle from which he starts eschews the sense of direct protest and the vision of our release from the repercussions of history as our only means of escape. His approach works on the level of a morality and internal psychology that turns on a confrontation with self. This is not to say that Walcott does not allow for the effects of the historical experience in aggravating the problems of the environment but, rather, that he does not see this as the main feature standing in the way of self-realisation. A typical example of his approach is his analysis of the kind of megalomania that finally defeats the hero of "Junta" (*The Gulf*). He begins with the observation of the kind of illusions that the carnival psychology is fraught with. As the hero marches through in the guise of Vercingetorix, there is already a premonition that for him this fantasy is in dead earnest, and the illusions of power are being engendered in the very spirit of carnival:

> He fakes an epileptic, clenched salute,
> taking their tone, is no use getting vex,
> some day those brains will squelch below his boot
> as sheaves of swords hoist Vercingetorix.

The ironic approach here retains its sympathetic poise, but almost unobtrusively Walcott shows how this fantasy finds its way through the political outlet of the junta, and the curious twist it takes in leaving the coup, which is to prove his undoing, just as much a matter of fantasy for Vercingetorix. What had been for him a symbol of fulfillment retains the emptiness of an over-desperate and rash gesture, without the authentic purpose of the coup to give it direction:

> . . . He clears his gorge and feels the bile
> of rhetoric rising. Enraged, that every clause
> 'por la patria, la muerte' resounds
> the same, he fakes a frothing fit and shows his wounds,
> while, as the cold sheathes heighten, his eyes fix
> on one black, bush-haired convict's widening smile.
>
> "Junta," *The Gulf*

These insights finally turn upon an intense type of confrontation with self. Walcott's humanistic concern leads him to explore this kind of delusion as a condition ultimately arising from shortcomings within the individual consciousness—although they arouse sympathy, as in the case of Vercingetorix in showing how vulnerable man really is. In other words, his approach shifts the emphasis away from the external targets that Brathwaite keeps in view. One notices how the turbulent political atmosphere is brought in almost as a matter of course; and in fact, Walcott's approach does carry its environment with it as inevitably. But in bringing the irony to bear directly on the processes of his mania, Vercingetorix' disoriented state becomes a matter of private tragedy for which he alone is, ultimately, responsible. This is the peculiar achievement of Walcott's approach, and it is closely related to his dogged pursuit of a personal hold on reality.

Brathwaite, however, does opt now and again for the stability of traditional morality as a tentative avenue of 'liberation'. This is proposed every so often as he returns to the theme of Mammon as another major source of the disruption of possible order and the good life:

> when only lust rules
> the night . . .
> when men make noises
> louder than the sea's
> voices; then the rope
> will never unravel
> its knots; the branding
> iron's travelling flame that teaches
> us pain, will never be
> extinguished . . .
>
> (**"Islands,"** *Islands*)

He seems to concede intermittently, therefore, that some sort of poise between the protesting consciousness and a moral vigilance will show the way out of the morass. This moral responsibility, summarily included in his mission of protest, is the very dimension on which Walcott concentrates. One last comparison between the two will serve to underscore this point: their treatment of carnival, an indigenous cultural feature. Brathwaite sees carnival as an expression of a positive and vital impulse, instinctual in the race. So that, in his presentation of Tizzic's case, he denounces the tyranny of a foreign imposition such as Christianity that robs Tizzic of its powers of enrichment: Through carnival's 'stilts of song' Tizzic comes near to attaining the seventh heaven, but he is doomed to failure:

> In such bright swinging company
> he could no longer feel the cramp
> of poverty's confinement, spirit's damp;
> . . . But the good stilts splinter-
>
> ed, wood legs broke, calypso steel pan
> rhythm faltered. The midnight church
>
> bell fell across the glow, the lurch-
> ing cardboard crosses. Behind the masks, grave
>
> Lenten sorrows waited. Ash-
> Wednesday, ashes, darkness, death.
>
> After the *bambalula bambulai*
> he was a slave again.
>
> ("Tizzic," *Islands*)

Brathwaite's mission of protest leads him to this kind of expose of the hopelessness of Tizzic's thraldom, held as he is within the fastnesses of an alien religion. He seems to be offering carnival as a possible outlet. In a poem like "Mass Man" (*The Gulf*) Walcott harbours no such illusions about it. As he watches the frenetic gaiety behind the carnival extravaganza, he is conscious of the emptiness behind it all; and the sensuality, devoid of any significance beyond the most philistine type of self-indulgence, assumes sinister resonances. So that the child 'rigged like a bat', far from experiencing any genuine merriment, is aware of the absurd scene of its isolation:

> But I am dancing, look, from an old gibbet
> my bull-whipped body swings, a metronome!
> Like a fruit-bat dropped in the silk-cotton's shade
> my mania, my mania is a terrible calm.

All this must end in a dispirited sense of negation and futility, Walcott thinks with misgiving. His manner of expressing this latter has tended to mislead a number of his readers into thinking that he is merely judging from a sickeningly orthodox and self-righteous viewpoint, based on an acceptance of the Christian religion. His reference to Ash Wednesday is primarily figurative, hinting at the violation of sensibility, the kind of self-desecration that this attitude involves. He continues to stress this sense of aberration with metaphorical intensity:

> some mind must squat down howling in your dust,
> some hand must crawl and recollect your rubbish,
> someone must write your poems.

Put beside Brathwaite's view as champion of such cultural features, Walcott's seems to be hopelessly negative. Yet his diagnosis of the carnival psychology in the decadent urban atmosphere of Port-of-Spain where the gesture serves mainly as a means of license, does uncover an authentic aspect of present day carnival. The morality that informs his sardonic appraisal does arise from a genuine humanistic concern, as his tableau of the child 'rigged like a bat' does show. It is the same approach which sees these shortcomings and deficiencies in terms of our own failures, places the onus of guilt upon us, and shows us to be victims of ourselves primarily. This is instinctively Walcott's purpose, and by comparison Brathwaite's notion of the liberating influences of carnival seems curiously half the truth, if not altogether off the mark. It presupposes a kind of 'innocence' which we have quite lost; and this is what Walcott is fundamentally realistic about. This is the peculiar strength of his approach. Yet Brathwaite's attempt to draw attention to such indigenous cultural features and his move to preserve them through his artistic medium remains an important undertaking. If, in his enthusiasm to retain what is our own—and this relates closely to his larger purpose of creating Black aesthetic—he gets carried away into half-truths, much shall be overlooked, because he hath meant well . . . . At the same time, it is exactly here that the two become complementary. In dwelling on his peculiar emphases, Walcott takes such cultural features for granted; while Brathwaite's mode of protest brings them to the fore and points to the importance of preserving them. Walcott is not proposing a rejection of carnival, but denouncing the vulgarization resulting from our unwholesome attitudes towards it. Yet without Brathwaite's attempt, its presence as an indigenous feature worth salvaging from this unwholesomeness might well be glossed over . . .

The different positions of these two poets does, however, assume peculiar relevance when viewed within the larger context of liberation. Walcott's humanistic approach, in its insistence on searching within for the attitudes of mind that will set us free, signifies this: he accepts himself, in his time and place as a man who, with the ravages of history behind him, is willing to rise above any surviving fetters by a courageous expression of his intrinsic stature as a man. There is this spirit of independence in his approach, completely unselfconscious, that shows him to be altogether free of that historical legacy, a sense of inferiority—a point from which the movement of protest does start. The significance of his 'acceptance' of the Western Word is closely related to this attitude: it has availed him of a strategy for consciousness that, having been absorbed and modified in his environment over the centuries, becomes as much his property as that of the former masters. So that he feels free to mould it, bend it to his own purposes, now to expose its shortcomings, now draw upon its strengths—as competently as the original possessors. This is the sense of freedom that makes him recognise the positive aspects of the double-heritage of the West Indies, fraught as it is with all the contradictions that precipitate the crisis of liberation. Nor is it merely a matter of an abdication of the historical sense on Walcott's part. It suggests instead of a man, who, realising that there is no turning back, believes that the destiny of the West Indian peoples must depend on the resources they find within themselves for acting with confidence towards what has been left, negative as well as positive. Only with this attitude, can we begin to make them ours. Moreover, this is not to be derivative and beholden, or to deem ourselves secondary in status. The very confidence and tenacity of his approach challenges and defies any such notions of inferiority. His reaction to the Southern States, in "The Gulf" (*The Gulf*) is revealing in this respect. He recoils instinctively from the negro's condition there, his 'secondary status as a soul'. Its strangeness communicates an uncanny sense of fear to him. Somehow Walcott has managed to achieve a sense of self-mastery, and it begins with the attitude of a mind that makes the most strenuous demands upon itself, and takes for granted its right to do so. This is the peculiar strength of his personal quest, and it is, in its own way, *a most powerful gesture of assertion.* Yet perhaps not all can rise to the level of courage that he represents. He stands out curiously among his contemporaries in this respect, in his refusal to leave the West Indian setting. It is finally a refusal to see the area as confining, or as a secondary order of existence. The attitude he stands for is a valid and acceptable one, though difficult for it opens up a definite possibility, even through the elusive reflections of such a medium as poetry.

This is one mode of assertion, and the next most effective is through protest such as Cesaire's: an outright insistence on the intrinsic stature of the Black man that aims at exploding the myth of his inferiority, and makes an absurdity of all the lingering effects of that myth. There is just so much poetry can do and no more, however committed it is to such a cause. Cesaire's gesture represents the rousing call to manhood and defiance that epitomises this kind of commitment. This spirit is finally lacking in Brathwaite, and it is a direct result of his peculiar conception of his artistic purpose. Concerned to create Black poetry first and last, he depends on the painful lyricism of Black suffering for the anguish of protest. Protest itself remains a subordinated theme, accordingly, and the elegiac mood that pervades it tends to weigh too heavily upon us to leave us in any positive attitude. There is not, in its brooding lament, the defiant will to strive. It is for this reason that his protest, even taken on its own terms remains weaker, in the final analysis, than Walcott's kind of assertion. Yet what he has achieved in missing the mark is indeed valuable, even though it seems to offer more

of an escape into its rhythmical movements. If we can resist the lotus-eating atmosphere of the appeal they tend to exert—Brathwaite's attempt to draw attention to the latent possibilities of these rhythms as modes of awareness, is indeed a positive and timely contribution.

Notes

1. "The Historian as Poet," *The Literary Half-Yearly* Vol. XI No. 2, July 1970, p. 178.

2. "Walcott and the Audience for Poetry," *Caribbean Quarterly* Vol. 14 Nos. 1 and 2, March-June 1968, pp. 22-24.

3. "The Historian as Poet," *The Literary Half-Yearly* Vol. XI No. 2, July 1970, p. 178.

4. "The Poetry of Edward Brathwaite," *Jamaica Journal* Vol. 2 No. 3, September 1968, p. 24.

5. "Meanings," *Savacou No. 2,* September 1970, p. 51.

6. *The Rites of Passage* (Translated from the French by M. B. Vizedom and G. L. Caffee), London, Routledge and Kegan Paul, 1960.

7. "The Poetry of Edward Brathwaite," *Jamaica Journal* Vol. 2 No. 3, September 1968, p. 25.

8. "West Indian Poetry, a Search for Voices," seminar sponsored by the Extra-Mural Department, U.W.I., 14 March 1965; fifth in a series on "The State of the Arts in Jamaica."

9. The present writer has heard him make this comment at several seminars on West Indian poetry at the U.W.I.

10. *The Chosen Tongue* (London, Longmans, 1969), p. 36.

11. "The Historian as Poet," *The Literary Half-Yearly* Vol. XI No. 2, July 1970, p. 174.

Lloyd Wellesley Brown (essay date 1978)

SOURCE: Brown, Lloyd Wellesley. "The Cyclical Vision of Edward Brathwaite." In *West Indian Poetry*, pp. 139-58. Boston: G. K. Hall & Co., 1978.

[*In the following essay, Brown traces a communal voice through Brathwaite's collections* Rights of Passage, Masks *and* Islands, *which the author claims demonstrates "the cycles of black New World culture in time and space."*]

It has become a custom in West Indian criticism to discuss Walcott and Brathwaite as opposites.[1] Walcott himself ventured some scepticism about the Walcott-versus-Brathwaite debate, preferring (as he did during a visit to the University of Southern California in 1974) to emphasize the similarities between himself and Brathwaite. The interest in drawing comparisons and contrasts between the two is inevitable, given the fact that they have been easily the most dominant and significant West Indian poets, especially since the 1960's. And by a similar token, Walcott's impatience with the emphasis on the differences between himself and Brathwaite is understandable since there has been a tendency to describe them in exclusive terms—Walcott as the Western-oriented craftsman and individualist and Brathwaite as the epic poet and master seer of the black diaspora. In fact there are enough similarities to justify Walcott's impatience. From a general historical point of view their works are the culmination of major developments in modern West Indian poetry—an intensified ethnic awareness, a growing national consciousness that seeks to accommodate the cultural diversity of the West Indian's cultural sources, and a complex perception of the destructive energies and creative aftermath of the past. They also write well within the major directions of contemporary West Indian poetry in that their work reflects a highly self-conscious preoccupation with the artist's identity and role in the national culture: they both share with other poets an ambivalent vision of the West Indian's Middle Passage history, perceiving it as a symbol of dispossession and death but simultaneously transforming it into the symbol of a continual odyssey for new beginnings. And in this connection both poets share historical perspectives and cultural symbols that are interwoven with a New World ethos. Finally the West Indian's moral and nationalist odyssey in the New World is symbolized by the artist himself.

There are differences too, of course. But these should be considered in relative rather than absolute terms. Brathwaite's trilogy, *Rights of Passage, Masks,* and *Islands,* constitutes an epic of sorts on the black West Indian's history and culture.[2] But neither is Walcott indifferent to black ethnicity as such: indeed it is integral to his perception of the West Indian's hybrid cultural personality. Brathwaite also underscores that duality, in a rather different context. In Walcott's work black ethnicity is tempered by an emphasis on his personal closeness, by way of his white grandfather, to the white Western fact. In Brathwaite the West lacks this personal immediacy, but there is a correspondingly intense awareness of the nuances of being black in the West *and* in Africa. Walcott's Africa is a mere memory, often vague and beyond physical or psychological reach. But Brathwaite's Africa is presented as a personal encounter and as an immediate fact. Walcott's white grandfather and his English memories (inherited from the ambience of his grandfather's world) come easily to the surface of his work. Brathwaite has had a fairly substantial experience of Africa (especially West Africa), having taught in Ghana from 1955 to 1962

after graduation from Cambridge University. Moreover his academic career as historian at the University of the West Indies and in his island home, Barbados, has extended his intellectual immersion in Africa and in the black diaspora. And altogether this personal experience informs the poetic memories of the continent in his trilogy. On the whole Brathwaite's work reflects his far greater interest in the cultural transmissions from West Africa to the New World, and in the organic links between the West Indian and the West African experience, past and present. But he can be as sensitive as Walcott to the nuances and literary significance of the Western dimension in Afro-Caribbean culture. Hence *Islands* is dominated by echoes of Western poetry and religion, especially by way of Eliot's *Wasteland,* just as much as the modes of Akan culture dominate the language and perception of *Masks.*

Finally, although both poets clearly address themselves in a positive way to the ethnocultural experience in the West Indian's nationalism, their approaches are shaped by their respective interests in group versus individual. Walcott's preoccupation with isolation as a universal and persistent condition does not allow him Brathwaite's relatively optimistic assumptions about the realization, or possible realization, of an ongoing ethnic group experience. In Walcott the reader is ever aware of the primary needs, self-conflicts, and self-acceptance of the individual: the individual stands outside the group experience, especially if he is the artist himself, and at its closest his relationship with the group is symbolical or analogical. The group experience is not unimportant but its primary significance is derived from the extent to which the group symbolizes, contributes to, or is an analogy of, the private experience of the individual. Brathwaite's work reflects a more immediate, less reserved reaction to the burgeoning black ethnicity of the 1960's. His poetry does not dispense with individuals as such, but the greater emphasis is on archetypes who are intrinsically bound up with, and lead the reader directly into the group experience of which they are a part. Both poets are sceptical about the facile rhetoric and built-in delusions of much ethnic politics and many national postures, but Brathwaite is more committed than is Walcott to the exploration of ethnic and national consciousness in terms of their group manifestations. This distinction between both poets is also pertinent to their perception of the poetic role. As already suggested, Walcott's highly individualized themes are an extension of his preoccupation with the poet as private person: his themes evolve from the more archetypal dimensions of the castaway poet in earlier works to the decidedly autobiographical framework of *Another Life.* His poet remains a private individual with public significance rather than the artist who is totally defined by the public function of his art. But in Brathwaite the artistic identity is a composite or collective persona. The "I" of his trilogy seldom, if ever, acquires the private identity of

Walcott's poet. In *Masks,* for example, the "I" represents (1) the precolonial African on the historical quest from old kingdom to new worlds in West Africa (2) the African river over which the migrating African must cross, and (3) the West Indian who visits West Africa as an ethnocultural pilgrim of sorts. Brathwaite's "I" is the communal voice speaking out of and demonstrating the cycles of black New World culture in time and space—in the West African past and present, and in the New World past and present.

I RIGHTS OF PASSAGE

Rights of Passage concentrates on blacks in the Americas, moving from the West Indies to the United States and back. The second book, *Masks,* reverses the Middle Passage voyage by returning the reader to Africa. Finally, *Islands* is both a return to the contemporary West Indies and a symbolic retracing of the original voyage of enslavement. The odyssey or journey motif of the trilogy dramatizes the nature and function of the artistic imagination in the black experience: art is a journey through time as well as space; it is an act of memory, discovering and imitating the cycles of history, and in the process both creating and demonstrating a heightened new awareness of the past in the present. Consequently the work song with which *Rights of Passage* opens exemplifies art as an act of memory:

> Drum skin whip
> lash, master sun's
> cutting edge of
> heat. . . .

> (p. 3)

As West Indian folk art the song re-enacts the black New World history of hardship and pain. The skin of the drum imitates the beaten skin of the slave; but the image of heat not only recalls the suffering of the plantations in the West Indies, it also re-experiences the suffering of those precolonial West Africans searching for new homes on the continent, and subsequently, the disaster overtaking those new homes when they were burnt down by the slavetraders. Conversely, art as memory moves in the opposite direction in time, recollecting the Middle Passage journey which followed the slavetrader's raids. Here it is the gospel song motif that is dominant, emphasizing the Christian forms which Afro-West Indians have incorporated into their culture and which were betrayed by the white Christians in order to establish the slave sources of Afro-West Indian culture:

> How long
> how long
> O Lord
> O devil
> O fire
> O flame

> have we walked
> have we journeyed
> to this place

> (p. 8)

That reference to movement or journey not only underscores the theme of exile in the history of the black diaspora. It also dramatizes the migratory role of the exile's memory and of the artist's imagination. On a technical level it also complements the manner in which Brathwaite's structure is itself an outward representation of art as movement, as a creative, suggestive fluidity: the poem's form flows from the hard, driving drum rhythms of the work song to the melodious lament of gospel music. The easy movement from one art form to another therefore reflects that imaginative movement or journey which is memory or art itself; and in historical terms, the movement imitates the remembered journeys of the past. But it is also a stream-of-consciousness technique, or more accurately, a stream-of-consciousness experience which is centered on a succession of archetypes. The first of these archetypes is Tom, appropriately so since the popular association of Uncle Tom with an abject servility allows for a typically smooth transition, within the stream-of-consciousness format, from the slavery of the past to a traditional servility. In turn, that transition is underscored by the physical (half-white, half-black) as well as the mental dimensions of Tom's personality. Like the cotton of the slave plantation itself, he is the growth from the seeds of his (white) father's (sexual and economic) needs. But the circumstances of Tom's conception and birth are actually ambiguous. The slave mother's union with the master might have suggested a surrender or an act of apostasy; but it was also fraught with a subversively tenacious commitment to survival and to covert resistance. Appropriately enough, then, the poem's structure shifts to a blues format in the introduction of Tom himself, for the blues is the quintessence of that tenacious commitment. Simultaneously, the total movement from Caribbean work song, to gospel song, to blues corresponds with the gradual expansion of Brathwaite's New World context, from the Caribbean to the Americas as a whole. Conversely, the symbols of black history in the Americas—gospel, blues, the slave plantations, and the Uncle Tom archetype—have been concentrated in the black West Indian consciousness that stands at the center of Brathwaite's themes in *Rights of Passage*: Uncle Tom and the West Indian experience which the archetype represents are linked by their common New World experience.

In more specific terms Tom represents the usual deference and the self-hating acceptance of myths about the racial inferiority of blacks. But considered as a whole Tom is as ambiguous as the circumstances of his conception. His habitual self-negation is actually a thinly disguised mode of defiant survival. The capacity to survive and to create art (music, song, and dance) is integrated with the will to remember the implications of his racial condition. The Uncle Tom mask is the *surface* acquiescence of the singer, the clown, and the carnival calypsonian; but his heart represents a more complex, less servile response:

> So I who have created
> nothing . . .
> who have forgotten all
> mouth "Massa, yes
> Massa, yes
> Boss, yes
> Baas."
> and hold my hat
> in hand
> to hide
> my heart.

(p. 14)

As an archetype Tom's composite language echoes the West Indian mouthing "Massa," the black American's "Boss," and the black South African's "Baas." In terms of time the cyclical implications of the archetype are emphasized by the fact that Tom the rebel-child of the master must now cope with his own scornfully militant children:

"All God's Children"

> They call me Uncle
> Tom and mock me
> these my children
> mock me.

(p. 16)

In dealing with the young militants Tom demonstrates the real complexity of his character by his awareness of the actual weaknesses of a certain kind of black militancy which, in its own way, is a kind of Tomishness; for it actually panders to the subhuman expectations of whites about black violence and black sexuality:

> "Cut the cake—
> walkin', man; bus'
> the crinoline off the white woman,
> man; be the black buttin' ram
> that she makes you
> an' let's get to hell out'a Pharaoh's land!"

(p. 20)

Within the memory's cyclical patterns of past and present the ambiguities of an older generation of Uncle Toms have been juxtaposed with the ambiguities of the latter-day militant. The archetypal mode itself reinforces the cyclical pattern. Hence the Uncle Tom archetype brings together both past and present in his person, in that his old-fashioned deference and the bolder "hustles" of the younger, militant generation are both methods of

subversion and survival in a white world. The geographical cycles (Tom as West Indian, black American and black South African) have therefore been integrated with the cycles of time and the archetypal mode. Finally, the poem's exploration of these cycles of being relies on a structure that is really a cyclical succession of black folk art forms—from work song, to gospel and spiritual, then on to the shuffle of the sardonic young militant hustler.

In keeping with the multiple cycles of Brathwaite's structure and vision Uncle Tom and his militant child are succeeded by the black "spade" who combines the ambiguities and tensions of both. The spade's angry sense of identity is compromised by a contemptuous disregard of history, including his own history:

> just call my blue
> black bloody spade
> a spade and kiss
> my ass.

(p. 28)

He is the contemporary urban Black whose self-awareness is punctuated by a sarcastic parody of white perception of the mere "Negro"; but that self-awareness is diluted by the extent to which that parody actually reflects some of his real insecurities. The rhetoric of angry pride masks a basic sense of vulnerability—a striking reversal of the Uncle Tom posture. Hence there is a gradual shift from the hard, declarative style to the moan of a hurt child ("I feel / bad mother"). Altogether the diverse rather than one-dimensional, ways of black folk are demonstrated both by the variety of Brathwaite's archetypes and by the ambiguities and self-conflicts which he attributes to each archetype. And this diversity is the direct outcome of the complex awareness and the multiple images of reality which the poet derives from his cyclical approach to his subject. But the cyclical mode is also complemented by a sense of evolution or progression that promises some kind of maturing consciousness. Thus the boogie-woogie beat with which Brathwaite concludes his description of the spades is laced with the rhythms of a railworker's song: those rhythms reaffirm the continuous, albeit slow, journey towards a robust ethnicity.

The journey motif of the poem is therefore a dual one. It not only describes the cyclical movement of memory and artistic imagination through past and present, but in another, psychologically defined, dimension, it also describes the progression of a certain kind of ethnic psyche groping towards self-definitions that are rooted in humane criteria. This kind of progression has an accumulative effect in that, like the cyclical movement, it brings together the groups and experiences of the New World black—the dreams of Panama boys (West Indian migrant workers at the Panama Canal), the language of the urban black American, and the images of West Indian slums. But unlike the cyclical movement, the progressive structure sets forth these groups and experiences in a sequential pattern. That is, even as one mode (the cyclical) impresses us with the essential repetitions and circularity of the black experience in Africa and the New World, the other mode (a sense of progression) suggests that the archetypes representing those repetitions also establish a clearly defined movement towards a certain kind of perception, as they pass before the reader in succession—Uncle Tom, the black spade, and then the Jamaican Rastafarian (Ras).

This psychic progression is usually underlined in the poem by a corresponding shift in language, a strategy which demonstrates Brathwaite's formidable versatility in handling a variety of musical and colloquial rhythms. Consequently the cool, hip bluster of the black spade's American ghetto gives way to the stately flow of Ras' language:

> rise rise
> leh we
> laugh
> dem, stop
> dem an' go
> back back
> to the black
> man lan'
> back back
> to Af-
> rica.

> (p. 42)

The impressive impact of the language transforms the usually self-deluding Back-to-Africa argument with a new forceful energy: the theme now connotes a racial or cultural rebirth rather than a literal return to Africa, and on this allegorical basis the theme reflects an expanding and aggressive, rather than merely self-defensive or angrily insecure self-consciousness. This moral and emotional incisiveness which distinguishes Ras from the earlier archetypes is heightened by a style which combines the spiritual fervor of the gospel song with the rhythms of the language of Jamaica's urban poor. In one sense the weight of Ras' ethnic awareness and the thrust of his moral outrage do go hand in hand with the pathetic wish fulfillment of an impotent rage—especially when he calls down flames of retribution on an unjust social order:

> from on high dem
> raze an' roar dem
> an' de poor dem
> rise an' rage dem
> in de glory of the Lord.

> (p. 44)

But in another sense, notwithstanding that element of wish fulfillment, the mere fact of Ras' anger represents a real threat to the future of Babylon (the established

order), particularly since Ras' rage, unlike that of the spade's, expresses a fairly coherent and consistent sense of ethnic integrity.

Once again the sense of a progression (represented here by Ras' ethnicity) is linked with the cyclical structure of historical repetition. Thus the threat of a destructive flame in Ras' contemporary Jamaica recalls the fires of death and destruction in the slavetrader's raids of the past. If Ras' consciousness represents a progression of awareness, the flame motif underlines the cyclical persistence of the conditions against which he is striking. Moreover these dual movements of cycle and progression are incorporated in Ras' personality and style. His Back-to-Africa platform repeats a long-lived black dream in the New World, as old as the black presence in the New World; the gospel-song echoes of his language recall the style of Uncle Tom. But, on the other hand, the old Back-to-Africa theme is integrated with the new urgency of a psychological journey of discovery into one's self; and in this vein the contemporary dialect of the urban Jamaican poor expresses the new urgency and a new militancy. Style and structure have become psychological experiences within the poem. This is the kind of dual movement that informs the role of the calypso in the description of West Indian poverty and social injustice. The calypso is a sardonic salute to deep-rooted inequities: "*Some people doin' well / while others are catchin' hell*" (p. 48). On this level its function is cyclical, for it is really a reminder that the injustices of the present, postindependent period actually repeat the harsh brutality through which the modern West Indies were born: "The islands roared into green plantations / ruled by silver sugar cane" (p. 47). But while the calypsonian's song demonstrates the historical cycles of West Indian poverty and injustice, as folk art it is a corrosively satiric insight that represents an attitudinal and strategic progression from Uncle Tom's guileful but self-protective deference.

"The Return" which concludes *Rights of Passage* should therefore be read in the dual context of cycle and progression which Brathwaite has been developing throughout the work and which is so well integrated in the figure of Ras and in the role of the calypso. The physical return of the West Indian migrant from his North American exile represents a full psychic cycle, in terms of memory and in terms of the artistic imagination. For the Caribbean to which he returns is marked by the age-old problems of colonial, or neocolonial, violence (the United States versus Cuba), racial exploitation and anger (Black Power riots in Aruba and Trinidad), national leaders who are under attack for having merely substituted themselves for the old colonial masters, and at the bottom of the pile as usual, the poor who are now beginning to "catch their royal asses" (pp. 61-62).

Here too the cyclical experience is integrated with the sense of a progression in the individual's, or more precisely the archetype's, perception. The returning exile therefore communicates a matured consciousness, in contrast with the limited militancy of the spade, for example. That consciousness is manifest in the overview of the Caribbean to which he returns: in other words, the very ability to comprehend the cyclical patterns of West Indian history and culture represents a significant progression from the spade's angry indifference to history. This level of awareness is also implicit in the intensely felt identification with the poor folk, not merely by way of the rhetoric of moral indignation, but also by way of that easy slide into the colloqualism of the folk ("catch their royal asses"): in a work in which shifts in language and style are so closely patterned on subjective experience, that slide into the language of the folk is significant. Moreover this kind of perception is really identical to the perspectives of folk art and Brathwaite's own poetry: it shares with the poetic imagination the creative memory which traces historical cycles, the moral energy to generate a sense of psychic progression, and as a result of all these the ability to see the West Indian situation by being aware of its repetitive inequities as well as its creative energies.

At this point in his maturation our returning exile is ready to re-evaluate Uncle Tom:

> No one
> knows Tom now, no one cares.
> Slave's days are past, for-
> gotten. The faith, the dream denied,
> the things he dared not do, all lost, if unforgiven.
>
> (p. 72)

Tom's reappearance heightens the impression of Brathwaite's cyclical structure. The re-evaluation of his character represents the moral and intellectual progression of the exile. That progression is also implied by the more complex view of history itself: the old self-hate and the more recent insecurity of the bellicose spade have given way to a realization that black history can be perceived positively as a creative process rather than as mere "nothing." Creation is the most important kind of historical heritage that there is, especially the kind of creation that is rooted in a growing sense of one's humanity. In this sense history as creation must be distinguished from history as building things through slavery, through the "love- / less toil" of others: it is love, less toil (p. 80). Like Walcott's castaway figure and like the redefiners of West Indian history in modern West Indian poetry, Brathwaite's creators are really analogous to the artistic imagination. And, finally, Walcott's West Indian Adam who bestows new names and identities on the old nothingness of the New World is succeeded in this work by Brathwaite's Noah, that second Adam who stands as a "fully aware" West Indian

in the ruins of an old tradition contemplating the possibilities of the new order that must be created, and realizing that there is "no turning back" (p. 86).

II *MASKS*

Masks, the next work in the trilogy, is also rooted in the strategy of developing a full awareness through the cyclical course of memory and art. Here the persistent journey motif describes the West Indian's cultural pilgrimage to West Africa. That pilgrimage is a literal and physical one. But it is also psychic, linking the West Indian's modern return to his Akan beginnings with the period in which his ancestors were torn from West Africa by the slave trade and with that even earlier period when those precolonial ancestors sought new homes for the first time in West Africa. The total effect of this simultaneous perception of time cycles is to re-emphasize time itself as an essentially cyclical, or circular whole. It is therefore appropriate that the work opens with a ceremony of libation that celebrates the cycle of time in the year that has "come round / again" (p. 5). Moreover, this impression of a cyclical wholeness also rests on the continental dimensions of Africa, the cultural affinities between its distinctive regions, and most important that cyclical perception of time and experience which the poet shares with his Africans: "all Africa / is one, is whole" (p. 3).

The making of the drums which follows the libation therefore becomes not simply the production of an artifact in the Western sense, but a ritual which confirms simultaneously: the cyclical wholeness that Akan culture perceives in experience; the manner in which that sense of wholeness has been transmitted to Afro-West Indian culture; and a reflection of that wholeness in the actual making of the drum. Consequently, the construction of the drum requires the union of male (the skin of a goat) and female (the hollowed wood of the duru), and this union re-enacts the timeless, universal principle of life and fertility. The combination of the duru wood with the goatskin rather than with the more traditional elephant-skin, represents the continuity of West African and Afro-West Indian cultures since the goatskin drum is characteristic of Brathwaite's Caribbean. The cultural significance of the drum in both Akan and Afro-West Indian culture therefore underscores the poet's sense of continuities—the birth of West Indian culture out of the enslavement of the West African, the creation of the drum itself out of the death of goat and tree, and in all these the continuous cycle of life, death, and re-creation. Finally this organic relationship between the drum and the created world emphasizes that art is not separate from society and experience but is the very essence of both: art and artist speak out of and on behalf of a communally perceived experience in which the drum can be the voice of Odomankoma the Creator himself.

The drum, itself a symbol of history's cycles, now represents the artistic imagination of the poet himself in his vision of West African and West Indian history. The main thrust of that vision in *Masks* is to bridge the gulf, in the popular imagination, between the West Indian present and its West African sources, and to demonstrate the dependence of a vital West Indian identity on an acceptance of the general wholeness of black history. To these ends the poem evokes the past and the present cycles of West African (Akan) culture in highly immediate and concrete terms. Consequently the precolonial West African of *Masks* is never presented solely with reference to that precolonial history. The drum's recall of the Akan past is the West Indian's memory of the periods of slavery and colonialism and the West Indian's impressions of the West African present. The arrival of the ancestral "pathfinders" to new homes in West Africa is therefore described in terms that evoke memories of the white slaver's incursion and the modern West Indian's return:

> well have you walked
> have you journeyed
> welcome.
> You who have come
> back a stranger
> after three hundred years. . . .
> So beware
> cried Akyere
> beware
> the clear
> eyes, the near
> ships. . . .

> (pp. 37, 41)

Whereas the full awareness into which the archetype grows in *Rights* depends upon accepting the cycles of New World history, in *Masks* that progression is now integrated with an awareness of the cycles of West African and New World history. To grasp the West African past in its totality is to come to terms with the complex nature of the West Indian identity, black history, and the nature of history itself. The West African market with its flies "clotting" the entrails of the meat stalls and with its trinkets pulls the memory back to the slaver's trinkets which led to the blood-clotted birth of the West Indies. The fallen trees of Nyame the African Creator have given way to the Christian cross, and the Christian's bells have silenced the drums of the African God; but in contemplating these West African endings in the present, the West Indian also acknowledges a sense of kinship, which signals the new beginnings of his self-identification:

> My scattered
> clan, young-
> est kinsmen,
> fever's dirge
> in their wounds,
> rested here.

> (p. 47)

The return of the West Indian is therefore a total immersion into both his past and present, or to borrow Brathwaite's imagery, he has returned "eating time like a mud-fish" (p. 51). And this kind of immersion is emphasized by the poet's language. His contemporary English is endowed with rhythms and with a metaphoric texture that recaptures the cadence of the Ashanti king's ceremonial exchange with his subjects:

> When the worm's knife cuts
> the throat of a tree, what will happen?
> It will die
> When a cancer has eaten the guts
> of a man, what will surely happen?
> He will die.

> (p. 58)

In invoking the cadences of the Akan language, Brathwaite creates a linguistic symbol of his West Indian's immersion into the West African sources of his identity. In turn that immersion confirms the essential connections between things, beings, and eras in the wholeness of experience, connections that are celebrated here by the precise network of question-and-refrain between king and subjects. And the West Indian's immersion into the African's ceremonial reminder of life-and death is essential to the West Indian's rebirth into a renewed cultural identity. This too is the function of the mask. In donning the Akan mask the West Indian assumes the spiritual and cultural significance that is inherent in the mask as it is in the drum:

> . . . I return
> walking these burnt-
> out streets, brain limp-
> ing pain, masked
> in this wood, straw
> and thorns, seek-
> ing the dirt of the com-
> pound where my mother
> buried the thin breed-
> ing worm that grew
> from my heart.

> (p. 65)

In effect, his cultural self-exploration by way of the art of the mask exemplifies the function of art as memory.

III *ISLANDS*

The circular movement of art and memory also takes us back, in the other direction, to the Caribbean starting-point of *Rights of Passage.* And this return is the main subject of *Islands,* the final book of the trilogy. The major divisions of this work are centered on the growing consciousness with which the West Indian returns from the memories of, and journey to Africa, **"New World"** therefore represents both the New World ambience of the West Indian and the new possibilities that are inherent in the West Indian's recreated consciousness; **"Limbo"** recalls the legendary roots of the dance as an exercise for slaves immediately after disembarkation from the slave-ships, and in so doing it celebrates the West Indian endurance despite slavery; **"Rebellion"** offers reminders of the old plantation systems, emphasizes their continuation under new, post-colonial disguises, into the present, and by virtue of those reminders its title becomes a prophecy or threat; **"Possession"** picks up the rebellious, transforming energies of **"Rebellion"** by offering the contrast between islanders as possessions and islands as symbols of a new dignity or integrity: "possession" as spiritual possession (in the manner of folk religions from Africa and the West) therefore celebrates the new, aggressive consciousness within Brathwaite's West Indian. And in a fitting conclusion to the circular structure of the trilogy as a whole, the carnival dance of **"Beginnings"** recalls the folk songs and dance with which *Rights of Passage* opens: in this concluding section the dance celebrates the beginnings of a national consciousness that has been derived from the total experience, or historical "rites," of the Middle Passage.

On the whole the return to the West Indies is marked by an awareness of African cultural traditions interacting with a dominant Western culture. The black musician's saxophone recalls Nairobi's male elephants uncurling their "trumpets to heaven." But the setting ("pale rigging") is decidedly Western, presided over by the North American God of "typewriter teeth" and glass skyscrapers (p. 3). But, in turn, that Western God coexists, in the West Indian's perception, with the African-derived Jah of Jamaica's Rastafarians and with Ananse, the West Indian folk hero who traces his lineage back to the spider-god of the Ashanti past. Ananse's webs are the visual counterpart of the "webs of sound" which are the musical and linguistic links between the West Indies and West Africa, past and present; and he is the emblem of the contemporary West Indian spinning webs of memory to fashion a new identity: he is the artist, existing at the center of the historical and communal patterns that represent his West Indian experience. Ananse as African archetype and Afro-West Indian artist is also counterbalanced by the symbols which Brathwaite adapts from Western literature to his West Indian themes. In the West Indian beach setting the one-eyed merchant-sailor of Eliot's *Wasteland* appears in the "bleached / stare of the one- / ey'd beach." The Caribbean fisherman repairing his nets recalls the life-death eternity of Eliot's Fisher King; and he is also endowed, by way of his blindness, with the poet-seer identity of Eliot's Tiresias:

> his eyes stare out like an empty shell,
> its sockets of voices, wind,
> grit, bits of conch, pebble;
> his fingers knit as the dark rejoices.

(p. 11)

The life-death cycle that is represented by the Fisher King and the cosmic perception of the artistic imagination are now being represented by Western versions of the African symbols through which Brathwaite has been examining his West Indian situation. And as an artist knitting the "embroideries" of his net the West Indian fisherman duplicates both Eliot's Fisher King and the figure of Ananse the Ashanti spider-god. Finally, the Dahomean deity, Legba, is both the vodun ("voodoo") God of Haiti and, by virtue of his lameness, the Fisher King archetype of life-and-death in Western mythology. In short the poet's imagination has transformed the Western wasteland into a fertile source of symbols and archetypes that duplicate or supplement the African sources of the West Indian's identity. These Western symbols are being transformed into modes of an Afro-West Indian consciousness, just as the chain-shackle emblems of Western slavery have become sounds of a joyous masquerade of self-affirmation: "Shackles shackles shackles / are my peace, are my home / are my evening song" (p. 19).

In musical terms, the Afro-Western synthesis is symbolized by the pocomania drums which recall the drums of the Akan god (*Masks*) who is dumb until the drum speaks, and which express the synthesis of Western and African religions in Afro-West Indian folk worship; and the steelband music of the carnival is another symbol of the synthesis—Afro-Caribbean rhythms pounded out of the oil drum discards of Western technology. In terms of ritual, the rites of the African drum in the Akan past have given way to the rites of cricket, one of the more enduring ceremonies of British rule. But the language and perception suggest that here too the inherited tradition has been transformed into a vital self-expressiveness:

> Boy, dis is *cricket*. . . .
> all de flies that was buzzin' out there
> round de bread carts; could'a hear
> if de empire fart.

(p. 45)

On the one hand, the speaker's enthusiasm for cricket amounts to a wry tribute to the thorough effectiveness of the game as an imperial rite which subliminally encourages acceptance of the Empire itself. But on the other hand, the fervent partisanship (*our* West Indian cricketers versus the British *visitors*) takes us back to the central issue of the West Indian as rebellious Caliban, subversively adopting the inherited institutions of the Empire. The declarative "dis is *cricket*" implies an assertive kind of redefinition that wrenches "cricket" from the colonizer's polished "gentility" to a candid partisanship; the candor and the self-assertiveness are reinforced by that reference to buzzing flies, recalling as it does the ancestral memories of the West African market in *Masks*; and that ebullient mockery of empire ("de empire fart") carries with it the threat of a detached, even rebellious, perspective.

That rebelliousness is more fully developed in the cyclical motifs of the **"Rebellion"** section of *Islands*. The contemporary rumblings in Brathwaite's West Indies continue an established tradition of resistance to equally entrenched patterns of poverty and injustice. In this section the ritual of the wake sets the stage for the recall and celebration of the rebellious tradition. From a historical viewpoint, the slaves' wake for the dead acknowledges the death of freedom, but since the Afro-Caribbean tradition of the wake includes the sending of the spirit back to ancestral Africa then the ceremony is also a ritualistic act of memory, a cherishing of the idea of freedom, and therefore a covert form of resistance. Moreover, the destructive impact of slavery is counter-balanced here by the cultural continuity that is implied by the African memories of the wake. Finally Brathwaite's word-play (wake as death ritual and wake as awakening) reinforces the idea of a renaissance from psychological as well as physical slavery—a progression that has evolved through the cycles of black history. Conversely, those whose rebellion has been superficial rather than substantive have emerged as the new successors to the old colonial overlords:

> it is not enough
> to be pause to be hole
> to be void, to be silent
> to be semicolon, to be semicolony.
>
> (p. 67)

And by a similar token, an escapist zeal for the folk has nothing to do with a genuinely creative quest for a new life. Someone like Tizzic loves the carnival in this escapist sense, using it to get away from the confinement of poverty. But he is really a mere slave of the carnival's heady escapism. And when carnival is finished he is still a slave to the things which prompted the temporary escape: "After the *bambalula bambulai /* he was a slave again" (p. 105).

On the whole, then, the progression to a full ethnic consciousness in Brathwaite's work does not depend on the exclusive Westernisms of the "semicolon," the semicolonial mentality. Neither is it to be realized through a facile escape to a romanticized image of the folk and of the African heritage. Instead that full consciousness represents the usual West Indian preoccupation with harmonizing European, New World, and African sources. In effect, the progressive development of a mature cultural identity involves the acceptance of the cyclical wholeness of one's history. To grasp one's history and identity in this way is to be possessed, in a manner of speaking:

> A yellow note of sand dreams in the polyp's eye;
> the coral needs this pain. . . .

> And slowly, slowly
> uncurling embryo
> leaf's courses sucking armour,
> my yellow pain swims into the polyp's eye.
>
> (pp. 75, 77)

The painful metamorphosis from polyp to coral to island is an allegory of that progression which culminates in the spiritual possession of a full awareness. **"Possession"** in this sense contrasts with the status of possession—as slave or colonial possession. Viewed in this light the leopard which appears in the **"Possession"** section is Brathwaite's symbol of a collective West Indian consciousness. Its cage is a reminder of its status as a captive, as a possession. And in geographical terms the West Indian's island-identity offers similar reminders about his relationship with the West:

> Caught therefore in this care-
> ful cage of glint rock,
> water ringing the islands'
> doubt.
>
> (p. 87)

But the leopard's very awareness of what its cage means inspires a fierce determination to destroy its captivity: it is possessed by the need to be free. And this transformation from possession as subject to possession as purpose conforms with the central course of progressive growth in Brathwaite's work. The **"Beginning"** segment of *Islands* therefore marks both the end of the old experience of possession and the beginning of a new phase of awareness. In this context the carnival road march is no longer an escape, as it is for Tizzic and for Boysie, his counterpart in Walcott's "Mass Man." Instead it is the joyous celebration of new beginnings in which hearts, "no longer bound," are now making with their rhythms "some- / thing torn / and new" (pp. 112-113). The joyousness with which Brathwaite envisages the sense of beginnings, of progressive growth, provides his work with an artfully devised sense of resolutions. The device is not unconvincing: it flows naturally enough from the accumulative sense of progression or growth which the poet derives from a complex, cyclical vision of the West Indian experience.

The final note of joyousness suggests one of the central paradoxes of Brathwaite's achievement: the remarkable complexities which he discovers in the cyclical arrangement of his universe are never really complemented by equally complex emotional responses to that universe. Precisely because Brathwaite's art emphasizes a communal rather than individualized view of the artist's role, his poetry tends to elicit a limited response to his poetic experience as individual experience. He is always brilliant, and he is never simplistic. The carefully controlled vision and the carefully crafted design complement each other superbly, but the designer remains at a far more impersonal distance from the reader than does any other West Indian poet of major significance. This is not a defect in itself: the trilogy does deserve its reputation as the most important piece of West Indian literature on the relationship between the West Indian's Western and African sources. But it does suggest that Brathwaite still has further to grow as a poet, to allow for the development of an emotional complexity and immediacy that will match his formidable insights as poet-historian, and to permit the sense of contradictions which would, for example, balance the climactic celebration of beginnings with a realistic awareness of old attitudes.

Notes

1. See, for example, Patricia Ismond, "Walcott versus Brathwaite," *Caribbean Quarterly,* 17, 3-4 (Sept.-Dec. 1971), 54-71.

2. References to Edward Brathwaite's poetry are based on his *Rights of Passage* (London: Oxford, 1967); *Masks* (London: Oxford, 1968); and *Islands* (London: Oxford, 1969).

John Povey (essay date autumn 1987)

SOURCE: Povey, John. "The Search for Identity in Edward Brathwaite's *The Arrivants.*" *World Literature Written in English* 27, no. 2 (autumn 1987): 274-89.

[*In the following essay, Povey characterizes* The Arrivants *as a description of Brathwaite's personal search for identity that resonates with an overarching quest for a Caribbean identity.*]

> Once when we went to Europe, a rich old lady asked:
> Have you no language of your own
> no way of doing things
> did you spend all those holidays
> at England's apron strings?[1]

A central theme in Caribbean literature is the absence of a national or regional identity. History denied the residents of these islands the common process that formulates group cohesion. The iniquitous slave trade established African origins which constitute the ultimate inheritance, but that remains folk memory against which present experience is measured, rather than a system which can be adopted directly. A nearer impact derives from the consequences of white colonial behaviour reinforced by the impress of the English language and educational curriculum that produces an antagonistic tension. That sequence of African origin followed by slavery, cultural deprivation, economic exploitation and partial if resented assimilation is the cultural history of the Caribbean. It matches closely the history of American blacks. By deliberate policy in both regions, African religious and linguistic usages were forbidden, for they offered a unifying basis for a threatening resistance. For this reason, the subsequent development of an identifying culture needs to be assembled from limited retentions incorporated into the customs of the dominant system. The new would have to be the offspring of the foreign past.

In the Caribbean, white residents were a small minority and were later abandoned by an indifferent and declining mother country. Nationhood was possible as it could never be for black Americans, but, unlike other colonial territories, countries in this region did not, with independence, automatically re-acquire an indigenous culture that had tenaciously resisted imposed adaptation to European ways. There was a cultural void that needed to be filled with the construction of a specific Caribbean identity. This had to be woven from the three distinct threads that had influenced the growth of this society: an awareness of the African heritage, a vague but emotional sense of alliance with other blacks in the Americas and the inevitable continuance of the colonial social structure.

This excessive and generalized preamble brings me to the poetry of Edward Brathwaite. In this present context I will not make estimation of his qualities as a poet, although I believe him to be a good one. He is capable of exploiting an original and precise English diction for his purpose as effectively as the much admired Derek Walcott. In a manner which may well offend the precepts of the scholars of literature, I want to discuss *content* rather than form. That great axiom of departments of literature that "form and content are inseparable" must suffer temporary remission. The particular themes and *subjects* that stimulate a writer may be highly informative and reveal concerns which are crucial for understanding literary development. Subject alone cannot determine poetic consequence, but it may indicate the existence of pertinent agitations that hint at the direction future literary endeavour will follow.

It must be emphasized that this is a deliberately limited interpretation. Gordon Rohlehr in his impressive study *Pathfinder* (1981) has demonstrated the remarkable complexity and profundity of Brathwaite's work. This lengthy critical study unravels the depth of associative imagery the poet brings to bear in his lines. Against such detailed scholarship, brief and partial examination may appear trivial. But selection permits emphasis. It may allow Brathwaite's lines to throw light on the cultural and literary situation in the Caribbean without doing gross injustice to the many remaining elements which contribute to the technical distinction of his important work. Those other factors are set aside, only temporarily, to achieve a particular focus in the present paper.

In *The Arrivants* Edward Brathwaite exemplifies the bewildered and bitter sense of confused isolation which is so constant a topic in Caribbean writing. Its content was determined by his intention to explore alternative lives in those parts of the world which have influenced Caribbean behaviour. His venture is described in what amounts to a precise and imaginative diary. *The Arrivants* (1973) incorporates in a pre-determined trilogy three books of poetry originally published separately: *Rights of Passage* (1967), *Masks* (1968), and *Islands* (1969). This triple collection pursues an individual and cultural hegira in search of some personal accommodation to the different elements that have shaped his life. Implicitly his private discovery will provide the basis for the more general principles upon which a Caribbean culture could be formulated.

The sense of Africa is omnipresent in the poetry of Brathwaite. It defines his awareness both as a person and a writer, but it is tested against other Caribbean alternatives for acculturation. His first volume responds to the neo-African world in the first leg of what he calls "the triangular trade of my historical origins." The second, *Masks,* specifically draws upon his sojourn in Ghana. With *Islands* he returns, his vision illuminated by his explorations, and his rediscovery is the essential topic.

His first work constitutes both a personal and ethnic exploration. *Rights of Passage* is a pun on the ritual found in many regions of the African continent where the "rites" of passage represent a concrete transition, usually into maturity and manhood, with all the accompanying expectations of sexual awakening and initiation into conventional and established society. Brathwaite adds to this his "right" to discover his "birthright" denied by slavery. On a record cover he describes how his poem "is based on my own experience of that triple journey. In my case from the Caribbean to Europe to West Africa and back home again . . . to illustrate what home—or lack of home—means to those who up to now have been unable to afford the luxury of mythology."[2] That latter is a significant word because all poetry is ultimately based upon mythology, and only when this is established can it prove to be the basis for a national literature.

In this first collection Brathwaite comes of age as he advances into maturer awareness. The pun on "right" is linked to the West Indian admission that discovery of self or society requires "passage." Only absence from the islands can achieve that "distancing"—from which an understanding can come. Having come *from* Africa and having been occupied and administered by colonialists from overseas, only travelling *away,* a voyage matching or recapitulating those past enforced travels, can provide the Caribbean poet with the understanding from which the indigenous West Indian experience can

be re-encountered and absorbed into a personal and national future.

Brathwaite's *Rights of Passage* begins with memories. One can reverse the order of the opening stanza, called "**Prelude,**" to see the origin of his spirit, a compound of anger and despair out of which he develops an urgent poetic longing:

> I sing
> I shout
> I groan
> I dream
> about . . .
> Drum skin whip
> lash, master's sun's
> cutting edge of
> heat, taut
> surfaces of things. . . .
>
> (p. 4)

In "**New World A-coming**" there is some appeal to the earlier African glory, but the emphasis is on loss and the title thereby given ironic force. Brathwaite recalls the disasters that were inflicted upon the African heroes and goes on to the desperate rhetorical appeal:

> O who now will help
> us, help-
> less, horse-
> less, leader-
> less, no
> hope. . . .
>
> (p. 10)

Historical colonial government by "these hard men, cold / clear-eye'd" (p. 11) will provide no hope for them. No liberation can be expected from "no / Hawkins, no / Cortez to come . . ." (p. 10). No outsider, even by incest when "our blood, mixed / soon with their passion . . ." (p. 11), will create the alternatives for West Indians. From the poems, at this point, there is only an empty negation. Africa cannot be called upon to redress the enforcement of the colonial world, for on that continent too colonialists have imposed their domination. The penalties are recorded:

> Prempeh imprisoned,
> Tawiah dead
> Asantewa bridled
> and hung.
>
> (p. 10)

Finding no political sustenance, the poet turns to the heroes of the New World, seeking their power to redress the abasement of Africa and the present humiliation of the Caribbean:

> O who now can help
> us: Geronimo, Tackie,
> Montezuma to come.
>
> (p. 19)

The cry is to the Latin American revolutionaries who resisted and still were defeated. He cannot appeal directly to his own past since the present West Indians are themselves interlopers, savagely imposed upon indigenous Indian civilizations. They differed from the covetous European settlers because they came as possessions, not conquerors. They have joined the union of the oppressed, sharing closer ties with the dispossessed than with colonialists among whom they occupied their islands for centuries.

As Brathwaite contemplates the present situation, there is little cheer. The colonial inheritance has given the population an omnipresent sense of defeat.

> But help—
> less my children are
> caught leader-
> less are
> taught fool-
> ishness and use-
> lessness and
> sorrow.
>
>   (p. 14)

Brathwaite's angry frustration at deculturation persists, but he makes clear this is not the termination of experience. For him there remains a minimal but persistent optimism, the more sustaining because founded on a mood close to despair. He repeats Aimé Césaire's violent rejection of active success as the measure of civilized consequence. Like the French poet, Brathwaite appeals for an alternative standard to power:

> for we who have achieved nothing
> work
> who have not built
> dream
> who have forgotten all
> dance
> and dare to remember . . . the paths. . . .
>
>   (p. 13)

One memory which counters the limitations of contemporary history reaffirms the links of the Caribbean to Africa, the continent of origin. This remote inheritance is recalled by the poet, but his pessimistic rhetorical question indicates that only limited belief remains:

> we kept
> our state on golden stools—remember?
>
>   (p. 18)

He recognizes that salvation cannot lie in such distant association even when its memory has been allowed:

> Yes, I remember . . .
> but what good
> is recollection now
> my own mock
> me
>
>   (p. 18)

Cherished antecedents of historical glory cannot survive against the persistent colonial oppression that makes the cruel present:

> Boss man makes rules:
> who works, who jerks
> the rope, who rips
> the patient dirt.
> Boss man makes rules:
> I am his patient mule.
>
>   (p. 18)

A personal experience, oscillating between a memoried but irrelevant African glory and present humiliation, requires both a biographical and a psychological reappraisal. The examination can only occur outside these islands and necessitates painful exile. Sadly, almost petulantly, the poet inquires about the obligation of travel:

> These my children?
> God, you hear them? . . .
> When release
> from further journey?
>
>   (p. 21)

The answer to this plea is "Not yet," "Not now." Only after wide-ranging travel and experience can this supplicant explorer return to his own hearth, a different and more self-aware person. His acceptance is found in the deliberately colloquial term borrowed from the idiom of jazz, which incorporated the emotions of all New World blacks—"Didn't He Ramble." It is a wry comment on the formative years of the poet's development:

> So to New York London
> I finally come
> hope in my belly
> hate smothered down
> to the bone
> to suit the part
> I am playing.
>
>   (p. 22)

The pilgrimage was devoutly planned to inspect the non-Caribbean world that influenced his upbringing. The mood is of "hope in my belly." But the actual experiences do not fulfil the optimistic expectation of the discovery of cultural antecedents which drove him to this foreign inspection. The scene is violent and vicious. America offers no welcoming arms to the questing supplicant of a black allegiance:

> In New York
> nights are hot.
> In Harlem, Brooklyn,
>
>   . . . . .
>
> Police cars wail
> like babies
> an ambulance erupts
> like breaking glass.
>
>   (p. 54)

Temporarily settled in New York, he looks out at its harsh ugliness:

> In my small hired
> room, stretched out upon the New
> York Herald Tribune, pages
> damp from dirty lots, from locked
> out parks, from gutters: dark, tired,
> deaf, cold, too old to care to catch
> alight the quick match of your pity,
> I died alone. . . .
>
> (p. 22)

The vision of New York is grimy and gloomy. Hardships dismay the poet. Physical survival is a battle in a bitter world where "wind / cut my face with its true / Gillette razor blades" (p. 22). The suffering is more painful as he yearns for his tropic island "where the warm wind / blows" (p. 23). Psychologically more damaging is the disillusion that follows the personal encounters long anticipated as offering exciting confirmation. His American experience destroys the ignorance that sustained his optimistic expectation that escape from the Caribbean might lie in emulation of American black society, which shares the same history of slavery and segregation. Rather he saw sleaziness and greed as the consequence of racism:

> But my sons grow fat, grow
> fat, far from the slow guitar.
> See them zoot suits, man? Them black
> Texan hats? Watch false teeth
> flash: fake friendship. . . .
>
> (p. 23)

The culture which sustains these vulgar slickers is unconvincing and unsympathetic. Its emulation could bring the same spiritual nullity to his own islands, providing them with the same grasping mentality:

> it's now grab the can, grab all
> you can and give it to your
> selves. . . .
>
> (p. 23)

Brathwaite's experience of North America permits no enthusiasm for a unity postulated on blackness. There has to be an alternative for his inspection. After this New York encounter he does not return to the islands but "rambles on," experimenting with further personal and geographic exploration. He begins by pursuing the second element in the triple association of Caribbean society. England, the ex-colonial power, must now be experienced. He joins **"The Emigrants"** who have turned to England for their survival.

> So you have seen them
> with their cardboard grips,
> felt hats, rain-
> cloaks. . . .

> These are The Emigrants.
> On sea-port quays
> at air-ports
> anywhere. . . .
>
> (p. 51)

Many set out on this pilgrimage, but in this distant land, near in history but remote in climate, they encounter only day-by-day misery and rejection. "The men who lever ale / in stuffy woodbine pubs / don't like us much" (p. 55). Brathwaite rapidly recognizes that this second destination fulfils none of his hopes. He is driven to ask on behalf of others the rhetorical question:

> What do they hope for
> what find there
> these New World mariners
> Columbus coursing kaffirs. . . .
>
> (p. 52)

The bitter humour of the last line, ironically reversing the direction of colonial emigration, applies equally to the poet who shared this instinct to escape the islands. He recognizes this paradox and in confronting its implications, he finds a resolution. He must return, for the memory calls to him with irresistible strength: "But today I recapture the islands' bright beaches" (p. 57). He discovers the intensity of his commitment and inheritance: "We who are born of the ocean can never seek solace in rivers" (p. 57).

This may be true as a principle, but this traveller, like others returning "home," does not return to the idyllic dream of beaches that pervaded his dreams during temporary exile. The illuminating irony of the title **"O Dreams O Destinations"** suggestively contrasts delusive hopes and travel facts. He returns from Britain, but to no idyllic Caribbean utopia. World events have imposed themselves on the contemporary history of the region:

> But I returned to find Jack
> Kennedy invading Cuba
> black riots in Africa.
>
> (p. 60)

At some level the optimism of rose coloured memory is inevitably doomed to disappointment. Geography alone cannot provide spiritual freedom. But this discovery does not take place as an abstraction. It requires a personal familiarity which Brathwaite acknowledges in his poem **"Postlude/Home."** Sardonically he asks himself the unanswerable question that might be posed to him by the unsympathetic outsider:

> Where then is the nigger's
> home?
> In Paris Brixton Kingston

Rome? . . .
What guilt
now drives him
on?
Will exile never
end?

(p. 77)

For once the rhetoric can be answered, if in somewhat pompous phrases. When the guilt is assuaged, exile will no longer be necessary. This is the underlying reason for the poet's voyages and its resolution will be the discovery of the inner conviction of patriotism.

The concluding lines of *Rights of Passage* are revealing because they do not avoid the consequences of this exploration. They rather confirm its inevitable continuance:

of the future
to come?
There is no
turning back.

(p. 85)

Simply because the poet admits that he will not turn back, he is forced into further journeys. Neither the Afro-American society of New York nor the options available to West Indians in London provide guidance or fulfilment in his quest. A third element must be examined. The legendary and intimate association with Africa may supply him with the identity to reappraise his own culture. *Masks* examines the heritage of blackness through Ghana, where Brathwaite lived for several years.

The title may remind one of the subtle discrepancy between the external form—the social image—and the inner man who manipulates it and yet is shrouded from explicit appearance. That relationship between artist and audience becomes an important metaphor for the poet's new role. Like the African dancer, the poet seeks divorce from self and absorption into communality. His private activity must become public gesture. Contemplating Lake Chad, he senses "no peace in this world / till the soul / knows this dark water's world" (p. 105). He pursues the primary West Indian venture—to explore Africa as a source of origin, recognizing that only this discovery will bring a present harmony to a disconnected past. The first section is titled **"Pathfinders."** It suggests a bold task that artists must accept. He sees himself as a forerunner for others less aware of the consequences of indifference. It begins hopefully with a "libation."

Brathwaite's experience in Africa at first is encouraging. There is exhilaration in the new discovery of old truths. He learns of the seven kingdoms:

Songhai, Mali,
Chad, Ghana,
Tim-
buctu, Volta. . . .
comes
this song.

(p. 90)

The poet's vision of Africa covers the map. The titles record the epic empires, **"Axum," "Ougadougou," "Chad,"** and **"Timbuctu."** Their authority is impressive—dramatic in power and continuity. Yet, in **"Volta"** he poses a question that seems indicative of a deeper concern. Although taken somewhat out of context, it strikes the attention, indicating the nature of his enquiry and the question that African residence intends to resolve:

Can you expect us to establish houses here?
To build a nation here?

(p. 108)

In the sequence suggestively entitled **"Limits,"** the poet makes two comments. They are made in passing, but such thoughts begin to accumulate and indicate an underlying and persistent concern. "But the lips remember / temples, gods" (p. 113), is a line that, with its hint of "lip-service," indicates that these old temples and gods are not very convincing. Similarly, Brathwaite's comment on the desert:

. . . the desert
drifting certainties outside us

(p. 115)

separates the exterior certainties of the African landscape from the hesitant and indecisive inner search. It offers no confirmation of affiliation:

I travelled to a distant town
I could not find my mother
I could not find my father

(p. 125)

From these accumulating comments directed at his African experience, we recognize that the depth of the poet's cultural dilemma will not be resolved by examining African temples nor visiting African deserts. In **"Techiman"** the poet comments on the necessity of his search, even if it is not immediately productive:

But the way lost
is a way to be found
again.

(p. 119)

Later, with a specific and ultimately rather pathetic accusation concerning the pressures history imposes, the poet reaches a conclusion, in every sense of the word, to this part of his African travel:

This was at last the last;
this was the limit of motion;
voyages ended.

(p. 122)

The past is unconvincing and change is essential:

O new world of want, who will build the new ways,
the new ships?

(p. 122)

The conundrum is intended to be defiant and yet it remains unanswerable, as it is directed precisely at the heart of the Caribbean dilemma. If neither the old ways of Europe, the American connection, nor the African inheritance provides deliverance, "who will build new ways?" and in what direction? This sense of separation is reached only after a period of cogitation.

The poet's first reaction to Africa is of a happy discovery of racial identity. His reception is warm and unreflecting:

Akwaaba they smiled
meaning welcome . . .
welcome . . .
you who have come
back a stranger
after three hundred years. . . .

(p. 124)

The Africans recognize him affectionately as a long lost brother. After an initial delight, Brathwaite finds their response too natural and instinctive to satisfy the complex analysis that he was attempting. It was not the Africans who suffered the cultural dichotomy, and their instinctive generosity cannot assuage the substance of the poet's unanswered, and indeed unanswerable, Caribbean question, "Whose brother, now, am I?" (p. 126). His next question is more specific and apparently more negative in its sense of amazement and therefore separation: "Could these soft huts / have held me?" (p. 126). The lines carry a heavy weight of anxiety, for they challenge the ultimate connection with the racial past. There is some sense of affectionate responsiveness. Stronger is the feeling that the question cannot readily be answered by any simple agreement. Out of this anxious doubt comes the admission that the resolution will not be directly discovered in Africa. In **"Sunsum,"** he begins to talk of return:

. . . And I return,
walking these burnt-
out streets.

(p. 148)

There is no confidence in belonging. The exhilaration and the rich substance of Africa cannot convince him of identity. In a prose statement he writes of how he

"slowly, slowly, ever so slowly came to a sense of identification of myself with these people. I came to connect my history with theirs."[3]

But in his poems, he still probes the doubts rather than articulates any secure assurance. He is from elsewhere. For all its splendid vigour, Africa does not provide him with any certain sense of cultural identity. It rather forces him to acknowledge that he is a product of other worlds and other experiences, much as he might have preferred to settle any dilemma by embracing this continent. Africa is not his salvation, though it remains an affecting presence. He is compelled to follow his own racial history, back to the Caribbean. For this return to Africa must be denied, not as a continuing effect, but only as an absolute measure.

Exiled from here
to seas
of bitter edges,
whips of white worlds
strains of new
rivers,
I have returned
to you.
Not Chad,
the Niger's blood,
or Benin's
burning bronze
can save me now.

(p. 153)

In his recognition of otherness, with its attendant decision to return home, Brathwaite does not disdain the importance of the umbilical connection. There remains an element of supplication to the African oracles who "must" help and will sustain the adventures of their remote but attentive son:

Asase Yaa, Earth,
if I am going away now,
you must help me.
Divine Drummer, . . .
. . . you
must help me. . . .

(p. 156)

In the terminal lines, the acute new observation seems tentative and minimal but it is given emphasis in its repetition:

I am learning
let me succeed
I am learning
let me succeed. . . .

(p. 157)

Like *Rights of Passage, Masks* ends at dawn, a time linked to beginnings, to hopeful possibilities. Rohlehr summarizes the change of tone "in spite of the theme of disillusioned quest, one has the definite feeling that the poet is more confident of his ground."[4]

At this point Brathwaite's travels bring him back to the islands. His book *Islands* explicitly deals with his return to his birthplace. For him it is more than a convenient coming back. With some surprise he experiences a homecoming. Patriotism seems too definite and loaded a term, but he has tested and eliminated a series of alternatives and discovers home is the place of his origin.

Brathwaite does not arrive believing his renewed residence will produce automatic resolution of the divisions that sent him forth. He is, he admits, "a long way from Guinea" (p. 189). Even the poem called **"Home-coming"** does not describe any eager welcome. "No clan or kinsman turns my self respect. . . . In the yard the dog barks at the stranger" (p. 177). His attitude remains alertly cautious:

> to this new doubt
> and desert I return
> expecting nothing:
> my name burnt out.
>
> (p. 177)

There is an element of weariness at the cost of achieving this conclusion. An unspoken "even if" hovers at the beginning of his lines:

> If this is all
> I have
> if this is all
> I have
> I can travel no further.
>
> (p. 186)

He will stay, but he gains little local admiration for his explorations. Acquaintances seem indifferent to news of his adventures. What to him were significant discoveries, to others are merely travellers' tales. They are happily seduced by the tempting materialism of independence and affect indifference to information about "old immemorial legends / everyone but himself has forgotten" (p. 171).

This society has none of Africa's innocent continuity. A shiny new wealth evidences the latest form of colonial domination. International investment encourages greedy possessiveness while ignoring the production of staples on which human survival depends:

> and now I see these modern palaces have grown
> out of the soil, out of the bad habits of their crippled
>   owners
> and Chrysler stirs but does not produce cotton
> and Jupiter purrs but does not produce bread.
>
> (p. 191)

His concern increases as he witnesses the unthinking satisfaction these meretricious enterprises have engendered. Scornfully he comments on the new forms of the old domination:

> Unrighteousness of Mammon
> hotels for tourists rise on the sites
> of the old empire. . . .
>
> (p. 216)

This kind of surface prosperity does nothing for the urgent needs of the majority. It repeats and expands their historic dispossession:

> Looking through a map
> of the Antilles, you see how time
> has trapped
> its humble servants here. De-
> scendants of the slave do not
> lie in the lap
> of the more fortunate
> gods.
>
> (p. 204)

Like an impassioned Baptist preacher in the pulpit Brathwaite excoriates the sin of cultural indifference, erupting into the repetitions of public rhetoric. A dozen times he cries out "It is not enough" as he reprimands present unconcern for the honorable values:

> it is not enough to be free
> of the red white and blue
> it is not enough
> to be able to fly to Miami
> structure sky-scrapers, evacuate the moon-
> shaped seashore sands to build hotels, casinos,
>   sepulchres.
>
> (p. 223)

In his judgement the vaunted freedom from the Union Jack is an accident of politics unless it allows beneficial change. The sequence of useless construction concludes with a tomb. Such development buries the genuine Caribbean culture under a glamorous subjugation to an international elite.

This depressing recognition does not prevent him from feeling a part even of this temporarily debased society. Even the contemporary repetition of the devices of slavery does not daunt his commitment to the islands. It allows a further association: "shackles, shackles, shackles are my peace, are my home" (p. 178). From this assured base the poet plans to speak. "How then shall we succeed?" (p. 217). He feels, at first, his deficiencies, "My tongue is heavy with new language / but I cannot give birth to speech" (p. 221). He calls upon a new muse that will speak for all. Repeatedly in these late poems he talks of poetry; of its essential and urgent status in the new community. The task may need a vast effort for resuscitation. It needs **"Rebellion"** against the present lost state of the art:

> For the Word has been destroyed
> and cannot live among us . . .

For the Word is peace
and is absent from our streets.

(p. 212)

There is pessimism but no surrender as Brathwaite sees that he himself must become the poet who will expound the present experience and point the way to the future. He will compose his verse out of the social death:

But if to live here
is to die
I will sing songs of the skeleton.

(p. 219)

He calls the fifth section of his poem "a beginning," and it exposes the cyclic nature of the construction of this trilogy while it reflects the poet's own circular journey back to his origins. To invent these new "songs" language must be freed "from the skeleton." He attacks again the spiritual destruction, this time as it affects the crux of the poetic art, **"The Word."** Like citizens, language also must be freed from its servitude to the surrounding materialism. In a series of appeals he demands some alternative to the debasement of communication when it serves only "to pray to Barclay's bankers on the telephone / to Jesus Christ by short wave radio" (p. 223). Words are vital and serious because they do not merely reflect, they create:

I
must be given words to shape my name . . .
I
must be given words to refashion futures.

(p. 223)

It is not only the present that the poet observes. He will make his poetry a means to advance the destiny of these islands. That can only be achieved when

The Word becomes
again a god and walks among us . . .
on this ground
on this broken ground.

(p. 266)

The original foundations have crumbled but Brathwaite's repetition indicates that it is over the same ground that the new culture must be erected, though now there appear insurmountable difficulties:

We seek we seek
but find no one to speak
the words to save us.

(p. 212)

Brathwaite's *Arrivants* in total makes a fervent beginning that reflects the Caribbean more than the impress of the world that has offered these islands so little in the past. The trilogy establishes the philosophical and technical basis for important books that follow. Their success required Brathwaite's effort to determine a new identity from which poetry could forge a national regional originality. *Arrivants* cleared away the external barriers to a new creativity. Let us allow the poet, as is always appropriate, the last word.

To hell
with Af-
rica
to hell
with Eu-
rope too,
just call my blue
black bloody spade
a spade and kiss
my ass, o-
kay? So
let's begin.

(p. 29)

Notes

1. *The Arrivants* (London: Oxford University Press, 1973), p. 55. Further references are incorporated in the text.

2. Quoted in Gordon Rohlehr, *Pathfinder* (Trinidad, 1981), p. 48.

3. "Timehri," *Savacou*, No. 2 (1970), p. 38.

4. Rohlehr, *Pathfinder*, p. 163.

Gordon Rohlehr and E. A. Markham (essay date 1987)

SOURCE: Rohlehr, Gordon, and E. A. Markham. "Rohlehr on Brathwaite." In *Hinterland: Caribbean Poetry from the West Indies & Britain*, edited by E. A. Markham, pp. 109-16. Newcastle on Tyne, UK: Blood-axe Books, 1995.

[*In the following interview, Rohlehr, an authority on Brathwaite's poetry, expresses admiration for Brathwaite's growth as an artist and reflects on the critical reaction to Brathwaite's work, especially among Caribbean writers.*]

There are a number of possible ways I might have gone about it. I could have selected a number of concerns in the **Trilogy** [*The Arrivants*], for example, spoken about imagery. I felt that as a first exploratory work on the **Trilogy** I should retrace in my criticism the journey which the **Trilogy** was about. The **Trilogy** is about a journey, or several journeys, which are all tributaries of a single journey. And it's interesting when you take that line, how many things come together. For example, I used that word tributaries, right away you've got the river, and the image of several branches coming in to form a stream, and you've got the idea of the trail. Then you've got that central image in the Trilogy of Anancy, the spider's web. You can see the spider's web, the trail, the river, the strands, the themes, all come together in such an intricate way that what you have is a network or a web; several tissues or strands joining together.

There is a remarkable coherence in what Eddy was doing in the **Trilogy**. One exciting way of approaching Eddy would be to jump in anywhere, or you might take a single word or a single image and see what has happened to this throughout the thing, and you find yourself moving in all kinds of directions. I decided that I'd take the chronological approach poem by poem, right through to the end. On the other hand I decided that I must also capture something of the sense of growth and the dimension that you gain as you move through the **Trilogy**.

You ask me about the criticism of Eddy's work. One of the things I have found is that for all the acclaim that his work has got, there isn't really much authoritative statement on the work. You've had this mixture of admiration and reservation, a grudging kind of admiration, particularly among Caribbean critics. There are some who have been in many ways overtly or covertly really quite hostile. Now you find that there is much less written about *Masks* even though there is Maureen Warner-Lewis's special work on *Masks*. She digs into all the sources on what he has done, in fact I deliberately said in my study that I am not going to do that in *Masks* because it has already been done by Maureen.

The general reaction in the Caribbean is one of not really wanting to open themselves up to the African experience. The African experience has been censored out of us, and we have learned to censor ourselves. You say Africa, you say black, and the minute you say those words, there is a sense of, why am I going on about this? Or, why am I preoccupied with the past? These notions immediately arise, and you feel that you shouldn't talk about it. Not much was said about *Masks*. Almost nothing was said about *Islands*; you can pick up ten articles but they don't say anything. So here I was feeling that the poetry is gaining in dimension, growing with every book. The words, the images and that the very 'superficiality' of which Eddy was overtly or covertly accused in *Rights of Passage,* had disappeared by the time we got to *Islands*. By that time the same people who might have criticised superficiality were not prepared to go through the effort of discovery and self discovery which was necessary if you were to come to grips with the new dimensions in *Islands*.

It struck me that this was very typical of us, that there are levels at which we are very superficial people. We talk about writers without knowing the writers. I mean there is very little autobiography in the West Indies. We literally talk about people we don't know. It is something which we need to contemplate, when we are contemplating this whole business about a biography or autobiography in the Caribbean: the concealed self, the layers and layers of *Masks,* or whatever that we create to protect us. Is this the result of some strategy which we as a people designed because our real selves were so frequently under attack? I mean parents don't tell us about the past, they don't tell us about the immediate family. You have no sense of the last generation. Our writers have been preoccupied by history; they have been preoccupied by autobiography, maybe for that very reason, that this was already an allusive thing. We grew up in the present moment, without having been given this dimension, this sense of a linkage with the past. I went into sketching the pattern of his ideas as he had expressed them in his various non-poetic statements: in his essays, in his reviews, in his articles, seeing how that mind was developing before *Rights of Passage* had begun.

Nobody in the Caribbean wants to reassess the African presence, even those who talk about it. I mean if you go into the libraries of our colleges, you'll see that the books on Africa are largely unread. They don't know anything about it. The books on India are also largely unread. The point about this is that where knowing that past and knowing that self becomes hard work you're pretty certain that nobody wants to do it.

Islands has that dimension because having gone into Africa, Brathwaite gets a way out, he gets another eye. The eye was always there, but he didn't know. So another eye is opened. He can now, for example, approach an image from two cultural angles. So the cross becomes not only the Christian cross but the crossroad and an icon. If you look at my book *Pathfinder* you'll see that the cover is black, that black on the cover represents the black ground. The names are largely in white, that white represents the white language, which is an image taken from the book too, you see.

The ground is black, the ground of being is black. The language which has been imposed on you is white. You use that language but you are using it on a black ground, which is actually a total reversal of the European image of making black marks in the white snow.

Then you will see on the cover a circle cut by a cross. Now that represents the beginning, that is the central icon. Then there is the God, the crippled God, the old man who stands at the gate at the point of intersection of the crossroads. And he has to be invoked to open the barrier, to open the gate before you can begin anything. The circle is the central image in the sense of moving in four different directions, the sense of moving away from an origin or moving back to an origin if you like— everything there is icon.

Now if **Masks** projected us into the past, **Islands** is projecting us towards the future. Now the question of refashioning the future is fascinating because it suggests that the future has already been mapped out; we are already headed for something that needs to be changed, that needs to be refashioned. So, it's a concept again of the poets, the artists, a rule of constant redefinition, remaking. He's saying that unless we have an energy of consciousness which we inject into the present, we remain with a future which is already pre-determined for us. It's pre-determined for us by the people who have made us what we have been from the past. It is pre-determined for us by the moles, by the categories and prisons that they have created.

Before we look at the second Trilogy [comprised of **Mother Poem, Sun Poem,** and **X/Self**] let's look at what came in between. You had **Other Exiles** (1975), which is going back to some of his earlier work between 1948 or 1950, when he was at Cambridge. He has some interesting portraits of Europe and Europeans.

The poems which came out in **Black and Blues** (1975) were written between 1969, 1970, 1971, and 1972. Now if you talk about a silence about **Islands,** there has been an almost total silence about **Black and Blues.** Poems like 'Starvation', are severely focussed on the Kingston of the early 1970s. We are dealing with a phenomenon of terrifying violence. They are a response to the nakedness of now, the terror of now, with what we have become through the constant corrosion of being urban people in a ghetto, unemployed, and being in a sense trapped in that post-emancipation arrangement, by which we were not to be accommodated, by which we were never to possess the world into which we have supposedly been set free.

The dry season in the Caribbean is when the bushes burn. It's also when the hibiscus blooms. There are times when the place has been so dry, that the silver birch drops all of its leaves and you have this white skeleton of stems with a flower at the end of it. There's just not sufficient moisture to sustain the tree. That is the ambiguity running through **Black and Blues.** The ambiguity of drought and a life which was there. The ambiguity of the bareness and bleakness.

Brathwaite spent his first extended stay in Barbados for nearly 20 years, in early 1975/76. What I think it did was to free him from the kind of mental oppression that is part of the Jamaican experience. Now I'm not saying this against Jamaica, but you live there in a society which is under pressure, under stress. The mid-70s was period of a lot of raping. The poem 'Spring Blades' is about raping, at least part of it is about that. It's a place that set fire to an old ladies home, a place which gunmen made children go back into. So that there is grimness there, which obviously is lifted off when you get to Barbados.

On the other hand, of course, I remember George Lamming saying that Barbados was stable—the stability of the cemetery. So that you can get the other sense in Barbados of the place being stable as well as static. I think though that what Barbados did was to give his mind an ease, and he began now to explore the Barbadian landscape.

Now, **Mother Poem** is autobiography. So is **Sun Poem,** and so to a certain extent is **X/Self.** The question is how do we see these three very different poems as part of a trilogy. If they are part of a trilogy, what kind of trilogy? They're certainly not the same kind of trilogy as **Rights of Passage, Masks,** and **Islands.** It is possible to see **Mother** and **Sun** poems as being two sides, two ways of looking at the Barbadian experience, **Mother Poem** being essentially the experience of the women, obviously as seen through the eyes of a man. Though the voices in **Mother Poem,** apart from the narrator's voice, are all those of women. **Sun Poem** is about the male experience. And, the images or central symbols are different. In **Mother Poem** you're dealing with the land, the women, and not so much the sea, you know, the sea becomes your existence towards the end, and I think there is a really marvellous poem about the sea towards the end of **Mother Poem.** Some of the best writing about the sea I know anywhere; where the actual pulse and rhythm of the poem is the long heave of the sea. Now we get hints of this early in the poem, like you know when you're in Barbados in the night and there is less traffic, and if you're close to the coast, you sometimes just hear the sea. And there is that poem about the land talking about what has happened to the consciousness of the ordinary Barbadian, who has been told to accommodate himself to tourism. And so he becomes maybe a beach-boy, or a bus-boy.

Although **Mother Poem** is autobiography, it is not autobiography in any simple way. There is a kind of process by which Brathwaite distances himself, but it is not autobiography for example in quite the same way as, say, Walcott's *Another Life;* even there there is distancing. The people who appear in **Mother Poem** are all voices for something much larger than themselves. They are voices for the landscape; they are voices for the whole historical process; they are voices of the psyche or consciousness, protesting at what is happening to it. And they are voices of the women coming into a consciousness of themselves, and into a kind of visibility which is quite similar to the apocalyptic movement in their arrivance. In other words in **Mother Poem** the women are moving from accepting their position in the room, you know, the domesticity to that voice in 'Cherries' which rebels.

These women are also located in history, because Brathwaite is very much aware that there was and is women's oppression. So that passage at the centre of **Mother**

Poem is historical; it deals with the confrontation of the plantation between the slave girl and the mistress. In other words it's not just simply that men oppress women, which is the formula we sometimes get. Oppression has got to be seen as part of a system, which includes women oppressing each other. So it includes a class dimension, a race dimension, as well as a gender dimension. *Mother Poem* I think is a very important poem.

Sun Poem is dealing with boyhood. It's more closely autobiographical. But the rituals are different. The rituals of the men are rituals of male confrontation, fighting on the beach, winning your spurs, and this kind of thing. That autobiographical strain is interrupted somewhere in the middle too, by a movement back to the past. Because Brathwaite is really interested in what has happened to the male archetype. Why is it that we don't have any heroes that look like ourselves? What was done to the male? What was destroyed when we destroyed the male archetypes in this society? He does this in the poem called 'Noon', in which he looks at the movement of the sun-god across the East Coast of Barbados. That East Coast is rugged; it's quite different from the other part of Barbados. He creates a myth, the dying of the god, but the dying of that god is also equated with the dying of Christ; the three hours of darkness, so that it is a dying of a male archetype.

The mother is not only a woman but the land, looking at the destruction of spirit and consciousness in her children, particularly in her sons. It is done in terms of the sea surging, that surge of the sea becomes more insistent. And then there is also the sense of trying to get the shape of the landscape in the movement of the verse, which is remarkable towards the end of *Mother Poem.* Barbados exists in terraces, the whole country can be seen as a series of steps, you move from one plateau right up to the other and then at the core of it there is this fairly hard rock, the rest of it is like stone.

There are all these caves because of the limestone, with water seeping through. Barbados is literally an island which has as its centre a womb of water. *Mother Poem* makes fantastic use of this geological fact. So the caves become wombs, become consciousness. The water is the fertility, the life, which is always springing there; but it's under the surface; you've got to get below these layers, you've got to get down into the caves before you discover Barbados. And that is seen as an almost archetypal female presence in the island. Mind you the real mother lives under a system of oppression, oppression on the job. Not only that, they are on the tail end of a system of oppression because when their man is oppressed they are oppressed too. And so at the beginning of *Mother Poem* you've got the monologue, there's a long monologue in which she is looking at her husband and what has happened to him. He has worked in a warehouse and it just mashes him up. But what is fascinating about that monologue is that it turns, it changes halfway through and she begins to contemplate that this is what my work has become. She's talking about what his work has done to him, and she's saying that that is all they give him, they didn't even give him a little gratuity, a little sense for all the work he had to do, in the morning. So that she is a rebel voice in the poem.

And of course there is the other archetypal thing of placing the poem in the framework of the sun, or of mythology. So that is the *Sun Poem,* but it ends, like *Mother Poem,* with a promise of rebirth: the sun goes down, the sun comes back up. So that cycle of death is also a movement towards rebirth. *Mother Poem* ends with the sea surging and the land is pulsating so that we get the sense that she isn't dead at all; she's become part of the process. So we get these two *Mother* and *Sun* poems becoming two ways of looking at Barbados. And there's a precision. Brathwaite tends to be geologically precise when he talks about the terraces and the steps and the movement up, they're there. So the thing is precise on a visual level, on a geographical level, as well as on a level of image and archetype.

In *X/Self,* what Brathwaite is doing and what links it with *Mother Poem* and *Sun Poem* is that it is his intellectual autobiography. In other words it is telling us that to understand where I am coming from you have to understand all of those things. So it is going to pose a lot of problems partly because the range and the scope of what it brings together is so wide. It has a lot to do with redefining the way in which we see. It is using the other eye to look at European history up to the point where Europe became involved with Africa creating the world we know today. So in a sense it is an autobiography of the mind, and of the development of the mind. But it is not done in an easy way. The eye for example is a Roman, an Emperor, or a Tribune. The eye is sometimes, just a black presence. And there is this sense of contrasts for example between Europe and Africa. *X/Self* is an attempt to explain why it is that Europe has been able to create the society it has created, and Africa has had a great deal of problems with the same thing. And what he is really saying is that Europe has done it because Europe has drained the resources of Africa. So that I think the central statement there is 'Rome burns and our slavery begins', because it begins to see the disintegration of the Roman Empire, particularly through the movement of Islam into the Iberian peninsula and into North Africa. He seems to see that as something which drove Europe back on itself which destroyed feudal Europe and created the Europe of the Compass, the Europe of Columbus, the Europe which moved out of Europe again in a sort of new wave of imperialism, which now included the 'dark continent'.

Now, saying that is one thing, but trying to look at how he worked that vision out in the poetry is another. I find a lot of the earlier European poetry that he wrote, some of which you get in **Other Exiles,** I find some of the style of that is there. A very relaxed style. At the same time I find this has added a kind of witty, almost comic style. I mean he's doing all sorts of things with words. He's laughing all the time. But it's a fun which tends to reduce the grandeur. A punning which reduces, which cuts down, which tries to see this thing in a new way.

The "X" is the unknown quantity, suggesting what you cannot contain in any single image or metaphor. The central vision is that of the confrontation between Europe and Africa, but not only Africa, it brings in a lot more of the new world, the American Indians; so it is really dealing with the frontier situation; with the question of conquest, and in its latter pages with apocalypse.

Simon Gikandi (essay date summer 1991)

SOURCE: Gikandi, Simon. "E. K. Brathwaite and the Poetics of the Voice: The Allegory of History in 'Rights of Passage.'" *Callaloo* 14, no. 3 (summer 1991): 727-36.

[*In the following essay, the author examines "Rights of Passage" as an example of a poem "in which oral languages take revenge against institutionalized poetic forms."*]

> At the beginning was the shout—the beginning is, for us, the time when Creole was created as a means of communication between the master and his slaves. It was then that the peculiar syntax of the shout took hold. To the Antillean the word is first and foremost a sound. Noise is a speech. Din is a discourse.
>
> Edouard Glissant, "Free and Forced Poetics"

Like many other poets in the Caribbean, Edward K. Brathwaite began his writing career under the anxiety of cultural identity and a crisis of writing. He was brought up in a colonial tradition which emphasized the hegemony and desirability of European culture at the expense of the Antillean tradition, which slavery and colonial domination had tried to repress or deny. The West Indies was not perceived as the source of meaningful cultural expression; on the contrary, it was a scene of fear and rejection, a place devoid of those forces that trigger poetic beginnings. "I was a West Indian," Brathwaite was to observe years later, "roofless man of the world. I could go, belonging everywhere on the worldwide globe. I ended up in a village in Ghana. It was my beginning" (quoted in Rohlehr 3).

The importance of Brathwaite's "return" to Ghana to the language and structure of his poetry has been documented by Gordon Rohlehr in his definitive study of *The Arrivants*: the discovery of Asante culture forced Brathwaite to reconceive or revise his own understanding of poetics, not only by enabling him to textually realize African as a precondition for what Rohlehr calls the "wholeness and self-knowledge of Afro-Caribbean man" (3), but also by endowing the poet with the knowledge that those African forms which white cultural imposition had tried to repress (worksongs, gospel, blues) were indeed valid forms which the poet could use to produce a poetics of resistance, one directed at dominant cultural practices.

In a more specific sense, Brathwaite was to discover the centrality of voice and sound in African forms of self-expression, a discovery which was to lead him to what has become a life-long desire to establish a poetics of the voice in the Caribbean.

The importance of this turn away from scriptured forms to oral ones cannot be emphasized enough, for more Caribbean poetry has developed in response to a crisis of the written word, an awareness of the opposition, in Edouard Glissant's words, "between an idiom which is used and a language which is needed" (96). When a community cannot express itself directly, in this case because of the constraints of cultural imperialism under slavery and colonialism, it develops what Glissant calls a "forced poetics," one in which the true meaning of words "is hidden from the master's ear by the non-meaning of the noise and staccato, which is the true meaning. This nonmeaning hides and reveals a hidden meaning" (97). Denied a public forum of self-expression under colonialism, Caribbean peoples developed a secret language, a pact of noise and sound which both challenged the master-codes of the plantation system and, at the same time, sustained a symbolic or semiotic system of cultural resistance.

Brathwaite has traced this process in his monograph, *History of the Voice,* but it is his mentor, Glissant, who expresses the nature and function of the secret language which African slaves developed in the plantations most vividly:

> What Creole transmitted, in the world of Plantations, was above all a refusal. From there, we could define a mode of linguistic structuration which would be "negative" or "reactive," differing from the "natural" structuring of traditional languages. In this, Creole appears as if organically linked to the world-wide experiences of cultural relationship. It is literally a consequence of cultural interface, and did not exist prior to this interface. It is not a language of Being, but a language of Relatedness.
>
> (98)

We cannot fully comprehend the dimensions of Caribbean poetics without understanding the doubleness in Glissant's postulate: for if, on one hand, Creole literatures function as acts of refusal, it is a refusal which, on the other hand, is constructed at the point of interface, at the junction where the European language meets the African voice. What happens when these two faces meet is the key to understanding Caribbean poetics.

I will now turn to Brathwaite's **"Rights of Passage"** as an example of a poem that is generated by the tensions between the hegemonic European language and Africanized forms of poetic expression, a poem in which oral languages take revenge against institutionalized poetic forms, as Glissant had predicted. Moreover, I want to read **"Rights of Passage"** as an exemplar of what Bakhtin calls "ambivalent writing," a mode of discourse in which language is appropriated by the individual as "a form of practice" (151). Following Julia Kristeva's formulation, we can see textual ambivalence as the capacity of poetic language to insert history into the text and the text into history (68): it also implies the poet's ability to enter into an intertextual relationship with the already written: "Dialogue and ambivalence are borne out as the only approach that permits the writer to enter history by espousing an ambivalent ethics: negation as affirmation" (Kristeva 69).

Indeed, Brathwaite finds such an ambivalent ethics of language at the heart of Afro-American expression, especially in the structure and ideology of jazz: by adopting the jazz musician's "double-language," the Caribbean poet believes he can move away from what Susan Willis has aptly called "a cultural middle passage" (619), and hence, in Brathwaite's words, find a "possible alternative to the European cultural tradition which has been imposed upon us and which we have more or less accepted and absorbed, for obvious historical reasons, as the only way of going about our business" ("Jazz and the West Indian Novel II" 39). But where does the poet start? By confronting the authority of history itself or by excavating a new space of original invention?

Beginnings are never easy: like most of Brathwaite's other poems, **"Rights of Passage"** is a poem generated by an acute anxiety about the authority of the marginalized voice, doubts about beginning and intentions. To establish the authority of the Creolized voice, Brathwaite, unlike his contemporary Derek Walcott, shuns invention, preferring instead to confront Caribbean history as it has been represented in European texts, while seeking to maintain the integrity of the poet's voice as a figure of alterity and subversion. Brathwaite's model for his new poetics of voice is undoubtedly jazz, because as he noted in one of his famous *Bim* essays, "Jazz and the West Indian Novel," the poetry of Caribbean cultural resistance has sought a space of representation analogous to New Orleans at the beginning of the jazz tradition:

The West Indian writer is just beginning to enter his own cultural New Orleans. He is expressing in his work of words that joy, that protest, that paradox of community and aloneness, that controlled mixture chaos and order, hope and disillusionment, based on his New World experience, which is at the heart of jazz. It is in the first place mainly a Negro experience; but it is also a folk experience; and it has (or could have, depending on its own internal integrity, as we have seen with jazz), a relevance to the "modern" predicament as we understand it today.

(279)

Brathwaite is attracted to jazz for several reasons: its capacity to use the voice to subvert the logic of hegemonic cultures, its ability to represent paradox and to interpolate what appear to be radically opposed world views, and most importantly, its capacity for improvisation. Jazz is indeed the matrix for "forced poetics," for it rejects the mastery of established forms not by dismissing them from its repertoire, but by constantly using them as a point of reference, and then sublimating their canonical meanings under the power of unpredictable sounds and idioms.

Thus, for Brathwaite, the history of the voice is not derived from any canonical meanings it exudes, for spoken history in the Caribbean has always been that of the marginal; rather, the authority of the voice lies in its ability to situate and disperse codified forms while concealing its own powers behind a mask; in other words, what we think we know about the Caribbean, what appears so obvious on the surface of things, is couched in more ominous cabalistic signs and double-meanings.

The opening of **"Rights of Passage"** is a case in point: "Drum Skin Whip / lash, master's sun's / cutting edge of heat" (4)—one can't find a simpler image of the slave experience: the whip has become an innate symbol of slave labor and violence in the islands. But Brathwaite's meaning is doubled-edged: the skin that produces the whip (the figure of violence and repression) is also the skin that produces the drum (the figure of the voice and hence true identity).

Indeed, a few lines later, we see how the slaves' weapon against the regimen of the whip is their ability to utter through the "taut / surface of things: I sing / I shout / I groan / I dream" (4). The utterance of the slave is, of course, imprisoned in structures of domination which Brathwaite presents through images of waste and destruction: the desert, the stalled waters of the world, and "The hot / wheel'd caravan carcasses" (4). So, in a sense, history as seen from the margins is a negative process of displacement and repetition; indeed, to recover the meaning of this new history we need to seek, not its monuments of glory, but its ruins; what time leaves behind is a tree stump "ravished / with fire / ruined with its gold" (5).

The meaning of experience in Brathwaite's poetry hence lies in the reader's ability to reverse common structures of address and images which have become reified with time; where we expected gold to lead to happiness, it has left behind evidence of greed. Here, too, ruins mark the temporariness of things, for as J. Hillis Miller has observed in another context, the effect of ruins on things "is to introduce visible evidence of the eroding effect of time" (365). And yet for Brathwaite, it is out of the ruins left behind by the conquerors that new habitats and cultures emerge:

> mud walls will rise
> in the dawn
> walled cities
> arise
> from savanna and
> rock river bed:
> O Kano Bamako
> Gao.

However, these lines express the deliberately mixed nature of Brathwaite's verse: on one hand there is the certainty of regeneration, the spectacle of mud walls rising at dawn is an expression of hope; but on the other hand, what the poetic speaker sees at dawn could just be the walls of destroyed cities. Kano, Bamako, and Gao are indeed monuments of black civilizations in Africa, but their meaning is complicated by the apostrophe at the end of the stanza, which suggests an absence rather than a presence. Indeed, if we accept Jonathan Culler's assertion (in his "Changes in the Study of the Lyric" 40) that the "O" in the apostrophe is the figure of emptiness, then Brathwaite seems to write about solid things to foreground the absence of any semantic reference to that which is most critical in black histories in the new world—images of Africa.

Invariably, the improvisation of history involves challenging the linear movement of time, subverting the authority of chronology. How does Brathwaite expose the lineality of history and hence the authority of chronos? Essentially by setting up binary oppositions which are then undermined and exposed in the course of the poem, or by reversing poetic figures in such a way that they don't convey any determinate meanings.

A good example of this process of reversal appears in the title of the first part of **"Rights of Passage," "Work Song and Blues,"** where the two musical forms that frame the poem would appear to be opposites: the African work song is traditionally conceived as a signifier of unalienated labor, a mark of the self's identity with its work; the blues, on the other hand, as Amiri Baraka (LeRoi Jones) notes in *Blues People,* is the mark of the slave's history of alienation, a figure of dissonance (25). But in Brathwaite's poem, and indeed within the context of the plantation system, there is no essential difference in the economy of the two musical

forms—they both signify the slaves' alienation from the means of production.

Similarly, there is an important duality in the images the poet uses to (re)present history: flames are marks of destruction because they "scorch, crack, / consume the dry leaves of the hot / house" (7); but Flame is also a "red idol" the source of revolutionary power: "Flame, / that red idol, is our power's / founder: flames fashion wood . . ." (8). Thus the overture to **"Rights of Passage"** ends with a deliberate confusion of the flame image and the ideology of power that it supplements: "Flame is our god, or last defense, our peril. / Flame burns the village down" (8); the flame destroys and saves.

My argument here is that the authority of the voice in Brathwaite's poetry is contingent on the poetic speaker's deconstruction of previous representations of history. Indeed, where many Caribbean writers (including poets as diverse and different as Walcott and Guillèn) conceive their engagement with history as the quest for the principles which, in Edward Said's apt phrase, "authorize writing" (23), Brathwaite's allegories of history are contingent on "molestation," Said's term for the converse process. Rather than appropriate and hence re-establish the laws that institute the logic of history, Brathwaite's poetic speakers conceive history as absolute negation, tempered only by its repetitive structures.

In **"New World A-Comin',"** the subjects of history have been inscribed into Western history as an absence, as figures of negation ("Helpless like this / leaderless / like this, / heroless" 9); in the New World, the imprisoned slaves have no horses, no leaders, no hope. Their discourse on absence is structured around the binary opposition between historical figures who appear as the balancing marks of negation and of definitive historical affirmation:

> . . . no
> Hawkins, no
> Cortez to come.
> Prempeh imprisoned,
> Tawiah dead,
> Asantewa bridled
> and hung.
> O who now can help
> us: Geronimo, Tackie,
> Montezuma to come.
>
> (10)

Here, the structure of the poem (re)presents history as an entity which is stablized by figures who represent opposed ideological interests: thus, the Europeans, Hawkins and Cortez, are the figures of negation, ranged against Tawiah and Asantewa, the Asante heroes of liberation, while Geronimo, Tackie, and Montezuma are signifiers of New World liberation. On closer examination, however, these distinctly different figures share something in common: they are all absent from the scene; they are in different ways absent marks of history; a history which is represented not by the perceptualizing figures we thought were so apparent on the surface of the poem, but by the figure of hypotyposis, which entails engagement with absent things.

I want to extend my thesis further by making the following claim: what is at issue in Brathwaite's concern with the forms in which history is represented is not so much the meaning of that history, nor its value, but how that history (Western history, if you want) functions as a means of repressing the language of the black self. In this sense, what the poet seeks is not a language of Being but what Glissant (in the quotation above) identified as the language of Relatedness: the relations of power as they are manifested in linguistic structures. There is hence a struggle, in **"Rights of Passage,"** between the written word and the voice, here posited as signifiers of two opposed ideological positions.

I think we can understand this tension more clearly if we look at history and writing, in the Western tradition, as synonymous entities. A collapsing of these two terms is etymologically justified: the OED, for example, defines history as "A written narrative constituting a continuous methodical record, in order of time, of important and public events," and as a branch of knowledge dealing with past events "as recorded in writings or otherwise ascertained."

The voice, on the other hand, signifies the shapes and consciousness of that which has not, and cannot, be institutionalized. To create a space in which oral forms of history can be authorized as the true depositories of black cultures, Brathwaite (re)presents written history as a metonymic process which negates its own claims to ascent, to knowledge and fulfillment. Very early in **"Rights of Passage,"** the experience of slavery is represented as a journey "down / valleys down slopes," a journey into fire, a journey that links the subjects in "a new / clinked silence of iron" (11).

Traditionally, the validity of history lies in the ability of the subject to realize itself in a temporal situation; indeed, the meaning of history is revealed by time. But for Brathwaite's slave subject, time engenders uprootment: "It will be a long time before we see / this land again" (11). Instead of leading to the fulfillment of desire, and to an absolute knowledge of self, time becomes a signifier of indefiniteness and postponement—any hope that the African slaves will return home again, "will create new soils, new souls, new / ancestors" (11), lies in a period beyond the measure of time. In the meantime, the slaves must maintain the power and integrity of their own voices.

This combination—of the remoteness of return to the source and the need to sustain the memory of the past—creates a double movement in the poem: European history is displaced from its graphic pedestal, while what Brathwaite calls the history of the voice is inscribed as a secret language that is passed from generation to generation. Brathwaite's influence here is undoubtedly Baraka who, in *Blues People,* misappropriates the Western idea of graph as a written form (the *OED* [*Oxford English Dictionary*] tells us that *graphic* in Greek means drawn or written), and asserts that the blues are a graph of black social history (65). So, for Brathwaite, the voiced graph is the repressed that returns to haunt the written graph.

We see this process at work in the section called **"Islands and Exiles"**: the title of the section establishes the framework in which Caribbean identity has been sought; the island being the place in which New World black culture seeks its new groundings; exile being a metaphor of the call of the other, of Europe or the United States. The islands are represented by a stone that "had skidded arc'd and bloomed into islands" (48). The image of the stone appears to be a simple reference to the geology of the islands; the gesture of the stone blooming into the island would appear to be a reference to the unexpected survival and regeneration of culture in the slave community. What we have here, then, is a set of dialectical relationships which the poet uses to represent the two forces at work in Caribbean history: the islands roar "into green plantations / ruled by silver sugar cane," and this is counterbalanced by the "sweat and profit / cutlass profit" (48).

But let us beware of such neatly structured processes of history, for in keeping with his deconstructive rhetoric, Brathwaite has here cast the history and geography of the islands in the subversive form of the Calypso ode. He has put many dissonant words and phrases in the melodic line to put the dialectical movement of the poem into question. Listen to the kaiso version of slavery:

> And of course it was a wonderful time
> a profitable hospitable well-worth-your-time
> when captains carried receipts for rices
> letters spices wigs
> opera glasses swaggering asses
> debtors vices pigs.
>
> (48)

Indeed, this is one instance when meaning seems to have been sacrificed to what Eroll Hill calls meaningless "speech rhythms" (74); rhythms and noises that mask the meaning of the poem.

As a matter of fact, this ostensibly "meaningless" play with words presents an excellent example of what happens to European structures of meaning when they are (re)presented in Afro-Caribbean modes of speech. In his brief but important study of the Calypso ode, Hill argues that the extension of the melodic line and the use of polysyllabic words, of the kind which we see in the example above, "tended to sink the calypso into a morass of elaborate verbosity rattled off with unintelligible speed" (74). And yet it is that improvisorial and unmastered dimension of the calypso that Brathwaite uses to parody existing versions of the islands' history: the slave master's claims to "civilization" has been "cut" by being reduced to the ribaldry of a bar scene.

Thus, instead of presenting us with an elevated poetic consciousness, Brathwaite falls back on the *la bètise* of the Calypso to show how the Afro-Caribbean voice, by reducing the old order of things to babble, parodies the other's version of the Caribbean experience:

> And what of John with the European name
> who went to school and dreamt of fame
> his boss one day called him a fool
> and the boss hadn't even been to school . . .
>
> (49)

John thought he had mastered the master's modes of expression, but in the Calypsonian ode he is reduced to just another slave. And if a mastery of European forms (the school is a symbol of these) does not reconcile the black self to the other, then the poetic speaker is content to reduce his or her utterance to babble and doodle, to meaningless verbal play:

> Steel drum steel drum
> hit the hot calypso dancing
> hot rum hot rum
> who goin' to stop this bacchanalling?
>
> (49)

But there is something more at stake in this kind of verbal play: what the figure of the voice represents is not the utterance of an individual; rather, what this poem sustains is the integrity of communal structures of address. Indeed, anyone who tries to develop a description of the poetic speaker in **"Rights of Passage"** is bound to be very disappointed. The verbal play of the calypso singer has here become a mask of communal voices which, because of their marginalization, can express meanings only through indirect modes of address. For these subjects, history is not the archetypal journey to self-knowledge, but the ultimate form of displacement. For this reason, instead of functioning as a reflection of the quest for identity, which is what the concept of *rites de passage* entails, Brathwaite's poem is a meditation on the word "rights": it is generated by the poet's anxiety about the entitlements which black people have in the Americas; identity and rights have become almost synonymous.

In a sense, Brathwaite's poem presents a variety of black figures, but they have one important thing in common—they are all moving in search of their rights. We have Africans moving from the Sahara to the Ocean, American blacks moving from the South to the North, and Caribbean peoples "migratin' overseas" (50). What is of particular note about these journeys, however, is their repetitiveness: even when they have been cast in different time frames and contexts, they mirror each other. Thus, both the migrants moving from the United States' South to the North, and the Caribbean peoples moving from the islands to Europe, share a common temporal desire: at the end of their journeys, it is hoped, the self will not only recover its natural "rights," but move onto a level of self-consciousness, a positive sense of selfhood, an important cognizance of its own subjectivity.

In reality, the migrants' journey is one of reversal, repetition, and displacement: they are headed for clearly defined geographical entities (Canada, the Panama Canal), but these places are also fantasies, hence the poet's conclusion that the migrants don't know where they are going. Indeed, the journey to nowhere is posited as a mimicry of the journey of "discovery," and the migrating blacks are burlesqued as "these New World mariners / Columbus coursing kaffirs" (52). Columbus, too, had followed his "charted mind's desire" and invented the West Indies to compensate for his error, but what was the meaning of his discovery? Through a process of ironic reversals, the new discoverers are confronted with temporality not as an allegorical process that leads to the recovery of self-identity, but as a negative knowledge of the self, an awareness that they are defined by the gap between desire and demand:

> Once when we went to Europe, a rich old lady asked:
> Have you no language of your own
> No way of doing things
> did you spend all those holidays
> at England's apron strings?
>
> (55)

Thus, the moment of failed reconciliation with Europe, as Cesaire showed so passionately in his *Cahier,* is the moment when the subjects realize, in Paul de Man's words, that they can relate to their source "only in terms of distance and difference" (222).

In fact, we can push the argument further and argue that **"Rights of Passage"** is not a poem about the anthropological transition of the self to higher stages of consciousness; rather, it is a poem about the failure of consciousness, of its entrapment in hostile and hegemonic cultural structures. Brathwaite begins with the assumption that black or Caribbean identity cannot be found in a reconciliation between the alienated self and its Euro-American figures of desire; rather than seek to overcome this gap, the self must come to terms with the history of its repression, like a mental patient who cannot be cured until he or she has spoken the trauma of childhood.

At the end of **"Rights of Passage,"** both the Afro-Caribbean migrants and the black Americans have been brought back to the repressive past they sought to escape. Their journeys were intended to transcend the negativity engendered by the plantation system; instead movement from the scene of the trauma has only led to the accentuation of reification. The only form of knowledge the poetic subjects have, now, is of their own negativity and the failure of their self-invention, hence the re-echo of Césaire's famous line: "we / who have cre / ated nothing, / must exist / on nothing" (79).

This cognizance of negativity is important for two reasons: First, by discovering the nature and depth of their reification in the world of the other, the black subjects have rejected any positive mode of consciousness that may be predicated on identification with the other; they realize that rites of passage don't lead to any rights. Second, at the end of the poem, these subjects have fashioned a language which they can now use to express their negativity; they have indeed invented forms of selfhood that are "nothing," but in the process they have hallowed a space which offers the possibility of authentic self-representation, which is indeed the subject of the other two parts of *The Arrivants.*

Works Cited

Bakhtin, Mikhail. *Problems of Dostoevsky's Poetics.* Tr. R. W. Rotsel. Ann Arbor: Ardis, 1973.

Brathwaite, Edward. *History of the Voice.* London: New Beacon, 1984.

———. "Jazz and the West Indian Novel," *Bim* 11 (1967): 275-84.

———. "Jazz and the West Indian Novel II," *Bim* 12 (1967): 39-51.

———. "Rights of Passage." *The Arrivants.* London: Oxford UP, 1973.

Culler, Jonathan. "Changes in the Study of the Lyric." *Lyric Poetry: Beyond New Criticism.* Eds. Chaviva Hošek and Patricia Parker. Ithaca: Cornell UP, 1988. 38-54.

de Man, Paul. "The Rhetoric of Temporality." *Blindness and Insight: Essays in the Rhetoric of Contemporary Criticism.* Minneapolis: U of Minnesota P, 1983.

Glissant, Edouard. "Free and Forced Poetics." *Ethnopoetics.* Eds. Michel Benamou and Jerome Rothenberg. Boston: Alcheringa, 1976. 95-101.

Hill, Eroll. *The Trinidad Carnival.* Austin: U of Texas P, 1972.

Jones, LeRoi. *Blues People: Negro Music in White America.* New York: Morrow, 1963.

Kristeva, Julia. *Desire in Language: A Semiotic Approach to Literature and Art.* Ed. Leon S. Roudiez. Tr. Thomas Gora, Alice Jardine, and Leon S. Roudiez. New York: Columbia UP, 1984.

Miller, J. Hillis. "The Two Allegories." *Allegory, Myth, and Symbol.* Ed. Morton W. Bloomfield. Cambridge, Mass.: Harvard UP, 1981. 355-71.

Rohlehr, Gordon. *Pathfinder: Black Awakening in the Arrivants of Edward Kamau Brathwaite.* Tunapuna, Trinidad: Gordon Rohlehr, 1981.

Willis, Susan. "Caliban as Poet: Reversing the Maps of Domination," *Massachusetts Review* (Winter 1982): 615-30.

Mary E. Morgan (essay date autumn 1994)

SOURCE: Morgan, Mary E. "Highway to Vision: This Sea Our Nexus." *World Literature Today* 68, no. 4 (autumn 1994): 663-68.

[*In the following essay, Brathwaite's sister reflects on the importance of the Caribbean Sea as an influence on her brother's poetry. She attempts to show how the movements of the sea are reflected in the rhythms of Brathwaite's work.*]

1. We were brought up by the sea. I do not mean merely that as island people we saw the sea always there, but that our home was actually *by* the sea; the Round House where we grew up looked out on Brown's Beach and Carlisle Bay. And we came to appreciate, and to learn, the movement of the sea, which forms so much a part of Kamau's work. The sea, our highway out (migration, to study),[1] our wave-ride back—back to what Brathwaite calls "the centre," after England and Ghana: "I had, at that moment of return, completed the triangular trade of my historical origins."[2]

The sound and rhythm, the movement, the restlessness, and indeed the changeable nature of the sea are constantly reflected in his work, especially in *Mother Poem* [*MP*] (1977) and *Sun Poem* [*SP*] (1982), his two long works about growing up in Barbados.

> up the slope of the beach a crab pauses
> flickering white beads of ground stone spotted with
>   coral
> in a day lazy with sea-wrack and glisten, the richness
> of the day's candle wind burning with iron and blue
>
> the crab pauses
>
> raising its flat seeds of eyes
> listening down to the thunder coming up from the
>   curve of the bay

then sideways to scuttles, making necklace of dots on
    the day
and a wave follows, sweeping[3]

I remember how the beach used to change from being a
small beach to no beach at all and then later again to
the wide expanse of white sand where the boys would
play cricket. Sometimes during the hurricane season a
storm would suddenly blow up, and we would watch
from the back windows of our house as the waves rolled
in from far out.

and he had seen far away where sky was low a big
bright wave that was standing still . . . but was build-
ing up and was getting bigger and he tried to run . . .
and his sister screamed and his mother held her close
as she turned her back to the cruel sea and the world
was falling like the power of babel . . . as he opened
his eyes to his mother sprawled . . . and her yellow
bathcap bobbin[4]

2. The sound of the waves would punctuate our sleep,
and next morning some of the small fishing boats that
were moored offshore would be wrecked on the beach.
Or sometimes there would be no beach and the waves
would be lapping against the breakwater on which our
beachgate and paling (sea fence) were built. Then we
would run down the stone steps from the pantry and
dive right into the sea from our gate. In a few weeks
the sea would recede, and we again had a beach behind
our house; and there were times, our mother told us,
when the sea went out as far as—indeed beyond—the
place where the fishing boats now lie at anchor, so that
once upon a time there was cultivated land where the
sea now was. In the poem **Soweto** (1979), of all places,
Kamau transforms this into "and we are rowing out to
sea / where the woman lived / with her pipe and her
smoke // shack . . . / and we are rowing out to sea /
where there were farms."[5] It taught us, among other
things, the importance of breakwaters, of protection
against this sea that we loved but which could change
so easily, so dangerously. It was from this that my
brother developed his notion of Caribbean "tidalectics,"
a way of interpreting our life and history as sea change,
the ebb and flow of sea movement; and with the sug-
gestion of surf comes the contrapuntal sound of waves
on the shore: "the peace of the lord is upon her // lost:
they will single her out / hurt: they will balm her /
afraid: she will find their flicker underneath her door"
(**MP**, 113).

The sea was also the means by which we all, "the
people who came,"[6] came to our islands, became fused,
smelted in the encounter of fire blood sun lust hate
tyranny servitude . . . love. And the awareness of this
fusion is everywhere in Brathwaite's work, echoes of
the stories that Mother and Cousin Jeanie Stuart used to
tell: family stories, some of them about slavery days;
dream stories[7] (the image I just quoted from **Soweto**),

and others. For instance, Mother felt convinced that she
was a reincarnation of an Ethiopian or Egyptian
princess; so she read all she could about Egypt and
Ethiopia and passed this on to us at night when she was
sitting ironing.[8] That's how we knew that the pharaohs
were black while everybody else assumed they were
white (as they were pictured in "the books"); and we
always had this joke about the Sphinx's nose—that the
English "discoverer" had broken it off so that the flat-
ness wouldn't show!

E-
gypt
in Af-
rica
Mesopo-
tamia
Mero-
ë
the
Nile
silica
glass
and brittle
Sa-
hara, Tim-
buctu, Gao
the hills of
Ahafo, winds
of the Ni-
ger, Kumasi
and Kiver
down the
coiled Congo
and down
that black river
that tides us to hell
Hell
in the water
brown
boys of Bushongo
drowned in the
blue and the bitter
salt of the wave-gullied
Ferdinand's sea
Soft winds
to San Salvador, Christoph-
er, Christ, and no Noah
or dove to promise us, grim
though it was, the simple sal-
vation of love.[9]

and

my mother sits above these on her mountain
curl, leaf of dreamer
drift plantations away
I remember ancient watercourses
dead streams, carved footsteps
and my mother rains upon the island with her loud
    voices
with her grey hairs
with her green love

(**MP**, 3)

There were duppy stories too. Gordon Rohlehr and Bob Stewart have spoken about Kamau's concept of the circle and its spiritual significance: "they will light wicks to honour her circle / standing all night to hinder her ghosts from rising from surface of mirrors / through the long wax of stars and the blood's surfage" (*MP,* 113).

3. Also significant in Brathwaite's work is the image of the stone, with so many different nuances: the stone as creation and beginning and vision, as in **"Calypso"** (from *Rights of Passage,* 1967); the stone as instrument of destruction, as used against Mikey Smith in the poem **"Stone";**[10] and often the stone as catalyst and agent of change ("out of the living stone, out of the living bone of coral").[11] Inevitably there is a connection between the stone and the circle. When we were children running on the beach behind our house, Kamau and his friends used to skim the surface of the sea with a stone. I could never do it well, but they could, so that you could follow the flight of the stone with your eye—in a dead straight line or in a beautiful curving arc, which sometimes, like our archipelago itself, seemed about to close a circle. But whatever the pattern, as the stone tipped the water each time, it rippled out into a circle, into circles, widening, sparkling, in the sun—which eventually becomes Kamau's alternative, as he puts it, to Wordsworth's "Daffodils": "The stone had skidded arc'd and bloomed into islands: / Cuba and San Domingo / Jamaica and Puerto Rico / Grenada Guadeloupe Bonaire" (*A* [*Arrivants,*] 48).

4. *Shar—Hurricane Poem* came out of Kamau's traumatic experience of the ravages of Hurricane Gilbert on his home in Irish Town, Jamaica, in September 1988, and also out of his involvement in the last few months of my daughter Sharon's life (1990),[12] echoing memories of his own wife Doris's end (he called her "Mexican") in 1986.

> out of the dry river grande of pain
>   . yes. yes. yes. yes.
> & pouring west. towards the years of wrest
> & wreck & space & time between the stone
>   & Maya & the Aztec & the
>   te & teh & touch of your face
>   *Tetemexticlan*[13]

The images come with the power and passion of the storm itself.

> And what. what. what. what more. what more can i
>   tell you
> on this afternoon of electric bronze
> but that the winds. winds. winds. winds came straight
>   on
> & that there was no stop. no stop. there was no stopp.
> ing them & they began to reel. in circles.
> scream. ing like Ezekiel's wheel
> & that the valley of destruction filled with buzz.

> with kite tails wild. ing
> tug & tear & rip & tatter up & like old women laugh.
>   ing

The "scissors-howl" wind, like a copper kettle "boiling over into your years," while you hoard its sound "like a thimble of thunder." Then at last the calm of acceptance, the stone become/ing song:

> faces that must eat, that must eat, that must drink, that
>   must sleep
> beside these waters.
> that will open their doors again & again to a wet
> leaf tomorrow despite any sodden or sorrow
>   Un/til
>   at last
>   *stone*
>   lone/ly
>   at first
>   &
>   slow/ly
> out of the valleys. smoke. trail. trial. song
>   · · · · ·
>   from stone not echoing shell
>   from bone not timbrel of pestilence
>   *song* at last *song*

5. *Mother Poem* and *Sun Poem* are replete with echoes of childhood; not all are truly autobiographical, but many are recognizable. "Occident," for example, captures our warm, loving, almost overpowering upbringing round our mother, with her concerns, her worries, her aggressions, her angers, her visions, her dreams, her determination concerning our education and future. I can just remember the teacher on his bicycle who opens this passage: "Chalkstick the teacher / dreamer of desk- // coteque and dais" (*MP,* 22). Of course, what Kamau is doing here also is "punning into" and "modernizing" the story of our growing up: "crinkled his bicycle bell with the sound of ice in a bucket / . . . // my mother heard and opened the door of the mountain" (*MP,* 22). Earlier there had been "mohammet," the teacher, who "had come to [her] black / mountain" (*MP,* 19). This passage gives a pretty good idea of the forces involved in Bajan education—and an aspect of our mother's personality in her prime:

> this planter's puncher
> looked in at her window
> from his plantation into her plot
>
> he did not know what pots were on her fire:
> eddoes and yam in the kitchen
>
> he did not know if there was pumpkin vine
> running wild all over her backyard
>
> if the gate-door creaked
> if red crabs crawled in her rock
>
> garden

>   (*MP,* 22-23)

That "backyard," the creaking "gate-door," the red crabs in the "rock garden" are all from that area where we ran down the "back steps" to the beach. The "gate-door" creaked because its hinges were constantly singed with sea-breeze: "but he knew the mam looking at him: // squint-eye front-frown / keen glance made keener by glasses: gold // framed . . . / . . . / the cool flat voice of her iron" (**MP**, 23), round which, as noted earlier, we heard her tales of Africa.

> getting hotter and hotter
> as the galvanized roof of the red-shingled castle
>
> crinkled and stretched in the daylight
> its waves of tin going tick tick tick in the white sheet-
>   shine
>
> the kettle lips boiling to buse him, you hear,
> if he didn't take care to be care-
>
> ful, to be po-
> lite, to be bow-
>
> tie
> to defuse her ticking stare
>
> the fear he would not listen
> showing where she did not smile:
>
> that the boy would be a *lux*
> *occidente*: her great light riding from the west
>
> that even if she had to pick her way through sticks
>   and
>   broken pathways for
> him
>
> there would be the time, there would be the place,
>   there would be the day.

> (**MP**, 23-24)

Our father, on the other hand, was a very quiet person—not "marginal," as the textbooks say Caribbean fathers are supposed to be, but just quiet. Our mother, among other things, was, as far as we were concerned, a great quarreler. Our mother, among other things, was, as far as we were concerned, a great quarreler. Our father was not. Refusing to quarrel, he just walked away. Kamau captures this in what I have always regarded as one of the finest tropes in his poetry.

> fish
>
> was a sign of peace inside our house
> we listened in the dark to how our mother quarrelled
>   all night long like surf
> lines on the other shore: he never angered we could
>   hear
>
> though sometimes coughed and sometimes terrible to
>   fear: what
> would become of us: said

> he would go back out and *stay* back out: our mother
>   bawled
>
> then silence
>
> at last the crickets chirped the bull frogs bulbed
> the night wind nestled in the black leaf tree
>   · · · · ·
>
> the next day
> fish

> (**SP**, 90)

6. Mile & Quarter, St. Peter, where our father came from, was also a significant "other shore"-not surf-sound here, but the sea-sound of canefields and "country people." That place, a mile and a quarter from Speights-town,[14] has as much influence on Brathwaite's poetry as the sea outside Round House, Bay Street, Bridge-town.

> the window in the little redwood gallery where I'd sit
>   for hours
> watching the canefields groan the blackbirds march
>   across the road
> the sun swing downwards to the shakshak
> tree the mulecarts creak/ing home the way
> the donkey dung was trod and round and burst like
>   pods along the golden ground
>
> and nighttime when the crickets became stars
> and comets smoked high up among the betujels and
>   jewels of orion and the flare of mars
> the lighthouse distant beyond distance beyond fields
>   · · · · ·
>
> searching for salt for dead souls . . .

> (**SP**, 92)

And at the center of it all, our grandfather, his sister-in-law, our Aunt May Agard, his brother-in-law Bobby O'Neale (Bob'ob, who becomes Ogoun in Brathwaite's poetry), and "all the aunts and uncles" we remembered in our prayers each night.

> Every Friday morning my grandfather
> left his farm of canefields, chickens, cows,
> and rattled in his trap down to the harbour town
> to sell his meat. He was a butcher.
> Six-foot-three and very neat: high collar,
> winged, a grey cravat, a waistcoat, watch-
> chain just above the belt, thin narrow-
> bottomed trousers . . .

> (**A**, 239)

The actual, wonderful now-fading photo portrait of "Granpa" still hangs on the sitting-room wall at Mile & Quarter: "He drove the trap / himself: slap of the leather reins / along the horse's back and he'd be off / with a top-hearted homburg on his head: / black English country gentleman" (**A**, 239).

In addition to this open "trap," there was also a great assortment of horses, cows, lorries in various stages of repair or disrepair, including the magical ruin of a V-8 Ford: "the car had two horns: black bubble bugle: *paa paa paadoo* / and the round electric button nose inside the steering wheel: / *aa aa aaoooooga*: which we all preferred" (**MP,** 110). Next door to Granpa was Bob'ob—his home upstairs, where he and his two daughters the musicians Miriam and Mabel lived; downstairs was the carpenter shop, now famous in Kamau's poetry (though the house and shop no longer exist) through the poem "Ogun."

> My uncle made chairs, tables, balanced doors on, dug out
> coffins, smoothing the white wood out
>
> with plane and quick sandpaper until
> it shone like his short-sighted glasses.
>
> The knuckles of his hands were sil-
> vered knobs of nails hit, hurt and flatt-
>
> ened out with blast of heavy hammer. He was knock-
> kneed, flat-
> footed and his chip clop sandals slapped across the concrete
>
> flooring of his little shop where canefield mulemen and a fleet
> of Bedford lorry drivers dropped in to scratch themselves and talk.
>
> (**A,** 242)

Like our mother and Granpa's sister-in-law Aunt May Agard, who told "us stories / round her fat white lamp," Bob'ob also told us stories—of the Emperor Haile Selassie, of Mussolini and the Abyssinian War, of Marcus Garvey, the Sphinx, the pyramids and pharaohs, Africa. The closing stanzas of "Ogun" reveal how Brathwaite remembered, nourished, and transformed these things into his now well-known images of Middle Passage / reconnection.

> And yet he had a block of wood that would have baffled them.
> With knife and gimlet care he worked away at this on Sundays,
> explored its knotted hurts, cutting his way
> along its yellow whorls until his hands could feel
> how it had swelled and shivered, breathing air,
> its weathered green burning to rings of time,
>
> its contoured grain still tuned to roots and water.
> And as he cut, he heard the creak of forests:
>
> green lizard faces gulped, grey memories with moth
> eyes watched him from their shadows, soft
>
> liquid tendrils leaked among the flowers
> and a black rigid thunder he had never heard within his hammer

> came stomping up the trunks. And as he worked within his shattered
> Sunday shop, the wood took shape: dry shuttered
>
> eyes, slack anciently everted lips, flat
> ruined face, . . .
>
> . . . . .
>
> . . . the heavy black
>
> enduring jaw; lost pain, lost iron;
> emerging woodwork image of his anger.
>
> (**A,** 243)

7. We were all writing in the late 1940s and early 1950s: in school magazines, in newspapers, in school newspapers like the one started by Kamau and friends at Harrison College. Thanks to Frank Collymore, Kamau's work, like that of Derek Walcott in St. Lucia, starting appearing in *Bim,*[15] while others of us were successfully entering newspaper competitions (Kathleen McCracken, later Drayton, in the *Trinidad Guardian*; Slade Hopkinson and myself in the *Barbados Advocate*). Apart from the encouragement from our "home" editors, we were stimulated by lectures given under the auspices of the British Council by people like H. A. Vaughan (poet, historian, judge), Judge Chenery, Crichlow Matthews, and Frank Collymore himself. Small wonder then that by the end of the war (1945-46) we felt our region to be a zone of excellence, though not of peace, because memories of the war still clung: the Dutch merchant ship *Cornwallis* had been torpedoed in Carlisle Bay, straight across the water from our back door,[16] and the *Oumtata* had gone down spectacularly in Castries harbor, St. Lucia.

Yet the boys still played "cowboy and crook" up and down the stairs of the Round House, under the cellar, and on the beach. Everybody could swim out to the liners in the bay, but I found it rather scary the one time I tried. Then the boys would come in from the beach to eat and listen to music—jazz, classics, the blues. Kamau had a gramophone and a formidable collection of records (he still has!) by the time he reached sixth form, bought mostly from saved lunch money: Dizzy Gillespie, Harry James, Sinatra, Ella Fitzgerald, Sarah Vaughn, Woody Herman, Charlie Parker. His poem **"So Long Charlie Parker"** echoes the very notes of the sax itself. Here it is in the version called **"Bird"** in *Jah Music.*[17]

> The night before he died
> the bird walked on and played his heart out
> notes fell like figure forming pebbles
> in a pond[18]. he
> was angry. and we
> knew he wept to know his time had come
> so
> soon
> so

little had been done
so
little time to do it
in
he wished to furl the night from burning all time long
    . . . . .

but time
is short
& life
is short
& breath
is short
& so
he slurred
&
slowed
&
stopped
his fingers fixed
upon a minor
key
then slipped
his bright eyes blazed & bulged against the death in
    him then knock
ing at the door
we watched
as one will watch
a great clock striking time
from a great booming midnight bell
the silence slowly throbbing in behind the dying bell
        . . . . .

The night before he died
the bird walked on through fear through faith through
    frenzy
that he tried to hide
but could not stop that bell

8. As the movement of the sea has shaped so much in Kamau's poetry, so the music of it has influenced his writing—powerful imagery, lyrical beauty, magnificent symphony of "song. song. song. / syllable of circle. pellable of liquid contralto / tonnelle of your tone into fire / & the songs of crossing the river & the dead & sea / of the morning & the brass & bells of the water" (**Shar**). So that the syllable the stone skids full circle and becomes "there in the rise & rise of the sorrel horizon / & sing. ing / & sing. ing / the song of the morn/ing" (**Shar**). Both Sharon & Doris loved to sing. . . .

Notes

1. Edward Kamau Brathwaite left the island for England by ship, out there in the bay "before they built the deep-water harbour, sinking a whole island to do it," so that we had to go out to the liner by launch; and when we were on board, we could look straight "back to the land and the house where [we] lived" (*Sun Poem* [subsequent references are abbreviated as *SP*], Oxford, Oxford University Press, 1982, p. 17), right there on the beach, and I remember that when our mother discovered that his passport and other important papers had been left behind, I had to run back down the gangway before the launch steamed back to shore, run from the Pierhead up Bay Street to the Round House, to retrieve the folder with the papers, and get back to the ship. But I was lucky getting back. I caught sight of our neighbor, Captain King the pilot (he appears as "Mr Queen" in *Sun Poem*), on the beach outside, just about to step into the small rowboat that would take him out to his "Pilot Boat." I called out to him, ran down the back steps, and was lifted by his men into the rowboat, and so arrived in fine style back at the gangway of the French ship *Gascoigne*. Ten years later, our brother returned home from England and Ghana, again by ship.

2. Kamau Brathwaite, in *Contemporary Poets of the English Language,* London, 1970, p. 129.

3. Kamau Brathwaite, *Mother Poem,* Oxford (Eng.), Oxford University Press, 1977, p. 115. Subsequent references are abbreviated as *MP*.

4. Kamau Brathwaite, *SP*, p. 77. Originally in *The Boy and the Sea,* an unpublished novella completed while he was at Cambridge University in England in the early 1950s. The variant which appears in *SP* uses quite a lot of material from this novella, where we also find the breakwater, the boys playing cricket on the beach where Bebe appears as, among other things, the champion beach-cricketer, "the great breakwater bat." In *SP* Bebe is now part Batto, and the beach-cricket appears in part only in "Rites" (*Islands,* 1969).

5. Kamau Brathwaite, *Soweto,* Mona (Jamaica), Savacou, 1979, p. 3 (unnumbered).

6. The title of a three-part book textbook for schools edited and coauthored by Kamau Brathwaite, first published in 1968, 1970, and 1972; revised edition 1987, 1989, and 1993.

7. Kamau Brathwaite, *DreamStories,* Harlow (Essex), Longman, 1993.

8. Our mother tended to do her ironing while sitting rather than standing, because even then she was suffering from "her feet"—what we now know was a diabetic effect.

9. Edward Brathwaite, *Rights of Passage,* Oxford, 1967. Reissued as part of *The Arrivants,* London, 1973, pp. 35-36. Subsequent references to *The Arrivants* use the abbreviation *A*.

10. "Stone: for Mikey Smith" first appeared in *Jah Music* (Mona, Savacou, 1986).

11. Edward Brathwaite, *Islands,* Oxford, 1969, p. 34; the collection was reissued as part of *The Arrivants* in 1973. I understand that Pam Mordecai, at the University of the West Indies in Mona, Jamaica, is working on a thesis that explores this very image—the stone and pebble.

12. *Shar* (Mona, Savacou, 1990) is dedicated by Kamau to Sharon, my daughter, who spent the academic year 1989-90 between our home in Jamaica, hers in St. Lucia, and the University Hospital back at Mona, where she died in July 1990 after a triumphant fight with non-Hodgkins lymphoma—triumphant because of her shining faith (she sustained her pregnancy through chemotherapy) and the miracle of the birth of her second son, Richard (March 1990), beyond the expectation of her doctors.

13. Brathwaite, *Shar,* n.p. Kamau's account of Doris's death in 1986 is contained in *The Zea Mexican Diary,* Madison, University of Wisconsin Press, 1993.

14. Barbados has four towns: Bridgetown, the capital; and Speightstown, Holetown, and Oistin, which when we were growing up were little more than villages.

15. Derek Walcott first appears in *Bim,* 10 (June 1949), with the poem "A Way to Live." Kamau's first publication is in *Bim,* 12 (June 1950), the poem "Shadow Suite." Between 1950 and 1972, when Colly was editor, Kamau published some seventy-five poems in *Bim.*

16. The *Cornwallis* incident is recorded in George Lamming's book *In the Castle of my Skin* (London, 1953) and in even greater detail in Kamau's unpublished novella *The Boy and the Sea,* since after the torpedoing, he and his friends used to swim or row out to "the wreck in the harbour." It was there for years, tilted onto the sea floor, and there was this great gaping hole of horror in its side where the torpedo had struck, blowing its way through the submarine nets that stretched on huge buoys right across the mouth of the harbour from Pelican Island to Needham's Point. For months the boys from our beach went out there, diving into that black hole and bringing up cans of corned beef, sardines, and all sorts of tar-sticky goodies.

17. Kamau Brathwaite, *Savacou,* Mona (Jamaica), 1986, pp. 12-13.

18. A variation on the image of the "circles" from pebbles skidding on Brown's Beach water. The "ponds" are those we used to play among at River Bay in St. Lucy.

H. H. Anniah Gowda (essay date autumn 1994)

SOURCE: Gowda, H. H. Anniah. "Creation in the Poetic Development of Kamau Brathwaite." *World Literature Today* 68, no. 4 (autumn 1994): 691-96.

[*In the following essay, Gowda praises Brathwaite for creating a national language and for moving "from the margins of language and history, from the peripheral realm of 'the other exiles,' to the center of civilization, effecting a renaissance of oral poetry and remaking the poetic world."*]

> *dry stony world-maker, word-breaker,*
> *creator . . .*
>
> Edward Brathwaite, **"Ananse"**[1]

There are not many historians who have distinguished themselves as poets and prose writers, who can recite poetry with rhythm and melody, not many who have endeavored to create "nation language" and make poetry truly native. Kamau Brathwaite, who has now become the Neustadt Prize laureate for 1994, has all these attributes and accomplishments, as well as the great honor of freeing poetry in English from the tyranny of dying of ossified main tradition. In his 1982 lectures at the Centre for Commonwealth Literature and Research in Mysore, India, he emphasized a "true alternative to Prospero's offering." "What happened in Shakespeare," he said, "what happened to Caliban in *The Tempest* was that his alliances were laughable, his alliances were fatal, his alliances were ridiculous. He chose the wrong people to make God. And if he had understood the nature of the somatic norm, it is possible that he would have chosen a different set of allies for his rebellion. So that is the first thing I want to present to you, the notion of the alternative, the image of the alternative, which resides in the figure of Caliban, not the Caliban who is concerned with metaphysical revolt, the revolt of the spirit, the reconstitution of the mind, which is something that becomes much more crucial in the development of the Third World than simple physical revolt."[2] He considered Sycorax, Caliban's mother, "a paradigm for all women of the Third World, who have not yet, despite all the effort, reached that trigger of visibility which is necessary for a whole society" (*CE* [*The Colonial Encounter: Language Speeches by Kamau Brathwaite*], 44).

This is the main theme that underlies the prose and poetry of Brathwaite, a major Caribbean poet with a large reputation and world stature. He insists on the sense and value of the inheritance of the West Indies and continuity with Africa; he is keen on discovering the West Indian voice in creative arts and emerges a creator of words. He has waged a war against the English language, which had allowed itself to be shackled into a verse system borrowed from the Latin language which did not go in for hammer blows of the West Indian Creole. His legacy was to work in "the English which is so subtly deformed, so subtle a subversion of English." Hence he draws freely on all the riches of the Caribbean multicultural inheritance and has created "the semantic image, where you begin to conceive of the metaphor, also an alternative to that of Prospero." His essays and speeches offer very interesting insights into his own creative writing and the situation of the writer in the Third World and newly independent nations. He has evolved a critical system using critical values different from what one would find in the *Times Literary Supplement*. As a historian, he traces the background to the evolution of West Indian writing and its structural conditions and the diversity of languages in a plural society. He wants the language, the new language, to embody "the syllables, the syllabic intelligence, to describe the hurricane, which is our own experience."[3]

The early Walcott, Brathwaite, and others have endeavored to create a nation language and confidently communicate with the audience. They use language in its most intense, rich, nuanced, and vital forms, outgrowing the sophisticated and artificial language of the colonizers. They use dialect and local detail and express the voice of the community. In their hands we see the strangeness of the English language. We are aware of Walcott's use of speech rhythms—"O so Yu is Walcott? / You is Robby brother? / Teacher Alix son?" (*Sea Grapes,* 1976)—but this mission is up to a point in Walcott, who seems alternately ardent and cold in the desire to be *outside* English literature—English literature in a hierarchical sense. The angst of the important poems "The Spoiler's Return" and "North and South" in *The Fortunate Traveller* suggest an American infection. But it is zeal that makes him return to the Caribbean in theme and vocabulary in his epic *Omeros* (1992), which demonstrates his philosophy to "ground with West Indian people." Salman Rushdie in 1982 argued that the English language "grows from many roots; and those whom it once colonized are carving out large territories within the language themselves."[4] It is the genius of the English language that it adapts to strange climates and strange people.

Brathwaite, who has not wavered in his determination, is very close to Indian poets who try to make their content Indian, even while their drapery is English. In his views on "nation language," exploration and exile, and the drudgery and loneliness of Negro slaves, he seeks and seeks "but finds no one to speak," and prayers do not go "beyond our gods / or righteousness and mammon."[5]

Brathwaite, who now rides the tide of literary innovation freeing poetry "from the tyranny of the pentameter," is distinguished in his use of nation language. He is deeply immersed in writing about the frustration of a West Indian and of his critical experience of the black sage and the New World. In 1970 he said, "The problem of and for West Indian artists and intellectuals within this fragmented culture, they start out in the world without a sense of wholeness."[6] Having mastered and bent Prospero's language to suit his purpose, as a poet he concentrates on "Europe coming to the Caribbean,"

or what he calls "the after-Renaissance of Europe coming with an altered consciousness" (*CE,* 52). Therefore his poetry deals with the Maroon, the artist, the Negro slave, the reconstruction of fragments into something much more humane: a vision of a man-world (*CE,* 61). Brathwaite's ability lies in discovering the sense of wholeness. He has produced a metaphor for West Indians as a dispossessed people and has tried to invent his own esthetics for representing the Caribbean consciousness.

How does Brathwaite, who feels the need to liberate himself from inherited colonial cultural models, seek to distance his work from the pentameter of Chaucer? By attempting to develop a system that more closely and intimately approaches the experience common to all ex-colonies. He has expanded the treasures of his native talent in adapting and deepening his hold on the English language, making of it an instrument upon which he is able to play to perfection a greater variety of melodies than any other West Indian.

The West Indies, like many Third World countries, has colonial problems, but unlike India, the region does not have a long and rich literary heritage. In spite of many invasions, India retained her cultural riches; she was neither humiliated nor dispossessed even when ruled by foreigners. In the New World, on the contrary, blacks and West Indians had to endure slavery, indentured labor, and also an apparent discontinuity with their native cultures in Africa and India: "We have had a history of slavery and colonialism for the last four hundred years and very little else" (*CE,* 43). In such a situation a heavy burden is placed on the writer. He must create not only awareness but a tradition, what Eliot termed "the historical sense-indispensable." Hence Brathwaite endeavors hard to create a usable past for his fragmented region.

Having lived in Ghana for nine years and felt his stay there to be something of a homecoming, Brathwaite sees "its" culture as continuous with the West Indian diaspora. In order to drive home this important point, he uses the words of a revolutionary and composes poetry characterized first and foremost by its self-conscious and formal lexical contrast to standard English. He uses "music and rhythm" as bases of his verse, and also "kinesis and possession." *Kinesis* is a term which refers to the use of energy, and it derives here from the African religious culture, where worship is best expressed in kinetic energy. The idea is that the more energy "you can accumulate and express, the nearer you will come to God" (*CE,* 71). The poet's heart bleeds at the predicament of the Negro slave in the New World. His prayers are the common prayers of all who underwent imperialism but still possess the "mother's milk of language to fall back on."

Brathwaite began his poetic career on the assumption that he was cut off from civilization, that he was in exile. He even gave his earliest poems the suggestive collective title *Other Exiles.*[7] A desire for change in social values is evident there in the juxtaposition of folk images and historical elements: "he watched the seas of noon-dragged aunts and mothers / black galley slaves of prayer // but all his thoughts were chained / which should have sparked and hammered in his brain" (**"Journeys"**).

In many multilingual countries creation in a foreign language is considered inferior to creation in one's mother tongue. Unlike India, which possesses a rich cultural heritage and a strong epic tradition, the Caribbean had no alternative to Prospero's offering. Hence Brathwaite's attempts to overcome that obstacle, to "leap the saddle" and "reach the moon" (**"Journeys"**). The medium is English but the subject is Caribbean. Very early the poet discarded the classical meters of English verse as incapable of effectively expressing, for example, the havoc of the hurricane. In **"Arrival"** he speaks of how his islands inspire him, and he hugs them, "stuffed away in his pockets / the fingers tightly clenched, / around a nervousness."

Brathwaite conceives of ancestral cultures from the Caribbean perspective—that is, the American culture, the European culture which formed the modern Caribbean beginning in 1492, and the cultures of Africa and Asia which constitute the basis of Caribbean society. One culture impinges on the other. Therefore, he says, "he unpacked the wired apparatus of his eyes // So that he could assess not only surfaces / but doubts and coils" (**"Arrival"**). His images are distinct. In one of his early poems, **"Cat,"** he writes that the poet must create with the sensitivity of the cat, an integral element of African history which imparts authenticity to the Caribbean. The sensibility of **"Cat"** yields to a new type of poetic sensibility which adumbrates the folk culture of the slaves; that folk culture, in turn, contributes a certain continuity to the development of modern-day society. As a historian, Brathwaite asserts that the folk culture of the ex-African slaves still persists in the life of contemporary folk.

The Arrivants: A New World Trilogy [A]—comprising the earlier collections *Rights of Passage* (1967), *Islands* (1969), and *Masks* (1968)—is an epic which explores the pathos and frustration of a nation on an epic scale. Its opening lines are suggestive:

> Drum skin whip
> lash, master sun's
> cutting edge of
> heat, taut
> surfaces of things
> I sing
> I shout

> I groan
> I dream
> about
>
> Dust glass grit
> the pebbles of the desert
>
> (*A*, 4)

The short lines and strong rhythm express pain and anguish.

African migration to the New World and the consciousness of the slaves become integral elements in the poetry of Kamau Brathwaite. They form the underlying basis of *Rights of Passage,* which is considered an epic of a civilization. **"Prelude,"** whose first twelve lines are cited above, is characteristic of Brathwaite's effort in composing new verse for the consciousness of an ignored soul. That poem continues:

> sands shift:
> across the scorched
> world water ceases
> to flow.
> The hot
> wheel'd caravan's
> carcases
> rot.
> Camels wrecked
> in their own
> shit
> resurrect butter-
> flies that
> dance in the noon
> without hope
> without hope
> of a morning.

Brathwaite's verse deals with the history of rootlessness, folk aspirations, and exile. Hence it is a kind of an "Iliad for Black People."[8] *Rights of Passage* demonstrates Brathwaite's preoccupations not only with the poetic form but also with content: the experiences of the black diaspora and its links to the new archetypal themes of exile, journey, and exploration of the New World. Of the Maroon he says: "The Maroon is not an antiquity, lost and forgotten, an archeological relic. Maroons are alive and their patterns are still there for us to learn from. You can still learn the art of carving from Maroons. You can still learn the poetry of religious invocation from the Maroons. You can still learn techniques, if we need them, of guerrilla warfare from the Maroons, so that we have a very living alternative culture on which we could draw" (*CE,* 58). Therefore he says in **"Tom"**:

> the paths we shall never remember
> again: Atumpan talking and the harvest branch-
> es, all the tribes of Ashanti dreaming the dream
> of Tutu, Anokye and the Golden Stool, built
> in Heaven for our nation by the work
> of lightning and the brilliant adze: and now nothing
>
> (*A* 13)

This reference to heritage is relevant to all Third World countries where an older or existing civilization is destroyed by imperialism. There is a correspondence between the poet's sense of tradition and his vision which gives *The Arrivants* its epic quality. "Tom" the old slave is a symbol of the continuity of the tradition of the poet as visionary and as representative voice in all oppressed Third World countries.

> not green alone
> not Africa alone
> not dark alone
> not fear
> alone
> but Cortez
> and Drake
> Magellan
> and that Ferdinand
> the sailor
> who pierced the salt seas to this land.
>
> (*A* 16)

The mask is also an important symbol in Brathwaite's poetry. It can conceal the real nature behind it, but it can also act as a bridge. *Masks* (1968) contains elegiac poetry. The adventure of an epic character through "tunnelling termites," "monuments, graves," and **"The Making of the Drum"** through ruins and cities ends on an interrogative.

> So the god,
> mask of dreamers,
> hears lightnings
> stammer, hearts
> rustle their secrets,
> blood shiver like leaves
> on his branches. Will
> the tree, god
> of path-
> ways, still
> guide us? Will
> your wood lips speak
> so we see?
>
> (*A* 131)

The poet's voice and concerns are those of all West Indians. Like most poets of the Commonwealth, Brathwaite seems to have been influenced early by English poets, for several of whom he has expressed clear admiration: "What T. S. Eliot did for Caribbean poetry and Caribbean literature was to introduce the notion of the speaking voice, the conversational tone" (*HV* [*History of the Voice*], 30). Soon he outgrew this influence, however, and developed his own forms and style of expression. In his 1968 essay "Jazz and the West Indian Novel" he delineated what he saw as a new and more relevant esthetic for the assessment of West Indian writing.[9]

Brathwaite is of the earth, earthy, and creates a history which links the West Indies to Africa. As we read the three constituent parts of *The Arrivants,* we see the

Maroons resurrected and given a voice as "the first alternative settlers in the Caribbean, the first successful alternative communities in the Caribbean" (*CE,* 57). We hear of the untold sufferings of the slave, the Maroon, the peasant, and the unemployed; we are taken into the Caribbean past, into West Indian culture as represented by the calypso singer, the Rastafarian, and the black radical. In **"Volta"** (from *Masks*) we read:

> I know, I know.
> Don't you think that I too know
> these things? Want these things?
> Long for these soft things?
>
> Ever since our city was destroyed
> by dust, by fire; ever since our empire
> fell through weakened thoughts, through
> quarrelling, I have longed for
>
> markets again, for parks
> where my people may walk,
> for homes where they may sleep,
> for lively arenas
>
> where they may drum and dance.
> Like all of you I have loved
> these things, like you
> I have wanted these things.
>
> But I have not found them yet.
> I have not found them yet.
> Here the land is dry, the bush
> brown. No sweet water flows.
>
> Can you expect us to establish houses here?
> To build a nation here? Where
> will the old men feed their flocks?
> Where will you make your markets?
>
> (*A,* 107-8)

In Brathwaite we find a unique combination of poet, historian, and creator of critical theories. *Mother Poem* (1977), all about "my mother, Barbados," is an attempt to document his native island in verse and place it in the context of the historical experience of tribal Africa and of the deracinated African in the New World. For Brathwaite the historian, his poetry is to a considerable degree an abstract of racial and historical experience. History seems to reinforce and fulfill the poetry. As he says in the preface to *Mother Poem,* Barbados is the "most English of West Indian islands, but at the same time nearest, as the slaves fly, to Africa. Hence the protestant pentacostalism of its language, inter-leaved with Catholic bells and kumina."[10]

Compared to the other islands of the West Indies, Barbados is plain, ordinary, unexotic, even dry. *Mother Poem* begins in the southerly parish, with its wide, bleak, wind-beaten plain; the opening lines of the very first poem, **"Alpha,"** suggest the mood: "The ancient watercourses of my island / echo of river, trickle, worn stone, / the sunken voice of glitter inching its pattern to the sea, / memory of form, fossil, erased beaches high above the eaten boulders of st philip // my mother is a pool" (*M* [*Mother Poem*], 3). The poet makes a kind of grim sense of the country when he goes on to speak of his mother's "grey hairs" and "green love" and her association with nature: "she waits with her back / slowly curving to mountain / from the deeps of her poor soul" (4).

In political terms Brathwaite's ability to envision a wholeness amid the fragments of postcolonial societies can be clearly seen here. The landscape of Barbados becomes a vehicle of his mood to depict "[slavery's] effect upon the manscape." The island's history is condensed for us in the story of Sam Lord, a kind of English pirate, in lines that echo the Twenty-third Psalm: "The lord is my shepherd / he created my black belly sheep // he maketh me to lie down in green pastures / where the spiders sleep" (8). The images contained in such titles as **"Bell," "Fever," "Lix,"** and **"Cherries"** evoke the various African cults of the West Indies and their permutations over time, and the poems document the experience and practices of the slaves who kept such traditions alive, often within the confines of their cabins and always in spite of their "unhappiness" and servitude. In one hymn it is suggested, "let unhappiness come / let unhappiness come / let unhappiness come" (49). The plague of 1854 killed about 20,000 in Barbados alone. To describe the havoc of such events, the poet cleverly uses the image of a black dog "blinding the eye balls" and "prowling past the dripping pit latrines" (80). In such lines and poems Caribbean culture and history are vividly brought to life.

Mother Poem is an exhilarating exploration of the land and people of Barbados, in a vocabulary that blends standard English and "Bajan," but in a larger sense it represents the poet's continued movement toward a concept of West Indian identity. In almost kinesthetic terms he says, "so she dreams of michael who will bring a sword / ploughing the plimpler black into its fields of stalk, / of flowers on their stilts of future rising / who will stand by the kitchen door and permit no stranger entrancement" (112).

Sun Poem (1982) has the ring of authority and the sureness of rhythm of *The Arrivants*. It supplements *Mother Poem*, exploring the male history of Barbados. The opening poem, **"Red Rising,"** seems to be universal in the broadest sense of that term: "When the earth was made / when the wheels of the sky were being fashioned / when my songs were first heard in the voice of the coot of the owl / hillaby soufriere and kilimanjaro were standing towards me with water with fire."[11] There is a change in the method here, for the lines can be set to music. The swiftly growing "sun" moves from one

generation to the next, from grandfather to father to son, the relationships realized through the imagery of the seven colors of the rainbow. With sprinklings of Barbadian dialect, the clearly fascinated poet describes sunsets and sunrises around the world. *Sun Poem* shows Brathwaite's ability to recast biography into poetry; it is built principally around his childhood and youth and his relations with his father: "this pic- / ture shows him always suited dressed for work hat / on his head no light between his him and me" (*S* [*Sun Poem*], 87).

The collection has poems in both prose and verse, all suggesting a certain naturalness. On seeing the Krishnaraja Sagar illumination at Mysore, Brathwaite expressed the thought that some civilizations create things for the enjoyment of others whereas some are selfish, money-minded. What strikes one most is how flexible and beautiful Brathwaite's writing often is, and how different in word and feeling individual pieces are from one another. *Sun Poem* deals with Rastafarianism and Ethiopia, with Yoruba traditions and the black New World God, with landscapes both African and Caribbean. Truly the historian is seen here as a poem of great authenticity. "History, after all," wrote Carlyle, "is the true poetry. Reality; if rightly interpreted, is greater than Fiction; nay, even in the right interpretation of Reality and History does genuine poetry lie." This statement seems to find a true exponent in Kamau Brathwaite. Neither history nor poetry is repudiated at the cost of the other in his work, as *Sun Poem* amply illustrates.

Brathwaite, who has used the metaphor of Caliban to depict the subjugation of the West Indies, is now like Prospero, whose "charms are all o'erthrown," supplanted by the sweetness and harmony of **"Son,"** where "my thrill- / dren are coming up coming up coming up coming up / and the sun // new" (*S*, 97). The later Brathwaite writes a bare kind of poetry, with lines that are austere but images that are real, as in this selection from *Jah Music,* a collection of poems of incomparable music and rhythm:

> He grows dizzy
> with altitude
>
> the sun blares
>
> he hears
> only the brass
> of his own mood
>
> if he could fly
> he would be
> an eagle
>
> he would see
> how the land
> lies softly

in contours
how the fields
lie striped

how the houses fit into the valleys

he would see cloud
lying on water
moving like the hulls of great ships over the land

but he is only
a cock
he sees[12]

Brathwaite has faced the problem of creating a nation language and has worked steadily to arrive at a solution. The problem is one which has beset many countries as they have thrown off the yoke of English imperialism. Indian poets have moved from Toru Dutt and Sarojini Naidu to Nissim Ezekiel, Leel Dharma Raj, A. K. Ramanujan, and other moderns whose work is characterized by quick, deft touches and a style that renders native idiom and nuance perfectly. Nissim Ezekiel's hymns are distinctively native. The late Ugandan writer Okot p'Bitek, the unique author of the long dramatic monologue *Song of Lawino,* gave voice to the dispossessed, the urban vagrant prisoner, and the ubiquitous *malaya* (Swahili for prostitute) and became a social reformer in verse. In New Zealand both Maori and Pakeha (white European-descended) poets have searched for a broad "symbolic language" natural to the indigenous people of the land. Thus writers of the new lands have gone beyond the inherited modes of English and modern European poetry and have de-educated themselves, escaping the tyranny of the sonnet in an effort to be more genuine, more true to their medium and milieu. The new poetry of the Commonwealth is no longer the prisoner of the colonizer but instead has found the rhythmic audacity and wherewithal to express local realities and, in so doing, has become a part of world poetry. Kamau Brathwaite, a towering poet, has moved from the margins of language and history, from the peripheral realm of "the other exiles," to the center of civilization, effecting a renaissance of oral poetry and remaking the poetic world.

Notes

1. Edward Brathwaite, *The Arrivants: A New World Trilogy,* Oxford (Eng.), Oxford University Press, 1973, p. 167. Subsequent citations use the abbreviation *A* where needed for clarity.

2. Kamau Brathwaite, *The Colonial Encounter: Language Speeches by Kamau Brathwaite,* published as *Power Above Powers 7,* ed. H. H. Anniah Gowda, Mysore (India), Centre for Commonwealth Literature and Research, University of Mysore, 1984, p. 46. Subsequent citations use the abbreviation *CE.*

3. Edward Kamau Brathwaite, *History of the Voice: The Development of Nation Language in Anglophone Caribbean Poetry,* London, New Beacon, 1984, p. 8. Subsequent citations use the abbreviation *HV.*

4. Salman Rushdie, writing in the *Times Literary Supplement,* 14-20 September 1990.

5. *Comparative Approaches to Modern African Literature,* ed. S. O. Asein, Ibadan (Nigeria), University of Ibadan, 1985, p. 134.

6. Edward Brathwaite, writing in *Savacou,* 2 (September 1970), p. 36.

7. Edward Kamau Brathwaite, *Other Exiles,* Oxford (Eng.), Oxford University Press, 1975. The individual poems collected in this volume date as far back as 1950.

8. Gordon Rohlehr, "Blues and Rebellion: Edward Brathwaite's *Rights of Passage,*" in *Caribbean Literature,* London, Allen & Unwin, 1978, p. 63.

9. Kamau Brathwaite, "Jazz and the West Indian Novel," in his *Roots,* Ann Arbor, University of Michigan Press, 1993, pp. 55-110. *Roots* was originally published in 1986 by Casa de las Américas in Havana.

10. Edward Kamau Brathwaite, *Mother Poem,* Oxford (Eng.), Oxford University Press, 1977, "Preface," n.p. Subsequent citations use the abbreviation *M.*

11. Edward Kamau Brathwaite, *Sun Poem,* Oxford (Eng.), Oxford University Press, 1982, p. 1. Subsequent citations use the abbreviation *S.*

12. Edward Kamau Brathwaite, *Jah Music,* Mona (Kingston, Jamaica), Savacou, 1986, p. 16.

Norman Weinstein (essay date autumn 1994)

SOURCE: Weinstein, Norman. "Jazz in the Caribbean Air." *World Literature Today* 68, no. 4 (autumn 1994): 715-18.

[*In the following essay, the author, a noted jazz critic, provides examples of poems showing how Brathwaite's love of jazz is a strong influence on his poetry, a claim made by Brathwaite himself. In particular, the author finds the influence of such jazz geniuses as Duke Ellington, John Coltrane, Charlie Parker and Sonny Rollins.*]

If one could assemble in imagination an ultimate jazz band to honor the literary achievement of Kamau Brathwaite, one could not do better than to choose the four musicians his poetry heralds: Sonny Rollins, John Coltrane, Albert Ayler, and Duke Ellington. This jazz quartet particularly noteworthy in Brathwaite's poetic world has as much to do with the heroism Brathwaite finds in their lives as with the rich intellectual and spiritual rewards he has discovered in their music over the decades. Without hyperbole, one could look upon Rollins, Coltrane, Ayler, and Ellington as primary sources of poetic inspiration, "muses," or, even more strikingly, archetypal poetic figures. While it is belaboring the obvious to state that jazz has been a lifetime influence upon Brathwaite's poetry, it is perhaps a revelation to discover just how central the lives of these four musicians have been to his evolving notion of his role as a poet as well as to the forms of his poetry.

In an interview with the American poet and editor Nathaniel Mackey, Brathwaite described his adolescent experiences as a jazz deejay:

> It [jazz] was regarded as devil music in Barbados, especially bebop, which I grew up on in the fifties there. We had a radio program as schoolboys—Harrison College, you know, the elite school of the island—and when we went on the air that first evening, the one and only evening, the people flooded the station with phone calls demanding the incarceration of the perpetrators, the, as they saw us, *cultural traitors.* Instead of Mozart or Rogers and Hart we were playing, I think, "Oop Bop s'Bam" or "Shaw Nuff" or "Ornithology," certainly something hard by Dizzy and Bird, followed by Thelonious Monk.[1]

Several facets of this early jazz memory deserve illumination. Bop, a jazz style favoring extravagant thematic improvisation based upon reformulating the structures of pop tunes, was Brathwaite's first embraced jazz style. Further, it was the first jazz style to wholeheartedly integrate Afro-Cuban rhythms, sacred and profane, thus bringing jazz listeners close to the African roots of this originally American music. And bop's most heroic single figure, "Bird," Charlie Parker, offered Brathwaite the image of a master saxophonist whose art and life-style were in opposition to bourgeois Caribbean societal standards, a true "cultural traitor" who, if he would play a Rodgers and Hart tune, would only do so by deconstructing its chords and accelerating its original tempo into the stratosphere.

Parker's saxophone style influenced virtually every major saxophonist of the fifties. It is not surprising to discover that the earliest recordings of Rollins, Coltrane, and Ayler, to differing degrees, all bear the stamp of Parker's influence. It was only in the 1960s, when the three saxophonists fully matured into highly individual styles, that the Parker sound fell away from their recordings. Brathwaite's poetry about these three appears to focus exclusively upon that period in the sixties when their true artistic voices crystallized.

One particular image of Sonny Rollins haunts Brathwaite: that of the saxophonist practicing alone on a catwalk on the Williamsburg Bridge, over New York's East River. Rollins did this repeatedly in 1959 during a period when he retired for a few years from public performance in order to rethink his musical direction. Brathwaite's first mention of the Rollins image occurs in **"Jah,"** a key poem in *Islands,* the third book in the trilogy *The Arrivants* [*A*]. Here are the poem's first two stanzas, with Rollins introducing himself symbolically in the second.

> Nairobi's male elephants uncurl
> their trumpets to heaven
> Toot-Toot takes it up
> in Havana
> in Harlem
>
> bridges of sound curve
> through the pale rigging
> of saxophone stops
> the ship sails, slips on banana
> peel water, eating the dark men.[2]

The surreal layering of unlikely imagery juxtaposed from Africa and the Americas creates a violently vivid set of impressions of urban life. Federico García Lorca's *Poet in New York* and Hart Crane's *The Bridge* are two book-length poems that come to mind when reading **"Jah."** The opening stanza plays on the cliché of "the city is a jungle," the locale where a Harlem jazz trumpeter's sound resonates with the ancient African jungles. But it is in the second stanza, where the image of Rollins playing saxophone on a city bridge is symbolically declared, that the power of jazz is illuminated. In one of many shocking puns that fill his poetry Brathwaite plays with multiple meanings of the word *stop*. Stops are the holes in the body of a saxophone, opened or closed by keys the player digitally controls. *Stop* is also utilized in its common meaning of "desist."

Brathwaite's second stanza is a striking compression of images, a knotty mass of complementary meanings. First, without mentioning Rollins by name, he is evoked by "bridges of sound curve / through the pale rigging / of saxophone stops." Simply juxtaposing the bridge and the saxophone will conjure the image of Rollins for almost any modern jazz fan. But Brathwaite takes the Rollins bridge imagery further than simply dropping an aside about a very unorthodox and talented player. Punning on "bridge," he compels us to hear Rollins's jazz as a bridge, a path to spiritual transcendence. The poem, like Rollins's jazz, is that artfully constructed bridge which allows us a view from the heights (metaphysical if not physical). In the poem's ninth stanza the reader is offered a divine gaze: "But here God looks out over the river / yellow mix of the neon lights / high up over the crouching cottonwool green / and we float, high up over the sighs of the city, / like fish in a gold water world" (*A,* 163).

It is not that the jazzman performing on the city bridge is God per se. That would entail the quite human saxophonist having the power *literally* to stop the sailing ships that eat dark men, as Brathwaite graphically and symbolically described the marine commerce that brought us the horrors of capitalism and slavery. What Rollins as a saxophonist is able to offer in the poem is an image of artistic and spiritual power which can at least *interrupt* "business as usual" in an oppressive urban center. It is a transitory interruption, quick as a saxophonist's finger pressing a key to stop a hole, but a wholly meaningful gesture, an act of rebellion against economic and political forces transforming the earth into a dead mass of commodities for sale. The closing lines of **"Jah"** are a woeful reminder of that world: "The sun that was once a doom of gold to the Arawaks / is now a flat boom in the sky" (**A,** 164). If the gods will not allow this to happen, they must cry through a saxophonist's horn, as they do through Rollins's, and through Brathwaite's dramatization of Rollins assuming a godlike stance over the East River.

Pessimism about the earth's fate—and about the artist's capacity to offer alternative scenarios for the earth—can be found in a poem written nearly two decades after **"Jah."** In **"And now a soft commentaries from Angelo Solimann Africanus the Neumann,"** from the book *X/Self,* Sonny Rollins on the bridge is once again evoked, but this time more directly and more darkly than in **"Jah."** In a catalogue of horrifying imagery describing a greed-driven world gone mad sometime in the near future we discover: "there will be / no more sonny rollins // practising his tenor sax among the spires of the brooklyn bridge."[3] It is curious that Brathwaite chose to rewrite the Rollins incident by having him on the Brooklyn Bridge rather than on the Williamsburg. While both span the East River, it is the Brooklyn Bridge that was heralded as a symbol of urban American's decadence by the poets García Lorca and Hart Crane, a symbolism perhaps prompted by the fact that the Brooklyn Bridge, unlike the Williamsburg, is exactly on the edge of New York City's financial district.

Sonny Rollins and John Coltrane recorded together in the fifties. The album was released under the title of *Tenor Madness,*[4] suggesting that both saxophonists allowed themselves highly abandoned and free-form improvising. The recording suggests nothing of the kind. It sounds like two young saxophonists who had not yet found their signature styles, playing with reserve, careful to stay out of each other's path. It is unfortunate that no recordings are available of Rollins and Coltrane playing together in the sixties after they had found their mature voices; that might have created a recording truly worthy of a title like *Tenor Madness.* Rollins and Coltrane grew into sharing more musical ideas during the sixties, working independently of each other, than they did sharing a bandstand in the fifties. They never appear together in a Brathwaite poem, though, like Rollins, Coltrane makes frequent appearances, both as a heroic figure and as an artist whose art builds bridges between Africa and the Americas.

The image of Coltrane in **"Trane,"** a poem from Brathwaite's 1976 collection *Black and Blues,* is straightforward: "Propped against the crowded bar / he pours into the curved and silver horn / his old unhappy longing for a home."[5] The poem's concluding fourth stanza reprises the first stanza quoted above: "and pours his old unhappy longing for home." Whether that "home" the saxophonist is longing for is Africa or some Christian dream of heaven is never made explicit. That is the gist of Coltrane's depiction on the surface of the poem: the jazz man pours out his soul into his instrument to declare this longing for home.

The connection to Coltrane's life and music, however, is far more subtle than what can be quickly read on the surface. The second stanza introduces some obvious end rhymes: "the dancers twist and turn / he leans and wishes he could burn / his memories to ashes like some old notorious emperor." The rhyming continues in the third and fourth stanzas, quite obvious and quite musical. Since rhyming is used rarely in most of Brathwaite's poetry, when it does occur the reader should be alert to the reasons for it. The poem moves in and out of conventional (rhymed) poetic shape—in much the same fashion that Coltrane's famous renditions of "My Favorite Things" move in and out of conventional song structure. The shape of "Trane" actually enacts what the saxophonist became famous for: the ability to deconstruct conventional artistic forms creatively and subversively for the sake of adding spiritual dimensions to the performance of superficially banal art works.

Still, for all the artistic splendor Coltrane executed by articulating his longing for home through his music, Brathwaite's poem insists that the saxophonist could expect little reward. "This crowded bar . . . holds all the fame and recognition he will ever earn / on earth or heaven," claims Brathwaite. But when the image of Coltrane resurfaces in the poem **"Noom"** a few years later, Coltrane gets his just recognition—in the heavens. In an incantation to the power of the sun (again, Brathwaite is punning on "sun" and "son"), Coltrane is transformed into a *loa,* a divine spirit in Haitian voodoo, akin to the Yoruba god Shango: "sun who has clothed arethas voice in dark gospel / who works on the railroad tracks / who gave jesse owens his engine / who blue coltranes crippled train."[6] As was the case with Rollins, Brathwaite compresses multiple references to the saxophonist in a few knotty lines. Coltrane is joined to a pantheon of African American heroic figures, real as well as folkloric ("John Henry" is suggested by the mention of the railroad work, which simultaneously evokes the Yoruba god Shango). It may seem peculiar that Brathwaite has included the Olympic athlete Jesse Owens with musicians on the order of Aretha Franklin and John Coltrane. Yet by forging this association, Brathwaite is reminding us of the physical strength necessary to play saxophone as Coltrane did. Think of the sheer stamina, the pushing of lungs and nerves required to improvise for over an hour on the melody of "My Favorite Things." It was an "olympian exercise" of body and mind, and perhaps, like Owens's performance at the Nazi-saturated Olympic Games of 1936, an act of artistic beauty to fly in the face of a racist society.

Puns once again abound in Brathwaite's poetry. **"Blue"** refers to Coltrane's roots in the blues, to the title of an album, *Blue Train,* on the "Blue Note" label. Hearing the poem read before examining it on a printed page, one could easily hear "blue" as "blew," implying that the power of the sun blew through Coltrane's saxophone as he recorded *Blue Train,* an album which marked a turning point in the saxophonist's career. There is also Shango's symbolism brought into play by the title of Coltrane's album, since locomotives are associated in West African and Caribbean mythology with Shango. Coltrane was referred to by fellow musicians and fans as **"Trane,"** an allusion to how often he played with locomotive energy a long unraveling train of thought. An additional linkage of Coltrane to Shango, the Yoruba god linked not only with railroads but more commonly with extreme bursts of rage against dishonesty and injustice, occurs in **"Word Making Man,"** a poem from Brathwaite's *Middle Passages.* [*MP*] The word *Coltrane* seems now to transcend mere reference to a divinely inspired jazz musician; Coltrane is now a common noun referring to a force of nature: "& the sea between us yields its secrets / silver into pellables into sheets of sound / that bear our pain & spume & salt & coltrane."[8]

Coltrane viewed his jazz as chiefly a spiritual exercise once he discovered his mature voice on saxophone. That view of jazz as a *kind* of religion links him partially to Rollins (who has moved in and out of highly commercially compromising situations in the last two decades), but it links him totally to the other major saxophonist of the sixties, Albert Ayler. More radical in his musical thinking than either Rollins or Coltrane, Ayler developed a highly dissonant and free-form style of saxophone playing which ran counter to all saxophone styles of previous eras. At the heart of Ayler's style was an extremely unconventional sense of how musical time could progress in a composition. While Rollins and Coltrane were known for "swinging" saxophone solos—a rhythmic momentum hard to define but easily felt by how one's body moves while listening to certain patterned relationships between long and short notes—Ayler's music never "swung." It seemed to issue forth in asymmetrical waves of pure sound, impossible to indicate on paper using conventional music-scoring notations. Ayler's saxophone playing seemed to defy any *regular* time measure. Metronomes and clocks seemed to have no reality in his music or life. Yet, of course, he lived in the world that accepted their absolute reality.

The contrast between Ayler's sense of time and that of conventional society is at the heart of Brathwaite's poem **"Clock,"** dedicated to Ayler. The opening lines present the saxophonist as a kind of surreal flower blooming through plate-glass barriers, with roots anchored in the solid and nourishing mud of the earth. What uprooted him was the "clock / ground up / to tick / the time."[9] Ayler is seen as attempting through his art to counter the mechanizing impact of commercially defined uniform time by telling liberating tales through his saxophone.

```
                    skill
       of the
       horn
       in its cradle of   alarms
                tell
       ing what
       ever tale
       was
               tocked

                                              (33)
```

The shape of the poem suggests bursts of staccato notes rapidly executed, a favorite stylistic trait of Ayler's. The poem looks like an attempt to score an Ayler solo for the page.

The tales that Ayler told on his saxophone, however, were stopped by the musician's possible suicide or murder. His body was found in the East River, the same river Sonny Rollins towered above on a bridge a few years earlier. Brathwaite does not offer a theory concerning Ayler's demise; he lets the image of the clock dramatize it: "the / clock / stopp. / & the rock of his skull fall down" (35). This "Poe-like" conclusion seems also to introduce the image of the heart as a jazzman's time regulator. It is Brathwaite's bleakest image of the jazz saxophonist. There is no hint of transcendence through his art. But there is a potent image offered which is as applicable to Brathwaite the poet as to any of these jazz artists: they are the ones whose art sounded *alarms.* That is why we need to heed their cries.

Brathwaite's poem of tribute to the artistry of Duke Ellington, **"Duke Playing Piano at 70"** (from *Middle Passages*), lets more than saxophone cries resound. Female vocalists (Bessie Smith, Ivie Anderson), percussionists (Sonny Greer, Sam Woodyard), and a broad assortment of brass and reed players are heralded. They attain significance in the poem as they constellate about the radiantly central figure of the elder Ellington, their pianist and band leader. The poem opens with the haunting lines "The old man's hands are alligator / skins" (*MP,* 21), conjuring the image of the crocodile in Egyptian mythology, a creature embodying ancestral wisdom. But the evocation of this ancient mythic realm superimposed upon Ellington suddenly shifts to a summoning of Bessie Smith's power in wailing the blues. This is then followed by one of several starkly written lists of nouns. The first is a catalogue of places where African Americans confronted racism most dangerously: "Watts / St Louis / Selma Alabama / Chicago / Montgomery Bus Boycott / Cairo" (23). The second catalogue, which sets up a call-and-response pattern in the poem, is a list of Ellington's original compositions: "Caravan / Perdido / Cotton-tail / . . . / Creole Love Call" (25). The final list is of Ellington's star soloists, whose instrumental styles so colored his compositions, among them Paul Gonsalves, Harry Carney, and Sam Nanton.

What all these names of places, musicians, and compositions suggest is jazz embodying a moral vision. In lines echoing that other great poet of the Americas closely associated with jazz, Langston Hughes, Brathwaite writes: "*[It] is a matter of hope of keep hope alive of the right to continue the / dream / about our rightful place at the table*" (*MP,* 24). Ellington's way of establishing "the right to continue the dream about our rightful place" was through jazz informed by a strong historical racial consciousness. "We must be proud of our race and our heritage, we must develop the special talents which have been handed down to us through generations," wrote Ellington.[10] Ellington's musical vision not only encompassed generations but also continents. He composed extended jazz suites to celebrate the statehoods of Liberia and Togo, wrote jazz tunes to celebrate African women and African flowers, and even composed pieces to herald the Afro-Caribbean cultural world. In the concluding stanzas of his poem Brathwaite notes the range of Ellington's musical vision: "the old man's hands are striding through / the keyboard sidewalks alleyways & ages // from / Shakka spear and guinea Bird // to / Caribbean stilt dance / vèvè / masquerade" (27).

By concentrating on Ellington the pianist, Brathwaite focuses upon an artist with a highly percussive and rhythmically surprising style, drumlike at times, evoking the thunder of African ancestors. And Ellington often conducted his band from his vantage point as the group's pianist, his percussive keyboard attacks calling forth rapturous responses from reeds and brass. Those hammering hands of Ellington the pianist, as wrinkled with age as a crocodile's skin, undergo a transformation in the closing lines of Brathwaite's poem: "& look / the old man's alligator hands are young" (28). By presenting the great jazz composer as a creator who can defy

even aging, Brathwaite puts Ellington in that sacred pantheon where he places Coltrane in **"Noom,"** in the holy and timeless realm of African spirits.

The value that the adolescent Brathwaite sensed in jazz recordings has become for the mature poet a vibrantly inspiring driving force and knowledge source for his poetry. In Ellington, as in Sonny Rollins, John Coltrane, and Albert Ayler, African spirits have found ways to communicate their messages in New World settings. Brathwaite's poetry touching upon jazz sharpens our awareness of these African voices singing in the Caribbean air.

Notes

1. Nathaniel Mackey, "An Interview with Edward Kamau Brathwaite," *Hambone,* 9 (Winter 1991), p. 57.

2. Edward Brathwaite, *The Arrivants,* Oxford (Eng.), Oxford University Press, 1973, p. 162. Subsequent references use the abbreviation *A.*

3. Edward Kamau Brathwaite, *X/Self,* Oxford (Eng.), Oxford University Press, 1987, p. 59.

4. Sonny Rollins, *Tenor Madness,* Original Jazz Classics compact disc OJC-124.

5. Edward Brathwaite, "Trane," *Black and Blues,* 1976; reprinted in *The Jazz Poetry Anthology,* Sascha Feinstein and Yusef Komunyakaa, eds., Bloomington, Indiana University Press, 1991, pp. 17-18. References are to the anthology reprint, since Brathwaite's book is currently out of print in the U.S.

6. Edward Kamau Brathwaite, *Sun Poem,* Oxford (Eng.), Oxford University Press, 1982, p. 53.

7. See Brathwaite's explanatory notes to *X/Self,* p. 130.

8. Kamau Brathwaite, *Middle Passages,* New York, New Directions, 1993, p. 6. References use the abbreviation *MP.*

9. Art Lange and Nathaniel Mackey, eds., *Moment's Notice: Jazz in Poetry & Prose,* Minneapolis, Coffee House, 1993, p. 33.

10. Barry Ulanov, *Duke Ellington,* New York, Da Capo, 1975, p. 190.

Timothy J. Reiss (essay date autumn 1994)

SOURCE: Reiss, Timothy J. "Reclaiming the Soul: Poetry, Autobiography, and the Voice of History." *World Literature Today* 68, no. 4 (autumn 1994): 883-90.

[*In the following essay, Reiss links the structure of Brathwaite's poetry to seventeenth-century England by positing that the poet's work often has an underlying structure derived from iambic pentameter, a meter that Brathwaite has tweaked to reflect the historical changes that have led to the postcolonial culture of Barbados.*]

Through Kamau Brathwaite's work run three favorite metaphors. The earliest uses the iambic pentameter that had become a norm in English poetry from roughly the seventeenth century. The second represents the Caribbean Islands as the result of a child's (or god's) skipping stones in a great curve across the ocean from the coast of Guyana to the tip of Florida. The third transforms the waters buried deep in the porous rock that is Barbados into the welling of a buried culture whose very concealment has made it the more vital to the life above. The first concerns the constitution, practice, and differentiation of a poetic voice; the second holds an individual's sense of a home place; the third captures something like a collectivity's living cultural and political consciousness.

At the same time, each one works and plays with the other two. More than tropes in language, the finest metaphors are alive and capture vital actualities. Such are these. Barbados *is* rock of the sort Brathwaite takes for his image. Beneath and in it *is* the fresh water making life on the island possible. As the poet/historian has also been able to show, Barbados *does* have a hidden culture, living remnant of Igbo consciousness. Then too, Barbados is geologically unique among the islands, and the more-than-metaphor grasps that singularity as it simultaneously situates it among its companion islands geographically, historically, and culturally. Lastly, the skipping stones, as well, offer not just an image of place but a rhythm and the curving shape of an imagination.

They ground a different poetry and a consciousness not best rendered by that pentameter whose exemplar Brathwaite finds in the English eighteenth century: "The Cúrfew tólls the knéll of párting dáy." He observes that before Chaucer no such dominant meter was to be found, but that since then poetic effort in the anglophone world has had to be expended in its terms. (Whitman sought to overcome it by noise, "a large movement of sound," Cummings by fragmenting it, Moore "with syllabics.") Yet it stays. And that rhythmic inertia is a dilemma, for "it carries with it a certain kind of experience, which is not the experience of a hurricane. A hurricane does not roar in pentameters. And that's the problem: how do you get a rhythm which approximates the *natural* experience, the *environmental* experience?"[1] That rhythm, of course, is grounded and trammeled in the skipping stones and rock-concealed water, both bearing spirit of place. But that is not the only problem. With experience of place bound in form goes a bond of culture.

In the essay just quoted, Brathwaite did not dwell on Thomas Gray's celebrated poem, and for good reason:

he wanted to get on to the forms of a new voice. Here, though, we may grant it a bit more attention, and I would like to quote its beginning at a little more length:

> The Cúrfew tólls the knéll of párting dáy,
> The lówing hérd winds slówly ó'er the léa,
> The plówman hómeward plóds his wéary wáy,
> And léaves the wórld to dárkness ánd to mé.
>
> Now fádes the glímmering lándscape ón the síght
> And áll the áir a stíllness hólds,
> Save whére the béetle whéels his dróning flíght,
> And drówsy tínklings lúll the dístant fólds.

If you look at where the accents fall in the first stanza, you see how the long vowels echo tolling bell and "lowing herd." Fading landscape at dusk, evening quiet of late summer, wheeling beetles, tinkling sheep bells, the later "ivy-mantled tow'r," "mopeing owl," "rugged elms," "yew-tree's shade," and "swallow twitt'ring from the straw-built shed" are stereotypes meant to summon the image of an age-old country England to frame the elegy on humble folk that is the principal weight of the poem: "the short and simple annals of the poor" (l. 32). They frame a nostalgic musing on those who might have been great churchmen, rulers, or musicians, except only that "Knowledge to their eyes her ample pages / Rich with the spoils of time did ne'er unroll" (ll. 49-50). So these remain a gem unknown in ocean cave (53-54), a flower "to blush unseen" and "waste its sweetness on the desert air" (55-56), "a village-Hampden," a "Cromwell guiltless," or "some mute inglorious Milton" (57-60).

The marching, endlessly expansive pentameter, then, contains a very particular history and cultural experience. "The madding crowd's . . . strife" may be called "ignoble" (73), but the nostalgia grounding the poem's theme depends entirely on the achievements of those who supposedly formed and sprang from that crowd. Indeed, the Hampdens, Miltons, and Cromwells, who, lost in poverty, misery, and illiteracy, never did share the expansive culture, would have done so if only they had had the wealth and learning to give them the necessary competitive edge. Gray glories in a "loss" that proves the depth of English culture, with its myriad putative conquerors, preachers, and poets scattered about the countryside. The Hampdens, Cromwells, and Miltons raise before us the image of those great churchmen, rulers, and artists who were *not* silent or "wasted" in the desert or under the seas; those who *did* "wade through slaughter for a throne" and "shut the gates of mercy on mankind" (67-68), whether at home on those of a different class, abroad on those of a different race, or everywhere on those of a different sex.

We may also perhaps be permitted to see how the marching linear pentameter (or its equally normative counterpart in the alternating masculine and feminine rhymes of the French alexandrine, with its more or less clearly set caesura) corresponds to a broader cultural reality, one anchored both in political theory and in historical actuality. I mean the argument that what makes a "healthy" state, society, and culture is expansion. The notion dates at least from Machiavelli's suggestion that the reason a society needed to think constantly of outward expansion was clear in its image as a place composed of endlessly active animals that would turn destructively against one another if not directed elsewhere. Bacon thus thought of war as the health-giving exercise of nations; so did Hobbes, Locke, and many other successors. The individuals whose threatened warring necessitated the founding covenant of civil society provided the very image and model of the states that those individual societies were to become. Reason, knowledge, will, and power to act became their organizing axioms. The order of reason matched that of the world, the accumulation of material knowledge allowed such reason instrumentally to adjust the world to its own benefit, will urged one to it, and power gave the tools to make intervention sure.

What came to be termed "literature" participated in these changes, adopting what I have elsewhere called "epistemological," "ethical," "aesthetic," and "political" roles—the last being initially the most important. It confirmed a (sometimes complicated) politics of singular authority, however embodied; it claimed to be ordered by a syntax that was both that of right language and that of universal reason; it portrayed and asserted an ethics of individual interest whose virtue lay in simultaneously benefitting the community; and it placed beauty in a personal "taste" that echoed general reason.[2] Literature's "guarantee" of political claim and historical practice ultimately helped "universalize" these developments, so that the assertion of a right to intervene in others' histories and cultures became grounded in Europe's claim to being the vanguard of human progress, with no less than an obligation (God- or History-given) to put others in the way of such progress.

We do this, of course, only with the deepest regrets and the most profound awareness that something has been lost. Gray's mid-eighteenth-century nostalgia was quite typical of that of many others: Oliver Goldsmith's, for example, in poems like *The Deserted Village* or *The Traveller*. And that such as Samuel Johnson made fun of the linguistic archaisms used by Gray changes not a whit the significance of the nostalgia. Alexander Pope had put it perfectly in his *Essay on Man* not so long before (1730-34) of the "lurking principle of death" that dwells within the body: "The young disease, that must subdue at length, / Grows with his growth, and strengthens with his strength / . . . cast and mingled with his very frame" (1.134-37). This death lurking in the heart of expansive Enlightened Reason finds its modern currency among such as Max Horkheimer, The-

odor Adorno, Edmund Husserl, Martin Heidegger, Georg Lukács, and many others, who have argued that within such Reason lies a virus destructive not just of the European—Western—world and its culture, but of all civilizations. Some think it means the need to find something quite new; others to complete an unfinished, unperfected Enlightenment; yet others a rediscovery of what came before, of some supposed wholeness with the universe.

Whatever the solution, golden age or Eldorado lost meant golden age or Eldorado had to be found. With or without regret, expansive Europe would have to march out in file and find it. Death could not be allowed its victory. And whatever they might be, right reason and knowledge would first be Europe's. Others, Asian, African, or American, untutored like those inglorious Miltons and guiltless Cromwells, poor like Gray's "rustic moralist" (84) or "hoary-headed Swain" (97), without power and the knowledge of right reason, would justly be put in order by the vanguard. For after all, as James Thomson put it in the artful pentameters of his rewritten *Summer* of 1744:

> Ill-fated race! the softening arts of peace,
> Whate'er the humanizing Muses teach,
> The godlike wisdom of the tempered breast,
> Progressive truth, the patient force of thought,
> Investigation calm whose silent powers
> Command the world, the light that leads to Heaven,
> Kind equal rule, the government of laws,
> And all-protecting freedom which alone
> Sustains the name and dignity of man—
> These are not theirs.[3]

One can but admire these "softening arts of peace" that, by teaching us that we alone rightfully possess "the name and dignity of man," so readily justify the manipulation of those who therefore do not.

I am not—need I say?—suggesting that pentameters create (or in themselves are) a tool of oppression, a title of hegemony. Nor, of course, was Brathwaite. Language and style alone no more make hegemony than revolution. Yet they confirm and guarantee them. They are nonetheless the form of a particular pattern of thought, bearer of certain structures of feeling, and expression of specific kinds of practice. Those, too, are crucial to this experience that never had to learn to roar with the notes of a hurricane, to curve with stones skipping across the ocean, to limp with the life of Legba or dance with the rhythm of Shango. In his 1992 "Columbus poem" Brathwaite aims Colón westward into the future as a linear missile whose sure systems become less assured when he looks out upon the changed history and geography for which he has been willy-nilly responsible. Not for him the view of Keats's Cortez in Darien. Both the rhythm and the typography of the poem are aimed to undermine the patterns, structures, and practices which Columbus was to come historically and culturally to embody and exemplify.

The move is essential. Voice, language, forms of expression, we know, capture and colonize the mind no less surely than more overt ways of seizure. As James Joyce's Stephen Dedalus put it in a famous passage: "His language, so familiar and so foreign, will always be for me an acquired speech. I have not made or accepted its words. My voice holds them at bay. My soul frets in the shadow of his language."[4] Brathwaite has inevitably put the matter rather differently: "It was in language that the slave was perhaps most successfully imprisoned by his master, and it was in his (mis-)use of it that he perhaps most effectively rebelled. Within the folk tradition, language was (and is) a creative act in itself."[5] Again, language is not and cannot be separated from a whole culture, and the West Indian case was graver still than such a one as the Irish to which Dedalus referred. The modern peoples of the islands never had a tongue alive in and imbued with the place where they dwell, for they were forcibly brought to lands whose own peoples had been destroyed. Further, the languages whence they came were both robbed of their source and shattered to fragments. The language Dedalus holds at bay is their only possibility: a language bent first to a victimizer's will, desires, and interests.

Brathwaite argued the consequences in 1963, characterizing anglophone Caribbean prose writers as producing, at home or abroad, "the same story, expressed in the same rhythms and a similar technique: frustration, bewilderment, lack of a centre, lack of faith in the society into which they were born or in which they find themselves."[6] It was a story of endless emigration, no matter the direction in which it went. In this regard, one reads now, with the surprise that even a mere twenty years of changed awareness can bring, the pride with which Kenneth Ramchand viewed such emigration in 1971: "Since 1950 . . . every well-known West Indian novelist has established himself while living [in the English capital]. London is indisputably the West Indian literary capital."[7] One recognizes economic and cultural pressures that still drive a Caryl Phillips to "establish himself" in London and indeed to tell the same story of exiled "frustration, bewilderment, lack of a centre, [and] lack of faith in [their] society," as that to which Brathwaite earlier addressed himself.[8] The point, though, was the *pride* Ramchand could then take in such emigration.

In a very real way, one may characterize Brathwaite's own work as historian, storyteller, cultural archivist, educator, essayist, and poet as a lifelong effort to take up the gauntlet he threw down in his criticism. The effort to find a poetic form that would not just pick at or disrupt the dominant pentameter but use a quite different rhythm, one from another place, another environment, another experience, was just the earliest of the

shapes that work took. It has also led him from the rock of Barbados and the curving stones of its habitat, through Europe to Africa, and eventually back to the Caribbean. Its aim has been to discover, to invent (in that word's double sense of finding *and* making: *invenire*) that Caribbean—especially his own Barbados—as a *home,* not as a displacement or a surrogate for something else, be it "little England" or robbed Africa.

The first part, and understanding, of that geographic and historical story was told in the ***Arrivants*** trilogy. There, ***Rights of Passage*** "tells the story" of the passage from Africa to the Caribbean as a displacement that remains a displacement, simply the obverse, in a sense, of the coin that had Europe as center and exile on its other face. Indeed, that particular passage was quite evidently part of the same story. ***Masks*** then tells the further tale of a modern poet's return to Africa, less as a search for "roots" than as a way to compose cultural remnants into something more "whole," whose masks become successive distancings from a self that will ultimately be thereby able to become part of a collectivity. Can this itself be shipped back, as it were, to the poet's home in the "islands" whence he came? ***Islands,*** the third book of the trilogy, seems to answer this question with another one: the remnants that Africa may "put together" can surely only remain remnants in those displaced islands? But it is as remnants, pieces fit for recovery, creation, building, that they can be fitted into a cultural space that is, precisely, Caribbean—a *home* space.

Brathwaite's poetry has never sought any easy answers. There was certainly no hope here for one. This last "conclusion," if it was not to remain only a pious wish, demanded considerable and wide cultural work. Already in the late 1950s, Brathwaite had started writing criticism of Caribbean literary work, and it has always accompanied his poetry and, equally importantly, his work as a historian. That latter work was clearly essential: to understand the place that was and is Barbados and its island companions, and the European, African, and American history in which it and they participated. This is not the place to examine the details of that work. What is important here is how it informs the poetry and criticism, infusing it with that very sense of an "environment," a place, of particular historical experience, which is and is not that of Europeans—or Africans, or other Americans (although it may be worth noting that the effort to make anew a culture's voice is seconded by an educative one, where he has made his scholarly work the basis of textbooks for schoolchildren of the Caribbean).

Suffice it to say, as the three metaphors with which I began suggest, that this work has always explored issues similar to that found in the poetry and criticism.

One way to get at this, perhaps, is to suggest that the ten years Brathwaite spent in Africa (mainly Ghana) enabled him to make a passage akin to that expressed by George Lamming's Trumper, who comes back from the United States having discovered his group identity as a black. Memory, a sense of place, and above all a culture-consciousness are embodied for Trumper in this recognition, so that the old "big bad feeling in the pit of the stomach," the dizziness and emptiness are forgotten: "A man who knows his people won't ever feel like that."[9] Brathwaite came close to paraphrasing these sentences in the characterization we saw of the anglophone Caribbean novel. In West Africa he found both the possibility of such group belonging and a place which grounded many of the fragments he had found and was to find in the Caribbean. But that was assuredly not to say, as some critics have, that he set aside Europe. "West Indian literature" had to be seen, he wrote in 1967, in its "proper context of an expression both European and African at the same time." It is to say, however, that fragments of the one had to be set against, recovered from, built into the "imposure" of the other.[10]

Brathwaite was now prepared to go beyond both those he had once criticized and his own criticism. He would seek the home from a discovery of Caribbean geography and its meaning in history (the skipped stones and their fall; the rock hiding vital waters; windstorms of Africa, the Saharan harmattan, that are now—after him— understood to affect the December-February droughts that strike the islands and the aforementioned hurricanes) by reconstructing the shards of fragmented cultural memory, by historical recovery, folk recall, and exploration in a poetry that would set out to find not only a Caribbean "content," but its own form of expression, its own rhythms and music. This last he would eventually draw from his work on jazz forms, his sensitivity to local sounds and images, and his deep awareness of the cultural importance of drumming rhythms. But he would also explore the wider and more general possibility of "nation language": a language that would itself echo "the environmental experience."

For one—disastrous—way for the colonized mind to face down its colonizer is to do what some did to the normative pentameter: fragment it, take it apart, break it up—even though, as Brathwaite argues, to do so still leaves it as the only hegemonic form. And what the fragmenter risks getting, and indeed gets in the end, is "a frantic impoverished dialect." This is to quote Wilson Harris describing the speech of one of his protagonists, Hassan, in *The Far Journey of Oudin.* He is matched by Kaiser, who had but "a few words of formal English." Neither of them can possibly come close to grasping the "unearthly delicate writing on the sky." And to Hassan's imagined wish to go back to India, Kaiser responds by protesting: "What language had he save the darkest and frailest outline of an ancient style and tongue? Not a blasted thing more." "You have no language," says another; "you have no custom." That is why the Hindus' Indian father feels so distanced from them: "we got to forgive he," says one of them, "for the strict unfathomable way he got of looking at we like if he grieving for a language. In ancient scorn and habit at the hard careless words we does use. But is who fault if the only language we got is a breaking-up or a making-up language?"[11]

One cannot just "create a language" or "rescue . . . the word" from its possessors, as Eduardo Galeano writes. No doubt a writer's feel for "his or her people—their roots, their vicissitudes, their destiny—and the ability to perceive the heartbeat, the sound and rhythm of the authentic counterculture" must be intense.[12] But what and where is such "*another* culture"? How can one recognize its "authenticity"? To say so much leaves yet unsaid the matter of *how* one might create or rescue language and word. One does neither *ex nihilo*: one uses, combines, fuses, and recombines myriad elements from the varied sources that forge everyone's homes or home. These elements already always exist, doing so in cultural experiences and environments whose ramifications may often escape notice. Whatever impoverishment is theirs, they remain remnants of a particular culture, and will do so until we know enough of *that* experience and ours to be able to use them otherwise. "Collective identity is born out of the past and is nourished by it."[13] We must know the working of the elements composing that past and the identities which arise from it. To think one can adopt them without preparation, as if they were neutral, is almost surely to fall back into the patterns customary to the words one supposed one was rescuing: not—perhaps— impoverished, but still colonized.

Brathwaite traced those difficulties—with anger—in *Black and Blues.*[14] There the angry breaking away from the consequences of colonization and oppression, of cultural "imposure," made use of his gradual uncovering of jazz forms, local sounds and images, the rhythm of the drum—the fragmented shards, as I said, of cultural memory—to recombine them into something potentially new. Anger, while it is surely the only appropriate response to the theft of a language and a culture, clearly risks rejecting altogether the very elements it must of necessity use: "like a rat / like a rat / like a rat-a-tap tappin // like a rat / like a rat / like a rat-a-tap tappin // an we burnin babylone" (**"Conqueror,"** pp. 19, 23). These lines were to be repeated in *Sun Poem* (1982), where they signal even more emphatically Caliban's revolt. *Black and Blues* then takes the reader through a triple sequence of understanding.

The opening anger emphasizes the dismay and disgust of the poet who has been forced to pick through the "fragments" marking the loss of his own culture and the sinister "gift" of the pieces permitted by another only to serve its own interests. Then comes the outrage of **"Drought,"** facing the consequences of oppression: Caliban as "victim of the cities' victory" (30), Madrid or Paris, Amsterdam or London; Caliban, too, confronting visions of a place that "is no white man lan' / an' yet we have ghetto here" (32). This yields to the further outrage of being forced to violence to avenge what has been taken (a violence that usually destroys its own), and at the adulteration of African memories: "a forgotten kingdom" (43), a yearning still borne in pain. Yet, at the last, we find the hopefulness of **"Flowers"**: the rediscovery of fragments, African and Caribbean, based in firm geography of place: "the seas drummers // softly softly on sound . . . / it is a beginning" (**"Harbour,"** 83); in the symbol and existence of **"Crab,"** who holds memory and geography together; and in the final hope of **"Koker,"** with its "coastline" lying beneath "the sounds of stretched light . . . the don drumming light, against / sky that is their living monument" (90).

Black and Blues captured the dismay, frustration, bewilderment, decentering, and grief of Harris's characters in their linguistic and cultural deprivation, but found a way to tap new rhythms, a confident history, and a solid sense of place(s) to start making something otherwise. In a way, it repeated in concentrated little the movement of *The Arrivants*. We seem to be shifting here from what we may once more call, again after Ngũgĩ wa Thiong'o, a decolonizing of the mind, toward something that may be considerably harder, something that requires remapping the terrain, reclaiming the soul. Brathwaite's second trilogy, consisting of *Mother Poem, Sun Poem,* and *X/Self,* furthered these themes. The first was, so to speak, a discovery of the *place* of Barbados. The poet's quest to know and remember his mother became a rediscovery of Barbadian geography, imbued with the Atlantic call of Africa and Europe, but essentially now *itself,* its own, with its own no longer buried culture as well. Out of the submerged coral of the island come its waters of life as out of various cultural practices, now *seen* for the first time, come submerged but ever less fragmented cultural forms, completing the hope expressed at the end of *Black and Blues*. The poet himself gets a grounded (new, but also culturally old) name.

Sun Poem next pursued the poet's paternal "genealogy," confirming his place in the land less "mythically," through the family grounding of grandfather, father, son, and memories of the boy's childhood. The son's name of Adam symbolized this rooting, discovery, and, no doubt above all, the poet's *invention* of the new. *X/Self* finally explored the poet's now affirmed grounding in past and present, in Europe and Africa, in violence and oppression as well as in tact, grace, and renewal. The islands have become, too, a place of and for their *own* people: "not fe dem / not fe dem / de way

caliban / done // but fe we / fe a-we."[15] This poem was to be reworked, rewritten, and lengthened as **"Letter Sycorax"** in *Middle Passages,* where the poet himself became and superseded the old Caliban of a past that still depended on fragments tied to a particular hegemonic memory.[16] Answering (for example) Galeano's dilemma, this shift may prove as important a one for the Caribbean imagination as was Roberto Fernández Retamar's replacement of José Enrique Rodó's Ariel by Caliban himself. The negation, aggression, and denial with which Rodó's "Uncle Tom" was finally rejected yield here to new cultural creation.

Not for nothing did Brathwaite finish the second trilogy by rewriting **"Shango,"** a poem that came toward the end of *Black and Blues*. There the poem had started: "huh / there is a new breath here // hah / there is a sound of sparrows" (75). **"Xango"** begins: "*Hail* // there is new breath here // *huh* // there is a victory of sparrows" (*X* [*X/Self*], 107). The more European-like "hail" (befitting conquering Rome of the beginning of *X/Self*) was now combined with the thunder god's "huh"; noncommittal "sound" became the more optimistic "victory"—still, perhaps, not altogether freed of indecent hegemonies, for those "sparrows," after all, are the New Testament birds whose fall God would heed as much as a human's. Their victory risks being understood as a version of a central tenet of a text crucial to the European imagination: "And the meek shall inherit the earth."

Yet at this end, even if only momentarily, the poet of the second trilogy seemed to have found a moment of that "tact and selfless grace" he found necessary for such peace and balance in the much earlier *Contradictory Omens* (61). It is in light of this that we should read the humorously expressed sense of hope maintained in *Middle Passages* (even after the most catastrophic losses, personal and intellectual): "*is a matter of hope of keep hope alive of the right to continue the dream / about our rightful place at the table,*" he wrote in **"Duke: Playing Piano at 70"** (*MP* [*Middle Passages*], 24). Of this collection, Fenella Copplestone observed: "Its menace is real, its compassion touches the deepest springs of sadness, and its mythology is potent and frightening. People die in his world."[17]

But people also live there, and if the world has menace, it is to those whose control is overthrown by it. For here death is not the lurking disease, at least momentarily endemic to Enlightened Reason, recorded, as we saw, in unthreatening (?) expansive linear pentameter. Death plays its accepted and unfearful part in the ineluctable rhythm of life, the balanced experience of tact and grace. The "menace" of this poetry (poor, but revealing, word) is of a site composed from fragments no longer just remnants of things lost, but living crystals recombined and fused into consciousness of a place that does now capture fully "the *natural* experience, the *environmental* experience" of which Brathwaite was writing ten years and more ago.

It touches the deepest springs of sadness because the people who die there are vital, crucial to the remaking; their loss—one loss, anyway—is incomprehensible disaster: "without reason," he wrote in the dedication of *X/Self,* "all you hope gone / ev'rything look like it comin' out wrong. / Why is that? What it mean?" But these lines come from the last part (**"The Return"**) of *Rights of Passage,* first book of a trilogy whose last word was of hope—"making / with their // rhythms some- / thing torn // and new"[18]—so that the loss itself was now tied to the sense of place. Geography, poetry, self, history come together. The "missile" that was Columbus, that was the whole mighty power of an expansive culture imposed on Africa and the Americas, has yielded to a changed rhythm, a changed voice, the networked circle of Shango hidden in the watered rock beneath the still ongoing destructions of multinational capital.[19] Another major impingement of Europe on the Caribbean was of a different missile: a German torpedo sinking the *Cornwallis* in Bridgetown Harbour—but that was fifty years ago. Here too, marks of European aggression were quickly swallowed by Barbadian waters, becoming a plaything for local boys (*BP*, [*Barabajan Poems*], 153-54, 347-61). This swallowing may also be a harbinger of creation and hope.

Now, the poet returns to his uncle's workshop of his youth, to his limping Bob'ob. In the ruins of the old workshop he discovers that Bob'ob had carved a forbidden African image; as surprising and mysterious as the carving itself is its survival over the years in the ruins of Bob'ob's home (*BP*, 155). Limping Bob'ob, holding a lost past of Africa but also opening it unbeknownst to the poet, can be recognized as Legba, "the limping / crippled African god of the crossroads of beginnings & opening doors—as Bob'ob as Toussaint Louverture— the Liberator or 'Opener' of S Domingue into Haiti— himself a cripple—*fatras baton* they once called him . . . and whose French sobriquet—'Louverture'—was surely a direct translation of the Dahomey Legba (Open/ Doorway) & why not?" (172). And what of the poet himself? New **"Adam"** of *Sun Poem,* inventor of new names, opener of culture, finder of lost presences, sewer of remnants—may he not fill the same role? And why not? He discovers too that Bob'ob's ruined workshop has become a Zion meeting hall, a place of worship for a fundamentalist "Christian" group not happily accepted by authorities (166).

Listening outside, the poet hears the rhythm of their worship, their singing/chanting, and their movement/ dancing slowly change, "the sound of their voices has gradually gone through an alteration of orbit & pitch. they are into the pull of an alteration of consciousness as if the tides of their lives have paused on the brin(k) of falling onto our beaches & instead have slowly lifted themselves up up up so that the cries that should have been breaking from their crests do not move anymore but glisten in the deep silence of their throats until they begin to sweep slowly backwards like away from our shore from our trees from our hills away from Barbados" (181-82). The rhythm changes, the motion changes, the dance becomes the hoarse rhythmic deep breathing of Shango's visitation. The Christian hymnal pentameters give way to a different syncopated drumbeat, that is also the echoed blues and jazz rhythms of the old trains, "*sulphur and fire into a sibilant & quiet acceptance of her trans-formation like Aretha coming home in* Pullin*" (196-97).[20] "*Until there is at last what there always was /* SHANGO */ as she struggles to name almost names him the train comin in / comin in / comin in wid de rain*" (200-1; see also *Mother Poem,* 98-103).

Barabajan Poems is, for the moment, the culmination of the movement I have been seeking to trace. Bringing together the three metaphors with which we started, it transforms them into the vital essence of a culture. Legba, Shango, the rhythms, voice, and history that together make a whole have come together with other shards of other cultures: steam trains and blues, Christian hymns and jazz, the "rattle and pain" of loss and deprivation (*BP*, 201) with the vivid hope of new names and endless depth of proverbial orality (268-83). Brathwaite is here far indeed from Pope, Thomson, and Gray—not to mention the falling snow of his Cambridge youth. He is also very distant from those bewildered tales of emigration typical of the Caribbean writers of his youth—and still perfectly usual, we saw: both are, we have of course been suggesting, aspects of the *same,* very partial and interested, history—and place (which is not—not just, and not first—Caribbean). *Barabajan Poems* confirms the hopefulness of the lighted living coastline that ended *Black and Blues* and affirms the embedded collective "self" of *X/Self* into what seems a quite new cultural, natural, environmental surety.

Galeano wrote that "a literature born in the process of crisis and change, and deeply immersed in the risks and events of its time, can indeed help to create the symbols of the new reality, and perhaps . . . throw light on the signs along the road."[21] Brathwaite, poet, historian, and critic, has brought us—and himself—somewhere else, into a "web," it may be, as Wilson Harris puts it, "born of the music of the elements."[22] The poet offers a reply of grace and tact to inertias of a European literature whose forms still by and large correspond to needs fixed four centuries ago and query them, sap them, only with a great tentativeness of difficulty, striving against political, economic, and cultural forces whose interests lie in pursuing and retaining a familiar and customary history into the present (pretending its conflicts over).[23] He has found/created experience natural to the place that is his, itself made (into a) whole from what had been the blighted fragments he recorded in earlier poetry. This is, we suggested, to go beyond decolonizing the mind, becoming aware of the forms and content of colonization, so as to remove—or at least see past and between—the accretions of alien "imposure." It is to remap an environment, a history, a geography, a culture, and an experience. It is to reclaim the soul.

Notes

1. Edward Kamau Brathwaite, *History of the Voice: The Development of Nation Language in Anglophone Caribbean Poetry,* London/Port of Spain, New Beacon, 1984, pp. 9-10. I thank Patricia J. Penn Hilden for her attention to this essay.

2. Timothy J. Reiss, *The Meaning of Literature,* Ithaca, N.Y., Cornell University Press, 1992. Others of these matters are in Reiss, *The Discourse of Modernism,* Ithaca, N.Y., Cornell University Press, 1982, 1985.

3. James Thomson, *The Seasons and the Castle of Indolence,* James Sambrook, ed. [1972], Oxford (Eng.), Oxford University Press, 1984, pp. 61-62 (ll. 874-84).

4. James Joyce, *Portrait of the Artist as a Young Man* [1916], New York, Viking, 1960, p. 189.

5. Edward Brathwaite, *The Development of Creole Society in Jamaica, 1770-1820,* Oxford (Eng.), Oxford University Press, 1971, p. 237.

6. Kamau Brathwaite, *Roots: Essays in Caribbean Literature,* Havana, Casa de las Américas, 1986, p. 36.

7. "Introduction" to C. L. R. James, *Minty Alley,* London/Port of Spain, New Beacon, 1971, p. 5. The novel itself first appeared in 1936.

8. See e.g. Caryl Phillips, *The Final Passage,* Harmondsworth (Eng.), Penguin, 1985.

9. George Lamming, *In the Castle of My Skin* [1953], New York, Schocken, 1983, pp. 300-1.

10. Kamau Brathwaite, "Jazz and the West Indian Novel," in *Roots,* pp. 62-63. The term *imposure* comes from Brathwaite's *Contradictory Omens,* Mona (Jamaica), Savacou, 1974, p. 61 and passim.

11. Wilson Harris, *The Far Journey of Oudin* [1961], in *The Guyana Quartet,* London/Boston, Faber & Faber, 1985, pp. 179-82, 155.

12. Eduardo Galeano, "In Defense of the Word," in *We Say No: Chronicles 1963-1991,* tr. Mark Fried et al., & New York, Norton, 1992, pp. 141-42, 138.

13. Ibid., p. 138.

14. Edward Kamau Brathwaite, *Black and Blues,* Havana, Casa de las Américas, 1976. References to this work in this paragraph and the next are indicated directly in my text.

15. Edward Kamau Brathwaite, *X/Self,* Oxford (Eng.), Oxford University Press, 1987, pp. 84-85. Subsequent references use the abbreviation *X.*

16. Kamau Brathwaite, *Middle Passages,* Newcastle (Eng.), Bloodaxe, 1992, pp. 76-88; New York, New Directions, 1993, pp. 93-116. Subsequent references use the abbreviation *MP.*

17. Fenella Coppleston, review in *P.N. Review* 89, 19:3 (January-February 1993), p. 61.

18. Edward Brathwaite, *The Arrivants: A New World Trilogy,* Oxford (Eng.), Oxford University Press, 1973, pp. 69, 270.

19. Kamau Brathwaite, *Barabajan Poems 1942-1992,* Mona (Jamaica)/New York, Savacou/Savacou North, 1994, p. 187. References to this work are henceforth indicated directly in my text and use the abbreviation *BP* where needed for clarity.

20. I cannot, needless to say, hope here to capture completely Brathwaite's typographical play, echoing visually the changing sounds of voice and rhythm of dance.

21. Galeano, p. 139.

22. Harris, *The Guyana Quartet,* p. 7.

23. I refer here to the "Epilogue" of my *Meaning of Literature,* pp. 338-47, and to work in progress.

J. Michael Dash (essay date 1995)

SOURCE: Dash, J. Michael. "Edward Kamau Brathwaite." In *West Indian Literature, 2nd Edition,* edited by Bruce King, pp. 194-208. London, UK: McMillian Education Ltd., 1995.

[*In the following essay, the author claims that Brathwaite views himself through the Modernist assumption of the poet as divine interpreter, an individual with the power to give one voice to multiple identities and histories. In the case of Brathwaite, this power is used to give voice to the Islands' African ancestry and colonial history.*]

Probably the best introduction to the poetry of Edward Kamau Brathwaite is his largely autobiographical essay entitled 'Timehri'. In this account of his own experiences and how they combined to form an awareness of certain literary and cultural problems, the poet attempts to situate himself in terms of the evolution of West

Indian writing. In tracing various tendencies among his fellow-writers, Brathwaite isolates two important phases in a gradual movement from an initial sense of dispossession and fragmentation towards a more recent attempt to go beyond this sense of disintegration and to envisage the positive forces of creolization in the Caribbean context:

> The problem of and for West Indian artists and intellectuals is that having been born and educated within this fragmented culture, they start out in the world without a sense of 'wholeness'. . . . The achievement of these writers was to make the society conscious of the cultural problem. The second phase of West Indian and Caribbean artistic and intellectual life, on which we are now entering, having become conscious of the problem, is seeking to transcend and heal it.[1]

There is no attempt by Brathwaite to disown any of the writers who preceded him and whose preoccupations he sees as different from his. What he is taking care to outline is a crucial shift in sensibility within recent West Indian writing. The evolution is away from that obsessive sense of loss, that once fed the violent protest or inveterate cynicism of the earlier phase, towards a newer, more speculative vision of 'wholeness' in the Caribbean situation. He not only identifies closely with the second phase but sees it as a way of resolving the problems posed in the work of his literary forebears.

Indeed this notion of estrangement from one's community and landscape becomes in Brathwaite's various critical articles or surveys of West Indian writing the main criterion for judging individual Caribbean writers. For instance, Claude McKay's ability to visualize Bita Plant's reintegration into Banana Bottom makes him a precursor of the second phase. In contrast to the vision of V. S. Naipaul, McKay presents a positive world from which one was not tempted to escape. In this progression Wilson Harris emerges as the artist whose work represents a conscious investigation of the previously overlooked creolizing forces or 'native consciousness' in the Caribbean experience.[2]

An insight into Brathwaite's formative literary experiences can be had from the early poems published in the literary journal *Bim* in the 1950s. In what must be one of the first poems published by Brathwaite, **'Shadow Suite'**, we have a private, contemplative mood which has obviously drawn on the abstract metaphysical brooding of T. S. Eliot for inspiration:

> You who expect the impossible
> Know that here you will see
> Only what you have already seen
> What you hear
>   is only what you have already heard
> For life is an eternal pattern.[3]

This sombre, meditative verse does not indicate the poet's alienation from reality; it illustrates the introspec-

tive quality present in his early period of literary apprenticeship which also directly informs his later vision of the New World.

A pattern emerges from this poetic contemplation of the human condition. What the poet seems to be doing is linking a fundamentally religious notion with the process of artistic creativity. Brathwaite seems to consider reality in general in terms of a world fallen from grace; the poet's special role revolves around his awareness of this fall and his capacity to recapture the lost state through his vision. For instance, the poem **'South',** which first appears in *Bim* in 1959 (and is later included in an edited form in **Rights of Passage**), concerns the poet's ability to transform this fallen world through his creative imagination. The poem's first line indicates the difference between the vision and the ordinary world: 'But today I recapture the islands.' This poetic fantasy comes to a climax with: 'And gulls, white sails slanted seawards, / fly into the limitless morning before us.' The restoration of a state of grace is seen as fragile and tentative in the 1959 version. The ending, which he later removed, suggests a world which easily relapses into its former state as the vision fades:

> Night falls and the vision is ended.
> The drone of the groaners is ended.[4]

The same is true of the poem **'The Leopard'** which, when it later appears in *Islands,* can be made to suggest the Black Panther organization and certainly a more militant context. The caged animal in the first version of **'The Leopard'** becomes a metaphor of betrayal with obvious religious overtones. It connects with the poet's concern for a world heedless of spiritual values and vainly attempting to tame or shut out a deeper dimension to human existence:

> We breed our haggard rages
> And lock Christ up, a leopard
> in cold unheeded cages.[5]

A final illustration of this quality in Brathwaite's early work is seen in the short poem **'The Vision'**. This might be considered a poetic manifesto, as it stresses the need for restoring that lost hallowed quality to the world, what he would later term 'wholeness'. The poet's role in this process of recreating a sense of wonder before reality is made explicit here:

> Without fear or faces. There
> should be places where the roots
> can grow, where green shoots
> Sing, where the gold blown pollen
> Blossoms. But feet that walk
> the rootless walk, find no way here
> No water. And so the blind eyes, wells,
> Lack tears, lack pity, lack their proper use.[6]

The poem is a prototype for the world of Brathwaite's trilogy. The very images of roots, pollen, green shoots are to recur in the later work as symbols of a world restored. The blind eyes that 'lack their proper use' relate to the inhibited and insensitive world that has lost its sense of the fantastic which can only be regained through a poetic consciousness.

The *Other Exiles* completes the pattern we have been examining. This collection of miscellaneous poems has no dominant theme. Many of the poems are largely personal poems of his early period, and their inclusion seems to be based on their success in evoking certain impressions or moods. For instance, a love poem such as **'Schooner'** reveals Brathwaite's ability to use sustained imagery to suggest, in this case, a relationship between two individuals. The collection is given some coherence by being enclosed by two poems that allude to the theme of re-creation and that awesome moment of wonder in which communion is made with the spiritual. The first poem, **'Ragged Point',** refers to the east coast of Barbados where the landscape is untamed and is easily linked with the idea of freshness associated with the dawn light, and the new year:

> We watched what there was to watch
> saw the cold rocks come clearer
> sky rise.

The vision cannot be sustained:

> Next morning the weather was clear
> we'd forgotten our notions.

The final poem, **'New Year Letter',** symbolizes the same moment of intense revelation:

> So softly now this moment fills
> the darkness with its difference.
> Earth waits, trees touch
> the dawn.[7]

Brathwaite's work can be seen as a slow progression towards this moment when the vision of 'wholeness' is established.

In his early work Brathwaite conceives of the poetic imagination as a superior way of perceiving the world. The poetic reconstruction of the world could redeem reality from its fallen state. In another early poem in *Other Exiles* Brathwaite expresses the need for 'words to refashion futures like a healer's hand'. The same line recurs in the trilogy as the poet is attempting to liberate the region from its sterile fallen state. The poet's public voice has its roots in this early recognition of the role of art as a means of discovering unconscious figurative meanings behind the concrete and the visible. What was essentially a private literary quest for the young Brathwaite later becomes the point of departure for an aesthetic exploration of the Caribbean that transcends the historical stereotype of pluralism and fragmentation.

Even though Brathwaite situates himself in a new vanguard of West Indian writing, his actual career and experiences are not unlike those of the generation of the 'first phase'. Born in Barbados in 1930, he follows the familiar pattern of metropolitan exile and an eventual return to the West Indies. He receives his higher education in Cambridge in the early fifties and becomes in his own words 'a roofless man of the world' before returning to the Caribbean. As is the case with most artists who underwent this sequence of experiences, the odyssey served to heighten the poet's sensitivity to the dilemma of alienation which plagued West Indian intellectuals in exile.

During this period of exile Brathwaite's work reflects his various experiences. For instance, **'The day the first snow fell'** (1953) is basically about the poet's disappointment at discovering his estrangement in Britain from a world which he thought he could possess. The frustration normally expected at this point in the career of the exiled artist, when all worlds appear strange to him, never really emerges in Brathwaite's work. We have an important departure from the sense of dispossession that comes with exile, in the poet's eight-year stay in Ghana (1955-62). It is here that he discovers that sense of the sacred so crucial to the poetic imagination. He discovers a world which he cannot adopt but one which seems to retain a communion with the mysterious and numinous which is absent in the historically disadvantaged New World. His awareness of the customs and language of the Ghanaian people is seen in his adaptation of *Antigone* to a Ghanaian context in *Odale's Choice* (1962). This does not represent an original project since the adaptation of classical drama to local situations was not unknown, but it does show a closeness to the environment in which he found himself, which is central to his dramatization of this experience in his trilogy.

Brathwaite returned to the Caribbean in 1962 and began work on the trilogy, *The Arrivants,* which meant a coming-to-terms with his European and African experiences. The earlier, more introspective mode would now yield to an epic reconstruction of the cultural and historical situation of the Caribbean. The first section of this long work, *Rights of Passage* (1967), evokes the sterility and dispossession inspired by his own experiences growing up in Barbados and his awareness of Caribbean history. *Masks* (1968) draws heavily on the world observed during his stay in Ghana and is in marked contrast to the fragmented and desecrated world of the previous section. The final part, *Islands* (1969), treats the poet's physical and spiritual return to the Caribbean and attempts to restore that vision of grace that was absent in his first negative picture of waste and sterility.[8]

When one considers the epic and dialectical structure of Brathwaite's trilogy, a comparison is inevitable with

Aimé Césaire's *Cahier d'un retour au pays natal.* Essentially the same pattern emerges in both these poets, from an initial evocation of devastation in the Caribbean, the poem moves to a concluding vision of renascence. This progression can be shown by the following examples.

The *Cahier* first presents the islands 'shipwrecked in the mud of this bay' and later returns to the islands as 'scars upon the water . . . waste paper torn and strewn upon the water'. The movement is from the static and pathetic to an image which, while retaining the sense of absurdity and tragedy, suggests new possibilities. Brathwaite in his long poem locates the progression in his work in the same way. The cabin presents Old Tom as a casualty of history, his suffering forgotten by his descendants. The later section, *Islands,* contains the poem 'Anvil' which evokes a less resigned Tom: 'But from the edge / of dark, defeated silence, / what watchful patience glitters.' Césaire's poem could easily have had some influence on Brathwaite. The *Cahier* is an unprecedented attempt to deal with the Caribbean region on such a scale and with such insight. Indeed, solely on the evidence of the literary activity in *Bim* in the 1950s, there was obviously an awareness of the literary renascence in the French-speaking Caribbean. Translations of Haitian and French West Indian poets are present as early as 1953, and in a review of Harris's poetry in 1960 Brathwaite mentions the influence of Césaire and French West Indian poets on modern French writing.[9] Yet it would be a simplification to present *The Arrivants* as an English version of the *Cahier.* The *Cahier* may have presented identical issues a few decades earlier than Brathwaite's poem and was in general a shaping force on the younger poet, but the latter work can be more usefully interpreted in terms of a response to certain issues raised within Anglophone West Indian writing.

These issues touch on two important areas—the history of the New World and the problems of the literary imagination in such a context. V. S. Naipaul, because of his outspoken views, can easily illustrate what these ideas meant. The tension between Naipaul and Brathwaite has been overworked but it is important to see the distance between these writers in order to state the point of departure of *The Arrivants.* The two stereotypes that emerge in Naipaul's essays hinge upon a particular attitude to the absurdity of the New World situation. In *The Middle Passage* the Caribbean is presented as uncreative and philistine:

> The history of the islands can never be satisfactorily told. Brutality is not the only difficulty. History is built around achievement and creation; and nothing was created in the West Indies.[10]

Brathwaite's trilogy can be conceived as a demonstration of how the writer can emerge from such a despairing attitude to the Caribbean. The second notion which follows on this one concerns the enormous difficulty faced by the writer who attempts to use such an environment as a source for literary creation. Naipaul is perceptive on the question of the problems faced by such a writer attempting to repossess this experience and landscape:

> Fiction or any work of the imagination, whatever its quality, hallows its subject. To attempt . . . to give a quality of myth to what was agreed to be petty and ridiculous . . . required courage.[11]

Brathwaite as a writer of the second phase saw it as his duty to resolve this question. For him George Lamming started this process with *In the Castle of My Skin* (1953) in his attempts to 'hallow' the commonplace and the petty. *The Arrivants* can be read as a metaphor of the literary process, namely an attempt to redeem through literary means a world thought to be trivial and debased. This latter preoccupation neatly ties in with the attempts to retrieve a communion with the spiritual values present in Brathwaite's earlier work. The poet's own literary development is now tied in with our ideological debate and is the prime motivation for the literary and psychic journey traced in his trilogy.

The poems of *Rights of Passage* are clustered around the theme of spiritual dispossession. They are an attempt to remove the amnesia about historical events in the West Indian psyche and create an awareness of the historical injustice perpetrated in the region and the blind materialism of the present. In this instance, the actual historical events in the New World are symbolically related to the Fall of Man; one of the most effective fantasies describes the arrival of Columbus in the West Indies. This arrival is an important hieroglyph for the poet, as it marks the transition from a state of grace to a desecrated and profane reality. It is one of the few instances when images of decay and waste are not used to describe the Caribbean. Columbus first sees an untainted world:

> Columbus from his after-
> deck watched stars, absorbed in water,
> melt in liquid amber drifting.

'Liquid amber' suggests a state of sustained harmony existing before Columbus's intrusion. The latter is portrayed as an innocent, not fully aware of the horrors this encounter would precipitate:

> What did this journey mean, this
> new world mean: dis-
> covery? Or a return to terrors
> he had sailed from, known before?

Brathwaite's reconstruction of this moment is not done as a strident protest against the European conquest, but rather he imagines it in terms of a process of desecration that makes the Spaniard no different from self-seeking politicians, from Mammon.

This section is devoted to a recall of the violations that are part of the New World heritage. In the same way that Césaire shattered the picture of an exotic, fun-loving Caribbean, Brathwaite undermines such superficiality with a sustained tableau of absurdity and frustration. This is interestingly done in 'Calypso' as the tragic consequences of the Imperialist Adventure emerge. The contrast lies between the glorification of the adventure and the awesome truth of what took place. The light-hearted jingle of the following lines emphasizes the irony of what is suggested:

> O it was a wonderful time
> an elegant benevolent redolent time
> and young Mrs P.'s quick irrelevant crime
> at four o'clock in the morning.

This picture of 'the hurt of history' is continued in the numerous references to the historical suffering of the black race. This is a repeated theme of the negritude writers and the Harlem Renaissance; Brathwaite adds his voice to tracing the journeys of 'the wretched of the earth' or in his words, 'Columbus' coursing Kaffirs'. Poems such as 'Didn't he ramble', 'The journeys', 'The Emigrants', all suggest the sufferings and humiliations of the black diaspora.

The images that dominate *Rights of Passage* convey the atmosphere of desolation the poet sees around him. In **'Prelude'** these images are introduced as engraved in the landscape:

> Dust glass grit
> the pebbles of the desert:
> Sands shift
> across the scorched
> world water ceases
> to flow.

These lines recur in **'Epilogue'** with the same suggestion of a sordid, barren world: 'desert / sands still shift'.

The religious associations of this sterile world become clear in a poem such as **'Mammon'.** The title is significant in itself and the poem deals with a profane world trapped in a blind materialism. The Caribbean of the present makes no attempt to retrieve the spiritual, or to establish traditions, but forges 'brilliant concrete crosses'. This ties in with the general picture of a paralyzing materialism in the Western world not unlike the dry, sterile Europe of Senghor and Césaire. New York epitomizes this tendency, 'soilless, stainless, nameless'.

The following sequence, *Masks,* is a contrast to the first in that it is an evocation of serenity and reverence totally absent in the violated New World. It is tempting to locate Brathwaite's vision of Africa as part of the mythical, nostalgic picture evident in such poets as Senghor, to cast Brathwaite in the role of the prodigal son returning to his roots. However, it is significant to note the section is entitled *Masks* and not 'Africa' and to see the extent to which we witness something more complex than blind romanticizing of the ancestral past.

What Brathwaite does is situate his quest for a hallowed world in the Ghanaian experience. There he makes contact with a world where there is still communion with the spiritual. So *Masks,* as the word implies, represents a borrowed way of interpreting the world, of making contact with the numinous:

> So for my hacked
> heart, veins' mem-
> ories, I wear this
> past I borrowed.

Three hundred years have made him a stranger and the agony of this recognition is felt in a poem such as **'The New Ships'.** *Masks* is not a reintegration into the African past. It is a significant stop on the way back to the New World.

Masks is also used to provide a corrective to the traditional myth of savagery and primitivism in African societies. It describes the kingdoms of Ghana, Mali, Songhai and the growth of these civilizations with the historian's eye for setting the record straight. Central to *Masks,* however, is the poet's encounter with this universe and his initiation into a world of rituals and mystery. 'The Forest' describes such a recognition of a hallowed state. The images of desolation in the previous section are replaced by a sense of awe and calm appropriate to an unfallen world, the poet's 'wom'd heaven':

> This
> was the pistil journey in-
> to moistened gloom. Dews
> dripped, lights twink-
> led, crickets chirped and still
> the dark was silence, still
> the dark was home.

This vision of 'wholeness' is not permanent. It is the preparation for the final stage of the poet's return. It is the attempt to restore such a moment of stillness and contemplation in his own broken landscape that represents the fundamental movement of the trilogy.

The analogy with Césaire's *Cahier* is useful in discussion of the final phase, *Islands.* In the Martinican poet's work we find that the process of return and fashioning a new poetic vision draws on Rimbaud and Surrealist technique as literary antecedents. The *Cahier,* even more than an ideological *prise de position,* is an attempt to dislocate the traditional meanings of words so as to set the poetic imagination free. It was through such directed anarchy that language could be cleansed and become the poet's miraculous weapon for reconstructing the world after the flood. This is precisely what the poet is referring to when he speaks of 'the madness that sees'. Brathwaite's 'the eye must be free / seeing' also suggests this feature of modern poetry as he wishes to reach beyond the static and sterile to retrieve his world through his poetic vision. In this, an important literary ancestor is T. S. Eliot.

Eliot is as important to Brathwaite's creative imagination as the overwhelming moment of revelation in the African experience. To this extent Eliot's poetry almost becomes the literary pretext for the Caribbean poet's trilogy. This is not to say that Brathwaite supports Eliot's religious and ideological dogma; what he does endorse is the latter's plea for the restoration of the numinous and his indictment of man's enslavement to materialism. In the same way that Eliot criticizes modern man's attempt to fix time—indeed, his servitude to linear time, 'the enchainment of past and future', and the accompanying notions of material progress—so Brathwaite attempts to defy such a view of the New World which would make it an uncreative adjunct to Imperial expansion.

At this point Brathwaite the poet upstages Brathwaite the historian, in that he feels the need to go beyond the formal recorded history to a more open and speculative view of the New World experience. This is one way to avoid the knowledge that falsifies, to rediscover in myth a new, liberating sense of self and of possibilities in the Caribbean. When this intense moment of revelation is attained, the poet begins to see his community and landscape for the first time. It is his poetic vision that has the redemptive force of defying the tragic, mutilated, historical stereotype. Brathwaite is alluding to this moment of quasi-mystical illumination when he explains:

> Like a worshipper possessed at shango or vodun, as with a jazz musician, time past and time future speak to the community in the trapped and hunting [sic] moment of awareness.[12]

The artist/shaman in this creative trance becomes a medium, the community's link with a world of mystery which involves a new potency for change.

Islands casts the poet in such a role and can be seen as the *raison d'étre* of the trilogy. It begins by restating the sterile, materialistic world of **Rights of Passage**. In **'Homecoming'** this initial state is made explicit:

> To this new doubt
>
> and desert I return,
> expecting nothing.

The universe to which the poet returns represents a harsh encounter with a lifeless, secular reality: God 'is glass with his type- / writer teeth'; the land 'has lost the memory of the most secret places' and the people 'float round and round . . . without hope of the hook / of the fisherman's tugging-in root'. This state is poignantly evoked in the epigrammatic poem **'Pebbles'** which in a sustained image presents a world which is barren and unheeding:

> But my island is a pebble.
>
> . . . . .
>
> It will slay
> giants
>
> but never bear children.

The humpbacked turtle of **'Francina'** is a symbol of the past, of the sacred (like Eliot's river in 'The Dry Salvages') which is ignored and unpropitiated by an insensitive, complacent world. Francina's quiet, daring act of retrieval is mocked by a world that cannot comprehend such an act.

For the poet to accomplish his mission he must find the poetic equivalent to Francina's act. He must reinstate a sense of the sacred in this empty, destructively secular world. Ideology and political solutions are not adequate for this level of restoration. Yet this spiritually impoverished world resists the poet. The poetic word in its full literary and religious significance is the only means of redemption but the poet is daunted by the task. The 'word has been destroyed / and cannot live among us', and the poet has difficulty restoring the word to its real importance. The way in which this strange, desecrated waste land defies the poet is referred to in such lines as 'the stars / remain my master's / property' and 'they'd rob the world I ruled'. The world is at least temporarily possessed by the Other. It can only be retrieved by an imagination and a language that have been set free.

Some of the poems in *Islands* can be seen as an allegory of the poetic act, namely the act of retrieving and renaming the landscape. A poem such as **'Veve'** suggests this process of 'hallowing' as the fisherman's net or poetic vision falls gently over reality and retrieves it. The lyricism of the poem revolves around the invoking of this state of 'wholeness' and images of rebirth: 'The black eye travels to the brink of vision: / look, the fields are wet, / the sea sits gentle on the dawn.' Significantly placed towards the end of *Islands,* this poem represents the end of the quest, the attainment of this transcendental vision. The final poem, **'Jou'vert'**, is more than an attempt to re-use a local ritual—the carnival. It also represents the dawn of the risen god/ word and the poetic vision retrieved with all its positive and healing resonances.

Brathwaite has included himself in the 'second phase' of West Indian writing because his work is so deeply involved in an aesthetic renascence. It is interesting to see how this vision of salvation for the Caribbean has certain implications for the poet's role. The relationship of the poet to his community becomes more complex than that of a poet-politician. It is no longer a question of a readily accessible ideal of commitment which would inspire some collective action. Central to Brathwaite's conception of the poet is the element of possession. Even though he identifies closely with his community, his superior vision inevitably isolates him. Each metaphor of the artist as he appears in Brathwaite's work is presented in terms of a sensitive but essentially lonely figure. For instance, **'Ananse'** suggests such characteristics, 'creator / dry stony world-maker, word breaker' who survives with his memories in the 'dark attic'. The same is true of **'Littoral'** with the frequently-used image of the solitary fisherman/artist; 'his head / sleeps in the surf's / drone, his crossed / legs at home / on the rough sand'. He shares the same spiritual resources as Ananse—a voice in the dark—'his fingers knit as the dark rejoices / but he has many voices'. The distance between this creative consciousness and the materialistic world around it is made clear in **'Ogun'**. Ordinarily he appeared to be nothing but a carpenter making 'what the world preferred' but secretly he is a divine craftsman shaping the block of wood 'that would have baffled them . . . breathing air . . . still tuned to roots and water'. This sombre communion with the spiritual has little to do with the rhetorical gesture and iconoclasm of protest poetry. The contemplative state which frees the creative imagination creates an overwhelming kind of self-awareness in the poet. As the trilogy progresses, Brathwaite focuses more intensely on the relocation of his vision of the Caribbean in an artistic consciousness and not in the external history of the region.

So far we have treated literary preoccupations in Brathwaite's work and the emergence of a poetic self-consciousness. Such a resumé of his poetry would seem adequate if he simply saw himself as a cerebral poet, but even the most casual reading of Brathwaite's verse would reveal different or even conflicting voices in his work. The voice we have examined so far is easily recognized as the product of various literary concerns of his initiation into poetry. The other voice that is apparent is more direct and closely linked to the speech patterns and rituals of the folk.

Along with the use of sustained visual imagery and the dislocation of words, Brathwaite favours the use of speech patterns for purposes of irony or to bring immediacy to what he is saying. These intonations that often relieve the apparent plainness of his verse are frequently drawn from local dialects. This has both ideological and literary implications. Brathwaite accepts the need for a writer to be part of a tradition, indeed to be its growing edge. He has sought such a tradition in the creolized cultures of the Caribbean. The use of

dialect (like the use of various deities and rituals) is his articulation of the consciousness of those who survived in the New World. The literary significance of what the poet is doing presents a more complicated problem.

The use of dialect in poetry is never considered just another literary device which a poet can exploit to dramatize certain features in his work. It has traditionally been seen as part of an anti-intellectual rejection of formalism in poetry. The spontaneity and simplicity of folk poetry did not seek academic acclaim—in the case of Langston Hughes it meant a defiance of the literary establishment—and so was apparently exempt from critical evaluation. However, it would be a simplification to see Brathwaite's use of dialect as a gratuitous rejection of formal poetic devices, especially with his own closeness to the conventions of modern poetry. The seriousness with which he considers this issue is revealed in a series of articles written in 1967 entitled 'Jazz and the West Indian Novel'. The analogy between the novel-form and jazz may be overdone but the point is that Brathwaite sees Caribbean writing in terms of literary improvisation, which explains the comparison with music. This improvisation is also part of a general shift away from traditional literary models towards the articulation of indigenous cultural forms. Repeatedly stressed is the need to bring the literary work closer to speech and the community experience. What are never really discussed are the inevitable differences between speech and the language of poetry.[13]

Essentially any language in poetry is subjected to the conventions of the genre in that the language of everyday speech undergoes a process of transformation. The language of poetry moves beyond the familiar to a new mode that brings new ambiguities, new clusters of resonances and a certain atemporality to what is expressed. Brathwaite in his more successful poems subjects the English language to this process. The same should apply to his use of dialect. Brathwaite's better dialect verse is subjected to enough of a formal re-ordering and control that it rises above the commonplace to become the language of poetry. The poem **'Dust',** which recounts the explosion of Mont Pelée in Martinique in 1902, effectively captures a feeling of deep-seated terror as well as the notion of a world that has become contingent, where bewildering things occur 'widdout rhyme / widdout reason'. The metaphor of the dust from the volcanic eruption is used with its full biblical resonance to suggest a world where the people 'can't pray to no priest or no leader / an' God gone and darken the day'. Similarly the cricket-match of **'Rites'** is more than a celebration of a certain community ritual. It becomes an insight into a debilitating passivity which afflicts the crowd. When a poet uses a language in his work he makes it his own. Dialect is a tool for exploring the Caribbean landscape and is moulded by the poet's creative authority. It is in this way also part of the conscious process of repossession.

Any attempt to extract either cultural or political prescriptions from Brathwaite's work takes us on to treacherous ground. The poetic concept of 'wholeness' and the importance of myth and ritual can become distorted when converted into ideological formulae. Brathwaite does not opt for the simplification of cultural decolonization and does not see the colonial past as a complete void. He has attempted to discover tangible evidence for his essentially poetic perception of reality in the investigation of the continuing process of creolization in Caribbean society. His historical work, *The Development of Creole Society in Jamaica (1770-1820)*, is original in its attempts to substantiate the integrating Creole features which he sees at work in Jamaican society. He has more recently returned to this refutation of cultural plurality in his monograph, *Contradictory Omens: Cultural Diversity and Integration in the Caribbean.*[14]

This work, which sets out to be an objective account of the creolizing forces in the Caribbean, becomes somewhat impenetrable as the language moves further away from historical documentation towards the poetic imagination. Brathwaite's main thesis is that

> In spite of efforts to socialize individuals into separate racial groupings as demanded by the ethos of slavery, the ramifications of personal relationships . . . brought new, unexpected exchanges into each group's repertoire of behaviour. This slow uncertain but organic process (from initiation/imitation to invention) . . . is what we mean by creolisation.

Art sometimes offers a way of seeing reality which may be left out of account in other kinds of investigation. *Contradictory Omens* is an attempt to combine poetry and history. The difficulties of such an endeavour are apparent in the obscure and paradoxical nature of this text.

In contrast to this monograph, Brathwaite's *Mother Poem* is a more appropriate medium for articulating his intuition of an authentic Creole presence in the Caribbean. The monograph ends 'Unity is submarine' and the main theme and dominant imagery of *Mother Poem* are drawn from this idea. This is the continuation of the process begun in *Islands* as the poet returns to Barbados to discover the 'ancient watercourses' secreted in its limestone landscape. The collection presents a specific focus on Brathwaite's own beginnings and the landscape of Barbados. To this extent it is different from the more panoramic trilogy. We have a narrowing-down of the same act of retrieval, the same desire to transcend a dehumanized, materialistic world and restore a sense of the past and a sense of 'wholeness'. The mother, however, is neither Europe nor Africa; the Caribbean poet is no longer a provincial. The image of 'black Sycorax', like the old Amerindian women of Wilson Harris's stories, is that of an ancestral, hidden symbol of survival from which the poet derives his vision.[15]

To conceive of Brathwaite as either a folk poet or a political poet is to limit and even distort what has emerged from his creative imagination. Perhaps the most important single idea behind Brathwaite's work is the rejection of man as a product of ideology. His ability to shift back and forth between a palpably desolate world and the realm of the imaginative, and his consistently anti-materialistic position suggest that for him art has provided a way of liberating the individual from the confining grip of privation and brutality that cloud the documented, external history of the New World. It is this subversion of the traditional myths of an uncreative past and fragmented present that provides the crucial transition to the 'second phase' and enables the artist to conceive of the possibilities of growth and an authentic Creole culture in the Caribbean experience.

Mother Poem is the beginning of another poetic cycle, a seventies sequel to his earlier trilogy. This time, however, the focus is shifted away from the black diaspora as a whole towards Brathwaite's own island home, Barbados. The Barbados that emerges in this largely autobiographical phase in Brathwaite's work is not a sentimentalized or nostalgic one. It is a world of eroded memory, and silent suffering.

This 'tear shaped island' is a space of unresolved conflicts. The island-mother is a far cry from the healing, restorative force of that other mother, Africa, of *Masks.* Here, the image of the island-pebble of *Islands* is extended to describe an entire landscape of harsh limestone and dried-up water courses. Perhaps, even more than in his earlier works, Brathwaite gives free rein to his considerable dramatic skills in the multiple voices heard in *Mother Poem.* The Barbadian female condition appears in diverse forms—from the nagging matriarch to the hapless prostitute; from the stoic victim to the maternal figure of black Sycorax. As the epigraph from Wilson Harris implies, there is in all this a 'porous underside', the silent dreaming of these women suggests crucial but latent possibility.

In the final section of *Mother Poem,* entitled **'Koumfort'**, Brathwaite imagines the possibility of spiritual renewal. Coined from the Haitian Creole word for temple, *houmfor,* the title of this section suggests ways in which African connections are preserved despite appearances. For instance, **'Angel/Engine'** reenacts a victimised female's capacity to reach back through Christian worship to the god Ogoun whose hissing presence is evoked as the poem closes. In the final poem **'Driftword'** a fertile union of sea and land allows for a vision of coherence and wholeness as the ancient water-courses are flooded again and rush down to foaming beaches of Barbados's Atlantic coast.

With each book in the second trilogy the need for convulsive resolution grows more insistent. In giving meaning to Caribbean landscape, Brathwaite chooses as his focal point the violent and the explosive. In the rugged, scarred topography of Barbados's eastern shoreline, he locates the ideal terrain for defiance, negation and marronnage, always reminiscent of the Césairean image of the volcano. The Eliot-derived moments of transcendental stillness of early verse have been replaced by an almost Whitmanesque celebration of primal energies.

In his meditation on the male image in the second book of the trilogy *Sun Poem* (1982), Brathwaite more than ever longs for an ideal of convulsive potency. This is suggested in the poem's title. The sun is here the male principle. As in all his work, Brathwaite seeks to bridge the personal and the universal. In *Sun Poem* the poet looks at how boys turn into men in terms of his own memories of boyhood. Childhood is evoked in passages of lyrical prose as the central persona, significantly called Adam, grows in a 'shower of green light'. Childhood is a fragile bubble, however, and the world intrudes, preventing him from growing 'down to the dark soil of himself'.

The idyll of boyhood yields to the eclipsed masculinity of **'Clips',** of 'the afternoon of fathers growing grey'. The fathers evoked by Brathwaite are a pathetic parade of negritude denied. It is all summed up in his lament over 'this death / of sons, of songs, of sunshine;' in the Caliban poem of *Islands.* If Caliban lives at all it is in the dim memory of the rebellious slave Bussa or in the sexual and racial potency of Rastafarianism. Like *Mother Poem, Sun Poem* ends with the retrieval of the life-force, of **'Inam'.** In the rainbow image, the play of light on water, the poet rediscovers the powers of dreaming, of light and song. The triumphant image of the rainbow is not one of flaccid reconciliation, but the dawning of mobilized and boundless energy.

The final work in the trilogy *X/Self* (1987) contains few surprises. Brathwaite moves away from the personal to concentrate on the theme of empire. This book is a passionate indictment of capitalism and materialism. The impatience of the visionary voice is more emphatic in these poems, which are shriller because of a feeling of failed revolution in the Caribbean—from Haiti to Grenada. The villain of the piece is Europe, Babylon is located in Mt Blanc. Everywhere, from the gas of Nazi extermination-camps to the chemical disaster of Bhopal, the poet sees the wheeling vultures of imperialism. The poet's visionary voice articulates new possibilities of rebellion in the Soweto riots and the muse of black rebellion in **'Xango'.** Brathwaite here celebrates the

body electric as he invites an apocalyptic redemption in the embrace of Xango, the 'Pan African god of thunder'.

Two aspects of Brathwaite's work in the eighties become increasingly apparent: the frustration of the demiurgic voice in its project to create a Caribbean negritude and a growing tension between the poet as sacrificial figure at the mercy of the philistine and uncaring 'status crow'. Both are naturally related and have much to do with the changing ideological scene of this decade. On one hand the poet's quest for Calibanesque reversals of Prospero's mischief leads to one disappointment after another. In two collections in 1986, *The Visibility Trigger* and *Jah Music,* a number of poems are dedicated to murdered artists and revolutionaries. The killing of Mikey Smith and George Rodney as well as Brathwaite's own personal misfortune lead to almost hysterical shrieks of isolation and gloom. This sense of catastrophe pervades his hurricane poem *Shar* (1990).

He may well be the last poet to believe with such fervour in the Modernist legend of the artist as priest or divine interpreter, favoured by the Gods and a victim of the System. Brathwaite, nevertheless, defiantly pursues his belief in 'The Voice' and not in the multiple voices that would be the preferred mode in contemporary writing. The title of his essay *History of the Voice* (1984) is telling in this regard. Familiar dichotomies emerge in this essay as the Western pentameter is opposed to Caribbean 'nation language'. This revival of the old negritude belief in the white voice as opposed to the black voice reveals Brathwaite's deep interest in performance poetry, in sound and freeing the poetic line. The new graphic presentation of his poems could be seen not as eccentric doodles but as an attempt to integrate the acoustic into the written text.

Perhaps it is still useful to locate Brathwaite on that threshold between the everyday and the abstract, between island reality and ancestral presence. However, this posture seems to have become increasingly precarious. An inexhaustible fluency is evident in his work as old themes and fragments of poems are combined to reappear in new publications. His *Middle Passages* (1992) is characteristic of this tendency. These must be aimed at a new international audience as they do not address some of the current issues in Caribbean writing. *Zea/Mexican Diary* promises to be a personal response to the uncaring Caribbean, demonstrating how problematic the relations between artist and community have become. No one can doubt Brathwaite's powerful influence on what he called the 'second phase' of Caribbean writing. Perhaps the problem now is that this phase is coming to an end.

Notes

1. *Savacou* 2 (September 1970) 36.

2. See 'West Indian Prose Fiction in the sixties', *Critical Survey* (Winter 1967), 169-74.

3. *Bim*, 3, 12 (1950), 325.

4. *Bim*, 7, 28 (1959), 191.

5. *Bim*, 9, 33 (1961), 18.

6. *Bim*, 10, 40 (1965), 250.

7. *Other Exiles* (London: Oxford University Press, 1975).

8. *The Arrivants* (A New World Trilogy). (London: Oxford University Press, 1973). It is the subject of Gordon Rohlehr's *Pathfinder: Black Awakening in the Arrivants* (1981).

9. *Bim*, 8, 30 (1960).

10. *The Middle Passage* (Harmondsworth: Penguin, 1969), p. 29.

11. *The Overcrowded Baracoon* (Harmondsworth: Penguin, 1972), p. 26.

12. *Savacou* 2, p. 43.

13. *Bim*, 44/45/46 (1967-68).

14. *Savacou*, monograph no. 1 (1974).

15. *Mother Poem* (London: Oxford University Press, 1977). *Black and Blues* (Havana: Casa de las Américas, 1976) won the Casa de las Américas poetry award for 1976. It is a compilation of material old and new which tends to restate themes raised in the trilogy.

Mervyn Morris (essay date 1995)

SOURCE: Morris, Mervyn. "Overlapping Journeys: *The Arrivants*." In *The Art of Kamau Brathwaite*, edited by Stewart Brown, pp. 117-31. Melksham, UK: Cromwell Press, 1995.

[*In the following essay, a poet praises* The Arrivants *as "a major document of African reconnection" that "draws attention to Caribbean continuities out of Africa."*]

Of the many useful and interesting discussions of *The Arrivants*[1] or of individual books in the trilogy, there are two I am anxious to recommend. Maureen Warner-Lewis' *Masks: Essays & Annotations*[2] and Gordon Rohlehr's *Pathfinder*[3] are of value not only for their critical judgements but also for the wealth of information they provide about the contexts of the poetry. Inter alia, Warner-Lewis guides us through West African detail, and Rohlehr elucidates many allusions to jazz and other manifestations of Africa-related New World

culture. Anyone studying *The Arrivants* should make early contact with these two items, and will no doubt wish to explore the rest of the bibliography.

The present essay is introductory, offering a very brief outline of the trilogy, its origins, its shape, its main concerns, and a glance at some of its techniques.

In an autobiographical essay called 'Timehri'[4] Brathwaite describes himself as a Barbadian "from an urban village background, of parents with a "'middle-class' orientation" who made friends "with boys of stubbornly non-middle class origin". From Harrison College, "originally founded for children of the plantocracy and colonial civil servants and white professionals", Brathwaite won one of the prestigious Barbados scholarships "that traditionally took the explanters' sons 'home' to Oxbridge or London". It took him, "a potential Afro-Saxon", to Pembroke College, Cambridge, to read History. He wrote poems, most of them rejected by the Cambridge magazines. He felt neglected and misunderstood.[5]

> Then in 1953, George Lamming's *In the Castle of My Skin* appeared and everything was transformed. Here breathing to me from every pore of line and page, was the Barbados I had lived. The words, the rhythms, the cadences, the scenes, the people, their predicament. They all came back. They all were possible. All the more beautiful for having been published and praised by London, mother of metropolises.[6]

After graduation, he applied for jobs all over the place. "I was a West Indian, roofless[7] man of the world. I could go, belong, everywhere on the world-wide globe. I ended up in a village in Ghana. It was my beginning". He began to feel connected to Africa.

> Slowly, slowly, ever so slowly; obscurely, slowly but surely, during the eight years that I lived there, I was coming to an awareness and understanding of community, of cultural wholeness, of the place of the individual within the tribe, in society. Slowly, slowly, ever so slowly, I came to a sense of identification of myself with these people, my living diviners. I came to connect my history with theirs, the bridge of my mind now linking Atlantic and ancestor, homeland and heartland. When I turned to leave, I was no longer a lonely individual talent; there was something wider, more subtle, more tentative: the self without ego, without I, without arrogance. And I came home to find that I had not really left. That it was still Africa; Africa in the Caribbean.[8]

Brathwaite returned to the Caribbean in 1962. "I had, at that moment of return," he writes, "completed the triangular trade of my historical origins. West Africa had given me a sense of place, of belonging; and that place and belonging, I knew, was the West Indies".[9]

Like many other publications by Brathwaite, *The Arrivants* draws attention to Caribbean continuities out of Africa, which a European overlay may sometimes obscure, and argues that the psychic wholeness of Caribbean black people requires fuller recognition of our African heritage. As Damian Grant wrote in an early review article:

> The theme, over the three books, might be summarized as the rediscovery of Africa; a rediscovery that has to be made by the twentieth-century Negro, a condition of his own proper freedom, selfhood and political independence. Brathwaite offers in fact to define and articulate the modern Negro consciousness, seen as a complication of past experience, present problems, and future possibilities.[10]

In response perhaps to talk about the trilogy's public mission, Brathwaite was emphatic in an interview: "This trilogy as a whole, is concerned first of all with *my* own experiences. I am trying to come to terms with being a West Indian who has travelled to Africa".[11] But he is trying also to present "the self without ego" and to express "an awareness and understanding of community, of cultural wholeness, of the place of the individual within the tribe". In *The Arrivants* he speaks through a series of personas or masks or, to put it differently, through a shifting persona who represents black experience in various manifestations. As Brathwaite notes, in *Rights of Passage* the persona, Tom, "undergoes a series of transformations—from ancestor to slave to prophet to Uncle Tom, and is finally translated into an image of the past out of which the future springs".[12] With reference to *Masks,* Warner-Lewis writes:

> The poet found that he could not get to the heart of his questionings unless he became other people and felt as they did at the crucial points of their existence: the slave, the ancestor, the king, the villager, the pioneer and clan-founder, and he himself, Brathwaite, the descendant and inheritor of all these. But the poet needs at times the detached mask of an onlooker, an outsider, the scholar with history at his fingertips.[13]

The Arrivants brings together "three long poems that . . . deal, in their different ways, with journeys".[14] "Time's walking river is long" (*The Arrivants,* 120). The order in which the books appeared is part of the point: the African book is the centre of the trilogy; and though the journeys never end, the poem leaves us in the Caribbean. The final book signs off with a series of present participles, whose suggestion of a continuing process is reinforced by the absence of punctuation after the final word:

> now waking
> making
>
> making
> with their
>
> rhythms some-
> thing torn
>
> and new[15]

(*The Arrivants,* 269-270)

In *Rights of Passage* we meet personas of the New World Negro, the dislocated African, forever on the move and with little memory of ancestral Africa. "Where then is the nigger's / home?" "Will exile never // end?" (*The Arrivants,* 77). According to the author, "*Rights of Passage . . .* is about the black diaspora: the shattering journey out of Africa into New World plantation slavery, the song and dance of illusory emancipation, and the first recognition of identity. *Masks* is the necessary and countervailing journey: ingathering of the multitudes: return of scattered psyches to the ancestral homeland: a movement from hurt to heart"[16] The epigraph to *Masks* is an Akan proverb: "Only the fool points at his origins with his left hand" [i.e. disrespectfully]. In the first half of the book, we travel through sections of African history and culture; in the second half, an African returns from the New World, in unavailing search of his buried navel string. Though the attempt at reconnection has been fraught with disappointment, contact with Africa has strengthened the persona. He will rise and stand on his feet. In *Islands* we are in the Caribbean, mostly, exploring Africa forgotten and retained; and, through a series of Afro-Caribbean figures, considering "the certainties/ uncertainties of the Caribbean, taking up the theme of 'the gains and the losses', implicit in *Masks*".[17] As understanding deepens, there is movement towards correcting the cultural imbalance of the colonial heritage which has tended to privilege Europe. Near the end of the trilogy, in **'Vèvè'**, when the Word is invoked (*The Arrivants,* 266), Legba—"the Dahomean / Haitian god of the gateway"[18]—emerges from St John chapter one. "Christ will pray / to Odomankoma // Nyame God / and Nyankopon" (*The Arrivants,* 267). As Rohlehr puts it, "Christ and Odomankoma are recognized as different names for the same concept of God as communicable immanent force in the universe and incarnate Word."[19]

Rights of Passage, Masks and *Islands* were republished together as *The Arrivants* in 1973. Reprints from 1978 at least have included a new and closely relevant epigraph.

> Well, muh ol' arrivance[20] . . . is from
> Africa . . . That's muh ol' arrivants family. Muh
> gran'muddah an' muh gran' fadda. Well, they came
> out here as slavely . . . you unnerstan'?
>
> Well, when them came now, I doan belongs to
> Africa, I belongs to Jamaica. I born here.
>
> Well, muh gran'parents, she teach me some of the
> African languages an' the rest I get it at the
> cotton-tree root . . . I take twenty-one days to get
> all the balance . . .
>
> So I just travel right up to hey, an' gradually
> come up, an' gradually come up, until I experience
> all about . . . the African set-up . . .
> Kumina Queen, Jamaica

The epigraph foregrounds African ancestry; and slavery as the reason African ancestors came to the Caribbean. It makes a point which is extensively explored in *Masks*: the speaker, a leader in an Africa-derived religious ritual, says plainly that she does not belong to Africa, she belongs to Jamaica, she was born here; and that she has been taught some African lore by her ancestors and has received some of it by intuition or by supernatural means ("at the cotton-tree root"). There is a direct connection with various concerns in the trilogy. The trauma of slavery is evoked in all three books. In *Masks* the African returning from the New World is forced to recognize that he no longer belongs in Africa. *Islands* examines manifestations of Africa in the New World, finding ancestral memory retained to some degree in religious ceremony (**'Shepherd'**, **'Wake'**, **'Eating the Dead'**, **'Negus'**, **'Vèvè'**, for example) and the intuitive gropings of art (as in **'Jouvert'** and **'Ogun'**).

Each book is divided into parts, each part into sections, some sections into numbered subsections. The transitions are often introduced by connectives (such as "and now", "but", "so", "for") which strengthen the appearance of continuity. Many sections seem to be poems complete in themselves, and some have indeed been published separately. But meaning in the trilogy is partly a function of placement, as passages extend or modify ideas introduced earlier and as their music plays against the movement of other passages. Acknowledging the influence of T. S. Eliot, Brathwaite has said: "The tone, the cadence and above all the organization of my long poems (and all three poems of my trilogy are long poems, not collections of poems) owe a great deal to him".[21]

Brathwaite also shares with Eliot a recurrent concern with memory and time. "And the wheel turns / and the future returns / wreathed in disguises" (*The Arrivants*, 168).[22] History repeats itself. As Mark McWatt has observed, "the reality one confronts in the poems, however clear or 'raw', is always coloured, as it were, by a sense of historical time, an overlay of reverberations from past events and personalities which cause in the reader a kind of mental or imaginative shift toward a historical perspective".[23]

For example, there is a sense in which the West Indian emigrants travelling to Europe in the 1950s replicate Columbus in the fifteenth century travelling in the other direction.

> What do they hope for
> what find there
> these New World mariners
> Columbus coursing kaffirs
> What Cathay shores
> for them are gleaming golden
> what magic keys they carry to unlock
> what gold endragoned doors?

2

> Columbus from his after-
> deck watched stars, absorbed in water,
> melt in liquid amber drafting
>
> through my summer air.

(*The Arrivants*, 52)

So too in *Masks* "the omowale/ex-african reverses the movement of the poem (ship to heartland rather than heartland to ship) and undertakes a journey of re/ discovery of origins"[24] In the third part of *Masks,* at a moment centuries ago, the Africans captured for slavery reach the sea, where "voyages ended; / time stopped where its movement began;" (122) and at the beginning of Part IV (which follows) the persona recently arriving in West Africa is welcomed as a stranger: "you who have come / back a stranger / after three hundred years // welcome" (124).

Images merge cinematically, as again in **'Littoral'** (170-173), near the beginning of *Islands.* In section one the blind fisherman (whose head is like a mask) is weaving a net, "his fingers knit as the dark rejoices / but he has his voices . . .". Section two presents one of those voices, a woman singer who "travels far back, explores / ruins". When the poem was published in 1960 the singer was Billie Holiday;[25] but in the immediate context of *Islands* she is an African ancestral memory, becomes Yaa Asantewa, "warrior and queen and keeper of the tribe". Between sections two and three we make another leap through time: from the blind fisherman on a Caribbean beach more or less now, into the hold of a slave-ship long ago.

>   He hopes
> that light will break in the clearing
> before her song ends . . .

3

> But no light breaks under the decks
> where the sails sing

The trilogy is held together partly by patterns of recurrent imagery. Journey, movement, time, river, sea; dust, sand, dryness, pebble, stone, rock, earth, soil, water, tendril, pistil, green, tree, hurricane; sun, moon, night, fire, sleep, awakening, dawn, morning, day, light, dark, womb, birth, blindness, sight; speech, shout, whisper, silence; drum, mask, dance, circle, music, song; gold, silver, black, red, whip, lash, iron, shackle, clink, clank, Uncle Tom; spider, fisherman—these are some of the images and some of the ways they cluster. They are of multiple significance, they inter-relate variously, they develop and change. So the spider, for example—Ananse, "the spider-hero of the Akans; earthly trickster, but once with the powers of the creator-gods"[26]—is both positive and negative, is used to suggest diminished memory of Africa ("Creation has burned to a spider", 164), is an agent of rebellion (heard by Tacky and L'Ouverture), is both untrustworthy and supremely creative ("stony world-maker, word-breaker, / creator", 167), and connects with the blind fisherman weaving "nets, embroideries" (170), the fisherman whose "fine webs fell softly" (263). The fisherman in turn shades into a mask: "his eyes stare out like an empty shell" (170): which reminds us of "his- / tory bleeds / behind my hollowed eyes" (148) and connects with many other references to masks, masking, role-playing, disguise.

Or take, for example, pebble, stone. "It will slay / gi-ants // but never bear children" (196). Its potential in battle is acknowledged, but the emphasis here is on sterility. When "my island is a pebble" (196), when lightning strikes a "world of stone" (268) the main implications are negative. In **'Negus',** on the other hand, "stone" is more positive, the instrument of existential rebellion: "fling me the stone / that will confound the void" (224).

There are references throughout to the drum, a central symbol of African culture. "God is dumb / until the drum / speaks" (97). **"Drum"** is the very first word of *The Arrivants,* and it is there at the end in **'Jouvert'.** Wrenched from Africa, the New World blacks still remember the talking drum, "Atumpan talking and the harvest branch- / es" (13). The angry man in **'Folkways'** feels "like a drum with a hole / in its belly" (31), an image later associated with Tom, in whose cabin there is "A rusted / bucket, hole kicked into its / bottom" (70, 248). The Rastafarian in **'Wings of a Dove'** summons us to "beat dem drums / dem" (44). The poet-persona in the **'Prelude'** of *Masks* invokes creative power: "Beat heaven / of the drum, beat" (91). Near the beginning of *Masks* we share in a ritual of creative preparation, **'The Making of the Drum'** (94-97). The "quick drummer" (162) is part of the jazz scene in **'Jah'.** Drums are crucial in **'Shepherd',** helping towards possession: "the room rumbles / clouded with drums" (185), "the drum trembles" (186), "the drum speaks" (187); and when the Shepherd senses an ancestor, "can smell / his sweat / his musk of damp and slave // ships", the Shepherd himself becomes metaphorically a drum with which the ancestor communicates: "his heat hurts / me, my belly is tight / his hands hit // me into sound" and "Slowly / slowly / slowly / the dumb speaks" (188), the form of words suggesting—since "God is dumb / until the drum / speaks" (97)—that the drum and the Shepherd are divine instruments. Drums are important also in the voodoo ritual, "*Att / Att / Attibon // Attibon Legba / Attibon Legba / Ouvri bayi pou' moi / Ouvri bayi pou' moi . . .*" (224), open the gate for me. In **'Vèvè'** the gods will arrive "welcomed by drumbeats" (265). There are also the drums of steel band music, the booming bass drum and the ping pong tenor pan as in "flowers bloom / their tom tom sun // heads raising / little steel pan // petals to the music's / doom // as the ping pong / dawn comes // riding / over shattered homes" (269).

Rhythmic patterns recur in various contexts. For example, the "It / it / it / it is not" (222) and "*Att / Att / Attibon // Attibon Legba . . .*" of **'Negus'** (224) recall the beginning of **'Tano'** (151), "dam / dam / damirifa / damirifa due . . .", each clearly suggesting drumbeats. But *damirifa due* is "an Akan cry of pity and sorrow meaning 'condolences'";[27] the soul of the returning African is gathered back into the ancestral fold. **"Attibon Legba"** moves in the opposite direction: it is an invocation to the gateway god, Legba, who facilitates access to other gods. The drumbeats return in **'Shepherd'** ("Dumb / dumb / dumb", 185-187) but, through possession, there is reconnection with ancestors, and "Slowly / slowly / slowly / the dumb speaks" (188). Here "Slowly / slowly / slowly"—also recalled in **'Timehri'**—reminds us of Osai Tutu, royal founder of the Ashanti Confederation, rising in ceremonial dignity (141).

The Arrivants is richly allusive, connecting a range of detail in the history and culture of various communities. Each volume has its prevailing tone, created partly by the diction, the rhythms of speech, and partly by allusions to music. We hear in *Rights of Passage* a New World soundtrack—worksong, Negro spiritual, various styles of jazz, calypso, ska; in *Masks,* Akan drum rhythms, and jazz; in *Islands*—centred in the Caribbean—jazz again, and aural motifs of steel band, limbo dancing, Jamaican folksong, Haitian drums. Some of the music allusions[28] are to the words of songs—"just call my blue / black bloody spade / a spade" (29), for example, echoes "What did I do / to be so black an' blue". Some are to the titles of tunes, such as **'New World A-Comin'** (9) which alludes with irony to a Duke Ellington composition. There are musicians mentioned by name or nickname (such as Charlie Parker's, **'Bird'**). Some of the allusions assume an intimate knowledge of the music.[29] Here, for example, is Brathwaite in response to an enquiry about the final pages (82-85) of *Rights of Passage.*

> I'd never be able to write "bird calls" . . . without having Parker in mind: especially since there is an LP of that name. So when I wrote it I heard that saxophone in addition to what I was really talking about: Noah's dove after the rain: which is again connected with Coltrane's greatest lyric 'After the Rain': which derives its beauty not only from itself, but also from its juxtaposition to his greatest storm, 'Impressions'.[30]

The music allusions are not just cultural background. They are often an important element of the meaning, as again, for example, in section two of **'Folkways'** (33) which ends:

> rat tat tat
> on the flat-

out whispering rails
on the quick
click
boogie woogie
hooeeee
boogie woogie
long long
boogie woogie
long long
hooey long
journey to town.

Pointing out "the connection between this passage and traditional railroad blues", Gordon Rohlehr has argued that Brathwaite is here "establishing the connection between Jazz and Journey; seeing jazz as yet another gift of the archetypal tribal experience in Africa, and its counterpart in the New World".[31]

Sometimes Brathwaite will more or less mimic the music or imitate rhythms as in that brilliant passage, or in "*Kon kon kon kon / Kun kun kun kun*" (98), or "Come-a look / come-a look / see wha' happen" (240), patterned on a Jamaican folksong. More often, however, there is a subtle tension between the speaking voice and the music reference, as in these lines which parody Caliban's drunken song (*The Tempest,* Act II, Scene ii) and also suggest the syncopation of road march music in Trinidad carnival:

Ban
Ban
Cal-
iban
like to play
pan
at the car-
nival;
pranc-
cing up to the lim-
bo silence
down
down
down
so the god won't drown
him
down
down
to the is-
land town

(*The Arrivants,* 192)

But Brathwaite does not insist that the speaking voice always be equal or dominant. He sometimes gives absolute priority to the music rhythm. In **'Wings of a Dove'**, for example, the emphatic rhythm is sometimes expressed in normal creole syntax, but at other moments normal syntax is ignored. "So beat dem drums / dem, spread // dem wings dem, / watch dem fly // dem" is normal speech; "soar dem / high dem" (44) is not.

This seems to be a choice he makes from time to time: to let the music rhythms take charge. When he prefers to, he convincingly represents speech. Indeed a major

area of Brathwaite's achievement in *The Arrivants* is his flexible command of speech rhythms. His ear allows him to register various accents, including American and African:

See them zoot suits, man? Them black
Texan hats?

(*The Arrivants,* 23)

Akwaaba they smiled
meaning welcome
akwaaba they called
aye kooo

well have you walked
have you journeyed

welcome

(*The Arrivants,* 124)

He captures many West Indian voices, from standard English as in **'Mammon'** (73-76) to Barbadian creole (he says "nation language")[32] in **'Cane'** (225-229) and **'Tizzic'** (260-261), Jamaican Revival preaching in **'The Stone Sermon'** (254-256), Rastafarian speech in **'Wings of a Dove'** (42-43). In section two of **'Francina'** (215) standard English modulates into creole. In **'The Dust'** (62-69), one of our finest poems in creole, he presents Barbadian women talking about their world and its worries, moving without strain into ultimate questions about the meaning of life.

An' then suddenly so
widdout rhyme
widdout reason

you crops start to die
you can't even see the sun in the sky;
an' suddenly so, without rhyme,

without reason, all you hope gone
ev'rything look like it comin' out wrong.
Why is that? What it mean?

(68-69)

'Rites' (197-203; a prose version had been published earlier[33]) is a West Indian classic, our quintessential cricket poem. It is clear from the cricket-loving tailor's lively monologue that the test match is, as Orlando Patterson has argued, "not so much a game as a collective ritual".[34] When things are going well for their side, spectators feel empowered. "All over de groun' fellers shakin' hands wid each other // as if was *they* wheelin' de willow / as if was *them* had the power" (200). When the batsman is doing well, a spectator brings a votive offering, as to a god—"a red fowl cock // goin quawk quawk quawk in 'e han'". A man who for twenty-five years has been "lickin' gloy / pun de Gover'ment stamps" (200-201) is transformed, noisily calling for blood. But when the game begins to favour the invading English, there is silent consternation—"could'a hear de empire fart" (202)—then a babel of advice. The moral is drawn explicitly:

> when things goin' good, you cahn touch
> we, but leh murder start
> an' ol man, you cahn fine a man to hole up de side
> . . .

(*The Arrivants,* 203)

The umpire/empire pun is characteristic of *The Arrivants.* Wordplay abounds. "Miss- / issippi painfields" (51) is typical. The pun is arguably an aspect of the jazz technique, the literary analogue of the blue note (the flattened third or fifth or seventh), a note that makes you hear an adjacent semitone. In "Boss man lacks pride: / I am his hide // of darkness" (19) the Hyde is emphasized by the line break: I am his Hyde, his other self, the self of darkness. In "to hell / with Eu- / rope too" (29) we get: to hell with you, and with the rope as well. Sometimes the lineation visually reinforces meaning as in:

> the wise
> are di-
> vided

(*The Arrivants,* 130)

or:

> O who now will help
> us, help-
> less, horse-
> less, leader-
> less, no
> hope, no
> Hawkins, no
> Cortez to come.

(*The Arrivants,* 10)

Some early readers of *Rights of Passage* were disconcerted by the frequent division of words, by passages such as

> E-
> gypt
> in Af-
> rica
> Mesopo-
> tamia
> Mero-
> e

(*The Arrivants,* 35)

especially as the division was often not aurally detectable in Brathwaite's own reading of the verse. Lineation is far less obtrusive in *Masks* and *Islands.* But *Rights of Passage,* Brathwaite has explained, was "a tale of deprivation, paradoxically balanced upon a sense of hope, of continuity and of unity: fragments that still

held secrets of the whole. And this paradox came to be expressed in the poem in the counterpoint between the broken lines of the verse, and the shifting but basic rhythms of its impetus".[35]

The Arrivants is a major document of African reconnection. Brilliantly, it charts a set of overlapping psychic journeys to, from and within the New World and Africa, acknowledging achievement and some painful realities, examining self and community, past and present. The final lines of the trilogy celebrate awakening consciousness and the creative growth of the artist-persona and other Caribbean black people:

> hurts for-
>
> gotten, hearts
> no longer bound
>
> to black and bitter
> ashes in the ground
>
> now waking
> making
>
> making
> with their
>
> rhythms some-
> thing torn
>
> and new

(*The Arrivants,* 269-270)

Notes

1. Pronounced ar-RIVE-ants. Edward Kamau Brathwaite, *The Arrivants* (London: Oxford University Press, 1973), comprised of *Rights of Passage* (1967), *Masks* (1968) and *Islands* (1969). For other works by Brathwaite and a selection of Brathwaite criticism, see the bibliography at the back of this book.

2. Maureen Warner-Lewis, *E. Kamau Brathwaite's Masks: Essays & Annotations* (Kingston: Institute of Caribbean Studies, 1992): a reissue of *Notes to Masks* (Benin City: Ethiope Publishing Corporation, 1977) with a revised version of 'Odomankoma 'Kyerema Se', an essay published in *Caribbean Quarterly* 19: 2, June 1973.

3. Gordon Rohlehr, *Pathfinder: Black Awakening in The Arrivants of Edward Kamau Brathwaite* (Trinidad: private publication, 1981).

4. Edward Brathwaite, 'Timehri', *Savacou* 2, September 1970, 35-44. For a slightly different version see Orde Coombs ed., *Is Massa Day Dead?* (New York: Doubleday/Anchor Press, 1974), 29-44.

5. 'Timehri', *Savacou* 2, 36-37.

6. Ibid.

7. In *Is Massa Day Dead?* "rootless", 33. The word as in *Savacou* is much richer, playing against "rootlessness" earlier in the paragraph, and suggesting "unaccommodated man" and a Barbadian pronunciation of "ruthless".

8. Ibid., 38.

9. Rosalie Murphy & James Vinson eds., *Contemporary Poets of the English Language* (London: St James Press, 1970), 129.

10. Damian Grant, 'Emerging Image: the poetry of Edward Brathwaite', *Critical Quarterly* 12:2, Summer 1970, 186-187.

11. *The Poet Speaks* Record Ten, ed. Peter Orr (London: Argo, 1968).

12. Edward [Kamau] Brathwaite, Record Notes to *Rights of Passage* Record One (London: Argo, 1968).

13. Maureen Warner-Lewis, *Masks: Essays and Annotations,* 15.

14. Edward [Kamau] Brathwaite, Record Notes to *Islands* (London: Argo Records, 1973).

15. The concluding lines of *Rights of Passage* and *Masks* also emphasize process—each marks a stage in the psychic journey—but with a full stop at the end of the one, an ellipsis at the end of the other. Images of journey, dawn and music figure in the final pages of each book.

16. Edward [Kamau] Brathwaite. Recorded Notes to *Islands.*

17. Ibid.

18. *The Arrivants,* 273 (Glossary).

19. Rohlehr, *Pathfinder,* 314.

20. "Ol' arrivance" would be the same sound as "whole arrivants", meaning all my ancestors here (as well as my old ancestors or ancestry).

21. Rosalie Murphy & James Vinson eds., *Contemporary Poets of the English Language,* 129.

22. Cf. the opening lines of T. S. Eliot's *Burnt Norton:* "Time present and time past / Are both perhaps in time future, / And time future contained in time past."

23. Mark McWatt, in Daryl C. Dance ed., *Fifty Caribbean Writers* (Newport: Greenwood Press, 1986), 60.

24. Edward [Kamau] Brathwaite, Record Notes to *Masks* (London: Argo, 1972). The *omowale* is one who returns.

25. Rohlehr, *Pathfinder,* 192.

26. *The Arrivants,* 272 (Glossary).

27. Maureen Warner-Lewis, *Masks: Essays and Annotations,* 93-94.

28. See Gordon Rohlehr, *Pathfinder,* 333-340, Appendix One, 'Black/Ground Music to *Rights of Passage*'.

29. "Knowing precisely what music is being alluded to, one can fruitfully explore the hidden network of allusions beneath the taut or casual surface of things", Rohlehr, *Pathfinder,* 333. In a passage at the beginning of *Masks* (90-91, "Gong-gongs / throw pebbles in the rout- / ed pools of silence . . ." etc), Jimmy Carnegie hears a John Coltrane solo. "Brathwaite," he writes, "has accomplished an almost impossible feat of 'transcription'." (J. A. Carnegie, 'The Face's Soul', review of *Masks, Public Opinion* (Kingston, Jamaica), August 2, 1968.

30. *Pathfinder,* 55.

31. Gordon Rohlehr, review article on *Islands, Caribbean Studies* 10:4, 178.

32. See Edward Kamau Brathwaite, *History of the Voice: The Development of Nation Language in Anglophone Caribbean Poetry* (London: New Beacon Books, 1984).

33. Edward [Kamau] Brathwaite, 'Cricket', in Andrew Salkey ed., *Caribbean Prose* (London: Evans Brothers, 1967), 61-67.

34. Orlando Patterson, 'The Ritual of Cricket', *Jamaica Journal* 3:1, March 1969.

35. Edward [Kamau] Brathwaite, Record Notes to *Rights of Passage* (London: Argo, 1968).

Silvio Torres-Saillant (essay date 1997)

SOURCE: Torres-Saillant, Silvio. "Kamau Brathwaite and the Caribbean Word." In *Caribbean Poetics: Towards an Aesthetic of West Indian Culture,* pp. 93-122. New York: Cambridge University Press, 1997.

[*In the following essay, examples of the Caribbean language, religion, and culture are teased out of Brathwaite's poems, leading to the conclusion that "Brathwaite insists on a theory of language, culture, and on a philosophy of history that have strong political implications insofar as they aim to liberate the Caribbean mind from the throes of a colonial heritage."*]

. . . isn't it odd that the only language I have in which to speak of this crime is the language of the criminal who committed the crime?

Jamaica Kincaid (1989: 31)

Few *oeuvres* stress Caribbean literature's deep concern with language as sharply as that of the Barbadian Kamau Brathwaite. A poet, historian, fiction writer, and critic, Brathwaite became known in the archipelago starting in the early 1950s primarily through his contributions to *Bim,* then the leading cultural journal in the Anglophone West Indies. He had already gained distinction as one of the leading producers of intellectual discourse in the area when, in 1967, his first published volume of poetry brought him quick recognition throughout the Third World. His more recent honors include the 1986 Casa de las Américas Prize for a collection of essays entitled *Roots,* which was republished in the United States seven years later by the University of Michigan Press (Brathwaite 1993c). He also won the 1987 Commonwealth Prize for Poetry, granted by the London-based Commonwealth Institute, received the 1994 Neustadt International Prize for Literature, and had the Autumn 1994 number of *World Literature Today* (Vol. 68 No. 4) devoted to his life and work. Today his prestige as a major contemporary poet has spread through Africa, the Caribbean, England, and the United States. A glance at the large body of criticism generated by Brathwaite's literary production reveals a common thread that normally points to the element of sound in his texts. Decades ago a reviewer in England referred to Brathwaite's **Rights of Passage** (1967) as "very much a 'script' for recitation," and over twenty years later a West Indian critic has observed that "acoustic effect and phonetic play have always been an important element in Brathwaite's poetry" (Lucie-Smith 1968: 100; Dash 1987: 88).

The pages that follow provide a wide socio-aesthetic and cultural frame within which to view the implications of the sonority identified by critics in the poetry of Brathwaite. The recitative element, the acoustic effect, the phonetic play, the centrality assigned to sound in his texts, form part of a complex vision of art, culture, and society. That vision, as we shall see, corresponds to an overall philosophy of language with aesthetic implications for virtually all facets of Brathwaite's literary practice. His poetry, prose fiction, historiographical essays, and literary criticism, all reflect a scheme of thought wherein language is seen as a means of communication, a vehicle of cultural identity, a potential instrument of liberation from the vestiges of colonial education, and the principal ingredient of an aesthetics that delves into the sociohistorical specificity of the Caribbean to uncover the elements of an authentic manner of utterance.

CULTURE AND THE INDIVIDUAL TALENT

Brathwaite's idea of language is inextricably linked to his notion of culture and the artist's relationship to the community in a given sociocultural context. His 1957 essay "Sir Galahad and the Islands" described what he

perceived as a dichotomy in the attitudes of literary artists in the Caribbean regarding their native "island cultures." He distinguished those writers who choose to remain in the West Indies, whom he called "Islanders," from those he dubbed "Emigrants," the ones who feel they must leave "whether that migration is in fact or by metaphor" (Brathwaite 1957: 8). Among the former, he spoke positively of those who in their writings absorb their surroundings by claiming a "heritage." They reflect an attitude of alliance with the folk, the peasant tradition, evincing their recognition that they do "depend on" people, and in so doing augur a bright future for Caribbean letters (8, 11, 13). George Lamming would later reinforce that view by claiming that the West Indian novel at its best is essentially rooted in peasant life (Lamming 1978: 25).

Although Brathwaite privileged the "Islanders" over the "Emigrants," he made a significant reference to the latter's peculiar use of language. Speaking of the fiction writers, he praised their use of narrators who "speak what is practically a West Indian language" (1957: 8). Brathwaite furthered this point in his 1960 review of the anthology *Voices of Ghana* prepared by Henry Swanzy. There he hailed the compiler's effort for "bringing in the voices of the people of the new nation making patterns of sound in hammer, engine, power saws, and the movement of earth and water" (Brathwaite 1960a: 131). He particularly stressed the fact that the texts collected in the book were written in English by young Ghanaian writers "whose native language is not English" and who face the challenge of converting their "own forms and speech-rhythms into English," producing a sort of English which "while retaining its peculiar West African flavor" may be deemed "acceptable at any level by the critical intelligence." What Brathwaite referred to as "the power and certainty of the writing," primarily "the way it celebrates and takes confidence from the culture and traditions of the land" in the Ghanaian anthology, appeared to him to have exemplary implications for West Indian writing (131-2).

Brathwaite's early criticism was prescriptive along the lines suggested by the above dichotomy. He applauded, for instance, the achievement of the Jamaican Victor Reid's novel *New Day* for its capture of "a feeling for the poetry of the spoken word, and an imagination capable of giving those spoken words life," an element he found lacking in the novels of Edgar Mittelholzer (Brathwaite 1960b: 207). Mittelholzer's novels, in Brathwaite's view, also lack "the actions of *people* in a given, recognizable society, acting under compulsions that we can understand" (206). Brathwaite requires in literature a "sense of social and moral values." The perceived absence of those values caused him to see a failure in John Hearne's *The Autumn Equinox,* and their perceived presence made him hail the "peculiar distinction" of *A Quality of Violence* by Andrew Salkey

(1960c: 217; 1960d: 219). Likewise, despite his good words in praise of the "intuition" in Wilson Harris's poetry, he found it "limited through its inability to communicate at the level of religious significance" (1960e: 114).

The judgments Brathwaite has passed on the literary artists of the archipelago are all linked directly or indirectly to his conviction that the "value of the artist's work is in the inter-communication between himself and his special public" (1960b: 206). In the essay "The New West Indian Novelists," he argued that writers have their native public that will best appreciate their style. When one writes as an "Emigrant" one becomes divorced from one's natural literary habitat and suffers the lack of "that special criticism and appreciation" that only the writer's own *home* public can provide (1960b: 206). Brathwaite declared in effect that "the final responsibility for the future and achievement of West Indian literature lies in the sympathy and sense of proportion of the West Indian reading public" (1961a: 280).

Brathwaite's early critical writings made the ability to communicate a part of the merit of literary artists. There must be a correspondence between the literary text, which is a cultural product, and the society and culture that inform it. A literary text, consequently, has its autochthonous audience, whose human drama it must address if it is to be considered authentic. V. S. Naipaul's *A House for Mr. Biswas* earns praise from Brathwaite because in it the novelist exhibits an acute awareness of the predicament of his own sociocultural community, the East Indians of the Caribbean, "first brought here as indentured labor after Emancipation in 1838" (1963a: 16; 1968: 159). But the relationship between writers and their people must be genuine and not based purely on aesthetic and intellectual gymnastics. His essay "Roots" decries the practice of those West Indian novelists who derive their folk talk and rhythmic prose style from Anglo-American literature, "the Lawrence-Steinbeck-Hemingway tradition," contending that their use of "the people's speech" is not authentic since it does not arise from a real contact with the people (1963a: 20). Because practically none of the writers referred to by Brathwaite could earnestly be said to form part "of the people," belonging as they do to the middle class, he conjectures that these writers' use of *folk* rhythms might actually be "a sign *and* symbol of their rejection of society" (20). Thus he proposes "a *prose* style which can catch the varying shifts and shades of narrative, action, and speech" in the West Indies in light of his conviction that a literary text that lacks an authentic relationship between writer and society cannot succeed artistically. Following that line of reasoning, he deems *The Scholar Man,* a novel by O. R. Dathorne, "a failure at all levels" (1965: 68). At the same time, he praises Derek Walcott's *The Castaway*

because there the St. Lucian poet succeeds in addressing "our great dichotomy: the split in most of us between Africa and Europe" without exhibiting the "frustration" or the "bitter choice" that seems to beset so many when confronted with the same realization (1966a: 140). Characteristically the aesthetic valuation focuses persistently on the writer's relationship with the people, the society, the cultural habitat informing the creation of his or her text.

In Search of the Word

Brathwaite's literary practice as a creative artist during this early part of his career accords with the socioaesthetic doctrine he had been expostulating in his critical writings. A short story entitled "The Black Angel" published in 1955 presents us with characters whose destiny follows the ups and downs in the town's factory, the sole source of employment for the people. Although the town remains unnamed, the narrator's descriptions, even at the topographical level, place the setting unmistakably in the Caribbean. More importantly, the protagonist wins his battle against the unknown through the strength derived from the wisdom of the *folk,* symbolized here in Ta Mega, the "high priestess." Guardian of the spiritual well-being of the townspeople, she uses her "necromancography" to help him fight the forces of evil (1955a: 84).

The narrative tension of Brathwaite's early fiction piece "Law and Order" is maintained basically through the cultural distance between the young sweethearts Emma and Horace, the main characters. The action takes place in a Ghanaian village where she is a native and he a foreigner. While strolling down the beach, they are harassed by a group of Ga fishermen, and it is up to Emma to confront the marauders, communicate, and negotiate with them. Though feeling that "after all this was a *man's* palaver," Horace has to stay out of it because "he couldn't understand the language" (Brathwaite 1955b: 197). Here as elsewhere in the story what amuses the most is the crisis of communication between Emma and Horace: her efforts to translate her culture to him, his almost unavoidable misconstruing of her rendition, and, consequently, their failure to say anything meaningful to each other. Here, as in "Cricket," a story published years later, language acquires centrality as a means through which to measure cultural authenticity. "Cricket," told almost entirely in West Indian dialect, re-creates an eventful match in the recent history of West Indian cricket. By enacting an encounter between a Caribbean team and a British team, the story symbolically dramatizes a colonial confrontation. The British invented cricket and brought it to the islands just as they brought the English language during the colonial transaction. Rendered mostly via a dialogue among the Creole-speaking characters, the dynamics of the match evoke the need felt by colonial people to prove their worth at the former masters' own game, "de very game they invent" (Brathwaite 1973a: 66).

When the Caribbean players excel in the cricket game, they demonstrate their appropriation of the formerly British sport. Parallel to this, when the characters tell the event in the West Indian vernacular we are witnessing the nativization of English, that is, the appropriation of the formerly British language. At the linguistic level too we see a colonial confrontation. Resorting to dialect means asserting the local culture, the culture of the folk. How the relationship between the colonial language and its nativized counterpart can affect human interactions in the Caribbean is suggested in an episode from the 1961 story "Christine." The contrapuntal effect of the dialogue between the two main characters, Adam and his teenage girlfriend Christine, dominates the narrative flow. They speak in a demotic language using recognizable forms of West Indian dialect. Playfully and with an unmistakable tenderness, the conversation revolves around their elders' supposed opposition to their romance. The one time Adam feels the need to scold Christine, we hear him say: "Don't you know you shouldn't jump down like that from the branch of a tree?"—the only standard English sentence we hear him utter in their whole dialogue (Brathwaite 1961b: 249). This switch from the nativized speech to standard English insinuates the characters' deep understanding of the linguistic codes available to them and their societal implications. Adam seems to sense that to sound for a moment rigidly prohibitive, he can do no better than to step outside the aura of intimacy and love that has been established through their Creole communication. To achieve a momentary distance from his sweetheart he reverts to the official language of the establishment, the standard English of the schools and the upper classes.

Brathwaite's theatrical writings illustrate his preoccupation with language and cultural authenticity no less than his prose fiction and his criticism. He wrote plays primarily while serving as an education officer in Ghana, a country with a complex linguistic situation. "English, the major language of education in this country, is not indigenous," says S. Addo in his introduction to four plays by Brathwaite (Addo 1964: iii). These plays, intended for primary schools, evoke the emblematic texture of Medieval mystery plays and derive much of their dramatic tension from their incorporation, in both form and content, of the linguistic situation and the sociocultural reality of the people of Ghana. The collection includes *The Children's Gifts,* a reworking of the Nativity in an African setting, *Rabbit at the Well* and *Ananse and the Dinner Drum,* both of which draw on moralistic animal fables from African lore, and *The People that Walk in Darkness,* a recreation of another moment from the Nativity. The playwright allows for "improvisation sections" meant to be filled with words spoken by the children acting in their own mother tongue, as he recommends to future producers in his preface (Brathwaite 1964a: v). Three of the four plays feature a character who goes by the name of "the Linguist." In a characteristic scene from *The People that Walk in Darkness,* the birth of Mary and Joseph's child, made possible after defeating personified Darkness, is announced to a group of fishermen who are able to rejoice in the glorious news because the message is brought by angels who speak to them "in their own language" (38).

Brathwaite's book-length play, *Odale's Choice* (1967a), takes up the Antigone story. The story here preserves the ethical dilemma and the existential predicament facing the heroine in the play by Sophocles that so delighted the mind of Hegel, who thought of it as "the most excellent and satisfying work of art" (Hegel 1962: 74). For the German philosopher, Creon and Antigone "stand fundamentally under the power of that which they battle, and consequently infringe that which, conformably to their own essential life, they ought to respect" (72). Hegel further observed that the play dramatized a clash between the two highest moral powers: "family love, what is holy, what belongs to the inner life and to inner feeling, and which because of this is also called the law of the nether gods," collide terribly with "the law of the State" (325).

But, by placing the action against the backdrop of a tangible neo-colonial setting, Brathwaite manages to incorporate into the drama a sociocultural dimension and to season it with the conflict of varying linguistic codes. The social stratification of the characters is revealed in that the soldiers speak dialect while the higher ranking members of the power structure speak standard English. Thus, when the sergeant comes to Creon with the news that his edict has been violated, the head of state demands to be addressed in the official language: "For God's sake speak the language man! Don't talk to me in that damn pigeon all the time! Speak the language" (Brathwaite 1967a: 23). There is the suggestion also that Odale's challenge to the power structure may have the unexpressed support of people in the lower social ranks as represented in the character of Musa. Brathwaite's plays, like the other genres he has practiced, seek to localize all human experience within very discrete historical circumstances. The characters have conflicts that correspond to the demands of a given society and their actions are colored by distinct cultural variables. Language, whether it be imposition of an official code or affirmation of an alternative one, occupies a central position in the people's grappling with history, society, and culture. Even when dealing with an African setting, the plays bear relevance for the Caribbean and could probably be hailed for their "essentially West Indian or even suggestively regional" nature, to borrow the words of a reviewer (Marshall 1965: 71).

Poetry and Cultural Centeredness

Brathwaite's poetry continues and expands the socio-aesthetic paths suggested by his texts in the other genres, particularly since the publication of *Rights of Passage,* his first book-length poetic work to appear in print. His verse production before 1967 appeared in *Bim* and in various anthologies (Murphy 1970: 129). A good many of these early poems have found their way into the poet's subsequent volumes. One could easily concur with Brathwaite's own assessment that his "verse until 1965 had no real centre" (cited in Murphy 1970: 129). For him, the "centre" of his poetry came about only after he completed "the triangular trade" of his historical origins—that is, the passage from Barbados to England, from England to Ghana, and from Ghana back to the West Indies. His verse developed a definite direction, he affirms, after he acquired a "sense of belonging." And although he acknowledges a "European" influence through T. S. Eliot, he insists that his "major influence was perhaps the West Indian novelists who from the very beginning have been putting the speech of our people into our ears" (cited in Murphy 1970: 129). His explanation of how his verse production arrived at a point of aesthetic coherence clearly suggests a link in Brathwaite's mind between literary creativity and an awareness of one's sociohistorical ontology.

Rights of Passage is the first part of a poetic trilogy that subsequently appeared under the title *The Arrivants* (1973b). Divided into four sections, the poem announces its theme in its epigraph from *Exodus* (16: 1), which, in telling of the peregrination of the "children of Israel" upon their departure from Egypt, brings to mind the idea of journey, which pervades the text. The first section, **"Work Song and Blues,"** begins with a **"Prelude"** that sets the predominantly epic tone of the poem. Despite its peculiar line arrangement, the first stanza preserves a distantly perceptible echo of the Virgilian proemium: "Drum skin whip / lash, master sun's / cutting edge of / heat, taut / surfaces of things / I sing / I shout / I groan / I dream / about" (1973b: 4). *The Aeneid* is the story of a historic voyage, one which traces in mythopoetic terms the origins of the people for whom the poem is written. In *Rights of Passage* one is presented with "an impression of the centuries of migration Westward across the Sahara, from Egypt to the West Coast of Africa," thus preparing the reader for the historic travel of the African people to their New World experience, which is a central concern of the poem (Rohlehr 1981: 23).

Early in *Rights of Passage* we come upon Brathwaite's stylistic exploration of a distinct sound quality to his subject matter. Passages such as "Here clay / cool coal clings / to glass, creates / clinks, silica glitters, / children of stars" (5) draw on phonetic resources to convey meaning. Scholars have identified this practice as a

common feature of Brathwaite's poetic production (D'Costa 1968: 25; Rohlehr 1980: 15-31). The preference for language that highlights sonority has thematic implications. The poet often uses sound to suggest an antidote to the destructiveness of silence. In the poem, the fight for life, for survival, is frequently seen as a charge against silence. Silence evokes the predominance of desolation in the African soil where the slaves were first seized: ". . . Flies / nibble and ulcer: / tight silver- / back swarms bringing / silence, the slender / proboscis of rot" (Brathwaite 1973b: 6). Images of death and destruction accompany silence: ". . . until sudden burst, / the buzzing black ones that were / silence, swirl through the / sunlight" (6). Toward the end of the **"Prelude,"** the first person singular that opened the poem transforms itself into a collective voice, saying: "Flame is our god, our last defense, our peril" (8), enacting the bewailing of the slaves when faced with impending doom before the Middle Passage. This switch from singular to plural suggests a Protean conversion of the voice that occurs at various points throughout the poem. Implicit in this practice is Brathwaite's notion of the harmony between the one and the many in a social group as the ideal relationship between an individual and his or her community.

The speaker in the poem, **"Tom,"** has a very clear sense of sociohistorical identification, a definite idea of his origins, and a complete understanding of his place in his community. Derived from the central figure in the novel *Uncle Tom's Cabin* (1852) by Harriet Beecher Stowe, the character of Tom has been seen, particularly among African-Americans, as archetypical of the individuals who passively submit to oppression and who become champions of the interests of their masters (Malcolm X, 1966). This poem, however, presents us with a view of Tom that shows the character's human depth and obdurate dignity. His apparent servility and submissiveness conceal a profound sense of resistance, to "mouth 'Massa, yes / Massa, yes / Boss, yes / Ba as' and hold my hat / in hand / to hide / my heart / hoping my children's eyes / will learn" (15-16). Lloyd Brown has correctly pointed out that "considered as a whole Tom is as ambiguous as the circumstances of his conception. His habitual self-negation is actually a thinly disguised mode of defiant survival" (Brown 1984a: 150). Tom's use of the first person plural indicates a clear awareness of his unique history as well as of his sociocultural alterity vis-à-vis those in relation to whom he must live in subservience: "we who have achieved nothing / work / who have not built / dream / who have forgotten all / dance / and dare to remember" (Brathwaite 1973b: 13).

"The Spades," the second part of *Rights of Passage,* also begins with a **"Prelude."** It explores the various transformations of the African descendant in the New World and Europe and surveys some of the many human types that have arisen from the African diaspora. The multiple vocal characterizations that surface here have struck Mervyn Morris as a "lack of unity of tone" (1967: 64). It would seem more reasonable, however, to interpret these vocal shifts as an attempt by the poet to represent the "typical transformations of the Negro," as Edward Baugh put it, or, in the words of Gordon Rohlehr, as "the several faces, masks, poses, and voices of the deracinated African in the New World" (Baugh 1967: 66; Rohlehr 1978b: 64). This part of the book, at any rate, concerns itself less with historical reminiscence and more with an assessment of the contemporary descendants of the African slaves. Their presence is undeniable in the cultural centers of Africa, the Americas, the United States, and France: "in the fall we reached De- / troit Chicago and Den- / ver; and then it was New / York selling news- / papers in Brooklyn and Harlem. / Then Capetown and Rio; remember how we / took Paris by storm: Sartre, Camus, Picasso and all?" (Brathwaite 1973b: 36).

The text entitled **"Folkways"** explores some of the known stereotypes constructed around African descendants, including their sometimes demeaning self-characterizations. But most evident here is the concern with the music of the folk: "o' this work-song singin' you singin' / the chant o' this work chain" (32). Through the allusion in the title and in the text to Folkways Records, the concern established by Alan Lomax to promote American Negro music around the world, we are reminded that music has often been one of the avenues of survival used by the African descendants. In lines such as "quick bugle / train, black / boogie- / woogie wheels / fat / boogie / woogie waggons / rat tat tat" (33), the language clearly aims to reproduce onomatopoeically what has been called "train blues." Also, the somber languor of the blues is intended in these characteristic lines: "Ever seen / a man / travel more / seen more / lands than this poor / land- / less, harbour- / less spade" (39). That these echoes of specifically Negro musical forms are central to Brathwaite's aesthetic plan in this book has been thoroughly demonstrated by Rohlehr (1980b: 32-40).

But certainly music has not been the only vehicle of survival. There has also been outright resistance in more militant terms. **"Wings of a Dove,"** whose speaker identifies himself as a Rastafarian, covers this aspect of the New World experience of the African. Here the speaker recounts the plight of his people, their articulation of the oppressor in ethnic terms, and their appeal to a favorable god. The text begins with stanzas spoken in standard English, but as the speaker reproduces the voice of what he calls "my people," the tone of protest is heightened and a drastic change occurs in the morphology of the words: "Rise rise / locks- / man, Solo- / man wise / man, rise / rise rise / leh we / laugh / dem, mock / dem stop / dem, kill / dem an' go / back

back / to the black / man lan' / back back / to Af- / rica" (Brathwaite 1973b: 43). Here is certainly an instance of what Louis James in a review of ***Rights of Passage*** referred to as Brathwaite's deliberate fracturing of "the conventional English cadences" to awaken the reader's attention to "the cadence of Caribbean speech" (James 1967: 41). But the practice has thematic implications as well. It presents language as being closer to the expression of the folk the farther it is from the standard forms of the schools and the upper classes. It insinuates also that the folk utter their wish for liberation in more militant terms than do those in the higher sectors of society. Marcus Garvey, one of the most intransigent leaders the black liberation movement has known, came from the folk. Similarly, Malcolm X, the most influential proponent of black nationalism in the United States, came from the lowest ranks of society. Perhaps those at the bottom, those suffering oppression in its crudest form, are quicker to speak an authentic speech of liberation. That possibility, at least, seems to be behind the switch in linguistic codes from standard English to Creole forms in the above lines.

The last two sections of the book, **"Islands and Exiles"** and **"The Return,"** dramatize the condition of dispossession of people in the Caribbean and their condition of permanent exile. A text suggestively entitled "The Emigrants" describes the lot of Caribbeans who for want of a productive existence in their lands often opt for testing their luck abroad. In the other Americas, the United States, and Europe, Caribbean people retrace the route initially charted by Columbus, but inversely, and find that those shores do not hold in store for "these New World mariners" the wealth and the prestige that awaited the Admiral in the fifteenth century. It is only rhetorically that the speaker asks: "What Cathay shores / for them are gleaming golden / what magic keys they carry to unlock / what gold endragoned doors?" (Brathwaite 1973b: 52). These deracinated Caribbeans do not often fare well abroad, especially in the Christian West, where they are often met with outright hostility: "Once we went to Europe, and a rich old lady asked: / Have you no language of your own / no way of doing things / did you spend all those holidays / at England's apron strings?" (55).

What is left for Caribbean people seems to be the option chosen by the speaker in **"South."** There he turns his eyes back to the archipelago, declaring: "But today I recapture the islands' / bright beaches" (57). He rejoices in the natural beauty of the region and extracts from nature's very elements a source of historical hope: "And gulls white sails slanted seaward, / fly into the limitless morning before us" (58). That hopeful evocation of the area's potential gives the strength needed to assess realistically the otherwise hopeless situation of the West Indies as perceived by the speaker. He can then see the Caribbean soil as an intricate mixture of hope and frustration. From a picture of desolation, "the landscape with the broken homes" (61), in the poem **"O Dreams O Destinations"** we move to **"The Dust,"** where we find a moving portrayal of the wisdom of the folk. While evincing a measure of sociohistorical misunderstanding about themselves as a people and about their affinity with the people who "speak so / in they St. Lucia patois" (66), and while mouthing the conformism that often comes with Christian religious devotion, they instinctively sense things happening "widdout rhyme widdout reason" and feel dissatisfied with the prevailing order of things. Far from explaining their sorrows away, as their biblical training would encourage, they give vent to their doubt: "Why is that / what it mean?" (69). Because of its sensitive delving into the experience of the folk, **"The Dust"** has been called a "near perfect expression of the life, music and philosophy of the people" (Pollard 1980: 41).

When looking panoptically at the region, the speaker in **Rights of Passage** does not fail to pass judgment on the disciples of Mammon among African descendants, those with a strong proclivity to imitate their former masters when governing themselves in the Caribbean. Through mass education, they preserve the same patterns of thought fostered by the former slave-owners. Imitating the manners of the British and relishing their books, they, deprived of selves, go to school to learn how to be good British subjects. The pertinent question here seems to be: Where is the home of those who have been trained to be other than themselves: "In Paris Brixton Kingston / Rome? / Here? / Or in Heaven?" (Brathwaite 1973b: 77). The text poses a disturbing question and promises no easy answer. The speaker's historical past has not been easily visible to him and its legacy has often given cause for self-mockery and shame: "the old / unflamed remains / of Tom we sometimes / joke / about" (78). He seems to see no other alternative but to seek to define himself by his dispossession, which he, oddly enough, construes as an avenue of self-affirmation.

Rights of Passage closes with an **"Epilogue"** in which the speaker, after examining the journey of the children of the diaspora and their various legacies in the New World, declares that: "There is no turning back" (85). The conclusion is neither sad nor happy but crudely true. Uprooted from their African abode, the slave descendants became deracinated through the colonial transaction. Living now for centuries in the New World, they cannot truly call Africa their home. Any true search for a constructive existence in the present must begin with the conviction that the Middle Passage is irreversible. Clearly, we can read here an utter dismissal of the alternative proposed by Garvey's "Back-to-Africa" movement in the early twentieth century. This should not be seen, however, as a negation of the past in the search for origins, the valuation of cultural authenticity, and the coinage of an efficacious language. The point

here, instead, seems to be that Africa provides not a *home* to which one returns but rather a source from which one draws understanding in order better to grasp the meaning of one's life in the Caribbean setting. As would later be said of the third volume of Brathwaite's trilogy, Africa becomes here a "fructifying interlude in the long task of finding a language and a ritual" befitting the Caribbean experience (Moore 1970: 186). One could infer from this the teleological notion that home is where one ends up, as opposed to the etiological proposition: "Home is where one starts from" that we read in the "East Coker" section of T. S. Eliot's *Four Quartets* (1971: 129). In Brathwaite destination takes precedence over origins, although the ability to go forward presupposes the empowerment that comes from knowing where one came from. For someone who has to contend with an ignominious past of slavery, dehumanization, and dispossession, home is not "where one starts from" but rather a stage to which one *arrives,* after one has survived the misery of the earlier stages. The collective title of Brathwaite's trilogy is called, not incidentally, **The Arrivants.**

THE AFRICAN QUEST

The use of Africa as a source from which to draw understanding forms the core of **Masks** (1968), the second volume in Brathwaite's **The Arrivants.** "Only the fool points at his origins with the left hand," says the Akan proverb that serves as epigraph to the book. The book is divided into seven parts. Its first part, **"Libation,"** begins with a "Prelude" that identifies the geographical and historical setting of the poem: "Out / of . . . the seven / Kingdoms: / Songhai, Mali, / Chad, Ghana, / Tim- / buctu, Volta, / and the bitter / waste was / Ben- / in, comes / this shout / comes / this song" What we have here is a lyrical—though not romanticized—exploration of the African past from the ancient empires of old to the arrival of the Europeans. **Masks** has been the subject of various close readings, chiefly by Rohlehr (1981) and Maureen Warner Lewis (1977a). The reading here focuses primarily on the poem's emphasis on tying the search for origins to a preoccupation with language and communication against an aura of religious significance.

Throughout **Masks** we find an emphasis on sounds and the rejection of its antithesis: silence. Particularly meaningful in this respect is **"The Making of the Drum,"** which enacts the stages involved in the construction of the drum in ancient African culture. The ceremony surrounding the creation of the instrument symbolizes the awareness of these traditional people with regards to the need for an antithesis to silence. This is clear when we hear of the exigencies around the choice of wood for the barrel of the drum. It has to be the kind of wood whereby "we hear the sounds / of the rivers; / vowels of reed- / lips, pebbles / of consonants,

/ underground dark / of the continent" (Brathwaite 1973b: 95). In her reading, Warner Lewis has found that sound (speech, song, music) and water are images of life and attainment whereas "silence and dumbness betray inactivity and death," consistently revealing a clear dichotomy throughout the poem and occasionally appearing as a juxtaposition (Warner Lewis 1977: 19, 40). If one accepts this dichotomy as mythopoetically plausible, the meaning of this particular part of the poem emerges clearly. We can see that the drum is the most valuable object of these traditional people's craft because it is the vehicle through which the divine order can communicate with them. "God is dumb / until the drum / speaks," we hear (Brathwaite 1973b: 97). The drum serves as the language of ultimate communication. This first section concludes with "Atumpan," a text in which the actual sounds of the drum are reproduced ("kon kon kon kon / kun kun kun kun") to conjure Odomankoma, the sky-god Creator, who in turn speaks through the sounds of the drum (98).

In general, the sonorous quality of *Masks* is achieved by a combination of onomatopoetic reproduction of drumming vibrations, the incorporation of ritual song forms and hymns, the introduction of various Akan words and phrases, as well as the exploration of Akan syntactical structures in English. One critic at least has, in an otherwise favorable review, objected to passages in the book that she finds more functional in sound than in sense, suggesting that the poem is bound by its rhetoric and exterior dimension (Risden 1968: 147). However, the more common view agrees with another critic for whom in Brathwaite the use of "sound itself" constitutes "another extension of the literary uses of language" (New 1978: 368). Warner Lewis, for her part, sees sound and sense in the poem as inextricable, proposing that, even in such instances as when the text is dominated by the "drum," sounds cohere into the overall "voice" of the poem (1977: 60). Even when the result appears to be what a critic calls "a hybrid prosody," the diction, syntax, and rhythm in *Masks* contribute to what Edward Baugh once called the "one-ness of overall tone" (Lieberman 1969: 56; Baugh 1968: 209).

In the second section of *Masks,* "Pathfinders," the text entitled "Ougadougou" (referring to the capital of Upper Volta, West Africa) significantly illustrates an important technique employed by Brathwaite. The words here are spoken by the Niger state as a persona. Talking in the first person as a character in a play, the speaker recalls in a spirit of self-recrimination the coming of warring visitors to the land: "Our errors before them; too soft, / too blandished, too ready for peace and for terror" (Brathwaite 1973b: 104). The states of Chad and Timbuktu also join the *dramatis personae,* and they too regret their lethal passivity. Finally, Volta, the personified river, symbol of the civilization that once flourished on its banks, speaks of a longing for the ancient glory of the empire (109). In every case, the speaker (state, river, or person) comes summoned by the *mmenson,* the orchestra used on state occasions to relate history in ancient Akan tradition, to "recount now the gains and the losses" (107), the past events of the land and its people. Through these various speakers, the poet allows himself the opportunity to rehearse diverse forms of telling in the text.

"Limits," the third section of *Masks,* explores the desolation of the ancient lands and their inhabitants. The collective memory, in desperation for a better time, appeals, for spiritual refuge, to the Egyptian past: "But the lips remember / temples, gods and pharaohs, / gold, silver ware; imagination / rose on wild unfolded wings" (113). The speaker, however, reflects on the futility of overestimating a past which may also be filled with cruelty: "And Ra, / the sun / god's gold, / demanded blood / to make it sacred" (114). It is, therefore: "Time to forget / these kings. / Time to forget / these gods" (114). One can read into these lines the suggestion that one must, when assessing the past, sort out the recoverable values from those that are to be rejected. Much has certainly been lost, abused, and misused, but, as the speaker in "Techiman" affirms, "the way lost / is a way to be found / again" (119). The hope remains that the errors of the past can be averted in the future. Nor is it too late for repair because "Time's walking river is long" (120).

The next two sections of the poem, "The Return" and "Crossing the River," are particularly important because they enact the return of a New World African descendant to the original soil of the West African coast. The speaker evokes a pathos-filled encounter with the ancestral land and people. Their meeting becomes the most touching when it comes to verbal communication. When the New World Negro looks at the ancestral Africans, he sees their "white teeth / smooth voices like pebbles / moved by the sea of their language" (124). They, of course, speak to him in the mother tongue: "*Akwaaba* they smiled / meaning welcome / *aye koo*" (124). He is treated ceremoniously according to the demands of traditional hospitality. They realize that he has come "back a stranger / after three hundred years" and would wish to activate his memory: "here is a stool for / you; sit; do / you remember?" (124). He does not recognize them and their manner any more than they remember him. Here as elsewhere, the poem dramatizes the near amnesia that separates the survivors of the diaspora from their ancestral ways, as Warner Lewis has appropriately observed (1973: 96).

The speaker here does not succeed, as Alex Haley in *Roots* (1976) presumably would, in tracing his beginnings to an original progenitor in the African continent. The return to the ancestral land leaves him with a sense of his disconnection. He utters this recognition: "I travelled to a distant town / I could not find my mother / I could not find my father / I could not hear the drum / whose ancestor am I" (125). The disconnection from people and from the land manifests itself also in language (Warner Lewis 1977: 56). For the fall of the glorious tribe in the past, as told by the speaker in **"The Golden Stool,"** can be expressed as triumph of silence and death over the reign of the living word: "the priests cried: / die. Let the tongues, / lips' labials, rot; / withering words in the hot / wind. If / you must speak, / wear a black mask / of silence; ask- / ing *no* elder to lead you / again through the branch- / es, through the path- / ways of prayer, / to Onyame's now / leafless air" (Brathwaite 1973b: 145).

The final section of *Masks,* **"Arrival,"** continues to dwell on the loss, but this time the speaker, who continues to be the New World African descendant, addresses contemporary African interlocutors. The arrival of the Europeans to the West African coast and the subsequent misery endured by their captives from the moment of uprooting through the various stages of the colonial transaction have colored the intervening centuries. Reddened by the legacy of bloodshed and darkened by the oblivion resulting from the obliteration of ancient cultural traditions, history for the African descendant can hardly evoke pride and joy: "I wear this / past I borrowed; his- / tory bleeds / behind my hollowed eyes" (148). The ancestral land also shows as much desolation as the New World abode: "Beginnings end here / in this ghetto" (149). The African soil cannot help, nor can the ancient household gods since they, when the invaders came centuries ago, did "not save us from pride, / foreign tribes' bibles / the Christian god's hunger" (149). Too long the machinery of destruction has prevailed, undoing the African people's sense of self and their creations, in the long colonial domination of the Europeans. In other words, "the termites' dark teeth, three / hundred years working, / have patiently ruined my art" (150).

Despite the irreparableness of his separation from the ancestral landscape and its people, however, the New World African descendant and his counterparts in the old continent preserve a deeper memory that makes itself felt at the level of language: "welcome your brother now / my trapped curled tongue / still cries" (148). Reference is made here to a sort of communication that transcends the centuries of uprooting and depredation. Perhaps the yearning for reconnection expressed implies a reliance on the oneness of the peoples of the black diaspora with those who remained in the ancestral lands. This sense of an urge for communication between Africans and the children of the diaspora may have to do with a human experience that encountered equal misery at both ends of the Middle Passage. The last words in *Masks* are "I am learning /

let me succeed" (157). Spoken in the context of an invocation to Asase Yaa, the Akan earth goddess, those words would insinuate that it is in the areas of communication and understanding that the contact with the ancestral heritage can best equip the New World slave descendant. In this sense, the African journey of *Masks'* narrator justifies itself in the end as a journey of enlightenment and as a prelude to a "rediscovered voice" (Grant 1970: 187).

On Language and Home

Brathwaite's *Islands* (1969) completes the poetic trilogy *The Arrivants* and significantly brings to closure the poet's "triangular trade." Just as the previous volumes dramatize the plight of the West Indian "emigrating" from the New World soil, going to Europe and then searching for "roots" in Africa, *Islands* brings the speaker back to the Caribbean. Divided into five sections, the poem begins with a part entitled **"New World"** that fathoms the spiritual climate of the region. The first text, called **"Jah,"** the name the Rastafarians of Jamaica use for God, illustrates this religious concern. The initial impression bespeaks a blatant spiritual poverty prevailing in the area: "the land has forgotten the memory of the most secret places" (Brathwaite 1973b: 164). Then follows a prodding into the slave past to gather the remnants of a strong religious cosmology. We come upon the evocation of **"Ananse,"** the Protean "spider-hero of the Akans; earthly trickster, but once with powers of the creator-gods" (272). The epithets associated with the divinity ("dry stony word-maker, word-breaker, / creator"), whose close relationship with language is made evident, suggest to a significant extent that the search for a spiritual tradition in the area is not disconnected from the search for an authentic speech.

It becomes clear in **"Shepherd"** that, as far as the speaker is concerned, the local milieu, despite the initial appearance, is rich in spirituality. "The streets of my home have their own gods / but we do not see them," he regrets (189). All it takes to "see them," it would seem, is to enter into a sort of communion with one's surroundings so that one may be attuned to the language they speak. For they do try to communicate since: "the drum praises them / and the rope that loosens the tongue of the steeple; / they speak to us with the voices of crickets, / with the shatter of leaves" (190). The speaker utters his predications as a "shepherd" in the religious sense and more specifically as a "leader of the *pocomania* and other religious groups in the West Indies," as Brathwaite's **"Glossary"** explains (275). His words, therefore, carry the weight of a collective regional voice. The general title of the second part of *Islands,* **"Limbo,"** also sheds light on what we see here as an attempt to emphasize expressions which, like the religion of the folk, can be considered authentic Caribbean forms. For "limbo," a very popular kind of performance in Caribbean night clubs, was created in the area. Brathwaite's glossary describes it as:

> a dance in which participants have to move with their bodies thrown backwards and without any aid whatsoever under a stick which is lowered at every successfully completed passage under it, until the stick is practically touching the ground. It is said to have originated—a necessary therapy—after the experience of the cramped conditions between the slave decks of the Middle Passage.

(274)

"Caliban," another text in the second section of the book, contains implications for Caribbean religion and language. Inherited from Shakespeare's *The Tempest*, Caliban here becomes a spokesman for the region who clearly sees himself in contradistinction to the interests of the colonial power structure of the West. Curiously, *Une tempête,* Césaire's adaptation of Shakespeare's play in which Prospero appears as "le colonisateur" and Caliban as "l'esclave nègre révolté," appeared in print the same year as Brathwaite's *Islands.* At any rate, Brathwaite's Caliban begins with a bitter assessment of the dismal condition of people in the Caribbean: "Ninety-five percent of my people poor / ninety-five percent of my people black / ninety-five percent of my people dead," he says (191). A panoptic look at the region's history draws his eyes to pivotal moments which are also violent ones, and he asks: "How many bangs how many revolutions?" (192). His survey of contemporary events yields a no less problematic picture. Present complexity is symbolized here by two opposing poles. The "limbo stick," on the one hand, smacks of sociohistorical alienation: "stick is the whip / and the dark deck is slavery" (194). The music, on the other hand, points to those elements in the local setting that contain the stuff of survival: "out of the dark / and the dumb gods are raising me / up / up / up / and the music is saving me" (195).

To resist his indentured existence, Caliban must fight off a history that has deprived him of many of the symbols of his human integrity. Spiritual elevation becomes a potential vehicle of his liberation. But implicit in the choice of the Shakespearean character, who wields the ability to curse as a weapon of resistance against Prospero's domination, is the realization that his rebellion must also occur in the sphere of language. The choice of Caliban as a *persona* presupposes a confrontation which is no less dramatic than the one enacted in **"Rites,"** a reworking in dialect verse of the short story "Cricket." In **"Rites,"** as Kenneth Ramchand has pointed out, dialect and cricket are used in conjunction to suggest the drama of the islands (1976: 139).

In the third part of *Islands,* **"Rebellion,"** the connection between history, spirituality, and language is articulated in ways that are deeply meaningful for cultural authenticity in the Caribbean. The first text here, **"Wake,"** which a scholar describes as "a highly formalized poem whose function is to summarize this journey from negation to self-affirmation," presents us with a speaker who seeks sociocultural self-assurance through the spiritual equipment contained in language (Rohlehr 1981: 239). We hear him beg: "mother me with words, / gems, spoken talismans of your broken tongue" (Brathwaite 1973b: 210). It is in the absence of "the Word" that the moral poverty of the islands is most deeply felt. "For the Word is love / and has been absent from our butterflies. / For the Word is peace / and is absent from our streets" (212). The Word here, apart from its religious connotation, refers also concretely to language. As Rohlehr has indicated, it is for language that the speaker begs his Ibo ancestors, whose "incarnation must result in poetry" (1971: 196). For the speaker in **"Naming"** it seems an unequivocal equation that the absence of language necessarily amounts to an absence of meaning, for: "What is a word to the eye? / Meaning" (Brathwaite 1973b: 217).

Languageless peoples lack the power to name things and, in a certain sense, to make things happen: "The tree must be named. / This gives it fruit / issues its juices" (217). The magical possibilities here attributed to naming recall the creative power of the Word in the African concept of *Nommo* as expounded by Janheinz Jahn in *Muntu* (Morris 1970: 19). Similarly unproductive is the use of language that cannot be called one's own. For the speaker in **"Eating the Dead,"** this can lead to confusion and, eventually, to muteness, marking the triumph of silence: "My tongue is heavy with new language / but I cannot give birth to speech" (221).

The political implications of the need and the quest for an authentic language are explored most meaningfully in **"Negus."** The title of this piece alludes to "one of Haile Selassie's titles which Rastafarians freely employ as a substitute for Jesus" (260). The persona, placing himself in a postcolonial moment, speaks decidedly from the vantage point of one opposed to colonialism. In the modern period, the most overt signs of classical colonialism have been removed. But certain mental structures that get translated into cultural expressions still obey the command of a colonial social order. It is quite clear to the speaker, in that sense, that "it is not enough to be free / of the whips, principalities and power / where is your Kingdom of the Word?" (222). To direct one's destiny one must first be able to control one's language. Language is the ultimate confirmation of decolonization. Decolonization entails a possession, an appropriation of language. Therefore, the speaker declares: "I / must be given words to shape my name / to the syllables of trees / I / must be given words to refashion futures" (223-4). For Negus, as Rohlehr has aptly put it, "Independence must mean a new language, a redefinition of self and milieu" (1971: 197). The last line of **"Negus,"** which ends in an invocation of Attibon Legba, the vodou god of the crossroads, suggests that the struggle for the affirmation of "self and milieu" in the Caribbean has simultaneously political, linguistic, and religious dimensions: "fill me with words / and I will blind your God. / *Att / Att / Attibon*" (Brathwaite 1973b: 224).

The fourth and the fifth sections of *Islands,* **"Possession"** and **"Beginning,"** offer an inventory of the historical legacy of the West Indian region with the purpose of determining what can rightfully be owned. Toward the end of the poem one gets a suggestion of the youthfulness of Caribbean culture in the eyes of the poet and how such a view informs his artistic project. The emphasis on the past supposes an effort to create new possibilities for the future. One picks up the fragments of the lost heritages in order to better build a durable tradition. In this sense, a time that is past is an announcement of a beginning. Reconnection with one's surroundings and possession or appropriation of language must mark that beginning which corresponds to the refashioning of one's future.

The speaker recognizes that the region has created various forms and types. In **"Tizzic"** we find an individual who recalls the lumpen-proletariat. Indigenous to the sociohistorical condition of the area, this individual enjoys a sort of alienating freedom that tends to perpetuate his oppression (Rohlehr 1981: 302). There is also **"Vèvè,"** sign of the vodou religion and, consequently, symbol of the most authentic cultural forms forged by the Caribbean experience. The following lines are suggestive: "For on this ground / trampled with the bull's swathe of whips / where the slave at the crossroads was a red anthill / eaten by moonbeams, by the holy ghosts / of his wounds / the Word becomes / again a god and walks among us" (Brathwaite 1973b: 265-6). This is no mere resuscitation of the Western Logos, but a refashioning and validation of it via the power of Nommo as inscribed historically in the human experience of the people of the Caribbean. The revitalizing potential of this spiritual legacy has to do with the fact that, having survived the Middle Passage and the inhumanity of the colonial transaction, people here are just beginning.

Islands closes with a piece entitled **"Jou'vert."** The word refers to the dawning of each Carnival Monday in the West Indies (Rohlehr 1981: 313). In re-creating the atmosphere of that festivity, the text suggests a possibility for synthesis between the liberated expression of certain regional types and the observance of authentic Caribbean forms. It proposes the grounds for a marriage between Tizzic and Vèvè under the aegis of the traditions of the folk. The carnival, an authentic expression of the creativity evident in what Brathwaite calls "the little tradition" of the folk, can serve for Tizzic as

an outlet to his hedonistic energy, since this expression uses music and dance. Simultaneously, since carnival employs religious symbols and forms of worship, it can induce Tizzic into contact with native spirituality in a way that demands less sanctimonious sobriety than would be possible in **"Vèvè"** (Rohlehr 1981: 313 et passim). The location of these texts, at the end of the poem's last section, which is suggestively entitled "Beginning," indicates that it is from these autochthonous types and forms that one must start any attempt to appraise authentic Caribbean culture. Cultural authenticity alone can provide the arena wherein there can be: "hearts / no longer bound / to black and bitter / ashes in the ground / now waking / making / making / with their / rhythms some- / thing torn / and new" (Brathwaite 1973b: 268-9). Brathwaite's review of Faustin Charles's volume *The Expatriate* draws parallels with his own *Islands.* He observes in closing that: "Both books, published late in 1969, are concerned with the possession of the Caribbean through word, metaphor, and symbol" (Brathwaite 1970a: 65).

Brathwaite's editorial success with *Rights of Passage, Masks,* and *Islands,* and their collective republication in 1973 in one volume as *The Arrivants,* had little precedent for a poet of the region. Kenneth Ramchand credited the publication of Brathwaite's trilogy with having "at last brought poetry to the attention of the West Indian populace as something related to their lives" (1974: 197). The acclaim and popularity Brathwaite has enjoyed with an audience that encompasses readers from diverse class strata reveals the wisdom of the search for cultural authenticity. The trilogy brought him to the forefront of artistic discourse throughout the Third World, and his international reputation as a major poet rests largely on *The Arrivants.*

Shortly after the publication of the trilogy in one volume, three books of poetry by Brathwaite appeared in quick succession: *Other Exiles* (1975a), *Days and Nights* (1975b), and *Black and Blues* (1976). These lack the aesthetic cohesion of *The Arrivants,* their composition being in general less oriented by a systematic aesthetic program. *Other Exiles,* for instance, simply gathers shorter poems spanning a period of twenty-five years of Brathwaite's poetic career. In general, the tone of the book is subdued. The voice sustains a predominantly personal vantage point and at times engages itself in questions pertaining to the drama of the individual artist. Despite the absence of a sustained thematic core, however, geographically the *locus* is the Caribbean. Likewise, although the systematic exploration of language as a vehicle of cultural authenticity hardly surfaces here, one could detect in the sonority of the words a music which "is euphony related to, and expressive of, meaning" to use the words of a reviewer (Silken 1977: 230). Also, a good many of the poems included in the volume treat subjects related to local Caribbean history.

Days and Nights, containing basically a variation on a sequence of the same title that would appear in ***Mother Poem,*** the long poem Brathwaite was working on at the time, is a casual publication that ought to be seen as a fragment from a major poetic endeavor. ***Black and Blues,*** which competed for and won the Casa de las Américas poetry prize in Cuba in 1976, is also a gathering of shorter poems, many of which had appeared in earlier volumes while others would find their way into later ones. But despite the assortment of texts in ***Black and Blues,*** the organization of the collection gives it thematic unity. The experience evoked here is Caribbean and so are the voices through which the evocation happens. The voice that dominates the book at times speaks West Indian dialect, assuming the collective sound of the folk. Sometimes, inversely, a choric "I" expresses the sentiment of a collective consensus. Shango and Caribbean religion, Caliban and the history of the region, the tropical landscape, scarcity and dryness, beaches and sand, flora and fauna, the thirst for the word—most of the salient symbols of the local milieu are here. The following lines from **"Harbour"** evoke "self and milieu" in a way that evinces the contingent texture of the area's sociohistorical make-up: "yet here in the cup of my word / on the lip of my eyelid of light / like a star in its syllable socket / there is a cripple crack and hopple / whorl of colour, eye / it is a cool harbour" (Brathwaite 1976a: 82). The speaker's tone is, as in the conclusion of ***The Arrivants,*** optimistic. The optimism derives from the realization that the existence of multiple options provides the opportunity for a creative future. At any rate, "it is a beginning" (83).

The Woman's Caribbean

The next major poetic text published by Brathwaite, ***Mother Poem*** (1977a), as the first volume of yet another trilogy, tackles the Caribbean experience with a focus on the plight of women. Localized in one specific island, Barbados, the text centers around the speaker's mother, who typifies women generally in Barbados as well as throughout the Caribbean. At the same time, the mother is also Barbados itself, a discrete historical *locus* in time and space, as well as all the other islands, "pebbles" floating in the unharvested sea of the Caribbean. Held together by a narrative voice that recounts the travails of the woman and the anxiety of her relationship with men (husband, son, preacher, boss, God), the poem occasionally intersperses monologues spoken by the mother herself. In general, the poem assigns the mother the role of preserver of culture, hope, humanity, and the word, anticipating the role given to Sycorax in Brathwaite's later work. Approximately one-half of the bulk of the book is written in dialect, "partly

to create a voice for the speakers" and evoke the collective persona of the folk against the backdrop of a "search for an organic cultural tradition" (King 1980: 130).

At the beginning of ***Mother Poem*** the child-narrator speaks of the island-mother as a fountain of fertility: "my mother is a pool" (Brathwaite 1977a: 30). Though having endured depredation, she has kept her hope. Among her various calamities, she has suffered the dehumanization of her man, for whom she pathetically bewails: "My husband / if you cud see he / fragile, fraid o'e own shadow" (6). The official religion has not helped, so her telling of her present misery and grim future incorporates the language of Psalm 26 in a way that contradicts its biblical message: "and I will dwell in the house of the merchant for never" (9). Her history has made her privy to her country's conflicting spiritual legacies. While attending to the requirements of Catholicism, she must also answer the calling of the more autochthonous form of worship. She appeals to the bell, a symbol of official Christianity, to gain access to the depths of the vodou cosmology: "is the bell, pastor john / leh me racket / is the bell, pastor john. / leh me wreck it / till uh pour sounn in the Vèvè" (15).

The mother's sense of sociocultural self-recognition is clear. She sees herself in contradistinction to the colonizing legacy of the Christian West. She fears her children might get lost in the pit of alienating Western education, seduced by the crafty "Chalkstic the teacher" promising that for them "there would be the day" in order to beguile "another black hostage / of verbs" (24). Yet, she must remain occupied, ensuring the survival of the household by going to the "market bawlin' for fish" (25). She, who now goes "selling half-sole shoes in the leather / department" (36) as another way "of keeping her body and soul- / seam together" (36), has been on the go since she, as a youngster, "left school / taking up sewing since she was fourteen" and now has to keep selling anything she can find to make a living (38). The overall ambiance of poverty and suffering re-created in this part of the poem is set against sociohistorical and cultural opposites, with the Judeo-Christian capitalist tradition on one end and the native possibilities on the other. Brown, in alluding to these polarities in the poem, has termed them "cultural complexities," that is: "standard English and island creole, Christianity and Afro-West Indian religious forms, the symbols of a deep-rooted, persistent colonialism and the musical modes (calypso, work-songs) of a vital, uncorrupted sensibility which the poet attributes to his Afro-West Indian folk" (Brown 1984a: 167-8).

The sequence entitled **"Woo/Dove"** juxtaposes thoughts on the ways of the creator "who calls the lightning down," recalling the Lord's vaunting of his own almighty power when asked about the fairness of his designs in *The Book of Job* (Brathwaite 1977a: 41). Such is the background for a scene in which the mother, pressed by economic necessity, has to implicate herself in the virtual prostitution of her own child, whom she tries to soothe by saying things like: "it int hard, leh me tell he you / jess sad / so come darlin chile / leh me tell he you ready you steady you go" (44). The fate that befalls the mother and her children is really a microscopic representation of the lot of the people of the island. For, "all the peaks, the promontories" included, "there is more weed than food in the island" (46).

The desolation which castrates the West Indian's potential to become more fully human, as Paulo Freire would say, is associated in *Mother Poem* with a human disruption that comes with capitalist exploitation. In that context, even the people's proclivity to love themselves or their land finds itself impeded since "the broken lives, broken eyes / shattered syllables of leaves / cannot love you" (49). This desolation the mother, as a speaking persona, traces back to historical origins rooted in colonialism, whose remnants she sees in "the man who possesses us all / who has broken the heart of my father's hands" (54). The mother, who has somehow managed to preserve a potential for rebellion, refuses to accept passively the docility of her men. She urges them on, assuring: "i will carry the wit twitching rag / bearing your face, conveying you futureless race / in its burst bag of balls to your doorstep" (80).

The section of the poem entitled **"Driftwood"** suggests the possibility for the people of the region, the mother's children, to arm themselves with new strength, new meaning, freshly carved words. In essence, "they will wait: cutting their reeds / jagged eared knives working on wood / wreathing their own words" (113). The mother evinces her self-recognition as the voice of a community which defines itself by its subversion against a dominant order. The resources used by the poet in the text combine to highlight the contingent nature of the place, the situation, and the people appearing in the poem, what is called here "the manscape." The contingency pervading the texture of *Mother Poem* has been noted by Warner Lewis, for whom the techniques of "line-internal rhymes," a certain "Biblical lyricism," the "oratorical crescendo of noun phrase accumulation," and the echoing of "the phraseology of Rastafarian speech" all contribute to underline "the idiom of this anti-Establishment poetry." The critic connects this element of socioaesthetic subversion to Brathwaite's nationalistic position which, as in Chinua Achebe and Ngũgĩ wã Thiong'o, comes into view primarily through "an immersion in the language structures" of the metropolis and their recasting in the language of the people (Warner Lewis 1985: 111-12, 114).

Mother Poem closes with the speaker's recognition of the possibility of empowerment for people in the region. There is reference to a recovery of water, antidote to the gloom contained symbolically in aridity, paralleled by a recovery or possession of the word, antithesis of silence, to announce the rebirth and replenishment of the long crushed vitality of the mother and her children, the land and its people. Thus, "let it be hand and clap and tambour / and she will praise the lord / so that losing her now / you will restore her silent gutters of wordfall / slipping over her footsteps like grass / slippering out of her wrinkles like rain" (117). With its hopeful spirit and the expectation of a creative future for the "manscape," the poem's conclusion signals an insistence on identifying human potential in the midst of pervading ruins.

The optimism typical of Brathwaite's idiom derives from the poet's belief in the indomitability of the folk, represented in *Mother Poem* by the persona of the mother, whose "soul goes marching on" (104), agent of resistance that she is. In a subsequent poem, *Soweto* (1979a), which deals with the moral annihilation to which the black majority in South Africa was put by the white regime, the speaker manages to see beyond the devastation of the human landscape to point to existing—albeit not conspicuous—sources of liberating productivity: "and we know, somewhere, there / there is real fire" (Brathwaite 1979a). Another poem published in the same year, written as a tribute to Cuba's national poet, the late Nicolás Guillén, illustrates Brathwaite's tendency to express the possibility for hope in terms of Caribbean people's access to what could be considered culturally authentic. Addressing Guillén as "the *sunsum* of our ancestors," Brathwaite sings his solidarity with the Cuban poet intimating a linguistic commonality that goes beyond the limitations of English and Spanish: "and the sea between us yields its secrets / silver into syllables into sheets / of sound that bear our pain" (Brathwaite 1979b). Brathwaite's choice of title, **Word-Making Man,** for the poem to Guillén is worthy of note, since he appears to have inverted the title of the anthology of Guillén's poetry, *Man-Making Words* (1975) edited by Roberto Márquez and David A. McMurray. These anthologists in turn had taken the phrase from a sentence in Ralph Waldo Emerson's *Journals*. Brathwaite's inversion gives to human beings power over words.

The Caribbean and Manhood

Brathwaite's **Sun Poem** (1982a), the second volume of the trilogy that begins with **Mother Poem**, stresses the connection—indeed, the continuity—between the plight of women and that of men. Using Barbados as its geographical focus, **Sun Poem** covers the same ground as **Mother Poem** but from the point of view of a voice that aims to capture the male experience in the island. The poem begins *ab ovo,* as it were, with a first-person narrator reminiscing the experience of things being born, stretching as far back as the beginning of time:

"When the earth was made / when the wheels of the sky were fashioned / when my songs were first heard in the voice of the coot and the owl / hillaby soufrière and kilimanjaro were standing towards me with / water with fire / at the center of the air" (Brathwaite 1982a: 1). The main character in **Sun Poem** is a boy called Adam, which brings to mind the Creation in the Hebrew tradition.

The setting of the poem is recognizably West Indian. Most of the action recounted here takes place around Browns Beach, a clearly defined Barbadian setting. Likewise, most of the text consists of the boy's personal memories. He recalls discovering the sea on "that bright afternoon" (8), his compulsion to master the water by making it go "chow" as it did when the expert "beach-boys jumped / and the water wore wreaths where they disappeared" (12), his need to test his mettle before his peers by facing Batto "the shark of the sea-egg / season" (15), his final self-assertion against Batto (18), his boyish dreams induced by the sea (21), and his wish to transcend the respiratory limitations of humans so he could breathe under water like a fish (29).

The greater bulk of the material in **Sun Poem** centers around Adam's *Bildung,* his upbringing and coming of age in the island, his bitter-sweet passage to adulthood. Growing up inexorably entails a loss of innocence, and for Adam the bitter reality of his surroundings must speed and increase the sadness of the loss. "Looking back to the land / you would see that only the tallest trees were still / standing / but they were losing their colour / but they were losing their names / they didn't toss light anymore" (41), he says, recalling a world of physical decay. The picture of an environment marred by deterioration is perhaps paralleled by the memory of a corresponding dismalness in the human landscape: "the afternoon of fathers going grey / soft in the head / in the belly / in the heart / and where it hurts him most / is filled with looking out of windows / waiting for the bells to ring / bring news of recognition" (66).

There is much in the poem that could be read as autobiography, with Adam serving as the voice through which Brathwaite does his remembering. The sequence entitled **"Fletches,"** in which the speaker reflects on two family photographs, has an unmistakably autobiographical tone. The speaker uses these photographic impressions as a vehicle through which to recapture the memory of his father (87-8). In **"Indigone"** his "inward eye" relives the experience of seeing his father grieving the death of his "further progenitor" (94). Another sequence, the one entitled **"Return of the Sun,"** reproduces in verse form the chapter called "Christine" from Brathwaite's unpublished novel *The Boy and the Sea,* which Warner Lewis has described as an autobiographical text (1977: 1).

To say that the poem is largely autobiographical, however, does not limit the scope of its significance to the personal history of an individual. Here we find a practice that is typical of Caribbean writers, the tendency to connect personal experience with social observation. The picture re-created, remembered in **Sun Poem** is one of many men living in an oppressive social order, men who, powerless to extricate the root of their oppression, resort to behavioral patterns that connote forms of oppression, particularly against their women: "There is also the version of fathers / those who live on the dub side of mujeres" (Brathwaite 1982a: 69). The use of the word "dub," which probably means "money," as we gather from the *Dictionary of Jamaican English* authored by Cassidy and LePage (1980: 162), points to Caribbean men's economic exploitation of women. The very allusion to the genesis of everything at the beginning of the poem would bring to the fore the larger implications of Adam's recollections. In this respect, a critic has accurately stated that

> by identifying the man's cycle of existence with the heavenly cycle of the sun, Brathwaite universalizes the autobiographical details and avails himself of a cosmic imagery of light and color which transfigures character, event, and situation and shifts the authority and effect of the poem from the autobiographical to the archetypal.
>
> (McWatt 1986: 64)

There is in **Sun Poem** a meaningful marriage between personal memories and historical reflection. The mountains mentioned as central to the creation, for instance, would indicate an intent on the part of the poet to present the beginning in more global terms than are offered in the *Old Testament.* In referring to Hillaby (Barbados), Soufrière (St. Vincent), and Kilimanjaro (Tanzania), these "landmarks of the Third World" (98), the text incorporates into the large cosmic scheme of the Hebrew scripture a geographical scope which is more consistent with the world as we have known it in postbiblical times. At the same time, growing up for Adam entails his seeing himself as part of a larger community, a discrete people in a given regional reality and within specific historical, cultural, and spiritual legacies. The speaker learns of the time when "the *loa* came out of the sea" (51) and of his own closeness with the local pantheon. "Sun have you forgotten my mother / sun who gave birth to shango my uncle / who was fixed in his place by ogoun the master of iron" (53), he says in acknowledging his spiritual heritage of the archipelago's folk religions.

Adam grows not only "up" but also "down to the darker soil of himself fitting himself to new feelings," coming to terms with the realization that, while "noisy on top," he "was silent having no words to nourish that darker feeling" and "finding for the first time that there was other sea behind the high hills of the island's other shore" (39). Growing up (and "down"), then, leads to a historical "prise de conscience." He recognizes the legacy of past events, whose repercussions connect him with people back in slavery times. "Soon after the blacks arrived plantations prospered" (53), he reflects. The reflection leads to an understanding of past sorrow, past subjection, past dehumanization, which must necessarily bring to mind the resulting history of rebellion, from the contemporary forms of anti-Establishment resistance symbolized in Rastafarianism ("an we burnin babylone"), to the more traditional forms of subversion represented by Caribbean preachers who used the pulpit to speak "brave words" (55, 61). His sense of connection with a tradition of resistance makes him see himself linked with Hannibal, revered by the speaker as a courageous, if pathetic, ancestor (63). Hannibal, having challenged the military might of the Roman legions in antiquity, may, especially given his African origin, serve as a handy symbol if one is looking for alternatives to the hegemony of the traditions inherited from Western imperialism.

From the allusions to a legacy of resistance, the speaker moves to the precognition of a future with potential for reconstitution and creation. The poem ends, in effect, with a further evocation of genesis. Instead of chronicling a completed event in the remote past, however, the vision of creation is rendered by means of the present continuous tense, highlighting, thus, the notion of present beginning and future possibility. The closing lines, "and my thrill- / dren are coming up coming up coming up / and the sun / new" (97), decidedly look forward in a spirit of hope. The use of the word **"Sun"** here, as in the title of the poem, suggests through phonetic association a threefold meaning: "Son" corresponds to the male child whose experiences are narrated in the poem; "Son" refers to the Afro-Cuban folk song form that is evoked in the last text in the book; and "sun" is the heavenly body that keeps us warm and in the poem is associated with the Afro-Caribbean divinity Shango. The word "thrilldren," found in the texts that open and close *Sun Poem,* suggests both "children," marking beginnings and potentialities, and the "thrill" connoted by the moment of creation either human or cosmic. Through the association of personal, historical, spiritual, and cosmic levels of significance and the contextualizing of language in the Caribbean experience, Brathwaite achieves here a harmonious fusion of "manscape" and words.

MEETING OF WORLD HISTORIES

Brathwaite's second trilogy, still without a collective title, ends with the volume *X/Self* (1987). Suggesting the indefiniteness of the voice, that speaks neither for a he nor a she, the text features a collectivized self— hence "X"—which strikes one as an attempt to circumvent the pitfalls of individualism. An implication of the

indistinct nature of the voice is that it conjures a speaker who reflects a condition of what Paulo Freire has called "dialogical" action, a state in which one has resolved the I/Thou contradiction and entered into a relationship of communion with one's fellow humans, all of whom become I's: "Subjects who meet to *name* the world in order to transform it" (Freire 1986: 167). Appearing four years after *Third World Poems* (1983a)—a volume which, consisting for the most part of poems gathered from his earlier books, does not merit a separate discussion—*X/Self* follows the historical explorations evident in parts of *Sun Poem.* But its tenor encompasses a wider spectrum, the Third World, and exhibits a more clearly subversive attitude vis-à-vis the Western tradition.

The voice that dominates the text in *X/Self* starts from a Caribbean reference point. But the vision of sociohistorical connection expands to the vast panorama of which the Caribbean is but a component. "Rome burns / and our slavery begins" says a refrain that recurs throughout the poem. The refrain suggests an indefectible link between developments in the history of the West and the events that have shaped the destinies of the people of the Third World. From the start, the superimposition of various slices of historical experience, sometimes chronologically distant and, on the surface, disparate moments and events within a boundless geography, becomes evident in passages such as this: "there are no olives left in lebanon / in the camp of the visigoths vercingentorix the arven in creole / chieftain / has met che has met kismet has met young doctor castro / liberators are being guillotined from heaven / along the ho chi minh trail / caesars daughter is pompeys wife" (Brathwaite 1987: 6). The layers of historical experience here pasted together, as it were, give us a sense of the temporal connectedness of events one has grown used to seeing as separate and isolated from each other.

One has grown used to seeing the human experience encircled within very limited geographies and has often failed to see either the links or the parallels that evince a global commonality among peoples in the world. Lines such as the following show a junction of human experience in the past along a geographically horizontal line of relationship: "cry babylon / galileo galilei is free / far out across the lake of galilee / the aztecs wheel around their painted whips" (9). The technique used here, as the author himself explains, is that of perceiving history as "one single, unfolding episode in montage: one image running into, echoing, continuing and extending another" (122). At times the geography serves as a unifying arena to combine stages of past time, as is the case with the characters of Hannibal, Patton, and Rommel (17), all of whom coincide in having led military campaigns in Africa. Arranged vertically in time and horizontally in space, the montage serves to expand the boundaries of chronology and geography. The thematic implication of this measure is that we can no longer see the experience of mankind in terms of a narrative that reduces everything to the history of the West, ascribing to all other human experience a merely tangential importance. Brathwaite's montage serves to reveal a picture showing a larger and more multifaceted mass of humanity than is made manifest in our history books, in which the "ascent of man" often appears to be equivalent to the rise of the West.

The expanded rendition of human history in *X/Self* sets the tone for critical analysis and occasional indictment. The sequence entitled "The fapal [*sic*] state machinery" explores the incestuous relationship of the Christian church and the powers of violence and exploitation through the centuries. It is the empire's adoption of Christianity as the religion of the state that comes to mind when we hear that: "in rome / god and his armies have become identified with each other" (17). In **"Mont Blanc,"** for instance, we come upon a reflection on the flourishing of Western technology and capitalism that recognizes modern advancements as indissolubly linked with the refinements of the forces of destruction: "industry was envisioned here in the indomitable glitter / . . . / there is more wealth here than with the bankers of amsterdam / more power than in any boulder dam of heaven / volt crackle and electricity it has invented / buchenworld nagasaki and napalm / it is the frozen first atomic bomb" (31).

Certainly the historical re-reading that we get in *X/Self* seeks to dissect some of the most cherished cultural myths of Western civilization. We get here a rendition of the story of Charlemagne, unifier of Christendom and first Holy Roman Emperor, that is very far from the saintly nobility with which he is depicted in *La chanson de Roland*. In Brathwaite's poem, **"Charlemagne,"** "hope / of the christians / destroyer of muslims / defender of rome" (24), made the glory of his name on the grounds that "he saved eu / rope from the so / called sterile fate of mulattoes" (24). Fountainhead of the Christian West which would later evolve into the stage of capitalist imperialism, Charlemagne as a cultural symbol could be seen as antithetical to the aspirations of the people of the Third World. The introduction of Caliban here, contrapuntally to the words of the Emperor, brings to the fore the contingent nature of the Western project. For the West becomes the West fundamentally through its self-differentiation from non-Christian cultures and peoples.

It is very significant that Charlemagne, portrayed here "dying at aachen" and prophesying "the downfall of the empire," should foresee the imperial demise in terms of the destabilization of the language of domination: "the dialect of the tribes will come beating up against the crack / foundation stones of latin like the salt whip speechless lips / of water eating the soft stones of venice" (29). Implicit in highlighting the relationship between the predominance of the Latin language and the hegemony of the imperial legacy of Rome in the Middle Ages is the unearthing of a precedent for the subversive overtones perceptible in certain uses of language in the Third World, particularly in the Caribbean. Drawing on morphological variation, rhythmical devices, and a sonority that often rests upon semantic transmutations, *X/Self* aims to present language in a way that is divergent from the language of domination. "The poem's language, sometimes verging on incoherence, articulates the pathos of the two-way linguistic inheritance of the West Indies: the givens of an alien, dominant lexicon (the imported, educated *langue de culture*) and the remnants of African usages still existing in the islands," says Joan Dayan in this respect (1988a: 506).

In **"Dies irie [*sic*],"** the speaker, clearly a voice of resistance, invokes the forces of justice in these terms: "day of thunder day of hunger / bring me solace bring me fire / give me penance give me power / grunt me vengeance with thy word" (Brathwaite 1987: 39). The word, we see, assumes the power of a weapon of redress. Consistent with that rationale, we see that those who are perceived as fighters for liberation earn the epithet of "sooth say / ers," as Malcolm X, Marcus Garvey, Martin Luther King, and Mahatma Ghandi are called in **"Mai Village"** (69). In many respects the spirit of resistance to a power structure that seeks to undermine their sense of humanity is what most clearly connects the various peoples whose experiences figure in the poem. In Africa (**"Nam"**) and in the Caribbean (**"Cap"** and **"Citadel"**) people have had to struggle to maintain their dignity. The following invocation: "vieques porto bello choc guantanamo bahia O / black cat nany nanahemma do not desert us now" (94) appeals to the legacy of subversion against empire as it has taken place in the Caribbean region. Resistance takes place in the spiritual arena as well, and the speaker in "Sun song," appealing to the local cosmology, invokes the restorative powers of the "spirit of the fire." He conjures thus: "i summon you from trees / from ancient memories of forests / from the uncurling ashes of the dead / that we may all be cleansed" (98).

As *X/Self* draws to a close, there seems to be an increasingly perceptible relationship between spirituality, history, and language. First, the narrative voice recognizes the dual power of language to describe reality and virtually construct it. It is in language that "virgil invents aeneas as they set out for civilization," and it is in language that, the speaker complains, "you make of me mysteries foundationless histories" (102). The word, therefore, ought to be appropriated by those whom it must serve. But that word must be changed, recast. It must be revitalized with the legacy of the folk, represented at one point by the figure of legendary jazz trumpeter Bunk Johnson, so that it may, its sense of justice restored, set history aright: "word / and balm / and water / flow / embrace / him / he will shatter outwards to your light and calm history / your thunder has come" (111).

Characteristically, the volume ends in a hopeful outlook. Having appropriated the word, the central voice in the text offers a credo of empowerment. Abounding in historiographical and literary allusions, *X/Self* may be said to compare with Dante's *Divina commedia* and *The Cantos* of Pound in the wealth of its references. The text presents another stage, a global and more encompassing glance, in an aesthetic exploration that has marked Brathwaite's entire literary career. Twenty years ago a critic noted that Brathwaite's "most serious opposition is aimed at the Western Word, and his craft works carefully at expunging it from black modes of feeling and expression" (Ismond 1971: 58). Today that appraisal continues to seem valid, although one should probably warn that in Brathwaite blackness too undergoes a process of creolization. Nommo too is nativized by the Caribbean experience as much as Logos. This caveat should also ward off the temptation to construe Brathwaite strictly as the spokesman of the African heritage, with Walcott, as champion of European values, representing his polar opposite (Ismond 1971: 59). In keeping with the argument in the previous chapter, Brathwaite and Walcott reflect two of the ideological options available to Caribbean thinkers in their attempt to tackle the awesome dilemma of culture in the archipelago. Clearly, *X/Self* draws from diverse intellectual and cultural traditions just as Walcott's *Omeros* (1990) does. A fair treatment of this subject would avoid dichotomies. Reading **The Arrivants,** for instance, as "essentially a record of the stages of Brathwaite's life from feelings of exile," as does King (1980: 131), tends to undermine the public tenor and epic breath of the trilogy and reduces its meaning. Similarly, focusing on the aesthetic distinction between the two major West Indian poets to celebrate Walcott and to slight Brathwaite's accomplishments, as does Walsh (1973: 63-5), is essentially an aberration. Avoiding extremes, one should instead explore the aesthetic and philosophical creeds behind the differences that mark the works of the two poets off from each other, starting, perhaps, with glossing the significance of Brathwaite's collective "we" and Walcott's personal "I," as Anne Walmsley once proposed (1970: 157).

Independently of the relationship with Walcott, Brathwaite the poet continues to see himself as a builder of the sociohistorical reality in which he lives. Through a remodeling of the official language of the Establishment, he undertakes to recompose the fragments of a scattered history with the intention of chronicling the experience of his people in a manner that may be deemed culturally authentic. That is the program which informs the various facets of his literary creativity, and it is that program that provides the prism through which he looks at the works of others. One may note that three decades ago, he praised two anthologies of the literature of the archipelago by Coulthard (1966) and Howes (1966) for their contribution to expanding communication throughout the Caribbean, thus helping to break "down the barriers of language, politics and custom that separate us" (Brathwaite 1966b: 223). More recently, his various entries on individual Caribbean poets for a dictionary of contemporary poets (Vinson 1980) indicate a persistence of his view of the literary artist as a griot through whom the community speaks. In reviewing Dionne Brand's *Winter Epigram,* Brathwaite has continued to assign value to literary works in proportion to the writer's effort to reconstruct his or her reality with an eye on empowering the voiceless sectors of society (1985a). In that respect, I can hardly concur with a reading by Dash that depoliticizes the poet by stating that any "attempt to extract either cultural or political prescriptions from Brathwaite's work" could lead to treacherous ground, insisting on the "rejection of man as the product of an ideology" as presumably "the most important single idea behind Brathwaite's work" (Dash 1979: 226-7). My reading suggests, instead, that Brathwaite insists on a theory of language, culture, and on a philosophy of history that have strong political implications insofar as they aim to liberate the Caribbean mind from the throes of a colonial heritage.

Velma Pollard (essay date 2001)

SOURCE: Pollard, Velma. "Francina and the Turtle and All the Others: Women in EKB." In *For the Geography of the Soul: Emerging Perspectives on Kamau Brathwaite,* edited by Timothy J. Reiss, pp. 43-50. Trenton, N.J.: Africa World Press, 2001.

[*In the following essay, Pollard examines the allusions and rhythms of Brathwaite poems that depict women as rescuers.*]

FRANCINA

He chooses Francina, a simple woman. She who "used to scale / fish in the market." He makes her save the "humpbacked turtle with the shell-fish eyes . . ." (*IS* [*Islands*] 215).

Brathwaite, railing against the destruction of a park, something precious reserved for the use of the people, chooses a woman to be the rescuer. The turtle she saves is a symbol of what is dearest to him, to all people of similar mind-the island with all that is natural to it.

The poem rails against "the Mayor and Council / thin brown impressive men." We meet them in the act of destroying the park to build a dance hall and a barbecue. We share the poet's outrage. The lake has become a parking lot. A macaw, monkeys and the "humped hundred /-year old turtle" must go. Francina rescues the turtle. She is the opposing symbol to what the city officials represent. A woman with no resources at all takes pity on the turtle which represents the real values of the islands. The city officials loudly declare that they will build

> the island; hotels where there were pebbles,
> casinos where the casuarinas sang,
> and flowing fields of tourists for our daily bread
>
> (*IS* 214)

This progress, this building of the island is in fact the island's undoing. Francina's act of rescue is an indication of some small hope; if any one will follow it up. While it is significant that she is poor:

> . . . How she think she could spare
> nine dollars an' thirty-five cents
> for a wrinkle-face monster you can't
> even eat, when she can't keep
>
> she body an' soul-seam together—
> I can't unnerstand it . . .
>
> (*IS* 215),

it is even more significant that Francina is woman, nurturer, protector of the future for the next generation. It does not matter that she is not strong enough to fight powerful corporate men effectively. What is important is that she tries. The excuse, suggested with what sarcasm the poet can muster in these circumstances, is predictably not convincing:

> . . . I suppose
> she got a nose for slimy things
> like eels an' red-tail lobsters
> though muh eyes can't see
> what she want wid a turtle that too old
> to be yuh father. . . .
>
> (*IS* 215)

Her act remains heroic. The poem is **"Francina"** from the collection, *Islands,* third book of Brathwaite's first trilogy, *The Arrivants.* He selects for the task of saving a civilization, a simple woman, an outcast of society really, scorned by most men. The creature she rescues is a turtle. The shell ensures its protection and survival beyond the century it has already lived. The lines exude the gratitude her poet creator feels towards Francina and wishes the reader to feel as well. There is deep warmth and affection here.

BEFORE HER

Before Francina (at least in order of publication) were the wise women gathering at evening in the small goods (grocery) shop in the village in **"The Dust,"** a poem which has become a true classic, appearing in most Caribbean anthologies. These women represent the people who, in Brathwaite's own words in another context, "from the centre of an oppressive system have been able to survive, adapt, recreate; have devised means of protecting what has been so gained" (*Contradictory Omens* 64).

They speak the language of the West Indian street-an anglophone creole (here a Barbadian version). It is what Brathwaite labels "nation language." These women love, respect, care for each other. The latest arrival greets each one by name and immediately addresses problems:

> Evenin' Miss
> Evvy, Miss
> Maisie, Miss
> Maud. Olive,
>
> how you? How
> you, Eveie, chile?
> You tek dat Miraculous Bush
> fuh de trouble you tell me about?
>
> (*RP* [*Rights of Passage*] 62)

Life is not easy. Times are hard. Nature is sometimes unkind. But they have forged philosophies which allow them to endure hardship without complaining, propped up by the support they receive from each other and by their faith in God to whom they constantly give thanks:

> we got to thank God
> fuh small mercies.
>
> Amen,
> Eveie, chile . . .
>
> an' agen
> I say is Amen.
>
> (*RP* 63)

There is no hopelessness here. The main speaker among the women names each blessing, lest we regard them as commonplace and pass over their value. They include the possibility of a child for the man you love, healthy offspring and a piece of land which is small but productive and your own. Perhaps most important is the faith and hope they find in the unfailing progression of time where nature's cycle repeats itself:

> ev'ry day you see the sun
> rise, the sun
> set; God sen' ev'ry month
>
> a new moon. Dry season
> follow wet season again
> an' the green crop follow the rain.
>
> (*RP* 68)

This is the hope which allows them to endure the inexplicable tantrums of nature which make crops fail and visits other tragedies upon them.

These women bring to the world a message of survival in spite of misfortune, beauty in spite of ugliness and hope where one expects despair. This is the same message as that contained in the detailed description of Francina's saving the turtle. The difference is that where their actions are personal, protecting themselves and each other, hers is public. She is saving a world.

AFTER HER

After her is a catalogue of women in *Mother Poem,* the first book of Brathwaite's second trilogy. Here he celebrates the endurance of woman who must nurture husband and children and on a grander scale, celebrates the Mother his island—Barbados.

"Calypso" (*Rights of Passage*) begins by explaining how the Archipelago of Caribbean islands came into being:

> The stone had skidded arc'd and bloomed into islands
>
> . . .
> . . . curved stone hissed into reef
> wave teeth fanged into clay. . . .
>
> > (*TA* [*The Arrivants*] 48)

But when the stone does not skid it connects with the water and forms quick concentric circles around itself. The mind can draw an imaginary line from the stone center to the circumference of the farthest circle, a line that unites them all. Francina is the stone at the centre. The largest circle is the island-Barbados; the circles in between are all the women of *Mother Poem.* And all are linked ingeniously to Francina and in some way to the women in the evening grocery shop.

The cycle/circle in ". . . Dry season / follow wet season again" reasserts itself in *Mother Poem.* Rohlehr points out that mother is, "ultimately, a principle of renewal and rebirth" (*Shape* 191). Later, he comments that the sea is the major presence through which the perpetual ongoing movement of the life force is conveyed, and notes another cycle implied in the portraits of women ending with the death of the grandmother (193).

Francina is the kernel, the nam which is expanded into this major celebratory poem of woman. She has rescued the turtle, the symbol of the island and its future. There is hope if anyone follows the lead she has provided. In **"Hex"** (*Mother Poem*) we get a feeling of (temporary) despair. The poet loudly laments the signs of Francina's failure, on the body of the island:

> all the peaks, the promontories, the coves, the glitter
> bays of her body have been turned into money . . .
> for master for mister for massa for mortal baas . . .
>
> > (*MP* [*Mother Poem*] 46)

And the Mayor and Council men, the evil male figures of destruction return here, in the various guises of plantation authority figures. They are embodied in the figure of Money/Mammon which breaks the land and breaks people. Through the complaints of women we find that he haunts the futures of children. Brathwaite's women, these wives and mothers, lament his effect on their husbands, watching with tears how he breaks them just as the council men broke the future of the Island. He is the "thin skinned merchant" who, in **"Alpha,"** represents ". . . the world Columbus found / . . . the world raleigh raided / . . . the plantation ground" where the husband works to death while the caring woman, the mother

> sits and calls on jesus name
> . . . waits for his return
> with her gold rings of love . . .
>
> > (*MP* 4)

He is the Mammon who breaks the courage of the husband of the woman who in **"Twine"** is full of regrets as she compares his past with his present:

> I know when I did first meet e
> he did strong . . .
>
> but if you look pun e now
> fragile, 'fraid o' e own shadow

and explains that after all what made him so: "he never get no pension from de people" (6). He is the merchant the woman in **"Bell"** sings about:

> the merchant own me husband
> an me husband never home
>
> > (*MP* 12)

She curses and blames him for her husband's illness. She too notes the pensionless condition:

> not a cent
> not a bline bloody cent
> not even a dollar a year for the rock he was wrackin
> not even a placket to help pay de rent
>
> > (*MP* 14)

Predictably the poet records her resilience. She complains. This is not what she expected. But "to help enns meet," she gets out and goes to work, "sellin shoes in de white people shop." She becomes a worker like the other women in *Mother Poem.*

Like **"Miss Own"** who keeps "body and soul-seam together" singing "sign a bill here" as she sells "calico cloth on the mercantile shame / rock" (15), or the woman in **"Horse Weebles"** who sells "biscuit an salt-fish in de plantation shop at pie/corner so she can keep "body and soul-seam together" (38), this woman is a prototype of mother. She sells in the shop full time but she also is doctor and seamstress for her family and she still finds the time and the energy to express the concern which links her to all other women in late night grocery shops, repeating accordingly the lines of an earlier poem:

evenin' miss
evvy, miss
maisie, miss
maud, olive
how you? how
you, eveie, chile?
yu tek dat miraculous bush
fu de trouble you tell me about?

                                             (*MP* 38-9)

Eventually the woman becomes old and tired. In "Moth-air" she has worked too long and too hard. Her sigh comes from deep within her:

boy me feet heavy

de tiredness passin
like water clouds carryin

rain . . .

                                             (*MP* 86)

She is gravely ill. The doctor comes around prescribing diet and pills. What folk wisdom says about dying is happening to her. Her whole life passes through her mind: her own mother's illness, her lifelong service to children and husband, her feeding the children coming home from the beach, rushing them off to "sabbath day school," her bearing with silent endurance her husband's infidelities, all the while pretending not to know: "dese men doan know what a wo-/man does know . . ." (89). Near her end now there is no one to return nurture to her:

. . . she turns
alone to the o-

ven burn-
in burn-

in world
without

without
end

amen

                                                  (93)

This is her end. The lines mark as well the endlessness of this kind of suffering that is the thankless reward for a life of sacrifice and hard work. There is a kind of passionate empathy here from the poet to this woman who is all women.

But *Mother Poem* will not end on a note of hopelessness, for Brathwaite is above all a poet of hope. Out of every "falling" situation he creates a "rising": future out of past, birth out of death. The line "the midwife encircles us all" (**"Mid/Life"** 111) is perhaps his most eloquent expression of this way of seeing. **"Kounfort,"**

the final movement of **Mother Poem,** indicates ways of comfort additional to those mentioned earlier, bound to the *hounfort* where world and spirit meet. In **"Angel/ Engine,"** for example, the woman finds her comfort in the church/*hounfort,* an Afro-Caribbean version where the prayers are loud and there is breathless trumping:

praaze be to
praaze be to
praaze be to gg

                                                  (98),

and where the faithful are assured a seat on the Zion train.

Finally in **"Driftword,"** the last poem of the collection, all the mothers become one with the mother that is the island. The prototypical mother is drifting away. Through her "dead sea eyes" she sees the future generations who will save the island: those who

. . . will say no to distortions
who will pick up the broken stones
sloping them with chip and mallet out of the concave
   quarries . . .

                                                  (112)

Because of this kind of hope she is at peace at her death-"she knows that her death has been born", and so is everyone else. On the page, that sense is achieved with Brathwaite's usual economy. He simply juxtaposes opposing notions:

so that *losing* her now
you will slowly *restore* her silent gutters of word-fall

                                          (17: my emphasis)

I like to think that the composite woman at the end of **Mother Poem** is the transformed Francina who goes gently out

. . . into the sunlight
towards the breaking of her flesh with foam

                                                  (117)

Mark A. McWatt (essay date 2001)

SOURCE: McWatt, Mark A. "Looking Back at *The Arrivants.*" In *For the Geography of the Soul: Emerging Perspectives on Kamau Brathwaite,* edited by Timothy J. Reiss, pp. 59-65. Trenton, N.J.: Africa World Press, 2001.

[*In the following essay, the author looks back at* The Arrivants, *in which one can detect "subtle displacements and perturbations caused by the gravitational tug of the author's academic discipline."*]

My first publication after arriving at Cave Hill as a very green Assistant Lecturer in the mid-70s was a review of Kamau Brathwaite's **Mother Poem** in *Bim* magazine. The first paragraph of that review was not lacking in effrontery:

> As a whole the poem sustains the reader's interest and there is much in it that is effective, but by some reverse alchemical process the golden poetic voice of the earlier poems has been transformed into that of a baser metal. . . .

(137)

At that time I had not yet met the poem's author, but someone suggested to me that he would be very displeased to read that and a few other sentences in the first paragraph of my review. This bothered me and I consulted my most approachable colleague at the time, Michael Gilkes, asking him what he thought. Michael said that he had not yet read the review but that Kamau was one of the most important and celebrated of Caribbean poets and why did I think he would care two hoots what was said about his work by a young Assistant Lecturer in his first published review. This advice was meant to console me, of course. Two days later Michael Gilkes came up to me and said: "I've now read your review and the first paragraph is not so much annoying as puzzling: after the negatives of that introductory paragraph you go on to show precisely why **Mother Poem** *is* a wonderful volume of poetry." He then went on to give me a good piece of advice: "In future, don't worry with introductory rhetorical flourishes, just get down to the practical criticism." I hope I've been able to follow his advice since.

Gilkes had seen through me—realized that the offending paragraph was mostly insincere rhetoric and was there more because of the precious alchemical image than anything else. Fortunately for me its point was lost as the review moved on to an appreciation of the poems themselves. The pretentiousness and posturing of youth? Certainly, but I also consider now that part of the problem may have been my inordinate love and admiration for the first trilogy—*The Arrivants*—which is something I still feel and is why I want to look back here at **The Arrivants,** in an attempt to assess something of what those poems have meant to me over the years.

Before that, however, I should say that I have long since come to consider **Mother Poem** [*MP*] one of Kamau's finest volumes of poetry, probably the one I most enjoy teaching, particularly to Barbadian students, and that, having got to know Kamau quite well (soon after the *faux pas* of my first review), I have found him to be entirely tolerant, helpful and generous, not only in encouraging my academic writing (on himself as well as on other Caribbean writers) but also my own efforts at writing poetry.

I read **Rights of Passage, Masks** and **Islands** [*IS*] as separate volumes during my undergraduate years at university in Toronto and they were an important part

of my own self-discovery as a West Indian and a great influence on my thinking about the West Indies and its history. For me **The Arrivants** is still the most important of Brathwaite's works. In this trilogy the reader encounters most of the poet's major themes and obsessions and many facets of complex imagination and craft. Perhaps the foremost theme is history itself. Everything that Kamau writes is touched and coloured by a sense of history; sometimes this is very subtle—particularly when the poems are excerpted or appear in anthologies, taken out of their context in the trilogy—but if you read attentively you can always detect, in the orbit of each Brathwaite poem, subtle displacements and perturbations caused by the gravitational tug of the author's academic discipline, and this often makes for a mysterious, numinous quality in the poems and great richness of meaning and emotional impact.

The first volume of the trilogy, **Rights of Passage** [*RP*], begins with two poems which trace, in a rapid and highly evocative way, the large historical movements of a people across the continental desert to the west coast of Africa, and then the journey in chains across the sea to the new world. Here is the first stanza of the first poem, **"Prelude"**:

> Drum skin whip
> lash, master sun's
> cutting edge of
> heat, taut
> surfaces of things
> I sing
> I shout
> I groan
> I dream
> about . . .

(*RP* 4)

Thus are we introduced to the history of the New World Black man. The drum controls the rhythm of the poem as it does the rhythm of the life of the people, but in this poem it also reverberates with historical references: the stretched skin that is the percussive surface of the drum is or becomes also the skin of the black man which feels the slaver's lash and the fierce heat of tropical plantations. Thus the drum and its rhythm become part of the identity of the black man and, at the very beginning of the first journey, proleptically suggests the slave plantations many miles and years away. I can still remember vividly the excitement with which those drumbeat lines were read by me and probably by many of my generation in the late sixties. Now the technique is well known and ears well tuned to this poetic line and this rhythm (there are many imitators of Kamau among younger West Indian Poets), but then we were all like Keats looking into Chapman's Homer, savouring the wonder and newness of the poetry. However much the cruder Afro-Centrics and Cultural Nationalists among us may have beaten the African drum into a tiresome cliché, there's no denying the original power and freshness with which it was associated in those first Brathwaite volumes of poetry.

The other aspect worth pointing out in that first stanza quoted above is the way in which Brathwaite attaches an emotional freight to the historic references, indeed to history itself. The poetic form rescues the historical past from the dust-dry aloofness of the academic subject and reconnects it to the human subject in terms of fears and feelings. The four consecutive verbs at the end of the quoted paragraph—"I sing / I shout / I groan / I dream"—do not just fill in the emotional content of the particular historical reference, but also insist upon the varied and even contradictory nature of those emotional responses, as the verbs together indicate celebration, exuberance, pain and longing all at the same time. The dull continuum of historical time is thus compressed and conflated and its effects concentrated into paradoxical expressions and experiences. This is one of the aspects of Kamau's poetry that I value most—its sense of emotional and moral balance, achieved through its inclusiveness, through its paradoxes and seeming contradictions.

The first stanza of the second poem, **"New World A-Coming,"** is as follows:

> Helpless like this
> leader-
> less like this
> heroless,
> we meet you: lover,
> warrior, hater,
> coming through the files
> of the forest
> soft foot
> to soft soil
> of silence:
> we met in the soiled
> tunnel of leaves.
>
> (*RP* 9)

Note the seeming contradiction in the sequence of nouns "lover, / warrior, hater" which nevertheless captures accurately the serial masks of the European in Africa, his various roles over time and the modulation of emotional responses from attraction to conflict to rejection. Perhaps this is how we arrive, at the end of the stanza, at "the soiled / tunnel of leaves," where the very landscape or location has become morally tainted by the infamous acts that took place there. It's interesting the way the repetition of soft sounds reinforces the bitter leap from the soft physical soil of Africa to the harsh notion of the way in which the particular human encounter is "soiled" in a metaphysical sense—tainted for all time. Also the "tunnel of leaves," suggestive of forest pathways where the encounters took place, also conjures up the morally darkened tunnels that led from the slave forts (like Elmina) to the ships of the middle passage. Such moments, when ordinary language leaps

into extraordinary referential plenitude because of historical resonances, are frequent in Brathwaite's poetry, particularly in **The Arrivants.**

It is worth remarking that the pain of these historical memories does not lead Brathwaite to proclaim implacable enmities. The poetic techniques we have been looking at ensure that the scope and vision of the poems are always larger than the individual hurts they may contain. As with Walcott at the end of "Ruins of a Great House," there's an inevitable movement towards compassion and understanding and a desire to learn from the experience. Hence we have the Uncle Tom figure in **Rights:**

> hoping my children's eyes
> will learn
>
> not green alone
> not Africa alone
> not dark alone
> not fear
> alone
> but Cortez
> and Drake
> Magellan
> and that Ferdinand
> the sailor
> who pierced the salt seas to this land.
>
> (16)

This passage at the end of the poem **"Tom,"** apart from indicating the generosity of Tom's dream that his children will acquire from their bitter experiences the skill and technology to master the physical world in which they live, lifts the mood of the poem out of the helplessness it expressed earlier, the way the frustrations and the despair of the **"Spade"** in **"Folkways,"** are alleviated and transcended by the rhythm of the "boogie woogie" train in the second section of the poem. This too is typical of Kamau and one of the reasons for cherishing these poems which taught a generation how to live with a painful past.

I'm suggesting that one discerns in **The Arrivants** the way drum rhythms, as well as phrases, themes and other aspects of content build into patterns which transcend individual poems or passages. The first two poems of **Rights** are about journeys across the desert and across the sea. Later on, in **"The Emigrants,"** we see the Black man on the move again:

> These are The Emigrants.
> On sea-port quays
> at air-ports
> anywhere where there is a ship
> or train, swift
> motor car or jet
> to travel faster than the breeze . . .
>
> Where to?
> They do not know.
>
> (51)

These later journeys contain thematic, verbal and circumstantial echoes of the earlier journeys and come eventually to create an inevitable pattern of journeying and to suggest drift and placelessness. In this way Brathwaite achieves a more powerful emotional impact that transcends all individual historical moments. I cannot but feel myself that this is where history should go, to the level of large patterns and designs which are entirely comprehensible in terms of how they came about and what they mean to a people, but are free of niggling scholarly disputes, individual hurts and dry dates and other particularities. To enjoy *The Arrivants* is to celebrate Kamau Brathwaite *as historian* as much as poet; by packaging history in poems, he teaches West Indians about themselves painlessly and without shrill polemic. (Perhaps if other prominent Barbadian historians had chosen poetry as the medium in which to educate their countrymen about history and historical figures, much recent controversy might have been avoided and fewer reputations called into question.)

Another aspect of *The Arrivants* that has always interested me is the persona, the voice we hear in the poems. Of course there are times when the voice comes from historical or archetypal figures, like **"Tom,"** literary and "folk" figures like **"Caliban"** and **"Ananse,"** and from contemporary figures of town or village, like **"Tizzic"** or the women in **"The Dust."** But the voice is also that of a frequently undramatized but protean persona, who speaks to us throughout. What has always struck me is the range and the protean nature of Kamau Brathwaite's poetic voice in the trilogy. It can speak for a whole people, as in **"Jah"**; it can become the voice of the drum, as in **"Atumpan"** or, perhaps more interestingly, in **"Tano"**:

> dam
> dam
> damirifa
> damirifa due
> damirifa due
> damirifa due
> due
> due
> due . . .
>
> (M 151),

or can express personal memories, as in **"Ancestors"** or **"Ogun."** There are times when the voice stutters and claims to be unfamiliar with speech, as in **"Eating the Dead"** (suggesting strategies of resistance or for recovering lost modes of expression), and times when it gushes Nation Language like a river in spate, as in **"The Dust"** or **"The Stone Sermon."** But one senses that behind this voice lie years of silence, of voicelessness. The poetry gives a people their history, but also their voice: the strategies for expression and self-discovery, for emerging from the "soiled" tunnel of the past. There's a sense in which the voice, the *breath* of the poems, is itself the interpellated subject, the one

called into being or constructed by the specific ideological and discursive machinery that we all acknowledge, and this subject speaks for us all, with a voice that is our own, for, as Ashcroft, Griffiths and Tiffin contend:

> Although ideology serves the interests of the ruling classes, it is not static or unchangeable, and its materiality has certain important consequences. For while ideology is dominant, it is also contradictory, fragmentary and inconsistent and does not necessarily or inevitably blindfold the 'interpellated' subject to a perception of its operations.
>
> (*Key Concepts* 222)

Brathwaite's poetic voice transmits its perceptions and strategies to its people.

Finally, there are times when the voice seems to be simply that of, if not Kamau Brathwaite, then "the Poet," the one planning future voices. To illustrate and celebrate this, I end with a passage from **"Dawn"** which seems to point, in terms of subject, rhythm and feeling, towards the second trilogy, especially towards *Mother Poem* and *Sun Poem*:

> Till the sun enters fine, enters fine, enters finally its growing circle of splendour
> rising
> rising
>
> into the eyes of my father,
> the fat valley loads of my mother
> of water, lap-
> ping, lapping my ankles, lap-
>
> ping these shores with their silence:
> insistence of pure
> light, pure pouring of water
> that opens the eyes of my window
>
> and I see you, my wound-
> ed gift giver of sea
> spoken syllables: words salt on your lips
> on my lips . . .
>
> (*IS* 238)

FURTHER READING

Criticism

Asein, Samuel Omo. "Symbol and Meaning in the Poetry of Edward Brathwaite." *World Literature Written in English* 20, no. 1 (spring 1981): 94-104.
    Examines symbols in Brathwaite's poems, especially symbols of circularity in individuals and civilizations.

Brown, Stewart. "Sun Poem: The Rainbow Sign?" In *The Art of Kamau Brathwaite*, edited by Stewart Brown, pp. 152-62. Melksham, UK: Cromwell Press, 1995.

Sun Poem is given a close reading to reveal Brathwaite's use of rainbows as symbols and metaphors of healing.

Chukwu, Augustine. "Bridging the Gulf: The Ancestral Mask and Homecoming in Edward Brathwaite's 'Masks.'" *UFAHAMU* 11, no. 2 (fall-winter 1981-82): 131-39.

Discusses Brathwaite's use of imagery in his poem "Masks," especially in representing the poet as a "living diviner" who connects the past and present and Africa and the Caribbean.

Cobham, Rhonda. "K/Ka/Kam/Kama/Kamau: Brathwaite's Project of Self-Naming in *Barabajan Poems.*" In *For the Geography of the Soul: Emerging Perspectives on Kamau Brathwaite,* edited by Timothy J. Reiss, pp. 297-315. Trenton, N.J.: Africa World Press, 2001.

Brathwaite's transformation from "Edward Brathwaite" to "Kamau Brathwaite" is traced through his collection *Barabajan Poems.*

Dawes, Kwame. "Kamau Brathwaite." In *Talk Yuh Talk: Interviews with Anglophone Caribbean Poets,* edited by Kwame Dawes, pp. 22-37. Charlottesville: University Press of Virginia, 2001.

Discusses the role of the writer in the Caribbean and themes like exile.

Ezenwa-Ohaeto, "From a Common Root: Revolutionary Vision and Social Change in the Poetry of Brathwaite and Chinweizu." *Journal of Caribbean Studies* (1991): 89-104.

Ezenwa-Ohaeto applies a Marxist reading to the poetry of Brathwaite and the Nigerian poet Chinweizu.

Grant, Damian. "Emerging Image: The Poetry of Edward Brathwaite." *Critical Quarterly* 12, no. 2 (summer 1970): 186-92.

Grant describes several themes running through the three volumes of *The Arrivants,* focusing primarily on the effects of memory and rediscovering African roots among the African diaspora.

James, Louis. "The Poet as Seer: Kamau Brathwaite." In *Caribbean Literature in English,* pp. 185-91. New York: Longman, 1999.

Brathwaite's use of stone and mother images is shown to be present throughout his career.

Pagnoulle, Christine. "'Labyrinth of Past/Present/Future' in Some of Kamau Brathwaite's Recent Poems." In *Crisis and Creativity in the New Literature in English,* edited by Geoffrey Davis and Hena Maes-Jelinek, pp. 449-66. Atlanta: Radopi, 1990.

Pagnoulle examines Brathwaite's "essentially ludic (though also extremely serious) attitude to language and reality" that helps him break down the walls between past and present.

Pattanayak, Chandrabhanu. "Brathwaite: Metaphors of Emergence." *The Literary Criterion* 17, no. 3 (1982): 60-8.

Discusses how Braithwaite's poems are informed and enriched by his use of history, aesthetics, and music.

Warner-Lewis, Maureen. "Africa: Submerged Mother." In *The Art of Kamau Brathwaite,* edited by Stewart Brown, pp. 52-61. Melksham, UK: Cromwell Press, 1995.

Brathwaite's poems are given a close reading and shown to contain many examples of African words used in the contemporary context of Barbados.

Williams, Emily Allen. "Whose Words Are These? Lost Heritage and Search for Self in Edward Brathwaite's Poetry." *CLA Journal* 40, no. 1 (September 1996): 104-08.

Discusses the continuities of the past in the present as found in Brathwaite's poetry.

Wilson-Tagoe, Nana. "Edward Brathwaite and Submerged History: The Aesthetics of Renaissance." In *Historical Thought and Literary Representation in West Indian Literature,* pp. 182-222. Gainesville: University Press of Florida, 1998.

Brathwaite's poetry is described through the writer's endeavor to find "community and image through a drama of consciousness . . . ."

Additional coverage of Brathwaite's life and career is contained in the following sources published by the Gale Group: *Black Literature Criticism Supplement*; *Black Writers,* Eds 2, 3; *Concise Dictionary of World Literary Biography,* Vol. 3; *Contemporary Authors,* Vol. 25-28R; *Contemporary Authors New Revision Series,* Vols. 11, 26, 47, 107; *Contemporary Literary Criticism,* Vol. 11; *Contemporary Poets,* Ed. 7; *Dictionary of Literary Biography,* Vol. 125; *Discovering Authors Modules: Poets*; *Encyclopedia of World Literature in the 20th Century,* Ed. 3; and *Literature Resource Center.*

René Char
1907-1988

(Full name: René-Emile Char) French poet, essayist, and philosopher.

The following entry presents criticism of Char's poetry from 1948 through 2001.

INTRODUCTION

In his poetry, Char emphasized hope in the face of struggle, rejected compromise, and acknowledged desire as the center of inspiration. Char offered an influential and dominant literary voice during the post-World War II era. Although he was by no means a regional poet, Char's native region of Provence provided the backdrop for many of his literary treatments of the universal conflicts of good versus injustice and resistance in the face of oppression.

BIOGRAPHICAL INFORMATION

Char was born in the town of L'Isle-sur-la-Sorgue on June 14, 1907. His father, a businessman and the local mayor, died when Char was only ten years old. This pivotal event is seen as an influence on his work by many critics, not as the subject of poems, but as a contributing factor to the sense of dispossession and solitude that these critics find as an underlying theme in much of Char's poetry. Although he was well-schooled, Char did not complete his secondary studies with the *baccalaureat* but chose instead to attend business school in 1925. He fulfilled his military obligation with an artillery unit from 1927 to 1928. During this time he published his first small collection of poems, *Les Cloches sur le coeur* (1928; "Bells on the Heart"). This was the only work published under his given name, René-Emile Char.

In 1929 Char published a second volume of poetry, *Arsenal,* and shortly thereafter, he moved to Paris to join the Surrealist literary movement. One of his significant contributions to Surrealist poetry was the volume *Ralentir travaux* (1930; *Slow Under Construction*) which was written collectively with prominent French Surrealist writers Paul Éluard and André Breton. Through the early 1930s Char remained closely affiliated with Surrealism, publishing poems in Surrealist reviews and participating in political protests. He also

established ties with numerous avant-garde painters of the day, Surrealist and otherwise, establishing foundations for his later collaborations and poetic writings on art.

By 1935, Char was no longer a public participant in the political activities of the Surrealists, though he remained friends with Eluard and others. He had married in 1932, and by mid-decade he returned to his hometown to take over the business affairs of his father's former company. Serious illness caused him to resign in 1937, and he moved to the village of Céreste to recover. Some years later, during World War II, Char would return to this place to form a resistance unit in the fight against Nazism. The last major collection of Char's poetry to appear before the outbreak of World War II was *Dehors la nuit est gouvernée* ("Outside the Night is Governed"), which was published in May 1938. Although it was not overtly political, the work foreshadowed the darkness that was about to affect all of Europe under Hitler's influence.

Once France entered the war, Char set literary aspirations aside in favor of political and military commitment. He first served his country in a heavy artillery regiment, and later, after the occupation by Germany and the installation of the French Vichy authority, he went underground and became an active participant in the French Resistance movement. He did not publish works during the occupation but he did continue to write. One of his major works of the wartime years was *Feuillets d'Hypnos* (*Leaves of Hypnos*), a poetic journal of the war. Written between 1941 and 1944 and published in 1946, this volume established Char as an authentic resistance writer who had, to a greater extent than many of his literary peers, risked his life to stand up to Nazi and Vichy oppression.

During the post war years of 1950 to 1962, Char's reputation as an influential literary figure expanded, and he enjoyed the respect of fellow artists, musicians, and writers, which resulted in collaborative and cooperative works featuring art and music. In the 1960s, Char turned his political energy toward the issue of nuclear missile silos in France and continued to collaborate on creative works for small presses and artistic printers. In 1971 he published *Le Nu perdu* ("Nakedness Lost"), for which he assembled poems written since 1964. Although this was his last large compendium of works, Char continued to write and publish steadily throughout the mid-1980s, pursuing projects that fed his desire to support creativity as a form of intellectual resistance against the many inhumane and oppressive aspects of the modern age. Char's final volume of original verse was published posthumously, having been submitted to the publisher several months before his death on February 19, 1988.

MAJOR WORKS

Char wrote and published prolifically from 1928 until just before his death in 1988. Throughout his long career, first in association with the Surrealist movement and later as an active participant in the French Resistance, and still later as a supporter and proponent of artistic expression in the face of economic oppression, Char consistently addressed universal themes such as justice versus injustice and resistance as a moral imperative. When circumstances required, civic action took the place of literary endeavor. From his early works throughout the final volumes of new work that were published after his death, Char embraced the notion that art, literature, and music are reciprocally linked as necessary expressions of resistance—necessary to preserve the humanity of individuals and the morality of society.

Among Char's vast output, three volumes are considered particularly significant. These works raised Char's profile as a vital force in French intellectual and creative circles. The first of these is his war journal, *Leaves of Hypnos,* which was written during his years of active service on behalf of the French Resistance and published soon after the war's end. Even more influential to his literary career was *Fureur et mystère* (1948; "Furor and Mystery"), a collection of poetry that offers readers a poetic roadmap of the journey from a prewar sense of impending disaster in the 1930s through the rigors of occupation and resistance in the early 1940s, to the return of life-giving creativity after the destruction of war. Finally, Char's *Les Matinaux,* published in 1950 (translated to English in 1992 as *The Dawn Breakers*), confirmed Char's position among the elite of postwar French poets. While *Fureur et mystère* focuses on the contrasts between love and war and resistance and oppression, *The Dawn Breakers* decisively depicts the return to peace.

While Char's next large collection, *La Parole en archipel* ("The Word as Archipelago"), appeared in 1962, the previous years had also seen the publication of numerous smaller volumes; among them was the critically noted *La Bibliothèque est en feu* (1956). The works of the 1950s and 1960s display Char's use of verbal landscape and his employment of specific geographic settings, particularly his home region of France, to symbolize universal experience. In 1971, Char published *Le Nu perdu* which was his last major compendium of work, though it was by no means his final volume of new poetry. Even with the 1983 publication of Char's *Oeuvres complètes,* his writing days were not yet over. In 1985, Char's penultimate collection, *Les Voisinages de Van Gogh* ("In Van Gogh's Territory"), appeared. Two years later, only months before his death, he submitted another volume of new works to his publisher, but he did not live to see it in print. Although Char's posthumous collection, *Eloge d'une Soupçonnée* (1988), is brief—containing only thirteen poems—it is considered by critics to be one of the significant works of his career, for it offers a capstone to the poet's life and work. Throughout his life, Char preferred to maintain a separation between his personal life and his professional work, and thus did not welcome or indulge queries about his life. However, observers note that the opening poem of this final collection, "Riche de larmes," reveals that Char saw his career as a lifelong devotion to poetry.

CRITICAL RECEPTION

Char earned the respect of critics and fellow literary artists throughout his career. Following the poet's death in 1988, Mark Hutchinson wrote that "Char's vision . . . is at once aristocratic . . . democratic . . . and egalitarian." He further noted that Char was "that rare thing in a country as intellectually sectarian as France, a poet whose work was universally admired." Through three generations, Char's literary peers and friends included such luminaries as Albert Camus, André Breton, Paul Eluard, Octavio Paz, and William Carlos Williams. In 1952, French novelist Albert Camus, calling Char a "tragic optimist," hailed him as France's "greatest living poet." In 1968 critic Paulène Aspel noted that Char had "remained remarkably faithful to his themes" of resistance, rebirth, and reconciliation throughout what was then a forty-year career as a poet. Several years after Char's death, critic Michael Bishop praised the poet as one "who, caught between naming and unnaming, senses the profound mystery of things being in the first place."

PRINCIPAL WORKS

Poetry

Les Cloches sur le coeur 1928
Arsenal 1929
Artine 1930
Ralentir Travaux [Slow Under Construction] (with André Breton and Paul Éluard) 1930
Le Tombeau des secrets 1930
Poèmes militants 1932
Le Marteau sans maître 1934; revised 1945
Moulin premier 1936
Placard pour un chemin des écoliers 1937
Dehors la nuit est gouvernée 1938; revised 1949
Le Visage nuptial 1938
Seuls demeurent 1945
Feuillets d'Hypnos [Leaves of Hypnos] 1946
Premières alluvions
Le Poème pulvérisé 1947
Fureur et mystère 1948; revised 1962
Le Soleil des eaux 1949; revised 1951
Les Matinaux [The Dawn Breakers: Les Matinaux] 1950; revised 1964
À une sérénité crispée [To a Tense Serenity] 1951
A la santé du serpent 1954
Poèmes des deux années 1955
Recherche de la Base et du Sommet 1955; revised 1971
La Bibliothèque est en feu 1956
Hypnos Waking (poetry and prose) 1956
En trente-trois morceaux 1956
Jeanne qu'on brula verte 1956
Les Compagnons dans le jardin 1957
Poèmes et prose choisis 1957
Sur la poésie 1958; revised 1974
La Montée de la nuit 1961
La Parole en archipel 1962

Commune présence 1964
L'Age cassant 1965
Retour amont 1966
Les Transparents 1967
Dans la pluie giboyeuse 1968
Le Nu perdu 1971
La Nuit talismanique 1972
Aromates chasseurs 1975
Poems of René Char 1976
Chants de la Balandrane: Poèmes 1977
Fenêtres dormantes et porte sur le toit 1979
Oeuvres complètes 1983
Les Voisinages de Van Gogh 1985
Eloge d'une Soupçonnée 1998
Selected Poems of René Char 1992
This Smoke that Carried Us: Selected Poems of René Char 2004

Other Major Works

Correspondance 1935-1970 (with Jean Ballard) (letters) 1993

CRITICISM

Kenneth Douglas (essay date fall-winter 1948)

SOURCE: Douglas, Kenneth. "René Char." Yale French Studies 1, no. 2 (fall-winter 1948): 79-84.

[In the following essay, Douglas assesses the evolution of Char's reputation in post-World War II France.]

It is time to speak of Char. He has been writing since 1927, and since the Liberation has aroused a fervent interest within France. His novitiate served in the seminaries of Surrealism, and having published jointly with Breton and Eluard, from that dogmatic chaos he emerged gradually (and without apostasy) to affirm his own poetic truth.

For truth is his concern. Not the mirage of yet another imaginary world, not the dexterous patterning of words and echoes. Truth in, through, and about poetry, which thus reflects self, as so often before it has done (traditional invocation of the "Muse," and compare the like attitude of those who pray that they may be shown how to pray), but sinks itself, too, in other objects—even Narcissus, after all, had to purchase a mirror—for example the poet's relations with others, their relationship to him, the problem of his death, the line of filiation of this momentary and momentous activity, his striving for authentic expression, with the deeds which thereafter he will perform. Or, to put it more concretely, his poetry is not a nostalgia for the past or the impossible, is not exclusively a delighting in the present, but while realising intensely the presence of the present is directed also towards the future. And his fellow-men! Even that wretched creature, the reader, is envisaged—a contrast with Baudelaire's degraded accomplice or butt which he shocks into registering a hit—as a companion possibly in the exploring and making of the real world. "Poetry is creation productive of the real." "Greetings for him who marches by my side to the end of the poem. Tomorrow he will pass *upright* beneath the wind."

Let us question René Char's poetic labors as to their fundamental significance. Patent is the failure of purely objective explanations of the universe and man's place in it, flagrant, the unsubstantial gratuitousness of all subjectivism. Must we choose between this sterile solipsistic play and "the barrenness of the merely correct" (Jaspers), of partial truths? Suffer impalement on the dilemma's one or other horn? The skilled athlete can evade the danger, the *razeteur* of the sport popular in Char's own Southern region, who running diagonally across the bull's path possesses himself of the cockade which, attached to both horns, had graced the animal's forehead. The poet as *razeteur,* the prize he has snatched on his oblique course mysteriously pendant from the twin horns of subjectivism and objectivism—such, it may be, is the poet's part, with this aspiration he may shorten the birth-pangs of new meaning in a universe that has lost all meaning, and help to reintegrate therein men become aliens. After the rationalism of René Descartes, after the preoccupation with self of François-René, Viscount of Chateaubriand, the bridge-building or cockade-snatching exploits of René Char? It might be so. To be *rené* is to be reborn, and possibly, we have suggested, to assist in a new birth.

Lest the misconception arise: Char is not the author of *Fin de Satan,* of *Dieu.* Lacking Victor Hugo's megalomania, he does not regard himself as a source of universal and total salvation. What can one man do for another? At most, with a word or gesture, unveil momentarily a possible path, or as briefly retain, between thumb and forefinger, a wriggling, a slippery, a vanished reality: he cannot give eyes or hands. This "most" Char offers. Yet, and thereby he assumes the trappings of omnipotent deity, the means by which he realises his intentions are hard to discover: for while he inhabits a coherent poetic landscape, the barren or intermittently fertile regions of the *Midi* (the Vaucluse is his birthplace), the pressings of grape and olive have filtered into various receptacles. Dominant in his recent work is the aspect of prose. He has also employed free verse; and the "versicle," that is to say the deep-lunged, robust Claudelian line; and almost regular rhythms, though with the avoidance of rhyme. This exclusion il-

lustrates his tendency, reaching right up to the supreme *cockade* of which we have spoken, to base prosody (as does Paul Claudel, in theory and practice), and all else, on the reconciliation of opposites rather than on repetition, on echo. (Sameness and difference, like all antitheses they too reciprocally determine one another; but either may be accentuated.) A poem, with Char, consists on occasion of a short phrase that, like much considerable poetry, will by many be judged "not poetry at all." He aims at the maximum density, not of imagery alone, but of meaning. A sequence of these self-contained blocks can form nevertheless a larger unit, as discrete rumbles of thunder build a storm. Thunder, maintained Heraclitus, governs all things. Or, when a poem has a greater apparent unity, something other subtends than a logical or narrative sequence, to ensure validity.

These notes constitute the *heralding* of Char, they are not a thorough study or even an introduction. What follows attempts, mainly, to convey his tone, an entire comprehension may not be attained. It goes with Char as with Heraclitus, whom so greatly he admires: first comes the shock of recognition, cognition lags behind. There is no cult of obscurity, nor technical incompetence—the horseshoe of authentic poetry must of necessity be hammered out of glowing metal. Authentic, essential. If assurance of immediate surface comprehension were the Medean law, only the superficial, discursive, peripheral would have unfailing right of entry. But enough of reflection, here is the reflected in person, the bridge, anvil, wheelbarrow, salvo, iridescence, etc., of Char's poetry.

"Pure eyes in the woods—Search weeping for the inhabitable head." Found, with a variant which has no equivalent for "weeping," in two early collections. A Surrealist image and something more: multiple meaning. Instead of the element of fear in Goethe's "The oak tree stood in garb of mist—Towering up a giant there,—Where darkness out of the undergrowth—Looked with its hundred ebon eyes," there is longing, love, and the hope of that love's satisfaction, a turning to the future as well as immobilization, in the poem, of the present. Union of self and outside world is desired, a union which for Victor Hugo was already consummated: "Oh madman, who believest I am not thou!" Or Char's lines may be regarded as a visual variant of the notion, expressed by Rainer Maria Rilke and many others, that the poet lends his voice to the world and to natural things, which otherwise must remain mute. And Jorge Guillén exclaims "The world invents me!—I am its legend!" With Char the sought and sightless object is the human head, and the eyes belong to the world—already an interpenetration of opposites. Compare (for there is not so much a total newness in recent poetry as the more radical exploitation of age-old spells, and a shunning of the non-poetic), compare the spatially paradoxical exchange and containment of lovers' hearts in the "metaphysical" verse of John Donne. Again, most simply, Char's couplet can be taken to express the desire for that not yet encountered, for the divined and miraculous She. Its few words compete with the expansive resources of a Japanese paper flower (simile adapted from Proust).

Below are brief quotations, most of them presented in the original as relatively independent units, for the most part dealing with poetry and the poet, and taken from the whole range of Char's productivity. It would be tempting to comment further on many things; on his faithfulness to Surrealism (maintaining with a surer judgment than Breton and others the balance even between, more sovereignly fusing the worlds of dream and wakefulness) and his avoidance of its pitfalls; on the doctrine he offers of poetic *commitment* (my translation of "engagement"), which at the same time rescues the notion from the Gehenna where Breton would plunge it and crashes through the barrier which Sartre rather too summarily has erected between the unescapable commitment of the prose writer and the alleged freedom of the poet to play with words as with pebbles (reflections of Valéry's theories persist, even on waters hostile to him); on Char's own share in armed resistance, and the resultant precipitation in his *Feuillets d'Hypnos*; on—but Char is entitled to speak for himself.

(1)

The poem is furious ascent; poetry, the sport of barren hillsides.

(2)

The poem is the consummated love of desire which remains desire.

(3)

Sing your iridescent thirst.

(4)

Oh truth, mechanical infanta, remain earth and murmur amidst the impersonal stars!

(5)

The very spirit of the castle

Is the drawbridge.

(6)

Poetry is of all clear waters that which tarries the least at the reflections of its bridges.

Poetry, future life within requalified man.

(7)

The poet is the man of unilateral stability.

(8)

The poet, this torrent with serene mud.

(9)

If we inhabit a lightning flash, it is the heart of the eternal.

(10)

Produce what knowledge wishes to keep secret, knowledge with its hundred passageways.

(11)

The poet, inclined to exaggeration, evolves correctly under torture.

(12)

The poet cannot long remain in the stratosphere of the Word. He must coil himself in fresh tears and push on farther in his realm.

(13)

In poetry, it is only upon the communication and the self-determination of the totality of things among themselves through us that we find ourselves committed and defined, in a position to acquire our original form and our probative qualities.

(14)

The poet must hold the scales even between the physical world of waking and the redoubtable ease of sleep, the lines of the knowledge wherein he lays the poem's subtle body passing without distinction from one to the other of these different conditions of life.

(15)

Sometimes his reality would lack meaning for him did not the poet influence in secret the narration of the exploits of others.

(16)

Escape into one's fellows with immense perspectives of poetry one day perhaps will be possible.

(17)

Set beside fate resistance to fate.

(18)

To every crumbling of the proofs, the poet responds with a salvo of future.

"Threshold"

When man's barrage crumbled, sucked in by the gigantic fissure of the abandonment of the divine, words far away, words which did not want to be lost, tried to withstand the excessive thrust. There the dynasty of their sense was decided.

I have run to the outlet of this diluvian night. Braced in the quivering dawn, my belt filled with seasons, I await you, oh my friends who are going to come. Already I divine you behind the blackness of the horizon. My hearth does not exhaust its good wishes for your dwellings, and my stick of cypress wood laughs with all its heart for you.

Bibliography

Le Tombeau des secrets, Nîmes, A. Larguier, 1930.

Ralentir Travaux, Paris, Editions Surréalistes, 1930. In collaboration with André Breton and Paul Eluard.

Placard pour un chemin des écoliers, Paris, GLM, 1937.

Dehors la nuit est gouvernée, Paris, GLM, 1938.

Le Marteau sans maître suivi de Moulin premier, 1927-1935, Paris, Corti, 1945.

Seuls demeurent, Paris, N.R.F., 1945.

Feuillets d'Hypnos, Paris, N.R.F., 1946.

Premières Alluvions, Paris, Fontaine, 1946. His earliest poems.

Le Poème pulvérisé, Paris, Fontaine, 1947.

Georges Mounier, *Avez-vous lu Char?,* Paris, N.R.F., 1946.

Gilbert Lély, *René Char,* Paris, Variété, 1947

Maurice Saillet, "Le Poème pulvérisé," *Le Mercure de France* CCCI, No. 1010 (1er oct. 1947), 319-22.

Gaëtan Picon, "René Char et l'avenir de la poésie," *Fontaine* II, No. 63 (nov. 1947), 826-34.

Translations in *View* VI, Nos. 2-3 (March-April 1946), 21, 40.

Wallace Fowlie (essay date 1958)

SOURCE: Fowlie, Wallace. "Rene Char and the Poet's Vocation." *Yale French Studies,* no. 21 (1958): 83-9.

[*In the following essay, Fowlie discusses Char's treatment in his poetry of the work and calling of the poet, an endeavor that comes with a disparaging price—"the daily assumption of peril."*]

M. Char has never written in any of the usual ways about his understanding of the poet's vocation. But it becomes more and more clear, as his work continues to grow, and as the significance of this work continues to deepen, that the particular calling of the poet is his major theme. The poet's life unfolds within the limitations of man's mortal nature. Mortality and poetry are so conjugated in the writings of Char that one provides the setting for the other, that one is finally indistinguishable from the other. René Char has moved away from the esoteric place assigned to the poet by Mallarmé in order to stand today in the humanistic center of his close friend Albert Camus. The familiar picture of Char as Resistance leader, with his companions in the maquis of the Basses-Alpes, in Céreste, is still remembered as we read his poetry, not only **Feuillets d'Hypnos,** composed during the Occupation years, but the subsequent volumes as well, and even the recently published **Les Compagnons dans le jardin,** of 1957.

Does this mean that M. Char's poetry is an example of the new "engaged" literature advocated by Sartre? Not, certainly, in any literal sense. Poetry, according to Char, does not seem to be committed to any cause unless one calls life itself a cause and a reason for commitment. Poetry is not in the service of an idea or a party or a movement. It is that which is at the very heart of whatever is a human reality, a human problem, a human commitment. In France today, in all countries for that matter, in the midst of overwhelming problems and insurmountable obstacles, the voice of the poet is heard as one of the few voices left, faithful to the truth which man represents and seeks, to the continuing mysteriousness of his dignity, to the belief that man's noblest efforts are salutary for himself and for humanity.

The verses of Char, the aphorisms which abound in his work, and the brief condensed tales which appear in company with the aphorisms, all speak of the nature of poetry. It is that which is lived, for Char, experienced with the penetrating realization of submitting to human destiny. It is a comparatively easy matter to describe a literary work which is about life. But such a definition would not apply to the poetry of Char. This poet looks upon his art as an assault on life and an embracing, an animation of life. He answers, in the writing of his poem, not some outside command, but the uprising surge of his nature and his feelings. No cause which can be defined as such will move him as much as the proportions of his own human nature, with its contradictions and its puzzling enigmas.

The word "risk," for example, applies to Char's conception of life as well as to his conception of poetry. The outside world in which he lives, almost as a poacher lives invading someone else's forest, is the natural world of constant change, a flowering river of things such as his favorite philosopher Heraclitus had described. But this is the site of risks and provocations. The things he sees there are not poems, but they discover their reality in poems. The poetic act is a finding of a form for things which otherwise would never emerge from their abyss or their silence or their possibility. It is difficult for Char to elaborate on the principles of poetry because for him poetics and poetry are hardly separable. It is unusual for a French poet not to bequeath texts on poetics and technique. Char's answer is his entire existence as poet. The poet, he would say, has no other place to be except within poetry.

The risk of poetry is precisely this responsibility of the poet in the action of drawing poetry from the poet's sleep and from his subconscious.

The risk of poetic creation is admirably transcribed in the striking antitheses of so many of M. Char's poems. The new poems, published in 1955, entitled *Poèmes des deux années 1953-1954,* contain examples of the contrast which Char establishes between solidity and fragility, between a sense of security and a premonition of the evanescence of things. The state of the world is so often established in these terms of contrast by Char that the poems themselves are seen finally to be constructed in a similar tension between strength and weakness. In **"Le Bois de l'Epte,"** for example, the poet is seen following on foot a valley stream. He comes upon two wild rose bushes bending into the water. The brilliance of a single rose in the water awakens in the poet an awareness of the earth and he sees the wood of Epte beginning just ahead.

> Le rauque incarnat d'une rose, en frappant l'eau,
> Rétablit la face première du ciel avec l'ivresse des
>   questions,
> Eveilla au milieu des paroles amoureuses la terre.

The poem, **"La Chambre dans l'Espace,"** announces an antithesis in its title. Within the poem, the poet compares himself with a piece of earth calling for a flower.

> Je suis un bloc de terre qui réclame sa fleur.

The title, **"Le Rempart de Brindilles,"** is another antithesis and the poem itself begins in the form of a definition of the function of poetry, but the definition is so highly charged with antithesis that it is the poem. The poet is made sovereign, we read in this important poem, by making himself impersonal and by reaching the fullness of what had only been sketched or deformed by the boasting of a single man. The opposites are thus established of sovereignty and impersonality, of fullness and deformity.

> Le dessein de la poésie étant de nous rendre souverains
> en nous impersonnalisant, nous touchons, grâce au
> poème, à la plénitude de ce qui n'était qu'esquissé ou
> déformé par la vantardise de l'individu.

The second verse of the poem is perhaps the supreme antithesis in Char's work. It is the contrast between a poem and death, between incorruptibility and corruptibility. Poems are particles of the incorruptible part of our existence which we hurl into the jaws of death. They fall back into the world which is the name for unity.

> Les poèmes sont des bouts d'existence incorruptibles
> que nous lançons à la gueule répugnante de la mort,
> mais assez haut pour que, ricochant sur elle, ils tombent
> dans le monde nominateur de l'unité.

The title of this poem, **"Rampart of Twigs,"** establishes the fundamental antithesis between the world and poetry, between the fragile and the everlasting, between the mortal and the immortal. Multiple are the bonds this poet discovers existing between himself and nature, but the lesson is harsh to assimilate because it is inevitably a picture of a threatened and perishable nature he perceives.

The purity and the conciseness of Char's language make it appear more primitively faithful to his reactions, to his first responses. He has sustained in his style, which is devoid of the usual poetic rhetoric, something of the secret meaning of his reactions. One remembers easily that his first adherence was to surrealism. And yet in this will to record and explain his reaction to the world and to human experience, he places himself quite centrally within the tradition of French moralists. With his ever-increasing understanding of life, Char the poet and Char the moralist both denounce the vanity of life. Poetry is both a critique of poetics and a critique of illusions. The new poems, like aphorisms, are brief and elliptical. The white spaces around them—like the silences which precede and follow speech—have their own message and their own suggestiveness.

The poet's vocation is felt in its very special insistency, in the need it creates in the poet to write. If what he writes has both fury in it and tragedy, the poet is struck by the silence of the ink on the page. The oxymoron is there at the start: in the silence of the hieroglyphic characters and in the rage of the sentiments expressed. The poet is within a curse, Char writes, in *Recherche de la Base et du Sommet.* "Il est dans la malédiction." He could not exist if it were not in accord with some mysterious law of apprehension. There is a price to pay for feeling deeply and for writing as a poet. That price is the daily assumption of peril. The ordinary man is able to fix the source of evil in the world: he traces it back to some event or to some cause. But the poet knows that evil comes from farther back than he can remember, from farther back than he can ever believe. The horrors he encounters in the world he is unable to simplify. That is the function and the activity, again, of the non-poet. But the horrors have simplified the poet. They have made him into a man unable to be anything save the poet.

The strong stylistic and moralist claims made by this new poet designate him as the heir both of symbolism and surrealism. He is surrealist in the way in which he feels an event. He is symbolist in the distance he knows exists between the occurence of the event and its narration. He actually speaks of the enigmas of poetry as often as Mallarmé did, but he defines the actions of the poet as the results of these enigmas.

> Les actions du poète ne sont que la conséquence des
> énigmes de la poésie.

> (*A une sérénité crispée*)

Mallarmé would call the poet the creator of enigmas. Char would agree with Mallarmé in calling a poem a quintessence, but in the straining of Char's language, in the tension of each poem and each aphoristic utterance, he defines the natural movement of poetry as a revolt.

In the tributes written to his friends, René Crevel and Paul Eluard, Char exalts human life in its relativity, in all the attacks man has waged against injustice and deception, in man's love of the sun, and simply in the power he feels in accomplishing an action. He will forego any pleasure to be derived from vengeance or from persecuting others even if this means the resumption of uncertainty in life. Some of the humanistic definitions of man, found in Char's most recent publication, *Les Compagnons dans le jardin,* complete earlier definitions. He sees man's place as a coalition. He is a flower held down by the earth, cursed by the stars because he is unable to rise to them and solicited by death which is his constant fate.

> L'homme n'est qu'une fleur de l'air tenue par la terre, maudite par les astres, respirée par la mort; le souffle et l'ombre de cette coalition, certaines fois, le surélèvent.

Here again is stated, in fresh terms, the prevailing paradox of Char's work: man seen as tenderness in the surge of his spirit and as an Apocalyptic figure in his end. The pessimism of Heraclitus was not difficult to discover in the early work, *Feuillets d'Hypnos.* The myth of tragedy is man's principal heritage, but it may accompany a lifetime of revolt against this fate. This revolt is the subject matter of some of the greatest prose writers of modern France: Malraux, Saint-Exupéry, Camus. It is not only the subject matter of Char's poetry, it is the poetry itself. The poetry is his life lived as a maquis fighter and as a disciple of the philosopher of Ephesus. Char can no more cut himself off from the action of men, from cohabitation with men, than he can cease meditating on the tragedy of man's fate in a world of change and flux.

Char's vision of the world in which he lives, of the world where all men live, is one of his most fertile themes, but this vision is often cast into the abstract terms of a poet-philosopher. He calls it, in one passage, that which is inconceivable. But it is also that which has luminous points of reference, dazzling signs.

> Nous sommes dans l'inconcevable, mais avec des repères éblouissants.
>
> **(*Recherche de la Base et du Sommet*)**

Thus, in a single line which is a poem by virtue of its image and power, the world of tragedy is juxtaposed with the burning revolt of man's spirit living that tragedy. The violent contrast is at times softened: In the garden of men exist the future forests.

> Dans nos jardins se préparent des forêts.
>
> **(*Les Compagnons dans le jardin*)**

In the survival of man there is visible a better survival.

> O survie encore, toujours meilleure!
>
> (*ibid.*)

The walker, the man who is bound to the earth and who walks on its surface, is granted some knowledge of the secret existence of things, secrets of the wind, of trees, of water. At moments in history when total destruction seems inevitable, man is unable to believe that the world, which has always been redeemed in the past, is facing its death in the very presence of man. In the future, Char may be looked upon as the apocalyptic poet of our day, as the poet the most persistently oppressed by the Apocalypse aspect of the mid-century.

The thought of Heraclitus has undoubtedly encouraged Char's philosophy to state that no matter how inherently noble truth is, the picture we have of this truth is tragedy. But there is a relationship between the nobility of truth and the noble character of tragedy. This is the source of what we have been calling the antithesis or the oxymoron in Char's poetry. Man's ever increasing awareness of his fate is equivalent to what Char calls the continuous presence of risk felt by the poet. This risk maintains the poet in a lofty position of attentiveness, of freedom of attitude and action. The risk represented by each poem is best understood by comparing it with the risk each day of living, with the threat involved in each decision of each hour in every man's life.

During the richest years of the surrealist movement in France, 1930-1934, René Char was initiated to poetry and to a search for what the surrealists called "énigmes." Char, who has never disavowed his debt to surrealism, has undergone since that time many changes. The quest for enigmas, for example, would no longer be applicable to his present discoveries. But there are images in his newer writing which bear strong reminiscences of surrealism. A phrase in *A une sérénité crispée* describes the dual character of man, which we have seen repeatedly stressed in Char, but in a surrealist coupling of terms.

> L'oiseau et l'arbre sont conjoints en nous. L'un va et vient, l'autre maugrée et pousse.

A surrealist habit of looking at the world, of joining seemingly unrelated objects, has helped Char to express some of his deepest convictions on the nature of man and the universe.

As Char's writing has become more and more visibly affected by the events of his time, he has made the effort in his poetical work more and more consciously to transform what he sees and feels. But his age seen in an image is both transformation and interpretation. It is the understanding of the essence of things, an abstraction which, when successful, is the container of opposites. His poet's journal, *Feuillets d'Hypnos,* clearly states that he is opposed to the static, that if the alternative is the absurd, he will choose that, because thereby he will move closer to the pathos of the world:

> Si l'absurde est maître ici-bas, je choisis l'absurde, l'antistatique, celui qui me rapproche le plus des chances pathétiques.

How lucidly the poet's vocation emerges from such a text! He is intransigent and refractory. His work is provocation and defiance. His system is unclassifiable because it contains all the opposites of our nature, all the dimensions of the absurd.

Despite the fact that René Char is a difficult poet in almost every sense, he has today reached an eminent degree of fame. The danger is now that he will be enshrined and not understood. To read Char, a new mechanism of sensibility is necessary. A mere knowledge of Char's commitments and an awareness of his literary affiliations will never reveal his poetic excellence.

The best way to approach Char is a study of those moments in his writings when he is aware of the poet's vocation. They are the moments of natural perception when he greets the world. This poet is essentially an analogist. The experience he relates in his books is not beyond the understanding of anyone who has looked intently and lovingly at the world.

Char initiates his readers first to his vigorous, sensuous life in nature. But from nature he moves quickly to the moral and the intellectual order. The final line of *Feuillets d'Hypnos* states the ultimate reign of beauty in the world: "Toute la place est pour la Beauté." There is really no poet, in Char's system, there is only poetry. He is consciously bent on bringing back into poetry the strength of living men.

The vigor of this poet's mind puts him into a separate poetic world. We are moved by the vitality of his thought, but especially by the vitality of his concreteness. The truths of the world as he sees them are constantly demanding his allegiance. (This trait in Char would be more easily understood in a frankly religious poet.) He is a poet characterized by the habit of seeing things charged with meaning—an ordered meaning regarding the relationships between nature and men.

Times Literary Supplement (review date 21 October 1965)

SOURCE: "Back to the Novice He Once Was." *Times Literary Supplement,* no. 3,321 (21 October 1965): 941.

[*In the following review, Char's* Commune présence *is considered and praised for the way Char "regroups the poems in a coherent whole so that we can see their underlying unity."*]

All but a few of the poems in this selection have appeared before, but even for those already familiar with the poetry of René Char it will look like a new book. He has chosen them mainly from eight volumes published since 1934, though he has also included the final text of one complete poem (**"Lettera Amorosa"**, first printed in 1953) and a sprinkling of poems from a new volume, not yet published but presumably in preparation, **Retour Amont.** The poems are grouped in eight sections, not by the books in which they first appeared but according to their themes and moods. M. Char's most characteristic and telling effects owe much to his careful juxtaposition of images, and the arrangement of the poems he has now chosen as representative of his best work gives the whole body of it a new freshness, a more easily comprehensible unity and a more pointed significance. But let it be said without further ado that, as an aid to understanding what that significance is, Georges Blin's introduction is disappointing. M. Char's poetry is not inaccessible. Its impact is direct and only deadened by explanation. M. Blin's essay lacks illumination and creates as many difficulties as it removes.

If you look up "CHAR, *René*" in *Who's Who in France* you will find the entry: "*Carrière*: toute entière consacrée à la poésie". This is less than the whole truth. For M. Char, poetry is infinitely more than a literary form and much more than a career. It is hard to believe that he has ever managed to live by it or on it, but there is no doubt that he has always lived with it. Even during the war, as a resistance fighter, he was living a life of poetry in action. But poetry and the poem are not interchangeable terms. Poetry is the poet's inner world, possessing him as much as he possesses it, a way of life of the spirit, a personal ethic, an intimate religion with its own values and ritual. Essentially, the poet is a missionary. His conviction of the reality and validity of his own inner world and his faith, born of humility, that others have their inner world too and can therefore share in his, impel him to communicate what he can of it. The act of communication is the poem.

This conception of poetry was vaguely adumbrated by the Romantics; and if M. Char had been writing a hundred years ago he would have been a Romantic poet. In the twentieth century the stream of poetry has carved new channels for itself and the sacred river now runs through caverns hitherto measureless to man. French poets, to continue the metaphor, were the first to discover this unsuspected network of underground watercourses and to explore and extend it. The "new poetry" has spread far beyond France, but France is still its spiritual and intellectual home. It has, of course, its charlatans and parasites. It has also its dedicated exponents and authentic voices, and René Char is one of these. They use a common language, images, to record and interpret their subterranean voyages, but it is a language with many dialects. Eventually the poet has to return to the surface, and the images he uses are those he finds at the point of time and place where he regains the upper air. He may emerge under the palms of an oasis or through a manhole out of a Parisian sewer. The point where M. Char breaks surface most often is in his own familiar Provence.

More precisely, it is L'Isle-sur-Sorgue in the Vaucluse where he was born fifty-eight years ago. The first poem in the book, **"Déclarer son Nom"**, establishes his credentials by putting him in his own setting as a child:

> J'avais dix ans. La Sorgue m'enchâssait.
> Le soleil chantait les heures sur le sage cadran des
>   eaux.

M. Char has a wide range of images. He draws them freely from the glowing but austere *provençal* landscape, its craggy horizons, its olive trees, its flora and fauna, its birds and reptiles, and sometimes from its curious traditional human figures. Everywhere there is the smell of much loved soil and time-honoured husbandry. The significant images are those which denote rapid movement and instant perception, the lightning flash, the loop of a swift in flight, and, recurrently, water, especially the mountain stream before it swells into a river:

> L'eau est lourde à un jour de la source.

The poem cannot be bogged down by the passage of time. It consists essentially of transfixing a moment and snatching it out of time:

> Si nous habitons un éclair, il est le coeur de l'éternel.

Poetry being, for M. Char, what it is, a poem can hardly be other than fragmentary. One of the great virtues of the present book is that it regroups the poems in a coherent whole so that we can see their underlying unity. Each section has a central theme. The first evokes the poet's childhood, the last is mainly about death. The sections in between are concerned with love, friendship and the comradeship of like minds. The last one is entitled *L'Ecarlate,* the vivid colour symbolic of poetry itself. It is a kind of *art poétique,* though this is basically something that can be said about the whole book. In one way or another, implicitly or explicitly, by imagery or by aphorism, all the poems add up to an unmistakably positive affirmation, a spirited as well as spiritual defence and illustration of poetry as a mystical calling, as a way of life conducive to a state of mind in which the hidden forces of creation and the common ancestry of even the most incongruous things can be perceived and, at least in part, communicated to others. His *art poétique* is also an *art de la vie.* Poetry cannot exist without love or without liberty; and both, in poetry,

are eternally unassailable. Poetry is truth in its utmost simplicity, reality without the meretricious trappings of appearance:

> La poésie est de toutes les eaux claires celle qui
> s'attarde le moins aux reflets de ses ponts.

Poetry overcomes death:

> La poésie me volera ma mort.

It is central to life itself:

> La seule signature au bas de la vie blanche, c'est
> la poésie qui la dessine.

It can be said the other way round: René Char lives in his poems. *Commune présence,* the title of the book, is also the title of an early poem first published in 1934. It is a kind of self-administered lecture on how to be a poet. It is an endearing touch, suggestive of great humanity, that the nearly sexagenarian poet should go back more than thirty years to the novice he once was for a name for so much of his life's work. *Commune présence* suggests also the common ground between the poet and his public. René Char's presence in his poems can be felt almost palpably, reaching out to his readers. They may not be many in this country, but they will surely be greatly rewarded.

Paulène Aspel (essay date spring 1968)

SOURCE: Aspel, Paulène. "The Poetry of Rene Char, or Man Reconciled [1968]." *World Literature Today* 63, no. 2 (spring 1989): 205-08.

[*In the following essay, which was originally published in 1968, Aspel comments on Char's career as a poet, observing how the poet uses certain symbols to portray the "opposite, ambiguous human behaviors."*]

At the age of sixty, with twenty volumes of poetry published, René Char is considered by more and more critics in France as the greatest living French poet. Albert Camus had made such a claim for him as early as 1951, in *L'homme révolté,* when he greeted him as "poète de notre renaissance," and in the preface he wrote for Char's *Dichtungen,* an anthology compiled in Germany in 1959, he declared that no such voice had been heard since the pre-Socratics. In 1962 Char was placed among the constellations whose "feux sont sûrs et durables," and in 1966 he was awarded the Prix des Critiques for his latest volume of poems, *Retour amont.* A film was made by the Télévision Suisse de Genève the same year. Last August his prominent position was highlighted by a "Soirée René Char," an event that took place at the Fondation Maeght's new fine-arts center and museum. Char is now achieving international recognition as well, with translations and critical anthologies published in a dozen European countries, in the United States, Canada, Argentina, and Japan.

The poet's life is spent chiefly between Provence and Paris. Near L'Isle-sur-Sorgue, his birthplace and the cradle of his family, is Les Busclats, a white Provençal house surrounded by a large garden of cosmos, hollyhocks, and lavender. A short distance away, one has a view of the Mont Ventoux, whose summits have a prestigious presence in Char's poetry. Three miles west, at Fontaine-de-Vaucluse, where Petrarch lived and wrote, the soaring Sorgue, with its heavy cubelike waters, springs from a vertical rock. The swift river has been for the poet, since his childhood, an infinite source of inspiration.

Although several American universities have invited him to read or discuss his poetry, he has declined. It seems that he wants above all to preserve his freedom and independence. Meanwhile, Les Busclats is becoming a high place, with Char sought out by a growing number of visitors from the world of art and literature. When Heidegger came to France in 1955, the two individuals he wanted to meet first were René Char and Georges Braque.

Today, when we look back over forty years of production, the striking constant we can observe is Char's fidelity. From his early books *Arsenal* (1929) and *Le marteau sans maître* (1934), an enigmatic, unoriented, but radiant current which hammered down the author's young beliefs with even more rage than *Fureur et mystère* of fifteen years later (1948), to his latest volumes *Retour amont* (see *BA* 41:1, p. 56) and the 1967 reedition of his plays, *Trois coups sous les arbres* (see *BA* 42:2, p. 236), Char has remained remarkably faithful to his themes. If a continuous line of major trends can generally be seen in every great writer, the fact is indeed especially true of Char, who has not zigzagged between political affiliations and would not let himself be enslaved by the most tempting ideologies. He parted from his surrealist *bons compagnons de révolte* only after five years of comradeship when he found André Breton becoming too dogmatic and, later, his best friend Paul Eluard turning into a hopelessly committed communist. Moreover, two important breaks in Char's life, which could have developed into a complete change of outlook, in the end were not ruptures. Rather, they helped him elaborate and reinforce the themes he had already anticipated in his early works. The first break was in 1936-37, a septicemia followed by a long recovery. The other was *la grande épreuve de Céreste* (1941-44) when, hemmed in by Vichy police, he organized and directed the Maquis in Basses-Alpes. In each case Char was engaged in a struggle against monsters, disease or oppressor; he went through "l'halucinante expérience de l'homme noué au

Mal, de l'homme massacré et pourtant victorieux." Char's merit was, in the course of a perilous moral itinerary comparable to Camus's of the same time, to have reconciled two opposite, demanding truths: revolt and happiness. It was to wager in favor of man when man everywhere sank, to speak up for beauty when beauty was obscured by darkness. Char was to emerge from the Résistance as a genuine moralist and a greater poet.

His first major works then, *Seuls demeurent* (1945) and the famous journal of a Résistance fighter, *Feuillets d'Hypnos* (1946), reveal his important themes. These appear with mixed ethical and poetic concepts, in long poems as well as in simple little ones close to nature and daily life. They are tightly interwoven, sharing their brilliant, challenging images. Poetry, the making of the poem, the poet's function, is regarded by all Char's exegetes as his predominant, richest theme. Char says in **"Mirage des aiguilles,"** a poem in *Retour amont*: "Fidèle à son amour comme le ciel l'est au rocher." Tender loving expressions, such as *mon amour, l'Amie, ma martelée, la Rencontrée,* apply most often to poetry in this poet's world, and not to woman, as more than one unaware reader has been misled to think. The decisive, magic encounter between poetry and poet had already taken place in childhood: "Tout enfant, j'ai senti, réellement, quelqu'un, qui se tenait à mon côté, invisible—qui n'était pas Dieu." The theme runs through many different kinds of texts in prose and verse, in poems and even in pamphlets, letters, or homages to other poets, like those in a book which can be said to represent Char's credo: *Recherche de la base et du sommet.* This theme is also the very topic of special long poems made up of short numbered sequences, which can be read as a series of aphorisms or a continuous poem, such as *Partage formel* (1945), *A une sérénité crispée* (1951), *A la santé du serpent* (1954), *L'âge cassant* (1965). One characteristic Charian definition in the fifty-five dazzling sentences of *Partage formel* presents the poem as a free unifying force of ethics and esthetics: "Cette forteresse épanchant la liberté par toutes ses poternes, cette fourche de vapeur qui tient dans l'air un corps d'une envergure prométhéenne que la foudre illumine et évite, c'est le poème, aux caprices exorbitants, qui, dans l'instant, nous obtient puis s'efface."

In *Arrière-histoire du poème pulvérisé,* which consists of comments added to a 1947 plaquette called *Le poème pulvérisé,* Char explains how a poem is born: "J'ai pris ma tête comme on saisit une motte de sel et je l'ai littéralement pulvérisée: de cette illusion atroce est né 'J'habite une douleur,' plus quelque calme. C'est là, je crois, l'un de mes poèmes les plus achevés." Hence the nature of Charian poems, which indeed bear traces of this pulverization, somehow become *fragments* scattered over the world, but paradoxically remain solid, resistant entities. These fragments are island-poems, made of small blocks, prose paragraphs, boldly emerging from silence. In fact, the entire work of the poet is in the form of an archipelago. *La parole en archipel* (see *BA* 36:4, p. 393) is the title of a book published in 1962, but it had been Char's program long before that date. Moreover, the compact quality of the fragment is all the more striking because so many polyvalent images are condensed in it. The word is taut with poetic charge, or, in Char's terms, "La constellation du solitaire est tendue." Immense perspectives and opposite metaphors in a short, elliptic sentence constitute the Charian explosive aphorism. In brief, it can be said that the chief theme of Char is a complete monography of the Poem, its genesis, form, function, and aims. A passage written by Maurice Blanchot in *La part du feu* and often quoted since it was first published in 1946 sums up the poet's originality and work: "L'une des grandeurs de René Char, celle par laquelle il n'a pas d'égal en ce temps, c'est que sa poésie est révélation de la poésie, poésie de la poésie, et comme le dit à peu près Heidegger de Hölderlin, poème de l'essence du poème."

The second essential theme in Char's poetry is that of rebirth, a theme which has been somewhat neglected by criticism but will demand more and more attention since it has gained more importance in the poet's latest works. Frequently it appears together with hymns to nature and spring life, as in **"Le bois de l'Epte,"** or it borrows the paths of his ars poetica, as in **"La bibliothèque est en feu."** The theme is confirmed and amplified in *Retour amont,* a book which is, as defined by the author, "a tentative crossing beyond springs," "vers ce qui permet aux sources de se refaire." In a central piece, **"Le nu perdu,"** the instant is revealed when the living, the creators, "those who will bear boughs," are touched by the down of black night that precedes the lightning flash of illumination.

The theme of rebirth is generally apprehended in its full scope, as the dialectical operation of destruction and renaissance. It is supported, in the tradition of mythology and alchemy, by multiple images of fire. Fire is the one of the four elements which lends itself best to symbolizing opposite, ambiguous human behaviors, a large variety of which can be found in Char's poetry. The word *feu* achieves indeed a high frequency, which is surpassed only by the word *soleil.* The terms have many related ones, such as wheels, stars, peacocks, light, dawn, warmth, the famous lightning, et cetera. Numerous references are also made to their opposites, shadow and light. The "feu-chaleur" is associated with the expression of friendship and brotherhood, whereas *l'éclair,* the quick happening of which lasts a little longer for the privileged poet, brings knowledge, uncovers a brilliant and beloved country, and finally becomes *le cœur de l'éternel.*

Fire is so precious, however, that we want to preserve, condense it in a form and space as small as possible. What could such a compact dynamic entity be? Bird, of course. A variety of birds, as well as the word *oiseau,* appear in numerous texts. Above all of them flies the eagle. In a typical taut Charian metaphor, "l'aigle solaire," encompassing the two main types of fire, represents the thinker Heraclitus, whose "exaltante alliance des contraires" has forever inspired the poet.

Both closely related major themes of regeneration and the essence of the poem are essential in forming the meaning of one of the greatest poems by Char: **"La bibliothèque est en feu"** in *Poèmes et prose choisis* (1957). The flawless *poème en archipel* also combines three other chief Charian themes: the problems of knowledge and time, and especially the beautiful and frail fraternity among men of this earth. The poet dances with his fellow man: "Torche, je ne valse qu'avec lui." Man, "le bel homme déconcertant et fragile," has been for Char an object of long-range attention and care. The poet often seems to imply that his preferred friends are "les amis au sol," his Vauclusian compatriots, who partake of qualities of earth itself, serenity, solidarity, warmth, and who can also understand the language of the Provençal sun. The native soil is rarely used as topic itself for a poem, but it pervades all works, with its mountains, rivers, and fauna contributing their own personalities to that of the poem, the geographic elements being thus transcended and humanized. The *pays* leads one to other regions, especially the *Pays* with a capital *P,* which is poetry land.

Knowledge, with its traditional meaning of a vast, baffling, and misleading endeavor, is also for Char "la connaisance aux cents passages," a dispenser of vertigo to the one who has climbed it up to its crest and is fascinated by the abyss. Another type of knowledge, however, one which is more specifically Char's, aims at being productive, ultimately resulting in the poem itself. It can be at the same time defined by a strange aspect of unpredictability. Events are always surrounded with mystery, and a few unexpected encounters are truly privileged moments in Char's world. It is, for instance, at the turn of a road, a girl walking on a country trail after picking mimosas during the day: profiled against sunset, her figure appears as a lamp of perfume, ("Congé au vent"); but the apparition could have been poetry herself. Knowledge and poetry are sisters, even if, according to Heidegger, they like to live on separate summits. In **"La bibliothèque est en feu,"** one day in winter, poetry manifested itself, with another one of its touching ways, as bird down on the windowpane; it announced spring and a life of writing: "Comment me vint l'écriture? Comme un duvet d'oiseau sur ma vitre en hiver."

Most Charian happenings take place in an absolute present. By the emphasis given to the use of that tense and time in his work, Char reveals himself as a true existential poet. Georges Poulet, who has made a thorough study of Char's time, has stressed the compact, tense, full quality of a "présent essentiel," that culminates into instant. Things are given very little time "pour faire leur entrée dans le champ de la conscience." Many metamorphoses, many contradictory events are accomplished in no time at all, in what Char himself calls "raccourci fascinateur." Hence the continuous trembling of a crowded instant under the pressure of such forces; hence the constantly explosive quality of this poetry.

Among the many polyvalent images, *l'éclair, le serpent, la rose, l'oiseau* offer probably the richest symbols. Among all birds, unique is the eagle, which can be said to combine and condense the main Charian themes. It is a small, live fragment, endowed with a furious power, that of creation, of the poet himself. He is freedom as well as free encounter of knowledge with all its frailty; but he never means escape. On the contrary, watching is his concern and duty; his view and views are sharp. Proudly flying high, or staying on summits, he is closer to the sun than anyone else; but dwelling in rocks, he draws links between sun and earth, thus symbolizing the dynamic unified man. Finally the eagle is to come, and, like the Nietzschean superman, only in the future will he be ideally realized.

* * *

In the past twenty years Char's poetry has challenged the foremost critics to write an ever-increasing number of penetrating analyses; but for all the excellent decoding they have done, Charian studies are only beginning. For instance, no stylistic study has yet been made on the famous aphorism, allegedly inherited from Heraclitus, but which also bears resemblances to those of several French moralists. In numerous homage poems, recently thoroughly classified by the author in *Commune présence* (1964) and the second edition of *Recherche de la base et du sommet* (1965), the poet has acknowledged his debt to Heraclitus, Rimbaud, Mallarmé, and Nietzsche, among others, and also to his great friends of the postwar period, Albert Camus and Georges Braque. Criticism so far has merely repeated these opinions. It has insisted on Heraclitean as well as surrealist influences but has hardly touched the Nietzschean. That influence, however, will undoubtedly be found far greater and more durable than the others. A study should compare Char and the author of *Also sprach Zarathustra*. Let us remember, for example, the latter's interrogation to the sky after hearing the cry of an animal: "And behold! An eagle was sweeping through the air in wide circles, and from it was hanging a serpent, not like a prey, but like a friend, for it was coiled around the eagle's neck." "The proudest animal under the sun and the wisest animal under the sun" appear in Char's poetry with similar and even richer

implications. Among all known serpents in mythologies and poetries, Char's snake is indeed the most akin to Zarathustra's. The eagle occupies the privileged place we know. Concerning the "unvollständiger Nihilismus," which is one of the evils confronting our human condition, as also denounced especially by the existentialists, the poet repeatedly challenges us to perform the necessary task of destroying harmful, worn-out values. *La parole en archipel* echoes Nietzsche's "fragmentary language" which urged us first to reduce the universe to crumbs. Thus numerous tentative questions posed by the philosopher are tentatively answered by the poet. To the madman's burning one, why earth and sun are being tragically divorced, several poems, among them **"La bibliothèque est en feu,"** do indicate the way to reconciliation. The reconciliation is also symbolized by the eagle of the summits and the terrestrial snake as friends. The poet himself participates as a "liana" of the sun.

This reconciliation, however, goes further than Nietzschean or existential philosophy, by its encompassing and understanding of the unknown. Char does not feel any nostalgia or anxiety about it. Char, "poète du devenir," praises it as being "l'inconnu équilibrant." He recommends it, in fact. The **"Argument"** of *Poème pulvérisé* begins with these words: "Comment vivre sans inconnu devant soi?" The unknown might well be the region where brilliant rebirth will take place after the darkness of our lives, where miraculous fragments of poems can be collected, love for the fellow man reach its zenith, and man his unity. The firm young voice of the great poet achieves indeed an "Umwertung aller Werte," the striking change in life which our times demand. His poetry teaches the way to reconciliation: "En poésie, devenir c'est réconcilier."

Virginia A. LaCharité (essay date 1968)

SOURCE: LaCharité, Virginia A. "Conclusion: 1962-1966: A Poetics of Renewal." In *The Poetics and the Poetry of René Char,* pp. 195-206. Chapel Hill, N.C.: The University of North Carolina Press, 1968.

[*In the following essay, LaCharité develops an interpretation of Char's poetic philosophy and the poet's works from 1962 to 1966.*]

René Char's poetics and poetry form an integral whole which reflects the development of his discovery of the cosmic totality which characterizes all existence. His work from *Les Cloches sur le coeur* to *La Parole en archipel* elucidates this fusion of opposites through the examination of man, nature, and the role of the poet. In his examination of each subject, Char finds that Poetry contains the solution, that is, Poetry overcomes contradiction and fragmentation. Poetry is the common fact of truth and being; it is the principle of unity, the "commune présence" in which each element and each individual participate.

Char's sixth stage of development dates from 1962 to 1966 and includes only three works: *Commune présence* (1964), *L'Age cassant* (1966), and *Retour amont* (1966). In these three volumes, Char undertakes a profound investigation of his poetics and poetry from 1923 to 1966. His painstaking and rigorous review of his aesthetic journey through life leads him to a renewal of confidence in his discovery that Poetry is the macrocosm of all existence. Char finds that his efforts to reveal this singular truth are attained in his own creative acts. His vision of the fusion of life and poetry is represented by his own being.[1] In the study and evolution of René Char, the man and poet, René Char concludes that his course justifies his own existence and that this course is the only one by which each individual may assert his dignity of being.

COMMUNE PRÉSENCE

Commune présence (1964) is the most comprehensive presentation of Char's poetics and poetry. This work consists of texts selected from all his collective editions, from *Le Marteau sans maître* (1934)[2] to *La Parole en archipel* (1961), and it includes 12 texts[3] from *Retour amont*.[4] The significance of *Commune présence* lies in the organization of the texts into eight sections.

Before *Commune présence,* Char's collective editions were organized according to a pragmatic method which is a common practice among poets. As soon as several small volumes of texts were published, he placed them in a larger and more accessible edition in the order of their publication although the order of the texts within any group was not strictly chronological. The title of each small volume became the section title for each group within the larger edition. This method of organization characterizes *Le Marteau sans maître* (1934), *Fureur et mystère* (1948), and *La Parole en archipel* (1961). *Poèmes et prose choisis* (1957), Char's major anthology prior to *Commune présence,* represents the first change in this organizational pattern because the poems are separated from the aphorisms. However, this departure from Char's usual method is not radical, for the texts are still arranged in order of publication. In *Commune présence,* Char disregards this organizational approach.

Each section of *Commune présence* is composed of texts selected from previous collective editions, rather than from small volumes,[5] and each text is placed according to the relation of its theme to the section title. All indications of the date of composition and that of

publication are obscured. *Commune présence* is not a collective work in the usual sense; it does not merely assemble a number of small volumes. *Commune présence* is a mosaic composition of diverse pieces which are combined for the formation of an integrated whole. Earlier collective works are disarranged; texts are displaced from their established position and rearranged in a new pattern. Char "pulverises" his original structures and forges a new order with the fragments. The configuration of *Commune présence* parallels Char's theory of constructive destruction. He risks the unity of his work in order to give concrete evidence of the unity of Poetry: "Essaime ta poussière / Nul ne décèlera votre union."[6]

Although the organizational structure of *Commune présence* is strictly non chronological, the arrangement of the eight sections follows an architectural order which seems chronological. These sections reflect and summarize the evolution of Char's poetry: 1) *Cette fumée qui nous portait,* 2) *Battre tout bas,* 3) *Haine du peu d'amour,* 4) *Lettera amorosa* (definitive text), 5) *L'Amitié se succède,* 6) *Les Frères de mémoire,* 7) *L'Ecarlate,* and 8) *Vallée close.*

Cette fumée qui nous portait begins with an evocation of Char's childhood and adolescence in Isle-sur-Sorgue and describes the poet's personal experiences of communion with nature. His early awareness of the possibility of reconciling man with his world leads him to the singular discovery that the human and the elemental participate in a "commune présence" of existence. His desire to communicate this vision of a harmonious universe appears early in his life. The event of war[7] precipitates him into participation with men of varying individual traits, yet men who are willing to risk their individuality in the struggle against an immediate danger. In the revolt of fraternal action, the poet discovers that each man has a mystery of being, "une fumée," which enables him to survive despite the constant threat of destruction. This inexplicable "fumée" causes man to act, and it justifies his existence. He becomes "l'homme debout."

In *Battre tout bas,* the poet examines "l'homme debout" and finds that when man fails to risk his being he ceases to communicate with others; he returns to his illusion of isolation and estrangement. The poet must dispel this illusion, "battre tout bas," and show man the totality offered by poetic truth. The individual has an immediate means with which to end his isolation; through a sexual union with woman, he obtains the strength necessary to act, to accept the risk of exposure which characterizes "l'homme debout." Moreover, man's union with woman prepares him for an exchange of self-knowledge with others.

The theme of love is continued in *Haine du peu d'amour.* The cause of man's alienation from the world lies in his past failure to act creatively. The act of love is the human expression of the poetic act. The celebration of exchange in the present, the only time which exists for action, guarantees human continuity because the desire to reexperience the totality of union projects man into the future. The fusion of man and woman is no different from that of poet and the written word; the act of living is synthesized with the act of poetry in *Lettera amorosa.*

L'Amitié se succède brings together the first four sections by expanding the role of exchange. Union with woman leads to fraternal communion; it also enables man to understand the external world, nature. When man acts constructively toward nature, he finds that the role of exchange and its ensuing vision of totality are equally attainable in the world. Man and nature are mutually dependent for a meaningful existence; man needs nature in which to be threatened to act, and nature needs man to enrich its possibilities. Only creative activity can reconcile the individual with his world.

Creative activity is no longer restricted to the poet; it includes all men who fuse an act of living and an act of poetry. The poetization of man enables each individual to become one of *Les Frères de mémoire* and participate in artistic immortality. Any expression of art is an expression of Poetry:

> L'Art est une route qui finit en sentier, en tremplin, mais dans un champ à nous.[8]

In *Les Frères de mémoire,* Char pays hommage to those artists who have accepted the risk of creativity in order to guide man to an understanding of himself and an acceptance of his world. The efforts of these artists endure beyond death. In this section, Char includes not only well known figures (Corot, Courbet, Mozart, Giacometti, and Braque) but also the unknown caveman whose sketches on the walls of the Lascoux grotto defy time. Art, not history, expresses man's heritage of survival; the individual who acts creatively overcomes death, "se réfléchissant . . . dans le miroir de notre regard, provisoire receveur universel pour les yeux futurs."[9]

Because Poetry, that is all forms of artistic expression and representation, offers a guide for man's conduct, the poet's method serves man. *L'Ecarlate* is a concise summary of the poet's role and responsibility. Although he is aware of the baser side of man, he also knows that man's inner resistance can be channeled into a constructive revolt against his condition. The poet's "épidémie de feu"[10] combines apparent contradictions within man and his world into one harmonious reality in which each individual has unlimited possibilities to act, to become, to live creatively, poetically. Poetry gives man self-confidence in his present and hope in his potential:

> Porteront rameaux ceux dont l'endurance sait user la nuit noueuse qui précède et suit l'éclair. Leur parole

> reçoit existence du fruit intermittant qui la propage en se délacérant.[11]

Poetry not only unifies the cosmos, but also constricts and humanizes it in order that each member of the human community may understand his part in the *Vallée close,* the oneness of all existence. Poetry demands the risk of activity; man and poet alike must maintain a constant state of response in order to assault the destructive forces and construct a better present:

> . . . à la poursuite de la vie qui ne peut être encore imaginée, il y a des volontés qui frémissent, des murmures qui vont s'affronter et des enfants sains et saufs qui *découvrent.*[12]

There can be no respite from the risk of confrontation: "la poésie vit d'insomnie perpétuelle."[13] Man's essential dignity lies in his creative acts of living, which permit him to discover his integral place in the "vallée," the world. Furthermore, this "vallée" is "close" because "le poète est *combinable*";[14] he fuses absence and presence, the concrete and the abstract, the past and the future, that which is solid and that which is becoming, object and emotion, being and destruction. Without Poetry, man is isolated, and his existence is fragmented. Through Poetry, his dignity and justification for being are made manifest to him. Because he can fuse an act of living and an act of poetry, he realizes his own possibilities and participation in the unity of the cosmos. Man's reality and cosmic totality form one order of existence; "la poésie, c'est le monde à sa meilleure place."[15]

Commune présence demonstrates the unity and continuity of Poetry, the theme of the whole body of Char's work. Each text reveals one aspect of the oneness of Char's poetic universe. However, it is significant that Char's deliberate disregard for chronological organization in *Commune présence* results in a succinct presentation of the evolution of his poetics and poetry. Each of the eight sections of *Commune présence* evokes a given stage of thematic concern which characterizes Char's quest for the discovery and communication of poetic truth. Each section contains at least one text or phrase which refers to Char's historical existence.[16] Char's poetic evolution is one of resolution, which follows a deliberative course of development. One problem is overcome before another is undertaken, and each problem raised is one that has its foundation in Char's personal experience. The non-chronological structure of *Commune présence* is paradoxically chronological. Char has constructed an orderly and well-integrated work in which dates of composition and publication are obscured only to affirm the successive stages of his own poetic development.

CHAR'S PRESENT POSITION

Char's subtle confirmation of the stages of development of his poetics and poetry in *Commune présence* provides the main theme of *L'Age cassant* (1966) and *Retour amont* (1966). These two volumes summarize Char's present position. He reviews in detail his aesthetic evolution, previously presented as a successive but integrally unified whole in *Commune présence.* In this self-examination, Char finds that he has reached a time of poetic maturity, "âge cassant." The very arrival at this positive time of life imposes upon him the personal demand and the artistic summons that he reaffirm the value of the poet's risk to discover and reveal the fusion of life and poetry. *L'Age cassant* contains Char's frank admission that a reassessment of his poetry justifies his right to continue his task. *Retour amont* presents his serious reflections on his own past efforts. This reexamination leads him to a renewal of confidence in his chosen vocation and its possibilities for all men and the immediate future.

A second major characteristic which shows the interrelationship between *L'Age cassant* and *Retour amont* and further identifies them with *Commune présence* is the use of "je." It becomes increasingly more difficult to distinguish between the "je" of Char the poet and the "je" of Char the man. In *L'Age cassant* and *Retour amont,* there seem to be examples which refer to incidents and impressions of a personal or historical nature and others of a more general aspect. Prior to 1962, that is prior to the first publication of texts from *Retour amont,* Char's use of "je" had evolved to the point where it included every man involved in creative activity. In *L'Age cassant* and *Retour amont,* Char goes beyond this fusion of man and poet; indeed, no fusion is necessary. Poet and man were never opposite elements or contradictory forces to be fused into a single entity. On the contrary, Char's retrospective self-study shows that the poet and the man are one and the same. Each experience and insight known by the man are essential to the poet, and each artistic effort and discovery is significant in the growth of the man and his response to his world: ". . . j'entrai dans l'âge cassant."[17] It is Char who has attained this point in space and time; it is neither Char the man nor Char the poet; it is the harmony of these elements and experiences, personal and aesthetic, which identify René Char. Life and poetry are inseparable; if life determines poetry, Poetry determines life; it is this latter vision which Char emphasizes in these two volumes. If each man will look back upon his past, "retour amont," he will discover that the same "commune présence," the same harmony of life and poetry, reside within him. By describing the evolution of his "je," Char reveals the poet and the role of poetry in each individual.

A third significant trait which links *Commune présence* to *L'Age cassant* and *Retour amont* is found in the dates of composition and arrangement. Although *Commune présence* is an anthology which covers Char's creative development from 1934 to 1962, it also contains 12 of the 30 texts of *Retour amont.* This indicates that much of the composition of *Retour amont* coincided with the preparation of *Commune présence.* More importantly, it shows that Char had conceived of the need for such a retrospective and cogitative work before 1962, when two texts were published separately with the reference *Retour amont* inédit. It is probable that as soon as *La Parole en archipel* (specifically *Quitter* and *Au-Dessus du vent*) was completed Char began *Retour amont* as a concrete demonstration of his poetics of the totality of life. *L'Age cassant,* although most likely undertaken after the completion of *Commune présence,* was composed concurrently with *Retour amont.* In fact, *L'Age cassant* is the companion work to *Retour amont* and places the inner experience and reflections of *Retour amont* in their proper perspective.

L'Age cassant consists of 43 aphorisms which summarize Char's present aesthetic position. In this volume, he affirms the value of his poetry and his poetic direction. The tone of the work is one of authority and decisiveness; it is the voice of one who has made no concessions in his search to justify life and who has succeeded. The quest has been difficult, at times turbulent and seemingly without direction, but the end result is worthwhile.

In *L'Age cassant,* Char reiterates and reemphasizes previous themes. He warns against complacency: "Confort est crime" (**"XIV"**). He praises the threat of destruction, the lack of security, and the necessity of crispation: ". . . nous apprenons à n'être jamais consolés" (**"V"**). The poet, that is the one who has accepted the writing of poetry as a means to guide man, must make man see that he must not be patronized: "L'histoire des hommes est la longue succession des synonymes d'un même vocable. Y contredire est un devoir" (**"XXII"**). Life must be continually assaulted and confronted:

> "Je me révolte, donc je me ramifie." Ainsi devraient parler les hommes au bûcher qui élève leur rébellion.
>
> (**"XXXIV"**)

Man must be in a constant state of action: "Nul homme, à moins d'être un mort-vivant, ne peut se sentir à l'ancre en cette vie" (**"XXI"**); there is no excuse for inactivity. Moreover, man must not look to the future; he must concentrate on the present:

> Ce qui fut n'est plus. Ce qui n'est pas doit devenir. Du labyrinthe aux deux entrées jaillissent deux mains pleines d'ardeur. A défaut d'un esprit, qu'est-ce qui inspire la livide, l'atroce, ou la rougissante dispensatrice?
>
> (**"XXIII"**)

Acceptance of the risk of being in the knowledge of human fragility and mortality is essential in the construction of a better present.

In addition to a review of the main themes of his poetry, Char reviews his own course of development. He justifies his efforts to liberate poetry and man:

> Qui oserait dire que ce que nous avons détruit valait cent fois mieux que ce que nous avions rêvé et transfiguré sans relâche en murmurant aux ruines?
>
> (**"XX"**)

He evokes his childhood in Isle-sur-Sorgue: "L'aubépine en fleurs fut mon premier alphabet" (**"XIII"**). Nature and the important lessons she contains are stressed in several aphorisms, notably "Venasque."

L'Age cassant is Char's poetics of life. In his reaffirmation of the major tenets of the whole body of his work, he demonstrates the compatibility of his life and poetry. He has attained his "âge cassant" historically and aesthetically through a constant assault on life: "J'ai de naissance la respiration agressive" (**"VII"**). Others can attain this point of maturity and self-justification by accepting his lead:

> Se mettre en chemin sur ses deux pieds, et, jusqu'au soir, le presser, le reconnaître, le bien traiter ce chemin qui, en dépit de ses relais haineux, nous montre les fétus souhaits exaucés et la terre croisée des oiseaux.
>
> (**"XLIII"**)

In *L'Age cassant,* Char presents a positive and forceful resumé of his poetics. The reason for his absolute confidence in his work is found in *Retour amont.* The title of this volume reflects the more important aspects of its 30 texts. In the first place, *Retour amont* means literally the action of returning upstream, that is of movement in the direction of the source. In the second place, it refers to an inner voyage of self-examination.

Char is going back to the original source of poetry, his own formation. He is strongly influenced by his native region of Provence and the specific references to this area are numerous: Luberon, Vaudois, Mérindol, Vaucluse, Thouzon. It was here that he first felt within him the stirrings of poetry and here that he first became aware of the vital lesson of homogeneity that nature holds: "Notre figure terrestre n'est que le second tiers d'une poursuite continue, un point, amont."[18]

The term "amont" is taken from the world of nature, a significant factor in all of Char's work. It is from nature that he has learned the constructive role of destruction. When the river Thouzon overflows, it damages the surrounding area; but, when its waters recede, the result is enrichment: "Dans le creux de la ville immergée, la corne de la lune mêlait le dernier sang et le premier limon."[19] From the fig tree described in **"Devancier"** comes the knowledge of nature's cyclical process: being-nothingness-being. Char poses the rhetorical question: "La terre est quelque chose ou quelqu'un?"[20] It is;

it exists and daily surrounds man. It is composed of menacing elements and peaceful, beneficent ones; each serves the other. "Retour" means repetition and reciprocity; it refers directly to the process of recurrence in nature.

Man is a part of this homogeneous framework and he must participate fully in this world: "Dans le ciel des hommes, le pain des étoiles me sembla ténébreux et durci, mais dans leurs mains étroites je lus la joute des étoiles; j'en recueillis la sueur dorée, et par moi la terre cessa de mourir."[21] This demand for struggle and action is also inherent in the title, for it is considered more difficult to go upstream than downstream, that is to go in the opposite direction, to contradict the usual course of movement. It is a risk to act in an opposing fashion, but the risk must be accepted as necessary for a meaningful existence: "Qui a creusé le puits et hisse l'eau gisante / Risque son coeur dans l'écart de ses mains."[22] This risk of action must occur in the present: "Lâcher un passé négligeable."[23] The present is man's only time of being for acting:

> Le passé retarderait l'éclosion du présent si nos souvenirs érodés n'y sommeillaient sans cesse. Nous nous retournons sur l'un tandis que l'autre marque un élan avant de se jeter sur nous.[24]

The use of the verb "retourner" indicates that the past has a contributive role. Study of past activity explains certain problems of the present; one of these problems is liberty. Char recalls his participation in "la drôle de guerre" in **"Les Parages d'Alsace"** and in the maquis in World War II in **"Faction du muet."** While there is no immediate and easily identifiable outside threat of destruction, man's tendency towards complacency can undo in the present the successful risks and acts of the past: ". . . le loriot . . . / Au lieu de faim, périt d'amour."[25] This symbol of peace and liberty must be vigilantly and actively maintained: "Le vin de la liberté aigrit s'il n'est, à demi bu, rejeté au cep."[26] Man's inactivity can return him to adversity. Moreover, the reason that the present is better than the past is found in the courageous acts of the past. If this present is to be better, man must act now: "Revers des sources: pays d'amont, pays sans biens, hôte pelé, je roule ma chance vers vous."[27]

Char's going back in space and time in *Retour amont* is an additional example of his negation of temporality and spatiality. In his travel backwards, he is actually going forward; it is this very return to an examination of the past that renews his confidence in himself and in his work to challenge the future: "J'ai renversé le dernier mur . . ."[28] In his inner journey he finds that he carries within him the past, that he belongs to the present, but that he is also future; he is a "convergence des multiples" as is his poetry: "Des années de gisant s'éclairèrent soudain sous ce fanal vivant et altéré de nous."[29] In **"Célébrer Giacometti,"** Char emphasizes the survival of man's creative acts. His poems have hopefully helped man to understand his essential dignity of being: "Tu es une fois encore la bougie où sombrent les ténèbres autour d'un nouvel insurgé."[30]

Char's search for the discovery and possession of the knowledge of being unfolds in *Retour amont*. This serious and careful self-investigation confirms his belief in the whole body of his poetry. Scrutiny of his own formation and the course of his subsequent development justifies his work and his life. *Retour amont* offers demonstrable proof that his risk and all risk is worthwhile, that man's possibilities of fulfillment lie in his own creative acts, and, most importantly, that life and poetry spring from the same source. From this vantage point, Char acknowledges the truth of his discovery of unity:

> Le point fond. Les sources versent. Amont éclate. Et en bas le delta verdit. Le chant des frontières s'étend jusqu'au belvédère d'aval.[31]

This is the message of Char's poetics and poetry and the meaning of his life.

Notes

1. Further evidence that this sixth period is one of review and self-examination is found in Char's decision to reassess, revise where necessary, and republish his previous major collections: *Fureur et mystère* (1962), *Le Marteau sans maître* suivi de *Moulin premier* (1964), *Les Matinaux* (1964), and *Recherche de la base et du sommet* (1965).

2. *Commune présence* contains texts from *Le Marteau sans maître,* a work not included in any of Char's anthologies, particularly *Poèmes et prose choisis* (1957), before 1964.

3. A thirteenth poem, "Effacement du peuplier," was published in *L'Arc* (été 1963), p. 48.

4. *Commune présence* also contains one text, "Avec Braque, peut-être, on s'était dit . . . ," which was not previously published; this text is included, however, in the section on Georges Braque in *Alliés substantiels* in *Recherche de la base et du sommet,* 1965.

5. The exception is *Retour amont*.

6. "Commune présence," *Cette fumée qui nous portait* in *Commune présence* (Paris, 1964).

7. In *Cette fumée qui nous portait,* 15 of the 24 texts refer to World War II.

8. "Avec Braque, peut-être, on s'était dit . . . ," *Les Frères de mémoire.*

9. "Célébrer Giacometti."

10. "La Récolte injuriée," *L'Ecarlate.*

11. "Les Parages d'Alsace."

12. "Jacquemard et Julia," *Vallée close.*

13. "Les Dentelles de Montmirail."

14. Pierre Berger, "Conversation avec René Char," *La Gazette des lettres* (11 juin 1952), p. 13.

15. *Ibid.,* p. 9.

16. The most frequent references are: Névons, Sorgue, Moulin du Calavon, Thor, Vosges, Alsace, and "partisan."

17. *L'Age cassant,* I (Paris, 1966).

18. "Lenteur de l'avenir," *Retour amont* (Paris, 1966).

19. "Chérir Thouzon."

20. "Pause au château cloaque."

21. "Lutteurs."

22. "La Soif hospitalière."

23. "Traversée."

24. "Pause au château cloaque."

25. "Lied du figuier."

26. "Pause au château cloaque."

27. "Aiguevive."

28. "Lenteur de l'avenir."

29. "Le Banc d'ocre."

30. "Servante."

31. "L'Ouest derrière soi perdu."

Virginia A. LaCharité (essay date spring 1976)

SOURCE: LaCharité, Virginia A. "Beyond the Poem: René Char's *La Nuit talismanique*." *Symposium: A Quarterly Journal in Modern Foreign Literatures* 30, no. 1 (spring 1976): 14-26.

[*In the following essay, LaCharité focuses attention on Char's* La Nuit talismanique *while exploring the relationship between Char-as-poet and Char-as-painter.*]

Any examination of the whole body of Char's work reveals a variety of written modes: regular verse poems (sonnet, ballade), free verse texts, prose poems,[1] aphorisms, diary notations, prefaces, essays, introductions to art catalogues, radio scenarios, theater, and ballet. One aspect which these multiple forms of written expression have in common is Char's interest in the plastic arts, for some mention of an artist[2] is found in all of his writings. In fact, in his aphorisms and poems Char acclaims Georges de La Tour as one of his major sources. Moreover, besides the many contemporary artists mentioned in his work, Char has written numerous verse and prose poems on Georges Braque[3] as well as a lengthy essay, *Flux de l'aimant* (1965), on Joan Miró.[4] In addition, *Recherche de la base et du sommet* (1965) contains a complete section, *Alliés substantiels,* on practitioners of plastic form.

Because of his writings on artists and, more important, because of his constant references to La Tour and homages to Braque, Char seems to fall into that general category of modern poets who collaborate with painters because of the affinities between the poem and the painting. Certainly, many of Char's works have been illustrated by the leading artists of this century. His first volume of poems, *Les Cloches sur le cœur* (1928), was illustrated by Louis Serrière-Renoux, and many of his subsequent volumes and plaquettes have been accompanied by drawings by Braque, Giacometti, V. Hugo, Kandinsky, Matisse, Miró, Picabia, Picasso, and others.[5] From this point of view, Char does indeed appear as one more in the pantheon of poets whose vision is complemented by plastic representation.

However, René Char is more than vitally interested in painting and its adjuncts. He is himself a practicing painter who has illustrated some of his own poems, such as "L'Une et l'autre" (1957), "Élisabeth petite fille" (1958), "La Faux relevée" (1959), "Traverse" (1959), "Deux poèmes" (1960), "Éros suspendu" (1960), and "L'Issue" (1961). But these "minuscules" with sketches by the author are not readily available, and, until the publication of *La Nuit talismanique* in 1972, Char as a practicing artist was relatively unknown. And, simultaneously, *La Nuit talismanique* brings to a head a fundamental critical question: is there a difference between Char the poet and Char the painter? An analysis of the mechanics of meaning in his latest venture into plastic creative activity indicates a previously undetected non-verbal poetics; with *La Nuit talismanique,* the Char of day and expression in word forms gives way to Char as a poet of night and silence, for Char the painter not only complements the poet but also brings to his multiple poetic forms a new dimension beyond the poem.

The format of *La Nuit talismanique*[6] is curious. In one sense there are three parts: an introduction and two main divisions: *Faute de sommeil, l'écorce* . . . (1955-1958) and *La Nuit talismanique qui brillait dans son cercle* (1972), which is subdivided into two parts.[7] Moreover, thirty-seven drawings (a count which includes the picture on the cover) accompany these texts. However, closer examination of the format of the volume reveals the following inner arrangement: the introduction consists of three drawings, a "Frontispice," an explanatory preface on the personal crisis which occurred in 1955-1958, the reproduction in longhand of an aphorism from *Les Compagnons dans le jardin* (*La Parole en archipel,* 1962), and a revised form of the poem "Sur une nuit sans ornement"[8] with six paragraphs omitted from the 1954 version and a new one added (and dated 1972 by the author) at the end.

The section, *Faute de sommeil, l'écorce* . . . can be viewed in several ways. The simplest one is to say that the section consists of 25 drawings and 4 previously published poems: "L'Inoffensif," "L'Issue," "Nous tombons," and "Éros suspendu" (*La Parole en archipel*). Moreover, four other poems[9] are also reproduced in their entirety but superimposed on drawings; there are a total of twenty-three aphorisms, of which four are reproduced in longhand (just as all eight poems), twelve are in italics, and seven are superimposed on drawings.[10] Hence, there seem to be three forms in this section: poem, aphorism, and drawing, as well as an obvious interrelationship between the written word and the illustration. The most striking text in this respect is perhaps "L'Oiseau spirituel," originally published in *Hommage à Georges Braque* (1958). The black and light-grey sketch depicts a chain of mountains at the bottom; to the right, and going up the entire side, is an impressionistic rocky crag, cliff, or bush; fully three fourths of the drawing is cloudy sky on which is superimposed in black ink in Char's hand the text—the text becomes the bird and completes the sketch. It is neither the poem nor the picture but the conjunction of the two, wherein the poem receives its actual significance and takes on meaning before it is read. Like a painting, the poem first is grasped as a whole and the details follow this initial experience. The picture is a poem, and the poem a picture.

The same is true of the other three poems superimposed on drawings: "Obéissez à vos porcs qui existent . . ." (originally published as "Contrevenir"), "Aubépine,"[11] and "Je ne suis pas seul . . ." (whose original title is "La Grille," one of the "Neuf merci" texts). But the omission of the titles of two of these short poems, "Contrevenir" and "La Grille,"[12] gives them the appearance and quality of the aphorism. Instead of maintenance of the usual Char distinction between two formal modes, namely the poem as application of the general truth of theory which is expressed by the aphorism, we find that all previous differentiation between poem and aphorism disappears. Conversely, the same applies to the seven aphorisms which are superimposed on drawings: they emerge as poems. For example, on the top of page 32, there is a colorful drawing of a bird's nest in the branch of a leafy tree; in the nest are several eggs; handwritten, again in black ink, across the drawing is this aphorism from *Les Compagnons dans le jardin*: "Le réel quelquefois désaltère l'espérance. C'est pourquoi contre toute attente l'espérance survit" (p. 32).

With the effacement of the stylistic distinction between poem and aphorism, attention to the drawings in *Faute de sommeil, l'écorce . . .* reveals that not one of the sketches is free from the written word; all of the remaining drawings which do not have writing superimposed on them are accompanied either by an aphoristic statement or a title.[13] The drawing attracts attention first, then the words of the title or accompanying statement come into view. The first sketch in *Faute de sommeil, l'écorce . . .* (p. 19) is a red and black criss-crossing of lines; it portrays a dense thicket from which there is no relief except for a rosy globule on the left side. The accompanying statement is: "Sortir de l'Histoire se peut. En dynamitant ses souterrains. En ne lui laissant qu'un sentier pour aller." The explanation of the drawing suddenly seems evident: the dark confusion created by plurality and contradiction can be cleared up through a refusal of historical linearity and a revolt against the condition of determinism through art. Such an interpretation would be consistent with Char's notions of pulverization and crispation. But in this case, the statement, which is a means of grasping the visual drawing, is not complete without the title of the illustration: "Bulle d'air dans l'étang: le poème." The drawing is not a thicket, but a pond, and the dominant red and black coloration fades before the rosiness (hope and trace) of the poem—but this poem is not a poem in that it is not limited to verbal composition. On the contrary, it is the visual experience of the drawing in interaction with the written word which creates the poem. And, what is more, it is formless—beyond both the written word and its plastic representation.

There is an additional topographical curiosity in *Faute de sommeil, l'écorce . . .* which is germane to this discussion of the inner arrangement of the section. There are eight texts which are unaccompanied by illustrations and are written out in longhand: four poems and four aphorisms (to use a simple but no longer virtual distinction). These texts stand by themselves with the visual impact of a drawing, but it is only in retrospect, at the end of the volume, that this distinction between print and script emerges as a significant topographical and typographical characteristic.

The section entitled *La Nuit talismanique qui brillait dans son cercle* offers several striking contrasts to *Faute de sommeil, l'écorce. . . .* In the first place, the number of drawings greatly diminishes; there are a total of nine, seven in the first subsection and only two in the second. Moreover, only three of the nine are in color, as compared to 19 in color in *Faute de sommeil, l'écorce. . . .* Although each subsection begins and ends with an illustration, an arrangement which emphasizes somewhat the position of the drawings and underscores their importance, one is struck by the dominance of the printed word.

The first subsection contains one introductory prose text, "Dévalant la rocaille aux plantes écarlates," and six additional texts, whose form is closer to the aphorism than to the prose poem composed in separate paragraphs. There is inner cohesion from one paragraph or entry to the next, just as there is in *Moulin premier, Partage formel,* and *Rougeur des Matinaux.* But unlike previous aphoristic groupings, the six texts of *La Nuit I* can be read without any point of reference, for even the titles are autonomous entities. To enter these texts is comparable to entering an art gallery; it does not matter which way one begins the tour, in which room or along which side of the wall; any direction will eventually yield the artistic experience. Of course, with the printed text, grammar forces one to follow a prescribed direction: left to right, top to bottom, for unlike a painting the written text reveals its details first and its whole second. But despite the fact that the texts of *La Nuit I* physically determine our first reading, we remain at the end without a composite whole of any one text. Each detail is in itself a whole, each paragraph is a painting, and each fragment is a complete island of the archipelago of visual experience.

The only statement which accompanies a drawing in either subsection is found in *La Nuit I,* and it succinctly summarizes the esthetic operation of these texts: "Entre l'exprimé et le décrit, j'offre la fleur de sauge" (p. 66). The illustration, "La Sauge des villages," is a wax bas-relief of a salvia plant; each of the component parts of the flower is isolated as though it had been taken apart and laid out on a board or table in order to show its actual plurivalent nature. It is not a salvia plant in its usual state and is neither expressed nor described as such. It is evoked, and in its evocation it provokes the viewer into expression and description. The viewer even supplies the color, scarlet, for the bas-relief is reproduced in black and white. In this case, the illustration betrays the usual nature of painting; it does not give the whole first and then the details; rather, it presents the various parts and the whole comes afterwards, just as the printed text functions.

The same pattern occurs in the other six illustrations of *La Nuit I.* In these remaining drawings, the details strike the observer first, in direct opposition to the "wholeness" of the drawings of *Faute de sommeil, l'écorce. . . .* Even the final illustration of the subsection (p. 74) attracts the eye by its details; it is a face on a pebble which in turn is attached to a rock or piece of pipe; the face, particularly the eyes, is the first aspect seen, not the whole which sets the face in relief and gives it its rugged singularity. The reversal of the laws of perspective of plastic art are in turn reversed for those of the printed text.[14] Hence, the six texts of *La Nuit I* should be regarded as paintings which are coming into being, as Char proclaims in the introductory text: "Soudain nous surprend l'ordre de halte et le signal d'obliquer. C'est l'ouvrage" (p. 57). A new direction is indeed indicated: "C'est le peu qui est réellement tout" (p. 62).

La Nuit II consists quite simply of 13 poems in free verse and prose and only two drawings. Here we seem to return in both texts and illustrations to the original distinctions between written and plastic art that precede the publication of *La Nuit talismanique.* It seems that Char has elected the printed word over plastic form; in a sense he has, in another sense there never was any "choice" to be made; but in his plastic venture, primarily in *Faute de sommeil, l'écorce . . . ,* he retains the plastic experience that projects the printed form beyond the confines of the page. As Jean Starobinski notes, "la parole poétique cherche à transposer l'apparence visible en une nouvelle essence, puisque parler, nommer les choses tend à prolonger (sinon à achever) l'œuvre de sauvegarde qui dans le regard reste toujours inachevée et précaire."[15] Through "un peu," a detail, a trace of the whole, Char abolishes all formal distinctions of expression by showing that cause and effect are synonyms—the effect of a painting or text on its viewer is the cause. As the talismanic night prepares for the morning experience of sunlight, the effect of dark is the cause of light and the cause of dark has the effect of light. In the same way, the final illustration in *La Nuit II* (p. 93) is a talisman which concretely demonstrates the convergence of plastic and written expression. On a jet black background there is a round white pebble on which there are some red tracings and eight small black spots. The cryptic appearance of the pebble immediately leads one to an attempt at decipherment. It is a sign (the title of the illustration is "Signe sur caillou"), but of what? It is silent, as is all matter, and yet one is compelled by its invitation to find a message. Its markings hint at a starry constellation in reverse, the pure essence of the stars being captured in the impurity of stone. Time and its human form, history, are non-existent; so is space; it is impossible to establish its temporal and spatial origins. It is there in its muteness as testimony to the poetic experience which unifies the celestial and the terrestrial: "La poésie qui va nue sur ses pieds de roseau, sur ses pieds de caillou, ne se laisse réduire nulle part."[16]

But the volume, *La Nuit talismanique,* does not end with the mysterious pebble. There is an epigraph in longhand: "Hirondelle, active ménagère de la pointe des herbes, fouiller la rose, vois-tu, serait vanité des vanités" (p. 95). The abrupt reappearance of a text in script recalls the conjunction of text and illustration in *Faute de sommeil, l'écorce . . .* in the same way that the

"Signe sur caillou" conjoins earth and sky. Type is machine-made and impersonal, while script is human and individual. Through a juxtaposition of illustration, print, italics, and script, Char safeguards and projects man's creative power of magic intervention in his world in order to "écouter le récit de ce qu'il voit" (p. 70). Secondly, the face on a pebble which in turn is on a piece of crystallized gypsum on the cover of the volume provides an additional ending to the work, an ending (effect) which is also the springboard (cause) for the experience of the volume.

A key to this work is found in the dual referentials of night and silence as preparation for speech or communication. As George Steiner observes, two means of transcendence "to make language commensurate with the manifold truths of the experienced world" by which the insensate speaks and man assumes "privileged singularity in the silence of creation" are light and music.[17] Steiner goes on to name a third mode of transcendence in which language ceases and borders not on radiance and sound, but on night. This "election of silence" is what Char earlier visualizes in *Les Compagnons dans le jardin*: "Un poète doit laisser des traces de son passage, non des preuves. Seules les traces font rêver" (p. 84). In *La Nuit talismanique,* he demonstrates how the traces alone open the way to action: "Nos traces prennent langue" (p. 58). Silence is the anticipatory and necessary prelude to language: "La beauté naît du dialogue, de la rupture du silence et du regain de ce silence. Cette pierre qui t'appelle dans son passé est libre. Cela se lit aux lignes de sa bouche."[18] The mute stone in the first and last illustrations of *La Nuit talismanique* initiates the poetic dialogue which begins and ends in silence. It may indeed be seen as a talisman whose effect is its cause, whose magical powers enable man to become a poet and intervene in his world.

The pebble as illustration or text acts "comme un filtre qui s'interpose entre nous et la conscience rigide que nous avons du réel, pour que, la magie aboutie, nous soyons la Source aux yeux ouverts."[19] The return to the source of origin, silent matter, is a return to night. In the conversation between a painter (Braque) and a poet (Char), the role of night alone binds together the plastic and written approaches: "Je remonte simplement à leur nuit, à leur nudité premières. Je leur donne désir de lumière, curiosité d'ombre, avidité de construction. Ce qui importe, c'est de fonder un amour nouveau."[20] Night is the cradle of light, and without night light has no meaning. Light is dependent upon contrast with shadows, but night, unlike light, is autonomous: "La nuit ne succède qu'à elle" (p. 16). In contrast to day or light, night is endless, for it is neither limited by horizon, "toute lumière, comme toute limite" (p. 64), nor subject to time: "La lumière a un âge. La nuit n'en a pas" (p. 34). Hence, while light may take the form of a poem, night is beyond form and is poetry.

Char's very desire to insure the prestige of night and its adjunct silence leads him to find an "allié substantiel" in the seventeenth-century painter Georges de La Tour,[21] and it is in La Tour's painting, "Le Prisonnier," that Char clearly exalts silence in its transcendence of language: "Le Verbe de la femme donne naissance à l'inespéré mieux que n'importe quelle aurore. Reconnaissance à Georges de La Tour qui maîtrisa les ténèbres hitlériennes avec un dialogue d'êtres humains."[22] In the anthology, *Choix de Poèmes,* this painting is reproduced with the following comment by Char: "Cette image est la Poésie même et, mieux qu'aucun manifeste, elle dit."[23] The painting is of a woman, who, with a candle in one hand, is standing and speaking to a bearded unkempt prisoner, who, in contrast, is gaunt in appearance, half-clad, and seated on a stool. The unspoken (and unwritten) words are the ones which the poet hears: "des mots essentiels, des mots qui portent immédiatement secours."[24] Silence, "la signification qui ne s'évalue pas,"[25] initiates dialogue, just as night goes towards action: "La couleur noire renferme l'*impossible* vivant. Son champ mental est le siège de tous les attendus, de tous les paroxysmes. Son prestige escorte les poètes et prépare les hommes d'action."[26]

The unspoken dialogue of painting becomes a poetic structure which maintains the beneficence of night. As in the case of two earlier volumes,[27] a personal crisis reverses the prestige of night and the poet turns to plastic expression: "***Faute de sommeil, l'écorce*** . . . date d'un temps où la nuit qui m'avait tant servi se retira de moi . . . Je sus alors que la nuit . . . seule abreuve et irrigue, et pour m'assurer contre ce passage difficile, je rassemblai mes précaires outils" (p. 11). Not unlike the primitive man of the Lascaux grotto wall drawings, Char uses unsophisticated materials for plastic expression; he picks up what is more or less on hand, not an easel and palette, but ink, sealing wax, birch bark, feathers, knives, nails, blotters, and his drawings in appearance and texture reflect a primal quality. The dominant color is black—"couleur noire qui renferme l'*impossible* vivant"—black lends depth and solidarity to the illustrations, and the black script of texts in longhand, either superimposed on illustrations or set apart from them, commands the eye from page to page.

Hence, Char is not the poet of white space, but of black traces across the void. The illustration of the saffron sun (p. 44) which depicts an intensely orange-yellow circle against a background of the same color in a lighter hue is accompanied by a protest against light: "Beauté, est-il encore des mains discrètes pour dérober ton corps tiède à l'infection de ce charnier?" The pen and ink sketch of a black crow (p. 47) as the image of peace further meta-morphosizes light into dark ("Corbeau s'exerçant à la paix des colombes"). ***Faute de sommeil, l'écorce*** . . . significantly ends with a text in black script, "Éros suspendu," and the final phrase of this poem seems to evoke light: "au chant de ma trompette rouge" (p. 51). But this reference is not a contradiction. By the end of ***Faute de sommeil, l'écorce*** . . . , the restorative powers of night have been reconquered through the silent medium of plastic art.[28]

Thus, in the second half of the volume, ***La Nuit I*** and ***II,*** the number of illustrations dramatically decreases, as the poet sets aside his "précaires outils" and returns to the text. This return to the medium of the written word remains within the dual referentials of silence and beneficent night. Although the title of this section is ***La Nuit talismanique qui brillait dans son cercle,*** which reverses ***Faute de sommeil, l'écorce*** . . . , the title of the volume and of the first illustration (the cover) is ***La Nuit talismanique,*** a title which significantly contains no modifying clause which refers to light. Light is known only through night. Char's night, not his day, incarnates freedom ("La liberté naît, la nuit," p. 59), innocence ("Nuit au corps sans arêtes, toi seule doit être encore innocentée," p. 78), perseverance ("Riche de nuit je m'obstinais," p. 89), and the vital element of poetic existence ("Êtreau-monde est une belle œuvre d'art qui plonge ses artisans dans la nuit," p. 69). It is the silence of the ascendancy of night which is initial, rather than the rising of the morning sun: "Parole de soleil: 'Signe ce que tu éclaires, non ce que tu assombris.' Se saurait-il soleil?" (p. 70). Night protects against and prepares for the harshness of day: "Dans la nuit se tiennent nos apprentissages. . . . Fertile est la fraîcheur de cette gardienne!" (p. 15).

Char's election of silence and night is a recurrent pattern of esthetic practice with regard to his poetry as well as to the plastic arts. As he inverts form, dialogue, and light, he returns to "le cœur de l'éternel"[29]; it is not a matter of looking upward, of aspiring to the stars, but of looking downward, to earth, in order to negate space and time. The paintings of the caveman of Lascaux and Georges de La Tour reaffirm birth rather than propose completion: "Un autre âge se reconstitue tout autour, et sa plénitude est celle du premier jour, et son oeuvre, la première étincelle dans l'enfance du temps. L'avènement n'a pas de fin."[30]

Char does not pretend to raise man to the celestial through some mythological celebration; on the contrary, he seeks our self-sufficiency. The last printed text in ***La Nuit talismanique*** is entitled **"Sommeil aux Lupercales."** This Roman fertility rite in honor of the rural deity, Lupercus, was a rather licentious celebration, but the key word in the title of the poem, *sommeil,* indicates that man has no need to honor the gods, for he has the same powers over himself and his world as they are assumed to have. The final strength of the talismanic night is its conquest of determinism in all forms; creative power, the "divine" ability to intervene in the world, is the human privilege of art.

The "geste solitaire" which begins **La Nuit talismanique** becomes "solidaires," as the singular *je* of **Faute de sommeil, l'écorce** . . . moves from the aridity of sand and insomnia to the fertile *nous* of spacelessness and restorative sleep: "Nous nous suffisions, sous le trait de feu de midi, à construire, à souffrir, à copartager, à écouter palpiter notre révolte, nous allons maintenant souffrir, mais souffrir en sursaut, fondre sur la fête et croire durable le succès de ce soulèvement, en dépit de sa rapide extinction" (pp. 92-93).

In one sense, **La Nuit talismanique** may be considered linear; there is a definite progression from *je* to *nous,* insomnia to sleep, isolation to fraternity, reprinted texts to original texts, night to day, artificial to natural light, predominance of illustration to predominance of printed text. However, such a point of view denies the inherent circularity of the volume. The geometrical figure of the circle is the primary shape in the illustrations as well as in the texts. It is to the round pebble of the cover that the reader-viewer returns at the end, and only by this return to the beginning do the illustration on the cover and the volume as a whole gain their full significance. Secondly, Char begins this work encircled by night which has lost its restorative power and is countered only by the small circular light of the "électricité haïssable" (p. 12); he moves to the circle of flame cast by a candle to the full circle of the sun at noon, "feu de midi" (p. 92), which is possible because night reasserts itself as a talisman whose primary attribute is to bring happiness. Moreover, the appearance of the final line of the volume in script recalls the dominance of script over type in *Faute de sommeil, l'écorce.* . . .

Yet, implicit in the circularity of **La Nuit talismanique** is its quality of solidity. Char is often described in terms of aerianness, fugacity, and ephemeralness, but these characteristics of his work are structurally contingent upon his usage of terms of hardness, weight, and density, such as rock, mountain, earth, almond, coral, tree. These objects of opaque solidity are actually the base of his poetry, while the ephemeral ones are the summit, just as the efficaciousness of day and light is inextricably dependent upon the beneficence of night. In **La Nuit talismanique,** circle, opacity, and hardness come together and are visually objectified by the round, hard, dense stone. It might perhaps be argued that the Char image which fuses this *base et sommet* is dust: "Fils, cette nuit nos travaux de poussière / Seront visibles dans le ciel."[31] However, dust in Char's work ascends in its lightness from its hard and circular base, earth: "Voici que dans le vent brutal nos signes passagers trouvent sous l'humus, la réalité de ces poudreuses enjambées qui lèvent un printemps derrière elles" (**La Nuit talismanique,** p. 80).

The flash (*éclair*) which lights up the poet's traces endures through his magical talisman, the poem. These are the traces which "font rêver" in the same way as Hierle's portrait of Char's father transmits "dans le présent de son regard un rêve qui ne lui appartient pas mais dont nous sommes ensemble l'Écoutant" (p. 9). It is not a Proustian "lanterne magique" which lights up the fundamental unity of our reality, but a "buvard magique" (p. 67), which obscures in order that the viewer may listen to the unity he sees. Hence, "Le Serpent" (p. 36) becomes on the blotter a bird in flight. The portrait on the small hard stone on the cover of **La Nuit talismanique** immediately expresses the durable and solid fusion of man and nature, yet it is undeniably a work of art, a poem. But a poem which must go beyond its own form, just as the mysterious pebble of "Signe sur caillou" leads from earth to sky. To bring the poem and the painting into opposition is to pose the unity of poetry.

Notes

1. Within Char's three major forms of poetic expression, namely the free verse poem, prose poem, and aphorism, there are considerable differences which further demonstrate the multitude and plenitude of his written form. For example, "Le Nu perdu" (*Le Nu perdu,* 1971, p. 31) is a short, one-paragraph text in prose, while "Nous avons" (*La Parole en archipel,* 1962, pp. 143-45), consists of 13 prose sentences, each one forming a separate paragraph so that at first glance the poem appears as a group of aphorisms. The opposite occurs when one first sees "Dans la marche," which follows "Nous avons" in *La Parole en archipel* (pp. 146-47); the eight prose paragraphs of "Dans la marche" are aphorisms despite the asterisk division into three parts. The verse poems display a similar variety, from the formal metric patterns of *La Sieste blanche* (*Les Matinaux,* 1964, pp. 24-54) to the free verse forms of "Quatre fascinants" (*La Parole en archipel,* pp. 30-33) and the "calligramme" form of "Dansons aux Baronnies" (*Le Nu perdu,* p. 27).

2. I have used the term "artist" to refer to any practitioner of plastic form.

3. Char has written more on Braque than on any other painter, including Georges de La Tour. Moreover, Braque has illustrated more of Char's work than any other artist.

4. Due to the number of Char's works which Miró has illustrated and because of the quantity of pages Char has written on him, Miró occupies second place among contemporary artists in Char's work.

5. Other artists are Charbonnier, Domingo, Fernandez, Grenier, J. Hugo, Lam, Laurens, Reichak, de

Silva, Staël, Zao Wou-ki. Some works were republished as special art editions and contain illustrations by artists such as Arp, Ernst, Léger, Sima, and Villon, but these are "ornamental" editions for collectors and friends rather than textual ones. There are also several collaborative works, such as *Rêves d'encre (1945)*. In addition, P. A. Benoît has done the photography for some of Char's work. For an excellent sampling of Char's work as illustrated by others, see *Exposition René Char* (Paris: Fondation Maeght, 1971).

6. René Char, *La Nuit talismanique* (Geneva: Albert Skira, 1972). All references are to this edition unless otherwise stated.

7. In order to facilitate the discussion, I have used *La Nuit I* to refer to the first subdivision of the section entitled *La Nuit talismanique qui brillait dans son cercle* and *La Nuit II* to refer to the second subdivision.

8. René Char, *La Parole en archipel* (Paris: Gallimard, 1962).

9. *Ibid.* In the Table of Contents for *La Nuit talismanique,* only the four poems which are not accompanied by illustrations are listed as texts ("Table des matières," p. 97); the rest are listed in the "Table des illustrations" (p. 98) as sketches. Such an editorial division, however, does not negate the fact that four other complete poems are republished in *La Nuit talismanique.*

10. In counting the aphorisms, I have included the one on page 30, "Le céleste, le tué." This phrase is used as an aphoristic statement and as part of the title of the sketch on that page; it is taken from "Lèvres incorrigibles," *Recherche de la base et du sommet* (Paris: Gallimard, 1965), p. 54. The original sentence, which refers specifically to Braque's painting, "Nature morte au pigeon," is "Demeure le céleste, le tué."

11. The original title of this text in *Hommage à Georges Braque* (Geneva: Engleberts, 1958) is "Aubépine"; in *La Parole en archipel,* it appears under the title, "Ligne de foi."

12. The sketch for "Obéissez à vos porcs . . ." is given its original textual title, "Contrevenir." On the other hand, the textual title of "La Grille" is not restored to the title of the illustration.

13. A possible exception to this format is found on the bottom of page 20, where the title of the design, "La Pirogue de fruits," does not appear on the page itself.

14. The immediacy of the laws of painting is stylistically captured by Char's verbal condensation and brevity. The texts of *La Nuit I* are particularly elliptical in the suppression of articles and use of the present tense.

15. Jean Starobinski, *L'Œil vivant* (Paris: Gallimard, 1961), p. 15.

16. René Char, XI *Sur la poésie* (Paris: Gallimard, 1958).

17. George Steiner, *Language and Silence* (New York: Atheneum, 1970), pp. 33, 37, 39, 48.

18. René Char, "Le Bulletin des Baux," *Fureur et mystère* (Paris: Gallimard, 1962), p. 195.

19. René Char, *Flux de l'aimant* (Paris: Gaston Puel, 1965), pp. 24-25.

20. René Char, "Sous la verrière," *Recherche de la base et du sommet,* p. 51.

21. Georges de La Tour is first mentioned in Char's work during the war in IX, *Partage formel* (*Fureur et mystère* [Paris: Gallimard, 1962], p. 69), where La Tour is coupled with Heraclitus. It is interesting to note that the three artistic sources which Char consistently claims, namely Georges de La Tour, Heraclitus, and Arthur Rimbaud, are linked by a plastic vision. La Tour is the only one of the three who is a painter, but much has been written about Rimbaud's visual imagery (for a discussion of the impact of Rimbaud on Char, see my "The Role of Rimbaud in Char's Poetry," *PMLA* [*Publications of the Modern Language Association of America*] 88 [1974]: 57-63). In the preface to *Trois contemporains* (Paris: Gallimard, 1955), Yves Battistini states: "Héraclite . . . *voit* ce qu'il pense: les mots, pour lui, vivent et sont aussi réels que des objets, ils en ont toutes les qualités sensibles" (p. 15); it was for the original edition of Battistini's translation of Heraclitus (Paris: Cahiers d'Art, 1948) that Char wrote "Héraclite d'Ephèse," *Recherche de la base et du sommet,* pp. 90-2. Moreover, in *Language and Silence,* George Steiner credits Heraclitus as the first writer to elect silence (p. 48).

22. René Char, 178, *Feuillet d'Hypnos* in *Fureur et mystère,* p. 139. It is important to note that the earliest illustration in *La Nuit talismanique* dates from 1944 and is entitled "La Lune d'Hypnos" (p. 57), a clear indication of a relationship between *La Nuit talismanique* and Char's wartime discovery of the expressivity of nonverbal forms. Certainly, Char was sensitive to plastic art prior to the war; his two earliest poems on painters, "Une Italienne de Corot" and "Courbet: Les Casseurs de cailloux" were published in *Dehors la nuit est gouvernée* (Paris: G. L. M., 1938), and his first prefaces to art catalogues also appeared before the war years. However, it is not until after 1945 that Char's interest in the plastic arts emerges as a major aspect of his poetics. *Art bref* (1950) is his first collection of prefaces to art catalogues, which

were later grouped with other critically interpretative art commentaries in *Alliés substantiels* (*Recherche de la base et du sommet,* 1955 and 1965). His association with Georges Braque began in 1947 with *La Conjuration,* which along with *Le Soleil des eaux* (1949), *Fête des arbres et du chasseur* (1949), *Claire* (1949), *L'Homme qui marchait dans un rayon de soleil* (1949), and *L'Abominable homme des neiges* (1956) represent his experiments with "theater" and more visual forms of expression. During these same years, most of his works are accompanied by sketches, and he also begins to include his own designs; the works published between 1947 and 1960 are particularly rich in the drawings which accompany them.

23. René Char, *Choix de Poèmes* (Mendoza, Argentina: D'Accurzio, 1953). La Tour's "Le Prisonnier" is also evoked in the subtitle, "L'Emmuré," of "Gravité" (*Fureur et mystère,* pp. 56-7); this subtitle was not added to the text until it was moved from the 1938 *Dehors la nuit est gouvernée* edition to the 1945 volume of *Seuls demeurent,* that is, it is related to Char's wartime experience.

24. René Char, 178, *Feuillets d'Hypnos,* p. 138.

25. Char, 16, *Feuillets d'Hypnos,* p. 95.

26. Char, 229, *Feuillets d'Hypnos,* p. 153.

27. *Dehors la nuit est gouvernée* and *Feuillets d'Hypnos.*

28. The eight poems and over one-third of the aphorisms in *Faute de sommeil, l'écorce . . .* are not original to *La Nuit talismanique* and most can be found in *La Parole en archipel.* On the other hand, all of the texts of *La Nuit I and II* are original, including the final epigraph in longhand, which is the only text in script which is original to this volume.

29. René Char, "A la santé du serpent," *Fureur et mystère,* p. 208.

30. René Char, *Flux de l'aimant,* p. 11.

31. René Char, "Courbet: Les Casseurs de cailloux," *Dehors la nuit est gouvernée.* See also "Commune présence," *Le Marteau sans maître suivi de Moulin premier* (Paris: José Corti, 1963), p. 146: "Essaime ta poussière / Nul ne décèlera votre union."

Mary Ann Caws (essay date 1977)

SOURCE: Caws, Mary Ann. "Poetics and Morality." In *René Char,* pp. 13-34. Boston, Mass.: Twayne Publishers, 1977.

[*In the following essay, Caws discusses expressions of morality in Char's poetry.*]

I Life and Early Text

In his preface to *La Nuit talismanique* (*Talismanic Night*) Char describes the psychological atmosphere of his childhood, presenting an unforgettable picture of his parents: "My father had courteous, shining eyes, good and never possessive. . . . My mother seemed to touch everything and to reach nothing, at once busy, indolent, and sure of herself. The strong lines of their contrasting natures clashed with each other, their intersection catching fire." (*La Nuit talismanique,* p. 9)[1] The ten year old saw his father returning more and more exhausted each evening from the family plaster factory: he died after a long illness, in which "a forest of oaks was burned in the fireplace." From the powerful effect of this page, one gesture stands out: the father laying his hand on the boy's shoulder with a weight which seems to carry into the present. And in one portrait by Hierlé, the father's look seems to show a similar extension into the time of our reading: Char points out "in the present of his gaze a dream which is not his alone, but whose listener we are together" (*NT* [*La Nuit talismanique*], 9).

I shall sketch rapidly the few lines of Char's history which are essential, and of which each reader is himself a listener, together now with the poet. Then the poetry takes its own route with its own marked and unmarked points, according to an interior dynamics of its own, in the spirit of Char's definition:

> Le poème est l'amour réalisé du désir demeuré désir.
> The poem is the fulfilled love of desire as it remains desire.
>
> (*Sur la poésie,* p. 10)[2]

For enthusiasts of biographical and geographical anecdote, there is no dearth of detail. For example, the poem **"Jouvence des Névons"** recounts the poet's childhood in a deserted village where the men are away at war. "The child, a stream, and a rebellious nature converge in one single being, modified according to the years. It shines and fades by turn, according to the event, on the horizon's steps" (*Les Matinaux* [*The Matinals*], 1st ed.)[3] Accompanying the scene, a cricket is still and yet all the more present for its stillness. The tone of that one poem could be considered characteristic of much of Char's writing, whether it deals with childhood, adolescence, manhood, or an advancing age: personal and vaguely mysterious, placed in a distant time and yet informing the moment of writing and all the subsequent moments of reading.

From the next period comes the collection *Arsenal,* of major importance for the understanding of the poet's future work. A copy of the collection was given to Eluard,[4] whose enthusiasm caused him to present Char to the Surrealist group, with which Char was associated from 1930-1934, the period of *Artine* and the poems in

Abondance viendra (*Abundance Will Come*), among others. From this arsenal, where sufficient weapons for all future skirmishes are stored, we might consider just the poem **"Voici"** (**"Here Is"**) as an example of the possible interior linking of life and text.

> Voici l'écumeur de mémoire
> Le vapeur des flaques mineures
> Entouré de linges fumants
> Etoile rose et rose blanche
>
> O caresses savantes, ô lèvres inutiles!
>
> Here is memory's plunderer
> The mist of minor pools
> Surrounded by steaming linen
> Rose star and white rose
>
> Oh knowing caresses, oh useless lips!
>
> (*Le Marteau sans maître* [*The Hammer with No Master*],
> p. 30)[5]

If we compare this text with a far longer one from *Le Tombeau des secrets* (*The Tomb of Secrets*) (an early volume, some of whose few poems are taken up and revised in *Arsenal*), the difference is startling, seemingly indicative of a sharp reduction in sentimentality. This particular development will determine the course of much of Char's writing and of his life, in both of which the containing force of the personality prevents any prolonged lapse into self-pity or any tendency to shed *lacrimae rerum* either from nostalgia or from a lucid observation of the world around. As is true of Char's method in general—that "enlèvement-embellissement" or removing-in-order-to-beautify of which one could be tempted to say too much, thus ruining the point—the details of the original anecdote drop away, leaving only a condensed remainder, all the more forceful for the brevity of its trace.

Compare these lines from the longer, unpublished first version (twenty-three lines in all), called **"Flexibilité de l'oubli"** (**"Flexibility of Forgetfulness"**), which include the starting point for the poem quoted above:

> Sans mille bras pour plonger dans les pores
> Tâter le suc de la douleur
> O souvenir aigu des soirs sans riposte
> Sans le claquement d'un adieu
> Chargé à blanc de repentir
>
> Sans l'écumeur de mémoire
> Avide de ce qu'il ne comprend pas
> Vorace de ce qu'il redoute
>
> . . . . .
>
> Boule élastique ce coeur
> Percé de flaques mamelles
> Poches soudées sans espoir de déséquilibre
>
> Les putains aux portes cochères
> Eteignent leurs ombres

> Se lancent leurs linges fumants
> Etoile rose et rose blanche
> Candélâbres en mains les étreignent
> En caresses savantes
> O lèvres inutiles
>
> . . . . .
>
> Without a thousand arms to dive into the pores
> To try the sap of pain
> Oh sharp memory of evenings with no retort
> Without the slam of a farewell
> Loaded with the blanks of repentance
>
> Without the plunderer of memory
> Avid for what he does not understand
> Voracious for what he fears
>
> . . . . .
>
> Elastic ball this heart
> Pierced with breasts aslack
> Pockets soldered with no hope of unbalance
>
> The whores at gateways
> Extinguish their shadows
> Hurl at one another their steaming linen
> Rose star and white rose
> Candlesticks in hand embrace them
> With knowing caresses
> Oh useless lips
>
> . . . . .

As the poem continues, a dead woman's body appears at each ring of the doorbell: all these elements, the picturesque (girls squabbling), the sensual (caresses of meadows, of undergarments), and the sentimental (repentance, farewells, nostalgia in the evening) together with grotesque deformations (the rubber ball and the breasts) disappear to leave only the quintessence of the experience. The presentation, marked as such by the self-reflecting title: **"Voici,"** gives in fact only that which is sufficiently enduring as a résumé of the past moments: the knowing caresses are generalized beyond the grasp of their original donors, and the uselessness now stretches beyond the domain of the lips alone to imply, or so it would appear, the final futility of language itself.

Not just an example of textual condensation, this definitive alteration can also be seen as a model of the poetic and personal development Char manifests throughout his more than fifty years of poetic production. In each period the raw matter of the future text is observed, explored, and condensed.

Artine, a long prose poem on dream, and the densely beautiful prose poems of *Abondance viendra* date from Char's Surrealist period, when he was particularly close to Breton and to Eluard: the language of these poems somewhat resembles in image and tone many poems of other Surrealists, for instance, the violent refusal of commonplace diction, and the will to attack, which characterize even the title *Le Marteau sans maître,* relieved by an occasional lyric gentleness. Furthermore, the crystal transparency of Artine, who is also a river, and all the alchemical themes are familiar to the readers of Surrealism. Char's affection and companionship are deep, once he has chosen his friends, and it cannot have been easy for him to make a formal break with some of his Surrealist companions—but individual conscience and conscious individual work had finally to triumph, for him, over collective production, and commitment even over friendship. In a letter of 1963, he explains: "Because what we were seeking was not discoverable by many, because the life of the mind, a single-strand life, contrary to that of the heart, is only fascinated—in a poetic temptation—by an unapproachable object which shatters in fragments when, having overcome the distance, we are about to grasp it" (*Recherche de la base et du sommet* [*Search for the Base and the Summit*], p. 45).[6]

But the "common" or "shared" presence with other poets and other friends which is described in **"Commune présence,"** the final poem of *Le Marteau sans maître,* makes it clear that the new urgency is highly individual even though the concern is more general:

> Tu es pressé d'écrire
> Comme si tu étais en retard sur la vie
> S'il en est ainsi fais cortège à tes sources
> Hâte-toi
> Hâte-toi de transmettre
> Ta part de merveilleux de rébellion de bienfaisance
> Effectivement tu es en retard sur la vie
> La vie inexprimable
> La seule en fin de compte à laquelle tu acceptes de
>   t'unir
> Celle qui t'est refusée chaque jour par les êtres et par
>   les choses
> Dont tu obtiens péniblement de-ci de-là quelques frag-
>   ments décharnés
> Au bout de combats sans merci

. . . . .

> You are in a rush to write
> As if you were of a slower pace than life
> If this be so accompany your sources
> Hasten
> Hasten to transmit
> Your portion of wonder rebellion good-will
> In truth you are behind in life
> Life inexpressible
> The only one you accept at last to join with
> Alone refused you every day by beings and by things
> Whence you take laboriously here and there a few
>   fleshless fragments
> After implacable struggles

. . . . .

(*MM* [*Le Marteau sans maître*], 145)

Aware now of his individual task—the neighborly and collective venture of poetry—Char finds even in the center of this common presence, an uncommon singularity: the poet elected both by his peers and by the gods

is not unaware of his election.[7] The necessity of writing and of acting, the choice and the moral urgency combined can be said to involve the man as poet whose presence is unique as well as dominant.

Now the first part of the poem **"Commune présence"** begins with an illumination quite different from the hermetic and alchemical gleam of the earlier poems— included in *Le Marteau sans maître* for example, in *Abondance viendra.* The light is rather open than veiled; in fact, the sun appears as a messenger herald-ing the coming day: "Eclaireur comme tu surviens tard" ("Light-bearer how late you come"). This poem, with its sense of urgency of a mission felt and accepted, can be seen to play the same role for what we might call the first period of Char's poetic life as does the poem **"A***,"** written in 1953, for another period.

The "common presence" of the title indicates not only the now renewed present of the poet in the world, and the presence of the poet in the text he shares with us, into which the record of his life is intricately interwoven, but again the exterior companionship developing coextensively with the inner experience—as if, in fact, exterior and interior presence were to depend on each other. And yet as the poem ends, the reader is conscious that this common presence is not to be fully shared after all, that there will always remain a part of mystery: "Nul ne décelera votre union" ("None will divulge your union"). Suddenly the question arises as to what other sort of presence Char may have had in mind, what other union, whose outline we are only permitted to glimpse. This very strong sense of withdrawal is constant in Char's work, where reticence finally prevails over self-expression. As he phrases it elsewhere, the poem is the only refuge of privacy for his "too exposed face." Thus a poetry opening onto a space common to all although set apart, closed to any facile gaze, may not reveal the secret "union" of the poet, while nevertheless taking its strength from that union.

II SHARED PRESENCE

A poet's moral position may often seem to bear little relation to his work. Discussions of commitment, of political attitude are of value only in specific cases and rarely insofar as concerns the text itself. It goes without saying, furthermore, that the critic's own position can unconsciously influence his attitude, try as he may to prevent any leakage between personal belief and profes-sional analysis. From an outsider's point of view, the comments may thus invalidate themselves. For example, Michel Carrouges, a devout Catholic, author of one of the best books on Breton and Surrealism,[8] was finally attacked by the Surrealists for venturing to speak of them before an audience of Catholic intellectuals: his "prejudice" may not seem obvious in his remarks, but the Surrealists' viewpoint is consistent with their theory.

In general, I would heartily disagree with the narrow-minded position that would have only churchgoers speak of Claudel, only Marxists speak of Marx, and only practicing Surrealists speak of Surrealism—to say nothing of only French critics writing on French poets. In the writing on René Char, a greater openness than usual is felt. For example in the large volume devoted to him by *Les Cahiers de L'Herne,* the testimonies of his fellow *résistants* in the Vaucluse are found side by side with those of his fellow poets and writers, and an assortment of critics and students of his works, French and non-French,[9] of widely differing attitudes.

Poetics is taken here in its widest sense, that of *poiein,* "to make," so that the working out of a theory should be valid not just for the writing of poems but for living and acting in general. Much the same extension must be applied to all of Char's statements, which are at once directed toward an individual self—privileged because responsible—and a world of unique beings, themselves chosen by the simple choice they have made to read these formulations and to welcome this kind of poetics. Here, poetry is redefined:

> Poésie, la vie future à l'intérieur de l'homme requali-
> fié.
> [Poetry, future life within requalified man.]
>
> (*SP* [*Sur la poésie*], 10)

In Char's view, a poem is never intended as an ornament to living but is meant to function within its universe. In each successive volume, a few statements on poetry are gathered into a series, so that the definitions accumulate. Elsewhere, we have compared the style of these aphorisms to the *éclats* or flashes of a luminous whole, furnishing an uneven illumination. What is true of the successive groups of aphorisms on poetry we shall be discussing is true of all the series of brief statements making up what we think of as Char's poetics. Of this aphoristic form compared by Jean Starobinski to the Baudelairean *Fusées,* spurts of poetic prose,[10] Char says that it is like a button suited to a buttonhole: if it fits, it fits exactly. Or that it is like an answer to an emptiness, individual each time; and finally, that it is like a tiny morsel of bread hardened in the pocket: it lasts, and it nourishes, if it responds exactly to the hunger one has. Somehow, the aphorisms in general seem to answer needs both poetic and moral; each statement made for poetics holds also for morality, hence the title of the present chapter.

The aesthetic judgments Char makes are usually in favor of a contemporary version of the golden mean, to be more closely identified with perfect measure than with puritanical restraint: he terms the process, as we have already seen, an aesthetic trimming ("enlèvement-embellissement") and compares it to a gardener's task, or to that of a tree pruner. The branch removed permits

the others a greater range; the limited number of sprigs on a plant augments their chances. Char's own work, as revealed in his manuscripts, makes this process clear and proves the aesthetic point. When reduced in number from their original profusion, the images lose their possibly "precious" tinge to take on a more necessary character. Writing becomes a moral work also, not merely in its message but in its difficult stylistic being.

The first statement of a consistent poetics appears in **Moulin premier** (*First Mill*), appended to **Le Marteau sans maître,** and so entitled perhaps because it is the first harvest of wheat which must then be processed into flour. It is noticeable that the image includes a human construction, whereas the previous **Premières alluvions** (*First Alluvia*) had not. Here in **Moulin premier,** even if under a different metaphor, the alluvia are gathered up once more, and the harvest yields grains of different sizes and usefulness. Of these, three, which can be extracted and compared, are of particular importance to us and should be considered before moving on to the complete series.

> LXIII. We are sure that a poem *functions* when its formula is found to work, and this is so, in spite of the unknown quality of its dependencies.
>
> LXV. That at any demand a poem can efficiently, as a whole as in fragments, throughout its course, *be confirmed,* that is, match its divagations, proves to me its ineffable reality. . . .
>
> LXVI. That at any demand a poem must necessarily *be proved* implies for me the episodic moment of its reality.

So the poem must be seen as coherent: here we think of Char's later statements on the essential order of its parts, whatever their apparent freedom of disposition. Char will call this an "insurgent order." How does the poem express itself—to the outside, or only to the inner vision? The successive statements answer this only half-rhetorical question by successive clarification and differentiation, since poem and poetics must adapt themselves, as surely as the poet himself, to circumstance. "You must be the man of rain and the child of fine weather" (**MM,** 140). It is a matter of knowing how to adjust.

In fact, **Moulin premier** opens with the lines of a long prose-like sentence with the typographical form of verse, on the subject of a "productive knowledge of the Real." There we can discern the inexorable geological ordering of certain eccentric island-like formations which obscure the voluptuousness of love, and certain skeletons hinting at ancient epochs of species, geographically scattered, which explains the word play on "espaces/espèces." The latter is reminiscent of other word plays such as the "sleep washing the placers" in the poem **"Croesus"** in the **Poèmes militants** of 1932:

the original expression "placer" being at once the ore deposits in a stream (which explains the title figure, Croesus, whom we associate with gold) and the Spanish word for pleasure. Thus sleep is regarded as the bringer of riches and the purifier of carnal pleasures.

The serious point in this opening text is that the knowledge must be collectively satisfying; nevertheless, the text ends with the poet's individual invocation of light as the other member, with him, of a couple to be granted the experience of reality. This opening poem joins immediately with the first paragraph of the prose maxims which follow: "An inhabitant of globes. The childish ambition of the poet is to become a living being of space. Backward from his own destination" (*MM*, 123). This theme, already present in 1934, becomes, or remains, a major element in the subsequent works, wherein Char will compare himself to a meteor falling to earth, then reabsorbed in the atmosphere as a constellation, of Orion or of Orpheus returned to the heavens: the end of *Le Nu perdu* (*Nakedness Lost*) predicts the Orion poems of *Aromates chasseurs*[11] for its texts are clearly arranged like the stars in that constellation. As a first step in the poetic operation, it is essential to accept, even to welcome, a certain fragmentation without permitting this separation of parts to destroy one's own personality. On the metaphoric level, the operation is clear: the invasion of space must be submitted to, as traditionally, the logical coherence of the personality can be invaded by moments of inspiration, as a considered series of acts can be penetrated by a spontaneous flash. For a visual equivalent, we might consider Hugo's celebrated image of the beggar's cloak riddled with holes, through which the stars shine. That is, against—or through—the fabric black like night, comes an intermittent illumination, all the more precious for its contrast with the obscure. Thus the regular is made valuable by the irregular, the constant by the inconstant, and dark by light, in a reversal of expectation closely related by its tone and its meaning to Mallarmé's themes of shipwreck, constellation, and poem. The image of the cloak with holes becomes rich or diamantine, as absence changes to presence, so that the metaphor of reversal has a material and a moral component. In Char's maxim, to "suffer" or permit an invasion such as that of space is to take an active role in one's own deconstruction and reconstruction, while, on the other hand, it is to oppose one's own destruction. Thus the initially active desire is altered to a passive acceptance before a final return to a strongly active mode with a warning attached. The dialectical development is manifest even in the grammar: ambition de devenir → subir → "se démanteler sans se détruire" (ambition to become → to suffer → to take oneself apart without destroying oneself).

If I have gone into such lengthy detail over one maxim, unambiguous in appearance, it is for at least two

reasons. First, the systematic positive reevaluation of certain functions which might ordinarily be considered negative ones is characteristic of Char's way of seeing; and secondly, as stated above, the theme itself is stressed in Char's future work. A coherent center is implied within these statements in which, as Char points out in the next part of the maxims, "to impose itself all the more, logic takes on the traits of the absurd" (*MM*, 124).

On the formal level, appropriately, the seventy prose fragments of *Moulin premier* themselves resemble the taking apart of the self, the white of the page dividing the verbal matter into segments; the separate statements show up as black holes on a white page or then as partial illuminations against an emptiness. The reversal is akin to the one already suggested in affinity with the poetry of Mallarmé: a constellation interpreted one way or the other, page and sky, writing and stars.[12] Elsewhere, we read: "La quantité de fragments me déchire" ("The quantity of fragments tears me apart"), and we cannot tell whether the poet or the poem is speaking. In either case this negative is more positive than it might seem.

"L'étincelle dépose" ("The spark deposits"). So reads one of the next fragments. The poet can declare martial law, if he so chooses, electrifying or magnetizing the fields of words, like Breton's and Soupault's *Champs magnétiques* (*Magnetic Fields*), as if sending to battle the warring partners, the opposition of substance and space, gleam and emptiness, the dark of ink and the white of the page, reflection and, most important, intuition, which wins out by arousing all the echoes and resonances possible, giving birth to all the possible forms of poetry. The referential background is particularly dense here, even more so than in the later statements on poetry. The "occult properties of phosphorus" and the opaque waters, the "transfusion of the sun" and the coffin's "fecundation," various male and female images, all these betray the poet's fascination with alchemy, while the image of the phoenix nourished on cinders is related to the traditional fire burning the imagination: "the poet needs more to be 'passionate' than to be taught" (*MM*, 132).

Even after Char's Surrealist period, he will continue to prize the imagination above all else for its total grasp of what may seem only passing but which nevertheless conveys the eternal, as opposed to pedestrian reason and its prudence: "To the despair of reason, the poet never knows how to 'return home . . .'" (*MM*, 133). He dwells often in the moment, as if it were an interior place, and the choice of that place over an external one is not without risk, not only of the miscomprehension of others, but also of his own disappointment. For the moment passes also with all other matter into the mill, to be prepared for the eventual nourishment of the poet and of his companions. Thus the image of the "poème pulvérisé," the poem ground into powder for a future utilization.

III REFUSAL

In 1942, Char ("le capitaine Alexandre") was in charge of the Resistance movement in the Basses-Alpes region in southern France. The records and the testimonies of this period reveal the intense courage of the men participating at once in the "furor and mystery" of the epoch, developing throughout a series of experiences often recounted.[13] More significantly for us, the poet's wartime notebook, **Feuillets d'Hypnos,**[14] describes the state of mind as well as of the surrounding universe, interior and exterior conditions. The tone is now and again bitter ("infernal duties"), quietly despairing ("We wander near well-rims from which the wells have been removed" [**FM, Fureur et mystère,** 110]), and vigorously determined ("Belong to the leap. Don't belong to the banquet, its epilogue" [**FM,** 138]).

Above all, the uncompromising nature of the man stands out, somewhat in the same vein as Breton's "Haughty Confession": "Absolutely incapable of accepting the fate meted out to me . . . I am careful not to adapt my own existence to the derisive conditions of all existence *here.*"[15] Char's equally firm statements have a double resonance: "I shall write no poem of acquiescence" (**FM,** 114). The tone carries through to a later text, of a parallel brevity, called **"Contrevenir"** (**"Contravening"**): "Nous restons gens d'inclémence" ("We remain men for inclemency.") (**LM** [**Les Matinaux**] 201). Whether it be the inclement weather of the maquis or the vicissitudes of a poet's life lived in large part against the current of the Parisian mainstream, the statement remains a true description of the poet himself: René Char, who claims even now the position of a marginal poet, found in the climate of the Resistance his definitive tone.

The poems of 1938 to 1944, grouped under the title, **Seuls demeurent** (*There Remain Only . . .*) already a title of monumental isolation, show a profound realization of what will from now on be seen as poetic morality. Initially this is developed against the background of a terrible experience suffered through: "On the ridge of our bitterness, the dawn of consciousness advances and lays down its silt" (**FM,** 19). Spain's tragedy too is part of the bitter acquisition of experience. "Punishment! Punishment!" As the sensibility of a whole generation is developed during these years, so is a companionship based on continuing collective struggle. "I've traveled to exhaustion" (**FM,** 45), explains Char in **"Vivre avec de tels hommes"** (**"To Live With such Men"**), and he speaks not just for his own wartime experience but for what was to come after. Just so, the ending of another

prose poem—called by a title which seems to set us at some distance from an understanding of the text: **"Ne s'entend pas"** (**"Unheard"**)—applies to much of the future work: **"No renunciation"** (**FM,** 42). Such a tone chooses to annihilate, for the time it lasts, the line commonly thought to hold between text and life: this is not a literary statement, but rather, a moral declaration.

But the **"Refusal Song"** which marks the "Début du partisan," or the beginning of a committed personality and action, sketches the outline of what appears to be a retreat from that common presence. "The poet has returned for a long span of years into the naught of the father. Do not call him, all you who love him. . . . He who worked suffering into bread is not visible in his glowing lethargy" (**FM,** 48). It is impossible to consider the maquis of the Resistance as only a place of political commitment, where necessary action is carried out. How not to see it also as an image of a necessary removal from the too open sight as in the passage already quoted: "You are, poem, the repository of darkness on my too exposed face." Moreover, it forms a parallel to Char's conception of poetry itself. A place committed and yet apart, where action and concealment depend on one another and where the difficulty of the moment seems to strengthen the entire duration of the work: it would be hard to find a better definition of the poem as Char conceives of it. This is a privileged example of the exterior and interior geography to be discussed later.

As the **"Refusal Song"** ends, a collective performance is once more envisaged, at the instant of liberation: the poet calls again for a "shared presence," stressing the term, lest we take it too lightly as a mere physical manifestation. From now on, creative privacy joins awareness of number; individual refusal and choice reinforce general commitment. The opinions of Char the partisan and of Char the poet are mutually strengthening.

Poetry consists of action, as Rimbaud said: it consists of judgment also, for poetry is neither to be bought nor facilitated. Among Char's comrades, all of them men destined to face inclemency, the poet, like his poem, endures at once "solitary and multiple," keeping his margin about him and yet joining with others. His paradoxical temperament is apparent here as elsewhere, visible in substance and in style: "We are torn between the avidity of knowing and the despair of having known" (**FM,** 96). Or again, "Wed and do not wed your house" (**FM,** 94), a statement reminiscent of the tragic poem called **"The Swift,"** the bird who circles about the house and yet is not identified with it, in a flight mediating between the sky's freedom and the inner intimacy. He is felled, like the human heart, for even the least imprisoned among us may be a prisoner to something, if only to doubt: "Doubt is at the origin of all greatness. Historical injustice wears itself out trying not to mention it. That doubt is genius" (*FM*, 140). But here the poet is careful to distinguish between the genius of doubt and the weakness of uncertainty, which he defines as a wearing away of the senses. Doubt seems to imply for him strength and youth, whereas uncertainty is on the side of the jaded, of that which lingers too long.

And befitting that viewpoint on the importance of time, the best poem will be brief, as are the excerpts in this journal, for practical reasons which luckily coincide with stylistic ones. "I write briefly. I can scarcely *absent myself* for long." Poetry is rapidity of perception—another lesson from Rimbaud—and a complete absence of that paralysis which overtakes the too self-conscious writer. "Poetry is, of all clear waters, the least likely to linger at the reflection of its bridges," we read in *A la santé du serpent* (*Here's to the Snake*). The tone prepares such images as that of the meteor appearing in the **"Météore du 13 août"** (**"Meteor of August 13"**) and thereafter throughout Char's work. The path of the meteor has a brilliance and an ephemeral quality which makes it an appropriate representation, in its passing, of the poet's own version of his being: "La voie d'or du météore" ("The meteor's golden path") can also be read, by a slight shift, as "la voix d'or" ("the golden voice"). The metaphors are of brightness and speed: "At the second when you appeared my heart had the whole sky to brighten it. It was noon by my poem" (*FM*, 202). Thus, in *Feuillets d'Hypnos* (*Leaves of Hypnos*), the poet observes, records, and preserves the "infinite faces of the living," all the while protesting against injustice and capitulation. Political attitude and poetics are meant to merge. The stance taken is to be Char's most familiar one: obstinate, concerned, standing against a time of mediocrity.

In this period, **Partage formel** (*Formal Division*) is a deeply optimistic ars poetica ("The poet answers each crumbling of proofs by a volley of future" [*FM*, 78]), which balances *Feuillets d'Hypnos,* the journal of the embattled poet who writes only briefly, because he does not care to *"absent himself"* for long (*FM*, 94). In like manner, the inner and the outer works find no definite dividing line but rather a juncture. In René Char's unbending attention to the combined problems of poetics and morality, there dominates, from the beginning, his refusal of an easy renown: to claim a special monumental position because of one's past heroic acts would be as reprehensible as taking a facile road when the other, more arduous, is there for the choosing. The description attached in 1948 to the collection *Fureur et mystère* (*Furor and Mystery*) begins with the words "The poet, as we know, combines lack and excess, goal and past history. Whence the insolvency of his poems. He is in malediction, that is to say, he takes on perpetual and renascent perils, just as surely as he refuses, with

his eyes open, what others accept with theirs closed: the profit of being a poet" (*RBS* [*Recherche de la base et du sommet*] 35). Poems, he continues, cannot exist without provocation, nor poets without watchfulness, both moral and aesthetic. "The poet is the part of a man stubbornly opposed to calculated projects." He may not even consent to a poetic martyrdom, will not die necessarily "on the barricade chosen for him."

The drastic metaphor must not blind us to the real position taken here, lest it be thought that we would situate René Char in one stance, reducing poetic ambiguity. This is a tricky point, and a sensitive one, which bears thinking about. For, reading Char's aphorisms, many of which have a lofty resonance, we might be tempted to consider the poet only in his heroic guise, for instance, in the position of a man tied to his past, filled now with exactly the same fury and searching for exactly the same mystery as formerly, devoted to exactly the same combination of the two: we might thus take the *Fureur* and the *Mystère* to be eternal entities, in eternally lasting proportions. Witness a critic writing on Char's aphoristic style recently: he lamented the poet's attachment to his past at the price of his present.[16] Which is to say that he disregarded—or then found that Char disregarded—the other half of the maxim just quoted about the poet who combines his past with his future goal. We must, of course, permit René Char, insofar as he wishes it, to give the precise weight he chooses to his wartime past. The effect on him was great and the memory has proved ineradicable. Having to abandon all nuance, every shade of hesitation in the face of an actual decision, this necessity changed him forever: ". . . I want never to forget that I was forced to become—for how long?—a monster of justice and of intolerance, a simplifier, shut off and enclosed, an arctic personage without interest in the fate of anyone who isn't leagued with him to down the dogs of hell" (*RBS,* 10). But then, afterward, the other seasons replaced that limit-situation, that crisis which, while unforgettable, was not to be resurrected.

"After the conflagration, we believe in effacing its marks, walling up the labyrinth. An exceptional climate cannot be prolonged" (*RBS,* 15). When Char refused to testify at the trials of war criminals, he proved himself to have mastered that "generosity in spite of oneself" (*RBS,* 14) that he wanted to acquire. And here he gives us the example of a friend who, the evening after returning from two years in a concentration camp, preferred walking quietly with his dog to denouncing the man who had reported him. This man is plainly one of the few beings the poet would always choose to accompany him, among his multitude of friends, present and absent. And this statement, written as a "Note to Francis Curel," is of such capital importance for Char's moral position—toward poetry as toward life—that we include it in its entirety here. He considers it, in fact, to be "the most complete statement and comment" upon his poetry, and calls it a letter "in which I have defined, at a crucial moment of my existence, my relation to action, to society, and above all, to poetry, a text furthermore addressed to a man who accompanied my youth, and who survived many years in a German concentration camp" (Letter to author, October 23, 1975).

Note to Francis Curel (1958)

In the months which followed the Liberation, I tried to put some order into my ways of seeing and feeling which—against my will—a little blood had spotted, and I strove to separate the ashes from the hearthstone of my heart. Like the Ascian, I sought the shade and reinstated that memory which was anterior to me. Refusal to sit in the Court of Justice, to accuse my fellow man in the daily dialogue as it was resumed, a reaffirmed decision to oppose lucidity to well-being, a natural state to honors, those evil mushrooms proliferating in the crevices of drought and in corners tainted after the first spattering of rain. The man who has known and dealt violent death detests the agony of the prisoner. Better by far a certain depth of earth, fallen in the fray. Action, in its preliminaries and its consequences, had taught me that innocence can, mysteriously, pierce through almost everywhere: innocence deluded, innocence unknowing by definition. I am not holding out these attitudes as exemplary. I was simply afraid of being mistaken. Yesterday's fanatics, those creators of a new type of "continuous murderer," still nauseated me beyond all possibility of punishment. I envisaged only one use for the atomic bomb: eliminating all those, judiciously assembled, who had joined in the exercise of terror, in the application of Nada. Instead, a trial[17] and a disturbing qualifier in the texts of repression: genocide. You know all this, having lived for two years behind the barbed wire of Linz, imagining all day long your body scattered into dust; on the evening of your return among us, you chose to walk in the fields of your countryside, with your dog at your heels, rather than answer the summons from the magistrate wanting to expose to your sight the excrement who had denounced you. To excuse yourself, you said this strange thing: "Because I am not dead, *he* doesn't exist." In truth, I only know one law which befits the purpose it assigns itself: martial law in the instant of adversity. In spite of your emaciated and other-worldly appearance, you are willing to agree with me. Generosity in spite of oneself, that was our secret wish, measured by the exact timekeeper of our conscience.

There is a meshing of circumstances which must be intercepted at whatever cost: we must practice a cheerless clairvoyance before it becomes the underhanded consequence of impure alliances and compromise. If in 1944 we had, as a general rule, punished rigorously, we would not blush at meeting every day those dishonored beings, ironic wretches not in the slightest discomfited, while a colorless crowd fills the prisons. Someone may object that the nature of the misdeed has changed, since a merely political frontier always lets evil slip by. But we cannot revive the dead whose tortured bodies were reduced to mud. The man shot by the occupant and his helpers will not awaken in the land next to the one where his head was blown to bits. The truth is that compromise with duplicity has been considerably reinforced among the governing class. Those barnacles are laying in provisions. Does the enigma of tomorrow call for so many precautions? We do not think so. But take care lest the pardoned, those who had chosen to side with crime, should become our tormentors once more, thanks to our levity and a culpable oblivion. They would find a way, over time, to slip Hitlerism into a tradition, to make it legitimate, agreeable even!

After the conflagration, we believe in effacing its marks, in walling up the labyrinth. An exceptional climate cannot be prolonged. After the conflagration, we believe in effacing its marks, walling up the labyrinth, and renewing the sense of civic responsibility. The strategists are not in favor of that. The strategists are the scourge of this world, its evil-smelling breath. In order to foresee, to act, and to correct, they need an arsenal which, lined up, would stretch several times around the globe. Prosecuting the past and securing full power for the future are their sole preoccupations. They are the doctors of agony, the boll-weevils of birth and death. They call science of History the warped conscience permitting them to decimate the joy of a forest in order to set up a subtle work camp, projecting the darkness of their chaos as if it were the light of Knowledge. They will new crops of enemies to rise before them, lest their scythe rust and their enterprising intelligence become paralyzed. Deliberately they exaggerate the fault and underestimate the crime. They destroy harmless opinions and replace them with implacable rules. They accuse the mind of their fellow man of sheltering a cancer analogous to the one they harbor in the vanity of their hearts. They are the whitewashers of putrefaction. Such are the strategists who keep watch in the camps and manipulate the mysterious levers of our lives.

The sight of a bunch of little animals demanding the slaughter of a prey they had not hunted, the consuming artifice of a macabre demagogy, the occasional imitation by our men of the enemy's mentality in his comfortable moments, all that led me to reflect. Premeditation was transmitted. Salvation—how precarious!—seemed to lie only in the feeling of supposed good and outdistanced evil. I then moved up a notch in order to mark the distinctions clearly.

For my lack of enthusiasm in vengeance, a sort of warm frenzy was substituted, that of not losing one essential minute, of giving its full value, at once, to the prodigy of human life in all its relativity. Yes, to restore to their natural fall the thousands of streams that refresh men, dissipating their fever. I wandered untiringly on the edges of this belief, I rediscovered little by little the duration of things, I bettered my seasons imperceptibly, I dominated my just gall, I became daily once again.

I did not forget the crushed visage of the martyrs whose look led me to the Dictator and his Council, his outgrowths and their sequel. Always Him, always them, united in their lie and the cadence of their salvoes! Next came some unpardonable wretches whom we should have afflicted in their exile, resolutely, since the shameful luck of the game had smiled at them. Justice invariably loses out, given the conjunction of circumstances.

When a few sectarian spirits proclaim their infallibility, subjugating the greater number and hitching it to their own destiny to perfect the latter, the Pythia is condemned to disappear. Thus do great misfortunes begin. Our tissues scarcely hold. We live on the slope of a mortal inversion, that of matter complicated infinitely to the detriment of a savoir-vivre, or a natural behavior, both monstrously simplified. The wood of the bush contains little heat, and the bush is chopped down. How preferable an active patience would be! Our own role is to have an influence such that the vein of freshness and of fertility may not be turned away from its land toward the definitive abyss. It is not incompatible, in the same instant, to resume one's relation to beauty, to suffer in oneself, and to be struck, to return the blows and to vanish.

One who possesses some human experience, who has chosen to side with the essential, to the extreme, at least once in his life, is occasionally inclined to express himself in terms borrowed from a teaching of legitimate defense and of self-preservation. His diligence, his distrust are relaxed with difficulty, even when his discretion or his own weakness makes him disapprove this unpleasant leaning. Is it known that beyond his fear and his concern, he aspires to an unseemly vacation for his soul?

So Char returned to peacetime existence, readjusting to a daily cycle, understanding its worth: like the narrator in the prose poem **"L'Inoffensif"** (**"The Inoffensive One"**), he learned to control his righteous indignation and to accept the turning of the seasons and the change they inevitably bring, as opposed to the one single moment of crisis. Here we think of the harvest poem, **"Redonnez-leur . . ."** (**"Restore To Them . . ."**), at once a poem of the tragic acceptance of failure and of a sure triumph. "I bettered my seasons": the cycle assures continuity and a profound awareness.

IV THE MOUNTAIN

Char is, with a few others, one of those who have "chosen the essential, to the extreme . . ." (**RBS,** 17). That expression conveys his deepest sense of morality, manifest in his style. Even the terms "essential" and "extreme," chosen rather than some diluting formula such as "in some measure" or "often," reveal Char's absolute and unequivocal, unmodified position. As for the metaphors of morality, he speaks usually of mountains, of climbing and rigor, of the ascent in self-denial necessary to an eventual perspective from the peaks. There is a strong correlation between the elevated sparseness of the setting—the upland bareness so often recurring, particularly in *Le Nu perdu*[18]—and this moral refusal of facile accumulation so that the poor and dry land is made equivalent to a rigorous self-discipline. As the climber divests himself of all his heavy belongings before the final ascent, so the poet is seen to have, or at least to acquire, the nature of an ascetic as well as that of a lover of the earth.

The balance of sparse and abundant, of dry and flowing texts, is quite as marked as that between darker and lighter shades, as, for instance, in *La Nuit talismanique* (*Talismanic Night*), where the talismanic notion suggests no less mystery than the obscurity of night itself, as opposed to, or rather complementary to, the idea of **Les Matinaux** (*The Matinals*) in all its illumination and in its hope of an always new beginning. At last, the moral fervor itself is sufficient to do away with even the metaphors privileged to describe it. Speaking of the volume that includes most of this prose and of its title, which is at the basis of the present discussion— *Recherche de la base et du sommet* (*Search for the Base and the Summit*)—Char explains: "Base and summit, provided that men bestir themselves and diverge, crumble rapidly. But there is the tension of the search. . . ." Now that tension and that search, in their unceasing moral concern, are sensed as the essential elements in the metaphor, and, as we have seen, Char opts for those elements in their most extreme form. Even the metaphor of the mountain parallels the concern and the extreme choice and reinforces their effect. We shall see its profile rising throughout Char's work, standing out literally against the sky of the Vaucluse, but also figuratively, in the effort and in the bareness sought, in the space of a life and of a work.

V INVOLVEMENT

"I am concerned about what is accomplished on this earth, in the laziness of its nights, under its sun we have forsaken" (RBS, 8). As opposed to history, which "ruins our existence with its veils," the poet chooses the most active contemporaneity. Char in fact appears to identify poetry with presence itself. Thus the duty of the poet is more human than sublime, more present than transcendental: "The poet has no mission; on the whole, he has a task. I have never proposed to build up anything which, once the euphoria had passed, was likely to crash" (**RBS,** 152).

Which is certainly not to say that poetry operates in forgetfulness of the past. Many texts deal with events of the moment and are meant to consecrate them to memory: for example, such poems as **"Par la bouche de l'engoulevent"** (**"Through the Mouth of the Whippoorwill"**): "Children who riddled with olives the sun sunken in the wood of the sea, children, oh wheaten fronds, the foreigner turns away from you, from your martyred blood, turns away from this water too pure, children with eyes of silt, children who made the salt sing in your hearing, how can we resign ourselves to no longer being dazzled by your friendship?" (**FM,** 44). Or again, the poem **"L'Eclairage du pénitencier"** (**"Lighting of the Penitentiary"** [**FM,** 46]) or, in particular, **"Le Bouge de l'historien"** (**"The Hovel of the Historian"**), whose titles are significant in relation to our discussion about the past and remind us of **"L'Historienne"** in *Le Marteau sans maître*. The latter poem reads in part: "The pyramid of martyrs obsesses the earth. . . . Last, in order to love still more what your hands of former days had only brushed lightly under the olive tree too young" (**FM**, 47). The effect of many of these poems, where the poet's indignation at injustice is combined with a gentle lyricism, is based on certain recurring patterns such as "water too pure," "olive tree too young": these elements too extreme, untouched as yet by suffering, therefore innocent as to the ways of grief—the opposite of the furrowed valley of suffering—make up a typical setting in which innocence is threatened and finally defeated. "Mirror of the mureno! / Mirror of yellow fever! Manure of a flat fire held out by the enemy!" (**FM**, 47). The violence of Char's language is also evident throughout these poems, as in his moral condemnations of an epoch, seen in **"Mirage des Aiguilles"** (**"Mirage of the Peaks"**):

> They take for clarity the jaundiced laughter of shadows. They weigh in their hands death's remains and exclaim: "This is not for us." No precious viaticum embellishes the mouth of their uncoiled snakes. Their wife betrays them, their children rob them, their friends mock them. They see none of it, through hatred of darkness. Does creation's diamond cast oblique fires? Quickly a decoy to shroud it. They thrust in their oven, they place in the smooth dough of their bread just a small pinch of wheaten despair. They have settled and they prosper in the cradle of a sea where glaciers have been mastered. Be warned.
>
> (*NP* [*Le Nu perdu*], 17)

The language stands out sharply against that of the lighter poems, for instance, those of *Les Matinaux,* which are traced by only a slight rosy wound, a tinge of suffering, whereas these more violent poems permit no nuance.

The fervent belief in poetry as a moral stance lends a special significance to the tone of Char's poems and to his poetics—whose general outline only we have sketched so far and to which we shall return in the following pages. Few writers have taken greater care to situate their attitude in relation to moral matters: it is perhaps in this care above all that his importance for the majority of readers lies. Char speaks for the poet in general, whose moral purpose we might come to share.

Notes

1. NT—*La Nuit talismanique.*

2. SP—*Sur la poésie.*

3. LM—*Les Matinaux.* Annotation in Doucet library.

4. A—*Arsenal.*

5. In the Fonds René Char-Yvonne Zervos of the Bibliothèque littéraire Jacques Doucet. MM—*Le Marteau sans maître.*

6. RBS—*Recherche de la base et du sommet.*

7. As Hölderlin puts it, the gods choose to hurl their lightning toward the being they privilege. See the later discussions on Hölderlin and the gods' elec-

tion of the poet, in chapter 2 and *passim.* The information on Hölderlin comes principally from *Friedrich Hölderlin, Poems and Fragments* (Ann Arbor: University of Michigan Press, 1967), ed. and tr. Michael Hamburger.

8. Michel Carrouges, *André Breton et les données fondamentales du surréalisme* (Paris: Gallimard, 1950).

9. Cahiers de l'Herne, no. René Char, 1971. For instance, among the most valuable and touching comments are those by William Carlos Williams, who also contributes a poem.

10. Jean Starobinski, "René Char et la définition du poème," Courrier du Centre International d'Etudes poétiques, 66, Maison Internationale de la poésie, Brussels. Reprinted as the preface to *Ritorno sopramonte*, Vittorio Sereni's translations of Char's poems under the title *Retour amont* (Lo Specchio: Mondadori, 1973).

11. AC—*Aromates chasseurs.* (Not yet translated.)

12. In *The Presence of René Char* we discussed at some length the transposition of Char's "Parole en archipel" ("word as archipelago") to its reverse image in the nighttime sky.

13. FM—*Fureur et mystère.* Originally the title of this volume, perhaps Char's best-known work, was to be translated as *Rage and Mystery,* but it was decided, by the poet, that *fureur* has more properly the sense of fury or of furor.

14. Translated as *Leaves of Hypnos* by Jackson Matthews in *Hypnos Waking* (New York: Random House, 1956).

15. André Breton, *Les Pas perdus* (Paris: Gallimard, 1924), pp. 7-8.

16. Pierre de Missac, "Situation de l'aphorisme," *Critique,* no. 323 (April, 1974).

17. The Nuremberg trials. The extent of the crime renders the crime unthinkable, but its science perceptible. To evaluate it is to admit the hypothesis of the criminal's irresponsibility. Yet *any man,* fortuitously or not, can be hanged. This equality is intolerable. [René Char's footnote.] (*RBS,* 13-18)

18. NP—*Le Nu perdu.*

Mary Ann Caws (essay date 1977)

SOURCE: Caws, Mary Ann. "From Fury to Recollection." In *René Char,* pp. 35-57. Boston, Mass.: Twayne Publishers, 1977.

[*In the following essay, Caws traces relationships between life experience and literary expression in the works of Char.*]

I Matinal Light

Throughout the course of Char's work, the poet's personal involvements find their texts, grave or joyous, quiet in tone or more ringing, as reflections of his own moral commitment: they mirror the changing perception of the work undertaken, are determined or depressed, according to the mood of the speaker. Of his Resistance poems—"resistance" taken in all its senses—Char says:

> "Il te fut prêté de dire une fois . . . les chants matinaux de la rébellion. Métal rallumé sans cesse de ton chagrin, ils me parvenaient humides d'inclémence et d'amour.
>
> Once it was granted to you to recount the matinal songs of rebellion. Metal ceaselessly relit from your sorrow, they came to me damp with inclemency and love.
>
> (*AC* [*Aromates Chasseurs*], 43)

As for later "events"—those occurrences supposed to be marked in capital letters in one's life and in one's biography—after 1944 and the end of wartime, their external profile would have to include Char's reactions to the postwar political trials[1] and his praise of the Resistants, his friendship with poets and philosophers and artists,[2] his defense of various positions concerning natural preservation,—all of which are consistent with his general outlook of a "marginal" thinker. As an example in his later years, he has participated in, and led, a movement whose focus was both political and ecological, protesting atomic installations on the plain of Albion in the Vaucluse (see **"La Provence Point Oméga"**) and endeavoring in general to save whatever sites mark a rich heritage.

This is perhaps after all the point: that a poet's protests and involvement count for all of us, that his considered and passionate positions matter for the vigor of their intention, in spite of their local interest and their apparent practical "uselessness." In the long run, the fact that old Catharist sites like Thouzon are vandalized or that trucks can literally carry away the stones forming the old *bories*—those prehistoric stone dwellings found on the land near the poet's home—represents a larger concern.

René Char himself mentions a dividing line in his life at the moment when he was forced to kill another human, becoming "a monster of justice and intolerance, a simplifier . . ." (*RBS* [*Recherche de la base et du sommet*] 10). The fury of those years is unforgettable, even if the poet refuses all acts of revenge, and it lies unceasingly at the heart of all his perception in the same way as the "absent brother" in the poem of the same name resides like a crucible burning "at the center of unity." Impatience is frequently sensed in the man as in the writing: to what extent it originates in the war experience we would not hazard a guess. But the incontrovertible evidence remains, in the text as in the life: an extreme tenderness alternates with irritation, a tragic and benevolent perception is balanced by anger. The inner outline and the outer continue to correspond.

A. Rougeur des matinaux (Redness of Matinals)

Now Char takes up again the image of the meteor, glimpsed this time in a negative light: "I have fallen from my brilliance . . ." (*LM* [*Les Matinaux*], 81). Or perhaps it is simply that the dawn's redness has subsided. Nevertheless, in spite of such moments (which he refers to elsewhere as the "low cycle"), the characteristics of Char's meteor remain unchanged: first, its intensity with its accompanying mystery. "Intensity is silent. Its image is not. (I am fond of what dazzles me, then accentuates the obscurity inside me)" (*LM,* 76). Here we think of Tristan Tzara's statement of 1917, in a "Note on Poetry": "Obscurity is productive if it is a light so white and pure that our neighbors are blinded by it."[3] And second, even more important, the uncompromising uniqueness of the passage in which each profile is preserved as distinct from all others: Char warns us again against a too great resembling, grouping our uniqueness with the crowd's similarity: "Wisdom is not to conglomerate, but, in the creation and the nature common to us, to find our number, our reciprocity, our differences, our passage, our truth, and this bit of despair which is its goad and its moving mist" (*LM,* 76). We might compare the image of the mountain peaks, separate in the morning crimson, with the poet's acerbic statements against a town in which the least folds have been smoothed out, and all citizens conform. In such a "ville sans plis," only a coward would choose to live. (See also the poem "Mirage des aiguilles," in which Char attacks the idea of a civilization free of enigma, where even the snakes lose their mysterious coils.) The meteor—or "the cock's enemy"—remains mysterious; a useful mystery, as Valéry might say.[4]

B. La Bibliothèque est en feu (The Library is Afire)

The poet wills himself sufficiently alone to preserve his space, his freedom, and his *passage*: he should leave traces of his passing, Char says, but no proofs. The insistence on the obscure remains constant. "Free birds do not permit us to observe them," he remarks, and, in another text bearing witness to the same spirit: "Birds do not sing in a bush of questions." Poets leave a margin about them, that demanded by Hölderlin's Empedocles who dismisses Pausanias, by Rimbaud as he "requires everything of us," and even that we take leave of him ("Tu as bien fait de partir, Arthur Rimbaud"; "You did well to leave"), and by Gide, dismissing his reader ("Et maintenant, Nathanaël, jette mon livre"; "And now, Nathaniel, cast my book away"). It is finally of all of us that the poet will require this necessary distance.

From meteor to constellation, the solitariness of the poetic work persists as essential. Here we read a statement which will recur in the series of poetic aphorisms called *Sur la poésie* (*On Poetry*). "The constellation of the Solitary is taut" ([JG], *LM*, 146). The image of the constellation is that of the poet, singular in his setting and yet collective, an object of general perception and nevertheless unique, solitary like a diamond, or like a star, even when extended against the heavens. We think of the constellation of the hunter Orion as we see it first suggested in the poem **"Seuil"** (**"Threshold"**)—"I have run to the outcome of this diluvian night. Standing firm in the quavering daybreak, my belt full of seasons . . . [JG]" (where the belt of Orion might be seen) and then, less obviously, in *La Nuit talismanique.*

The same vision links the poems of the recent *Aromates chasseurs,* where the myth of Orion blinded by Diana (as in Poussin's famous canvas, *Orion aveuglé*) and turned to a constellation, forms the background, and occasionally the foreground, for the entire work. A meteor and the king of the bees, Orion (in **"Réception d'Orion"**) makes his honey of the earth and then ascends once more to the heavens, so that the myth of blinding and radiance, or descent and ascent, merges with the celestial and mysterious figure of the meteor and the useful animal presence of the bee, whose buzzing is felt here in a poem of the morning, intense and strident like a red color.

Equal attention is given to the actual art of writing. A meditation on the advantages of error, of ambiguity, leads to a eulogy of multiplicity: for the greatest diversity of interpretation depends on an initial imprecision, which poetry will not try to eliminate. And then, on the other side of the paradox, Char insists that his work is one of precision, of the point and the prow: his intricate, often ambiguous, and yet essentially clear poetry confirms this. Once the library of ancient works is set afire, as in the title, we can start over in our recreation of literature, as in our re-reading it.

C. Le Nu perdu (*Nakedness Lost*)

The first text of poetic aphorisms in this volume opens with space or pause like that suggested in its title **"Pause au château cloaque,"** with another consideration of time, a fascination at the very heart of the volume, which treats returning upland as a temporal climb, in which the past unobtrusively supports us. The determination to throw off useless baggage which might weigh us down for our final climb toward bareness does not entail the absolute exclusion of memory; it only insists on jettisoning a useless nostalgia: "The past would retard the blossoming of the present if our eroded memories did not sleep there ceaselessly. We turn back to one while the other has a fresh spurt of energy before leaping on us" (*NP* [*Le Nu perdu*], 22). The climb is clearly marked, even in this pause near the beginning: "Race. First mountain pass: clay weathered away" (*NP,*

22). Others have been here before, using up the earth, on this rise which is also interior for each of us. We remember Char's frequent descriptions of the poet as mountain climber, to whom there is granted an exceptionally aggressive breathing. The ascent leads finally to the tomb dug in the air, that "dry house" built again, further up, like the dwelling constructed further upstream in **"Recours au ruisseau."** The profound series called **"Lenteur de l'avenir"** (**"Slowness of the Future"**) begins with a climb characterized as both mental and physical by its juxtaposition of nouns: "You have to scale many dogmas and a mountain of ice." Next, verbs of triumphant action: "I have demolished the last wall," echoed a few poems later by the definitive motion out of the confines of a dwelling: "Without ceremony, I step across this walled-up world" (*NP,* 46), and concludes with another statement concerning the three ages of past, present, and future, arranged vertically: "Our terrestrial figure is only the second third of a continuous pursuit, a point, upland" (*NP,* 38). The climb represented by the *retour amont* is slow, lasting a lifetime. But at the lookout points along the way—these pauses like the "Pause au château cloaque"—the bare upland is seen as illuminated: "amont éclate" ("upland breaks forth"). In his notes to the Italian version of the volume, *Ritorno sopramonte,* Vittorio Sereni comments that a reddish brightness is always seen above the peaks toward which the movement leads. He reminds us of Char's expression: "un brisant de rougeur" ("a breaker of redness"), a presence of light which is, in fact, felt throughout the darkest of visions.

The climb which the poetry represents is not intended only for the poet alone, and not only for one season; it takes place, no matter what the conditions ("we remain men for inclemency"): *"Where shall we spend our days at present? . . . Let us stay in the quarried rain and join to it our breathing"* (*NP,* 51). The aggressive respiration of the mountain climber joins the animal breathing of those continually exposed to downpour, snow, and sun: *"we shall hold together under the storm become forever familiar"* (*NP,* 51). Sereni points out a passage in which the poet identifies himself with the plant and animal life in answer to the alienation of contemporary affections. **"Aliénés"** begins: "From the shadow where we were . . ." (*NP,* 110). Thus in the following poem whose title we have already commented upon, **"Buveuse"** (**"Drinker"**), the plant absorbing endless water is allied also to the poet who has been discouraged with the devastation of nature by the warlike installations of men: "why should we still liberate the words of the future of the self now that every speech soaring upward is the mouth of a yammering rocket, now that the heart of every breathing thing is a stinking cascade?" (*NP,* 53).

In **"Le Terme épars"** (**"The Scattered Term"**), each of whose flashes is brief or sparse, Char reminds himself, and us, of our commitment to generosity and forgiving, on this upward path which is also that of the mind: "Give always more than you can take back. And forget. Such is the sacred path" (*NP*, 55). "The evening frees itself from the hammer, man stays chained to his heart" (*NP*, 55). Compare another text from *Le Nu perdu*: "Generosity is a facile prey. Nothing is more frequently attacked, confused, defamed. Generosity creates our future executioners, our retrenchments, dreams written in chalk, but also the warmth which receives once and gives twice" (*NP*, 91). The text ends on a streak of red light in the distance, representing the future, a silence free from our present doubt and misgivings as they are tied to our words: "How uncurious truth would be bloodless if there were not this breaker of redness in the distance where the doubt and the saying of the present are not engraved. We advance, abandoning all speech in promising ourselves that sight" (*NP*, 56). The profound silence is, like the space the poet demands about him, a denial of everyday triviality at the final height. Significantly, the next series of *fusées* has to do with both silence and motion: "we would have only liked to answer mute questions, preparations for movement" (*NP*, 58). In the title the poet includes Maurice Blanchot, a well-known critic whose advocacy of silence and the poetic mystery are closely associated with Char's own. Char speaks for them both, then, in this ascent at once temporal, spatial, and moral: "The time is near where only that which could remain unexplained will be able to summon us" (*NP*, 58). That ideal bareness we cannot really recreate is akin to silence and to mystery: all three converge in the poetry and the "irresolute and misunderstood infinite" which is said to surround it (*NP*, 58).

As we look in succession at the texts of *Le Nu perdu*, the distance up the mountain seems measured out like the **"Tide Ratio"** of *Les Matinaux*; here the flux is no longer only that of water, but also of space and time. From the **"Pause"** and the **"Slowness"** we arrive at the **"Tables of Longevity,"** where we read, still in relation to the infinite, a future couched in a present tense: "When there is less and less space between the infinite and us, between the libertarian sun and the prosecutor sun, we are aground on night" ([JG] *NP*, 61). But it is some time before the "bell of pure departure" will signal the triumphant end of the battle upland: "True victories are only won over a long time, our forehead against the night" (*NP*, 65). The struggle is again that of upstream as well as upland and is openly marked as being so. A beautiful series of aphorisms called **"La Scie rêveuse"** (**"The Dreaming Saw"**) moves from an initial line of understatement and blossoming ("To be sure of one's own murmurs and to lead action as far as its word in flower") through an invocation to the river to whose modest murmur we were listening ("Law of the river . . . , of losses compensated but of torn sides, when the ambitious house of the mind crumbled, we recognized

you and found you good" (*NP*, 69) to the final statement of persistence in spite of difficulty, toward the recapturing of a true identity ("Alone among the stones, the stone of the torrent has the reverie-like contour of the face finally restored") (*NP*, 70).

This text comes from the collection *Dans la Pluie giboyeuse* (*In the Quarried Rain*), from whose heavy and nourishing fall the torrent was created, to whose animal intensity the poet hunter or the poet as his own prey has joined his breathing and his fate: that hunter who is associated with the flower called Orion's dart, with the unicorn in **"L'anneau de la licorne"** (**"Ring of the Unicorn"**), as well as the poem **"Seuil"** (**"Threshold"**), as we have seen, will later appear in a "mute game," then at last in his own constellation before redescending to earth in *Aromates chasseurs* as Orion Iroquois. The path upland leads through all the texts, for in the constellation glimpsed within the poem **"Possessions extérieures"** (**"Exterior Possessions"**) traces of many myths might be seen to merge, for example, Orion the hunter, changed to a dove, a bee, and then a star, and Orion blinded—as in Poussin's canvas *Orion aveuglé*, already mentioned, which telescopes two legends[5]—but by his own radiance. The blinding or the self-blinding ray resembles the single horn of the animal in **"The Ring of the Unicorn,"** in *La Nuit talismanique*. Here Orion, not named but no less present, chews a leaf of a virgin flower, a hunter never satisfied with his prey: "He had felt jostled and lonely at the border of his constellation, only a little town shivering in tempered space. To the questioner: 'Have you finally met her? Are you happy at last?' he did not deign to reply, and tore a leaf of guelder-rose" (*NT* [*La nuit talismanique*], 83). But this Orion remains as tragic as he is lucid; "The more he understands, the more he suffers. The more he knows, the more he is torn. But his lucidity has the measure of his pain and his tenacity, that of his despair" (*NP*, 89).

Orion will reappear, assuming in himself all the rising of a return upland and the falling of a meteor, all the scattered brilliance of *La Parole en archipel* (*The Word as Archipelago*) and the clustered radiance of his own constellation, bridging the heavens and the earthly streams for both senses of the return upland, human as well as mythic. To the path of the return, a mystery is still assigned. "The roads which do not promise the country of their destination are the roads most loved" (*NP*, 91). Upland in all its bareness must remain open to interpretation; it will never be reduced to one landscape, neither that of the Vaucluse nor that of the heavens. Similarly, to join the figure of Orion, already the convergence of so much legend and of so many myths, there now comes another hero, Hölderlin's *Hyperion*—"The best son of the old solar disk and the nearest to his celestial slowness" (*NP*, 95).[6] Hölderlin himself, stricken with madness by the gods as if by a lightning bolt, and thus singled out as a poet, is a chosen figure of René Char. Heidegger's essay on Hölderlin ("Hölderlin and the Essence of Poetry") comes close to the spirit of Char's poetics, as do many of Heidegger's writings, with their emphasis on being-toward-death and its relation to being-in-this world. (Some of Char's most moving prose has to do with his friendship with Heidegger, which can be called poetic as well as philosophic.)

The breaker of redness has now become a crepuscular light, itself said to be bare like older times, magnified like a torrent swollen with rain, and as peremptory as the lightning which apparently chooses the poet. These terms are used by Char to describe his night of fire, resembling Pascal's terrible night to whose brief, jagged, and unforgettable "mémorial" Char's most intense passages now bear such a strong likeness.[7] These texts have about them a suddenness and yet a gravity which set them apart. The very violence of that night marks the culmination of the path upward toward what is no longer a simple line of daybreak, magnetic in its attraction, but a passionate light of conflict, where even the word *brisant* becomes active rather than descriptive, changing from a noun ("the breaker") to a verb: "se brisant de toutes ses artères contre nous" ("breaking with all its arteries against us") (*NP,* 97).

That passionate vision prepares a quieter illumination. After the breaking down of walls and the scaling of heights, the poet goes once more inside, having acknowledged all along that the path of returning was interior, as the summit is finally an invisible one: "I have lived outside, exposed to all sorts of inclemencies. The hour has come for me to return, oh laughter of slate! into a book or into death" (*NP,* 106).

II Outlook: *Recherche de la base et du sommet (Search for the Base and the Summit)*

Often, as we know, a poet's theory is most clearly seen in his essays on other writers or artists—more clearly, indeed, than in his essays centering on his own poetics. Char's recently published volume of commentary on the major artists whose world he values—*Le Monde de l'art n'est pas le monde du pardon (The World of Art is not the World of Pardon)*—shows a range of writings from diverse epochs and concerning equally diverse creations. His comments, for instance, on Georges de La Tour, Miró, Braque, de Staël, Vieira da Silva, as well as on Baudelaire, Rimbaud, and Nietzsche, together with his conversations with Heidegger and his remarks on Camus, indicate the ways and depth of his thought. Even the intonation can prepare us for Char's own poetry. For instance, in describing Miró's achievement, Char finds the evocative phrase: "the taste of springs and of their flight," (*RBS,* 83), a formulation applicable

to many of his own poems. The elements of water and air, the motions of beginning and soaring, the suggestion of an entire cycle—all are complete in that one line. Miró, says Char, indicates, without spelling out or proclaiming: that is also a good description of the essential concern characteristic of his own work in the graver moments. "We recognize the painter's gesture by that gravitation toward the sources which, as they appear, turn the images aside from their end. As if breathed in by the movement seizing them, they contract" (*RBS,* 83). The description might well be that of the intense expectation and occasional massing of Char's own images, under the sometimes hidden weight of an idea, felt to press even on the movement of the poem itself.

Or a passage on Nicolas de Staël, which by chance serves as a useful reference point for Char's own play on the abominable snowman. Char, in discussing the illustrations of de Staël for some of his poems, writes that they "appear for the first time on a field of virgin snow that the sunlight . . . will try to melt" (*RBS,* 93). De Staël and he are not, he says, abominable snowmen, "but we sometimes come nearer to the unknown than is permissible, and to the empire of stars." Like that of Char, de Staël's art is the contrary of long-winded; it is rather, like his, of a lapidary simplicity and shows a natural ellipsis. Of all the artists with whom Char has been allied, de Staël seems—to this reader—the closest to him, along with Braque.

Concerning theory, the latter seems of the closest temperament:[8] we have only to read their conversations, as Char relates them here, or to consider the similar humanity of their characters. Indisputably, André Breton's writings on and his admiration of Picasso or Matta reveal Breton's way of thinking as nothing else can, for instance, Breton's essays in *Le Surréalisme et la peinture* on Picasso's venture across the abyss or on his juxtaposing of objects, and on Matta's reshaping the entire universe to fit his own vision and to make way for chance. Just so, Char's writings on Braque further our understanding of the poet as much as of the artist. To take an example corresponding to the one just related from Breton and Picasso, Char says of Braque the following: "Children and geniuses know that there is no bridge, only the water allowing itself to be crossed. Thus in Braque's work the spring is inseparable from the rock, the fruit from the soil, the cloud from its fate . . ." (*RBS,* 57-58).

Char describes in his work the "incessant going and coming from solitude to being and from being to solitude": this sure convergence of the natural, the human, and the universal on one hand and of this alteration from the one being to the being-in-the-world is constant in Char's writing. We have only to think of his essay on the artist Sima, in which he discusses the junction of the four elements and the situation of man-in-the-world: "I am not separated; I am among" (*Se Rencontrer paysage avec Joseph Sima*).[9] Braque knows how to "judge an enigma, how to revive for us its fortune and its benumbed brilliance" ("son éclat engourdi") (*RBS*, 67). When the poet despairs, as in the phrase already quoted: "Je suis tombé de mon éclat . . . ," the artist, above all others, can render to him his inspiration. For he symbolizes continuity: Braque's work of one day, maintains Char, if it were to be suspended over the abyss in the evening, would carry over like a projection toward the morrow's work. Char finally likens these germs of the next day's work—"a multiplier in the expectation of its multiplicand" (*RBS*, 87)—to a threatened candle which the sun would soon replace. In *La Nuit talismanique,* the poet warns us not to substitute for the flickering chiaroscuro of candlelight, its flame rich in imaginative possibilities and ambiguities (that "éclat nourri de sa flamme"), the steady brightness of day.[10]

Braque, like Char, "recreates his candle" every evening, never sacrificing the indispensable mystery in favor of what is at best only clear. The candle in several of La Tour's canvases around which the other masses are grouped,[11] makes a fitting image for an observation as quiet as the flame: "Action is blind, it is poetry that sees." Similarly, we might observe the lighting in Char's major poems as an example of poetic interiority. These two kinds of light serve to nourish one another, like Breton's image of the communicating vessels of day and night; for Char, poetry and action will be the interdependent "vases communicants." So the contemplation of the flame and the daytime motion ("Emerge on your surface . . . ," *RBS*, 168) are joined.

Among the philosophers whose poetics are close to Char's own, Heraclitus seems one of the nearest. The fragments which have survived from his writing are like poems, each chosen by chance to endure above all that has been submerged. For Char, convinced that our only certainty for the future is an ultimate pessimism ("the accomplished form of the secret where we come to refresh ourselves, to renew our watchfulness and to sleep," *RBS*, 117), Heraclitus represents a solar eagle. He is a profound predecessor, and an uncompromising one: "He knew that truth was noble and that the image revealing it is tragedy." Likewise, Char's own poetry is not sad; it is exhilarating, complicated, forceful, and often tragic.

Two other poets—for Heraclitus is, for Char, as much a poet as a philosopher—lend a psychological strength and a nourishing unrest to his language: Baudelaire and Nietzsche are Char's "water-carriers," sources of his poetry and of his disquiet. He defines poetry now as "the wound that shines where the sentence effaces itself" (*RBS*, 139) and finds Nietzsche's "seismic anguish" close to his own.

Rimbaud is a significant predecessor as many critics have pointed out. "But if I knew what Rimbaud meant for me, I would know what poetry is before me, and I would no longer have to write it . . ." (*RBS*, 130). One of Char's numerous commentaries on Rimbaud indicates sufficiently his particular importance: "we must consider Rimbaud in the single perspective of poetry. Is that so scandalous? His work and his life are thus revealed to be of an unequaled coherence, neither because of, nor in spite of, their originality. . . . We are fully aware, outside of poetry, that between our foot and the stone it weighs upon, between our gaze and the field traversed, the world is null. Real life . . . is only found in the body of poetry" (*RBS*, 127). Poetry has, for Rimbaud, for Char, possibly for all true poets, no other reason for being than being. Rimbaud's famous statement quoted by Char is infinitely applicable to the latter's own poetry: "I meant to say what it says, literally and in all senses" (*RBS*, 127).[12] Rimbaud was, like Char, a lover of nature, seen as a luminous force, joining with the language of the poem for a lasting creation. His spirit pervades Char's notion of the three ages, recurring in the title of *Le Nu perdu* and in a text of *Aromates chasseurs,* which are, respectively, the story of simplicity and unfeigned spiritual nakedness—that is, the golden age—as they are lost in an industrial age, and that of a middle time we must find again, by retaining the value of the past and predicting the future. "Rimbaud escaping[13] locates his golden age in the past and in the future. He does not settle down. He has another epoch come forth, either in the mode of nostalgia or in that of desire, only in order to fell it instantly and to return to the present, that target with the *center* always hungry for projectiles, that natural port for all departures." This spatial description of past and future and present serves to map the three ages, already mentioned; Rimbaud's rhythm, many of his conceptions, and his dynamics are Char's also: "In the motion of an ultrarapid dialectic, so perfect it does not arouse *panic,* but rather a whirlwind, fitting and precise, he pulls us along, he dominates us, carrying everything with him . . . as we consent" (*RBS*, 131). Not only is there to be no settling down in comfort for poetry, but no permanent attachment to what we have most loved: "The urgency of his word and its scope espouse and blanket a surface that language before him had never attained nor occupied." In fact, Rimbaud is perhaps best known, in Char's works, for his uncompromising departure, to which we have already referred. Char defines poetry as "the song of departure": how, he asks, could such a poet as Rimbaud have been satisfied with less than complete separation? For "poetry is the distanceless solitude among everyone's bustling, that is, a solitude which has the means of expressing itself." Our aloneness, even our loneliness should be as refreshing for us as the fountain nourishing the brutality of a poet: "To drink shivering, to be brutal, restores" (*NP,* 82).

III NIGHT AND REFLECTION

The volumes now to be discussed are turned towards an inner realm: towards a "talismanic night," a gathering of reflections about the deepest aspects of poetry, and, finally, a constellation.

A. *LA NUIT TALISMANIQUE (TALISMANIC NIGHT)*

These texts are each a witness to solitude and to a contemplation both cosmic and minute. Some add or strengthen aspects which we had not clearly seen before: for instance, concerning the importance of the small and the minimal, less as a plea for modesty than as an insistence on our *perception* and on our reordering of values. In line with this attitude, Char praises the man who takes care of his working instruments, in full knowledge of their value. We must assign the proper place to things and gather about us all we might use, in time of drought. (The importance of water in the austere landscape of the Vaucluse can hardly be overstated: thus the chosen images of scarcity and aridity.) This volume is turned toward the interior, as a kind of challenge to the mind. Since no movement in Char's work is entirely simple, there will be an extension outward subsequent to this introspective stage: "The night brings nourishment, the sun refines the nourished part" (*NT,* 15). Just so, this talismanic night provides the temporary halt and the renewing source for later works.

Again we hear the plea for space to be created about the poet: "The obligation, without pausing to breathe, to rarify, to hierarchize beings and things intruding on us" (*NT,* 72). The multilated giant who will finally take on the traits of Orion is subject to laws outside himself over which he has no intellectual command, but here he controls the space of his own contemplation, choosing its light and "inventing" his own sleep. He concentrates on the flickering of one candle, on its circular dance, triumphing over the partitioning of days (as in the "divided" time or "cloisons" of an earlier poem, **"Faction du muet"**): "As night asserted itself, my first task was to destroy the calendar viper knot where the start of each day sprang to sight. The aboutface of a candle-flame prevented me. From it I learned to stoop over and to straighten quickly in the constant line of the horizon bordering my land, to see, nearing, a shadow giving birth to a shadow through the slant of a luminous shaft, and to scrutinize it" (*NT,* 87). The text is called **"Éclore en hiver" ("To Blossom in Winter")**, and the deepest meditation in its inward flowering is encouraged by just this close scrutiny of a minimal event, requiring careful attention.

One of the more interesting lights to cast on this volume is a light of difference, in a comparison of these texts with the brief opaque splendor of Mallarmé's *Igitur,* built around the expectation of one gesture, the breath which will extinguish a candle at midnight. The consequence of that annihilation of being by the breath is ambiguously positive: the creation of shadow and the union of word and act. For here the breath which has served in speech serves then as destruction; the observation is of especial interest for us, in view of the wide scope and extraordinary frequency of the images of breathing in Char's writing, from the earliest volumes. The complex awareness of certain extremes ("the presence of Midnight," the absolute presence of things) and of absolute emptiness (a "vacant sonority," "reciprocal nothingness") is echoed by another violent contrast shared in the common space of the two poets. The poles of dark ("shadows disappeared in obscurity") and of a flame, of chance and necessity, of ancestral apparitions hanging over the quiet yet lucid meditation of an open book on a table surrounded by mystery, all these find their place within the shadows of Char's talismanic night.[14] Both texts depend on a temporary suspension of breath before the candle is extinguished, with the extinction of the text as its necessary corollary. Even the old gods storming outside the room where the poet plagued by insomnia keeps watch over the candle and the page remind us of Mallarmé's "dieux antiques." It is as if René Char had assembled his writing and drawing instruments on the table where Igitur's book is open, in a space no less haunted by presences: "Another hand protects the oval flame," and the presence is as mysterious as that other presence of midnight. "The heart of night was not to be set afire. The obscure should have been the master where the dawn's dew is chiseled" (*NT,* 16). Valéry points out "The usefulness of mystery." "The best work is the one that keeps its secret longest."[15]

The volume bears witness to the "desert sand" of insomnia, where the waters of night nourish like the redemption by water in **"Le Visage nuptial" ("The Nuptial Countenance")**. Igitur closes the book and blows out the candle "with his breath that contained chance," while the poet stands fast in his nocturnal quiet, until the daybreak described earlier in the poem **"Seuil,"** where the figure of Orion may be seen to make his appearance against the horizon. Yet that interior meditation retains the hospitality of the hearth:

> J'ai couru jusqu'à l'issue de cette nuit diluvienne. Planté dans le flageolant petit jour, ma ceinture pleine de saisons, je vous attends, ô mes amis qui allez venir. Déjà je vous devine derrière la noirceur de l'horizon. Mon âtre ne tarit pas de voeux pour vos maisons. Et mon bâton de cyprès rit de tout son coeur pour vous.

> I have run to the outcome of this diluvian night. Taking my stand in the trembling dawn, with my belt full of seasons, I am waiting for you, my friends who will come. Already I divine you behind the black of the horizon. My hearth's good wishes for your homes never dry up. And my cypress walking-stick laughs with its whole heart for you.

> ([JG] *FM* [*Fureur et mystère*], 181)

Char's nocturnal meditation accommodates all of the landscape outside, taking within its range harvest, sun, the wind of the mistral, the river, and the land beyond. From the candle he watches, this "sedentary flame" itself containing the household gods propitious to our contemplation, he moves to an observation of the stars, of the human sky as it is matched to the universe beyond man. Thus the talisman, whether held by the poet's hand or that of another, serves as a guide to whatever is beyond the contemplation of any one night or any series of texts with its single or multiple source.

B. *Sur la poésie* (*On Poetry*)

In **Sur la poésie** Char collects several previous statements on poetics written between 1936 and 1974. The statements will be referred to according to their proper order, so as not to falsify the evolution once chosen, which is then reexamined by the poet in his reprinting of these texts. They begin by an echo of **Moulin premier**: "I admit that intuition reasons and gives orders from the moment that, as a bearer of keys, it does not forget to set the embryonic forms of poetry in motion, crossing through the high cages where the echoes are sleeping, those elect precursors of miracle which, as the forms pass by, steel and fecundate them" (**SP** [**Sur la poésie**] 71). As in the text **En trente-trois morceaux** (*In Thirty-three Pieces*), the fragments chosen and reassembled, taking on a different order, find a new coherence; the definitions of poetry itself may appear differently lit in this rereading of poetry as the realized "love of desire remaining desire" or as the future life of "requalified man." Now the previous image of wool strands extended ("laines prolongées") joins with that of a spiderweb on the same page, form replying to like form, as well as with the other images of making and of long enduring, through a dialectic of presence and passing: "The vitality of the poet is not a vitality of the beyond but an *actual* diamantine point of transcendent presence and pilgrim storms" (**SP**, 13).

And this dialectic is balanced by another, that of the torment and the happiness of the poet as they are always intransitive, the poet drawing "unhappiness from his own abyss" (**SP**, 17). It is important here to make a distinction between the writer in general and the poet in particular, for Char's morality and poetics are specifically fitted to the "métier du poète," his chosen location in space and time to the "logement du poète," his passion for life to the "vitalité du poète." For example, the following statements do not start, and could never have done so, in Char's universe, with the words "Être écrivain" ("To be a writer"), but rather, with the words "Être poète." Near the outset Char reconsiders the poet's own place ("The poet cannot remain for a long time in the stratosphere of the Word") (**SP**, 8) and his mission ("The poet, keeper of the infinite faces of the living") (**SP**, 9). "To be a poet is to have an appetite for an unease whose

consummation, among the whirlwinds of the totality of things existent and intimated, provokes happiness just at the moment of conclusion" (**SP**, 13). The poetic function actively liberates, at its source, the only wealth found valuable: the verb *tourmenter* carries perfectly in both languages the double sense of a creative disturbance strong enough to arouse and of an inspiration sufficient to realize all that was only potential. In short, it indicates a *troubling activity,* both positive and negative: "The poet torments with the help of immeasurable secrets the form and the voice of his fountains" (**SP**, 14). It will be noticed that even the source is individual, not general.

Above all, these statements manifest a vivid faith in continuity, even when the poet leaves whatever he might consider as the base of his too prosaic safety for the risk implied in this conception of the poetic. He does not choose to remain untouched by his involvements: "Lean over, lean over more," he reminds himself—and us (**SP**, 15). Typically, rather than merely speaking the "truth," he maintains that he must live it (**SP**, 19). Now he takes advantage of the miraculous enduring of the smallest things, like the poor man profiting from an olive's eternity, as he phrases it elsewhere. Or again, at every disappointment in the expected—for in a "profession of risk," nothing can really be counted on but the certainty of that risk—this "magician of insecurity" (**SP**, 18) responds with a confidence whose foundation is often far from evident to us, and all the more affecting: "To each crumbling of proofs, the poet replies by a salvo of futures." And later: "Poetry will steal my death from me" (**SP**, 20).

The situation of the mind turned-toward-the-future is closely allied to the metaphors of climbing toward a height from which the poet, called a "summit of breath in the unknown" (**SP**, 16), can see forward and around at a great distance, leaving behind him the feats already accomplished of which he is no longer a simple reflection. He is no longer to be compared to others since he fits neither their norms nor their hopes, neither is he tied down to possessions. He thus occupies a perfect position for superior or future action. "The serene town, the unperforated village is before him" (**SP**, 16). The statements surrounding this one are noticeably full of increase and of upward growth. Everywhere the relation of the exterior or the physical to the moral and mental is clear, as in our chapter title "exterior and interior architecture." The text directly following the one just quoted begins with a simultaneous description of the poem and of its poet: "Standing erect, increasing throughout its course, the poem . . ." (**SP**, 17). The initiator of verbal action is also the arranger, not of a placid still life, but of an "insurgent order" which is inscribed in the future, rebellious to past tranquillity and even to past truth. "You cannot begin a poem without a parcel of error about yourself and the world

. . ." (*SP,* 21). So the spirit of contradiction or at least of ambivalence remains. Many of Char's more profound statements are structured along those lines: for example, "poetry is the fruit we hold, ripened, joyously in our hand, at the same moment it appears to us on the frosted stem, within the flower's chalice, of an uncertain future" (*SP,* 21). Living amid truth makes one a liar, claims Char (*SP,* 19), and exactly that spirit of ambivalence and dialectic moves us beyond individual pettiness and pride to a certain impersonality. There is, however, no coldness to the term, rather a feeling like that in the poem **"The Extravagant One,"** in which a frost grazes the surface of the wanderer's forehead, "without seeming *personal*" (*FM,* 182).

The perception of contrasts is often a matter of outlook and of patience in examining detail: ". . . il est permis enfin de rapprocher les choses de soi avec une libre minutie . . ." (". . . we are finally permitted to bring objects near us with a free exactness . . .") (*En trente-trois morceaux,* April 8, 1956).

By a paradoxical twist, just as the aphoristic generalizations which we discuss here under the heading of morality may seem to have a particular application, so the observation of the smallest objects, the juxtaposition of which composes the universe of Char's daily observation, may appear to find the widest scope. To give only one example of the rapid expansion of perspective, let us take, in *La Nuit talismanique,* the line: "Fourche couchée, perfection de la mélancolie" ("Pitchfork laid down, perfection in melancholy"). The eye, and with it the mind, travels from the object to its announced position, to the representation of the mood or its emotional effect, and then to an implicit question as to situation. Why the halt? Will the work halted continue? The answer is, in all probability, positive, and the reason, temporal: "Successives enveloppes! Du corps levant au jour désintégré, . . . nous restons constamment encerclés, avec l'énergie de rompre" ("Wrappings, one after the other! From the rising body to the day disintegrated . . . we remain constantly surrounded, with the energy to break off") (*NT,* 65). The phenomenon is somewhat reminiscent of Pascal's celebrated statement on the meeting of extremes: Char's contrasting wide and narrow focus are equally important for our understanding of his overall perspective. We might compare this stretching of the imagination to other mental exercises: first to one of Char's own observations on vertical extremes, already quoted, applicable to these roughly horizontal extremes of focus: "Base and summit . . . crumble rapidly. But there is the tension of the search. . . ." Here the value is placed on an effort surely as much moral as physical, in this "Recherche de la base et du sommet." The ability to take in the distance between two extreme points and to juxtapose them nevertheless, to grasp the complex relation between them, all that is essential for poetic understanding.

Moreover, we might see in the extraordinary proliferation of all varieties of contrasts the same mental athletics required of the reader, if he would follow the work with any fidelity.

Now the balance of opposing terms requires a movement between the components of the individual statements which can properly be called dialectic, in that the statement itself serves as the final term. In turn, a series of statements can be seen as moments in the temporal advance toward an integral statement on poetry, necessary movements in themselves, whose individually contradictory and yet eventually resolved terms accumulate in a balance sensed as delicate and complete.

We saw above an example of the relation of one moment to the next, where a description of the poet as the "summit of breath in the unknown," whose being cannot be tied down or measured, led to the expression: "Standing erect, increasing throughout its course . . ." by way of the metaphors of height and increase, and an earlier example, where the "prolonged wool strands" into which the poet transforms each potentially dying object led to the image of a spiderweb hung in the sky—or with its concentric circles reaching from line to line. Such relations can often be traced through a few moments in succession, each adding to the preceding information without altering its own dialectical progress. For example, a series of three statements on death makes up a whole, evidently related to other statements and yet still sufficient unto itself. Each statement shows its own obvious exterior and interior contradiction and subsequently, its own more subtle resolution; it should be noted, parenthetically, that we are still following Char's own order for these aphorisms, so that the sequence of discussion is first of all controlled by his arrangement of texts.

> To make a poem is to take possession of a nuptial beyond, which is found well within this life, closely attached to it and nevertheless in near proximity to the urns of death.
>
> * * *
>
> Poetry, unique ascension of men, which the sun of the dead cannot obscure in the perfect and burlesque infinite, perfected and ludicrous.
>
> * * *
>
> Poetry is at once speech and the silent, desperate provocation of our being, exigent as it is ("être-exigeant") for the advent of a reality which will be without rival. It is incorruptible—imperishable, no, for it is exposed to common dangers. But the only one which visibly triumphs over material death.
>
> (*SP,* 24-25)

The moments are not only joined together in theme—what conquers death and gives value to life?—but also, in form. The construction is strong, or, to use a musical description, the opening attack is vigorous. The set of three terms is joined to the subsequent fragment by implication of the death theme: "The only signature at the bottom of the blank sheet of life is traced by poetry" (*SP,* 26), and to the preceding parts by such definitions as the following: "Poems are incorruptible bits of existence which we hurl toward death's repugnant muzzle, but high enough so that, ricocheting onto it, they fall into the nominative world of unity"(*SP,* 22). (This concept is closely related to Heideggerian thought.)

Since poetry is necessarily a situation of disquiet, value attaches not to calm but to unrest, to the rebellious intellect, "refractory to calculated projects." For, "Poetry lives on perpetual insomnia" (*SP,* 26). The contradictory attitude itself corresponds perfectly to that state of unease and nonprogression which it magnifies. It is genuinely an exciting venture: not a pseudoheroic escapade, but rather one to be taken seriously, or not attempted at all. "In poetry, you only dwell in the place you leave, you only create the work you are detached from, you only obtain duration by destroying time" (*SP,* 28). Again, on the next page: "The act of writing, poignant and profound when anguish raises itself on one elbow to observe and when our happiness thrusts itself uncovered into the wind of the path" (*SP,* 29). The play of one concept against another, while it allows both stability and flexibility, prevents stagnation.

In the most recent part of the book, some previously unpublished statements are gathered under the dedication: *A Faulx contente* (*To Your Scythe's Content*). We think, in reading this title, of the opposite melancholy of the pitchfork laid to rest at evening in *La Nuit talismanique.* The image of the scythe serves as a metonymy for the ideal of pruning and trimming, for the sacrifice of what is unessential; it is therefore, unlike the pitchfork, not laid to rest.

We are still following a marked path along *Sur la poésie,* that of the contradictory and finally resolved terms of much of Char's writing, exemplified in another image of anguish: a path chosen by the poet leads, he says, only "to one's own bloodied heart, the source and the sepulcher of the poem" (*SP,* 33). Above all, the point of a poem, its beginning and end, is *not* exterior representation, which Char would associate with prose. The poet is of a sensitivity such that the extremes touch within each text, occasionally far inside: sometimes his writing expresses a quiet ambivalence, sometimes the clash of opposing forces. The next to the last statement reads: "the poem lays us in a postponed grief, making no distinction between the cold and the ardent" (*SP,* 34). The adjectival terms even in their opposition show a slight unbalance, for we would expect either frigid/ ardent or cold/hot. But "ardent" is precisely the term which matters here, for a multiplicity of reasons. A poem is, for Char, ardor expressed or suggested,

intuition at its highest point; yet it is at the same time the product of a clearheaded and rational process; it thus represents emotional weight and imaginative spirit.

The complexities and ambivalencies of the opposing terms are seen with some of their prolongations in the final statement of the volume, where the role of the poet now assumes the functions of freeing and joining: "The poet bursts the bonds imprisoning what he touches; he does not teach the end of linking," reads the last statement in the book (*SP,* 35). The linking of element to element can be perceived in a form identical with the essential and traditional double nature of all profound relationships. The relations of poetic elements will not be simple, and therefore continue despite the conclusion of each poem, or of each series of statements, each slight imbalance encouraging the extension of thought.

From each twist of the "prolonged strand" of the poet's thought, there comes another possible one, joining a literal to a figurative, a physical to an emotional term. The same bifurcation can be seen in many words: for an example, the French word *source* has an extension far beyond its English usage, as seen in the double definition: "source and sepulcher of the poem." For the source is equally the liquid origin and the inspirational *spring,* at once figurative and geographic, moral and actual. Thus the specific word "source" renews itself, in one more prolongation, by its own ambivalence, through all the endless links a poem creates. We read, in a retrospective extension from **"A Faulx contente,"** the title of the poem **"La Faux relevée ("Scythe Lifted Again")**: "Fontaine, qui tremblez dans votre étroit réduit, / Mon gain, aux soifs des champs, vous le prodiguerez" ("Fountain, trembling within your narrow nook, / My gain you'll spread bounteous to fields athirst") (*LM,* 184), as if this were also a source, a spring of poetic ambivalence and abundance, of poetic enduring, in correspondence with the poetics which always underlies it. Finally, all Char's meditations, whether on aesthetic or moral matters, could be entitled: ***Sur la poésie.***

C. AROMATES CHASSEURS (AROMATICS HUNTERS)

These poems follow an inward path, made up of meditations on political and moral problems, on poetry and survival in the present world, and yet the path remains in direct and strongly sensed correspondence with one constellation in the sky, that of Orion. The volume takes up and expands the brief texts from *Le Nu perdu* on the relation between poet and destiny, expressed by the image of stars against blackness, with the play of bright and dark fully as complex as that of Baroque poetry. The architecture, with its columns leading from earth to sky—four corresponding texts of Orion—will be referred to again in the chapter on **"The Elements of**

the Poem," since each has its own element. This architecture seems particularly close to that of Mallarmé.

The four great Orion poems which form the pillars of the volume are inserted in the constellation, at once the archipelago from which Orion descends because of a thirst for earth in the initial poem, **"Evadé d'archipel"** (**"Escaped from the Archipelago"**), and the sky to which he finally returns, garbed in an "infinity" of luminous points. They are set in the series of radiant islands as a structure—visible and implied—to whose light each bears a brief witness. The volume itself joins all the elements, as the aromatic smoke returns the hero to his heaven, to build there the giant pontoon bridges under which we can pass safely, after our swim "in the icy waters" connected to the earth. Orion Iroquois, a builder in steel and at great heights, is the figure corresponding to the hunter Orion blinded and received on high (**"Réception d'Orion"**), these two figures forming the two central pillars or columns of the book, the first and last poems of Part II. Just so, the first and last poems of the volume correspond, for in **"Evadé d'archipel,"** Orion has put down his arrow and his sickle, and in his meteoric fall, his traits are blackened with crude celestial ore, like those of the laborer in the early poem **"Fréquence"** or those of the maquisards in the Resistance poems, all in *Fureur et mystère*. And the last poem, **"Eloquence d'Orion,"** will answer this one, by its own resistance songs: "les chants matinaux de la rébellion. Métal rallumé sans cesse de ton chagrin, ils me parvenaient humides d'inclémence et d'amour" ("matinal songs of rebellion. Metal relit ceaselessly from your pain, they came to me damp with inclemency and with love") (*AC*, 43). The suffering and the fire are implicit, merged with the morally unforgiving nature: we remember the earlier refrain: "We remain men for inclemency" from **"Contrevenir."** In this last moment of eloquence, Orion would choose to be, in all simplicity, by a river and in a poem, before his departure:

> Tu t'établirais dans ta page, sur les bords d'un ruisseau, comme l'ambre gris sur le varech échoué; puis, la nuit monté, tu t'éloignerais des habitants insatisfaits, pour un oubli servant d'étoile. Tu n'entendrais plus geindre tes souliers entrouverts.

> You would settle in your page, on the bank of a river, like ambergris on the seaweed adrift; then when night had risen, you would depart from the unsatisfied inhabitants for a forgetfulness serving as a star. You would no longer hear your half-open shoes complaining.

(*AC*, 43)

Notes

1. See the "Note to Francis Curel" in Chapter One.

2. For example, see the large volume of original works by his friends the artists and the accompanying texts: *Le Monde de l'Art n'est pas le monde du pardon* (Paris: Maeght, 1975). Preface by Jacques Dupin.

3. Tristan Tzara, "Note sur la poésie," in *Sept manifestes Dada, suivis de lampisteries* (Paris: Pauvert, 1963).

4. Paul Valéry, *Oeuvres*, vol. I, Pléiade edition (Paris: Gallimard, 1957), p. 862.

5. Ibid.

6. E. H. Gombrich, "The Subject of Poussin's Orion," in *Symbolic Images: Studies in the Art of the Renaissance* (New York: Phaidon, 1972), in particular, pp. 121-22. See also Claude Simon, *Orion aveuglé* (Geneva: Skira, 1970).

7. See Sereni, (Chapter One, note 10). All the notes in this book are invaluable.

8. Thomas Hines, "L'Ouvrage de tous les temps, admiré: *Lettera amorosa*/René Char and Georges Braque," *Bulletin du Bibliophile*, no. 1, 1973.

9. *Se rencontrer paysage avec Joseph Sima*, exhibition Château de Ratilly, June 23 to September 16, 1973.

10. Mallarmé's *Igitur*, referred to above in the same connection, is an excellent example of the shadowy play of ambiguity. The comparison with the table and its open book, the candle about to be snuffed out, and the atmosphere of midnight is worth considering. "C'est le rêve pur d'un Minuit, en soi disparu, et dont la Clarté reconnue, qui seule demeure au sein de son accomplissement plongé dans l'ombre, résume sa stérilité sur la pâleur d'un livre ouvert que présente la table . . ." (Pléiade edition, p. 435). In Char and in Mallarmé, the figures of the unicorn and the ancient gods, and in both breath and life play against the dark, as speech against silence and chance against necessity: "Il ferme le livre—souffle la bougie—de son souffle qui contenait le hasard . . ." (Ibid., p. 442).

11. Sereni, p. 217: "Le Tricheur à l'as de carreau," "Rixe de musiciens," "La Diseuse de bonne aventure," "Le Vielleur," are the four works of Georges de La Tour to which Char refers here. "For the oppositions and on the cohabitation of a 'diurnal' painter and a 'nocturnal' one (two times, two manners and thus two languages) the scheme of distinctions essential in the art of Georges de La Tour . . . ," Sereni refers us to the catalog of the La Tour exhibition in the Orangerie (May 10 - September 25, 1972).

12. This statement is a response to and consolation for any translator or critic about to lose one of the meanings of a poem: Char uses it in just that way.

13. See "Evadé d'archipel" in *Aromates chasseurs,* in which Orion represents the figure of the poet, who escapes eventually both from his constellation and from our earth; he is essential, and not to be pinned down to one locality.

14. See note eight above.

15. Valéry, p. 562.

Paulène Aspel (review date spring 1980)

SOURCE: Aspel, Paulène. Review of *Fenêtres dormantes et porte sur le toit. World Literature Today* 54, no. 2 (spring 1980): 250-51.

[*In the following review, Aspel provides an overview of* Fenêtres dormantes et porte sur le toit.]

"Le Temps" ("Time") bears a capital *T* six times. From his early poems on, René Char (see *WLT* [*World Literature Today*] 51:3, pp. 349-403) has often capitalized the first letter of key words for the purpose of conjuring or praising. The uppercase *T* in **"Dormant Windows and Door onto the Roof"** must and will exorcise time, for the latter is "bloody"; it only holds power and secure position. The poet also calls it "recidivist." "Do not glance at it. Ignore it," he warns. "It must not be seen, or felt, still less measured. Time, however, can be defied by the poet's will and stubbornness: "I banged against it with my flash, my fear, among ruins where my obstinacy is still grating."

Poetry intervenes, bold and brave, though modest. It "dares to say what no other voice dares to confess to bloody Time." Called a number of affectionate names, as in previous books, a "fervent worker," the "ravishing," a rose whose wound "equals that of the poet," the she-wolf worrying about her cub leaping ahead, this "magnifying poetry," master of all absurds, is sized up, defended, commended in many texts, especially in the two longest poems, **"Faire du chemin avec . . ."** (**"To Share the Way with . . ."**) and **"Tous partis"** (**"All Gone"**). We are reminded that poetry itself is the main theme in Char's works. In two other long poems, **"Vieira de Silva, chère voisine, multiple et une . . ."** (**"Vieira da Silva, Dear Neighbor, Manifold and One . . ."**) and **"Se rencontrer paysage avec Joseph Sima"** (**"To Become Landscape on Meeting Joseph Sima"**), words, phrases continue to contribute an analysis of poetry. Words exchange their past for our present. They consent or resist: "Somewhere a word suffers with all its meaning within us." Thus confirmed once more is the significant fact that the long prose poem is the locus of poetry par excellence, that it is a trademark of René Char.

First published in 1976, **"To Share the Way with"** bears striking similarities to **"The Library Is on Fire,"** its elder by twenty years. It is the same length, thirty-eight and thirty-seven diversified paragraphs separated by large blanks, where we "bounce from fragment to fragment"; it has the same vibrant, firm aphoristic style, sometimes becoming proverb-like sentences cast in alexandrines: "on se vide de vie, on s'emplit de pardon" (emptied of life, filled with forgiveness). Two major themes of Char emerge: that of poetry, and that of the fellowman, the brother, the same: "How many are infatuated with mankind, not man! To elevate the former, they lower the latter." With man, *la vie,* "the grace of going each time farther" is celebrated, as well as the life given by poetry versus death: "I shall know how to go to the Fate Sisters with the necessary leap which severs regret, neglecting survival, staying with life." "The Matinals would live even if night, if morning no longer existed." But this life is threatened, and **"To Share the Way with"** engages into a bitter, jagged criticism of twentieth-century utopias and totalitarianisms. Little windows open on certain landmarks of the poet's oeuvre. The mention of **Les matinaux,** a book published in 1950, is one. The allusion to the concepts of explosions and fragments cuts out a second window: "Before being pulverized, each thing gets ready and meets our senses," which echoes the "Why 'pulverized poem'?" of **"The Library Is on Fire."** Inserting a picture in a picture, a device often used by painters in their "Studios," is a way for the poet to emphasize important aspects of his esthetics. Painters? Char reasserts his delight in encountering them or watching them paint in section two of the book, appropriately called **"A Whole Day Without Debate."** Seven of the nine artists mentioned have been lauded in other books. A long, elaborate text is devoted to Picasso on the occasion of his death. Char also quotes insights into him as told by Braque, the poet's close friend of many years.

Other old acquaintances are present. Twelve birds add a background of color and wisdom. Oriole, nightingale, the firebird were met before. The angry hoopoe, the sedge warbler are newcomers. The latter is depicted on a familiar "reed shaken by the wind." We remember the birds who, like men, entrust their frailty "to a shock of reeds" in **"The Library Is on Fire."** Thanks to the same poem, we also know that birds and windows are secretly linked, because writing came to Char "like bird's down on [his] windowpane in winter." In the fourth section of **Fenêtres dormantes** the poet "listens by the pane," through his muted memory, to his first, shy "song of the frost."

So those dormant windows are not really asleep after all. A fixed fanlight, a *dormant*—the poet playing on the word—yields even more life. A lot of it is passing through, back and forth. A pane also leads to a stone in the wall beyond, thus participating in the quiet history of a home: "At the end of the whirling steps, the door has no lock: here is the roof. . . . My pain is no longer employed." The poet has stated it clearly in the first poem of the book: he has not committed the "crime of upland." On the contrary, he will continue to go, to go up, to climb, to hoist himself despite the difficulty. A voice against iniquity speaks stronger. And finally, a joy, a plain if frail joy emanates from the sixteen moving poems which comprise the part titled **"Effilage du sac de jute"** (**Fraying the Jute Sack**; 1978-79). These are portraits of a man "walking without foulness," "dressed in jute," a "grinning flame," the poet. Death is being envisaged more and more weightlessly. The wounded rose, in **"Libera II,"** offers the poet "une mort apparentée" (a kindred death).

James R. Lawler (review date spring 1984)

SOURCE: Lawler, James R. "'Not to Renounce': René Char's *Oeuvres complètes.*" *World Literature Today* 58, no. 2 (spring 1984): 222-24.

[*In the following review, Lawler lauds the publication of René Char's* Oeuvres complètes, *explaining how the poet's work "is not of easy access and demands the reader's active participation. The poem is this enigma that does not narrate or confide."*]

The Pléiade **René Char** [*Oeuvres complètes*] is without any doubt a major literary event.[1] The edition, elegant in form and composition, shows the guiding hand of the poet himself. It brings together the fruit of his many collections that have appeared since 1926; presents pieces hitherto unpublished, including several written in the last few years; contains an admirable new dialogue on the practice of poetry. For a good number of texts there are useful, at times precious notes that explain an allusion by adducing a complementary passage or original version or set of variants. In addition, a few friends offer their recollections of René Char as they came to know him in his thirties—his relationship to his native Vaucluse, his service in the maquis—while half a dozen critics of the same generation as Char (Jean Beaufret, Maurice Blanchot and Georges Blin, among others) contribute fragments of previously known and now classical essays. As for the introduction, it is a discriminating commentary by Jean Roudaut, to whom we owe vigorous studies of baroque and modern French literature. The volume is, then, an indispensable resource for our enjoyment of René Char; but, above all, it allows us for the first time to gauge in moving detail the full range of one of the great voices of our century.

"We who write in order to live . . .": passionate urgency infuses the work from one end to the other. The chronological order demonstrates a continuing inventiveness of songs, proverbs, aphorisms, free verse, plays, prose. René Char's most typical mode is the prose poem adopted first and foremost from Rimbaud, who showed its huge imaginative potential; but Char develops the genre in ways that Rimbaud's earlier followers have not approached, not even the stylistically subtle Claudel of *Connaissance de l'Est*. His structures can possess the brevity of "Congé au vent," the spaciousness of "Sur une nuit sans ornement," the rigor of "Allégeance," the anaphoric insistence of "Jacquemard et Julia," the binary patterns of *Contre une maison sèche,* the implicit musical line of *Lettera amorosa.* Yet whatever the chosen form, the poetic energy gives a unique tonus or *dyne* (as Char might say) to this work of fifty years. No poetry more than his creates a forward movement which, if it can never reach its goal of total integration, "furiously," "inclemently" strives toward it. The opening poem of the first collection bears the significant title **"La Torche du prodigue,"** which is the firebrand that burns all barriers in its haste to go beyond; and the final one, from the most recent collection dated 1982 ("A qui s'informe d'une impasse"), is the exorcism of stagnation.

Roulements, jurons, désunion!

Dans la ville nouvelle tout s'accourcit sans rite,
Notre-Dame du Lac voit ses pierres soustraites;
Ne révoquant pas le passé,
La bougie s'affaisse et meurt.

Lors que la beauté naît détruite
Dans le blâme des yeux ouverts,
Faites-vous l'otage du givre,
Le jamais las du bien de vivre.

(Rumblings, oaths, disunion!

In the new city all is shortened without ritual,
Our Lady of the Lake sees her stones carried off;
Because it does not revoke the past,
The candle sinks and dies.

When beauty is born already destroyed
In the blame of unclosed eyes,
Become the hostage of hoarfrost,
Never tired of life's sweetness.)

The conflict, external and internal, is the furor provoked by our time (*ce siècle épouvantable*): in a single exclamation the first three words designate turmoil, violence, isolation. The old harmony is lost; poetry is out of joint; the candle is spent. Men have chosen to live without due commitment, despoiling sacred places, obeying lifeless precedents. But a rhythm is heard that takes up the octosyllabic measures of the title and the first line: the meter that had served to point to error articulates in the second quatrain a principle of conduct so that an ultimate rhyme is achieved rather than imposed. Among the ruins of a cruel age that would betray the imperatives of love and awe, the poet counsels a bond with nature, a dependency with regard to the humblest of images. To submit to hoarfrost is to give oneself to an ardent expectancy. Submission becomes the way to the poem no less than to a vital discipline, like that of René Char's artist of the ice-age caverns who makes of hoarfrost his home and point of departure: "que deviendrai-je m'est d'une chaleur presque infinie" (*what shall I become* is for me almost infinitely warm). The metaphrastic function is inseparable from a moral statement; and the idea of beauty— "La Beauté, la Beauté hauturière, apparue dès les premiers temps de notre cœur. . . ." (Beauty, noble Beauty of the high seas, that appeared from the earliest times of our heart)—involves the quest for ontological wholeness.

Yet can this intention be expressed other than by indirections? René Char's language is not of easy access and demands the reader's active participation. The poem is this enigma that does not narrate or confide. We are at furthest remove from confessional or descriptive literature, equally far from didacticism: "Supprimer l'éloignement tue. Les dieux ne meurent que d'être parmi nous" (To suppress distance is to kill. The gods die only from being among us). The words are a discontinuity by virtue of which the poem is first and foremost a mystery for the poet himself. They come with their evident rhythm and tone, yet their sense lies in paradoxes that hold reason at bay: "Remarquez que je ne brûle pas les relais, mais que je les élude" (Note that I do not rush through the halts but rather I avoid them). By a sequence of ellipses, at the end of an oblique course, the moment of Orphic recognition occurs—"une prairie irriguée un soir d'été," "le campanile percé par l'orgie du vent" (a field irrigated on a summer evening, a campanile traversed by the wind's orgy). A conversation with France Huser dated 1980 and published in the Pléiade edition for the first time treats in lyrical manner the art of composition, "a game full of ruses and invention," like an act of seduction. The title *Sous ma casquette amarante* refers to René Char's dark red cap but also to the autumn flower which, in the way of the poem, "does not wither." Fire and water, moon and sun, beauty and truth conjoin in the substance of the text whose culminating figure is the woman, a shimmering Diana sensual and transparent, who was loved with the eyes of a Provençal adolescent, and loved and loved again under other names as poetry itself: "Je venais d'avoir quatorze ans et Diane n'avait que l'âge du désir qu'elle suscitait" (I had just turned fourteen and Diana was only as old as the desire she awakened).

Vaucluse was, and has remained, the living source of René Char's lyricism—a landscape of arid heat, mistral, spring waters; of aromatics, wheat, vines. Char does not depict it as such but, rather, its code of concrete wisdom, its alliance of sensuous charm and symbolic meaning. His verse echoes deeply in us like that of few other poets: "Je suis épris de ce morceau tendre de paysage". . . ."; "Comme tendrement rit la terre. . . .";

"Rivière trop tôt partie, d'une traite, sans compagnon. . . ."; "O le blé vert dans une terre. . . ."; "Pures pluies, femmes attendues. . . ." It is plain that nature in the later collections takes on a particular spareness: no less central, it is graver, less jubilant: "La douleur est le dernier fruit, lui immortel, de la jeunesse" (Pain is the last fruit—an immortal one—of youth). On the other hand, the will is still as strong to turn to its refreshment, which is identified with consolation and reborn desire. **"Se réchauffer l'ardeur"** was written in December 1981.

> Dans le froid, le vent, lancées vers vos montagnes,
> Se confiant à leur rougeur,
> Point d'ailes comme les vôtres, mes grives en décembre;
> Moi je baisse la tête et j'amarre à la rive,
> Coureur des eaux vertes originairement;
> Oui, nous sommes pareils lorsque la peur nous crible
> De son savoir jamais usé.
>
> Le soleil disparut sur sa palette étroite
> Taisant son lendemain fatal.
> Nous ouvrîmes de guerre lasse
> Sur la terre enfantine l'écluse d'un bref sommeil.
>
> (In the cold, the wind, darting toward your mountains,
> Confident in their redness,
> No wings like yours, my December thrushes;
> I lower my head and moor by the bank,
> Originally a runner of green waters;
> Yes, we are alike when fear fills us
> With its ever powerful knowledge.
>
> The sun disappeared on its narrow palette
> Concealing its fatal tomorrow.
> Wearily we opened
> Over the earth of childhood the sluice of a short sleep.)

The irregular rhythm moves to an alexandrine balance, then to a series of even-syllabled lines, predominantly octosyllabic; and this evolution corresponds to a change from the forceful description of a December flock of birds whose redness is promise to a sober return to the self. By daring grammatical inversion the energy of the thrushes is caught in the first three lines, which contrasts with the subsequent pause of the boatsman who from experience knows the risks, and deceptions, and deadly lures. Yet his halt is not surrender but necessary respite, and the sluice waters of sleep offer a renewal secretly parallel to sunrise. Nature is this ever efficacious land of childhood: the heart has not lost its ability to find joy in birds, stream, sun, which it transforms into spiritual vitality like Rimbaud's "Million d'oiseaux d'or."

Nevertheless, if this poetry is attached to its native earth, it is also nurtured by age-old languages to which it pays large tribute. Few books are as generous as *Recherche de la base et du sommet* (originally published in 1955 and, since, much augmented) in the naming of poets, painters, friends—Substantial Allies,

Grand Compellers; and the recent *La Planche de Vivre* (1982), a series of English, American, Spanish, Italian and Russian poems translated by René Char in collaboration with Tina Jolas, is further proof of his openness. But these encounters are not stylistic, or thematic, but ontological: the game of poetry is a perilous one and the stakes are high. "Je vous écris en cours de chute" (I write to you in free fall), he says; again, speaking of the poet: "Ne te plains pas de vivre plus près de la mort que les mortels" (Do not complain that you live closer to death than mortals); again, of the poem that is at once the sudden vision of tree and harp: "Contrepoint du vide auquel je crois" (Counterpoint of the emptiness in which I believe). It is this integrity of thought and feeling, this combination of disabusement and beauty, that gives his work such power, for it assumes past and present while remaining faithful to threatened hopes. We think of René Char's interpretation of "La Bête innommable" in the Lascaux frieze as the eternal mother—"Wisdom with tear-filled eyes"—misunderstood, compassionate like the poem; we think too of the latest of all the texts included in the Pléiade volume, which is an untitled prose poem dated August 1982.

> Comme les larmes viennent aux yeux puis naissent et se pressent les mots font de même. Nous devons seulement les empêcher de s'écraser comme les larmes ou de refouler au plus profond.
>
> Un lit en premier les accueille: les mots rayonnent. Un poème va bientôt se former, il pourra, par les nuits étoilées, courir le monde, ou consoler les yeux rougis. Mais pas renoncer.
>
> (As tears well up to our eyes, then appear and hurry forth, so do words. We must only prevent them from being crushed or repressing innermost depths.
>
> A bed welcomes them first of all: the words are radiant. Soon a poem will be formed that will, on starry nights, be able to race across the world or to console reddened eyes. But not to renounce.)

Other poets have compared tears to poetic language; thus, Valéry comes to mind when he writes in one of his notebooks: "Et comme viennent les larmes aux yeux de l'ému, ainsi les paroles divines et *plus qu'exactes* du poète. . . ." (And as tears come to the eyes of an emotional man, so do the divine and *more than accurate* words of the poet). Yet in René Char the development goes, beyond a reference to the immediate sensibility, to an act of will, an act of love, a dynamic effect. The involuntary event is a prelude to the poet's husbanding care: the words find a familiar place, are brought to a bed of intimacy. Now a new conception and birth takes place which is the poem whose action in the world is multiple, its accompanying stars like crystalline tears; it traverses space as unfettered being, or—here the text comes full circle—brings comfort to tear-stained eyes. The piece might end here, but, in a manner typical of René Char, we find an unexpected

conclusion. The three words, "Mais pas renoncer," are a sign of the courage that is infused in his language as he escapes from formal and thematic symmetry. Like the tear, indeed like the collection of poetry as a whole, his poem is a statement whose ultimate veracity lies in its moral resoluteness, leaner today but no less exigent than in his early years. As he promised us four decades ago: "I shall not write a poem of consent."

Note

1. René Char. *Oeuvres complètes.* Jean Roudaut, intro. Paris. Gallimard (Bibliothèque de la Pléiade). 1983. lxxxvii + 1,364 pages. $45. On Char see also *WLT* 51:3, pp. 349-403.

John Porter Houston (essay date September 1985)

SOURCE: Houston, John Porter. "Modes of Symbolism in René Char's Poetry." *French Forum* 10, no. 3 (September 1985): 339-54.

[*In the following essay, Houston examines themes, images, and symbols in selected works of René Char.*]

The three most helpful books on Char's work are concerned with tracing the evolution of his poetics, themes, and images.[1] I intend to focus here on poetic structures, how symbols inform them, and the attendant problems in reading. The poems discussed all date from *Fureur et mystère* (1948) on and are mostly prose poems. I have left aside the aphorisms and do not attempt to fit the poems into any historical pattern, although a careful reader of Char can readily sense the existence of one. Since the Orion myth in Char has received much attention, I have not concerned myself with it. On the other hand, I have tried to discuss as many difficult texts as seemed feasible. The publication of the Pléiade edition of the *Oeuvres complètes* in 1983 (ed. Jean Roudaut [Paris: Gallimard]) has provided readers with some new material in its notes and variants, which I have made use of. For those who wish to refer to the poems in other editions, I have indicated the source for each piece: *FM* (*Fureur et mystère,* 1948), *LM* (*Les Matinaux,* 1950), *PA* (*La Parole en archipel,* 1962), *NP* (*Le Nu perdu,* 1971).

* * *

A useful preliminary approach to Char's symbolism is to analyze his use of female figures, for they are abundant in Char's poetry and their significance and mode of being vary considerably. In some poems, we encounter a woman in her ordinary human and sexual identity. Such is the case of **"Léonides"** (*FM*), where the repeated phrase "Es-tu ma femme" suggests the basic natural relation of the couple. At first she is sleeping; her "hypnose du phénix" implies she will reawaken, as does the ivy (a symbol of the recurrence of life, as well as of the feminine need for protection), with which the stone or sleep of time has surrounded her. She is told of the poet's progress: combat and the rose of his violence (with the positive sense of revolt it often has in Char) have yielded them their land, where bees and "pain naïf" denote plenty and creativity; a "Fête" awaits them (which the shooting stars of the title would seem to allude to). Amid all this symbolism, much of it familiar and recurrent in Char's poetry, "ma femme faite pour atteindre la rencontre du présent" keeps her human and material quality. She is simply the poet's authentic companion, whereas his conquests are metaphorical. Likewise, in **"Biens égaux"** (*FM*) the poet's garden of poetry differs distinctly from the woman he meets, who has pointedly "emerged" from a hymn or imaginative plane into reality, the concreteness of the latter being stressed by the explicit reference to sexual intercourse, after which the poet meditates, in regard to the woman's unresponsiveness, on disunity and unity.

The balance between the impression Char creates of a literal woman (though not, of course, necessarily of any one specific woman in real life) is sometimes a matter of detail. In **"La Minutieuse"** (*PA*) the poet walks through a flooded landscape with "Toi et cette Autre qui était Toi." We learn shortly that one of the figures stays behind in a village and represents the woman's childhood, but to obviate any suggestion of abstraction, the poet holds in his hands both women's breasts, which seem not so much to imply spiritual nourishment as to sexualize the figures. The trees of memory are finally reached, and the temporal symbolism of the flood, which appears to threaten no one, becomes clear. But when the poet asks the remaining figure her "eternal name," she replies "la Minutieuse," a term which suggests the method of the poem with its largely paratactic succession of details. Thus the identification of woman and poem extends to the kind of imagination involved, not merely to the basic subject matter.

A woman's imagination explicitly envelops the poet in **"Envoûtement à La Renardière"** (*FM*), where she makes the blue-ringed eye of the air blink at her light, although no one has ever seen her face before except the poet at this moment when the wheel of life's alternations reaches a stopping point in its phases ("classes"). The abundance of symbolic expression is countered finally by words susceptible of a more concrete reading: the poet's memory has since known the "monsters," a word Char uses almost exclusively to designate the enemy in World War II, and he has also "survived" the woman of this "Chant de Vous" and taken on a new role ("sosie"). Of course, we could allegorize the poem in the most abstract way and say that Char records here his giving up poetry during his Resistance years, but

that seems a bit crudely reductive. However, the connotations of the female figure do go far beyond the human and sexual. In a very short poem, **"Maison doyenne"** (*FM*), the face which is seen in the winter "water flowers of the grass" and in the forest achieves a perfect ambiguity between the memory of a woman and an inner force associated with summer. "Mon amour" in the long, symbolic **"Les Trois Sœurs"** (*FM*) is connected with victory (the poem dates from the *drôle de guerre*) and, naturally, because of her sex, with the demonic child who is born in this time of upheaval. Nevertheless, like the woman in **"Chaume des Vosges"** (*LM*), written in the same circumstances, she need not be seen as a cause in any abstract sense.

The use of allegory in Char's poetry encompasses the range from poems in which abstract or thematic words or even statements provide an element of interpretive commentary, to those in which an action must be worked out solely in terms of narrative configurations or traditional symbols. A curious example of both kinds of poems in one is **"Faim rouge"** (*NP*), which in its first version had an epigraph designating the dead woman as revolution. In the poem's definitive form, it is something of an enigma: a woman associated with the poet dies, yet follows him, and a man who once slept with her contentedly dines. The earlier version, by the words "boulevard extérieur," also made clear that the woman was a prostitute. While **"Faim rouge,"** as it is printed today, makes almost impossible demands on our powers of reading, **"Congé au vent"** (*FM*), with only the vaguest suggestion of self-contained commentary, employs classic symbols which, by extension, are easily interpreted. In the absence of wind (that is, change, process) a girl comes from the mimosa harvest. Crops often suggest poetry in Char, and yellow mimosa corresponds to the sun in its meaning of eternal life. Walking away from the setting sun, she appears to be approaching a previously mentioned village. The poet finds it would be "sacrilegious" to speak to her; she is like a lamp with a "halo." The question which concludes the poem suggests, in condensed form, everything that is antithetical to the girl and field: "Peut-être aurez-vous la chance de distinguer sur ses lèvres la chimère de l'humidité de la Nuit?" Village and night betoken society, rest, sexuality, and above all mortality. The question is whether there is a connection between the poetic vision, for which Char uses Christian symbolism like so many post-Christian poets, and man's ordinary life or the poet seen in his purely human capacities. Char's themes work by implication and sometimes antithesis: poetry implies a poet, who is usually seen as one with his art, but here a gap is sensed between the mode of existence of poetry and that of the poet. If it is not quite a thorough-going antithesis, the disparity still generates wonder and uncertainty.

At times our reading may legitimately hesitate between the symbolic and the literal. The brief **"Dot de Maubergeonne"** (*NP*) speaks of a bride, the traditional symbolic herbs she has received, and the "rejoicing of roads" before her nuptial chamber. The speaker wishes a windy day for her when she emerges. The association among roads, moving onward like the wind, and imagination is frequent in Char's work, but should the bride be seen as a symbol or as a woman for whom a rich future is hoped? We have here a real crux. If **"La Dot de Maubergeonne"** is, however, too slight a piece to merit much concern, the remarkable **"Eclairage du pénitencier"** (*FM*), placed among war and Resistance poems in *Fureur et mystère,* presents a more complex problem. The poem is initially addressed to a *toi,* whose night the poet has wished to be short, in order to deceive "ta marâtre taciturne." Day—by virtue of the title—and nature—with its unwanted cyclic alternations—could be referred to, but the poet's subsequent dreaming of himself "à ton côté" suggests more that *toi* is a woman, for whom he would be an "être fugitif harmonieux," an escapee from the prison and associated with roads. As daylight dwindles, other expressions consonant with the figure of the poet are used. Although he is "exclu" and a prisoner, he is also "comblé" by a vision of "beauté planeuse," which he addresses as *vous.* Usually, Char distinguishes *vous* and *tu* not by number or degree of intimacy, but to make clear that different persons or things are being spoken to. "Beauté" can either be abstract or designate a woman—or even something else. Perhaps here it means evening light, real or imagined like a woman. In any case, the poet feels contentment, although he realizes that his imprisonment is not yet at its worst: there is a poetic wind blowing over his yoke and lightening the sensation of it, as opposed to what will come later. The prison could have a social, political, or even psychological meaning, yet this does not disturb one so much as the fact that the antithesis to prison is rendered with complete ambiguity. In a symbolic convention in which women give off light and light represents the outside world where women are, we can scarcely eliminate polysemous readings, especially given the further frequent association of women with poetry and of poetry with the natural world.

I have spoken of antitheses as representing either complementaries or antagonisms in Char's poetic discourse. If man and woman are often complementary, man as poet is opposed to non-poets, and these may include women. A rather unusual modification of Char's familiar patterns occurs in **"La Passe de Lyon"** (*PA*), which tells of the poet's meeting a prostitute, "dans le répit des filatures," in the Place Bellecour. She has unexpected associations with imagination: her eyes "voyagent," her light is exchanged for that of meteors. Whether this is an ironic description of her allurements or a parody of Char's gallant manner is hard to say, but the poet characterizes himself with seeming serious-

ness: "Avec mes songes, avec ma guerre, avec mon baiser, sous le mûrier ressuscité. . . ." The poet is interested in "isolating" his "conquest" from her previous encounters with men and scarcely cares how many men she will have sex with afterward, provided that his experience becomes a "chef-d'œuvre"—poetic or otherwise, it is not clear. The conclusion consists of an apostrophe to his sexual desires, which function almost autonomously, with little regard for him as a whole. This woman is clearly incidental to the poetic vocation.

In **"Joue et dors"** (*LM*), which contains a characteristic kind of social allegory of good-humored oppressors driving a couple into a desert, thereby reducing their love to a purely "mortal" good fortune, the poet opposes his thirst for the tokens of imagination (aromatic herbs, clouds over the sea) to the necessity of not exposing his companion to danger by escaping with her. Woman as hindrance is most elegantly conveyed in **"Le Gaucher"** (*NP*), whose speaker regrets that an "odorante main" in his does not keep him from ravines, thorns, social pressures and other unpleasant sides of life, but does take away from him the "consolation" of contemplating evening light and sunset. The crepuscular image, fairly unusual in Char's work, may suggest more precisely a consolation for aging and death. (The fact that being left-handed, unable to hold another's hand properly, is a lifelong condition may be only an irrelevant association.) Finally, in **"Les Lichens"** (*LM*) the road, so often indicative of imagination, becomes a road of life in a wasteland, where a couple separates *à l'amiable.* We reach again the point where the female figure does not cause, represent, or participate in visionary experience, but is merely his opposite in one aspect of the poet's life.

The handling of feminine figures suggests some of the gamut of effects in Char's poetry. One particular device we have seen that Char exploits in poems which contain no overt commentary or abstract, thematic words is contrast. Antithesis in expression or bipartition in structure tend to generate meaning, even if they are too schematic to constitute an articulated argument in the traditional fashion. For example, the speaker of **"Cur secessisti?"** (*FM*) has withdrawn to a stone dungeon, where he addresses the winter sun and tells it of his sons on the hills: "mes fils qui sont incendiaires, mes fils qu'on tue sans leur fermer les yeux, s'augmentent de votre puissance." The parent-child relation summons up the analogy of poet-poem, and, unlike Char's usual poet figures, this one is not free, but has channeled his liberty into his work, so that he and his progeny stand in an antithetical relationship. Combativeness and incendiary violence are indeed more often the property of poems than of their authors, to whom these attributes are given by hypallage, as elsewhere in Char's work. However, the title of this poem is not answered; we do not know why the poet has withdrawn, a piece of information which would have perhaps raised the antithesis to an argument.

In **"Mirage des Aiguilles"** (*NP*), which is longer, the antithesis is more elaborate. A substantial collective portrait opens the poem, in which we see cheerful, self-contented men who do not care to be aware that they are systematically robbed and deceived by those around them. Moreover, the images of their inadequately seasoned bread and of the hastily concealed "diamond of creation" indicate that these are inferior poets. The discouraged novice of the second part of the poem faces a plain of sinister fire, unlike the inviting, open spaces drawing other poet figures in Char's work. The present is a "massacre d'archers," and thus the red plain is also a "trésor de boucher, sanglante à un croc." The power of the poem lies partly in the very imperfection and, therefore, unexpectedness of the antithesis as far as imagery goes. If the thematic content offers exact opposition, a vision of red scarcely corresponds to the preceding portrait in the manner of light to darkness or of other imagistic counterparts. Interestingly enough, however, the two sections are in syntactic contrast: there is only one main finite verb in the rather nominal second part, whereas the first consists almost entirely of normal whole sentences.

There is only one poet, but two kinds of poetry in **"Aiguevive"** (*NP*). A carefully protected spring has been sending its water, marked with a "provident" face, to the garden of the poet's enemies. He resolves to abandon his usual inviting water poetry and seek his inspiration in the dry and austere back country: "La faute est levée." This brief moral and esthetic allegory relies on a familiar symbol and its antithesis, but the running water of **"L'Abri rudoyé"** (*NP*) is said to share the poet's affection with grass, "qu'une charge de pierres arrête comme un revers obscur met fin à la pensée." If this is an opposition of free movement to patient growth, it suggests Char's two symbols of creativity, movement into the distance and dogged work, but the final simile evokes more the contrast of life and death. Traditional symbolism does not dispel the ambiguity, as it does, for example, in Char's bestiary poems, where one can usually detect, even with little commentary, which qualities of the animal and its enemy are relevant.[2] Thus in **"Le Vipereau"** (*PA*) the snake's role as outsider relates him to the poet. **"La Rainette"** (*NP*) preserves herself in water while the wind whips the bushes against the sky in its "aberration." Of course, as we approach such emblematic descriptions, we move into a realm where we are obliged to make a self-conscious exegesis; we are using a different mode of reading from that we employ when merely perceiving the imagistic oppositions of poetry which lacks a literal level of meaning. It is idle to debate the merits of the two kinds of allegory, but in the one the tension between literalism and symbolism forces us into intellectual reflection of a kind that encourages unnecessary ingenuity and risks making the commentary too imposing for the poem.

Char's range of stylistic techniques is vast, and in some poems the presence of distinctions is more readily felt than easily demonstrated, so intricate is the language. In **"Permanent invisible"** (*NP*), for example, we know, reading back from the end, that a "double jardin," two distinct, yet related things, is covered by the title phrase, and we can roughly perceive them as poetry and sexuality. "Invisible" is not always a literal term in Char: it implies enduringness (and so the title is slightly redundant), as well as a higher mode of being or feeling than that of routine pleasures. The difficulty in reading lies in the metaphoric overlay of references to hunting. "Chasse," of course, is so ordinary a figurative term as not to cause a problem, but "gibier" is more precise: "boire frileusement" suggests something one might do while literally hunting, and "être brutal répare" could also fit the allusion. On the other hand, "Proche, proche invisible et si proche à mes doigts" suits poetic creation, and "novice corps à corps" strongly evokes the sexual (as might "boire" and "être brutal" as well). In between the references to "proche invisible" and the "corps à corps" occurs the phrase "distant gibier." It is very difficult in this context of shifting, slithery connotations to point out exactly at what point in the poem the distinction is found between poetry and sexuality, for, while assimilated to each other to a considerable degree by the title, they also constitute separate "gardens." (The variants, in this case, suggest some modification in the speaker's attitude in the course of reworking, but do not constitute a necessarily clearer version.)

Another uncommon structural pattern occurs in **"Fenaison"** (*FM*), where, as in much of Breton's poetry, the sentence forms are plain, with only modest hypotaxis, but a new image is introduced in each one, so that we are constantly confronted with problems of relation and sequence. A general narrative configuration can be perceived: the speaker, who has had only the "appearance" of a night of felicity after the death of the evil and deceiving "faneur," goes through a struggle, defined in terms of work, and concludes that he is of too late and decadent an age to succeed in his undertaking. After lamenting that he is unable to "translate" his Sister from childhood into a galaxy, he recognizes that a strong companion will lead him to the end of the poem and triumphantly march off the next day. The words pertaining to night ("félicité," "oiseaux," "désir," "Sœur"), to work ("pelle," "sueurs," "chantourne sa langue"), and to the poet's heritage (the Pythian or prophetic knighthood) are suitable for poetic activity, and the poem alludes to itself at its end. Nevertheless, the harvest or "fenaison" does not seem to have its usual sense of achievement, and the "Faneur" who has led the poet to this point in a cursed journey, appears to be not so much a reaper as a witherer or destroyer, in accordance with the other sense of the verb *faner*. Some details are clear, such as the poet's desire to huddle anonymously on the ship of life, an act of renunciation. The Sister from "les temps purs" is not at all sexualized, and the companion is perhaps another self or part of the self. Still, a number of words and phrases resist commentary ("mon front aux moulinets d'une lampe d'anémone"), and the poem seems much closer than most of Char's mature work to the Surrealist esthetic of his youth, where the desire for surprise and discontinuity is stronger than the concern for coherent symbolism. Mystery and intermittent clarity join.

The fondness for bipartition largely replaced the Surrealist kind of image sequence in Char, but the relation between the two parts of a poem is not necessarily antithetical. In **"Fréquence"** (*FM*), for example, Char links a distorted image of forging (the smith hammers the ground and extracts metal) to that of the smith cooling his arm in water and reaching for the deep "cold bell" of water plants. (An anecdote in the notes to the Pléiade edition clarifies the relation of forging to the traditional barrel of cooling water and to the river.) The images represent two aspects of poetic creation which tend to be separated elsewhere in Char: repeated labor (whence "fréquence") and the quest.

"Fréquence" brings us closer to unitary imagery, and certain poems embody it even more fully. The brief **"Tracé sur le gouffre"** (*NP*) presents someone or something as suffering, turning into a river, then a road, and crossing through death. Since "it" has a secret, I presume, the poet's life is the relevant analogue, but with no defining, contrastive image, the poem is rather elusive. The figure in **"L'Absent"** (*FM*) was opposed to society's lies and confusion; he has vanished, but remains the "fourneau" or burning center of "unity," apparently the unity of the speaker's world or being. The poet's former self (with whom violence and other traits of "l'absent" are connected in certain retrospective poems) would seem to be an acceptable answer to the implicit enigma of the piece. The twin beggar-roses of **"Le Jugement d'octobre"** (*NP*) have become a slight puzzle by the omission of material included in the variants, but the banality of the symbolism (late roses and hope) is not likely to detain the reader. A far greater example of a poem centered on one figure demands our attention.

If a unitary subject is unsupported by symbolic conventions, traditional or peculiar to the poet, it can, according to the degree of literalness of the language, give rise to a poem of monolithic difficulty. One of what I think are Char's two finest poems pertaining to the Resistance is cast in a form of expression which, had Char not briefly indicated elsewhere its subject, would risk making it all but incomprehensible. **"L'Extravagant"** (*FM*) is not an allegory in the

ordinary sense of using metonymic or analogical terms; rather, tone and turn of phrase veil the horrifying episode described, about which Char would say only that it was a "marche au supplice," evidently the execution of one of his fellow *résistants*.[3]

Something is amiss or idiosyncratic about the idiom of the poem right from the beginning: "Il ne déplaçait pas d'ombre en avançant. . . ." This fussy circumlocution evidently means that the figure is walking erect and not swaying from side to side, even though "son pas fût assez vulgaire," a rather supercilious observation quite in keeping with the tone of the almost *précieux* speaker. It is next suggested that those who get up after little sleep may be "tentés par les similitudes." We do not know for sure if the speaker is one of those who are up at an unaccustomed hour—his speech is too indirect for such a blunt statement—but he proceeds immediately into metaphor, including this periphrasis for snow: "cristaux à prétention fabuleuse que la morne démarche du quotidien sécrète, aux lieux de son choix, avec des attouchements de suaire." This flower of rhetoric, in which we see a penchant for abstractions and verbal nouns suggestive of both Neoclassical and late 19th-century "decadent" styles, leads us to a negative comparison, here an idle-seeming embellishment: "Tel n'était pas ce marcheur. . . ." We begin to see that the economy of movement of the walking figure stands in contrast to the lavish phrase-making of the speaker, who is "l'extravagant," overflowing with rhetorical invention.

By a kind of transference or hypallage, the icy wind whipping the figure's face is said to be "impersonal," but of course it is the condemned man who is losing his person and identity. Beneath the flowery idiom we can sometimes distinguish meanings other than the surface one: the night is clean, that is, the snow untrodden, because the night "était commune à la généralité des habitants de l'univers qui ne la pénétraient pas." Other men have abandoned the doomed figure or refuse to be aware of him. His detachment from life is insisted on in an ambiguous phrase: "Il avait perdu tout lien avec le volume ancien des sources propices aux interrogations." The "sources" can be springs, symbolic of the future in Char, which one may question about one's own life, or else a figurative book of matters about which his tormentors have interrogated their prisoner under pressure. He has also lost touch "avec les corps heureux qu'il s'était plu à animer auprès du sien lorsqu'il pouvait encore assigner une cime à son plaisir, une neige à son talent." "Corps heureux" follows the Buffonesque model of using a very general term and adding an ennobling adjective; the generality of "animer" in turn permits it to apply both to sex ("plaisir") and to social relations ("talent," in a somewhat old-fashioned absolute sense). "Neige" is an elegant variation for "cime." Somewhat strained idiom continues: "La terre avait faussé sa persuasion," that is, lost its charm. The fact that the man was not necessary to anyone else's life becomes "l'utile ne l'avait pas assisté, ne l'avait pas dessiné en entier aux regards des autres." This "comédien," who like all actors is detached from his personal life while performing, finally "tourne à jamais le dos au printemps qui n'existe pas," the most eloquent phrase in the poem. His death is a final act of indifference to life.

The language of **"L'Extravagant"** is at times distant, almost as if the speaker did not know what was happening. The insipidity of his idiom, which is "literary" in the most pejorative sense, heightens the horror of what is being narrated. At the same time, the attenuating periphrases seem to render the gradual psychological emptying and vanishing of the actor's individuality. The intentional choice of a tone and style that are not, by ordinary criteria, suitable to the matter presented can be a rare and covertly eloquent device, making a virtue of that disparity between expression and subject which we normally associate with inept writers. It was part of Voltaire's array of mordant resources, and Baudelaire also used it in prose, notably in "Le Mauvais Vitrier." There are a few other places where Char uses special styles as an integral part of his design, but in contrasting patterns. Thus **"L'Inoffensif"** (*PA*) presents two poets' descriptions of sunset and the disappearance of a loved one: the first is an unctuous, luxuriantly "poetic" evocation of the clichés of evening melancholy; the second is a terse, violent, authentic rendering of the same material. Style takes on moral as well as psychological and esthetic values. In **"Bienvenue"** (*NP*) glorious visions of the poet's afterlife sound like a parody of some of Char's more exultant poems, while the conclusion bluntly points out that an engraved stone, that is, silence and the written word, are what the poet will be reduced to. The images and aphorisms of **"Contre une maison sèche"** (*NP*) are arranged in pairs so that the style of the second often corrects and comments on the first.

Stylistic indirection is also marked in Char's allusions to religion. Aside from one overt reference to Christ's inadequacy in the events of the war (**"Carte du 8 novembre"** [*FM*]), these are generally somewhat veiled and ambiguous, despite genuine vehemence. The simplest, because of its use of traditional imagery, is to be found in **"Violences"** (*FM*). The allegory begins with the poet's lantern, his quest, which leads him to a prison courtyard, where eel fishermen come nightly to gather the few sparse herbs the place has to offer to bait their lines with. The symbolism is rich: fishing for eels, a treacherous, devious prey, is a perversion of the Christian pursuit of the wholesome fish or *ichthys* ("Jesus Christ, Son of God, Saviour") in the lifegiving sea, a contrast marked in the phrase "pègre des écumes," applied to the eel-fishers. The speaker disdains a life spent with these nighttime prisoners and enters the garden of the dead. Its flowers, however, are "servile" traitors, the "companions of men," but also the "ears" of a remote, forbidding Creator, with whom communication goes only one way.

Elsewhere the symbolism is less overt, and we are aware primarily that there is some sinister force which cannot be clearly ascribed to the social or political domain. In **"Calendrier"** (*FM*) a turbulent sequence of images includes references not only to a beneficent female presence, "spacious force," rising movement, moral consolidation, and the disarming of equinoctial storms, but also to an enslavement to the oracle, which the poet is now free of. "J'éprouve ou non la grâce" is his ironic comment—grace in his sense, but not in that of others. The beach which winter had strewn with "légendes régressives" and thorny sibyls is now cleared and smoothed over. Char's fondness for terms from métiers unexpectedly shows up at the end of the poem: "Je sais que la conscience qui se risque n'a rien à redouter de la plane." The poem's language is like a kind of symbolic shorthand in its dense use of brief allusions to imagery and themes developed elsewhere in Char's work; however, all the varied positive images are clearly grouped against a single coherent strain of negative references (oracle, backward legends, and sibyls), which, under a classical guise, designate Christianity. Much more cryptic is the allusion in **"Note sibérienne"** (*NP*), where, in a "Nordic" land remote from Char's usual settings, a new, hostile kind of snow has been falling and the suffering inhabitants repeat in protest that "nous sommes une étincelle à l'origine inconnue qui incendions toujours plus en avant." The divine origin and immortality of the soul is alleged in the face of a world gone wrong, but the soul eludes all proof of its existence: we cannot even hear it "râler et crier" at the moment of our death.

With **"Les Inventeurs"** (*LM*), we find a perfectly clear and elegant narrative about a people who irrigate, plow, and build in contentment, while "les forestiers de l'autre versant," who come to warn them of a cyclonic storm predicted by their ancestors, thrive rather on a crude life dominated by terror and superstition. The allusion to religion seems to me fairly evident, and a somewhat similar poem, **"Les Seigneurs de Maussane"** (*LM*), has a comparable suggestion. These poems are very different from the ones where dark political forces threaten, but there is one piece which seems to combine the idea of the supernatural and the political. In **"Fossile sanguinaire"** (*NP*) the conquering enemy brings torments "dont il n'était ni l'auteur ni l'inventeur." The enemy is merely the agent of a "supplice dont la décision provenait on ne sait d'où." The point of the poem is perhaps that the surviving ("demeurant") old speaker resists the invasion, as do the "providential" young, but the mysterious origins of the evil descended upon the land have an analogy in certain conceptions of original sin.

Finally, **"Dyne"** (*NP*), a very difficult text, appears to me to refer to Christ in "l'homme transpercé," whom the poet passes by in order to find his own "Verbe" and faith. The poet's paradise turns out to be an austere desert, but one of his own making, in contrast to the "sites immémoriaux" graced by "la lyre fugitive du père." The "Verbe" is more specifically referred to in **"Seuil"** (*FM*). When mankind's dam breaks because of the "abandon du divin," words try to rescue themselves. "Là se décida la dynastie de leur sens." This would seem to allude to the fact that a post-Christian poet like Char necessarily uses a vocabulary rich in Christian resonances, even though it has been purged of any theological reference. Roads, morning, springs, and other symbols derive from centuries of Christian figurative use, just as Christian expression drew, in its origins, on antecedent imagery. In a characteristic shift, the words become "friends" in the second part of the poem—there is bipartition without antithesis—and they are welcomed by the poet's "laughing" cypress staff, which rejoices over being freed from the cemetery, where traditional usage kept the cypress.

Not only are Char's references to religion infrequent, but also, as a result, they employ language which does not form part of his usual symbolic vocabulary. In a number of other poems we find, in addition to familiar categories of imagery, expressions which seem cryptic or terms whose customary figurative associations are altered. For example, in **"Affres, détonation, silence"** (*FM*), the memorial poem for Roger Bernard, the phrase "la foudre au visage d'écolier" alludes at once to death and poetry, since Bernard was a poet; "visage d'écolier" is not so much an odd iconographic conception of death as a reference to the fact that Bernard was still quite young when he was killed. In **"Le Banc d'ocre"** (*NP*) the glowworm symbolizes death beckoning, in ghost-like fashion, to the aging couple. The ash tree in **"Sous le feuillage"** (*NP*) is the poet's proper shelter because ash trees cannot be burned or destroyed by lightning, and *foudre* is what emanates from him ("frapper du regard" is a figurative thunderbolt). **"L'Ouest derrière soi perdu"** (*NP*) alludes to the old association between the west and the darkness of death; in winter the west has disappeared, but returns in spring as an ordinary landscape. **"Pénombre"** (*FM*) suggests the symbol of the center or place outside banal space and containing an essential, almost magic reality; the distant stars appear hostile because they represent the laws and fate of the ordinary world. The "non lumineux" of **"Mutilateurs"** (*NP*) is the revolt which did not take place, as a result of which the fountain of poetry and the future is defaced and life (called "time" by metonymy) limps. The "vitrail" of **"Force clémente"** (*FM*) represents poetry, and the elliptical absolute construction means "I create poetry if. . . ." The "Fête" of **"Grège"** (*LM*) seems at first to betoken love or life; however, the death with which it is contrasted is figurative, lying both before and after the *fête* (cf. "retour à la mort"). Actually, the *fête* appears to be creativity, of which love is but one aspect, and must be abandoned triumphantly before the poet's powers wane and his aspirations become "irréalisables."

Two poems are built around terms which seem to shift in meaning in the course of them. "Mon amour" in **"Allégeance"** (*FM*) is not a woman, but the poet's love, a part of him personified, which is not clear until the end of the poem, where we learn that his love was once loved, an expression which explains the title. A somewhat misleading line also opens **"Le Mortel Partenaire"** (*PA*), which is an allegory based on boxing. The first words are "Il la défiait." Despite the feminine pronoun, this is not some banal "battle of the sexes" or much less "bed," as one commentator puts it. Char is very careful that we do not form some kinky image of a couple in boxing gloves and trunks. The second boxer becomes "l'adversaire," then "le second" and then "celui-ci." While the masculine noun *adversaire* can be used of women, it is unidiomatic to make sustained reference to a woman with masculine nouns and pronouns. In spite of the feminine suggestion of "une virginité agréable," Char is blurring and shifting his imagery, the technique we have noted in "Permanent invisible." The second boxer ultimately kills the first, and we are still uncertain about the detail and sense of the piece. The early pronoun *la*, ringing ambiguously in our memory, is finally caught up in the commentary on the allegory, where we encounter the feminine noun *vie*. Certain men try to get to the secret of life: "elle les tue." Life is often personified in the feminine (life is a bitch; *quelle chienne de vie*), but with no particular iconographic associations, so that Char's peculiar allegory exploits ambiguities of image and gender.

The symbols I have just discussed are of the occasional type, but Char's customary arsenal of images should not be conceived of as functioning like the words in an elementary language textbook, which have only one meaning and are used in only limited ways. Char's symbols are more like the words in the *OED* [*Oxford English Dictionary*] or the "big" Robert, where whole columns are needed to chart their vagaries of sense and use. The normal associations of Char's symbols are subject to being recombined for new effect. Sometimes this is fairly unobtrusive, as in **"La Compagne du vannier"** (*FM*), where the basketmaker is not settled in a workplace like **"Louis Curel de la Sorgue"** (*FM*), but moves steadily onward ("Aller me suffit") in contrast to people who have "round" or circumscribed imaginations. His "compagne" is appropriately described in terms of outward nature and vast inner spaces ("ton domaine"), to which a kiss on the mouth ("chiffre") gives access. The speaker's métier serves primarily to motivate the image of controlling or enclosing despair in the space of a small wicker basket or poem, like the dark one immediately proceding, **"Violences."**

Whether love is a part of imagination or imagination part of love in Char's poetry is a nice question, and the relation of the two can perhaps best be defined only in regard to individual poems. If "désir" is associated with poetry in **"Force clémente"** (*FM*) and **"Fenaison"** (*FM*), the lovers of **"Les Premiers Instants"** (*FM*) are borne by one of Char's floods (the symbolism of which varies considerably) on the "arc tout-puissant de son imagination," where the couple is, further, "poncé jusqu'à l'invisible," just like a poem—or just like poetry and sexuality taken together in "Permanent invisible." There is ambiguity in **"Vermillon"** (*PA*), where something which could be a woman, poetry or water is summoned up; it scarcely matters here, because the point of the poem, expressed in colloquial rhythms after the alexandrines of the invocation, is that, whatever is being called on, it does not come. If more terms in **"Vermillon"** seem appropriate to a woman than to poetry or water, the same group of associations in **"Médaillon"** (*FM*) is perhaps dominated by poetry, because "foudre" begins the poem and "électricité du voyage" closes it.

Combined references to poetry and to unpleasant social or political realities appear to be more frequent in Char's later work. The dying poet of **"Chérir Thouzon"** (*NP*) has become mute as a flood recedes, opening an "ère rigoureuse" of "audace nouvelle," both expressions being highly pejorative in this context. The character of the flood is suggested by the fact that it leaves behind it not only mud, but also traces of blood. In an entirely different vein, **"Le Requin et la mouette"** (*FM*) joins the seemingly incompatible images of a perfect moment ("ni éternel ni temporel," as Char entitles another poem about a moment) with the imagery of indefinite movement forward. A simple juxtaposition suffices to connect "un jour de pur dans l'année," when shark and gull communicate in nature's noontide unity, with the "fiévreux en-avant" of a ship for whom all ends are new departures.

If Char's associations of images or themes present problems only when one begins to reflect on them, his disassociation of things that frequently go together are sometimes startling in the general context of his œuvre. The poets of **"Le Nu perdu"** (*NP*) collectively endure existence before and after the moment of illumination ("éclair," "fruit," "entaille," "signe") and hoist from its well the "jarre du ralliement." Solitude or a society of two is the normal condition of the poet in Char, and mankind at large is usually his antagonist rather than the object of "ralliement." Even more surprising is the disassociation in **"Front de la rose"** (*PA*). The poem first evokes a room in which the scent of a rose, the

memory of a woman, cannot be dissipated, and the poet experiences it with desire, as if for the first time. This languorous note is unusual in Char, who employs the word *rose* often enough elsewhere, but without the suggestion of heady, enervating odor. The second part of the poem represents a man marching soldier-like through rain and hostile parts, with the warning that "s'il s'arrête et se recueille, malheur à lui . . . il vole en cendres, archer repris par la beauté." Marching is disengaged from its usual sense of a poetic quest in which beauty would normally play a role. Evidently the point is to distinguish a certain form of beauty, perhaps a certain aspect of women, from the rigor and austerity of the poet's calling and achievement. The freshwater poetry and the wasteland poetry distinguished in **"Aiguevive"** offer an analogy.

Differing kinds of poetry are again suggested by **"Eclore en hiver"** (*NP*). Summer, sun, and outdoor spaces are common correlatives of poetic creation in Char, but night, winter, and a room with a candle here produce the "ouvrage," which paradoxically is full of "force intacte et clairvoyance spacieuse." The poet epitomizes the sunny day which dawns and his own nighttime work as "Brocante dans le ciel: oppression terrestre." As he had earlier referred to the sun's divine harness, the superficial meaning of "brocante" is worn mythological trappings, but by extension it refers to all clichés and insubstantial glitter. Poems like this one take on their full force in the whole context of Char's poetry, where a piece on the sun like **"Force clémente"** (*FM*) is an exact contrary. Char is an aphorist as much as a poet, and the art of the aphorist presupposes nuance, contrast, and discontinuity, as opposed to the smoothness, consistency, articulation, and development of systematic exposition.

One of the normally unfissile unities in Char's thematics is that among the esthetic, the moral, and the physical. Thus we find complexes such as poetic vision in the esthetic domain, freedom in the moral realm, and open spaces or eroticism in the physical order. In **"L'épi de cristal égrène dans les herbes sa moisson transparente"** (*FM*), however, we find what looks at first like the poet stripped of his concern with poetry—only the word *chant*, used in the metaphoric sense, belongs in any precise way to the field of poetry. The rather sexual-sounding title anticipates the union of a woman with the "donneur de liberté," an expression which is exceptionally repeated, as if to underscore the dominant aspect of this figure. The woman is, at first, "son amour," then merely dative "lui," or included in "ils"; she has only the most shadowy existence in contrast to her lover. After telling her of his legendary exploits, the latter vanishes to "se confondre avec d'autres naissances, une nouvelle fois." The words "alchimie du désir," "leur mère" (suggestive of "matrice," "matière mère"), and "naissances" (in the alchemical sense) confer a distinctly allegorical character on the sexual act, as do the "moisson transparente" of the title and the simile "semblable à . . . la création d'un fluide par le jour." The obtaining of freedom by a moral act seems to be the sense towards which alchemy and sexual union (which are symbolic equivalents) point, and we find the same notion, accompanied by legend-like imagery, in **"Ne s'entend pas"** (*FM*): "nous nous faisions libres tous deux. Je tirai d'une morale compatible les secours nécessaires." This removal of freedom from the practical domain to invest it with the unassailable character of a state like grace is characteristic of Char's ethical attitudes.

I earlier referred to the way Char at times uses something like a symbolic shorthand. This aspect of his language is notable in certain poems which are not in themselves symbolic structures, or at least not in the same sense as most of the poems I have been discussing. There are some pieces which are recollections, contrasting the past to the present, such as **"Rémanence"** (*NP*), **"Sommeil aux Lupercales"** (*NP*), and **"Vétérance"** (*NP*); at least one reflective monologue, **"J'habite une douleur"** (*FM*); narratives like **"Anoukis et plus tard Jeanne"**; and brief epitomes or reminiscences of the *drôle de guerre* and Resistance. In all of these poems we observe that Char deploys images similar to those of his allegories: "Voici que dans le vent brutal nos signes passagers trouvent, sous l'humus, la réalité de ces poudreuses enjambées qui lèvent un printemps derrière elles" (**"Vétérance"**). In this remarkable sentence we find references to present poems, past youth, oppressive physical or social conditions, and life as a quest. The non-symbolic poems often demand the same care in reading as texts like **"Calendrier"** or **"Médaillon."**

* * *

In Char's poetry we encounter virtually all the techniques (and consequent problems) relevant to allegory or dense symbolism: ambiguity of symbols, intermittent literalness, reliability or uncertainty of thematic words or statements, personification, enigma, implication as opposed to overtness, imperfect antithesis, non-traditional or occasional symbols, and symbols in isolation. Moreover, the associative groupings of symbols contain widely divergent images or ideas. To take only the major symbolic grouping in Char, that pertaining to poet, creation, and poetry, we find its constituents vary in frequency of use and stability of sense. Besides space, roads, *voyages,* and freedom, there are the notions of sunlight, morning, and invisibility. Water appears as ocean, river, stream, spring, or fountain. Combat, violence, and revolt are easily related, but work, harvest and bread seem heteroclite to them, although, curiously enough, Char manages to link the ideas of battle and repetitive labor in **"Louis Curel de la Sorgue"**

(*FM*). Lightning, fire, and storms are logical opposites of certain symbols of the same grouping. A tremendously subtle, and varied imagination produces from all this heteroclite material a symbolic language which is coherent and readable, but more like a living tongue in its shadings and occasional surprises than like an abstract or entirely rational system.

The coherence of Char's language is related to another very distinctive aspect of his œuvre subsequent to the surrealist phase. His work frequently reminds us of the old genres that used to be called didactic: not only allegory, but also *allegoria,* or a shorter statement in an image, often used in proverbs ("Tant va la cruche à l'eau qu'enfin elle se casse"); maxims or aphorisms; the bestiary; the emblem or enigma; the fable even or parable (such as **"Masque funèbre," "Aliénés," "Recours au ruisseau,"** or **"Chanson du velours à côtes"**); finally, the moral portrait (**"Yvonne"** is a good example). A whole literature that to taste formed by the lyric appeared foreign to poetry is reflected, with greater or lesser fidelity, in Char's work. This is one respect in which he differs notably from other abundant users of symbols.

Finally, Char's symbolism stands out for the distinctive way in which it often suggests and sometimes even demands readings that encompass the esthetic, ethical, sexual, social, physical, and political domains. My comments on his poems have not done justice to the multivalent character of his symbology, since I was concerned with more rudimentary problems in interpretation, but this aspect of his work separates him from those poets who, if we are to believe their critics, write about nothing but the imagination. Char is decidedly not in that category.

Notes

1. Mary Ann Caws, *The Presence of René Char* (Princeton: Princeton Univ. Press, 1976); Virginia A. La Charité, *The Poetics and the Poetry of René Char* (Chapel Hill: Univ. of North Carolina Press, 1968); and James R. Lawler, *René Char: The Myth and the Poem* (Princeton: Princeton Univ. Press, 1978).

2. I have not commented on the most famous bestiary poems, those of "La Paroi et la prairie," in *La Parole en Archipel,* because James R. Lawler has made a detailed study of them, pp. 51-107.

3. "Le sujet de ce poème est une affreuse circonstance que je ne veux pas décrire, une marche au supplice. Hypnos rompit le rêve et découvrit le cauchemar." René Char, *Arrière-histoire du poème pulvérisé* (Paris: Jean Hughes, 1953), p. 31. Curiously enough, a commentator in 1976 wrote about this poem: "And the poet hunter, extravagant in

the strictest sense of wandering outside (extra-vaguer) founds his anguished wisdom here on a cold and lucid solitude, striding along under the luminous veil of these aromatic colors that will guide his final ascent to the place, no longer that of the Minotaur, but of Orion . . ." (Caws, p. 206).

Virginia A. LaCharité (essay date 1989)

SOURCE: LaCharité, Virginia A. "The Conflicts of Art: René Char's *Placard pour un chemin des écoliers*." In *Rewriting the Good Fight: Critical Essays on the Literature of the Spanish Civil War,* edited by Frieda S. Brown, Malcolm Alan Compitello, Victor M. Howard, Robert A. Martin, pp. 185-97. East Lansing, Mich.: Michigan State University Press, 1989.

[*In the following essay, LaCharité discusses the effects of war on the evolution of Char's early poetic development.*]

> Poetry . . . goes forward in order to indicate the movable road.[1]

The Spanish Civil War is the artistic and historical event that definitively marks the end of René Char's affiliation with Surrealism and the beginning of his adoption of a poetics of response. Char's identification with the events in Spain in 1936 and early 1937 is both personal and aesthetic. Among Char's close friends in the Surrealist group were the Spanish painters Picasso, Miró, and Dali,[2] and he had visited Spain three times, twice in 1931 with the poet Paul Eluard and again in 1932 with his childhood friend, Francis Curel. Familiarity with Spain, admiration for the Spanish avant-garde, a growing awareness of the ominous political events in Europe, and a life-threatening case of blood poisoning came together for Char the man with the outbreak of the Spanish Civil War and confronted Char the poet with the conflicts of art.

As an active member of the second generation of Surrealists, Char participated enthusiastically in their artistic and political activities in the early 1930s in order to place Surrealism "at the Service of the Revolution." His own work during these years, collected in the volume *Le Marteau sans maître* (1934), is characterized by an aggressive language, provocative images, a hatred of absurdity in the world, hostility toward all forms of authority, explosive phrases, even violence. Nevertheless, *Le Marteau sans maître* is a disturbing work, for underlying the tone of insolence and rage, especially in the section *Poèmes militants,* there is the suggestion that the Surrealist demand for revolution is not a synonym for action but is rather the embracing of

an attitude which separates action from art, an attitude which exalts scandal, insists on an aesthetic of emotionalism, ignores the social response value of language, denies common sense, and favors total revolt—the utopian dream of a world in which anything and everything is potentially marvelous and the pleasure principle reigns supreme. While the Surrealists were avowedly against external authority in all forms (anti-fascist, anti-religious, anti-bourgeois)—stances which led them to celebrate the establishment of the Spanish Republic in 1931 and then later, in 1936, to identify with the anarchists (the POUM and FAI factions)—during the 1930s they gradually abandoned their original attitude of revolt as insubmission and moved closer and closer to a somewhat mythical concept of the self: revolt in the name of absolute freedom, disorder, and fulfillment of desire. Marx's "transform the world" and Rimbaud's "change life," the two basic tenets of Surrealism, nearly cease to be constructive rallying cries in the Surrealists' efforts to effect their "revolution" through political commitment. In fact, they were openly viewed as dilettantes by the very political group they sought to join and "serve." The basic Surrealist love of the irrational borders on nihilism and is astutely analyzed by Albert Camus in his *Actuelles I* and *L'Homme révolté.*[3]

As the Surrealists themselves disagreed over how to accomplish their own revolution, they found themselves electing Rimbaud over Marx, choosing to defend an attitude of all or nothing and refusing in the process a historical response to the human condition. While André Breton always insisted that love was the value and the moral, that the freedom of the individual would somehow lead to that of all of society, he, nonetheless, viewed art as the expression of man's inner self and desires, not as a response that confronts reality in the name of mankind. The problem of the Surrealist "personal self" in opposition to the non-Surrealist "collective self" is a leitmotif in René Char's *Moulin premier* (1936), a group of seventy aphorisms and two poems which subvert the Surrealist aesthetic of separating art from action, history from revolt. Throughout this work, Char begins to view poetry as a possible response to history: "Earth, becomingness of my abyss, you are my bathtub for reflection" (*OC* [*Oeuvres complètes*], 62).

Moulin premier is marked by a vocabulary and phraseology of reflection, control, rationalism, responsibility, and lucid protest. Char refuses total revolt or revolt for the sake of revolt; instead, he indicates that language can correct the world, lead to order, even alleviate moral suffering; the poet has the responsibility not to confront a real which is a construction of the mind but to classify the real and refuse to accept its arbitrary conditions: "The Poet precedes the man of action, and when he encounters him, declares war on him.

the parvenu had at least promised to be present in his perilous fights!" (*OC,* 67).

Char's aesthetic and personal movement away from Surrealism evolves gradually and naturally. He never had an outright break with Breton or with the group. Yet, his selection of the title of his first theoretical writings on the role of poetry in the contemporary world, *Moulin premier,* strongly suggests by the numerical term *first* that he has already passed beyond Surrealism although he has not yet identified a second *mill* for his writing. At this moment of artistic transition, Char was taken dramatically ill with a nearly fatal case of blood poisoning. The illness brought Char the man face to face with his own mortality and made him intimately aware of death as an inalienable historical aspect of the human condition.

During the months of his recovery, he corrected the proofs for *Moulin premier,* which offered him a review of his Surrealist adventure, and he read Nietzsche, whose nihilism and lack of a human value system repudiated Char's admiration for the Heraclitean theory of flux and becomingness. At the invitation of René Roux, an aspiring young poet and painter who was the schoolmaster at the Collège de L'Ile-sur-Sorgue, Char's native town, Char spent the month of August 1936 in Céreste, "a village lost in the hills of Provence" in Haute-Provence (*OC,* 1116). René Roux had three younger brothers, "small schoolboys from 12 to 14 years old" (*OC,* 1116), who accompanied Char every afternoon on long walks in the area. Describing at length the youths' joys at spending so much time with Char, Georges-Louis Roux testifies to Char's interest in children and adolescents, the marvelous stories he related, and how the summer of 1936 must have been for Char a "moment of relaxing and of happiness, a fleeting respite" (*OC,* 1122). It was shortly after this period of respite and reflection that Char undertook *Placard pour un chemin des écoliers,* which he dedicated to the children of Spain and had illustrated by Valentine Hugo.[4] The effects of his recognition that he had evolved aesthetically away from Surrealism and his personal period of recuperation, of contact with nature and the Roux family children in Céreste, undeniably form the underpinnings of *Placard.*[5]

The theme of childhood which characterizes much of Char's work does not emerge as one of his major subjects until the publication of *Placard* in 1937. Prior to this work, Char tends to treat childhood in a typical Surrealist fashion: the child is not yet tainted by societal inhibitions and prejudices, the child enjoys using freely his imagination and intuition, the child believes that creations of the mind are real. With *Placard,* and, indeed, since 1937, the child for Char represents innocence, health, happiness, and human potential for rising above man's terrestrial circumstances. Like the poet,

the child precedes the man of action—a form of matinal light and a source of illumination.

Written during the winter of 1936-37,[6] *Placard* consists of an introductory prose text, **"Dedication,"** and seven verse poems which are written in a language and style that directly oppose Char's former Surrealist practice. The texts of *Placard* are basically conventional in form and share a sense of anguish and social protest against suffering. Throughout the small volume, the tone is one of a melodic continuum, which consistently expresses a poetic belief in the potential of the text to respond to objective reality. In many ways, *Placard* reflects the moral and spiritual crisis experienced by Char the man and Char the poet in 1936. In a letter written to André Breton, explaining why he cannot participate in the Surrealist exhibition in 1947, Char observes that "I am not the one who simplified things, but horrible things made me simple" (*OC,* 660).

Awareness of the horrors wrought by the events of the Spanish Civil War is summarized for Char in the suffering of the children of Spain, and yet these very same children offer him insight into man's refusal to be reduced to his historical circumstances. In an introduction written in 1949 to the second edition of *Placard pour un chemin des écoliers suivi de Dehors la nuit est gouvernée,* Char expresses his personal and aesthetic agitation over the events in Spain that foreshadowed World War II and its atrocities: "I ran" (*OC,* 85). Indeed, the highly personal tone of this 1949 text dramatizes Char's awareness of the importance of the inner crisis he experienced in 1936. And this 1936 crisis, which was physical, moral, aesthetic, and spiritual, continues to resurface throughout his work. In 1956, for example, his preamble to *En trente-trois morceaux* recalls *Placard* as one of four capital poetic turning points in his work (*OC,* 772). In 1979, his attack on nuclear weapons echoes the events that triggered *Placard*: "How many [people] fall in love with humanity and not with man!" (*OC,* 578). Telescoping the human tragedy of the Spanish Civil War into an evocation of the children in only seven texts in *Placard* becomes a preferred Char structure of condensation in his poetry, as the fragment bears witness to the whole: "Since the operation of totalitarianisms we are no longer tied to our personal self but to a collective self assassin, assassinated" (*OC,* 579).

The shift to an optic beyond the self and the recognition of the need to become involved responsibly with the outer world are expressed by the word *placard* of the title: a written opinion publicly posted to make a specific announcement. The phrase, "a road for schoolboys," is typical of Char's post-Surreal period. While the Surrealists frequently and humorously used proverbs and clichés in their effort to purify language and return it to its original source, Char's adoption of common phrases and terms goes beyond the confines of the page to create new exchanges between words, lines, poems, and the experience of poetry. On the literal level, the phrase evokes a roadway frequented by schoolboys, not unlike the path taken each afternoon in Céreste in the summer of 1936 by Char and the Roux children. The warm, fraternal, and innocent image of a peaceful scene is not disrupted by the public posting of a sign along this particular road. But, *écolier* in French does not refer only to a pupil or schoolboy; it also refers to anyone who is not skilled in his profession, a learner, one who is at the beginning of a given experience. The very choice of the word *écolier* takes the title and the volume beyond the confines of a single event and opens up the volume to a more universal level of meaning. On the figurative level, the French expression for the longest road is "le chemin des écoliers" ["the road for schoolboys"], and, with this reading, the title takes on its ultimate significance. It is an announcement that reality is harsh, history limits human activity, and the poet must protest against his time, give it form, and bear witness to the future. The title is a conscious declaration to revolt against all limitations, but it also recognizes that such an action will not be without its hardships, struggles, setbacks, and sacrifices. The nature of that revolt is not clearly outlined in *Placard,* but the reasons for that revolt are the subject of the volume.

The **"Dedication,"** written in March 1937, is provocative in its use of capital letters to describe the children of Spain as victims of the war around them: "RED." They are dead, thrown into a common ditch and covered with mud, in contrast to the poet's memories of his bucolic childhood, which was marked by World War I. But that war took place on the frontiers and in distant battle zones; it did not disrupt and overturn his everyday existence. By contrast, the Spanish Civil War affects the daily lives of children, whose "école buissonnière," or playing hooky, is a school of death, not of life. The **"Dedication"** ends with a second address to the "Children of Spain" and a salute to their "matinal eyes," which is the earliest appearance of the term *matinal* in Char's work. Char the man begs for their forgiveness; Char the poet cries out that he has written the work "With my last reserve of hope."

The discovery of hope in the atrocities suffered by children ties together the seven poems that make up *Placard.* Each poem bears witness to love as the only possible means for dealing with the oppressiveness of daily horror. Daytime is evoked as bitter, a time of schism, deception, distress, and anguish, while night is seen as a time of peace, renewal, unity, and promise. The historical determinism of day is countered by the affirmative reconciliation of night. The nihilism of Nietzsche is already giving way to Char's postwar predilection for Heidegger and a poetics of pulverization and crispation. The "loyal adversaries" of Char the

man and Char the poet emerge in their first form in the seven texts of *Placard.*

In a very real sense, *Placard* is a volume of a poetry of circumstances, inspired by a specific external event and written to deal with the particular circumstances of that event. But, as an examination of the title alone shows, *Placard* is not circumstantial in its attitude of response. Throughout Char's subsequent work, *Placard* reemerges in different forms, as Char the man and Char the poet accept the world as it is and find in it values worthy of admiration and expression. To the redemptive quality of love, which is perhaps the most important carryover from his Surrealist days, Char will later add the redemptive quality of courage (**Feuillets d'Hypnos,** 1946). Still, in *Placard* there come together for the first time in his work the two ends of his poetic bow: "obsession with the harvest" takes the form of the value of mankind as represented by the children of Spain, and "indifference to history" is affirmed in commitment to the artistic value of creation. *Placard* refutes the agony of the historical circumstances in a blunt declaration that hope is possible only through poetic action: "my last store of hope."

The question that continues to confront the reader of Char's work in general and *Placard* in particular is: why Spain? Why did the Spanish Civil War serve as such a catalyst for Char the man and Char the poet? The answer does not lie in Char's trips to Spain nor in his deep friendships with Spanish painters, but it is clearly articulated by Camus in *Actuelles I,* which is dedicated to Char: "The first weapons of the totalitarian war were soaked in Spanish blood. . . . We delivered to Franco, on Hitler's order, Spanish Republicans . . . who raised his voice? No one. . . . We are responsible" (244-46). Char's physical condition prevented him from directly participating in that war, but among his Surrealist contemporaries only one, Benjamin Péret, actually took up arms in an effort to prevent the Nationalists from delivering Spain to an oppressive dictatorship. The French Surrealists were notably absent from the war despite their admiration for the Republican cause. Writing in *L'Amour fou* in 1937, Breton expresses regret that he did not join Péret and participate in the war because he was waiting for the birth of his daughter: "I did not have the courage."[7] Yet, reason, not the irrational, demanded a response in 1936. It may very well be that the Surrealist movement lost its momentum because of the Spanish Civil War, that the breakup of the group, which occurred in 1940 and 1941 at the onset of World War II, was already underway in 1936. Certainly, those Surrealists who remained in France and joined the Resistance were never able again to embrace the Surrealist election of the pleasure principle over reality. In point of fact, those who did not go into exile had aesthetically moved beyond the Surrealist attitude by the mid-1930s. It may even be speculated that without World War II the events of the Spanish Civil War would have sufficed to trigger in Paul Eluard, Robert Desnos, and others what Louis Aragon had already determined and what René Char would later describe as the discovery that "It must be admitted that poetry is not sovereign everywhere. . . . The poet, susceptible to exaggeration, evaluates correctly in agony" (*OC,* 207, 212).

In *Placard,* the text becomes for Char a dialectic between "a subjective assessment" and "an objective choice" (*OC,* 162). The poem is no longer situated in inner space, "intimate space in which our imagination and our feelings play," but it is instead situated in time, what Char describes as circular space, "that of the concrete world" (*OC,* 509). What was lacking aesthetically in the texts of *Le Marteau sans maître,* time or circular space, becomes the structuring principle of *Placard pour un chemin des écoliers*: "Terror surrounds us and an artistic anti-life takes possession" (*OC,* 700). Poetry must "indicate the mobile road" (*OC,* 734).

While the image of *chemin* pervades Char's work, nowhere does it more fully bring together a volume of poems than in *Placard.* The word *chemin* indicates the process of artistic creation, the promise of "the next" vista, turn, a very human form of Char's notion of the immediate future. A road suggests motion, the probable encounter with others, a common concrete space that exists in human terms. A road occupies space, yet it denies the limitations and restrictions of that space, actually contradicts the confines of that area in its invitation to advance, continue, all the while never abandoning the notion of redistributing those limits. A road is an element of life, not death, and offers the possibilities of better pursuits. A road summons up human values in space and in time and the creative process beyond all time and place: circular space. A road bears witness to man's refusal to die, to his lucid revolt against fixity in the name of freedom and opportunity to travel, seek happiness, and respond to a need to continue to live. A road is a corrective to a given terrestrial condition.

The road in *Placard* is an apt image for the poet's physical, mental, spiritual, and artistic journey. Each text contributes to his discovery that historical terror, suffering, and injustice may be effectively opposed through artistic counteraction. The poet should not serve history, but refuse it. Hence, in *Placard,* Char's obsession with the harvest, a filtered and refined Surrealist pattern, encounters on the road of his own inner turmoil and conscience the need for becoming indifferent to the limitations of history.

Placard pour un chemin des écoliers is by no means representative of a mature René Char, nor can the work be considered one of his major volumes of poetry. However, in looking at all of Char's writing, the volume

is pivotal for an understanding of his self-distancing from Surrealism and the adoption of a poetics that will risk its very existence and expression in order to be provocative in its refusal to acquiesce. In *Placard,* the Char poem is not pulverized, crisped, or matinal. It is not a double that tautly balances "fury and mystery," hope and anguish, the immediate and the essential, word and silence, fragmentation and unity, prose and poetry, "the child of beautiful weather and the man of rainy weather" (*OC,* 76). The tension between incompatibilities, which characterizes the mature Char text, is almost jarringly absent in *Placard,* perhaps explaining why most Char studies tend to overlook the work, causing the volume to fall unfortunately into the misleading and rather pejorative category of circumstantial poetry. Yet, examination of the work reveals that it is in tone, subject, and aspiration pure Char—it simply is not written in what we have come to identify as the indisputable Char text of the archipelagic structure in language and form. *Placard* is not a work of poetic traces; it cannot even be described as a work of proaction, for the texts are firmly rooted in personal and poetic reactions. But all of Char's texts are in some way a form of reaction and protest; all of his poems combine elements of the man and the poet, elements which provide the basic tension in his poetry from *Le Marteau sans maître* to the present, especially *La Nuit talismanique* (1972).[8] It is in the recovery of these elements, recognition of the inner crisis in which Char the man and Char the poet confront each other for the first time, that the reader grasps just how pivotal to Char studies and to contemporary French poetry in general these seven texts and their introductory poem are.

In *L'Homme révolté,* Camus pays homage to Char as the "Poet of our rebirth" (127). As the twentieth century begins to draw to a close, it becomes increasingly evident that René Char towers over contemporary French poetry. The clues to how and why Char is the poet of man's renaissance are in *Placard,* the work which places Surrealism in a finished perspective—poetic activity and reaction—and opens the way to matinal poetic action and proaction in his World War II resistance participation and the texts of *Fureur et mystère* (1948), leading eventually to *La Parole en archipel* (1961), in which the mature Char poem holds together apparent contradictions by creating a new totality in the present, what "We have" (*OC,* 409-10). The humanly alive poetry that marks Char's work is not descriptive, but evocative and provocative—the fragments or word clusters that result create the text of maximum reader freedom and response in a "formal sharing." On every page, there is a road to follow, a path that links extreme reference points, and on that road is a warning sign that risk lies in the adventure. It is never a safe, secure, complacent journey. It is always a difficult poetic quest, a non-ending search for contact. The Char text is a process to evoke response, a "common presence," never a procedure to manufacture a given product.

Accordingly, Char's language is elemental, drawn from the familiar outer world of people, places, and things, especially nature. His structures repress transitions, as he rejects traditional discursive elements of language. The text sets relationships, enacts them, and gives the reader a new way of participating in the world. Encounter and exchange take the form of union through words: word with word, poet with poem, man with woman, man with men, reader with text. To think is to feel, to share is to participate in the direct comprehension of absolute reality. The base is the summit, as Char links together the concrete and the abstract, the solid and the emerging, the object and the emotion. The impossible is possible. As the flower justifies the plant, poetry justifies man's existence in its affirmation that man's nobility is discovered in art, not in history. Poetry as creative action can determine the quality of life.

A major key to the Char text, thematically and stylistically, is love: love on the erotic level, love of mankind, love of nature, love of written expression in all forms, love of plastic art. While love as beauty, freedom, and truth may have its roots in Surrealism, love, for Char, is not limited to the expression of individual desire. Rather, it is an action that conjoins opposites, brings about an order, and unifies the whole of human experience. Love is not restricted to the individual level, but is the principle of human and aesthetic cohesion. Love is life, and the Char text is always a lived poetry, lived in the present, the eternal moment experienced along the road.

Love is the principal theme in *Placard*. The ugly reality of the historical events of the Spanish Civil War, vividly evoked in the **"Dedication,"** are effectively juxtaposed, nearly contradicted, by the poetic discovery that love offers hope—hope for all. Love ends isolation, brings about a sense of immediate fulfillment, makes the intolerable present acceptable, and cannot be limited by time, space, or history. Love is not a state of being, but an action which links together contradictions and opposes all restrictions. Love will not be denied, not even by brutality and cruelty. Love is the concrete world at its best, circular space. Love testifies to man that he is alive and that his life is worth living. Art confers value and offers assurances of "a fervent dawn" (*OC,* 92).

The seven texts end on the word "resistance," which only the act of love is able to posit in a world in which children suffer, bleed, and die. The schoolgirl of **"Schoolgirl's Company"** denies her father's fears; she is confident that her lover's eyes hold "the promise / Which I made to myself / I am mad I am new" (*OC,* 99). The queen in **"The Queen's Bearing"** recognizes how only "the couple entwined with the word heart"

refuses to acknowledge a bleak and hostile environment and time. Even in **"Exploit of the Steam Cylinder"** and **"The Sea Urchins of Pégomas,"** love is viewed as a "valid revolt" (*OC,* 97). In the text **"The Confidant's Alley,"** Char finds that "Daring little girls, / It's good to be imprudent / But for love" (*OC,* 93), while **"Four Ages"** expresses sadness over the isolation of the individual when he lacks love.

The final text, **"Provisions for the Return,"** completes the **"Dedication"** in its demonstration of how the love act during the darkness of night prepares for the bitterness of day and prefigures the beneficent role of night in *Dehors la nuit est gouvernée* (1938). Love renews, revitalizes, and inspires; it strengthens through its moment of union for the coming diurnal struggle, the longest road of living through a historical catastrophe, all the while offering dignity and nobility to those who must travel that road.

Throughout *Placard,* language takes the form of a social response. The emotional is social in that the indignant tone of the **"Dedication"** gives way to the confident declaration at the end. Hope is transmogrified into resistance, as action and art fuse. To write is to act and to requalify the reader. Faith in man to resist his historical circumstances, belief in the text to discover, reveal, and communicate value, and confidence in poetry to justify man's existence in a continual process constitute the ultimate testimony of *Placard pour un chemin des écoliers.* The exchange of energy between the terms *hope* and *resistance* takes place only under the aegis of Poetry, as Char the man and Char the poet resolve their conflicts and merge into the master architect of twentieth-century man's renaissance: "Art ignores History but makes use of its terror" (*OC,* 651).

Notes

1. René Char, *Oeuvres complètes* (Paris: Gallimard, 1983), 743. All Char quotations are taken from this edition, identified in the text as *OC.* The translations are my own.

2. Picasso illustrated Char's *Dépendance de l'adieu* in 1936, "Enfants qui cribliez d'olives" in 1939, and the second edition of *Le Marteau sans maître* in 1945. Dali illustrated *Artine* in 1930, while Miró has illustrated nearly a dozen of Char's works.

3. Albert Camus, *Actuelles I* (Paris: Gallimard, 1950); *L'Homme révolté* (Paris: Gallimard, 1951); quotations from these editions are identified in the text. The translations are my own.

4. Valentine Hugo was a member of the inner circle of Surrealists from 1930 to 1940; best known for her black and white illustrated visions, she visited Spain in 1928 and is described by Char as able to capture "fire under the snow."

5. For a detailed account of this episode in Céreste in 1936, see Georges-Louis Roux, "René Char, Guest in Céreste," in *OC,* 1115-31.

6. It must be remembered that Char wrote *Placard* before the bombing of Guernica and the incarceration of the poet Machado, events which deeply disturbed the French avant-garde.

7. André Breton, *L'Amour fou* (Paris: Gallimard, 1937), 137.

8. *La Nuit talismanique* was also triggered by a personal crisis and posited for Char the man and Char the poet another series of conflicts of art. See my "Beyond the Poem: René Char's *La Nuit talismanique,*" *Symposium* 30 (1976): 14-26.

Charles D. Minahen (essay date fall-winter 1989)

SOURCE: Minahen, Charles D. "Disclosures of Being in René Char's 'Riche de larmes.'" *Dalhouse French Studies: De Duras et Robbe-Grillet à Cixous et Deguy* 17 (fall-winter 1989): 55-61.

[*In the following essay, Minahen examines the opening poem of Char's* Eloge d'une soupçonnée.]

Char's description of Vincent as *"sans abord réel"*[1]—the phrase is underscored by a change of type in the title-poem of *Les Voisinages de Van Gogh*[2]—echoes unmistakably (and no doubt intentionally) the difficulty of access encountered in any attempt to apprehend the phenomenon of being. Vincent's *tableaux,* like Char's poems, record such attempts and prove the point that the artist must do violence to conventional modes of perception in order to break through numbing clichés of the real, i.e., the experience of everyday things (*res*), to dis-cover being in the fullness of its presentation to consciousness. These explosions of being, experienced as overwhelming and all-consuming presences, have little in common, beyond a superficial resemblance, with the world of recognizable referents, which are too ordinary and familiar and thus deprived of the wonder suddenly restored when the visionary artist or poet fractures and reforms the vehicle of apprehension (the graphics of the painting or poem), catalyzing conditions that allow the disclosure of being to occur.

But even though our familiarity with things has rendered them inconspicuous, they are the objects of consciousness that enable it to be conscious, since, as the phenomenologists insist, consciousness is consciousness of some*thing*. No wonder that modern poets have affirmed the importance of things, even taken the side of things, since in our contempt for the familiar we are all too likely to overlook not only the thing but also the being

that it attests. For the poet, like Char or Ponge, the thing is the "point de départ" and the "point culminant" of the poetic utterance, which often requires an escape from the real into the surreal in order to gain a perspective on things by getting outside of them. The mode of the surreal, free of the restrictions of conventional concepts of space, time, grammar, syntax and other such offspring of the logos, conduces to the unrestricted apperception of being, seized in the full free play of possibilities, as in dreams, where meanings emerge, converge and connect spontaneously and polysemously to reveal being in all its plenitude and complexity.

The thirteen texts of *Eloge d'une soupçonnée,* the last work Char delivered to his publisher before his death on February 19, 1988, are in all cases the disclosures of being that Heidegger associates with *aletheia* (in Greek "truth"), which connotes literally "unhiddenness", a discovery of what was covered up, an "unforgetting" or retrieval of meaning from oblivion. The opening poem, **"Riche de larmes",** is a particularly eloquent attempt at such disclosure. Comprising thirty sections, divided into two parts, it is a microcosm of Char's *ars poetica,* containing twenty-six prose strophes and four verse strophes[3] that together evince a veritable panoply of prevalent and even obsessive Charian themes, techniques and images.

The first part opens Genesis-like with an evocation of dark and light, although the sequence is reversed, as the poet envisions an imminent envelopment of the self in night, an approaching death, which prompts the despondent query, "A quoi bon s'éclairer, riche de larmes?" This despair occurs in the context of a realization of achievement ("s'achève") in the French sense of completion, but not a full or altogether satisfying completion, since death interrupts our course on the "chemin qui conduit du bas jusqu'au sommet et que nous n'avons pas le temps ni la force de parcourir en entier" (16). We are too weak and our lives too short for us to realize the full expectations of our desire, and our accomplishments are all the less significant since they are made in the obscurity of private, individual lives, "à l'insu de notre âge" (1). The bitter fact is that "La Passante-Servante, tantôt frêle tantôt forte" (2), Char's metaphor perhaps for the fleeting passage of life and of a poet's intermittently strong and frail service to an ideal of enlightenment of being through art, can only hope to "perce[r] l'ombre", sparkle briefly in a flash of brilliance before fading back into the vast oblivion of the dark.

Not only do we find ourselves caught between opposing postulations, symbolized here and ubiquitously in Char by light and dark and the mountain's summit and base, but our movement through time is frustrated by a nostalgia for the past (an impossible desire to return to the source) and a fear of the future's only certain promise, death, or, as the poet puts it in strophe 3, "nous nous tenons, notre existence durant, à mi-chemin du berceau séduisant et de la terre douteuse". Moreover, the self itself is divided ("nous nous tenons"), and the human dilemma of living on "l'entrouvert" (*OC* [*Oeuvres complètes*] 411)[4] between antinomous forces of the exterior world is further aggravated by an inner dichotomy and estrangement, since "Je" indeed "est un autre".

But there was a primordial epoch, the poet suggests in the closing strophe of part one, when divisions were not merely antagonistic and man was wondrously one with himself and the world, like Lascaux's hunter-artist wedded to the beasts he stalked through the intimacy of mortal combat and sacred symbols of reverential awe:

> Merveilleux moment que celui où l'homme n'avait nul besoin de silex, de brandons pour appeler le feu à lui mais où le feu surgissait sur ses pas, faisant de cet homme une lumière de toujours et une torche interrogative.
>
> (4)

Modern humanity, alienated from production by the very instruments of technology meant to ease the burdens of survival, can only marvel at this enigma of synthesis and fulfillment. Contact with nature was not mediated, like flint to the production of the flame. Fire, Heraclitus' primary element, was in and of man, inseparable from the Logos; matter and spirit emanated brilliantly and harmoniously in this magnificat creature so innocent and authentic in his curiosity about the world. That golden age has passed, irretrievably, a paradise lost never to be regained.

As if to sublimate his sense of loss and recuperate it through the sonorous beauty of the lyric, Char opens the second part of "Riche de larmes" with two verse strophes that transform the poetic vision articulated in the first part into pure symbol and sound. In one of the strophes, a dialectic of "Dépliement" and "Repli" is evoked in the image of a branch from which the cracked bark ("this mortal coil") seems on the verge of being blown off by the wind. In the other, the opposition is incorporated in the juxtaposed images of wet dew and parching salt:

> Lacrymale la rosée;
> Vespéral le sel.
>
> (6)

The antithetical structure of the couplet is underscored by the contrasting feminine and masculine grammatical modes, but the water of the dew combines with the salt to produce the synthetic admixture of tears shed in the vesperal twilight of a waning life. Nonetheless, the richness of the sonorities, brimming with assonance and alliteration, embues the lament with the plaintive beauty of a requiem ("Lacrimosa dies illa").

These and all the ensuing strophes are marked by a preoccupation with dialectical antithesis and synthesis, always typical of Char, but presented here with an unrelenting sense of urgency. The fragmented, aphoristic nature of the discrete utterances, replete with oxymorons, also casts them in a decidedly Heraclitean mold. If one theme predominates, it is the motif of "souffrance" intimated in the poem's title, hinted at in part one and now thematicized overtly in strophes 6-10, from the evocation of lachrymal dew through allusions to suffering associated with time: "cette souffrance a duré toute ma vie" (7). In all cases, the suffering is related to a fragmenting and frustrating disunity, involving self ("à mon corps et à mon esprit défendant"), otherness ("à l'écoute de l'interlocuteur") or the experience of time:

> Nous sommes désunis dans nos mille motifs.
> Demain ne nous suffit pas,
> Demain devrait suffire.
> Douloureux sera demain,
> Tel hier.
>
> (8)

In this indictment of sheer endurance without satisfaction, underscored by the three repetitions of *demain* ("tomorrow and tomorrow and tomorrow . . .") with the drumbeat of repeated d's sounding a dirge, the poet situates human being at the juncture of two infinities, past and future, the one receding irretrievably, the other approaching relentlessly and uncertainly and always "before its time" (3). No mention of the present, for it, like the consciousness that inhabits it, is merely a site, continuously occupied and abandoned, a catch-all of becoming ineluctably wedged between intangible and uncontrollable extremes. Strophe 14 very pithily sums up the poet's cynical opinion of "la condition humaine":

> L'homme n'est-il que la poche fourre-tout d'un inconnu postnommé dieu? Pressenti, jamais touché? Tyran et capricieux?

If, in its pitiful state, humanity harbors intimations of immortality and an absolute divinity, such a whimsical tyrant, the poet implies, is neither knowable nor worth being known.

In Char's Heraclitean cosmos of flux and contradiction, however, the dialectic must produce occasional, if fleeting, expressions of the one. In fact the poet celebrates, in an earlier work, the presocratic philosopher's "exaltante alliance des contraires", adding that

> Il voit en premier lieu en eux la condition parfaite et le moteur indispensable à produire l'harmonie . . . Le poète peut alors voir les contraires—ces mirages ponctuels et tumultueux—aboutir, leur lignée immanente *se personnifier*, poésie et vérité, comme nous savons, étant synonymes.
>
> (**"Partage formel"**, *OC* 159)

In **"Riche de larmes"**, the outlook is much less enthusiastic and optimistic. The exalting alliance personified as truth in the poem has become "La brusque alliance de l'âme avec des mots en butte à leurs ennemis" (10). When soul and words come together to produce the poem's burst of harmony, the alliance is "brusque", that is, rude, brutal, unexpected, the product of toil, suffering and an all-too-fickle muse. It does provide a release from the prison of contradictions and from all the obstacles that block and frustrate the creative act, but "Cette levée d'écrou n'est qu'un passage" (10). Poetry for Char has always been a deliverance ("La seule liberté, le seul état de liberté que j'ai éprouvé sans réserve, c'est dans la poésie que je l'ai atteint" [19]), but it is the brevity of the reprieve that the poet emphasizes in this late work.

Consider the following two strophes:

> L'art est fait d'oppression, de tragédie, criblées discontinûment par l'irruption d'une joie qui inonde son site, puis repart.
>
> (17)

> Laissons l'énergie et retournons à l'énergie. La mesure du Temps? L'étincelle sous les traits de laquelle nous apparaissons et redisparaissons dans la fable.
>
> (18)

In Char's pessimistic presentation of the human plight, lack of freedom ("oppression") and inescapable fatality ("tragédie") are the givens that are ironically "riddled" by scattered and spontaneous invasions of quickly dissipating joy. So it is with human being, caught in the cycle of inviolable natural laws like "the conservation of energy", a fully determined process in which lives are mere sparks of electricity flashing and fading in an electromagnetic field of constant kilowattage. And it is the poet's painful awareness of his own waning, cracking, deteriorating self—"le front souffrant, strié, comme un tableau noir d'école communale"—that gives urgency to his desire to create, even in the face of impending doom: "Vite, il faut semer, vite, il faut greffer, tel le réclame cette grande Bringue, la Nature; écoeuré, même harassé, il me faut semer" (9). Time presses, is running out ("Un sablier trop belliqueux se coule" [30]), but seed once sown still needs time to germinate, take root, mature. Production of the text, moreover, is arduous ("La zone d'écriture si difficile d'accès" [20]), an "unending combat" between the referent and the sign, reality and its representation ("le nom sans la chose" [24]); and the poetic consciousness, a nothingness ("Je suis cet absent") seeking being, inhabits that gulf, a threshold of relentless present becoming, where future meets past and the idea the thing, to spark the poem's sudden illumination of being.

It is not surprising, then, that the aging poet, for whom "le deuil est à peu près constant" (29) and whose paranoia amid hostile forces has made him feel "en-touré d'ennemis" (25) and thus suspicious of others, turns inward ("Je me suis immergé" [23]), seeking solace in sleep: "Terre arable, sommeil intelligent et prodigue jusqu'au sang, s'il désire s'échapper" (22). This sleep, though, evinced repeatedly in the closing strophes, proves not to be an escape, but rather a slow and steady surrender to extinction, as death indifferently and inexorably takes hold. The poet, helpless and yet painfully conscious, can only wait and watch nervously, suspiciously, as the body clings to life, slipping in and out of sleep, until it finally fails to awaken: "J'endure lorsque j'étouffe et que tu rentres au sommeil. Epiage" (27). This penultimate moment is symbolized (in the penultimate strophe) by one last allusion to fire, which contrasts markedly with the earlier celebration of ancient man's enlightening torch: "la bougie s'écoeure de vivre" (29). It's not enough that the flame must flicker and die unwillingly before its term, but consciousness must also witness the decline and the body suffer through the agony of its undoing, until a point of utter disgust with living is reached that yields astonishingly, if inevitably, to a pain-relieving thanatos.

"Riche de larmes" thus involves not only disclosures of being but, in particular, of being-toward-death and of its concomitant anxiety. Although one of Char's darker introspections, it does illuminate the decline toward death, the poet valliantly transmuting his own raw experience into an essence-revealing epiphany. It is in this sense a testament, not only to the tragedy of human entrapment in time and bewildering uncertainty, but also to the tenacity of the creative will that turns adversity into verses and finds richness in tears.

Notes

1. René Char, *Les Voisinages de Van Gogh* (Paris: Gallimard, 1985), p. 39. Numbers appearing in parentheses not preceded by a siglum are to the thirty strophes of René Char's "Riche de larmes", *Eloge d'une soupçonnée* (Paris: Gallimard, 1988), pp. 7-11. The other works cited in this article are identified by sigla. OC: René Char, *Oeuvres complètes,* Ed. Pléiade (Paris: Gallimard, 1983); V: Jean Voellmy, "Comment lire René Char", in three parts, *Les Lettres romanes* 34, 1 and 2-3 (février, mai-août 1980): 3-191.

2. Michael Bishop's study of this volume, "Ce peu qui nous tient éveillés: *Les Voisinages de Van Gogh*", *Europe* 66, 705-06 (janvier-février 1988): 112-19, is highly recommended. This issue features several other interesting pieces devoted to Char, including Daniel Leuwers' "Repères chronologiques" (120-24), which updates the poet's life and works to 1987. Another recent and important contribution to Char studies is the special issue of *Sud,* "Actes du colloque de Tours" (1985), which joins the well-known special

numbers of *L'Arc* (1963), *Liberté* (1968), *Cahiers de l'Herne* (1971) and *World Literature Today* (1977). In addition to the established studies of Char by Blanchot, Bataille, Rau, Richard, La Charité, Caws, Lawler, Cranston, et al., the following are some notable recent analyses: Nancy Piore, *Lightning: The Poetry of René Char* (Boston: Northeastern University Press, 1981); Jean Voellmy's article cited in the previous note; Jean-Claude Mathieu, *La Poésie de René Char ou le sel de la splendeur,* 2 vols. (Paris: Corti, 1985), which contains an excellent bibliography; Roger Payet-Burin, *René Char, poète de la poésie* (Paris: Nizet, 1985).

3. Since the text is a hybrid of verse and prose poetry, a problem of vocabulary arises concerning the appropriate term to describe the individual sections. The term "paragraph" is obviously inadequate, since there are versified stanzas, and even the French "aliéna" ("aliena" in English would seem to be the obvious neologism for it), although certainly preferable to "paragraph" for the description of the indented units of a prose poem, is not appropriate for the non-indented verses. For lack of a more adequate general term, I shall use "strophe", which stresses the poetic nature of the divisions. Prose poetry since Rimbaud is decidedly more poetic than prosaic, as Voellmy affirms in his description of modern poetry as "antiprose": "Il y a belle lurette que nous savons que tout ce qui n'est point prose est vers, et tout ce qui n'est point vers est prose. Mais le fait que la poésie moderne est l'antiprose, un discours où le code de la langue est violé pour fonder un nouvel ordre linguistique sur les ruines de l'ancien, n'est pas encore entré dans tous les esprits" (V 8).

4. In "Dans la marche" the poet writes: "Nous ne pouvons vivre que dans l'entrouvert, exactement sur la ligne hermétique de partage de l'ombre et de la lumière".

Michael Worton (essay date 1992)

SOURCE: Worton, Michael. Introduction to *The Dawn Breakers Les Matinaux*, pp. 11-45. Newcastle Upon Tyne, England: Bloodaxe Books, 1992.

[*In the following excerpt, Worton offers a thematic commentary and introduction to his translation of Char's* Les Matinaux.]

René Char (1907-88) is often described as a poet of nostalgia who is essentially concerned with his own childhood in Provence and with the pre-industrial and pre-nuclear world. His poems have also often been described as hermetic, as "difficult" or "intellectual". Internationally recognised as one of the most important French poets since the Surrealists, perhaps even since Paul Valéry, he is respected as a poet-philosopher but he has never become a popular poet. This says much about what many modern, urban readers expect from contemporary poetry: they want to encounter both familiar, "relevant" images and a language which corresponds to what they know and speak, hence the commercial success of such different poets as Prévert, Brel, Betjeman and Larkin.

Char does not seek to please his readers but to make them more aware of their own lives, and this he does by capturing and crystallising brief moments of existence which may aid readers to understand their own experiences. However, his imagery is drawn from a direct and sustained contact with Nature in Provence, a region which most of his readers will not know at all or will know only as tourists rushing from one celebrated site to another. And yet when we discover in the poetry reference to Vaucluse villages or sites such as Le Thor, Maussane, Thouzon, Les Dentelles de Montmirail, the Fontaine de Vaucluse, these names do not exclude us but resonate in a magical way—and even those who know the Vaucluse well must recognise that the poet has transformed a specific, physical geography into a universal, mythic geography. Char's sense of place is both acute and emotional: the topography of this land can be verified and has an intense physical presence but, more importantly, it is a world traversed by the enigmatic *Transparents* or *Clear-seeing Ones* who remind us of a time when our relationship with Nature was intimate, a world inhabited by the *Matinaux* or *Dawn Breakers* who live in and between night and day. Like Michaux's poetry, Char's work has an extraordinary visual force, an 'evidence'. But whereas Michaux creates imaginary countries in order to comment on the nature of reality, Char chooses to present his native region in order to reveal the truth that lies within reality.

Throughout his life, from his lonely childhood days until his last years when he chose to lead a secluded life near his birth-place L'Isle-sur-Sorgue and far from the literary and political feudings of Paris, Char found his inspiration in his long walks through the Vaucluse countryside and in his quiet, questioning observation of plants, animals, birds, rivers and meteorological changes. Many of his finest poems result from his determination to see fully in order to understand, to see in solitude in order to offer others the possibility of finding their own vision: for him, seeing authentically is a necessary first step towards the establishment of a sense of what I shall for the moment call 'being-in-the-world'.

However, in Char's poetry Nature is not a mere pretext for some late-come Romantic poetry. When Char looks at flowers, he uses his vision in a different way than did Wordsworth coming upon his 'crowd or host of golden daffodils'. When he writes of the river Sorgue which rises at the Fontaine de Vaucluse and runs through his home town, he is not imitating Petrarch who, fascinated by the isolated and enclosed Fontaine de Vaucluse, composed there many of his poems on Laura. Nor is he following Lamartine who gazed in narcissistic melancholy on his celebrated lake. The natural world around him provides no excuse for projection of his own moods and anxieties or for pathetic fallacy. Rather, he seeks to see fully, to *receive* the natural world and thence to discover oneness in difference always maintained as difference.

The focusing on individual objects is a feature of much modern French poetry. Yves Bonnefoy, for example, repeatedly portrays a salamander in order to meditate on presence and absence, and Francis Ponge writes sequences of poems on a pebble or a block of soap in order to offer a post-Cubist image of their quiddity or "thingness". Char's procedure is somewhat different—he seeks to show that no single object, be it animate or inanimate, can or should be perceived and interpreted in isolation but must be recognised as part of some vaster plan. For instance, in **'Complainte du lézard amoureux'/'Lament of a lovesick lizard'** in *Les Matinaux/The Dawn Breakers,* the lizard is presented as a commentator, as a mediator who 'sees everything from his low wall' and can therefore 'tell the secrets of the earth'. For Char it is essential that we realise that all things, all beings have an autonomous existence and also function as revelatory *images*. His readers may well live in an environment in which there are no lizards or vipers, no crickets or cicadas, no Mistral winds, no high jagged mountains, no saxifrage or lavender, but the images hit home because they are offered as examples, as *paradigms*. Char should not be seen as a regional poet, but as a poet-thinker who universalises what he knows and sees personally, as a 'tragic optimist' who seeks to remind us that the past is always with and within us. In *La parole en archipel/ The Word as Archipelago* (1962), there is a sequence of four poems inspired by the prehistoric Lascaux cave-paintings. Each text refers us to an individual painting, yet the poetic act consists not in giving a verbal equivalent but in offering an interpretation of past images that we need to think about if we are to avoid simply admiring them as tourists. When writing of the painting of a young horse, Char marries his memory of this one image to references to African cults of the White Woman (a goddess of maternity) and to Georges de la Tour's paintings of Mary Magdalene (a symbol of repentance, death—and hope). The Lascaux painting is evoked but, more importantly, it is made the site of interpretation and appropriation. And the past, like the specific location of the Vaucluse, is shown to be both specific in its otherness or distance and universal in its present emotional and metaphysical value for us.

All of Char's poems articulate the experiences of a man confronting the physical world in a state of heightened emotion, be it as a lover, as a Resistance fighter, as a walker through the Provence landscape, as a 'Green' militant against nuclear power stations and the industrial polluting of rivers, as a spectator of paintings or as a reader of past writings. In many ways Char's poetic position is very close to that of the Thirties poet and critic Christopher Caudwell who stated that 'poetry is an adaptation to external reality. It is an emotional attitude to the world'. All Char's poems are highly personal (in *Fureur et mystère/Furor and Mystery,* 1948, he affirms that 'The poem is always married to someone'), but they never seek to impose a purely subjective truth. Rather, they use language and images to urge readers into a sense of wonderment at, and a questioning of, the essence of existence.

Char's work should not, however, be seen as ontological or metaphysical in the sense that only scholars or philosophers can understand it. He himself said in an interview in 1948: 'I have my own personal critic. He's a poacher. When I've written something, I read it to him, and I can't help but laugh when people say that I'm hermetic, because he immediately understands, and says "Yes, you've got that right" or "You should change that word, and this one".' Another revelatory anecdote relates to Char's work in the Resistance. An officer sent from de Gaulle's headquarters in Algiers found it difficult to follow the imagistic language of Char's men. The poet explained that while slang is merely picturesque, the language shared by the Provençal Resistance fighters was metaphorical because of their intimate, direct contact with Nature, and he added that he used images in his dealings with them because 'when an image once strikes home, it is never ever forgotten'.

Char's poetry is extraordinarily visual even, as I say, for those who have never climbed the Provençal mountains or walked along the River Sorgue, but it also testifies to an almost mystical belief in the power of language. Words are our companions, our supports and our adversaries as we live out our lives, so we must be careful with them: as Char said in 1968, 'My love of words is so great that I cannot bear to squander them.' Char's poems are characterised by crispness and tension, but the individual terms employed are neither crisp nor fixed: each poem is like a limpid pool into which words have been dropped like pebbles, radiating out circles of connotations which never come completely to rest: in this poetry, words do not have single denotational meanings nor even "mere" ambiguity; they have etymological and connotational resonances and ultimately function as *echoes* of the lost language of a violent harmony.

For Char, poetry should not be categorical or didactic; it should lead readers to a state of lucidity in which they can perceive for themselves the meaning of the contradictions which fill and define the world. Yet no poet has full control over organised language and even less over individual words—which will always mean something different to different readers each of whom brings to their readings a personal (and often anxious) response to terms such as 'father', 'mother', 'love', and 'home'. Char is aware of this phenomenon, which, in a sense, is at the heart of his poetic project.

In his first collection *Les cloches sur le cœur/Bells on the heart* (1928), he used an imagery reminiscent of that of earlier French poets such as Laforgue and Apollinaire, an urban imagery of taxis, show-girls and electricity, but he later repudiated this volume and bought up and destroyed most of the 153 copies. While more than 50 years later the poet was to incorporate and rewrite fragments from this volume in some of his last works, this act of self-censorship, of what one might call poetic self-mutilation, is important for an understanding of Char's development. As he himself recognised, this volume is the work of a poet who is in search of his own voice—and who has not yet liberated himself from the influence of near-contemporaries or from the demands of formal poetic structures. Furthermore many of the texts are haunted, even scarred by his anguish at the deaths of his father and grandmother. They speak of a very private universe, of a childhood that could not be properly incorporated intohis poetry until he had exorcised the ghosts and found a voice which was both individual and universal. Hence the repudiation of the volume.

The poems in *Les cloches sur le cœur/Bells on the heart* were written between 1922 and 1926, the year in which Paul Éluard published *Capitale de la douleur/ Capital of suffering*. Char's discovery of this volume was to be decisive for his poetic career. He found there a contemporary voice which married the personal and the universal, the simple and the complicated, violence and harmony, love and disappointment (even anger). It was a book that ceased to look to the past for models and inspired Char to explore new ways of writing. In 1929 and at his own expense he published *Arsenal/ Arsenal,* a collection which heralds the true Charrian voice. Here there is much violence but most of the images are now drawn from Nature and the poet has discovered the complex virtue of simplicity, as in this poem:

"L'amour"

Être
Le premier venu

"Love"

Being
The first to come along

Char sent a copy of **Arsenal** to Éluard who immediately went to L'Isle-sur-Sorgue to meet the young poet and to invite him to Paris to meet other Surrealists such as Breton and Aragon. Char consequently joined the Surrealist group at the same time as Dalí and Buñuel and in 1930 published **Ralentir travaux/Slow down men at work,** a text written collectively with Éluard and Breton. For the next five years he was an important member of the group, co-signing many tracts and open letters. More importantly, he began to read such major Surrealist precursors as Rimbaud, Lautréamont, the pre-Socratic philosophers and the great alchemists. He also engaged actively, and occasionally belligerently—with his fists—in their political battles. These were times of friendship (notably with Éluard, a surrogate elder brother), times of reading and self-examination, but Char was already more concerned with poetry as a way of dealing with the world than with Parisian and international quarrels about details of political ideology. During his membership of the Surrealist group, he above all explored different ways of being free, yet he could never fully accept that the unconscious should be privileged over the conscious, as the Surrealists as a whole did. The most important lesson that Char learned from Surrealism was that poetry can and must violate the comfortable rules of society and syntax. A consequence of this is that aggression can be poeticised in such a way that neither subject nor object is destroyed. Both are maintained in a state of creative, prospective suffering. Formal logic has no place in this thinking; what is privileged is *lived* experience and an often aggressive engagement with the Other, by which I mean anything outside of himself. While Char is primordially committed to writing about the Other, his poems testify to an aggression toward the object, be it an image or a poem he has created, a woman he loves, the reader, the text, language generally—or even himself. His poetry is profoundly sadomasochistic in its play with aggression and passivity. But he seeks not to destroy either subject or object but to maintain both in a state of suffering and heightened awareness. Char's exploration and presentation of the subject-object relationship as an interaction, as a *dialogue,* distinguishes him from the other Surrealists whose work is often generated by narcissism, by an obsessive need to define and describe everything in terms of their own fantasies and political positions. Char rejects this (willed) identification of subject and object which characterises most Surrealist poetry, especially that of André Breton, preferring to articulate his own sense of aggression in order to establish a new sense of (warring) harmony. Even in his love poems where he inevitably speaks of himself, we find an *expansive* rather than a *retracted* narcissism, that is to say he expresses his own deeply personal emotions in order to engage fully with some absolutely *other*—who is always both the beloved and the unknown reader.

Much later, in *À une sérénité crispée/Towards a tense serenity* (1952), he explicitly confronted the problem of narcissism, writing: 'You should have drunk of the water, Narcissus, and not looked at yourself'. Narcissus, as mythic figure and as psychic structure, is finally perceived as culpable. By preferring his self-image to the nourishing and ever-changing transparency of the water, he has risked more than narcissistic imprisonment: he has denied freedom and even immortality both to the self and to the Other. In his love poem **'Lettera amorosa'** (1953, definitive version 1964), Char most fully reveals how he has learned to incorporate images of violence and fantasies of death and resurrection into a tender but brutally honest text. This long poem warns against the dual temptations of idealisation and aggressiveness and proposes that reflection must be more than a narcissistic gazing at the self: we must both see our uniqueness and allow the world and other people to become part of ourselves and of our self-images.

All of Char's later poetry bears the traces of his contact with the Surrealist group, notably in his creation of juxtapositional images, but even during his period of allegiance to Surrealism he was seeking to write with moral seriousness and with simplicity (he rarely indulged in the linguistic firework-displays dear to Breton, Desnos and Queneau). Furthermore he always insisted on the creative control of the conscious: all of his poetry is firmly tied to the world and communicates a commitment to lucidity as the touchstone of existence. This is what led to his official break with the movement in December 1935 when he wrote in a public letter that 'Surrealism has committed itself to a course which is bound to lead it to the Retirement Home for Belles-Lettres and Violence'. Angry, cruel words—generated by his disappointment with colleagues who had in his view betrayed the ideal of fraternity and poetry. Although Char was reluctant to speak about his Surrealist period, whenever he did he would express his irritation with those who 'did in fact rather bore me'. But at the same time he would also insist on the importance of the lessons he had learned and especially the life-long friendships he had formed, notably with Éluard, Braque and Picasso.

In 1936, history—both social and personal—coincided with a literature of violence when the Spanish Civil War broke out and the poet contracted an acute case of septicaemia which almost led to his death. His rage against the senseless killing of children led to **Placard pour un chemin des écoliers/*Sign towards the long way round*** (1937) in which he re-enacts his own childhood, now perceived in the context both of the Spanish child-victims and of his narrow escape from death. Yet

already here we find his refusal to write poems which are too closely tied to individual events: for Char, if we are to be fully human, we must constantly engage in acts of resistance but we must also look beyond the specific aspects of individual events and atrocities in order to perceive their universality. Only then can we realise that oppression is always with us. In 1952 he wrote, 'Our most insidious enemy is what is happening today', by which he means that the defeat of a Hitler, a Franco or a Saddam Hussein is never enough: there will always be other—less obvious—oppressors, such as the State, the Church, even the education system. So, he insists, we must never at any moment allow ourselves to relax into thinking that human liberty has been assured once and for all.

The 1930s were a crucial decade in Char's moral, political and poetic development. He rejected Surrealism and what he called its 'clever but artificial' obsession with alchemy and Rimbaud's notion of verbal alchemy (which for some Surrealists merely meant language-games). He came close to death and was outraged by the atrocities committed during the Spanish Civil War. Later, he made a personal discovery of the horror of the Nazi persecution of Jews and 'communists': his first wife, Georgette Goldstein, was a Jewess and he was officially declared to be a Communist in 1941. These various factors lead him to join the Resistance forces and, known as 'le capitaine Alexandre', he initially masterminded sabotage attacks on the occupying Italian army and against the Nazis and then took charge of the SAP (Section Atterrissage Parachutage/landing-parachuting organisation) in Southern France. During his struggle against the occupying forces, he continued to write, although he did not show to his comrades his brief, passionate notes—which he agreed to publish only after the war. These **Feuillets d'Hypnos/Leaves of Hypnos** (1946) are a precious historical, moral as well as poetic document. They say much about how Resistance activity aided men to find themselves, about how deaths can be witnessed impotently, from a distance, and yet ultimately be perceived as a means of understanding life and what it should be. Many of these texts blaze with rage, especially when Char talks of intimate friends who were executed or sent to concentration camps and when he writes of his angry refusal of any and every tyranny. Yet scattered throughout these 237 notes are many highly moral, self-controlling, almost religious exhortations to go beyond rage, fury and hatred in order to continue effectively the struggle against oppression and to prepare for the future creation of a better world. In this respect, it is important to note that after the Liberation Char spent much time helping to establish dossiers which proved that his Resistance comrades had been true 'maquisards', but that he refused to participate in the shameful witch-hunt of alleged collaborators which he considered to be nothing more than 'a copy of what our enemy did when it was in power'. 'We must triumph over our rage and our disgust . . .' he wrote, 'in order to make both our actions and our morality nobler and more far-reaching.'

However, the demands of warfare and leading a Resistance group led Char to make difficult decisions which were to haunt him for the rest of his life. In 1946, he wrote a darkly mysterious poem **'L'extravagant'/'The act of madness,'** published in *Le poème pulvérisé/The pulverised poem* (1947), which ends with the statement that 'Spring does not exist'. Of all his texts, this was the one which for years he refused to discuss. 'You are forbidden to touch this poem—it's mine and mine alone,' he stormed at one critic and friend when pressed for an explanation. This refusal is a surprise when one remembers the poet's usual insistence that no text 'belongs' to its author once it is published. But in this case his reasons were understandable in that the poem does not speak of an extravagant or mad person but of an excessive *act*. In 1983 he finally explained to Paul Veyne that **'L'extravagant'/'The act of madness'** was born out of his anguished decision to execute two young traitors, one of whom had betrayed forty-five of his comrades to the Gestapo who then shot them; the other was a dangerous collaborator. While Char has said that individual lives cannot have the same value in wartime as they do in peacetime, he was haunted by these executions, especially in the immediate post-war years when he was nauseated by the way in which both the Right and the Left in France were exploiting the Liberation. The actual poem makes no explicit reference to the executions, but this very silence is revelatory: it reminds us that poetry must always be about transformation—whatever details we may glean of its genesis, the text itself should remain as a trace of lived experience and, more importantly, as a metamorphosis of that experience.

Through his contact with the Surrealists, Char had discovered the communicational possibilities of a language which bypassed the rational, the conscious, the socially-determined; his experiences in the Resistance, when revolt had to be expressed in deeds rather than in words, taught him to beware of the temptation of merely playing with language. In his war notebooks he repeatedly articulates his awareness that words—and even poetry—become marginal when events demand active commitment, yet he also could not but continue to write, in secret, when not engaged in Resistance work. As he says in a revelatory note: 'I write briefly. I cannot *be absent* for any length of time. Saying all I wanted to say would become obsessive. The adoration of the shepherds no longer makes any sense for our planet.' By this he means that we cannot today permit ourselves either to indulge in self-centred expression or to be naïve, passive worshippers at any shrine: we need to be aggressive and even violent. So the problem of the place of poetry in the modern world was posed for

him in a much more urgent way than for Hölderlin or even for Heidegger. In moments of danger, actions must take precedence over words, he recognises—but only words can both maintain and interrogate the memory of these events in and for future years.

All of Char's later work is shaped by his war-time experiences with language and silence, but it is also marked and enriched by an event which gave an anxious reality to the Surrealists' mystical, utopian view of language as magical. During his Resistance activity the code-word for one of the parachute drops was 'La bibliothèque est en feu' (The library is on fire). One of the containers exploded and set fire to the forest, illuminating the horizon, with the result that Char's group only just escaped with the other containers before the Gestapo arrived. Char's reaction was immediate: he contacted London to demand that the code be changed because 'I believe in the magic and in the authority of words'—since paper is made from wood, the code fatally determined that the forest should burn. Whatever we may individually wonder about such beliefs in the prophetic power of language, it is certain that Char was convinced that words can have a direct effect on the material world. This conviction can be traced back beyond his Surrealist period to the folklore of his childhood. For instance, he was familiar with the Provençal custom of setting out a glass of water in order to placate the 'returning spirits' and stated that he believed in ghosts even though he had never actually seen one. In both his Surrealist and his post-war periods, he wrote texts which tell of encounters which appear to be supernatural. This belief in a world beyond the physically verifiable links Char to pre-Christian thinking. His opposition to all religions that name their gods arose out of a deep mistrust of organised Christianity yet he nonetheless always retained a sense of the real possibility of transcendence. He might insist that 'It is fatal to abolish distance. The gods die only when they live amongst us'; yet his work is haunted by references to Christian figures and to Provençal and Classical mythologies. The latter may be familiar but for many readers the Provençal allusions are problematic.

One example from *Les Matinaux* is the use of *calendes* in **'Fête des arbres et du chasseur'/'Celebration of the trees and the hunter.'** For many years I assumed that this referred to the Calends, the first day of any month in the Roman calendar and consequently I had problems understanding the full significance of the verse. French dictionaries and encyclopaedias were of no help, and none of the French writers I consulted could shed any light: I was left puzzling over why Char had used the term. Then, purely by chance, when chatting one day with a friend in Avignon, I discovered that in Provençal *calendes* means New Year (and in popular folklore is associated with the return of the dead). The meaning of the verse was suddenly clear, but this discovery was more than just a problem solved. It helped me to understand that when Char uses unfamiliar or archaic words, he does not intend to confuse or deter his readers. Rather he is reminding us that words mean different things in different contexts and that they often have a hidden history. Convinced that we increasingly need today to learn from the past which is all too swiftly disappearing from our ken, Char offers us enigmas to solve—in order to oblige us to construct a new and personal sense of presence. . . .

. . . . .

THE RELATIVITY OF POETRY

Full of merit, yet poetically
Man dwells on this earth

FRIEDRICH HÖLDERLIN

Merit in poets is as boring as merit in people

WALLACE STEVENS

All poetry is about a passionate, if sometimes despairing, relationship with the world. In Char's case, this relationship is one of anger as well as one of hope. If he often castigates humankind for its cowardice and lack of commitment to others, he also repeatedly uses images of growth (the chrysalis which will become a butterfly or the seed which will become a plant, the flower which will become a fruit). He loves his fellow-beings, without pity, without any illusions or delusions . . . and always determinedly. As I have said, he lives and writes in a state of 'tragic optimism', in a state where pessimism and optimism are not so much at war as succeeding each other in a cycle that moves him and us on towards the creation of a world which will finally recognise its inherent transcendence. Yet the poet is always writing for someone else, for the unknown reader. Therein lies his grandeur—and his solitude.

Traditionally the love poem is seen as the celebration of a relationship, whether this relationship be consummated or not, real or imaginary. In his love poems Char hymns sexual and emotional complicity (**'L'amoureuse en secret'/'Loving him secretly'** and **'Recours au ruisseau'/'Recourse to the river'**), laments absence (**'Le carreau'/'The window-pane'**), warns against jealousy (**'Corail'/'Coral'**); he speaks of the necessity of sharing the experience of a fleeting love with others, be they friends or readers (**'Anoukis et plus tard Jeanne'/'Anoukis and later Jeanne'**); he challenges the narcissism which is at the heart of much loving and much poetry (**'À la désespérade'/'At the Désespérade'**). All this was lived by the poet; all this has much in common with the work of such major French love poets as Ronsard, Baudelaire and Éluard. However in Charrian love poetry the beloved is never the sole focus or pretext for his thinking and writing but is always part of his desire to understand and describe existence in its manifold differences. From his childhood discovery of the beautiful whiteness of his Italian nanny's breast until his death, Char loved and was loved by many women—indeed one of his friends has written that *la sua lista* was longer than Casanova's! Loved and loving women were essential to the poet's personal life and well-being, but in his writing they become poetic *figures* whose function is similar to that of animals, rivers, plants and trees: they remind the reader that all aspects of our lives are intertwined, that every relationship is ultimately about our indwelling.

While Char loved often and passionately, his poetic presentation of Woman is marked by a certain male chauvinism. ***Le Visage nuptial**/The Nuptial Countenance* (1938) ends thus: 'This is the sand dead, this the body saved: / Woman breathes, Man stands upright'. Like the field in **'Louis Curel de la Sorgue'**, the body is saved and the male lover is upright, while the female lover 'breathes', is horizontal and passive. There can be no doubt that Char considered women to be inferior, his sexism being as calm and assured as it was absolute. He saw himself as the liberator of all those he loved, giving them the freedom of poetry as well as the freedom of eroticism, and above all freeing them from the constraints of society's rules and expectations. When Char writes of love, it is always about desire which must *remain* desire and not slide into repetition, fidelity, marriage, and certainly not into parenthood: like Baudelaire and Sade, he cannot love woman's procreative potential, and indeed his conception of desire is an essentially male one. For him as for many of the Surrealists, encounters are best when fleeting—like a lightning-flash: therein lies their intensity and their permanence. 'The friend who stays,' he writes, 'is no better than the friend who leaves. Fidelity is a usurped territory.' There are echoes here of the parable of the Prodigal Son but above all a sense that sexual fidelity is irrelevant, whereas fidelity to moral principles is paramount.

'Anoukis et plus tard Jeanne'/'Anoukis and later Jeanne'is one of Char's most beautiful and resonant love poems and one of his most revelatory. A celebration of love, **'Anoukis'** is traditional in that it sings the praises of a beloved whom the poet wants to share 'poetically' with others. It is typically Charrian in its insistence that love leads to a coincidence with Nature and with folklore. In Provençal mythology, Anoukis is both the goddess who watches over river-bends and a figure of destiny who kills her victims by embracing them. The poem's full force, however, can be realised only when one knows a little of its source. In conversations with Char, Paul Veyne discovered that Char did indeed have a chance with an Anoukis figure (Jeanne) and that he swiftly passed to a sexual relationship with her. More worryingly, Veyne gives some details of the end of this encounter. One of Char's painter friends saw her and made the following request: 'René, give her to me, I love her too much'. Char 'gave' her to him!

Poetic sharing is admirable; actual sharing of women by "giving" them to friends is problematic or, rather, shameful, in that it pre-supposes that men actually have proprietorial power over women and can dispose of them as they will. The anecdotal basis of the text is disturbing to anyone committed to sexual equality, and many of us will be shocked by the fact that Veyne has no information to offer about the woman's reactions. However, the poem itself articulates a transcendance of individual experiences. Anoukis is Jeanne, his best friend's sister, a goddess, his destiny, all women in one, an incarnation of women. She can be loved and hymned in a poem only because she can be, *has been,* discarded—and has been made into a figure, a symbol. All too often, Char's love poems, like those of Baudelaire, have been (mis-)interpreted as being for and about individual women, but a close attention to his work reveals that his first and last beloved is poetry—which transforms the anecdotal or biographical into the archetypal and the mythic. At the heart of his poetic, intellectual and erotic thinking lies his conviction that 'the poem is the consummation of a love which maintains desire as desire'.

Poetry, Beauty, Nature, love, desire, justice: these are the forces which structure Char's universe. And each of them involves violence. The poet experienced violence from the moment he could see and relate to the world: the emotional violence of his mother, the physical bullying of his elder brother, the necessary violence of the ploughman 'wounding' the earth, the regretful violence of the hunter who kills birds 'to keep the tree for himself', the natural violence of snakes, animals, birds and insects, of sun, storm and snow. The natural world is full of predators and preys whose warrings are necessary to the balance of nature. This Char discovered as a child who initially identified with the role of victim. However his reading of the pre-Socratic philosophers, notably Heraclitus and Empedocles, led him to recognise that conflict is a cosmic force and ultimately a moral force. Heraclitus declares that the universe consists of a struggle, that justice is a conflict and that all existence is determined by discord. He insists on the creativity which springs from a balanced strife between opposites. If conflict is natural and inevitable, Man/the poet must always respond by an act of resistance: 'I will never write a poem of acquiescence' (*Fureur et mystère*/*Furor and Mystery*).

Char's angry revolt is directed outward at a world in which innocent children are killed, oppressors torture and tyrannise, and past traditions and beliefs are replaced by the selfishness of materialism. At times we must withdraw temporarily in order to find our strength,

we must 'desert' as he urges in **'Conseil de la sentinelle'/'The Guard's advice,'** in other words, reject the entire system of oppression until we have rebuilt our ability to rebel. In this, there is no cowardice, rather a recognition that vulnerability is inherent in us all and that it can be creative and progressive only when it is allied to an active aggressivity.

The poet himself is both aggressor and aggressed—as is his poetry. And given the fact that his poetry is driven by an erotic desire for violent union with Woman, with Nature and with Poetry, we may go so far as to describe his poetry as sadomasochistic. Char's godmother Louise Roze was a descendant of the Marquis de Sade's lawyer and as an adolescent Char discovered in her library some autograph letters of the 'divine marquis' (or the 'violet man' as he calls him). This led him to read Sade's work and to discover not the social philosopher that many praise today, but a champion of erotic desire as violent, multiple and often self-contradictory who had an almost nihilistic conception of Nature as the victim of man's ferocity. While the Sadean obsession with orifices, real or created, finds no place in Char's writing, the presentation of eroticism as a reversible process of cruelty haunts several of his early poems. After his Surrealist period he abandoned much Sadean thinking, perceiving both harmony and the potential for rebirth in both love and Nature, but the concept of reversibility was to inform all of his mature work.

Like his Surrealist friends in the 1930s, he became fascinated by the work of Freud which offered a theoretical validation of the mobility both of his poetry and of his emotional and intellectual positions. For Char, the poet must assign himself an object which is both victim and 'dangerous'. This is why I describe his work as sadomasochistic—not because of any writing about sexual 'perversion' but because of the way in which it functions as poetry. For Freud, activity and passivity are universal characteristics of sexual life and the libido dictates all of our actions and decisions. If Char can exalt the love-making of praying mantises, in which the female bites off her partner's head at the moment of full consummation, he must see himself as the 'active' male and also as the 'passive' victim of erotic violence. However the Freudian active/passive opposition is used by the poet mainly as a theoretical model for a poetry in which meaning emerges from the tension which always exists in language as in life: in all of Char's work, there is a creative struggle between fraternal duty and individual desires, between the erotic and the moral, between the emotional and the intellectual, between the realistic and the metaphysical.

Violence and delicacy work together and against each other in his texts and slowly the poetic Word, the *logos,* reveals itself as an ardent force. For Char, the sun is a source of violence, burning, evaporating, killing; but, more importantly, it is a noble counter-aggression liberating the persecuted from the 'plague of false knowledge'. Since this 'false knowledge' is monovalent certainty, humans need liberation, not liberty. Like Gide and Sartre, albeit in a different way, Char believes that freedom is a *process,* never a fixed state won and retained once and forever.

Paradoxically perhaps, liberation comes from an active acceptance of difference rather than from a single conviction of what is right and just. In the universe described in **Les Matinaux/The Dawn Breakers,** birds illuminate our world and are killed, trees provide a warming shade and are set alight by the hunter's cartridge (**'Fête des arbres et du chasseur'/ 'Celebration of the trees and the hunter'**); dogs are faithful and tormented (**'Les Transparents'/'The Clearseeing'**); windows are openings and mirrors (**'Le carreau'/'The window-pane'**); mountains are hostile and generous, rivers hide and reveal, are sterile and productive, but their violence is always magical (**'Cet amour à tous retiré'/'This love lost to all'**). In an open letter to Georges Bataille in 1950, Char asserted that the modern world will never rediscover 'a relative harmony, its burning diversity' until the 'problem of incompatibilities' is seriously posed. Earlier in a brief essay on Heraclitus, he speaks of 'the exhilarating union of opposites' which is 'the indispensable creative foundation of harmony'. This abiding concern with opposites, with dialectics, although reinforced by his reading of Heraclitus, Sade, Hegel, Freud and Heidegger, has its roots in Char's childhood observations of the natural world.

Nowhere is this better seen than in **'Fête'/'Celebration,'** composed for four Catalan 'maquisards' or Resistance fighters who could not return to Spain after the Liberation of France. Stylistically simple so that these modern-day troubadours could easily remember and sing it, the poem presents a series of images that underline the warring contradictions of Nature, and—crucially—the figure of humankind. The 'melancholy hunter' inadvertently destroys the forest that he loves and that is the habitat of his prey. While the poem has often been interpreted as an indictment of human interference in Nature, **'Fête'/'Celebration'** says and does something more: a characteristically Charrian allegory, it speaks as much of poetic creation as of the violence and the killing which mark so much animal and human behaviour. The hunter is melancholy not because he intends to kill in order 'to keep for himself the tree and its long-suffering gloom' but rather because he dares to take no truly decisive action and so release the creativity inherent in all existence.

When he finally fires, his cartridge accidentally sets fire to the forest. Yet the blaze, though consuming, is above all illuminating. Like the gnomic utterances of the **Clear-seeing Ones,** this allegory refuses and challenges the rigidity of traditional allegory, offering a transcendence of received logic. Like Goethe's butterfly which dies and is transfigured in the candle-flame, Char's poetry transforms matter into blazing light and destroys the world in order to recreate it in a more beautiful form. Throughout his work we find this central image of the blaze, whether it be the fire in the father's room which suddenly blazes up and inspires him to write, the lightning-flash which is simultaneously ephemeral and eternal and lights up our darkness, the forest-fire which by illuminating defers death, or the burning of the harvested fields which ensures a new and stronger growth. In *À une sérénité crispée/Towards a tense serenity,* he affirms: 'Beauty sets fire to everything in our sheaf of darkness which must be set alight'; in **'Note sibérienne'/'Siberian note'** (*Aromates chasseurs/Hunting herbs,* 1975), he asks: 'Why then this repetition: we are a spark of unknown origin and always set fire ahead. This fire, do we hear it wheeze and cry out at the very moment when we are consumed? Nothing, except that we were suffering, so much that in its centre the vast silence was splitting'; in *Le poème pulvérisé/The pulverised poem,* he hymns the 'Nomadic spark which dies in its fire'. Life and death are not perceived as a simple cycle: while Char's imagery is drawn from Nature, he is never satisfied with the life-death-resurrection cycle that Western culture has installed as the most optimistic description of existence. If his poetry and thinking are radical, this is because he sees that existence is not—or at least should not always be—bound by the tyranny of Time. From the past, we must retain only moments of transcendance and transfiguration, recognising that the Christian tradition tells us that Christ's Transfiguration not only reveals his divinity but prefigures his mortal death. Memory is 'death's great ally', for it prevents us from looking onward performatively to moments when sequential time may be crossed by vertical, eternal time, when the world is ablaze with illumination. This is the form of harmony which Char finds, advocates and creates in his poetry, hence his insistence on such images as the plateau which is a *continuous* summit not a temporary high point or the lightning-flash which reveals the permanence of illumination in the split-second of its occurrence.

In **'La Sorgue'/'The Sorgue: a song for Yvonne'** (from *La fontaine narrative/The narrative fountain* of 1947), he hymns the 'River where the lightning ends and my house rises / Rolling to the steps of oblivion the rubble of my reason'. Running from the Fontaine de Vaucluse and encircling L'Isle-sur-Sorgue on three sides, the Sorgue is both a reality and a mythic figure but above all it is a constant presence which reminds the poet that all things are multiple and that we must maintain a position of simultaneous revolt and fraternity. For centuries the Sorgue supported the entire town which lived from fishing but it was later punished by the industrial pollution of a paper-making factory; its waters are still astonishingly transparent but are now dangerous; it is a symbol of death and survival. The poem ends with an invocation to the Sorgue which resumes Char's moral attitude: 'Keep me violent and the friend of the bees on the horizon'.

Poetic language is the most challenging and disquieting of all languages, in that it both juxtaposes differing stances and self-consciously explores and proclaims its own silences, inadequacies, redundancies and possibilities. At the same time, it is always inscribing itself inescapably but voluntarily into a history of previous thinking. Modern French poetry is perhaps more explicitly intertextual than any since the Renaissance, in that the past is woven into the present with both gratitude and a certain aggression, as poets seek to delineate their own space. Char's implacable stance occasionally led him to attack poets who had in his view slipped into mere word-play. For him, poetry should be essential, that is to say, central to our lives rather than a marginal decoration. For this reason, he insists on repositioning poetry in contemporary culture by urging us to read differently and so to relearn the lessons of past moral thinkers. If there is one statement which illuminates Char's attitude to our shared heritage, it is his favourite fragment by Heraclitus which prefigures much of Heidegger's thinking on sameness and difference: 'You never step twice into the same river.' Each experience we have, be it of love, Nature or poetry, is always a repetition yet always an innovation.

Hölderlin's crucial question, brilliantly considered by Heidegger in his oracular 1946 lecture on Rilke, 'Wozu Dichter in dürftiger Zeit' (What are poets for in a destitute time?) is an anxious question that Char repeatedly poses both to himself and to his readers. Like Hölderlin, he thought of the poet as 'the priest of the invisible'; like Heidegger, he conceived of poetry as a renovation of experience and as the site of truth or, more accurately, of *aletheia* (unveiling or unconcealedness). However, while the sacred is ever-present in his work and while he too merits the appellation given by Heidegger to Hölderlin of the poet of the Time Between, Char's insistence on the value of poets and on our need for them has a political edge. Poets must unveil truth and in so doing must challenge all the systems of oppression which shape the world in which they live and write. The poet is someone who must have moral courage, integrity (and indeed ferocity) and must consequently judge. Yet this social merit must also be traversed by moments of illumination, by colourful play with the lexicon and with folklore. Char essentially agrees with Hölderlin's view of the difference between merit and poetry, but he is also close to Wallace Stevens' position, believing that authentic merit is not propriety but must be splashed through by vivid

personal experiences. This is one reason why he so admires such artists as Picasso, Braque and Arpad Szenes, in that their paintings marry intellectuality to emotion, graphism to colour. Above all, poetry must use its potential to disquiet. As he says in the last statement of **'Rougeur des Matinaux'/'Redness of the Dawn Breakers'**: 'In short, if you do destroy, let it be with nuptial tools'.

Seamed through by references to past works and past thinking, Char's poetry demands a reading that includes but also goes beyond local, personal knowledge, a reading that accepts that we can understand fully only if we attend to what has been prepared for us. In **'Cet amour à tous retiré'/'This love lost to all'** from *Les Matinaux* we find the following stanza:

> The violence was magical;
> A man sometimes died,
> But as death seized him,
> A trace of amber would seal his eyes.

Violence, death, magical transformation: these Charrian thematic constants are presented here, simply, in one stanza that poses no interpretative difficulty for the reader. Except . . . why the amber? Most of us vaguely recognise its ritual importance, yet Char's usage is calculated to activate its multiple cultural resonances. Since Thales in 600 B.C., we know that amber (*electron* in Greek) has magnetic properties—it absorbs excess electrical charges from the person rubbing it. The tears of amber shed by Apollo when expelled from Mount Olympus symbolise his nostalgia for a lost paradise and the promise of Elysium. Prehistoric insects have been preserved (and made beautiful) in amber, hence the Egyptians' use of amber in their embalming processes. Both the Celts and Christians saw amber as a symbol of spirituality and sanctity. Like so many of the symbols that Char uses, amber is plurivalent and intercultural. This means that readers can never fix on one single meaning and will in each successive reading privilege one or other of the possible connotations. Such a dismantling of the notion of textual authority is characteristic of Char's work in that he both accepts that the reader is the co-creator of his poems and also wishes to push the reader into an exploration of his or her own responses to superficially simple texts which are in fact creatively unstable. Although Char disliked the term *aphorism,* preferring the neutral 'short text', his poetic utterances do have the contestatory force of pre-Socratic aphorisms in that they juxtapose the explicit and the implicit, continuity and discontinuity. His writings therefore demand that readers accept that they are both the victims and the operators of a 'nuptial' violence (and create problems for any translator!).

If Char's imagery is often taken from his native Provence, his thinking is far from Eurocentric, largely perhaps because of his encounters with France-based painters from other continents, such as Wilfredo Lam and Zao Wou-Ki. With someone as widely read as Char, it is always difficult to know exactly whom he had or had not read, but it is interesting that his poetics, like his philosophical thinking, is very similar to that of Octavio Paz, who wrote in *The Bow and the Lyre*:

> Poetic creation begins as violence to language. The first act in this operation is the uprooting of words. The poet wrests them from their habitual connections and occupations: separated from the formless world of speech, words become unique, as if they had just been born. The second action is the return of the word: the poem becomes an object of participation. Two opposing forces inhabit the poem: one of elevation or uprooting, which pulls the word from language; the other of gravity which makes it return. The poem is an original and unique creation, but it is also reading and recitation: participation. The poet creates it; the people, by recitation, re-create it. Poet and reader are two moments of a single reality. Alternating in a manner that may aptly be called cyclical, their rotation engenders the spark: poetry.

Char's poetry begins in violence—in his just anger at all betrayals of freedom and in his determination to release language from the straitjacket of conventional usage. It ends in the (never-ending) work of reading which necessarily recognises that the universe exists as multiple by virtue of division and oppositions.

THE COMPLICATIONS OF SIMPLICITY

Art is the only thing that can go on
mattering once it has stopped hurting.

ELIZABETH BOWEN

Life may change, but it may fly not;
Hope may vanish, but can die not;
Truth be veiled, but still it burneth
Love repulsed,—but it returneth!

SHELLEY

If Char's relationship with himself and his subjects may be defined as sadomasochistic, the workings of his texts are no less violent, albeit in a different way. Thematically, his work is dominated by suffering, woundings, deaths, all of which are for him potentially creative, a source of transformatory radiance—as all farmers, fisherfolk and hunters intuitively know. A child of the Vaucluse countryside, Char realised this from an early age and wrote of what he saw. And he wrote as he saw, hence his definition of the poet as 'a man of simplicity'. However, his vision or *inseeing* is not, as I have suggested, that of modern urban, industrialised man; although his poacher friend could immediately grasp the meaning of his poems, most modern Europeans have lost the ability to see the world around them. So poetry must be more than a mirror of reality and must re-open our eyes.

The twentieth century is above all the age of the image, of the spectacle, yet the barrage of images which daily assails us has had the effect of blinding us to the fact that true seeing is an act of active engagement and interpretation rather than one of passive reception. When in 1938 Char sent to his friend Christian Zervos, the editor of *Cahiers d'art,* two poems he had composed on paintings by Courbet and Corot, he spoke in his covering letter of 'the complications of poetry . . . the simplicity of painting'. His thinking then, as throughout his life, was not determined by Platonic or Hegelian hierarchies but by a belief that language has a duty to be 'complicated' in order to lead us on toward a new vision—like that of Rimbaud who wished to reinvent language so that we could once more see authentically. His was no intellectual project, as was that of Valéry whose difficulty is a strategy to ensure concentration on the workings of his poetry—Char frequently proclaimed that he was not an intellectual but 'a man of desire'. Rather, his poetry works to remind us that language must speak again of our primal roots. But the poet can achieve this only be reminding us that language, though the prism through which we can (hope to) apprehend reality, is necessarily also the vehicle of centuries of cultural accretion; consequently the poet must work both with and against history. If Wordsworth can write of 'intimations of immortality', Char cannot but write of 'intimations of origin'. However, sentimental nostalgia must be resolutely refused and the origin must constantly be made present as the future towards which we strain: 'To live is to obliterate a memory', as Char said in an interview. The past is consequently not to be rewritten or recuperated in purely personal terms; it is to be discovered, new and different, as a 'shared presence'.

The project is idealistic, but it is also problematic in that even today reading is still a somewhat elitist activity: what is shared? how much knowledge is needed? why bother? and should we bother? One answer offered by Char is the distinction between the poem and poetry which he established during the Resistance: 'The poem is a furious ascension; poetry, the play of arid riverbanks' (*Feuillets d'Hypnos/Leaves of Hypnos*). In other words, we must attend to each individual text and not to a culturally approved mode of writing. A further answer is proposed in another wartime statement: 'If the absurd reigns here on earth, I choose the absurd, the antistatic, or whatever brings me close to the possibilities of pathos and empathy. I am a man of the riverbanks—of erosion and swelling—since I cannot always be a man of the roaring stream.' These two statements articulate important thoughts on poetry, but they use the same image of the riverbanks (berges) to express radically different ideas. This does not mean that Char's poetics is incoherent or contradictory, but that he is committed to rethinking his position constantly, to maintaining it in a state of creative flux.

Char describes Heraclitus as 'this proud, stable and anxious genius who sees truth as noble and the image which reveals truth as tragic'. All that Char admires in Heraclitus is to be found in his own poetry, notably the anxiety about how one can possibly express or, more accurately, *unveil* the beauty of truth. The truth, however, for both these thinkers is neither serene not stable: like existence itself, it is a *becoming,* a discovery of harmony through and in discord, through and in struggle. Heraclitus asserts that the fundamental principle of existence is Strife (also translated as Hate or War) which is an external force and that Love is a unifying force *within* the world. These two forces are engaged in an eternal struggle which is the foundation of all becoming. The notion of struggle is crucial, in that it is a question not of a simple cycle in which Hate and Love succeed each other. It is a question of a creative co-existence of opposites: a process which, to paraphrase Char, involves both a straining towards the future and a remembering of the past.

The Ancient Greek idea of existence as flux had particular resonance for those who had experienced World Wars and had come to recognise that unity of thought is a fantasy created by the particular society in which we live. Furthermore, and crucially, the thoughts of Heraclitus, Empedocles and Parmenides have been left to us in *fragmented* form. Char is fascinated by the concept of fragmentation. For him, both life and poetry are tragically (though potentially creatively) structured and defined by splitting, by lack of coherence, by a principle of difference and constant differing, hence his insistent privileging of the individual poem over poetry. His own texts are usually brief and may appear to be separate, autonomous entities, yet there is in his work as a whole a continual interweaving of terms whereby ideas and images are re-presented and rethought. His preferred image for fragmentation is the archipelago. One of his volumes is called *La parole en archipel/The Word as archipelago* and all his poems and images relate to each other as do the islands in an archipelago, which, though apparently, *superficially* distinct, are linked each to the other by a hidden submarine landmass. The reader thus becomes an explorer who must both scan the sea-surface of the poems and plumb the depths of the waters which separate the various texts in order to establish some kind of map of Char's work.

The archipelago is a central notion for Char, but he also uses another significant metaphor as the title for one of the poems in *Les Matinaux,* that of the cento. In Latin, a cento is a patchwork garment made of scraps of material, but the term has come to mean a poetic composition made up of passages selected from the work of great poets of the past. Most of the fragments which make up this poem were in fact written by the poet himself. However, what is most important is that they have the aphoristic quality of much Ancient Greek writ-

ing and *could have been written* by Heraclitus or Empedocles—with the difference that statements of moral philosophy are here made subjectively, in the first person. While Char is a highly individual poet, his work constantly refers back to past writers and especially to past conceptions of harmony—in order to make us think creatively about the destructively fragmented present in which we live today.

Char is sometimes described as a 'precious' poet in that he occasionally uses both unusual or highly specific words and syntactic structures that are 'old fashioned' or 'pedantic'. But he is also radically modern, even 'postmodern' in his insistent poetic use of fragmentation, collage and incorporation of references to the past. He is also above all an archaeologist of language who reminds us that words have a history, whether we know it or not, and that these words need to be found again, dug up, uncovered, resurrected . . . This concern with the past is not nostalgic, or at least not simply so: Char is preoccupied by the problems of absence and presence, both of these being bound up into a meditation upon time and history, and all of his work may be seen as an interrogation of the very movements and constructs that are nostalgia's. If he frequently returns to the notion that we still hold the 'old gods' within us, this does not mean that he is advocating a return to paganism or even pantheism. Rather, he is aware that the past is simultaneously gone and *present,* albeit in a fragmented and often unrecognised form. Hence for example his insistence on transcribing the language of the Provençal *Transparents* in order to remind us that even today there are those whose discourse ambiguously conjoins the metaphysical and the concrete.

For Char, poetry is necessary, *central,* in that only poetry can (dare to) speak truth. This truth is, however, not an absolute, immutable truth, but an *aletheia.* In his 1956 essay on Rimbaud, Char states categorically that 'without poetry [. . .] the world is and means nothing. True life, that unimpeachable colossus, finds its meaning only in the flanks of poetry.' While it is interesting that here as elsewhere he conceives of poetry as feminine (flanks) and of true life as masculine (colossus), what is crucial is that truth can be found only in an acceptance of difference and interaction, in the warring harmonies offered by poetry. Each individual poem is part of a patchwork, a fragment of an eternal and universal discourse that is half-lost to us— and so as readers we must engage in a kind of archeological activity. Char's occasional use of archaic syntax and of unfamiliar words taken from Provençal is neither elitist nor exclusive; rather it serves to remind us that we must seek to refind the original meaning of words in order to reposition ourselves fully in the present. Yes, many of us may sometimes need to use dictionaries or encyclopaedias when reading his poems, but this is part of the poet's committed strategy to make us reconsider the past so that we may re-encounter and rethink the complex simplicity of vision of our predecessors, be they pre-Socratic philosophers, clear-seeing wanderers, fisherfolk, farmers or poachers—or poets.

In his 1985 volume *Les voisinages de Van Gogh/In Van Gogh's territory,* which in its subtle and erudite allusions to Provence offers an interesting counterpoint to *Les Matinaux/The Dawn Breakers,* the vocabulary is more recondite and the references more problematic for the uninitiated reader, but the concern with the past's relation to the present is just as dominant. The first, programmatic text is called **'L'avant-Glanum'/'Before Glanum',** referring to the quarry where Van Gogh was painting when he had his first serious fit of madness. But Char's allusion is more complex in that the Roman ruins for which Glanum is now famous were not discovered until the 1921 excavations, that is to say more than 30 years after Van Gogh's death. What matters for Char is that although Van Gogh could not possibly know of the subterranean ruins, his eye was that of the in-seeing artist who intuitively senses the past in the present—and so his painting created a link between the mountain's natural arch and the hidden town which would later be uncovered.

It is this complex web of past, present and future which underpins all of Char's poetry wherein origins lie not only in the past but also as future destinations. Through art we can uncover the truth of existence, the simple truth that all is complicated, that there are links between all things.

THE SOVEREIGN CONVERSATION

Echo answers echo; everything reverberates.

GEORGES BRAQUE

Char's poetry is profoundly aware of the past which is our shared heritage, the 'common wealth' that in **'Anoukis and later Jeanne'** permits him to understand that all experiences are repetitions. This is especially true of experiences of love which, though often presented as singular, as unique, have their full meaning because they are commemorations which rewrite the past in order to promise a new harmony in the future. This poetry is undoubtedly difficult in its moral and philosophical speculations and affirmations, but it also has a vigorous immediacy, precisely because it speaks of the problems and conflicts which have preoccupied human beings since time immemorial. Char is firmly, even aggressively, explicit on issues of social justice. He is however questioningly suggestive when writing about his individual emotional experiences which he perceives as simultaneously deeply personal and characteristic of all human behaviour. Our passions are not simply the product of our own psyches and libidos: they are always partially determined by the culture in

which we live, hence Char's conscious and unconscious dialogue with past and present writings, paintings and music.

If the creation of poetry is necessarily a solitary and individualistic activity, the reading of poetry is collaborative. We each bring to texts our own thoughts, hopes and especially our memories. We try out our own histories against those of the poet, and the marvellous miracle occurs: we recognise that what poets say reveals more about ourselves than it does about them.

When Char wrote, it was always alone, whether in the necessary solitude of every poet or in the brief 'absence' of the Resistance fighter, yet in all of his moments of creation he was accompanied by other artists with whom he silently dialogued, notably Heraclitus, Sade, Hölderlin, Rimbaud, Éluard, Heidegger, Braque, Picasso—and Georges de la Tour. Throughout the War he kept pinned to his wall a colour print of de la Tour's *The Prisoner* which depicts a woman speaking to a captive. All of de la Tour's luminescently candle-lit paintings fascinated Char but *The Prisoner* had a particular significance for him during the War because, as he says, this representation of a dialogue between human beings 'defeated and brought under control the manifold darkness of Hitlerism' (*Fureur et mystère/Furor and Mystery*). This is one of the rare examples where Char privileges the decoding of content over emotional response. Usually he strives to transcribe and to generate an experience of *happening*. This happening is a form of *aletheia* whereby we discover that we both belong to the past and are different from it. In his essays on artists, he often insists on his sense of belonging (in an ambivalent way) to a tradition, and his choice of epigraphs from writers as diverse as Heraclitus, Empedocles, Shakespeare, Monteverdi, Blake and Melville further underlines his anti-historical commitment to discovery of the past as a recognition but also as a becoming, a moving-onwards. The Tradition is for Char what Paz has called a tradition of discontinuity. This explains his reluctance to write fully-argued theoretical essays, preferring to offer short aphoristic texts which allow his readers space to interpret, to reposition themselves in time—and above all to create their own meanings.

Throughout the work of this tragic optimist, of this darkly luminous poet burns one constant light: the beacon of hope in our individual and collective capacity to surmount oppression. All of the Dawn Breakers, be they human or animal, are therefore to be respected and cherished, for they are our models in a world of moral poverty. Char's work may point up the gloom which shrouds contemporary existence, yet always there is a sense that progress will be made. In his 1979 volume *Fenêtres dormantes et porte sur le toit/Sleeping windows and door on the roof,* he restates unequivocally this belief that informs all the poems in *Les Mat-*

inaux: '*The Dawn Breakers* would go on living, even if there were no more evening, no more morning.'

Jean Starobinski (essay date 1994)

SOURCE: Starobinski, Jean. "René Char and the Definition of the Poem." In *Figuring Things: Char, Ponge, and Poetry in the Twentieth Century,* edited and translated by Charles D. Minahen, pp. 113-27. Lexington, Ky.: French Forum Publishers, 1994.

[*In the following essay, Starobinski discusses the poetics and aesthetics of Char's writings.*]

There is no poem, no line of René Char that does not give us a feeling of opening. An increased space appears before us, lights up within us. This space offers itself to our open eyes. It does not have the facile qualities of the dream: it is the harsh and expanding volume of our earthly sojourn, the instant of our present breath, revealed to their fullest extent. Something immense, intense, announces itself imperiously. We are made sensitive to its fullness through a fit of emotion which will not be felt distinct from great, natural energies: we recognize the advent of the "matière-émotion instantanément reine" ["matter-emotion instantaneously queen"]. But the feeling of opening that we experience when reading René Char comes not only from this devastating increase of the present site and instant. The poem, so neatly traced before our gaze, makes us feel its two shores of silence; it develops between a past and a future, it tears itself away from an original space, it is pointed toward a distance that can only be sensed and that is destined to remain inaccessible. The poetic word surrounds itself with a here and a there which are neither attained nor named, but which the energy of the poem never ceases to designate. The feeling of opening, more than just resulting from the expanse offered to the domination of our gaze, stems from the way René Char, in giving the present and presence their full force, safeguards the integrity of the distant and the absent. The great alchemy of the poem consists of implicating in the present tense of language, in the present movement of the word, a vigilant relationship with that which lets itself neither possess nor name, which announces itself and slips away in the absolute interval. To the admirable definition "le poème est l'amour réalisé du désir"[1] ["the poem is the realized love of desire"] can be added these more recent words: "Supprimer l'éloignement tue. Les dieux ne meurent que d'être parmi nous" (767) ["Removing the distance kills. The gods only die from being among us"].

The opening, we see, does not limit itself to the positive conquest of a vast horizon offered for contemplation. It apprehends negatively that which is taken from us. It arises from the dramatic contrast between a here and an elsewhere, between present dazzlement and unreachable ground against which it stands out. The function of poetry, as Char never ceases to repeat, is to maintain this confrontation of opposites, to reap its suffering and its fruit: the poet can thus appear to us in the double role of wounded one and conciliator.

The aphorisms of René Char offer the perfect example of the amorous and bellicose commerce that contraries maintain. These texts of extreme awakening are not written in a different ink than the rest of his work. These are poems that rush to declare the universal; in them, as Maurice Blanchot so well puts it, "poetry is revelation of poetry . . . poem of the essence of the poem . . . poetry faced with itself and rendered visible in its essence through the words that seek it out."[2] In their so strong and imperious writing, the aphorisms seem at first to close upon a definition, to circumscribe a truth, to enclose a precept. But let us give them our full attention: little by little we will see the answer turn interrogative; absence, future, distance take their places at the heart of this apparently closed form and crack its shell; the definition put into service of the undefinable, and the precept enjoining only to set free. Having chosen, among all the modes of expression, the one that supposes the greatest constraint, Char makes from it the key of a liberation. The contraction of the word engenders the expansion of its sense. The aphorism authoritatively enunciates the order of the world, but, according to Char's own very beautiful expression, it is an "ordre insurgé" ["insurgent order"].

> Le poète transforme indifféremment la défaite en victoire, la victoire en défaite, empereur prénatal seulement soucieux du recueil de l'azur.
>
> (155)
>
> [The poet transforms indifferently defeat into victory, victory into defeat, prenatal emperor concerned only with gathering the azure.]
>
> Magicien de l'insécurité, le poète n'a que des satisfactions adoptives. Cendre toujours inachevée.
>
> (156)
>
> [Magician of insecurity, the poet only has adopted satisfactions. Ash always incomplete.]

These texts, to which the Baudelairean term "rockets" would so well apply, carry their own reserve of supplemental energy, the very principle of their bursting in the illuminated heights. The formal contraction of the aphorism is in a relation of opposition to an unlimited space which is foreign to it only in order to become more perfectly complementary to it. "L'intensité est silencieuse. Son image ne l'est pas. (J'aime qui m'éblouit puis accentue l'obscur à l'intérieur de moi)" (330) ["The intensity is silent. Its image is not. (I like what dazzles me then accentuates the obscure within me)")]. The instant flashes; it rends the silence and the night of waiting. Then the night recomposes itself. This is but one image among many of the surging of the poetic event: the poet is the master of designating as he pleases (and according to the grace that grants him the world) this instant that will remain like an overwhelming trace. And what borders this instant, on the two shores of past and present, is too elusive not to call the play of the most varied images. Whence is the poem born? To what horizon is it destined? The poem implicates this origin and this end in its internal tensions and its liveliest assertions. The image of the night, without fail, recurs insistently, associated with the image of humus, of the rock, of winter, of anguish. One should reread above all the admirable poem entitled **"Sur une nuit sans ornement"** (392-93) [**"On a night without ornament"**]. Numerous are the other poems where an obscure depth lets itself be seen, a dolorous anxiety "beneath the text." Let us just as soon add that it is a fought anxiety, an anxiety become fecund because it feeds the impulse that repudiates it. We feel strongly the tenebrous silence from which many a poem tears itself; and we also perceive the silence that after having been accomplished each sentence leaves behind, a silence comparable to a stagnant, black water, where burgeoning life ferments.

But René Char is not a poet of nostalgia. He is not fascinated by the origin and temptation of the retrospective look. If he evokes the nocturnal places of the beginning, it is because they belong "basically" to movement which uproots itself. The work of Char, in its most general character, manifests itself as an *uprising* that, leaving behind a nocturnal region, points across the sharp clarity of the day toward an ulterior risk. But the poetic event does not assure continuity of duration: it is not the transition point where the past flows lazily towards the future. Temporality manifests itself there in the form of rupture, disjunction.

* * *

An *uprising* of the word. Uprising, in its multiple meanings, is indeed the appropriate term here. It applies first to the images of climbing, so numerous in Char's poetry; it indicates the movement of that which raises itself—the surging of a volcanic archipelago, the shock of the wave, the leap of the heart, the ascending flight of the eagle; it also denotes the elevation of language to its full sense, to its dominating height, region in the breast of which the entire literality of words is revealed to be compatible with their widest metaphorical aptitude (in the exchange of powers between the abstract and the concrete). The poetry of René Char is once again uprising, in the sense of insurrection, seditious impulse, revolted energy. The image of uprising permits us therefore to see the cardinal virtues of René Char's poetry: anguish mobilized, heights attained, the

adversary defied. These are the virtues of a living person at the same time as those of a work. Here the poet is the exact contemporary of his word: if one could have said, with regard to Char, that the poet is given birth by the poem, one would just as soon have to add that the poem is the peril consented to, into which a man disappears to be reborn a poet. There is someone at the origin of the uprising, who will not be the same on the "crest of knowledge" where his movement takes him. This is to say that the poetic act is inseparable from a confrontation: anguish, height, adversary, René Char has felt them all to their most intense degree, in the concrete struggle as well as the imaginary dimension. Height is the glorious attribute of the poem and is at the same time the region where the double sun of love shines ("chemin de parélie," 341 ["parhelion way"]); as for anguish, it is in facing the worst, in defying in the maquis the most monstrous of real adversaries, that the poet has answered for his rebellious word.

I have just evoked the secret region that one senses at the origin of the poem, its prenatal space: night, earth, anguish, rock. But an antagonistic principle is immediately at work; it is a principle carrying concentrated energy and capable of *opposing*, sometimes by patient effort, sometimes in a sudden way. Char communicates to us evidence of it through images of a significant diversity: the seed in the earth, the source in the rock, the lightning bolt in the night, the sparkling of stars against a tenebrous background. (In a way that really reveals the always extreme demands of René Char, the image of the constellation or of the swarm of meteors manifests the opposition of the luminous flash and the darkness, in terms of a *multiple* flash struggling with the monotonous *uniformity* of the night sky; the contrast of light and night redoubles, so to speak, in that of plurality and unity.) The movement, henceforth irrepressible, issues from a shock of bellicose and amorous adversaries, whose theater is neither the "exterior" world nor the isolated "conscious," but their common belonging. For whoever knows how to listen, there is, behind many a poem of Char, a fecund couple, a play of antagonists or even incompatibles, who lend mutual support in view of a tearing, a springing, a forwardness that henceforth will no longer be able to stop before having spent all the motor energy that the commotion of their origin has charged them with. In the beautiful, luminous poem **"Déclarer son nom"** [**"Declaring One's Name"**], where Char evokes his childhood, the generating couple are *insouciance* and *pain*. As soon as these two terms are evoked, an acceleration is produced.

> J'avais dix ans. La Sorgue m'enchâssait. Le soleil chantait les heures sur le sage cadran des eaux. L'insouciance et la douleur avaient scellé le coq de fer sur le toit des maisons et se supportaient ensemble.

Mais quelle roue dans le cœur de l'enfant aux aguets tournait plus fort, tournait plus vite que celle du moulin dans son incendie blanc.

(401)

[I was ten. The Sorgue was enshrining me. The sun was singing the hours on the wise clockface of the waters. Insouciance and pain had sealed the iron cock on the roof of houses and were supporting (suffering) one another. But what wheel in the heart of the watchful child was turning more forcefully, turning more quickly than that of the mill in its white fire.]

One perceives at the beginning of this poem, the *slowing* typical of images of memory, and particularly memories of childhood. Elsewhere, a rapid and quasi-instantaneous movement carries the poem from its origin to its peak, from its initial surging to its "point diamenté actuel" ["immediate diamond point"] where the precarious and sharp-edged present illuminates us. And often, as we have seen, the multiple instant, the bouquet of sparks, the cluster and the swarm—plural figures where the unity of the present shatters in pieces—are, in René Char, privileged themes. But one would be hard pressed to name a poet as free as Char in obsessively repeating a course and a dynamic scheme. How many poems, in this work, do not speak to us of flight delayed, of patience, of endurance in the heart of a hostile element (nocturnal duration, inclement and unjust time), an element rendered fertile by the *vigil* that inhabits it and awaits its issue? "Porteront rameaux ceux dont l'endurance sait user la nuit noueuse qui précède et suit l'éclair" (431). ["Those whose endurance knows how to use up the gnarled night that precedes and follows the lightning will carry branches."] And in the uprising of the word, it is not only the origin and the summit that count for the poetic experience: René Char knows the entire cost that must be accorded to the threshold, the edge, the border, the breach—to all the places where the decisive outcome is accomplished, between the dark origin and the unformulated term. The poet, he tells us, is a "passer of justice," a "passant *appliqué* à passer" (334) ["passer-by *determined* to pass"]. Now if he is among the number of "early risers," it is not only because he is there at first light, but also because he knew, in the middle of night, to watch for the reddening of the dawn. The point of passage is not one where conflict nullifies itself: the opposites remain faced off, the tragedy of opposition rests complete, but an impulse is produced, to which the poet acquiesces:

L'état d'esprit du soleil levant est allégresse malgré le jour cruel et le souvenir de la nuit. La teinte du caillot devient la rougeur de l'aurore.

(329)

[The state of mind of the rising sun is cheerfulness despite the cruel day and the memory of the night. The tint of the clot becomes the redness of the dawn.]

Nous ne pouvons vivre que dans l'entrouvert, exactement sur la ligne hermétique de partage de l'ombre et de la lumière. Mais nous sommes irrésistiblement jetés en avant. Toute notre personne prête aide et vertige à cette poussée.

(411)

[We can live only in the half-opened, exactly on the hermetic line of sharing of the shadow and the light. But we are irresistibly thrown forward. Our whole person lends aid and dizziness to this push.]

All surging crosses a limit, clears an obstacle, risks itself in an unforeseen space: the *first instants* of the poem, of love, or of the river are linked together by powerful analogies. They carry within them the revelation of the passage. And if there are privileged places and objects—let's say even sacred—in Char's universe, they are those where the trace of passage is inscribed: the stone of the threshold, the gorge that a conquering force traverses, the rock of the *Fontaine de Vaucluse,* or that ambiguous *carreau* (310) [*window pane*], which unites and separates and where the outside and the inside mark their joint border.

At the extreme limit of poetic uprising, we find a new but forbidden threshold, which cannot be crossed. The summit is not a goal conquered and possessed. Should the poem leap to its highest altitude—and it happens that it does with dazzling speed—it finds itself less rich for its acquisition than thirsty for what it lacks and slips away again. The summit is but an instant, where unknown, future, silence manifest themselves by their very withdrawal:

Après l'ultime distorsion, nous sommes parvenus sur la crête de la connaissance. Voici la minute du *considérable danger*: l'extase devant le vide, l'extase neuve devant le vide frais. (753)

[After the ultimate distortion, we have arrived at the crest of knowledge. Here is the minute of *considerable danger*: the ecstasy before the void, the new ecstasy before the fresh void.]

Whatever the image the poet proposes to us for the term attained—height of pleasure, delta of the river, crest of the wave, zenith of the arrow or the star—victory inverts itself gloriously in defeat. In this way, instructed as to his limits, but obstinately refusing to submit to them, the poet finds himself driven back to the limitless night of his origins, to the source of his springing forth.

The high point, in René Char, excludes possessive accumulation. Between an abolished past and an "unpredicted future," the most lively crest of the present—where vigilance, transport, emotion, thought, vertigo join—is not the place for a possible stay. The dynamics of the poetic act, for René Char, do not allow finding rest on the heights: "Notre arche à tous, la très parfaite, naufrage à l'instant de son pavois. Dans ses débris et sa poussière, l'homme à tête de nouveau-né réapparaît. Déjà mi-liquide, mi-fleur" (344) ["The ark of us all, the very perfect one, shipwreck at the instant of its flag. In its debris and dust, man with a newborn's face reappears. Already half liquid, half flower"]. When he was enduring the night, the poet was watching for the instant of passing; but the word, at the extreme point of its trajectory, is forbidden to stay. "La poésie vit d'insomnie perpétuelle" (413) ["Poetry lives by perpetual insomnia"]. The poet faces the unknown. "Comment vivre sans inconnu devant soi" (247) ["How can one live without the unknown before one"]. This aphorism from Char, to which Maurice Blanchot has dedicated an admirable commentary,[3] situates life—thus poetry—on the front line of a confrontation. The unknown: that which I am not master of, that whose call does not cease to keep me awake, that which surrounds and provokes me, the *adverse part* that besieges me, the inaccessible horizon where my destiny foments. But the unknown does not stay neutral and faceless any more than the poet remains inactive. It is going to reveal itself to us in the *event* which has just broken the immobile watch. From the heart of the unknown, the occurrence surges, and the poet has the duty to retort. Destiny *produces itself,* and the poet must *produce* in response "l'inextinguible réel incréé" (155) ["the inextinguishable uncreated real"]. From the still unqualified horizon, where the reserve of the unknown stays intact, here come the delegates of the unknown: misfortune and risk—or luck. An attack—or a gift. The tormentors and the monsters—or unhoped-for beauty, always awaited. The poet proceeds to meet them, with the appropriate response.

Everywhere in Char's work, we find the scansion, the two times of a provocation of the world and a response of the poet. Unless in reverse order the human act precedes the world's reply: the hunter shoots, the forest blazes (281-88); in **"Le Soleil des eaux"** [**"The Sun of the Waters"**], the fishermen blow up the barricade, "*puis l'eau s'échappe en bouillonnant, l'eau que l'explosion a délivrée, l'eau encore dans les secrets de sa source*" (1053) ["*then water escapes bubbling, water that the explosion set free, water again in the secrets of its source*"]. The violent instant, the brief syllable of the explosion is followed by a long syllable, the tumultuous reply of nature delivered to the punctual and pure act of human revolt.

Matched with the unknown, the poet is thus dedicated to the duel and must adjust his response to the provocation of the world. When history is burdened with too many crimes, the just response is in the muffling of the voice, in the "sleep" of poetry. Man then moves on to acts and lets poetry occupy a marginal position, where the essential is preserved. The *Feuillets d'Hypnos* [*Leaves of Hypnos*], of which "un feu d'herbes sèches eût aussi bien été [l']éditeur" ["a fire of dry herbs might

also have been (the) editor"], serve as witness: the poet saves the truth of poetry by taking it back as close as possible to silence, by gritting his teeth before spilled blood. "J'ai répliqué aux coups" (144) ["I replied to the blows"], he will write. The texts from the period of the maquis are traces of the absence and hibernation of the poet, required by his "infernal duties." But they are at the same time the guarantors of a "shared presence," promised in the future, and already anticipated in the ordeal. It would not have been appropriate to sing out loud. Only, at that moment, is muteness capable of giving the right measure of hope; muteness, or these notes close to silence, that bespeak the waiting and watching in the darkness.

To live a vocation of opposing in so generous, so truthful, so intransigent a way is possible only for a man capable of experiencing in himself the power of opposition. The unknown, the adversary, are present in him in his relationship with language, in his duel with poetry: "Au centre de la poésie, un contradicteur t'attend. C'est ton souverain. Lutte loyalement contre lui" (754) ["At the center of poetry, a contradictor awaits you. He's your sovereign. Fight loyally against him"]. "Que le risque soit ta clarté" (756) ["Let risk be your clarity"], says René Char again. We are at the point where risk turns and shows its other face, which is luck; where, consequently, retort must take the name of welcoming and defiance change into confidence. The possibility of the poem, it too, is an event, that is to say, a presence come to us from the depths of the unknown. Thus it is that the unknown itself is present in the response the poet gives to the unknown: "Comment me vint l'écriture? Comme un duvet d'oiseau sur ma vitre, en hiver. Aussitôt s'éleva dans l'âtre une bataille de tisons qui n'a pas, encore à présent, pris fin" (377) ["How did writing come to me? Like a bird's down on my window, in winter. Just as soon there rose in the hearth a battle of brands which has not yet presently ended"]. Declaration of an astonishing richness, where opposites lend support to one another; the outside and the inside, the cold of winter and the warmth of the hearth, the softness of the feather and the violence of battle. On the temporal level, the antagonism is that of the *instantaneous* apparition on the window and of the *interminable* battle—brief syllable and long syllable.

One ordinarily sees in Char a poet of violent energy and conflict. But one too often omits to add that it is precisely that which enables him to be a love poet. Violence and tenderness, far from being mutually exclusive, must ally themselves to respond to the unknown when it comes to us in the miraculous form of luck and favor. Luck announces itself in people, in the living, in faces: it is no longer a neutral horizon, it is a being offered in its carnal singularity: "Le poème est toujours marié à quelqu'un" (159) ["The poem is always wed to someone"]:

Il n'y a que mon semblable, la compagne ou le compagnon, qui puisse m'éveiller de ma torpeur, déclencher la poésie, me lancer contre les limites du vieux désert afin que j'en triomphe. Aucun autre. Ni cieux, ni terre privilégiée, ni choses dont on tressaille.

Torche, je ne valse qu'avec lui.

(378)

[There is only my likeness, the female or male companion, who can awaken me from my torpor, release the poetry, hurl me against the limits of the old desert so that I triumph over it. No other. Not skies, nor privileged earth, nor things one thrills about.

Torch, I only waltz with it.]

The answer is thus one of fraternity or love, not without the mixing in of at least the semblance of violence. Isn't the happiness of the couple "guérilla sans reproche" (343) ["guerilla warfare without reproach"]? For the female companion, the loved one, is always mandated by the unknown: she is luck born of the mysterious depths of the world. She arouses our grateful impulse, but she does not allow herself to be captured. "Saisir" ["seizing"] the beloved head can only be a "convoitise comique" (346) ["comic coveting"]. The unity of love is not accomplished in the fusion of likenesses, but in the asymmetrical relationship where our desire faces the part of the unknown and of absence that, in the chance offered, never ceases to slip away from us. No matter how close he may be to his likeness, to his companion, the poet remains the man of "unilateral stability." The interval must be safeguarded; we must welcome our luck, our beloved adversary, with all the regards due to a foreign guest. One could not emphasize enough the fact that the intensity of the encounter, in René Char, is linked to respect for an irreducible distance. The proof is found most clearly manifested in an illustrious poem, **"Congé au vent"** (130) [**"Leave to the Wind"**]; but one could find it in many an other poem. Hence, in **"Le Bois de l'Epte"** (371) [**"Epte Wood"**], the sudden apparition of "deux rosiers sauvages," "venus du mur d'angle d'une ruine laissée jadis par l'incendie" ["two wild rosebushes," "sprung from the corner wall of a ruin left long ago by fire"]: the encounter is the signal of an upsetting awakening; but it is in retracing one's steps, "sur le talon du demi-tour" ["on the heel of an about-turn"], that the poet conforms to the exigencies of poetry.

Two wild rosebushes: the dual relationship of the poet and the world, here the world offers him the redoubled image of it: "Il s'y devinait comme un commerce d'êtres disparus, à la veille de s'annoncer encore" ["One divined there a kind of commerce of vanished beings, on the verge of appearing again"]. The double vegetal presence repeats, in the moving evidence of a sensitive allegory, the couple that the poet forms with the unknown. "Lettera amorosa," poem of the absent loved

one, ends with the image of "deux iris jaunes dans l'eau verte de la Sorgue" ["two yellow irises in the green water of the Sorgue"]. In **"Le Jugement d'Octobre"** [**"October Judgment"**], "deux gueuses dans leur détresse roidie" ["two wretched women in their stiffened distress,"] two late-season roses, erect an emblem of loving perseverance:

Une nuit, le jour bas, tout le risque, deux roses,
Comme la flamme sous l'abri, joue contre joue avec
  qui la tue.

(434)

[A night, the day low, all the risk, two roses,
Like the flame under cover, cheek to cheek with who
  is killing it.]

In fact, the true couple is not the one the rose forms with her too similar sister, but the one she forms with the mortal cold and the imminent night. This fundamental assymetry of love is still more evident if one passes from the plant universe to the admirable bestiary of René Char. The animal does not make a couple with its likeness: in **"Complainte du lézard amoureux"** (294) [**"Complaint of the Amorous Lizard"**], it is the goldfinch that the lizard is in love with; and it is with the seagull that the shark communicates on the day of the "neuve innocence" (259) ["new innocence"]. An even closer link matches the animal with what threatens and kills it. The swift is stalked by "un mince fusil" (276) ["a thin rifle"]; the solar bull dies "cerné de ténèbres qui crient" (353) ["surrounded by shadows that shout"] beneath the sword of its ritual murderer; the lark, "extrême braise du ciel et première ardeur du jour" (354) ["extreme ember of the sky and first ardor of the day"], finds death in the mirror that amazes it; the beast of Lascaux loses its entrails beside the hunter who has perished for its capture (351). Pushed to the limit, the love-agony relationship is the one that links the living thing to the space that surrounds it—space offered to flight, but inhabited by peril. René Char's bestiary is the burgeoning symbol of the freedom of the heart and its essential risk. The animals that fascinate him are creatures that know no master: they live in the pure intimacy of the elements—like **"La Truite"** (353-54) [**"The Trout"**] in its river, or the slow worm in the earth, or again the vanished wolves with which the poet feels fraternally conjoined. Free, noble, they are altogether "incorruptible" and vulnerable—exposed to death by the very fact of their sovereignty.

* * *

That this bestiary, these olive trees, and these reeds are from a particular region of Provence; that the forests, mountains, villages (whose names often appear in the very titles of Char's poems) can be located on the map in the vicinity of *L'Isle sur Sorgue,* clearly indicate a fidelity to the native land, but it is, once again, from the perspective of the union of contraries that the acknowledged links must be understood. For no other poet is, on the other hand, as free of any dependence, more resolved to assert himself in a today without past, without hereafter, and without lineage. Between this belonging to every trial, and great freedom without limit, a vehement dialogue remains engaged: fidelity and freedom accentuate their difference in order to fortify each other mutually, like the "base" and the "summit," like downstream and upstream. The poet is from the latter place, in order better to face what is from no place. He is not from this land, from this "closed valley," to live there separated, immobile, but to experience there movement and passage:

> Se mettre en chemin sur ses deux pieds, et, jusqu'au soir, le presser, le reconnaître, le bien traiter ce chemin qui, en dépit de ses relais haineux, nous montre les fétus des souhaits exaucés et la terre croisée des oiseaux.
>
> (768)

> [To take to the road on one's own two feet, and, until evening, press it, recognize it, treat it well this road which, in spite of its hateful stages, shows us the wisps of wishes fulfilled and the earth crossed by birds.]

The "earth crossed by birds," the walk on the immutable road, or again: the course of the river. There are so many exemplary images, sensitive precepts that teach alliance between fixity and movement, rootedness and flux. The poet finds in the world great figures which mirror back to him his destiny of quartered victim and conciliator, and whose poem will have to duplicate the tracing. Deciphering the world will be, to a large extent, disclosing the events that carry in themselves *the analogy of the poem*—so that telling the world, proferring the poem and telling the essence of poetry (that is, elevating the spoken word to the poem of the poem) will be but one and the same gesture.

Thus, in one poem, the effacing of the poplar will tell the effacing of the poet himself: a marvelous way of repeating that "en poésie, on n'habite que le lieu que l'on quitte, on ne crée que l'œuvre dont on se détache, on n'obtient la durée qu'en détruisant le temps" (733) ["in poetry, one inhabits only the place one leaves, one creates only the work one detaches oneself from, one obtains duration only by destroying time"]. Let's reread **"Effacement du Peuplier"** (423) [**"Effacing of the Poplar"**], that so laconic and spacious text, where not only the four elements find their place, but again truth and lure, violence and tenderness, nature and man unite:

> L'ouragon dégarnit les bois.
> J'endors, moi, la foudre aux yeux tendres.
> Laissez le grand vent où je tremble
> S'unir à la terre où je croîs

Son souffle affile ma vigie.
Qu'il est trouble le creux du leurre
De la source aux couches salies!

Une clé sera ma demeure,
Feinte d'un feu que le cœur certifie;
Et l'air qui la tint dans ses serres.

> [The hurricane strips the woods,
> I lull to sleep the lightning with tender eyes.
> Let the great wind where I shake
> Unite with the earth where I grow
>
> Its breath sharpens my lookout.
> How turbid the hollow of the lure
> From the source to the soiled strata!
>
> A key will be my abode,
> Pretense of a fire that the heart certifies;
> And the air which held it in its claws.]

The hurricane is freedom unleashed, with the inexhaustible flow of wind and the burning of lightning. But the enduring tree, in its obstinate growth, lulls to sleep the lightning: it is named "the lightning with tender eyes," gentleness *mixes* with violence. If we listen to the injunction of the tree, the moving fury of the hurricane *will unite* with the immobile earth. The tree belongs at once to the air and the earth. The conflict of the elements inflicts on it its passion, but it is at the same time its conciliator. It is standing, moored to stable ground, and it shakes at the whim of the hurricane. Its quivering is an indication of its double belonging. For shaking is a static movement, where obedience to the earth and obedience to the wind are expressed simultaneously. Thus the poplar participates in the vagabond flow and remains prisoner of its site. In its agitated verticality, by its top raised up in the heart of the aerial tumult, the poplar refuses the idle destiny of the source: the sign of altitude wide-awake ("the lookout") opposes itself to the image of a turgid origin mixed with humus. (The figure of the tree raised up in the tumultuous air connects with other figures of freedom: notably that of the oar in the ocean.)

"A key will be my abode." The word spoken by the tree here becomes the poet's. For the poet is the man of opening, the one who refuses to establish himself. "A key will be my abode": this utterance may seem enigmatic; Char's terseness rejoins the emblem and the motto; the word does not immediately allow its singular side or universal reach to be deciphered. It only awaits, though, patience and support from our gaze to be illuminated. And one discovers that it defines the *place* of poetry and that it makes an appeal, once again, to the union of opposites. Char tells us emphatically that the only abode of the poet is the instrument of passage, this means by which a threshold can be crossed. ("Epouse et n'épouse pas ta maison," 183 ["Marry and do not marry your house"], he says elsewhere.) The poem is this key—a key that liberates us readers—while the poet remains assigned to his watch. Now the key has taken the form "of a fire that the *heart* certifies," and, then again, it also belongs to the sovereign force of the *wind* ("which held it in its claws"). What better way to say that the poem, feigned thing, imaginary object, has for guarantor of its truth the interior fire of man and the exterior royalty of the wind? That thus, under this double auspice, the poetic word cannot lead us astray, however far it may take us from our idle lodgings? The poem, slender and strong key, gives us an ampler abode under the common sky; it makes us accede to this instantaneous home "où la beauté, après s'être longtemps fait attendre, surgit des choses communes, traverse notre champ radieux, lie tout ce qui peut être lié, allume tout ce qui doit être allumé de notre gerbe de ténèbres" (757) ["where beauty, after having made itself long awaited, rises out of common things, crosses our radiant field, links all that can be linked, lights up all that must be lit from our sheaf of shadows"].

Notes

1. René Char, *Oeuvres complètes* (Paris: Gallimard "Pléiade," 1983), 162. Page numbers in parentheses refer to this volume.

2. Maurice Blanchot, *La Part du feu* (Paris: Gallimard, 1949), 105.

3. "René Char et la pensée du neutre," *L'Arc* 22 (Summer 1963), 9-14.

Michael Bishop (essay date 1994)

SOURCE: Bishop, Michael. "Char's Mysticism." In *Figuring Things: Char, Ponge, and Poetry in the Twentieth Century,* edited and translated by Charles D. Minahen, pp. 175-89. Lexington, Ky.: French Forum Publishers, 1994.

[*In the following essay, Bishop offers a thematic analysis of mysticism in Char's work.*]

Laissons l'énergie et retournons à l'énergie.

(*ES* [*Eloge d'une Soupçonnée*] 7)[1]

DIFFICULTY, REBELLION, AND INNOCENCE

In a poet whose work has to such a compelling degree stressed actuality and engagement, the difficulties and divisions of history, and the need for ethical, even political intervention *à ras de terre,* it may seem more than paradoxical to invite consideration of his *œuvre* as an "act and place" of what I have termed mysticism. Certainly, like Rimbaud—I am thinking of his *brouillon* from *Une Saison en enfer,* "Bonr"—Char can swiftly dismiss, as he does in **"Eaux-mères"** from *Le Marteau*

sans maître, a certain concept of the mystical: "Il n'y a rien de miraculeux dans le retour à la vie de cet enfant," he writes; "Je méprise les esprits religieux et leurs interprétations mystiques" (*OC* [*Oeuvres complètes*] 52). And, of course, behind Char's entire poetic project there lies an important sense of individual difference, heroic resistance and "sovereign" action and telluric re-creation, faced as he is/we are with the "subordination" and "terrors" of those many "totalitarianisms" and other bloodinesses threatening our collective, planetary existence (cf. *AC* [*Aromates chausseurs*] 20). His refusals and high revolt seem not, perhaps, to allow readily for some ultimate recuperation by the esotericism and serene contemplation we may imagine pertinent to mystical states and endeavors.[2]

There is, however, from the outset in Char a level of perception of not only possible modes of being but, much more crucially and immediately, quotidian experience that permits an influx, into this model of radical existential problem and struggle, of factors that significantly shift emphasis away from the kind of one-dimensional morality and philosophy that a strictly and conventionally binary logic of good and evil can generate. Already, in *Seuls demeurent,* Char thus speaks of "une innocence où l'homme qui rêve ne peut vieillir" (*OC* 132), an innocence of being and action liberating the mind and the emotions from seemingly rigid existential grills and cumbersome sociological transformations, opening the self to what only appears to be utterly withdrawn but which, in effect, already enjoys a certain status of reality within consciousness. Thus is it that, in **"Qu'il vive,"** from *Les Matinaux* (*OC* 305), Char not only perceives—the initial perception remains part of the unidimensionality evoked, arguably—the earth as a "countertomb," but brings tumbling down his own edifice of terror, abomination, and "disaster" by insisting, once again, upon the latter's essential lack of malignancy: the inner intentionality, despite external evidence to the contrary *and* despite our own efforts to act upon such evidence—the inner intentionality of being is not predicated upon some intrinsic *mal,* but upon—one might presume, based upon other texts of Char—principles of improbable benignity, harmlessness, even love. Does not *La Parole en archipel* speak of "un mystère plus fort que leur malédiction innocentant leur cœur"? (*OC* 410). Such a sense of ontic innocence, I should argue, sets Char's poetics at some important remove from platitudinous verification of personal and collective trauma and the inevitable resistance we may seek to apply to such trauma.

KNOWING AND FORGETTING

Should Char turn out to be, in any conceivable sense of the term, a mystic, it seems reasonable to maintain that he would have to be engaged in some process of (self-)initiation. Now, if it is clear that such a search or mental movement in no way propels him towards religious forms and rites—even oriental: I shall return to this—it is equally clear that his work depicts a powerful and generalized impulsion towards what he terms in **Moulin premier** "la connaissance productive du Réel" (**OC** 61), towards an encounter with what he has elsewhere called *le grand réel* (*OC* 665): being in all its modes, sensory to psychic, phenomena as apparently separate as soupspoons, wind upon wheatfields, dream, feeling, intuition: reality as actuality, felt possibility, achieved creation. The human being, in this process of endless (self-)initiation into what is at once everything and "merely" our individual traversal of something, thus becomes "[cette] lampe de toujours et [cette] torche interrogative" of which he speaks in **Eloge d'une Soupçonnée** (7). Thus does Char's both pragmatic and cosmically attuned "mysticism" imply a moving, unfixed and unfixing initiation into the known and the given, the received and the imposed. Such mysticism demonstrably demystifies at a certain level, while recognizing the power of myth and symbol at another—and fully appreciating that the entire process of knowing and (self-)initiation remains linked to what, in **Chants de la Balandrane,** Char emphasizes as a crucial optic according to which specific, systematized search—science, he declares in **Le Nu perdu,** is no more than "un phare aveugle" (*OC* 467)—may be distinguished from other modes of consciousness (cf. **"Sans chercher à savoir,"** *CB* [*Chants de la Balandrane*] 67).[3]

It is here that we can see to what degree Char's (self-)initiatory gesture merges with a certain skepticism or *soupçon*—"ma réserve," he succinctly calls it in **Dehors la nuit est gouvernée** (*OC* 111)—which renders Char's writings, despite their aphoristic and apophthegmatic high-mindedness, delightfully open, fresh, unpretentious. "Soyons avares de crédulité," he writes in the same collection, "comment se montrer aux autres et à soi autrement que hardi, modeste et mortel?" (*OC* 85). The impulse to know, to discover, to live in that light emanating both from within and without, thus remains delicately articulated, anchored in a belief in the virtues of "[les] chemins muletiers," as Char characteristically puts it in **Chants de la Balandrane** (72): rocky, rugged, plural paths of knowing, earthy and meandering: paths for all seasons, reversible, unassuming. That said, however, Char never loses sight of the relativity of the real, its malleability, the consequent need for availability in order to distinguish, in what we may think of too hastily as the opaqueness of being, those teeming "births" or creations that, in effect, constitute it (cf. *AC* 34)—and which, without our precise "seeking to know" (cf. *CB* 67), constantly found our knowing, constantly initiate. No doubt this accounts for Char's, and our, "faithfulness" in the midst of "excessive vulnerability" (cf. *OC* 215), the kind of "tacit consent" to what is, to what surges forth, unknown, knowable, of which he speaks in **Les Matinaux** (*OC* 311). Such sought/

unsought knowledge or initiation into *le grand réel* is visceral, intuitive, brought about by some "ardor of soul," as he suggests in **Fenêtres dormantes et porte sur le toit** (84). This does not mean that effort is excluded: "Il faut souffler sur quelques lueurs," he suggests in **"Rougeur des matinaux,"** from **Les Matinaux,** "pour faire de la bonne lumière" (*OC* 331); but it does mean that cause-effect thinking is not banally privileged (cf. *OC* 159) and that some "faith" is given, beyond reservation, to what Char terms, in **Fureur et mystère,** "une lampe inconnue de nous, inaccessible à nous, à la pointe du monde" (*OC* 147). Knowing, for Char, is thus always caught up in meaning beyond reductive evaluation: it involves "l'intelligence avec l'ange, notre primordial souci," as he says in **Feuillets d'Hypnos** (*OC* 179). Such (self-)initiatory knowledge and (inner) sensing cannot, of course, result, despite all appearances in Char, in a writing predicated upon absolute truth or revelation. Writing, for him, is rather the blossoming of some exquisite but ephemeral convolvulus, "liseron élevé audessus d'une vie enfin jointe, liseron non invoqué en preuve" (*CB* 30). Does not Char, already in **Seuls demeurent,** delightfully deem poetry to be "un point diamanté *actuel* de présences transcendantes et d'orages pèlerins"? (*OC* 154): an act and place now, yet both plunged into the *movingness* of our "pilgrimage" and *beyond* blatant presence. A "sacred way" of ontic *dépense* à la Bataille, an initiation into (self-)knowledge predicated upon giving and receiving—and letting go, moving on, "forgetting" so as to remain available to the swarming "births" of (our) being: "Donne toujours plus que tu ne peux reprendre," Char writes in **Le Nu perdu,** "et oublie. Telle est la voie sacrée" (*OC* 446).

HINGING AND EQUILIBRIUM

The late volumes of Char often strike us for their suddenly surging signs of a deep love of life in this "gueux de siècle, ventre et jambes arrachés" (*CB* 13) and thus seem to apply an apt poetic closure to an *œuvre* whose beginnings, too, operate endless and precarious equilibrium, shifts, changes, and paradoxical convergence of optics we might think relatively immutable: **Le Marteau sans maître** speaks from its outset of "l'homme massacré et pourtant victorieux" (*OC* 3) and evokes that Charian—yet universal—"hésitation" experienced between "l'imprécation du supplice et le magnifique amour" (*OC* 3). Now, while such complementarity may be readily appreciated at a conceptual level, it is more difficult to live. There can however be little doubt, I should argue, that this early and continuing sense, in Char, of paradox, and the deep meaning of paradox, explains the great and delicate appeal of his work and constitutes a plain but yet subtle further mark of what I am terming Char's mysticism. The phenomenon of wedding "praise" to "mockery" (**FD** [**Fenêtres dormantes et porte sur le toit**] 73), *éloge* to *soupçon,* or perceiving in the coffin—as in the 1933 "Eaux-mères"—"cet objet *creux destiné à être longuement fécondé*" (*OC* 51, Char's italics) may be a phenomenon we all know at some level, but it is also a phenomenon few persist in exploring as a deeply meaningful ontic complementarity, central to our purpose and to our spiritual possibility.

"Evidence mutable," Char writes in *Dehors la nuit est gouvernée* (*OC* 116): being's signs pointing in many directions, always through us, our own individual and collective mutations, infinite in time and in space; being's signs rooted in our thought and emotion (I shall return to this), our sense of *fureur,* of immanent involvement both political and private, and our sense of *mystère,* of depth and transcendence albeit in "presence" and "pilgrimage." And, given the Charian logic of complementarity, slippage, interpenetration, even fury acquires its mysteriousness: exile and fulfilment—"Je suis l'exclu et le comblé," Char declares in *Seuls demeurent* (*OC* 145)—become reciprocally pertinent, caught up in that love of "twin mysteries" he confesses in *Les Matinaux* (*OC* 310). The compelling consciousness of death will thus not drown out a sense of equilibrium and equivalence Char can term, after Baudelaire, unity (cf. *OC* 359), any more than his alertness to *hasard* and accident will swamp his abiding intuition of life's indefinable meanfulness (cf. *OC* 228). Such a hinging of absurdity to the resilient (il)logic of love—which we see explicitly in, say, the *Chants de la Balandrane*—creates a fragile but sure "order" of global completeness, of psychic—and *real*—"alliance" (cf. *CB* 23). Sarcasm and "inner fright" do not, in consequence, unhinge a critical residual sentiment of "grace," as he calls it in *Fenêtres dormantes et porte sur le toit* (43). Equilibrium, continuity, imbrication, and oneness are never discarded as sadly irrelevant. A mysticism of—an unknowing but intuitive (self-)initiation into—what Bonnefoy might term *l'improbable,* never ceases to inform Char's thinking and feeling. Reality may be distressing fact, but it is also both improbable enchantment and beset by its intrinsic ontic implications, the very mystery of the being of what may distress or enchant. Existential frailty, ephemeralness, and mortality are underpinned by what I have called elsewhere, "*ce* qui nous tient éveillé/e/s." "La Voie où nous étouffons," as he writes in *Les Voisinages de Van Gogh* (9), remains a Way, a place of unique, inimitable going through a nearness and an invisibility that, as Char suggests in *Le Nu perdu,* may well be coincident (cf. *OC* 459). Such a sense of being merges that persistent demand for the splendors of what, in its broadest perspective, we can call *le surréel,* and that much admired Reverdyan urge for *justesse*: distance and proximity, *l'intelligence de l'ange* and immanence, deep ontic and psychic obscurity flickeringly illuminated and the simple light of ethical consciousness.

FALLING AND BUOYANCY

In the 1979 *Fenêtres dormantes et porte sur le toit* Char tells us in fairly plain terms that "je vous écris en cours de chute. C'est ainsi que j'éprouve l'état d'être au monde" (52): being or being-in-the-world entails not only what we might be tempted to think of as a classic nineteenth-century obsession—one thinks of poets as divergent as Vigny, Baudelaire, Hugo, and Rimbaud—with original fall and its consequent multicolored ethico-spiritual tensions, but, further, a more radical sensation of unattachment, uprootedness and free fall "down" through the very onticity that, nevertheless, allows Char to speak, in the first place, of being *in* the world. The sensation, then, is one of undoubted slippage, comparable to the sense of horizontal, temporal movement; it implies an experience, presumably physical and not just psychical—and certainly not purely conceptual, as it turns out was Sartre's "experience" of *nausée*—of abyss, of hollowness, of crumbling and insecurity. Yet, paradoxically, such falling takes place, is felt as taking place, within something—experience of being-in-the-world—which possibilizes the sensation of falling. And, indeed, falling is feasible only because depth is understood both conceptually and experientially.

Beyond even the ontic spaciousness and depth through which falling occurs, there is in Char's poetics a further critically compensating factor which involves his sense of the buoyancy of being, of those myriad but perhaps synonymous forces that render possible human—and phenomenal—going and doing, feeling and thinking. Buoyancy is the endless, teeming, imbricated surging forth—*jaillissement,* Jacques Dupin terms it—of being's phenomena, of our consciousness thereof. Buoyancy possesses an implicit and intuitive logic of non-void, of filling, of "birth," of creation. Buoyancy suggests that absence is purely notional, "replacement" or "filling" being actual. "Il n'y a pas d'absence irremplaçable," Char writes in *Poèmes militants* (*OC* 35); "l'inextinguible réel incréé" constantly flooding in where void might have been thought feasible, imaginable (cf. *OC* 155)—a logic applicable to all domains, moreover, material, moral, emotional, intellectual, or psychical. Buoyancy ensures a seamless continuity, a possibility where probability may have induced thoughts of rupture, finality, separation. "Cette fumée qui nous portait," which Char evokes in *Les Loyaux Adversaires,* from *Fureur et mystère* (*OC* 241), seems to be an easily dispelled presence, but rather does it bear up, barely visible in itself, a presence which, intrinsically, it is not—or rather does not seem to be. Like the *si peu* of "Te devinant éveillé pour si peu" (*VVG* [*Les Voisinages de Van Gogh*] 27), Char's *fumée* is at once mortality and eternity, it is that which constantly and infinitely floods into being, inflating and buoying its possibility and its actuality. It is, therefore, not just the action of "Vert sur noir" that Char so exquisitely conjures up in *Aromates chasseurs* (39-20); it is, too, that "Haute fontaine" of *Chants de la Balandrane* (53-54), that source and action of vital onticity ceaselessly spurting forth, emanating from depth and, yet, what we can call abyss, but meeting the "fall" of being, shoring it up, allowing it to float upon its creative possibilizing impulse, letting it be-in-the-world. Buoyancy is, indeed, a force well known to the poet Char. Does he not speak so tellingly in *Seuls demeurent* of "le glissement des abîmes qui portent de façon si anti-physique le poème"? (*OC* 159). And does he not call up within himself, both as poet and man, in *Fenêtres dormantes et porte sur le toit,* that power of fullness of being ever available to him—no matter how the world may be characterized, believed to be: "Si le monde est ce *vide,* eh bien! je suis ce plein"? (*FD* 54). And there is, too, that remarkable account of something akin to an out-of-body experience, where, in the midst of a serious accident, Char's entire being, physical and psychical, is caught by that very ontic buoyancy at issue, so that "*everything* happened outside of me" (*OC* 211), as being seemingly displaced, absent, yet utterly present, utterly supportive.

GOD, GODS

"Dieu faute de Dieu n'enjambe plus nos murs soupçonneux," Char declares in *Le Nu perdu* (*OC* 466): an individual and collective skepticism—that Char espouses, as we have seen—which shuts off the banalities and the terrors of dogma and fanaticism, and which shuts out, too, the absolutism, the dispossessing monolithism of some reductive and imposable structure of the Divine. Before and after "Dieu l'accrêté," Char argues more recently, our being was and is (cf. *CB* 30): the kind of "miracle" or ontic buoyancy referred to in *Abondance viendra* (*OC* 52)—his own accident just evoked (cf. *OC* 211) is equally pertinent—does not need a religiously restrictive grill placed upon it for us to appreciate the delicate workings of grace and marvel at play in being. Any sense of life's divineness may, and should, arise within the self, where it can be honored and meditated in freedom. "[Les] dieux puissants et fantasques qui habitent le poète," as Char writes in *Seuls demeurent* (*OC* 165) are thus neither pure fiction, metaphorical rhetoric, nor elves, dryads, kobolds. They are the recognized energies and modes of being and (self-)creation Char chooses to celebrate, energies he can project—fancifully but purposely, imaginatively but really—into some dreamed world "ému par le zèle de quelques dieux, aux abords des femmes" (*OC* 186). In this personalized sense of the divine, language's very origins may be deemed to bathe in an energy and a spirituality (cf. *OC* 255) that, certainly, somehow is locked into his perception of *poiesis* and whose dispersal writers like Bernard Noël or Yves Bonnefoy or Michel Deguy varyingly denounce. If "les dieux sont dans la métaphore," as Char says in *A Faulx contente* (*OC* 783)—with the metaphor's logic of unity within

difference, *com-parution,* as Deguy would say, compassion, love, and so on—then we should not imagine that Char feels coming immediately a new age of poetico-spiritual (self-)transformation, even though *Aromates chasseurs* seeks to usher in something of this kind. The "gods," rather, are retiring, "withdrawing" from our cyclically atrophied grasp, he suggests in *Le Nu perdu* (*OC* 467), and those that are fully incarnate, like, for Char, Baudelaire, Melville, Van Gogh, or Mandelstam, retain a "hagard" look about them (cf. *FD* 17).

For all that, with the "failure" of God, the "gods" of Char remain a "tonic" presence, as he emphasizes in the same "Faire du chemin avec . . . ," from *Fenêtres dormantes et porte sur le toit* (18). No doubt this is, in part because Char, the poet of intervention, commitment, and self-assumption, views divineness less as some exteriorized force and not at all as a force utterly removed from the self's collaboration: "Nuls dieux à l'extérieur de nous," he goes so far as to assert in *Aromates chasseurs* (25): the self thus becomes the essential locus for all and any divinity upon the earth's human way, for, as Char already writes in *La Nuit talismanique qui brillait dans son cercle,* such gods as we know, as traverse us, as we are, are the "least opaque expression of ourselves" (cf. *OC* 502)—though perhaps the expression most difficult to formulate. This does not mean that Char denies the divineness of what Bonnefoy terms "les choses du simple": "Grimpereau, charmeur des soupçonnée," he notes in *Les Voisinages de Van Gogh,* where the notion of *charm* may be read according to its fullest range of significance; and, in *Fenêtres dormantes et porte sur le toit,* he speaks of "mes dieux à tête de groseille [qui] ne me démentiront pas, eux qui n'ont figure qu'une fois l'an" (66). Rather may we see divineness as always to be assumed within the self, privately, intimately, simply, unpretentiously; as something to be recognized as crucial to the consciousness of our and all being, but within that center of being—the self—whose esotericism should not concern, but, rather, delight us, confirming our staggering uniqueness of perception of the divine—and thereby multiplying, infinitely, the latter. In **"Gammes de l'accordeur,"** from *Chants de la Balandrane,* Char quotes from Hilarion de Modène: "Les dieux, habitez-nous! / Derrière la cloison, / Nul ne veut plus de vous" (58). Char's own text proper goes beyond this deliberately echoed call for our collective assumption of what lies divine within all of being: his further, passing, symbolic call urges upon us a state and action wherein humanity and divinity remain in balance within the optic of what he feels is our brief telluric "apprenticeship" (cf. *CB* 59). To forget the divineness buried deep in our humanness; to forget our human depths in the light of the remembrance of our divinity: two contradictions, but held in equilibrium by the fact of our merged learning of twinned lessons in the simplicity of our incarnated movement.

Going, Continuity

Char, poet of presence, as has often been said, and rightly so; poet of "la gloire navigable des saisons" (*FD* 17), of the sufficiency of going, of *this* traversal of being and going: "Aller me suffit," he declares in **"La Compagne du vannier,"** from *Seuls demeurent* (*OC* 131), and it would not be outrageous to articulate a Charian mysticism of immanence, somewhat Hugolian or Nervalian in its root implications but Bonnefidian in its contemporary bareness, its level of understatement. Such a mysticism would reside in the sufficiency of givenness and the self's givingness, the inimitable appropriateness of our—perhaps any: we would return to the earlier logic of innocence—existential traversal. Such a "going" is caught, however, inevitably—it is inherent in the poetics of all movement—between the Charian logic of quest, *chasse,* rebellion, and desire, which may imply conceptual exceeding of the immanent, and that of strictest adherence to the going at hand and refusal of the prestige of what, in *Fenêtres dormantes et porte sur le toit,* Char calls, "devant nous, haut dressé, le fertile point qu'il faut se garder de questionner ou d'abattre" (19). The consciousness of our going may thus be immediately focused or it may widen to an intuition still essentially part of this immediacy yet conceptually overflowing it, or even to pure speculation, an avenue rarely appealing to Char. One's going, however, is inevitably seen in the context of origin and end, and is inescapably framed by notions of purpose and absurdity, choice and blockage, temporality and eternity. Going, for Char, clearly fuses these seemingly competing perspectives, as he characteristically indicates in *Seuls demeurent*: "J'ai, captif, épousé le ralenti du lierre à l'assaut de la pierre de l'éternité" (*OC* 137): any mysticism here, of course, merges transcendence with immanence and suggests that the interlocking is not merely temporal, linear, sequential, but predicated, too, on factors of equivalence and simultaneity. Thus is it that persistence *hic et nunc* is synonymous with a movement "beyond" the latter; going is both traversal of, and immersion in, itself, and implicitly, movement towards what such traversal and immersion are not.

In effect, Char's work is shot through with a sense of the continuity of being beyond what we might term life or death. "Mourir," he writes in *La Nuit talismanique,* "c'est passer à travers le chas de l'aiguille après de multiples feuillaisons. Il faut aller à travers la mort pour émerger devant la vie, dans l'état de modestie souveraine" (*OC* 496). The earthly form of our presence would seem, then, to be caught up in the buoyancy of some larger going and presence. In *Le Nu perdu,* Char similarly argues this more cosmically attuned continuity of being, "notre figure terrestre n'[étant] que le second tiers d'une poursuite continue, un point, amont" (*OC* 435)—a movement, or so our spatio-temporal imagination would have us believe, always showing us at once the exquisite specificity of ephemeral experience and "la chose qui continuait, / Opposée à la vie mourante, / [Qui] à l'infini s'élaborait," as Char writes in *Les Matinaux* (*OC* 324). Little wonder that he can remind us, as he has also with respect to our fused divineness and humanity, that humankind is to be deemed "neither eternal nor temporal" (cf. *OC* 460): the privileging of either dimension risks breaking that magic spell that holds us intact—and keeps us on course, in a going for and beyond itself. If Char's sense of being "loin de nos cendres"—a phrase apparently meditated for most of his life (cf. *OC* 807-18)—seems, then, to plunge his consciousness deeply back into the passingness of *présence,* it aptly evokes more transcendent modes of being: states and actualities where humankind's eternal "common language" may be perhaps spoken (cf. *OC* 105); where, as he writes in *Seuls demeurent,* from *Fureur et mystère,* "l'évasion dans son semblable, avec d'immenses perspectives de poésie, sera peut-être un jour possible" (*OC* 169); where some new "visibility" beyond the mere optimism of philosophy may be feasible (cf. *OC* 269); where "ce qui sut demeurer inexplicable pourra seul nous requérir" (*OC* 447). For Char's going offers both a lived essentialness of the passing, the endeavored, and the felt essentialness of the unaccomplished (cf. *AC* 23).

Being

To speak, as Char does in *Seuls demeurent,* of "l'éternité d'une olive" (*OC* 167), is to oblige us to rethink the very structure and quality of (our) being, which, in effect, assumes a "spacious strength" we can often too readily deny it (cf. *OC* 133). To realize the fullness of our (place of) being, the streaming timelessness that floods through its very ephemeralness, its apparently mere ontic flash or *éclair* (cf. *OC* 266), it is helpful to begin with the most modest of steps, allowing us to sense both difference and the non-emptiness, the depth, of what is: "cesse de prendre la branche pour le tronc," he suggests in *Les Matinaux,* "et la racine pour le vide. C'est un petit commencement" (*OC* 331). Our being may be of unknown origin and of unknown end—perhaps absolutely synonymous with going, with an incessant creation-now—but this being of fire is also a being of light, as Char writes in *Aromates chasseurs* (34), a consumption that is an arising, a passing equally, coincident with, an emergence. Moreover, partly for these reasons but also because our individuality or difference of being is always experienced *in situ,* being, for Char, is never a being-in-separation: "Je suis *parmi,*" he affirms in *Fenêtres dormantes et portes sur le toit* (26). And, in the same volume, he goes even further in articulating the swarming ontic multitudinousness of what might only appear singular, unidimensional: "Cent existences dans la nôtre enflamment la chair de tatouages qui n'apparaîtront pas" (63).

Such elliptical, often decontextualized, yet firm declarations constantly point to a conception—an on-going meditation—of being that is complex, intuitive, visionary in a post-Rimbaldian sense, caught in respected obscurity, yet pushing relentlessly towards (self-)illumination. Certainly, for Char, being exceeds mortality, as we have seen, death offering access, he even suggests in *Aromates chasseurs,* to a "space" perhaps our primordial locus of being (cf.*AC* 21). Evocations of Tibetan mystics—and activists—such as Milarepa and Marpa (cf. *OC* 815-16; *FD* 32), or of our constant immersion in ontic energy, regardless of our state of being—"laissons l'énergie et retournons à l'énergie," he writes in the posthumous *Eloge d'une Soupçonnée*—such evocations prepare us well, as we tack back and forth in our contemplation of Char's mystical proclivities, for the kind of exquisite ontological conundrum we find for example, in *Le Nu perdu:* "Sois bien, tu n'es pas" (*OC* 436). Being seems, thus, at once relative and absolute, achieved and unachieved, livable, experienceable, and yet ever future, ever more fully "to be." *Présence* seems, thus, at once inviolate, utterly authentic, yet rethinkable as part of existential or ontic dimensions we are, at times, with Char, conscious of, though incompletely. "Les plus pures récoltes," he notes in *Feuillets d'Hypnos,* "sont semées dans un sol qui n'existe pas" (*OC* 195): in a framework or *présence* that is no doubt a psychic or psychological structure or gestalt. Thus is it that poetry has "nothing in it," as he argues in *Le Poème pulvérisé,* "that doesn't exist elsewhere" (*OC* 247): like life itself, poetry is creation of being: all corresponds to the infinity and depth available in being; all is, and this mysterious isness is at once irreplaceable and imbricated with structures and modes of being seemingly belonging to the realms of pure emotion, pure thought, pure imagination, pure fiction. Thus is it that fiction and reality merge, equal, equivalent, same, in Char's wider perception of being's "spaciousness." Thus is it, too, that, though life and poetry may be deemed "absurd" (cf. *FD* 63), being doubly recuperates them: both in the many ways we have seen Char elaborate, but in that mathematics that would have two negatives yield being by virtue of their mysterious and teeming multiplication together.

MYSTERY, EMOTION, THOUGHT

Poetry, Char tells us in *Dehors la nuit est gouvernée,* is "une marche forcée dans l'indicible, avec, pour viatique, les provisions hasardeuses du langage et la manne de l'observation et des pressentiments" (*OC* 85): it thus moves through the ineffable, riding upon those multiple mysteries of which we are barely conscious as such: effort, utterance, sensory and mental, especially intuitive, perception. Poetry may, indeed, as already in *Le Marteau sans maître* Char would stress, not "traffic in sacredness," to the extent that poetry eschews the pretensions of religious dogma and tendentiousness,

seeking its pathos rather within the open attachments of the self; yet it clearly engages "furiously" with "mystery" and its *indicible* manifestly plunges it into the most secret recesses of (one's) being and the most visionary gestures of (self-)initiation. The mystery of being, for Char, is ever "new" and "sings in your bones": it is good reason for him to urge us to "develop [our] legitimate strangeness" (cf. *OC* 160), or, as he puts it in **"Encore eux,"** from *Loin de nos cendres,* "make, barefoot, a mystery of [ourselves]" (cf. *OC* 816). Mystery, meaning, function, and purpose lie deep within, buried in materiality, in geneticity, but available, too, via their assumption within us, by virtue of the further mystery of consciousness, choice, emotion. To "feel awakening the obscure plantation" within, as Char writes in *Seuls demeurent* (*OC* 152), is to accept a sacredness, a divineness, without name or creed, rites or conceptual fixity other than those the self might obscurely articulate. "J'aime qui m'éblouit puis accentue l'obscur à l'intérieur de moi," we read in *Les Matinaux* (*OC* 330), and certainly essential to any appreciation of Char's poetics is the persistent desire to develop insight concomitantly with an intense reverence for the obscureness, the mysteriousness, of all manifestations of being. Life is secret (cf. *OC* 363) and the private though joined (the logic of being-*amongst* never dissolves) world of the self is infinitely, inimitably deep (cf.*AC* 43), psychologically, emotionally, intentionally.

Char, I should argue, is one of those rare writers who, caught between naming and unnaming, senses the profound mystery of things being in the first place. Emotions and thoughts, in effect, are not simply remarkable in their diversity or in that flowingness, paradoxicalness, and balance of which I spoke earlier; they are mysterious in themselves, in the very fact of their being (cf. *OC* 188). Char's "mysticism," here, may be said to revolve about his, and our, belief in consciousness, impulse, intuition, obscure but lived "truth(s)." Central remains a sense of meaning—*sens,* going, ontic orientation—not of meaning as specifiable, reducible fact or mechanism, but rather as an inalienable sense—the sense(s) we inalienably have, at once fleshy and psychical—of some infinite project, individual and collective, that buoys us up and constitutes our being. Such a feeling and thinking of the world—and the word, for the poet—may embrace the "meaning" of love and the "meaning" of doubt or skepticism or atheism, for it would imply the essential *mysteria* of all experience, the lived, at once revealed and undivulged, nature of our being. In this sense, the *mysteria* of existence are self-generated; whether lived "negatively" or "affirmatively," all is (self-)creation, (self-)affirmation. "Tu tiens de toi tes chemins," Char writes in *Chants de la Balandrane* (78), and mystery, "mysticism"—with any accompanying skepticism or hesitation—arise upon, as, these paths of blinding/illuminated being: emotions, thoughts, well up within us as our sense/*sens,* our felt and mentally projected goingness. They are the guides, the creators, and the definers of our going; they are our entry to "[le] grand réel"; they can sense and think our meaning, our *sens,* our sufficiency of going (cf. *OC* 131). And they are predicated upon a never-closing of themselves, for Char's "mysticism" widens, opens, seeks ever to, as he writes in the liminal 1938 **"Argument"** of *Fureur et mystère,* "déborder l'économie de la création, agrandir le sang des gestes, [comme] devoir de toute lumière" (*OC* 129). Such a self-initiatory seeing, as he emphasizes in *Feuillets d'Hypnos,* is, if not implacably then crucially, psychological and affective: "Si l'homme parfois ne fermait pas *souverainement* les yeux, il finirait par ne plus voir ce qui vaut d'être regardé" (*OC* 189). The mystery of being may be everywhere, but it is nowhere if not within.

Notes

1. The following abbreviations are used in reference to Char's work: *ES: Eloge d'une Soupçonnée* (Paris: Gallimard, 1988); *OC: Oeuvres complètes* (Paris: Gallimard "Pléiade," 1983); *AC: Aromates chasseurs* (Paris: Gallimard, 1975); *CB: Chants de la Balandrane* (Paris: Gallimard, 1977); *FD: Fenêtres dormantes et porte sur le toit* (Paris: Gallimard, 1979); *VVG: Les Voisinages de Van Gogh* (Paris: Gallimard, 1985).

2. Of the recent major Char criticism—I am thinking of: Mary Ann Caws, *The Presence of René Char* (Princeton: Princeton UP, 1981); Mary Ann Caws, *L'Œuvre filante de René Char* (Paris: Nizet, 1981); Christine Dupouy, *René Char* (Paris: Belfond, 1987); Danièle Leclair, *Lecture de René Char: Aromates chasseurs et Chants de la Balandrane* (Paris: Lettres Modernes, 1988); Daniel Leuwers, ed., *René Char, Sud* (1984); Jean-Claude Mathieu, *La Poésie de René Char ou le sel de la splendeur,* 2 vols. (Paris: Corti, 1984); Tineke Kingma-Eijgendaal and Paul J. Smith, ed., *Lectures de René Char* (Amsterdam: Rodopi, CRIN, 1990); Serge Velay, *René Char: qui êtes vous?* (Lyon: La Manufacture, 1987); Paul Veyne, *René Char en ses poèmes* (Paris: Gallimard, 1990); Michael Bishop, *René Char: les dernières années* (Amsterdam: Rodopi, 1990); Jean Voellmy, *René Char ou le mystère partagé* (Seyssel: Champ Vallon, 1989); Eric Marty, *René Char* (Paris: Seuil, 1990); Philippe Castellin, *René Char, traces* (Paris: Evidant, 1989); *René Char,* special issue of *Europe* (1988); Daniel Leuwers, *René Char, dit-elle, la mort* (Bourges: Amor Fati, 1989)—few texts broach in a direct manner the issues of Char's "mysticism," though many implicitly wrestle with elements pertinent to my argument. In particular, I would note Hughes Labrusse's essay in Leuwers (1984), various sections of Marty (1990), as of Velay (1987) and Voellmy (1989).

3. For an analysis of "Sans chercher à savoir," see Bishop (1990), 56-57.

Van Kelly (essay date winter 1995)

SOURCE: Kelly, Van. "The Elegiac Temptation in Char's Poetry." *L'Esprit Créateur* 35, no. 4 (winter 1995): 59-70.

[*In the following essay, Kelly addresses the tension in some of Char's poems between past and future in perspective and focus.*]

Laissons l'énergie et retournons à l'énergie. La mesure du Temps? L'étincelle sous les traits de laquelle nous apparaissons et redisparaissons dans la fable.

—René Char, **"Riche de larmes"**

Life and death vie fiercely in *Fureur et mystère* (1948), especially in the section subtitled *Le poème pulvérisé,* which contains a number of texts written from the Munich crisis through the Purge.[1] Virginia A. La Charité notes that a paradox informs this era in Char's creation: "To live is to act, but every act appears menaced by the flux and destruction of the world."[2] The poems **"Les Trois Soeurs," "Donnerbach Mühle,"** and **"Seuil"** manifest Char's labor to make his poetry adequate to the dialectic which endangerment and death entertain with life forces. A text from *Feuillets d'Hypnos* (1946) expresses the model concisely: "Nous voici abordant la seconde où la mort est la plus violente et la vie la mieux définie" (fr. 90).[3]

Exceptionally, the poem **"Affres, détonation, silence,"** also from *Le poème pulvérisé,* exhibits a traditional elegiac stance: the word is not an inspiring confrontation with danger, it is a memorial of past association and intimacy. Char incorporates the present in his discourse only to instill perspective on bygone tragedy. The focus on mortality renders the poem melancholy.[4] This conflict—between an elegiac, retrospective linkage of life and death, and an ecstatic economy where the two sustain a manichean but invigorating battle—remains acute in Char's later poetry, although differently than in the 1930s and 1940s, and as such furnishes a criterion for evaluating shifts in his artistic profile.[5] In **"Riche de larmes,"** the opening poem in Char's last collection, *Eloge d'une soupçonnée,* the poet eschews the enthusiasm of poems like **"Les Trois Sœurs,"** yet he refuses to furnish an unmitigated elegiac retrospective on his life as it wanes.

"Affres, détonation, silence" explicitly accepts elegiac conventions. The poet laments the demise of the resistance fighter Roger Bernard, executed by the SS near the village of Céreste in the Luberon, where Char commanded a group of partisans.[6] Menace and death assume mythopoetic guise: "Roger Bernard: l'horizon des monstres était trop proche de sa terre." The poet creates a lack and a deathlike quietness in the landscape: "A leur tour les présages se sont assoupis dans le silence des fleurs." The future ("les présages") is abolished, so that we may meditate on the past. In a prose eulogy, **"Roger Bernard"** (*Recherche de la base et du sommet*), Char recounts his protégé's execution: "C'est durant un aller au P. C. de Céreste, chargé d'une mission de liaison, qu'il tombe aux mains des Allemands, le 22 juin 1944"; "Il est fusillé peu après sur la route, ayant refusé de répondre aux questions qui lui sont posées" (646). Char witnessed Bernard's execution from afar but decided not to intervene, fearing Nazi reprisals against the nearby village harboring his group (*Feuillets d'Hypnos,* fr. 138). According to Paul Veyne, the poet carried his conscious abstention heavily: "Après la Libération, René se présenta à la veuve de Bernard pour lui rendre des comptes, qu'elle admit."[7] Char's several texts on Bernard attest how difficult it was to resolve the grief.[8]

In *Feuillets d'Hypnos,* Char has begun crafting Bernard's death scene: "Il est tombé comme s'il ne distinguait pas ses bourreaux *et si léger, il m'a semblé, que le moindre souffle de vent eût dû le soulever de terre*" (fr. 138, emphasis added). **"Affres, détonation, silence"** amplifies this mingling of body with environs, and, in order to accomplish this, Char raises an empathetic description of the event to the level of intense poetic metamorphosis and formal elegy. Bernard, a breeze among canyons, is changed into storm cloud, then into naïve lightning, unslaked yearning, echoes of friendship, a mourning that cannot be put to rest: "Ne cherchez pas dans la montagne; mais si, à quelques kilomètres de là, dans les gorges d'Oppedette, vous rencontrez la foudre au visage d'écolier, allez à elle, oh, allez à elle et souriez-lui car elle doit avoir faim, faim d'amitié."

Bernard's shade induces Char to celebrate and perpetuate the loyalty and solidarity which his friend and others incarnated: "Pour qui œuvrent les martyrs? La grandeur réside dans le départ qui oblige. Les êtres exemplaires sont de vapeur et de vent" (*Feuillets d'Hypnos,* fr. 228). Roger Chaudon, another *maquisard,* exemplifies an elegiac construction where heady perseverance against the catastrophes of history is validated: "Peu de jours avant son supplice, Roger Chaudon me disait: 'Sur cette terre, on est un peu dessus, beaucoup dessous. L'ordre des époques ne peut être inversé. C'est, au fond, ce qui me tranquillise, malgré la joie de vivre qui me secoue comme un tonnerre . . .'" (*Feuillets d'Hypnos,* fr. 231). Death conjures its twin, "la joie de vivre," the latter powerful like thunder, but intermittent and often submerged by the greater course of oppression ("on est un peu dessus, beaucoup dessous"). Emile Cavagni, "tué dans une embuscade à

Forcalquier," "mon meilleur frère d'action," exemplifies *élan vital* that thrives in crisis and inspires commitment and solidarity: "Il portait ses quarante-cinq ans verticalement, tel un arbre de la liberté. Je l'aimais sans effusion, sans pesanteur inutile. Inébranlablement" (*Feuillets d'Hypnos,* fr. 157).

These figures of life despite death sign the countryside, they are poetic landmarks inscribed as reminiscences in the earth—Cavagni freedom tree, Chaudon joyous thunder, Bernard schoolboy lightning. Epithets configure Bernard, Chaudon, and Cavagni into the verbal landscape as artifacts and echoes that endure beyond the death of individuals: "La parole soulève plus de terre que le fossoyeur ne le peut" (**"Trois respirations,"** *Recherche,* 652). A well-wrought poetic sign relies on the multiplication of converging traces and intangible symbolic associations to evoke its referent, yet similar to death it markedly places its object, the referent, at a distance, thus affording a very effective and moving representation of grief.[9]

Char, in **"Affres, détonation, silence,"** creates a nexus of ethical tensions that enables us to relive the meaning of Bernard, whose bivouac was a world of joyous violence and excess: "Le Moulin du Calavon. Deux années durant, une ferme de cigales, un château de martinets. Ici tout parlait torrent, tantôt par le rire, tantôt par les poings de la jeunesse." The poetic detonation is at least a dual trace of the past—the sounds of camaraderie and loyal combat as much as the report of the executioner's weapon. Silence after the tragedy honors Bernard yet makes him fragile and tremulous like life—he is a fitful wind in the canyon, across lavender fields. "Affres, détonation, silence" represents life forces that drove Bernard, but it also depicts a stillness that translates the difficulty of working through absence. The poem conforms easily to the elegiac canon.

"Affres, détonation, silence" lingers, a flashback and sad remembrance. Char's ecstatic poetry, typified in **"Donnerbach Mühle,"** **"Les Trois Sœurs,"** and **"Seuil,"** is by contrast a flash-forward and a severance from the past. These three Dionysian poems, which share a scenario of imminent, unregretful confrontation with death, are psychologically innovative. They accept, even celebrate, the burning of former emotional sites, after which they move on expeditiously. They contrast with the vaporous ambiance of the Roger Bernard cycle, in that they furnish through their own forward motion a therapeutic against melancholy and depression. Char places us right on the line of passage from mourning into a renewed future, and the exhilaration that courses through these ecstatic poems does not truly satisfy elegiac expectations.

In **"Les Trois Sœurs,"** the limit between catastrophe and exhilaration is born. Love produces a child who is projected into a field of contraries, hope and despair, life and death. The prologue recounts the primal love, both the height of passion ("Mon amour à la robe de phare bleu, / je baise la fièvre de ton visage") and post-coital melancholy ("Hors de toi, que ma chair devienne la voile / qui répugne au vent"). The rest of the poem consists of three scenes, the first of which portrays the conception of the mythical, elemental child ("Dans l'urne des temps secondaires / L'enfant à naître était de craie") as well as his birth ("la fleur apparue").

The following scene places the child, now a "chasseur," under the governance of the second of the three Fates, as Veyne suggests (272):

> La seconde crie et s'évade
> De l'abeille ambiante et du tilleul vermeil.
> Elle est un jour de vent perpétuel,
> Le dé bleu du combat, le guetteur qui sourit
> Quand sa lyre profère: "Ce que je veux, sera."

The tutelary goddess animates this world, reveals its contours, and allows momentarily for harmonious interaction between young inhabitant and habitat. Moreover, the second Fate who cries out in her flight represents time, both brevity and duration: she is the instant ("la seconde"), which, multiplied, becomes "un jour de vent perpétuel." She decrees the moment when one should strengthen oneself against the pull of an uncertain future that approaches too quickly:

> C'est l'heure de se taire
> De devenir la tour
> Que l'avenir convoite.

The hunter and friendly prey ("Son gibier le suit n'ayant plus peur"), to the contrary, abandon their vigilance. Naïvely confident in their surroundings and in each other, they take the bucolic world at face value, unaware that their inadequate language dulls perception of the tensions that striate nature and endanger them:

> Leur clarté est si haute, leur santé si nouvelle,
> Que ces deux qui s'en vont sans rien signifier
> Ne sentent pas les sœurs les ramener à elles
> D'un long bâillon de cendre aux forêts blanches.

In the third scene, the child's language ("la parole qui découvre") cannot rescue his unique gifts (his "yeux singuliers") from the catastrophe which engulfs this world. A prophetic voice tries to ward off disaster:

> Cet enfant sur ton épaule
> Est ta chance et ton fardeau.
> Terre en quoi l'orchidée brûle,
> Ne le fatiguez pas de vous.

The interlocutors, the earth excepted, are difficult to specify Perhaps the third Fate addresses the poet, who is urged to foster and defend his talents ("ta chance et ton fardeau") despite a hostile universe. The conditions of communication might be reversed, too: it could be the poet who apostrophizes Fate (second person singular) not to abandon the child to a bad destiny, after which he confides the child to Gaia, the earth mother. Although the child is a chance for the future (a short-lived orchid), circumstances may waste its intense bouquet; therefore, the poet implores the earth ("vous") to remain "fleur et frontière," but also "manne et serpent"—a diversity within which the child may flourish, challenging multiple limits.

The prophetic warning, perhaps because it addresses a split audience, *tu* and *vous,* proves ineffectual. Events surpass this enigmatic voice from the desert. The shoulder upon which the child perches breaks to reveal death whose threat puts life into high relief. The child's life narrative shifts abruptly into devastating, unlinked image bursts that dislocate adjective and noun, verb and subject—"Violente l'épaule s'entrouvre," "Muet apparaît le volcan." Syntax in the last stanza cannot be properly characterized as paratactic. It is elliptical, and even the relation between clauses is questionable. The earth is described and directly addressed, then, as if simultaneously, its vaporization is expedited and confirmed without lingering regret: "Terre sur quoi l'olivier brille, / Tout s'évanouit en passage."

This last scene institutes a conflict of interpretation that cannot be resolved, because the two processes, life and death, sustain each other antagonistically in the present, between unavoidable destruction and brilliance, immediate poetry and crisis. Char's language evolves in both vivid and catastrophic registers. In the first stanza of this last scene, the orchid burns ("Terre en quoi l'orchidée brûle"): imminent peril for beauty and language, cataclysmic earth. In the final stanza, to the contrary, an olive tree ignited by the lava burns brightly, "brille": this is only partially a nihilistic fire, to the point that Veyne (276-78) understands the conclusion as a biographical representation of Char's mixed feelings of contentment and solitude, once he had completed a poem and abandoned it to the reader. The child, mortally wounded, produces a burst or flash of poetry amid disaster. The urn has become volcano. Poetry, which is an allegory of life, issues from the crucible and is seized in an image which cries out like fate, then flees like time, "crie et s'évade." Veyne rightly considers this third scene a representation of poetry, which tends to "s'abolir triomphalement dans sa propre naissance" (267).

The poet initially retained classical evocations of death and of life's brevity (the Fate who, as instant, evades our grasp), but the images in the conclusion express their own paroxysmal, instant autonomy. The child has disappeared, displaced by the poet who thrives now amid the debacle, He revels in the power of his

apocalyptic language: it ignites self-contained, gratu-
itous images in the present, and it destroys memories of
primal origins ("l'urne des temps secondaires") and of
pastoral utopias.

The line between life and death acquires a less
enigmatic sense in **"Donnerbach Mühle,"** which Char
began while stationed in Alsace. Nathan Bracher has
analyzed the "bombardement qui est évoqué en fili-
grane d'un bout à l'autre du texte," from the presence
of the German "donner," in the title, to its translation
and incineration in "tonnerre" at poem's end.[10] From the
start, Char adopts an elegiac tempo: "Novembre de
brumes, entends sous le bois la cloche du dernier sen-
tier franchir le soir et disparaître. . . ." Wistfully,
autumn trails into winter during the *drôle de guerre*.
Beneath nostalgia for the dying season, other borders
are infringed. The cliché of seasonal change has been
rerouted into a conflict of limits between sound, echo,
and final silence: "[entends] le vœu lointain du vent sé-
parer le retour dans les fers de l'absence qui passe."[11]
The major boundary transgressed is historical, since the
bell tolls for a world whose time has expired and whose
pleasant symbols ("animaux pacifiques," "filles sans
méchanceté") historical change is annulling ("j'entends
les monstres qui piétinent sur une terre sans sourire").
The metallic resonance of the bell evokes cannons on
the front (Bracher 431), but this funereal "glas" doubles
as a call to arms, and we might see it, finally, as a
revocation of elegy.

Despite death's shadow—the lake becomes a bier ("un
lit de profondes cendres") for summer's "doux feu
végétal"—the seasonal cycle persists, and the poet sud-
denly awakes, reborn to an ecstatic world that parellels
the volcano burst in **"Les Trois Sœurs"**:

> Tracée par le canon,
> —vivre, limite immense—
> la maison dans la forêt s'est allumée:
> Tonnerre, ruisseau, moulin.

The poet, in this last stanza, abruptly discovers the
poem's hidden unity: his former sites, his *loci amoeni*,
are burning in the fires of history.

The sentence "la maison dans la forêt s'est allumée" is
a striking equivocation. The poem takes its title from a
place which Char visited to relieve the frustration of the
Phony War:

> alors qu'artilleur dans le Bas-Rhin, je me morfondais
> derrière des canons mal utilisés, chacun de mes loisirs,
> de préférence la nuit, me conduisait avec un camarade
> au lac de Donnerbach Mühle, à trois kilomètres de
> Struth, à la maison forestière, où nous prenions un
> frugal mais combien délicieux repas, servi par le couple
> de forestiers.[12]

Prosaically, night falls and the people in the house light
lamps. Poetically, the house in the forest, which is struck
by enemy cannon fire, or perhaps illuminated by nearby

cannon which are firing at the enemy, combusts, and
the silvan image releases its symbolic energy: the elegy
for a dying world has become a paean to diffident,
combative values. This paradoxical limit is too immense
for one habitat. The experience of precariousness, of
being on the verge of an irremediable transgression of
limits between past and present, peace and war, life and
death, imparts breath to this closure and expands the
site beyond its forest confines. The sentence that carries
the illuminated-incinerated house arrests breathtakingly
to designate the limit it is crossing: "—vivre, limite im-
mense—. . . ." Past and present are equally excessive.
The old world was "trop aimé," the new one demands
high rage: "Ma sœur vermeille est en sueur. Ma sœur
furieuse appelle aux armes." Poised on a demarcation
line, however, the poet chooses to reject nostalgia, and
he accepts the coming struggle.

The renewal of poetry, with history or despite it, is
implicit in Char's recurrent accentuation of the limit
between life and death. The structure of **"Seuil"** centers
on the breaking of nocturnal dams, on the infringement
of inhibitions. The poet participates in an apocalypse,
where forceful poetic language is revealed.[13] **"Seuil,"**
replicating the pattern in **"Donnerbach Mühle,"**
portrays a time that moves in infinite bursts beyond a
tensile limit:

> Quand s'ébranla le barrage de l'homme, aspiré par la
> faille géante de l'abandon du divin, des mots dans le
> lointain, des mots qui ne voulaient pas se perdre,
> tentèrent de résister à l'exorbitante poussée. Là se dé-
> cida la dynastie de leur sens.

The poet senses in the maelstrom the fabrication of
renewed words: "je vous attends, ô mes amis qui allez
venir. Déjà je vous devine derrière la noirceur de
l'horizon." The confrontation with disaster produces a
dynasty of new expressions which the poet greets as he
would his intimates: "Mon âtre ne tarit pas de vœux
pour vos maisons." Beyond the flood imagery that first
establishes the poem's tenor ("barrage," for example),
pyrotechnics reminiscent of **"Les Trois Sœurs"** and
"Donnerbach Mühle" reappear in **"Seuil"** as this
hearth ("âtre"), which leads the poem to its conclusion.
Beside the hearth, the poet places a piece of cypress,
crafted semantically into an odd, captivating personifica-
tion: "Et mon bâton de cyprès rit de tout son cœur pour
vous." This stick of cypress is not wholly a death's-
head, since it embodies enthusiasm for the new poetry
that is being generated in the crisis. The wooden image
traces our border with death, but it does so in order to
redefine our sense of life, just as the destruction of the
old dynasty restructured language away from divine
transcendence. Char has situated us within several
figures of the limit—"le barrage de l'homme," "faille
géante," "nuit diluvienne"—but the "bâton de cyprès"
is perhaps the most universal and exemplary of them
all. Char could not have stated more forcefully than

with this cypress cane that death imparts urgent tension to the experience poetry affords us within language, and conversely that life for the poet and his readers ecstatically transgresses the limits with which death surrounds them. The life-and-death struggle polarizes the poet's image fields and gives his language a "sprung," highly stressed quality.[14]

This tensed frontier between life and death recurs in a paradoxical mode at the end of "Riche de larmes," the opening poem of *Eloge d'une Soupçonnée*: "A présent que la bougie s'écœure de vivre, l'écoute rougeoie aux fenêtres / Un sablier trop belliqueux se coule dans un Temps ancien et non sans retour" (11). The time flow is reversible ("non sans retour"), since the poet recuperates it in a new dawn; but the hourglass, despite its reversibility, empties itself too quickly—it is "trop belliqueux"—and the candle in the room expires. To understand this paradox, we need to review its prior construction. The poem consists of a variable horizon line, arrayed into two questions and an answer of sorts.

"Riche de larmes," like **"Donnerbach Mühle,"** begins with a wistful nightfall. The poet then asks for the lesson behind the image of night: "Quand s'achève au vrai la classe que nous continuons de fréquenter à l'insu de notre âge, il fait nuit sur soi. A quoi bon s'éclairer, riche de larmes?" (7). The incendiary anticipation of **"Les Trois Sœurs," "Donnerbach Mühle,"** and **"Seuil"** becomes a futile, utopian longing in the first moments of **"Riche de larmes"**: "Merveilleux moment que celui où l'homme n'avait nul besoin de silex, de brandons pour appeler le feu à lui, mais où le feu surgissait sur ses pas, faisant de cet homme une lumière de toujours et une torche interrogative" (7). Time since that ideal moment—Lascaux or youth—has become monotonous, it has lost its ecstatic qualities: "Douloureux sera demain, / Tel hier" (8).

In the middle of the poem, Time is again questioned, but the poet no longer can distinguish east from west: "Le secret, serait-ce le lendemain non ramené à soi? Ce qui grandit semble s'unir de plus en plus étroitement pour une nuit inspirée tout autant que pour un jour façonné" (9). The uncertain horizon may reveal "lacrymale la rosée" or "vespéral le sel" (8), so chiastically are the limits of life and death, dawn and vespers linked. Nevertheless, time manages, in this instance, to escape mundane duration and to become productive. The poet crafts death into eulogies to Nicolas de Staël and Ossip Mandelstam, in order to reach a higher plateau that indeed recalls the poet's ecstatic site in **"Seuil"**: "L'art est fait d'oppression, de tragédie, criblées discontinûment par l'irruption d'une joie qui inonde son site, puis repart" (10). The poet's "brusque alliance" with language—that is, his inexplicable seizure of the combination of words that properly evoke an image—allows him to formulate a vivid definition of artistic

creation as discontinuity and rupture, as a "lendemain non ramené à soi." Poetry represents the possibility of an escape from duration and self-pity.

At the end of this itinerary, however, the poet appears to fall back into depression. Such reversal is perhaps inevitable in a poetics where elation plays a preponderant role. Edouard Morot-Sir, discussing Char, asserts that "poetry cannot avoid the fact of language slowing down . . . and breaking the stream of writing."[15] The temptation of elegy pulls the image stream back toward death and melancholy. While Char, in an undeniably elegiac gesture, has just designated poetry and love as his only consolations in life—"le seul état de liberté que j'ai éprouvé sans réserve, c'est dans la poésie que je l'ai atteint, dans ses larmes et dans l'éclat de quelques êtres venus à moi de trois lointains, l'amour me multipliant" (10)—he then moves toward his conclusion by mitigating the degree of solace that they offer: "Il faut savoir que le deuil est à peu près constant sitôt la fête mise bas, démâtée" (11). We have returned to the lesson of darkness which opened the poem, that is, the lesson of ongoing grief.[16]

The poet, in the penultimate line of **"Riche de larmes,"** defiantly reorients us by resurrecting a classical topos of the *aubade*: the candlelight fades in dawn's first light. Char's candle dies in the moment when it becomes a personification: it loses the heart to live ("s'écœure de vivre . . .") as it pales from sight. The poet's accompanying image of rebirth is also a complex figural exchange. Sight, implied by the candle, is replaced by hearing, "l'écoute." It would be more exact to say that sight and hearing fuse while the candlelight dies: "la bougie s'écœure de vivre, *l'écoute rougeoie aux fenêtres*" (my emphasis). One process is incited while the other wanes. Beyond synesthesia of sight and hearing, the force of the image derives, too, from the concurrent use of hypallage: the act of tinting the windowpanes is not attributed to the real agent, the rising sun, but to the concentrated attention, or "écoute," that the poet pays to dawn, which has just paled the candle. The hypallage places us on both sides of the windowpane and expands our consciousness of the scene. This intricate figural array underscores the interdependency of candle's waning and sun's rebirth, but the poet also shows here his sensitivity to the rivalry between elegiac and ecstatic modes, since the poem becomes a dawn song, or the hint that such a revival is still possible. Char has momentarily reinvigorated the younger archetype of the fire that burns the forest house in pure expenditure. We would ask if this furnishes an answer to Time's enigma, but at least for a brief second the delicate image of the poet between candle and sun seems to resolve, through its own example, the paradox of a "Temps ancien" which nevertheless is "non sans retour."

In **"Riche de larmes"** Char produces, in a sense, his own eulogy. By imagining a new dawn, the poet exhibits the force or conflagration that inspired his best poetry. The rising sun burns off some of the vapors and regretful mists which darkened much that preceded. The poem becomes a last resistance against the elegiac temptation, a final effort to work through grief and against melancholy. The concluding sunrise defers the plaintive questions we found at the beginning and midpoint of the poem, metaphysical questions which were not merely rhetorical but, of course, unanswerable.

The final scene in **"Riche de larmes"** is a victory of sorts, stubborn even if it is tenuous. As Char writes in "A une sérénité crispée," "Je suis l'imbécile des cendres bien froides mais qui croit à un tison quelque part survivant" (**Recherche,** 761). In **"Riche de larmes,"** he admits that his resistance against the passage of time is "trop belliqueux," that his dawn is more than a little obstreperous and out of place. Nevertheless, through this closure, which eschews the explosive awakening to immensity of **"Les Trois Sœurs," "Donnerbach Mühle,"** and **"Seuil,"** Char relights and softly thrives in the poetic values of brinksmanship that he battled throughout his career to establish. The poet cannot accept unreservedly the death mask of elegy proper, even at the time of his own waning. Instead he chooses to offer us, at the last instant, this sunrise.

Notes

1. I quote Char's texts as published in *Oeuvres complètes* (Paris: Gallimard-Pléiade, 1983). Page numbers, and fragment numbers of *Feuillets d'Hypnos,* refer to that edition, except for "Riche de larmes," where references are to *Eloge d'une Soupçonnée* (Paris: Gallimard-NRF, 1988).

2. *The Poetics and the Poetry of René Char* (Chapel Hill: University of North Carolina Press, 1968), 77.

3. See Jean-Claude Mathieu, *La Poésie de René Char ou le sel de la splendeur* (Paris: José Corti, 1984-1985), 2: 263, 282-85, and Louis Bourgeois, *Poètes de l'au-delà d'Eluard à René Char* (Lyon: Presses Universitaires de Lyon, 1984), 12-37.

4. S. F. Fogle, "Elegy," *Princeton Encyclopedia of Poetry and Poetics,* ed. A. Preminger et al., 2nd ed. (Princeton: Princeton Univ. Press, 1974): "A lyric, usually formal in tone and diction, suggested either by the death of an actual person or by the poet's contemplation of the tragic aspects of life. In either case, the emotion, originally expressed as a lament, finds consolation in the contemplation of some permanent principle." The author distinguishes elegy proper ("lament for the dead") and elegiac tone ("meditative and reflective verse").

Henri Bénac, "Elégie," *Vocabulaire de la dissertation* (Paris: Hachette, 1949), gives this definition: "Poème triste qui peu à peu s'enrichira de toute la philosophie romantique: Ex. *Le Lac* de Lamartine. De nos jours, l'élégie est avant tout un poème qui exprime la mélancolie."

5. Strains of Char's elegiac voice are certainly audible prior to *Fureur et mystère,* in *Placard pour un chemin des écoliers,* for instance. Elegiac and eulogistic tones, if not elegy proper, permeate several postwar poems—"Le pas ouvert de René Crevel" (399), "Rémanence" (457), "Excursion au village" (514), "Ibrim" (619), for example. *Recherche de la base et du sommet* contains many eulogistic texts, among them "Dominique Corti," "Antonin Artaud," "René Crevel," "A la mort d'Eluard," and "Au revoir, Mademoiselle."

6. For the historical and biographical context of this poem, see Mathieu 2: 199-220.

7. *René Char en ses poèmes* (Paris: Gallimard, 1990), 206.

8. Bernard was also a poet, Char's metaphysical double (*Recherche,* 646). The text "Roger Bernard" prefaces the postwar edition of Bernard's poetry, *Ma faim noire Déjà* (*Cahiers d'art,* 1946; Seghers, 1976), while "Affres, détonation, silence" is its *envoi.* Mathieu (2: 240) remarks Char's insistent rewriting of this death scene.

9. On mourning and melancholy in *Feuillets d'Hypnos* and "Affres, détonation, silence," see Mathieu's perspicacious remarks (2: 217-18, 240-41).

10. Nathan Bracher, "Au-delà du mot: métaphore et métonymie dans 'Donnerbach Mühle' de René Char," *French Review* 64 (1991): 429, but the article throughout delves into the title of the poem. For Bracher, the alternation of past and present, "jouissance et dépérissement," relates to problems of trace and absence (435; see also 430).

11. See Bracher: " . . . 'séparer le retour' signifie que le bruit du vent empêche la propagation de l'écho" (432).

12. René Char, "Arrière-histoire du *Poème pulvérisé*" as quoted in *Oeuvres complètes* 1247, notes to "Donnerbach Mühle."

13. See Eric Marty, *René Char* (Paris: Seuil, 1990), 213-14.

14. In a similar vein, see Georges Poulet, "René Char: De la constriction à la dissémination," *L'Arc* 22 (1963): 40-42.

15. Edouard Morot-Sir, *The Imagination of Reference: Meditating the Linguistic Condition* (Gainesville: Univ. Press of Florida, 1993), 153.

16. See Daniel Leuwers, *L'Accompagnateur: Essais sur la poésie contemporaine* (Marseille: Sud, 1989), 18-19; Michael Bishop, *René Char, les dernières années* (Amsterdam: Rodopi, 1990), 101.

Van Kelly (essay date 2001)

SOURCE: Kelly, Van. "Suffering and Expenditure: Baudelaire and Nietsche in Char's Poetic Territory." In *Baudelaire and the Poetics of Modernity,* edited by Patricia A. Ward, pp. 172-86. Nashville, Tenn.: Vanderbilt University Press, 2001.

[*In the following essay, Kelly analyzes Char's poem, "Baudelaire mécontente Nietzsche."*]

René Char's poem **"Baudelaire mécontente Nietzsche"** (**"Baudelaire Irritates Nietzsche"**), which appeared in the 1972 collection *La Nuit talismanique,* begins with a contrast:

> C'est Baudelaire qui postdate et voit juste de sa barque de souffrance, lorsqu'il nous désigne tels que nous sommes. Nietzsche, perpétuellement séismal, cadastre tout notre territoire agonistique. Mes deux porteurs d'eau.
>
> (Char *OC* [*Oeuvres complètes*] 495-96)

[Baudelaire from his boat of suffering postdates and sees things with justice when he describes us as we truly are. Nietzsche, ceaselessly earthshaking, maps out all our strife-ridden land. My two water-bearers.][1]

Paulène Aspel noted in 1968 that Char had devoted pieces to Rimbaud, Camus, Heraclitus, and others, but not to Nietzsche, with whom the poet seemed to "entertain, to prolong an intimacy" (1968, 166).[2] **"Baudelaire Irritates Nietzsche"** thus fills gaps in a longstanding chronology of influences.

Other texts imply that Char's two "water-bearers," or provisioners, flank and complement Rimbaud at the confluence that defines modernity.[3] The essay "In 1871" clarifies Rimbaud's middle position in this series of partial intersections. Char associates Rimbaud's poetic revolution with the fall of the Second Empire: "A contemporary of the Commune, and with a similar vengefulness, he punctures like a bullet the horizon of poetry and of sensibility" (Char *OC* 727). Rimbaud breaks the dam standing against modernity, while Baudelaire and Nietzsche inhabit opposite sides of the divide: "Romanticism has dozed off and dreams aloud: Baudelaire, the entire Baudelaire, has just died after he moaned with true pain. . . . Nietzsche readies himself, but he will have to return each day a bit more lacerated from his sublime ascensions" (726). In "1871," Baudelaire lingers behind, straddling the divide between

Romanticism and modernity, whereas Nietzsche, yet to arrive, represents futurity. **"Baudelaire Irritates Nietzsche,"** by contrast, asserts that Baudelaire "postdates" rather than just completes a dying era.[4] In this version, he survives Romanticism's catastrophe and accompanies Nietzsche into the future.

Char's temporal perspective on Baudelaire and Nietzsche is thus paradoxical, as is the case for Rimbaud. There is a "before" life and an "after" life through philosophy or poetry. Char states enigmatically that "Nietzsche détruit avant forme la galère cosmique" ("Nietzsche, destroyed prior, forms the cosmic galley" [**"Page d'ascendants pour l'an 1964,"** Char *OC* 711]). If Baudelaire postdates, Rimbaud is "ahead of the wave." He is temporally unfinished, "the first poet of a civilization yet to materialize" and cannot be defined precisely, but he is crucial to Char's poetic vein: "If I knew exactly what Rimbaud meant to me, I would know what poetry remains ahead of me, and I would no longer need to write it" (732). Char's characterization of Baudelaire, Rimbaud, and Nietzsche as radically forward-looking responds to what de Man sees as the prototype of modernity: "Modernity exists in the form of a desire to wipe out whatever came earlier, in the hope of reaching at last a point that could be called a true present, a point of origin that marks a new departure."[5] Commenting specifically on Baudelaire's essay *The Painter of Modern Life,* de Man notes that modernity has a predilection for ideas and representations that "illustrate the heroic ability to ignore or to forget that this present contains the prospective self-knowledge of its end" (158-59). This general propensity is quite evident in Char's poetry—"Action is virgin, even when repeated," (*Feuillets d'Hypnos,* no. 46, in *OC* 186)—but his *grands astreignants* (great models who include, significantly, Heraclitus and Georges de La Tour) also tend to annul duration and deny the erosion of newness within his own works, through the mechanism of an artistic, philosophical, and poetic community situated paradoxically as if it were entirely in the present, despite the passage of time. De Man argues his definition of modernity along similar lines: "This combined interplay of deliberate forgetting with an action that is also a new origin reaches the full power of the idea of modernity" (162).

Unlike de Man, Char incorporates Baudelaire hesitantly into his modern continuum, as the title **"Baudelaire Irritates Nietzsche"** implies. The displeasure or irritation signals a conflict, yet the qualities that Char attaches to Baudelaire and Nietzsche in the opening stanza of the poem seem complementary rather than mutually exclusive: lucidity amid suffering does not necessarily annul a vigorous struggle to conquer adversity. Char deepens the enigma when he mentions explicitly neither Baudelaire nor Nietzsche in the rest of the poem, creating thereby a gap that our interpretation of the poem must bridge: the title implies a conflict of influences, but the opening stanza implies their compatibility. This opening gambit or paradox creates more problems than it solves, but it conceals, too, the defense of a position on modernity which the rest of the poem plays out stylistically and allegorically.[6] What does Baudelaire's skiff of suffering, and Nietzsche's seismic mapping or registry, represent for Char?

SKIFF OF SUFFERING

Claude Pichois depicts Baudelaire as "plagued throughout his life by what he called his *guignon*—the evil spirit of misfortune and disaster," and Baudelaire is certainly an icon of personal misfortune in Char's view (Pichois and Ziegler 1989, xi). This offers the basic outline for an interpretation, yet the skiff of suffering which postdates and sees things with justice leads to a rich zone of Baudelairean imagery. Cargo's concordance to *Les Fleurs du Mal* lists no use of the word *barque* ("bark," as in Charon's bark or ferry), whereas *vaisseau/vaisseaux* (vessel/vessels) occurs nine times, *navire* (ship) four times, and the synecdoche *mâts* (masts) five times. The various usage of boat images form a neat dichotomy as well. In one set of Baudelairean poems, woman is represented as a ship on a trip toward pleasant, idyllic countries as in **"La Chevelure,"** where the lover's hair, at first a "noir océan" (black ocean), becomes a "pavillon de ténèbres tendues" (shadow-filled sail), or in **"Le Serpent qui danse,"** where she is compared to "un fin vaissseau / Qui roule bord sur bord" [a gossamer ship, / Swayed by ocean swell] (*OC* 1:26-27, 29). **"L'Invitation au voyage"** and **"Parfum exotique"** prolong this idyllic utopia. By contrast, the vessel, like woman in Baudelaire's world, has strong contrastive associations, and they are more pertinent to Char's "barque de souffrance." **"L'Héautontimorouménos"** pointedly echoes the line from **"Le Beau Navire,"** where desire, "[like] a beautiful . . . vessel putting out to sea," finds not an idyllic land but the victim or self-torturer's experience (*OC* 1:78). This establishes the double, antithetical register of the ship: symbol of pleasurable exoticism or hellish journey.[7] **"Le Voyage"** refers insistently to the suffering that inner enemies or complexes inflict. The soul, "un trois-mâts cherchant son Icarie" [a three-master seeking its utopia], encounters at home and abroad "le spectacle ennuyeux de l'immortel péché" [the monotonous spectacle of immortal sin].[8] Baudelaire concludes: "Amer savoir, celui qu'on tire du voyage" [Journey's bitter fruit], but he departs in Death's ship, heedless of good or evil. Suffering does not postpone the trip.

The elements associating vessel and suffering coalesce in Baudelaire's **"La Musique,"** where the figure of the poet becomes a ship:

> Je sens vibrer en moi toutes les passions
> *D'un vaisseau qui souffre,*
> Le bon vent, la tempête et ses convulsions
>
> Sur l'immense gouffre
> Me bercent. D'autres fois, calme plat, grand miroir
> De mon désespoir.

> (*OC* 1:68, emphasis added)

[I feel tensed within me, like passion, all the lurch and tremblings *of a ship that suffers,* the downwind, the storm and its convulsions lull me over the vast abyss. In other moments, flat seas, endless mirror for my despair.]

Other poems drift from ideal toward spleen. In **"L'Irrémédiable,"** all sense of adventure has disappeared from the image of the ship: "Un navire pris dans le pôle, / Comme en un piège de cristal" [A ship immobilized in polar ice, / As in a crystal trap] (*OC* 1:75). Char states, by contrast, that Baudelaire sees things justly despite suffering ("voit *juste* de sa barque de souffrance," emphasis added): in this sense his vessel encounters despair but elation, too, in a less fatal mix of spleen and ideal than in **"L'Irrémédiable,"** something closer to the melancholic if harsh adventure in **"La Musique"** and **"Le Voyage."**

Char strongly connects creation and suffering. Poets of all eras, from his perspective, have purveyed harsh truths and have been persecuted (before and after 1857):

> Think about the suspicion and torture to which Villon, Baudelaire, Nerval, Rimbaud, Mandelstam, or Maria Tsvetaeva were subjected . . . Do not forget that poets have always received fireworks in the chest, their internal and external enemies having placed them in a target zone.

> (*Sous ma casquette amarante,* in Char *OC* 856)

For Char, poetry is conspiratorial yet triumphant: "From the Inquisition to modern times, temporal evil clearly did not get the better of Theresa of Avila nor of Boris Pasternak . . . The statute of limitations has expired there where poetry flares up, resides . . ." ("Arthur Rimbaud," *OC* 727-28).

When Char comments on the image of suffering offered by Baudelaire—"I am the wound and the knife, / The victim and the executioner"—he infers the lesson that "at such a degree of suffering and flight, the poet is brother to all the earth and its misfortune" (*OC* 858). Poetry espouses a lucid violence that resists all compromise with oppressors: ("One of the noble aspects of violence . . . is its ability to pay off the victim's debt and deliver him from that plague: false knowledge, the nursemaid of shipwrecks, of capitulations," *OC* 857.) Char echoes this ethical reading of **"L'Héautontimorouménos"** with a stylistic one.

Competing moments of lucidity and frenzy inform poetry. Char finds the "ardent Nuance" (his own aesthetic ideal) in Baudelaire's poetry, too:

> Nuances and violence are in close combat. Through their mediation, the conflicts and tempers slowly but steadily counterbalance, and through them poetry disseminates, like water through limestone . . . Nuance and ardor raise and lower the horizon line, morning and evening, stimulating the spectrum.
>
> (*OC* 857)

Nuance is another form of violence, because it battles ardor to form poetry: "Poetry likes that double, mad violence and its double taste which listens at the doors of language" (*OC* 858), a violence in which Baudelaire's poetry shares. Char, significantly, interprets **"L'Héautontimorouménos"** not as a depiction of Baudelaire's psyche but as an allegory of poetry itself and of the poet's role in history.

The positive meaning of the skiff of suffering in **"Baudelaire Irritates Nietzsche"** becomes clearer: struggle is a necessary ingredient of self-accomplishment, and the good struggle (to write the poem or to resist oppression) elates the poet. Char associates the ship or the boat with the exhilarating struggle in his poem **"Faction du muet,"** where the word *barque* confirms but diversifies the Baudelairean images of suffering. The shift from Baudelaire's *vaisseau, navire* and *mâts* to Char's bark may be explained partly by the effort to translate a marine image, reminiscent of Baudelaire's journey to the Indian Ocean, into a fluvial world centered around representations of the Sorgue, the river that flows through Char's native town. A *barque* is a smallish vessel, used on inland waterways or employed in seaports to unload merchandise from a larger ship. In **"Faction du muet"** (*Le Nu perdu,* 1971), the poet, reminiscent of his counterpart in Baudelaire's **"La Musique,"** becomes a skiff gliding over the transparent riverbed of human experience. The journey enriches poetry, sometimes violently through the shock of life's contradictions, at other times sympathetically through identification with human foibles and tragedies: "Je me suis uni au courage de quelques êtres, j'ai vécu violemment, sans vieillir, mon mystère au milieu d'eux, j'ai frissonné de l'existence de tous les autres, *comme une barque incontinente au-dessus des fonds cloisonnés*" [I allied myself with the courage of some people, I have violently lived out my mystery among them, never aging, I have trembled to the existence of all others, *like a boat shifting above the cloisonné of a riverbed*] (*OC* 429, emphasis added). The experience of the Other stimulates the poet and energizes him. This kind of ecstasy contrasts with the desperation of Baudelaire's leave-taking in **"Le Voyage"**—"Pionger au fond du gouffre, Enfer ou Ciel, qu'importe?" [Plunge to the bottom of the abyss,

whether it is Hell or Heaven]. Suffering often appears in Char's poems, but a mysterious exhilaration usually gives it tone. Something resembling exhilaration fills the poet's sails in Baudelaire's **"La Musique"** ("I feel tensed within me, like passion, all the lurch and tremblings / Of a ship that suffers"), though there is only partial satisfaction: Baudelaire's "good winds" die to reveal the "calm mirror" of his despair. Char and Baudelaire become allegorical vessels of Poetry, each "shivers" or "suffers" in the wind, but each to different effect.

Differing attitudes toward despair, self-doubt, regret, and remorse furnish Char's rationale for placing Baudelaire on the near side of modernity, as its precursor, rather than at its point of origin:

> Baudelaire is the most *humane* genius of all *Christian* civilization. His song incarnates that civilization in its conscience, in its glory, in its remorse, in its malediction, at the moment of its beheading, of its loathing, of its apocalypse. "*Poets,*" writes Hölderlin, "*are usually revealed at the beginning or the end of an era.*"[9]

This remark occurs in the essay "Arthur Rimbaud," but it is crucial to Char's view on poetic modernity, and it attaches a caveat to the reception of Baudelaire's work: Baudelaire brings a premodern era of poetry to its end and represents an apogee prior to modernity's clean slate and new inscription. What survives the tabula rasa is Baudelaire's empathy with human suffering, less sin and remorse which are foreign to Char, who would certainly be irritated by the sense of guilt and self-deprecation in the conclusion of **"Un voyage à Cythère"**: "—Ah! Seigneur! donnez-moi la force et le courage / De contempler mon cœur et mon corps sans dégoût!" [Oh Lord! Give me the force and courage / to consider my heart and body without disgust!] (*OC* 1:119). In moments of suffering, Char does not feel remorseful but anxious, as in **"Baudelaire Irritates Nietzsche"**: "What is, our greatest cause of suffering? Worry" (*OC* 496); in other words, our anxiety lacks a religious, eschatological foundation in God's redemptive or damning gaze. Personal instinct or difference, rather than belief, founds resistance to the world's weight, to its thrusts and currents: "We are born in the same torrent, but we roll differently amid frenetic stones. Worry? Follow instinct" (496). Char sees suffering not as an apocalypse that reveals or subverts godhead, but as a self-affirmation and instinctive resistance to phenomenal change.

Baudelaire's sense of suffering as Char portrays it in **"Baudelaire Irritates Nietzsche"** implies a religious sense, even if that sense manifests itself as Cain's revolt against God. Char rejects the postlapsarian aspect of Baudelairean suffering, and through this rejection the figure of Baudelaire begins to migrate through the poem, after the initial stanza introducing the two precursors. Humanity is part of a purely materialistic universe: "Sons of nothing and destined to nothing. . . . What we hear during sleep is our heartbeat and not the outbursts of our soul at leisure" (496). The only redemption and rebirth is in the poet's work. "The work, unique, in the form of a broken shutter" is the sole agent of "the sense of its own renewal" (496).[10] Suffering pervades the house of poetry with its broken shutter, yet this results not in divine transcendence but only in the renewal of our participation in a world that is either a chaos or an impersonal determinism: "Whether we defy order or chaos, we obey laws we have not intellectually ratified. We approach with the step of a mutilated giant" (496). We struggle violently, as if Titans, against the assault of senseless material forces—this is one of the lessons that underlies Char's fragmentary style—but here mythology evacuates theology and relegates it to the realm of metaphor for the blind forces of nature.[11] Char's poetry, which cultivates rupture and discontinuity, cannot assimilate Baudelaire's "ardent sanglot qui roule d'âge en âge" [ardent sob that rolls from age to age] and which dies—futilely or with redemption—at the feet of God's eternity (**"Les Phares,"** *OC* 1:14).

Char willfully effaces the divine, but his fragmentary style also saps the poetic conventions of wholeness and unity that typify Baudelairean verse (the open-ended succession of quatrains and artists of **"Les Phares,"** for instance, or the interweaving typical of the sonnet and pantoum). **"Baudelaire Irritates Nietzsche"** typifies Char's fragmentary style. The poem consists of eight prose stanzas, and the links from one to the next are "eluded" if not "burned," to use Char's own terms for describing transitions.[12] His poetry points through its form to the lack of an overarching principle, immanent to the universe and to language, which would make the movement from moment to moment and stanza to stanza self-evident. The poet presents fragments without apparent coherence, or with a unity that the poet senses incompletely, and the reader must join in this search beyond catastrophe for renewed wholeness. Char confirms the idea that poetic modernity, in the lineage of Rimbaud, is joined to the annulment of theology, since poetry is "toujours en chemin vers le point qui signe sa justification et clôt son existence, à l'écart, en avant de l'existence du mot Dieu" [always in transit toward the point that signs its verdict and closes its existence, well ahead of the existence of the word God].[13] Deprived of religious finalities, the poem crafts and imposes an immanent linguistic justification upon the surrounding chaos or oppressive order of things. Char's poetry, by its form, indicts the coherence of a universe it confronts and intends to conquer.

Char's version of poetic modernism is founded on the death of god, or, as Virginia La Charité says, "Poetry has the position that religion assigns to God" (1974,

57). Char suggests this again, but elliptically, in **"Faire du chemin avec . . ."** (*Fenêtres dormantes et porte sur le toit,* 1979): "Baudelaire, Melville, Van Gogh are haggard gods, not readings of gods" (*OC* 580)—that is, Baudelaire's poetry of misfortune and resistance to spleen inspires Char, but he rejects the detour through religious finality that *Les Fleurs du Mal* implies. Baudelaire survives the collapse of Romanticism but in a secular, de-Christianized form: "Baudelaire forges the wounds of the heart's intelligence into a pain that rivals the soul" (**"Page d'ascendants pour l'an 1964,"** *OC* 711).

THE SEISMIC REGISTRY: NIETZSCHE

What then does Nietzsche carry on Char's journey? Nietzsche, too, signals the existence of oppression and suffering, since he plots Char's "territoire agonistique," but pain derives in this case from a voluntary struggle and from the swords of battle. Commenting on **"Baudelaire Irritates Nietzsche,"** Paul Veyne interprets the "séisme nietzschéen" as the destruction of social conformity, or "valeurs établies," and this includes conformist institutions and conventional language.[14] Critics have also pointed out that Char appropriates Zarathustra's eagle to symbolize the poetic summit, sovereign independence, and human overcoming without the aid of God or gods (Aspel 1968, 180-81; Mathieu 1984-85, 1:121 n. 75). Char adopts Nietzsche partially because of the latter's rejection of the divine: "Creation—that is the great redemption from suffering, and life's growing light"; "Away from God and gods this has lured me; what could one create if gods existed?" says Zarathustra (Nietzsche 1968, 199), echoing the madman in *The Gay Science*: "Gods, too, decompose. God is dead. God remains dead. And we have killed him" (Nietzsche 1974, 181). Char's journey, too, is an ascension instead of the sea voyage that informs his interaction with Baudelaire. The ascension of man involves the annulment of God—"God, the arranger, could not but fail," Char declares—yet this lays the ground for a modern humanism, namely the cultivation of the "intermittent gods" who "pervade our mortal amalgam without ever going beyond us."[15] Char uses the philosopher-poet Nietzsche against the poet-philosopher Baudelaire, because in Nietzsche the philosophical and poetic project replaces religious teleology.[16]

As Aspel remarks, Char's "open attitude toward chance" echoes Zarathustra's claim that he has liberated the world from "the slavery of goals or ends."[17] Otherworldly redemption, or even blasphemy, gives way to an affirmation of the intrinsic value of the world and of the individual's path through it: "Let your will say: the overman *shall* be the meaning of the earth! I beseech you, my brothers, *remain faithful to the earth*," says Zarathustra, although it could just as well have been

Char, so close are the thought and instinct (Nietzsche 1968, 125, author's emphasis). Although he praises Baudelaire and has more indulgence for pity than does Nietzsche, Char's version of self-renewal closely emulates Zarathustra's praise of going under in order to overcome adversity:

> Man, says Zarathustra, is a rope tied between beast and overman—a rope over an abyss. A dangerous across, a dangerous on-the-way, a dangerous looking-back, a dangerous shuddering and stopping.
>
> What is great in man is that he is a bridge and not an end: what can be loved in man is that he is an *overture* and a *going under*. I love those who do not know how to live, except by going under.[18]

In **"Baudelaire Irritates Nietzsche,"** Char likewise denies otherworldly redemption while he espouses renewal through strictly human creativity. The human condition demands neither faith nor salvation but self-reliance. Char emphasizes renovation and a despiritualized transcendence, where the beginning point is the self and the culmination a self refashioned through its agonistic contact with *this* world: "To die is to go through the eye of the needle after several burgeonings. One must traverse death in order to emerge in front of life," but "in a state of sovereign modesty" as an individual self-sufficient, content to live without the self-importance imparted by notions of divine providence or of revolt against divinity (*OC* 496). Ascension toward personal sovereignty and elation also entails a plunge into the deepness of the world. Nietzsche's dialectic of overture and going under harmonizes with Char's supreme indifference to the divine, unless divinity is redefined as the vitality of nature, the ceaseless shock and metamorphosis of contraries without any transcendence beyond process.

Nietzsche's depiction of secular agony differs fundamentally from Baudelaire's striving between spleen and ideal. For Char, as for Nietzsche, risk and endangerment are fundamental categories. Life is a dangerous crossing over the abyss. Poems from the collection *Fureur et mystère,* published in 1948 but written from roughly the Munich crisis onward, grant an important place to these ideas and explain why Nietzsche, for Char, is "perpétuellement séismal." The idea that going under may result in destruction and not rebirth is accentuated in the poem "Les trois sœurs," where the poet beseeches the earth to safeguard "that child on your shoulder," whose allegorical sense is not yet clear—endangered innocence? human vulnerability? Disaster strikes, however, and a volcanic eruption engulfs the child, yet the child is poetry and the cataclysm only ignites the olive tree on the slope, here a symbol of the poetic image itself and its renewal through creativity (*OC* 250-51). In **"Seuil"** (**"The Edge"**), the Nietzschean denunciation of metaphysics and the images of cata-

clysm conjoin. The human figure in the poem confronts "the gigantic fault line of the abandonment of the divine," which has broken down the "dam of humanity." The reaction to catastrophe is not a political philosophy, or a philosophy of the will, but a language: "distant words, words that did not wish to be lost, mounted a resistance to the exorbitant thrust" (*OC* 255). Paul Veyne interprets this as a rejection of the Nietzschean overman in favor of the poet who sees in language, and not in metaphysics, the only valid project (316-17), but the ecstatic, wide view of **"Seuil"** suggests a reform of the ontological environment: when the downfall of God threatens humankind, the poet steps forth to await new words but also to remake the universe out of the surrounding chaos. Being, and not just language, is at risk here, though language, to be sure, is the agent of salvation. The dawn after the catastrophe signals the birth of a new poetic language, but the consequences surpass language and poetry alone, indeed this enriched threshold alludes to all of life— "life, immense limit," as Char asserts (**"Donnerbach Mühle,"** *OC* 252). The world is not an expiation for the sin of existence ("le châtiment du devenir," in the terms Bianquis uses in 1938 to translate Nietzsche's evaluation of Anaximander). It is, rather, "la justification de l'être" (Nietzsche's synthesis of Heraclitus: the sanctification of being), an apt description of Char's poet in **"Seuil,"** who, his belt "full of seasons," stands before the flood to welcome the rebirth of poetry after the quake, amid change.[19] As Aspel says, "Char's poetry sings reality, 'noble' reality, and seeks to attain it beyond the very idea of the unknown, and one may accurately call this exaltation Dionysiac" (172; see also 182).

Char's poetry in general, takes noble endangerment as its unspoken ground.[20] From violent risk issue words with the hard edge and urgency that contemplation of death imparts, and this is the sense of the characterization in **"Baudelaire Irritates Nietzsche"**: "Nietzsche, always earthshaking, maps out all our strife-ridden land" (*OC* 495-96). The devastated site, traversed by flood, volcanic eruptions, and tremors, produces, through struggle against the tragic sense of life, poetry at its most intense and its most exhilarating.[21] Against this background, and with reference to Baudelaire's remorseful apocalypse, Char espouses a Nietzschean "gaspillage sans frein," a relentless going under in order to overcome the world's resistance to poetry, philosophy, and justice.

The Anagogical Sense: Baudelaire's Return

The end of **"Baudelaire Irritates Nietzsche,"** however, should cause hesitation. Baudelaire is not easily repressed; he returns despite Nietzsche's displeasure.[22] Once Char rehearses his two provisioners' itinerary, he suddenly cannot choose between the two. Poetic language trembles in the confrontation:

Qui appelle encore? Mais la réponse n'est point don-
née.
Qui appelle encore pour un gaspillage sans frein? Le
trésor entrouvert des nuages qui escortèrent notre
vie.

                                        (*OC* 496)

[Who calls out once more? But no answer is given.
Who calls out once more for a relentless expenditure?
The open treasure of the clouds that escorted our
life.]

"Relentless expenditure" is the Nietzschean release of
the poet's and Zarathustra's "wild dogs" (1968, 155), of
his Dionysian urges toward fusion, toward the testing of
limits, and toward devastated orders and sites. The clos-
ing sentence of **"Baudelaire Irritates Nietzsche,"**
however, could be read as an allusion to Baudelaire's
prose poem "L'Etranger" (*Le Spleen de Paris*): "Well
then, what do you like, extraordinary stranger?—I like
the clouds that are passing! down there! down there!
the marvelous clouds" (*OC* 1:231).[23] Char opposes this
"open treasure" to "relentless expenditure," not as reten-
tion opposes prodigality, since the treasure, too, is
opened up/"entrouvert," but as serene contemplation
and recollection contrast with, and nuance, an ecstatic
and tragic vision of life—in other words, as Apollonian
serenity tempers Dionysian frenzy in Nietzsche's early
works on the origins of philosophy and tragedy (one of
Char's early contacts with Nietzsche's work).[24]

Char's "open treasure of the clouds" echoes the
interplay of distance and intimacy that marks not just
"L'Etranger," but Baudelaire's "Harmonie du soir," too,
with its concluding metaphor of the sunset and a
memory:

> Un cœur tendre, qui hait le néant vaste et noir,
> Du passé lumineux recueille tout vestige!
> Le soleil s'est noyé dans son sang qui se fige . . .
> Ton souvenir en moi luit comme un ostensoir!

                                        (*OC* 1:47)

[A tender heart, that hates the vast black nothingness, /
from the shining past collects all remainder! / The sun
has drowned in its clotted blood . . . / Your memory
glints in me as if a gilded monstrance!]

By contrast, a Dionysian sunset—one that insists on
violence and expenditure rather than on retention and
nostalgia—marks Char's **"Le Visage nuptial"**: "The
eagle's claw funnels high the blood" (*OC* 151), an ag-
gressive painting of the crepuscule that clashes with the
more serene, contained violence of "Harmonie du soir,"
where the clotted sun of the penultimate line is held by
coming darkness just as the poet captures the ray of
memory.[25] The union of disparate parts, and an inner
distance or serenity essential to contemplation, are even
more evident in **"Correspondances,"** where the mix of

elements moves toward unity, not toward clash and
disintegration. A number of Baudelaire's poems do
focus on dissolution ("Une charogne," "Le Masque,"
"La Destruction") or Orphic mutilation ("L'Albatros,"
"L'Héautontimorouménos"), but poems that accent
disruption often occur against a background of calm-
ness, as in "Harmonie du soir" and similar poems that
convey Baudelaire's predilection for a simultaneous
picture of spleen and ideal. "La Cloche fêlée" establishes
the poet's flaw through such counterpoint: the soul's
broken moaning ("râle épais") punctuates an Apollonian
vastness ("faraway memories" and bells that sing
through the mist). In **"Baudelaire Irritates Nietzsche,"**
Char's own conclusion among the "open treasure of the
clouds," however, accentuates what suffering could not
annul in Baudelaire's poetic vision, namely serenity and
contemplation as in "Recueillement": "Ma Douleur,
donne-moi la main . . . / . . . Vois se pencher les dé-
funtes Années, / Sur les balcons du ciel . . ." [My Pain,
give me your hand . . . / . . . See the dead Years lean
over / The balconies of the sky . . .], a serenity set
against (and despite) the frenetic search for pleasure
taking place in the city streets below.

At the end of **"Baudelaire Irritates Nietzsche,"** when
Char evokes both the philosopher's "relentless expendi-
ture" and the poet's "open treasure of the clouds," he
reaffirms his need for a contrast between ecstatic
violence and serene contemplation, distance and fusion.
Char refuses to exclude from modernity either Nietzsche
or Baudelaire, furor or mystery, fusion or distance,
dismemberment or order. This poem is not a Ni-
etzschean monologue. Baudelaire postdates Nietzsche:
he remains a valid marker and companion on Char's
poetic journey through the desert or through the
archipelago, and he is not brutally annulled. Instead
Baudelaire contests, by his *ennui* and pessimism, but
also through his sense of passive contemplation, Ni-
etzsche's harsh yet enthusiastic going under. Baudelaire
is put under erasure but returns in Char's poetry as the
supplement of suffering that maintains pity on the
horizon, though this does not lead Char to remorse or to
condemnation of the self's deep urges.

I have left for last the second strophe of **"Baudelaire
Irritates Nietzsche,"** because we must seek the true
rather than the apparent place of each of Char's stanzas
within the heterodox and fragmented order of his poem.
This stanza demonstrates, too, Char's inclination to
adopt a worldview more fundamentally Nietzschean
than Baudelairean, though the Nietzschean element
never governs uncontested. Encounter, conflict, and
influence renew poetic language and assure its continu-
ity: "Duty, before one takes another breath, to rarify
and hierarchize people and things that impinge on us."
Pollen, deprived of a future, "smashes into the rocky
partition." Char allows Baudelaire and Nietzsche, suf-
fering and untold generous expenditure, to inflect his

poetry. Pollen, or the word, is thus triple—Baudelaire and Nietzsche interact with Char, constrain him momentarily with their own original limits, pollinate his poetry, open it to change and growth beyond his solitude. Char's praise for his provisioners is not funerary rhetoric or banquet praise—it is not eulogistic or elegiac properly speaking—so much as it is a creative stimulus for further poetry. Nietzsche justifies, in similar terms, his own search for models of thought and life among the Presocratics. "Let us leave the tombs in peace, but make ours whatever is eternally lively. Humanity grows only when it venerates what is *rare and great*." "Adopter un style de rêve ou de légende," says Nietzsche in a French version which Char had read (Nietzsche 1985, 168, 171; Mathieu 1984-85, 2:90 n. 4). The poet has taken this advice and crafted a dialectic of Baudelairean clouds and Nietzschean dam breaking, but within the hidden design of a Nietzschean genealogy of influences.[26] Char's choice of clouds to symbolize Baudelairean poetics should be read as an allusion *both* to strophic poems such as "Harmonie du soir" (where the pantoum relies on the obsessive return of sentences and images in order to evoke the memory of lost love) *and* to the prose poems like "L'Etranger," freed from rhyme and strophic measure. In *Le Spleen de Paris,* Baudelaire attains a modernity and a freedom from convention that tie more directly to Char's vein of formal experimentation.[27]

In Char's poetry, Baudelairean stasis, ambiguity, and suffering contest alternative moments of vertigo, frenzy, and empowerment. Baudelaire remains a veiled reference in Char, although Nietzsche retains preponderance as the more modern one, less attached to a past morality and style. **"Dans la marche"** (*La Parole en archipel*) anticipates **"Baudelaire Irritates Nietzsche"** and illustrates the bind: "We can only live in what is opened up, precisely on the hermetic dividing line of shadow and light," says Char. This is stasis, penumbra, calm before dawn or dusk. "But we are irresistibly thrown ahead. All our person aids and spins this thrust" (*OC* 411). Expenditure indicts stasis but cannot avoid its moment.

Notes

1. Subsequent references to Char *OC* are to his *Oeuvres complètes,* 1995. No further page references will be given for "Baudelaire Irritates Nietzsche."

2. Char, in successive editions of his *Recherche de la base et du sommet,* first published in 1955, systematically developed the cult of his "grands astreignants." "Pages d'ascendants pour l'an 1964" contains a later list of "astreignants" and of "alliés," the latter term reserved for the *beaux-arts* (*OC* 711-12).

3. Prose texts in *Recherche de la base et du sommet* make it clear how central Rimbaud is to Char's view of the modern. See Char, "In 1871," "Réponses interrogatives à une question de Martin Heidegger," but especially "Arthur Rimbaud," an essay which originally served as Char's preface to the edition of Rimbaud published in the 1956 by the Club de l'Honnête Homme (*OC* 726-36). For a thorough analysis of Char's writings on and attitude toward Rimbaud, see La Charité, "The Role of Rimbaud."

4. Char states this banally in his response to a poll of contemporary poets ("Pour ou contre Baudelaire," *Les Nouvelles littéraires*): "Baudelaire's place in contemporary knowledge and sensibility is that of a very great poet whose genius and meaning have not stopped growing in the last one hundred years. Only today can we measure the degree of his undeniable sovereignty and universality."

5. *Blindness and Insight,* 148. For Char, Rimbaud remains unique, nevertheless, in that he represents life's supremacy over poetry (see Char's poem "Tu as bien fait de partir, Arthur Rimbaud," in *Fureur et mystère*). De Man ties the possibility of surpassing or abandoning literature to the concept of modernity: the "continuous appeal of modernity, the desire to break out of literature, toward the reality of the moment" is how the writer shows that literature exists in history, within time, instead of in the contradiction of endless newness (1983, 162).

6. For two more recent views on Baudelaire's modernity, see Compagnon 1990, 7-78, 177-80, and Meschonnic 1995, 469-82.

7. See Compagnon 1996 on Baudelaire's images of the good and bad seas.

8. The expressions "trois-mâts barque" and "la barque de Charon" are noted in *Heath's Standard French and English Dictionary,* 2 vols. (London: D. C. Heath, 1959).

9. *OC* 731-32, author's emphasis. The idea of a Baudelaire still enmeshed in Christianity corresponds to Breton's views in the 1930 *Second manifeste du surréalisme,* which Char signed. Char also clearly shares Breton's rejection of Claudel's Christian reading of *Illuminations* (without following Breton's shift toward a rejection of Rimbaud on the grounds, more or less, of religious ambiguities; see Breton 1988, 782-87). On Baudelaire and religion, see Ruff 1955, especially 281-366; *L'Année Baudelairie* 2 (1996), devoted to death and spirituality, but especially, in that issue, Milner, "Le paradis se gagne-t-il?," who critiques Ruff's Jansenist thesis; Lawler, *Poetry and Moral Dialectic,* who offers a balanced view of the place of the crucial section "Révolte" in *Les Fleurs du Mal* (16-25, 153-57, 182-88).

10. The broken shutter also appears in the poem "Le Ramier" (*Le Nu perdu* 1971): "Nous rallions nos pareils / Pour éteindre la dette / D'un volet qui battait / Généreux, généreux" (*OC* 448). On Char's linkage of creativity and transcendence, see Marty 1990, 159-228.

11. Char's mutilated giant also refers to another "grand astreignant," Poussin, through the figure of Orion, who is the protagonist of Char's 1975 *Aromates chasseurs* (*OC* 507-28).

12. "[J]e ne brûle pas les relais, mais je les élude," referring to his own remarks to the interviewer, but very pertinent to his poetry (*OC* 854-55). On Nietzsche and Char's aphorisms, see Aspel 1968, 168-70, 173.

13. "Réponses interrogatives à une question de Martin Heidegger," *OC* 734. See also Char's "A la question: 'Pourquoi ne croyez-vous point en Dieu?'" ("To the Question: 'Why do you not believe in God?'"): "If by some rare chance death did not end it all, we would probably find ourselves in front of something other than this God invented by men, in their image and adjusted for better or worse to their contradictions. Imagining a square of white linen, traversed by a sun ray, is nostalgically childish" (*OC* 658).

14. Veyne 1990, 318, and see for further comment his entire chapter, entitled "Héraclite, Heidegger et Nietzsche" (302-32).

15. "Faire du chemin avec . . . ," *Fenêtres dormantes et porte sur le toit,* in *OC* 580; "Peu à peu, et puis un vin silcieux," *La Nuit talismanique,* in *OC* 494. On Char's secular and metaphorical use of imagery of the gods, see Starobinski 1992.

16. Plouvier (1997) compares Nietzsche and Char as to their common rejection of history in favor of art.

17. Aspel 1968, 174, see also 179, on the "nécessité bienfaisante du hasard" in Nietzsche and Char. The article appeared before the publication of "Baudelaire Irritates Nietzsche" but is still very useful.

18. Nietzsche 1968, 126-27, author's emphasis. See also Zarathustra's speeches against suffering and pity in Nietzsche 1968, 143, 287.

19. Nietzsche 1985, 44. The English translations of the French are my own. See also Plouvier, who remarks on Nietzsche and Char's common sense of "lightness" and "marvel" in their confrontation with the world (1997, 218, 221-22).

20. See "Riche de larmes" (Rich with tears), one of Char's last poems: "Art is made of oppression and tragedy, themselves punctured occasionally by the onslaught of a joy which floods art's site, then leaves again" (*Eloge d'une soupçonnée, OC* 841).

21. See Char's "Nous avons" (*La Parole en archipel,* 1962), where a volcanic cataclysm kindles the poetic image and instills tension within freshness: "Notre parole, en archipel, vous offre, après la douleur et le désastre, des fraises qu'elle rapporte des landes de la mort, ainsi que ses doigts chauds de les avoir cherchées" [Our word, in the form of an archipelago, offers you, after pain and disaster, strawberries that it brings back from the moors of death, fingers still warm from the picking] (*OC* 409).

22. Historically, Nietzsche approved of Baudelaire in a way, as his letter to Peter Gast, dated 26 February 1888, makes clear in the context of the public reception of Wagner's music: "Wagner himself . . . surpasses a thousand times the understanding and the comprehension of the Germans. Does he surpass that of the French as well?" Nietzsche had often mused that the Frenchman most likely to appreciate Wagner "was that bizarre, three-quarters lunatic Baudelaire, the poet of *Les Fleurs du Mal.* It had disappointed me that this kindred spirit of Wagner's had not during his lifetime discovered him; I have underlined the passages in his poems in which there is a sort of *Wagnerian sensibility* which has found no form anywhere else in poetry (Baudelaire is a *libertine,* mystical, 'satanic,' but, above all, Wagnerian)" (author's emphases). Nietzsche then tells Gast of his discovery of the existence of a letter from Wagner to Baudelaire (see Nietzsche 1996, 286-88). See Delesalle, who refers in passing to this letter ("Eugène Crépet," 8 n. 16). Char seems unaware of these documents, but the thrust of "Baudelaire Irritates Nietzsche" goes to other issues.

23. Contrast "L'Etranger" with another poem in *Le Spleen de Paris,* "La Soupe et les nuages" (*OC* 1:298), where the poet becomes a useless "marchand de nuages" (cloud merchant). Remorse and self-deprecation return, like obsessions, to line the clouds.

24. See Veyne 1990, 313; Mathieu 1984-85, 1:121 n. 75, 2:90 n. 4. See also Nietzsche 1992, 63, among many other passages on the Apollonian and the Dionysian.

25. See La Charité on the crucial interplay of night and day in the collection *La Nuit talismanique*: "While light imagery may indeed tend to dominate Char's work, the creation of the active diurnal text is dependent on the order and prestige of night" (1973, 278). Some of the poems in the original edition of *La Nuit talismanique* were illustrated by Char, though not "Baudelaire Irritates Nietzsche." On the relation of image to text in this collection, see La Charité (1976), "Beyond the Poem."

26. We find an aesthetic pantheon in "Les Phares," but the notion of verse as sacrifice or defiance laid at God's feet goes against Char's impulse.

27. See de Man 1983, "Lyric and Modernity," 184.

FURTHER READING

Criticism

Baker, Peter. "Postmodern Poetics of Community: Perse and Char." In *Obdurate Brilliance: Exteriority and the Modern Long Poem,* pp. 65-75. Gainesville, Fla.: University of Florida, 1991.
  Comparison of works of Saint-John Perse and René Char.

Bracher, Nathan. "History, Violence, and Poetics: Saint-John Perse and René Char." *Studies in Twentieth Century Literature* 15, no. 2 (summer 1991): 317-34.
  Similarities and differences in the works of Perse and Char.

Caws, Mary Ann. *The Presence of René Char,* Princeton, N.J.: Princeton University Press, 1976,

Thematic and aesthetic overview of the works of Char.

LaCharité, Virginia A. "René Char and the Ascendancy of Night." *French Forum* 1, no. 3 (September 1976): 269-80.
  Examines the motif of light in Char's works.

Lawler, James R. *René Char: The Myth and the Poem,* Princeton, N.J.: Princeton University Press, 1978,
  Critical analysis of Char's poetry.

Noland, Carrie Jaurès. "The Performance of Solitude: Baudelaire, Rimbaud, and the Resistance Poetry of René Char." *The French Review* 70, no. 4 (March 1997): 562-74.
  Char's adoption of the poetics of solitude and resistance.

————. "Messages personnels: Radio Cryptography, and the Resistance Poetry of René Char." In *Poetry at Stake: Lyric Aesthetics and the Challenge of Technology,* pp. 141-62. Princeton, N.J.: Princeton University Press, 1999.
  Exploration of the influence of wartime communication technology on the aesthetics of Char's poetry of resistance.

Additional coverage of Char's life and career is contained in the following sources published by the Gale Group: *Contemporary Authors,* **Vols. 13-16R;** *Contemporary Authors New Revision Series,* **Vol. 32;** *Contemporary Authors—Obituary,* **Vol. 124;** *Contemporary Literary Criticism,* **Vols. 9, 11, 14, 55;** *Dictionary of Literary Biography,* **Vol. 258;** *Discovering Authors Modules—Poets;* *Encyclopedia of World Literature in the 20th Century,* **Ed. 3;** *Guide to French Literature,* **Vol. 1789 to the Present;** *Literature Resource Center;* *Major 20th-Century Writers,* **Eds. 1, 2;** **and** *Reference Guide to World Literature,* **Eds. 2, 3.**

Dafydd ap Gwilym
c. 1320-c. 1380

Medieval Welsh poet.

The following entry provides criticism on Dafydd's poetry from 1978 through 1995.

INTRODUCTION

Dafydd ap Gwilym is recognized as one of the most innovative European poets of the Middle Ages. His refined and erudite verse introduced a unique brand of poetry into the turbulent society of Wales during the aftermath of its loss of independence. While drawing on the contemporary elements of bardic poetry, his themes of love and nature embedded in original metric forms was a revolutionary technique. Though his work is relatively obscure outside of Wales today, largely due to difficulties in translation, Dafydd is still recognized as a radical poet of great significance in his era.

BIOGRAPHICAL INFORMATION

Much of the information known regarding the life of Dafydd ap Gwilym has been inferred from his own poetic writings and those of his contemporaries. Verifiable historical data is scarce from this period, but it is estimated that Dafydd was born circa 1320 at Brogynin in Wales. A few years later, he and his parents moved to nearby Llanbadarn Fawr, Aberystwyth. His father, Gwilym Gam ap Gwilym, traced his ancestry to Gwynfardd Dyfed, who is reputed to have sired numerous families in southwest Wales. Dafydd came from a family of fair wealth that included several high government officials under the English crown. As such, he was a self-described member of the "clêr," or peripatetic intellectuals of affluent families, never possessing nor needing a steady occupation. He appears to have traveled extensively throughout Wales and Anglesey visiting friends throughout his life; however, only one poem, centered in Chester, indicates he ever journeyed beyond the borders of the country. Much of his work suggests he generally remained near Aberystwyth for the greater part of his life, very close to where he spent his childhood. Dafydd was known to have been closely acquainted with contemporary poets Gruffudd ab Adda, Madog Benfras, and Gruffudd Gryg, among others. However it was his uncle, Llywelyn ap Gwilym, who is credited as having the greatest influence on Dafydd's development as a writer. The constable of Newcastle Emlyn, Llywelyn was responsible for his early education as well as his introduction to traditional bardic work and romantic Anglo-Norman poetry—the amalgamation of which comprised Dafydd's later work and gained him his infamy. Dafydd died around 1380 and was buried at Strata Florida monastery, near Pontrhydfendigaid. Though the building itself is now in ruins, a slate memorial remains there, dedicated to the native poet.

MAJOR WORKS

Dafydd ap Gwilym is best known for his utilization of *cywydd,* or a contemporaneous form of metric poetry consisting of couplets of seven-syllabled lines, rhyming asymmetrically. As one of the greatest proponents of what was a newly-developed style, he played a vital role in its rapid evolution into a popular and accepted form of praise-poetry, gaining timeless esteem. Dafydd generally tailored his own *cywyddau* to thirty to sixty lines, almost always focusing on his two passions: love and nature. These themes have become synonymous with his work, appearing most often together in scenarios of romantic affairs taking place in idealistic woodland settings. His characteristic plot entails his building a shelter of leaves or branches to which he retreats with his lover—generally the golden-haired Morfudd or the dark-haired Dyddgu—as a haven from the conventions of society. In these poems, it is very difficult to distinguish to what extent Dafydd is speaking of reality or his imagination, as it is believed that much of his work was fantasies on his own love life. However, ultimately it is the forest setting itself which is his true focus. Dafydd often invented "love-messengers" in the form of various woodland animals or natural forces, in which he incorporated the stylistic technique of *dyfalu,* or a protracted depiction of an entity through an extended string of similes or comparisons, also closely linked to the development of *cywydd.* Through these heralds, Dafydd was able to fully convey his ardor for nature and exploit his creative imagery. In one of his most famous poems, "The Wind," thirty of the poem's thirty-five lines are devoted to the personification of the title "character" while persuading it to fly faster to the poet's mistress. Dafydd's contribution to *cywydd* and *dyfalu* was a true revolution in fourteenth-century Welsh poetry, inspiring contemporaneous poets to rise to a new level of imagination and style.

CRITICAL RECEPTION

Dafydd's critical reception in his own time may only be deduced from elegies composed for him by his contemporaries, such as Gruffudd Gryg, Iolo Goch, and Madog Benfras. His work was initially condemned for its departure from traditional verse and its introduction of irrelevant and inappropriate personal sentiments. However, following a lengthy heated written debate among his contemporaries, Dafydd was finally recognized as the master of a new love poetry, deemed an "architect of words" and an "architect of song." Today, Dafydd's work has not been widely acclaimed outside of Wales primarily due to difficulty in translation. Alteration of the metric flow of the poetry as well as loss of meaning through inexact phrasing has caused the English version to dull the brilliance of the original text, written over six centuries ago. However, those modern critics who have successfully analyzed Dafydd's writing have extolled it for its considerable ingenuity and comparative importance in the historical development of European poetry, especially in the areas of love poetry, informal addresses to fellow poets, and objective verse.

PRINCIPAL WORKS

Poetry

Barddoniaeth Dafydd ab Gwilym (edited by Owen Jones, William Owen, and Edward Williams) 1789

Cywyddau Dafydd ap Gwilym a'i Gyfoeswyr (edited by Ifor Williams and Thomas Roberts) 1914; revised edition 1935

Gwaith Dafydd ap Gwilym (edited by Thomas Parry) 1952; revised edition 1979

The Oxford Book of Welsh Verse [contributor] (edited by Thomas Parry) 1962

Principal English Translations

Fifty Poems (translated by H. I. Bell and David Bell) 1942

A Celtic Miscellany [contributor] (translated by K. Jackson) 1951

The Burning Tree (translated by Gwyn Williams) 1956

Medieval Welsh Lyrics [contributor] (translated by J. P. Clancy) 1965

The Penguin Book of Welsh Verse [contributor] (translated by A. Conran) 1967

The Oxford Book of Welsh Verse in English [contributor] (edited by Gwyn Jones) 1977

Twenty-five Poems by Dafydd ap Gwilym (translated by Nigel Heseltine) 1982

Dafydd ap Gwilym: A Selection of Poems (translated by Rachel Bromwich) 1985

House of Leaves (translated by Rachel Bromwich) 1993

Dafydd ap Gwilym: His Poems (translated by Gwyn Thomas) 2001

CRITICISM

Helen Fulton (essay date May 1978)

SOURCE: Fulton, Helen. "The Love Poetry of Dafydd ap Gwilym." *Aumla,* no. 49 (May 1978): 22-37.

[*In the following essay, Fulton compares and contrasts the poetry of Dafydd ap Gwilym to that of Chaucer, suggesting that while both are creative yet traditionalist, Dafydd distinguishes himself with his unique praise-poetry of love and nature.*]

In retrospect, the literary scene in fourteenth century Britain seems dominated by the figure of Chaucer. His poetry marked a new phase in the native tradition, reviving it with new blood from France, and establishing the English language finally as a major literary medium. But in another part of Britain, a poet writing in a different language was simultaneously making a vital contribution to the poetic tradition of his own people. He was the Welsh poet Dafydd ap Gwilym.[1]

Just as Chaucer was both conservative and innovatory in his contribution to English poetry, so Dafydd continued and yet modified the existing poetic models of Wales. Unlike Chaucer, however, he inherited a centuries-old tradition of formal praise-poetry, composed by a socially important class of professional bards writing for royal and aristocratic patrons.[2] Conservative and backward-looking by nature, the bards continued to use the same metres and themes as their predecessors even after the fall of the royal families and the loss of Welsh independence. By the time Dafydd was writing, about 1350 to 1360, Wales had been under the jurisdiction of the English crown for nearly a century, and Dafydd and his contemporaries were composing their poems for a new class of noblemen, the *uchelwyr.* Dafydd himself belonged to one of these aristocratic families, whose members often held important office as administrators of the Principality. The background to Dafydd's poetry, therefore, is as aristocratic as that supposed for the author of *Sir Gawain and the Green Night,* or even, though on a smaller scale, that of Chaucer himself.

The innovations made by Dafydd ap Gwilym (literally, David son of William) are, broadly speaking, in the areas of metre and content. Expertise in the use of a large variety of complex metres was an essential attribute of the professional bards. While Dafydd was obviously proficient in the metres considered appropriate for serious poetry, he chose to use a simple metre, the *cywydd,* borrowed from popular poetry, for the majority of his poems.[3] His subject matter is also a departure from the traditional eulogies and elegies: inspired in part by the dominant theme of *amour courtois* in French poetry, Dafydd's work is largely lyrical and subjective, extolling love and nature with a freshness and sensitivity which brought a new mood to medieval Welsh poetry.[4]

Of the one hundred and fifty poems attributed to Dafydd ap Gwilym,[5] well over a hundred are love poems. The pursuit of love, its success or failure, had a tireless attraction for him, and presumably appealed also to his aristocratic audiences of friends, hosts and guests. His poems reflect an assortment of moods associated with love—the bliss of being with his lover, the despair after rejection, the sometimes comical disgust over a thwarted meeting, or the hope with which he sends a love message to a girl he admires. Throughout all these experiences, his tone is philosophical, often lighthearted, never bitter, and he himself emerges as a charismatic figure, full of an unquenchable joy and vitality. This is surely an impression of the poet himself, and not merely one of the persona he sometimes uses to exemplify a particular experience.

The logical counterpart of this commitment to earthly pleasures is a spontaneous appreciation of the natural world, and this Dafydd also evinces with genuine exuberance and pleasure. In fact, love itself is seen in the context of nature, with the countryside providing the natural (in both senses of the word) surroundings for the poet's encounters. His joy in seeking love is exactly paralleled by his delight in nature, in every bird, tree, plant and animal which form part of his beloved countryside. Here Dafydd is much more recognizably a successor of the earliest Welsh bards, whose affinity with nature and evocative expressions of nature imagery are endemic to Celtic poetry in its entirety.[6]

These two themes, then, love and nature, preoccupy Dafydd above all, and they are inevitably and inextricably combined in many of his poems; one is interpreted through the other. Sometimes this relationship is quite explicit, as in the poem **"I Wahodd Dyddgu"** ('Invitation to Dyddgu'), in which Dafydd imagines a woodland dwelling which his lover can share with him:

> Nid addawaf, da ddiwedd,
> I'm aur ond eos a medd;
> Eos gefnllwyd ysgafnllef

> A bronfraith ddigrifiaith gref.
> Ygus dwf, ac ystafell
> O fedw ir, a fu dŷ well?
> Tra fôm allan dan y dail,
> Ein ceinnerth fedw a'n cynnail.
> Llofft i'r adar i chwarae,
> Llwyn mwyn, llyna'r llun y mae.

> (*GDG* [*Gwaith Dafydd ap Gwilym*] no. 119, 13-22.)

[I can promise nothing (a happy ending) to my golden girl but a nightingale and mead; a grey-backed clear-voiced nightingale and a sturdy thrush of cheerful song. Is there a growth, and a room of fresh birches, which could be a better house? While we are out beneath the leaves, our fine strong birches contain us. A loft for the birds to play in: a gentle grove, behold the picture it makes.]

Here the countryside in all its natural beauty is evoked specifically as the most fitting place to meet his lover, and his joy in these surroundings reflects his anticipation of the projected meeting. A room provided by the trees, and sustenance from the bird-song, are infinitely preferable to any man-made provisions; all the necessities of life and more can be supplied by nature's own creations in the wood.

This enjoyment of earthly pleasures in simple, natural surroundings reflects Dafydd's preference for all things natural, and a corresponding rejection of artificiality. This includes the appearance of the girls he admires; in one poem he criticizes the use of jewels as ornaments, telling his lover:

> Gwell wyd mewn pais wenllwyn wiw
> Nog iarlles mewn gwisg eurlliw.

> (*GDG* no. 49, 37-38.)

[You are better, in a fitting pale petticoat, than a countess in a golden dress.]

Characteristically, throughout his love poetry, Dafydd praises a woman's eyes or mouth or hair, hardly ever her dress or jewelry or superficial appearance. A woman can be compared to a jewel, as a symbol of flawless beauty, but the only ornament she need wear is a garland of flowers.

Dafydd's rejection of artificiality extends to the form of the poetry itself. This conforms to the complex patterns of rhyme and alliteration known as *cynghanedd,*[7] an essential element of medieval Welsh poetry, yet avoids the conventional exaggerations of the courtly love tradition; the imagery is as simple and unstrained as the natural world from which it is often drawn. Compare this stanza of Chaucer's with one of Dafydd's:

> Hide, Absolon, thy gilte tresses clere;
> Ester, ley thou thy mekenesse all adown;
> Hide, Jonathas, all thy frendly manere;
> Penalopee, and Marcia Catoun,

Make of your wif hode no comparisoun;
Hide ye youre beautes, Isoude and Heleine:
My lady cometh that all this may disteine.[8]
Mal eiry y rhiw, lliw llywy,
Wyneb bun; mi a wn pwy.
    Ffynhonnau difas glasddeigr,
    Yw gloywon olygon Eigr,
Aeron glân, dirperan' glod,
Eurychaeth Mab Mair uchod.

(*GDG* no. 30, 19-24.)

[Like mountain snow, a bright colour, is the maiden's
face; I know who. Deep fountains of pale tears are the
bright eyes of Eigr, fair maid of Aeron: they deserve
praise, gold-craft of the Son of Mary above.]

The superb construction of Chaucer's stanza, and the
formality and dignity of his words, make it a very strik-
ing piece of poetic art. The repetition of *Hide,* the
invocation of beautiful women from past history,
contrast with the present tense of *My lady cometh,*
conveying pride and confidence, and emphasising her
greater beauty. There is subtlety in his *Make of your wif
hode no comparisoun*: he is implying that there can be
no comparison because his lady is by far the superior,
yet at the same time he is suggesting the comparison
himself. Dafydd's stanza does not attempt a similar
double meaning, or employ the same elevated diction,
but his figurative language gives a richness to what is
basically a simple range of words. He also compares
his lover with a legendary heroine of renowned
beauty—Eigr, the mother of Arthur—but his phrasing is
less rhetorical, less conscious of being a poetic conven-
tion, and consequently more subjective and sympathetic.
Whereas Chaucer achieves his effect through the ac-
cumulation of a number of names belonging to the same
category, Dafydd relies on a variety of simple compari-
sons and metaphors to place his girl in the world of
nature, which is also the world of God. The image of
the girl's eyes as worked gold with Christ as the
goldsmith is a skilfully controlled metaphor which
implies Dafydd's worship of both the girl and of Christ
who created her.

Dafydd's sense of comfort and fulfillment in a woodland
setting is reinforced by a contrasting mood which is
often associated with a domestic or urban environment.
His rueful and ironically humorous accounts of failures
or frustrations in love are inevitably set against the
mundane background of a house, village, or even
church, places where the poet feels confined and
disadvantaged. The poem **"Trafferth Mewn Tafarn"**
(**'Trouble in a Tavern'**; *GDG* no. 124) is an amusing
saga in the *fabliau* tradition of Dafydd's disastrous at-
tempt to keep an assignation made in a tavern, and
exemplifies the ineptness and gaucherie often attributed
by Dafydd to himself, or perhaps to a caricature of
himself, when conducting his courting within four walls.
The imagery reflects the disreputable nature of the

projected affair, with references to articles of an
unromantic and domestic flavour, such as the meal
which Dafydd consumes while making the assignation,
and the variety of stools, tables, pots and dishes with
which he involuntarily comes into contact while search-
ing for the girl's room at the dead of night. A similar
mood is created in **"Tri Phorthor Eiddig"** (**'The Three
Gatekeepers of the Jealous Husband'**; *GDG* no. 80)
in which Dafydd is kept at bay by a fierce dog, a creak-
ing door, and an old hag: these all combine to prevent
him meeting his lover, who is married to *Yr Eiddig,* the
stock figure of the 'Jealous Husband.'[9] In contrast to
these two poems is the mood evoked in **"Campau
Bun,"** (**'The Maiden's Virtues'**; *GDG* no. 56). Here
the setting is similarly domestic, but suggests comfort
and nobility rather than the more plebeian context of
the previous poems. The scene is still associated with
failure in love, as Dafydd sorrowfully laments his rejec-
tion by his girl while he sits sleepless by the fire. Thus
settings other than the woodland have a definite func-
tion in Dafydd's poetry, to provide opportunities for hu-
mour and irony, or grief and regret, and also to empha-
sise his preference for the countryside beyond the
confines of the town.

Often in Dafydd's poetry, praise of nature is seen as a
means to an end: just as he makes use of the birch trees
for his own purposes, so he rarely hesitates to appropri-
ate the birds, animals, and elements of the natural world
in order to further his pursuit of love. There are poems
to the moon, the stars, the wind, and to a large variety
of birds, many of whom are enlisted as his *llatai,* or
love-messenger, and are entrusted with a message of
praise and love for his girl. These poems characteristi-
cally begin with a sparkling description of the subject
whose very essence is captured through a lively ac-
cumulation of imagery, metaphor and personification—a
technique perfected by Dafydd and known as *dyfalu.*
This, for example, is how he describes the *ceiliog bron-
fraith,* the thrush:

Y ceiliog serchog ei sôn
Bronfraith dilediaith loywdon,
Deg loywiaith, doe a glywais,
Dawn fad lon, dan fedw ei lais,
Ba ryw ddim a fai berach
Plethiad no'i chwibaniad bach?
Plygain y darllain deirllith,
Plu yw ei gasul i'n plith.
Pell y clywir uwch tiroedd
Ei lef o lwyn a'iloyw floedd
Proffwyd rhiw, praff awdur hoed,
Pencerdd gloyw angerdd glyngoed.
Pob llais diwael yn ael nant
A gân ef o'i gu nwyfiant,
Pob caniad mad mydr angerdd,
Pob cainc o'r organ, pob cerdd,
Pob cwlm addwyn er mwyn merch.

(*GDG* no. 28, 1-17.)

[The thrush, pleasant its sound, thrush of pure accent, clear-bright, fair bright language—yesterday I heard, a merry talent, his voice under a birch tree; is there anything which could be sweeter plaited than his little whistling? Matins, he reads the three lessons, feathers his chasuble, in our midst. Far above the land is heard his cry from a grove, and his clear call. Hill prophet, great author of longing, bright poet of passion of the glen-wood. Every excellent voice in the brow of the brook, he sings from his beloved vivacity; every song a happy metre of passion, every tune of the organ, every musical art, every fine trill for the sake of a girl.]

A complex interweaving of brief images is the basis on which our impression of the thrush is constructed. Yet throughout this passage, Dafydd describes virtually nothing except the voice of the thrush, starting with its quality and leading on to the places where the bird sings, and the kind of music he makes. The thrush is personified briefly as a priest, there is the merest allusion to him as prophet and poet *par excellence*. But inevitably Dafydd sees him as one of his own kind, a poet singing in praise of love, a substitute virtuoso for Dafydd himself.

Obviously Dafydd's use of the theme of nature in love poetry is not unique or original. He was to some extent developing this combination of the two themes used by the *gogynfeirdd,* the twelfth and thirteenth century bards of Wales,[10] but he was probably influenced also by French lyrics of the period, by the techniques of Provençal troubadours and *chanson populaire,* in which the growth of love was associated with the springtime flourishing of nature.[11] However, his poetry indicates very strongly that he took this convention only to interpret it according to his own priorities, and the result is a very subjective view of Dafydd's sense of oneness with the natural world. For most English poets of the period, on the other hand, the theme of nature never became more than a conventional motif, a recognized means of establishing a particular atmosphere. Chaucer's use of nature imagery for the purposes of his narrative art in *The Canterbury Tales* is highly specialised and skilful; but this lyric poem from early fourteenth century England aims to do no more than illustrate the spring *topos* by means of a list of simple images:

The rose raileth hire rode,
The leves on the lighte wode
Waxen all with wille.
The mone mandeth hire ble,
The lilye is lossom to se,
The fennel and the fille.
Wowes this wilde drakes,
Miles murgeth huere makes,
Ase strem that striketh stille.
Mody meneth, so doth mo;
Ichot ich am on of tho
For love that likes ille.

('Lenten is come with love to toune', 13-24)[12]

The poem is relieved by its unpretentiousness and the variety of the imagery, but it lacks the subtlety and sophistication with which Dafydd ap Gwilym relates nature and love. Here the two are simply juxtaposed, with the earthy references to the *wilde drakes* and *miles* prefacing and contrasting with the poet's confession of failure in love. Compare this extract from Dafydd's poem to the month of May:

Dillyn beirdd ni'm rhydwyllai.
Da fyd ym oedd dyfod Mai.
Harddwas teg a'm anrhegai,
Hylaw ŵr mawr hael yw'r Mai.
Anfones ym iawn fwnai,
Glas defyll glân mwyngyll Mai.
Ffloringod brig ni'm digiai,
Fflŵr-dy-lis gyfoeth mis Mai.
Diongl rhag brad y'm cadwai,
Dan esgyll dail mentyll Mai.

(*GDG* no. 23, 7-16.)

[Poets' perfection, he would not deceive me, good fortune to me was the coming of May. A fair handsome youth who would bring gifts to me, a handy man, great and generous, is May. He sent to me true wealth, green slices of fair gentle twigs of May. Florins of tree-tops would not displease me, fleur-de-lis of the wealth of the May-month. Smooth, from treachery he would save me, under wings of foliage of May's mantles.]

All the conventional aspects of May—its beauty, mildness, and abundant new growth—are captured in striking images, of the handsome youth instead of the usual feminine personification, and of the bright new buds appearing like freshly minted coins. The normal extension of springtime as the season for loving is made obliquely through Dafydd's implications that May is his ally and supporter, more trustworthy and generous than any of his female lovers. Later in the poem there are brief references to a maiden whom he must appease, and to May as a love-messenger, but the whole notion of love is thoroughly integrated into the seasonal imagery so that the poet has no need to spell it out for us in the manner of the English poem.

There is another aspect of Dafydd's response to the natural world which helps to reinforce his deeply felt affinity with it: this is his habit of criticising various natural phenomena and blaming them when the course of love does not run smoothly. Thus he apostrophises the mist which descends to spoil his assignation with a girl, saying *rhestri gleision i'm rhwystraw,* 'rows of whey to hinder me', and *toron gwrddonig tiredd,* 'boorish cloak of the country' (*GDG* no. 68, 16 & 30). In another seasonal poem he compares January unfavourably with May as a blight on the normal activities of lovers:

Annhebyg i'r mis dig du
A gerydd i bawb garu.

(*GDG* no. 69, 31-32.)

'Unlike the black angry month, which punishes everyone in love.' He is not above chastising one of his love messengers either if the hapless bird is at all dilatory, as in the opening to **"Cyrchu Lleian"** (**'Fetching a Nun'**):

> Dadlitia'r diwyd latai,
> Hwnt o'r Mars dwg hynt er Mai.
> Gedaist, ciliaist myn Celi,
> Arnaf y mae d'eisiau di.
>
> (**GDG** no. 113, 1-4.)

[Shed your rage, hard-working love messenger: yonder from the Marches, take a course for May. You left, you flew away by Heaven—I have need of you!]

In yet another poem, **"Cyngor y Biogen"** (**'The Magpie's Advice'**), Dafydd and the magpie engage in an acrimonious argument about the futility of Dafydd's pursuit of love. The magpie is brutally honest, and maddeningly practical:

> Gwell yt, myn Mair air aren,
> Garllaw tân, y gŵr llwyd hen,
> Nog yma 'mhlith gwlith a glaw
> Yn yr irlwyn ar oerlaw.
>
> (**GDG** no. 63, 37-40.)

[Better for you, a wise word by St. Mary, to stay by the fire, you old grey man, then here amidst dew and rain in the green grove with the cold and wet.]

There is an amusing contrast between Dafydd's imagery before this interruption, of fresh new-leaved trees and heavenly birdsong counterpointing his mood of sweet self-pity, and his spirited retaliation against the bird's advice:

> Mwtlai wyd di, mae't liw tyg,
> Mae't lys hagr, mae't lais hygryg.
>
> (**GDG** no. 63, 57-58.)

[A motley thing you are, with your fine colour and your disreputable following and your croaking voice.]

The ease with which Dafydd personifies the woodland inhabitants reflects his complete communion with them, a relationship founded firmly on respect and love. He feels at home in natural surroundings, able to be himself and follow his own desires. He has no scruples about recruiting the aid of anything at hand, be it bird, tree, season or weather, but at the same time he is looking for approval and support from the countryside, an acknowledgement that nature is his ally and refuge. The occasional realization that natural forces cannot always be manipulated at his will is both a source of wonder to him and a cause for complaint.

Dafydd ap Gwilym's love poetry therefore has some affinities with the mainstream of medieval European lyric poetry, in his use of conventional nature *topoi* and a subjective view of love; but his approach to the theme of nature in connection with the pursuit of love is strikingly original and fresh. Similarly, he has been influenced by some of the concepts of *fin amor,* as is shown by his occasional comparisons of girls with the sun or the moon, and his use of recognizable metaphors such as being wounded by the shaft of love. But again, he takes these conventions only to mould them to his own ideals of the nature of love and its place in his life. He is neither the swooning love-servant nor the courtly lover nobly suffering the pangs of unrequited love, both of whom appear in Chaucer's poetry. Rather than addressing doleful poems to the object of his love, he vents his emotions on the world of nature, using it as a go-between, and his polished use of this technique sets him apart from his contemporaries, both within and outside Wales.

The second major departure in Dafydd's poetry is his method of incorporating a religious theme into much of his work. None of his poems are purely devotional in the manner of many Latin, French and English lyrics of the Middle Ages, but love of God is as pervasive in his work as his enjoyment of secular love. In fact, by linking both kinds of love to his appreciation of nature, Dafydd manages to imply an equation between the two which is audacious but never blasphemous. Just as he regards the woodland as the natural place to meet his lover, so he sees it also as the most fitting place to worship God, in preference to man-made churches and orthodox doctrine. He uses God's creations as a medium through which he can reach God himself, as well as a medium for the expression of secular love.

This dual function of nature is clearly expressed in one of his most famous poems, **"Offeren Y Llwyn"** (**'The Mass of the Grove'**). In this, a grove of birch trees is imagined to be a form of church, a sacred area of worship, and a thrush is personified as the priest, but also as a love-messenger:

> Pellennig, pwyll ei annwyd,
> Pell ei siwrnai'r llatai llwyd.
> Yma y doeth o swydd goeth Gaer,
> Am ei erchi ò'm eurchwaer,
> Geiriog, heb un gair gwarant,
> Sef y cyrch, i Nentyrch nant.
> Morfudd a'i hanfonasai,
> Mydr ganiadaeth mab maeth Mai . . .
>
> Mi a glywwn mewn gloywiaith
> Ddatganu, nid methu, maith,
> Darllain i'r plwyf, nid rhwyf rhus,
> Efengyl yn ddifyngus.
>
> (**GDG** no. 122, 7-14, 21-24.)

[From far away, discretion his nature, far the journey of the holy love-messenger. He came here, from Carmarthen's rich county, because he was asked by my golden girl—wordy, without one word of safe-

conduct—to this very spot, to Nentyrch brook. Mor-
fudd had sent him, a metre of singing of a son of May's
nurture. . . .

I heard in bright language a chanting, without faltering,
for a long time; a reading to the people, not too spirited,
of the gospel, without mumbling.]

The status of the thrush is immediately evident in *Ilatai
llwyd,* 'holy love messenger'. The adjective *llwyd* can
also mean 'grey', referring to the colour of the bird,
and even suggesting the robes of a monk. He is sancti-
fied because he sings in the service of God, but also
because he carries a sacred message from Dafydd's girl,
Morfudd. Thus, by extension, Dafydd's love is also
exalted and glorified, so that he obtains the approval
not only of the natural world, but of God himself.

This element of self-justification and self-interest is a
pervasive part of his love poetry, symbolized by his
easy appropriation of God's creations for his own
purposes. He tends to interpret religious doctrine and
the will of God in ways which are most favourable to
his own interests on earth rather than to the securing of
a place in Heaven. He sees religion as an inherent part
of his lifestyle, and not a separate activity confined to
Sundays in church. Religious imagery is inseparably
bound to his perceptions of nature, just as the world of
nature is the ever-present setting for his love encounters,
so that religion, nature, and love are but three aspects
of the same response to the world. When Dafydd is
walking in the darkness thinking of his lover, he praises
the moon as his only source of light, referring to it as
afrlladen o nen y nef, 'mass wafer from the roof of
heaven', and *dysgl saig y saint,* 'feast cup of the saints'
(*GDG* no. 67, 28 & 30). Similarly, the lark is personi-
fied as a chorister, a preacher of God—*cantor o gapel
Celi,* 'singer in the chapel of Heaven' (*GDG* no. 114,
27)—in order to express the poet's pleasure in the bird
as a potential servant of his own, to carry a love-
message to his girl.

So convincing is Dafydd's imagery that even to his
listeners there seems nothing incongruous in his ap-
plication of religious terminology to his purely secular
concerns. Moreover, he goes further than borrowing
church property for his metaphors and God's creations
for his love messages, and actually appeals to saints,
monks and nuns to assist him. In **"Galw ar Ddwyn-
wen,"** ('**Appeal to Dwynwen'**; *GDG* no. 94) he asks
the patron saint of lovers, Dwynwen, to intercede for
him with his lover Morfudd, using all the conventional
religious devices of prayers, offerings and appeals to a
saint, in an attempt to move Morfudd by heavenly
means when earthly ones have failed. This procedure is
at least orthodox and acceptable, whereas Dafydd's
determination to obtain a nun from the convent in
another poem (**"Cyrchu Lleian,"** ['**Fetching a Nun'**;
GDG no. 113]) is bold to the point of blasphemy.

Dafydd, however, has a genuine love of God that
precludes deliberate and direct blasphemy. He may find
the rigid approach to worship as exemplified by monks
and nuns, and even communal services in church,
restricting and remote from his own conception of God,
but he nonetheless possesses a very fundamental belief
in the enveloping presence of God, a presence which he
finds reflected in the natural world. His love of nature
therefore has a two-fold basis, being an earthly paradise
on the one hand where he can woo his lovers, and at
the same time a means of de-mystifying God, of bring-
ing God into his own secular world rather than attempt-
ing to reach up to God through monasticism and
religious doctrine.

His stance is made explicitly clear in **"Y Bardd a'r
Brawd Llwyd,"** ('**The Poet and the Grey Friar**'; *GDG*
no. 137) in which Dafydd converses with a monk and
defends the orthodoxy of celebrating love. The monk
represents the critics of Dafydd's love poetry, real or
imagined. He says:

> Mi a rown yt gyngor da:
> O cheraist eiliw ewyn,
> Lliw papir, oed hir hyd hyn,
> Llaesa boen y dydd a ddaw;
> Lles yw i'th enaid beidiaw,
> A thewi â'r cywyddau,
> Ac arfer o'th baderau.

> (*GDG* no. 137, 20-26.)

['I will give you some good advice: if you have loved
the foam-coloured one, colour of paper, for a long time
until now, lessen the pain of the day which is coming;
there is benefit for your soul if you cease, and are silent
with your rhymes, and practise your prayers.']

This is the kind of attitude that Dafydd rejects most
strongly in his love poetry, the idea that secular love
and religious devotion have no place together and
should be rigidly separated; and also the notion that a
preoccupation with secular pursuits automatically closes
the gates of Heaven. He replies in witty rhetoric which
challenges the Friar's own ability to sermonize:

> Nid ydyw Duw mor greulon
> Ag y dywaid hen ddynion.
> Ni chyll Duw enaid gŵr mwyn
> Er caru gwraig na morwyn.
> Tripheth a gerir drwy'r byd:
> Gwraig a hinon ac iechyd . . .

> O'r nef y cad digrifwch
> Ac o uffern bob tristwch.
> Cerdd a bair yn llawenach
> Hen ac ieuanc, claf ac iach.
> Cyn rheitied i mi brydu
> Ag i tithau bregethu.
> A chyn iawned ym glera
> Ag i tithau gardota.
> Pand englynion ac odlau

Yw'r hymnau a'r segwensiau? . . .

Amser a rodded i fwyd
Ac amser i olochwyd,
Ac amser i bregethu,
Ac amser i gyfaneddu.

(***GDG*** no. 137, 37-42; 49-58; 63-66.)

['God is not as cruel as old men say. God will not lose the soul of a gentle man for loving a woman or a maiden. There are three things loved throughout the world: a woman, and fine weather, and good health . . .

From heaven is obtained pleasure, and from hell every sadness. It is poetry which brings more joy to old and young, sick and well. It is as necessary for me to compose verse as for you to preach, and as fitting for me to wander as a minstrel as for you to seek alms. Are not the hymns and sequences but englyns and odes? . . .

There is given a time for food and a time for prayer, a time for preaching and a time for entertaining.']

Thus Dafydd defends his profession as a poet and his obligation to entertain with his songs and poems, using a diction and syntax which is strongly reminiscent of biblical oratory. The oppositions of Heaven and Hell, old and young, sick and whole; the list of the three things universally loved; the rhetorical question—these are all devices of learned rhetoric used in formal speeches and sermons. In addition, the sequence using the repetition of *amser,* 'time', is surely a brief allusion to the famous passage in Ecclesiastes 3, beginning 'A time to be born, and a time to die.'

Dafydd has clearly beaten the Grey Friar on his own ground, and his clever use of rhetoric and imagery make his argument very convincing, despite its essential tenuousness. It is partly a matter of his adopting the pleasanter of two lifestyles, a choice which he attempts, successfully, to justify by expressing his conviction, based on supreme optimism rather than definite proof, that God does not disapprove of his enjoyment of earthly love. Dafydd is therefore able to satisfy himself, and his listeners, that his association of the natural world and the spiritual world as interchangeable elements in his imagery of secular love is entirely orthodox and praiseworthy.

This same poem provides another example of Dafydd's creative adaptation of a conventional poetic mode to something out of the ordinary. Debate or dialogue poems are common in medieval France and England, both in Latin and the vernacular. These are either secular, in which a lover converses with his lady, or religious, often involving a debate between the body and the soul, or perhaps between Jesus and one of his disciples.[13] Another kind of debate poem is that in which the respective merits of poet or scholar and a soldier or

knight are argued, and Dafydd has also written a poem on this theme.[14] But the combination of the religious and the secular, as in **"Y Bardd a'r Brawd Llwyd,"** is not handled so wittily elsewhere; the idea of opposing a man of religion and a poet devoted to the pursuit of worldly pleasures did not occur to the minstrels and poets of Europe. Dafydd's poem has a particular relevance within the context of his own poetic corpus, but it reinforces the fact that he was not composing his poetry in a vacuum and indeed was able to make original contributions to the established poetic traditions of Europe.

In Dafydd ap Gwilym, then, we find another fourteenth century poet, whose output was large, and whose name was well-known within his own country, translating contemporary European poetic conventions into his own language and into the context of an already established native tradition. For these reasons alone, Dafydd merits a place in any overview of medieval poetry. Moreover, his poems in themselves are works of art, the result of an innate harmony between language and metre. He has been called a love poet and a nature poet, but to classify him as one is to negate the simultaneous presence of the other, for the two themes are virtually inseparable. Secular love and religious worship are intimately connected with his love of nature and, unlike other medieval poets, Dafydd enjoys the natural world as much for its own sake as for the possibilities it provides for secular and spiritual love. His is a personal philosophy, not the mere reflection of a school of thought, and through images of nature and devotion and worldly love he states his basic need for freedom to pursue earthly joy on his own terms, and thereby to find the spiritual support on which he depends so greatly.

Notes

1. For the life of Dafydd ap Gwilym, see Rachel Bromwich, *Dafydd ap Gwilym,* Writers of Wales series, University of Wales Press, Cardiff, 1974.

2. See J. Lloyd-Jones, 'The Court Poets of the Welsh Princes', *Proceedings of the British Academy* vol. 34 (1948), 167-197; H. I. Bell, *The Development of Welsh Poetry,* Oxford, 1936; H. I. Bell, *The Nature of Poetry as conceived by the Welsh Bards,* Taylorian Lecture 1955, Oxford, 1955.

3. For an introduction to bardic metres and *cynghanedd,* see Thomas Parry, *A History of Welsh Literature,* translated by H. I. Bell, Oxford, 1955, pp. 121-126, 133-149; and Gwyn Williams, *An Introduction to Welsh Poetry,* Faber & Faber Ltd., London, 1953, pp. 232-247.

4. The nature of Dafydd's contribution to fourteenth century Welsh poetry is discussed by Rachel Bromwich in *Tradition and Innovation in the Poetry of Dafydd ap Gwilym,* University of Wales Press, Cardiff, 1967; reprinted 1972.

5. I refer to the definitive edition of Dafydd's poems by Thomas Parry, *Gwaith Dafydd ap Gwilym,* University of Wales Press, Cardiff, 1952; second edition 1963. This edition (1963) is henceforth abbreviated to *GDG,* and all quotations are taken from it, using Parry's numbers.

6. The earliest Celtic nature poetry, both Welsh and Irish, was often gnomic in character; these are discussed and translated by K. H. Jackson in *Early Celtic Nature Poetry,* Cambridge, 1935; reprinted Folcroft Library Editions, Pa., 1974 (limited edition). For a wider view, see J. Glyn Davies, 'The Welsh Bard and the Poetry of External Nature', *Transactions of the Honourable Society of Cymmrodorion* (1912-1914), 81-128.

7. See note 3.

8. This extract is taken from R. T. Davies (Ed.), *Medieval English Lyrics,* Faber & Faber Ltd., London, 1963, p. 134.

9. For a translation of these two poems, and others by Dafydd, see J. P. Clancy, *Medieval Welsh Lyrics,* Macmillan, London, 1965. Dafydd's motif of the Jealous Husband may well have its origins in 'Le Jaloux' of the *Roman de la Rose:* for a discussion of the character see John V. Fleming, *The Roman de la Rose, A Study in Allegory and Iconography,* Princeton University Press, 1969, p. 154 ff.; Henry Ansgar Kelly, *Love and Marriage in the Age of Chaucer,* Cornell University Press, 1975, p. 39 ff.

10. In particular, poems of the *gogynfeirdd* ('quite early poets') known as *gorhoffedd* or 'boasting' poems, illustrate most clearly the native tradition which influenced Dafydd. See, for example, a poem of the twelfth century prince of North Wales, Hywel ab Owain Gwynedd, beginning

> I love a fine hillside's shining fortress,
> Where a fair girl loves watching a seagull,

in J. P. Clancy, *The Earliest Welsh Poetry,* Macmillan, 1970, p. 129.

11. For examples of this, see Peter Dronke, *The Medieval Lyric,* Hutchinson University Library, London, 1968, especially the love poem by the twelfth century Guillaume of Aquitaine, p. 115, and the chapter on the *alba,* p. 167 ff. Other examples can be found in J. J. Wilhelm, *Seven Troubadours, The Creators of Modern Verse,* Pennsylvania State University Press, 1970, pp. 48-50; and L. T. Topsfield, *Troubadours and Love,* Cambridge University Press, 1975, pp. 74-78. Rachel Bromwich discusses the possible influence of the *Roman de la Rose* and *reverdie* poems on Dafydd in *Tradition and Innovation in the Poetry of Dafydd ap Gwilym* (op. cit.).

12. Davies, *Medieval English Lyrics* (op. cit.), p. 84.

13. For a survey of secular debate poems in Latin, see the section on 'The Poetical Debate' in F. J. E. Raby, *A History of Secular Latin Poetry in the Middle Ages,* vol. 2, Oxford, 1934; second edition 1957, pp. 282-308. Raby mentions the most popular types of debate—e.g. between summer and winter, knight and clerk, death and man—and gives examples of several, especially love debates. Examples of dialogue poems in Middle English and Provençal poetry can be found in Davies, *Medieval English Lyrics* (op. cit.), p. 75 (between Judas and Christ), and J. J. Wilhelm, *Seven Troubadours* (op. cit.), p. 80 (a pastoral poem by Marcabrun describing an encounter between a nobleman and a shepherdess).

14. *GDG.* No. 58, *Merch yn Edliw Ei Lyfrdra,* 'A girl reproaches his Cowardice'. Other debate or dialogue poems by Dafydd include No. 77, *Amau ar Gam,* in which Dafydd questions Morfudd's love; and No. 141, *Ei Gysgod,* 'His Shadow', which is similar to a debate between body and soul.

Rachel Bromwich (essay date 1979)

SOURCE: Bromwich, Rachel. "The Earlier *Cywyddwyr:* Poets Contemporary with Dafydd ap Gwilym." In *A Guide to Welsh Literature,* pp. 144-60. Wales: Christopher Davies Ltd., 1979.

[*In the following excerpt, Bromwich analyzes the metre of the works of Dafydd and his contemporaries, and its societal and artistic implications.*]

The following lively fragment describing a horse is quoted in each of the four early versions of the Bardic Grammar as an example of the metre *cywydd deuair hirion,* which was to become the increasingly favoured medium of fourteenth-century poets:

Breichffyrf, archgrwn, byr ei flew,	Strong of foreleg, round-chested, short-haired,
Llyfn, llygadrwth, pedreindew,	Sleek, keen-eyed, thick-haunched,
Cyflwydd coflaid, cyrch amcaff,	Victorious darling, greedy for oats,
Cyflym, cefnfyr, carn geugraff,	Swift, short-backed, firm and hollow-hoofed,
Cyflawn o galon a chig,	Fulfilled in spirit and in flesh,
Cyfliw blodau'r banadlfrig.	One hue with the flower-tips of the broom.

This is evidently an excerpt from a poem of request or thanks for the gift of a horse, but beyond this the authorship and provenance of the fragment are equally unknown. If we knew by whom and at what time the lines were composed, this knowledge would be of the greatest value towards elucidating the origin of the *cywydd.* Metrically, these lines are a crude and inadequate illustration of the metre as it came to be developed by Dafydd ap Gwilym and his contemporaries. Only the first and the third of the three couplets of which it is composed have end-rhyme between accented and unaccented syllables, such as later became obligatory, and *cynghanedd* appears only in an incipient or rudimentary form most evident in the alliterating initial words of the last four lines. Apart from the predilection for compound words in describing the horse, there is little that can be related to the art of *dyfalu* as this was developed in the poetry of Dafydd ap Gwilym.

Yet the lines are a fair example of the verse-type known as the *traethodl,* which was practised by the poets of subordinate status called the *clêr* (the *clerici vagantes*), to whom Dafydd ap Gwilym, as has been seen, acknowledged a somewhat ambivalent allegiance. The *cywydd* came into being in direct descent from the *traethodl,* by the endowment of the latter with full *cynghanedd,* and the tightening up of the rule as to the a-symmetrical final rhymes. Except in occasional instances, such as his dialogue with the Grey Friar, which is composed in the looser form of the *traethodl,* the *cywydd deuair hirion* was Dafydd's choice for all those kinds of verse which departed radically in their subject-matter from the older tradition of praise-poetry—for verses of familiar personal address to friends and to his patron Ifor Hael, and above all for poetry concerned with the love-theme in its various aspects, most characteristically set against a background of wild woodland scenery. Yet with hindsight we can see that the literary development in fourteenth-century Wales, which was at least as far-reaching in its consequences as were Dafydd's thematic innovations, was this very transference into the medium of the *cywydd* of all the traditional apparatus of praise-poetry, as this had been practised by previous generations. Without this development, which secured lasting prestige for the *cywydd,* the poetry of love and nature might not itself have persisted, in the way that it did, to remain a lasting and recognisable constituent in the poetic tradition of Wales.

Since Dafydd ap Gwilym adhered to the traditional *awdl* for his 'genuine' praise-poems and elegies, he cannot with any probability be regarded as the innovator responsible for the adaptation of the *cywydd* to *canu mawl.* Some other powerful influence must be postulated as having lain behind the emergence, in the middle years of the fourteenth century, of *cywyddau* paying tribute to patrons, and re-creating within the new medium all the inherited concepts of the *awdlau* of the *Gogynfeirdd.* The verse of five poets needs to be considered in relation to that of Dafydd ap Gwilym, if we are to obtain anything approaching to a correct perspective of his achievement. These were Iolo Goch, Llywelyn Goch ap Meurig Hen, Gruffudd Gryg, Madog Benfras and Gruffudd ab Adda, all of whom appear to have been closely contemporary with each other and also with Dafydd himself. References in contemporary legal documents place this beyond reasonable doubt in the case of Madog Benfras and Gruffudd Gryg, showing that they may be presumed to have reached man's estate by the year 1340: these two, in addition to Gruffudd ab Adda, were certainly known personally to Dafydd. It is a significant and striking fact that all five of these pioneer poets of the *cywydd* belonged to north or to northeast Wales: not one of them, like Dafydd himself, belonged to the south. Iolo Goch came from the Vale of Clwyd, Gruffudd Gryg from Anglesey, Llywelyn Goch ap Meurig Hen from Meirionydd, Madog Benfras from Marchwiail near Wrexham in Powys, and Gruffudd ab Adda also from Powys. The likelihood that all five were closely contemporary with Dafydd himself has been obscured by the fact that whereas there are no certainly datable poems by Dafydd composed after the 1350s, Gruffudd Gryg was still composing in the 1370s, and probably later, while Iolo Goch and Llywelyn Goch, whose earliest *cywyddau mawl* of certain date belong to the 1350s, were still active in the final decades of the century: both speaking of themselves in their last poems as being very old men. These two, it would seem, may actually have survived to reach their eighties—a remarkable attainment in the fourteenth century. All five had passed away before the end of the century, and did not live to witness Glyndŵr's revolt.

All of these poets composed love-poems in the *cywydd* form. Indeed, all the main types of *cywyddau* composed by Dafydd ap Gwilym are represented in the work of one or other of them: by all there are *cywyddau* of love and of love-complaint addressed to girls; there are poems showing affinity with the Continental *fabliaux* (Madog Benfras and Iolo Goch), *llatai* or love-messenger poems (Gruffudd Gryg and—probably—Llywelyn Goch) and poems abusing friars (Iolo Goch), besides religious *cywyddau* (all of them but Madog Benfras and Gruffudd ab Adda). The poetry that has been preserved in the name of each of these poets is very much smaller in quantity than is the accepted canon of Dafydd ap Gwilym. Of the five, Iolo Goch has by far the largest number of poems ascribed to him, and is second in stature only to Dafydd himself, though very different from him in the main features of his verse. On the existing evidence, Madog Benfras is the least distinguished of the five, though it is he who is the most plainly under the influence of Dafydd ap Gwilym, without distinctive inspiration of his own. But much of his verse, and indeed of that of the others, may be presumed to have been lost, or may perhaps in a few instances be recoverable among the 'apocryphal' *cywyddau,* now rejected by Dr Parry as belonging to the canon of Dafydd ap Gwilym's own work. There exists in the manuscripts the same kind of confusion with regard to the authorship of individual poems by these poets as is the case with Dafydd himself, and their verse—again like his—has in the main survived only in late copies which have suffered all the vagaries of both scribal and earlier oral corruption.

Yet among the poems which may with confidence be ascribed to these poets there have come down a handful of highly original and exceptional *cywyddau* which deserve to be placed on a par with Dafydd's finest work: Gruffudd Gryg's *cywyddau* 'To the Moon' and 'To the Wave', Gruffudd ab Adda's poem to the Birch-tree uprooted and placed as a may-pole in the town of Llanidloes, Iolo Goch's praise of the labourer or plough-man, his dialogue between the Soul and Body (which effectively burlesques the old convention of such dialogues, to describe a *taith clera* or bardic circuit between the homes of his patrons), and his vivid description of the miseries of a sea-journey in his satiric *dyfalu* of a ship. There is also Llywelyn Goch's celebrated *marwnad* or lament for his beloved Lleucu Llwyd, to which I shall return later. Mutual influences are discernible in a marginal degree between all these poets, yet all but the one mentioned show strong and impressive originality. In addition to these poems, which may indeed, like Dafydd's *cywyddau*, be classified as 'personal poetry', three of the five poets composed *cy-wyddau* of a kind which is quite unparalleled in Dafy-dd's work: that is, *cywyddau mawl* and *marwnad*, or formal praise-poems addressed to patrons, including also a *dadolwch* or placatory poem asking forgiveness for offence from patrons who were also relatives (Gruffudd Gryg), and poems of asking and thanks for the gift of a horse, a dagger, and for generous hospital-ity (Iolo Goch) and for a greyhound (probably by Lly-welyn Goch, but of uncertain authorship). These are all verse-types which are attested at an earlier date in the *awdlau* of the *Gogynfeirdd*. Metrically, the verse of these poets tends to be 'couplet-structured' more often than it is 'sentence-structured' with tmesis (*torymadrodd*—with *sangiadau*), in the manner favoured by Dafydd ap Gwilym. Where the device of *dyfalu* oc-curs, it is almost always used 'pejoratively' rather than 'positively' by these poets (whereas Dafydd ap Gwilym employs it in both ways), and mainly with the purpose of satirizing the various impediments to love's game. A notable exception, however, is Iolo Goch's remarkable 'positive' *dyfalu* of the Plough in his *cywydd* to the La-bourer:

A cradle which tears the trailing broom,
a gentle creel which yet can shred the plain.
Dear is his praise, a holy relic,
a heron who opens a quick furrow.
A basket of the wild land, which will now be cultivated
with a coulter in wisely-ordered state.
A gander of the untamed acres,
true it is that grain will be had from his skill.
He drives forth crops from the heavy tilth,
a splendid creature, biting the ground.
He must have his knife and his food

and his table under his thigh.
He goes unwillingly over small stones—
a lad who flays with leg outstretched.
His snout is active daily
in a fair hollow beneath the oxen's feet.
He would often sing his hymn—
his wish is to follow the plough-chain.

But this is in every respect a remarkable poem: the fact that it is unmatched in the work of any other of the early *cywyddwyr*—except by Dafydd ap Gwilym himself—in its 'positive', rather than negative and 'pejorative', use of the device of *dyfalu,* lends force to my earlier suggestion that the main origin of this device is to be found in the elaborately figurative language of bardic satire—witness, for instance, Dafydd ap Gwi-lym's satire of Rhys Meigen. Iolo Goch was apparently inspired to compose his praise of the Labourer by the words of the *Elucidarium,* a popular twelfth-century theological treatise, which was translated into Welsh in the *Book of the Anchorite of Llanddewifrefi* and ap-peared in 1346. In a well-known passage of this work the author assigns the *clêr* (meaning, in this case, poets in general) to perdition, and contrasts them with the humble tillers of the soil, who shall be blessed because they feed the populace by the sweat of their brows. Iolo paraphrases the text of the *Elucidarium* (*Lusudarus hwylus hen* or 'fortunate old Lucidarius' is for him a person) when he quotes this authority as saying: 'Blessed is he who from boyhood holds the plough with his hands'—and he goes on to expand upon the virtues of the Labourer—he trusts in God, he pays his tithes and receives God's bounty in recompense; he is hospitable and generous to all; he does not utter an opinion on any subject but one which concerns his own craft; he dislikes all disputation and all warfare; he does not rob anyone or claim the least thing unjustly; he prefers humbly to follow the plough, rather than to be an 'Arthur' despoiling castle towers. And yet *nid by-wyd, nid byd hebddaw ef* ('there is no life, nor world without him'). As in Dafydd ap Gwilym's *cywydd* to the Wind, the picture of the Labourer is built up by a series of negative statements: the Labourer's virtues are expressed mainly by a list of the things he does *not* do. In both poems the catalogue of negatives indicates a deftly implied criticism of their opposites: in **"The Wind"** this is aimed against the 'restrictive practices' of the alien officers who administer the foreign legal system; in Iolo's poem it is obviously directed against those in high places who rob and persecute, pursue unjust claims, fail to dispense charity and hospitality, are too ready with their opinions—or interference—in matters which do not concern them, and above all, who prosecute warfare. These are the sins which are proper to the great and powerful ones of the earth, and it is surprising to find such a minutely detailed list in the work of a poet who was a pioneer in composing *cywyd-dau mawl* to just such temporal magnates as might in some cases with some justice be accused of committing them. Yet no doubt Iolo's idealized portrait of a character who embodied the opposite of all these sins was intended for a clerical rather than for a secular audience. The poem 'Piers Plowman' by the English poet Langland invites an obvious comparison; it appeared about 1370, but we have no means of knowing whether or not Iolo's *cywydd* preceded it in date of composition. The social upheavals consequent upon the Black Death are likely to have been a contributory cause behind both poems.

Another characteristic of the verse of these poets which is also significantly characteristic of Dafydd ap Gwilym's poetry is their use of personification. In the passage which has been quoted from Iolo's *cywydd* to the Labourer the plough is personified as *gŵr* and *gwas*, 'a man' and 'a lad', and 'he must have his knife and his food, and his table under his thigh'. For Gruffudd Gryg the Moon is *mursen* ('a coy wench'), while Gruffudd ab Adda's Birch-tree is poignantly addressed as if it were a sentient and suffering creature:

> Green birch-tree with bedraggled tresses, you have been long exiled from the hill-side; a lovely tree in the forest where you were reared, green-mantled, you are now a traitress to the grove. Your enclosure made a lodging for me with my darling in the short nights of May . . . Now no longer do you meditate on love, and your branches up aloft stay dumb. In your entirety, and at whatever cost, you have gone from the green slopes where you were once a miracle, to the town—a swift exchange. Though your favoured monument may seem good, in Llanidloes town, where crowds assemble, yet may I not approve, my birch-tree, either your abduction, or your present company, or your home; it is no good place for you, with long face, to bear forth new leaves. Every town-garden is able to have feathery green—was it not rash, birch-tree, to bring about your fading there—a wretched pole, beside the pillory? Have you not come, at the very time of putting forth leaves, to stand at the barren centre of the cross-roads? Although they say that your station is pleasant, birch-tree, yet it were better by far to be a roof above the brook. No bird sleeps or sings, with slender voice, in the fair precinct of your topmost branches, owing to the great clamour of the people about your tent, sister of the shady trees . . . You have been made over to bartering, and you have the look of a selling-woman; everyone will point his finger at your suffering, with joyful chatter, as you stand in your grey dress and your worn fur, amidst the trivial merchandise of the fair . . . You will no longer shelter the April primroses; no more will you have thought or care for the valley's birds, though once their fair protector . . . Choose one of the two, captive branches—your burgess-hood is a folly—either to return home to the woodland, or to wither yonder in the town.

Here again, as in Iolo Goch's *cywydd* to the Labourer, the undertones are all but audible: beneath the sensitive evocation of the birch-tree's beauty in its natural woodland setting, which is rarely matched even by

Dafydd ap Gwilym, lies a general suspicion and rejection of the crowded life of the boroughs, with their often predominantly alien population ('your burgess-hood is a folly'), and again at an even deeper level there is the poignant realization of beauty's frailty and life's transitoriness.

Another characteristic which more than one of these early *cywyddwyr* share with Dafydd ap Gwilym is an expertise in the embodiment of colloquial dialogue in their verse, undaunted by the restrictions imposed by *cynghanedd* and by the *cywydd*'s obligatory rhyme-scheme: good examples are Iolo Goch's 'Dialogue between the Soul and the Body' or the poem in which he abuses his beard ('like a hedge-hog's coat') for acting as an impediment to his love-making. Yet a third feature which is also characteristic of Dafydd is their manner of presenting themselves as leading actors in their poems of incident, as does Madog Benfras in his *fabliau* poem 'The Saltman' and Iolo Goch when—again like Dafydd—he tells how he was pursued by *Yr Eiddig*, the stock figure of the 'Jealous Husband' as the result of a game of fortune-telling with the man's wife, played with nuts.

A recent critic of the contemporary literary scene in England (John Burrow) has pointed out that a relaxed and 'un-grand' style, tending to irony and humour and self-depreciation—and therefore very obviously comparable with these features in the style of Dafydd and his contemporaries—is a characteristic of the informal manner shared in common by Chaucer and other late fourteenth-century English poets, who as a group have been designated the 'Ricardian' poets.

We do not know how these poets stood in relation to each other with respect to the early development of the *cywydd*. Any conclusions which are to be reached concerning this must be based upon the poets' own statements, and in particular upon what they have to tell us concerning their own attitudes towards Dafydd ap Gwilym. Some indication of these may perhaps be deduced from the 'elegies' composed for Dafydd by Gruffudd Gryg, Iolo Goch, and Madog Benfras, and—more importantly—from the eight *cywyddau* of the *ymryson* or poetic controversy which took place between Dafydd ap Gwilym and Gruffudd Gryg. This poet came from the commote of Llifon in the west of Anglesey. Evidence brought to light from a legal document some years ago by Mr E. D. Jones would place the probable date of Gruffudd's birth several years earlier than was hitherto supposed, and this earlier dating puts a somewhat different light upon the controversy between the two poets than that in which it had been regarded previously. No longer do we have a young poet from Gwynedd, the stronghold of the poetic 'establishment', challenging the poetic innovations made by his senior from the more volatile south; but instead an argument between two contemporaries relating to differences in the basic assumptions of each concerning the subjects proper to be celebrated in poetry. There can be no mistaking the import of Gruffudd Gryg's initial attack upon Dafydd's verse: he accuses him of monotony of theme and of obvious and blatant 'untruth' by his exaggeration of the plight to which the spears and arrows of his love for Morfudd have reduced him over the last ten years. Such exaggeration would have outraged the conventional standards of truth as recognized hitherto in bardic praise-poetry, and Gruffudd claims that missiles of this kind would have been quite sufficient to kill any other man, even the great Arthur himself. Implicit in this charge is an even deeper one: that of departing from the formal restraints imposed by the *rhieingerdd* convention, in order to introduce improper and irrelevant personal feelings into his poetry. Dafydd retorts with a much-discussed couplet in which he defends the new kind of verse practised by him as being at least equal in value with that which belonged to the familiar old tradition: *Nid llai urddas, heb ras rydd / No gwawd, geuwawd o gywydd* ('No less the honour (though) without free favour / Than a praise-poem, a *cywydd* of false praise'). A '*cywydd* of false praise' means Dafydd's own love-poetry: the phrase is employed with similar meaning by Llywelyn Goch [. . .]. He asserts that Gruffudd is merely *cynnydd cerdd bun unflwydd* ('the product of a maiden-song of a single year')—which is as much as to say that he is a newcomer to the practice of love-poetry, compared with Dafydd himself. In obscure and even cryptic language but with striking imagery, Dafydd then asserts that the mature technical accomplishment of his own *cywyddau* is such that it would give distinction even to the meanest of antiquated worn-out harps, if such a one were to accompany it, or to the tattered pages of the most ragged song-book in which such verses as his own might be written: without the harp's accompaniment of song, or the barely legible love-poetry inscribed in the book, both of these would by themselves be valueless. Adopting attack as the most satisfactory form of defence, Dafydd then introduces another issue into the argument: he claims that Gruffudd lacks originality, that he takes his subject-matter from the verse of others, including Dafydd's own poetry, and that in doing so he debases it—*gwyrodd â'i ben gerdd y byd* ('his mouth has distorted everyone's song'). Gruffudd replies by hotly denying that Dafydd is his teacher with respect to the content of his verse, and he asserts confidently that his own high attainments are fully recognised in his own country: 'Though my voice may stammer (*cryg*), by Mary, there is no stammering in any word of my verse.' Nevertheless, he concedes that in the past Dafydd's poetry had introduced a major novelty into Gwynedd: *Hoff oedd yng Ngwynedd, meddynt / Yn newydd ei gywydd gynt* ('A favoured novelty in Gwynedd, they say / his *cywydd* was when new')—it was a short-lived

wonder which caused as much stir at the time as did two other similar marvels: the wooden hobby-horse (an adjunct of the morris-dance) and the new organ in Bangor cathedral—but these too have long since become familiar and are no longer of particular remark. In his second *cywydd*, Dafydd refuses to withdraw his charge of plagiarism and issues a challenge: since both contestants are *prifeirdd*, or established and qualified poets, let them grapple together in a word-contest in the traditional manner of their craft—a fitting test, indeed, as to the high degree of technical accomplishment to which each laid claim. The last two *cywyddau* by both poets consist of a series of charges and counter-charges, elaborated with richly vituperative invective. There is much obscure allusion and innuendo in the argument which inevitably escapes us, but the scurrilous claim made by both contestants to be the 'father' who has begotten the other is perhaps no more than a crude metaphor reverting to their basic difference: the argument as to the real parentage of the *cywydd bun* or new love-poetry, in whose composition Dafydd was plainly acknowledged by his opponent to be preeminent. The controversy breaks off without any clear decision having been reached either as to Gruffudd's charge of exaggeration, or Dafydd's of imitation. Clearly there was a serious and important issue underlying the *ymryson,* in so far as it concerned the clash between the older established poetic modes and Dafydd's thematic innovations—though from the point-of-view of metrics, the major poetic innovation of the fourteenth century is completely left aside from the argument, both poets tacitly accepting the *cywydd* as the natural medium for their discussion; as indeed it was for them for all kinds of personal and 'untraditional' poetry.

An 'elegy' composed by Gruffudd Gryg to Dafydd ap Gwilym regularly follows the *ymryson* in nearly all the manuscripts, and is best regarded as a poem composed to form a gracious termination to the controversy. Gruffudd forgives Dafydd for his harsh words, expresses regret for their dissension, admits that he himself has been partly in the wrong, and acknowledges his debt to Dafydd—*Disgybl wyf, ef a'm dysgawdd* ('I am his pupil, he instructed me'). Dafydd is *paun Dyfed* ('the peacock of Dyfed'), he is in the direct line of descent from Taliesin, Myrddin, Aneirin, and the most famous of the *Gogynfeirdd*; and Gruffudd claims that he would prefer satire from Dafydd's lips rather than praise from those of any other poet. It is clear that Gruffudd regarded Dafydd as a master of the *cywydd serch* or new love-poetry, yet none the less he placed him within the central tradition of Welsh poetry, as one who worthily perpetuated the tradition inherited from the *Cynfeirdd* or earliest poets. A parallel attitude is expressed by Iolo Goch and by Madog Benfras in their *marwnadau* for Dafydd: for both he was *pensaer yr ieithoedd* ('architect of words', literally 'languages'), and *pensaer gwingerdd* ('architect of song'), he was *athro pawb* ('everyone's teacher'), and by his death, according to Iolo, the *cywydd* will be reduced to a sorry state. Madog Benfras describes Dafydd as *digrif* ('amusing'), and as *tegan rhianedd* ('the darling of girls'), and prays that Mary and Jesus will forgive his levity; yet he too describes Dafydd as a worthy transmitter of the traditions of Aneirin and Taliesin. None of these poets offer any suggestion that they regarded Dafydd as the *inventor* of the *cywydd*; indeed, Iolo Goch appears to give pride of place to Llywelyn Goch ap Meurig Hen in this respect, describing him in another so-called 'elegy' as *primas cywydd Ofydd* ('the primate of Ovid's *cywydd*'), to be praised above all for his love-poetry: when a court-audience requests a song, no other *cywydd* but one by Llywelyn Goch will satisfy it, and in his verse no single word is misplaced; he is compared to the prophet David, who like Llywelyn, was a sinner in love who afterwards repented. The force and immediate application of all these compliments and innuendos would surely have been lost had not their subject been still alive to take note of them, and I think it is only natural to conclude that it was to the living Dafydd, or Llywelyn, that all these poems were addressed. This is no less obviously the case, I think, with the *cywyddau marwnad* addressed by Dafydd to Gruffudd Gryg, Madog Benfras, and Gruffudd ab Adda: the presumption is, indeed, that all such 'elegies' addressed during the early *cywydd* period by one poet to another are 'fictitious' elegies, addressed to men who were still living. The choice of the *cywydd* for compositions of this kind is an indication that they are not serious, but that they are to be regarded as friendly and admiring compliments to their subject, for almost invariably they contain touches of humour which betray their fundamental levity. They subscribe to certain recurrent conventions; one is the expression of regret that such-and-such a despised poet (a certain unknown 'Bleddyn' is alluded to in this way in Gruffudd's elegy for Dafydd) was not removed from the world instead of the subject of the elegy; another is a prayer for divine forgiveness for their subject for his frivolity in composing love-poetry. As in much medieval poetry, levity goes hand-in-hand with seriousness (in this case with genuine admiration and affection), as when Dafydd ap Gwilym in his 'elegy' for the poet-musician Gruffudd ab Adda follows up his marvellously sustained image of a nightingale singing enchantingly in an orchard, only to be struck wantonly by an arrow, with the abrupt assertion that the poet was killed with just such a 'discourteous' blow (*pond oedd wladeiddrwydd?*) as if one were striking off the head of a goose. Even Gruffudd Gryg's poem to the Yew-Tree above the grave of Dafydd ap Gwilym comes under suspicion for similar reasons, and on grounds of general probability: the poem echoes closely Dafydd's own *cywydd* to that other evergreen, the Holly; of both trees it is claimed that they will provide secure 'houses' for the poet, and both will share the additional advantage that

their leaves will not be nibbled away by goats! And even Iolo Goch's comparison of Llywelyn Goch, in his eloquent tribute to him, with the prophet David who also sinned in love and subsequently repented, has on the whole a greater ring of authenticity if we are to believe that the poet was at the time still in the land of the living. These early *cywydd* poets were not as yet fully enfranchised from an inherited tradition, in that the *awdl* still retained for them the *aura* of its ancient prestige as the preferred medium alike for formal elegy and for the expression of genuine grief in bereavement, as I have already suggested in discussing Dafydd ap Gwilym's employment of the two media. The same probability that a *cywydd marwnad* enshrines a familiar personal tribute to a living friend is applicable to Dafydd ap Gwilym's address to Rhydderch ab Ieuan Llwyd; and very probably also, as Mr Dafydd Bowen has suggested, to Gruffudd Gryg's 'elegy' for Rhys ap Tudur of Penmynydd.

This convention of addressing elegies to the living, which appears so strange to present-day readers, seems to have been employed primarily for the purpose of making familiar, semi-humorous addresses by one poet to another. Outside this relatively well-defined category, there is frequently no possibility of distinguishing among the compositions of fourteenth-century poets between the 'fictitious' and the genuine *marwnad*. Already by 1356 we have Iolo Goch's *cywydd marwnad* to Sir Rhys ap Gruffudd, securely dated by the death of its subject in that year. This was followed after twelve years by the same poet's *cywydd marwnad* to Tudur Fychan of Penmynydd (1367), and later again by his elegy to Tudur's sons Ednyfed and Goronwy (1382), and by his dramatic and moving elegy to his friend and principal patron Ithel ap Robert, archdeacon of St. Asaph—a poem which Mr Saunders Lewis has acclaimed as one of the poetic masterpieces of the century. There can be no doubt but that all these are sincere and genuine elegies, each one a formal composition in honour of a man who wielded great power and authority, whether local or national. These are praise-poems which in their language, metaphors and concepts—in everything but in their metrical form—reproduce the traditions of the *canu mawl* of previous generations, employing the linguistic archaisms and all the familiar imagery of the traditional *awdlau*. Like Dafydd ap Gwilym, Iolo is believed to have been a man of good birth and standing who had taken minor religious orders. It is evident that he possessed deep learning and wide knowledge of biblical and classical sources, of divinity in translation (the *Elucidarium*), as well as of all branches of the native Welsh tradition as expressed in earlier poetry, in triads and romances, in saints' lives, in genealogy and in heraldry. There is also that 'subtle over-plus' of poetic vision which is characteristically his own: a remarkable power of evoking atmosphere and of conveying with intensity the sense of an impressive occasion; as in his portrayal of the immensely long funeral *cortège* which accompanied Ithel ap Robert to his burial, led by the high cross waving like a ship at anchor in the March gale of rain and wind, or his description of the darkness which overcast all Anglesey upon the death of the sons of Tudur of Penmynydd.

No less strong an affiliation with the whole range of techniques of the Gwynedd court poets who were his predecessors is apparent in Iolo Goch's many other *cywyddau mawl*: ironically enough, the earliest of these whose authenticity is without doubt may well be his remarkable *cywydd* in praise of Edward III (composed after 1347), in which after praising the king for his victories in France and Scotland, including Crécy (1346), Iolo takes it upon himself to impress upon the king his responsibilities, urging him to undertake a crusade to the Holy Land. It seems incongruous to meet here with all the age-old formulas: Edward is described as *anian Bedwyr* ('of the nature of Bedwyr'); he is the defender of Windsor, a lion, a boar, and a leopard. From every point-of-view this is a surprising poem: why was it composed at all? Mr Dafydd Bowen suggests that this may perhaps have been due to the instigation of Sir Rhys ap Gruffudd, a strong supporter of the king, to whom Iolo's *marwnad* attests his allegiance: one wonders, however, in what form, if at all, its import was ever communicated to the king. But here, in what may well be the earliest of all *cywyddau mawl,* is a poem of assured technical accomplishment and of unquestionably serious intention; the earliest extant example (to be followed later by Iolo's urgent advice to Sir Roger Mortimer on the occasion of his coming-of-age) of a succession of *cywyddau* in which poets ventured to offer weighty ideological, practical, or political advice to their patrons.

Iolo's gift for selecting the essentials of a scene and projecting them with an almost photographic immediacy is to be seen no less in certain of his praise-poems than in his elegies. It is most noticeable, however, in those of his *cywyddau* in which praise is offered to a patron by means of praising the splendour of his home; as in Iolo's minutely detailed description of Owain Glyndŵr's court at Sycharth, or his description of Cricieth castle when 'Sir Hywel of the Axe' was its constable. This is a poem-type which has an illustrious ancestry, leading as far back as the ninth-century 'Praise of Tenby' in the *Book of Taliesin,* and precedents for it in the older metres must presumably have been known to Iolo. Yet he gives to this type of poem a new orientation by presenting his description of Cricieth in the form of a dream, and in doing so he evokes in the plainest terms the closely similar description of the heroine's home at Caernarfon, seen in a dream, which occurs in the tale of *The Dream of Maxen*:

> I see in the first place, truly, a fair large fortress yonder by the sea; a splendid magnificent castle, with men at tables, a rampart, and a blue sea against a wall of comely stone. There are sea-waves about the womb of the dark and gloomy tower; music of flutes and pipes; a lively warrior and a man of note; sprightly maidens weaving pure and shining silk; proud men on the fortress's floor playing chess and backgammon on a dais. And a grey-haired man, a very savage Twrch Trwyth in battle, passing from his hand to mine a gold-chased goblet containing sweetly-tasting wine, with a fair tall black standard on the turret-top, bearing three identical white flowers with silver leaves—he was indeed a noble warrior.

The main cause for the transference in Gwynedd of the traditional techniques of court-poetry from *awdl* to *cywydd* must be sought in the rapid social changes which followed the conquest, but the obscurity which surrounds the successive stages in this change is thrown into relief by the fact that whereas Iolo Goch composed a *cywydd marwnad* to Tudur ap Goronwy of Penmynydd (d. 1367), his younger contemporary Gruffudd ap Maredudd was at the same time composing an elegy to him in the form of an *awdl*; also that Llywelyn Goch ap Meurig Hen (another of the pioneers of the *cywydd*) addressed an *awdl* to the powerful magnate Sir Rhys ap Gruffudd, whose death in 1356 was subsequently celebrated by Iolo in a *cywydd marwnad*. The possibility can certainly be excluded that Iolo Goch's *cywyddau mawl* owe anything initially to the example of Dafydd ap Gwilym: indeed, the date assigned to the earliest of these, appearing as they do in mature and assured form in the middle years of the century, is by itself sufficient to discredit it. The only possible influence which would need to be considered would be that from Dafydd ap Gwilym's four polished *cywyddau* to Ifor Hael, as to whose relative date in relation to Iolo's *cywyddau mawl* we can do no more than conjecture. And the Ifor Hael poems offer no sufficient explanation: the *cywydd* was for Dafydd the obvious medium for such poems of familiar personal address to a generous friend and patron; three of the four were composed, apparently, in response to particular incidents of a trivial nature: a journey planned or deferred, the gift of money in the fingers of a glove. Their whole manner and tone is entirely different from that of the genuine *cywydd mawl*: their originality consists in the way in which recognisable concepts from the new love-poetry have been blended with the inherited praise-formulas—the mutual dependence of poet and patron, praise of the patron's home, the poet's deserved reward compared with that given by Urien Rheged to Taliesin. It is, on the other hand, with the formal *awdl* which Dafydd addressed to Ifor that Iolo Goch's *cywyddau mawl* and *marwnad* deserve rather to be compared—with the essential difference that Iolo has transferred into the new medium all the traditional techniques known to him from the *awdlau* addressed to the Gwynedd princes. Nor does it appear that any other of the earliest group of *cywyddwyr* but Iolo Goch composed sincere and genuine *mar-*

wnadau in the form of the *cywydd* (the only other questionable example being Gruffudd Gryg's supposed *cywydd marwnad* to Rhys ap Tudur—a 'fictitious' *marwnad,* in all probability, as has already been seen, and one whose penultimate lines link it with the Ifor Hael poems rather than with genuine elegy). We have no evidence that Iolo Goch had any predecessor in making the transference of serious praise-poetry from *awdl* to *cywydd*: as far as our existing knowledge will take us, the *cywydd mawl* originated with Iolo Goch in Gwynedd, just as the *cywydd serch* originated with Dafydd ap Gwilym in Dyfed. Both innovations were of equal magnitude, and were comparable in their far-reaching implications.

Stephen Knight (essay date March 1981)

SOURCE: Knight, Stephen. "Welsh Poetic's Well-Shaped Art." *Journal of European Studies* 11, no. 41 (March 1981): 18-28.

[*In the following essay, Knight highlights the key attributes of Dafydd's work within the context of various translations and their ensuing repercussions.*]

This paper discusses problems and possibilities in translating a poem by Dafydd ap Gwilym, widely regarded as the greatest Welsh poet. The wit and beauty of Dafydd's themes and the subtlety of his poetic form make his work both fascinating and difficult to translate—impossible to translate, in the opinion of some Welsh poets and critics. Various attempts have been made in the past, however, and I believe they can be improved upon in a number of ways.

Dafydd ap Gwilym was writing in the fourteenth century; 1320-80 is usually accepted as an estimate of his life span. He came from a fairly noble family, closely connected with the Anglo-French administration of South Wales; his father's name Gwilym, the Welsh form of Guillaume, goes back a good way in his pedigree and may imply some French blood. Poetry was also in the family; Dafydd's uncle Llywelyn ap Gwilym was constable of the castle at Castellnewydd Emlyn and also, according to Dafydd, a fine and learned poet.[1] It was presumably he who educated Dafydd in the themes and forms of Welsh versification, which reached back in unbroken, self-conscious tradition to the *cynfeirdd,* the early bards, of the later sixth century A.D. But while Dafydd wrote some poems fully in accord with the aristocratic tradition of elegy and eulogy, using the time-honoured *awdl,* a long-lined monorhyming stanza form, much of his poetry deployed forms and themes which had not previously been so fully acceptable to the highly structured and convention-conscious Welsh bardic tradition. About a hundred and

fifty of Dafydd's poems have survived; the exact number is uncertain because doubts remain about some poems attributed to him, though Thomas Parry has settled most of these problems in his authoritative edition.[2] The bulk of these poems are about love and nature, and some are sharply ironic and comic to the point of vulgarity. Like many major artists Dafydd drew into a "high-art" context material which formerly had been regarded as popular or improper; modern research suggests he was not the only Welsh poet of the period to be doing this, but he did it with such force and particularly with such formal mastery that he gave this new type of poetry special status. The resemblance to Chaucer in this, as in other ways, is striking.

The formal power, so crucial to Dafydd's authority and so problematic for the translator, lies in his easy mastery of the intricate Welsh systems of rhyming and *cynghanedd.*[3] In the *awdl* Welsh poets had long developed a system of internal rhyme, assonance and alliteration which bound words together into strikingly harmonious patterns. Dafydd in particular adapted this system to the more popular measure of seven-syllable rhyming couplets, called the *cywydd.* The following illustration of *cynghanedd* is from the first six lines of the poem I will be discussing, entitled by Parry **"Trafferth mewn Tafarn" ("Trouble in a Tavern")**. Each line has seven syllables, and the rhyming pattern is on-stress, off-stress. That is, in each rhyming pair one rhyming syllable is stressed, the other unstressed. The stress in Welsh falls regularly on the penultimate syllable except in compound words, so a pair of rhymes like "badell" and "ymhell" can occur: "ymhell" is the compound. Apart from these complexities of rhyme, the lines all contain varieties of *cynghanedd*; the features and the names of the types are set out beside the lines:

			Cynghanedd Type
Deuthum i ddinas dethol	d.. th	d.. th	traws ('over')
A'm hardd wreangyn i'm hol.	m.. h	m.. h	traws
Cain hoywdraul, lle cwyn hydrum	C.. n.. h.. dr	c.. n.. h.. dr	traws
Cymryd, balch o febyd fum,	yd	f.. yd.. f	sain ('harmonious')
Llety urddedig ddigawn	ig	ig	llusg ('trailing')
Cyffredin, a gwin a gawn.	in	g.. in.. g	sain

The third line only just misses providing the one remaining type of *cynghanedd,* described as "croes", that is "cross". In *cynghanedd groes* all the consonants of the first half line repeat in sequence in the second half line except the final consonant or consonant cluster in each half-line. The title of this paper, "Welsh poetic's well-shaped art", is an example of such a pattern, as the devoiced final consonant of "shaped" repeats the /t/ in "poetic". In line three above, it is the initial "lle" of the second half-line which prevents it being *cynghanedd groes*: the absence of this type in the opening of the poem is, I will suggest later, no accident.

This intricate and exclusive set of patterns is mastered by Dafydd and many other Welsh poets, though some of Dafydd's imitators verge on incoherence through the exigencies of the form. This intricacy is, of course, the major reason why Welsh readers consider Dafydd impossible to translate, and I do not know of any translators who have attempted to imitate or recreate the formal intricacy in English. Before considering in detail if this is possible, it will be instructive to look at the published translations of **"Trafferth mewn Tafarn"**. Again, the first six lines will be used as a sample.

In *A Celtic Miscellany* Kenneth H. Jackson offers a prose translation:

> I came to a choice city with my handsome squire in my train, a place of liberal banqueting, a fine gay way of spending money, to find a public inn worthy enough, and I would have wine—I have been vain since childhood.

Jackson has changed the syntactical shape of the original to make a more fluent English prose, but he is scrupulously accurate.

In *Medieval Welsh Lyrics,* Joseph P. Clancy offers this:

> I came to a choice city,
> Behind me my handsome squire.
> High living, a festive place,
> I found, swaggering youngster,
> A decent enough public
> Lodging, and I ordered wine.

Clancy has maintained the seven syllable count but abandoned rhyme and *cynghanedd*. He is careful to catch the shape of the Welsh lines, notably the feature called *sangiad,* that is a syntactically separate comment—"swaggering youngster" for example. This feature is characteristic of Dafydd and other Welsh poets: it enables the poet to bring in vocabulary from a wide range, so facilitating the *cynghanedd,* but Dafydd in particular also uses it to create a commentary in the poem on the events of the poem. Clancy represents well the basically colloquial vocabulary and the rhythmical variety of the poem, and he successfully hints at the self-conscious narrative tone.

An earlier translation of Dafydd was by H. I. and David Bell, *Dafydd ap Gwilym: Fifty Poems.* Harold Bell knew a great deal about Welsh poetry; he was the author of the first major book in English on the topic, *The Development of Welsh Poetry* and he and his son tried to convey the "poetic" quality of Dafydd's work. This is David Bell's version of the poem under discussion:

> I and my servant on travel came
> To a city of good repute and name,
> And since I am a Welshman bred
> It seemed as for my pleasure made.

> I took a lodging in the common inn
> And straightway called to bring me wine.

The third line here, which corresponds to line four in the Welsh is actually based on a now rejected reading: "Cymro i'r byd o febyd fûm", "A Welshman to the world from youth I was". This line probably derives from oral repetition of the poems—*cynghanedd sain* has been preserved, though not in Dafydd's own version.

Bell sought a part Georgian, part-Browningesque effect, but the rhyme and rhythms seem rather uncertain: the original has been altered considerably to obtain a satisfactory effect in the new medium and form.

I have dealt with these three translations in this order because they seem obvious examples of the three types of translation that Dryden and other translators have described: Jackson offers a metaphrase, a word-for-word account of the sense; Clancy gives a paraphrase, trying to be as accurate as is concordant with a general idea of the tone of the original; Bell is seeking an imitation, what Goethe called a metamorphosis. In terms of their aims, it seems that Bell is clearly the least successful, choosing a largely inappropriate analogy and failing to make it intrinsically effective in any case. If it is desirable for translation to give some account of the poetic nature of the original, then Clancy's version is more satisfactory than Jackson's. But Clancy still falls a good way short of the original; I feel translation can come closer, can represent the poem's form more accurately.

Literary criticism of recent decades has asserted forcefully that the form and the content of literature are inseparable, that a writer will convey meaning through stylistic implication, through formally created tone and through the structure of the work itself. In Dafydd's poetry this is so. The extreme complexity of the form is not merely a dazzling piece of poetic exhibitionism; it is also integral to the meaning of the poem.

The more emphatic, self-proclaiming *cynghanedd* effects in the poem are usually associated with the more self-conscious and self-satisfied remarks by the persona: there is a formal correlation between an elaborate style and the persona's own high self-esteem. And when he recognises his folly and prays for forgiveness in the last line, there is no *cynghanedd* at all. But the variations of *cynghanedd* also shape the movement of the poem outside the specific presentation of the persona, building up to several climaxes, crystallising the mood of the poem and the persona together. [The Welsh text and its translations are reprinted here.]

> Deuthum i ddinas dethol,
> A'm hardd wreangyn i'm hôl.
> Cain hoywdraul, lle cwyn hydrum,

Cymryd, balch o febyd fûm,
Llety urddedig ddigawn
Cyffredin, a gwin a gawn.

Canfod rhiain addfeindeg
Yn y tŷ enaid teg.
Bwrw yn llwyr, liw haul dwyrain,
Fy mryd ar wyn fy myd main.
Prynu rhost, nid er bostiaw,
A gwin drud, mi a gwen draw.
Gwarwy a gâr gwŷr ieuainc—
Galw ar fun, ddyn gŵyl, i'r fainc.
Hustyng, bûm wr hy astud,
Dioer yw hyn, deuair o hud;
Gwneuthur, ni bu segur serch,
Amod dyfod at hoywferch
Pan elai y minteioedd
I gysgu; bun aelddu oedd.

Wedi cysgu, tru tremyn,
O bawb eithr myfi a bun,
Profais yn hyfedr fedru
Ar wely'r ferch; alar fu.
Cefais, pan soniais yna,
Gwymp dig, nid oedd gampau da;
Haws codi, drygioni drud,
Yn drwsgl nog yn dra esgud.
Trewais, ni neidiais yn iach,
Y grimog, a gwae'r omach,
Wrth ystlys, ar waith ostler,
Ystôl groch ffôl, goruwch ffêr.
Dyfod, bu chwedl edifar,
I fyny, Cymry a'm câr,
Trewais, drwg fydd tra awydd,
Lle y'm rhoed, heb un llam rhwydd,
Mynych dwyll amwyll ymwrdd,
Fy nhalcen wrth ben y bwrdd,
Lle 'dd oedd gawg yrhawg yn rhydd
A llafar badell efydd.
Syrthio o'r bwrdd, dragwrdd drefn,
A'r ddeudrestl a'r holl ddodrefn;
Rhoi diasbad o'r badell
I'm hôl, fo'i clywid ymhell;
Gweiddi, gwr gorwag oeddwn,
O'r cawg, a'm cyfarth o'r cŵn.
Yr oedd gerllaw muroedd mawr
Drisais mewn gwely drewsawr,
Yn trafferth am eu triphac—
Hicin a Siencin a Siac.
Syganai'r gwas soeg enau,
Araith oedd ddig, wrth y ddau:

'Mae Cymro, taer gyffro twyll,
Yn rhodio yma'n rhydwyll;
Lleidr yw ef, os goddefwn,
'Mogelwch, cedwch rhag hwn.
Codi o'r ostler niferoedd
I gyd, a chwedl dybryd oedd.
Gygus oeddynt i'm gogylch
Yn chwilio i'm ceisio i'm cylch;
A minnau, hagr wyniau hyll,
Yn tewi yn y tywyll.
Gweddiais, nid gwedd eofn,
Dan gêl, megis dyn ag ofn;
Ac o nerth gweddi gerth gu,
Ac o ras y gwir Iesu,

Cael i minnau, cwlm anhun,
Heb sâl, fy henwal fy hun.
Dihengais i, da wng saint,
I Dduw'r archaf faddeuaint.

Turning up at the choicest town
my suave young servant in my train,
for living lavish and refined
I, finely proud and youthful, found 4
a reasonable resting house—
a common one, but wine for us.
I glimpsed a graceful pretty girl
in that house, the darling soul, 8
and bent my eyebrows to appraise
that sunshine ray, my slender prize.
I bought a roast, but not to boast:
the wine and wench were both the best. 12
I made the moves young men adore
and motioned to my modest dear;
I boldly whispered then a pair
of words, I swear, with occult power; 16
no lazy lover, I agreed
to find that fond and fairest maid,
dark black her brows, when the platoon
of others to their rest had gone. 20

When sleep had slipped—a troubled trip—
its trance upon the travelling troupe,
I tried to tread, wise and wary,
where her bed lay—it went badly. 24
I collected—clarion howl—
a fearful fall—clumsy fool—
more easy rising—misery's scowl—
clumsily than with climbing skill; 28
I had thumped, by fumbled jumping,
my shin—the laggard leg is limping—
on a stupid ostler's stool,
my ankle's sting is killing still. 32
Rising—a wretched resumé—
aloft—ah, the Welsh all love me—
I battered (bad is luscious lust,
I found my feet were fettered fast 36
within a trip and tackle trap)
my topknot on the table tip.
Then rang a rattling tenor tin,
a brazen basin's baritone: 40
I tumbled into trestle trouble,
the raging room a roaring rumble.
The pan demonically yelled
upon me; I heard—manacled 44
both by noise and by the legs—
the basin baying, and the dogs.
Stuck by the wall, stinking bad,
three Saxons in their brackish bed 48
bothered bad about their packs—
Hickin, Jenkin, Jack, three pigs.
Jack with slobbered slack lips makes
secret mutters to his mates, 52

"There's a Taffy, tough and tricky,
treading round with treachery:
there'll be crime unless we catch him,
look out keenly, let's keep watching." 56
All the hosts of ostlers rose
(a sorry story it portrays):
frowning, they all failed to find me,

fumbling, bumbling round so blindly. 60
And I, by direst destiny
silent where no soul should see,
I prayed, not the bravest deed,
in secret like a fear-sick maid, 64
and from the power of prayer so blest,
and with the love of our lord Christ,
I slipped at last—sleep was lost—
love-less to my lair of lust. 68
I'd got away, dear gracious heaven:
I pray to God I am forgiven.

I came to a choice city
with my lovely squire behind me.
Fine enjoyment, place of liberal dining,
I took—proud of youth I was—
a respectable enough lodging-house,
a public one—and I got wine.

I saw a maiden, slim and fair,
in the house—my lovely dear.
I cast fully—colour of the eastern sun
my thought on the pure one, my slim treasure.
I bought a roast—not for boasting
and expensive wine, I and the fair one yonder.
I played as young men love to do,
I called the girl, modest creature, to the bench,
I whispered—a bold earnest man I was—
true is this—two words of magic;
I made—love was not idle—
a compact to come to the gay girl
when the hordes would have gone
to sleep: a dark-browed maid she was.

After the sleeping—sad journey—
of all except me and the girl,
I tried dexterously to find
the girl's bed: grief it was.
I got—then I made a noise—
a bad fall—it was not good skill—
easier to rise—cruel wickedness—
awkwardly than very swiftly.
I struck—I did not jump well—
the shin—and woe to the leg—
against the side—because of an ostler—
of a loud stupid stool, above the ankle.
Coming—it was a sorry tale—
up—the Welsh love me—
I banged—bad is too much lust—
(there I was given, with no free step,
many a trap of foolish blows)
my forehead on the table top,
where was a basin a long time loose,
and the noise of a brass pan.
They fell from the table—ferocious room—
and the two trestles and all the furniture.
There came a shout from the pan
after me, it was heard afar;
a clang—I was a helpless man—
from the basin, and the dogs barked at me.
There were, beside the thick walls,
three English in a stink-sour bed,
worrying about their three packs—
Hickin and Jenkin and Jack.
The slush-mouthed boy muttered,
words were angry, to the two—

"There's a Welshman, the disturbance of deceit,
creeping here very treacherously.
He's a thief, if we allow it,
beware, be on guard against him."
Arose all the hosts of ostlers
together, and a dire tale it was.
Squinting they were around me,
searching to find me all about me,
and I—ugly hideous pain—
was silent in the dark.
I prayed—not a bold manner—
in hiding—like a girl with fear—
and from the power of wondrous dear prayer
and from the grace of the true Jesus
I got—a knot of sleeplessness—
without benefit—my own old lair;
I escaped, dear good saints,
to God I ask forgiveness.

In lines 1-20 the *cynghanedd* is restrained, depending basically on the less ostentatious types *cynghanedd draws* and *cynghanedd lusg*. The more ornate *cynghanedd sain* occurs in lines 4, 6 and 10 where the first person singular is also present and the persona's conceit is suggested.

Line 16 introduces the richly consonantal *cynghanedd groes* for the first time and in lines 17-20 the complex harmony of *cynghanedd sain* occurs three times. Through lines 21-26 the *cynghanedd* increasingly depends on *cynghanedd sain,* and this growing intricacy is brought to a head in the splendidly elaborate lines 28-32, the last of which is both *cynghanedd sain* and *cynghanedd draws*. In this way an organically developing complexity in the poem also makes dramatically authoritative both the knockabout comedy and noisy disasters of the plot and also the self-conscious frustration of the persona.

From this point the style quietens, moving easily on through comic action. An exceptional flurry of artifice authorises in style the brief passage displaying the hostility of the English—and the form itself partly neutralises them, as Dafydd encloses in Welsh poetic the three Saxon names: in line 50 "Hicin a Siencin a Siac" is a model of *cynghanedd sain*. Apart from this, the formal climax of the second half of the poem is in the very full intricacy of lines 65-69, where the persona prays, aware of folly and failure. The repetitive structure of lines 65-66 imply a more secure tone, less mobile and uncertain than the earlier movement. But a plainer veracity and security is suggested in the final line, where the repeated consonants, almost wilfully it seems, do not form any *cynghanedd* pattern for the first time in the poem; the persona and the poem finally speak a simple Christian truth without artifice or self-conscious art.

In this way, a close reading of the poem reveals its power to create meaning in form. The problem for the translator is to represent this power. Clearly, the handling of the *cynghanedd* is a central part of it, though the subtle nature of the rhyming and the strict syllable count are also important. It is possible to imitate *cynghanedd* in English—Gerard Manley Hopkins used the effect a good deal, sometimes in strict form (and he also wrote at least two poems in Welsh, neither of which is much applauded by native critics). Returning to the first six lines of **"Trafferth mewn Tafarn"** as a test-piece, here is a strictly imitative translation:

> I attained a choice township,
> my handsome squire at my hip;
> dainty spot, dinner tasty,
> taking—proud, youth's making me—
> rooms that seemed to be decent,
> public—classic wines were sent.

This version has a seven-syllable line, on- and off-stress rhyming, and the *cynghanedd* patterns of the original (though the stress patterns associated with the *cynghanedd* have proved, to me at least, impossible to imitate exactly). The problem is that the translation quite lacks the natural and colloquial fluency of Dafydd's Welsh. In being a portrayal of form it is a betrayal of tone.

In this second attempt I have kept the *cynghanedd* and the rhyming pattern but have abandoned the seven-syllable requirement, so making the sense clearer and the movement a little more fluent:

> I turned up at a choice township,
> my handsome squire behind my hip;
> a dainty spot for dinner tasty,
> and taking—proud, youth's making me—
> rooms that seemed to be quite decent,
> public—but classic wines were sent.

This also seems something of a travesty. It is still not fluent enough and though the slightly arch quality of the third line does reflect the flowery word-compounding of the Welsh, the passage seems a failure. It is also very hard to do, I might add, and seems intrinsically wrong-headed because the Welsh forms derive from native linguistic features that English does not share. Penultimate stressing, natural in Welsh polysyllables, gives a ready store of off-stress rhymes to match the stressed rhymes deriving from monosyllables or compounded words. English has no such resources. And the extreme variety of English stress makes a strict syllable-count metre unnatural compared with a stress-count pattern. *Cynghanedd* in itself is not so specifically related to Welsh linguistic features, but it is certainly true that the small group of familiar prefixes and the absence of unpronounced consonants make it easier to find and feel the presence of *cynghanedd* in Welsh than in English. From these considerations there emerges what administrative echelons would call a policy decision. Rather than painfully and sometimes cryptically imitating the Welsh form, the translator who wishes to convey the

formal properties of the Welsh will be better advised to aim for effects which are natural and familiar in English, and which can be used as analogues to the effects in Welsh.

Half-rhyme can be used to give the tentative linking conveyed by the restrained, stress-varied rhyme of the Welsh. It seems wise to avoid the restriction of a syllable count and to make the number of stresses equal, using variation of syllable count or stress weight to match effects that Dafydd obtained either through pauses that are not always imitatable or, harder still to match, in passages where he varies the intensity of sound and sense within his set length. And since *cynghanedd* provides many of these effects but is both painful to imitate and not immediately evident, in a printed English text especially, it should be represented in its varying character by varied patterns of assonance, alliteration, internal rhyme and half-rhyme. As a result of these decisions, the translation set out [previously] was developed. This is juxtaposed with the original text and a literal translation, in order to illustrate both the formal character of the Welsh and the liberties taken with the sense to achieve an adequately representative translation.

There are a number of arguments I would offer to defend my practice in changing the sense of some of the original text. By adopting the premise that the translation should give some idea of the nature and quality of the original, rather than being a strict metaphrase, I have already built into the translation an assumption of certain structural changes. In trying to find a way of recreating the formal property of the poem, I moved further away from the original in selecting formal analogues. To change the sense at times, especially when it is for formal purposes, merely continues the movement in the direction of rewriting the original. Now this may well seem outrageous in terms of a positivistic idea of the sanctity of the text. But how much sanctity does a text have? It is changed simply by our cultural distance from it, as Borges has authoritatively observed in "Pierre Menard, author of the Quixote".

Even to reproduce a text invokes socio-cultural change, and this is much more sharply the case with translation. The translator cannot help being a redactor, naturally making a whole set of linguistic changes and often working in a period and place different from the original context. The nature of the target language and the target culture may well necessitate changes of emphasis to achieve the same effect—notions implicit in the other culture may need to be clarified, old jokes may have died. All but the most mechanical translation rewrites, and there is no special sin in rewriting the sense when this is appropriate. Obviously the translator who takes this approach, who judges this appropriateness, requires more skill, tact and imagination than if the translation were merely an attempted metaphrase or a timid paraphrase. Equally, this approach is the only way to make the text live in a new and particular cultural context. The adaptive translation may well be itself limited by its particularity and its innovations, but it is the only way to give the translation any real chance to let the reader penetrate a culture different from his or her own—and perhaps go back to the original. To translate in this way is to work at the level of "imitation", according to Dryden, or "metamorphosis" in Goethe's terms, and it is because Harold and David Bell at least attempted this with Dafydd that I admire their intention—without feeling it was very successful.

If we feel that an adaptation of an early poem violates it, then we are giving that original a status its author would not have expected. Our culture's idea of a text is reified, based on accurate mechanical reproduction, laws of copyright and specific money remuneration for the artist. That is our cultural situation, of course, but there is no reason why we should fail to communicate with the past because of it. Translation of the sort I am advocating is etymologically sound because it bears across from the past material in living form; metaphrase and many paraphrases merely exhibit curious mummies that once had life. Especially when a culture has been as isolated and oppressed as Welsh, it is important that its communications should be vital ones. I believe that lively modern translations of poets as good as Dafydd will lead some people to read him in Welsh; but if it merely leads others to grasp his qualities in a modern medium, then that too is something of a victory for Welsh culture that has not often been won.

Notes

1. An excellent account of Dafydd's life and work is Rachel Bromwich's *Dafydd ap Gwilym* in the Writers of Wales series (University of Wales Press, Cardiff, 1974). See also the Dafydd ap Gwilym number of *Poetry Wales,* viii, no. 4 (spring, 1973).

2. *Gwaith Dafydd ap Gwilym,* ail argraffiad (reprint, revised) (Gwasg Prifysgol Cymru, Caerdydd [University of Wales Press, Cardiff], 1963).

3. The patterns of *cynghanedd* are set out most fully in John Morris-Jones, *Cerdd Dafod* (Oxford University Press, London, 1925). A helpful discussion in English is appended to the chapter on Dafydd in T. Parry's *A History of Welsh Literature,* trans. by H. I. Bell (Clarendon Press, Oxford, 1955). See also the first appendix to Gwyn Williams's *An Introduction to Welsh Poetry* (Faber, London, 1953).

David Johnston (essay date summer 1983)

SOURCE: Johnston, David. "The Serenade and the Image of the House in the Poems of Dafydd ap Gwilym." *Cambridge Medieval Celtic Studies* no. 5 (summer 1983): 1-19.

[*In the following essay, Johnston comments on the significance of the house and its prominence in Dafydd's narrative serenades.*]

A serenade is a poem addressed by a lover to his beloved as he stands outside her house begging to be let in. Dafydd ap Gwilym's work contains only one example of the genre, **"Dan y Bargod"** (89).[1] There are however a number of poems describing Dafydd's nocturnal visits to the girl's house in the past tense, which might be called narrative serenades. I shall discuss the following poems: **"Amnaid"** (40), **"Y Ffenestr"** (64), **"Tri Phorthor Eiddig"** (80), **"Dan y Bargod"** (89), **"Y Rhew"** (91), and **"Caru yn y Gaeaf"** (145).[2] The house itself is of central significance in all these poems. On no occasion does Dafydd succeed in entering it. Its role is an ambiguous one, ranging from that of hostile fortification to that of potentially sheltering sanctuary. This ambiguity is closely connected with the wide variety of tone which is to be found both within the serenade group as a whole and, particularly in the case of **"Caru yn y Gaeaf,"** within the individual poem. Broadly speaking, the tone is at its most humorous when the girl is welcoming and the house acts as a hindrance separating the lovers. More serious undertones are noticeable when the girl is unwelcoming. Dafydd is then a homeless outcast exposed to the harsh weather, and the house becomes a desired sanctuary, a place of physical and emotional warmth. Although all six poems deal with the same basic situation, no two contain precisely the same tone. Each must be approached individually. After discussing these six poems in detail I shall briefly consider other poems by Dafydd in which houses figure prominently. But first a consideration of possible sources and influences will serve to throw into relief the individuality of Dafydd's treatment of the serenade theme.

"Dan y Bargod" has often been cited as an example of Dafydd's use of Continental literary genres.[3] This is somewhat ironic, since examples of serenades in medieval literature before Dafydd's period, the fourteenth century, are surprisingly difficult to find. According to Jeanroy there is nothing in French before the fifteenth century.[4] The only Middle English example known to me is a four-line lyric preserved in a manuscript of thirteenth- to fourteenth-century English sermons:[5]

> So longe ic have, lavedi,
> yhoved at thi gate,

that mi fot is ifrore, faire lavedi,
for thi luve faste to the stake!

I have waited so long at your gate, lady, that my foot is frozen, fair lady, for your love fast to the post!

But it seems reasonable to assume with Chotzen, and more recently Professor R. Geraint Gruffydd in his article on Llywelyn Goch's *Marwnad Lleucu Llwyd,* that the serenade was common in popular tradition throughout the Middle Ages, being based upon actual customs of wooing.[6] Professor Gruffydd points out that Dafydd may be making use of the serenade genre in his *marwnad* to his uncle Llywelyn ap Gwilym (13), when he says to the dead man (line 8): 'Agor i mi, y gŵr mud' ('Open for me, dumb man'). Llywelyn Goch's elegy for Lleucu Llwyd[7] is certainly based on the serenade, more appropriately since it is addressed to a girl. The fact that the serenade could be used for such a purpose shows that it must have been a well-known genre in fourteenth-century Wales.[8]

However, although no lyric serenades are to be found before Dafydd ap Gwilym, Chotzen points out[9] that in *Le Roman de la Rose* of Guillaume de Lorris[10] Amors, in his advice to the dreamer, describes a lover visiting his lady's house at night. There is already quite convincing evidence for Dafydd's knowledge of *Le Roman*,[11] so this passage may well have influenced his serenades. I therefore quote it here in full:

Lors t'en iras en recelee,
Soit par pluie, soit par gelee,
Tot droit vers la maison t'amie,
Qui se sera bien endormie
E a toi ne pensera guieres;
Une eure iras a l'uis derrieres,
Savoir s'il est remés desclos,
E jucheras iluec defors,
Toz seus, a la pluie e au vent;
Après vendras a l'uis devant,
E se tu trueves fendeüre
Ne fenestre ne serreüre,
Oreille e escoute par mi
S'il se sont laienz endormi;
E se la bele, senz plus, veille,
Ce te lo je bien e conseille
Qu'el t'oie plaindre e doloser,
Si qu'el sache que reposer
Ne puez en lit por s'amitié:
Bien doit fame aucune pitié
Avoir de celui qui ensure
Tel mal por li, se mout n'est dure.
Si te dirai que tu doiz faire
Por l'amor dou haut saintuaire
De quoi tu ne puez avoir aise:
Au revenir la porte baise;
E, por ce que l'en ne te voie
Devant la maison n'en la voie,
Gar que tu soies repairiez
Ainz que li jorz soit esclairiez.

(lines 2513-43)

[Then you will go in secret, whether through rain or frost, straight to the house of your sweetheart, who will be sound asleep and scarcely thinking of you; first you will go to the back door to see if it has been left unlocked, and you will perch there outside, all alone, in the wind and rain; then you will come to the front door, and if you find a chink or a window or lock, put your ear to it to hear if they are lying asleep; and if the fair one alone is awake, I strongly advise you that she hear you lamenting and groaning, so that she may know that you cannot rest in your bed for love of her: certainly any woman ought to have pity on one who suffers such pain for her sake, if she is not most hard-hearted. Now I shall tell you what you should do for love of that high sanctuary, because of which you can get no rest: on departing kiss the door; and, lest anyone see you in front of the house or in the street, make sure you are gone by daybreak.]

The chief importance of this passage, assuming that Dafydd was familiar with it, is that it establishes the nocturnal visit to the girl's house as a standard thing for the lover to do. *Le Roman de la Rose* was enormously influential in the Middle Ages, being regarded almost as a textbook upon love. This passage therefore goes some way towards explaining the frequency of the serenade in Dafydd's work. But Guillaume de Lorris's tone differs markedly from that which Dafydd normally adopts in describing his nocturnal visits. To the French lover the girl's house is an 'haut saintuaire' which he approaches with reverence. His aim is not to get inside the house, but simply to let the girl know that he is there so that she will realise his devotion. Dafydd's intentions, on the other hand, are never in doubt, and he expresses his frustration at being shut out in curses upon the house.

There is, however, one exception, **"Amnaid"** (40), a poem which is quite close in tone to the French passage, and completely different to Dafydd's other nocturnal visits.[12] Dafydd is wandering around the girl's house at night, and manages to catch sight of her through a glass window. They converse without being heard, but exchange no more than three words before parting. The poem ends with Dafydd swearing that he will never reveal her name.

Like the lover in *Le Roman de la Rose* Dafydd is content just to communicate with the girl. He specifically says that he sought nothing more:

Ni cheisiais wall ar f'anrhaith,
Pei ceisiwn, ni chawswn chwaith.

(lines 25-26)

[I did not tempt my darling; if I had, I would not have succeeded.]

The glass window has the effect of making the girl into a rather aloof figure, visible yet unattainable.[13] And she is further distanced by the comparison with the traditional heroine Branwen in line 14. Although the house is referred to in line 8 as a 'thick fortress' (*tew gaer*), a central image in the other serenades, the idea is not developed here. More in keeping with the tone of the poem is 'llys Eiddig a'i briod' (line 5), 'the court of the Jealous One and his spouse'. Though the term *llys* may be used ironically, it does connect up with the image of the girl as one set apart, to be admired from afar.

Dafydd does not make himself look in any way ridiculous in **"Amnaid."** Despite being shut out he retains his dignity by the sly secretiveness of the ending. Whilst secrecy is of great importance in Continental love literature, it normally plays little part in Dafydd's poetry. It is interesting to note that in the passage quoted from *Le Roman de la Rose* Amors ends by stressing the importance of secrecy on the part of the serenading lover. It would be going too far to assert that Amors's advice to the lover is a source for **"Amnaid,"** but it can at least be said that the two are very close in tone. If Dafydd's other serenades bear any relationship to the French passage it can only be as parodies.[14] In **"Dan y Bargod"** (89) he hammers on the door, making enough noise to wake up the whole neighbourhood. In **"Y Rhew"** (91) his suffering from the harsh weather is so extreme that it excludes all thought of the girl. In **"Y Ffenestr"** (64) he is able to talk to the girl through a window easily enough, but that is not the limit of his intentions. In **"Tri Phorthor Eiddig"** (80) the furtive visit turns into an outright attack on the house. And in **"Caru yn y Gaeaf"** (145) Dafydd comes drunk from the tavern and in his efforts to attract the girl's attention wakes up the husband.

Again, it is difficult to prove that Dafydd is directly parodying the passage from *Le Roman de la Rose,* but it is reasonable to assume that he must have known other poems which took the devotion of the serenading lover seriously. However, the possibility of influence from Ovid is also worth bearing in mind.[15] There is only one *paraclausithuron* in Ovid's work, *Amores,* I.vi, but the figure of the shut-out lover is common in both the *Amores* and the *Ars Amatoria,* always in a humorous light, showing the humiliating effect which love can have upon a man. For instance, Ovid says of himself in *Amores,* III.viii.23-24:

Ille ego Musarum purus Phoebique sacerdos
     ad rigidas canto carmen inane fores.

[Whilst I, the pure priest of Apollo and the Muses, sing an empty song to the unyielding doors.]

Dafydd may therefore be drawing directly upon Ovid rather than parodying the serious treatment of the serenade as found in *Le Roman de la Rose.* Of course, a third possibility, as Dr Bromwich points out,[16] is that he has no source at all, but is simply drawing upon his own real or imagined experience.

Le Roman de la Rose may, however, have influenced the portrayal of the house in Dafydd's serenades. Towards the end of Guillaume's unfinished work Jealousy builds a castle in which to immure the rose. Jean de Meun's continuation tells, among other things, how the lover besieges the castle and eventually wins the rose. The idea of the girl's house as a hostile castle which the lover besieges forms the basis of **"Tri Phorthor Eiddig"** (80). The three porters are a guard dog, which attacks Dafydd as he approaches the house, the door, which makes a noise as he opens it, waking the third porter, an old serving woman, who warns the husband that someone is trying to get into the house. His first attack having been repulsed, Dafydd retreats and fires arrows of love through the wall at the girl, who returns fire. The poem ends with Dafydd asserting that although the husband can exclude him from his house, God has given him the freedom of the woods and fields.

A suggestive parallel between this poem and *Le Roman de la Rose* is the fact that Jealousy builds the castle in the French poem, whilst Dafydd besieges the 'castle' of *Yr Eiddig,* the Jealous One. And furthermore, Jealousy appoints three gatekeepers, Fear, Shame, and Danger, with Evil Tongue as a fourth commanding them (lines 3867-910). When Friend is advising the dreamer how to assault the castle he speaks of 'ces treis portiers' (line 7562).

But again, Ovid is another possible influence. The idea of the lover besieging the girl's house occurs in *Amores,* I.ix.19-20, where Ovid compares the lover to the soldier:

Ille graves urbes, hic durae limen amicae
     obsidet. Hic portas frangit, at ille fores.

[The one besieges grim cities, the other the doorstep of his hard-hearted mistress. The one breaks down gates and the other doors.]

And in the *paraclausithuron, Amores,* I.vi, Ovid asks the *ianitor,* the equivalent of the Welsh *porthor*:

Urbibus obsessis clausae munimina portae
     prosunt: in media pace quid arma times?

                                                          (lines 29-30)

[Besieged cities are defended by barred gates: why do you fear weapons in peacetime?]

However, Ovid's lover is entirely dependent upon the girl's favour to obtain entry into the house. He only besieges the house in the sense that he waits outside it. In **"Tri Phorthor Eiddig,"** on the other hand, the girl herself is perfectly willing for Dafydd to come in; it is her husband and his porters who prevent him. Dafydd is therefore able to develop the metaphor more fully than Ovid, since the house does act like a hostile castle preventing him from reaching the girl.

In addition to these possible literary sources for the siege metaphor we must bear in mind the prominence of the Norman castles in fourteenth-century Wales. This has been discussed, with particular reference to **"Tri Phorthor Eiddig,"** by Mr D. J. Bowen in his article 'Dafydd ap Gwilym a'r Trefydd Drwg'.[17] But the direct source for the metaphor may perhaps be indicated by this description of stone houses in Pembrokeshire by Iorwerth C. Peate:

> In construction the houses are greatly influenced by the castle-building technique as found in Pembrokeshire. The thick stone walls with deeply recessed windows, the arched doorways, the stone staircases and benches, especially when considered in toto are strongly reminiscent of the Norman builders' technique.[18]

If Dafydd was familiar with houses which actually looked like miniature castles, then the siege metaphor would have been a very obvious one.

Mr Bowen points out that the office of porter applied not only to the gates of the castle, but also to those of the towns which developed around them.[19] Dafydd is perhaps thinking of the house itself as the castle and the surrounding outhouses (from one of which the dog attacks him) as the town. At the end of the poem he says that Eiddig is able to exclude him from his *tai* and his *tyddyn,* where the former word seems to refer to the whole collection of buildings,[20] and the latter to the house itself. This ending may contain an oblique reference to the exclusion of the native Welsh population from the castled towns.[21] Dafydd's claim that he still has the freedom of the woods and fields could be taken as an assertion of Welsh independence under the English oppression which the castles both enforced and symbolized.

Although the castle metaphor does not appear in **"Y Ffenestr"** (64), the house plays much the same role as in **"Tri Phorthor Eiddig,"** its solidity preventing Dafydd from reaching the girl. Dafydd arrives at the girl's house at night, and asks for a kiss through a small window, but she refuses. He then explains that they were unable to kiss because of the narrowness of the barred window, and the poem ends with a curse on the window and the carpenter who made it.

The contrast between this barred window and the glass one of **"Amnaid"** (40) is an indication of the different significance of the house in the two poems. Although there would be even less chance of kissing through glass, its principal purpose is not to keep people out or in, as the bars do, but to let in light. The barred window of **"Y Ffenestr"** is more like a castle window (note the 'deeply recessed windows' of Peate's description of Pembrokeshire stone houses quoted above), and this impression is strengthened by the comparison with the window through which Melwas climbed at Caerlleon to reach Gwenhwyfar, the daughter of Gogfran Gawr (lines 19-26).[22] Dafydd's poem is the only reference to Melwas climbing through a window, but in Chrétien de Troyes's version of the story, *Le Chevalier de la Charrette,*[23] the same exploit is attributed to Guenièvre's rescuer Lancelot (lines 4574-715). Like Dafydd, the French lovers curse the bars for keeping them apart:

> De ce que ansanble ne vienent
> lor poise molt a desmesure
> qu'il an blasment la ferreüre.
>
> (lines 4594-96)

[They are so extremely distressed at not being able to come together that they curse the iron bars.]

But whereas the bars ultimately pose no problem for Lancelot, impotent cursing is all that Dafydd is capable of. The sense of frustration which the lovers feel is effectively expressed by the long sentence from lines 32 to 38, the reference to the kiss itself being delayed by asides (*sangiadau*) and subordinate clauses, giving the impression of futile straining. Dafydd's frustration is made worse by the fact that the girl is so near and yet still unattainable. This situation of the two lovers on either side of the wall is expressed in an important idiom in lines 27-28:

> Cyd cawn fod pan fai'n odi
> Hwyl am y ffenestr â hi.
>
> [Though I was able to be on the other side of the window to her for a while when it was snowing . . .]

The idiom *am . . . â,* meaning 'on the other side of . . . to',[24] occurs in all the other poems which I am discussing. In **"Dan y Bargod"** (89) Dafydd says:

> Mau wâl am y wialen
> Â thi, rhaid ym weiddi, wen.
>
> (lines 13-14)

[My bed (is) on the other side of the wall to you, I have to shout, dear.]

In **"Tri Phorthor Eiddig"** (80) and **"Caru yn y Gaeaf"** (145) a whole line is repeated. In the former, having failed to get into the house, Dafydd says:

> Digrif oedd ym, ni'm sym serch,
> Am y maenfur â meinferch.
>
> (lines 55-56)

[It was pleasant for me, love does not disappoint me, on the other side of the stone wall to a slender girl.]

And in the latter he comes from the tavern:

> I geisiaw, mawr fraw fu'r mau,
> Gweled serchawgddyn golau,

Drwy goed y glyn, ni'm syn serch,
Am y maenfur â meinferch.

(lines 11-14)

[to try, great was my fear, to see a bright loving girl, through the wood of the valley, love does not surprise me, on the other side of the stone wall to a slender girl.]

The idiom appears in a slightly different form in **"Amnaid"** (40):

Daethom hyd am y terfyn
Ein dau, ni wybu un dyn.

(lines 21-22)

[The two of us came up to either side of the boundary, not a single person knew.]

And in a different form again in **"Y Rhew"** (91):

Gofyn, o'i glud gofion glân,
Am y mur o'm gem eirian . . .

(lines 9-10)

[My bright jewel asked from her lasting pure memories, on the other side of the wall . . .]

The situation of the two lovers separated by a wall is common to all the poems, but it is clear that Dafydd's attitude to this situation varies considerably. In **"Amnaid"** he is happy just to talk to the girl on the other side of the wall. In **"Tri Phorthor Eiddig,"** even though he has been repulsed from the house, he specifically says that it was pleasant for him to be on the other side of the wall to the girl, and that love does not disappoint him. The metaphor of the arrows of love which he fires through the wall conveys the idea of love overcoming physical separation. At this point the tone of the poem changes from humorous self-mockery to triumphant self-assertion, which is continued in the defiance of the ending. In **"Caru yn y Gaeaf"** he expects the situation to be the same, which is perhaps why he uses the same line again. The verb at the end of the previous line is changed from *sym*, 'disappoint', to *syn*, 'surprise'. Love does not surprise him because he is used to this kind of situation, on the other side of the wall to the girl. As we have seen, **"Y Ffenestr"** contains much more of a sense of frustration at being so near to the girl and yet unable to reach her. There is no idea of love overcoming physical separation in that poem. But his situation is at its most pathetic in the examples from **"Y Rhew,"** where the girl is secure inside the house whilst Dafydd is freezing outside, and **"Dan y Bargod,"** where he complains that because of the wall he has to shout to make himself heard. This latter contrasts tellingly with the lovers talking secretly on either side of the wall in *Amnaid.*

The crucial difference which distinguishes **"Dan y Bargod"** and **"Y Rhew"** from these other poems is the attitude of the girl. In all the poems we have looked at so far she is sympathetic to Dafydd. In **"Y Ffenestr"** she does refuse to kiss him at first, but it is the barred window rather than the girl's unwillingness which causes the problem. In **"Dan y Bargod"** and **"Y Rhew,"** however, she is totally unsympathetic and refuses to allow him in.[25] **"Dan y Bargod"** is a dramatic monologue spoken by the excluded lover, who complains of the harsh weather to which he is exposed on account of the girl. He reproaches her for failing to keep her promise, and thus the poem rather inconclusively ends.

The dramatic serenade is a necessarily limited genre, since it is difficult to present action in a monologue. We see Dafydd attempting to overcome this problem in lines 8-12, when he bangs on the door:

Taro trwy annwyd dyrys
Tair ysbonc, torres y bys
Cloedig: pand clau ydoedd?
Ai clywewch chwi? Sain cloch oedd.

[I struck three blows in a wild passion, and the bolted latch broke; was it not loud? Do you hear? It was the noise of a bell.]

He rather unnecessarily tells the girl that he has banged on the door in order to make this clear to the audience. In fact, this could be regarded as an aside to the audience up to 'cloedig', and perhaps also 'sain cloch oedd'.

The difficulty of presenting action may have discouraged Dafydd from using the dramatic serenade more than once (it is interesting to note that Ovid also uses the genre only once, *Amores,* I.vi). But in **"Dan y Bargod"** the excluded lover's inability to act forms one of the main themes of the poem. It is brought up first by the reference to the jail in Caernarfon castle:

Ni bu'n y Gaer yn Arfon
Geol waeth no'r heol hon.

(lines 27-28)

[There was never in the castle in Arfon a jail worse than this yard.[26]]

The primary meaning of this comparison is simply that his situation is extremely uncomfortable, but it also contains the suggestion that he is no more able to change his situation than if he were in Caernarfon jail. He is in fact imprisoned outside the house. Such is also the point of the clever lines:

Yna y mae f'enaid glân,
A'm ellyll yma allan.

(lines 39-40)

[There (inside the house) is my pure soul, and my ghost is here outside.]

'Enaid' is a play on the primary meaning of the word as 'soul' and its secondary meaning 'friend, darling' which developed from that.[27] As long as his darling is inside the house his soul is there with her, and he is unable to leave. That part of him which remains outside is deprived of the will to act. In view of Dafydd's inability to depart the poem's ending is necessarily inconclusive. Ovid's *Amores,* i.vi also contains no action, but Ovid gives it a conclusive ending by bidding a formal farewell to the girl's door. That may be a more elegant ending, but the ending of Dafydd's poem more effectively conveys the utter helplessness of the excluded lover.

"Y Rhew" (91)[28] uses the narrative mode, but it describes exactly the same situation as **"Dan y Bargod."** The girl does appear briefly, but only to make a heartlessly sarcastic comment. She asks Dafydd from inside the house whether he enjoys suffering the cold and whether he is human. He replies that he was human that day, but now he is so cold that he does not know what he is. Dafydd then falls into a frozen pond, making a great deal of noise. This is followed by a long passage of *dyfalu* describing the ice and the pain it causes Dafydd. He ends by wishing for the sun to come and melt the ice, since he is excluded from the house.

The lover's exposure to the harsh weather is a standard element of all serenades, serving to emphasize his devotion to his lady. It occurs with that purpose at the beginning of the passage quoted from *Le Roman de la Rose*— 'soit par pluie, soit par gelee'—and similarly in **"Dan y Bargod"**:

> Ni ddown i oddef, od gwn,
> Beunoeth gur, bei na'th garwn.

> (lines 31-32)

[I would not come every night to suffer pain, indeed, if I did not love you.]

But in **"Y Rhew"** the discomfort is so extreme that the object of the visit is quickly forgotten, and by the end of the poem Dafydd's only concern is to find some release from his suffering.[29] Yet, although the girl is not mentioned after the brief conversation at the beginning of the poem, there is an implicit reproach to her in:

> Gan na chaf, geinwych ofeg,
> Le mewn tŷ liw manod teg,
> Yn ôl hawl anial helynt,

> (lines 63-65)[30]

[Since I cannot have, splendid speech, a place inside a house the colour of fine snow, according to the right of a desert wandering, . . .]

It is because of the girl's coldness in refusing to let him in that he is exposed to the cold weather. The same connection between emotional and physical coldness is to be found in **"Y Cyffylog"** (115), one of the 'love-messenger' (*llatai*) poems. Dafydd tells the woodcock to seek shelter from winter in the girl's house, which he describes thus:

> Dyred, na ddywed ddeuair,
> Lle y mae a garaf, lliw Mair,
> Lle gofrwysg gerllaw gofron,
> Lle claer tes, lle y clywir tôn,
> I ochel awel aeaf,
> O ras hir, i aros haf.

> (lines 13-18)

[Go, say not two words, to the place where is the one I love, the colour of Mary, cheerful place by a slope, bright warm place where song is heard, to shelter from the winter wind, by a long respite, to wait for summer.]

He asks the bird to find out whether the girl is faithful to him, but it immediately tells him that she is not. It significantly prefaces its revelation with a statement about the weather:

> Eres hyd y bu'n oeri,
> Aeth arall hoywgall â hi.

> (lines 47-48)

[Remarkable how long it has been getting cold, another swift shrewd one went off with her.]

It is Dafydd rather than the woodcock who will be excluded from the shelter of the girl's house because of her faithlessness.

The role played by the house in **"Dan y Bargod," "Y Rhew,"** and **"Y Cyffylog"** is the complete opposite of the role which it plays in **"Tri Phorthor Eiddig"** and **"Y Ffenestr,"** where it is envisaged only as a restriction separating two lovers. With the emphasis on the harsh weather, the house becomes a place of warmth and shelter, from which Dafydd is excluded not by its impregnability but by the coldness of the girl. Whilst in **"Tri Phorthor Eiddig"** the girl inside the house is seen as shut away inside a castle, in **"Dan y Bargod"** it is the lover stuck outside who complains that his situation is worse than in the dungeons of Caernarfon castle.

The vulnerability of the excluded lover is the main theme of the most complex of Dafydd's nocturnal visits, **"Caru yn y Gaeaf"** (145),[31] which is another poem set in winter. Dafydd comes drunk from the tavern to the girl's house and taps on her window to attract her attention, but wakes up the husband instead, who thinks that Dafydd is after his money. He and a crowd from the town pursue Dafydd, who flees to the woods, hoping to find shelter there. But he finds that winter has deprived the trees of all their leaves and there is no shelter to be had. Like **"Y Rhew"** the poem ends with Dafydd wishing for summer to come.

The harsh weather in **"Caru yn y Gaeaf"** does not have the effect of making the house into a symbol of warmth and shelter, as it does in **"Y Rhew,"** but rather the weather joins force with the house to enhance its hostility. The thick ice under the roof adds to its solidity:

Tew oedd dan frig y to oer
Rhywlyb bibonwy rhewloer.

(lines 19-20)

[The very wet icicles of the frost moon were thick
under the edge of the cold roof.]

And in line 26 the icicles are said to be 'pyrs addail'
('leaves of the porch') as if they were actually growing
from the house. The house is therefore even more
menacing than in **"Tri Phorthor Eiddig."** But whereas
when he is forced to flee in that poem he has the shelter
of the woods, here he is deprived of even that consola-
tion. The comparison with **"Tri Phorthor Eiddig"** is
made particularly pointed by the curious passage (lines
49-56) where Dafydd says that he expects to find the
woods as he knew them in the summer. This could
almost be a comment on the claim at the end of **"Tri
Phorthor Eiddig,"** showing it to be only a half-truth
taking no account of the possible hostility of nature
itself.

Up to the point at which Dafydd flees to the woods the
tone of **"Caru yn y Gaeaf"** is humorously self-
mocking. But with his realisation that the trees have
been stripped of their leaves, the tone becomes much
more serious:

Nithiodd y gaeaf noethfawr,
Dyli las, y dail i lawr.

(lines 61-62)

[Great bare winter had winnowed down the leaves, a
green weaving.]

The pursuers are completely forgotten, even though
Dafydd has found nowhere to hide, and the theme of
the poem is now the destructiveness of winter, which
not only blends with the house of stone, but also
destroys the house of leaves. The use of the image 'pyrs
addail' (line 26) to describe the icicles now appears
extremely ironic. These are the only leaves which winter
can produce.

The variant readings for the poem's final couplet contain
a significant image which seems to me to be much more
powerful than the rather weak reading of the printed
text. Dr Parry gives:

Dyn wyf ni châr âr aeaf
Ar hir hawddamor i'r haf.

[I am a man who does not love the land of winter, with
a long greeting to summer(?).]

But thirteen of the sixteen manuscripts read: *Dyn wyf
yngharchar dan aeaf*[32] ('I am a man imprisoned under
winter'). Dr Bromwich has pointed out the prominence
of the prison image in Dafydd's work.[33] We have already
seen it used in **"Dan y Bargod"**:

Ni bu'n y Gaer yn Arfon
Geol waeth no'r heol hon.

And it also occurs as a *sangiad* in **"Tri Phorthor Eid-
dig,"** again referring to the surroundings of the house:

Carchar bardd, a mi'n cyrchu
Yn ddigyngor y ddor ddu.

(lines 27-28)

[Poet's prison, as I was heedlessly making for the black
door . . .]

In both cases it is paradoxically applied to the lover
outside the house. And the paradox is even more
extreme in **"Caru yn y Gaeaf,"** if we accept the read-
ing of the majority of the manuscripts. Without shelter
anywhere, Dafydd is still imprisoned. Indeed he is
imprisoned precisely because he is without shelter. A
prison is looked upon as the complete opposite of a
dwelling place. In **"Tri Phorthor Eiddig"** Dafydd was
only imprisoned in the environs of the house, but in
"Caru yn y Gaeaf" he is imprisoned as long as the
winter reigns. Having begun as a humorous fabliau, the
poem ends on an extremely sombre note, dwelling on
the vulnerability of the excluded lover.

The central point of this discussion has been the
significance of the house. Dwelling-places of various
kinds are also at the centre of a number of other poems,
which provide some interesting comparisons and
contrasts.

"Yr Adfail" (144)[34] is the only one of Dafydd's poems
which has a house as its direct subject. Dafydd ad-
dresses a ruined house, recalling its former state. The
situation which he remembers is not that of the
serenades, but of himself and the girl making love inside
the house, which provided them with warm shelter:

Dy gongl, mau ddeongl ddwyoch,
Gwely ym oedd, nid gwâl moch.
Doe'r oeddud mewn gradd addwyn
Yn glyd uwchben fy myd mwyn.

(lines 33-36)

[Your corner, my release of two cries, it was a bed for
me, no pigsty. Yesterday you were in a fine state snug
above my tender darling.]

But whereas in the serenades the house is seen as solid
and impenetrable, here it is vulnerable to the elements.
The ruin itself says:

Ystorm o fynwes dwyrain
A wnaeth gur hyd y mur main.
Uchenaid gwynt, gerrynt gawdd,
Y deau a'm didoawdd.

(lines 25-28)

[A storm from the bosom of the east battered along the stone wall. The sigh of the south wind, angry course, unroofed me.]

To which Dafydd replies:

Ai'r gwynt a wnaeth helynt hwyr?
Da y nithiodd dy do neithiwyr.

(lines 29-30)

[Was it the wind that did the late damage? Well did it winnow your roof last night.]

The image of winnowing connects up with that at the end of **"Caru yn y Gaeaf,"** where winter is said to winnow down the leaves from the trees. In that poem the house was unaffected by the weather, being itself almost a part of the wintry landscape. Here its roof is blown away as easily as leaves.

The retrospective image of the lovers secure inside the house is contradicted by the evidence that we have seen of Dafydd's attempts to get inside the girl's house. In fact, Dafydd is very rarely seen inside any real house. One notable case is **"Trafferth mewn Tafarn"** (124), where Dafydd meets a girl at an inn and agrees to come to her bed when everyone else has fallen asleep. He is completely out of his element within the confined space, managing to bump into all the furniture and wake up the other occupants of the inn. He is forced to creep ignominiously back to bed, the girl forgotten.

Another poem in which Dafydd is seen inside a house is **"Y Wawr"** (129). This belongs to the aubade genre, the dawn song of parting lovers, which was very popular in Continental literature, but not so in Welsh.[35] The girl urges Dafydd to leave the house before he is caught there, and he tries to persuade her that it is still night. Eventually he leaves, promising to return again if night ever returns. The aubade is in a sense the direct opposite of the serenade, the song of the successful lover who must leave rather than the unsuccessful lover who is excluded. It is therefore not surprising that Dafydd uses the genre only once, since except from the retrospective standpoint of **"Yr Adfail,"** the house invariably excludes him from the girl. Only in the freedom of the woods does he play the role of the successful lover.

In **"Lladrata Merch"** (135) he does manage to steal the girl away from the house to the woods while everyone else is in a drunken sleep, but Mr Bowen's suggestion that the poem is set in a tavern seems very likely.[36] Dafydd has learnt his lesson from his misfortune in **"Trafferth mewn Tafarn"**:

Sef meddyliais, ei cheisiaw
O'r gwâl drwg i'r gwiail draw.

(lines 29-30)

[My intention was to try to get her from that foul lair to the trees yonder.]

The image of the lover as a thief is quite common in Dafydd's work, and provides a contrast to the clumsy figure of the serenades, but **"Lladrata Merch"** is the only occasion on which it is applied to a specific incident. In **"Trech a Gais nog a Geidw"** (72) he boasts:

Tramwyaf, lwyraf loywryw,
Trefi fy aur tra fwyf fyw.

(lines 37-38)

[I will frequent, fullest beauty, the dwellings of my treasure as long as I live.]

And a very similar couplet, this time from a retrospective standpoint, occurs in **"Llychwino Pryd y Ferch"** (81):

Tramwyais, hoywdrais hydreg,
Trefi y dyn tra fu deg.

(lines 35-36)

[I frequented, bold swift action, the girl's dwellings as long as she was fair.]

But he is never actually seen to fulfill these boasts. Poems such as **"Tri Phorthor Eiddig"** and **"Caru yn y Gaeaf"** can be looked upon as dismally unsuccessful attempts to do so.

An illuminating comparison can be made here with *Yr Halaenwr* by Madog Benfras, one of Dafydd's contemporaries.[37] Madog manages to get into the girl's house dressed as a salt-seller. He is mocked by the servants, but the girl recognizes him and summons him to her room, where he gleefully casts off his disguise. The success of Madog's cunning plan is in complete contrast to Dafydd's incompetence in his attempts to get into the girl's house.

It is also interesting to consider some of the poems printed in *Barddoniaeth Dafydd ab Gwilym*[38] which were rejected by Parry. There are six which are similar to, and quite probably imitations of, the authentic poems which I have been discussing. They are nos **"XCVI," "CXXXI," "CLII," "CLVII," "CLXV,"** and **"CLXXII."** In only one of these, **"CXXXI,"** does the poet fail to get inside the girl's house. In **"CLII"** she allows him in but then refuses his over-bold advances. In the other four he gets into the house and begins making love to the girl when her husband appears and he is forced to flee. All these poems contain humour at the poet's expense, but the house itself as a restriction to the lover is of no particular importance in the work of Dafydd's imitators.

Any discussion of the significance of the house in Dafydd's work must take into account the poems about the *deildy,* the house of leaves which Dafydd builds in the woods during the summer. We have already come across a reference to it towards the end of **"Caru yn y Gaeaf"** (145), where Dafydd flees to the woods hoping to find his 'lloches yr haf' (line 52). A full discussion of the *deildy* is beyond the scope of this article, but it is important to note that it is in direct opposition to the house of stone. In **"Y Deildy"** (121) this is made clear by paradoxes such as: 'Gwell yw ystafell os tyf' 'A room is better if it grows' (line 8). Whilst the sterile solidity of the *maenfur* keeps the lovers apart, the growing flexible branches provide them with protective shelter.

Saunders Lewis has argued that when Dafydd uses terms such as *llys,* 'court', to refer to the *deildy* he is deliberately opposing the 'house of leaves' to the noble dwelling as it appears in the traditional praise poetry (including poems by Dafydd himself, such as **"Basaleg"** [8]).[39] I consider such imagery to have a positive significance, establishing a threefold opposition. The *deildy* is compared to the lord's hall, the ideal image of welcoming shelter, and contrasted with *Eiddig*'s house, which is the complete antithesis of the lord's hall, shutting visitors out rather than welcoming them in. A striking illustration of this antithesis is provided by the following lines from Iolo Goch's *cywydd* in praise of Owain Glyndwr's court at Sycharth:

> Anfynych iawn fu yno
> Weled na chlicied na chlo,
> Na phorthoriaeth ni wnaeth neb . . .[40]

> [Very rarely was latch or lock to be seen there, nor was there any gate keeper . . .]

Mr Dronke has pointed out the remarkable range of genres used by Dafydd ap Gwilym.[41] This discussion of Dafydd's serenade poems has demonstrated the range of tone and theme to be found within a single genre. On the one hand **"Y Ffenestr"** and **"Tri Phorthor Eiddig"** are about the lover's attempts to overcome the physical obstacles presented by society, a theme common in medieval love literature. The tone here is self-mocking. On the other hand, **"Dan y Bargod,"** **"Y Rhew,"** and **"Caru yn y Gaeaf"** deal with the isolation and insecurity of the excluded lover. This theme is treated in a self-pitying rather than a self-mocking tone. Humour is still dominant, but there is always a serious undertone, which comes to the surface most clearly at the end of **"Caru yn y Gaeaf."**

All these poems provide an approach to the often raised question of the relationship between humour and seriousness in Dafydd's work. Dafydd has occasionally been charged with a lack of high seriousness,[42] a charge which can easily be answered by pointing to such thoughtful poems as **"Mawl i'r Haf"** (27).[43] But it seems to me that rather than dividing Dafydd's work into the frivolous and the profound more attention should be given to his distinctive mixture of humour and seriousness within the same poem. The mixture results from his ability to look at himself both objectively and subjectively, seeing how ridiculous the serenading lover appears, and at the same time feeling his plight as a shelterless outcast.

Notes

1. Titles and numbers of poems refer to *Gwaith Dafydd ap Gwilym,* edited by Thomas Parry, second edition (Cardiff, 1963). For translations see Rachel Bromwich, *Dafydd ap Gwilym: A Selection of Poems* (Llandysul, 1982); Richard Morgan Loomis, *Dafydd ap Gwilym: The Poems* (Binghamton, 1982) (cf. *CMCS,* 6).

2. A nocturnal visit to a girl's house also forms the starting point of "Y Mwdwl Gwair" (62) and "Y Cwt Gwyddau" (126), but his intentions are quickly frustrated in both cases. The real subject of the first is the haystack, and of the second Dafydd's humiliating escape from the husband by hiding among the geese.

3. For example by Ifor Williams in *Dafydd ap Gwilym a'i Gyfoeswyr,* edited by Ifor Williams and Thomas Roberts, second edition (Cardiff, 1935), p. xl.

4. A. Jeanroy, *Les Origines de la poésie lyrique en France* (Paris, 1925), p. 145.

5. Quoted by Peter Dronke, *The Medieval Lyric* (London, 1968), p. 147, from Rossell Hope Robbins, 'Middle English Lyrics: Handlist of New Texts', *Anglia,* 83 (1965), 47 (no. 3167.3).

6. T. M. Chotzen, *Recherches sur la poésie de Dafydd ap Gwilym* (Amsterdam, 1927), pp. 283-86; R. Geraint Gruffydd, 'Marwnad Lleucu Llwyd gan Lywelyn Goch Amheurig Hen', *Ysgrifau Beirniadol,* 1 (1965), 126-37.

7. *The Oxford Book of Welsh Verse,* edited by Thomas Parry (Oxford, 1962), no. 49.

8. It is interesting to note that in the last poem of Propertius' fourth book of elegies the dead Cornelia says to her husband: 'Desine, Paulle, meum lacrimis urgere sepulcrum: / Panditus ad nullas ianua nigra preces' (IV.xi.1-2)—'Paullus, no more besiege my tomb with tears: the black door opens to no prayers.' The *paraclausithuron* was a common genre in classical literature. See F. Copley, *Exclusus Amator* (Madison, 1956).

9. *Recherches,* p. 284.

10. Edited by Ernest Langlois, *Le Roman de la Rose par Guillaume de Lorris et Jean de Meun,* 5 vols, Société des anciens Textes Françaises (Paris, 1914-24).

11. See Rachel Bromwich, *Tradition and Innovation in the Poetry of Dafydd ap Gwilym* (Cardiff, 1967), pp. 28-31.

12. It should be borne in mind that Parry does point out a number of irregularities in the poem (*Gwaith Dafydd ap Gwilym,* p. 478), although he judges that style and cynghanedd adequately support Dafydd's authorship. The fact that the poem differs from Dafydd's other nocturnal visits is no additional reason for doubting its authenticity.

13. Compare Cynddelw's *Rhieingerdd Efa* (in *Llawysgrif Hendregadredd,* edited by J. Morris-Jones and T. H. Parry-Williams (Cardiff, 1933), p. 121), where the courtly maidens look at the poet through glass windows: 'Trwy fenestri gwydyr yt ym gwelynt' (line 14).

14. In her article 'Dafydd ap Gwilym: Y Traddodiad Islenyddol', in *Dafydd ap Gwilym a Chanu Serch yr Oesoedd Canol,* edited by John Rowlands (Cardiff, 1975), Rachel Bromwich points out Dafydd's tendency to treat his models in a highly individual, even frivolous manner, referring to "Y Wawr" (129), "Cyngor y Biogen" (63), and "Dan y Bargod" (89) as examples (p. 50). Note also how Chaucer makes fun of the serenading lover in the figure of Absolon in *The Miller's Tale.*

15. For evidence of Dafydd's knowledge of Ovid see Bromwich, *Tradition and Innovation,* pp. 24-28. On Ovid's use of the *paraclausithuron* see Copley, *Exclusus Amator.*

16. 'Dafydd ap Gwilym: Y Traddodiad Islenyddol', p. 50.

17. *YB,* 10 (1977), 190-220.

18. *The Welsh House,* revised edition (Liverpool, 1944), p. 139.

19. 'Dafydd ap Gwilym a'r Trefydd Drwg', p. 201.

20. See Peate, *The Welsh House,* pp. 113-14.

21. 'Dafydd ap Gwilym a'r Trefydd Drwg', p. 197.

22. On the story of Gwenhwyfar's abduction by Melwas see Rachel Bromwich, *Trioedd Ynys Prydein,* second edition (Cardiff, 1978), pp. 380-85 and 533, and Kenneth Jackson, 'Arthur in Early Welsh Verse', in *Arthurian Literature in the Middle Ages,* edited by R. S. Loomis (Oxford, 1959), pp. 19-20.

23. Edited by Mario Roques, Les Classiques Français du Moyen Age, 86 (Paris, 1969).

24. See Parry, *Gwaith Dafydd ap Gwilym,* p. 515.

25. Chotzen makes a distinction between visits to an unmarried girl and visits to a married woman. But we cannot assume that the girl is unmarried in "Dan y Bargod" and "Y Rhew" simply because there is no mention of a husband. There is no reason for the husband to be mentioned in either of these poems, since Dafydd's problem is the unresponsiveness of the girl, rather than the danger of discovery by the husband as in "Tri Phorthor Eiddig" and "Caru yn y Gaeaf." Chotzen's suggestion that "Dan y Bargod" has to do with the custom known as 'caru ar y gwely' is difficult to assess on the evidence of the poem (his suggestion also applies to other poems now rejected from the canon by Parry). For further information on this custom see *Eos: An Enquiry into the Theme of Lovers' Meetings and Partings at Dawn in Poetry,* edited by Arthur T. Hatto (The Hague, 1965), pp. 57-65.

26. This meaning of the word *heol* still occurs in parts of north Pembrokeshire, see *Geiriadur Prifysgol Cymru: A Dictionary of the Welsh Language,* edited by R. J. Thomas and Gareth A. Bevan (Cardiff, 1950-), p. 1854. I consider it to give better sense here than the more common meaning, 'road'.

27. See, for example, *Pedeir Keinc y Mabinogi,* edited by Ifor Williams, second edition (Cardiff, 1951), p. 14, line 1.

28. Eurys Rolant, 'Rhamant Hanes y Beirdd', *YB,* 3 (1967), 28-33, discusses this poem and compares it to "Dan y Bargod."

29. Dafydd's reaction to the cold weather is somewhat different in "Y Cyffylog" (61), where he fears that it will make him impotent (lines 16-24).

30. I have changed the punctuation of Dr Parry's text slightly in order to take line 65 with what precedes it rather than with what follows.

31. The manuscript evidence for the authenticity of this poem is not strong, and Parry says that it could easily be the work of one of Dafydd's imitators (p. 547). But unlike "Amnaid" (40) it is thematically very similar to Dafydd's other nocturnal visits—although it must be admitted that one would expect as much of an imitation.

32. This was the reading given by Sir Ifor Williams in *Cywyddau Dafydd ap Gwilym a'i Gyfoeswyr,* edited by Williams and Roberts, no. LII ('Dyn wy' 'ngharchar dan aeaf'). The last line of the poem is also difficult to make sense of in Parry's text. I prefer to read 'A'r . . .' with Sir Ifor Williams. Although *hawddamor* is not known to occur with the article, there does not seem to be any reason why it should not do so.

33. *Tradition and Innovation,* p. 45.

34. A most illuminating discussion of the background to this poem is given by R. Geraint Gruffydd, 'Sylwadau ar Gywydd "Yr Adfail" gan Ddafydd ap Gwilym', *YB,* 11 (1979), 109-15.

35. See *Eos,* edited by Hatto, in particular pp. 568-74, where Professor Melville Richards discusses "Y Wawr" and another aubade once thought to be by Dafydd but now rejected from the canon by Parry. It should be noted that Parry also has some doubts about "Y Wawr" (*Gwaith Dafydd ap Gwilym,* p. 537).

36. 'Dafydd ap Gwilym a'r Trefydd Drwg', p. 214.

37. *Oxford Book of Welsh Verse,* edited by Parry, no. 48.

38. Edited by Owen Jones and William Owen (London, 1789).

39. *Braslun o Hanes Llenyddiaeth Gymraeg,* I (Cardiff, 1932), p. 82.

40. *Cywyddau Iolo Goch ac Eraill,* edited by Henry Lewis, Thomas Roberts, and Ifor Williams, second edition (Cardiff, 1937), p. 38, no. XIII, lines 23-25.

41. 'Serch *Fabliau* a Serch Cwrtais', in *Dafydd ap Gwilym a Chanu Serch yr Oesoedd Canol,* edited by Rowlands, p. 1.

42. Dr Parry discusses this charge in his lecture 'Dafydd ap Gwilym', printed in *Y Traethodydd,* April 1978, pp. 73-74.

43. Discussed by J. Gwilym Jones, '"Mawl i'r Haf"', *Y Traethodydd,* April 1978, pp. 89-94.

Katharine T. Loesch (essay date 1983)

SOURCE: Loesch, Katharine T. "Welsh Bardic Poetry and Performance in the Middle Ages." In *Performance of Literature in Historical Perspectives,* pp. 185-90. Maryland: University Press of America, Inc., 1983.

[*In the following excerpt, Loesch provides a rough background of Dafydd and illustrates some of his most famous verses.*]

Dafydd ap Gwilym still stands as the greatest poet that ever wrote in Welsh and as one of the greatest of medieval poets. He lived from about 1320 to about 1380 and is said to be buried under the great spreading yew that still grows among the ruins of Strata Florida, the Cistercian Abbey where many of the princes and nobles of the south of Wales are buried and where many manuscripts were copied. He belongs to a period in Welsh history and medieval history generally which is both exciting and elusive.

Dafydd ap Gwilym was entirely a strict meter poet; the innovations in his poetry were in content rather than form. The innovations had mainly to do with love and with nature, often together. They may have been influenced by a lower stratum of non-bardic poets in Wales, or by the Provençal troubadours via Anglo-Norman, or perhaps by earlier occasional ventures of the *Gogynfeirdd.* Dafydd viewed love naturally, not romantically as in the courtly troubadour sense, and often even in a comic perspective, especially in winter settings where physical obstructions and jealous husbands could confound the lover's pursuits. Both love and nature in Dafydd's case are very humanly real, so that his own experience is felt as direct and immediate, whatever the operation of literary sources may have been in guiding or inspiring his expression.

Dafydd was not a Dante; he is most frequently compared with Chaucer of his own century. However, Dafydd was always a lyric, not a narrative poet—even when, as often, he had a tale to tell. He has been likened to Villon as another medieval lyric poet, but Dafydd has a much greater range both in choice of subject within the lyric mode and in the qualities of emotion expressed. His technical virtuosity and the quality of his voice—exquisite, tender, delicate, joyous, childlike, playful, yet capable of deep sorrow—can only be compared in nature if not in stature to another *sui generis* genius who practiced another art in another century—Mozart. Each was the inheritor of an extraordinary and highly technical tradition; each also set the high water-mark of that tradition. Though Dafydd cannot equal Mozart in sheer production, so far as remaining manuscripts can tell us, he is much like him in the combining of originality and virtuosity with extreme range of mood. He could reach the depths, but what we remember most is his delight in life and its beauty and his truly merry disposition. Like Mozart, his dominant mood is cheerful, even playful.

The time, place, and status of Dafydd's life had much to do with the creative freedom he enjoyed. He was a member of an aristocratic family among the landed gentry which had other bards in its lineage. In the Celtic technical sense, Dafydd was not a professional bard, trained as part of the order, paid and regularly employed. He did, however, have patrons who were his social equals, who gave him gifts, and who shared his dedication to the new poetry of love. And Dafydd, of course, was a professional in the sense of complete mastery of his craft and art. Although he was receptive to the ideas and techniques of lower grades of poets and performers, with most of whom he seems to have felt some degree of identification, he knew himself to be a chief poet. He was so recognized by the poets of his time.

It is also relevant to Dafydd's freedom and panache that even though born in mid-Wales, his special terrain was south Wales. He was known as "The Nightingale of Dyfed" and "The Hawk of the Women of the South." The south part of Wales had been largely dominated after 1066 by Anglo-Norman adventurers acting independently. By Dafydd's day, it had become more integrated under the English crown, and Dafydd's family had mingled with the Anglo-Normans for a long time. Integration was usual and does not appear to have affected Dafydd's sense of Welshness. Also usual in the South, in comparison with the North, were a more international outlook, a society less rigidly stratified, and a tolerance of other grades of poets than those who could be called bards. All these factors were part of the liberating influence which the South had upon Dafydd. They make clear "that the impression of the monolithic unity of the bardic order, which is given by the law books, and by much of the work of the poets themselves is largely illusory."[1]

The landed gentry to which both Dafydd and his patrons belonged were a learned class for their time. Some of them collected manuscript books written in Welsh, in English, and in French. Rachel Bromwich notes that a copy of a manuscript of Guillaume de Lorris's *Roman de la Rose,* which draws on Ovid, existed in Glamorgan in the southeast. Dafydd considered himself a disciple of Ovid, whom he mentions fairly often, though we cannot be sure how he came by his knowledge of him or how much knowledge he had. Bromwich does point out one close comparison with Ovid's *Amores.*[2]

Dafydd handled so brilliantly one of the many verse forms used occasionally by earlier bards and lesser poets that his bardic period was named for that form: the *Cywyddwyr* or masters of the *cywydd.* One feature of the *cywydd* is the way in which its lines, usually of seven syllables each, rhyme in couplets. Either one of the rhyming pair ends in an accented syllable and the other in an unaccented syllable. The following lines illustrate the rhyming scheme for *cywdd* couplets, here in the pattern of unaccented followed by accented syllabic endings:

> Night may dare not, my dearest,
> Shadow throw where she doth rest.
> Daylight round her shall dally,
> As sunshine on snow is she. . . .[3]

The above lines may also suggest another feature of *cywydd* verse. This one, however, is so complicated that it is beyond the full comprehension of anyone who has not studied how to hear multiple patterns in the sounds of Welsh poetry. This feature, of which Dafydd was a master, is named *cynghanedd.* It is an elaborate and regularized system of internal rhyme and alliteration in *cywydd* couplets.[4] Hints of this system in the above

lines are the matched alliteration of the first line, where the last three words repeat the starting letters of the first three, and the internal rhyme which the start of the third line makes with the opening of the first line, even while reversing the rhyming sounds: "Night may" and "Daylight." Such a glimpse of *cynghanedd* operating in the above lines may help illustrate Thomas Parry's famous statement of the Welsh bardic aesthetic: the "standpoint is that sound is as important as sense; that metre and *cynghanedd,* the whole framework of verse, are as much a part of the aesthetic effect as what is said."[5]

Perhaps the most remarkable thing about Dafydd ap Gwilym is that he developed and mastered the intricate formal aspects of the *cywydd* and its *cynghanedd* while sustaining a remarkable liveliness and spontaneity in his poems. Typical of his inventiveness was the *ymryson* or contest of *cywydd*-making he had with Gruffudd Gryg, another bard, in which Dafydd taunted.

> That Gruffudd, solemn in fear, does not sing
> (Complaining look) a *cywydd* like him.[6]

The second line illustrates Dafydd's amused way of talking about himself in the third person ("him"). It also contains an example of his use of *sangiad,* a parenthetical phrase here inserted for comic effect and sometimes elsewhere as a serious aside.

This same contest with Gruffudd spendidly illustrates the *joie de vivre* and sheer physical energy of Dafydd. He refers to himself as "I, of bright strong voice" and hurls this challenge at Gruffudd:

> Let's test each other if we're chief poets
> With two lovely poetry-hurling tongues,
> And two hostile songs, fine to mention,
> And two vigorous bodies,
> And a strong thrust on good handsome feet;
> And he who'd depart from the war, let him depart.[7]

Finally, there is perhaps no better example of the way Dafydd combined the audacity of his liveliness with the antiquity of the bardic system than these lines describing his beautiful brunette Dyddgu:

> There were faithful emblems there
> (Is this gift not God's painting?)
> In snow smooth as (heaped snowdrift)
> Her forehead, her husband says;
> The wings of the swift blackbird
> Like her brow (a spell's on me);
> The bird's blood after snowfall
> (Splendour of sun) like her cheeks.[8]

Even though the girl was just one of the many Dafydd pursued, most of whom also had husbands, the joyous poet elevated his contest of love from the domestic to the heroic by describing its prize in the Celtic emblematic colors of white, red, and black. Those, as we mentioned in the beginning, were part of the heroic heritage which came down to the Middle Ages from early Celtic and ancient Indo-European times. The vigorous Welsh bardic tradition, always oral and always celebrating performance, found a fitting climax in Dafydd ap Gwilym.

Notes

1. R. Geraint Gruffydd, "The Early Court Poetry of South West Wales," *Studia Celtica*, XIV-XV (1979-80), p. 103.

2. Rachel Bromwich, *Tradition and Innovation in the Poetry of Dafydd ap Gwilym*, rev. ed. (Cardiff: Univ of Wales, 1972), pp. 24-32.

3. Cited for the author from memory by Dr. R. Geraint Gruffydd, Librarian of the National Library of Wales. The lines, written in English by the modern Welsh poet T. Gwynn Jones, are discussed in part in [H. Idris Bell, *The Development of Welsh Poetry*, Oxford: Clarendon, 1936] pp. 35-36.

4. Eurys I. Rowlands, *Poems of the Cywyddwyr* (Dublin: Institute for Advanced Studies, 1976), p. xxvii.

5. [Thomas Parry, *A History of Welsh Literature*, trans. H. Idris Bell. Oxford: Clarendon, 1955], p. 48.

6. Thomas Parry, *Gwaith Dafydd ap Gwilym, The Works of Dafydd ap Gwilym*, 3rd ed. (Cardiff: Univ. of Wales, 1979); and Richard Morgan Loomis, *Dafydd ap Gwilym: The Poems* (Binghamton, N.Y.: Center for Med. and Ren. Studies, 1982), #148, 11. 41-42. The Loomis translations match the poem numbering in the Parry edition.

7. Parry and Loomis, #150, 11. 9, 39-44.

8. Parry and Loomis, #45, 11. 45-52. The translation is in Joseph P. Clancy, *Medieval Welsh Lyrics* (New York: Macmillan, 1965), p. 59.

Helen Fulton (essay date 1985)

SOURCE: Fulton, Helen. "Living the Good Life: A Medieval Fantasy." *The Anglo-Welsh Review* 80 (1985): 76-85.

[In the following essay, Fulton correlates Dafydd with Colin Muset, a thirteenth-century French poet and musician, citing similarities in their themes of the "good life" and their functionality in addressing social inequalities.]

Dafydd ap Gwilym and Colin Muset are two poets distanced in place and time. Colin Muset was singing in eastern France in the first half of the thirteenth century, while Dafydd was a Welsh bard composing in the second half of the fourteenth century.

The work of the two poets is comparable, however, in two ways—because of their similar status as entertainers, and because of their social contexts. Colin Muset was a professional *jongleur,* dependent on noble patrons for a living, and moving from court to town to entertain audiences. Little is known of Colin's life, but he addressed his poems primarily to the ranks of the urban nobility, rather than to the feudal aristocracy.

The *uchelwyr* class of which Dafydd was a member represented a similar social rank. The old native aristocracy of Wales had steadily declined since the conquest of Wales in 1284, and the new aristocracy comprised English and Norman overlords subject to the English crown. The *uchelwyr* were the educated Welsh upper class who administered the country for the English conquerors. Like Colin, Dafydd moved from courts to towns, entertaining noble audiences of his own social and cultural class.

The two poets also fulfilled similar functions in their social contexts. Both were composing verse at times of urban economic growth, marked by the emergence of an expanding class of laymen who were not directly involved with the agrarian economy. The purpose of their verse is to reinforce a corporate identity among this social group and to support its claims to noble status.

A brief look at the historical background will demonstrate the significance of the social context. In thirteenth century France, feudalism was still the dominant economic structure. The country was divided into provinces ruled by powerful dukes and counts, who were themselves vassals of the king. Within these provinces, there was often tension between the ruling noblemen and their subjects, creating opportunities for the direct intervention of the king. The token independence of the province could thus be undermined by the absolute authority of the king.

In order to administer the provinces, and to maintain some sort of justice between feudal overlords and their tenants, Louis IX of France (1226-1270) built up a network of professional administrators and public servants. Unlike feudal vassals, who owed allegiance to an overlord, the new bureaucracy were paid for their services, as part of a growing cash economy associated with increased commerce and urbanisation. The decline of feudalism began when overlords discovered that hired servants were more efficient than vassals as agents and public officials.

The emerging class of non-productive laymen is closely associated with the growth of towns and cities in France during the twelfth and thirteenth centuries. Many of the royal officials came from the ranks of the bourgeoisie, while others were already members of the lower nobility. As they acquired wealth and power from their administrative duties, they gradually became absorbed into the established land-owning aristocracy. The acquisition of land, through direct purchase or by judicious marriage, was an important stage in this upward mobility.

While courtly and chivalric literature, in the form of poetry and romance, expressed the concern of the knightly class and ratified their pursuit of power, the emerging class of public administrators required a literature which would reinforce their view of themselves as entrants into the nobility. *Chansons des gestes* and chivalric romances would have been accessible to them but not always directly relevant, with their emphasis on knightly prowess and martial skills. At the other extreme, humorous verse and *fabliaux* satirizes the lower bourgeoisie from whom the royal officials wanted to dissociate themselves.

The lyrics of minstrels such as Colin Muset provided a strong reinforcement of the kind of values to which the new class aspired. They wanted to be as noble and worthy as knights, so the figure of the courtly lover was still valid, but in a less overtly feudal environment. Women of superior birth and wealth were still an ideal passport to the ranks of the aristocracy, and the pursuit of ideal love a major theme of the lyrics. Rustic love, a poetic subject taken over from popular verse, provided an appropriate setting which was non-courtly and yet suggestive of the land-owning basis of the feudal aristocracy, as opposed to the urban environment of the bourgeoisie.

Colin's poetry is therefore composed for and about the members of a new bureaucratic money-based elite. This elite was intent upon ranking themselves with the knights and other noble land-owners by virtue of their public office, their proximity to the monarchy and royal government, and their acquisition of material wealth. As a professional singer dependent on patronage, Colin had a vested interest in supporting these aspirations.

The social content of Dafydd's poetry is analogous in some respects. In Wales, the monarchy of the English king was imposing a system of government on a country which had become a royal principality. The system was administered by an emerging class of native *uchelwyr*. Like the French officials, the *uchelwyr* consisted partly of hereditary noblemen, descendants of the Welsh princes, and partly of non-aristocratic families enriched by their service to the crown. The *uchelwyr* were also interested in expanding their powers and their material

wealth, and in asserting their superior status relative to the bourgeoisie of the towns. These were largely English settlements planted to ensure the growth of a cash economy.

The concern of the *uchelwyr* was thus to establish their position as the native elite, equivalent to the Anglo-Norman barons and overlords, and distinct from the emergent bourgeoisie. Their power-bases were their traditional courts and lands, and their operations as administrators of royal government. As a professional court bard, Dafydd was interested in affirming the nobility of the *uchelwyr* to whom he addressed his poems, and defending traditional Welsh rights to land and power against the inevitable growth of English borough towns and castles.

I am suggesting then that there are thematic similarities between the poems of Dafydd and Colin which arise not only from similar literary conventions but also from analogous social contexts and functions. Their poetry is intended to support and justify the social group for whom it was composed, and to reaffirm the exclusive privileges of the ruling class.

The canon of Colin Muset's work is far smaller than that of Dafydd's. In his edition of Colin's poems, Bedier attributes nine poems to Colin directly, and six others tentatively. The fifteen poems include topics such as appeals for patronage, praise of women, *reverdie* descriptions, love lament, debate, and *pastourelle* encounters, all of which are abundantly exemplified in Dafydd's poetry. I would like to examine two poems in particular from the point of view of shared themes and functions: Colin's *En ceste note dirai* (no. 2 in Bedier's edition) and Dafydd's **"I Wahodd Dyddgu"** (no. 119 in Parry's edition). . . .

The subject of both poems is a woodland meeting, in which the simple charms of the countryside reinforce the courtly nature of the love offered by the poet. In each poem, the girl is described as beautiful and courtly, the poet invites her to a rustic feast, and the woodland setting is described. The function of both poems is to identify the audience with the courtly refinement of the nobility—beauty, music, good food, an appreciation of the finer things of life. The two poems achieve this identification in different ways. Colin presents a persona of the courtly lover, and follows a series of conventions to establish this persona. He says that he suffers pain and sleeplessness because of his love, he prays to God to help him, he asks for a kiss, and he swears allegiance to his lady as if to a feudal overlord.

These motifs are echoes of Provençal *fin' amors* which created an analogy between the pursuit of courtly love and the pursuit of chivalric honour. Suffering for the sake of love was described in terms of the knight's suffering in battle on behalf of his feudal lord for the sake of honour. Appeals to God to help the lover are reminders of the knight's service to God as well as to his lord. The pursuit of physical satisfaction, represented here by the poet's desire for a kiss, led to a higher *joi* or bliss, just as a knight pursues glory and honour through the physical contact of battle, often in a single combat with a sword or a spear.

In Colin's use of these motifs, we can see a movement away from the chivalric metaphor of *fin' amors,* which is not so relevant to Colin's audience. Instead, the emphasis is on the courtly refinement and sensibility which the practice of *amour courtois* automatically confers on its exponents. By drawing on the literary conventions of *amour courtois,* already fully developed in French romance, Colin is suggesting an equation between the knightly class and his audience of administrators—if knights can achieve *courtoisie* through practising courtly love, so can they. To reinforce this notion of transferred *courtoisie,* the persona of Colin's poem is a representative of the audience to which it is addressed. He is not a knight, but a well-born layman who chooses the woodland, symbol of land-owning wealth and power, as an appropriate setting for a desirable and advantageous liaison.

The references to "good living" and "good service" reassure Colin's audience that they too are part of a noble class of royal servants, able to participate in the customs of the true aristocracy. The courtly love which ennobles the knights is also accessible to other classes of noblemen to reaffirm their status. By using conventions of courtly love, Colin equates his audience with knights, to whom courtly love lyric was originally addressed.

In Dafydd's poem, the emphasis is on the feast and the natural surroundings, rather than on the progress of courtship. The motion of courtly love as a means of proving knightly *curtoisie* or *corteza* is literally foreign to Dafydd's audiences. The knightly and feudal associations of courtly love are not relevant to the *uchelwyr* and are seldom referred to by Dafydd. When they do occur, in the form of conventional imagery such as swords and arrows of love, they help to identify the *uchelwyr* with the chivalric ideal of France, and thus with their Anglo-Norman rulers. French influences are reminders of the *uchelwyr* identification with the Anglo-Norman nobility, assuring the *uchelwyr* that they are equally noble.

In this poem, the courtliness of Dafydd's audience is reaffirmed by the description of the rustic feast. Dafydd describes the feast in negative terms, by what it is not. The list comprises non-courtly and boorishly rustic forms of celebration—the young reaper's feast, the farm labourer's dinner, the churl's feast of the shaving tool.

The reality and significance of these things in terms of the agrarian economy, the food-producing importance of the countryside, is ignored. As a contrast, bird-song representing the music which accompanies court feasts is used to create a mood of refinement appropriate to the noble status of Dyddgu and of the poet himself. So an apparently rustic feast, escaping from the restrictions of the court, actually emphasises the refinements of court life, the ability of the *uchelwyr* to appreciate beauty, their aesthetic sensibilities which are the hallmark of nobility. Furthermore, the extended metaphor of the trees as a house emphasises the equation between court and woodland. By describing the grove of nine trees as a dwelling—"a room of fresh birches", "a loft for the birds to play", "a green belfry above"—Dafydd is imposing the world of the civilized nobility upon the world of nature. On the one hand the poet rejoices in the beauty of nature as a fitting context for love, but on the other his appropriation of the woodland denies its inherently rustic and non-courtly environment, and sees it as an extension of noble and courtly life.

I would like to argue, therefore, that neither Dafydd nor Colin is describing the woodland tryst as part of a social reality. Instead, they are using the association of courtly manners and an apparently simple rustic beauty to confirm the noble status of an increasingly town-based audience. The rustic setting functions partly to emphasise the courtly appreciation of beauty and communion with God, and partly to remind the audience that land, and the peasants who work it, are a form of wealth, an emblem of noble status. This confirmation is expressed mainly through the theme of "living the good life". This is one of several "registers" of lyric poetry defined by Paul Zumthor in his book *Langue et Techniques Poétiques à l'epoque Romane* (Paris, 1963). Zumthor defines a *registre* as being constituted by a group of motifs, and lexical and rhetorical processes, which convey a particular tone of expression. He finds three coherent and strongly differentiated registers in lyric romance poetry—the "courtly request", a lover's plea for mercy; "idyllic love", or the joyous possession of love: and "the good life", characterized by an abundance of natural description, the rustic feast often accompanied by music, and the presence of a willing girl.

These motifs are present in both the French and Welsh poems. Colin makes a specific reference, "thus we will lead the good life". The kind of life suggested by the poems does not reflect a particular social reality, but serves to reinforce the image that the new nobility have of themselves. The delights of the countryside are merely transformations of those offered at court—pleasant surroundings, comfort, fine food, music, good company. The realities of the countryside—discomfort, damp, limited facilities, and above all the necessity to work the land in order to produce food—are conveniently ignored.

The wooing of a girl in the woodland as part of "the good life" represents a similar kind of transformation. In the poems, the girl is eligible, willing, passive—in some of Dafydd's woodland poems she is not present at all, only as a wish fulfilment. The natural surroundings evoke the benign presence of God, presiding over the ceremony of the rustic feast. The imagery brings in the notion of consummation and physical union—the grove of tall straight birches, the crooked circle, the full-blown rose, the flowering fruit tree.

All these things are a transformation of the reality of courtly marriage. The woman must be eligible, willing, passive or perhaps not present at all when the marriage is arranged. The marriage is blessed by God and celebrated with a feast. Consummation of the marriage, for the purpose of generating heirs, is an essential stage in the legitimation of the union.

It appears that to lead the good life is to escape from the trappings of noble society and to find a free love outside the complicated bonds of marriage. This is the fantasy that the poets are celebrating in these two poems. But the fantasy serves to mystify and displace the reality—the materialism, the power struggling, the political and economic unions—and conceals from the audience that these are their true goals. Such a displacement allows the audience to confront problems such as marriage and social mobility in a non-threatening way.

In various ways, then, the theme of the woodland tryst associated with the register of leading the good life is an endorsement of certain values held by the audience to whom these poems were addressed. Dafydd and Colin are confirming that their patrons are noble—they understand the conventions of courtly love, the values which comprise chivalry and *courtoisie,* the refinements of beauty and music, and the surroundings of court and castle. The countryside is seen as the display of wealth of the land-owning aristocracy, a symbol of their power. It is deliberately removed from the urban setting of houses and taverns, a setting which Dafydd uses in some of his other poems. The economic and food-producing aspect of the countryside is also ignored because of its associations with the churls who work on the land.

The poems also confirm the Church's attitude towards material wealth and its advocation of a simple way of life. The food and wine consumed at the rustic feasts are unpretentious and in keeping with the woodland setting. God's own creations provide the backdrop for the courtship rather than the ostentatious surroundings of a noble mansion or fortress. Nevertheless, the court set-ting is clearly evoked in the imagery—Dafydd actually refers to "a green court"—so that the presence of the court and its material trappings is superimposed upon the natural world, affirming the nobility and sophistication of the audience.

In these poems, the woodland trysts are a displacement of concerns essential to the noble classes. Love is presented as spiritually uplifting, masking the reality of marriage as a form of social and economic advancement. Physical consummation is desired as the culmination of joy, masking the social need to seal alliances and secure inheritance through the production of heirs. The simple beauties of the countryside symbolize the important connection between noble status and land ownership.

Leading the good life, with its implications of simplicity, lack of materialism, and spiritual worship, actually masks the exploitation of the land and the people who work it in order to supply the nobility with the goods they need. Evocations of the good life in association with woodland trysts confer a spiritual authorization of the tryst, just as the church authorizes marriage. Because a courtship is conducted among God's creations it must be approved by God.

The good life is therefore a means of reassuring the new nobility of their affinity with nature and with God, of their identity with the land-owning aristocracy, and of their ability to share the noble and courtly customs of the ranks to which they aspire. This reassurance itself imposes a false consciousness on the new nobility—they are made to believe in their own importance and superior status whereas in fact they are the servants of the upper aristocracy and royalty, whose power they are helping to maintain.

To summarize, then, I am arguing that these two poems share a similar social context and function. Their purpose is to support the claims to nobility made by an emergent group of royal officials and administrators. The poems achieve this through a group of motifs described as 'leading the good life', which focuses on a woodland tryst.

Colin emphasizes the courtly love associations of the tryst to confirm the courtliness of his audience. Dafydd concentrates on the natural beauty of the woodland setting to imply the courtly refinement of his audience, making an analogy between courtly pursuits such as feasting, hunting and music, and the delights offered by the woodland. He explicitly denies any connection between his audience and the peasants who actually work the land. Instead, the countryside is a reminder of the power of land-owners over the urban bourgeoisie.

The theme of leading the good life is a kind of fantasy, a transformation of reality, which allows Dafydd's and Colin's audiences of noblemen to confront social problems in a non-threatening way. In presenting the fantasy of the good life, the poems function in the same way as dreams, processing social preoccupations and anxieties into a controlled format.

Finally, the confirmation of a noble status offered by these poems in fact imposes a false consciousness on their audiences, concealing from them their true status as mere servants of power-wielding royal masters.

Helen Fulton (essay date 1989)

SOURCE: Fulton, Helen. "Dafydd ap Gwilym and Intertextuality." *Leeds Studies in English* 20 (1989): 65-86.

[*In the following essay, Fulton explores the concept of intertextuality, or the idea that writings refer only to each other and not directly to reality, and how it operates in Dafydd's work.*]

One of the unique aspects of Early English Literature and Language studies at the University of Sydney under the professorship of Leslie Rogers has been the promotion of modern English courses—including grammar and semiotics—alongside more traditional courses in Old and Middle English.[1] Such a combination has encouraged the practice of looking at medieval texts from the point of view of modern literary theory, rather than simply as philological curiosities or as 'words on the page' in need of close textual analysis. While acknowledging that the poems of Dafydd ap Gwilym amply reward a close reading, I would also suggest that a consideration of their wider social and literary context significantly expands the range of possible meanings available to us. The aim of this paper, then, is to examine the relationships between Dafydd's poems, other medieval literature, and contemporary Welsh society.

It is one of the central principles of current literary theory that texts construct their own reality.[2] This constructed reality refers only to other texts and not to the 'real world' outside literature. Something in a text can strike us as being 'true' because we know it has happened like that in other texts-books, poems, newspaper stories, TV documentaries, soap operas—and not necessarily because we know it happens like that in real life, from our own experience. An Emyr Humphreys novel such as *Flesh and Blood* (1974) can be described as 'realistic' in relation to the wider tradition of historical fiction, and in contrast to other non-realistic literary traditions such as medieval romance or folk-tale, the *Mabinogi,* for example. In other words, texts are defined in terms of other texts, not in terms of the real world that such texts supposedly reflect. This is the concept of *intertextuality,* the idea that texts refer only to each other and not directly to the real world.[3]

The concept of intertextuality operates equally well in the work of Dafydd ap Gwilym. The world constructed in the poems is not literally the real world of fourteenth-century Wales. Certainly, there are references to actual places, historical people, material objects such as castles, jewelry, fur coats, musical instruments, not to mention the various species of birds and animals which inhabit the poems. Such things must actually have existed, concretely, in medieval Wales. But the meaning which they assume in the poems is constructed by the text itself, and by reference to other texts, rather than to the real historical world.

Let us consider a poem full of references to real places in Wales, **"Taith i Garu"** ('**Journey for Love'**; *GDG* [*Gwaith Dafydd ap Gwilym*], 83).[4] The poet describes, in topographical detail, the overland journey he makes in order to meet his beloved, a journey which can easily be reconstructed by the modern reader with the help of an Ordnance Survey map. But readers and listeners of any period do not need to know or visualize the actual places of Celli Fleddyn, Pant Cwcwll, Nant-y-Glo, and so on, in order to understand and interpret the poem. Taken by itself, the poem constructs a context for these places, makes them exist, and gives them a function quite independent of their topographical reality (their function being to emphasize the poet's effort to see his beloved, as a kind of humorous hyperbole); taken in relation to other texts, the poem is drawing on a literary convention in which real places are used to locate and explain a poetic or narrative experience. We can compare the listing of place-names during the episode of the hunting of the boar, Twrch Trwyth, in *Culhwch ac Olwen,*[5] which functions to dramatize the chase and indicate the extent of Arthur's domain; or the pairs of place-names used in the Harley Lyrics ('the wisest from Wirral to Wye')[6] to intensify the exceptional qualities of the poet's beloved. Such reference to other texts—intertextuality—is one of the most important ways by which meaning is constructed in individual texts.

Though many of Dafydd's poems can be read and appreciated in splendid isolation, some knowledge of other related texts is crucial to a full understanding of his achievement. Without the concept of intertextuality, the meaning of his poems cannot be completely realized. Each individual poem becomes more meaningful when read in relation to the others, and all the poems become more meaningful when read with reference to other literary texts.

We need to consider, then, the literary context from which Dafydd ap Gwilym composed his poems, and within which his poems made sense to his audiences. Another consideration is the position we, as modern readers, need to adopt to find the poems meaningful, a position from which the assumptions and attitudes of the poems are perceived as 'natural' or 'right' or even 'obvious'. Finally, I would like to demonstrate the importance of the historical context and how this can be used to help us understand the poems.

There are three major areas from which Dafydd draws his poetic material. Firstly, there is the *cywydd* tradition of which he himself was a leading exponent.[7] The popularity of the *cywydd* metre rose as the old bardic order declined following the English conquest of Wales in 1282. Once the domain of lower-grade poets composing in an informal style, in contrast to the highbrow eulogies of the official court bards, the *cywydd* came to be the regular metre of the new 'all-purpose' poets such as Dafydd, who emerged after the conquest to serve the needs of the Welsh nobility under the Normans, the *uchelwyr.*

These poets could compose all types of verse, from the most formal eulogy to the most ribald anecdote, suiting the choice of metre and theme to particular audiences—influential patrons and their families, gatherings of other poets and peers, groups of clerics or monks wanting some secular entertainment. Though the *cywydd* was used for formal eulogy or religious verse, the majority of the numerous surviving *cywyddau* of the fourteenth and fifteenth centuries take secular love as their theme. Another characteristic of this type of poem is that they were composed for 'courtly' audiences—the new Welsh nobility—and yet owe a large debt to the traditions of popular song, invariably oral and therefore inevitably lost.

The strictly regulated form of the *cywydd,* with seven syllables to each line, the alternation between a polysyllabic and monosyllabic rhyme word, and the use of strict *cynghanedd* in every line, imposed significant constraints on the content, and in some measure dictated the characteristic style of *cywydd* poetry.[8] This is distinguished by its erratic syntactic flow, which sometimes proceeds undisturbed over several lines, sometimes breaks off for an intervening image or aside, sometimes is repeatedly and frequently ruptured by a virtually parallel syntactic structure moving along in alternate lines or half-lines. The pace of each poem is controlled by the skill of the poet, with varying degrees of success. But the demands of the metre require a great deal of ornamental and parenthetical words and phrases to supply the patterns of sound and rhyme fundamental to the *cywydd.* It is this factor which gives the *cywydd* its linguistic, aural, and thematic richness.

The tradition of the medieval *cywydd,* in its early flowering, is the main literary context for Dafydd's work. His skills as a *cywyddwr* have to be judged in relation to those of contemporary practitioners of the fourteenth century. In terms of meaning, his poems also have to be referred to the whole *cywydd* tradition, since his imagery, whether strikingly original or recognizably conventional, derives meaning from its difference from, or similarity to, other *cywydd* imagery. Furthermore, Dafydd's poems are self-referential, in that particular words or images or syntactic constructions acquire significance from the way Dafydd uses them: any juxtaposition of the name Dyddgu, for example, with adjectives suggesting light or brilliance, immediately recalls similar juxtapositions in other poems, each one enhancing the strength of the others. When the same adjectives are then associated with the name or identity of another girl, the connotations of Dyddgu's beauty and nobility are implicitly transferred to the new image.

The second area of intertextual reference is the old tradition of Welsh poetry which Dafydd and the *cywyddwyr* inherited from the *gogynfeirdd,* the court bards who dominated Welsh poetry before and during the English conquest of Wales.[9] From this tradition, Dafydd draws heroic references to warriors, the celebration of patriarchal virtues such as courage and leadership, the concept of the praise-poet who offers eulogies in return for payment, and, most fundamentally, the identity between ownership of land and ownership of women.

In the time of the twelfth- and thirteenth-century *gogynfeirdd,* when Wales was divided into separate kingdoms uneasily joined into shifting and unpredictable alliances, with each other and with the ever-encroaching Normans, ownership of land was the key to survival for the native Welsh dynasties. Along with their eulogies to individual princes and rulers, the *gogynfeirdd* celebrated the lands controlled by these rulers as an integral part of their identity and power. When they came to praise the beauty and nobility of the courtly women among their patrons, the poets often described them in close association with images of land and countryside. Women, too, were an important source of power and survival for patriarchal dynasties dependent on political alliances and the generation of heirs. In many cases, a prince who married into a wealthy family acquired not so much a wife as lands, possessions, and ultimately heirs, which would be crucial to his continued status.

It is not surprising, then, that we find many juxtaposed references to women and land in the praise poetry of the *gogynfeirdd,* for they both represent a significant and desirable kind of ownership. In Hywel ab Owain Gwynedd's celebration of warrior ownership of North Wales, women are included at the end of a list of the natural advantages to be found in his princedom:

> Caraf ei morfa a'i mynyddoedd
> A'i chaer ger ei choed a'i chain diroedd,
> A dolydd ei dwfr a'i dyffrynnoedd,
> A'i gwylain gwynnion a'i gwymp wragedd.
>
>   (*LH* [*Llawysgrif Hendregadredd,*], p. 315)[10]

[I love its sea-border and its mountains, and its fortress near its woods and its fine lands, and its watered meadows and its valleys, and its white sea-gulls and its fair women.]

At the beginning of his famous love-poem to Efa, daughter of Madog ap Maredudd, ruler of Powys, Cynddelw describes her as *cyfliw eiry gorwyn Gorwydd Epynt* (*LH*, p. 121), 'the same colour as bright snow on Gorwydd Epynt', linking the woman with the land to which she belongs, and which is also celebrated in the poem as an elaborate means of praising Madog, his patron. Another of the *gogynfeirdd*, Llywarch ap Llywelyn, weaves the imagery of battle and land together with love, three preoccupations central to the warrior aristocracy addressed by the court poets. He sends a stag as a love-messenger to Gwenlliant, *heb dymyr Tudur, tud o lysau* (*LH*, p. 289), 'past Tudur's lands, region of courts', and personifies the landscape as a woman:

> Neur arwedd dyfroedd yn eu dyfrlle
> Gwisc gwynddail, gwiail gwedd adarre . . .
> Neur dug wisc, cantwisc gan y godre,
> Dolydd Caer Llion, dail lliaws bre.
>
> (LH, p. 290)

[The waters in their river-bed wear a gown of fair leaves, twigs like a flock of birds . . . the meadows of Caer Llion wear a gown, a hundred gowns near the foot of the hill, a multitude of leaves at the top.]

Obviously this association of women with landscape imagery is not unique to the Welsh court poets, but occurs in literature of many periods and places. When the device is used, however, it reveals something about the social attitude towards women shared by the users of that literature, the way women are perceived, and the kinds of functions they are thought to fulfil. In the case of the *gogynfeirdd*, the praise of land and women in terms of each other reveals a fundamental association between them, in social and practical ways, something so 'obvious' and 'natural' to the warrior society of independent Wales that such imagery is perceived as entirely conventional.

This close connexion between women and land was one of the basic functions of praise poetry inherited by the *cywyddwyr*. Since the political situation had changed drastically in Wales by the fourteenth century, the dynastic importance of land-ownership had receded. However, lands were now acquired very often through marriage rather than through inheritance or warfare, so that as the cult of the warrior-prince declined, the cult of the eligible courtly woman increased. In *cywyddwyr* poetry, the overt identification of women with powerful land-holding dynasties is largely replaced with the convention of setting women in contexts suggestive of *uchelwyr* wealth and materialism, including pleasant tracts of rich woods and farmlands. Women are increasingly viewed as materially desirable assets for young *uchelwyr* seeking to maintain, restore, or establish the family fortunes in the wake of the English conquest.

This brings us to the third area of intertextual reference, that of French courtly literature, imported into Wales and England during and after the Norman Conquest.

Since large areas of South Wales and the Marches were handed over to Norman barons from the time of the Conquest, and Anglo-Norman lords ruled the whole of Wales from 1284, it was inevitable that the French language and its literature should make a considerable impact in Wales, as it did in England.[11] The Welsh court poets continued to compose in traditional metres using their own language, but the native nobility for whom they were now composing were increasingly familiar with various aspects of French culture—material possessions, music, literature—and expected to see these things reflected in their own native praise-poetry as confirmation of their equally noble status. The conventions of French poetry and romance, both popular and courtly, were quickly absorbed into Welsh literature to the point where, in Dafydd's time, it is impossible to separate features which would have been recognized as demonstrably 'foreign' from those which were accepted as part of the native Welsh tradition.

Courtly love literature in France grew up in the twelfth and thirteenth centuries in response to the social evolution of a new class of nobility, the independent knights. In the earlier stages of feudal society, knights were dependents of their feudal lords and had little economic power. But gradually knighthood came to acquire a status in its own right, and many knights rivalled their feudal lords in landholdings, inherited wealth, and the possession of vassals. Knights could acquire land as a reward for their services and could then pass this land on to their sons. For younger sons, who had no inheritance, the quickest route to economic power was often via marriage.[12]

It is no coincidence, then, that the prevailing type of medieval literature in France celebrated chivalry and courtly love and was directed at those immediately involved in these pursuits, the landowning nobility and those knights who sought to join it. The concept of chivalry, as defined in romance and lyric, confirmed the special status of knights and their right to enter the ruling aristocracy by virtue of their chivalric virtues—valour, generosity, dedication, spirituality. The literary conventions of courtly love installed the knights as perfect lovers and therefore as desirable marriage partners. The actual focus of courtly love literature is not the woman, who is remote, unattainable, often unnamed and depersonalized, but the courtly lover himself, whose words and actions are designed to win him the ultimate prize, an advantageous marriage, or, at worst, the patronage of a powerfully-placed (usually married) woman. The audiences for whom the literary conventions of love lyric and romance appear to be natural and right are the knights, the women who must marry them, and those who aspire to belong to the knightly class, particularly the emergent bourgeoisie of the later Middle Ages. Courtly love literature offers men the role models of chivalric knights who achieve worldly success through their own endeavours, while offering women the role models of noble beauties who by mere inactivity and passive acceptance of their lot will be rewarded by love and marriage.

The concerns of courtly love literature are therefore those of an influential class seeking to cement its position in the ruling hierarchy and to control the behaviour of its individual members by offering appropriate role models. The early troubadour lyrics of twelfth-century Provence were addressed to ambitious knights seeking advancement through marriage or patronage, while the lyrics and romances of northern France included the wealthy bourgeoisie among their audiences, an inclusion signified by the frequent references to material and consumer items, such as rich clothing and furnishings, and by the merciless satire of the lower bourgeoisie. Such references, almost entirely absent from troubadour poetry, were very consoling to those whose elevated social position depended more on wealth than on birth.

The position of the *uchelwyr* in fourteenth-century Wales was very comparable to that of the wealth-based nobility of northern France. Part of the reason why French literary conventions became so widely used in medieval Welsh poetry is that the messages they conveyed were as meaningful and relevant to the *uchelwyr* as they were to the French ruling classes. The whole ethos of courtly love stressed the courtliness of those who understood it, so the *uchelwyr* appreciation of courtly love poetry was an important way of identifying themselves with the Anglo-Normans who controlled their country. By supporting the composition of such poetry, the *uchelwyr* could demonstrate that they shared the same courtly tastes and practices, the same understanding of aristocratic values, as the Anglo-Normans, with whom they had to compete for power and status in Wales.

In fact, the *uchelwyr* as a social class corresponded almost exactly to the newly-established class of royal administrators and government servants which had grown up in France during the thirteenth century.[13] In both countries, this development accompanied a change in political organization: in France, the increasing power of the king in relation to his barons, and in Wales, the consolidation of Anglo-Norman, later English, control. With these increasingly centralized governments, a class of powerful administrators directly employed by the Crown emerged in both countries to oversee the implementation of uniform laws and institutions.

In Wales as well as in France, this emergent class needed to legitimate its status as a powerful elite. This was achieved partly by claims to noble descent, but more often through the display of material wealth—clothes, jewelry, furnishings, houses, and so on—which often rivalled and even surpassed that of the older established aristocracy. The administrators and wealthier bourgeoisie were usually based in or near large towns and therefore had access to the consumer items produced there, whereas the established aristocracy were land-owners living on their land without easy access to consumer goods and often without a supply of disposable cash either, since their wealth was more likely to be in the form of lands and vassals. It was the bourgeoisie, who dealt in cash services and trade, or the salaried administrators paid by the Crown, who increasingly came to acquire status through their money rather than through birth or land-ownership. Not uncommonly, rich townspeople would buy up lands belonging to impoverished noble families, or marry into such families, and so acquire land of their own, a desirable commodity.[14]

Dafydd's poems, addressed to *uchelwyr* audiences, have to be understood in this context of a relatively new social class seeking to legitimate itself within a wider framework of power. His use of themes and images traceable to Provençal or French or Latin lyrics—sickness, sleeplessness, dying for love, feeling the spears and arrows of love, the duality of love as both pleasure and pain, the indifference of the adored lady, and so on—depends not so much on a familiarity with these lyrics in the original, as on an understanding of what these conventions had to offer for his *uchelwyr* audiences. They were educated people who had some knowledge of continental literature, often in Welsh translations, enough to make intertextual connexions between non-Welsh texts and those which were composed specifically for them by Dafydd and the other *cywyddwyr*.[15] By adopting the language and imagery of continental courtly love poetry, Dafydd creates a courtly love hero who is entirely representative of *uchelwyr* values and locates this hero right in the place occupied by the chivalric knight of French literature. This is exactly the place where the *uchelwyr* wished to see themselves.

I have been discussing the major areas of intertextual reference in Dafydd's poetry and explaining the potency of these references for his audience. At the same time I have tried to indicate the subject position that modern readers are required to adopt in order to perceive the sentiments expressed by the poems as 'natural' and 'right'—that is, the position of a member of the *uchelwyr,* conscious of a noble Welsh past and of the need to consolidate a successful future as part of the ruling regime. It should also be obvious that the historical context of the poems is of major importance in understanding their particular function at that time. Though the poems construct their own reality, the historical and concrete reality need not therefore be dismissed as an irrelevance; on the contrary, it is the constant comparison of these types of reality which generates levels of meaning. It remains now for me to look at some individual poems from the corpus to illustrate and develop the ideas I have been outlining.

Dafydd's praise-poem to Dyddgu, noble daughter of Ieuan ap Gruffudd ap Llywelyn (*GDG,* 45), offers to its readers a complex tapestry of intertextual references. At the most simple level, Dafydd's allusions to his role as a court bard, to Dyddgu's role as a courtly love object, to her physical appearance, particularly her dark hair and pale skin, are greatly intensified by the frequent repetition of these motifs throughout the rest of his poetry. In **"Caru Merch Fonheddig"** (**'Loving a Noble Girl'**; *GDG,* 37), Dyddgu is *merch naf gwaywsyth,* 'daughter of a straight-speared lord', and *dyn eiry peilliw,* 'girl flour-white like snow'; in **"Morfudd a Dyddgu"** (**'Morfudd and Dyddgu'**; *GDG,* 79), she is *Dyddgu a'r ael liwddu leddf,* 'Dyddgu with the smooth black-coloured brow'; in **"Dagrau Serch"** (**'Love's Tears'**; *GDG,* 95), she has *duon lygaid a dwyael,* 'black eyes and eyebrows' and is *didaer lun o Dewdwr lwyth,* 'a gentle form, of Tudor stock', while the poet describes himself as *dy gerddawr,* 'your poet', and explicitly asks for payment in return for his praises.

The constant repetition of this kind of diction and imagery, all suggesting Dyddgu's nobility of birth, her physical appearance, and the poet's function as court bard, intensify the significance of each poem to Dyddgu, as well as poems to other women. When Dafydd describes a woman as *dyn wythliw ton,* 'a girl eight times the colour of a wave' (*GDG,* 82, l. 4), or *dyn fain wengain ewyngorff,* 'slim, white, elegant, foam-bodied girl' (*GDG,* 78, l. 43), the images are redolent of beauty, nobility, and courtliness because of the accumulation of such diction throughout Dafydd's poems (and the *cywydd* tradition in general).

This is why the same type of imagery can be used with comic or ironic effect in the non-courtly poems, such as **"Trafferth Mewn Tafarn"** (**'Trouble at the Tavern'**; *GDG,* 124), where the poet describes the girl he meets in the tavern as *lliw haul dwyrain,* 'colour of the rising sun', and *mau enaid teg,* 'my fair soul', and even *bun aelddu oedd,* 'she was a black-browed maiden', all courtly images which are humorously inappropriate in the context of this poem. But the humorous effect depends on cross-referencing with other poems where such imagery is used literally.

Another aspect of intertextuality in the poem to Dyddgu is the echoing of *gogynfeirdd* praise-poetry. Dyddgu's father is eulogized in the traditional bardic manner, using images whose precise significance must be constructed from *gogynfeirdd* texts, with all their implications of noble warrior heroism. The virtues attributed to Ieuan—bravery, generosity, leadership in battle—are almost anachronistic in terms of actual fourteenth-century Welsh society; they consciously belong to an earlier era when such virtues defined the ruling aristocracy. Yet Dafydd's listeners would have understood exactly the kind of man he was eulogizing and the qualities he admired in Ieuan: the real person, Ieuan ap Gruffudd ap Llywelyn, is reconstructed in Dafydd's poem and made into a warrior lord of pre-conquest Wales. To understand and admire this figure, the listener must refer to *gogynfeirdd* texts and their conventions of praise, not to the actual historical personage. In fact, the poem is not concerned with the real Ieuan but rather with its constructed figure of an archetypal heroic lord, whose poetic function is to symbolize Welsh martial glory and independence, and the noble ancestry from which Dyddgu is derived.

A third and explicit level of cross-referencing lies in the allusion in the Dyddgu poem to the story of Peredur.[16] Here again, the meaning of the poem has to be interpreted by drawing on knowledge of another text, beyond the poem itself. The more familiar the reader is with the Peredur story, the more meaningful and striking Dafydd's image appears to be. In addition, the reference to a courtly text automatically confers courtliness upon Dyddgu and, by association, the poet himself, who is implicitly identified with Peredur, an accomplished and illustrious Arthurian knight. Intertextuality works here to emphasize the function of the poem: to praise Dyddgu's extraordinary and almost supranatural beauty, and to suggest the poet's own knightly qualities which make him a worthy suitor.

Finally, the meaning of the poem also depends on a wider range of intertextual references, that is, the whole tradition of European courtly love poetry. When Dafydd's poem is placed in the context of troubadour and trouvère verse, it becomes at once more explicable and more original. Conventions in the poem such as the extravagant declarations of sickness and sleeplessness, the suggestion of dying for love, and the emphasis on Dyddgu's beauty and nobility, only appear to be appropriate and natural because the poem belongs to this larger genre of courtly love poetry, with its well-established conventions. Dafydd's own persona as Dyddgu's suitor as well as praise-poet also seems 'normal' in terms of other courtly love texts, where the poet is typically both poet and aspiring lover. On the other hand, it is only by reading Dafydd's poem in the context of the whole genre that we can begin to explain his particular achievement, his departures from convention, and his use of other literary references.

I am arguing here that it is virtually impossible to construct a meaning for the Dyddgu poem (or any other text) by referring only to concrete historical reality. Knowledge of a text's historical location is a valuable key to understanding, but a text cannot be read as a literal reflection of that reality. The meaning of the Dyddgu poem has been constructed from intertextual references—to itself, to other Dafydd ap Gwilym poems, to other Welsh texts, to European texts—and it must be deconstructed in the same terms if its meaning is to be fully realized. The possible historical reality of Dyddgu and her father does not affect any literary interpretation of the poem, since the historical personages are not part of the poem at all: Ieuan and Dyddgu are poetic constructs, the one symbolizing traditional Welsh heroic values, the other symbolizing noble feminine beauty, inherited wealth, and the desirability for a man to possess both.

Such an approach undermines the attempts by earlier scholars to reconstruct Dafydd's own historical life from the 'evidence' of his poems.[17] However convincing the historical evidence may be that Dyddgu and Morfudd—and of course Dafydd himself—were real people living in the fourteenth century, it does not alter the fact that the characters in the poems are poetic creations, and the poems can be interpreted without knowing whether these characters ever really existed. Whatever Dafydd's intention was when he composed his verse— autobiographical, confessional, purely commercial—the poems actually function to reveal not the precise social and sexual relationships between the 'real' Dafydd, Morfudd, Dyddgu, and the others, but the interests, concerns, aspirations, fears, and prejudices of the fourteenth-century *uchelwyr* for whom he composed. The 'real people' named in the poems are characters constructed from other texts, other literary conventions, which makes them recognizable to the audience and gives them a symbolic function. There is no difference, then, between the figure of Morfudd (possibly real and historical) and the figure of Eiddig, the jealous husband (a stock character of medieval literature).

Dafydd himself is no more 'real' in his poems than any of his other characters. Even though he consistently refers to himself in the first person, he constructs a poetic persona for himself to serve various poetic ends. Trying to analyze the 'real' Dafydd ap Gwilym on the basis of his poems is therefore a fruitless task, and in fact it is far more profitable to examine the poetic persona we are offered as part of an overall interpretation of each poem.

Dafydd's frequent representation of himself as a poet expecting his due financial reward corresponds to the troubadour persona of feudal knight in service to his liege-lord, that is, the woman herself. In exploiting the poet-patron relationship as a correlative of the lover-lady relationship, Dafydd is continuing a tradition begun with the *gogynfeirdd* in their *rhieingerddi* to noble-women of royal households in twelfth- and thirteenth-century Wales.[18] But unlike the *gogynfeirdd*, who were secure in their positions as part of a bardic and social hierarchy, Dafydd represents a new type of poet whose position was no longer taken for granted. The royal

households had disappeared after 1284, and poets had to seek patronage wherever they could find it, from the *uchelwyr*, from the Church, from English families serving the Crown in Wales.

Because of this relative instability and mobility of poets, Dafydd's assumption of the persona of traditional court poet is stylized and anachronistic in a way that it was not for the earlier *gogynfeirdd*. Moreover, Dafydd adopts a number of different personae in his poems, such as courtly lover, *clerwr*,[19] rustic suitor, adulterer, young squire, cleric, old man, and so on. This variety of authorial voices points to the fact that there was no unified and recognizable social position for poets in Dafydd's time, the old hierarchy of poets had fragmented into a whole range of composers, singers, and entertainers all dependent on the same patrons.

In his formal courtly love poetry, Dafydd uses his persona of traditional court poet to apply to his lady for reward, as a poet to a patron. In **"Dagrau Serch"** (**'Love's Tears'**; *GDG,* 95), for example, he says:

> Dêl i'th fryd dalu i'th frawd
> Dyfu yt wawd â'i dafawd

> [May it come into your mind to pay your brother for increasing your praise with his tongue.]

Such explicit connexions between praise and payment occur often in the poems and are obviously a conventional way of reminding *uchelwyr* patrons of their obligations to poets at a time when these obligations were no longer clearly understood by everyone. However, if the poet is also a lover, as he proclaims in his song, then the financial reward he seeks is a metaphor of sexual reward, a different kind of payment but just as material and earthly.

The purpose of Dafydd's eulogistic love poems is therefore twofold. By praising women in the style of continental court poetry, Dafydd is reinforcing their status, and consequently that of their families, as members of a noble and privileged class who share the traditions of the Anglo-Norman aristocracy; and by implicitly seeking sexual favours from the women he praises, Dafydd is acknowledging the importance of such women as marriage partners for young *uchelwyr* and those seeking entry to the ruling classes in Wales.

It is also a function of Dafydd's position as poet that many of his formal love poems have a moralistic attitude, particularly on the subject of fickleness and the need to fulfil obligations. Morfudd is often the target for these kinds of reproaches, as in **"Morfudd Fel yr Haul"** (**'Morfudd Like the Sun'**; *GDG,* 42), **"Gofyn Cymod"** (**'Asking for a Reconciliation'**; *GDG,* 52), and **"Y Cariad a Wrthodwyd"** (**'The Rejected Lover'**; *GDG,* 93). Since petitions to women are so often metaphors, or displacements, of petitions to patrons, it is hard not to read such poems in the general context of the relationship between poets and the *uchelwyr* in fourteenth-century Wales. In condemning women's fickleness, Dafydd is also reminding the native nobility of their duty to support their own Welsh culture and not to be seduced by the status and prestige of imported literary conventions and social structures. Some of Dafydd's courtly love poems, such as **"Cystudd Cariad"** ('A Lover's Affliction'; *GDG,* 90), **"Saethu'r Ferch"** ('Shooting the Girl'; *GDG,* 100), and **"Y Gwayw"** ('The Spear'; *GDG,* 111), are sufficiently hyperbolic and derivative to suggest a parody of familiar French courtly love imagery. At the same time, the wit and invention of these poems are the perfect advertisement for the superiority of the home-grown product.

Another area of influence from continental love poetry which Dafydd adapts to the native poetic tradition is the conflict between spiritual love and physical desire. In a sense, this is a conflict which Dafydd and the *cwyddwyr* necessarily inherited along with the whole courtly love convention, since the two are inseparable. The teaching of the Church was uniform and uncompromising on the subject of sexual activity in the medieval period. Love was to be consummated within marriage, and then only for the purposes of procreation. Yet medieval marriage was often for social or political reasons which had little to do with love. The troubadours interpreted love as the source of all higher (knightly) virtues, while acknowledging that love also implied physical consummation, a sin outside marriage. Individual poets dealt with this paradox in various ways without ever reconciling it, since it was irreconcilable. The frequent use of imagery describing the conflicting joy and pain of love also expresses the fundamental paradox of courtly love, the incompatibility of spiritual ennoblement with physical desire.

The imagery of love's suffering seems to have been particularly potent both for the *gogynfeirdd* and later for Dafydd and the *cywyddwyr.* Such imagery must have appealed partly because of its close association with a courtly context, but also because it symbolizes social tensions and conflicts already present in Wales. Like the knightly class of Provence, the *uchelwyr* needed to assert their status in order to emerge from the older Welsh aristocracy and to claim equality with the Anglo-Norman establishment. Women as marriage partners were a crucial factor in assisting the rise of the *uchelwyr,* just as they were for the knights, and the poetic sufferings of unrequited love provided a literary legitimation of men's pursuit of wealthy and well-connected women.

Dafydd ap Gwilym tackles the problem of the courtly love paradox in much the same way as the troubadours, by separating the two halves of the paradox into two different genres, courtly eulogy and humorous satire. In his courtly love lyrics, such as **"Dyddgu"** (*GDG,* 45), **"Talu Dyled"** ('Paying a Debt'; *GDG,* 34), and **"Caru Merch Fonheddig"** ('Loving a Noble Girl'; *GDG,* 37), the poet declares his love without referring directly to physical desire. Its place is taken by the poet's expressed desire for financial reward, a desire that is, as I have said, equally materialistic and earthly, but less offensive to Christian sensibilities. But in his ribald and satirical poems such as **"Y Rhugl Groen"** (**'The Rattle Bag'**; *GDG,* 125) and **"Y Cwt Gwyddau"** (**'The Goose Shed'**; *GDG,* 126), the lover's intention is more or less explicitly sexual, and he is shown to be punished by means of physical discomfort or humiliation. More clearly than in troubadour poetry, the message of Dafydd's poems is Christian and conventional: courtly love is a metaphor of bardic patronage and noble marriage, not of mere physical possession, while sexual activity outside marriage is a punishable offence.

However, unlike the troubadours, Dafydd does find a way to suggest a compatibility between spiritual love and physical desire, by locating love in a woodland setting. For this device he is dependent on popular types of lyric and love song common in medieval France (especially the *reverdie*) which also owe something to contemporary Latin lyrics and the earlier classical tradition. Dafydd is particularly renowned for his nature imagery, and it is clear from the work of other *cywyddwyr* that nature description and the theme of 'love in the woodland' had a special appeal for *uchelwyr* audiences.

Typical examples of Dafydd's use of the woodland as a trysting place include **I Wahodd Dyddgu** ('Invitation to Dyddgu'; *GDG,* 119), **Merch ac Aderyn** ('A Girl and a Bird'; *GDG,* 120), and **"Y Deildy"** (**'The Leaf-House'**; *GDG,* 121). In these, the countryside is idealized as a place of beauty, simplicity, and sensual delight, full of visual glory, bird-song, and the embracing presence of God. Above all, the woodland suggests freedom from social constraints, release from restrictive conventions of courtship, and a place where spiritual love and physical passion can blamelessly merge.

Dafydd's nature poems, like those of the French poets, share the ideological function of confirming the status of a new nobility. The trysts that Dafydd describes in his nature poems, even the countryside itself, are literary constructs, not a mirror image of real events and places. The most common motifs in both the Welsh and French poems of this type are the beauties of nature, the delights of the countryside and the encouraging sound of bird-song. But none of these things represents the reality of country life which, in the Middle Ages, meant discomfort, damp, limited facilities, and above all the labour required to work the land in order to produce food.

Instead, the woodland is described as a metaphor of the court. The comforts, luxuries, and privileges of wealthy society are re-located in an apparently rustic setting. Dafydd describes trees as houses, with all the appointments of a courtly mansion: bird-song exists merely to entertain and delight the lovers, just as minstrels play to noble audiences; the lovers' pastimes—walking together, sharing food and drink, plaiting flowers into garlands—symbolize the leisure pursuits of a moneyed class which does not need to undertake physical labour on the land to survive. Above all, the pursuit of courtly love in the woodland epitomizes the refinement of *uchelwyr* life and social institutions. Because they understand the significance of courtly love, the *uchelwyr* must, by definition, be courtly.

Dafydd's nature poems therefore work on two levels. On the one hand the poet rejoices in the beauty of nature as a fitting and 'natural' context for love, but on the other he appropriates the woodland as a variant kind of noble and courtly setting—the woodland court. In so doing he creates a location which is highly artificial, rather than 'natural', one which denies the inherently rustic and non-courtly realities of the countryside. This locating of courtly practices within an apparently simple and unspoiled rustic haven works to confirm the noble status of an increasingly town-based audience. The natural imagery evokes a spiritual appreciation of aesthetic beauty, which is felt to be characteristic of courtly audiences, but it also functions as a celebration of land and land-ownership as a mark of status. The land itself and the peasants who work it are a form of wealth, a symbol of nobility.

The wooing of a girl in the woodland is an important part of this celebration of courtly status. In the poems, the girl is eligible, willing, passive, sometimes not even present at all, except as a wish fulfilment. The natural surroundings suggest the benign presence of God, presiding over the ceremony of the rustic feast or tryst. The imagery itself implies the notion of consummation and physical union—the grove of tall straight birches, a crooked circle of trees, a bed of leaves.

All these things are a transformation of the reality of courtly marriage. The woman must be eligible, willing, passive, or perhaps not present at all when the marriage is arranged. The marriage is blessed by God and celebrated with a feast and music. Consummation of the marriage, for the purpose of generating heirs, is an essential way of legitimizing the union.

Dafydd's woodland poems therefore create an illusion which is particularly potent for his *uchelwyr* audiences. The illusion is that it is possible to escape from the trappings of courtly conventions and find a free love outside the complicated bonds of marriage. This illusion disguises the real aims and objectives of the *uchel-*

wyr as a class, which is to consolidate their power through land-ownership, the acquisition of wealth, advantageous marriage alliances, and the production of heirs. Through his poems, Dafydd is confirming the nobility of his audience—they understand the conventions of courtly love, the values of *courtoisie,* the aesthetic refinements of beauty and music, and the surroundings of court and castle. The countryside represents the display of wealth possible for the land-owning nobility and those who aspire to join it. The rural setting is deliberately kept apart from the urban setting of houses and taverns which is the world of the lower bourgeoisie from whom the *uchelwyr* want to dissociate themselves. Economic and agronomic aspects of the countryside are ignored, because these are irrelevant to the *uchelwyr* way of life.

This literary construct of the woodland, with its simplicity, lack of materialism, and spiritual uplifting, actually reinforces the materialism of *uchelwyr* life while reassuring them that they can participate in the courtly practices of the older Anglo-Norman aristocracy. But the illusion goes further—it encourages the *uchelwyr* to believe in their own importance and independent social status, while the political reality was that they were the servants of the English Crown and upper aristocracy, whose power they were helping to maintain.

In all these ways, then, the 'woodland court' offers a solution to the paradox of courtly love. The solution is in fact marriage, though the poems do not explicitly say this. But the tryst between lovers or the oath exchanged by them, presided over by the benign presence of God, represented by the birds and animals, symbolizes an idealized form of courtly marriage, stripped of its political and economic realities. Dafydd's poems suggest that the fusion of spiritual love and physical desire can be perfectly achieved in the woodland; in fact, such a fusion was the medieval definition of marriage. This is the social institution that Dafydd is actually offering, attractively packaged in the familiar imagery of romantic and courtly love, to people for whom marriage was a political and socially necessary practice.

The corollary to the importance of marriage among the nobility is their disapproval of non-courtly alliances and those which cannot lead to marriage. In the poems to Morfudd, who is supposed to be a married woman, Dafydd presents himself either as a noble courtly lover, who can never win Morfudd, or as a foolish suitor whose pursuit of her leads nowhere except to his own humiliation. The message of both types of poem is clear: relationships which do not have marriage as their goal mean nothing but trouble and suffering.

Dafydd also shares in a rich literary tradition of ironic and satirical verse aimed primarily at those who pursue sexual gratification without spiritual love—either outside marriage or within a non-dynastic and non-courtly marriage, such as that between Morfudd and Bwa Bach. Such a love is repeatedly shown to be worthless, sterile, and non-courtly; and the figure of the lover, and sometimes that of the husband as well, becomes ridiculous and debased.

This tradition of satire and irony, as the obverse of courtly love, is found in the fabliau stories and poems of France, the ribald songs of the troubadours and goliards, and the humorous tales of Chaucer. It is fundamentally an anti-feminist satire, a means of controlling the sexual activity of women and reinforcing the Church's view of women as responsible for men's sinful desires.

But it is also a class-based satire, aimed at those who pursue love in a non-courtly way and are therefore not themselves courtly.[20] The objects of Chaucerian satire are typically bourgeois figures such as the Miller, Absolon the clerk, Damien the young squire, and so on. Similarly in Dafydd's humorous poems, the targets for his mockery are characters such as the boorish Eiddig, Bwa Bach, and the poet himself, adopting the persona of brash young squire (**"Trafferth Mewn Tafarn"** [**'Trouble at the Tavern'**; *GDG,* 124]) or foolish rustic (**"Merched Llanbadarn"** [**'The Girls of Llanbadarn'**; *GDG,* 48]; **"Tri Phorthor Eiddig"** [**'The Three Porters of Eiddig'**; *GDG,* 80]). The humorous poems, then, do the same work as the serious courtly love poems and eulogies, drawing on existing conventions to affirm the values of an elite.

I have been trying to show that an intertextual reading of Dafydd ap Gwilym's work, taking into account the literary and social context within which he was composing, is an important way of releasing meaning for modern readers of medieval texts. It is not merely a matter of tracing sources and analogues for Dafydd's themes and motifs, interesting and fruitful though this process may be. Even the fullest understanding of the literary context has only a limited value without some sense of the social context in which literary conventions are perceived as conventional.

Literature as a construct is a function of society. The meaning of texts, whether in terms of individual words or intertextual references, depends on the consensus of a social group. Texts are not only the products of a social context, they are also a way of expressing the concerns of the social group which produce them. Literary conventions, such as courtly love, do not simply reproduce actual social behaviour, they re-interpret social practices in ways that make them appear comprehensible, familiar, reassuring, and natural. Indeed, this is the main function of conservative literature, to disguise the tensions and oppositions within a power-based society so that the prevailing social order appears to be 'natural' and therefore right.

In order to understand Dafydd ap Gwilym's poems, then, the reader has to adopt a position from which their literary conventions (courtly love, love in the woodland, the glory of the countryside, eulogy in return for payment, mockery of non-courtly lovers) and their implicit social attitudes (courtly lovers are noblemen who live in the country, boorish lovers frequent towns and taverns and smallholdings, women are passive or unreliable and need to be wooed persuasively) appear to be normal, right, and even 'real'. The literary conventions used in the poems are those associated with courtly love, bardic eulogy, and satire; the social practices fundamental to the poems are marriage, land-ownership, and the maintaining of power. The audience to whom these things appear real and natural are an elite class of Welsh nobles, the *uchelwyr,* striving to maintain their hereditary prestige while identifying themselves with the Anglo-Norman ruling aristocracy.

Although the poems are not simply a mirror image of any concrete or historical reality, but a way of constructing that reality into an acceptable literary form, knowing something of the historical background helps us to understand why this type of literature—the love poems of the *cywyddwyr*—was so significant for a particular social group. By relating the historical context of *uchelwyr* life, the material objects, the places, and people, to the constructed context of the poems, we can begin to understand the intertextual meanings and functions these realities acquire as a result of being 'textualized' into a literary form. The danger lies in trying to 'realize' ('make real') the historical context from any given text, trying to move directly from the world of the poems to the historical reality, when no such path exists.

Notes

1. Even more innovative, from my point of view, has been the gradual development and expansion of courses in Celtic Studies during the time of Leslie's professorship. It is in recognition of these two special achievements of Leslie's time as Professor of Early English Literature and Language—the development of comprehensive courses in Modern English and Celtic Studies—and in gratitude for the time I spent as Leslie's student and colleague, that I offer this contribution.

2. This idea of 'constructed reality' has its origins in the structuralist movement, which demonstrated that language does not reflect reality but produces it. See Terry Eagleton's discussion in *Literary Theory: An Introduction* (Oxford, 1983), pp. 107-08; also Terence Hawkes's convenient summary of Roland Barthes's work in *Structuralism and Semiotics* (London, 1977), pp. 106-22.

3. Intertextuality is described and discussed by (among others) Julia Kristeva in *Sémiotiké: Recherches pour une sémanalyse* (Paris, 1969).

4. All references to poems by Dafydd ap Gwilym refer to the standard edition by Thomas Parry, *Gwaith Dafydd ap Gwilym (GDG)* (Cardiff, 1952). The poems have all been translated by Richard Loomis, *Dafydd ap Gwilym: The Poems* (Binghamton, New York, 1982), who follows Parry's numbering of the poems.

5. A translation of this tale appears in *The Mabinogion,* edited by Jeffrey Gantz (Harmondsworth, 1976), pp. 134-76.

6. See *The Harley Lyrics,* edited by G. L. Brook (Manchester, 1956), p. 31.

7. On the *cywydd,* see D. J. Bowen, 'Dafydd ap Gwilym a Datblygiad y Cywydd', *Llen Cymru,* 8 (1964), 1-32; Gwyn Williams, *An Introduction to Welsh Poetry* (London, 1953). For examples of *cywydd* poetry (other than Dafydd's) in English translations, see Joseph Clancy, *Medieval Welsh Lyrics* (London, 1965) and *The Oxford Book of Welsh Verse in English,* edited by Gwyn Jones (Oxford, 1977).

8. Eurys Rowlands has a clear explanation of the *cywydd* metre and *cynghanedd* in his introduction to *Poems of the Cywyddwyr* (Dublin, 1976), pp. xx-xlix.

9. On the *gogynfeirdd* and their poetry, see J. E. Caerwyn Williams, *The Poets of the Welsh Princes* (Cardiff, 1978).

10. *Llawysgrif Hendregadredd,* edited by J. Morris-Jones and T. H. Parry-Williams (Cardiff, 1971).

11. For the history of medieval Wales, see Rhys Davies, *Lordship and Society in the March of Wales 1282-1400* (Oxford, 1978) and *Conquest, Co-Existence and Change* (Cardiff, 1987); Wendy Davies, *Wales in the Early Middle Ages* (Leicester, 1982).

12. The rise of the knights and its social implications are discussed by Georges Duby in *The Chivalrous Society* (London, 1977). See also Eric Koehler, 'Observations historiques et sociologiques sur la poésie des troubadours', *Cahiers de Civilization Médiévale,* 7 (1964), 27-51.

13. See Gerald A. Hodgett, *A Social and Economic History of Medieval Europe* (London, 1972).

14. The new wealth of the bourgeoisie in France is described by Edmond Faral in *La Vie quotidienne au temps de Saint Louis* (Paris, 1938).

15. French and Latin texts which were likely to have been available in fourteenth-century Wales have been discussed by Rachel Bromwich, 'Tradition and Innovation in the Poetry of Dafydd ap Gwilym', in her *Aspects of the Poetry of Dafydd ap Gwilym* (Cardiff, 1986), pp. 57-88.

16. The section of *Peredur fab Efrawg* relevant to this poem is in Gantz, *The Mabinogion,* pp. 232-33.

17. See, for example, E. B. Cowell, 'Dafydd ap Gwilym', *Y Cymmrodor,* 2 (1878) 101-132.

18. For examples of *rhieingerddi,* or 'songs to women', see the English translations by Joseph Clancy, *The Earliest Welsh Poetry* (London, 1970).

19. Literally, 'a member of the *clêr*', that is, a loosely constituted group of poets and singers without official patrons and usually educated as clerics, though not holding office. They are thought to be more or less equivalent to the continental goliards, or *clerici vagantes,* and may have been an important link between the popular song traditions of France and Wales.

20. The French tradition of satire aimed at the bourgeoisie has been examined by Jean V. Alter, *Les Origines de la satire anti-bourgeoise en France: Moyen Âge—XVIe siècle* (Geneva, 1966).

Morgan T. Davies (essay date 1995)

SOURCE: Davies, Morgan T. "'Aed i'r coed i dorri cof': Dafydd ap Gwilym and the Metaphorics of Carpentry." *Cambrian Medieval Celtic Studies,* no. 30 (1995): 67-86.

[*In the following essay, Davies traces the use of carpentry as a metaphor in various genres of literature, centering his argument around the way Dafydd ap Gwilym may have been influenced to use such a metaphor in his own works.*]

In the first *cywydd* of his *ymryson* with Gruffudd Gryg, Dafydd ap Gwilym responds to Gruffudd's opening attack with various countercharges of his own. Among the more substantive of these is his accusation that Gruffudd is derivative, a plagiarist, a poet who can only repeat poems composed by other bards. Thus, near the end of the poem, Dafydd terms his opponent 'craig lefair beirdd'[1]—'the echo-stone of poets'—a metaphor that suggests not only the passively imitative character of Gruffudd's poetry but also the inert, insentient character of the poet himself. But it is some twenty lines earlier, in a trope developed at much greater length and in much greater detail, that Dafydd levels this charge in the most interesting and far-reaching way:

Ni chân bardd yma i hardd hin
Gywydd gyda'i ddeg ewin,
Na chano Gruffudd, brudd braw,
Gwedd erthwch, gywydd wrthaw.
Pawb a wnâi adail pybyr
O chaid gwŷd a iechyd gwŷr;
Haws yw cael, lle bo gwael gwŷdd,

Siwrnai dwfn, saer no defnydd.
O myn wawd, orddawd eurddof,
Aed i'r coed i dorri cof.

(39-48)

[No poet sings here to fair weather a *cywydd* with his
ten nails [as accompaniment on the harp] without Gruf-
fudd singing, a serious test, with puffing face, the *cy-
wydd* back to him. Anyone could make a strong build-
ing if wood could be found, and the health of men; it's
easier to find, where the wood is poor (profound
journey) a carpenter than material. If he wants poetry,
the golden, cultured hammer-blow, let him go to the
woods and cut down matter.]

On the face of it, this looks like a straightforward
enough trope, and in discussions of this *cywydd* it is
usually overlooked in favour of the more striking, and
more problematic, metaphors of the harp and the old
manuscript that precede it in the poem.[2] But its
significance extends far beyond the bounds of this one
cywydd, and in fact it reverberates in some highly sug-
gestive ways throughout much of the corpus of Dafy-
dd's poetry. What I would like to do here is to consider
this trope in some detail, taking a fairly close look at
both its extremely rich heritage within the context of a
variety of different kinds of writing—exegetical,
philosophical, rhetorical, poetic—and its implications
within the context of Dafydd's own practice of poetry.
For here, as is so often the case, Dafydd is not just pas-
sively accepting a conventional metaphor as part of his
traditional poetic inheritance; on the contrary, he is
adapting it to his own specific needs, recognizing and
playing off its latent possibilities in a way that not only
instills new life in a well-worn figure,[3] but also reveals
a highly sophisticated and self-conscious conception of
what takes place in the act of *prydyddu,* of what is
involved in the relationship between the poet and the
world he evokes—or invokes—in his poems.

The Welsh background to this trope has been pointed
out by Ifor Williams, who notes that the Welsh poets
'were very fond of using terms of carpentry for their
composition of poetry',[4] and he has been followed in
this assertion by such scholars as Rachel Bromwich, Id-
ris Bell, and A. T. E. Matonis.[5] Such a metaphorical
development would be natural enough: the semantics of
poetry in Welsh, as in Irish, place poetry in the same
conceptual field (and, with qualifications, in the same
social field) as other crafts; and there is an equally
significant connection linking knowledge, especially
poetic or esoteric knowledge, with trees and wood in
the early Celtic cultures.[6] Unfortunately, neither Wil-
liams nor the other commentators who follow him have
documented this claim, and my own admittedly very
cursory and partial survey of pre-fourteenth-century
poetry has turned up only one rather equivocal example
of the trope in the earlier literature; in fact, it is only
with Dafydd and his circle of immediate contemporar-

ies that it seems to gain currency in Welsh poetry.[7] But
whether or not the trope of the poet as carpenter, seek-
ing his poetic materials in the figurative forest, has a
long history in Wales, it most certainly does have a
long and highly ramified history elsewhere in medieval
literature. And because the question of Dafydd's sources
and influences, of the extent of his reading and its ef-
fects on his own writing, must remain to some extent
an open one, it is worth briefly considering this history
for the light it may shed on Dafydd's use of the trope.[8]

In the first place, we should note that Dafydd's version
can be broken down into two distinct but related
constituents. The first of these is the metaphor of the
forest as a source of poetic building materials, set out
most clearly in the last couplet of the passage quoted
above: 'O myn wawd, orddawd eurddof, / Aed i'r coed
i dorri cof'. This metaphorical use of the word *coed*
finds a reasonably close equivalent in Latin writings in
the similar (though more varied) usage of the word
silva, the primary senses of which include 'an area of
woodland, forest, wood; plantation, grove', and which
also takes on the figurative meanings 'a mass of mate-
rial; the raw material of a literary work'.[9] *Silva* is used
at least implicitly in this metaphorical sense in several
places in Virgil's *Eclogues,* for instance, where 'the
woods sometimes seem to be not merely the place
where music is played, but its source'.[10] Allowing for
the difference between the composition of poetry and
the composition of scriptural interpretations, it is used
in a similar but more overtly figurative sense in
medieval exegetics, where the *silva* becomes the forest
of texts from which the exegete builds his interpreta-
tions: Hugh of St Victor, for example, writing in the
twelfth century, conceives of biblical study as a stroll
through the *silva* of Scripture, 'whose ideas, like so
many sweetest fruits, we pick as we read and chew as
we consider them'.[11] It occurs with the closely parallel
meaning of the source of the varied written materials
from which compilations are made: the preface to the
early-eighth-century Irish *Collectio Canonum Hibern-
ensis* describes the compilation that follows as having
been gleaned 'from a vast forest of writings',[12] and the
eighth-century Anglo-Saxon missionary St Boniface
describes his grammatical *compilatio* with an especially
ornate version of the trope, in which he promises to
glean what is 'best and most necessary' from 'the
ancient forest of grammarians' intricate density', 'the
woodlands of the grammarians'.[13] Classical and medi-
eval discussions of memory also use the term *silva* in a
similar metaphorical sense, although they tend to inflect
it with a somewhat more negative valence: the *silva*
here becomes the raw data of experience and learning,
a pathless forest of 'unrelated or disordered material'
upon which the conscious design of the memory is to
work its organizing or architectural magic;[14] something
like the same negative valence informs its occurrence in
the *Elucidarium,* where it is used to denote the trackless

forest of questions ('sylvam quaestionum') about the faith through which the believer must be taught a path, and whence it finds its way into Welsh vernacular writing in the fourteenth-century translation of this text.[15] Finally, *silva* occurs as a title or designation for a kind of written composition. Here the sense of profusion and variety characteristic of the forest is to the forefront, and the term seems to denote something like 'miscellany' or 'collection'. Statius' *Silvae* is the best-known example of this usage, but the term is used in more or less the same way by Aulus Gellius and others.[16]

Alongside the sense of *silva* as forest is the related sense of *silva* as the actual raw material provided by the forest, as the lumber or timber to be worked into the finished product of a poem, oration, scriptural interpretation, or well-trained memory. Indeed, it is not always easy to distinguish between these two senses: the title of Statius' miscellaneous collection of poems, for instance, may be intended to emphasize not only their variety but also the speed or extemporaneousness of their composition, their rough or unfinished quality; and the use of the term in classical and medieval analyses of the memory suggests both the disordered profusion of the untrained memory and the raw, unformed nature of such a memory's contents. In any case, this latter usage seems to be the more common, especially in rhetorical contexts: it appears, at times in a pejorative sense denoting undisciplined, impromptu, or unfinished composition, in Cicero, Quintilian, and, closer to home, Walter Map, among others.[17] Also related to this sense is the more philosophical meaning of raw matter, 'the concrete chaos of the primitive elements',[18] in which guise it appears in fully personified form as the character Silva in Bernardus Silvestris' *Cosmographia*; the term is also used in a similar way in Isidore's *Origines*, where this usage interestingly enough is attributed specifically to 'the poets'.[19]

Notwithstanding their variety, all of the examples I have cited depend on the figurative conception of the forest as a source of raw materials for essentially verbal constructions[20]—a conception that clearly lies behind the use of the metaphor by Dafydd ap Gwilym in his *ymryson* with Gruffudd Gryg. Of course, the raw material of the forest requires a craftsman to work it into useful shape, and this brings us to the second element of Dafydd ap Gwilym's trope: the poet as *saer* or carpenter. The notion of composition (or of interpretation, or of memorizing) as analogous to constructing a building is likewise a traditional one, with a venerable heritage. Philo, Gregory the Great, and Hugh of St Victor, among a great many others, all conceive of scriptural interpretation in terms of raising an edifice;[21] for Gregory, this process of building or edification takes place in stages corresponding to the traditional levels of biblical exegesis:

Nam primum quidem fundamenta historiae ponimus; deinde per significationem typicam in arcem fidei fabricam mentis erigimus; ad extremum quoque per moralitatis gratiam, quasi superducto aedificium colore vestimus.

[For first we lay a secure foundation of history; next through typological signification [allegory] we raise up in the citadel of faith a structure of our own mind [*fabricam mentis*]; on the outside as well through the grace of moral sense, we clothe as it were the superstructure of the edifice with colour.[22]]

As Mary Carruthers suggests, *mens* in Gregory's phrase 'fabrica mentis' means 'the educated or trained memory';[23] and in more thematic discussions of memory, both in the broader context of rhetorical treatises and in the *artes memorativa,* one of the most common methods recommended for memorizing is to dispose the items to be remembered systematically in the various rooms of an imaginary house constructed in the mind or memory.[24]

But of course the most relevant instances of this metaphor occur in the context of discussions of composition rather than of exegesis or memory; the best known of these is probably Geoffroi de Vinsauf's opening paragraph in the introduction of his *Poetria Nova*:

Si quis habet fundare domum, non currit ad actum
Impetuosa manus: intrinseca linea cordis
Praemetitur opus, seriemque sub ordine certo
Interior praescribit homo, totamque figurat
Ante manus cordis quam corporis; et status ejus
Est prius archetypus quam sensilis. Ipsa poesis
Spectet in hoc speculo quae lex sit danda poetis.

[If a man has a house to build, his hand does not rush, hasty, into the very doing: the work is first measured out with his heart's inward plumb line, and the inner man marks out a series of steps beforehand, according to a definite plan; his heart's hand shapes the whole before his body's hand does so, and his building is a plan before it is an actuality.

Poetry herself may see in this analogy what law must be given to poets. . . .[25]]

Geoffroi's treatise was an extremely influential one from the early thirteenth century to the fifteenth century, and this trope in particular had a wide and sometimes independent dissemination, appearing, for instance, in John de Briggis's *Compilatio de Arte Dictandi*, in Vincent of Beauvais's *Speculum Doctrinale,* and in Chaucer's translation of Boethius, as well as in the same poet's *Troilus and Criseyde*.[26]

It is also worth noting an instance of this metaphor which, if admittedly less influential than Geoffroi's, is nonetheless even more suggestive in the present context. It appears in the preface to Alfred the Great's Old

English translation—or version—of Augustine's *Soliloquies,* and it is one of the West Saxon king's original additions to Augustine's text:

> Then I gathered for myself staffs and posts and tie-shafts, and handles for all the tools I knew how to work with, and crossbeams and building-timbers for all the structures I knew how to build, the fairest wood, as much as I could carry. Nor did I come home with one load without wanting to bring home all the wood, if I could have carried it all; in each tree I saw something that I needed at home. So I advise everyone who is strong and has many wagons to seek out the same wood where I cut these posts, and fetch for himself more there, and load his wagons with fair sticks, so that he can weave many a fine wall and build many an unmatched house, and raise a fair dwelling; and there he may dwell pleasantly and tranquilly with kinsmen both winter and summer, as I have not yet done.[27]

The context of this passage, as the introductory description of a book that draws on patristic writings in order to provide spiritual guidance for the faithful, makes it clear that Alfred is concerned in his elaborate metaphor with 'the gathering of material from the forest of Christian knowledge for the building of one's heavenly habitation';[28] but however different may be both the timber he speaks of harvesting and the structure he intends to raise, this passage, with its yoking together of the metaphor of the forest as figurative source of compositional raw material and the metaphor of the writer himself as carpenter or craftsman, comes strikingly close to Dafydd's trope in the *cywydd* to Gruffudd Gryg.

Finally, a less closely related variant of this trope does appear in at least one Welsh text, the preface to the Welsh translation of the *Elucidarium,* which follows its Latin source in conceiving of compilation in architectural terms:

> Grwndwal ygweith hwnn aossodet ar garrec. Sef yw hynny. crist. Ar holl weith wedy hynny. ar pedwar piler. ar piler kyntaf adyrcheif awdurdawt yp[ro]ffwydi. Yr eil awastatta teilygdawt yr ebestyl. Ytrydyd agadarn-nhaa yr ysponnwyr. Ypedweryd piler. a sefuydla kall gywreinrwyd.

> [The foundation of this work was laid on a rock—that is, Christ—and the whole work after that on four pillars. And the first pillar the authority of the prophets lifts up; the second the merit of the apostles fixes; the third the commentators make fast; the fourth pillar wise art establishes.[29]]

This particular variant of the trope, with its careful articulation of different elements in the edifice, seems to draw on a version like that of Gregory the Great in the *Moralia,* quoted above. But however different it may be from Dafydd's rather more homely version, it does testify to the currency in fourteenth-century Wales of the same basic metaphorical field for composition; and

it is worth noting that the Welsh *Elucidarium* seems to have been known to a number of Welsh poets, beginning at least as early as Iolo Goch.[30]

While I have made no attempt to document fully the history and varied fortunes of this trope in earlier writing, the foregoing survey should make it abundantly clear that the metaphorical field on which Dafydd is playing in the *ymryson* with Gruffudd Gryg is an especially rich one. And while I have no intention of arguing for Dafydd's dependence on any specific source or sources for this trope, its status as a commonplace in such a wide variety of classical and medieval contexts, taken together with the fact that it is only with Dafydd and his contemporaries that it seems to come into common usage in Wales, certainly raises the strong possibility that Dafydd's development of it is indebted to a source or sources outside Welsh poetic tradition. In any case, the preceding summary should provide us with a kind of context from which to assess Dafydd's intentions in employing the trope, and with this context in mind we can now return to the passage from the *cywydd* to Gruffudd Gryg with which we began.

In the first place, Dafydd does not seem in this passage to be attacking Gruffudd's technical proficiency. Elsewhere in the *ymryson,* and in this particular *cywydd,* he does make disparaging remarks about Gruffudd's craft, but here he appears to be granting Gruffudd's status as *saer.* Not that he attaches any great value to this status—anyone can put together a proper poem given the right materials ('pawb a wnâi adail pybyr / O chaid gwŷdd'). The problem is finding such materials, which are notably more scarce than the craftsmen or poets themselves ('Haws yw cael, lle bo gwael gwŷdd, / . . . saer no defnydd'), a claim which recalls the recurrent complaints among earlier poets concerning the proliferation of inferior versifiers.[31] In any case, *gwŷdd* here is clearly to be taken as something like poetic raw material—in fact, this passage is cited in *Geiriadur Prifysgol Cymru* as the earliest usage of the word in this sense[32]—and in the context of Dafydd's accusation that Gruffudd lacks all originality, the implication is clearly that Gruffudd is not harvesting his own poetic timber.

Or at least that he is not harvesting *good* poetic timber: Dafydd speaks of 'gwael gwŷdd'—poor or perhaps rotten wood—in a way that suggests that this is what Gruffudd has to work with. It is not entirely clear from this passage just how Gruffudd's material is to be considered inferior, but later on in the poem Dafydd refers to Gruffudd's poetry as composed of 'henwydd' or old wood. This reference points once again to the imitative or derivative nature of his work; it suggests, perhaps, that Gruffudd is recycling the used materials of others, including Dafydd. At the same time, because Dafydd assumes in this poem the mantle of defender of the *cywydd serch* against its detractors among the more entrenched, conservative, traditionalist school of poets—a school to which he seems to assign Gruffudd, whether accurately or not—it may be that we should take 'henwydd', and by extension 'gwael gwŷdd', as referring to the material of traditional praise poetry, which more than half a century after the Conquest may well have seemed superannuated in some respects to a poet as innovative as Dafydd.[33]

In any case, Dafydd concludes this passage with a word of advice. Since Gruffudd lacks sound material for poetry, what he should do is go to the woods to cut down his own stuff ('Aed i'r coed i dorri cof', line 48). The general sense of *coed* is clear enough here: it is the figurative forest in which one harvests the *gwŷdd* or raw materials of poetic composition, and it is worth noting that in using these two terms together in this way, Dafydd is recapitulating the ambivalence of *silva* as it appears in the same metaphorical range in Latin writings. The meaning of *cof* in this line is a little more complicated; its context within Dafydd's developing argument suggests that it is to be taken as more or less equivalent to *gwŷdd*, denoting something like the raw material of poetic composition. Such a usage is roughly in line with the narrower sense of *cof* as 'one of the three lores in which the poets were instructed in the bardic schools'—a meaning attested, with some variation, in the Bardic Grammars and in a seventeenth-century text in English known as the 'Three Antiquities of Bryttaen'.[34] But only roughly; the 'tri chof' are clearly the kind of traditional learning, concerned with genealogy, history, and the like, which was used as one of the basic materials of conventional praise poetry, and since Dafydd in the *ymryson* seems to be criticizing the imitative conventionality of Gruffudd's 'henwydd', and since he seems to be defending his own departures from convention against Gruffudd's charges—however he may have misconstrued those charges, intentionally or otherwise—it is almost certain that he is not using *cof* in quite this specific sense. The forest or *coed* in which Gruffudd is to seek his own *cof* is apparently not the forest of traditional sources from which one builds one's composition, as it is, for instance, for Alfred the Great in the passage cited earlier; it is something more like a forest of fresh, raw material—of virgin timber, so to speak. So Dafydd is clearly broadening the term's meaning—or at least the meaning assigned to the term by *Geiriadur Prifysgol Cymru*.

But of course neither should we rule out the more general meaning of *cof*: 'memory', both the faculty itself and its contents, that which is remembered. After all, the 'tri chof' are themselves memories of a sort— 'Records or Memorialls', in the words of the 'Three Antiquities of Bryttaen'. And it is worth bearing in mind that the same basic trope Dafydd is using here is prominent as well in classical and medieval discussions of the memory; the connections between memory,

poetry (or rhetoric), and the process of construction are an important facet of the trope's history in Latin writing. If we take *cof* as 'memory', then Dafydd is telling Gruffudd to go to the woods to cut down or harvest memory. But what can such advice mean?

In the first place, we can take this as counsel to follow the same course—at once both amatory and poetic— that Dafydd follows. After all, Dafydd's *cywyddau serch* are typically *cofion* set in a literal *coed*. Rather than continuing with his 'henwydd' as poetic material, Gruffudd should take to the woods with his sweetheart and harvest through his experience the kind of good wood or poetic raw material, in the form of memories, that Dafydd uses. This reading finds further support in Dafydd's reference to himself in **"Y Deildy"** (*GDG* 121) as love's axe: 'ac allor serch yw'r gelli / Yn gall, a'i fwyall wyf fi' ('and love's altar is the discreet grove, and I am his axe', lines 29-30). In terming himself the 'bwyall' or axe of love here in the sylvan setting of **"Y Deildy"** Dafydd casts himself in a rather aggressive metaphor as the harvester of those amatory experiences in the literal forest that make up the stuff of his *cywyddau serch*—an identification which suggests that when he counsels Gruffudd Gryg in the *ymryson* to go to the woods and cut down his own poetic timber, he is in fact advising him to glean the same kind of poetic raw material, in the form of romantic or sexual liaisons, that forms the basis of Dafydd's love poetry. The trope in the *ymryson* and these lines from **"Y Deildy"** thus gloss one another quite effectively, and in fact there is a couplet in another of Dafydd's poems that provides further warrant for such an interpretation. In **"Y Cyffylog"** (*GDG* 115), Dafydd cites a saying about the frustration of unrequited love for a (presumably married) woman that uses the figure of the axe in the same basic metaphorical sense: 'A tree in the forest: another man with an axe possesses it' ('Pren yng nghoed . . . / Arall â bwyall biau', lines 53-54).

In other words, if we take *coed* in a more or less literal sense, it is possible to interpret Dafydd's advice in the *ymryson* as a call to liberate poetry from pure, moribund convention, and to reground it in living experience— especially, perhaps, the experience of love. Of course, to judge from his surviving poems, which include a number of *cywyddau serch,* Gruffudd was already doing this—or at least purporting to do this—and it may seem odd for Dafydd to be advising Gruffudd to follow his own lead in a poem in which he is at the same time accusing Gruffudd of plagiarism; but since Dafydd seems intent on casting Gruffudd in the role of traditionalist defender of poetic orthodoxy in this *cywydd,* such advice does have a certain rhetorical appropriateness.

But perhaps the *coed* to which Dafydd is referring is not to be taken so literally after all. In a number of poems, Dafydd speaks of the woodland setting of his trysts in architectural terms: it is a *plas* or a *tŷ*, a *twr* or a *pentis*—a well-crafted edifice, square and plumb, generally built either by that *Saer Mawr* God or by his personified sub-contractor, the month of May.[35] Indeed, the *locus classicus* for this conceit is **"Y Deildy"** itself; here Dafydd describes the woodland bower in turn as 'caer', 'ystafell', 'tŷ', and 'adail', and in a passage ending with the lines quoted above, he goes into precise detail in setting forth the process of 'carpentry' by which it is constructed:

> Dwylo Mai a'i hadeila,
> A'i linyn yw'r gog lonydd,
> A'i ysgwîr yw eos gwŷdd,
> A'i dywydd yw hirddydd haf,
> A'i ais yw goglais gwiwglaf;
> Ac allor serch yw'r gelli
> Yn gall, a'i fwyall wyf fi.
>
> (24-30)

[The hands of May will build it, and his plumb-line is the calm cuckoo, and his carpenter's square is the forest nightingale, and his house-timbers are the long summer day, and his laths are the pain of the fine afflicted one; and love's altar is the discreet grove, and I am his axe.]

The highly metaphorical description of the *deildy* as a carefully constructed edifice makes it clear that there is something more going on here than just the straightforward representation of a real, literal forest, of the *actual* site of the poet's *actual* love affairs. This is a patently artificial construct, not a simple bit of mimesis. And the figure of the axe, too, is enriched when it is resituated within the context of the insistent architectural conceit governing the poem as a whole: it takes on the additional aspect of a tool for shaping wood as well as one for cutting down trees, a tool of carpentry as well as of forestry.[36] Finally, then, Dafydd may be love's axe not only because he harvests amatory experience in his woodland trysts, but also because he shapes or constructs in his poetry a fitting habitation for love—such as, of course, the *deildy* itself.[37]

Dafydd's reference to himself as an axe in **"Y Deildy"** thus invokes not only the obvious sexual or phallic connotations, but also the whole gamut of terms from carpentry and architecture used to describe the poet's craft—a lexicon which is precisely homologous with that used by Dafydd in poems like **"Y Deildy"** to describe the *locus amoenus* of his woodland rendezvous, and which appears with unparalleled frequency in the *marwnadau* exchanged between Dafydd and his colleagues. So Dafydd refers to Madog Benfras as 'canwyr y synnwyr a'r sôn' ('carpenter's plane of sense and sound', *GDG* 14.26) and to Gruffudd Gryg himself as 'ysgwîr mawl' ('carpenter's square of praise', *GDG* 20.12), and, in a poem rejected from the canon by Parry, the male blackbird is termed 'sgwir gwawd'

('carpenter's square of poetry').[38] And so in their own *marwnadau* to Dafydd, the poet's contemporaries refer to him variously as 'pensaer y ieithoedd' ('chief carpenter of languages') and 'trawst beirdd' ('rafter of poets'; thus Iolo Goch),[39] as 'pensaer y wengaer wingerdd' ('chief carpenter of the white fortress of wine-song'), 'pensaer y ffawd' ('chief carpenter of fortune'), and 'ysgwîr gwawd' ('carpenter's square of poetry'; thus Madog Benfras),[40] and as one who 'lluniai fawl wrth y llinyn' ('crafted praise by the plumb-line'; Iolo Goch again).[41] Indeed, in the *ymryson* itself, both Dafydd and Gruffudd continue to play off the metaphorics of wood and carpentry through several *cywyddau*.[42]

The close correspondence of some of the terms in these poems to terms used in **"Y Deildy"**—'llinyn' and 'ysgwîr', especially—is striking.[43] More striking still, however, is the broader conceptual parallel identifying both the woodland bower and poetry as consciously and carefully crafted structures, as architectural entities raised by precisely the same process of construction. This homology linking the construction of the 'deildy' and the construction of poetry suggests that the 'deildy' itself is less God's handiwork than a poetic construct, less an actual site than a *topos* of the mind, called into being through the creative, shaping, linguistic 'carpentry' of the *prydydd*. In effect, the 'deildy' *is* the poem in which it appears: not an actual woodland bower that is simply represented in the poetry, but a purely verbal edifice in which the poet houses—or even brings into existence—the experiences and the loves he purports to be recounting.[44] It is worth noting that earlier in his opening *cywydd* to Gruffudd Gryg, Dafydd refers to his own love poetry as *geuwawd*, the first element of which—*gau* 'false'—clearly suggests not only the fictive nature of the *cywyddau serch*, but also, and perhaps more importantly, the poet's conscious or even polemical recognition of this fictiveness. Dafydd's use of the metaphorics of carpentry is thus much more than just a conventional figurative allusion to the craftsmanly aspect of poetry; seen within the mutually informing contexts of both the *ymryson* and the love poetry, it becomes a kind of metapoetic comment on the world-invoking power of language—and of the poet.

The urge to find in Dafydd's poetry an essentially autobiographical significance has proved to be an almost irresistible imperative for even his finest critics. But surely the poet's own reflections on the nature of *prydyddu*—however allusive or glancing these reflections necessarily are—point up the limitations of such an approach. The trope of the poet as *saer*, both as it is developed explicitly in the *ymryson* to Gruffudd Gryg and as it informs much of the rest of Dafydd's poetry on a more implicit level, may well nod towards the necessity of regrounding poetry in lived experience, as my first reading of this trope has suggested; but at the same time it also reveals a highly sophisticated awareness that poetry is a transformative or even generative art rather than simply a matter of mimesis, that poetry authors or frames a world rather than simply representing *the* world. On this latter reading, the poet's stance with respect to his *silva* may seem to have less in common with that of the rhetorician, imposing order on the tangled forest of memory or of language, than it does with the more originary stance of the Neoplatonic *nous* imposing form and actuality on the chaos of cosmic *hyle*.[45] But of course such a claim would be far too extravagant; the notion of originary creation is no less problematic than that of mimesis in the context of Dafydd's poetry, a fact that becomes clear when we consider how heavily his poetry depends on the work of other writers. For despite his accusations concerning Gruffudd Gryg's lack of originality or plagiarism, Dafydd himself was perfectly willing to borrow from other poets—not least in his development of the woodland *locus amoenus,* which, as A. T. E. Matonis has amply demonstrated, draws on conventional *topoi* common in Latin and various vernaculars, if not in Welsh, well before Dafydd's time.[46] Which is to say that even Dafydd's poetic structures are built less of virgin timber than of 'henwydd' of a sort, and that the *silva* through which Dafydd strolled in search of poetic matter was also, like those of Hugh of St Victor and Alfred the Great, a forest of texts as well as a forest of experience. Perhaps this was Dafydd's point all along.

Notes

1. *Gwaith Dafydd ap Gwilym,* edited by Thomas Parry, second edition (Cardiff, 1979), no. 148.60 (p. 393). Except where otherwise noted, all quotations from Dafydd's poetry are taken from this edition, hereafter abbreviated *GDG*; subsequent citations will be identified parenthetically by Parry's poem numbers and lineation. An earlier version of this essay was read at the 29th International Congress on Medieval Studies at Kalamazoo, Michigan, in May 1994; I would like to take this opportunity to thank Colgate University for providing the funds that made my attendance at this conference possible.

2. cf., for instance, Saunders Lewis, 'Dafydd ap Gwilym', repr. from *Llên Cymru,* 2 (1952-53), 199-208, in *Meistri'r Canrifoedd: Ysgrifau ar Hanes Llenyddiaeth,* edited by R. Geraint Gruffydd (Cardiff, 1973), p. 54; Rachel Bromwich, *Aspects of the Poetry of Dafydd ap Gwilym* (Cardiff, 1986), pp. 46-47 and 69-70; E. I. Rowlands, 'Bardic Lore and Education', *Bulletin of the Board of Celtic Studies,* 32 (1985), 143-55 (p. 148). Parry includes an extensive note explaining the metaphors of the harp and the old manuscript (*GDG,* p. 549), but he has nothing to say about the metaphor of the *saer.* A. T. E. Matonis proves a rare exception; see her 'Later Medieval Poetics

and some Welsh Bardic Debates', *BBCS,* 29 (1982), 635-65 (pp. 645-46 and 659).

3. On the notion of the 'life cycle' of tropes, and on the possibilities of their revivification, see Michael Shapiro, *The Source of Grammar: Language as Semeiotic* (Bloomington, 1983), pp. 204-6.

4. *Cywyddau Dafydd ap Gwilym a'i Gyfoeswyr,* edited by Ifor Williams and Thomas Roberts (Cardiff, 1935; hereafter *DGG*), p. 190, note to no. 28.26. The passage is worth quoting in its entirety: 'Hoff iawn ydoedd y beirdd o ddefnyddio termau saer coed ar eu prydyddu. *Naddu* gwawd y byddent, etc., ac felly yn naturiol daeth safon y saer, yr ysgwir, yn derm hwylus ganddynt am ganu safonol, patrwm perffaith'. Compare also Williams's discussion in *Lectures on Early Welsh Poetry* (Dublin, 1944), p. 7: 'The second suggestive title for a poet is the Welsh *prydydd,* connected with *pryd* "shape, form", cf. Irish *cruth* "form", and *creth* "poetry". He sees and then sings, and his song has form, shape, the beauty of the shaped thing: it is not a formless, shapeless chunk of wood, but a carving, a piece of sculpture. The Welsh bards called themselves the carpenters of song, *seiri gwawd* or *seiri cerdd,* and claimed as their own all the tools and technical terms of the craftsmen in wood, e.g. the axe, knife, square. When a rival imitated their themes or methods they told him bluntly to take his axe to the forest and cut his own timber'. It is interesting to note that the earlier of these statements appears in a note to a word in a poem Williams attributed to Dafydd ap Gwilym, and that the later of them is quite clearly written with the example of Dafydd's use of the trope in *GDG* 148 in mind.

5. *Dafydd ap Gwilym: A Selection of Poems,* edited and translated by Rachel Bromwich, The Welsh Classics, 1 (Llandysul, 1982), p. 183, note to no. 48.25-26; H. Idris Bell, *The Nature of Poetry as Conceived by the Welsh Bards,* The Taylorian Lecture 1955 (Oxford, 1955), p. 10; Matonis, 'Later Medieval Poetics', p. 659.

6. See, among others, Eric P. Hamp, 'The Semantics of Poetry in Early Celtic', *Papers from the 13th Regional Meeting, Chicago Linguistics Society,* 1977, 147-51, esp. pp. 148-49, and Christian-J. Guyonvarc'h, 'Notes d'étymologie et de lexicographie gauloises et celtiques', *Ogam,* 12 (1960), 47-58 (pp. 49-58).

7. The one example is from the poem entitled *Buarth Beird* in the Book of Taliesin: 'wyf dur, wyf dryw, / wyf saer, wyf syw, / wyf sarff, wyf ferch' (*The Text of the Book of Taliesin,* edited by J. Gwenogvryn Evans (Llanbedrog, 1910), p. 7). The context of *saer* here hardly permits any conclu-

sion that the word is intended to evoke a traditional conception of the poet as carpenter. In addition to the Book of Taliesin, I have consulted the following editions: *Llyfr Du Caerfyddin,* edited by A. O. H. Jarman (Cardiff, 1982); *The Poetry in the Red Book of Hergest,* edited by J. Gwenogvryn Evans (Llanbedrog, 1911); *Llawysgrif Hendregadredd,* edited by John Morris-Jones and T. H. Parry-Williams (Cardiff, 1933). There is in the Red Book of Hergest an occurrence of the verb *adeilio* used to denote poetic composition (col. 1260.35), but this is at best a muted version of the trope, employed by the later-fourteenth-century poet Sefnyn; there are also in this manuscript instances of the figurative use of *saer,* but these refer not to the poet but to God or Jesus (e.g. 1295.34). I should emphasize that my search through these texts was necessarily quite superficial; I would certainly not hold it up as definitive. But if the manuscripts noted above are representative, then at least the purportedly wide currency of the trope among Dafydd's predecessors seems unlikely. For the sudden flowering of the trope among Dafydd and his contemporaries, see below, pp. 83-84 [elsewhere in the original text] and n. 42. Its appearances seem to cluster most heavily in the *ymryson* with Gruffudd Gryg and the various *marwnadau* exchanged between Dafydd and poets like Madog Benfras—that is, in those poems which thematize the craft of poetry itself, a context from which it is conspicuously absent in the earlier poetry. Interestingly enough, variants on the two main elements in Dafydd's trope appear in the *Elucidarium* and are carried over into its fourteenth-century Welsh translation, which was known to a number of Dafydd's contemporaries; see pp. 71 and 77 [elsewhere in the original text] and nn. 15 and 30 below.

8. On Dafydd's education and the sources of his poetry, see (above all) Bromwich, *Aspects,* and T. M. Chotzen, *Recherches sur la poésie de Dafydd ab Gwilym* (Amsterdam, 1927), both of which treat these questions extensively; cf. also Ifor Williams, 'Dafydd ap Gwilym a'r Glêr', *Transactions of the Honourable Society of Cymmrodorion,* 1913-14, pp. 83-204. Lewis, *Meistri'r Canrifoedd,* pp. 47-50, follows Chotzen (p. 228) and Williams (pp. 143-58) in taking Dafydd to have had some connection with the Church, either through his education there or through his having qualified for minor orders; but compare Bromwich's rather tentative qualification of Lewis's argument in 'Dafydd ap Gwilym', *Aspects,* p. 19.

9. *Oxford Latin Dictionary,* edited by P. G. W. Glare (Oxford, 1968-82), s.v., defs 1 and 5.

10. David F. Bright, *Elaborate Disarray: The Nature of Statius' Silvae,* Beiträge zur klassischen Philologie, 108 (Meisenheim, 1980), p. 37, citing as examples *Ecl.* I.5, II.4-5, IV.3, V.43-44, VI.1-2, and X.8. I have relied quite heavily on Bright's fine discussion of *silva* and its varied usages (pp. 20-42) in what follows; also worth consulting is *Statius Silvae IV,* edited by K. M. Coleman (Oxford, 1988), pp. xxii-xxiv.

11. *Didascalion,* V.5: 'cuius sententias quasi fructus quosdam dulcissimos legendo carpimus, tractando ruminamus'; quoted in Mary Carruthers, *The Book of Memory: A Study of Memory in Medieval Culture,* Cambridge Studies in Medieval Literature, 10 (Cambridge, 1990), pp. 164-65. The *Didascalion* has been edited by Charles H. Buttimer (Washington, 1939) and translated by Jerome Taylor (New York, 1961).

12. 'Synodicorum exemplarium inumerositatem conspiciens ac plurimorum ex ipsis obscuritatem rudibus minus utilem providens nec non ceterorum diversitatem inconsonam, destruentem magis quam aedificantem prospiciens, braven plenamque ac consonam de ingenti silva scriptorum in unius voluminis textum expossitionem degessi . . .': *Die irische Kanonensammlung,* edited by Hermann Wasserschleben (1885; repr. Leipzig, 1966), p. 1. I am grateful to Dr Huw Pryce for this reference.

13. 'ut antiquam perplexae silvam densitatis grammaticorum ingrederer ad colligendum tibi diversorum optima quaeque genera pomorum et variorum odoramenta florum diffusa, quae passim dispersa per saltum grammaticorum inveniuntur, ad cotidianum scilicet tui diligentis studii pastum et odoriferam coronam ingeniosae pubertatis et ut optima quaeque et necessariora quasi in unum cumulando farciens marsuppium coacervata et circumcisa tibi obtulerim' (Boniface, *Ars Grammatica,* edited by G. J. Gebauer and Bengt Löfstedt, Corpus Christianorum Series Latina, 133B (Turnhout, 1980), p. 9, quoted and translated by Martin Irvine, *The Making of Textual Culture: 'Grammatica' and Literary Theory, 350-1100,* Cambridge Studies in Medieval Literature, 19 (Cambridge, 1994), p. 302). In a similar context, Aldhelm speaks of the 'densa latinitatis silva' on which he bases his metrical treatise *De Metris* (Aldhelm, *Opera,* edited by Rudolf Ehwald, Monumenta Germaniae Historica, Auctores Antiquissimi, 15 (Berlin, 1919), p. 78, cited by Irvine, p. 437).

14. Carruthers, pp. 33 and 62.

15. *The Elucidarium and Other Tracts in Welsh from Llyvyr Agkyr Llandewivrevi,* edited by J. Morris Jones and John Rhys, Anecdota Oxoniensia,

Mediaeval and Modern Series, 6 (Oxford, 1894), p. 210; in the Welsh text, 'koet ygofuynnev' renders 'sylvam quaestionum' (p. 49).

16. Coleman, p. xxiii. For Gellius, see *Noctes Atticae*, Pr. 5-6: 'Nam quia uariam et miscellam et quasi confusaneam doctrinam conquisiuerant, eo titulos quoque ad eam sententiam exquisitissimos indiderunt. Namque alii *Musarum* inscripserunt; alii *siluarum . . .*' (*A. Gelli Noctes Atticae*, edited by P. K. Marshall, 2 vols (Oxford, 1990), I, 1-2); there are also ten books of *Silvae* attributed to Lucan, but nothing further is known of these (Bright, pp. 34-35). Bright points out (pp. 40-42) the close relationship between *silva* used in this sense and other terms 'suggesting growth in nature', of which *florilegium* comes to mind most readily in the medieval context; cf. also Irvine, pp. 243, 302, and 436-37.

17. Coleman, p. xxii. The relevant texts by Cicero are *De Inventione*, 1.34 ('quandam silvam atque materiam universam ante permixtim et confuse exponere omnium argumentationum': *Cicero: De Inventione, De Optimo Genere Oratorum, Topica*, edited by H. M. Hubbell, Loeb Classical Library (Cambridge, Mass., 1949), p. 70) and *Orator*, 12 ('omnis enim ubertas et quasi silua dicendi ducta ab illis [philosophorum disputationibus] est': *M. Tulli Ciceronis Rhetorica*, edited by A. S. Wilkins, 2 vols (Oxford, n.d.), II, 114); by Quintilian, *Institutio Oratoria*, 10.3.17 ('Diversum est huic eorum uitium qui primo decurrere per materiam stilo quam uelocissimo uolent, et sequentes calorem atque impetum ex tempore scribunt: hanc siluam uocant, repetunt deinde et componunt quae effuderant: sed uerba emendantur et numeri, manet in rebus temere congestis quae fuit leuitas': *M. Fabi Quintiliani Institutionis Oratoriae Libri Duodecim*, edited by M. Winterbottom, 2 vols (Oxford, 1970), II, 602). For Walter Map, see *De Nugis Curialium*, Dist. ii, c. 32: 'Siluam uobis et materiam, non dico fabularum sed faminum, appono; cultui etenim sermonum non intendo, nec si studeam consequar. Singuli lectores appositam ruditatem exculpant, ut eorum industria bona facie prodeat in publicum' (*De Nugis Curialium*, edited by M. R. James and revised by C. N. L. Brooke and R. A. B. Mynors, Oxford Medieval Texts (Oxford, 1983), p. 208).

18. Brian Stock, *Myth and Science in the Twelfth Century: A Study of Bernard Silvester* (Princeton, 1972), p. 100.

19. For the Latin text of the *Cosmographia*, see *De Munde Universitate*, edited by C. S. Barach and J. Wrobel (Innsbruck, 1876), an edition severely criticized by Winthrop Wetherbee in his own translation of this text, with extensive commentary, in *The Cosmographia of Bernardus Silvestris* (New York, 1973); see p. 63 for Wetherbee's criticism, together with a discussion of the manuscript sources used in his translation. Bernardus' formulation, in which *silva* has taken the place of Greek *hyle*, goes back ultimately to Plato's *Timaeus*, by way of Aristotle, Chalcidius, and Eriugena, among others; see the discussions of Bernardus' conception of *silva* and its sources in Wetherbee, pp. 29-45, and Stock, pp. 97-118, and cf. also Paul Piehler, *The Visionary Landscape: A Study in Medieval Allegory* (Montreal, 1971), pp. 75-77, who also notes the interpretation of *in silvam* in Bernardus' commentary on the *Aeneid* as 'in collectionem temporalium bonorum, umbrosam et inviam quia non est nisi umbra' (pp. 76-77). For Isidore, see *Etymologiae sive Origines*, edited by W. M. Lindsay, 2 vols (Oxford, 1911), I, 13, §3.1: 'Hylen Graeci rerum quamdam primam materiam dicunt, nullo prorsus modo formatam, sed omnium corporalium formarum capacem, ex qua visibilia haec elementa formata sunt. proinde et eam poetae silvam nominaverunt, nec incongrue, quia materiae silvarum sunt' (quoted by Bright, p. 25). Isidore's formulation closely echoes that of the fourth-century commentator Servius' gloss on *Aeneid*, I.314: 'quam Graeci *hylen . . .* vocant, poetae nominant silvam, id est, elementorum congeriem, unde cuncta procreantur' (quoted by Piehler, p. 75).

20. This claim must perhaps be qualified with respect to the use of the metaphor in the context of the *ars memorativa*, where visual images seem to play as prominent a part in the memory as language does. Compare, however, Carruthers, pp. 17-18, who notes that it is important to distinguish between the 'visual' and the 'pictorial'; the 'visual' memory can be (and often is) the memory of a written word as well as of an object or scene. The notion of an 'essentially verbal construction' might also seem to be problematic for the use of the term *silva* by Platonists like Bernardus Silvestris, but here, of course, the Christian perspective means that the *nous* which imposes order on the cosmic *silva* is to be identified with *logos*; cf. Stock, pp. 88 and 93.

21. For Philo, see *On Dreams*, 2.2.8, in *Philo*, edited by F. H. Colson and G. H. Whitaker, Loeb Classical Library, 10 vols (Cambridge, Mass., 1929-71), V, 445-47, and cf. Beryl Smalley, *The Study of the Bible in the Middle Ages*, third edition (Oxford, 1984), p. 5; for Gregory the Great, cf. *Moralia in Job*, in J.-P. Migne, *Patrologia Latina*, 75, 513c, and further below; for Hugh of St Victor, cf. *Di-*

dascalion (n. 10 above) and 'De Arca Noe Morali', *PL* 176, 618-80, translated by a Religious of C.M.S.V. in *Hugh of St. Victor: Selected Spiritual Writings* (London, 1962). All of these examples are noted by Carruthers, p. 43; see especially her discussion of Hugh of St Victor's 'De Arca' at pp. 44-45. As Carruthers notes, the motif may go back to scriptural passages like Proverbs 24, 3-4; also relevant, perhaps, is Luke 14, 28-30. The list above might be extended at much greater length; in his monumental *Exégèse médiévale*, Henri de Lubac devotes a full twenty pages to architectural metaphors in scriptural exegesis, citing an impressive variety of such us-ages by Ambrose, Rabanus Maurus, Aldhelm, and Bernard of Clairvaux, to name just a few: *Exégèse médiévale: les quatre sens de l'écriture*, 4 vols (Paris, 1959-64), IV, 41-60.

22. *PL* 75, 513c; the translation is Carruthers's. Gregory here echoes Philo, who in his exegesis of the dreams in Genesis 37, 7 and 9 outlines his methodology in similar terms: 'So much by way of a foundation. As we go on to build the super-structure, let us follow the directions of Allegory, that wise Master-builder, while we investigate the details of either dream' (Colson and Whitaker, V, 445-47).

23. Carruthers, p. 43: 'By *mens* in his phrase "fabrica mentis", Gregory meant the educated, trained memory; *mens* frequently is used by medieval writers to mean the whole complex of processes occurring in the brain, including memory, that precede understanding or intellection'. In a footnote, Carruthers goes on to cite Dante and Chaucer as supporting examples of such a usage—both, it should be noted, significantly later writers than Gregory.

24. Among the classical rhetorical treatises known to the Middle Ages, the clearest example is perhaps Quintilian's in the *Institutio Oratoria*, 11.2.17-22, although the best-known to the Middle Ages would have been in the *Rhetorica ad Herennium*, III.xvi-xxiv. For an example from a medieval analysis of memory, see Albertus Magnus, *De Bono, Tractatus* IV, *Quaestio* II 'De Partibus Prudentia', esp. *articulus* 2.7, *solutio* 10 (*Omnis Opera*, XXVIII, edited by H. Kuhle and others (Aschendorff, 1951), translated as Appendix B in Carruthers, pp. 267-80). Albert is responding here to the *Ad Herennium*. For discussion of this response, see Carruthers, pp. 137-43, esp. (for our purposes) pp. 138-39; for discussion of classical rhetoric's contributions to the *ars memorativa*, see also Francis A. Yates, *The Art of Memory* (Chicago, 1966), who provides a summary of the

relevant sections from the *Ad Herennium* (pp. 6-17) and a translation of the most relevant part of the *Institutio Oratoria* (pp. 22-23).

25. *Les Arts poétiques du XIIe et du XIIIe siècle,* edited by Edmond Faral (Paris, 1924), p. 198; the transla-tion is that of James J. Murphy, *Three Medieval Rhetorical Arts* (Berkeley, 1971), p. 34. Cf. the similar passage in St Augustine's *Enarrationes in Psalmos* on Psalm 44, 2: 'Hodie cor tuum, o homo, generat consilium, nec quærit uxorem: per consilium natum ex corde tuo ædificas aliquid; et illa fabrica, antequam siet in opere, stat in consilio' (*PL* 36, 496).

26. Murphy, p. 29; idem, 'A New Look at Chaucer and the Rhetoricians', *Review of English Studies,* new series, 15 (1964), 1-20; Marie P. Hamilton, 'Notes on Chaucer and the Rhetoricians', *PMLA* [*Publications of the Modern Language Associa-tion of America*], 47 (1932), 403-9; Karl Young, 'Chaucer and Geoffrey of Vinsauf', *Modern Phi-lology,* 41 (1943), 172-82; *The Riverside Chaucer,* edited by Larry D. Benson and others (Boston, 1987), p. 1030 (note to *Troilus and Criseyde,* 1.1065-71, where the clearest echo of Geoffroi occurs). It should be noted that Murphy concludes that 'the case for believing that Chaucer studied Vinsauf is less than convincing' ('A New Look', p. 15), and he argues that 'there is very little evidence of an active rhetorical tradition in fourteenth-century England', that 'the first concrete evidence of the teaching of formal rhetoric in English universities . . . does not appear until 1431, while lower schools apparently taught no rhetoric until the fifteenth century', and that 'there would seem little probability that any English writer of the period [the fourteenth century] would be influenced greatly by rhetoric in its several medieval forms' ('A New Look', pp. 2-5). Just what this means for the situation in Wales, and for poets like Dafydd ap Gwilym, is a matter for further consideration.

27. For the Old English, see *King Alfred's Version of St. Augustine's Soliloquies,* edited by Thomas A. Carnicelli (Cambridge, 1969), p. 47. 'Version' may be a more accurate designation of Alfred's work than 'translation' because of the many addi-tions, deletions, and revisions that characterize it; see Milton McC. Gatch, 'King Alfred's Version of Augustine's *Soliloquia*: Some Suggestions on its Rationale and Unity', and Ruth Waterhouse, 'Tone in Alfred's Version of Augustine's *Soliloquies*', in *Studies in Earlier Old English Prose,* edited by Paul E. Szarmach (Albany, 1986), pp. 17-45 and 47-85 respectively.

28. Gatch, p. 25.

29. Morris Jones and Rhys, p. 2, with minor changes; for the Latin, see ibid., p. 173.

30. On the poets' knowledge of this text, see Rowlands, 'Bardic Lore and Education', p. 148; Bromwich, *Aspects,* pp. 156 and 162; Morfydd E. Owen, 'Functional Prose: Religion, Science, Grammar, Law', in *A Guide to Welsh Literature,* edited by A. O. H. Jarman and Gwilym Rees Hughes, 2 vols (Swansea, 1979), II, 248 and 252-53. For references in the poetry, see *Gwaith Iolo Goch,* edited by Dafydd R. Johnston (Cardiff, 1988), no. 28.37-40 and notes (cf. also idem, *Iolo Goch: Poems,* The Welsh Classics, 5 (Llandysul, 1993), pp. 114-15 and 180); Evans, *The Poetry in the Red Book of Hergest,* pp. 141 (col. 1376.21; Dafydd y Coed) and 160 (col. 1415.39; Ieuan Llwyd ab y Gargam); *Cywyddau Iolo Goch ac Eraill,* edited by Henry Lewis, Thomas Roberts, and Ifor Williams, second edition (Cardiff, 1937), no. 119.7-10 (Gruffudd Llwyd).

31. See, e.g., Ceri Lewis, 'The Content of Poetry and the Crisis in the Bardic Tradition', in Jarman and Hughes, II, 88-111, esp. pp. 97-102.

32. *Geiriadur Prifysgol Cymru* (hereafter abbreviated *GPC*), edited by R. J. Thomas and others (Cardiff, 1950-), s.v. *gwŷdd*[1] 1(c). This usage of *gwŷdd,* taken together with the occurrence of *coed* and *defnydd* in the same metaphoric complex, brings that entire complex closely into line with the similar Latin usage of *silva/materia* (Greek *hyle*); cf. Bright. pp. 24-26; Coleman, pp. xxii-xxiii; and Stock, pp. 97-118.

33. There are problems with both of these interpretations. If Dafydd is accusing Gruffudd of plagiarizing his own work along with the work of other poets, then it seems odd that he would characterize Gruffudd's material as 'gwael gwŷdd'—a characterization that hardly redounds to Dafydd's glory. On the other hand, Dafydd himself wrote praise poetry, and Gruffudd's surviving work includes a number of *cywyddau serch,* so it might seem to make little sense for Dafydd to criticize Gruffudd's adherence to a hidebound tradition of panegyric. But compare the discussions of this point by Bromwich, *Aspects,* p. 65, and Eurys Rowlands, 'Dafydd ap Gwilym', *Y Traethodydd,* 122 (1967), 15-35 (pp. 26-27), the latter of whom argues for a more fundamental difference in perspective separating the two poets; for some of Gruffudd's *cywyddau serch,* see *DGG* nos 72 and 73 (pp. 131-34). *Henwydd* can mean 'pedigree' as well as 'old wood' (cf. *GPC* s.v., the earliest citation of which is from the *cywydd* under discussion

here), and Dafydd's use of the term may be intended to evoke not only the illegitimate paternity of Gruffudd's poetry ('Gywydd o'i henwydd ei hun') but also its basis in the traditional concerns of praise poetry, among which genealogy is of course quite prominent.

34. See *GPC* s.v., (b), drawing on *Gramadegau'r Penceirddiaid,* edited by G. J. Williams and E. J. Jones (Cardiff, 1934), p. 134, lines 23-28, which defines 'cof', together with 'kerdd' and 'cyfarwyddyd', as one of the 'tri pheth a berthyn ar wr wrth gerdd davawd', and which further subdivides 'cof' into three components: 'achav, arfav, a Ranndiroedd'. For the rather different definition in the 'Three Antiquities', see G. J. Williams, 'Tri Chof Ynys Brydein', *LlC,* 3 (1955), 234-39 (pp. 234-35): 'The office and function of the Bruttish or Cambrian Bards was to keepe and preserve *Tri chof ynys Brydain*: That is the Three Records or Memorialls of Bryttaen, or which otherwise is called the Bruttish Antiquitie which consisteth of three parts. . . . The one of the sayd three *Cof* is the History of the notable Acts of the kings and princes of this land of Bruttaen and Cambria; And the second of the sayd three *cof* is the languaige of the Bruttons for which thee bards ought to give accompt for every word and sillable therein when they are demanded thereof and to preserve the ancient tonge and not to intermix ytt wyth any forrayne tonge. . . . And the third *Cof* was, to keepe the genealogies or Descent of the Nob[il]itie, there Division of lands, and there Armes . . . .'.

35. Some examples in addition to "Y Deildy" (the list is not intended to be exhaustive): "Y Llwyn Celyn" (*GDG* 29, in which the architectural metaphor is pervasive); "Digalondid" (*GDG* 36.9-16); "Yr Het Fedw" (*GDG* 59.11-12); "Y Cyffylog" (*GDG* 61.11); "Rhag Hyderu ar y Byd" (*GDG* 76.23-24); "Canu'n Iach" (*GDG* 103.11-18); "Merch ac Aderyn" (*GDG* 120.33-44); "Offeren y Llwyn" (*GDG* 122.19-20); "Y Ceiliog Bronfraith" (*GDG* 123.1-18); "Y Bardd a'r Brawd Llwyd" (*GDG* 137.1-2); "Y Cleddyf" (*GDG* 143.35); "Caru yn y Gaeaf" (*GDG* 145.49-56). "Yr Adfail" (*GDG* 144) is also full of architectural references and would no doubt repay closer consideration in the present context.

36. On the axe as a tool of carpentry, see L. F. Salzman, *Building in England down to 1540: A Documentary History* (Oxford, 1952), pp. 330-48, esp. pp. 333-36 and 341-42. Salzman notes that 'pride of place in the ranks of the carpenter's tools, as with the mason's, belongs to the axe' (p. 341). The Welsh Laws also suggest the importance of the axe as a tool for building; compare, for

example, *Llyfr Iorwerth,* edited by Aled Rhys Wil-iam, Board of Celtic Studies, University of Wales History and Law Series, 18 (Cardiff, 1960), §§ 43.11 and 93.22. See also C. A. Hewett, 'Tool-marks on Surviving Works from the Saxon, Nor-man, and Later Medieval Periods', and P. Walker, 'The Tools Available to the Mediaeval Woodworker', in *Woodworking Techniques before A.D. 1500,* edited by Seán McGrail, British Archaeological Reports, International Series, 129 (Oxford, 1982), pp. 339-48 and 349-56 respec-tively; Julian Munby, 'Wood', in *English Medieval Industries: Craftsmen, Techniques, Products,* edited by John Blair and Nigel Ramsay (London, 1991), pp. 379-405, esp. pp. 384-86. For a comic Middle English verse debate on the relative merits of carpenters' various tools, see the fifteenth-century text edited by E. Wilson in 'The Debate of the Carpenter's Tools', *RES,* n.s., 38 (1987), 445-70.

37. Compare John Donne in 'The Canonization', with its implied pun on Italian *stanza* ('room'): 'We can dye by it, if not live by love, / And if unfit for tombes and hearse / Our legend bee, it will be fit for verse; / And if no peece of Chronicle wee prove, / We'll build in sonnets pretty roomes . . .' (*The Poems of John Donne,* edited by J. C. Grier-son (London, 1912), p. 15).

38. *DGG,* no. 28.26.

39. *GDG,* pp. 422-23, lines 25 and 35; edited more recently by D. R. Johnston in *Gwaith Iolo Goch* and *Iolo Goch: Poems,* no. 21.25, 35, who emends 'pensaer yr ieithoedd' to 'pensel yr ieithoedd'.

40. *GDG,* pp. 424-25, lines 5, 9, and 44.

41. *GDG,* p. 422, line 5; cf. Johnston, *Gwaith Iolo Goch* and *Iolo Goch: Poems,* no. 21.5, who emends to 'lluniodd wawd wrth y llinyn' and (in the latter book) translates 'he fashioned praise straight along the line'.

42. Thus, for instance, Gruffudd speaks of Dafydd's 'gwaith yng ngwŷd' having lost its novelty and gone out of favour (*GDG* 149.45-46), and in a more combative challenge refers to Dafydd as 'taradr cerdd' (151.46); Dafydd for his part al-ludes to his earlier satire on Rhys Meigen in refer-ring to himself as 'saer hoed' (152.62), and he characterizes Gruffudd as 'draenen gwawd' and 'eithinen iaith Gwynedd' (152.23-24)—echoes, perhaps, of his earlier suggestion that Gruffudd's poetry was composed of 'gwael gwŷd' (148.45). Finally, Dafydd also speaks of Gruffudd's going 'i west yrhawg / Ar Dudur' (150.23-24). The refer-

ence is to the otherwise unknown Tudur ap Cy-fnerth, from whom Dafydd accuses Gruffudd of having stolen poetic images (150.23-24), and it may be that here we have a marked allusion to that purported theft couched in implicitly architec-tural terms: to say that Gruffudd has long been lodging with Tudur—which is to say, occupying Tudur's house—may, given the metaphorical valence of houses and buildings in this context, be another way of saying that Gruffudd has long been occupying Tudur's *poetic* structures as well. Cf. *GPC* s.v. *gwestaf: gwest, gwesta, gwestu,* which gives 'to spend a night, sleep, rest; stay, lodge; visit, feast; borrow, beg; sponge (upon)'. Matonis has noted the 'cluster of "wood"-related images' in the *ymryson,* but without exploring it much further; see her 'Later Medieval Poetics', pp. 659 and 645-46.

43. It is worth noting that the first citation for this us-age of *llinyn* in *GPC* (s.v., 2 (a)) is Dafydd's in "Y Deildy." It is also worth recalling that Geoffroi de Vinsauf used the metaphor of the plumb-line in a similar context in the passage from the *Poetria Nova* quoted earlier—a suggestively close echo.

44. It is tempting to suggest another sense in which the *deildy* is to be taken as referring to a strictly literary construct rather than an actual place. While the meaning 'leaf, leaves (of a book)' is not at-tested in the *GPC* for *dail* until the beginning of the seventeenth century, it *is* attested for the synonymous re-formation *dalen* as early as the fourteenth; cf. *GPC* s.v. *dail* 2, *dalen* 1 (a). The *deildy* may thus be a house of leaves in a codico-logical sense—that is, because it exists only in the leaves of the manuscripts in which Dafydd's poetry is written. Such a possible allusion may be nothing more than a fortuity, of course; certainly the widespread position, articulated for instance by Bromwich (*Aspects,* p. 17), that Dafydd's poems were composed and preserved orally (at least throughout the fourteenth century) would suggest that this allusion could not have been intentional. But Rowlands, 'Bardic Lore and Education', pp. 147-50, makes a strong case, based on references in the poetry itself, that 'writing was an important element in the transmission of poetry and bardic learning in the late Middle Ages in Wales, and probably written sources had been used to some extent for centuries previously' (p. 150). Rowlands also suggests that the image of the old manuscript Dafydd uses in his first *cywydd* in the *ymryson*—the 'cwrrach memrwn' referred to in *GDG* 148.21-26—'refers to the writing of poetry,

and more than likely to the writing down of the satirical poem by Gruffudd Gryg which Dafydd ap Gwilym was answering' (p. 148).

45. See p. 73 [elsewhere in the original text] and nn. 18 and 19 above.

46. A. T. E. Matonis, 'Some Rhetorical Topics in the Early Cywyddwyr', *BBCS,* 28 (1978), 47-72 (pp. 47-56; see esp. p. 53). Compare also Bromwich's painstaking evaluation of Dafydd's possible non-Welsh literary sources in *Aspects,* pp. 68-88.

FURTHER READING

Biography

Bromwich, Rachel. "Dafydd ap Gwilym." In *A Guide to Welsh Literature,* edited by A. O. H. Jarman and Gwilym Rees Hughes, pp. 112-43. Wales: Christopher Davies Ltd., 1979.

Provides a lengthy background on Dafydd's life and work.

Criticism

Breeze, Andrew. "'Bear the Bell' in Dafydd ap Gwilym and *Troilus and Criseyde.*" *Notes and Queries* 237, no. 4 (December 1992): 441-43.

Discusses the metaphor "Bear the Bell," found in both *Troilus and Criseyde* and Dafydd's work.

———. "Dafydd ap Gwilym's 'The Clock' and *Foliot* 'Decoy Bird' in *The Owl and the Nightingale.*" *Notes and Queries* 238, no. 4 (December 1993): 439-40.

Analyzes the term "foliot" and its usage in "The Clock" and *The Owl and the Nightingale.*

———. "Chaucer's 'Malkin' and Dafydd ap Gwilym's 'Mald y Cwd.'" *Notes and Queries* 240, no. 2 (June 1995): 159-60.

Comments on the origins of the character names of "Malkin" and "Mald y Cwd."

Bromwich, Rachel. "Tradition and Innovation in the Poetry of Dafydd ap Gwilym." In *Aspects of the Poetry of Dafydd ap Gwilym,* pp. 57-88. Cardiff: University of Wales Press, 1986.

Weighs the magnitude of Dafydd's predecessors' influence in his work against his originality.

Conran, Anthony. "Welsh Poetry in Translation: A Review Supplement." *The Anglo-Welsh Review,* no. 75 (1984): 81-8.

Provides an addendum to a previous review of translations of Dafydd's poetry.

Crawford, T. D. "The *Englynion* of Dafydd ap Gwilym." *Études Celtiques* 22 (1985): 235-85.

Evaluates the authenticity of the *englynion* of Dafydd.

———. "The *Toddaid* and *Gwawdodyn Byr* in the Poetry of Dafydd ap Gwilym, with an Appendix Concerning the *Traethodlau* Attributed to Him." *Études Celtiques* 27 (1990): 301-36.

Following his essay on Dafydd's *englynion,* Crawford further concentrates his examination on the *toddaid* and *gwawdodyn byr.*

Davies, Pennar. "Review of *Dafydd ap Gwilym: a Selection of Poems.*" *Poetry Wales* 18, no. 4 (spring 1983): 107-09.

Review of Bromwich's *Dafydd ap Gwilym: a Selection of Poems.*

Fulton, Helen. "Dafydd's Poems of Humour and Irony." In *Dafydd ap Gwilym and the European Context,* pp. 186-227. Cardiff: University of Wales Press, 1989.

Considers the statements made regarding nobility and the bourgeois in Dafydd's satiric poetry.

Gruffydd, R. Geraint. "*Englynion y Cusan* by Dafydd ap Gwilym." *Cambridge Medieval Celtic Studies,* no. 23 (summer 1992): 1-6.

Comments on a previous article by Daniel Huws and provides an analysis and translation of *englynion.*

———. "*Englynion* to a Mill Attributed to Dafydd ap Gwilym." *Zeitschrift für celtische Philologie* 49-50 (June 1997): 273-81.

Disputes the ascription of a poem to Dafydd.

Huws, Daniel. "Translation of *This Cocotte, with a Quick Oath.*" *Delos* 1 (1968): 147-51.

Translation of three poems by Dafydd.

Jacobs, Nicolas. "Adjectival Collocations in the Poetry of the Early *Cywyddwyr*: A Preliminary Survey." *Cambrian Medieval Celtic Studies,* no. 31 (summer 1996): 55-70.

Investigates the characteristic adjectival compounds of medieval Welsh poetry as appearing in Dafydd's work.

Johnston, David. "Review of *50 o Gywyddau Dafydd ap Gwilym.*" *Poetry Wales* 16, no. 3 (winter 1981): 121-23.

Review of *50 o Gywyddau Dafydd ap Gwilym* by Alan Llwyd.

———. "Review of *Dafydd ap Gwilym: A Selection of Poems.*" *Cambridge Medieval Celtic Studies,* no. 6 (winter 1983): 97-9.

Review of *Dafydd ap Gwilym: A Selection of Poems* by Rachel Bromwich.

———. "*Cywydd y Gal* by Dafydd ap Gwilym." *Cambridge Medieval Celtic Studies,* no. 9 (summer 1985): 71-89.

In-depth analysis of *Cywydd y Gal.*

Klausner, David N. "Dafydd ap Gwilym in Translation." *University of Toronto Quarterly* 54, no. 3 (spring 1985): 284-85.

Evaluation of two translations of Dafydd in *Dafydd ap Gwilym: The Poems* by Richard Morgan Loomis and *Dafydd ap Gwilym: A Selection of Poems* by Rachel   Bromwich.

Knight, Stephen. "'Love's Altar is the Forest Glade': Chaucer in the Light of Dafydd ap Gwilym." *Nottingham Medieval Studies* 43 (1999): 172-88.

Compares Chaucer's work to that of Dafydd.

Mac Cana, Proinsias. "The Poet as Spouse of His Patron." *Ériu* 39 (1988): 69-85.

Discusses the topic of the poet as his patron's spouse as it pertains to Dafydd's *cywydd.*

A. D. Hope
1907-2000

(Full name: Alec Derwent Hope) Australian poet, essayist, critic, and editor.

The following entry presents criticism of Hope's poetry from 1962 through 2000.

INTRODUCTION

Hope is recognized as one of the most influential and celebrated Australian poets of the twentieth century. Critics classify him as a "classic poet," in that much of his work utilized traditional forms and rejected modernist and postmodernist poetic trends. He also incorporated mythology, legends, and fables in his verse. Despite the anachronistic nature of Hope's poetic oeuvre, commentators praise his biting satire, the clarity of his language, and sophistication of his poetic vision and view him as an important contributor to traditional prosody in contemporary poetry.

BIOGRAPHICAL INFORMATION

Hope was born on July 21, 1907, in Cooma, New South Wales, Australia, and spent most of his childhood in rural areas in New South Wales and Tasmania. He received his B.A. from Sydney University in 1928 and then went on to Oxford University for two years. He returned to Australia, working as a psychologist with the New South Wales Department of Labour and Industry. In 1937 he accepted a position as lecturer at Sydney Teachers' College, and then in 1945 at the University of Melbourne. In 1951 he was appointed the first Professor of English at Canberra University College, and held the position until his retirement in 1968. In his mid-thirties his poetry was starting to appear in periodicals, but it was not until 1955 that he published his first collection of poems, *The Wandering Islands*. After his retirement from teaching, he was appointed Emeritus Professor at the Australian National University. He was awarded the Robert Frost Award for Poetry in 1976, the Levinson Prize for Poetry in 1968, and the Myer Award for Australian Literature in 1967. He was awarded an Officer of the Order of the British Empire in 1972. He died on July 13, 2000 in Canberra, A.C.T, Australia.

MAJOR WORKS

Although Hope's poetry is regarded as stylistically conservative—he utilized the iambic quatrain—the

subjects of his verse were varied in scope. He is considered a major writer of erotic verse. Several of his early poems, such as "Phallus," reject the pleasures of sexual relationships and romantic attachment. Yet in later work, the beauty of the human body and the thrill of passion and erotic adventure become a central theme in many of his poems. In others he reflects on the dual nature of love; in "Imperial Adam," for example, Adam finishes a pleasurable sexual tryst with Eve only to visualize that their act has unleashed the first murderer, their son Cain, on the world. Hope is also viewed as a satirical poet, as many of his works poke fun at technology, conformity, and the absurdity of modern life. In "Australia" he notes the lack of culture and intellectual challenges to be found in Australian society. "The Return from the Freudian Islands" skewers the trend of psychological theorizing. Other poems explore such topics as creativity, nature, music, and the wonders of science. Hope's incorporation of myth and legend is viewed as a defining characteristic of his poems. "The End of the Journey" is an imaginative and bleak retelling of the Ulysses-Penelope story. "Paradise Saved" and "Imperial Adam" concern the Edenic myth. In other works Hope discusses the role of the artist in contemporary society and asserts his theory of poetic expression. His long poem, "Conversation with Calliope," investigates the status of epic poetry in our modern world.

CRITICAL RECEPTION

Much of the critical reaction to Hope's poetry focuses on his rejection of modernist and postmodernist poetic forms—particularly the free verse poem—and his utilization of traditional structure as well as classical mythology and legend. His poetic theory has led many commentators to view his verse as neoclassical, outdated, and too conservative—more in line with eighteenth-century poetry than twentieth century verse. However, in recent years, critics have reassessed Hope's verse, and have found much value in his formalized style. Critics have noted the lack of any identifiable Australian material in his work and perceive him as an outsider within the tradition of Australian literature. Thematically, commentators have traced his treatment of eroticism and sexuality, and have detected a vein of male chauvinism in many of his poems. His satirical verse has been a recurring topic of critical attention, and his nonconformist and biting viewpoint has attracted mixed reactions. Moreover, he has been derided for the self-pity, strident tone, and condescension in some of his verse. In general, however, commentators commend his poetic achievement and regard him as one of the most important Australian poets of the twentieth century.

PRINCIPAL WORKS

Poetry

The Wandering Islands 1955
Poems 1960
Collected Poems, 1930-1965 1966; revised as *Collected Poems, 1930-1970* 1972
New Poems: 1965-1969 1969
Dunciad Minor: An Heroick Poem 1970
Selected Poems 1973
A Late Picking: Poems, 1965-1974 1975
A Book of Answers 1978
The Drifting Continent and Other Poems 1979
Antechinus: Poems, 1975-1980 1981
The Age of Reason 1985
Selected Poems 1986
Orpheus 1991

Selected Poems 1992
A. D. Hope: Selected Poetry and Prose (poetry and criticism) 2000

Other Major Works

Australian Literature, 1950-1962 (criticism) 1963
The Cave and the Spring (essays) 1965; revised 1974
Midsummer Eve's Dream: Variations on a Theme by William Dunbar (essays) 1970
Native Companions: Essays and Comments on Australian Literature, 1936-1966 (essays and criticism) 1974
The Pack of Autolycus (essays) 1978
The New Cratylus: Notes on the Craft of Poetry (essays) 1979
Ladies from the Sea (play) 1987
Chance Encounters (memoir) 1992

CRITICISM

W. A. Suchting (essay date 1962)

SOURCE: Suchting, W. A. "The Poetry of A. D. Hope: A Frame of Reference." *Meanjin Quarterly* 89, no. 21 (1962): 154-63.

[*In the following essay, Suchting delineates the "frame of reference" in Hope's verse.*]

Every significant artist has a fundamental axis about which his work revolves, a basic perspective from which, in which, he sees the world and himself. (This is true even—perhaps especially—when the central attitude is composed of different, and maybe opposing elements.)

The aim of the following essay is to attempt to demarcate this 'frame of reference' in the poetry of A. D. Hope, as far as it has been published in *The Wandering Islands* (1955) and *Poems* (1960), and to discuss some of the implications of such a position.

I

The poem which gives its title to Hope's first collection expresses this basic perspective with simple directness: human isolation. 'Wandering islands' are by no means without points of possible, and sometimes even actual contact, but the meetings are in principle external, temporary only: for the ship-wrecked sailor there is no hope of rescue. (Compare here the island image in **'Ascent into Hell',** and also the penultimate stanza of **'X-ray Photograph'.**)

Because of its awkwardly yoked images, roughnesses of rhythm, because of its mode of statement which is at once too abstract and too explicit, this poem expresses only imperfectly the central attitude of isolation. The latter emerges in a clearer and poetically much more satisfying manner in what is doubtless one of Hope's finest poems, **'The Death of the Bird'.** The bird is a natural creature, a motif in its own right, and its destiny—its lostness and final death—natural to it. At the same time it may be seen as a concrete image of Hope's view of the 'human condition':

> A vanishing speck in those inane dominions,
> Single and frail, uncertain of her place,
> Alone in the bright host of her companions,
> Lost in the blue unfriendliness of space. . . .
>
> Try as she will, the trackless world delivers
> No way, the wilderness of light no sign,
> The immense and complex map of hills and rivers
> Mocks her small wisdom with its vast design.
>
> And darkness rises from the eastern valleys,
> And the winds buffet her with their hungry breath,
> And the great earth, with neither grief nor malice,
> Receives the tiny burden of her death.

The theme of isolation which appears in the above poem in a general form (though expressed in specific, concrete images) is particularized in numerous others.

It is seen in an estrangement from his own country, his image of which (in **'Australia'**) is not the traditional one of a young land of promise, but an immensely aged land, lacking any real future, its cities and people depleted and unoriginal, clinging to an alien soil.

He is estranged also from much of contemporary life, to various aspects of which he has devoted a number of satirical pieces: the husband-hunting female, and especially the mild and virtuous variety (**'The Brides', 'The Explorers'**), 'successful' men and 'Technocratic man' (**'Toast for a Golden Age', 'The Kings'**), vicarious emotions (**'Sportsfield'**), TV and advertising (**'A Commination'**), religion (**'Easter Hymn', 'The House of God', 'Lambkin: A Fable'**), levelling (**'The Age of Innocence'**), and even contemporary complaints about contemporary life (**'Standardization'**). There is no heroism in the poems included in *The Wandering Islands* under the rubric 'Sagas of the Heroes'. The 'Hero of our Time' (in **'Conquistador'**) who may

> With any luck, one day, be you or me

is an insignificant suburbanite who attains immortality by being made into a mat

> Tanned on both sides and neatly edged with fur

after an accident with a 'white girl of uncommon size' with whom he went to bed in a sudden break with his ordinary life.

The personal connection presented most frequently and in most detail by Hope is that centring in the relationship of woman to man. But it is precisely here, in this most intimate of interpersonal relationships, that the central isolation is present and is felt most intensely. In **'The Dream',** for example, the relation between the man and the woman is depicted as a refuge from a harsh alien world:

> Unable to speak, he touched her with his hand,
> Fingering the witnesses of cheek and breast.
> The bloody anguish breeding in the bone
> Told its long exile, told of all the lands
> Where the unresting heart, seeking its rest,
> Finds always that its language is unknown.

But by the end of the poem even this proves to be no refuge from human exile:

> Unable to speak, he rose and left her there;
> Unable to meet her eyes that gazed with such
> Anguish and horror, went out into the night,
> Burning, burning, burning in her despair
> And kindling hurt and ruin at his touch.

This isolation of man and woman is expressed, from a slightly different point of view, in the absence of presentations of fully-rounded love-relationships. Hope is rather a poet of eroticism. Indeed even eroticism tends to be reduced to its sexual aspect, the latter being abstracted from specifically human relations, personal feelings and attitudes, and considered in its physical directness, the other participant in the sexual act appearing rather as a source of sensations only, than as a genuine partner. From this point of view sex becomes

> A refuge only for the ship-wrecked sailor;
> He sits on the shore and sullenly masturbates,
>
> **'The Wandering Islands'**

In **'The Damnation of Byron'** the dead poet is depicted in the afterworld, surrounded by desirous women and enjoying them vigorously.

> And yet he is alone. At first he feels
> nothing above the tumult of his blood,
> while through his veins like the slow pox there steals
> the deep significance of his solitude.

The Hell to which he is condemned, in which he suffers, is just the contradiction between his obsessive eroticism, his inescapable desire for contact in the form of sexual relations, and his utter inability to make such contact in a way that penetrates to his inwardness. The result is an isolation and sense of nothingness that is constantly reproduced and intensified by his efforts to escape it, efforts that are condemned to futility.

Yet always to this nausea he returns
from his own mind—the emptiness within. . . .

II

But merely to establish, descriptively, the centrality of the idea and experience of isolation in Hope's poetry does not take us very far. If such a characterization is to be of any real significance in the criticism of his work, it must decisively assist us in the comprehension and evaluation of it in detail. Furthermore, the bare generalization in itself does not suffice to distinguish the poetry of Hope from the literary production of a practically indefinitely large number of writers over roughly the last hundred years, since isolation has been the central experience underlying the bulk of the serious literature of that period. However, a brief discussion of the general problematic of isolation will put us in a better position to apply the idea specifically to the poetry of Hope.

The loss of self-identification of men with a social whole—a loss that may be experienced with feelings ranging from indifference to active opposition—and the accompanying sense that life offers no objective guides for thought, feeling and action, which is at once a cause and an effect of isolation, has a dual—and contradictory—set of consequences. On the one hand, the individual experiences this state in 'dread', 'anguish', 'anxiety', inconsolable 'abandonment'. On the other hand, he feels an intoxicating sense of absolute freedom, of being thrown back entirely on himself for the norms of his being and action. Such a choice he must make, for he is 'condemned' to do so through the very fact of being a human being with the inalienable freedom that this implies. To choose to have no norms—to be a 'nihilist', or to commit suicide—is still to choose.

The attempt by the isolated subjectivity to find a firm principle in the sensible side of his nature alone is a vain one. The cycle of frantic search after sensation for its own sake, satiety, boredom, is an indefinitely repeated one, and offers no solid ground. The concentration on sensation and feeling, which is at once the most intense expression of isolation and one of the ostensibly fixed points of reference in a world with no objective axiological structure, leads to a dissolution of the contours of the personality, to inner chaos.

Alternatively, then, an attempt is made to find the Archimedean point in some purely rational factors, some set of abstract, formal norms to which the self may submit unconditionally and, as a result, gain an at least prima facie order, security, orientation. The norms may be derived quite literally from without, for example, from a Leader, an institution (Church, Party, etc.). Or the mind may be, in the absence of genuine extra-personal organizing forms, itself called upon to supply a principle of order. It thus differentiates itself, as it were, into two parts, the one clearly and explicitly subjective, the other prescribing norms for the first. What is gained thereby is, however, only a pseudo-objective principle of order, because it is objective only in the sense of being other than that aspect of the subjectivity which is clearly recognized as such; the relation of externality, which is one aspect of the idea of objectivity, is here located *within* the subject. An example of such a norm is the ideal of practising or enjoying art for its own sake only.

The main defect of the first attitude was the lack of any extra-subjective aim or order in the affective life of the individual, the norm of conduct being purely self-based. But the second attitude does not fundamentally alter this situation. Between the abstract, formal objectivity of the norms and their prescriptions, and the concrete, specific subjectivity of the real individual there is an unbridgeable gulf. The normative formalism can be united with any form of subjectivity, provided only that the latter does not, in its external expressions, interfere with general conformity to the norm. Thus this formalism has, as an opposite pole, an individualism which is limited, as far as possible, to the purely subjective, which does not interfere with the course of obedience to that formalism. But for this very reason, just because it is cut off from reason (here identified with essentially alien norms), this individual subjectivity is unregulated, inwardly unstable, full of resigned despair, of sentimental or frigid cynicism. (A profound portrayal of this fundamentally similar instability of both types of attitude is given by Thomas Mann in the figures of Christian and Thomas Buddenbrooks. Compare also the characterization of the second attitude with the figure of Gustav von Aschenbach in *Death in Venice*.)

A self is always a nexus of personal-social relations, a complex of subjective and objective elements in a mediated, developing bond. The stripping off, one by one, like the skins of Peer Gynt's onion, of the extra-subjective dimensions of the self leaves ultimately, not a peculiarly private world, but pure emptiness, nothingness. To try to give meaning to existence, or to discover it there, without stepping outside the limits of the isolated subjectivity is no more possible than the proverbial lifting of oneself off the floor by one's shoe-laces.

Aesthetic pseudo-authoritarianism in particular is no exception, though it may have, prima facie, a greater degree of plausibility, inasmuch as art seems to constitute a unique bridge between the objective and the subjective (the personal as objective in the artistic organization of experience). But insofar as this attempt at organization has no real foundation in the common, extra-subjective life and experience to which the principles of organization are being applied, the artistic subjectivity, oscillating between sensations at one pole, and form and reflection at the other, treads a void.

III

If the theme of isolation is clearly evident in Hope's poetry, that of the lack of any basic and positive guiding perspectives, and the resulting sense of bewilderment, which, as has just been seen is both a starting-point and terminus of the process of isolation, is not less obvious in, for example, the passage at the end of **'Observation Car'** beginning,

> I have lost my faith that the ticket tells where we are going.

and ending

> The future is rumour and drivel;
> Only the past is assured.

The attempt, within this condition, to find some firm points of orientation in either the sensible or the rational, which we have traced in very general form above, is traceable right through Hope's poetry in particular. The pole of the sensible is mainly represented by the eroticism already briefly discussed[1], that of the rational by the practice of art.

Hope's perception of the final consequences of a concentration on eroticism for its own sake has already been illustrated in the first part of this essay, particularly with regard to his poem on **'The Damnation of Byron'**.

Art is the theme of one of Hope's finest poems, **'Pyramis *or* The House of Ascent'** (which gives its title to the section of *The Wandering Islands* which contains it). The poem falls into three parts (though they are not marked as such). The first three stanzas depict in solid rhythms and images the building of the pyramids. In the desert wastes a whole nation is being driven to the task by the Pharaohs. The builder sees in imagination the inevitable decay of his work, but still cries, 'Let the work proceed!' The Pharaohs allow nothing to stand in the way of completion of the monument to them:

> If you lack slaves, make war! The measure of things
> Is man, and I of men. By this you live.

At the beginning of the fourth, essentially transitional stanza, the idea is made more explicit:

> No act of time limits the procreant will . . .

The final two stanzas draw explicitly the parallel already suggested in the first three and prepared for by the fourth. Here pyramid-building is seen as only one example of, or as an image of, the great art-monuments. (Compare here Horace's well-known line.) The makers of such monuments were

> . . . men who put aside
> Consideration, dared, and stood alone,
> Strengthening those powers that fence the failing heart;
> Intemperate will and incorruptible pride.

Thus the world of the creative individual, and in particular the artist, is the desert—the 'Waste land and homeless sea' as Hope puts it in **'Soledades of the Sun and Moon'**. He knows that time will deface his creations. But nevertheless he labours on, sacrificing all to his task, the lack of any real extra-subjective motive or purpose being supplied by a proud, unalterable stubbornness of aim, grounded solely in himself. (Compare here also the image of Dis at the end of **'The Return of Persephone'**, and **'The Pleasure of Princes'**.)

The basic themes of eroticism and art, while often handled separately, are sometimes closely combined. This is the case in, for example, **'Pygmalion'**, **'The Lamp and the Jar'**, and also perhaps in **'The Damnation of Byron'**. The images of darkness and light in their connection with love and art as illuminers may be studied in **'Invocation'**, in **'Sleep'**, and in the last section of **'An Epistle: Edward Sackville to Venetia Digby'**. Such a joint treatment is also present in **'The Trophy'**, which immediately precedes **'Pyramis'**. **'The Trophy'**, though much shorter and though by no means as easily apprehended, is, with its tight organization and economy, its poetical homogeneity of meaning and image, one of Hope's finest poems, and contains concentrated within its brief span his basic themes and their fundamental problems.

The structure of the poem is very similar to that of **'Pyramis'**, inasmuch as it is built up on a number of parallels, though in **'The Trophy'** the generality comes first and the concrete illustration (if it may be called that) follows, whereas in **'Pyramis'** this sequence is reversed. The poem falls into two main parts. In the first two stanzas two images are introduced: the 'builder' and the lover. The former is doubtless to be understood here (as in **'Pyramis'**) broadly in the sense of 'maker'. (This ties in with the etymological meaning of 'poet', just as 'art' in the eleventh line may be understood as referring to the Latin 'ars', the stem of which means 'to fit'.) Common to both is an unexpected feeling of horror, of emptiness, at the moment of consummation of their highest directed energies. (Compare here *The Wandering Islands,* pp. 35, 36, 39, 44, and the concluding stanzas of **'The Dream'**, partly quoted earlier.) In the second part there is what seems to be a meditation on what may be a vase-painting. The connection between the two parts is made explicitly in the penultimate line of the third stanza. The Roman soldier is anonymous: neither written records nor his stone monument reveals any information about even such a 'great captain'. The laurel, symbol of triumph, shades his tomb, but the laurel is 'bitter'. (This is doubtless to be taken in a metaphorical as well as a literal meaning.) The Roman captain has succeeded, by the sheer force of a proud will, in organizing his disordered soldiery, in subduing his fragmentary and refractory material, in moulding it into an instrument for producing a triumphant result, even in the face of defeat. But he has no inward relation to the object of his victory; the very greatness of his success only emphasizes the more its fruitlessness to him personally. His feeling of disgust and futility leads him to suicide. (This emptiness revealed by the success of activity carried on purely for its own sake, the futility intrinsic to the purely self-based will, is also hinted at in '**The Pleasure of Princes**'.) Thus the pure subjectivity, held together by proud will, to which a retreat is made as to a firm point d'appui in a meaningless world, finally dissolves into the same desperate chaos as that from which the attempted escape took place.

> Uns überfüllts. Wir ordnens. Es zerfällt.
> Wir ordnens wieder und zerfallen selbst.[2]

IV

The preceding consideration has been restricted, as far as possible, simply to analysis and elucidation. In conclusion something may be said in the light of the above, by way of evaluation, about two aspects of Hope's poetry which have attracted much attention— his satire and his erotic subject-matter.

Some critics seemingly consider Hope's greatest strength to lie in his satire. Certainly the satire is almost always well-turned, witty, and in general intellectually very pleasing. But it lacks many of the basic features of great satire. (That it could be so overrated is a comment on the state of satirical writing in contemporary literature.) The subjects of his satire (many of them already listed earlier) are certainly characteristic in many respects of our age, but few could be called basic; they are not analogous to the fundamental and burning issues with which an Aristophanes, a Swift, a Byron concerned themselves. Again, his satire lacks a certain passionate intensity, an indignation rooted in deep regard for human worth and dignity, which are among the marks of the satirist of the first rank. There is, indeed, at times (e.g. in '**A Commination**') a species of energy, but it is more the vigour of a spontaneous attack of vomiting than controlled, tensely directed power. The great satirist is deeply 'committed', certainly, but he also has a measure of detachment: he is at a sufficient distance from his subject not to feel immediate personal involvement. But, as Hope himself writes at the end of '**A Commination**', 'Sodom is my city still'. On the other hand, his satire is often reducible to a more or less harmless irony or fastidious puking. As a result of all this he lacks, in general, what he himself calls, in his poem on Yeats, 'the bitter, lucid mind of Swift', who

> Bred passion against the times, made wisdom strong;

The popularly controversial question about Hope's poetry is of course that concerning the sexual element in it. Indeed the importance of this is undeniable, even from the purely quantitative point of view: one critic has pointed out that more than half the poems in *The Wandering Islands* have direct or indirect sexual themes or references[3], and the proportion in *Poems* is roughly the same.

It practically goes without saying that this is, by itself, entirely without significance for the serious criticism of his work. It is not true that any subject at all is a suitable one for artistic purposes; but it is true that the criterion of fitness is not the lowest (or highest) common factor of conventional morality. What can, and indeed what must be in question in the case of a particular work, is the way in which the subject has been treated, the degree to which this treatment conforms to general aesthetic principles. The point at issue is that of the consequences of a particular attitude for the aesthetic worth of a work.

In considering the finest treatments of the erotic throughout the history of literature, it is clear that, almost without exception, the erotic is seen and portrayed primarily as an aspect of the total human situation, as a feature of personal and social relationships, and that, in particular, the purely physical aspects of the subject hardly appear: we look in vain for descriptions of the immediate erotic behaviour of Helen and Paris, Dido and Aeneas, Romeo and Juliet, Margaret and Faust, Julien Sorel and Mathilde, Anna and Vronsky, and the rest. This points to the common aesthetic insight that it is only from the point of view of whole human personalities, with all their relations, that the erotic has real aesthetic interest and significance. It is only in this way that the erotic, the purely physical basis for which has presumably persisted practically unchanged throughout most of human history, can illuminate a rich diversity of personalities and attitudes, can manifest a whole spectrum of unique modes of feeling and behaviour. It is an equal and opposite result that a concentration on the more exclusively physiological aspects of the erotic inevitably brings with it a certain monotony, a lack of possibilities of development—in short, the danger of sterility.

That Hope has produced poetry of power and beauty working along the latter lines is undeniable (e.g. '**Three Romances**'). It is equally undeniable that Hope does not always focus his attention on the more narrowly physical aspects of the erotic: there is present in his work a view of sex as an intensification of life as a whole, rather than as merely a source of intense and pleasurable sensations, of love as a source of general insights about life. In this connection one may point to '**Chorale**', and especially to '**An Epistle: Edward Sackville to Venetia Digby**' (though it may not be without significance that in the latter the lovers are irremediably separated). There is even in some poems what might be identified as a certain tension between love and sex, for example in **'Pygmalion'** and the ending of **'Chorale'**. (Compare in this connection the contraception theme in **'Massacre of the Innocents'**, **'The Walker',** and also the ending of **'Imperial Adam'.**)

The narrowness of subject and treatment in Hope's poetry and the consequent dangers of lack of avenues of development and sterility, despite the indisputably considerable poetical talent manifested, are matters which several critics have noted.[4] These are, I suggest, constantly present dangers for the writer isolated from the broad currents of social life which, reflected in what Hope's much admired Yeats called 'public themes', are an indispensable basis for sound, developing work, for work in accordance with what Hope himself has defined as 'the meaning of the poet's trade':

> To re-create the fables and revive
> In men the energies by which they live.[5]

Notes

1. The concentration on raw, not specifically erotic, sensation may be seen in 'Massacre of the Innocents', 'The Dinner' and 'Return from the Freudian Islands' (particularly stanzas 14-17). This presence, in the work of the same writer, of the world of crude and brutal feeling on the one hand, and of the world of the most refined aestheticism on the other, is by no means uncommon in the more recent literature. Rilke exhibits it in places, and Thomas Mann has brilliantly delineated the situation in *Dr. Faustus.*

2. Rilke, Eighth Duino Elegy.

3. C. Hadgraft, *Australian Literature* (London, 1960), p. 198.

4. See, for example, S. L. Goldberg, 'The Poet as Hero: A. D. Hope's *The Wandering Islands*', *Meanjin*, vol. 16, no. 2, 1957, and Vincent Buckley's essay on Hope in *Essays in Poetry Mostly Australian* (Melbourne, 1957).

5. 'An Epistle from Holofernes'.

Judith Wright (essay date 1965)

SOURCE: Wright, Judith. "A. D. Hope." In *Preoccupations in Australian Poetry,* pp. 181-92. Melbourne: Oxford University Press, 1965.

[In the following essay, Wright offers a thematic and stylistic analysis of Hope's poetry.]

As a poet, McAuley, in spite of his austerity, has sometimes seemed too gracefully nostalgic to present a firm front against the disregard and mere incomprehen-

sion that this commercial age and country accords to poetry. Its much more violent adversary has always been A. D. Hope. The two have at least this in common, that both insist on the imposition of order and metrical discipline on a poetic experience that seems to each to be chaotic. But Hope has often suffered from being as much his own adversary as that of the world; so that, instead of castigating the hypocrisy and insensitiveness of others, he seems rather to be preoccupied with enormous and half-real terrors which originate as much within himself as without—terrors of sexuality, of impotence, of cruelty and of decay.

Against these, and against the world's ignorance and spite, he has armed himself with a kind of half-hysterical cocktail-party wit, a conventional gift for caricature, and a repertoire of thrusts and parries that seems sometimes designed to conceal his real feelings even from himself. This manner, which has come to stand as Hope himself to superficial readers, can however modulate into its very opposite—a moving and rhythmical speech that rises at its heights into real nobility of form and content.

Hope is, in fact, as he has come to realize, a poet of two worlds and of at least two faces. His earlier work was much more given to a particular note of angry wit which gained him his reputation—much of it was a kind of defence-by-attack. Though for years he published little and did not earnestly seek the character of brilliant young man and alarming Swiftian critic, it is possible to trace a certain not wholly admirable enjoyment of the role, in his early reviews and poems.

It was tempting at that time to doubt whether any serious and passionate preoccupation with poetry, or even with criticism, would emerge from Hope's particular kind of distaste for the world. For one thing, his targets (though they have changed with the years) were not always those that most deserved martyrdom with arrows. Polemic can be admirable; Hope's has not always been so.

But, if his criticism has been sometimes one-sided, Hope has taken his poetry more seriously and responsibly than once might have been foretold. In fact, he has increased in stature so much that, in the ascendancy of University poets since the end of the war, he has become the most important figure. From a satirist, he has turned himself into a poet, and a poet with a vision of the world that is compelling and highly organized.

Nevertheless, Hope's world remains painfully dualistic. He is, more than any of our poets, torn between a loathed reality and a vision of eternal meaning. To his first world, he presents a frenetic puritan violence; of his second, until recently, he has not been able to speak with any certainty.

The difference between the two is perhaps best demonstrated in such poems as **'Observation Car'**. This appears in his first book, *The Wandering Islands,* but is not reprinted in his collection *Poems*. It is a very characteristic poem, however, with its bitter knock-about farce, its vulgar-postcard figures, its self-disgust projected on to the outer world, and its revealing self-pity. It is, in fact, a thoroughly self-conscious poem; and from the beginning Hope has been a poet of self-consciousness, and of the torture of the self exposed in a merciless limelight both to itself and to the outer world.

The central metaphor is itself revealing. It is of Hope as a small boy, put into the observation car of the train for his first journey alone—a journey which lengthens like a nightmare into the whole journey of life. The rhythm and construction of the poem lend themselves to a particular tone of hysterical wit:

> . . . I am bored and a little perplexed
> And weak with the effort of endless evacuation
> of the long monotonous Now, the repetitive tidy
> Officialdom of each siding, of each little station
> Labelled Monday, Tuesday—and goodness, what hap-
> pened to Friday?

The lonely bewildered child in the observation car has already begun to talk with one eye on the audience.

> . . . And the maddening way the other passengers
> alter:
> The schoolgirl who goes to the Ladies' comes back to
> her seat
> A lollipop blonde who leads you on to assault her,
> And you've just got her skirts round her waist and her
> pants round her feet
> When you find yourself fumbling about the nightmare
> knees
> of a pink hippopotamus with a permanent wave
> Who sends you for sandwiches and a couple of teas,
> But by then she has whiskers, no teeth and one foot in
> the grave . . .

By this time the kind of audience the writer is talking to seems to be established; and it is hardly likely to be an audience which wants to hear about the private agonies of a sensitive poet. So when Hope's switch from the cocktail-party to the confessional comes, it cannot help making us uneasy. Somehow it seems like trickery, to be suddenly buttonholed by the rueful poet, explaining how he 'planned to break the journey'

>   . . . to see
> My urgent Now explode continually into flower,
> To be the Eater of Time, a poet and not that sly
> Anus of mind the historian . . .

In the end, neither aspect of the poem is convincing; there is even a certain vulgarity about it, the vulgarity of the man who has misjudged his listener. Either we want to be amused, or we are interested in the private self-analysis of the poet; we cannot attend to both in the space of the one poem. One way or the other, the poem is a confidence-trick; our sympathy is demanded on false pretences.

Yet it is the note of the second personality, the despondent and ever-so-faintly maudlin self-analyst, that has deepened, changed and matured over the years since the poem was written, submerging the easy glitter and sword-play of the earlier Hope and finally turning him into someone far more important: into, in fact, one of the Eaters of Time.

In a society whose puritanism takes the form of making a more-or-less neat division between the less and the more respectable occupations of the normal man—a kind of vision-proof compartment as it were—Hope's unsuitable habit of confronting the flesh and the spirit has caused him to be regarded as outrageously taken up with sex, and, moreover, ambiguous in his attitude towards it. It is perfectly true that Hope's most obses-sive image of his first world, the world we call 'real', is in terms of sexual cruelty and sexual possession; just as his vision of the second world, the eternal verity, takes its rise from the image of sexual fulfilment. But in his best poems the imagery becomes, as Eliot said in another context, 'only a way of putting it'. In the worse poems, however, such as **'Massacre of the Innocents'**, **'Pygmalion'**, **'Three Romances'**, a certain kind of distaste is aroused in most readers which I think has a valid basis.

In these and other poems, what is really, and rightly, objectionable is not the nature of the imagery (though this of course adds to our dislike of the poems); it is rather that the imagery seriously overweighs what is actually being said—what the poem is about. This is an architectural fault, as much as a fault in taste. Poems as rococo as, for instance, **'Lot and his Daughters'**, simply cannot support their weight of emphasis on sexual detail; it becomes apparent that the poem is writ-ten for the sake of the detail, rather than the detail put in for the sake of the poem. Moreover, this particular fault in construction, which is excusable where a poem is over-decorated through sheer enjoyment of decora-tion, in that it enhances life, is inexcusable where it is mere Grand Guignol or where the object is just to 'make our flesh creep'. It is even more inexcusable where, as in **'Ascent into Hell'**, the poet's object is to emphasize his own anguish and self-pity, to blackmail the reader, as it were, into sympathy. This is the worst weakness in Hope's poetry; and from such poems we are right to draw back in distaste.

For we can seldom feel, in any of Hope's poems, that his immediate audience of admirers is dispensable. Rather, like his own Byron:

> through the Infernal Fields he makes his way,
> playing again, but on a giant stage,
> his own Don Juan . . .

—and playing to an audience that, in his best moments, he must at times have felt to be no less suffocating. Yet he cannot help assuming the tone, acting the part; and this is why in his worst poems he appears to be talking at, rather than speaking to us. Hope has his own self-occupied rhetoric:

> That breed is in my bones; in me again
> The spirit elect works out its mighty plan—
> Yes, but that birth is hard. In the grown man
> Habit corrupts the will with terror or pain . . .
>
> **('Invocation')**

It is the more admirable in Hope to have passed, in so many good poems (particularly in the later collection), beyond the temptations of his particular Slough of Despond. Cleverness and self-consciousness have spoiled more good writers than most other qualities, and simplicity and humility are difficult virtues for poets accustomed to use wit as a weapon.

Hope's present strength and maturity as a poet seem to have been reached, moreover, through a cultivation and exacerbation of his perception of his own loneliness and despair, a meditation on the moments that have seemed to offer a way out (such as the moments of love), and an enlightened submission to the necessities of poetry. Through these three aspects, he has found a basis for faith in some kind of universal process in which man is an instrument, not an end. This instrumentality is to be, curiously enough, through art and not through an increase in knowledge. If Hope cannot believe in Brennan's apotheosis of consciousness, he has at least had a glimpse of some kind of apotheosis of the creative side of man.

It is interesting that, whereas McAuley abandoned the notion of art as a saving and redeeming force, after writing his early poem 'The Blue Horses', Hope seems to have been led to it, and through it to a new vision of the possibilities of mankind, in his later years. In **'Pyramis or the House of Ascent',** what is celebrated is the 'great work', the pyramid that remains when the race is gone.

> Neglect and greed
> Have left it void and ruin; sun and frost
> Fret it away; yet, all foretold, I see
> The builder answering: 'Let the work proceed!'

This turns into a meditation on the builders,

> men who put aside
> Consideration, dared, and stood alone,
> Strengthening those powers that fence the failing
>   heart:
> Intemperate will and incorruptible pride.

This comparatively early poem shows Hope in a Nietzschean mood; for him, 'the builders', it would seem, worked for themselves alone and in defiance of the gods who must be 'overcome'. Yet his exemplars, Blake, 'Milton twice blind groping about his soul / For

exit, and Swift raving mad in his', would not have spoken so of their art or of its motives: Blake who insisted that he had written his Prophetic Books 'from immediate dictation, and even against my will'; Milton who lamented his blindness because it made useless 'that one talent which is death to hide', not for himself but 'to serve therewith my Maker'; Swift, who also understood that the world's sin and his own were not to be mended by strengthening 'intemperate will and incorruptible pride'.

The poem is in fact an emblem of Hope's failure in understanding; his emphasis on the achievement of the defiant ego, in the face of all else, is sheer modern *hubris,* the self-dramatization of the hollow self-occupied mind.

Yet the poem which, in his later volume, Hope chooses to put next to this, **'The Death of the Bird',** is an indication that he is capable of wider and deeper insights into the nature of the world. Where Hope is overtly or covertly self-occupied (and this happens in almost all his early work) his poetry is apt to be somewhat artificial in tone; his use of language can be flashily academic. In poems such as **'The Death of the Bird',** where he finds a metaphor that allows him to escape from himself and objectify his problems, the miracle is worked and simplicity comes easily:

> Season after season, sure and safely guided,
> Going away she is also coming home.
>
> And being home, memory becomes a passion
> With which she feeds her brood and straws her
>   nest. . . .

The theme—of division, of the two homes of the migrant bird—is one that Hope makes especially his own. No poet is more conscious of dualism, no poet more vehemently rejects the temptation of an artificial unification of the two sides of his and the world's nature; and perhaps no poet has gone farther in exploring his own oppositions. The challenge of black to white, of female to male, of evil to good, of flesh to spirit, and of life to legend, occupies him in all his work, and the problems of reconciliation are the more terrible for him in that he knows himself to contain all these opposites and to be at home nowhere and everywhere.

For a poet so deeply divided and so despairingly aware of division, the question of reconciliation must seem impossible, and the comparative peace of death must seem the only final answer. So, in **'The Death of the Bird',** there is a certain note of triumph as well as compassion in the very current of the last verses, with their piling up, first of despairs,

> Try as she will, the trackless world delivers
> No way, the wilderness of light no sign,

> The immense and complex map of hills and rivers
> Mocks her small wisdom with its vast design.

and then of elemental forces that by their strength justify her relinquishment of the struggle:

> And darkness rises from the eastern valleys,
> And the winds buffet her with their hungry breath,
> And the great earth, with neither grief nor malice,
> Receives the tiny burden of her death.

The death itself comes as relief, not as sorrow; the divided heart, Hope seems to be saying, can only find peace and unity here, where the earth from which the opposites spring reunites them in indifference.

This is the final message of *The Wandering Islands*; it is reiterated in the impressive poem **'The Return of Persephone'**. This re-creation of a legend of rebirth has a characteristically twentieth-century turn. Persephone has been the rebel bride of Dis; it is only when she leaves him to return to the world and the spring that, seeing him in despair and resignation,

> Foreknowing all bounds of passion, of power, of art,
> for the first time she loved him from her heart.

This deep recognition of the hopelessness of 'passion, of power, of art', this disillusion and search for the peace of death, is Hope's contradiction of his own assertion of the powers of the conscious self, the 'builder', the artist. It has always been in an ultimate refusal to believe in his own statements, a creative spark springing from the clash of one side of his personality on another, that Hope has found the strength and impulse to move on out of his insoluble dilemmas and pose fresh contradictions at a new level of insight. It is a painful method of progress and a bruising one, but for Hope it has been fruitful.

So in the more important new poems in his second volume, this deathward-turning denial, this vision of Persephone herself in love with resignation, finds its own answer in a new kind of statement of the 'bounds of passion, of power, of art', in a vision which for the first time allows of the entrance of eternity into mortality, of essence into existence, of the world of legend into the world of corruption. The new note of triumph sounds in the first poem of the book, **'Soledades of the Sun and Moon'**—a poem about the relationship, less of poets with each other than of poets to poetry, and of poetry to the 'immortal images', the archetypes and symbols of legend, typified in the constellations.

> The mortal hearts of poets first engender
> The parleying of those immortal creatures;
> Then from their interchange create unending
> Orbits of song and colloquies of light . . .
> . . . In the star rising or the lost leaf falling

> The life of poetry, this enchanted motion,
> Perpetually recurs.

The theme is taken up again in **'An Epistle'**—where again a man addresses a woman; the meditation this time is on the theme, not of poetry, but of love, denied yet triumphant:

> The soul sitting apart sees what I do,
>   Who win powers more than Orpheus knew,
> Though he tamed tigers and enchanted trees
>   And broached the chthonic mysteries.
> The gate beyond the gate that I found fast
>   Has opened to your touch at last.
> Nothing is lost for those who pass this door:
>   They contemplate their world before
> And in the carcase of the lion come
>   Upon the unguessed honeycomb . . .

This honeycomb is symbolic of a vision and knowledge beyond that of the flesh and time—a knowledge of the eternal images and their reality, which is far greater than that of individual man and individual love:

> As on the rough back of some stream in flood
>   Whose current is by rocks withstood,
> We see in all that ruin and rush endure
>   A form miraculously pure;
> A standing wave through which the waters race
>   Yet keeps its crystal shape and place,
> So shapes and creatures of eternity
>   We form or bear. Though more than we,
> Their substance and their being we sustain
>   Awhile, though they, not we, remain.
> And still, while we have part in them, we can
>   Surpass the single reach of man,
> Put on strange visions and powers we knew not of—
>   And thus it has been with my love . . .

This magnificent metaphor is perhaps the high point of Hope's thought so far. It makes most clear the new trend of his thought, both about the legend and about humanity's part in it; for humanity, like the rough chaotic stream, is that which, though bound by time, is now seen to sustain, even to make the fleshly incarnation of, that which is eternal and beyond time's limitations. Humanity, then, however its immediate manifestations may disgust and dismay him, has for Hope been redeemed and justified by its part in the creation and sustention of eternity. The breadth and splendour of this vision, even if Hope should carry it no farther, are in turn enough to redeem and direct his poetry and our own.

In the poem which concludes the first section of this volume, **'An Epistle from Holofernes',** the relation of the poet to this world of the eternal images, and the second world—that of the coarsely human temporality of event and action, where Love manifests itself as Lust and where compromise, habit and custom 'mask us from ourselves'—is set out and examined. The poet's function is to act as mediator between legend and actuality:

It is the meaning of the poet's trade
To recreate the fables and revive
In men the energies by which they live . . .

But in doing so he must not lose sight of that world, in which after all our salvation or damnation is worked out, and by ourselves: the fables must be truly re-created, not simply repeated.

If in heroic couplets then I seem
To cut the ground from an heroic theme,
It is not that I mock at love, or you,
But, living two lives, know both of them are true.
There's a hard thing, and yet it must be done,
Which is: to see and live them both as one.

This is, of course, also the task of all poets; but in Australia only Hope has seen and stated it so clearly. This may be because of all our poets Hope has thought most about the task of poetry. There is something in this concentration of consideration that reminds us of a French rather than an English habit of mind; like Mallarmé, like Valéry, his greatest gift to poetry has been as much his elucidation of the poetic task as his actual examples of poetry. With McAuley and Harold Stewart, he early theorized about the forms and subjects of verse; and like McAuley's, a good deal of his poetry since then has been about poetry. The visible sensuous world is not his starting-point—it enters his poems with sometimes startling impact, but it is more often used as an illustration and concretion of an intellectual or emotional insight, than as itself a provocation to poetry, or even as what Baudelaire called it, a 'forest of symbols'. For Hope, the poetry is the thing; it is the mediator between doomed time and saving eternity; its function must be clarified and defined, the poet must understand what it is that he is doing.

This new readjustment of our hitherto most contradictory poet to his task is, or ought to be, an important happening for poetry. Hope is what is called an 'intellectual' poet; he is neither a poet of humanity nor a poet of the senses and their objects. For 'intellectual' poets, there is seldom any escape from a basic confrontation with the problems of intellectual man—the solipsism, the second-hand mulling over of opinion, the abstraction of thought that, hypertrophied and self-generating, can lead only towards despair. The intellect is only of real use in poetry when it begins from a starting-point of faith—not necessarily religious faith, but simply belief in a meaning in the human world, a direction that governs the flow and eddy of event, an underlying and overriding destiny that is not confined to man's own conscious purpose and knowledge.

This faith seems to have come to Hope, rather as an intuitive perception than an intellectual conclusion. His long poem **'Conversation with Calliope',** a discussion of the situation of epic poetry in our present world, and incidentally of the situation of the poet as well, elaborates the idea behind it into a sketch of Hope's new world-view (though he is careful to emphasize that any such sketch must be regarded as a 'fable', not as an exposition).

In the beginning was the Word . . .
but though it *was,* it was not heard.

. . . And then the Word began to move,
Itself unmoved . . .

The endless edifice of love
Felt life's first step upon its sill,
And in that primal globule furled
Lay all the orders of the world.

These orders are then explained; the first is Life, the second consciousness. The third order, however, is beyond our grasp; it is a new creation through us as its instruments, the order of Art, and this, though we can see its products, we cannot fully understand:

The arts themselves propose the free
And unknown ends which they fulfil . . .
New modes of being, till their laws
Prevail, cannot be understood
Beyond the process and the cause . . .

But the modern flood of increasing population, increasing synthesization and mass-production, of 'Man disposing', is leading to Art's disappearance.

The Great Society produces
Only the arts it can afford,
Stamped, sterilized and tinned and tested
And standardized and predigested.

Even to this, however, the Muse can reply, though her answer may not provide much consolation for man as he now is; 'The Word withdraws', she says, 'but never fails'. Even in the coming barbarism, 'Small clans we choose, and hold apart. / Some few in whom the heavenly rage / Still blazes and keeps pure the heart,' and from these pilgrims the 'new forms of being' will still arise, though the poets of the present day (including Hope) may have to accept their own impotence.

The interest and importance of the new status Hope is postulating for art seems to me to lie less in the terms of his postulation than in the fact that, after years of self-disgust and disgust for the worse manifestations of humanity, he has, as it were, found a use for mortality that stretches all the way into eternity. Whether his readers can comprehend and credit the notion of the eternal images as a 'third order of being', higher than and incomprehensible by consciousness, is possibly beside the point. Indeed, he has himself carefully told us that we cannot grasp the notion of this 'third order', since we ourselves do not enter into it except as 'forming or bearing' the images that move above and beyond us. This means, in effect, that we act because of forces that move us beyond the comprehension of our own will and consciousness; that what we do has meaning in the state of eternity which it cannot have in the state of time, and which we therefore cannot believe in or even see in its full dimensions.

He himself gives the example of colour-vision, which may have arisen among a few while the mass of their fellows were still unable to perceive colour as such—no attempt at communication could make those who were unequipped for colour-perception understand or believe in the reality of colour for their fellows. (An even better illustration might be found in the fantasy **'Flatland',** where a sphere tries to bring to a one-dimensional world of flat circles the notion of extension in three dimensions. The circles dismiss him, however, as merely a circle which can make itself smaller or larger at will—since as he tries to demonstrate his own sphericity, he merely passes through their one-dimensional world.)

There is, decidedly, nothing new in the notion of forces that manifest themselves through us, though they themselves move on a different plane, and are incomprehensible to our senses and intelligence. But, as ever, what does have perennial interest and importance is that every now and then someone—like Hope—declares the discovery that they exist; and not merely as attenuated notions or universals, but as living and acting entities, 'orders of being'.

And there is a good deal in Hope's proclamation of them which recalls Rilke's even more painfully arrived-at perceptions: for Hope, as for Rilke, mankind exists for the sake of art, of transformation. For Rilke, this transformation is that of the material of everyday life, the simple images of the world around us:

> Are we, perhaps, *here* just for saying: House,
> Bridge, Fountain, Gate, Jug, Fruit-tree, Window,—
> possibly: Pillar, Tower? . . . but for *saying*, remember,
> Oh, for such saying as never the things themselves
> hoped so intensely to be . . .

> **('Ninth Elegy')**

For Hope, it is rather the archetypal images of human life—the images that already hang before our eyes in the constellations, and the legends and the myths from which the stars are named—that themselves take their life through and from us, requiring of the poet a continual reinterpretation and re-creation that they may in turn give life to man.

But, archetypal force or Angel, both require that man should be able to serve, perhaps even, unknown to himself, to harbour powers greater than he knows; and this is the conception which frees poetry at last from

the limitations of conscience and consciousness into which the rational and intellectual life of the eighteenth century first betrayed it, into the service of faith and praise of what is.

Fay Zwicky (review date 1986)

SOURCE: Zwicky, Fay. "The Prophetic Voice." In *The Lyre in the Pawnshop: Essays on Literature and Survival, 1974-1984,* pp. 246-52. Nedlands: University of Western Australia Press, 1986.

[*In the following review of* A Late Picking, *Zwicky discusses Hope's reputation as a poet in Australia and elucidates the central themes in his verse.*]

> The man alone digging his bones a hole;
> The pyramid in the waste—whose images?

When A. D. Hope asked this question in **'Pyramis or The House of Ascent'** in 1948, he was trying to reconcile the ambiguity of the creative consciousness in the image of the Egyptian Pharaoh: the artist/priest snagged in tension between the heart's passions and that clear-sighted perception of illusion which cuts him off from other human beings. In this early poem the artist's work becomes a monument to his self-assertion in a spiritual wasteland, and there was some admiration implied for 'those powers that fence the failing heart: / Intemperate will and incorruptible pride'. By invoking Blake, Milton and Swift and the hovering presence of insanity, Hope showed continuing awareness of the dangers and glories of over-assertive individualism to man as social being and as artist. Much of his earlier work kicked off from a dissociation and conflict within the personality; reason against passion, morality against desire, individual feeling against the collective organism. Had he, like Auden, been able to wield his wit in a sophisticated cultural context in which irony is a perfectly legitimate weapon and the pursuit of excellence part of the cultural fabric, he would never have been labelled 'alienated' or 'nihilistic' as he has been in the Australian context. His resistance to the glib insignia of grass-roots nationalism, his awareness and use of the whole European tradition, have often prejudiced his audience in this country, which equates sincerity with sloppiness, wit with barren ingenuity.

What, then, has become of that 'intemperate will and incorruptible pride' as part of the artist's equipment? What now bolsters the 'failing heart'? And was it such a failing heart after all? The appearance of this new collection would suggest that the heart has always been there and in a very healthy condition too, waiting its rightful season. In the best poems, the tensions from which all great poetry emerges still exist but without lash, strain, sweat and jolt; the opposing forces are integrated and fused in a state of wholeness and spontaneity. And the courage and distinction involved in the achievement demands humble and sympathetic recognition on the reader's part.

That it has not been a comfortable route is evident in a poem of 1971:

> The drug of custom helps us to adjust;
> If it did not, how could we possibly bear
> Our civilization for a single day?
> Although the edges of its knives are wet,
> The dripping red is easy to forget.
> Your own, or someone else's? Who can say?
>
> Just keep on putting one foot after another;
> The horror is blunted, like the ecstasy.
> Illusions of normal living serve us, brother,
> To keep the heart conditioned not to see
> What in his passionate age drove Goya wild;
> That old, mad god eating his naked child.

('**Under Sedation**')

If this is the mandarin recoil from reality of which Hope has so often been accused, then his critics have no eyes and no ears. The terrors have always been real enough, both from within and without. The torture of extreme self-consciousness in an alien environment produced work in the past expressive of frustration, hostility and shock against a world with which the younger man felt unable to come to terms. Hence, there was occasional faltering of tonal control and the release of cruelty in poems such as '**Observation Car**' and, to a lesser extent, '**Conquistador**'. The strong sexual overtones seemed, nevertheless, peripheral to the underlying network of guilt, repression, and recrimination shrugged off in brutally comic diction. The pain of this dualistic world lay in Hope's attempts to reconcile a powerful and self-conscious sexuality with a most intense idealism. He could only speak of the former with driven and often near-frantic puritanical violence, and has been (until this present collection) somewhat ambiguous in his expression of the latter.

It has become almost a cliché of Australian criticism to remark the prevailing melancholy of many writers, echoes of *Ecclesiastes* booming away in the spinifex like the mysterious 'boum' of the Marabar Caves.

> Then I looked on all the labours that my hands had wrought, and on the labour that I had laboured to do; and, behold, all was vanity and vexation of spirit, and there was no profit under the sun.

—*Ecclesiastes* 2: xi

A chill sense of loss animates Hope's awareness of desolation in a life of necessary compromises:

> Patch and mend, patch and mend;
> Borrow and scrape or lavish and spend

> As much good fortune as God may send:
> Naught shall avail you;
> All things shall fail you;
> Nothing shall profit you in the end.

('**Patch and Mend**')

—despair in the face of doom wrought by time and death. But Hope goes beyond wry homiletic pessimism in the best poems in this book—two wonderfully moving elegies for fellow poets whose Jewish fate might, but for the grace of God, have been his. Against the terrible odds of our century, he invests the memory of Gertrud Kolmar and Osip Mandelstam with stoic courage, an impersonality capable of being matched with the impersonal forces that destroyed them but not what they represented. The phrase, 'the grace of God' is no mere rhetorical figure to Hope—the search for grace, for closer connection with the God of suffering man, pervades these poems with a transcendent urgency directed towards learning 'the art of coming home'.

The Book of Job has always held a special place for poets of tragic persuasion, more especially for those whose experience has given them a sense of identification with the Jewish character. John Berryman (in his posthumously published autobiographical novel, *Recovery*), drawn to Judaism, found that 'no other nation of antiquity ever came to the point of regarding itself as chosen not for its own advantage but *for service*. A bearing attraction.' A particularly pertinent attraction to a writer trying to keep the artist's role in communal perspective for, like Hope, he too was aware of the potential *hubris* of the poet raging in the wilderness, forced into a secular prophethood by surrounding spiritual sterility. Berryman also referred in the novel to his 'unique devotion to *Job*'. Apart from the formal attractions of its dramatic presentation, Job's questioning of his creator becomes the questioning of a whole generation about the sense of its historic fate: 'Why do we suffer what we suffer?' The 'Why' is not a philosophical investigation of the nature of things but a religious concern with the ways of God, a God who contradicts His revelation by 'hiding His face' (13:xxiv).

> Where was He, too, that night you mused in the dark,
> Dog-tired, half-starved, the Terror just closing round,
> Taking incredible comfort from St Just's joke:
> 'Men perish that God may live'? Did His Covenant Ark
> Go before you to Auschwitz, his ram's-horn sound
> Till the gas-chambers of Jericho breached and broke?

The personal fate of Gertrud Kolmar becomes a universal issue:

> When they knocked you down and a jack-boot kicked in your teeth,
> Did you sing with Job: 'Though He slay me, yet will I trust'?
> Or did you remember St Just and the poem you made,

That gay, that terrible poem confronting death:
'We have always been Bluebeard's wives; we always
  must!'?
That was your answer to God and games he played.

('In Memoriam: Gertrud Kolmar, 1943')

The unquestioned assumption and affirmation of God's
presence is there from the beginning, as is the notion
that everything comes from God. In this compelling
poem, Hope never forgets the dripping edges of the
knives, makes passionate and direct identification with
those who have taught us 'that calm at the worst, when
the spirit goes free', acknowledges his debt to the dead:

Whistling past your cemetery in the black
Storm of our century of hate and dread,
I, who have lived in shelter all of my days,
Bring you, before the Lord of the Keys gets back,
Word from all those still doomed to those who are
  already dead,
Those able to recognize all and yet still able to praise.

('In Memoriam: Gertrud Kolmar, 1943')

The theme of approaching ripeness for death runs
through many of the poems: almost as if the moment of
death might be the only worthwhile moment of life.
Just as Job's protest may be interpreted as either the
greatest religious experience or the greatest blasphemy,
so ripeness can promise as well as threaten. Ripeness,
then, becomes equated with God—enclosing all,
answering all, justifying all:

God never speaks, they say, to a drunken man
Yet each of us proffers his draught of love to drain;
Each of us seeks in the other, as best he can,
    This respite from his pain.

('Under the Weather')

The first-born child in a world of horror knows its suf-
fering as determined by the archetypal example of
Isaac's preparation for death at his father's hands.
Especially if it is a product of that severe ethic which
feels responsibility to the gift of talent:

These cannot take life for granted as others do,
They shrink from kinship and kind; they have learned
  to greet
A kiss with caution, joy with a settled calm;
A celebration warns them they are taboo
And a caress reminds them that human meat
Torn at the summer solstice becomes a charm.

('The First-Born')

The lyric or elegiac tone predominates over the satiric
in most of these poems; the voices shored against his
ruins, haunting his inner ear, come from private and
personal sources, memories of the loved and the loving:

Who would suppose to view her then, the tender
Bloom and dazzle of wildfire, and the stance
Of unripe grace, the naked eloquent glance,

Time could so tame or age despoil her splendour?

('On an Early Photograph of My Mother')

On behalf of his son, he mourns the loss of heroes of a
simpler boyish fantasy world—Hercules, Samson, Ro-
land, and Robin Hood:

My unripe soul, groping to fill its need,
Found in these legends a food by which it grew.
Whatever we learned, the heroes were what we *knew*.
    We were fortunate indeed.

('The Sacred Way')

The same innocent romanticism is carried over into the
quest for love:

But where shall I find her? Where,
As I grope through these winter storms,
Is the house, the hearth, the stair
Where I held my love in my arms
And slept in the folds of her hair?

('Winterreise')

Parallel with this lyric strain runs the precocious articu-
lacy of the boy whose language ripened before his emo-
tions ever saw the light. This gives us playful, teasing
paradoxes of the intellect in poems like **'Exercise on a
Sphere'** or **'O Be A Fine Girl'**, [. . .] with a good deal
of heterogeneous yoking to keep his metaphysics warm.
It also gives us the very funny latter-day prophet of
'Country Places' crying 'Woe unto Tocumwal, Teddy-
waddy, Tooleybuc!', his rage de-fused in the wilderness
of his 'beautiful' 'prosperous' and 'careless' country,
the note of sadness never far away.

They have cut down even their only tree at One Tree;
Dust has choked Honey Bugle and drifts over Creeper
  Gate;

('Country Places')

The elegiac note is again sounded in **'Hay Fever'**
where, despite the skittish title, Hope effects a perfect
integration of his persistent dualism, a rich and deeply
moving affirmation of the stresses and resolutions of
birth and death—the complexity and order of man's
emotional and spiritual links with the natural world that
can't be stuffed into moral or political categories. It
implies an understanding, panoramic but exact, of the
interplay between images of Arcadia and of death and,
in the classical pastoral tradition, amounts to a state-
ment of accord between the notion of poetic immortal-
ity and time's threat:

Time, with his scythe honed fine,
Takes a pace forward, swings from the hips; the flesh
Crumples and falls in wind-rows curving away.
Waiting my turn as he swings—(Not yet, not mine!)
I recall the sound of the scythe on an earlier day:
Late spring in my boyhood; learning to mow with the
  men; . . .

I set the blade into the grass as they taught me the
    way;
The still dewy stalks nod, tremble and tilt aside,
Cornflowers, lucerne and poppies, sugar-grass,
    summer-grass, laced
With red-stemmed dock; I feel the thin steel crunch
Through hollow-stalk milk thistle, self-sown oats and
    rye; . . .

          . . . dandelion casts up a golden eye,
To a smell of cows chewing their cuds, the sweet hay-
    breath:
The boy with the scythe never thinks it the smell of
    death.

                                             ('Hay Fever')

In a late poem in his collection, *City Without Walls,* W.
H. Auden gave an autobiographical sketch which
included the lines:

    A childhood full of love
    and good things to eat:
    why should he not hate change?

                                             ('Profile')

They might have been Hope's words as the son/father
grows to painful acceptance of the God who 'provides
all', joy and suffering, continuing to hope that the 'next
vintage will not be too bad' ('Spätlese'). Because of
the social and cultural changes with which he is out of
sympathy, the public *persona* which he has maintained
with so much tact says less to his successors than the
voice beneath it, a prophet's voice, older and more
archetypal than the institutions to which he has given
worldly allegiance. We would do well to listen.

Peter Steele (essay date 1988)

SOURCE: Steele, Peter. "Peregrinations of A. D. Hope."
In *The Double Looking Glass: New and Classic Essays
on the Poetry of A. D. Hope,* edited by David Brooks,
pp. 170-80. St. Lucia, Australia: University of Queen-
sland Press, 2000.

[*In the following essay, which was originally published
in 1988, Steele examines the theme of voyage in Hope's
poetry, focusing on "the character of his quest."*]

Bad luck to *The Australian Pocket Oxford Dictionary*
(1st Edition) for leaving "peregrination" out of its
record, when it runs to "percoid"—"resembling a
perch"—and "perihelion"—"point in planet's orbit near-
est the sun". Perhaps they are mute witnesses to its
absence, both having to do with rovers as they do. But
peregrination too richly constellates meanings to be
easily spared. And if anything can naturally be a place
of lodgement for Hope, this may be it.

In the old days you could not be peregrine unless you
were both a quester and on the move: pilgrim blood
was the only type that counted. Spurred or stung by it,
you might make tracks towards the classic goals of
pilgrimage—Rome or Compostela or Jerusalem. The
cockleshell or the palm might boast your accomplish-
ment, but more importantly they were mnemonics for
the journeyings themselves. More drastically, there were
the courses adopted by those who, with devotion, in
penitence, or out of more obscure motives, went lifelong
on pilgrimage. The sea's shell or the land's tree could
not symbolise that for them, for they had already in
prospect left behind any place they might reach. As the
first Christians called themselves "followers of the
Way", these latter-day pursuivants were, through and
through, wayfarers.

They were themselves book-begotten, bibled into being.
Behind their trailings lay accounts of exodus and exile,
things mimed liturgically in annual cycles, incorporated
in homily or in mystical bricolage, teased out in patris-
tic speculation. Themselves mainly illiterate, they had
the day's slog counterpointed by the lyricism of that
small library which tradition had put between two cov-
ers. In turn, they engendered accounts, metaphors of
life as motion, in all the motley of travels fortunate and
unfortunate. And from a complementary tradition, Od-
yssean types learned new forms of tricksiness, new
destinations, new obsessions, exhilarations and angers.
Out of this peculiar stable, eventually, Rosinante
ambled, a thoroughly unappeasable figure on her back.

Later in the day, it is no surprise then that the work of a
poet of Hope's educated temper and unresting imagina-
tion should show the trope of travel. The eye running
down the contents of the **Collected Poems** or of other
work is taken repeatedly by revealing titles—**"The End
of a Journey", "Ascent into Hell", "The Return of
Persephone", "A Letter from Rome", "Crossing the
Frontier", "A Visit to the Ruins".** If this sort of thing
is not unusual nowadays, it is worth reflecting that
Hope's own ways have helped to habituate us to the
possibilities of the gambit. And my interest here is not
in codifying the travels which, to the casual attention,
are Hope's preoccupation, but in the character of his
quest. For peregrination, sunlit or shadowed as it may
be like the cheaper or more expensive seats in the bull-
ring, always trembles on disclosing something beyond
itself. Whenever the mind, whenever the imagination, is
much in use, there is an undeclared war between reduc-
tive and inductive forces. We want things to add up,
and we do not: the iconoclast wants his portrait painted,
the classicist dreams romantically, the hero of asepsis
longs for some honest dirt. The peregrinating mind,
legitimated on the face of it by some admirable goal,
but stirred by more comprehensive impulses which it
can neither entirely delineate or deny, "about must and
about must go", vaguely but urgently hopeful of change

beyond the calculable. Hope's titles, like the ones noted above, designate—usually ironically, be it noted—outcomes within the poems, but trail their coats into other transformations.

When Randall Jarrell writes, "Twice you have been around the world / And once around your life", his ruminating speaker is addressing a dead woman who awaits burial. She has been an original, cutting a figure among those who knew her: now, "today you look regularly erratic / In your great lead-lined cloak / Of ferns and flowers, / . . . As you lie here about not to leave / On the trip after the last".[1] The body which was one of her ways of being has now become her only way of being. It is not the mediatorial thing, fleshing itself out in nothing less than the travelled world, and converting that world into nothing less than intelligibility, but just a body, a residuum. It is a blank, which has the speaker saying after a while, "I feel like the first men who read Wordsworth. / It's so simple I can't understand it". And there is the poetical clue, as surely as it is the human rub. Faced with a vacuity, an unselving in the world, the speaker is carried into the *terra nova* of a wholly original imagination, that of Wordsworth, the world-breaker and world-donor. He is in effect embarked on that quest of mind and sensibility which has as many stations and monuments as there are distinctive lines of poetry, but which is not reducible to them. He is trying to find out how to be poetical.

That last expression may have a quaint look about it—"out of Aristotle, by Rilke", perhaps. But the reality is not quaint. It is in the end the thing that keeps the poet at his infuriating occupation, long after he has seen that many of the activities which once gave his art point are no longer required, or are better pursued by other means. Thinking that the sea-shanty is no place to take a Muse, or that lisping in numbers is good for addition but doubtful for transmutation, or that any world well-jingled into coherence is a world well-lost, the vexed dreamer has no resort but to keep worrying away at his art. Ultimately, that is what refuses to go away, however often it is dismissed by ideologues of the real or of the unreal. If the poetic word were merely a wheelbarrow for religious or scientific or sociological orthodoxies, tipped forward on the reader's demand and then trundled back for more of the same: or if it were nothing but a lamentation over its own frangibility, an instrument of unrealisation, it would not be worth more than a moment's attention, since to be the first is so intellectually clumsy and to be the second so intellectually perverse. No, we experience for experience's own sweet sake, think thoughtfully, see feelingly. Poetry is the evidence for this, as it is also its earnest. But what is being evidenced, and offered in earnest, is the shape-changing character of the poetical intelligence. Every

canto is a Mutability Canto, every move a shift. Going poetically, we are always finding out—or finding denied us—where and how to go.

Let us come to cases. In the *Collected Poems 1930-1970* it happens that **"The Wandering Islands"** (26) follows immediately after **"The Gateway"** (25). They are antipodal in claim or insight, the second in effect supplying a retort upon the first: to "Here I come home: in this unexpected country / They know my name and speak it with delight" there answers, ". . . The shipwrecked sailor senses / His own despair in a retreating face. / Around him he hears in the huge monotonous voices / Of wave and wind: 'The Rescue will not take place.'" Fair enough: it is not only upon lapidary inscriptions that one is not upon oath: makers of poems have forgotten, if they ever knew, how to take oaths. In any case, the peregrine writer may be interested less in what divides the poems than in what they share. One thing they share is their habit of leaving things behind.

We should not take that for granted, though we do. The principal feature of most speech, and of much writing, is simply its inertia. If the mind were not habitually slatternly and slobbish, not only could we not entertain the possibility of most advertisement, we could not pick up the newspaper, waggle fingers at the postman, give verdicts on the weather, betoken our love's hatreds, and bewilderments in boardroom or bar. Talk, as we ordinarily take it and want it taken, goes over the surface of our lives, leaving a smudge or a sheen, but in either case to let the substance of affairs be as it was before. Even the dramatic, performative, moments are as often as not the tickings in a column beside a narrative not to be changed. The general receiving the surrender of his foe is getting no new word, but merely a confirmation that he has had the last word: increasingly, given the fragility of the institutions within which the words are uttered, the marital "I do" or the forensic "I will" is dissolved into a deterministic "it does". Darwin, Marx and Freud gave us metaphors for mutation: but unfortunately each of them told us that it was an iron hand that was beckoning or impelling us forward. Well before them, the word passed on to the citizens of the West, and surely of the East as well, was principally one of stasis. The Bible begins with a starburst of creativity, but one could hardly be blamed for being caught in a lockstep of expectation, or of disconcertment, before many pages are turned. Later, philosophically, the bent of almost any thinker one can name from around the Mediterranean and its purlieus is towards the conclusive and, in large measure, the concluded. The virtuosi of the dead-end in our own intellectual season are perhaps the late, rank growth seeded thousands of years ago.

It would be folly to think that Hope is not attracted by all this. If you give him a wall, he may stand with his back to it, or attempt to scale it, or criticise its crumbling, or give it a certain amount of battering, but he knows that walls are walls, and that they are not going to go away, and that they have much to be said for them. Yet, to come back to **"The Gateway"** and **"The Wandering Islands"**, although the hastiest of readings of either would give us its theme, no such reading, and not many a more leisurely reading, would give us a live sense of Hope's metaphorical vivacity, the moving out which is also a moving-on. The lyricism of **"The Gateway"** can easily magick or musick the reader away from the metaphoric energies of these twelve lines— lines no one of which lacks direct reference to adaptation, issue, and emergence. The "gateway" of the title, without having that physical and emotional identity which is everywhere saluted in the poem, looks in practice as well to imaginative entree and exodus. In the same fashion, **"The Wandering Islands"**, often remembered as if it said in toto, "The Rescue will not take place", is a tissue of originated insights, kept under the famous Hopean discipline, but pacing out rhythmically towards further understanding. The fact is that Hope is both evocative and provocative—evoking those solidarities of human intellectual and emotional experience which he has articulated otherwise in his books of essays, and provoking new addresses to old appraisals. "Investing no fear in ultimate forgiveness" has, shadowing it, and however Hope came by it, the clouds of a hundred Reformation disputations: "a bursting mountain of spray" gives us a chill Vesuvius.

Is this, then, "how to be poetical"? It is and it is not. It is in that the heart leaps at the liveliness, the liveness, of the language. This is why we all hang around Shakespeare's grave, wondering why they should have put him seventeen feet down, yet oddly glad that it is so: we need to know where the body was buried, but can not afford to have so prepotent a figure looming. If the comparison between Hope and Auden has not often been made, it should have been, in that they are both inheritors and transmuters of the magistral touch— grateful and unscrupling when it comes to taking tips as to giving old matters new senses, pulling down the mighty from their thrones, clapping crowns of some cultural distinction on larrikin brows—and then, in the midst of it all, sweetening life's sourness as if hunger were made for nothing but song. That is how to be poetical, is it not?

It is and it is not. I go back to "The One Who Was Different". William H. Gass says, "If language is like consciousness in always urging objects on us, it is also always an emissary of the mind".[2] It was Jarrell's peculiar gift to be, even less than most of us, neither angel nor beast, and to be correspondingly more puzzled—puzzled in such a way that the language kept trying to do the sorting-out, trying to urge the objects on us, trying to be the mind's emissaries. It is almost the definition of critical ineptitude that the critic, or

interpreter, or reader, quits on one of these tasks—as it is almost the definition of a bad poet that he encourages his reader to behave in this way. Hope, when he is not about frolic or objurgation—and even sometimes when he is—will not take that path. It is as if, to Wittgenstein's "The world is all that is the case," he counterposes, "All that is the case *is the world*," meaning that the true aspires to englobe itself, to have its palpable and telling identity, to be its own say-so. But the fact is that, as Wittgenstein also suspected, most of the time we know what we may have either in seeing it fall behind us or having it loom in prospect. This, if recognised as commonplace by satirists and other moral commentators for more hundreds of years than we like to remember, has increasingly come to consciousness when we think about our very identity. The bitter-sweet gift made us by philosophical anthropology, as by other rueful benefactors, is that we are at best the pioneers of human appraisal. Hope, one of whose tastes is and always has been for the estimation of human (and suprahuman, and inhuman) identity, has at least the mercurial consolation of being able to be troubled by language itself into instructive stabilities and vindicated instabilities. Jarrell's dead woman—haunting, charming, other, mortal—has both circled the world and been of the world, is of her own life and is no longer of her own life: on both accounts she belongs in the company of the "worldly" and "unworldly" speaker. Hope, I think, is of her company. Of his diurnal affairs I know little and say nothing; but of that psychic affair in which he customarily awards, dissolves, and re-renders the affairs of the world, the poems are all we know or need to know.

These things he has said, and said better, at the culmination of **"An Epistle: Edward Sackville to Venetia Digby"** (*CP* [*Collected Poems, 1930-1970*] 165):

> Nature, who makes each member to one end,
>   May give it powers which transcend
> Its first and fruitful purpose. When she made
>   The Tongue for taste, who in the shade
> Of summer vines, what speechless manlike brute,
>   Biting sharp rind or sweeter fruit,
> Could have conceived the improbable tale, the long
>   Strange fable of the Speaking Tongue?
> So Love, which Nature's craft at first designed
>   For comfort and increase of kind,
> Puts on another nature, grows to be
>   The language of the mystery;
> The heart resolves its chaos then, the soul
>   Lucidly contemplates the whole
> Just order of the random world; and through
>   That dance she moves, and dances too.

The verse betokens ceremony, of course, Yeatsian word attended with Yeatsian plangencies; the bow is towards metaphysical coherences, teleologies, confections and resolutions. Momentarily, we have a world without waste and without loose ends; there are no Maenads to be rending at this dance. Yet Sackville's imagined finery of talk nowhere quite charms away the grave exordium of the poem: "First, last and always dearest, closest, best, / Source of my travail and my rest, / The letter which I shall not send, I write / To cheer my more than arctic night". The outreaching and overreaching of Nature, whether, as here, seen as ingeniously benign, or as elsewhere, where that natural oddity Man is concerned, as quizzical at best and disabling at worst, also lifts the stakes in the game of human comprehension, and of those feelings which aptly attend understanding. Designingly, or with flourish, or both at once, Hope's characteristic move is to move the mind on, not only from its lassitudes, but from its apparently legitimate settlements. When one is seized by this sense of his imagination and of his intellectual project, the temptation, a good one, is to cite it wherever it is to be found. So, at the conclusion of **"The Return of Persephone"** (*CP* 89), of Dis,

> Insuperable disdain
> Foreknowing all bounds of passion, of power, of art,
> Mastered but could not mask his deep despair.
> Even as she turned with Hermes to depart,
> Looking her last on her grim ravisher
> For the first time she loved him from her heart

as the second and last stanza of **"E Questo il nido in che la mia Fenice?"** (*CP* 166),

> But were I not that palm, and were the peasant
> To fell and faggot me for winter fuel,
> Still in the seasoned timber would be present
> Such passion, such desire for that renewal,
> That in my glowing embers he might see
> The burning bird and tree.

These are characteristic—and, better than that, free-standing. But Hope is not Shelley, nor was meant to be. The correlative note is there at the end of **"On an Engraving by Casserius"** (*CP* 226) where, the engraved dead woman contemplated in all her vulnerability, and the acknowledgement made that "The universals we thought to conjure with / Pass: there remain the mother and the child", the page is allowed to yield the words.

> The birth you cannot haste and cannot stay
> Nears its appointed time; turn now and rest
> Till that new nature ripens, till the deep
> Dawns with that unimaginable day.

Hope has no wide blue yonder—territory which, notoriously, one cannot tread. As peregrination always signals some circuitousness, the travail within travel, it is Hope's custom to be a way-maker as well as a way-taker. Twice around the world does not count without once around his life.

Gass, once more, with an apropos word: "The creature we choose to be on Halloween says something about the creature we are. I have often gone to masquerades

as myself, and in that guise no one knew I was there" (207). Nobody ever does, of course, not even ourselves. Unless we are tricked out in some comprehensible fashion—vestment, jeans and sloppy-joe, nakedness—no lines are to be had, no moves to be made. Take away my trappings and you leave me in the storm on the heath, as inaccessible to myself as either Lear or Poor Tom. The traditional pilgrim, wander however far he might, had pilgrim's kit, and could have food set before him or the dog set on him: happily or unhappily, he knew where he was. He also had a world about him which, however inadequately mapped, and however menacing at given points, had its adjacencies with the homeland. But as Hope says in **"The Wandering Islands"**, "The Mind has no neighbours"—something little alloyed by his scholarly judiciousness or pedagogical kindliness in other contexts. It is always a mistake to read his poetry as if, because invariably submitted to formal disciplines, it thereby makes common cause with the embourgeoisement of the imagination, the bitting of the mind. He says, dryly, in the ninth of the **"Sonnets to Baudelaire"**, "The voyage we do not take to the unknown / Becomes the poem that visits us instead" (*CP* 238), and the visitation is not sociable. It may too often be one of the most trivial pieces of psychobabble or socioprattle of our time to say that someone is looking for himself, but the locution is only waiting for an enabling imaginative touch to be wakened into vivid meaning. Hope's quest is for the apt verbal moment for the making of that move. He is, in the midst of storms of sensibility which he has himself heightened, still the pilgrim of the personal.

It is in that context that his manoeuvrings among the various personnel or personages of his poems should be seen. If you are playing the satirist, it not only pays to parade a derelict rabble past you—there is no other way of going about it. There is no such thing as a ludicrous solitary: bunchings give comedy, or nothing will. So *Dunciad Minimus* gives us the troubled ones at whose disarray we laugh, but over whom nobody could possibly lose any sleep; and so it goes with the rest of the rabblement out of whom Hope from time to time picks recruits for his satirical poems. But the rest of the time, whether it is Holofernes or Circe, Yeats or Totentanz, Susannah or Calliope, the figures chosen subtend a self in question, a self at quest. Somebody is blocking in the figure of A. D. Hope—always, in the Dantean fashion, "with the skill of the art, but a trembling hand."

"This will never do"—or so they say. The critic's, the pedant's splutter is part of everyone's repertoire, whenever there is a suggestion that those named figures, mythic or historic but in the poem always metaphoric, may have traffic with whoever it is that voices them. It seems to me an over-austere agitation. Surely we lend ourselves to the parts of the others, in hopes that they will lend themselves to ours. It is difficult to know with what sentiments the literal pilgrims of the past made their way or greeted their destination. What we do know is that well before and well after their time the physical world which we all traverse has been caressed, appealed to, invoked and sacrificed for as if it had the authority of the divine and the dearness of the human—it is a way of going "twice around the world". Similarly, more letters, lyrics, essays, paintings, sculptures and photographs than we can count betoken an impulse to know the personal—loved or hated—as the world's unique configuration. We are always in a state of stand-off or trade-off with "the others", those shadowy mirrors of ourselves, when we attempt to frame versions of the world. The price of self-knowledge is always emigration.

How to be poetical. . . . The preoccupation is not narcissistic, but one specification of the humane. Hope is a contemplative and a speculative poet, which is to say that he gazes both directly and obliquely at what interests him. The technical accomplishment, the being in a quiet way a maestro, gives him the resources for the second of these: it is a way of stealing up to what is to be known, a way of surprising and of being surprised—all the more so when the manner is faintly archaic: it is a poetry of patience. This is peregrination of a sort, a compliment to its object and, in its passage, a consolation to its exponent. For the first, for contemplation, there are perhaps no techniques: for, "Set on this bubble of dead stone and sand" (*CP* 222), or for, "All creatures seek their food, and ours is song" (*CP* 273), you simply wait and hope. Of course, as no reader of *The Canterbury Tales* will need to be reminded, there is plenty of room for the raffish and the roughcast in any extensive peregrination, and Hope has taken to those also with a will. But what he seems to have had from the first, and keeps still, is the spirit saluted in his poem for Akhmatova, **"For a Grave at Komarovo"**, "And did the Muse not smile at your reply: 'Sister, I went alone—but it was I'" (*A* [*Antechinus: Poems, 1975-1980*] 104).

Notes

1. Randall Jarrell, *The Complete Poems* (London and Boston: Faber and Faber, 1981), p. 316.

2. William H. Gass, *Habitations of the Word* (New York: Simon and Shuster, 1985), p. 83.

Philip Martin (essay date fall 1989)

SOURCE: Martin, Philip. "A. D. Hope, Nonconformist." *Journal of Popular Culture* 23, no. 2 (fall 1989): 47-53.

[*In the following essay, Martin asserts that although Hope is perceived as a conservative, almost archaic poet, he is in his own way an unorthodox and unique Australian poet.*]

Such savage and scarlet as no green hills dare
Springs in that waste, some spirit which escapes
The learned doubt, the chatter of cultured apes
Which is called civilization over there.

A. D. Hope, who will be eighty next July, is the son of a Presbyterian minister and his wife: of Nonconformists in the religious sense of the word. But he himself is a nonconformist in the other sense as well: one who does not conform to accepted opinions or attitudes. And though he by no means adheres to his parents' Christian beliefs it may well be that the religiously Nonconformist cast of mind helped to shape his character, helped to make him a nonconformist with a small "n". Even the need to break away from his parents' faith, in order to safeguard the freedom of his imagination, may have played its part in this formation. At any rate I think that his nonconformism has made Hope in his own way a very Australian sort of poet.

That may at first sound an odd thing to say, because when people think of Hope's poetry, and of the attitude to poetry expressed in his prose writings, many are likely to put him down as very *un*-Australian, and what's more, as conservative, formalist, "neo-Augustan", far from modernism, let alone postmodernism. Yet it may be that these last two are, in the wider perspective, only phases, and that Hope has put his trust in a view of poetry which will survive them both and to which poets and their readers will return.

In any case, that term "neo-Augustan" has never been inclusive enough to describe Hope's work. Already by the early 1960s we were noticing that along with his pronounced formalism went tendencies of a very different kind: post-Romantic, even modern. How many of those rhymed and metrical poems turn out to be a curious yoking of surface order and a vision of an often fierce, sometimes violent kind. Besides, while Hope does frequently write in heroic couplets, far more often he uses rhyming quatrains and more complex stanza forms.

In the 1960s many other Australian poets were turning away from the attitudes to verse and to life which Hope, along with his friend James McAuley, continued to uphold. In fact, many younger poets and some critics thought it almost scandalous that Hope should go on behaving as though poets like Eliot and Pound had never written. Hope went his own way, unperturbed by the changes taking place, antipathetic to the modernism of Eliot, who he frequently took issue with, earning himself with the reputation of a Dodo. What his critics didn't always notice, however, was that Hope wasn't ignoring that other great Anglophone poet of the century, W. B. Yeats, or that Hope's sense of life and of poetry was in many ways close to Yeats's: which surely suggests that Hope wasn't oblivious of the modern world, even if Hugh Kenner has, in a recent lecture, described Yeats as only "a part-time modernist".

As for Hope's notorious dismissal of free verse, one or two things need to be said. Personally I disagree with much that he has to say on this subject and I can see why in taking his stand against free verse he must strike many as fighting a long-lost cause. But as with most creative writers (Eliot, for instance), Hope's critical writing is often an apologia for his own practice as a poet. He knows that he needs strict form. Talking with him twenty years ago I remarked that he seldom wrote blank verse (and blank verse, after all, is hardly the freest kind of verse around). No, he said, he'd tried it, but the lack of rhyme led him to be too diffuse. (Since then he *has* published a number of blank-verse poems but I think these are among his best.) Traditional though this form is, it still seemed to him too unstructured, or too unstructuring. And notwithstanding my own liking for much free verse, from Whitman to a contemporary master like Galway Kinnell, I believe Hope's argument for retaining metre is a persuasive one. Metre, to him, is an essential "point of departure and return", and skilful verse combines metre and the prose rhythms of contemporary speech, those of the poet and of the age he or she lives in. Each good new poet who uses an old metre can both gain from it and refresh it, so that traditional metre is not, and can never be, exhausted. Because of this interplay between metre and speech rhythms, Pope's pentameters, for instance, are different from Shakespeare's . . . and, I would add, Hope's pentameters different again from Pope's, even when Hope is writing in his Augustan vein.

It also needs to be remembered that in keeping traditional metre he is far from alone on the contemporary scene. It's good to have had, on the one hand, Marianne Moore and William Carlos Williams, but also, on the other hand, Wallace Stevens, and more recent poets like Richard Wilbur and Anthony Hecht. It's worth remembering, too, that both Eliot and Lowell, while they sometimes employ free verse, also write just as powerfully in traditional forms. Pluralism, here as elsewhere, persists.

"Going his own way" is what Hope has always done, and in many respects. Conservative he certainly is, but, as a friend has just remarked, conservative in an unorthodox way. Temperamentally he seems to me to have a deep-seated reluctance to being pinned down. No one, and no literary vogue, can persuade Hope to do what he doesn't want to do. He is what is often called a "non-joiner". If he admires Dryden and Pope, for example, it's on his own terms: because of an affinity (one affinity among others) as opposed to subservience. And he has always strenuously refused to be committed to the point of view expressed in any one of his poems. Each poem, he believes, must have its say, which may not necessarily be *his* say. To quote the New Zealand poet James K. Baxter: "When I write, I do, not my own will, but the will of my poems". This is Hope's disposi-

tion too, and he has often spoken of how a poem he was writing has re-shaped itself, as it were despite his own intentions for it.

One further general point. Hope's nonconformism can be seen even in the fact that he didn't much enjoy his time as a student at Oxford, and left with only a third-class degree (not quite as distinguished as his contemporary, Auden, who got a fourth). This result, in Hope's case, was not for want of talent but for lack of trying. Given his love of English literature and European culture, one might have expected him to make more of an effort while at Oxford, and later to have visited England and Europe more often that he has. (In fact, he has probably spent more of his time overseas in the United States.) And in spite of his Europeanism he has lived most of his life in Australia and on the whole seems happy to have done so.

It's time now to look at some of his poems. The piece **"Australia"**[1] was written as long ago as 1939. Thirty-six years later he reminded an audience of this fact and added that he "would write somewhat differently of the country today". But how differently? I think that a good deal of what the poem says remains valid, and a valid statement of some of his abiding attitudes.

"Australia"

A Nation of trees, drab green and desolate grey
In the field uniform of modern wars,
    . . . . .
They call her a young country, but they lie:
She is the last of lands, the emptiest,
A woman beyond her change of life, a breast
Still tender but within the womb is dry.
    . . . . .

Whatever else, this is, it's a fine piece of poetic rhetoric: five measured and devastating stanzas against Australia, and then, with a command that is altogether typical of Hope, the poem wheels around and in two stanzas puts the opposite case. "Yet there are some like me turn gladly home": from what, to what? The answers, too, are characteristic. Rejection of "the lush jungle of modern thought" (Hope, a sensuous poet, elsewhere likes lush jungles but not this time), followed by the expression of a hope. Jungle versus desert: in 1939 (and later) it was common to hear Australia described as a "cultural desert". But to Hope it could be the Arabian desert from which prophets *may* still come as they once did in the Biblical times he has never forgotten from his Presbyterian childhood. There is a strong sense here, not of settling reluctantly from such a desert, but of a glad acceptance. And the poem ends with a whack at the Old World by whose standards it has previously judged Australia and found it wanting. Here, maybe, one will find

some spirit which escapes
The learned doubt, the chatter of cultured apes
Which is called civilization over there.

The tone of these lines is quite as savage as anything earlier in the poem: and, moreover, it has a strong affinity with certain mainstream Australian sentiments, independent, even republican.

Again, to see how much Hope's imagination is a characteristically modern one, take **"The Coasts of Cerigo"**: Hope's variant of the very old fable of the diver and the mermaid, but far from being a conventional treatment.

"The Coasts of Cerigo"

Half of the land, conscious of love and grief,
Half of the sea, cold creatures of the foam,
Mermaids still haunt and sing among the coves.
Sailors, who catch them basking on the reef,
Say they make love like women, and that some
Will die if once deserted by their loves.
. . . . .
But while in air they watch her choke and drown,
Enchanted by her beauty, they forget
The body of their comrade at her side,
From whose crushed lungs the bright blood oozing
  down
Jewel by ruby jewel from the wet
Deck drops and merges in the turquoise tide.

I could say a lot about his poem, pointing for instance to the power and majesty of the seascape in the second stanza: a seascape, incidentally, which suggests the Great Barrier Reef of Queensland. But to be brief, the main thing to stress has already been remarked on by the English critic William Walsh. While Hope, as Walsh says, is a traditional poet in the matter of "accepted patterns and rhythms",

he has also a pointedly contemporary gift—that of conducting the permanent functions of poetry through new classes of imagery, imagery particularly drawn from the sciences of biology and psychology.[2]

And as Walsh also points out, this poem presents us with "the implacable cruelty of a biologically determined life". Nothing Augustan there. Nothing Romantic either. This is a modern consciousness: and it's at work throughout the poem, subverting the expectations set up by the surface qualities of the verse which embodies the vision.

There is one more facet of Hope's nonconformism that I want to touch on. This is seen in the way he repeatedly takes a well-known attitude, or more often a well-known story, and by changing the focus or changing one crucial element, brings about a new way of seeing the thing, offers a new avenue for the imagination to pursue. In **"Standardization"** the aesthete and his ilk

are challenged in their detestation of mass production as *unnatural*. Stop a moment, the poem says: Nature herself, "The old, sound Earth", is the greatest standardizer of them all:

there is no manufacturer competes
With her in the mass production of shapes and things.
Over and over she gathers and repeats
The cast of a face, a million butterfly wings.

In two poems drawing on Biblical stories a similar reversal of the expected takes place. **"The Double Looking Glass"**, a version of the story of Susannah and the Elders, supposes that Susannah, there in her garden, conceives a sexual fantasy of her own. So that, technically (though in bad faith), the Elders are right in their accusation, and by implication Susannah is also guilty, in Christ's later terms, of committing adultery in her heart . . . though it has to be stressed that Hope neither approves of the Elders nor considers her guilty of anything. The shorter (and lesser) poem **"Paradise Saved"** proceeds from the question: "What if Adam *hadn't* eaten the apple?"

"Paradise Saved"

(another version of the fall)
. . . . .
Day after day he watched them in the waste
Grow old, breaking the harsh unfriendly ground,
Bearing their children, till at last they died;
While Adam, whose fellow God had not replaced,
Lived on immortal, young, with virtue crowned,
Sterile and impotent and justified.

I wouldn't claim that here one finds anything specifically modern, except the need to turn a traditional story around. But certainly this poem is the work of a deeply, a habitually, nonconformist imagination.

There is, as we all know, much pressure on us these days to conform; as Christopher Caudwell puts it, to become what society thinks we ought to be rather than to achieve individuation: to be a bank clerk rather than a person, your own person. Hope has resisted that pressure throughout his long career as poet, teacher and critic. In particular he is his own poet, not the one which "the age demanded": his own poet even in his love of the Augustans, and also in his keeping alive in his work those parts of the literary and human past which he values. And by choosing to live out his life in Australia, with just as much closeness to European civilization as he needs and no more, he has staked out his poetic territory. That desert has given him room to be himself, and only himself.

Note

1. The poems cited will be found in the *Collected Poems, 1930-1970*. Angus & Robertson (Publisher), Eden Park Estate, Waterloo Road,

North Ryde, N.S.W., Australia: "Australia", p. 13; "The Coasts of Cerigo", pp. 154-5; "Standardization", pp. 10-11; "The Double Looking Glass", pp. 167-73; "Paradise Saved", p. 219.

2. William Walsh, *A Manifold Voice* (1970), p. 131.

Chris Wallace-Crabbe (essay date October 1990)

SOURCE: Wallace-Crabbe, Chris. "True Tales and False Alike Work by Suggestion: The Poetry of A. D. Hope." *Australian Literary Studies* 14, no. 4 (October 1990): 415-24.

[*In the following essay, Wallace-Crabbe argues that Hope's poetry resists easy categorizations and investigates the poet's relationship to symbolism.*]

Attempts to characterise A. D. Hope's poetry fail very frequently because of a common tendency to see his oeuvre holistically. Simple caricatures emerge, portraying him in bold strokes as neoclassical, parnassian, art nouveau, anti-modernist, remorselessly iambic or whatever. All such categorisations underplay the extent to which Hope's poetry is strategically restless and subversive. The old tales he tells are nearly always undermined. The commonly bland critical prose sorts oddly with the poetic violence: indeed, much of his suaver criticism seems remote from the feminist high spirits of *A Midsummer Eve's Dream*. And the physical density of his compressed narratives is held with difficulty and at some cost between a declared thirst for glimpses of transcendence and the fear of non-being:

> The solid bone dissolving just
> As this dim pulp about the bone;
> And whirling in its void alone
> Yearns a fine interstitial dust.
>
> The ray that melts away my skin
> Pales at that sub-atomic wave:
> This shows my image in the grave,
> But that the emptiness within

Like Slessor—in most respects a very different poet—Hope practises a whole series of sleights against entropy, anomie, dissolution, silence.

The above stanzas, from **'X-Ray Photograph'**, epitomise one of the paradoxes available to poetry, in that they give syntactically coherent, formally shapely utterance to assertions of annihilation. In this they resemble much of the writing of Wallace Stevens. Stevens is a poet about whom Hope has always maintained critical silence, but I can remember a moralist colleague of mine years ago launching an attack on the American poet on the grounds that his metres continued to assert coherence while his overt discourse bespoke the dis-

solution of all certainties. Yet what he complained of is true of all writing which treats of destruction. No writer pursues the imitative fallacy all the way down to chaos.

We could say that if the above lines have an overt, constructive syntax, they also have an imaginatively powerful counter-syntax which runs, dissolving-dim pulp-void-yearns-melts-pales-grave-emptiness. The two information systems meet at the problematised noun, 'image', which is both what we clearly want from a poem and what is undermined by X-ray photography. This rhetorically compelling poem self-deconstructs all the way down the line.

Hope leaves his readers ill at ease. Often it is his double blow which disconcerts them, in that he both presents them with a myth or story which they believe, for ideological reasons, not to be accessible to contemporary readers and dismantles or vulgarises the tale as he tells it. The powerful **'Lot and His Daughters'** diptych is disturbing in just this way. It generates a chain of puzzled questions. Why take an Old Testament story? Why so obscure a one? Why focus on Lot, without his salted wife? Why write poems about incest? What is the point, for us, in Lot's forceful dream about spearing the lioness? How can the poetic voice end by endorsing 'that best wisdom, which is not to know'? Why are poems which drive from an instructive source so immoral? The Lot poems keep us scanning to and fro for comfort, trying to strike a balance between assertions of the Lord's will, the beautiful daughters' willingness, drunken assertions of moral truth and what it could possibly have meant to be the only just man in Sodom. And the narrative of these poems is so clear that a reader may well feel abashed at not being able to replace it with moral paraphrase, not being able to state firmly what wine, genital intercourse and God's word stand for in poetry which teases the allegorical sense.

Similar problems of stance, viewpoint and the possibility of judgement haunt a scattering of Hope's poems, among them **'Flower Poem'**, **'Easter Hymn'**, **'Rawhead and Bloody Bones'** and **'The Watcher'**. We do not know how much cultural baggage we are allowed, or expected, to bring to the poems. More common are the poems which seem to work to a coherent schema, proffering a lucidly coherent narrative which withholds nothing but its final significance. **'A Visit to the Ruins'**, **'Dragon Music'** and **'Crossing the Frontier'** all move to an ending by way of this modernist tactic of waived import. The last-named is a particularly striking example. Modern in setting, inhabiting the psychologised frontier world of Auden and Rex Warner, it baffles us as we try to place it on the intertextual map. The frontier is depoliticised after the first few lines; stanzas two and three suggest early Auden's transformations of Groddeck ('His father, rampant, nursed the Family Shame': here it seems as though we are waiting for the arrival of the Truly Strong Man); stanza four echoes the stillnesses of Edwin Muir (which brings to mind Seamus Heaney's recent suggestion that in the work of Muir and early Auden English poetry had its moment when it might have acceded to international Modernism); and at the climax melodramatic power exceeds the possibility of interpretation. If we contextualise the poem, turning back to the early **'Return from the Freudian Isles',** we may be tempted to read **'Crossing the Frontier'** as anti-Freudian, but nothing useful comes of that. Perhaps the cyclical message is that after the Oedipal rebellion, and despite it, the rescue will not take place. But such resignation does not account for the poem's power, either. Hope's poems resist reduction.

This resistance of the poems to interpretation leads us towards the question of Hope's relations to symbolism, and this is a track besmeared with red herrings and obscured by camouflage devices. They need to be cleared away. Hope has his place, too, in that distinguished line of Australians who have been fascinated by French symbolist poetry. But I shall come back to the traces of this after a few formalist observations.

For many readers, one of the problems in coming to terms with Hope's poetry is founded in his excessive reliance on the iambic quatrain. When you flick through a collection of his poetry, there you will see the quatrains over and over again, laid out down the page like motel rooms. It could be, and has been, said that Hope needs their steadying influence to contain and dramatise the violence of his apprehensions, but this is far from a general truth, I am sure. In his best poems of the 1940s—**'Imperial Adam', 'Conquistador', 'X-Ray Photograph', 'The Pleasure of Princes'**—it is possible to trace formally and syntactically how they work as little engines of narrative or as shock quanta. They seem inevitable, too, as the richly gilded, psychologically elaborate, *mise-en-abîme* love story of **'The Double Looking Glass'** acts itself out: readers need the mental comfort of steady forms as much in this poem as they do in **'Notes toward a Supreme Fiction'.** As in sung or recited ballads, the ABAB stanzas have each a little plot which combines into the overplot. Luring us on with rhymes, each stanza is lightly eroticised. Anticipation creates satisfaction. It is such dynamic coil and recoil that leads with seeming logic to the melodramatic shock of 'What beards, what bald heads burst now from the bush!' or 'And the first murderer lay upon the earth'.

Again, some of the poems resemble ballads more closely: **'The Watcher',** for example. But many readers have found, will find, too great a reliance on steady, rhyming quatrains in a number of other poems where the raw material seems almost to have been poured into a comfortable form. Moreover, some of these poems go

on for too long. The pitcher need not be taken to the fountain so many times. Such poems are the work of that Hope who wrote 'The Middle Way' and 'The Discursive Mode': this is the poet, partly genuine, partly a stalking horse, who stands farthest off from the disorders of Modernism.

Given the terms and concepts which were available to characterise modern art movements in Australia in the 1940s, Humphrey McQueen is right to have characterised the shock of Hope's earlier poetry in terms of its relation to surrealism. Attending properly to the element of radical excess in this poetry, McQueen writes in *The Black Swan of Trespass,*

> For all Hope's classical style, his poetry attacked the prevailing poetics far more profoundly than did any of the tricksy Modernists in *Angry Penguins.* The precision of Hope's materialism was built up through his granite hard images: . . . Such corrosive literalness horrified all those Surrealists, and other Romantics, who looked upon art as a dark cave in which "Life" could take refuge from life.
>
> Hope achieved what the Surrealists claimed to want, but were mostly afraid to touch. Many of his early poems inhabited a cannibalising bestiary in which severed limbs and unspeakable horrors were born from the promise of great joy.
>
> (86)

The reference to corrosive literalness here is a play upon James Gleeson's striking surrealist canvas of 1941, 'We Inhabit the Corrosive Littoral of Habit'. The reference to 'Hope's materialism' is in the one throw fruitful and misleading. It is true about poetic method, in that the poet's mimetic procedures constantly sought to fill his discourse with tangible substances which could be, as we have seen, some kind of stay against oblivion. It is misleading about belief systems, since Hope has never been at ease in a world which can be defined materialistically.

Hope's positions and assertions have always been hard for critics to smooth over and harmonise. In a very early poem, **'Pygmalion',** one can find these disconcerting lines:

> I want your suffering: the intense and bare
> Strain of your will. I want to see you dare
> This difficult thing, to walk with agony on
> The knives of my imagination, one
> I scarcely know—why even in your hands'
> Least moving something perfectly understands
> All I created you to feel and be.

Admittedly these are spoken by a version of Pygmalion, but they anticipate most gendered criticisms of Hope's poetry and most disapprobations of his assumption of poetic power. Here the Protestant work-ethic, that sexiest of ideologies, walks hand in glove (like

'The Lingam and the Yoni') with poetic heroism, as S. L. Goldberg has defined it. The artist-hero actually confesses—like any strong, uncompromised writer—that 'I want your suffering', but *want* also archaically means 'lack'; the creative artist can use pain, but is not so good at actually feeling it: because he is busy working, of course. The difficult middle clause calls for our attention: 'one I scarcely know' dangles, so that we do not know which of three referents it depends from. The woman may be effectively unknown to the artist, intent on his supreme fiction as he is; or he may find his imagination unknowable; or, most likely, it may be the whole 'difficult thing', the moral enterprise of living and surviving. The third interpretation sorts best with the kind of Protestant straining which is felt a few lines further down with 'And in myself this man I have willed to know / Wakes at long last'. But it should be added that **'Pygmalion'** is a most unusual poem since it is strenuously argumentative rather than narrative-symbolist in method.

For all that his explicit views and critical preferences have generally been as hostile to symbolist poetry as to Modernism, a concern of some kind for French symbolism has manifested itself again and again in Hope's writings. One source of this must lie in the line of French symbolist scholarship which has persisted in Sydney since the time of Brennan: John Passmore has observed that the study of modern French poetry has wider international recognition than any other aspect of the humanities in Australia. It should be added that Hope's younger friend, James McAuley, completed in 1940 a University of Sydney Master's thesis on 'Symbolism: an Essay in Poetics'. It can hardly be doubted that symbolist poetic theory and practice was a frequent topic of discussion between McAuley and Hope.

While it is in such early criticism as that to be found in 'Poetry and Platitude' and 'The Middle Way' that rationalist positions are created, positions which could allow no space at all for symbolism, it is not until *The New Cratylus* of 1979 that Hope the critic meets the French head-on. The result is very interesting. It is to be found in chapter eleven, 'Heresies of the Age'. Here Poe and to some extent Verlaine receive rough treatment; Mallarmé, however, a poet who is not mentioned in Hope's early criticism, appears in a very different light, for all that he contributed along the way to a cause which diminished the range of modern poetry. On pages 127 to 128 he is introduced with the paean, 'Mallarmé will last forever, except for a few poems which are no more than literary curiosities in a museum which can exhibit specimens from nearly all of even the greatest poets'. Twelve pages further on, Mallarmé's greatness is mentioned again, along with Baudelaire's. Soon afterwards he is called 'the master symbolist' and quoted at some length on allusion.

Let me add that in a previous chapter on the relation between poetry and the dream processes Hope records one of his own dreams in which he quoted Mallarmé's line, 'Un coup de dès jamais n'abolira la hasard' (a line which I have always found aurally displeasing, but that is another matter). Admittedly the dream quotation was immediately plonked by an interlocutor's nonsense line, 'Un chien qui manque de dents jamais ne pensera', but it remains striking that the original was so firmly lodged in the poet's consciousness-kitty.

Somewhat earlier, in an essay on Browning which was added to the second edition of *The Cave and the Spring* in 1974, Hope had written that 'It is this election for the moments of dramatic stasis, of events or characters poised excitingly in the balancing forces of an unresolved problem which illuminates what I believe to be Browning's real position as an intellectual poet'. This is itself most illuminating about Hope's idea of intellection, about the irresolvable balance of his own best poems and also about symbolist poetry in which the delineated components should always be 'Poised excitingly in the balancing forces of an unresolved problem'. It could fruitfully be brought to bear on some of his less celebrated poems: on **'The Bed'**—a poem which only Goldberg seems to have marked out for notice—on **'Three Romances'**, **'The Meeting'** and **'Dalla Sua Pace'**, for all its comic-ironic surface.

'Dalla Sua Pace', like a good many of Hope's poems, is queerly deceptive. It offers an easy version of itself, a textual surface which would appear to be straightforward secular subversion of one of the great European myths, that of Don Juan, who has with his tireless chutzpah desecrated the god that is in women. But the poem is concerned with absences: the wimp is onstage throughout but the Don is offstage after a brief flicker of swordplay. Ottavio-Fischblut keeps having his own life displaced by that of the absent Don Giovanni: thus at line four, 'One eye reflects a bed and one an urn' and, in the lovely mini-climax of the second stanza, 'Gently he turns the corpse upon its back / And finds the hand he holds a fist of stone'. 'Fischblut always wins' goes the poem's boast; attuned it may be to Don Ottavio's beautiful song, but a more famous aria, one with a nickname (like an old friend), takes over and the poem ends with the wicked verb, 'begins'. This points us back to the fact that to make his compact text Hope has debauched the chronology of the opera, not merely con-certinaed the sequence of events. Perhaps nobody wins at all. The lines of this fascinating little poem keep undermining one another.

The Hope poem which owes most to the French symbolists is **'The Double Looking Glass'**. Not only does it refuse us the comfort of moral resolution or even of psychological certainty, but the poet himself has declared its lineage. In his introduction to the selection of his poems made by Douglas Stewart in 1963—a particularly brilliant selection despite Stewart's earlier indifference to Hope, and despite the omission of **'Imperial Adam'**—he wrote that 'this subject or idea of a possible poem recurred to me at a time when I had the idea of writing a poem in a style suggested by certain poems of Mallarmé and Valéry'. He goes on to say that the poem changed its course somewhat in the writing; its narrative compulsion is typical enough of his own work. But its relation to 'L'Après-midi d'un faune' and, in lesser measure, to 'Le Cimetière marin', remains an important component in its peculiar power of tantalisation.

Essentially, though, the meaning of symbolism for an Australian writer had in some measure to be that of symbolism mediated by Christopher Brennan. Certainly the full scope and power of Brennan's speculations on French poetic theory could not have been felt until the publication of *The Prose of Christopher Brennan* in 1962 but, as I have already suggested, the main emphases of his thought had come down as an intellectual tradition at the University of Sydney.

Brennan believed that imagination gave one access to 'the unity which is our true spiritual being', that analytical language was too crude—or too 'pure'—a medium to have access to such wholeness, which could only be shadowed forth in the play of symbols and revelatory analogies. In 'Nineteenth Century Literature' some of his accounts of the symbol are such as to harmonise easily with Hope's poetic practice. Thus, 'The symbol is simply that image which, for the special purpose in hand, condenses in itself the greatest number of correspondences'. And again,

> A real symbol directs and governs its poem: it is at once starting point and goal, starting point as plain image, goal as symbol: the poem rises out of it, develops within its limits, and builds it up by successive correspondences.

Such observations could with point be read into **'The Pleasure of Princes',** or into **'The Coasts of Cerigo'** or **'Ascent into Hell',** for all the revenant narrative traction of the last-named.

Elsewhere in this essay we can find a more stubborn and challenging passage:

> To return to Mallarmé and his theory of style: the symbol governs the whole organism of the poem down to the syntax and what one might call the design of the sense; the phrase should model itself and bend itself to the rhythm of nature that gives the image. Thus in *Hérodiade,* what any English translation could not give you is the quality of the whole, a smooth dusky limpidity with still points of light here and there, like the jewels of Hérodiade reflected in her shadowy mirror. Or in the *Faun* the rhythm of the sense, here thronged

and pressed together and there escaping into a large sense of fulgency, is just the rhythm of sunlight and shade in the forest . . .

The second and third sentences of this passage are such lovely examples of criticism as prose poetry, scrumptious and ravishing, that they almost persuade us that what they are offering is a mimetic theory of poetry: until you actually ask yourself how language could ever begin to attempt to mime jewels reflected in a shadowy mirror. Impossible. So we have to turn back to the first sentence and its crucial, slippery phrase, 'the design of the sense'. It is this which points us to a sense of something like Significant Form at the heart of the symbolist project; to a gestalt which can be intuitively apprehended or which can be grasped by some developed aesthetic sense. It seems to me that Hope's poetry has never gone far along that track. His narratives or arguments are symbolically condensed, but his syntax is open, traditional and relatively even-paced, never attempting the grammatical elisions and metamorphoses which one finds in, say, John Tranter.

This has often, I think, been a source of readers' puzzlement with Hope's practice. One of his poems will put forward concepts which are disconcerting, even subversive, but will put them forward in a soothing, harmonious syntactical flow. The opening stanza of **'The School of Night',** an intriguing poem, will make my point well enough:

> What did I study in your School of Night?
> When your mouth's first unfathomable yes
> Opened your body to be my book, I read
> My answers there and learned the spell aright.
> Yet, though I searched and searched, could never guess
> What spirits it raised nor where their questions led.

Does the poem really need 'aright'? Does 'searched' have to be doubled? Both of these details are part of a conservative rhetorical tranquillity in the verse which cannot be said to be 'bending itself to the rhythm of nature that gives the image'. Or, to put it another way, we feel that certain habits of discursive language will not yield their authority to the imaginative gestalt.

When Brennan represents the symbolist task as heroic he stands far closer to Hope; as for instance when he writes in 'Fact and Idea' of the need

> To see ourselves *sub specie aeternitatis,* all human interests being united and the whole Human set over against the world, to take the last values and decide what it is that accords with Eternity—what it is that deserves to last; such is the reconciliation, such is our deliverance; the moment of Thought, no trimming of fear-bred tales.

This is very close to the spirit in which Hope chose as epigraph to **The Wandering Islands** the following lines ironically plucked out from McAuley's poetry:

Men must either bear their guilt and weakness
Or be a servile instrument to powers
That darken knowledge and corrupt the heart.

Both quotations could certainly find a lodging within a libertarian ethic of pride and freedom.

Brennan's account of visionary power, the motor of symbolic apprehension, as it is presented in 'Vision, Imagination and Reality', is also akin to that transcendent mode of apprehension which Hope dubbed 'the creative way' in the essay 'Three Faces of Love'. But I have discussed this in another essay.

A final meeting point for these two poets is to be found in their uses of Baudelaire. From the sexual and theological shock tactics of *The Wandering Islands* onward, one can find gestures and moods in Hope's poetry which are reminiscent of Baudelaire, though the rendered squalor of those Paris alleys and boulevards finds no equivalent. Brennan wrote of the French poet:

> It is because Baudelaire was morbid that poetry can again be healthy and glad. The romantics had infected their age with a vague melancholy and incapacity for living. Baudelaire took this on himself and lived it in its full intensity, so that what had been vague became precise and the malady, being thus exasperated, was taken away from us.

Under this rubric, Hope's most Baudelairean poem is **'The Damnation of Byron'**; it is there that the disputed territory between excitement and ennui is made precise and turned into a sort of fable.

But the work in which Hope makes his homage explicit is the **'Sonnets to Baudelaire'.** Using that difficult, slithery Elizabethan bag of tricks, the sonnet sequence, he hangs his poem on moments or aspects of Baudelaire's life (and even on the death of Pushkin). The method has very little in common with that of the addressee, and no affinities with later symbolists. One tends to read the sequence as a discontinuous narrative strung upon certain themes. It is also tempting to read it alongside, or against, **'The Planctus',** a contemporaneous sonnet sequence of some obscurity, but with strong, undeclared, personal components. In the end one slides off the tiles of both these sequences, fascinated but baffled.

The chief distinction between Hope's poetry and that of the symbolists surely lies in his reliance on narrative traction. It could be said that he has commonly wanted to preserve the concentric fizz, the concatenation, the éclat, of a symbolist poem while keeping the traditional channels of discourse open, sequential. In the circumstances plot becomes important. Things happen. One thing leads to another. We read on to find out what happens next, what monsters await us in the final stanza.

Where you have plot you have people, things and events located in time, even if the plot be miniature and the poem shortish. That which is temporally sequential is also consequential. But a symbolist poem is not like this at all. Its components are organised into—or held in—a harmonious stasis. Form holds them in a balance which suggests no more than the possibility of movement or the shadows of past movement. At its challenging purest, this suggestive inaction can be found in the last three lines of an untranslatable Mallarmé sonnet;

> Elle, defunte nue en le miroir, encore
> Que, dans l'oubli fermé par le cadre, se fixe
> De scintillations sitôt le septuor.

At other times, as with the Faun, the promise of possible action is stronger. After all, we need it to keep us interested: a poem should not be all resistance. It was to this end that Frank Kermode fixed on the figure of the dancer in his study of symbolism, *Romantic Image*. The dancer moves, but within enclosed space, and her dancing carves an abstract form in the air she breathes. Thus she can represent both movement and the stillness which ideal forms inhabit. How shall we know the body from the pirouette? Poetry makes nothing happen: symbolist poetry allows nothing to happen. It comes as no surprise, then, when Kermode refers to the 'life-in-death, death-in-life of the Romantic Image'.

More vulgar, more vitalist or it may be more Australian, Hope's poetry has commonly rejected the charms of such passivity. Even his reflective version of the Faun, Susannah, is finally bailed up by the baldheads from the bush. He cannot easily resist telling a story which will have an ending, however morally or cognitively obscure that ending may be. The impersonality of the symbolists can attract him, but not their sustained indeterminacy. Perhaps the poem which goes closest to the suspended, masque-like mood of symbolism is that high-spirited and frequently end-stopped poem, **'Pseudodoxia Epidemica',** the poem which Douglas Stewart placed at the head of the 1963 *Selected Poems*:

> Let reason ignore the reasons of the heart
> Pure knowledge is a sow that eats her farrow;
> But wisdom's children may hear mermaids sing
> In latitudes not found on any chart.
> Fledged without feet, to miss the hunter's arrow
> The bird of paradise keeps on the wing.

It is in the first stanza of the same poem that we can read the extremely comforting line, 'True tales and false alike work by suggestion'. We could add that the house of suggestion has many mansions.

Works Cited

Chisholm, A. R. and J. J. Quinn, eds. *The Prose of Christopher Brennan.* Sydney: Angus & Robertson, 1962. All Brennan excerpts are taken from this.

Heaney, Seamus. *The Government of the Tongue: the 1986 T. S. Eliot Memorial Lectures and Other Critical Writings.* London: Faber, 1988.

Hope, A. D. *The Cave and the Spring: Essay in Poetry.* 2nd ed. Sydney: Sydney UP, 1974.

———. *Collected Poems 1930-1965.* Sydney: Angus & Robertson, 1966.

———. *A Late Picking.* Sydney: Angus & Robertson, 1975.

———. *A Midsummer Eve's Dream: Variations on a Theme by William Dunbar.* Canberra: ANU Press, 1970.

———. *The New Cratylus: Notes on the Craft of Poetry.* Melbourne: Oxford UP, 1979.

Kermode, Frank. *Romantic Image.* London: Routledge, 1957.

McQueen, Humphrey. *The Black Swan of Trespass: the Emergence of Modernist Painting in Australia to 1944.* Sydney: Alternative Publishing Cooperative, 1979.

Mallarmé, Stephane. *Oeuvres complètes.* Ed. Henri Mondor and G. Jean-Aubry. Paris: Gallimard, 1945.

Wallace-Crabbe, Chris. *Melbourne or the Bush: Essays on Australian Literature and Society.* Sydney: Angus & Robertson, 1974.

David Brooks (essay date 1992)

SOURCE: Brooks, David. "The Ring of Isopata: *Orpheus* and *The Age of Reason.*" In *The Double Looking Glass: New and Classic Essays on the Poetry of A. D. Hope,* edited by David Brooks, pp. 274-80. St. Lucia, Australia: University of Queensland Press, 2000.

[*In the following essay, which was originally published in 1992, Brooks reevaluates Hope's reputation as a poet through an examination of his collections* Orpheus *and* The Age of Reason.]

I have long suspected that A. D. Hope's notorious traditionalism and poetic formalism have been generally misunderstood, and that, truistic as it has come to seem, the critical assumption that he is ultimately and perhaps simply an artist of inherent contradictions is reductive at best. The recent appearance of *Orpheus,* a new collection of his poems, has done nothing to change my thinking.

Even Nietzsche, iconoclast that he was, recognised the need for a pierpost—the need to have a system, a standard of measurement, arbitrary as it must be, by which to orientate one's thought: in a sea full of wandering islands, with no fixed point on the horizon, no one island can know its relative position or whether it has moved at all. And my understanding of A. D. Hope's formalism is something along these lines: that it represents a pierpost, a standard of measurement, or set of such standards—a fixed point in circumambient flux by and because of which one's position can be ascertained.

Of course, that it is a set of formal rules of verse, rather than a set of things that those who have written verse have said while observing them, may seem rather curious, as if Hope were perceiving some law, some set of rhythms within and of the machine itself, as having a value beyond what might go through the machine, beyond what might be said by those using it. It is, perhaps, a legacy of the *Symboliste* aesthetic—that aesthetic which held him for a good while early in his career, and from which in some ways he later tried to distance himself, but which has none the less been a part of him throughout—but it is also, and ironically, congruous with some aspects of Projectivist poetics on the one hand and, on the other, of those of the post-structural theorist Julia Kristeva, with her assertion of a "semiotic" the deeper rhythms of which erupt within and subvert those of the symbolic overlay. The language of the Father may figure large in Hope's poetry, but even he has his inbuilt checks against it.

There is, behind this, a paradox, or what some may see as a paradox (from another perspective it is only logical)—that the tenacity with which Hope holds to his formalism (it is, after all, a system of navigation, a pierpost in the mind only) is itself some measure of the *unc*ertainty, the *openness* of the seas upon which he ventures.

Increasingly the reputation of Hope's poetry and the poetry itself have been somewhat at odds. A few commentators have noticed this, as doubtless some sensitive readers, but again and again one still encounters the rather obfuscating notion of this poet as a staunch advocate of reason and enlightenment, the greatest eighteenth-century poet of our time. He himself has not helped, of course, in calling his 1985 collection *The Age of Reason.* In an age when Reason as an absolute has come in for a drubbing, such titles might well put off a number of would-be readers.

A pity, for the title was ironic enough (it was also a title of Sartre's!). In effect, Hope was there revisiting not only the eighteenth century, but reason itself with nostalgia. To speak of "the Age of" anything is surely to separate and delimit it, and to admit its relativity, and indeed, in his nostalgic revisiting, Hope's attention was not on reason itself but the gaps, the not-reason within and about it. Which is not to say the book was *about* not-reason, or *un*reason, but about reason's contexts, about its ineluctable relations with such things, its sometimes clearly *un*sovereign place amongst them. Amongst the most entertaining poems Hope has written, the eleven verse narratives of *The Age of Reason* are about the capricious, irrational, uncanny and mythical sides of the purportedly most rational of ages—Darwin's love life, Man Friday's suicide, Dampier's record of a Dantescan vision on the Isle of Aves, George III's chasing Fanny Burney through Kew Gardens, the supernatural explanation of Sir William Herschel's recovery of the planet Uranus—all presented with a view to further levels of Being and Explanation the rhythms of which erupt within and subvert those of Science and Reason.

In one of the poems (**"The Bamboo Flute"**) in the 1985 collection Hope has a Hindu artist say, in 1786, one hundred and ninety-nine years earlier,

> the poet should
> View nature, see into the heart of things
> And show them to themselves in all he sings
> . . . . .
> Each poem is a tryst with the unknown

A very *un*reasonable statement, I would think. And Hope, in something closer to *in propria persona,* says something like it again in the title-poem of *Orpheus*:

> Only much later in his life, they said,
> After Euridice died, forced to explore
> Twice hell in vain he learned, in his despair
> The ultimate measure of menace and of dread
> The world may hold for each of us in store
> And found another music to declare
>
> What the heart knows. And it was only then
> The whole world answered, hills and beasts and trees
> Danced . . .

In another long poem from *The Age of Reason* (**"Sir William Herschel's Long Year"**), Hope speaks of myth:

> The Enlightenment and all its cocksure heirs
> With their new sciences to conjure with
> Must bow in time to learn the truth of myth;
> And men must learn before it is too late
> Their "modern mind's" already out of date.
> Its views are temporary, on the way
> To others that may well ante-date today

Myth is one of the subjects of *Orpheus,* and it helps, in considering the volume, to consider what Hope might mean by the term. From a perspective which appeals very much to me, the kind of myth upon which Hope draws here stems from and registers a period of deep epistemological transition: we could call it the dovetailing of one way of knowing with another, of an earlier (as if it did not continue to exist!) with our own—in this case (Orpheus', but this is true of a great deal of Greek mythology), a shift which has been variously construed as the eclipse of the Dionysian by the Apollonian, the transition from a matriarchal to a patriarchal society, the beginnings of Orientalism, or the birth of modern consciousness in the breakdown of the bicameral mind. But, with an intriguing touch of C. J. Brennan in the tail, Hope himself says all of this, or subsumes it, in **"Sir William Herschel's Long Year"**:

> The legends of the ancients told this too
> With more prophetic insight than they knew,
> How, when the sky-god Zeus began to reign,
> Uranus vanished from the starry plain.
> Most primitive of gods, he married Earth,
> Gaia, his mother who had given him birth,
> And she, conceiving from his fruitful seed,
> Bore all the flowers, the grass, the trees, the breed
> Of beasts and birds and men, and bore again
> In his old age, from the same fertile rain,
> The cyclops and the Titans, till at last
> Saturn his son gelded his sire and cast
> His genitals and his sperm into the seas
> Whence Aphrodite sprang, Philommedes,
> She who loves all the tools of sex, whom still
> Men serve, adore and gladly do her will.
> In that new dispensation they forgot
> Uranus and their minds unloosed the knot
> That wedded him to Earth. He turned aside
> Into the night of things that brood and bide,
> Black Night from whom all other gods descend,
> And whom they all return to in the end.

The myth of Orpheus becomes thus that of one who, mourning his beloved, and singing her wherever he goes, sings *un*reason to the world of the reasonable, darkness to the world of the light, inclusiveness to the excluders, absence to presence, otherness to the familiar, and who is killed, accordingly, by Thracian women maddened by the wine-god for the purpose. (No matter that it was the wine god here who was being eclipsed: Pentheus, too, who had at first disparaged them, was torn apart by bacchantes, after he had himself become a bacchant. He seems to have been punished for his earlier misjudgement, just as it may be that Orpheus may be being punished as much for having tried to get Euridice back, or for not having stayed down with her.) Who sings woman, it seems, risks being torn apart by her. A patriarchal myth, if you like, to explain and explain away the haunting power of poetry.

If this seems to be the way that the twentieth century—through Rilke, say, or Apollinaire—has seen Orpheus, Graves, quite differently, tells us that Orpheus was killed because he had been preaching that Apollo, avatar of light and reason, was the god of gods. But no matter: it is the nature of myths—of these images from the brink—to be ambiguous. It's clear enough, in any case, that different ways and ideas of knowing (the Dionysian and Apollonian) are at issue here, and perhaps the ambiguity of the resolution suits Hope's own.

In some very clear senses his opening account of Orpheus in the poem of that name gives us a tale, a frame by means of which we can begin to draw the collection together. Here now is a poet who sings unreason as much as reason, a poet as much of the darkness as the light, and poem after poem bears this out. There is **"Conversation With Landor"**:

> Others may put themselves to bed
> When the coals fade between the bars;
> A poet seeks the cold instead,
> And steps outside to meet the stars.

There is **"On the Night Shift"**, in which he humorously but emphatically disclaims knowledge of the sources and meanings of his own poetry. And here, too, is a poet singing very evidently, and sometimes very specifically for his lost Euridice—or perhaps we should say Euridices, since *this* Orpheus (enter the biographers) has been "forced to explore / *Twice* hell in vain", and since we can see him, too, singing as much for the lost past, lost youth, as for the lost woman.

Here, too, to judge by some of the early critical reaction to the collection, we have a book (and poet? for can it be that Hope does *not* know this, has *not* allowed it to appear this way?) "torn apart" by bacchantes, or, rather, by its different images of women: the moving and deeply personal elegies (**"Tree"**, **"Orpheus"** itself) sitting with what, given this myth-structure, seems to be a calculated awkwardness beside the extravagance of a long, 'intellectual' elegy (**"Western Elegies"**), and, as the volume expands, what some have already claimed is a surplus of bawdry.

And here too, as in Rilke, is an Orpheus who, his overweening, ordering, presuming intellect humbled in the heart's fullness, sings (in **"A Gold Ring from the Tomb of Isopata"**) the withdrawal of discourse, things seen as they are:

> But leave its import now in mystery.
> Perfect in what it is, not what it tells,
> The grace of movement and the jutting breasts.
> These bodies leaning back put off the spells
> Of meaning and become themselves, set free,
> And what remains in its own beauty rests.

Orpheus, then, but which Orpheus? The one who mourns? The one whom "The whole world answered, hills and beasts and trees"? The one who sings things as they are? The one torn apart by bacchantes? The one who sings darkness? The one who sings light? The thrall of Hades? The servant of Apollo? Several interpretations are possible. The Discursive Mode is in abeyance here, in various ways, and the collection is the poet's most lyrical to date. But although is tempting to see it accordingly as a kind of retreat from reason, even a kind of apologia, I think that is to over-emphasise both the old allegiance and the subsequent remove. There is no real apostasy here. If the pendulum seems to have settled at one extremity, it is of an arc that has always been there, and the overall force of the collection is that this is right, this is the mythical balance, this is the way things have always been, this is the behest of the deeper rhythms, the rhythms beneath and about being.

My initial inclination—Hope having been all along the proponent of negative capability—is to accept all possibilities: the singer of light who sings also the circumambient dark; the poet who, pulled in different directions by Gaia or her daughter's daughters, would rather be torn than make a specious choice between them in defiance of what seems to have been a greater law.

"In his first youth", we read in **"The Progress of Poetry"**,

> each fire-new poet displays
> His talents of bright image and dazzling phrase.
> By toil his middle years achieve at last
> Fresh fusions of his present with the past.
> In his old age he lays aside his art
> And sings now from the fullness of his heart.

So be it. Athough I find, as I try rather vainly to round out my own thinking about this collection, two similar predicaments coming to mind—Pound, at eighty or so in Venice (city of Venus, on the water), unable to make it all cohere; and Yeats, in the rag and bone shop of his heart—I find myself also rejecting them, thinking that Hope has pegged out a place of his own, more humble than Pound's, somewhat more Rilkean than Yeats'.

Neal Bowers (essay date spring 1994)

SOURCE: Bowers, Neal. "Form as Substance in the Poetry of A. D. Hope." *Shenandoah* 44, no. 1 (spring 1994): 68-80.

[*In the following essay, Bowers contends that the defining characteristics of Hope's poetry—particularly his reliance on conventional forms and his rejection of modernism—have now come back into vogue in literary circles.*]

To identify A. D. Hope as an Australian poet and strict formalist is to employ terms he might well reject, the first on the grounds that true poetry transcends national boundaries, the second because it is redundant. In Hope's world, poetry is its own domain, and any poem lacking meter and rhyme is a mere sham. In an age when writers have eagerly indulged in chauvinism and free-form experimentation, such sentiments as Hope's seem decidedly old fashioned, even reactionary. Indeed, in Hope's own country, his almost total lack of interest in anything overtly Australian has disappointed some critics, and his open contempt for free verse has at times made him seem narrow-minded and anachronistic. In short, Hope has not been regarded as the Walt Whitman of his native land. And yet when viewed from the edge of a new millennium, and probably beyond the exhausted epoch of postmodernism, he seems to possess some of Whitman's prescience and a good bit of his self-assuredness.

Rather than a blinkered curmudgeon bent on reviving old forms and grumbling over the excesses of modernism, Hope may actually be something of an exemplar and a prophet. Certainly, his poetic agenda, fully elaborated by the early 1960s, seems markedly current: (1) a rejection of free verse and an adherence to traditional forms, (2) a general attack on modernist principles, (3) an insistence on the importance of verse narrative and (4) a determination to offer poetry to an audience outside the enclave of poets and critics. If these items seem familiar, it is because they have been advanced by a number of American poets over the last decade and stand at the center of an ongoing debate over the nature and future of poetry.

In an essay titled "Free Verse: A Post-Mortem," Hope proclaims his belief that free verse is "happily on the decline, and few serious poets now bother with it." By the time he chose to include this essay in his 1965 volume *The Cave and the Spring,* he must have known better, the news of postmodernism having reached even the English Department and Hope's office at Canberra, Australia. In all likelihood, he knew free verse was alive and well from the moment it occurred to him to perform its autopsy, and his assertion was a shrewd rhetorical strategy rather than an expression of ignorance. There is also a good amount of willfulness in it, because Hope would kill free verse if he could.

No one in the last forty years has argued more strenuously, through the insistence of his criticism and the example of his own poetry, for traditional formalism. Calling free verse "a very common cheap substitute for poetry," he has maligned its practitioners from Whitman forward and made a case for the reinstatement of every traditional verse form from the epic narrative to the heroic couplet. One hears in Hope's strident voice the uncompromising tone of an argument recently resurrected under the banner of the New Formalism by a younger generation of American poets. Strikingly, Hope, now nearing his ninetieth year, seems to have anticipated virtually all of their concerns and encapsulated their aesthetic in his own intransigent positions some thirty years ago. The parallels are all the more remarkable for Hope's geographical remoteness in Australia.

Characterizing the work of some of his contemporaries in *Australian Literature 1950-1962,* Hope makes the following observations: "What they have in common is a return to traditional forms and techniques of verse and a retreat from experimental methods, free verse, surrealist logomania, fragmentary imagism, dislocated syntax and symbolist allusiveness. They use traditional meters and rhymes, aim at lucid and coherent exposition of themes, and at poems which are intellectually and emotionally controlled and organized." It seems likely that the features Hope admires in the work of others are the ones he strives for in his own, so his statement may be taken as an indirect personal apologia.

As a specific example of the kind of poetry Hope advocates and practices, consider a selection from fairly early in his career (1944), **"Conquistador."** Almost any poem of Hope's would serve, but this particular one reveals him at his unabashed best, flirting with sexism and bad taste, all within the confines of tightly controlled iambic quatrains. In the poem, we are told that a character named Henry Clay, "a small man in a little way" loved "a white girl of uncommon size" and that his amorous adventures literally cost him his hide. (The hefty woman "squashed him flat" after making love and then transformed him into a bedside mat, "Tanned on both sides and neatly edged with fur.") Presumably, though, Henry Clay is happy, having "Planted his tiny flag upon the peak," and he even seems to derive some post-mortem masochistic pleasure when his weighty lover gets out of bed and steps on him: "The two glass eyes would sparkle in his head, / The jaws extend their papier-mache grin." The poem ends in mock moralistic fashion, observing that Henry Clay was "the Hero of our Time. He may / With any luck, one day, be you or me."

Our century hasn't been kind to any poem that manifests a sense of humor, and the "light" label often applied to Hope's work, as in the case of **"Conquistador,"** is both derogatory and dismissive. Art, after all, is deadly serious business. Knowing this attitude well, Hope frequently works to antagonize it and, no doubt, has many private laughs at the expense of his morose colleagues. But **"Conquistador"** is more than a sustained joke; it is an entertaining narrative poem connected to a mythological tradition. Henry Clay, the undersized mortal, falls for a woman who is literally larger than life (a goddess, if you will) and ends, as mortal heroes ensnared by goddesses typically end, transformed but much the worse for the encounter.

At work here is Hope's masterful determination to apply the traditional rules of poetry to his contemporary circumstances. His characters are not Venus and Adonis, of course, but neither are they Eliot's clerk and typist from *The Waste Land.* For while Eliot's characters are symbolic of a loveless, spiritless age and appear in a poem ostensibly constructed on a foundation of mythology, Hope's characters rise nearer to the level of myth. Moreover, they remind us not to take ourselves too seriously, a message not compatible with the precepts of modernism. Consequently, if this poem may be said to have a larger design, it is to antagonize and resist the modernist agenda while attempting to restore some of poetry's subverted elements.

Mainly missing in our age is a sense of proportion, the realization that we may all be small in a little way, and this absence of perspective is nowhere better viewed than in modern poetry. Whitman, whom Hope disdains, marks the beginning of a sensibility that has moved steadily from representations of the democratic self to preoccupations with the autocratic I. In his efforts to mythologize his own life, Whitman started a process that Hope intends to resist in his own work by shifting the focus away from the self. This is where myth and form come in, or come back in, having been displaced by Whitman's effusive self-inflations.

One of the abiding paradoxes of poetry (and art generally) in our century has been the exclusivity attending its pluralization. The more diverse poets have become, the less accessible their art. When Eliot gave many characters his own voice in *The Waste Land,* he altered Whitman's concept of a single voice representing multitudes, forcing the world to speak his words instead of striving for an oracular utterance of the world's manifold revelations. This alteration marked the death of myth, perhaps, and it also initiated a long process of attenuation and obfuscation, the development of which may be charted in the movement from modernist gamesmanship to confessionalism and finally to a solipsistic condition in which everyone speaks exclusively for and to himself.

Contrary to the introversion of modernism and postmodernism, Hope regards the poet's role as a public one, replete with societal responsibilities. In **"Conversation with Calliope,"** he has the muse lament, "There was a time the poet's mission / Was to give men their daily bread, / The crown of life, the timeless vision / Which linked the living with the dead." She goes on to say that in our time, however, only "schoolboys and the dons who breed / Their kind in every empty crater" know anything at all about the great poetic traditions, but they are unable to benefit from their knowledge, having had Pegasus "Boiled down for academic glue." Calliope's pessimistic assessment of the state of epic poetry, and poetry in general, is tempered by her prediction that "Some few in whom the heavenly rage / Still blazes and keeps pure the heart" will prevent the great forms from dying out entirely. Modestly (and probably ironically), Hope ends his poem with the muse consigning him to sleep and to the "lower slopes," suggesting that he is not among the chosen ones who will sustain the coals of tradition.

Nevertheless, Hope clearly thinks of himself as having a mission, and his zealous statements in behalf of formalism show how seriously he regards it. For him, poetry is not private prattle but a public duty, and the poet is charged with the dissemination of truth and vision. Implicit in his view is a belief in immutable principles and values that must be passed from one generation to the next. Poetic form is not merely a vehicle for such truths; it is itself truth. Hope's analogy for this relationship considers form at an atomic level: "Arrange atoms of carbon in one way and you will get black, greasy graphite; in another way and you will have the hard and brilliant diamond. The material is the same, the form is different."

For most of Hope's contemporaries, graphite has seemed an appropriate material for a world that gutters more than it shines and where diamonds are an anomalous perfection. However, it is a mistake to think of Hope as Pollyanna among the pragmatists, because his interest in formalism does not lead him to the simple packaging of maxims in attractive containers. In fact, among his most powerful poems are those suffused with uncertainty and personal angst, like **"X-Ray Photograph."** Notable for its vertiginous plunge, the poem begins with an x-ray of the skull, disclosing "the face my future wears / Drowned at the bottom of its pool," and moves to a chilling sense of nothingness: "The solid bone dissolving just / As this dim pulp about the bone; / And whirling in its void alone / Yearns a fine interstitial dust." No escape from the horrible perception of annihilation is offered or even suggested, and the poem ends with the recognition that our lives are as delusive as the light from a dead star.

A more compelling example of nihilism is difficult to find, and yet the poem's rhymed iambic tetrameter quatrains suggest order and control. Based on logic and intellect, the form counterpoints the poem's emotional free-fall into the abyss, giving the reader (and presumably Hope) something to grasp, as one suffering a spiritual vertigo can end the spiral into the void by grabbing a solid object. Just as the world argues for its own solidity and meaning, so does Hope's form.

Because art is necessarily a product of its time, no poet can work exclusively outside the prevailing cosmology. Should a resistant poet be lucky enough to attune himself to the hum of a new consciousness, his eccentricities will eventually be vindicated, but he will inevitably reveal attachments to his own era as well. Such was the case with Whitman, who anticipated the arrival of modernism. Inescapably, though, even a supremely innovative poet like Whitman could not entirely extricate himself from his own milieu, and we hear in his expansive lines an irrepressible optimism that marks him as an inhabitant of the 19th century. Similarly, Hope's exacting craft, although intended to resist the dissolutions of modernism, betrays a distinctly modernist preoccupation with art itself, making Hope, almost in spite of himself, a poet of his time.

Partly a result of his extreme critical assertions about form, a self-consciousness emanates from Hope's work, for everything he writes seems produced in direct opposition to the prevailing aesthetic, as if each poem were an object lesson in the virtues of formalism. This odd didacticism is powered by wit and general cleverness, aspects of the intelligence for which Hope is justly praised, but also manifestations of artifice. These strategies are readily seen in an elbow-in-the-ribs poem like **"To Julia Walking Away"**:

> Darwin's daughters have no tails,
> Yet a reminiscent motion
> Agitates the lovely frails
> At the seat of amputation.
>
> Charles called Eve and Adam lies
> And denied the garden state,
> Yet the gait of Paradise
> Could not wholly liquidate.
>
> Julia's coccyx never can,
> Swerving in delicious schism
> Now to the Descent of Man,
> Now towards Fundamentalism.
>
> Darwin, Paley, from the dust
> Argue in her ambulation:
> Was Eve genuine, or just
> A gorilla on probation?

Everything builds toward the poem's last line, which doesn't seem to be its finest moment and calls to mind Judith Wright's observation that Hope's poetry sometimes reflects "a kind of half-hysterical cocktail-party wit." Of course, there are other things to groan over, such as the sexist noun in line three and the pun in line seven.

Still, these apparent lapses in demeanor are part of a larger self-consciousness that characterizes this poem and is signaled by the title, which evokes Herrick's "Upon Julia's Clothes" and the tradition of the Cavalier lyric. Overtly, the poem playfully represents the debate over human (specifically female) origin. Simultaneously, though, the poem's form implicitly advances the creation/evolution dichotomy, arguing on the one hand for Herrick's traditional metrics (creation) and on the other for a modernization of them (evolution).

The first line, "Darwin's daughters have no tails," is notable for the way form reinforces content. Because the last trochaic foot is truncated, the line essentially lacks a metric tail, which is restored in line two as a "reminiscent motion." The unstressed syllable of the final foot disappears again in all four lines of stanza two where the biblical story of creation is confronted most directly, but returns in alternate lines of the final two stanzas, thereby sustaining a metrical counterpointing of the poem's central argument. While catalexis is frequently employed for metrical variation, Hope shows how it can be used to reinforce and even become meaning and, in so doing, brings form to the foreground.

The poem's central allusions are to Darwin and Paley and their argument, but the more subtle allusive pairing is of Hope and Herrick. They, too, are engaged in a debate or dialogue, as Hope represents his modern identity within the context of a tradition originally suited for a Renaissance sensibility. Because the tradition is only vestigial in him, he is obliged to consider the ambulation of his own lines as well as Eve's and Julia's gait, and his poem is as much concerned with the evolution of verse as it is with the origin and development of humankind.

One of the ways in which form sustains itself is through the infusion of new language from contemporary speech. According to Hope, "language itself provides continual new resources for rejuvenating the traditional patterns and providing them with new and yet traditional music." Certainly, his own poetry reflects this belief, and Hope's devotion to the old forms never leads him into the archaic. The final phrase of **"To Julia Walking Away"** is a good example. Because the caesura in the penultimate line is off-center, leaving only the two syllables "or just" for the coming enjambment, the poem's meter is altered, unless one forces a pause after "just." Read naturally, though, "or just a gorilla on probation" sounds like the poem's final line and results in a meter that doesn't scan neatly. The effect is that of a confidential, colloquial voice delivering the poem's punch line, and the broken metrics make it sound almost like prose. This effect is not ineptness but the result of Hope's attempt to create a "new yet traditional music." The trochaic tetrameter line is still there, though altered almost beyond recognition, the way evolution conceals a tail.

Elsewhere in Hope's work are abundant examples of poems dealing overtly with poetry as subject matter. One of them, **"Letter from the Line,"** finds the poet in mid-flight, returning to Australia from Los Angeles, musing in "comic horror, / To have seen the salaried Muses display their skill / In the universities of Sodom and Gomorrah: / Blind Homer, blind Harry treading corn at the mill." In **"Conversation with Calliope,"** the muse predicts:

> "Quite soon, let Observation view,
> As systems and their nostrums cramp us,
> The world from China to Peru,
> The wild from taïgá to pampas,
> The last tame bison in the zoo,
> The last tame poet on the campus
> Is all she'll find, poor Observation,
> Of all the former free creation."

Commenting on his 1958 trip to Canada and the United States, in an essay titled "Literature Versus the Universities," Hope notes, "A whole new industry and profession has grown up, that of the teacher of creative writing." And he goes on to express a fear that "the universities are beginning to move in, to take over, train and control writers—and that it will not be long perhaps before there are no wild writers left any more."

That Hope could have seen so clearly more than 30 years ago what has since become *fait accompli,* is astonishing. Moreover, his desire to preserve the "wild" poet, that person who learns his or her craft out in the world rather than in the college classroom, was not so much nostalgic as prescient of the growing anti-academic sentiment of the last decade. What worried Hope most was the fear that "the poet trained in a school of creative writing by academic critics and taking a job in the same atmosphere is more and more tempted . . . to produce work which, more or less unconsciously, is written in illustration of current critical theories; and thus reversing the proper order of nature in which the critical theories arise to deal with the independent raw material of the creative imagination." He couldn't have guessed how extensively critical theory and literature would become conflate or that creative writing programs would become an entity unto themselves, complete with their own kind of inbreeding. All the same, his prediction for the future of poetry was stunningly accurate.

At the base of Hope's concern is the expansion and greater availability of university education, which leads in turn to the demand for more teachers and the increased production of masters and doctoral theses and published research intended primarily "to help the researcher to qualify in the great rat-race." He didn't foresee it, but the same process has led to an equal or greater production of poems, stories, novels and nonfiction essays by creative writing students and teachers caught up in the same academic jog. The problem with expressing this worry is that it very quickly begins to sound elitist, as if one yearned for the old days when only the privileged could afford a college degree and university teaching was regarded as a genteel occupation requiring a pipe and a tweed coat but no portfolio. It also seems to imply that the proper condition for the poet is poverty.

However, Hope's vision of the future, because we have now fulfilled it, cannot be dismissed as a reactionary dream. The boundary between literature and criticism has indeed become difficult to distinguish, and those theorists lately insisting that their commentaries are the new literature are the culmination of a process begun, perhaps, when Eliot decided to append notes to *The Waste Land.* As modernist verse accommodated itself more and more to the critical apparatus designed to explicate symbols and abstruse language, criticism drew nearer to poetry and began, in some ways, to supplant it. This is certainly true of *The Waste Land,* which in

most texts is conspicuously secondary to the footnotes that dominate each page on which a few of the poem's lines are printed. All but lost in the chatter of seventy years of critical annotation, the poem is nearly impossible to read.

Obviously, this process has been aided and abetted by the university, which has become the patron of poetry and the promulgator of criticism, thereby making literature essentially a closed shop. In fact, the university has been an indispensable medium for the growth of modernism and postmodernism, and it is difficult to imagine what art in the 20th century might have been like without it, except to say that it might have been more accessible. For while universities, particularly the large land-grant institutions in this country, owe their extraordinary growth to populist ideals, they have paradoxically made an elitist business of poetry.

Although he was himself a university teacher until his retirement in 1968, Hope's position has always been that of the outsider, and it seems plain that his geographical distance from the principal centers of artistic change has afforded him a perspective unavailable to most. Speaking to his American counterparts in **"Letter from the Line,"** having departed from Los Angeles on the long flight home, Hope thinks of himself as Jonah escaped from the whale and says, "For you, my friends, are still in the monster's belly." Casting himself in the role of visionary or prophet, or perhaps just a fortunate escapee from the land of technology and its all-consuming appetite, Hope looks back with a kind of sadness for his swallowed friends.

Whether Hope's conception of the poet as someone apart derives from Australia's isolation is difficult to say. No doubt, calling and geography reinforce one another and contribute to his view of himself as someone privileged with a special vision and charged with the responsibility of disseminating it. In **"An Epistle from Holofernes,"** the spirit of the dead Captain describes the poet's role.

> It is the meaning of the poet's trade
> To re-create the fables and revive
> In men the energies by which they live,
> To reap the ancient harvests, plant again
> And gather in the visionary grain,
> And to transform the same unchanging seed
> Into the gospel-bread on which they feed.

The danger in the occupation is in trusting the fables too much and losing sight of the real world. Those who fall victim to this lure find themselves "damned upon infernal ground," the books on which they focus having become vampires to drink their blood. "They who feed vampires join the vampire's brood / And, changed to hideous academic birds, / Eat living flesh and vomit it as words." Clearly, the risk for the poet is greatest in the university, where the vampiric infection is epidemic.

Although in Hope's concept the poet is different from his fellow humans because of his calling, he is nonetheless in the best position to communicate with them. Regarding his mission as an almost sacred trust, he must share with others what he has seen and felt. This notion of the poet as a kind of priest or unacknowledged legislator of humankind is not modern, and we have special difficulty with it because of our belief that a poet is someone who successfully completes a university M.F.A. program. Hoards of them receive degrees each year and go on to produce, collectively, more work than anyone could possibly read, but the audience for poetry hasn't grown in even modest proportion along with its production. Perhaps this is because the number of poets has remained fairly constant or even declined a bit while the number of people writing poetry has increased astronomically. It is intriguing to speculate that this malaise might be cured by returning to an older notion of the poet's role. Obviously, Hope believes his efforts to restore poetic craft and poetic calling can make poetry more relevant and available to a wider audience.

Hope's desire to bring poetry back to the reader is reflected strongly by his interest in verse narrative, and the best examples of his work in this form are found in a 1985 collection, ***The Age of Reason.*** The rationable behind the poems, according to Hope, was a desire "to try my hand at the almost lost art of telling a story in verse and in a form of verse most favored in the 18th century itself: the heroic couplet modified to accept the rhythms of contemporary English and avoiding all conventional poetic devices apart from those of metre." His intent in these poems is to produce "narratives of a minor sort, chosen mainly for amusement or irony, mostly related to actual persons and events, but treated with a certain degree of fantasy."

Modernism and postmodernism have not been kind to narrative poetry, mainly because the lyric affords a more suitable medium for critical analysis. Compressed and packed with figurative language, the shorter lyric is mated to the exact dimensions of the critical machine. In direct opposition to this association, Hope's narratives are as anti-modernist as they can possibly be: lengthy, free of tropes and making absolutely no claims for themselves other than as entertaining stories. This is what Hope calls elsewhere, in an essay by the same name, the discursive mode: "that form in which the uses of poetry approach closest to the uses of prose, and yet remain essentially poetry." According to Hope, the discursive or middle style traditionally served as the poet's training ground, where he learned "the exercise and management of [his] craft" and from which he could launch himself toward more demanding poetic endeavors. In his efforts to revive the form, Hope ap-

parently means to remind poets of their technical obligations and to offer up examples of narrative verse that may prove Calliope's assessment of long narratives wrong: "Readers who give your poem a glance / Will settle for a police romance." Obviously, Hope wishes to make poetry competitive with prose by restoring both its abandoned narrative impulse and its accessible discursive language.

Throughout his career, Hope has remained obsessively dedicated to his vision of poetry and his notion of the poet's role in society. We can no longer dismiss him as old-fashioned, because most of his views have returned today and, expressed in the poetry and criticism of a younger generation, are helping shape the course of poetry as we approach the 21st century. The single problem with Hope, as with some of the younger poets, is a dogmatic certainty that tends to foreclose discussion; this is regrettable. On the other hand, no one provokes thought like the articulate devotee, so Hope's extremism may actually push some of us to think more cogently about what we do than we would otherwise.

Minus his haranguing tone, our contemporary concerns sound remarkably like the ones addressed decades ago by Hope: the excesses and biases of modernism, which have led not only to the exaltation of the figurative, free-verse lyric but also to the creation of a limited canon; the usurpation of literature by criticism; the professionalization of poetry through university writing programs; the diminishment of poetic craft; and the reduction of the audience for poetry. Even his more controversial insistence on the superiority of traditional metrics puts him in the middle of things today. In fact, it is Hope's preoccupation with form that makes him one of us, fellow citizen of a century during which the debate over form has shaped every aspect of our craft.

From Eliot to Olsen, this obsession has played itself out in factions and theories, but nothing seems ever to be finally resolved. The anti-academics of the 1950s and '60's have become the academics of the '80's and '90's Meanwhile, the former academic spirit has been reborn as the contemporary radical chic, and so A. D. Hope, for all his old-fangled notions, today aligns firmly with an avant garde that looks surprisingly traditional. More than a mechanic of forms, he is one of our most substantial poets.

Igor Maver (essay date 1997)

SOURCE: Maver, Igor. "The Baudelairean Decadent Strain in A. D. Hope's Verse." In *Readings in Contemporary Australian Poetry*, pp. 27-35. Bern, Germany: Peter Lang, 1997.

[In the following essay, Maver considers the links between the poetry of Hope and Charles Baudelaire.]

I

The Australian poet A. D. Hope never felt the particular need to stress the degree of 'Australianness' inherent in his poems; rather, as exemplified by his poem **"Australia,"** he would refer to "the Arabian desert of the human mind" in Australia. Hope is described by the critics as an academic and largely intellectual poet, because of his usage of traditional poetic forms and numerous allusions from classical literatures and cultures, which he considers the source of Western and also Australian culture. Although he did, in fact, find frequent inspiration in the English neo-classicist literary models and satirical impulses of the eighteenth century, Romantic and even Decadent content is to be found in a significant body of his poems. In this light, his literary affiliation with the French poet Charles Baudelaire is examined here.

Hope the poet, as opposed to Hope the critic, seems to be torn between the traditional and formal poetic impulse on the one hand, and Romantic despair over reality, over the concept of love as expressed through the images of deviant and unnatural sexuality and attitudes to women, on the other. His poems aesthetically very suggestively express this split, the dualistic contrast between a rational view of the world and an emotional, subjective response to it. Hope is labelled a 'University poet,' belonging to the loose group of poets, who in Australia in the fifties and sixties expressed great confidence in the intellect. Despite his adherence to classicist poetic heritage, his verse nevertheless displays a noticeable Romantic-Decadent strain, the characteristic all too often disregarded by the critics. Judith Wright is quite right in saying about sensuality in Hope's poems that his poetic world is explicitly dualistic.

> Nevertheless, Hope's world remains painfully dualistic. He is, more than any of our poets, torn between a loathed reality and a vision of eternal meaning . . . The visible sensuous world is not his starting-point—it enters his poems with sometimes startling impact, but it is more often used as an illustration and concretion of an intellectual or emotional insight, . . .[1]

In the case of Hope's poetry, it is possible to describe the specific literary affiliations or an intertextual relationship between texts. He is not merely steeped into the English neo-classical tradition of Alexander Pope, Samuel Johnson, Jonathan Swift and John Dryden, but is also affiliated with the Symbolist-Decadent tradition. James McAuley, the Australian poet, critic and Hope's friend was among the first to stress the Romantic-Decadent attitude as a diametrical feature of Hope's more evident 'classicism':

> I would observe also that this exploitation of various styles within the tradition is wide-ranging and renders misleading any characterization of the past as a

'classicist' or 'Augustan.' If one had to choose a word, I should think 'romantic' is in some of its important meanings a truer label.[2]

II

The Decadent strain in A. D. Hope's poetry can perhaps best be exemplified by the sonnet cycle dedicated to Charles Baudelaire, entitled **"Sonnets to Baudelaire"** and quite a few other poems (e.g. **"Flower Poem,"** **"Circe,"** **"Pasiphae,"** etc.). These poems describe a Decadent mixture of beauty, horror, death and putrefying disintegration, which can be found in Baudelaire's *Flowers of Evil* (*Fleurs du Mal*) and the works of some of the English *fin de siècle* poets such as Arthur Symons and Lionel Johnson. Hope himself admits that as a student he knew by heart many poems written by the French *parnassiens* (poets of the Parnassus movement in France), e. g. those written by Leconte de Lisle and José Maria Hérédia.[3] There are many Parnassian elements in Hope's verse: literariness, preciosity, allusiveness, and the like. Hérédia was the central poetic figure of the French school with his rhythmical and melodious sonnets *Trophies* (*Trophées,* 1893), together with Theophile Gautier and his *penchant* for art for art's sake.

It is known that the Parnassian school, as the sole outgrowth of Naturalism, decisively influenced Baudelaire's poems and thus the link with Hope can be established. Some of the main tenets on which Baudelaire's collection *Flowers of Evil* (*Fleurs du Mal,* 1857) is based are true also of Hope's poems: e. g. the expression of the ambivalence/duality of poetic experience on three levels. The poet is torn between "the divine and diabolic aspect of Beauty," between sensual and spiritual love as well as the double experience of loneliness (which is not so often present in Hope's poems). The poet attempts to flee these dualities through debauchery and dissipation, the Decadent attitude towards sexuality and through the quest of the 'cult of Beauty,' all of which are embodied in the morbid exaggerations of Decadent neo-Romanticism.

A contrastive analysis of the symbolism in Baudelaire's *Flowers of Evil* and Hope's poem **"Flower Poem"** illustrates this. Baudelaire describes "the suffering" of the flowers "cut" from the "ground," which means the loss of their source of life energy.[4] The speaker of the poem in Hope's **"Flower Poem"** suffers in the same way, because he feels like "a cut flower in the bunch." This metaphorically represents the separation of Australian culture from its European cultural roots and thus also from the source of energy, a concept so dear to A. D. Hope:

> Not these cut heads posed in a breathless room,
> Their crisp flesh screaming while the cultured eye
> Feeds grublike on the double martyrdom:
> The insane virgins lusting as they die!
>
> —A. D. Hope, **"Flower Poem"**[5]

The poet is explicitly concrete in his Decadent descriptions of the 'cut heads' in a stifling room (Australia?). On the one hand they are "screaming with crisp flesh," and on the other these "insane virgins" seem to enjoy their slow death and suffering. The presence of the Decadent sadomasochism is evident. Baudelaire's descriptions of the split between reality and ideal, evil and sensual stupor, spiritual void and death stand out clearly in the poem:

> Connoisseurs breathe the rose's agony!
> Between their legs the hairy flowers in bloom
> Thrill at the amorous comparison.

The first line of verse could be considered a real manifesto of a 'Decadent' poet such as was Baudelaire and such as appears to be Hope, at least in this particular instance: "connoisseurs" (probably including the speaker of the poem) sadistically enjoy in their agony and the cut flowers thus assume sexual connotations:

> Only transfusion of a poem's blood
> Can save them, bleeding from their civilization—
> Fresh seeding in some other dirty mind,
> The ache of its mysterious event . . .

Hope's flowers are "bleeding from their civilization," representing, of course, Australian civilization, which is, literally and metaphorically, cut off from its European roots and which could only be saved by the "transfusion of a poem's blood." The role of a poet in society thus reflects Hope's typically Romantic view of the poet's superiority and leading role in shaping the society by means of his verse. A. D. Hope concludes his **"Flower Poem"** with an image of sexually bored syrens ("the grinning girls"). These syrens had once enchanted Ulysses, but here and now in an Australia, cut off from European culture, there is no sign of him.

Hope in some of his poems, particularly **"The End of a Journey,"** compares himself with a latter-day Ulysses and thus reinterprets this classical Greek myth from the point of view of an Australian (artist), who, separated from it, wanders about the world in search of his native land Ithaca—Australia. The separation from the European Ulysses myth is stressed once again:

> The subterranean river roars, the troll's knife
> Winks on his whetstone and the grinning girls
> Sit spinning the bright fibre of their sex.[6]

The Ulysses myth is present also in the clearly Decadent poem **"Circe,"** for which Hope himself says he was inspired by a painting by the Italian painter Dosso Dossi. The description of the witch Circe is made in terms of sensual, almost animalesque sexuality, which reveals the 'classicist' poet Hope in quite a different light:

> She sits among her creatures motionless,
> Sees the best human shadow of despair

> Fade from the sad, inquisitive, animal eyes,
> The naked body of the sorceress . . .
>
>   —"Circe"[7]

In the poems **"Pasiphae," "The Meeting"** and **"The Coasts of Cerigo"** A. D. Hope further unites the images of beauty and horror (death). The poem **"The Coasts of Cerigo"** is strongly reminiscent of Baudelaire's "A Voyage to Cythera" ("Un Voyage à Cythère"[8]), since the islands Cerigo and Cythère (a small Greek island in the Aegean Sea) are very similar in the descriptions of "the dark island of sensual pleasures" savoured by "the goddess" (Hope) or "a nun" (Baudelaire). The omnipresence of death is in both cases equally notable: "the black seaweed drifting from her skull" in Hope, a silhouette of the gallows visible against the dark sky in Baudelaire. The Eros-Thanatos attitude towards love is typical of both poets:

> The Labra wallows in her bath of time
> And, drowned in timeless sleep, displays the full
> Grace of a goddess risen from the wave.
> Small scarlet-crabs with awkward gestures climb
> Through the black seaweed drifting from her skull.
> Her ladylegs gape darkly as a cave, . . .
>
>   —A. D. Hope, **"The Coasts of Cerigo"**

> What is this sad dark island? It is Cythera,
> They tell us, a famous country in songs,
> The banal Eldorado of all the playboys . . .
> It was not a temple with bosky shadows,
> Where the young priestess, lover of flowers,
> Walked, her body burning with secret fire,
> And her dress half opening in the passing breeze;
> But there as we grazed the coast close enough
> To disturb the birds with our white sails,
> We saw it was a three-forked gallows,
> Standing out in black from the sky, like a cypress.
> Ravenous birds perched on their prey
> Were ferociously demolishing a ripe body that had
>   been hanged, . . .
>
>   —C. Baudelaire, "A Voyage to Cythera"

Barry Argyle finds the poems **"Circe"** and **"Pasiphae"** shocking and labels them as poetic folly which says nothing new, an assertion difficult to agree with no matter how one looks upon it:

> But in **'Circe'** and **'Pasiphae,'** for instance, Hope's treatment adds nothing to what was already known, so that his treatment brings nothing new to what the myths were originally created to acknowledge. Such poems appear as Hope's follies, erected in the suburban city of Canberra to the consternation of its susceptible population, but a desire to shock suburban Australia fails on its own to invest such poems with any wider appeal. That they do shock is not in doubt: their waves carry as far as distant Queensland, where Cecil Hadgraft has counted Hope's references to 'sexual imagery' and 'the relevant anatomy.'[9]

The Australian poet and literary critic Vincent Buckley believed that Hope's "animalesque, fleshy" descriptions in the discussed poems reflect his "understanding" of the physical world.[10] Given the biological laws, the poet is aware of the disintegration and the decay of the physical world, which both attracts and repulses him.

The duality of the Decadent poetic experience therefore holds true. Charles Baudelaire in his *Fleurs du Mal* minutely depicts the physical aspect of Man that is bound to disintegrate, to die. He compares himself and his beloved with the putrefying carcass (Cf. "A Carcass"—"Une Charogne": "Et pourtant vous serez semblable à cette ordure, / A cette horrible infection, . . .").[11] In turn, Hope's attempts to create a perfect poetic form from the point of view of rhyme scheme and the traditionally prescribed forms cannot be solely understood as art for art's sake, which has been ascribed also to Baudelaire, but rather as an attempt to express the poet's innermost feelings in, to his mind, the most authentic manner. The content of his verse is, in the Structuralist sense, never separated from the form, which is complementary with the former. Henri Lemaitre's contention in the introduction to *Fleurs du Mal* is thus perfectly in order, even when applied to Hope, namely that despite appearances the form is here not a self-sufficient passive object, but a "true order of incarnation of interior ectasies":

> En tout cas, il n'a, malgré certaines apparences, rien de commun avec le formalisme de l'art pour l'art: la forme est ici non pas un objet impassible se suffisant à lui-même, mais véritablement l'ordre d'incarnation . . . des extases intérièures.[12]

A. D. Hope's **"Sonnets to Baudelaire"** reveal his explicit relatedness to Baudelaire's Symbolist/Decadent poetry, especially as far as his treatment of a woman as the *objet poétique* is concerned. The first of the twelve sonnets speaks for itself: Hope says Baudelaire laboured "our rotting paradise," grew "monstrous blooms" (possibly his 'shocking' poems) and taught his tongue poetic craft. This open acknowledgment of Baudelaire's literary influence, as well as the stressing of "Irony" (Hope) and "Beauty" (Baudelaire), is illustrative enough:

> These thoughts which I return you are your due
> Not so much that in origin most were yours,
> As that of all those spirits who know what laws
> Forge Irony to Beauty, it was you
> Drank deepest of that pure sardonic drought;
> You, naked, the first gardener under God,
> Who tilled our rotting paradise, from its sad
> Raised monstrous blooms and taught my tongue the
>   craft.

—**"Sonnets to Baudelaire"** (1968)[13]

However, as John Docker points out, A. D. Hope declaratively rejects Baudelaire's Romantic view of Woman ("That was one view of Woman I cannot share")

as a kind of *femme fatale,* who brings both life and death to Man.[14] Counter to Baudelaire's conception of Woman as the maleficent "womb" of earth, Hope offers a different version of woman-as-nature: to penetrate the womb means to explore the unknown, to enter the microcosm and consequently also the macrocosm:

> She is the earth: he digs his grave in her,
> The insatiate sea that drowns the tallest mast,
> The gorgon sky that stares his dream to stone,
> The mould that quietly eats him to the bone,
> The long, long night in which he sleeps at last.
> Was it your luck or genius to discover
>
> that living is this voyage among the dead,
> That poets have one task: to tell the brave
> How all his victories must be lost in bed
> And in the womb say to each unborn lover:
> The hand that rocks the cradle rules the grave.

—**"Sonnets to Baudelaire"**

Through images of women and sexuality A. D. Hope's poems express the concept of time and eternity. In **"Sonnets to Baudelaire"** Woman also symbolizes the seasons of the year, bringing summer and winter, life and death. As one giving birth, she also represents the cycle of life and death. However, it is true that women are very much depersonalized in A. D. Hope's poems, depicted almost as reified beings without any personality of their own, who through sexuality perform the invaluable function—to continue the human race.

Notes

1. Judith Wright, *Preoccupations in Australian Poetry.* Melbourne: Oxford University Press, 1965: 190.

2. James McAuley, *A Map of Australian Verse.* Melbourne: Oxford University Press, 1975: 182.

3. *Ibidem.*

4. "Charles Baudelaire," *Histoire de la littérature française,* Tome 2, Pierre Brunel *et al.* (ed.). Paris: Bordas, 1972: 481.

5. A. D. Hope, *Collected Poems 1930-1970.* Sydney: Angus and Robertson, 1972: 14.

6. Cf. James Wieland, "A. D. Hope's Latter-Day Ulysses," *Australian Literary Studies,* 10, 1982: 48-77.

7. A. D. Hope, *Collected Poems 1930-1970.* Sydney: Angus and Robertson, 1972: 71.

8. Charles Baudelaire, "Un Voyage à Cythère," *Flowers of Evil/Fleurs du mal,* W. Fowlie (ed.). New York: Bantam Books, 1963: 89.

9. Barry Argyle, "The Poetry of A. D. Hope," *Readings in Commonwealth Literature,* William Walsh (ed.). Oxford: Clarendon Press, 1979: 397.

10. Vincent Buckley, "A. D. Hope: The Unknown Poet," *Essays in Poetry, Mainly Australian.* Melbourne: Melbourne University Press, 1957: 134.

11. Charles Baudelaire, *Fleurs du Mal.* Paris: Garnier-Flammarion, 1864: 58.

12. *Ibid.*: 14.

13. A. D. Hope, "Sonnets to Baudelaire," *Collected Poems 1930-1970.* Sydney: Angus and Robertson, 1972: 234.

14. John Docker, *Australian Cultural Elites.* Sydney: Angus and Robertson, 1974: 48.

Xavier Pons (essay date October 2000)

SOURCE: Pons, Xavier. "Hope and the Apocalyptic Splendour of the Sexes." *Australian Literary Studies* 19, no. 4 (October 2000): 373-86.

[*In the following essay, Pons explores the erotic and chauvinistic dimensions of Hope's verse.*]

> I was then your music and you mine
>
> ('**Vivaldi, Bird and Angel**')

Among Australian poets, few owe a greater part of their inspiration to Eros than A. D. Hope. 'Love and desire have prompted some of his best poetry', Candida Baker noted, 'and some of Australia's most erotic poems' (Baker 162). This characteristic exposed him to much censure, both from those critics, like Max Harris, who regarded him as sex-crazed, or Vincent Buckley who thought him 'sexually obsessed, and obsessed in an unpleasant manner' (Hart 9; Brooks 46) and those who took him to task for his male chauvinism (see Docker 52 or Ann McCulloch in Brooks 264-65, 268). Oddly enough, however, the principal literary histories of Australia tend to ignore the erotic dimension of his writings.

Whether it censures or ignores his preoccupation with sex, criticism of Hope's verse too often presents a skewed vision of the part played by Eros in it. The spell of what he termed 'the sensual miracle' (Hope, *Collected Poems* [*CP*] 96)[1] is unmistakable, as can be seen from his repeated expressions of delight in the female form:

> The tapering trunk, the pure vase of the hips,
> The breasts, the breasts to which the hands go out
> Instinctive, the adoring finger tips.
>
> The thighs incurved, the skin misted with light,
> The mouth repeating its own rich circumflex . . .
>
> ('**The Damnation of Byron**' *CP* 3)

A woman's body, 'Eloquent through her clothes,'('**The Young Girl at the Ball**' *CP* 95) is an almost unfailing source of pleasure to him and, for all the classical rhetoric in which his verse is often couched, the sexual underpinning of this pleasure is made quite explicit. This is all the more striking as the most part of his production was written at a time when strict, narrow-minded censorship ruled Australian literature and anything that remotely smacked of the obscene was liable to be relentlessly prosecuted.[2] Of course, Hope's classical rhetoric provided excellent cover from the censor's guns. Metaphors derived from Greek and other ancient cultures offered respectability, and at the same time may have confused police brains as to what it all meant. When, addressing a female partner, instead of saying crudely 'open your legs, here I come', he put it thus: 'Stiffly my Wooden Horse / Receive into your Troy' ('**Phallus**' *CP* 31), he was making it possible for an Australian writer to deal with otherwise prohibited topics. He was also demonstrating the tongue-in-cheek combination of earthiness and lofty classicism which is one of the chief delights of his verse. The metaphors, perhaps, are not always of the highest originality, but they succeed in making the purely sexual acceptable, even palatable, to those who might object to the crudity of the theme, as in the following poem:

> When like the sun I warm her snow,
> She smiles above and melts below
> And my caress between her thighs
> Revives the dew of paradise.
>
> ('**When Like the Sun**' *CP* 256)

There may be echoes of Coleridge here, but the romanticism of the form stands in some contrast to the frankness of the subject-matter, reinforced by the reference, in the next line, to the 'glands of Bartholin'[3]. It is poems of this type, no doubt, that caused Norman Lindsay—of all people!—to call A. D. Hope's poetry 'intellectualized pornography' (Dutton 383).

For Hope, sex is as respectable as it is enjoyable—an attitude which was not terribly prevalent among Australian writers of his generation. 'I', he wrote, '. . . Draw from your loins this inexhaustible joy' ('**The Lamp and the Jar**' *CP* 79). Making love lifts human beings above their condition and brings a touch of paradise to their lives. The flesh, far from being sad as Rimbaud would have it ('La chair est triste, hélas . . .'), is something to exult in, and nakedness in the open air makes us like gods:

> Bare as the gods we must appear
> And as those blessed beings shine.
>
> A single, soaring flame shall bound,
> Frame and enfold our nakedness;
> And with that glory clothed and crowned
> Our souls shall want no other dress.[4]

Experiencing the body and its delights is not giving way to our baser instincts; on the contrary it is something uplifting and spiritual. Neither is the pleasure short-lived, and inevitably followed by sadness, as the classical adage averred (*triste animal post coitum*). The joy endures:

> You are a woman, I a man
> And nothing those two words entail
> Of ventured or unbidden joy
> Can time deny us or destroy

> ('Six Songs for Chloe' *CP* 250)

This unabashed celebration of earthly love, especially in its sexual aspects, is rare enough in the Australian context to be highlighted. In this respect, Hope seems to be the *rara avis* of Australian letters, the counterpart of so many prophets of doom and gloom for whom the body, rather than the mind, would seem to be the least of possessions, one to be left discreetly unmentioned for fear of appearing prurient or unnatural. To him, the 'apocalyptic splendour' (**'Splendour of the Sun and Moon'** *CP* 108) of the sexes calls for endless celebration. This is why it is difficult for later critics to agree with John Docker's contention that Hope 'is not interested in sex for itself, but for the ideological end behind it' (Docker 58). As we shall see, there is indeed more to sex for Hope than sensual pleasure, but that pleasure—'A mutual ecstasy of consenting love' (**'Vivaldi, Bird and Angel'** *CP* 276), as he put it—is fundamental, the cornerstone on which its other and not necessarily nobler functions rest.

The downside of his undisguised attraction to women, and to sex, is that early on he was called a male chauvinist, accused of treating women as if they were nothing but sex objects and of deriding them when they failed to satisfy.[5] And indeed, especially in his early poems, they are often the butt of his irony, as in **'Observation Car'**:

> The schoolgirl who goes to the ladies' comes back to
>   her seat
> A lollipop blonde who leads you on to assault her,
> And you've just got her skirts round her waist and her
>   pants round her feet
> When you find yourself fumbling about the nightmare
>   knees

> Of a pink hippopotamus with a permanent wave
> Who sends you for sandwiches and a couple of teas,
> But by then she has whiskers, no teeth and one foot in
>   the grave.

> (*CP* 22)

For all the long tradition to which it is heir, it is not hard to find this flippancy vaguely offensive—Prince Charming too has been known to grow a beer gut, lose his hair and succumb to brewer's droop. In the same

vein, Hope occasionally describes women as cold and calculating creatures who, in the sexual game, pursue goals that have little to do with passion or pleasure. Thus Louise, the American girl in Florence, who is wooed by Alessandro, and whose response is both entirely satisfactory and oddly disappointing:

> To his surprise, and more to his chagrin,
> She went to bed without the least demur.
> Passion expects resistance, and to win
> Without it on his passion cast a slur.
> He loved her voice, her eyes, her shape, her skin
> But found no answering response in her.
> She loved him, not for love however fiery
> But for providing data for her diary.

> ('A Letter from Rome' *CP* 139)

In a twist that recalls the underhand behaviour of Peter Carey's heroine in 'The Fat Man in History', Louise had not given herself up to an irresistible attraction for the young man: she had simply been doing field work for her research on the sexual behaviour of Italian males! Again, it is not unusual for writers to portray women as unscrupulous schemers, which feminists may not find all that funny, even though Hope is careful not to make this a general characteristic of womanhood. One can perhaps forgive the satirist for indulging his bent, and note that he is equally irreverent towards male academics in his *Dunciad Minor.* Besides, as far as sexual encounters are concerned, men do not always fare better than women in Hope's verse—witness the experience of Henry Clay destroyed by his huge partner:

> Her bulk of beauty, her stupendous grace
> Challenged the lion heart in his puny dust.
> Proudly his Moment looked him in the face:
> He rose to meet it as a hero must;

> Climbed the white mountain of unravished snow,
> Planted his tiny flag upon the peak.
> The smooth drifts, scarcely breathing, lay below.
> She did not take the trouble to smile or speak,

> And afterwards, it may have been in play,
> The enormous girl rolled over and squashed him flat;
> And, as she could not send him home that way,
> Used him thereafter as a bedside mat.

> ('Conquistador' *CP* 36)

If woman is the destroyer, it is perhaps because some men, by their very presumption, invite destruction. Or it may be that she is merely defending herself, and destroys her attacker by drawing on resources he did not suspect she might possess, as Little Red Riding Hood demonstrates to the unfortunate Wolf, who was preparing to bite off a lot more than he could chew.[6] While it is mostly true that, as Docker puts it, 'The women in Hope's poems are characteristically divorced from any social context' (Docker 45),[7] this observation applies to men as well: the poet, no doubt under the influence of his classicist preferences, tends to think in essentialist terms and, beyond the individual figures of whom he writes, to focus on 'Man' and 'Woman.' That he is not much of a social poet (except for satires such as **'The Brides'** or **'A Letter from Rome'**) must be admitted, but this does not *ipso facto* make him a male chauvinist.

In a more serious vein, though, Hope is a staunch defender of the rights of woman. She is in no way man's inferior and must be treated on a footing of full equality. Hope's woman is a free being, and the world is all the better for her freedom. He waxes indignant when he considers the indignities and tortures which patriarchal societies have visited upon refractory women:

> How many the black maw has swallowed in its time!
> Spirited girls who would not know their place;
> Talented girls who found that the disgrace
> Of being a woman made genius a crime;

> **('Advice to Young Ladies'** *CP* 207)

There is no flippancy in his treatment of this theme, no hint of irony in the classical references with which his plea for equality is studded:

> Historians spend their lives and lavish ink
> Explaining how great commonwealths collapse
> From great defects of policy—perhaps
> The cause is sometimes simpler than they think.

> It may not seem so grave an act to break
> Postumia's spirit as Galileo's, to gag
> Hypathia as crush Socrates, or drag
> Joan as Giordano Bruno to the stake.

> Can we be sure? Have more states perished, then,
> For having shackled the enquiring mind,
> Than those who, in their folly not less blind,
> Trusted the servile womb to breed free men?

> **('Advice to Young Ladies'** *CP* 208)

This is possibly not enough to acquit the poet of the charge of male chauvinism. One may express heartfelt indignation before major injustices and remain unaware of the smaller ones which, day after day, mar the lives of one half of the population and which add up to a very serious problem indeed. Yet Hope can also take up feminist positions, as Ann McCulloch acknowledges (Brooks 265), and should be credited with making an unambiguous stand for the social and intellectual equality of women. What becomes of this stand where sexual encounters are concerned is a slightly different matter, however.

Hope can be entirely sympathetic to the women who have unwelcome or unpleasant sexual attentions forced upon them, like Penelope when Ulysses eventually returned home:

> There at the last, his arms embracing her,
> She found herself, faith wasted, valour lost,
> Raped by a stranger in her sullen bed;

> **('The End of a Journey'** *CP* 1)

But he is also inclined to disparage women in a way that goes beyond the misogynistic mockery which occasionally drips off his pen, as when he refers to the 'taint of the pervading feminine' (**'The Damnation of Byron'** *CP* 5). The phrase may have ironical connotations to it, though they are far from obvious, but it expresses a derogatory view of women which is entirely in line with the great Australian tradition of mateship and which, surprisingly perhaps, would seem to place Hope's voice squarely among 'the chatter of cultured apes / Which is called civilization over there.' Too great an exposure to the company of women is debilitating for man. The joys of sex are no compensation, and eventually turn cloying and brutish. What a man needs, more than a woman, is in fact the company of other men. Such is the theme of **'The Damnation of Byron'**: after his death, the great poet is sent to the 'Hell of Women', which is peopled with innumerable attractive females all of whom, much to his happy astonishment, want to have sex with him:

> At first he moves and breathes in his delight
> Drowned in the brute somnambulism of sex.

> (*CP* 3)

The last phrase has disquieting overtones, and suggests that with sex the animal in us can take over, at the expense of the higher human qualities. The relentless pursuit of sex is the act of a sleepwalker, someone who is not aware of the incongruity of his actions and the grave dangers to which he exposes himself. It leads to a kind of life-in-death (as the word 'Drowned' suggests) in which lust replaces intelligence. This condition is in a sense an affront to human dignity, as Byron eventually realises. The force of his damnation

> Grows as the mind wakes inexorably
> The critic, the thinker, the invincible
> Intelligence at last detached and free
> Wakes, and he knows . . . he knows he is in hell . . .

> He seeks companions: but they only bring
> Wet kisses and voluptuous legs agape . . .

> He longs for the companionship of men,
> Their sexless friendliness.

> (*CP* 5)

It is not just Byron who is damned here, it would appear, but also sex and perhaps woman. The poem seems all the more damning as Hope was not yet thirty when he wrote it—this is not an embittered old man crying 'sour grapes'. But it would be inaccurate to read it as a blanket condemnation of sex and woman, if only because such a reading would be in stark contradiction with the far more positive views Hope has repeatedly expressed on those topics. Besides, Byron's last pilgrimage is to a land that bears very little resemblance to the real world, and with which it is not to be identified. He, the 'professional lover', is in Hell to be punished for his sins, and the punishment consists in letting him indulge his appetites to the point of surfeit—he is 'puni par là où il a péché', punished because of, and through, his inordinate lust. Hope's condemnation is of excess, not of sex itself, much less of women, as women critics have recognized.[8] He is aware of the many charges of destructiveness that have been levelled against them, and which he summarizes in his **'Sonnets to Baudelaire'**:

> Woman!
> She is the earth: he digs his grave in her,
> The insatiate sea that drowns the tallest mast,
> The gorgon sky that stares his dreams to stone,
> The mould that quietly eats him to the bone,
> The long, long night in which he sleeps at last.
>
> (*CP* 237)

But, as he points out at once, 'That was one view of Woman I cannot share' (*CP* 238). No woman-hater, Hope knows when to apportion blame to his own sex. Thus Byron is willing enough at first to turn himself into an animal, 'a great bull, stiffly, deliberately / Cross-[ing] his paddock, lashing his brutal tail' (*CP* 3), only to deplore this plunge into animalism when he remembers there is more to being a man than acting like a bull in heat. A sense of balance and of moderation are required if one is to lead a truly human existence. This, indeed, is Hope's message, one which is exemplified in his own works by the constant tension between classicism and romanticism, by the delicate balance between the pleasures of the intellect and those of the flesh. There is more to eroticism than giving a free rein to one's sexual drive, which can become a thoroughly alienating experience. Worshipping the Phallus—'the gods' god'—results in the obliteration of the self as

> It speaks in naked truth
> Indifference for me.
>
> My huge irrelevance
> Thought, passion, will, I know
> Mere words that serve to fence
> His obelisk of woe;
>
> (*CP* 31)

If left to his own devices, this tyrannical god (which Hope deflates by calling him a mere 'blood sponge') will reduce human existence to absolute dross, turning for instance love into nothing more than 'a romantic slime / That lubricates his way' (*CP* 31). Despite the 'Phallic Alec' tag, there is no mindless priapic celebration in Hope who, as a true epicurean, knows that reason

must control (though not deny) the animal impulse towards pleasure. While the latter is the supreme good and goal of life, it must be acknowledged that intellectual pleasures rank at least as high as sensual ones. Only through self-restraint, moderation, and detachment—that is through the exercise of reason—can one achieve the kind of tranquillity that is true happiness. The phallus must not be ignored, to be sure, but it must not be allowed to dictate our lives. To put it metaphorically, the tail must not wag the dog. Besides, the phallic god, for all its pride, needs a rest now and again, and it is wise to mix one's pleasures in order to avoid excess and satiation. Hence the poet's invitation to his mistress, 'Let us to dinner, Madam':

> Come now, for see the Captain of my lust,
> He that so stoutly fought and stiffly thrust,
> Fallen, diminished on the field he lies;
> Cover his face, he dreams in paradise.
> We, while he sleeps, shall dine; and when that's done,
> Drink to his resurrection later on.
>
> (**'The Elegy'** *CP* 58)

Besides, the pleasures of the flesh are not so easy to attain, trammelled as they are by a great many constraints, such as those of suburban, middle-class life, which Hope exposes with merciless irony in **'The Lingam and the Yoni'** (*CP* 39). And what about the flesh itself? What is so sexy about it when one remembers that it has to be fed, and that its continuing existence depends on the slaughter of myriad animals?

> The nakedness I had my arms about
> Was gorged with death
>
> (**'The Dinner'** *CP* 49)

the poet notes. But this is no more than the realisation that the flesh is subject to a great many limitations, and that there are distinctly unpleasant aspects about it. It is of the same order as Swift exclaiming half-disbelievingly that 'Stella shits'. The flesh resists our attempts to idealise it, and maybe this is just as well as it stops human beings from idolising it. It must be taken for what it is: a source of both pleasure and sorrow, an imperfect material with which to build a destiny, but an inescapable one which must be neither despised nor ignored in the name of higher realities. He who wants to play at being an angel will end up an animal, Pascal warned. And so, wisely, Hope attempts to make the most of this material, since none better is available. It may not be the best foundation stone one could have imagined to expand the bounds of the human condition but it does offers some exhilarating possibilities.

In Hope's conception, eroticism is an essential aspect of human existence because it provides a lifeline between otherwise isolated human beings. Aloneness is the rule, and 'You cannot build bridges between the wandering islands', to use his metaphor. But sex provides a temporary escape from this relentless isolation:

> An instant of fury, a bursting mountain of spray,
> They rush together, their promontories lock, . . .
>
> And then, in the crash of ruined cliffs, the smother
> And swirl of foam, the wandering islands part.
> But all that one mind ever knows of another,
> Or breaks the long isolation of the heart,
> Was in that instant.

('The Wandering Islands' CP 27)

Erotic relationships provide the only kind of epiphany available to human beings. Such moments are by their very nature short-lived. R. F. Brissenden convincingly analysed, in Hope's verse, 'the necessity of the condition of solitariness for that free play of the imagination and the intellect which alone can lead to creativity, and the necessity for recognising and accepting the solitariness and independence of each partner in the sexual act: a solitariness and independence which, if accepted, can be transcended, so that the intercourse of lovers, like the intercourse between the imagination and the material world, can become spiritually fruitful' (Brissenden 347).

This is a somewhat romantic conception, no doubt, but at least—and for a change in Australian literature—it offers a very positive image of sex. In striking antithesis to the biblical story of Susannah, sexual activity amounts to a kind of innocence: it takes us back to the days before the Fall, back to the Garden of Eden. Taking one's clothes off does not necessarily mean that one should feel ashamed of oneself.' On the contrary, to the extent that clothes serve to hide or embellish one's true self, nakedness is synonymous with honesty, candour, showing one's true colours. It is not just emperors who, without clothes on, appear as they actually are, devoid of all the trappings which confuse and mislead the onlooker. The removal of all clothing exposes our 'purged and primal selves' (**'Six Songs for Chloe'** *CP* 245), and in this act our nature puts off 'What parts it from the true divine'. Sex acquires here a spiritual aspect: the joining of man and woman in intercourse (as a staunch heterosexual, Hope pays little or no attention to homosexuality) results in a kind of bliss which helps us to transcend the limitations all flesh is heir to and gives a new dimension, a new completeness to the human condition. It is not so much a new version of the Platonic myth of the androgyne that he is proposing—the lovers do not fuse into a single entity so as to recreate the original complete being which Zeus in his anger split in two—as an epicurean art of living devoid of any true aspirations to transcendence but intent on making the most of human capabilities and limitations both.

Beyond this, Hope's erotic rhetoric suggests that there is something truly cosmic about the 'gallant game' (**'The Farewell'** *CP* 110), as he calls the pursuit of sex, which lifts it far above a mere hedonistic activity. This is made clear by some of the isolated metaphors he uses, as in **'The School of Night'** for instance:

> And dead sea scrolls that were my heart attest
> How once I visited your holy land.

(CP 254)

This gives an almost mystical dimension to the erotic experience referred to: sex is sacralised as a pilgrimage to the very sources of spirituality, and Eros gains his rightful place among the gods. Of course, Hope sometimes uses religious imagery with tongue in cheek to discuss sex, as when he refers to the phallus as 'the blood-sponge god'. But a more serious purpose is at work in this particular celebration. The image of the dead sea scrolls is the culmination of a metaphoric vein in which the body becomes a text ('the words made flesh') full of essential revelations. Hope thereby anticipates the Foucaldian insights into the inscription of textuality into the body. You, the poet tells the loved one,

> Opened your body to be my book, I read
> My answers there . . .

The book contains 'magic verse' which suscitates all kinds of strange visions and holds him captive. Reflecting on the Faustian themes in Hope's poetry, Kevin Hart noted the recurrence of 'The idea that the female body provides a privileged access to a visionary knowledge' (Hart 94). As the title of the poem **'The School of Night'** suggests, lovemaking is the best way to learn. But what is being taught? Some of the insights to be gained have less to do with religion than with the quest for pleasure, even though through its own metaphors the Bible equates intercourse with the acquisition (and dispensation) of knowledge, as in Genesis 4: 'And Adam knew Eve his wife; and she conceived.' Reading the lover's body means learning how to pleasure it:

> 'A blind man's fingers read love's body best;
> Read all of me!' you murmured in your dream.

But a more mystical intent pervades the poem, which is dotted with words such as 'spell', 'spirits', 'Delphic', 'magic', and this trend culminates in the last two lines with the reference to the lover's 'holy land'. The reference here is explicitly Christian, as are the connotations of the phrase 'The words made flesh' which, a tiny variation notwithstanding, inescapably recalls a way of designating Jesus. It can't be said, however, that Hope's purpose here is religious in the usual sense of the word. His world is wholly immanent, and the fate of his supposedly immortal soul does not seem to trouble him at all. The here and now is all that matters. Metaphors prevail over literality.

Much the same could be said of Hope's depiction of erotic relationships in cosmic terms. Thus he often describes woman in terms of geography or landscape. This metaphorical vein could be seen in **'The Elegy'** with the reference to 'your holy land'. Indeed, these geographical metaphors often concern women's genitals, as when he writes 'Her Bab-el-Mandeb waits' (**'Phallus'** *CP* 30), comparing the vagina to the strait that connects the Red Sea with the Gulf of Aden,[10] or when Susannah thus imagines a lover's embrace:

> For now his craft has passed the straits and now
> Into my shoreless sea he drives alone.

> **('The Double Looking Glass'** *CP* 172)

Other elements of the female body are treated in similar metaphorical way: the breasts of Henry Clay's gigantic lover are thus described as 'the white mountain of unravished snow' (*CP* 36). The whole body itself is apt to become a landscape through which the lover (himself under the spell of metamorphosis) will roam happily:

> O, let me be your bee and rove
> The heaths and tufted slopes of love,
> Gather that honey all day long
> And breathe its fragrance in my song.

> **('When Like the Sun'** *CP* 256)

Those landscapes are not always peaceful: erotic passion can be tempestuous and wild, resulting in a frenzy which makes it far more valuable than tamer expressions of love. Hence the poet's rather indignant remark to his lover:

> . . . would you dare to build
> A garden suburb of kindness where we piled
> Our terrible sexual landscape, heap on heap
> Of raging mountains?

> **('Pygmalion'** *CP* 10)

Hope has of course little patience with suburbs and the lifestyle associated with them: they lead to conformity, blandness—and a fear of sex in schoolgirls.[11] 'Suburban eroticism' would seem to be a contradiction in terms (John Updike notwithstanding), and the poet's yearning for more tormented landscapes is not surprising in view of the romantic vein that runs through his verse.

If woman is often seen as a landscape, sometimes the earth is conversely evoked in terms of woman, as in **'Toast for a Golden Age',** where he describes how modern man in his greed has been relentlessly destroying the natural environment:

> For the Earth, our mother, has at last found a master:
> She was slow and kindly, she laughed and lay in the
> sun—

Time strapped to his wrist, he made the old girl work
faster,
Stripping her naked and shouting to make her run.
He chopped the mantle of pines from her beautiful
shoulders,
He ripped her breasts for his vines, her belly for corn;
And she smiled and grew green again and did as he
told her,
And trebled the bounty of her plenteous horn.

> (*CP* 86)

But eventually such repeated rape wears the earth out and catastrophe ensues. Hope's concern for the environment can hardly be distinguished from his tender sympathy for women. This does not necessarily have an erotic side to it: earth as woman is not always sexy, as appears from **'Standardization,'** where, as may be appropriate in order to suggest a mother figure, the earth is embodied by an old woman:

> I see, stooping among her orchard trees,
> The old, sound Earth, gathering her windfalls in,
> Broad in the hams and stiffening at the knees,
> Pause and I see her grave malicious grin.

> (*CP* 10)

But the poet's sympathy for women is the underpinning of his eroticism. There is nothing exploitative about it, and the metaphorical linkage between woman and the earth suggests that an affectionate, mutually beneficial relationship should displace the all too common tendency among 'middle-aged, middle-brow male[s] of the middle-class'[12] to dominate and ravish where both women and the environment are concerned.

Woman is the earth and the earth is woman: the metaphor runs both ways. It is further developed to encompass man as well, and turn the lovemaking couple into a world of its own:

> Here's a new Genesis; the year is One;
> This bed and we a world, our lamp its sun.
> Love to its single dark dimension bound
> Rules its volcano kingdom underground:
> The feet at their remote antipodes
> Twine their smooth roots; at Capricorn the knees
> Nuzzle together; intershafted lies
> The amplitude of form and polished thighs;

> **('The Cheek'** *CP* 37)

Furthermore there are suggestions that this one world springing from the lovers' embrace is part of a wider cosmos and was brought into being by the conjunction of complementary elements, the male and the female principle, represented respectively by the sun and the moon:

> The moonbeam belly quaking in eclipse;
> The sunbeam belly on her tropic rests;

> (*CP* 36)

Making love is a most creative activity: not simply because this is how children are produced, but because elemental principles are brought into play, fulfilling some purpose of cosmic harmony and resulting in the 'new Genesis' referred to at the beginning of the poem. Sex not only makes the world go round—it brings new worlds into being. This opening onto the cosmic is facilitated by Hope's use of the feminine in his allegories, as in **'Soledades of the Sun and the Moon'**:

> Now the year walks among the signs of heaven,
> Swinging her large hips, smiling in all her motions,
> Crosses with dancing steps the Milky Valley.

> (*CP* 106)

Woman is consistently associated with the moon, whose cycle she shares, and which allows her to be in touch with the entire universe. Man, on the other hand, is associated with the sun (**'When like the sun I warm her snow'** *CP* 256). Other associations link woman with Venus, and man with Mars. The joining of man and woman in love is an expression of the creative forces which are at work in the cosmos.

It may be argued that in this joining woman is relegated to an inferior plane. The sun, with its traditional male associations, suggests power and majesty (as in the **'Sun-King'**), whereas the feminine moon—a mere satellite rather than a planet in its own right—enjoys far less prestige. But this would be a simplification of Hope's cosmic imagery. To the extent that woman is often equated with water[13] man can also be equated with the moon. Hence this evocation of Chloë's face,

> A face all women have in common
> When, lost within themselves, alone,
> They hear the demiourgos summon
> And draw their ocean like the moon.

> (*CP* 249)

John Docker has convincingly argued that, in Hope's poetry, women are 'phenomenal manifestations of universal processes of fertility and renewal' (Docker 46). But he goes on to say that the poet's attitude is arrogant and exploitative, since in his vision woman is necessarily man's inferior. The image of the sun and earth which he uses to suggest sexual intercourse has derogatory overtones for woman: 'Just as the sun in being above the earth is the normative condition of nature, the man must be above, as Hope says in the ninth sonnet to Baudelaire: "one is underneath and one above"' (Docker 52). But this is a misreading (and a misquoting) of the sonnet which actually describes the lovers in this way:

> Though one is underneath and one above,
> They are one body, one motion and one breath,

Where each caress becomes an act of faith
And every simile an act of love.

> (*CP* 238)

The indefinite pronoun 'one' does not allow the reader to conclude that man must systematically be on top. Indeed, the emphasis is not on some kind of hierarchical sexual position in which man and woman each plays an assigned and invariable part—man naturally dominating his partner—but, quite explicitly, on the fusion between the two lovers: they become one (however briefly), and this makes any hierarchy between the sexes irrelevant.

The refinement of Hope's erotic rhetoric, with its elaborate metaphorisations, is indicative of an erotic desire which is under control, but only just. Its imperial, carnal presence is tangible in his verse, yet the intellect never loses control. In Hope's verse, Apollo and Dionysus are a match for each other, and get on well together. The language ranges all the way from the brain to the genitals, which are shown to complement each other very nicely indeed. This may be the secret of the sheer quality of Hope's literary eroticism. If women allow him to achieve a kind of transcendence it doesn't follow that they are a mere instrument, and of no intrinsic worth. When someone says he finds a book thrilling or elevating, it does not imply lack of respect for that book, quite the reverse. Hope's point of view on erotic matters is clearly a masculine one—but should it be held against him? One might as well blame Marcel Proust for not adequately reflecting the proletariat's point of view. Hope's celebration of sensuality is not at the expense of women, and if he occasionally refers to them as man's helpmate, ascribing to them a position that seems hardly acceptable in this post-feminist age,[14] it means that he did share, unwittingly perhaps, some of the prevailing prejudices of his own time. On the credit side of the ledger, however, one must inscribe the fact that, in his own way, Hope is proclaiming much the same message as French poet Louis Aragon, namely that woman is man's future.

Notes

1. In subsequent references to this volume the abbreviation *CP* is used.

2. However, Hope was the victim of indirect censorship when Kenneth Slessor refused to include 'Imperial Adam' in the 1945 edition of *Australian Poetry* because the poem's sexual explicitness might jeopardize the whole anthology (see Dutton 383-90).

3. These glands lubricate a woman's private parts when she is aroused.

4. 'Six songs for Chloë III Going to Bed' (*CP* 245); also 'The Double Looking Glass':

> '. . . Man alone
> Cowers from his world in clothes and cannot guess
> How earth and water, branch and beast and stone
> Speak to the naked in their nakedness'
>
> (*CP* 168)

5. John Docker writes that for Hope, 'Women are non-intellectual and non-rational; they are only useful when young' (Docker 58).

6. See 'Coup de Grâce' (*CP* 166).

7. Note, though, that occasionally female characters are indeed presented against a fairly definite social background, such as suburbia in 'The Explorers.'

8. Ruth Morse comments that, 'A. D. Hope writes better about human sexuality than any poet in the Anglophone tradition with the possible exception of John Donne; it is part of his claim to greatness.' About 'The Damnation of Byron' she wrote: 'This is a powerful poem, however unfair to Byron, but certainly not anti-woman.' (See Morse 3)

9. See Genesis 5: 'And the eyes of both of them (Adam and Eve) were opened, and they knew that they were naked; and they sewed fig leaves together, and made themselves aprons.'

10. It may be a minor irony of this comparison that the name 'Bab-el-Manded' means 'the gate of tears' in Arabic, as Hope, who knew the language, was no doubt aware.

11. See 'The Explorers' (*CP* 11).

12. 'Toast for a Golden Age' (*CP* 87).

13. See 'The Double Looking Glass': 'lift of liquid breast . . . The nakedness of woman is a pool . . . I flow / Into the languid current of the day . . . I shall lie as still / As limpid waters . . .' (*CP* 167-72).

14. See 'Six Songs for Chloë-V' (*CP* 248):

> Night and the sea; the firelight glowing;
> We sit in silence by the hearth;
> I musing, you beside me sewing . . .'

Works Cited

Baker, Candida. *Yacker 3*. Chippendale, NSW: Pan, 1989.

Brooks, David, ed. *The Double Looking Glass*. St Lucia, Qld: U of Queensland P, 2000.

Brissenden, R. F. 'A. D. Hope's "The Double Looking Glass": a Reading.' *Australian Literary Studies* 6.4 (1974): 339-51.

Docker, John. *Australian Cultural Elites*. Sydney: Angus & Robertson, 1974.

Dutton, Geoffrey. '"Intellectualized Pornography": "Imperial Adam" and Kenneth Slessor.' *Southerly* 49.3 (1989): 383-90.

Hart, Kevin, *A. D. Hope*. Melbourne: Oxford UP, 1992.

Hope, A. D. *Collected Poems*. Sydney: Angus & Roberston, 1972.

Morse, Ruth. 'Woman in A. D. Hope's Verse', *Quadrant* 29.5, May 1985: 3.

FURTHER READING

Criticism

Brissenden, R. F. "A. D. Hope's *New Poems*." *Southerly* 30, no. 2 (1970): 83-96.

Evaluates Hope's literary achievements.

Brooks, David, ed. *The Double Looking Glass: New and Classic Essays on the Poetry of A. D. Hope,* St. Lucia, Australia: University of Queensland Press, 2000, 298 p.

Collection of critical essays that explore Hope's literary career.

Goldberg, S. L. "The Poet as Hero: A. D. Hope's *The Wandering Islands*." *Meanjin* 69, no. 2 (March 1957): 127-39.

Discusses Hope as an existentialist and an Australian poet.

Hart, Kevin. "Sexual Desires, Poetic Creation." *Raritan* 12, no. 2 (fall 1992): 28-43.

Investigates the ways in which the legends of Faustus and Don Juan influence Hope's verse.

Kane, Paul. "A. D. Hope and Romantic Displacement." In *Australian Poetry: Romanticism and Negativity,* pp. 119-40. Cambridge: Cambridge University Press, 1996.

Considers Hope's verse as a mix of romanticism and negativity.

King, Bruce. "A. D. Hope and Australian Poetry." *The Sewanee Review* 87, no. 1 (January-March 1979): 119-41.

Surveys the work of several prominent Australian poets, including Hope.

Mathur, Malati. "A. D. Hope's Ulysses and Kate Llewllyn's Penelope: Two Modern Voices from the Past." *The Commonwealth Review* II, nos. 1-2 (1990-1991): 86-95.

Explores Hope's use of the Ulysses myth in his verse.

McCooey, David. "'What Are We Doing Here?': A. D. Hope's 'Ascent into Hell.'" *Southerly* 61, no. 1 (2001): 112-16.

Describes "Ascent into Hell" as "a poem of inversion."

Wieland, James. "A. D. Hope's Latter-Day Ulysses: 'The End of a Journey' and the Literary Background." *Australian Literary Studies* 10, no. 4 (October 1982): 468-77.

Examines the structure and literary background of "The End of a Journey."

Additional coverage of Hope's life and career is contained in the following sources published by the Gale Group: *British Writers Supplement,* **Vol. 7;** *Contemporary Authors,* **Vol. 21-24R;** *Contemporary Authors New Revision Series,* **Vols. 33, 74;** *Contemporary Authors—Obituary,* **Vol. 188;** *Contemporary Literary Criticism,* **Vol. 3, 51;** *Dictionary of Literary Biography,* **Vol. 289;** *Encyclopedia of World Literature in the 20th Century,* **Ed. 3;** *Literature Resource Center; Major 20th-Century Writers,* **Eds. 1, 2;** *Poetry for Students,* **Vol. 8; and** *Reference Guide to English Literature.*

Kabir
c. 1440-c. 1518

(Also known as Kabīr-Dās) Indian poet, mystic, and religious reformer.

The following entry presents criticism of Kabir's poetry from 1915 through 1993.

INTRODUCTION

Kabir is considered a major figure among fifteenth-century Indian religious teachers. He rejected mainstream Hindu rituals and Muslim doctrines, yet his philosophies were influenced by both traditions, as well as by Sufi mysticism. A legendary figure in Northern India, Kabir is venerated as a social reformer of his day and a charismatic teacher whose works were adopted as sacred writings of the Sikh religion.

BIOGRAPHICAL INFORMATION

Kabir was born Varanasi Benares in Uttar Pradesh, India. The precise year and circumstances of his birth remain undetermined. Some sources say he was born before the beginning of the fifteenth century, circa 1398, while others set the date as circa 1440. The year of his death also oscillates between circa 1448 and circa 1518. Legends surrounding his birth and life variously describe him as the abandoned son of a widowed Brahmin woman and the product of a miraculous virgin birth to a young Muslim girl. He was likely raised by Muslim foster parents in a poor weaver's family. Although he rejected traditional Hindu rituals and strict Muslim practices, the influence of grassroots religious doctrine from each tradition is evident in his teachings. Calling himself "the son of Allah and Rama," he incurred the wrath of religious leaders who had no interest in the blurring of political or theological boundaries between the two traditions. Kabir's continued teaching of a monotheistic spirituality that was neither Hindi nor Muslim earned him the affection of many in Northern India who advocated tolerance and unity despite more than two centuries of conflict among numerous leaders intent on dominating the political and religious landscape. Kabir's legacy as the supposed unifier of two major and opposing traditions led to his legendary status as a holy man and teacher.

MAJOR WORKS

Although his poems and sayings are considered foundational to the development of religious thought throughout India, Kabir is believed to have been illiterate and thus unable to record in writing his own thoughts and ideas. The vocabulary of his poetry is rough and unpolished; the metrical forms reflect the popular dialects of the uneducated masses who came to revere him. His disdain for sacred Brahmanic language is seen in the lack of literary ornamentation of his works. The authorship of the large number of works attributed to Kabir cannot be verified with any degree of certainty, but it is believed that they were probably recorded by disciples during and following Kabir's lifetime. These works are found in four compilations. The first to attract the notice of Western scholars was the *Bījak* ("Account"), which was compiled after his death by members of the Kabirpanth. It was considered the most important of his religious teachings. A second volume, known as the *Granth* ("Book"), was assembled at the outset of the seventeenth century and became the sacred writings of the Sikh religion. The *Pamcvānīs* is a collection of sayings of five important teachers of the day, including Kabir. Finally, the *Sarbangī,* a compilation attributed to Rajjab, a later Indian poet, also includes a collection of Kabir's verse; it remains unpublished, however. Kabir's works have been translated and edited numerous times since the nineteenth and the early twentieth centuries. They are characterized by popular literary forms such as *padas*—short, rhymed poems adapted from religious use from folksongs—and dohas—popular dialect lyrical writings sung or recited by the common people.

CRITICAL RECEPTION

As influential as they have been in his native India, Kabir's works are not particularly well known to Western readers. In large part this is due to a lack of English translations of his verse and teachings. For much of the twentieth century, the primary translation available was the 1914 edition by Indian poet Rabindranath Tagore. American critic Paul Carroll notes that in this edition Kabir's words sound Victorian, "sober and didactic." By contrast, Carroll praises the appearance in the late 1970s of an edition of Kabir's works translated by American poet Robert Bly, in which the Indian poet's voice is that of "an ecstatic, generous saint." Carroll further comments that in the Bly rendition, the poems are "clear and direct and mean exactly what they say." Charlotte Vaudeville contends that it is inaccurate to portray Kabir "as an apostle of religious tolerance and of Hindu-Muslim reconciliation," noting that what the tolerance critics read into Kabir's teachings is "a kind of rationalism which rejects absolutely every revelation based on an authority extrinsic to the human soul." She acknowledges that "the greatest hurdle to be confronted by Kabirian scholars is the lingering uncertainty about the relative value and degree of authenticity to be accorded to any given verse." Commentator David C. Scott writes that Kabir's "immense popularity throughout the Indian subcontinent is due as much to his mystical perceptions as to his maverick nature."

PRINCIPAL WORKS

Poetry

Bījak [*Bījaks*] 1868

The Ādi Granth [*Gurū Granth*] [contributor] (translated by E. Trumpp) 1877

One Hundred Poems of Kabir (translated by Rabindranath Tagore, assisted by Evelyn Underhill) 1914

Songs of Kabir (translated by Rabindranath Tagore) 1915

The Bijak of Kabir (translated by Ahmad Shah) 1917

Kabir-granthāvalī 3 vols. (edited by S. S. Das) 1928

Kabir the Great Mystic (translated by Isaac A. Ezekiel) 1966

Kabir Granthavali (translated by Charlotte Vaudeville) 1974

The Kabir Book (translated by Robert Bly) 1977

Bijak of Kabir (translated by Linda Hess and Shukdev Singh) 1983

Mystical Poems of Kabir (translated by Swami Rama and Robert B. Regli) 1990

Couplets from Kabir (translated by G. N. Das) 1991

Songs of Kabir from the Ādi Granth (translated by Nirmal Dass) 1991

Love Songs of Kabir (translated by G. N. Das) 1992

Touch of Grace: Songs of Kabir (translated by Linda Hess and Shukdev Singh) 1994

Kabir: In the Light of Kriyayoga (translated and edited by Jogesh Chandra Bhattacharya) 1997

Selected Couplets from the Sakhi in Transversion: 400-odd Verses in Iambic Tetrameter Stanza Form (translated by Mohan Singh Karki) 2001

Other Major Works

Sayings of Kabir (translated by G. N. Das) (aphorisms) 1993

Maxims of Kabir (edited by G. N. Das) (aphorisms) 1999

The Thirsty Fish: Kabir bhajans (translated by Sushil Rao) (aphorisms) 2000

CRITICISM

Evelyn Underhill (essay date 1915)

SOURCE: Underhill, Evelyn. Introduction to *Songs of Kabir,* translated by Rabindranath Tagore, pp. 5-43. New York: Macmillan Company, 1915.

[*In the following essay, Underhill provides a historical context through which to consider Kabir's work, positing that the poet was "plainly a heretic" whose unorthodox view of the human relationship to God "was independent both of ritual and of bodily austerities."*]

The poet Kabīr, a selection from whose songs is here for the first time offered to English readers, is one of the most interesting personalities in the history of Indian mysticism. Born in or near Benares, of Mohammedan parents, and probably about the year 1440, he became in early life a disciple of the celebrated Hindu ascetic Rāmānanda. Rāmānanda had brought to Northern India the religious revival which Rāmānuja, the great twelfth-century reformer of Brāhmanism, had initiated in the South. This revival was in part a reaction against the increasing formalism of the orthodox cult, in part an assertion of the demands of the heart as against the intense intellectualism of the Vedānta philosophy, the exaggerated monism which that philosophy proclaimed. It took in Rāmānuja's preaching the form of an ardent personal devotion to the God Vishnu, as representing the personal aspect of the Divine Nature: that mystical "religion of love" which everywhere makes its appearance at a certain level of spiritual culture, and which creeds and philosophies are powerless to kill.

Though such a devotion is indigenous in Hinduism, and finds expression in many passages of the Bhagavad Gītā, there was in its mediæval revival a large element of syncretism. Rāmānanda, through whom its spirit is said to have reached Kabir, appears to have been a man of wide religious culture, and full of missionary enthusiasm. Living at the moment in which the impassioned poetry and deep philosophy of the great Persian mystics, Attār, Sādī, Jalālu'ddīn Rūmī, and Hāfiz, were exercising a powerful influence on the religious thought of India, he dreamed of reconciling this intense and personal Mohammedan mysticism with the traditional theology of Brāhmanism. Some have regarded both these great religious leaders as influenced also by Christian thought and life: but as this is a point upon which competent authorities hold widely divergent views, its discussion is not attempted here. We may safely assert, however, that in their teachings, two— perhaps three—apparently antagonistic streams of intense spiritual culture met, as Jewish and Hellenistic thought met in the early Christian Church: and it is one of the outstanding characteristics of Kabīr's genius that he was able in his poems to fuse them into one.

A great religious reformer, the founder of a sect to which nearly a million northern Hindus still belong, it is yet supremely as a mystical poet that Kabīr lives for us. His fate has been that of many revealers of Reality. A hater of religious exclusivism, and seeking above all things to initiate men into the liberty of the children of God, his followers have honoured his memory by re-erecting in a new place the barriers which he laboured to cast down. But his wonderful songs survive, the spontaneous expressions of his vision and his love; and it is by these, not by the didactic teachings associated with his name, that he makes his immortal appeal to the heart. In these poems a wide range of mystical emotion is brought into play: from the loftiest abstractions, the most other-worldly passion for the Infinite, to the most intimate and personal realization of God, expressed in homely metaphors and religious symbols drawn indifferently from Hindu and Mohammedan belief. It is impossible to say of their author that he was Brāhman or Sūfī, Vedāntist or Vaishnavite. He is, as he says himself, "at once the child of Allah and of Rām." That Supreme Spirit Whom he knew and adored, and to Whose joyous friendship he sought to induct the souls of other men, transcended whilst He included all metaphysical categories, all credal definitions; yet each contributed something to the description of the Infinite and Simple Totality Who revealed Himself, according to their measure, to the faithful lovers of all creeds.

Kabīr's story is surrounded by contradictory legends, on none of which reliance can be placed. Some of these emanate from a Hindu, some from a Mohammedan source, and claim him by turns as a Sūfī and a Brāhman saint. His name, however, is practically a conclusive proof of Moslem ancestry: and the most probable tale is that which represents him as the actual or adopted child of a Mohammedan weaver of Benares, the city in which the chief events of his life took place.

In fifteenth-century Benares the syncretistic tendencies of Bhakti religion had reached full development. Sūfīs and Brāhmans appear to have met in disputation: the most spiritual members of both creeds frequenting the teachings of Rāmānanda, whose reputation was then at its height. The boy Kabīr, in whom the religious passion was innate, saw in Rāmānanda his destined teacher; but knew how slight were the chances that a Hindu guru would accept a Mohammedan as disciple. He therefore hid upon the steps of the river Ganges, where

Rāmānanda was accustomed to bathe; with the result that the master, coming down to the water, trod upon his body unexpectedly, and exclaimed in his astonishment, "Rām! Rām!"—the name of the incarnation under which he worshipped God. Kabīr then declared that he had received the mantra of initiation from Rāmānanda's lips, and was by it admitted to discipleship. In spite of the protests of orthodox Brāhmans and Mohammedans, both equally annoyed by this contempt of theological landmarks, he persisted in his claim; thus exhibiting in action that very principle of religious synthesis which Rāmānanda had sought to establish in thought. Rāmānanda appears to have accepted him, and though Mohammedan legends speak of the famous Sūfī Pīr, Takkī of Jhansī, as Kabīr's master in later life, the Hindu saint is the only human teacher to whom in his songs he acknowledges indebtedness.

The little that we know of Kabīr's life contradicts many current ideas concerning the Oriental mystic. Of the stages of discipline through which he passed, the manner in which his spiritual genius developed, we are completely ignorant. He seems to have remained for years the disciple of Rāmānanda, joining in the theological and philosophical arguments which his master held with all the great Mullahs and Brāhmans of his day; and to this source we may perhaps trace his acquaintance with the terms of Hindu and Sūfī philosophy. He may or may not have submitted to the traditional education of the Hindu or the Sūfī contemplative: it is clear, at any rate, that he never adopted the life of the professional ascetic, or retired from the world in order to devote himself to bodily mortifications and the exclusive pursuit of the contemplative life. Side by side with his interior life of adoration, its artistic expression in music and words—for he was a skilled musician as well as a poet—he lived the sane and diligent life of the Oriental craftsman. All the legends agree on this point: that Kabīr was a weaver, a simple and unlettered man, who earned his living at the loom. Like Paul the tentmaker, Boehme the cobbler, Bunyan the tinker, Tersteegen the ribbon-maker, he knew how to combine vision and industry; the work of his hands helped rather than hindered the impassioned meditation of his heart. Hating mere bodily austerities, he was no ascetic, but a married man, the father of a family—a circumstance which Hindu legends of the monastic type vainly attempt to conceal or explain—and it was from out of the heart of the common life that he sang his rapturous lyrics of divine love. Here his works corroborate the traditional story of his life. Again and again he extols the life of home, the value and reality of diurnal existence, with its opportunities for love and renunciation; pouring contempt upon the professional sanctity of the Yogi, who "has a great beard and matted locks, and looks like a goat," and on all who think it necessary to flee a world pervaded by love, joy, and beauty—the proper theatre of man's quest—in order to find that One

Reality Who has "spread His form of love throughout *all* the world."[1]

It does not need much experience of ascetic literature to recognize the boldness and originality of this attitude in such a time and place. From the point of view of orthodox sanctity, whether Hindu or Mohammedan, Kabīr was plainly a heretic; and his frank dislike of all institutional religion, all external observance—which was as thorough and as intense as that of the Quakers themselves—completed, so far as ecclesiastical opinion was concerned, his reputation as a dangerous man. The "simple union" with Divine Reality which he perpetually extolled, as alike the duty and the joy of every soul, was independent both of ritual and of bodily austerities; the God whom he proclaimed was "neither in Kaaba nor in Kailāsh." Those who sought Him needed not to go far; for He awaited discovery everywhere, more accessible to "the washerwoman and the carpenter" than to the self-righteous holy man.[2] Therefore the whole apparatus of piety, Hindu and Moslem alike—the temple and mosque, idol and holy water, scriptures and priests—were denounced by this inconveniently clear-sighted poet as mere substitutes for reality; dead things intervening between the soul and its love—

> The images are all lifeless, they cannot speak:
>   I know, for I have cried aloud to them.
> The Purāna and the Korān are mere words:
>   lifting up the curtain, I have seen.[3]

This sort of thing cannot be tolerated by any organized church; and it is not surprising that Kabīr, having his head-quarters in Benares, the very centre of priestly influence, was subjected to considerable persecution. The well-known legend of the beautiful courtesan sent by the Brāhmans to tempt his virtue, and converted, like the Magdalen, by her sudden encounter with the initiate of a higher love, preserves the memory of the fear and dislike with which he was regarded by the ecclesiastical powers. Once at least, after the performance of a supposed miracle of healing, he was brought before the Emperor Sikandar Lodī, and charged with claiming the possession of divine powers. But Sikandar Lodī, a ruler of considerable culture, was tolerant of the eccentricities of saintly persons belonging to his own faith. Kabīr, being of Mohammedan birth, was outside the authority of the Brāhmans, and technically classed with the Sūfīs, to whom great theological latitude was allowed. Therefore, though he was banished in the interests of peace from Benares, his life was spared. This seems to have happened in 1495, when he was nearly sixty years of age; it is the last event in his career of which we have definite knowledge. Thenceforth he appears to have moved about amongst various cities of northern India, the centre of a group of disciples; continuing in exile that life of apostle and poet of love

to which, as he declares in one of his songs, he was destined "from the beginning of time." In 1518, an old man, broken in health, and with hands so feeble that he could no longer make the music which he loved, he died at Maghar near Gorakhpur.

A beautiful legend tells us that after his death his Mohammedan and Hindu disciples disputed the possession of his body; which the Mohammedans wished to bury, the Hindus to burn. As they argued together, Kabīr appeared before them, and told them to lift the shroud and look at that which lay beneath. They did so, and found in the place of the corpse a heap of flowers; half of which were buried by the Mohammedans at Maghar, and half carried by the Hindus to the holy city of Benares to be burned—fitting conclusion to a life which had made fragrant the most beautiful doctrines of two great creeds.

II

The poetry of mysticism might be defined on the one hand as a temperamental reaction to the vision of Reality: on the other, as a form of prophecy. As it is the special vocation of the mystical consciousness to mediate between two orders, going out in loving adoration towards God and coming home to tell the secrets of Eternity to other men; so the artistic self-expression of this consciousness has also a double character. It is love-poetry, but love-poetry which is often written with a missionary intention.

Kabīr's songs are of this kind: out-births at once of rapture and of charity. Written in the popular Hindī, not in the literary tongue, they were deliberately addressed—like the vernacular poetry of Jacopone da Todì and Richard Rolle—to the people rather than to the professionally religious class; and all must be struck by the constant employment in them of imagery drawn from the common life, the universal experience. It is by the simplest metaphors, by constant appeals to needs, passions, relations which all men understand—the bridegroom and bride, the guru and disciple, the pilgrim, the farmer, the migrant bird—that he drives home his intense conviction of the reality of the soul's intercourse with the Transcendent. There are in his universe no fences between the "natural" and "supernatural" worlds; everything is a part of the creative Play of God, and therefore—even in its humblest details—capable of revealing the Player's mind.

This willing acceptance of the here-and-now as a means of representing supernal realities is a trait common to the greatest mystics. For them, when they have achieved at last the true theopathetic state, all aspects of the universe possess equal authority as sacramental declarations of the Presence of God; and their fearless employment of homely and physical symbols—often startling and even revolting to the unaccustomed taste—is in direct proportion to the exaltation of their spiritual life. The works of the great Sūfīs, and amongst the Christians of Jacopone da Todì, Ruysbroeck, Boehme, abound in illustrations of this law. Therefore we must not be surprised to find in Kabīr's songs—his desperate attempts to communicate his ecstasy and persuade other men to share it—a constant juxtaposition of concrete and metaphysical language; swift alternations between the most intensely anthropomorphic, the most subtly philosophical, ways of apprehending man's communion with the Divine. The need for this alternation, and its entire naturalness for the mind which employs it, is rooted in his concept, or vision, of the Nature of God; and unless we make some attempt to grasp this, we shall not go far in our understanding of his poems.

Kabīr belongs to that small group of supreme mystics—amongst whom St. Augustine, Ruysbroeck, and the Sūfī poet Jalālu'ddīn Rūmī are perhaps the chief—who have achieved that which we might call the synthetic vision of God. These have resolved the perpetual opposition between the personal and impersonal, the transcendent and immanent, static and dynamic aspects of the Divine Nature; between the Absolute of philosophy and the "sure true Friend" of devotional religion. They have done this, not by taking these apparently incompatible concepts one after the other; but by ascending to a height of spiritual intuition at which they are, as Ruysbroeck said, "melted and merged in the Unity," and perceived as the completing opposites of a perfect Whole. This proceeding entails for them—and both Kabīr and Ruysbroeck expressly acknowledge it—a universe of three orders: Becoming, Being, and that which is "More than Being," *i.e.,* God.[4] God is here felt to be not the final abstraction, but the one actuality. He inspires, supports, indeed inhabits, both the durational, conditioned, finite world of Becoming and the unconditioned, non-successional, infinite world of Being; yet utterly transcends them both. He is the omnipresent Reality, the "All-pervading" within Whom "the worlds are being told like beads." In His personal aspect He is the "beloved Fakīr," teaching and companioning each soul. Considered as Immanent Spirit, He is "the Mind within the mind." But all these are at best partial aspects of His nature, mutually corrective: as the Persons in the Christian doctrine of the Trinity—to which this theological diagram bears a striking resemblance—represent different and compensating experiences of the Divine Unity within which they are resumed. As Ruysbroeck discerned a plane of reality upon which "we can speak no more of Father, Son, and Holy Spirit, but only of One Being, the very substance of the Divine Persons"; so Kabīr says that "beyond both the limited *and* the limitless is He, the Pure Being."[5]

Brahma, then, is the Ineffable Fact compared with which "the distinction of the Conditioned from the Uncondi-

tioned is but a word": at once the utterly transcendent One of Absolutist philosophy, and the personal Lover of the individual soul—"common to all and special to each," as one Christian mystic has it. The need felt by Kabīr for both these ways of describing Reality is a proof of the richness and balance of his spiritual experience; which neither cosmic nor anthropomorphic symbols, taken alone, could express. More absolute than the Absolute, more personal than the human mind, Brahma therefore exceeds whilst He includes all the concepts of philosophy, all the passionate intuitions of the heart. He is the Great Affirmation, the font of energy, the source of life and love, the unique satisfaction of desire. His creative word is the *Om* or "Everlasting Yea." The negative philosophy which strips from the Divine Nature all Its attributes and—defining Him only by that which He is not—reduces Him to an "Emptiness," is abhorrent to this most vital of poets. Brahma, he says, "may never be found in abstractions." He is the One Love who pervades the world, discerned in His fullness only by the eyes of love; and those who know Him thus share, though they may never tell, the joyous and ineffable secret of the universe.[6]

Now Kabīr, achieving this synthesis between the personal and cosmic aspects of the Divine Nature, eludes the three great dangers which threaten mystical religion.

First, he escapes the excessive emotionalism, the tendency to an exclusively anthropomorphic devotion, which results from an unrestricted cult of Divine Personality, especially under an incarnational form; seen in India in the exaggerations of Krishna worship, in Europe in the sentimental extravagances of certain Christian saints.

Next, he is protected from the soul-destroying conclusions of pure monism, inevitable if its logical implications are pressed home: that is, the identity of substance between God and the soul, with its corollary of the total absorption of that soul in the Being of God as the goal of the spiritual life. For the thorough-going monist the soul, in so far as it is real, is substantially identical with God; and the true object of existence is the making patent of this latent identity, the realization which finds expression in the Vedāntist formula "That art thou." But Kabīr says that Brahma and the creature are "ever distinct, yet ever united"; that the wise man knows the spiritual as well as the material world to "be no more than His footstool."[7] The soul's union with Him is a love union, a mutual inhabitation; that essentially dualistic relation which all mystical religion expresses, not a self-mergence which leaves no place for personality. This eternal distinction, the mysterious union-in-separateness of God and the soul, is a necessary doctrine of all sane mysticism; for no scheme which fails to find a place for it can represent more than a fragment of that soul's intercourse with the spiritual world. Its affirmation was one of the distinguishing features of the Vaishnavite reformation preached by Rāmānuja; the principle of which had descended through Rāmānanda to Kabīr.

Last, the warmly human and direct apprehension of God as the supreme Object of love, the soul's comrade, teacher, and bridegroom, which is so passionately and frequently expressed in Kabīr's poems, balances and controls those abstract tendencies which are inherent in the metaphysical side of his vision of Reality: and prevents it from degenerating into that sterile worship of intellectual formulæ which became the curse of the Vedāntist school. For the mere intellectualist, as for the mere pietist, he has little approbation.[8] Love is throughout his "absolute sole Lord": the unique source of the more abundant life which he enjoys, and the common factor which unites the finite and infinite worlds. All is soaked in love: that love which he described in almost Johannine language as the "Form of God." The whole of creation is the Play of the Eternal Lover; the living, changing, growing expression of Brahma's love and joy. As these twin passions preside over the generation of human life, so "beyond the mists of pleasure and pain" Kabīr finds them governing the creative acts of God. His manifestation is love; His activity is joy. Creation springs from one glad act of affirmation: the Everlasting Yea, perpetually uttered within the depths of the Divine Nature.[9] In accordance with this concept of the universe as a Love-Game which eternally goes forward, a progressive manifestation of Brahma—one of the many notions which he adopted from the common stock of Hindu religious ideas, and illuminated by his poetic genius—movement, rhythm, perpetual change, forms an integral part of Kabīr's vision of Reality. Though the Eternal and Absolute is ever present to his consciousness, yet his concept of the Divine Nature is essentially dynamic. It is by the symbols of motion that he most often tries to convey it to us: as in his constant reference to dancing, or the strangely modern picture of that Eternal Swing of the Universe which is "held by the cords of love."[10]

It is a marked characteristic of mystical literature that the great contemplatives, in their effort to convey to us the nature of their communion with the supersensuous, are inevitably driven to employ some form of sensuous imagery: coarse and inaccurate as they know such imagery to be, even at the best. Our normal human consciousness is so completely committed to dependence on the senses, that the fruits of intuition itself are instinctively referred to them. In that intuition it seems to the mystics that all the dim cravings and partial apprehensions of sense find perfect fulfilment. Hence their constant declaration that they *see* the uncreated light, they *hear* the celestial melody, they *taste* the sweetness of the Lord, they know an ineffable fragrance, they feel the very contact of love. "Him verily seeing and fully feeling, Him spiritually hearing and Him delectably smelling and sweetly swallowing," as Julian of Norwich has it. In those amongst them who develop psycho-sensorial automatisms, these parallels between sense and spirit may present themselves to consciousness in the form of hallucinations: as the light seen by Suso, the music heard by Rolle, the celestial perfumes which filled St. Catherine of Siena's cell, the physical wounds felt by St. Francis and St. Teresa. These are excessive dramatizations of the symbolism under which the mystic tends instinctively to represent his spiritual intuition to the surface consciousness. Here, in the special sense-perception which he feels to be most expressive of Reality, his peculiar idiosyncrasies come out.

Now Kabīr, as we might expect in one whose reactions to the spiritual order were so wide and various, uses by turn all the symbols of sense. He tells us that he has "seen without sight" the effulgence of Brahma, tasted the divine nectar, felt the ecstatic contact of Reality, smelt the fragrance of the heavenly flowers. But he was essentially a poet and musician: rhythm and harmony were to him the garments of beauty and truth. Hence in his lyrics he shows himself to be, like Richard Rolle, above all things a musical mystic. Creation, he says again and again, is full of music: it *is* music. At the heart of the Universe "white music is blossoming": love weaves the melody, whilst renunciation beats the time. It can be heard in the home as well as in the heavens; discerned by the ears of common men as well as by the trained senses of the ascetic. Moreover, the body of every man is a lyre on which Brahma, "the source of all music," plays. Everywhere Kabīr discerns the "Unstruck Music of the Infinite"—that celestial melody which the angel played to St. Francis, that ghostly symphony which filled the soul of Rolle with ecstatic joy.[11] The one figure which he adopts from the Hindu Pantheon and constantly uses, is that of Krishna the Divine Flute Player.[12] He sees the supernal music, too, in its visual embodiment, as rhythmical movement: that mysterious dance of the universe before the face of Brahma, which is at once an act of worship and an expression of the infinite rapture of the Immanent God.[13]

Yet in this wide and rapturous vision of the universe Kabīr never loses touch with diurnal existence, never forgets the common life. His feet are firmly planted upon earth; his lofty and passionate apprehensions are perpetually controlled by the activity of a sane and vigorous intellect, by the alert commonsense so often found in persons of real mystical genius. The constant insistence on simplicity and directness, the hatred of all abstractions and philosophizings,[14] the ruthless criticism of external religion: these are amongst his most marked characteristics. God is the Root whence all manifestations, "material" and "spiritual," alike proceed; and God is the only need of man—"happiness shall be yours when you come to the Root."[15] Hence to those who keep their eye on the "one thing needful," denominations, creeds, ceremonies, the conclusions of philosophy, the disciplines of asceticism, are matters of comparative indifference. They represent merely the different angles from which the soul may approach that simple union with Brahma which is its goal; and are useful only in so far as they contribute to this consummation. So thorough-going is Kabīr's eclecticism, that he seems by turns Vedāntist and Vaishnavite, Pantheist and Transcendentalist, Brāhman and Sūfī. In the effort to tell the truth about that ineffable apprehension, so vast and yet so near, which controls his life, he seizes and twines together—as he might have woven together contrasting threads upon his loom—symbols and ideas drawn from the most violent and conflicting philosophies and faiths. All are needed, if he is ever to suggest the character of that One whom the Upanishad called "the Sun-coloured Being who is beyond this Darkness": as all the colours of the spectrum are needed if we would demonstrate the simple richness of white light. In thus adapting traditional materials to his own use he follows a method common amongst the mystics; who seldom exhibit any special love for originality of form. They will pour their wine into almost any vessel that comes to hand: generally using by preference—and lifting to new levels of beauty and significance—the religious or philosophic formulæ current in their own day. Thus we find that some of Kabīr's finest poems have as their subjects the commonplaces of Hindu philosophy and religion: the Līlā or Sport of God, the Ocean of Bliss, the Bird of the Soul, Māyā, the Hundred-petalled Lotus, and the "Formless Form." Many, again, are soaked in Sūfī imagery and feeling. Others use as their material the ordinary surroundings and incidents of Indian life: the temple bells, the ceremony of the lamps, marriage, suttee, pilgrimage, the characters of the seasons; all felt by him in their mystical aspect, as sacraments of the soul's relation with Brahma. In many of these a particularly beautiful and intimate feeling for Nature is shown.[16]

In the collection of songs here translated there will be found examples which illustrate nearly every aspect of Kabīr's thought, and all the fluctuations of the mystic's emotion: the ecstasy, the despair, the still beatitude, the eager self-devotion, the flashes of wide illumination, the moments of intimate love. His wide and deep vision of the universe, the "Eternal Sport" of creation ("LXXXII"), the worlds being "told like beads" within the Being of God ("XIV," "XVI," "XVII," "LXXVI"), is here seen balanced by his lovely and delicate sense of intimate communion with the Divine Friend, Lover, Teacher of the soul ("X," "XI," "XXIII," "XXXV," "LI,'" "LXXXV," "LXXXVI," "LXXXVIII," "XCII," "XCIII"; above all, the beautiful poem "XXXIV"). As these apparently paradoxical views of Reality are resolved in Brāhma, so all other opposites are reconciled in Him: bondage and liberty, love and

renunciation, pleasure and pain ("XVII," "XXV," "XL," "LXXXIX"). Union with Him is the one thing that matters to the soul, its destiny and its need ("LI," "LII," "LIV," "LXX," "LXXIV," "XCIII," "XCVI"); and this union, this discovery of God, is the simplest and most natural of all things, if we would but grasp it ("XLI," "XLVI," "LVI," "LXXII," "LXXVI," "LXXVIII," "XCVII"). The union, however, is brought about by love, not by knowledge or ceremonial observances ("XXXVIII," "LIV," "LV," "LIX," "XCI"); and the apprehension which that union confers is ineffable— "neither This nor That," as Ruysbroeck has it ("IX," "XLVI," "LXXVI"). Real worship and communion is in Spirit and in Truth ("XL," "XLI," "LVI," "LXIII," "LXV," "LXX"), therefore idolatry is an insult to the Divine Lover ("XLII," "LXIX") and the devices of professional sanctity are useless apart from charity and purity of soul ("LIV," "LXV," "LXVI"). Since all things, and especially the heart of man, are God-inhabited, God-possessed ("XXVI," "LVI," "LXXVI," "LXXXIX," "XCVII"), He may best be found in the here-and-now: in the normal, human, bodily existence, the "mud" of material life ("III," "IV," "VI," "XXI," "XXXIX," "XL," "XLIII," "XLVIII," "LXXII"). "We can reach the goal without crossing the road" ("LXXVI")—not the cloister but the home is the proper theatre of man's efforts: and if he cannot find God there, he need not hope for success by going farther afield. "In the home is reality." There love and detachment, bondage and freedom, joy and pain play by turns upon the soul; and it is from their conflict that the Unstruck Music of the Infinite proceeds. "Kabīr says: None but Brahma can evoke its melodies."

III

This version of Kabīr's songs is chiefly the work of Mr. Rabīndranāth Tagore, the trend of whose mystical genius makes him—as all who read these poems will see—a peculiarly sympathetic interpreter of Kabīr's vision and thought. It has been based upon the printed Hindī text with Bengali translation of Mr. Kshiti Mohan Sen; who has gathered from many sources—sometimes from books and manuscripts, sometimes from the lips of wandering ascetics and minstrels—a large collection of poems and hymns to which Kabīr's name is attached, and carefully sifted the authentic songs from the many spurious works now attributed to him. These painstaking labours alone have made the present undertaking possible.

We have also had before us a manuscript English translation of 116 songs made by Mr. Ajit Kumār Chakravarty from Mr. Kshiti Mohan Sen's text, and a prose essay upon Kabīr from the same hand. From these we have derived great assistance. A considerable number of readings from the translation have been adopted by us; whilst several of the facts mentioned in the essay have been incorporated into this introduction. Our most grateful thanks are due to Mr. Ajit Kumār Chakravarty for the extremely generous and unselfish manner in which he has placed his work at our disposal.

Notes

1. Cf. Poems Nos. "XXI," "XL," "XLIII," "LXVI," "LXXVI."

2. Poems "I," "II," "XLI."

3. Poems "XLII," "LXV," "LXVII."

4. Nos. "VII" and "XLIX."

5. No. "VII."

6. Nos. "VII," "XXVI," "LXXVI," "XC."

7. Nos. "VII" and "IX."

8. Cf. especially Nos. "LIX," "LXVII," "LXXV," "XC," "XCI."

9. Nos. "XVII," "XXVI," "LXXVI," "LXXXII."

10. No. "XVI."

11. Nos. "XVII," "XVIII," "XXXIX," "XLI," "LIV," "LXXVI," "LXXXIII," "LXXXIX," "XCVII."

12. Nos. "L," "LIII," "LXVIII."

13. Nos. "XXVI," "XXXII," "LXXVI."

14. Nos. "LXXV," "LXXVIII," "LXXX," "XC."

15. No. "LXXX."

16. Nos. "XV," "XXIII," "LXVII," "LXXXVII," "XCVIII."

Charlotte Vaudeville (essay date 1963)

SOURCE: Vaudeville, Charlotte. "Kabir and Interior Religion." *History of Religions* 3, no. 1-2 (1963): 191-201.

[*In the following essay, Vaudeville links Kabir's spirituality with his status as a poor weaver, explaining that the poet's work is evidence of a "profound contempt joined with the most resounding indignation" for the influence and statutes of institutionalized religion.*]

Kabir (1440-1518)—from his true name Kabir-Dās, "the servant of the Great (God)"—is one of the great names of the literature and religious history of North India. He belongs to that first generation of poets of the "Hindi" language who composed couplets and songs for the people in a language which they understood: a mixed Hindi dialect, a kind of dialectal potpourri which is not amenable to the classifications of the linguists.

This jargon was first used by the innumerable itinerant preachers who at the time, as from all antiquity, traversed the country in all directions: Yogis covered with ashes, Muslim Sufis draped with picturesque patchwork robes, Jain ascetics dressed in white or only in "cardinal points," *sants* and *bhagats,* as one called the Vishnuite "saints" or "devotees"—all intoxicated with the Absolute or with divine love, all free and bold, exploiting without mercy the inexhaustible liberality of the poor Indian peasant. Kabir, who knew them well, often evoked them, and not without irony:

> Sweet is the food of the beggar! He collects all kinds of grains,
> He does not depend on anyone and, without distant expeditions, he is a great king!

If Kabir himself did not disdain to mingle with this motley crowd sometimes, he was, however, never an ascetic, nor a Yogi, nor even a professional "devotee." Born of a caste of weavers recently converted to Islām, a poor artisan lacking in culture, perhaps even illiterate as he boasted, he practiced the ancestral craft in a narrow alley in Kāshi, the modern Banaras. Banaras, the holy city of the "great god" Śiva was then, even more than today, the fortress of Brahmanic orthodoxy where the Pandits and the Pāndés, the Scribes and Pharisees of Hinduism, held sway as masters. For the Pandits and their holy Scriptures, for the Pāndés and their idols, for the immense mystification and exploitation of the ignorance and credulity of the masses, Kabir felt only a profound contempt joined with the most resounding indignation. He did not cease to pursue them with his sarcasm, in violent, often vulgar, language, in which bursts forth the rebellion of a proud soul against the venality, the baseness, and the hypocrisy of these so-called scholars, these sorry shepherds who with tranquillity lead a great multitude of defenseless sheep to their ruin:

> I am the beast and you are the Shepherd who leads me from birth to birth,
> But you have never been able to make me cross the Ocean of Existence: how then are you my master?
> You are a Brahman, and I am only a weaver from Banaras:
>   Understand my own wisdom:
> You go begging among kings and princes, and I think only of God!

The work of Kabir contains a resounding satire on Brahmanical orthodoxy and the superstitions of popular Hinduism. Not only does he condemn with finality worship of idols, these "lifeless stones," but he also rejects with contempt all the proceedings and ceremonies by which popular Hindu devotion manifests itself: purificatory bathings, ritual fasts, pilgrimages, and all sorts of practices:

> What is the good of scrubbing the body on the outside,
> If the inside is full of filth?

> Without the name of Rām, one will not escape hell,
> Even with a hundred washings!

This contempt is not inspired by his Muslim faith and there is no iconoclastic rage in it. If the Brahman and the Pāndé are his favorite targets, he feels scarcely more respect for the official representatives of the Islāmic religion, the Mullah and the Qazi, who are less venial but no less proud and pedantic, and who are still more intolerant:

> The one reads the Veda, the other does the *qutba,*
> This one is a Maulana, that one is a Pāndé:
> They bear different names,
> But they are pots from the same clay!
> Says Kabīr, both have gone astray
> And neither has found God. . . .
> The one kills a goat, the other slays a cow:
> In quibbles they have wasted their life!

This satire is brought to bear not simply on the vices and weaknesses of men but reaches in them and behind them to the systems themselves which they defend or pretend to represent. It is the authority of the Veda and the Qurān, as much and even more than the Pandit or the Qazi, that Kabīr attacks, or, more precisely, he rebels against the pretension of resolving by means of "books" or by way of authority the mystery of the human condition and the problem of salvation:

> Well! Pandit, by virtue of reading and reading, you
>   have become clever:
> Explain to me, then, your Deliverance!
>   . . . . .
> Well, Qazi! What then is this Book that you discourse
>   on?
> Night and Day you are jangling and wrangling,
>   And you do not understand that all systems are the
>   same.

The Paradise to which men aspire and the thought of which makes them forget their own mystery is but a snare:

> Everyone speaks of going there,
> But I do not know where that Paradise is!
> They do not understand the mystery of their own self
> And they give a description of Paradise!

It is therefore rather inaccurate to represent Kabīr as a reformer of Hinduism, or even as an apostle of religious tolerance and of Hindu-Muslim reconciliation. Undoubtedly, he loves to repeat that "the Hindu and the Turk are brothers," since God is present in all. But this reform is a final condemnation, and this tolerance is supported by a kind of rationalism which rejects absolutely every revelation based on an authority extrinsic to the human soul. In this, Kabīr follows the long nonconformist tradition which has its source in the Buddhist "heresy," if it is not still more ancient. In fact, a form of late Buddhism, mingled with practices and concepts of tantric

magic, had profoundly impregnated the lower layers of Hindu society in North India several centuries before Kabīr. Some recent researches have made it possible to establish the dependence of Kabīr on the tradition of tantric Yoga. The family of Kabīr belonged to a caste of married "Jogis" or "Jugis" recently converted to Islām. Many of these Jogis were, in fact, weavers. This family origin would explain Kabīr's irreducible opposition to Brahmanical orthodoxy as well as his ignorance of the Islāmic religion, which he seems to have known only from the outside.[1]

The schools and sects of tantric Yoga differ according to their "method" or "practice" (*sādhana*). The metaphysical basis always remains very nearly identical: it is characterized by a pure idealism and by a kind of dualistic monism. Whether Buddhists or Śivaites, the Yogis do not recognize any existence other than that of spirit, "the mental," and no field of experience other than that of the human body, which is itself considered a microcosm. All truth is experimental; it ought not to be discovered but "realized" within the body with the aid of psychological practices: concentration, control of breathing, sexual practices. For the Yogis the Absolute manifests itself under two aspects: negative and positive, static and dynamic, male and female. The supreme goal of their *sādhana* is a state of "non-duality" or of unity transcending the opposites, which ought to be "realized" by the Yogi at the end of a kind of process of regression: reabsorption of the states of consciousness in the consciousness and of the latter in the Undifferentiated. By thus overcoming the "mental" the Yogi attains the liberating trance, *samādhi,* which is conceived as "the great bliss," *mahāsukha,* of which nothing can be expressed. Through this *sādhana* the Yogi's body becomes incorruptible and the Yogi himself obtains immortality. The perfect Yogi claims to overcome death.

These conceptions form the background and, as it were, the terrain for the development of Kabīr's religious thought. However, in his time, two other currents had already penetrated the old substratum of popular Hinduism: that of Vishnuite devotion (*bhakti*), which had come from the South, and that of Islāmic mysticism, which had been spread by the Sufīs in Northwest India since the thirteenth century.

Contrary to Yoga, which is essentially technique, Bhakti is essentially faith, the adoration of a personal God, who is generally "manifested" in an anthropomorphic form, that of an *avatāra* or "descent." It is this visible form of a "qualified" (*saguṇa*) God which is the object of Vishnuite devotion. This God asks of his devotee ("bhakta") or of his servant (*dāsa*) nothing but faith, love, and trust. The attitude of the perfect bhakta, then, is one of humility and of totally giving himself into the hands of his chosen divinity, that is to say, of the divine

Form that he has chosen as the object of his worship. The bhakta expects his salvation only by grace, whatever may be his own moral faults. The invocation of the name of the divinity is enough to purify the devotee. In its purest and highest form Bhakti is *prapatti*, "abandon," the total self-surrender of the devotee to his Lord. The religion of Bhakti is one of a deeply felt love for a visible god, a love which suffices for everything and is its own recompense; Bhakti is constantly represented as the "easy path," a kind of *moyen court* which makes all asceticism unnecessary and which manifests itself by a kind of continual exaltation and an abundance of tears. As a religion essentially emotive, based on rather uncertain metaphysical foundations, but strongly monotheistic in its fundamental orientation, Bhakti appears remarkably in harmony with the religious needs of the Indian masses; one can say that it remains, to this day, the truly popular religion. The polytheistic forms which it continues to gather around itself have much less significance than one generally believes. It is remarkable that the entire Hindu tradition recognizes in Kabīr himself a "great bhatka," in spite of his fierce negations and his irreducible opposition to all kinds of idolatry and to all the divine "manifestations" adored by the Vishnuite bhaktas.

The mysticism of the Muslim Sufīs is based on a complete abandonment to the will of an all-powerful and merciful God—but this God is a completely spiritual Being, infinitely removed from all sensible manifestation. The man who discerns in creation a reflection of His Beauty is seized with a love for Him, a love which is above all the intense desire to meet Him, and he rushes toward Him by the path of detachment. Far from being strewn with flowers, this "path" (*tariqa*) is bristling with sorrows; the soul of the lover is tortured by desire for the inaccessible Beauty and by separation from his Beloved. Permanent union with his God is unattainable in this life and will be achieved only after death when the purified soul will be freed from the bonds of the body. But it sometimes happens that God makes himself in some way perceptible for some moments to that mysterious internal organ which is the "heart" (*sirr*) of man. The Sufī, like the Yogi, is turned inward in the quest for a superior Reality which manifests itself in the most profound depths of his soul. It may be pointed out, however, that the forms of Sufism which were widespread in North India at the time of Kabīr had already been influenced by Vedanta monism and had also assimilated some yogic methods, so much so that the Sufīs appeared to the people as a variety of Yogis. And one knows that Kabīr himself, although he was opposed to the Islamic practices and was rather suspicious of all pious mendicity, often associated with the Sufīs, numerous at the time in the west of the country.

The three currents of thought that we have attempted to define summarily agree on one point: the pre-eminence of the interior experience over any other source of religious and metaphysical knowledge. For the Yogi there is only experimental truth; he does not search for the truth and the Truth does not come to him: he "realizes" it, that is, he "makes" it, in proportion as he progresses in his *sādhana* (the word signifying both "method" and "realization"). The bhakta accepts in principle the postulates of Brahmanical orthodoxy, and recognizes at least theoretically the eternal truth of the Veda—but he cares very little about it, for he has no need of it in order to be saved. He needs a visible form or of a manifestation of the divinity in order to "pin" his devotion there, but in the choice of it he remains free to follow the desire of his heart and the inclination of his imagination: it is his own religious experience which largely determines the conception and the image that he makes of his God. The Sufī is apparently less free, since he acknowledges the Qurānic revelation and the principles of Islāmic orthodoxy—but he gets around this in his own way, by gnosis: without denying the validity of the traditional path, based on the Qurānic prescriptions, he willingly leaves it to the mass of believers, in quest of the joys of "Paradise." He chooses another way for himself, the way of love and of intimate experience of God, a way reserved for the initiates only; in this way he will come to a progressive illumination, symbolized by the rending of the veils which separate him from the perfect Beauty.

The blessedness to which the Sufī aspires is not the Islāmic paradise, but a kind of mysterious life in God, sometimes expressed as a veritable immersion or absorption in Him.

These various currents explain the genesis of the *sādhana* of Kabīr: it does not appear to have precise metaphysical bases, but seems rather to be an original synthesis of Bhakti and of medieval Yoga, with some elements borrowed from the Sufī tradition. Throughout Kabīr's work the accent is on interiorization: man ought to turn his attention away from the exterior world, from all sensible forms, in order to withdraw into the innermost depths of his conscience (undoubtedly analogous to the *sirr* of the Sufīs) where God dwells:

> They say that Hari dwells in the east and that Allah
>   resides in the west:
> Search in your heart, search in your heart—there is
>   his dwelling and his residence!
> I believed that Hari was far off, though he is present
>   in plentitude in all beings,
> I believed Him outside of me—and, near, He became
>   to me far!

The new Yogi has left there all his practices. Love (*prem*) henceforth is his only technique and his goal is the mysterious "meeting" with God:

Says Kabīr, in love, I have found Him,
Simple hearts have met Raghouraï. . . .

This meeting between the Lord and the soul in its depths
is a mysterious experience which Kabīr calls *paricaya,*
from a word which signifies "acquaintance by sight or
by contact." Kabīr liked to underline the ineffable and
transcendent character of this "experience":

In the body, the Inaccessible is obtained, in the Inac-
cessible, an access,
Says Kabīr, I obtained the Experience, when the Guru
showed me the Path.

Love has lighted the cage, an eternal Yoga has
awakened,
Doubt has vanished, happiness has appeared, the
beloved Bridegroom has been found!

Kabīr seems most often to interpret this union as an
ultimate absorption of the lover in the Beloved:

When I was, Hari was not—now Hari is, and I am no
more,
Every shadow is dispersed when the Lamp has been
found within the soul. . . .

The One for whom I went out to search, I found Him
in my house,
And this One has become myself, whom I called
Other!

Kabīr willingly borrows the language and metaphors of
Yoga in order to describe the conditions of the meeting;
this is possible only by the destruction of the "mental,"
and a final victory over "duality":

The lamp is dry, the oil is used up,
The guitar is silent, the dancer has lain down,
The fire is extinguished and no smoke rises,
The soul is absorbed in the One and there is no more
duality. . . .

Kabīr has lost himself; he has disappeared like salt in
meal, like a drop in the ocean:

You search, you search, O Friend—but Kabīr has
disappeared:
The drop is absorbed in the Ocean: how find it again?
. . . . .
By the touch of the magic stone, the copper is
changed,
But this copper, having become gold, is saved!
By the company of the saints, Kabīr is changed,
But this Kabīr, having become Rām, is saved!

The frequent allusions to the absorption of the soul in
God explain how Kabīr could be considered a monist
nirguṇī, that is, a partisan of the "non-qualified"
(*nirguṇa*) Absolute in opposition to the partisans of
Bhakti, worshipers of a personal and "qualified"
(*saguṇa*) God. But this monistic interpretation of the
thought of Kabīr is contradicted by the essential role

that love plays in his *sādhana* and by the nature of the
relation which he maintains with his God, Rām. The
principal difficulty of interpretation comes undoubtedly
from the fact that India, in its totality, conceives the
person as a limitation of Being, and cannot accept the
idea of a personal God who would not be anthropomor-
phic at the same time or in some way tainted with "illu-
sion." Now Kabīr formally rejected all the illusory
manifestations of the divine which are the object of
Vishnuite devotion, and he claimed to direct his love to
God, the unfathomable Being, "as He is in Himself."
For those who understand only sentimental devotion,
this love is a mystery: "Inexpressible is the story of
Love: if one told it, who would believe it?"

The attitude of *nirguṇī* Kabīr toward his God, to whom
he usually gives the Vishnuite names (Hari, Rām,
Govinda), is not that of the philosopher before a
metaphysical entity, but rather that of the devotee before
the God "who has bound his heart to His own with
gentle bonds." The weaver Kabīr entertains relations of
the most touching familiarity with this unfathomable
and ineffable Being. He retains an acute consciousness
of his own misery and looks only to the grace of his
Lord for his salvation, that is, the joy of meeting:

How shall I be saved, O Master, how shall I be saved?
Here I am, full of iniquities!
Weary, I stand at your royal threshold:
Who then, if not You, will care for me?
Let me see your face, open the door!

His confidence is complete; he belongs body and soul
to his Master:

I am your slave, you may sell me, O Lord,
My body and my soul and all I have, all is Rām's.
If you sell me, O Rām, who will keep me?
If you keep me, O Rām, who will sell me?

Rām is not only the companion and friend; He is more
than a father—He is a mother:

Whatever fault a son commits,
His mother will not have a grudge against him:
O Rām, I am your little child,
Will you not blot out all my faults?

Similar prayers and the sentiments which they express
are not rare in the Bhakti literature, even before Kabīr.
But the latter spoke of a completely spiritual Being,
which he endeavored to discover in the depths of his
own soul. Kabīr's devotion differs from Vishnuite
Bhakti not only in its object but also in its character.
Indeed, it does not consist only of the sentiments of
tenderness, trust, and abandon, of which the entire
Bhakti literature provides so many examples: it is also—
and above all—an ardent quest, a heroic adventure in
which he is completely involved, at the peril of his life.
Kabīr's conception of divine love seems to be an

original synthesis of the traditions of Yoga and of Sufīsm, the former exalting man's effort, the latter making of the yearnings, of the torments suffered by the exiled soul in its mortal condition, the necessary condition for every spiritual ascension. For Kabīr, Bhakti is no longer the "easy path," but the precipitous path where the lover of God risks his life:

> Bhakti is the beloved wife of Rām, it is not for
>   cowards:
> Cut off your head and take it in your hands, if you
>   want to call upon Rām!

Rām is the inestimable "Diamond" that one buys only with his life, and the love of Rām is "cutting as the edge of the sword," terrible as the fiery furnace; in the "tavern" of Love, the Tavernkeeper demands the blood price. Many are the verses which seem to paraphrase the Scripture: *"fors sicut mors dilectio, dura sicut infernus aemulatio, lampadae ejus lampadae ignis atque flammarum."*

The path which leads toward God is, then, a path of suffering, vigils, and tears, and there is no other. This suffering has its source in the separation—at least apparent—of the soul from its Beloved. As the wife whose husband is on a distant journey, she languishes in sorrowful and faithful vigil. This mysterious suffering that Kabīr calls *viraha,* "separation," is one of his favorite themes:

> I cannot go to You and I cannot make You come:
> So You will take my life, burning me in the fire of
>   separation!
>
> Kabīr, painful is the wound, and suffering continues in
>   the body:
> This unique suffering of love has seized my en-
>   trails. . . .

This suffering is itself a mystery, hidden from profane eyes. Nothing of it appears externally. He who loves "bleeds silently in the depths of his soul, as the insect devours wood." Only the Lord can understand it: "He who has opened the wound understands this suffering and he who suffers it."

He who loves does not, however, seek to avoid this torment, for he knows that this torment is the mark of divine election. The soul which has not known it will not have access to the true life:

> Do not revile this suffering: it is royal,
> The body in which it is not found will ever be but a
>   cemetery!

It seems that Kabīr, like certain Sufīs, such as the celebrated Mansur Hallāj, has come to love suffering itself, as a privileged path to God:

> Kabīr, I went out searching for Happiness and Suffer-
>   ing came to me,

Then I said: "Go home, Happiness—I no longer know anything but Truth and Suffering!"

The Yogis called the "living dead" (*jīvanmukta*) the ascetic who had succeeded in "conquering the mind" and thus freeing himself from his empirical self. Kabīr borrows this idea of the "living dead" from them and applies it to the mystic engaged in the Way of Love, who has sacrificed his earthly life. But this "death" is, in reality, the condition for the true "life" in God:

> If I burn the house, it is saved, if I preserve it, it is
>   lost,
> Behold an astonishing thing: he who is dead triumphs
>   over Death!
> Death after death, the world dies, but no one knows
>   how to die,
> Kabīr, no one knows how to die so that he will no
>   longer die!

This astonishing synthesis of such disparate elements shows the originality of Kabīr. Whatever the systems from which he was able to borrow, it is evident that all of his religious thought is ordered by an intimate experience, which may be properly called "mystical." If Kabīr happens to speak the language of Yoga, indeed, of Vedanta monism, it is difficult to misapprehend the import of some affirmation apparently tainted with monism or pure idealism. If Kabīr has a dogma, it is that of the immanence of the divine. God is the "milieu" of the soul, as water is the milieu of the water lily:

> Why do you wither, O Water Lily?
> Your stem is full of water!
> In the water you were born, in the water you live,
> In the water, you have your dwelling, O Water Lily.

The mystery is not that the "water lily" lives but that it dies. Death is the only true scandal; it is the perpetual defiance thrown in the face of God. The attitude of Kabīr with regard to the mystery of human destiny is essentially pragmatic, as that of the Yogis and of the Buddha himself: he seeks less to pierce the mystery than to triumph over death, in which he recognizes the fruit of a monstrous *separation* between the soul and its divine milieu. A man without culture but profoundly intuitive, when Kabīr tries to speak of this ineffable Reality that he has discovered in the depths of his soul, he quite naturally borrows a language of pure immanence which is that of the Yogis and Sufīs of his time. However, guided by his own intimate experience, Kabīr seems to presume the existence of a God who is *both* immanent and transcendent. While he is incapable of reconciling these two aspects, he holds firmly "the two ends of the chain," preferring the obscurity of paradox to the false clarity of a superficial systematization—and he keeps repeating that God is the Wholly Other, the Unknowable, the Ineffable, whose nature remains always inaccessible to created intelligence: "You alone know the mystery of your nature: Kabīr takes his refuge in You!"

For Kabīr, God is "the One," "the True," "the Pure," "the Mysterious." He feels only contempt for all those "makers of pious discourses" who pretend to speak of Him without having seen Him! Where is the truthful witness? What credence is to be given to these sages, to these prophets? All are dead and their bodies "burn with fire." And the gods also are dead! Who has ever defied Death? This world is only a see-saw on which swing myriads of beings given up to their ruin:

> Myriads of living beings swing while Death meditates:
> Thousands of ages have passed and it has never suffered a defeat.

For Kabīr, only God himself can meet the challenge of death. It is He, the "perfect Guru," who instructs his disciple in the depths of the soul and opens in him that mysterious wound from which life will emerge; the "Word" of the divine Guru is "the single arrow" which pierces the depths of the soul:

> When I found grace with the Perfect Guru, He gave me a unique revelation,
> Then the cloud of love burst with rain, flooding my limbs.

Then Kabīr, having unmasked the immense imposture of the false prophets, remains alone before his God, the unfathomable Being, at the same time near and far, immanent and inaccessible to the soul:

> O Madhao! You are the Water for which I am consumed with thirst.
> In the midst of this Water, the fire of my desire grows!
> You are the Ocean and I am the fish
> Which dwells in the Water and languishes with its absence.

Toward Him, there is no marked trail, no "way" other than the painful and faithful awaiting of an unforseeable illumination. God speaks only in the secret of the soul—but most men are incapable of hearing Him, and they run in crowds to their ruin "in the way of the world and of the Veda." This spiritual quest, this heroic effort toward a purely interior religion ends on a note of infinite despair. Through the grace of Rām, Kabīr and some "saints" have been able to cross "the Ocean of Existence," but the world is not saved, and will not be, for death remains unconquered and continues to reign over it.

"O Death, where is your victory?" This triumphant cry of St. Paul did not reach the ears of Kabīr. For him, hope is dead and no light can ever rise upon this world. The saint is he who does not yield, who does not resign himself, and who goes out alone, gropingly, in search of the true life, illumined by that unique Lamp which burns in the depths of his heart.

Note

1. The Tantric Yoga tradition seems to have profoundly impregnated the lower layers of society in North and Central India from the tenth century. In the north the most famous sect is that of the *Nāth-Panthīs* or *Kānphaṭṭa-Yogīs* ("the Yogis with pierced ears") who claim as a founder the fabulous Yogī Gorakhnāth. Besides the innumerable wandering Yogis, who were usually celibate and "unattached" (*Yogī bairāgī, avadhūtas*), there were numerous castes of married Yogis, called *Yogīs grhastīs* (also called *Jogīs, Jugīs*) and considered as beyond the pale of Hindu society, properly speaking. The majority of these Jogis seem to have been musicians, cotton-carders, and weavers. Many of these castes were superficially Islāmicized during the fourteenth and fifteenth centuries. Such seems to have been the case with the Julāhas of Banaras in the fourteenth century (cf. Ch. Vaudeville, *Au cabaret de l'Amour, Paroles de Kabīr* [Paris: UNESCO, 1959], Introduction, p. 24).

Paul Carroll (review date January/February 1979)

SOURCE: Carroll, Paul. "Paul Carroll: on Bly's *Kabir.*" *The American Poetry Review* 9, no. 1 (January/February 1979): 30-31.

[*In the following review, Carroll praises Robert Bly's translation of selected works of Kabir and considers the nature of God and faith as revealed in Kabir's poetry.*]

Kabir is one of the great poets of the love of God. He wrote his poems in old Hindi and Punji between about 1460 and 1518. He was the son of a poor basket weaver in Benares; early in life, he became a disciple of the great Ramanada and, in turn, attracted disciples himself, while raising a family through his work as a weaver of wool. So joyous, so deep, so radiant and so natural is the love embodied in his lyrics that reading them can be both awesome and frightening. If the reader feels moved to seek a comparable love he may well end terrified: the search could end in a revelation which would change his life forever. Yet many readers will probably feel tempted, as I certainly was, to abandon everything and take to the road, searching for Kabir.

Before Bly's superb translation, most readers knew Kabir only in the translation made in 1914 by Rabindranath Tagore, assisted by Evelyn Underhill. The Tagore translation presents Kabir as a rather stuffy, portentous Sufi educated at Victorian Oxford, sober and didactic. The Bly translation, on the other hand, offers an ecstatic, generous saint, speaking good, strong Midwestern, direct and intoxicated. (To the Alexandrine who might fidget, pointing out that Bly worked exclusively from the Tagore translation, which was itself based on a Bengali translation of the Hindu original, the poet's answer suffices: Admitting that many errors may well be built into his version, Bly says: "If anyone speaking Hindi would like to help me, I'll (do the poems) over.")

Bly earns the thanks of us all. I, for one, will reread **The Kabir Book** often—the way one takes *A Shropshire Lad* or *Duino Elegies* or *The Branch Will Not Break* or *Selected Odes of Horace* or the *Elemental Odes* or *The Poems and Songs of Burns* along to read during a walk along the lake or on a Sunday picnic in the forest preserve or on a reading tour.

Writing about Kabir is, at once, both tough and easy. The kind of love of God embodied in his poems is not within most of our experience. Thanks to St. John of the Cross and Kabir and a few others, we know something about the Eternal Bridegroom whose hair floats in the wind in the cell in Toledo, and the sound of the ecstatic flute inside the body and soul in Benares, and, thanks to Dante, we also know something about the *immensum pelagus essentiae,* the immense ocean of existence, the Great Rose of Being, and the Love that moves the sun and other stars. First-hand experience of such profound and joyous love, however, remains foreign to most of us. Even serious, loving reading about it is not enough, at least according to Kabir, who warns:

> The Sacred Books of the East are nothing but words.
> I looked through their covers one day sideways.
> What Kabir talks is only what he has lived through.
> If you have not lived through something, it is not true.

Kabir's poems are also easy to read and write about— that is, they are clear and direct and mean exactly what they say: like Christ's words of rebuke to his disciples when they tried to prevent children from getting his blessing: "Let the children be; do not keep them back from me; the kingdom of heaven belongs to such as these" (Knox translation).

At the core of Kabir's experience of the love of God is the revelation of the Guest, the Teacher, the Friend, the Holy One who appears at times as an old person living in a cheap hotel, is always inside of him. God is present, moreover, amid such beautiful things as: the sound of the flute of interior time, the structure of whose network of illuminating notes is as if "a million suns were arranged inside"; and the open flower near one's breastbone; and waves and the sound of big seashells and bells.

Such knowledge is as natural to Kabir as the oxygen he breathes. "The musk is inside the deer," he tells us, in an exquisite image, "but the deer does not look for it; / it wanders around looking for grass." And he shares the beautiful fact that in one's search for the Eternal Guest it is the intensity of one's longing that must do the hard work: "Look at me," he confesses, "and you will see a slave of that intensity."

Kabir reserves scorn and satire, on the other hand, for that seeker who is preoccupied by the superficial trappings and the gegaws of mysticism—the one who says his beads over and over, who paints "weird designs on his forehead," and wears his hair "matted, long and ostentatious," or who thinks that love comes from donning the orange robes of the Yogi. And to that seeker who insists that he must journey to Calcutta or Tibet or Boulder, Colorado in order to experience the divine, Kabir's advice is stunningly blunt: Stay at home. "One flower has a thousand petals. / That will do for a place to sit."

Scorn is also directed at the Manichaean who is, like the poor, always with us—the one who would make himself a eunuch, starving and flagellating and castigating his body for the sake of a kingdom of heaven populated, presumably, by ghosts of neuter gender:

> The idea that the soul will join with the ecstatic just
>   because the body is rotten—
> that is all fantasy.
> What is found now is found then.
> If you find nothing now,
> you will simply end up with an apartment in the City
>   of Death.
> If you make love with the divine now, in the next life
>   you will have a face of satisfied desire.

Kabir is, on the felicitous contrary, sensual, erotic, a lover of women and of the Holy One who hears "the delicate anklets that ring on the feet of an insect as it walks."

Most admirable of all is Kabir's humility. Despite the solid evidence in his lyrics that he knows what St. John of the Cross knew, what St. Francis of Assisi knew, what the St. Thomas Aquinas and the St. Philip Neri of the levitations knew, Kabir also knew that, although "I know the sound of the ecstatic flute / but I don't know whose flute it is."

(Kabir's translator shows an equal modesty. His afterword, which is excellent, states: "(Kabir) has, moreover, enigmatic or puzzle poems that no contemporary commentator fully understands." The afterword ends on a note of admirable, modest gratitude: "I love his poems, and am grateful every day for their gift.")

Linda Hess (essay date 1983)

SOURCE: Hess, Linda. Introduction to *The Bijak of Kabir,* pp. 9-24. San Francisco, Calif.: North Point Press, 1983.

[In the following excerpt, Hess offers a critical overview of the works of Kabir as a bhakti poet who, more than any other religious poet, challenges, unsettles, and shocks his audience.]

ADDRESS AND ASSAULT

In his mastery of the vocative, Kabir is unique among the *bhakti* poets. Not in the *saguna* devotees, not in *nirguna* Dadu or reformer Nanak, not in the radical Bengali Buddhist poets, the iconoclast Gorakh or the surreal Bauls, whatever else they may have in common with him, do we find the intense bearing down upon the listener that is so prominent in Kabir. It shows itself first in the array of addresses he uses to seize our attention: Hey Saint, Brother, Brahmin, Yogi, Hermit, Babu, Mother, Muslim, Creature, Friend, Fool! Many poems are simply directed at "you." But titles or pronouns of address are only the beginning. Kabir pounds away with questions, prods with riddles, stirs with challenges, shocks with insults, disorients with verbal feints. It seems that if one read him responsively one could hardly help getting red in the face, jumping around, squirming, searching, getting embarrassed, or shouting back.

For a taste of the style, here is a pastiche of lines from various poems:

Pandit, you've got it wrong.

Monk, stop scattering your mind.

Pandit, do some research
and let me know
how to destroy
transiency.

Now you, Mr. Qazi, what kind of work is that,
going from house to house
chopping heads?
Who told you to swing the knife?

Pandit, think
before you drink
that water!

Think! Think! Figure it out!

Saints and reverences—

Morons and mindless fools—

Enchanted madman—

Look in your heart!

You simple-minded people . . .

The vocative sabotages passivity. If someone shoots you a question, you immediately look for an answer. If someone sneaks behind your chair and whispers, "Why are you slouched over?" you will straighten your back before thinking about it. If someone calls you a lunatic you may be angered or amused, but you will certainly be interested. Addressed affectionately, you will soften and begin to trust—which may just prepare the way for a new, unexpected blow.

The vocative creates intimacy. "Where did two Gods come from?" might be a good opening to a polemical poem. But how different the effect when Kabir says, "Brother, where did your two Gods come from? Tell me, who made you mad?" (ś. 30). The vocative draws the reader, as participant, into highly charged dialogues:

Saints, once you wake up don't doze off.

(ś. 2)

Pandit . . .
tell me where untouchability
came from, since you believe in it.

(ś. 41)

Sometimes an intimate address turns out to be a brazen trick: "Where are you going alone, my friend?" the poet begins softly in ś. 99. A few lines later we realize he is addressing a corpse.

The address may become so aggressive that it must be called an assault, complete with abuses that no decorum moderates:

You go around bent! bent! bent!
Your ten doors are full of hell, you smell
like a fleet of scents, your cracked
eyes don't see the heart, you haven't
an ounce of sense.
Drunk with anger, hunger, sex,
you drown without water.

(ś. 72)

In one shocking opener Kabir calls his listener the "son of a slut." Then he steps out from behind this attention-getter and proceeds with his poem:

Son of a slut!
There: I've insulted you.
Think about getting on the good road.

(ś. 102)

Kabir's provocations often take the form of questions, skillfully inserted to ruffle us up or draw us out. Questions are used in a variety of ways—in openings or conclusions, singly or in series, as bait or goad, as funnel to point our inquiry. Sometimes a single question comes like a sudden jab: "When the pot falls apart, what do you call it?" (ś. 75). The jab may be just a setup: when we rise to it, a hard slap may hit us from another direction. Sometimes questions are shot in rapid series, like blows from a boxer, left, right, left, right, left, right. When they end we may find ourselves staggering:

Who's whose husband? Who's whose wife?
Death's gaze spreads—untellable story.
Who's whose father? Who's whose son?
Who suffers? Who dies?

(ś. 36)

Qazi, what book are you lecturing on?
Yak yak yak, day and night . . .
If God wanted circumcision,
why didn't you come out cut?
If circumcision makes you a Muslim,
what do you call your women? . . .
If putting on the thread makes you Brahmin,
what does the wife put on?
That Shudra's touching your food, pandit!
How can you eat it?
Hindu, Muslim—where did they come from?
Who started this road?
Look in your heart, send out scouts:
where is heaven?

(ś. 84)

In quieter poems questions are a way of approaching an experience that is not accessible to direct statement. In certain cases questions seem to open a space at the end of a poem that is wide and silent (for example, ś. 67, discussed on p. 24 below; and r. 7).

The intimacy created by Kabir's style is not always obvious or entirely conscious, because the audience would often prefer not to identify with his addressees. As readers or listeners, we are more inclined to identify with Kabir. When he conjures up a comic pandit, we laugh. When he exposes the greedy and hypocritical, we scorn. When he reveals the incredible blindness of people who won't face death, we applaud. The use of stock characters allows us to maintain a sense of detachment. We know what a Brahmin priest looks like: he has a shaved head, paints marks on his forehead, dresses in a white pleated loin-cloth, counts his beads, and sits among his paraphernalia of brass trays, sandalwood paste, scriptures and bells, exacting coins from hapless pilgrims. A yogi wears a patchwork cloak and drinks out of a cup made from a skull. A merchant sits amid his wares in the bazaar and holds up his scales, two round plates suspended from strings. These are not descriptions of *us*.

But gradually something begins to gnaw at our consciousness. It occurs to us that pandits can wear other costumes besides the white *dhotī* and rosary of *tulsī* or *rudrākṣa* beads, can sit under other umbrellas than those that front the Ganga at Varanasi. It is relatively easy to notice panditry in the universities, violence in government, greed in the marketplace, phoniness in religion. Then we can spot signals closer at hand, in the gestures and voices of our neighbors. But Kabir's power is most tellingly revealed when his words reverberate in our own skulls, and we see the succession of disguises under which we live our daily lives:

Dropped from the belly at birth,
a man puts on his costumes
and goes through his acts.

(r. 1)

RIDDLES AND SURPRISES

One set of formulas in Kabir clusters around the words *acaraj*—surprise or amazing thing—and *adbhut*—wonderful, marvelous, strange. Formula or not, the promise of amazement stirs up our interest and gives Kabir a further chance to play with us:

Saints, here's a surprise for you.
A son grabbed his mother
while a crazy virgin fell for her father,
dropped her husband but went
to the in-laws.
              Think of that!

(ś. 6)

Related to the "surprise" formula is the "Who will believe it?" formula:

Who can I tell?
And who will believe it?
When the bee touches that flower,
he dies.

The opening questions are teasers, designed to make the reader volunteer, "Tell *me*. *I'll* believe it!" The sudden injection of "that flower"[1] again elicits a curious response—"what flower?"—and the poet is set up for his main exposition:

In the middle of the sky's temple
blooms a flower. . . .

The poem could easily have begun at this point. But the experience is quite different when it begins with the rhetorical questions and the dramatic introduction of flower and bee.

From surprises and incredibilities it is a short step to the pure riddle. A number of poems are framed explicitly as riddles:

Think, pandit, figure it out:
male or female?

(ś. 44)

What will you call the Pure?
Say, creature, how will you mutter the name
of one without hand or foot,
mouth, tongue or ear?

(ś. 94)

Sadhu, that yogi is my guru
who can untie this song.

(ś. 24)

Is there any guru in the world wise enough
to understand the upside-down Veda?

(ś. 111)

As the last example suggests, from the riddling poems it is just another small leap to *ulaṭbāṃsī*, the "upside-down language" of paradoxes and enigmas that Kabir inherited from the Sahajiyas and Naths and adapted to his own purposes:[2]

> The cow is sucking at the calf's teat,
> from house to house the prey hunts,
> the hunter hides.
>
> *(ś. 31)*

> Sprout without seed, branch without trunk,
> fruit without flower, son born
> of a sterile womb, climbing a tree
> without legs . . .
>
> *(ś. 16)*

> It's pouring, pouring, the thunder's roaring,
> but not one raindrop falls.
> . . . . .
> frog and snake lie down together,
> a cat gives birth to a dog,
> the lion quakes in fear of the jackal—
> these marvels can't be told.
>
> *(ś. 52)*

There is a great diversity in the interpretation of the *ulaṭbāṃsī* poems. It has been questioned whether they are authentic, whether their symbols have the same meaning in Kabir as in the tantric tradition, or whether they have any meaning at all. For the purpose of our brief rhetorical inquiry it is enough to note that these poems fascinate while they perplex the reader, that the images stick in consciousness even when their meaning eludes the mind, initiating a dialogue not only between reader and poet but between the reader and himself, which may go on for years. Riddles and their extension, the paradoxes and enigmas of *ulaṭbāṃsī*, besides being effective rhetorical devices, are teaching devices, comparable to the Zen koan—a problem the student can't solve and can't escape, a matrix of verbal impossibilities in which a transparent truth lies hidden—or perhaps, as the Rigvedic hymn has it, does not.[3]

STRUCTURES

It is hazardous to analyze a *pada* by Kabir as if the structure had something inevitable about it. The same song might turn up in another collection in fragments, or with its stanzas reshuffled like a deck of cards. Still, certain principles of structure are apparent; once spotted, they can be recognized again and again. And many poems have a clear unity. They may consist of an extended metaphor, an unfolding argument, a dialogue, or a monologue. These structures reveal both how songs in general are organized for oral performance, and how Kabir in particular organized his utterances to produce the effects he wanted to produce.

Several typical patterns in Kabir depend on repetition with variation. Some poems comprise a series of negations whose syntax can be varied for pleasing effects in

sound and rhythm (ś. 43, r. 6). Some are built on anaphora—repetition of a word at the beginning of each line (rs. 3, 7; ś. 71). Or the repeated word may be scattered in different positions ("died" in ś. 45, "look" in ś. 104). The repeated element may be a grammatical structure, like the if-then clauses of śs. 40, 42, and 84, the parallel sentences of ś. 59, the jabbing questions of śs. 98 and 84.

Some poems are catalogues—of Vishnu's incarnations, famous sages, stereotyped fools (śs. 8, 12, 92, 38). One trick of Kabir's is to take a literary convention and turn it upside down. Other poets use the "ten-avatar" sequence to glorify Vishnu's descents; Kabir uses it to ridicule them (ś. 8). The rainbird (*cātaka*) is normally presented as a touching symbol of longing and devotion. Kabir conjures her up to point out her delusion (ś. 71).

Many poems are constructed as dialogues or monologues (śs. 103, 75, 62, 35). Sometimes a single figure is developed throughout a poem: the cow, the flower, the yogi, the con man (śs. 28, 63, 65, 36). Sometimes a series of parallel examples will be brought together in a conclusion, much as a sonnet may in successive quatrains give illustrations which are summed up in the sestet or couplet (e.g., the dog, lion, and elephant of ś. 76).

Perhaps the most consistent structural device in the lyrics is that of the strong "opener" and "clincher" lines that keep Kabir rhetorically in control. We have seen how proficient he is at seizing the audience's attention with intriguing, challenging, shocking addresses at the beginning. He is just as adept at twisting our noses at the end, summing up the poem in a peculiarly powerful way, turning things around unexpectedly, making a wry comment, or jamming on the brakes with a suddenness that sends us hurtling forward into the darkness.

A very simple example of Kabir's effectiveness in framing his song with rhetorical devices at beginning and end may be seen in ś. 43—a straightforward catalogue of negatives stating, in Upanishadic fashion, what the experience of truth is not:

> There's no creation or creator there,
> no gross or fine, no wind or fire,
> no sun, moon, earth or water,
> no radiant form, no time there,
> no word, no flesh, no faith,
> no cause and effect, nor any thought
> of the Veda. No Hari or Brahma,
> no Shiva or Shakti, no pilgrimage
> and no rituals. No mother, father
> or guru there . . .

The poem is musical and memorable, with the repetitious pattern finely modulated to avoid monotony. The whole piece could have been done in this style. But Kabir has another way. Characteristically, he opens with a sharp challenge: "Pandit, you've got it wrong" (literally, "your ideas are false"). Before we know what the poem is about, there is an engagement. We picture a pandit, Kabir's antagonist. He's got something wrong. What is it? From here on all the negatives also call forth the preaching of the pandit, who is fond of talking of creation, the elements, the heavenly bodies, Vedas, deities, karma, dharma. Behind the negatives is a shadowy foil, who is being continually silenced just as he is about to open his mouth.

The flowing pattern of negative statements is broken abruptly in the middle of the penultimate line with a shooting question: "Is it two or one?" The question snaps us out of the lyrical mode, enclosing in its few syllables the whole point of the dispute between pandits and what is beyond panditry. Without a moment's pause, Kabir concludes: "If you understand now, you're guru, I'm disciple." Now, in immediate response to "two or one?" you can understand what the gurus have wrong. To understand is to know very personally the meaning of the negatives: guru bows to disciple, identities are exchanged, distinctions erased.[4]

Actually these last paraphrases are lame, piling words on words. But the sharp formula, "You're guru, I'm disciple," remains in consciousness, revealing its meaning and appropriateness as the song is heard once, twice, or many times.

Ś. 41 provides a more complex example of a unified poem in which a single metaphor is developed to the point of allegory, and the poet plays certain tricks as he moves from opening to closing:

> Pandit, look in your heart for knowledge.
> Tell me where untouchability
> came from, since you believe in it.
> Mix red juice, white juice and air—
> a body bakes in a body.
> As soon as the eight lotuses
> are ready, it comes
> into the world. Then what's
> untouchable?
> Eighty-four hundred thousand vessels
> decay into dust, while the potter
> keeps slapping clay
> on the wheel, and with a touch
> cuts each one off.
> We eat by touching, we wash
> by touching, from a touch
> the world was born.
> So who's untouched? asks Kabir.
> Only he
> who has no taint of Maya.[5]

The first line presents a typical challenge which (as Kabir's openings are wont to do) cuts the props out from under the addressee. "Pandit, look in your heart for

knowledge"—not in your scriptures and commentaries, not in disputations with your friends. The pandit is crippled: if he follows this initial stricture, he won't be a pandit anymore. But Kabir goes on talking in a reasonable fashion. "Tell me where untouchability came from, since you believe in it." Another step is taken to lock the listener into the argument on Kabir's terms. "Well, yes, I do believe in it," the pandit is bound to say, which obliges him somehow to answer the question, "Where does it come from?" He is used to answering questions—that is his stock-in-trade—but here his usual mode of discourse has been cut off in advance by the injunction, "Look in your heart."

Ostensibly we have begun a dialogue; but in fact (as is often the case with Kabir), the primary speaker has a hammerlock on the argument. Or, to use another combative metaphor, the interlocutor receives two swift blows at the start. While Kabir continues the discussion in a leisurely tone, the pandit gasps, holding his solar plexus.[6]

The next couplet demonstrates the illusoriness of untouchability. All bodies are made of the same essential substances; each body is sealed within another body during its formation. At what point can touch, or defilement, take place? These verses create a very interesting picture of the emergent human being: a clay vessel, a string of lotuses. The lotuses are the chakras, which one almost has to imagine as luminous in the dark hollow of clay. They represent the uniqueness of the human being, the road of liberation, within a creature who is otherwise just an earthy paste of sperm, blood, and breath, like all other creatures.

From this image of an individual person's birth, the poet suddenly shifts perspective to the vast turning of births and deaths in the universe. Millions of clay pots crumble, all have been set up on the same stone wheel, and all are cut off with a touch. "Cutting off" is birth, the separation of the individual.[7] Now the meaning of touching widens. Everything we do in this world is touching, creation itself is a "touch." The word has come to denote duality: it takes two to touch.

The argument in this *pada* turns on Kabir's manipulation of the word *chūti* (modern *chūt*), which is used eight times in seven-and-a-half lines. Basically it means "touch," but in common usage it also means "defiled touch," thence untouchability. By playing on the whole range of possible meanings, Kabir seems to reverse himself. In the first half he says, "No one is touched"; in the second half he says, "No one is untouched." The common argument against untouchability—that everyone is made in the same way from the same stuff, and Shudras are therefore not polluted in relation to Brahmins—receives an uncommon twist. In the new and larger sense of the word *chūti*, the Brahmins are polluted, along with everyone else.

Coming and going, Kabir has proved a radical equality: not only of all people, but of all substances and interactions. The point he makes is no longer social or moral, but ontological. *Chūti* signifies the nature of phenomenal existence, transiency, desire, confusion of birth and death. The only way to be free of that defilement is to end one's contact with Maya.

Ś. 41 is only one of many *padas* whose metaphors and movements could be analyzed closely. Staying with the same general theme, we could find various poems whose imagery emphasizes the essential equality of all beings (all pots are made of one clay, all ornaments are made of one gold, all men and beasts have red blood).[8] Sā. 107 affirms that, as long as truth is not realized, "all four castes are untouchable." Ś. 47 again has a strong personal opening and closing, develops a central metaphor (the river), and works with "clay."

Ś. 75 operates on the audience in a particularly dramatic fashion. It is one of the most extreme examples of abrupt changes, rushing tempo, careening stops, barrages of words that land like blows, sudden questions that set you spinning and are followed (as you might be opening your mouth to reply) by assaults that turn you upside down.

> It's a heavy confusion.
> Veda, Koran, holiness, hell—
> who's man? who's woman?
> A clay pot shot with air and sperm.
> When the pot falls apart, what do you call it?
> Numskull! You've missed the point.

The diction as well as the structure is bruising; it *hurts,* it is designed to *break* something.

> It's all one skin and bone,
> one piss and shit,
> one blood, one meat.
> From one drop, a universe.
> Who's Brahmin? Who's Shudra?

This is not argument, but a direct assault on the structures of belief and self-image. The point that is being hammered across reaches its culmination in "From one drop, a universe." The line has several levels of meaning. It suggests not only a universal substance of creation (which is rather a remote, abstract idea), but also an event or experience that breaks through time: creation is instantaneous, a single act fills the universe, a single thought fills consciousness. Not giving the reader a chance to catch his breath after this climax, Kabir shoots another question: "Who's Brahmin? Who's Shudra?" The next verse may be temporarily comforting, for it is a rote repetition of the Hindu "party line" about the three *guṇas* (qualities of matter) and their association with the three gods: "Brahma *rajas,* Shiva *tamas,* Vishnu *sattva* . . ." But he has opened this line of thinking only to cut it off the more forcefully:

> Kabir says, plunge into Ram!
> There: No Hindu. No Turk.

If you reduce the universe to a drop, then remove (or plunge into) the drop, what do you have? Darkness. No distinctions.

KABIR AS THE GOOD PHYSICIAN

Stanley Fish, in *Self-Consuming Artifacts,* describes an aesthetic which he traces back to Plato and Augustine and demonstrates at length in the works of several seventeenth-century English authors.[9] Though Fish treats the metaphor of the good physician as "one of the most powerful in western literature and philosophy," the aesthetic he elaborates from it is universally applicable. Students of Kabir will vividly recognize their poet in Fish's account of the verbal good physician, who is characterized (in terms based on Plato's *Gorgias*) as a "dialectician" rather than a "rhetorician":

> A dialectical presentation . . . is disturbing, for it requires of its readers a searching and rigorous scrutiny of everything they believe in and live by. It is didactic in a special sense; it does not preach the truth, but asks that its readers discover the truth for themselves, and this discovery is often made at the expense not only of a reader's opinions and values, but of his self-esteem.
>
> . . . The end of a dialectical experience is (or should be) nothing less than a *conversion,* not only a changing, but an exchanging of minds. It is necessarily a painful process . . . in the course of which both parties forfeit a great deal; on the one side the applause of a pleased audience, on the other, the satisfactions of listening to the public affirmation of our values and prejudices.
>
> . . . The good physician may be philosopher, minister, teacher, or even deity, but whatever his status, his strategy and intentions are always the same: he tells his patients what they *don't* want to hear in the hope that by forcing them to see themselves clearly, they will be moved to change the selves they see.
>
> . . . The end of dialectic is not so much the orderly disposition of things in the phenomenal world, as the transformation of the soul-mind into an instrument capable of seeing things in the phenomenal world for what they really are (turning things upside-down). . . .[10]

So Socrates asks in the *Gorgias:*

> To which treatment of the city do you urge me? . . . Is it to combat the Athenians until they become as virtuous as possible, prescribing for them like a physician; or is it to be their servant and cater to their pleasure? . . .[11]

Fish comments that Socrates is here articulating the choice of motives that faces every would-be teacher, writer, or leader:

. . . whether to strive selfishly for a local and immediate satisfaction or to risk hostility and misunderstanding by pursuing always the best interests of his auditors. . . .[12]

Socrates' choice penetrated his acts as well as his words. With clear understanding he risked and incurred hostility, and finally died for his teaching.

Kabir's attitude is the same. He does not hesitate, in the holiest Hindu city, to attack the kingpins of Hindu society ("Saints, the Brahmin is a slicked-down butcher"); or, in a country ruled by Muslims, to ridicule the religion of the emperor (the Turk "crows 'God! God!' like a cock"). If someone tries to smooth over his insults, saying, "No offense," Kabir will cry like Hamlet, "Yes, but there is, and much offense too!"[13] And he will continue to offend. Though he did not, like Socrates, have to die for his outrages, he does speak of being beaten for telling the truth, and he often alludes to his isolation, the difficulty of finding anyone who will listen or understand. His constant effort was to strip away disguises, force confrontations, expose lies, promote honesty at every level. His social-satirical poems, his psychological probes, his poems about death, his crazy and paradoxical and mystical poems, do not inhabit separate categories. They are unified by a principle of radical honesty that sweeps through marketplace, temple, body and mind, that will no more allow you to delude yourself than to cheat others, to hack up the truth than to sever the head of an animal.

Kabir's abrupt and jagged style is a technique to jolt and shock people into facing things, to push them over the edge into an understanding that they fear and yet profoundly long for. It also corresponds to, and tones the mind up for, the actual experience of a sudden, unifying insight in the midst of chaotic temporal events.

Concluding Questions

A self-consuming artifact signifies most successfully when it fails, when it points *away* from itself to something its forms cannot capture.[14]

Kabir may seem to harangue in his more vehement poems against Hindu and Muslim hypocrisy, stupidity, violence, greed. Some of these poems are bound to be inauthentic, for the mode of satirical attack is one of the easiest to imitate. But the variety of Kabir's rhetorical modes and the integrity of the personality that informs them are not easy to imitate. In this rhetoric, the question is as important as the exclamation. We can assemble another pastiche of lines, this time all questions:

For one who doesn't know the secret,
what's the way out?

How to escape the spear?

On this riverbank, saints or thieves?

The three worlds whirl in doubt.
To whom can I explain?

. . . the sky is ripped.
Can a tailor mend it?

What color is a living being?

Where do the senses rest?

Where do the Ram-chanters go?
Where do the bright ones go?

. . . parrot-on-a-pole,
who has caught you?

At whom is Kabir shouting?

In his definition of the dialectical process, Fish describes a change in consciousness of a sort usually spoken of in religious contexts:

In a dialectical experience, one is moved from the first [discursive or rational way of thinking] to the second way, which has various names, the way of the good, the way of the inner light, the way of faith; but whatever the designation, the moment of its full emergence is marked by the transformation of the visible and segmented world into an emblem of its creator's indwelling presence . . . , and at that moment the motion of the rational consciousness is stilled, for it has become indistinguishable from the object of its inquiry.[15]

Though Fish avoids the troublesome word, what he is talking about is often called mystical experience. When the distinction between subject and object disappears ("consciousness . . . indistinguishable from the object of its inquiry"), the self disappears. We say this coolly, though in fact we have said nothing. It is an unabstractable, indescribable experience. That a person should drop, even for a moment, the conviction of separate selfhood, is the most unlikely eventuality in the world. Any author who can lead his audience to the edge of such an experience has proved himself skillful indeed.

Discussing Augustine, Fish further describes this transformation of consciousness:

The Christian rhetorician believes in a world everywhere informed and sustained by God's presence . . . a world that, because it is without parts, is without hierarchies, either of persons or of actions. Techniques for dividing and distinguishing, including the rules of rhetoric, are therefore antithetical to his purpose, which is not to persuade to a point, but to a vision in which all points are one (he works to turn the world, as we naturally know it, upside-down). . . .[16]

"Dividing and distinguishing" is the chief activity of the mind and its most powerful tool. It is also, in the view of Fish's authors, and of Kabir, the chief barrier to our understanding things as they actually are. The elaborate tension that Fish so skillfully illuminates in Herbert, Bunyan, and other English authors reflects the interesting fact that the mind is—or seems to be—the only means we have for understanding the truth, even if the truth we are reaching for includes the realization that the mind and its ways of perceiving are false. One thinks of Heisenberg destroying the myth of the precise observations of science by proving that the observations are irredeemably distorted by the interference of the measuring device. The dialectician (a word that sounds more rational than *mystic*) responds to the problem by trying to create awareness of the process of dividing and distinguishing, somehow causing the mind to mirror itself, so as initially to engender a doubt about the reliability of our perceptions, and ultimately to dissolve the tight network of divisions and categories in which we are ensnared.

It is one of Kabir's specialties to raise the problem of distinction. He asks, "Is it two or one?" He hovers over boundary lines, or imagined boundary lines—especially those that have to do with our sense of identity.

> Kabir says, how to work it out—
> I—he—you?
>
> *(sā. 312)*

> . . . if you understand now,
> you're guru, I'm disciple.
>
> *(ś. 1)*

He circles around the question of origin, differentiation, the existence of any separate entity, prodding us to determine priority. Which is greater? Which came first? To answer that we have to determine which is which. In ś. 112 he treats this profound metaphysical question as if it were the stuff of a children's argument:

> This is the big fight, King Ram.
> Let anyone settle it who can.
> Is Brahma bigger or where he came from?
> Is the Veda bigger or where it was born from?
> Is the mind bigger or what it believes in?
> Is Ram bigger or the knower of Ram?
> Kabir turns round, it's hard to see—
> Is the holy place bigger, or the devotee?

The questions all ask us to solve the problem of differentiation. At what point in consciousness is something "born"? When does it separate from "what it was born from"? Where is the line between knower and known? Mind and what is believed in? Outside (holy place) and inside (devotee)?[17]

In one *sākhī* he settles the question in an unsettling way:

> If I say one, it isn't so.
> If I say two, it's slander.

> Kabir thinks carefully:
> As it is,
> so it is.
>
> *(sā. 120)*

Where assertions are inescapably false, questions are conclusions. Kabir opens ś. 67 with a question to end questions:

> If seed is form is god,
> then, pandit, what can you ask?

If source is the same as realization, conception not separate from creation, and will or creator not separable either ("from one drop, a universe"), then . . . ? Kabir goes on with more questions, but now they seem like mere echoes of the pandit's untenable distinctions, borne away with the breath of Kabir's "where? . . . where?"

> Where is the mind?
> Where is the intellect?
> Where is the ego?
> The three qualities,
> *sattva, rajas, tamas*?

In the next line—"Nectar and poison bloom, fruits ripen"—the poet evokes the whole process of birth, death, karma, recalling lines from the first *ramainī*:

> No one knows this ineffable movement.
> How could one tongue describe it?
> If any man has a million mouths and tongues,
> let that great one speak.

Then, in the same sweeping, unexplained style, there is a reference to the possibility of freedom from the interlocking causes and effects of karma:

> The Vedas show many ways
> to cross the sea.

Finally, in a line that seems to focus on the pronouns "you" and "me," but where these are marvelously balanced, as a juggler balances balls, with other pronouns ("I . . . who . . . who"), the poet asks his most revealing and most conclusive question:

> Kabir says, what do I know
> of you and me,
> of who gets caught
> and who goes free?

Notes

1. The demonstrative pronoun *that* does not appear in Hindi; but the effect is much the same, as Hindi syntax allows the sentence to begin with *flower*.

2. See Appendix A for an account of the history of *ulaṭbāṃsī* in Indian tradition, and analyses of *ulaṭbāṃsī* poems by Kabir.

3. I refer to Rigveda X:129, sometimes called "Hymn of Creation." There are many translations. For example: A. L. Basham, *The Wonder That Was India* (London, 1954), pp. 247-48, reprinted in Mercea Eliade, *From Primitives to Zen* (New York: Harper & Row, 1977), pp. 109-11; *The Upanishads,* trans. Juan Mascaró (Baltimore: Penguin, 1965), pp. 9-10; *Sources of Indian Tradition,* ed. W. T. de Bary (New York: Columbia University Press, 1958), pp. 15-16.

4. There is another level of meaning for *jo aba kī būjhai*—"[the one] who understands now." Since the postposition *ki* cannot stand alone, the feminine noun *bāt* is mentally inserted after it. *Bāt* means matter, point, subject. "If you understand the 'matter of now'" can mean not only, "If you understand what I just said," but also, "If you understand *nowness.*"

5. See also ś. 41, n. 1.

6. Socrates, most famous of dialoguists, tends to have the same sort of hammerlock on his conversations. It often seems that his young interlocutors are there only to say, "Certainly, Socrates," "That is beyond doubt," or "It seems impossible to avoid that conclusion."

7. Indian readers will also be aware of the significance of saying eighty-four hundred thousand vessels: only once in that many lives does the *jīva* (living being) attain human birth, the unique opportunity to become liberated.

8. See śs. 30 and 70.

9. Berkeley: University of California Press, 1972.

10. Fish, pp. 1-7.

11. Quoted in Fish, p. 20.

12. Fish, pp. 20-21.

13. *Hamlet,* I.5.136-37 in *The Complete Works of Shakespeare,* ed. W. J. Craig (London: Oxford University Press, 1922), p. 1015. I have Americanized the spelling.

14. Fish, p. 4.

15. Ibid., p. 3.

16. Ibid., p. 39.

17. Another wonderful example of this sort of questioning discourse is in the *Granthāvalī, pada* 164, p. 107 in the Das edition:

> King Ram, I don't know how the unmanifest manifests.
> Tell me how to speak of your form.
> Was the sky first or the earth, lord,
> was the wind first, or the water?
> Was the moon first or the sun, lord?
> Which was first, all-knower?
> Was breath first or body, lord,
> was blood first or semen?
> Was man first or woman, lord,
> was seed first or field?
> Was day first or night, lord,
> was sin first or merit?
> Kabir says, where the pure one dwells,
> is there something there or nothing?

David C. Scott (essay date 1985)

SOURCE: Scott, David C. "Kabir's Religious Doctrines and Practices." In *Kabir's Mythology,* pp. 205-220. Delhi, India: Bharatiya Vidya Prakashan, 1985.

[*In the following excerpt, Scott explores the pathway to salvation that is set forth in the poetry of Kabir.*]

"BHAKTI"

> The *bhakti* of Rām is hard to obtain;
>   it is not for cowards.
> Sever your head with your own hands,
>   and then invoke *rām-nām.*[1]
> From the top of the pyre the *satī*[2] calls; Listen, friend Masan,[3]
> The people, mere wayfareres, have gone way, only you and I remain at the end.[4]
> The hero[5] taking spear in hand, donning the (ochre) robe of *sahaja*[6]
> Mounting the elephant of (supreme) knowledge, he is ready to die on the battlefield.[7]

For Kabīr, the way that leads to salvation is not, as most Vaiṣṇava(s) believe, an easy way. It is rather, an abrupt, rugged path which few can find and even fewer can follow. Real *bhakti* is conceived of a heroic[8] path, open only to those who have renounced the comforts and pleasures of this life, who have put behind themselves all desire or hope for bodily satisfaction and fulfillment and who strive stubbornly for the summit at the risk of their lives. For Kabīr, as for many *Sūfī*(s), the true lover, the seeker has a tryst with death. The soul striving for salvation is compared with the *satī,* the faithful wife who fearlessly leaves her home to climb the pyre[9] and be reunited in death with her beloved Spouse, or the Rājput *sūr,* who comes down to the battlefield in order to fulfil his pledge of fighting to the death. Indeed, Kabīr's imagination appears haunted by these two heroic figures, the *satī* and the *sūr,* who in the Hindu tradition embody the highest ideal of perfect love and [undaunted loyalty and who by their prior death gain release from the bonds of time and so cheat Death, personified as Yama.[10] Rām, or the mysterious *sahaja* state, which the tāntrics conceive of as *mahā-sukha,* the supreme or perfect bliss, for Kabīr is only to be had at the cost of one's life. Indeed, he who wishes to be a *jīvanmukta,*[11] "one liberated while living", must of necessity be *jīvanmṛta*,[12] "one dead while alive". But this "death" is in reality, the condition for the true "life" of the *jīvanmukta*.[13]

> The world is continually dying, but no one knows how to die;
> Kabīr, so die that you will not have to die again.[14]
>
> If I burn the house, it is saved; if I preserve the house it is lost.[15]
> I have seen an astonishing thing: a dead man has swallowed Death.[16]

The love symbolism of the *bhakti* tradition is common in Kabīr's poetry, but it is significant that the pleasurable aspect of human love is not considered an adequate symbol for the union of the soul with the ultimate Reality. Rather, it is the painful aspect, the pangs of separation, known in the *bhakti* tradition as *virah*, which suggest to the *julāhā* the painful longing of the soul who has not yet obtained the beatific vision of the divine Beloved.[17]

> There is no solace during the night or during the day, no solace even dreams;
> Kabīr, he who is separated from Rām finds no relief in sunshine or shade.[18]
> The eyes bring forth a torrent (of tears), the water wheel works day and night;[19]
> Like a *papihā* bird, I cry *piu, piu*[20] O Rām when will you come to me?[21]
> The *guru* lit the fire and the disciple was burnt, consumed in the fire of *virah*;
> The poor little blade of grass was saved by embracing the truss of hay.[22]

In the secular realm, *virah* is a favourite theme of poetry, especially of folk-ballads and folk-songs. The *virah-gīt*(s), sung by village women, mostly describe the painful longings and pitiful laments of a young wife waiting in vain for the return of her beloved spouse at beginning of the rainy season. Such songs are full of "messages" sent by the languishing wife to the oblivious husband, of sorrowful confidence to the heroine's girl friend, the *sakhī*, of tearful entreaties, with frequent allusions to the celebrated water birds whose pathetic cries over rivers and ponds at night are believed to the lovers' calls and which increases the torments of the *virahiṇī*.

Kabīr has evidently made use of these village songs: the pathetic *virahiṇī* of the folk-song becomes the symbol of the human soul wounded by "the arrow of the *śabd*",[23] and pining for the vision of her divine Spouse, Rām. The situation of the young girl married in infancy, who reaches adolescence without having ever met her Lord—a tragic situation, typically Hindu—is one of Kabīr's favourite symbols to suggest the situation of the *jīva* who, though already belonging to God and totally pervaded by his presence, has not yet been able to "meet" him: she longs for the meeting or Vision

which would consummate the union and make her at last a *suhāginī*, a happy wife.[24] But, here, it is no longer distance or the husband's forgetfulness that is the real obstacle—is in the real *virah-gīt*(s)—since the divine Spouse is always present within. The fault lies with the wife-soul herself since it is the impurity of her love that makes her spiritually blind. Only through enduring patiently the tormenting but purifying "fire"[25] of *virah* and ultimately giving up her life in that inextinguishable fire can the wife-soul obtain that total union of herself in her true Husband, Rām.

Kabīr's devotion, then, differs from that of Vaiṣṇava *bhakti* not only in its objects, but also in its character. It does not consist only of the sentiments of tenderness, trust and abandon, of which the entire *bhakti* literature provides so many examples. It is also, and all, an ardent quest, a heroic adventure in which the *bhakta* is completely involved at the peril of his life. Indeed, Kabīr's conception of divine love seems to be an original synthesis of the *yoga* and *Sūfī* traditions, the former exalting human effort, and the latter making of the yearnings, of the torments suffered by the exiled soul in its mortal condition, the necessary *sine qua non* of every spiritual ascension. For Kabīr, then, *bhakti* is no longer the "easy path", but the path of suffering, vigils and tears. Nor is there any other. This suffering has its source in the separation, at least apparent, of the soul its Beloved. However, the suffering itself is mystery, hidden from profane eyes. Nothing of it appears externally;[26] rather, he who loves "bleeds silently in the depths of his soul, as the insect devours the wood". Only God can understand the mysterious nature of the disease of *virah*.

> O Vaid,[27] return home; your cure is useless.
> He who created the body; he alone will cure it.[28]

In addition to the basic *bhakti* emphasis, we find in Kabīr's works the more important of its corollaries. There must be fear of God,[29]—though perhaps the word "awe" expresses this attitude more accurately—a recognition of His infinite immensity and of His absolute authority.

> Without fear[30] (of God) emotion[31] does not arise; without emotion there is no love;[32]
> When there is fear in the heart characteristic good sentiments pervade.[33]
> Fear (of God) is heavy and hard to bear; the wayward *man*, with its unrestrained expressions, is weak.
> He who carries the fear (of God) on his head[34] by the *guru*'s grace can bear its weight.
> Without such fear no one crosses (the ocean of existence),[35] but if one dwells in fear, to it is added love.[36]

The same sentiment of overpowering awe is the cause of Kabīr's humility in the presence of divine greatness.

In myself, there is nothing of mine, all there is Thine;
Whatever I offer to Thee is thine already, how can the
   gift be mine?[37]

There must also be complete surrender to God, an unconditioned submission in faith.

If a woman, said to belong to her beloved, keeps
   company with another,
If she keeps a paramour in her heart how can she find
   pleasure with her Lord?[38]

Without purity[39] how can a woman be a *satī*, O Pandit
   understand and ponder this in your heart.
Without love how can the relationship[40] remain
   steadfast; where there is selfish passion, there is no
   (true) relationship.
The devotee who loves the Lord[41] selfishly, that
   passion-seeking one will never meet the Lord, not
   even in his dreams.
She who devotes herself, body, soul, wealth and
   household, Kabīr calls that one a happy wife.[42]

Kabīr make the vermillion mark,[43] do not use col-
   lyrium;[44]
Have the Beloved ensconced in your eyes, do not
   permit another,[45]

Kabīr, I am the dog of Rām, "Mutiyā" is my name;
With Rām's chain around my neck, wherever He
   leads, I go.[46]

There must also be the singing of God's praises, a practice in which the *julāhā* is continually engaged.[47]

The limbs anointed with perfume, sandal paste and
   (sweet smelling) oils,
Shall be burnt with wood.
What is there praiseworthy in the body and in wealth?
After falling on the earth they cannot be resurrected.
They who sleep at night work during the day,
Who never for a moment utter Hari's Name,
Who rule[48] and who chew *pān*[49]
Shall at the time of death be as firmly bound as
   thieves.
They who under the *guru*'s guidance lovingly sing of
   the greatness[50] of Hari
They will become absorbed in Rām Himself and find
   joy.
He who graciously established His Name,
Has pervaded me with His sweet smelling odours,
Says Kabīr, think, O (spiritually) blind,
Rām is true and all worldly occupations are false.[51]

All these are aspects of traditional *bhakti* and they represent a significant area of agreement between the Vaisnava *bhakta*(s) on the one hand and Kabīr on the other. There are, however, in addition to those already discussed two basic differences separating them. In the first place, there is in Kabīr's works an explicit rejection of *avatār*(s).[52] Like the *Sant*(s) he addressed his devotion directly to God Himself, supreme and non-incarnated, not to any manifestation of intermediary. Secondly, there is Kabīr's understanding of the practical

expression of love, enunciated in his interpretation of *nām sumiran* or *nām japa*. This interpretation is of fundamental importance. It provides the heart of his discipline and in it we find his distinctive understanding of the believers' proper response.

"NĀM SAMIRAN"

Remember Rām, remember Rām, remember Rām, O
   Brother;
Without remembering the Name of Rām the majority
   drown (in the ocean of existence).[53]
Wife, son, body, house and pleasurable wealth,
None of these will be yours when Kāl finally arrives.
The wicked Ajāmila[54] and the prostitute did many vile
   things
But they crossed over (the ocean of existence) by
   repeating
Rām's name,
You have taken birth[55] from pigs and dogs, and yet
   you are not ashamed.
Why do you neglect the ambrosia[56] of Rām's Name
   and take poison instead?
Abandon the confusion of (ritually) prescribed and
   forbidden acts and take the Name of Rām.
By the grace of the *guru*, says the servant Kabīr, make
   Rām your beloved.[57]
Kabīr, remembrance is the essence,[58] all else is
   entanglement;
From beginning to end, I have searched everything all
   else I see is Kāl.[59]
Millions of actions are instantly erased by the slightest
   mention of the Name;
The merits acquired during endless ages, without (the
   Name of) Rām, will not get you anywhere.[60]

The divine order of things, as expressed in the law of *karma,* ensures that one must reap in accordance with what one sows. In order to banish the influence of committed sin the individual must sow the seed which bears not the baneful fruit of transmigration, but the blessed fruit of union. This seed is love of the divine Name.

But how does one "love the Name?" What is meant, in Kabīr's usage, by the expression *nām sumiran* or *nām japa*?

Nām has already been dealt with.[61] The divine Name is the revelation of God's being, the sum total of his attributes, the aggregate of all that may be affirmed concerning him. The two verbs which are normally attached to *nām* are *japanā* and *sumiran* neither of which can be adequately translated into English in the context of Kabīr's usage. *Japanā* mean "to repeat", and is used in connection with the recital of a divine name or *mantra*. In many contexts this literal translation is entirely appropriate, for mechanical repetition of this kind, often with the help of a rosary, was a very common practice. Mere mechanical repetition was not however, Kabīr's practice, even though some references might indeed suggest that Kabīr seems to adhere to the dominant Vaiṣṇava belief in the magical power of the invocation of the divine Name as a means of instant salvation.

> Through his previous wrong doings, man has collected a bundle of poison.[62]
> But millions of actions are instantly erased if he but takes (the Name of) Hari on his lips.[63]

Such examples, must however, be read in the context of Kabīr's experience of divine greatness and omnipotence. Here is a case of hyperbole, an effort to convey the immensity of God's power and not a claim that the mere mechanical mention of a single name or syllable is an assured path to salvation.[64] Indeed, we have Kabīr's own contention:

> Every one goes around saying "Rām, Rām, but Rām is not found in this way.[65]

Simple repetition of this kind is not enough, regardless of how devout the repetition may be or how sophisticated a system may be built around the practice. It is a pattern which can include the repetition of a chosen word or brief formula, but only if the emphasis is on the interiorizing of the utterance, upon the paramount need of understanding the word so uttered and of exposing one's total being to its deepest meanings.

Sumiraṇā, "to remember" or "to hold in remembrance", is more helpful, for "remembering the Name" is nearer to a description of Kabīr's practice than "repeating the Name".[66] It too, however, falls short of an adequate description. How then, is the practice to be described? Kabīr himself provides us with a definition.

> To repeat the Name of Rām is to establish Rām in the *man.*[67]

And the method whereby this establishment is carried out is meditation—meditation on the nature of God, on his qualities and his attributes as revealed in the Word (*śabd*).

> Kabīr, in this world meditate on Hari, since He pervades the whole universe:
> Those who meditate not on Hari's Name have been born in vain.[68]

> Meditate on Hari, my brothers
> Meditate peacefully so that the essential thing is not lost,[69]
> Make your body the churn. your *man* the churning stick;
> Into this churn put the *sabad.*
> Make meditation on Hari your churning
> So that by the *guru*'s grace you may produce the ambrosia.
> Says Kabīr, the devotee who fearlessly meditates thus
> Will with the aid of Rām's Name gain the (opposite) shore.[70]

The worship[71] which we offer is meditation[72] on the Name for without the Name there can be no (true) worship.[73]

This meditation on the nature and qualities of God is the core of Kabīr's religious discipline. The Word reveals the absoluteness of God. Meditate on this and make your submission before Him.

> As I meditate on Hari's perfections, I am pierced by many arrows
> I am pierced but I do not flee, Kabīr endures (the pain).[74]

The Word reveals the eternally stable permanence of God, the eternity of God. Reflect on this and abandon the fickle, fleeting world. The Word reveals the absolute freedom of God from all that is *māyā.* Meditate on this and so separate yourself from its deceits. The Word reveals the ineffable greatness of God. Reflect on this and humble yourself before Him.

> The Creator[75] possesses endless excellent qualities but not a single defect;[76]
> If I search my own heart, all the defects are in me.[77]

It is a meditation which must overflow in words and deeds which accord with the nature of the Name. It is remembrance of God *manasā, vācā, karmana*[78] in thought, word and deed.

This is the practical response which a believer is required to make. Meditate in love and you shall grow towards and into Him who is the object of your devotion and your meditation. It is a discipline whose roots are to be found in the Āgamic practice of *japa* as well as the Sūfī tradition of *dhikr* and after Kabīr, has been developed, interpreted and expounded again and not only by Nānak and his immediate successors but by devout Sikhs ever since,[79]

This meditation must be individual and it must also have a corporate application. Kabīr emphasized both.

> Says Kabīr, never cease meditating on the greatness of *rāmnām.*[80]

> Kabīr, in the company of a true believer,[81] love doubles day by day;
> But the Sakta is like a black rug,[82] wash it but it never becomes white.[83]

Indeed, the importance of the company of true believers (the *satsag*) as a vehicle of enlightenment is strongly stressed by Kabīr.

> Says Kabīr, if the benefit of saintly company is part of your destiny;[84]
> Through it salvation is obtained and the impassable gorge is not obstructed.[85]

The Creator who fashioned the universe and watches
   over it, dwells in every heart;
By the *guru*'s guidance He is made manifest in (the
   company of) true believers.[86]

Kabīr, the company of true believers ought to be
   sought daily;
They will drive away wickedness and show you wis-
   dom.[87]

Kabīr, blessed that day when you meet the saints;[88]
Embrace them intimately and sin will be washed
   away.[89]

The traditional figure of the sandalwood tree is also
used in this connection.

Kabīr, just as the fragrance of the sandal tree[90]
   pervades the *ḍhāk-palāś*;[91]
It has made all that surrounds it like itself.[92]

The activity of the true believer in the *satsag* is the
singing of divine praises rather than the function implied
by the word meditation, but *nām-sumiraṇ* covers both,
for both are concerned with God and with the individu-
al's approach to Him. Music has always been used and
the corporate singing of God's praise by His devotees is
something of which Kabīr heartily approved.

The purified believer who sings perfect qualities of
   Hari;
Such a devotee is extremely pleasing to me (says
   Kabīr).[93]

Meditation on the divine Name and the singing of
praises must have seemed easy to many, but Kabīr
declares them to be otherwise, as we have already
noted.[94]

Kabīr, it is extremely difficult to invoke Hari's Name:
As when performing (acrobatics) above a (impaling)
   stake, he who falls is lost.[95]

They are difficult, and few are prepared to make the
sacrifice which they demand. Those who do accept the
discipline, however find that the reward far outweighs
the sacrifice.

Kabīr. If i repeat the Name I live; if I forget it I die.
Repeating the *rām-nām* is hard, but if one hungers for
   it and partakes of it all sadness goes.[96]

This then, is the discipline. The human body is a field
in which the seed of the divine Name is sown. Cultivate
it with love, humility, fear of God, true living, purity
and patience, and thus you shall reap your reward.

Regard your body as a field, your *man* as the plough,
   your actions the ploughing and effort irrigation;
(In the fields) sow the Name as seed, level it with
   contentment, and fence it with humility.
Kabīr, let your actions be those of love, (the seed) will
   then sprout and you will cross the ocean of exist-
   ence.[97]

Love is the soil, holiness the water, and true and
   contentment the two buffaloes.
Humility is the plough, the *man* the ploughman,
   remembrance (of the Name) the watering, and union
   (with God) the seed-time.
The Name is the seed and grace the crop, while the
   world is wholly false.
Kabīr, if the Merciful One is gracious all separation
   (from Him) comes to an end.[98]

[. . .] our interest has been engaged by a man whose
immense popularity throughout the Indian subcontinent
is due as much to his mystical perceptions as to his
maverick nature, a synthesis which is the distinctive
religion and lifestyle of the *julāhā* from Banāras who
has long been hailed by all Indians as the "man for all
seasons", the universal man. What other human being is
hailed as a Hindu *bhakta,* a Muslim *pīr,* a Sikh *bhagat,*
an *avatār,* a champion of Hindu-Muslim unity, a bold
enemy of the superstition and empty ritual of orthodox
Hindus as well as the dogmatism and bigotry of
Muslims, an ardent foe of caste and class distinctions,
indeed of all forms of social discrimination? Surely,
Kabīr is the embodiment of true nonconformity. Surely,
Kabīr is one of those rare persons to appear on the
stage of human history, an embodiment of creative
spontaneity, of all that is "free, noble and challenging in
the Indian tradition".[99]

Notes

1. K. Gr., Sa. 14.18.

2. The feminine from of the Skt. *sat,* "truth", hence a
   true, chaste, faithful wife whose life is patterned
   on that of her namesake, the daughter of the sage
   Dakṣa, who took her own life on the sacrificial
   fire, *jwālā-mukhi,* when her husband Śiva was
   publicly insulted by his father-in-law. The term
   has come to be applied to all wives or widows
   who immolate themselves, as well as to the act of
   immolation.

3. *masān*: (H. *śmaśān*), "the cremation ground" is
   conceived of as a frightful place, haunted by
   ghosts and evil fiends. A vivid description of this
   may be found in the opening verses of the *Vetāla-
   pacaviśatika* of the *Bṛhatkathāsaritsāgara,* a
   marvelous English translation of which has been
   rendered by prof. J. A. B. van Buitenen in *Tales of
   Ancient India* (Chicago: University of Chicago
   Press, 1973). Though I could find no suggestion
   of it in the Indian commentaries, we cannot
   dismiss Dr. Vaudeville's contention that the *masān*
   addressed by the *satī* may well refer to the dread-
   ful goddess Masānī, also known as Śmaśāna-
   bhairavī, a form of the goddess Durgā.

4. K. Gr. Sa. 14.3.

5. *sūrai*: (H. *sūr*), lit. "a valiant" or "brave man",
   "hero", such characteristics are associated with the

martial *kṣatriya,* whose duty is to fight and for whom death on the battle field is the highest. The reference is, of course, to the soul.

6. *pahirā sahaj sajog:* lit. "wearing the apparel fit for *sahaja*", refers to the Rājput custom of a warrior, determined to die in last desperate fight, putting on the *sasajognyāsi*'s ochre robe as symbol of his voluntary renunciation of life.

7. K. Gr., Sa. 14.27.

8. In the *Kabīr-granthāvali* there is an *ag* or section each of *pad*(s) and sākhī(s) entitled *Suratan* or "Heroism".

9. The reader's attention is directed to some significantly suggestive sections of Prof. Willard Johnson's article, "Death and the Symbolism of Renunciant Mysticism", *Asian Religions/History of Religion, 1973 Proceedings,* American Academy of Religion Annual Meeting, pp. 12-22. One of the characteristics of Dr. Johnson's concept of "renunciant mysticism" is what he terms "the call of the funeral pyre", following Gaston Bachelard. Johnson goes on to quote from Bachelard's *The Psychoanalysis of Fire* a Passage which describes the death of mayflies attracted to burning logs, which he notes could just as well have been written on the image of the Indian funeral pyre.

> "Love, death and fire are united at the same moment. Through its sacrifice in the heart of the flames, the mayfly gives us a lesson in eternity. This total death which leaves no trace is the guarantee that our whole person has departed for the beyond. To lose everything in order to gain everything".

Johnson then observes: "One could hardly argue that ordinary men 'hear' the call of the funeral pyre. But as Indian mysticism developed, this old Vedic myth of death negation was adopted to the mystical path of escaping death. If one is 'already dead' one cannot die again: one has [a] further meaningful relation to death' (Johnson, op. cit., p. 14). See also K. Gr., Sa. 14.23; 14.24; 14.37; 14.41.

10. See supra, p. 208.

11. The final aim of the Nāth *siddha*(s) and other *haṭha-yogī*(s) is *jīvan-mukti* and it is this state of liberation which is synonymous with immortality. While other schools of thought regard the final dissolution of the physical body as indispensable for liberation, the *siddha*(s) seek liberation in a transformed or transmaterialized body, which [is called the] "perfected" body. See S. B. Dāsgupta, op. cit., pp. 251-255.

12. In addition to the idea of *jīvanmukta,* Kabīr also borrows that of *jīvanmrta,* from the Nāth *siddha*'s and applies it to the mystic engaged in *bhakti,* who has sacrificed his earthly life. See supra, p. 218, n. 197.

13. "The devottee makes the essential renunciation of the physical and consequently is released from its bondage to be participant in the immortal divine. . . . Mortality is transcended through the means of a symbolic death. . . . This kind of understanding of death sees it not as a fearsome loss of all that is dear, to be avoided at all cost, but rather as a powerful means of self-transformation, to be sought as a final resolution to the problem of mortality". (W. Johnson, op. cit., p. 14).

14. K. Gr., Sa. 19.1. In this and the following *sākhī* we have excellent examples of Kabīr's *ultabāsī*(s) or paradoxical poems, evidently patterned on the *sandhābhāṣā* of the tāntric Sahajiyā and Nāth-panthi masters. See supra, p. 29, n. 89 and also p. 48, n. 170.

15. i.e. if the gross body is abolished through the process of *yoga,* immortality in the *shahaja* is achieved, whereas if it remains as it is there is no hop of ending the natural round of *karma-sasāra.*

16. K. Gr., Sa. 19.12 *muā kāl kau khāi:* lit. 'the dead one ate Kāl." The "dead" man is the *jīvanmrta* who is the only conqueror of Kāl, Death.

17. In Kabīr's poetry and in the Sant tradition generally, the notion of *virah,* the tormenting desire of the soul for the absent Beloved, bears a resemblance to the Sūfī notion of *ishq,* the state in which "the Divine influence inclines the soul towards the love of God", and *shauq,* "the yearning to be constantly with God".

18. K. Gr., Sa. 2.15.

19. *rahaṭ:* the noria of a Persian water wheel. Though most Indian commentators see in the unending flow of water in the water wheel the ceaseless flowing of the lover's tears, Dr. Vaudeville sees the symbolism of *sasāra* in which "the helpless *jīva* ceaselessly passes from one body to another".

20. *papihā* is a popular name for the *cātaka* bird, the "Rainbird" (*Clamator jacobinus,* pied crested cuckoo), which in Hindu lore and legend is conceived as ceaselessly thirsting for the Svāti raindrop since it will drink no other water. The pathetic cry of the *cātaka* is: *piu, piu* "Beloved, beloved".

21. K. Gr., Sa. 2.48.

22. K. Gr., Sa. 2.50. *gali pūre kai lāgi:* because of the context one is inclined to follow Dr. Vaudeville in seeing *pūre* as the oblique from of *pūrā* (Tiwārī, *Kabīr-granthāvali* renders *pūlā* as an alternate reading) meaning a bundle of grass, rather than take *pūre* as *pūrṇa,* "full" or "plentitude", referring to the supreme Reality as some Indian com-

mentators do. In either case the meaning is clear enough: the *jīva* is saved by embracing the Absolute.

23. See K. Gr., Sa 1.7; 1.9; 1.12; 1.22; 2.35, 2.55. 14.5; 22.4; 22.15; etc.

24. See K. Gr., the *pad* section *Prem* and the *sākhī* section *Prem Virah Kau Ag* in their entirety but more especially Pd. 6, 11, 13, 15, 18; Sa. 2.9; 2.18; 2.23; 2.25; 2.31; 2.45 and also 9.7; A. G., Gauḍī 65; Sūhī 2.3.

25. e.g. K. Gr., Sa. 2.5; 2.8.

26. e.g. K. Gr., Sa. 2.7; 2.17.

27. i.e. a practitioner of the Ayurvedic system of medicine.

28. K. Gr., Sa. 2.14. P. N. Tiwārī notes an alternative reading for the last line. *jin yāh bhār ladāiyā; nirbāhegā soy,* i.e. "He who laid on the burden; he alone will cure it".

29. In Kabīr's works there is to be found evidence of two kinds of fear, with opposing attitudes to each. The first is the fear of being tempted by the world and the perdition which results from succumbing. The proper attitude here is *nirbhai* (H. *nirbhay*), K. Gr., Sa. 1.27; A. G., Sl. 5. or *anabhai* (H. *abhay*), A. Gr., Sl. 180, terms which belong to the vocabulary of tāntric *yoga. Abhayapada,* a state of absolute "fearlessness" belongs to the perfect *yogī* or *siddha,* whom nothing can move. It coincides with the perfect *sahaja* state from which there is no fear of falling back into the fetters of *sasāra.* Among the works attributed to Gorakhnāth by Dr. Mohan Singh is one called *Abhai-mantra;* see S. B. Dāsgupta, op. cit., p 374, n. 1. The second is the fear of God and it is an attitude to be cultivated.

30. *bhai* (H. *bhay*): has many meanings, including "fear" and "awe".

31. *bhāv* (H.): has numerous connotations, among them "intention", "emotion", "sentiment".

32. *prīti* (H.): indicates "satisfaction", "pleasure", "love".

33. K. Gr., Sa. 15:85. It is difficult to understand why Vaudeville renders the second line (*jab hirdai sau bhai bhayā, tab miṭī sakala rasa rīti*) as "When fear is not present in the heart, all other good sentiments vanish". Further, it is not clear why see opines, "This sakhi . . . was probably wrongly attributed to Kabīr", in spite of the fact that she acknowledges its appearance in the Pamcavāṇī literature of the Dādū-panthī(s), as well as the generally reliable Sarbāngī of Rajjabdās.

34. *man*: in this context is probably as a *double-entendre,* referring both to the *man* as well as to the thought faculty, situated in the head.

35. See supra, p. 214, n. 173.

36. K. Gr., Pd. 81.

37. K. Gr., Sa. 6.2.

38. *khasam* (H.): means both "husband", as well as "Lord", or "Master". K. Gr., Sa. 11.5.

39. *sat* (H. *satya*): lit. "true" or "pure".

40. *sneh* (H.): lit. "affection", partiality", friendship", hence relationship.

41. *sāhani* (H. *sāh*): lit. "gentleman" or "richman".

42. A. G. Gauḍī 23. *suhāganī* (H.): lit. "happy wife", is another example of Kabīr's commonly used soul/wife metaphor. See supra, pp. 233-34.

43. *sidūr* (H.): the vermillion, red lead, applied to the parting of a married woman's hair as a sign of marital fidelity.

44. *kājar* (H. *kājal*): lamp-black or antimony, used as collyrium on the eyes, is a poetic image of worldly attachments.

45. K. Gr., Sa. 11.13; cf. A. G., Gauḍī 69.

46. K. Gr., Sa. 6.1; cf. A. G., Sl. 74.

47. The majority of the verses of praise are concentrated in the K. Gr., Padāvalī sections 1 and 3, entitled "Satgurumahimā" and "Nau (*Nām*) Mahimā" respectively and in the *sākhī* sections 1 and 3, "Satgurumahimā kau Ag" and "Sumiraṇ Bhajan Mahimā". They are also to be found liberally sprinkled throughout the A. G., collections. See e. g. A. G., Gauḍī 17, 26, 48; Āsā 4; Dhanāsarī 5; Sūhī 3; Bilāwalu 3, 51, 119, 220, etc.

48. *hāthi taḍor,* lit. with a cord or string in hand. R. K. Varmā glosses this as "he who rules", which we accept for lack of any other adequate rendering.

49. *tambor* (Skt. *tāmbūla*), a betel leaf preparation, known also in North India *pān.*

50. *gun* (Skt. *guṇa*), lit. "quality", "attribute", hence greatness.

51. A. G., Gauḍī 16.

52. A. G., Dhanāsarī 1.

53. See supra, p. 214, n. 173.

54. *Ajāmela gaj*: Ajāmila was not an elephant, as Macauliffe would have it, but rather an evil (H. *gaj* "evil or undesirable person") *brāhman* who lived in open sin with a *śūdra* harlot and broke all the laws sacred to his caste. The prostitute bore him ten sons and Ajāmila was most fond of the youngest, named Nārāyaṇ (one of the names of

Viṣṇu). As the *brāhmaṇ* lay dying he called for his favourite son. Viṣṇu hearing his name, was bound to send his deputies in answer to the call. On arrival they found the emissaries of Yama already on the scene, but eventually persuaded him to recall them, and Ajāmila did. He did, however, repent of his sinful life and, taking *sanyās,* practiced austerities so fervently that he obtained *mokṣa.*

55. *sūkar kūkar joni bharme,* lit. "wander in the wombs of pigs and dogs".

56. *amirta* (Skt. *amṛta*): the ambrosia which bestows immortality so that one is released from the rounds of *sasāra.*

57. K. Gr., Pd. 20, cf. A. G., Dhanāsarī 5. This is an entire section of *sākhī* (s) in the *Kabīr-granthāvalī* dedicated to *nām sumiraṇ,* "Sumiraṇ Bhajan Mahimā kau Ag".

58. *sār:* (H.) "essence", i.e. the essential reality or the essential duty.

59. K. Gr., Sa. 3.14.

60. K. Gr.. Sa. 3.11. Cf. K. Gr., Sa. 3.10.

61. Supra, pp. 214 ff.

62. The bundle of poison in his bad *karma,* the accumulated weight of sinful actions committed in his previous existence.

63. K. Gr., Sa. 310. Tiwari notes *hoṭh* (H., lips) as an alternative reading. See also K. Gr., Sa. 4.13.

64. In the same third chapter (*aga*) of Kabīr-granthāvalī *sākhī* (s) (*Sumiraṇ Bhajan Mahimā*) several verses indicate that the salvific vision, which results from the invocation of Rām's name, is extremely difficult to obtain. For example:

> "Long is the road, distant is the house, rugged is the path, beset with dangers;
> O *Sant* (s), how can one obtain the inaccessible vision of Harī?"

> (K. Gr., Sa. 3.12)

65. K. Gr., Pd. 61 Refrain.

66. See supra, p. 49, n. 173.

67. K. Gr., Pd. 21 Refrain. *citu* (Skt. *citta*): see supra, p. 253

68. A. G., Sl 94, cf. A. G,, Basant (Hidola) 7.

69. *Hari kā bilovana bilobahu mere bhāī,*

> *Sahaji vilovahu jaise tatu na jāī.*

Literally:
> "Churn the churn of Harī, my brothers,
> Churn it gently so the essential thing is not lost."

Presenting his message in a familiar idiom, Kabīr here speaks of the body as a churn, from which salvation is obtained through the *śabd.* Haṭhayoga influences are abundantly clear in this piece.

70. A. G., Āsā 10. The reference here is to the crossing of the ocean of existence and reaching the opposite shore, i.e., salvation.

71. *pūjā.*

72. *bicārā* (H. *vicār*).

73. K. Gr., Pd. 26.3.

74. K. Gr., Sa. 14.22. The pain results from the mortal wound of *virah* which is caused by the "arrow" of the *śabd.* See K. Gr., Sa. 1.21.

75. *karatā* (H. *kartā*), "creator" here, as generally in Kabīr's works, does not refer to the god Brahmā, but to the supreme Divinity. Supra, p. 187.

76. See supra, p. 217, n. 186.

77. K. Gr., Sa. 6.5.

78. "*Bhakti* is adoration of Harī's Name;

> all else is endless pain.
> (Remembrance in) thought, word and deed
> is the essence of *sumiraṇ,* Kabīr."

> (K. Gr., Sa. 3.7)

79. J. S. Grewal, op. cit., pp. 160-61. This is but one of the more significant respects in which the tradition of Nānak and his followers is more truly heir to the religion of Kabīr than are the Kabīrpanthī(s).

80. K.Gr., Pd. 26.6.

81. *sāda:* see supra, p. 205, n. 116, as well as p. 44.

82. *kārī kābarī:* (H. *kālī kamari*) a kind of coarse rug or blanket made of undyed black sheep's wool. It is a proverbial simile which bespeaks something which cannot be changed, no matter how hard one tries.

83. A. G., Sl. 100.

84. *likhiā koi lilāṭ:* lit "written on the forehead", i.e. inscribed in one's destiny.

85. A. G., Sl. 231. *avaghhṭa ghāt:* lit. "a difficult" or "inaccessible landing" on the bank of a river or lake; "a difficult, narrow pass" as between two mountains, symbolic here of the *suṣumnā nāḍī* or the *brahmarandhra,* which provides the adept access to the ultimate state of *sahaja.* See supra, p. 203, n. 108.

86. K. Gr., Pd. 115.

87. K. Gr., Sa. 4.22. The entire fourth chapter of both *pad*(s) and *sākhī*(s) in the *Kabīr-grnthāvalī* are dedicated to the "praise of the saints".

88. *sant,* lit. "devotee", "pious person", hence true believer, see supra, p. 43, n. 145

89. K. Gr., Sa. 4.20. This *doha* is expressive of the Vaiṣṇava conviction regarding the value of *satsag,* the sanctifying power of the saint, even by mere touch or proximity. However, it is doubtful that Kabīr shared this quasi-magical view as he explicitly renounces such a view with relation to *nām japa.* See supra, p. 238.

90. *Santalum album* of the Santalaceae family.

91. *ḍhāka palāsa* (H. *ḍhāk-palāś*); two names for the same tree, *Butea frondosa,* also known as *kiśuk* in Hindi. It is known for its beautiful bright red flowers which bloom in March/April but seems to have no utilitarian value.

92. K. Gr., Sa. 4.1. As the fragrance of the sandalwood tree penetrates even the worthless *ḍgāk-palāś,* so the aura of devotion and virtue of true believer sanctify even the wicked who come near him.

93. K. Gr., Pd 30 refrain.

94. See supra, p. 239, n. 372.

95. K. Gr., Sa. 3.5.

96. K. Gr., Pd. 30.1-2.

97. Bj., Sa. 24.

98. Bj., Sa. 25.

Abbreviations

1. A.G. *Ādi Granth*

2. Bj. *Bījak*

3. H. Hindī

4. K. Gr. *Kabīr-granthāvalī* (Tivārī)

5. K. Gr. (Kāśi) *Kabīr-granthāvalī* (Śyamsundardās)

6. Pd. *pad*

7. Rmn. *ramainī*

8. Sa. *sākhī*

9. Sbd. *śabd*

10. Skt. Sanskrit

11. Sl. *ślok*

K. S. Ram (essay date 1989)

SOURCE: Ram, K. S. "Kabir, Surdas and Mirabai: A Note on Bhakti Poetry in Hindi." *The Literary Criterion* 24, no. 1-2 (1989): 147-52.

[*In the following essay, Ram provides a comparison of the works of three Bhakti poets in Hindi: Kabir, Surdas, and Mirabai.*]

Kabir, Mirabai and Surdas are three of the top four Bhakti poets in Hindi. The fourth is Tulsidas who, in terms of ranking, would probably come first but is excluded from the scope of this note.

'Bhakti' is a rather wide label under which each of the three poets discussed in this note has his or her own distinctness. For the sake of convenience and not on any criterion of merit, we could consider Kabir first.

The two significant factors of Kabir's world (XV Century) were: one, the shift of Vedantic religion to dry, abstract intellectualism; and two, the Hindu-Muslim quarrels which had become a sad fact of daily life. It was natural for the sensitive Kabir (fostered by Muslim parents and later a disciple of Guru Ramananda) to react to these two factors. His poetry is such reaction. A very common verse in many of his *Bhajans* is:

> *Kahat* Kabir *Suno bhai Sadho.* . . .
> Says Kabir, hearken good brothers. . . .

This line indicates an essential characteristic of Kabir's poetry: it is reformist.

To call Kabir a Bhakti poet is half-truth. He is as much a poet of Jnana. Much has been said of the Sufi influence on Kabir. While there are many indications of this in his poetry, what we often forget is that at the root of much of what looks like Sufi influence is the influence of Advaita Vedanta. Advaita thought is the reinforcement around which Kabir's poetry is cast. Sufism only confirmed Kabir's Advaita thought.

Vedanta having become so dry and intellectual as to discount Bhakti entirely, Kabir took to poetry to restore the balance. And hence flowed his *Bhajans.*

Bhajan is often loosely understood as a religious composition set to music. In Kabir, 'Bhaja' carries the same meaning as in Adi Sankaracharya's *Bhaja Govindam. Bhaja* is communion with God: the One, the All. It is to dissolve (albeit temporarily) one's individual ego in the Cosmic Unity i.e. *Bramhan.* This is an exercise in Advaita Vedanta which awakens in its practitioner equanimity of mind and happiness, not to speak of psychic powers. The practical form of such communion is to single-mindedly think on the One, the All, giving it aspects (*Saguna*) and to chant aloud His Name. A composition that helps in such an exercise is a *Bhajan.* Kabir's compositions were meant to be *bhajans* in this sense.

In the language of our Government, Kabir's poetry could be described as 'Vedanta for the Common Man.' Through similies, metaphors and images picked from everyday life Kabir can convey fundamental truths of *advaita* with masterly ease. Talking of the equation of *Atman* and *Paramatman,* for instance, he says:

> A pot in water, water-filled,
>   water within, without;
> The pot breaks, waters mingle. . . .

A point that Kabir repeatedly drives home is that Truth is not a thought to be comprehended by the intellect. Truth is an experience to be felt and lived. Hence self-study of books is not enough. You need a Guru to lead you to the experience of Truth.

> A single good in a pilgrimage.
>   In meeting a sage, four.
> *Satguru,* when found, Kabir,
>   Goods endless pour.

And he reminds vain intellectuals that thousands have passed away reading book upon book and yet they failed to become *pundits.* Ironically, to become a *pundit* you need to 'study' (*Paḍe*) a single syllable: love. (In the original it puts it more arithmetically: two and a half letters, *ḍhai akshar* of *Prem*).

The emphasis always is on the cultivation of mind. Outward make-up, *bhesh,* like, say, bathing or shaving of the head, mean little or nothing:

> . . . The sheep sheared again, again
>   discovers what heaven?
> . . . The fish washing perpetually
>   stinks any the less?

As for outward life a constant prescription is *fakiri,* voluntary poverty.

> My mind exults (*man laga*) in
> *fakiri.* The comfort (*Sukh*) that
> flows from *naam-bhajan,* where
> is it in wealth, *ameeri?*

In Surdas (XV-XVI Cent.; *Braj* dialect) we have a different form of Bhakti. There is a popular story that Surdas was in his earlier days given to wallowing in sensual pleasures. A rebuff from a prostitute when he failed to pay her changed him. In many of his poems there is a preoccupation with sin nowhere to be found in Kabir or Mirabai. These poems are supplications to God to forgive his trespasses (*av-gun*). He tells God not to discriminate because He is reputed to be equi-eyed (*Sama-darsi*) and it is necessary He should live up to His Name:

> One (thing of) iron is used in *pooja,*
> One in the butcher's house;
> The Philosopher's Stone no difference knows,
> of both alike makes Gold. . . .

A large number of his poems (and these are the ones most popular) deal with *bal*-Crishna, Krishna the child. These poems are pictures of Krishna in Nandgaon. Krishna's pranks are visualised with a fond love, *vatsa-lya.* Surdas is most reputed for his handling of this *rasa.* Krishna stealing butter and then lying to Yashoda; Krishna crying because his pigtail grows so slowly; Krishna complaining to Yashoda about Balram not involving him in piay; etc., etc. Poem after poem comes almost like an album of a growing child's action photographs. Surdas finds the greatest joy in drawing these pictures of Krishna. He can think of no other subject to portray. As he says in one of the poems, 'like a bird along with a ship on the sea', his mind makes short excursive flights and returns to Krishna. And why not, he asks 'whoever can let a Kamadhenu pass and go to milk a goat?'

The reaction against abstract Advaita can be seen in Surdas as in Kabir. In Surdas, however, it comes better in terms of art. This reaction is presented by Surdas in the context of the gopis' love for Krishna. These poems are in a series entitled *Bhramar Geet.* When Krishna left Nandgaon and went to Mathura at the instance of Kamsa, he came across a friend named Udhav who had a penchant for *Jnana* and dabbled in the talk of *Nirgun Bramhan.* Krishna (with a view to taming Udhav) suggests he go to Nandgaon and instruct the *gopis,* foolishly pining for him, in the science of *Nirgun Brahman.* Udhav confidently comes to Nandgaon and starts his discourses to the *gopis.* The *gopis* respond in their characteristic manner. They ask Udhav:

> To what land does Nirgun belong? . . .
> Who is his father? who his mother?
> Who is his beloved? who his maid?
> Is he dark? or fair? How does he dress?
> What is the sport, *rasa,* he enjoys most?

If he can answer them they will compare him to their darling Krishna and then decide and choose. Surdas says, hearing the above questions of the *gopis,* Udhav stood like one duped (*thago sau*), all his *jnana* shattered.

The *gopis* at another place request Udhav:

> Give us wisdom as us befits. . . .
> *Hum layak Seekh dijai.* . . .

There is in these poems a celebration of Truth in the physical (*Saguna brahman*) through single-minded Bhakti: a 'give all to love' attitude.

The same attitude is found in Mirabai, (XVI Century—Rajasthani dialect) a princess turned poetess. Krishna is the subject of Mira's poetry as in the poetry of Surdas. However, there is one major difference. In Mira's poems there are no *gopis,* no Radha. Mira is in herself a *gopi* and *Radha: her* love for Krishna is the sole subject of her poems:

> *Mere to* Giridhar Gopal, *doosaro na koyi.* . . .
> Giridhar, the Gopal for me; none other than he. . . .

Of Krishna, too, there is a particular form (*ishta-roop*) that she relishes: Krishna, the *Gopal,* shepherd:

> A peacock crown, yellow-robed,
> A garland of *baijanti* flowers. . . .

Of this Krishna Mira is crazy in love (*diwani, baavari*) and a serving devotee (*daasi*).

The poems of Mira are really songs. The *rasanubhava* is incomplete until these songs are *heard* sung to simple, enrapturing music. The songs are spontaneous and honest—honest in terms of art. The *baat* (colloquial for scandal) of her love for Govind has opened and spread 'like seed into a banyan tree'. This simple simile runs in many directions: her love is impossible to hide; it is firm, deep-rooted, alive, growing. . . .

Most of her songs are songs in ecstasy (better said: extasie). They celebrate her love. But there are moments of sudden fear and gloom:

> Seeing dark clouds I felt a fear. . . .

Dark clouds (*megh*) and Krishna (*shyam*) have traditionally been associated in Indian Poetry. In Mira's poem, too, dark clouds gathering in the sky remind her of Krishna. But soon the comparison reverses: dark clouds, thickening, become black (from 'shyam' in the first line they become by the third line *Kaari-Kaari*). And thoughts of love change to fear as she begins to feel forlorn in the heavy downpour. Looking to the sky she feels her Lord is there, somewhere far beyond (*Pardesh*) and she has been left here, drenched and waiting.

The pain of isolation repeats in her poems. It keeps her poems very human: she has her Krishna, of course, but in this world she is alone. Or worse, perhaps: an outcast. She has shed her shame (*Saj*) and become *prem-diwani,* crazy in love. And none understands her torment (*dard*).

At other moments she is more confident of herself. What she has shed is not *laj,* shame, but *lok-laj,* shame as the world knows it. She reminds herself: the way (*gati*) of swans (*hamsa*) is known only to swans; what can the crows (*Kaaga*) know of it?

The honesty of her poems referred to earlier manifests itself in terms of art through tone as well as bold images which are alive and operative rather than just witty and decorative. She says she has received upon her body (*tan*) and soul (*man*) love of Krishna 'like a Brahmin receiving the sacred thread':

> *Ju baman gal dhaga*

In how many directions does this simile operate? Apart from the connotations which are obvious, this implies that she is now a *dvija,* twice-born. Could there be a better way for Mira to explain her state to the orthodox world?

Lines like the above suggest a completeness of vision registered with a yogic ease and clarity. This is a feature common to all the three Bhakti poets discussed above. Poetry of their kind flows directly from a high life. It will have value so long as life continues to matter.

Charlotte Vaudeville (essay date 1993)

SOURCE: Vaudeville, Charlotte. "Selected Verses." In *A Weaver Named Kabir: Selected Verses with a Detailed Biographical and Historical Introduction,* pp. 131-47. Oxford, England: Oxford University Press, 1993.

[*In the following essay, Vaudeville discusses the authenticity and origin of verses and sayings attributed to Kabir.*]

The measure of authenticity to be attributed to the various recensions of the **Kabīr-vāṇīs** or **The Sayings of Kabīr,** is a particularly vexing one. Scholars agree that Kabīr, born towards the middle of the fifteenth century in Benares or in nearby Magahar, as a Muslim weaver, must have been illiterate—or at most half-literate. It is unlikely that he himself wrote down any of his compositions and even more unlikely that he composed any literary work. His famous utterances, couched in a form of old 'Hindui' must, therefore, have been transmitted orally at least one century before they were first written down.[1]

This oral mode of transmission naturally let the door wide open to all kinds of alterations, interpolations and additions—so that the number of verses attributed to Kabīr today may well run into the thousands:

> Like the leaves of a great tree, like the grains of sand
>   in the Ganga
> are the words which came out of Kabīr's mouth.[2]

Besides the numberless oral or written additions to the cherished treasure of **Kabīr's Sayings,** a number of composed works were attributed to him, especially by the sectarian *Kabīr-panthī*s, 'Kabīr's Followers'—a later sect—who claim to have been founded by Kabīr himself, their now divinized Guru.

THE EASTERN TRADITION OF KABĪR'S WORDS: *BIJAK*

The Kabīr-panthīs' treasure is the **Khās Granth,** whose original manuscript is said to be preserved in the 'Kabīr Chaurā Maṭh' (temple) at Benares, the main center of the Kabīr-panthī sect or 'those who follow the way of Kabīr'. The last book in that compilation, and by far the most revered by the Kabīr-panthīs, is a collection of Kabīr's verses called **Bijak,** literally 'seed' or 'chart' of sacred treasures. Several other manuscripts of that famed compilation are still in the possession of the 'Kabīr Chaurā Maṭh' and some other *maṭh*s belonging to other sections of the same sect elsewhere. However, the Mahants or 'authorities' of such *maṭh*s are reluctant to have them published. The 'original copy' of the *Bījak* in daily use and daily worship at the Kabīr-Chaurā *maṭh* appears to be an old lithographed copy of one of those manuscripts.

Supposed to represent the authentic Kabīr-panthī tradition of Kabīr's verses as prevalent in Eastern Uttar Pradesh and in Central India, the *Bījak* may be taken as representative of the 'Eastern' recension of the Kabīr-vāṇīs—as opposed to fairly ancient recensions of the same, current in Western India. The *Bījak* itself has come down to us in two main forms: a longer and a shorter form. Yet, even in its shorter form, the text cannot be accepted as totally genuine, as shown by Parashuram Chaturvedi and other Kabirian scholars: the *Bījak* not only includes a number of meaningless and obviously corrupt verses, but it also contains numerous references to the elaborate cosmogony and religious beliefs peculiar to the sectarian Kabīr-panthīs themselves.

The 'Bārābānkī' edition of *Kabīr's Words* includes 84 *rāmainī*s[3] and 115 *śabda*s, followed by an acrostic composition called *Bipramacautīsī*. Then follow 12 poems called **"Kahāra," "Basant," "Cancarī," "Belī," "Birahulī"** and **"Hindolā,"** evidently modelled on popular types of folk-songs. After the *pad*s or 'songs' comes a list of 353 *sākhī*s or *dohā*s.[4] The edition also includes a glossary and lists of interpretations relating to symbolical numbers, similies and allegorical allusions, which are found in the *Bījak* text as it has come down to this day. The 'Bārābānkī edition' has been reprinted many times with a modern Hindī paraphrase (*ṭīkā*): that *ṭīkā* was the work of a Kabīrpanthī scholar, who called himself Sadhu Abhilashdas.

The collection of satirical verses and paradoxical utterances called *ulṭabāmsī* in the *Bījak* are particularly striking. In spirit and style, they match rather well with similar utterances found in the other two main recensions of Kabīr's verses compiled in Northwestern India. But the *Bījak* verses have been largely interpolated: it has become a separate tradition, which we call the 'Eastern tradition' of Kabīr's verses.

As the major authoritative collection of Kabīr's verses in the hands of the Kabīr-panthīs, the *Bījak* early attracted the attention of Western missionaries and scholars, from the nineteenth century onwards. A first attempt at editing and translating some of it in English was made by the Reverend Prem Chand, as early as 1890; another English translation of the *Bījak* by the Reverend Ahmed Shah, a local clergyman who happened to be a Christian convert, appeared in 1917. None

of the first translators were very successful, and the result of their efforts is hardly understandable to the Western reader today. Yet, those early attempts at deciphering and translating Kabīr's purported *Sayings* were a witness to the newly-awakened interest for his teachings among the first generation of Christian missionaries in India.[5]

AHMED SHAH AND THE *BIJAK*

Ahmed Shah's own appreciation of Kabīr's religious and philosophical thought in his 'Introduction' is fairly balanced. Like other Christian writers before him, he believes that 'religious toleration and the brotherhood of mankind' were among the chief lessons that Kabīr had set himself to inculcate—but he does not commit himself on the question of a possible Christian influence. Yet, he underlines Kabīr's originality: "Though thoughts resembling his are to be found in the writings of Hindu philosophers, and also in the words of Muslim Sufis of all ages, yet the presentation of them is peculiarly his own".[6]

Ahmed Shah admits that Kabīr was brought up as a Muslim Julāhā, but he remarks upon the latter's considerable knowledge of Hindu concepts and practices, as well as of Puranic mythology, relying on a number of passages in the *Bījak*, which he evidently regards as representing the essence of Kabīr's authentic teachings. On the other hand, Ahmed Shah remarks on the scant knowledge of the doctrines of Islam revealed by Kabīr in the *Bījak*: for him, "the contrast between Kabīr's intimate acquaintance with Hindu thought, writings and ritual and his purely superficial knowledge of Moslem beliefs revealed in the *Bījak* are too striking to be ignored".[7]

The same author, therefore, seeks an explanation for Kabīr's expansive knowledge of Hindu tradition and beliefs in his contact with his purported Guru, Rāmānand, in whose company Kabīr is supposed to have spent a considerable time. In this, he agrees with the *Kabīrpanthī*s, or 'those who follow the path of Kabīr' and also with the Hindu tradition as a whole—in accordance with which he even admits that the weaver Kabīr was born a Hindu! Ahmed Shah suggests that it was because Indian Muslims welcomed Kabīr's efforts in combating idol-worship that they claimed him as a Muslim—and they went so far as acknowledging him as a *pīr*, a Muslim Sufi or saint, for his self-denying and pious life.[8]

Ahmed Shah's English translation of the *Bījak* was hailed by Grierson with enthusiasm, not so much for its literary achievement—which was rather poor—as for Kabīr's extraordinary personality:

> What a wonderful man Kabīr must have been! A lowly
> Muslim weaver who by a stratagem gained accession
> to a Vaishnav community—universally despised and

hated by both Mussalman and Hindu, maltreated by the Muslim emperor and persecuted by the Brahmanhood of Benares—with unparalleled audacity he dared to set himself face to face against both Islam and Hinduism, the two religions of the 15th century India, and won through. Each he attacked in its tenderest point—its shibboleths and its rituals—and over both rode triumphant, teaching and converting thousands who became his devoted followers. Not only did he found an eclectic monotheism that survives in India till the present day, but he became the spiritual father of Nānak who founded Sikhism.

The *Gurū Granth* or *Ādi Granth* of the Sikhs

The two other ancient and important compilations of Kabīr's verses originated from Northwestern India: in Panjab and Rajasthan. It is apparently in those areas that the **Kabīr-yāṇīs** made the greatest impact on both the Hindu and the Muslim masses, and that his teachings were enthusiastically received, assimilated and later written down. Several religious sects were founded in those regions, at least from the sixteenth century onwards, which were directly or indirectly influenced by Kabīr's teachings: such were the *Dādūpanthī* and the *Naranjanī* sects of Rajasthan, and the *Sikh Panth* in the Panjab. The latter, founded by Guru Nānak in the early sixteenth century, evolved into a religion independent from Hinduism proper.

The teachings of Guru Nānak and the four Gurus who were his immediate successors were gathered into a large compilation which was known as the *Ādi Granth,* literally 'The Original Book'. The *Ādi Granth,* the sacred scripture of the Sikhs, was later called *Gurū Granth.* It includes a collection of 243 *salokus* or *śloks* attributed to Kabīr.[9] It is a very important document and the only one which can be dated with precision: 1604. The *Gurū Granth* is free from the Kabīr-panthī sectarian element which imbues a part of the *Bījak,* and its authenticity is the best established of all. Yet, some *pads,* especially those which recall Kabīr's miraculous escapes from various attempts on his life, or the legend of the Vaishnav saint and martyr Prahlād, have a hagiographical character. Allusions to the mythical great Bhaktas (devotees) of yore, such as the holy bird Shukdev, the Vaishnav saint and martyr Prahlād and the learned monkey Hanumān, do not fit in with Kabīr's radical rejection of Brahmanical scriptures and Hindu lore.

According to Sikh tradition, the compilation of the *Ādi Granth* was completed in 1604 and the sacred Book was installed in the Sikh temple at Amritsar by Guru Arjan Singh himself.[10] A second recension of the *Granth,* including a few additions by Guru Bhai Banno, did not meet with Guru Arjan Singh's approval and remained, therefore, confined to its author's descendants. The third and final recension, including the sayings of the ninth

Guru, Tegh Bahādur Singh, was dictated to Mani Bhai Singh by the tenth Guru of the sect, Govind Singh, who died in 1708 A.D.

Before he died, Guru Govind Singh had passed the 'Guruship' of the Sikhs to the *Ādi Granth* itself, which then became known as the *Śrī Gurū Granth Sāhib* and was enshrined in the Golden temple at Amritsar. Govind Singh bode the Sikhs henceforth to obey the *Granth Sāhib,* held as identical with the 'visible body of the Guru'.[11] He is said to have refused to add his own compositions into the sacred Book—the only additions he tolerated being the verses composed by the ninth Guru. The Sikhs consider their *Śrī Gurū Granth Sāhib* as identical with the original Granth, the *Ādi Granth,* once compiled in the *gurumukhī* script by Guru Arjan Singh.

Besides the *pads* (songs) and the *salokus* (*śloks*), taken as an equivalent of *dohā,* and composed by the Sikh Gurus, the *Gurū Granth* includes a very large number of verses attributed to a number of ancient, (pre-Nānak), Hindu and Muslim saints: the latter are revered by the Sikhs, as some kind of spiritual precursors to the final revelation embodied in the compositions of Guru Nānak and the first Sikh Gurus. In the *Gurū Granth,* those saints are called *bhagats* (*bhaktas*) or 'devotees'. The Bhagats are staunch monotheists: they uphold the right type of *bhakti* or 'Devotion to the supreme God', without any concession to idol worship.

The 'Bhagats' mentioned in the *Gurū Granth* belonged to various times, but, as a whole, they may be dated from the fourteenth to the early sixteenth centuries A.D. The tradition gives Jaydev (or Jayadeva) as the earliest, but his time and location remain uncertain. Macauliffe believes that the 'Jaydev' who is held as the author of two hymns found in the *Granth,* is the same as the famed Sanskrit poet who composed the *Gīta Govinda,* in the second part of the twelfth century A.D.—but this appears very unlikely. As to *Rāmānand,* a high caste Brahman: according to the *Gurū Granth* tradition he was born around 1400 AD and lived in the early part of the fifteenth century, so that he may have been Kabīr's own guru, which however is very unlikely.

Farquhar believes that Rāmānand belonged to an ancient Ramaite sect in South India, and that he was the author of the *Adhyātma Rāmāyaṇ.* Neither Grierson nor Parashuram Chaturvedi, however, accept Farquhar's view about Rāmānand—the latter being sometimes represented as Kabīr's own guru, and sometimes as a dealer of magic spells. The present Rāmānandīs, as high caste Brahmans, composed books in Sanskrit.[12] Two Hindi *pads* compiled by the Dādū-panthī Rajab, are found in the *Sarvāgnī* and one of them found its way in the *Gurū Granth.*[13]

SOME PARTICULARITIES OF THE *GURU GRANTH*

In the *Guru Granth,* as written by the scribe Bhāi Gur-dās under Guru Arjan's dictation, the words were not divided off, as is customary in Indian manuscripts. Modern editions are now printed under the supervision of the Gurudvārā at Amritsar, both in the Gurmukhī and the Nāgarī characters. In all those editions, the original disposition is rigorously kept—but for the division of the words: the *verse numbering* and even the *page numbering* always remain the same. The cutting of the words, however, appears sometimes doubtful. Another difficulty stems out of the composition of the *Guru Granth* itself, whose intricacies make it difficult for the non-initiate to discover and pick out the verses of the Bhagats—or, for that matter, of any particular Guru. Indication of the page number is, therefore, necessary when referring to a particular verse.

In the *Guru Granth,* the distichs (*dohās*), called *salokus* (Skt *ślok*) are found listed together in a continuous series, without any classification according to the theme—and the *saloku*-list occurs after the *pads* of the last *rāg*.[14] In the treatment of the *dohās*, the *Guru Granth* recension agrees with the *Bījak* (in which the *dohās* are called *sākhīs*, lit. 'witnesses'), but it contrasts with the *Kabīr-granthāvalī* recension, in which the *sā-khīs* are classified into *agas* or chapters, according to the subject-matter.

As to the poems (*pads*) *Guru Granth,* they are found classified under thirty-one different *rāgs*, or musical modes, beginning with *sirī rāgu* (*Śrī rāg*) and ending with *jaijāvantī rāgu.* At the end of each *rāg,* the poems to be sung by the Bhagats in that particular *rāg* are listed immediately after the last of the poems composed by the Sikh Gurus.

The near totality of the *salokus* attributed to Kabīr in the *Guru Granth* begin with the name of the presumed author, Kabīr, accompanied by the so-called *bhanitā* 'Says Kabīr'.

It is apparently to alleviate the difficulties encountered by non-specialists, and to make the *Guru Granth* collection of Kabīr's verses available to Indian students that R. K. Varma published a collection of his verses, entitled *Sant Kabīr* (Allahabad, 1947), together with an Introduction in Hindī.[15]

Within the collection of poems attributed to the *Bhagats* in the *Guru Granth,* the 'Words of the Bhagat Kabīr' are invariably listed first, Kabīr taking precedence even over the older saint Nāmdev.

As we have seen, poems attributed to Kabīr in the *Guru Granth* are found classified in seventeen different *rāgs.* As to the longer compositions attributed to him, they are found at the end of *gaurī rāgu,* the second and the longest section in the whole of the *Guru Granth.* A composition in the form of an acrostic poem called *Bā-van akharī,* literally 'The fifty-two letters', also includes *tithi* (list of lunar dates) and *vār,* or 'Weekdays'. What makes the use of the *Guru Granth* even more puzzling to the non-initiate is the confusion in terms. Short poems known as *pads* in Hindī poetical tradition are also referred to as either *śabda* or *pāurī,* the latter liter-ally meaning the 'rung of a ladder'. But various compositions with a given *rāg* are classified according to the number of *pads* they include, as *dupade* (two *pads*), *tipade* (three *pads*) and so on—the longest being the *aṣṭapadī* (eight *pads*) and the *solhā* (sixteen *pads*).

Most of the *pads* attributed to Kabīr in the *Guru Granth* are made of two to four stanzas, including a refrain. Each given stanza is made of either two long lines rhyming together or four short lines and two rhymes.

The refrain itself, *rahāü,* is usually made of two short lines, or one short and one long line rhyming together. The refrain is invariably included in the first stanza and is never numbered separately, so that it constitutes either the two first lines or the two last lines of the poem. All those peculiarities, plus a number of unwarranted varia-tions within the general pattern, may well drive the non-specialist (and even the specialist) to despair, and drive him to resort to the Macauliffe translation! Yet those short, naive utterances have a charm of their own:

> O Madhao! In water, I couldn't quench my thirst:
>> in that water, a huge fire has sprung up
> You are the Water, and I, the little sea-fish,
>> in water I live, yet, for Water I pine!

THE *KABIR-GRANTHAVALI* RECENSION

The so-called *Kabīr-granthāvalī* recension essentially coincides with the *Dādū-panthī* tradition of Kabīr's sayings—a tradition which developed in Rajasthan, and may also be called the 'Rajasthani' recension of the *Kabīr-vānīs.* This tradition goes back to Dādū-Dayāl, a low-caste Muslim like Kabīr. He was a *dhuniyā* or cotton-carder from Ahmedabad, who settled in Rajast-han and flourished in the second half of the sixteenth century. The recorded *vānīs* of Dādū Dayāl show a close dependence on Kabīr's thought and style. Besides Ka-bīr, their purported founder, the Dādū-panthīs hold Nāmdev, Ravidās and Haridās as their most revered saints.

The *Pañc-vānī* literature composed by the Dādū-panthīs of Rajasthan is based on the words of the 'Five Saints' among whom the most prominent (apart from the founder Dādū himself) is Kabīr. It was found that the two manuscripts on which Shyam Sundar Das based his edition of the *Kabīr-granthāvalī* closely followed the texts found in the *Pañc-vānīs* of Rajasthan. Both, therefore, are considered as belonging to the same tradi-tion.[16]

The standard edition of the so-called *Kabīr-granthāvalī* is the above-mentioned S. S. Das edition (often referred to in India as 'the *Sabhā* edition'), which was reprinted a number of times. This edition, which we have referred to as *KG1* includes 811 *sākhī*s (or *dohā*s) classified into 59 *aga*s, 'parts' or 'chapters', whose length may vary from 2 to 62 *sākhī*s. The *KG1 pad* collection, placed after the *sākhī*s, includes 403 *pad*s, classified under 16 *rāg*s—each of which may include any number of *pad*s. The third and last section of *KG1* also includes a very large number of *ramainī*s: a case of *inflation galopante*! It is not possible to ascertain the number of such *ramainī*s and the so-called *pad*s within the *ramainī*s are not numbered.

Clearly, the 'standard edition' of the *Kabīr-granthāvalī* (*KG1*) compiled by S. S. Das was of little value: the editor had done little more than reproducing his first manuscript (*ka*), adding in the footnotes the extra verses found in the second manuscript (*kha*). In the Appendix are listed the verses (*sākhī*s, *pad*s and *ramainī*s) found in the *Gurū Granth* and nowhere else. But references to the text are not given.

Though the first of the two manuscripts on which S. S. Das based the 1928 edition is not as ancient as he himself thought, it is a valuable manuscript which, when compared with the *Pañc-vāṇī* manuscripts, gives a fair idea of the contents of the Dādū-panthī or Rajasthani tradition of the Kabīr-vāṇīs. The comparison, however, was not undertaken by S. S. Das himself and the title he gave to his edition: *Kabīr-granthāvalī*, was somewhat misleading, since it only gave the text of the first *Nāgarī Pracāriṇī Sabhā* manuscript, with variant readings found in the second manuscript in the footnotes. This edition, which for a long time, remained the only printed text of the main tradition of Kabīr's verses, was reprinted a number of times. Later, different *ṭīkā*s or paraphrases of the S. S. Das text appeared, published by various Indian scholars. None of such *ṭīkā*s, unfortunately, is of much help.

Another important compilation of Kabīr's verses is that found in the *Sarbāgī* of the poet Rajab, from Sanganer in Rajasthan, who was the foremost disciple of Dādū Dayāl in the middle of the sixteenth century. The *Sarbāgī* compilation includes sayings of sixty-six Siddhas and saints, whose verses are divided, according to the subject, into 144 *aga*s (chapters). The collection of verses found in the *Sarbāgī* includes 337 verses: though it is much shorter than the Pañc-vāṇī manuscripts, it clearly belongs to the same tradition. The *Sarbāgī* seems to contain an epitome of what is generally called the Dādū-panthī or Rajasthani tradition of Kabīr's verses.[17]

The first, and so far the sole attempt at a critical edition of Kabīr's verses, was the work of a young scholar of the Allahabad University, Dr. Parasnath Tiwārī. His edition was first published in 1961, by the University of Allahabad under the same title: *Kabīr-granthāvalī*. It is the P. N. Tiwārī edition of the *Kabīr-granthāvalī* that we refer to as *KG2*.[18] The method adopted by the author was to retain and include, in his own edition, *all the verses* he found in *two* or *more* independent *pāṭh*s, (i.e. readings), giving the references in the footnotes and classifying the numerous variants found in the texts. This enormously painstaking effort was only partly successful: some of the eleven *pāṭh*s obviously were not worth much (especially the older printed compilations)—and not to be treated on a par with the *Bījak*, the *Gurū Granth* and the best manuscripts in the Rajasthani tradition. This methodological error led to the acceptance, in *KG2*, of a large number of verses of doubtful authenticity.

The comparison of the three recensions of the Kabīr *vāṇī*s, namely the Eastern recension (represented by the *Bījak*) and the two Western recensions, (namely the Panjabi *Gurū Granth*) and the Rajasthani (called *Kabīr-granthāvalī*) recensions, clearly brings out the fact that, on the whole, the tradition of the *sākhī*s and *ślok*s of Kabīr, is better established and more coherent than that of his *pad*s. The comparison between the three recensions also brings out the fact that, the shorter the poem, the more likely it is to be found in two—or even in all the three recensions. This tends to confirm the presumption that the original verses composed by Kabīr were either in the form of distichs (*sākhī*s or *ślok*s), or in the form of short compositions (*pad*s), probably not exceeding four or five rhyming verses, in which the first or the last line was used as a refrain. It becomes clear that the longer poems found in one or the other of the three recensions are either spurious or heavily interpolated.

In the *Bījak* and the *Gurū Granth,* the *dohā*s (whether called *sākhī* or *saloku*) are found jumbled together without any apparent order. In the Dādū-panthī or Rajasthani recession, they are classified into *aga*s, i.e. 'chapters', according to the subject matter—such as 'Guru kau ag', 'Viraha kau ag' etc. P. Chaturvedi is of the opinion that this division might have been an innovation introduced by Rajjab.[19] Yet precedents can be found in ancient Indian literatures: in the *Dhammapada*, a Pali text belonging to the Buddhist canon, the so-called *gāthā*s are classified into *vaggo*s (Skt *varga*) according to the subject. In Indian medieval poetry, the short lyrics known as *pad*s are traditionally classified according to the *rāg*, the type of melody in which they are to be sung. In the *Gurū Granth,* each *rāg* includes first the *pad*s composed by Guru Nanak—by far the longest list—then the words composed by the other Sikh Gurus, and finally those composed by holy men, the *Bhagats*. In the *Bījak,* the poems, called *sabad*s (*śabda*s), meaning 'holy utterances', are also chanted, though the *rāg* is not indicated in the text. The 'Dādū-panthī' or Rajasthani tradition seems to hesitate: the *pad*s are sometimes classified under a particular *rāg,* as in the **Gurū Granth,** and sometimes treated as non-musical utterances. The **Bījak** includes a large number of so-called 'Ramainīs' and 'Shabads' (*śabda*) composed in the *caupāī* metre. Such *ramainī*s mostly appear in didactic compositions. Besides the *sākhī*s, *śabda*s and *ramainī*s, the **Bījak** includes a few long poems with particular rhythms, named after popular folksongs and dances, such as **Basant, Camcar** (or **Carcari**) and **Hindola**: those songs are meant to impart spiritual teachings in the form of simple village songs or short rhymed ballads. It is difficult to ascertain whether such compositions can be ascribed to Kabīr. They are only found in the **Bījak.**

Experience has shown us that the greatest hurdle to be confronted by Kabirian scholars is the lingering uncertainty about the relative value and degree of authenticity to be accorded to any given verse. Another hurdle consists in the non-existence of cross-references between the main recensions: for instance, a Hindī scholar trying to read the Kabīr *ślok*s in the **Gurū Granth** text has no way of knowing if a particular verse is found anywhere else attributed to Kabīr, and under which form. If he manages to lay his hand on the **KG2** edition, he cannot ascertain whether a particular verse finds a correspondent in the **Gurū Granth** or in the **Bījak** recensions, since lists of the few verses common to all the three recensions are nowhere to be found.

In presenting in a single volume the three principal texts of the **Kabīr-vāṇīs,** our intention has been to make those treasures available to the scholars concerned and to all 'Friends of Kabīr'. But such a compilation would have been of limited value without fairly reliable Concordance-Tables. The author, therefore, endeavoured to establish such Concordances, which are printed at the end of the volume.

We sincerely hope that our endeavour will not be in vain and that it will encourage Indologists with an interest in Indo-Aryan literatures and/or medieval Hinduism to attempt a direct approach to the **Sayings of Kabīr,** the most quoted—and also the most misquoted—of all the great Indian poets and mystics.

Notes

1. Cf. P. N. Tiwārī, *Kabīr-vāṇī-sagraha,* Allahabad, 1970, p. 120.

2. *Bī. sā.* 261.

3. 84 is a sacred number in Indian tradition.

4. *Sākhī* means 'testimony': it is an equivalent of *ślok* or *saloku,* a two-lines utterance; *dohā,* or *duhā,* an equivalent of *sākhī,* means 'a couplet'.

5. K. F. Keay, as well as other Christian missionaries did not believe that Kabīr himself came into contact with Christians or knew anything of Christian teachings, but he considered as 'almost certain' that the Bhakti movement as a whole, to which (according to him) Kabīr belonged, was influenced by Christian ideas. His views were accepted by George Grierson. See F. E. Keay, *Kabīr and his Followers,* Calcutta, 1931, p. 172.

6. Ahmad Shah, *The Bijak of Kabir,* Hamirpur, 1917, p. 36.

7. *Ibidem,* p. 40.

8. The desperate efforts of Ahmed Shah, himself Muslim-born, and some others, to prove that Kabīr was indeed Hindu-born, appears puzzling. But the fact is that, as a convert, it is more difficult to be a Hindu convert than a Muslim convert, at least in India.

9. The 243 *saloku*s attributed to Kabīr in the *Gurū Granth* (pp. 1364-1377) are immediately followed by the 130 *saloku*s attributed to the famous saint Shaykh Farīd (pp. 1377-1384).

10. Cf. Teja Singh and Ganda Singh, *A Short History of the Sikhs,* vol. 1, p. 33.

11. Quoted in S. S. Kolhi, *A Critical Study of the Ādi Granth,* Delhi, repr. 1976, p. 19.

12. Cf. Vaudeville, *Haripāth,* pp. 74-76, 'Nivṛtti et la Religion du Nom'. In the Maharashtrian tradition, Rāmānand is supposed to have been the Guru of Viṭṭhalpanth, (Jñāneshvar's father) in Kashi.

13. *Basant,* 1, p. 1195.

14. *Rāg* or *rāgu* refers to a specific mode of singing.

15. Unfortunately, the comparison of R. K. Varma with the text shows a fantastic amount of copying—or printing—mistakes. As to the added *ṭīkā,* it is only a popular one, and the author made no attempt to elucidate the obscure passages in the text. Moreover, references to the relevant page numbers in the *Gurū Granth* (1364-1377) are missing.

16. The date ascribed by S. S. Das to his first manuscript (*ka*) has been disproved (Vaudeville: 1974, pp. 19-20), but it is a valuable manuscript of the so-called Rajasthani tradition.

17. Four manuscripts have been critically studied and partially translated into English by Winand M. Callewaert: *The Sarvāgī of the Dādūpanthī Rajab,* Leuven, 1978. The *Sarvāgī* means: 'all the *aga*s', brought together by Rajab.

18. In opposition to the S. S. Das edition: *KG1.*

19. Chaturvedi, *KSP,* p. 78.

FURTHER READING

Biography

Keay, F. E. "Kabir." In *A History of Hindi Literature,* pp. 21-5. Calcutta, India: Y.M.C.A. Publishing House, 1960.

> Offers a brief overview of the life and works attributed to Kabir.

Machwe, Prabhakar. *Kabir,* New Delhi, India: Sahitya Akademi, 1968,

> Biographical and literary overview of Indian poet Kabir.

Criticism

Bahadur, Krishna P. *A New Look at Kabir,* New Delhi, India: Ess Ess Publications, 1997, 288 p.

> Critical assessment of the works of Kabir.

Jha, Ashok Kumar. "Kabir in Tagore's Translation." *Indian Literature,* no. 113 (May-June 1986): 48-60.

> Assessment of Rabindranath Tagore's treatment of Kabir in translation.

Saraswati, Baidyanath. "Notes on Kabir: A Non-literate Intellectual." In *Dissent Protest and Reform in Indian Civilization,* edited by S. C. Malik, pp. 167-84. Simla, India: Indian Institute of Advanced Study, 1977.

> Discussion of Kabir's religious teachings and their historic and cultural evolution.

Topa, Ishwara. "Self-Culture." In *The Social Philosophy of Kabir: A Study of His Thought-World,* pp. 59-78. Buxiper, Gorakhpur, India: Sahitya Sansar Prakashan, 1975.

> Traces Kabir's writings about the philosophy of "wakefulness."

Additional coverage of Kabir's life and career is contained in the following sources published by the Gale Group: *Literature Resource Center*; **and** *Reference Guide to World Literature,* **Eds. 2, 3.**

How to Use This Index

The main references

Calvino, Italo
1923-1985 .... CLC 5, 8, 11, 22, 33, 39,
73; SSC 3, 48

list all author entries in the following Gale Literary Criticism series:

AAL = *Asian American Literature*
BG = *The Beat Generation: A Gale Critical Companion*
BLC = *Black Literature Criticism*
BLCS = *Black Literature Criticism Supplement*
CLC = *Contemporary Literary Criticism*
CLR = *Children's Literature Review*
CMLC = *Classical and Medieval Literature Criticism*
DC = *Drama Criticism*
HLC = *Hispanic Literature Criticism*
HLCS = *Hispanic Literature Criticism Supplement*
HR = *Harlem Renaissance: A Gale Critical Companion*
LC = *Literature Criticism from 1400 to 1800*
NCLC = *Nineteenth-Century Literature Criticism*
NNAL = *Native North American Literature*
PC = *Poetry Criticism*
SSC = *Short Story Criticism*
TCLC = *Twentieth-Century Literary Criticism*
WLC = *World Literature Criticism, 1500 to the Present*
WLCS = *World Literature Criticism Supplement*

The cross-references

See also CA 85-88, 116; CANR 23, 61;
DAM NOV; DLB 196; EW 13; MTCW 1, 2;
RGSF 2; RGWL 2; SFW 4; SSFS 12

list all author entries in the following Gale biographical and literary sources:

AAYA = *Authors & Artists for Young Adults*
AFAW = *African American Writers*
AFW = *African Writers*
AITN = *Authors in the News*
AMW = *American Writers*
AMWR = *American Writers Retrospective Supplement*
AMWS = *American Writers Supplement*
ANW = *American Nature Writers*
AW = *Ancient Writers*
BEST = *Bestsellers*
BPFB = *Beacham's Encyclopedia of Popular Fiction: Biography and Resources*
BRW = *British Writers*
BRWS = *British Writers Supplement*
BW = *Black Writers*
BYA = *Beacham's Guide to Literature for Young Adults*
CA = *Contemporary Authors*
CAAS = *Contemporary Authors Autobiography Series*
CABS = *Contemporary Authors Bibliographical Series*
CAD = *Contemporary American Dramatists*
CANR = *Contemporary Authors New Revision Series*
CAP = *Contemporary Authors Permanent Series*
CBD = *Contemporary British Dramatists*
CCA = *Contemporary Canadian Authors*
CD = *Contemporary Dramatists*
CDALB = *Concise Dictionary of American Literary Biography*
CDALBS = *Concise Dictionary of American Literary Biography Supplement*
CDBLB = *Concise Dictionary of British Literary Biography*

CMW = *St. James Guide to Crime & Mystery Writers*
CN = *Contemporary Novelists*
CP = *Contemporary Poets*
CPW = *Contemporary Popular Writers*
CSW = *Contemporary Southern Writers*
CWD = *Contemporary Women Dramatists*
CWP = *Contemporary Women Poets*
CWRI = *St. James Guide to Children's Writers*
CWW = *Contemporary World Writers*
DA = *DISCovering Authors*
DA3 = *DISCovering Authors 3.0*
DAB = *DISCovering Authors: British Edition*
DAC = *DISCovering Authors: Canadian Edition*
DAM = *DISCovering Authors: Modules*
   DRAM: *Dramatists Module;* **MST:** *Most-studied Authors Module;*
   MULT: *Multicultural Authors Module;* **NOV:** *Novelists Module;*
   POET: *Poets Module;* **POP:** *Popular Fiction and Genre Authors Module*
DFS = *Drama for Students*
DLB = *Dictionary of Literary Biography*
DLBD = *Dictionary of Literary Biography Documentary Series*
DLBY = *Dictionary of Literary Biography Yearbook*
DNFS = *Literature of Developing Nations for Students*
EFS = *Epics for Students*
EXPN = *Exploring Novels*
EXPP = *Exploring Poetry*
EXPS = *Exploring Short Stories*
EW = *European Writers*
FANT = *St. James Guide to Fantasy Writers*
FW = *Feminist Writers*
GFL = *Guide to French Literature,* Beginnings to 1789, 1798 to the Present
GLL = *Gay and Lesbian Literature*
HGG = *St. James Guide to Horror, Ghost & Gothic Writers*
HW = *Hispanic Writers*
IDFW = *International Dictionary of Films and Filmmakers: Writers and Production Artists*
IDTP = *International Dictionary of Theatre: Playwrights*
LAIT = *Literature and Its Times*
LAW = *Latin American Writers*
JRDA = *Junior DISCovering Authors*
MAICYA = *Major Authors and Illustrators for Children and Young Adults*
MAICYAS = *Major Authors and Illustrators for Children and Young Adults Supplement*
MAWW = *Modern American Women Writers*
MJW = *Modern Japanese Writers*
MTCW = *Major 20th-Century Writers*
NCFS = *Nonfiction Classics for Students*
NFS = *Novels for Students*
PAB = *Poets: American and British*
PFS = *Poetry for Students*
RGAL = *Reference Guide to American Literature*
RGEL = *Reference Guide to English Literature*
RGSF = *Reference Guide to Short Fiction*
RGWL = *Reference Guide to World Literature*
RHW = *Twentieth-Century Romance and Historical Writers*
SAAS = *Something about the Author Autobiography Series*
SATA = *Something about the Author*
SFW = *St. James Guide to Science Fiction Writers*
SSFS = *Short Stories for Students*
TCWW = *Twentieth-Century Western Writers*
WLIT = *World Literature and Its Times*
WP = *World Poets*
YABC = *Yesterday's Authors of Books for Children*
YAW = *St. James Guide to Young Adult Writers*

Literary Criticism Series
Cumulative Author Index

Allan, Sidney
See Hartmann, Sadakichi
Allan, Sydney
See Hartmann, Sadakichi
Allard, Janet .... **CLC 59**
Allen, Edward 1948- .... **CLC 59**
Allen, Fred 1894-1956 .... **TCLC 87**
Allen, Paula Gunn 1939- ..... **CLC 84; NNAL**
See also AMWS 4; CA 112; 143; CANR 63; CWP; DA3; DAM MULT; DLB 175; FW; MTCW 1; RGAL 4
Allen, Roland
See Ayckbourn, Alan
Allen, Sarah A.
See Hopkins, Pauline Elizabeth
Allen, Sidney H.
See Hartmann, Sadakichi
Allen, Woody 1935- .... **CLC 16, 52**
See also AAYA 10, 51; CA 33-36R; CANR 27, 38, 63, 128; DAM POP; DLB 44; MTCW 1
Allende, Isabel 1942- ... **CLC 39, 57, 97, 170; HLC 1; SSC 65; WLCS**
See also AAYA 18; CA 125; 130; CANR 51, 74, 129; CDWLB 3; CWW 2; DA3; DAM MULT, NOV; DLB 145; DNFS 1; EWL 3; FW; HW 1, 2; INT CA-130; LAIT 5; LAWS 1; LMFS 2; MTCW 1, 2; NCFS 1; NFS 6, 18; RGSF 2; RGWL 3; SSFS 11, 16; WLIT 1
Alleyn, Ellen
See Rossetti, Christina (Georgina)
Alleyne, Carla D. .... **CLC 65**
Allingham, Margery (Louise) 1904-1966 .... **CLC 19**
See also CA 5-8R; 25-28R; CANR 4, 58; CMW 4; DLB 77; MSW; MTCW 1, 2
Allingham, William 1824-1889 ...... **NCLC 25**
See also DLB 35; RGEL 2
Allison, Dorothy E. 1949- .... **CLC 78, 153**
See also AAYA 53; CA 140; CANR 66, 107; CSW; DA3; FW; MTCW 1; NFS 11; RGAL 4
Alloula, Malek .... **CLC 65**
Allston, Washington 1779-1843 .... **NCLC 2**
See also DLB 1, 235
Almedingen, E. M. .... **CLC 12**
See Almedingen, Martha Edith von
See also SATA 3
Almedingen, Martha Edith von 1898-1971
See Almedingen, E. M.
See also CA 1-4R; CANR 1
Almodovar, Pedro 1949(?)- .... **CLC 114; HLCS 1**
See also CA 133; CANR 72; HW 2
Almqvist, Carl Jonas Love 1793-1866 .... **NCLC 42**
al-Mutanabbi, Ahmad ibn al-Husayn Abu al-Tayyib al-Jufi al-Kindi 915-965 .... **CMLC 66**
See also RGWL 3
Alonso, Damaso 1898-1990 .... **CLC 14**
See also CA 110; 131; 130; CANR 72; DLB 108; EWL 3; HW 1, 2
Alov
See Gogol, Nikolai (Vasilyevich)
Al Siddik
See Rolfe, Frederick (William Serafino Austin Lewis Mary)
See also GLL 1; RGEL 2
Alta 1942- .... **CLC 19**
See also CA 57-60
Alter, Robert B(ernard) 1935- .... **CLC 34**
See also CA 49-52; CANR 1, 47, 100
Alther, Lisa 1944- .... **CLC 7, 41**
See also BPFB 1; CA 65-68; CAAS 30; CANR 12, 30, 51; CN 7; CSW; GLL 2; MTCW 1

Althusser, L.
See Althusser, Louis
Althusser, Louis 1918-1990 .... **CLC 106**
See also CA 131; 132; CANR 102; DLB 242
Altman, Robert 1925- .... **CLC 16, 116**
See also CA 73-76; CANR 43
Alurista .... **HLCS 1**
See Urista (Heredia), Alberto (Baltazar)
See also DLB 82; LLW 1
Alvarez, A(lfred) 1929- .... **CLC 5, 13**
See also CA 1-4R; CANR 3, 33, 63, 101; CN 7; CP 7; DLB 14, 40
Alvarez, Alejandro Rodriguez 1903-1965
See Casona, Alejandro
See also CA 131; 93-96; HW 1
Alvarez, Julia 1950- .... **CLC 93; HLCS 1**
See also AAYA 25; AMWS 7; CA 147; CANR 69, 101; DA3; DLB 282; LATS 1; LLW 1; MTCW 1; NFS 5, 9; SATA 129; WLIT 1
Alvaro, Corrado 1896-1956 .... **TCLC 60**
See also CA 163; DLB 264; EWL 3
Amado, Jorge 1912-2001 ... **CLC 13, 40, 106; HLC 1**
See also CA 77-80; 201; CANR 35, 74; CWW 2; DAM MULT, NOV; DLB 113; EWL 3; HW 2; LAW; LAWS 1; MTCW 1, 2; RGWL 2, 3; TWA; WLIT 1
Ambler, Eric 1909-1998 .... **CLC 4, 6, 9**
See also BRWS 4; CA 9-12R; 171; CANR 7, 38, 74; CMW 4; CN 7; DLB 77; MSW; MTCW 1, 2; TEA
Ambrose, Stephen E(dward) 1936-2002 .... **CLC 145**
See also AAYA 44; CA 1-4R; 209; CANR 3, 43, 57, 83, 105; NCFS 2; SATA 40, 138
Amichai, Yehuda 1924-2000 .. **CLC 9, 22, 57, 116; PC 38**
See also CA 85-88; 189; CANR 46, 60, 99; CWW 2; EWL 3; MTCW 1
Amichai, Yehudah
See Amichai, Yehuda
Amiel, Henri Frederic 1821-1881 .... **NCLC 4**
See also DLB 217
Amis, Kingsley (William) 1922-1995 ...... **CLC 1, 2, 3, 5, 8, 13, 40, 44, 129**
See also AITN 2; BPFB 1; BRWS 2; CA 9-12R; 150; CANR 8, 28, 54; CDBLB 1945-1960; CN 7; CP 7; DA; DA3; DAB; DAC; DAM MST, NOV; DLB 15, 27, 100, 139; DLBY 1996; EWL 3; HGG; INT CANR-8; MTCW 1, 2; RGEL 2; RGSF 2; SFW 4
Amis, Martin (Louis) 1949- .... **CLC 4, 9, 38, 62, 101**
See also BEST 90:3; BRWS 4; CA 65-68; CANR 8, 27, 54, 73, 95; CN 7; DA3; DLB 14, 194; EWL 3; INT CANR-27; MTCW 1
Ammianus Marcellinus c. 330-c. 395 .... **CMLC 60**
See also AW 2; DLB 211
Ammons, A(rchie) R(andolph) 1926-2001 ...... **CLC 2, 3, 5, 8, 9, 25, 57, 108; PC 16**
See also AITN 1; AMWS 7; CA 9-12R; 193; CANR 6, 36, 51, 73, 107; CP 7; CSW; DAM POET; DLB 5, 165; EWL 3; MTCW 1, 2; PFS 19; RGAL 4
Amo, Tauraatua i
See Adams, Henry (Brooks)
Amory, Thomas 1691(?)-1788 .... **LC 48**
See also DLB 39
Anand, Mulk Raj 1905- .... **CLC 23, 93**
See also CA 65-68; CANR 32, 64; CN 7; DAM NOV; EWL 3; MTCW 1, 2; RGSF 2

Anatol
See Schnitzler, Arthur
Anaximander c. 611B.C.-c. 546B.C. .... **CMLC 22**
Anaya, Rudolfo A(lfonso) 1937- ...... **CLC 23, 148; HLC 1**
See also AAYA 20; BYA 13; CA 45-48; CAAS 4; CANR 1, 32, 51, 124; CN 7; DAM MULT, NOV; DLB 82, 206, 278; HW 1; LAIT 4; LLW 1; MTCW 1, 2; NFS 12; RGAL 4; RGSF 2; WLIT 1
Andersen, Hans Christian 1805-1875 .... **NCLC 7, 79; SSC 6, 56; WLC**
See also CLR 6; DA; DA3; DAB; DAC; DAM MST, POP; EW 6; MAICYA 1, 2; RGSF 2; RGWL 2, 3; SATA 100; TWA; WCH; YABC 1
Anderson, C. Farley
See Mencken, H(enry) L(ouis); Nathan, George Jean
Anderson, Jessica (Margaret) Queale 1916- .... **CLC 37**
See also CA 9-12R; CANR 4, 62; CN 7
Anderson, Jon (Victor) 1940- .... **CLC 9**
See also CA 25-28R; CANR 20; DAM POET
Anderson, Lindsay (Gordon) 1923-1994 .... **CLC 20**
See also CA 125; 128; 146; CANR 77
Anderson, Maxwell 1888-1959 .... **TCLC 2, 144**
See also CA 105; 152; DAM DRAM; DFS 16; DLB 7, 228; MTCW 2; RGAL 4
Anderson, Poul (William) 1926-2001 .... **CLC 15**
See also AAYA 5, 34; BPFB 1; BYA 6, 8, 9; CA 1-4R; 181; 199; CAAE 181; CAAS 2; CANR 2, 15, 34, 64, 110; CLR 58; DLB 8; FANT; INT CANR-15; MTCW 1, 2; SATA 90; SATA-Brief 39; SATA-Essay 106; SCFW 2; SFW 4; SUFW 1, 2
Anderson, Robert (Woodruff) 1917- .... **CLC 23**
See also AITN 1; CA 21-24R; CANR 32; DAM DRAM; DLB 7; LAIT 5
Anderson, Roberta Joan
See Mitchell, Joni
Anderson, Sherwood 1876-1941 .. **SSC 1, 46; TCLC 1, 10, 24, 123; WLC**
See also AAYA 30; AMW; AMWC 2; BPFB 1; CA 104; 121; CANR 61; CDALB 1917-1929; DA; DA3; DAB; DAC; DAM MST, NOV; DLB 4, 9, 86; DLBD 1; EWL 3; EXPS; GLL 1; MTCW 1, 2; NFS 4; RGAL 4; RGSF 2; SSFS 4, 10, 11; TUS
Andier, Pierre
See Desnos, Robert
Andouard
See Giraudoux, Jean(-Hippolyte)
Andrade, Carlos Drummond de ..... **CLC 18**
See Drummond de Andrade, Carlos
See also EWL 3; RGWL 2, 3
Andrade, Mario de .... **TCLC 43**
See de Andrade, Mario
See also EWL 3; LAW; RGWL 2, 3; WLIT 1
Andreae, Johann V(alentin) 1586-1654 .... **LC 32**
See also DLB 164
Andreas Capellanus fl. c. 1185- .... **CMLC 45**
See also DLB 208
Andreas-Salome, Lou 1861-1937 ... **TCLC 56**
See also CA 178; DLB 66
Andreev, Leonid
See Andreyev, Leonid (Nikolaevich)
See also DLB 295; EWL 3
Andress, Lesley
See Sanders, Lawrence

Arnold, Matthew 1822-1888 ..... **NCLC 6, 29, 89, 126; PC 5; WLC**
See also BRW 5; CDBLB 1832-1890; DA; DAB; DAC; DAM MST; DLB 32, 57; EXPP; PAB; PFS 2; TEA; WP

Arnold, Thomas 1795-1842 .... **NCLC 18**
See also DLB 55

Arnow, Harriette (Louisa) Simpson
1908-1986 .... **CLC 2, 7, 18**
See also BPFB 1; CA 9-12R; 118; CANR 14; DLB 6; FW; MTCW 1, 2; RHW; SATA 42; SATA-Obit 47

Arouet, Francois-Marie
See Voltaire

Arp, Hans
See Arp, Jean

Arp, Jean 1887-1966 .... **CLC 5; TCLC 115**
See also CA 81-84; 25-28R; CANR 42, 77; EW 10

Arrabal
See Arrabal, Fernando

Arrabal, Fernando 1932- ... **CLC 2, 9, 18, 58**
See Arrabal (Teran), Fernando
See also CA 9-12R; CANR 15; EWL 3; LMFS 2

Arrabal (Teran), Fernando 1932-
See Arrabal, Fernando
See also CWW 2

Arreola, Juan Jose 1918-2001 .... **CLC 147; HLC 1; SSC 38**
See also CA 113; 131; 200; CANR 81; CWW 2; DAM MULT; DLB 113; DNFS 2; EWL 3; HW 1, 2; LAW; RGSF 2

Arrian c. 89(?)-c. 155(?) .... **CMLC 43**
See also DLB 176

Arrick, Fran .... **CLC 30**
See Gaberman, Judie Angell
See also BYA 6

Arriey, Richmond
See Delany, Samuel R(ay), Jr.

Artaud, Antonin (Marie Joseph)
1896-1948 .... **DC 14; TCLC 3, 36**
See also CA 104; 149; DA3; DAM DRAM; DLB 258; EW 11; EWL 3; GFL 1789 to the Present; MTCW 1; RGWL 2, 3

Arthur, Ruth M(abel) 1905-1979 ..... **CLC 12**
See also CA 9-12R; 85-88; CANR 4; CWRI 5; SATA 7, 26

Artsybashev, Mikhail (Petrovich)
1878-1927 .... **TCLC 31**
See also CA 170; DLB 295

Arundel, Honor (Morfydd)
1919-1973 .... **CLC 17**
See also CA 21-22; 41-44R; CAP 2; CLR 35; CWRI 5; SATA 4; SATA-Obit 24

Arzner, Dorothy 1900-1979 .... **CLC 98**

Asch, Sholem 1880-1957 .... **TCLC 3**
See also CA 105; EWL 3; GLL 2

Ascham, Roger 1516(?)-1568 .... **LC 101**
See also DLB 236

Ash, Shalom
See Asch, Sholem

Ashbery, John (Lawrence) 1927- .. **CLC 2, 3, 4, 6, 9, 13, 15, 25, 41, 77, 125; PC 26**
See Berry, Jonas
See also AMWS 3; CA 5-8R; CANR 9, 37, 66, 102; CP 7; DA3; DAM POET; DLB 5, 165; DLBY 1981; EWL 3; INT CANR-9; MTCW 1, 2; PAB; PFS 11; RGAL 4; WP

Ashdown, Clifford
See Freeman, R(ichard) Austin

Ashe, Gordon
See Creasey, John

Ashton-Warner, Sylvia (Constance)
1908-1984 .... **CLC 19**
See also CA 69-72; 112; CANR 29; MTCW 1, 2

Asimov, Isaac 1920-1992 ..... **CLC 1, 3, 9, 19, 26, 76, 92**
See also AAYA 13; BEST 90:2; BPFB 1; BYA 4, 6, 7, 9; CA 1-4R; 137; CANR 2, 19, 36, 60, 125; CLR 12, 79; CMW 4; CPW; DA3; DAM POP; DLB 8; DLBY 1992; INT CANR-19; JRDA; LAIT 5; LMFS 2; MAICYA 1, 2; MTCW 1, 2; RGAL 4; SATA 1, 26, 74; SCFW 2; SFW 4; SSFS 17; TUS; YAW

Askew, Anne 1521(?)-1546 .... **LC 81**
See also DLB 136

Assis, Joaquim Maria Machado de
See Machado de Assis, Joaquim Maria

Astell, Mary 1666-1731 .... **LC 68**
See also DLB 252; FW

Astley, Thea (Beatrice May) 1925- .. **CLC 41**
See also CA 65-68; CANR 11, 43, 78; CN 7; DLB 289; EWL 3

Astley, William 1855-1911
See Warung, Price

Aston, James
See White, T(erence) H(anbury)

Asturias, Miguel Angel 1899-1974 .... **CLC 3, 8, 13; HLC 1**
See also CA 25-28; 49-52; CANR 32; CAP 2; CDWLB 3; DA3; DAM MULT, NOV; DLB 113, 290; EWL 3; HW 1; LAW; LMFS 2; MTCW 1, 2; RGWL 2, 3; WLIT 1

Atares, Carlos Saura
See Saura (Atares), Carlos

Athanasius c. 295-c. 373 .... **CMLC 48**

Atheling, William
See Pound, Ezra (Weston Loomis)

Atheling, William, Jr.
See Blish, James (Benjamin)

Atherton, Gertrude (Franklin Horn)
1857-1948 .... **TCLC 2**
See also CA 104; 155; DLB 9, 78, 186; HGG; RGAL 4; SUFW 1; TCWW 2

Atherton, Lucius
See Masters, Edgar Lee

Atkins, Jack
See Harris, Mark

Atkinson, Kate 1951- .... **CLC 99**
See also CA 166; CANR 101; DLB 267

Attaway, William (Alexander)
1911-1986 .... **BLC 1; CLC 92**
See also BW 2, 3; CA 143; CANR 82; DAM MULT; DLB 76

Atticus
See Fleming, Ian (Lancaster); Wilson, (Thomas) Woodrow

Atwood, Margaret (Eleanor) 1939- ... **CLC 2, 3, 4, 8, 13, 15, 25, 44, 84, 135; PC 8; SSC 2, 46; WLC**
See also AAYA 12, 47; AMWS 13; BEST 89:2; BPFB 1; CA 49-52; CANR 3, 24, 33, 59, 95; CN 7; CP 7; CPW; CWP; DA; DA3; DAB; DAC; DAM MST, NOV, POET; DLB 53, 251; EWL 3; EXPN; FW; INT CANR-24; LAIT 5; MTCW 1, 2; NFS 4, 12, 13, 14; PFS 7; RGSF 2; SATA 50; SSFS 3, 13; TWA; WWE 1; YAW

Aubigny, Pierre d'
See Mencken, H(enry) L(ouis)

Aubin, Penelope 1685-1731(?) .... **LC 9**
See also DLB 39

Auchincloss, Louis (Stanton) 1917- .. **CLC 4, 6, 9, 18, 45; SSC 22**
See also AMWS 4; CA 1-4R; CANR 6, 29, 55, 87; CN 7; DAM NOV; DLB 2, 244; DLBY 1980; EWL 3; INT CANR-29; MTCW 1; RGAL 4

Auden, W(ystan) H(ugh) 1907-1973 . **CLC 1, 2, 3, 4, 6, 9, 11, 14, 43, 123; PC 1; WLC**
See also AAYA 18; AMWS 2; BRW 7; BRWR 1; CA 9-12R; 45-48; CANR 5, 61, 105; CDBLB 1914-1945; DA; DA3; DAB; DAC; DAM DRAM, MST, POET; DLB 10, 20; EWL 3; EXPP; MTCW 1, 2; PAB; PFS 1, 3, 4, 10; TUS; WP

Audiberti, Jacques 1900-1965 .... **CLC 38**
See also CA 25-28R; DAM DRAM; EWL 3

Audubon, John James 1785-1851 . **NCLC 47**
See also ANW; DLB 248

Auel, Jean M(arie) 1936- .... **CLC 31, 107**
See also AAYA 7, 51; BEST 90:4; BPFB 1; CA 103; CANR 21, 64, 115; CPW; DA3; DAM POP; INT CANR-21; NFS 11; RHW; SATA 91

Auerbach, Erich 1892-1957 .... **TCLC 43**
See also CA 118; 155; EWL 3

Augier, Emile 1820-1889 .... **NCLC 31**
See also DLB 192; GFL 1789 to the Present

August, John
See De Voto, Bernard (Augustine)

Augustine, St. 354-430 .... **CMLC 6; WLCS**
See also DA; DA3; DAB; DAC; DAM MST; DLB 115; EW 1; RGWL 2, 3

Aunt Belinda
See Braddon, Mary Elizabeth

Aunt Weedy
See Alcott, Louisa May

Aurelius
See Bourne, Randolph S(illiman)

Aurelius, Marcus 121-180 .... **CMLC 45**
See Marcus Aurelius
See also RGWL 2, 3

Aurobindo, Sri
See Ghose, Aurabinda

Aurobindo Ghose
See Ghose, Aurabinda

Austen, Jane 1775-1817 ...... **NCLC 1, 13, 19, 33, 51, 81, 95, 119; WLC**
See also AAYA 19; BRW 4; BRWC 1; BRWR 2; BYA 3; CDBLB 1789-1832; DA; DA3; DAB; DAC; DAM MST, NOV; DLB 116; EXPN; LAIT 2; LATS 1; LMFS 1; NFS 1, 14, 18; TEA; WLIT 3; WYAS 1

Auster, Paul 1947- .... **CLC 47, 131**
See also AMWS 12; CA 69-72; CANR 23, 52, 75, 129; CMW 4; CN 7; DA3; DLB 227; MTCW 1; SUFW 2

Austin, Frank
See Faust, Frederick (Schiller)
See also TCWW 2

Austin, Mary (Hunter) 1868-1934 . **TCLC 25**
See Stairs, Gordon
See also ANW; CA 109; 178; DLB 9, 78, 206, 221, 275; FW; TCWW 2

Averroes 1126-1198 .... **CMLC 7**
See also DLB 115

Avicenna 980-1037 .... **CMLC 16**
See also DLB 115

Avison, Margaret 1918- .... **CLC 2, 4, 97**
See also CA 17-20R; CP 7; DAC; DAM POET; DLB 53; MTCW 1

Axton, David
See Koontz, Dean R(ay)

Ayckbourn, Alan 1939- ...... **CLC 5, 8, 18, 33, 74; DC 13**
See also BRWS 5; CA 21-24R; CANR 31, 59, 118; CBD; CD 5; DAB; DAM DRAM; DFS 7; DLB 13, 245; EWL 3; MTCW 1, 2

Aydy, Catherine
See Tennant, Emma (Christina)

Barbour, John c. 1316-1395 .... **CMLC 33**
See also DLB 146
Barbusse, Henri 1873-1935 .... **TCLC 5**
See also CA 105; 154; DLB 65; EWL 3;
RGWL 2, 3
Barclay, Bill
See Moorcock, Michael (John)
Barclay, William Ewert
See Moorcock, Michael (John)
Barea, Arturo 1897-1957 .... **TCLC 14**
See also CA 111; 201
Barfoot, Joan 1946- .... **CLC 18**
See also CA 105
Barham, Richard Harris
1788-1845 .... **NCLC 77**
See also DLB 159
Baring, Maurice 1874-1945 .... **TCLC 8**
See also CA 105; 168; DLB 34; HGG
Baring-Gould, Sabine 1834-1924 ... **TCLC 88**
See also DLB 156, 190
Barker, Clive 1952- .... **CLC 52; SSC 53**
See also AAYA 10; BEST 90:3; BPFB 1;
CA 121; 129; CANR 71, 111; CPW; DA3;
DAM POP; DLB 261; HGG; INT CA-
129; MTCW 1, 2; SUFW 2
Barker, George Granville
1913-1991 .... **CLC 8, 48**
See also CA 9-12R; 135; CANR 7, 38;
DAM POET; DLB 20; EWL 3; MTCW 1
Barker, Harley Granville
See Granville-Barker, Harley
See also DLB 10
Barker, Howard 1946- .... **CLC 37**
See also CA 102; CBD; CD 5; DLB 13,
233
Barker, Jane 1652-1732 .... **LC 42, 82**
See also DLB 39, 131
Barker, Pat(ricia) 1943- ...... **CLC 32, 94, 146**
See also BRWS 4; CA 117; 122; CANR 50,
101; CN 7; DLB 271; INT CA-122
Barlach, Ernst (Heinrich)
1870-1938 .... **TCLC 84**
See also CA 178; DLB 56, 118; EWL 3
Barlow, Joel 1754-1812 .... **NCLC 23**
See also AMWS 2; DLB 37; RGAL 4
Barnard, Mary (Ethel) 1909- .... **CLC 48**
See also CA 21-22; CAP 2
Barnes, Djuna 1892-1982 .... **CLC 3, 4, 8, 11,**
29, 127; SSC 3
See Steptoe, Lydia
See also AMWS 3; CA 9-12R; 107; CAD;
CANR 16, 55; CWD; DLB 4, 9, 45; EWL
3; GLL 1; MTCW 1, 2; RGAL 4; TUS
Barnes, Jim 1933- .... **NNAL**
See also CA 108; 175; CAAE 175; CAAS
28; DLB 175
Barnes, Julian (Patrick) 1946- . **CLC 42, 141**
See also BRWS 4; CA 102; CANR 19, 54,
115; CN 7; DAB; DLB 194; DLBY 1993;
EWL 3; MTCW 1
Barnes, Peter 1931- .... **CLC 5, 56**
See also CA 65-68; CAAS 12; CANR 33,
34, 64, 113; CBD; CD 5; DFS 6; DLB
13, 233; MTCW 1
Barnes, William 1801-1886 .... **NCLC 75**
See also DLB 32
Baroja (y Nessi), Pio 1872-1956 .... **HLC 1;**
TCLC 8
See also CA 104; EW 9
Baron, David
See Pinter, Harold
Baron Corvo
See Rolfe, Frederick (William Serafino
Austin Lewis Mary)
Barondess, Sue K(aufman)
1926-1977 .... **CLC 8**
See Kaufman, Sue
See also CA 1-4R; 69-72; CANR 1

Baron de Teive
See Pessoa, Fernando (Antonio Nogueira)
Baroness Von S.
See Zangwill, Israel
Barres, (Auguste-)Maurice
1862-1923 .... **TCLC 47**
See also CA 164; DLB 123; GFL 1789 to
the Present
Barreto, Afonso Henrique de Lima
See Lima Barreto, Afonso Henrique de
Barrett, Andrea 1954- .... **CLC 150**
See also CA 156; CANR 92
Barrett, Michele .... **CLC 65**
Barrett, (Roger) Syd 1946- .... **CLC 35**
Barrett, William (Christopher)
1913-1992 .... **CLC 27**
See also CA 13-16R; 139; CANR 11, 67;
INT CANR-11
Barrie, J(ames) M(atthew)
1860-1937 .... **TCLC 2**
See also BRWS 3; BYA 4, 5; CA 104; 136;
CANR 77; CDBLB 1890-1914; CLR 16;
CWRI 5; DA3; DAB; DAM DRAM; DFS
7; DLB 10, 141, 156; EWL 3; FANT;
MAICYA 1, 2; MTCW 1; SATA 100;
SUFW; WCH; WLIT 4; YABC 1
Barrington, Michael
See Moorcock, Michael (John)
Barrol, Grady
See Bograd, Larry
Barry, Mike
See Malzberg, Barry N(athaniel)
Barry, Philip 1896-1949 .... **TCLC 11**
See also CA 109; 199; DFS 9; DLB 7, 228;
RGAL 4
Bart, Andre Schwarz
See Schwarz-Bart, Andre
Barth, John (Simmons) 1930- ... **CLC 1, 2, 3,**
5, 7, 9, 10, 14, 27, 51, 89; SSC 10
See also AITN 1, 2; AMW; BPFB 1; CA
1-4R; CABS 1; CANR 5, 23, 49, 64, 113;
CN 7; DAM NOV; DLB 2, 227; EWL 3;
FANT; MTCW 1; RGAL 4; RGSF 2;
RHW; SSFS 6; TUS
Barthelme, Donald 1931-1989 ... **CLC 1, 2, 3,**
5, 6, 8, 13, 23, 46, 59, 115; SSC 2, 55
See also AMWS 4; BPFB 1; CA 21-24R;
129; CANR 20, 58; DA3; DAM NOV;
DLB 2, 234; DLBY 1980, 1989; EWL 3;
FANT; LMFS 2; MTCW 1, 2; RGAL 4;
RGSF 2; SATA 7; SATA-Obit 62; SSFS
17
Barthelme, Frederick 1943- ...... **CLC 36, 117**
See also AMWS 11; CA 114; 122; CANR
77; CN 7; CSW; DLB 244; DLBY 1985;
EWL 3; INT CA-122
Barthes, Roland (Gerard)
1915-1980 .... **CLC 24, 83; TCLC 135**
See also CA 130; 97-100; CANR 66; DLB
296; EW 13; EWL 3; GFL 1789 to the
Present; MTCW 1, 2; TWA
Barzun, Jacques (Martin) 1907- ..... **CLC 51,**
145
See also CA 61-64; CANR 22, 95
Bashevis, Isaac
See Singer, Isaac Bashevis
Bashkirtseff, Marie 1859-1884 .... **NCLC 27**
Basho, Matsuo
See Matsuo Basho
See also PFS 18; RGWL 2, 3; WP
Basil of Caesaria c. 330-379 .... **CMLC 35**
Basket, Raney
See Edgerton, Clyde (Carlyle)
Bass, Kingsley B., Jr.
See Bullins, Ed
Bass, Rick 1958- .... **CLC 79, 143; SSC 60**
See also ANW; CA 126; CANR 53, 93;
CSW; DLB 212, 275

Bassani, Giorgio 1916-2000 .... **CLC 9**
See also CA 65-68; 190; CANR 33; CWW
2; DLB 128, 177; EWL 3; MTCW 1;
RGWL 2, 3
Bastian, Ann .... **CLC 70**
Bastos, Augusto (Antonio) Roa
See Roa Bastos, Augusto (Antonio)
Bataille, Georges 1897-1962 .... **CLC 29**
See also CA 101; 89-92; EWL 3
Bates, H(erbert) E(rnest)
1905-1974 .... **CLC 46; SSC 10**
See also CA 93-96; 45-48; CANR 34; DA3;
DAB; DAM POP; DLB 162, 191; EWL
3; EXPS; MTCW 1, 2; RGSF 2; SSFS 7
Bauchart
See Camus, Albert
Baudelaire, Charles 1821-1867 . **NCLC 6, 29,**
55; PC 1; SSC 18; WLC
See also DA; DA3; DAB; DAC; DAM
MST, POET; DLB 217; EW 7; GFL 1789
to the Present; LMFS 2; RGWL 2, 3;
TWA
Baudouin, Marcel
See Peguy, Charles (Pierre)
Baudouin, Pierre
See Peguy, Charles (Pierre)
Baudrillard, Jean 1929- .... **CLC 60**
See also DLB 296
Baum, L(yman) Frank 1856-1919 .. **TCLC 7,**
132
See also AAYA 46; BYA 16; CA 108; 133;
CLR 15; CWRI 5; DLB 22; FANT; JRDA;
MAICYA 1, 2; MTCW 1, 2; NFS 13;
RGAL 4; SATA 18, 100; WCH
Baum, Louis F.
See Baum, L(yman) Frank
Baumbach, Jonathan 1933- .... **CLC 6, 23**
See also CA 13-16R; CAAS 5; CANR 12,
66; CN 7; DLBY 1980; INT CANR-12;
MTCW 1
Bausch, Richard (Carl) 1945- .... **CLC 51**
See also AMWS 7; CA 101; CAAS 14;
CANR 43, 61, 87; CSW; DLB 130
Baxter, Charles (Morley) 1947- . **CLC 45, 78**
See also CA 57-60; CANR 40, 64, 104;
CPW; DAM POP; DLB 130; MTCW 2
Baxter, George Owen
See Faust, Frederick (Schiller)
Baxter, James K(eir) 1926-1972 .... **CLC 14**
See also CA 77-80; EWL 3
Baxter, John
See Hunt, E(verette) Howard, (Jr.)
Bayer, Sylvia
See Glassco, John
Baynton, Barbara 1857-1929 .... **TCLC 57**
See also DLB 230; RGSF 2
Beagle, Peter S(oyer) 1939- .... **CLC 7, 104**
See also AAYA 47; BPFB 1; BYA 9, 10,
16; CA 9-12R; CANR 4, 51, 73, 110;
DA3; DLBY 1980; FANT; INT CANR-4;
MTCW 1; SATA 60, 130; SUFW 1, 2;
YAW
Bean, Normal
See Burroughs, Edgar Rice
Beard, Charles A(ustin)
1874-1948 .... **TCLC 15**
See also CA 115; 189; DLB 17; SATA 18
Beardsley, Aubrey 1872-1898 .... **NCLC 6**
Beattie, Ann 1947- ..... **CLC 8, 13, 18, 40, 63,**
146; SSC 11
See also AMWS 5; BEST 90:2; BPFB 1;
CA 81-84; CANR 53, 73, 128; CN 7;
CPW; DA3; DAM NOV, POP; DLB 218,
278; DLBY 1982; EWL 3; MTCW 1, 2;
RGAL 4; RGSF 2; SSFS 9; TUS
Beattie, James 1735-1803 .... **NCLC 25**
See also DLB 109

Brodzki, Bella ed. .... **CLC 65**

Brome, Richard 1590(?)-1652 .... **LC 61**
See also DLB 58

Bromell, Henry 1947- .... **CLC 5**
See also CA 53-56; CANR 9, 115, 116

Bromfield, Louis (Brucker)
1896-1956 .... **TCLC 11**
See also CA 107; 155; DLB 4, 9, 86; RGAL
4; RHW

Broner, E(sther) M(asserman)
1930- .... **CLC 19**
See also CA 17-20R; CANR 8, 25, 72; CN
7; DLB 28

Bronk, William (M.) 1918-1999 .... **CLC 10**
See also CA 89-92; 177; CANR 23; CP 7;
DLB 165

Bronstein, Lev Davidovich
See Trotsky, Leon

Bronte, Anne 1820-1849 ..... **NCLC 4, 71, 102**
See also BRW 5; BRWR 1; DA3; DLB 21,
199; TEA

Bronte, (Patrick) Branwell
1817-1848 .... **NCLC 109**

Bronte, Charlotte 1816-1855 ...... **NCLC 3, 8,
33, 58, 105; WLC**
See also AAYA 17; BRW 5; BRWC 2;
BRWR 1; BYA 2; CDBLB 1832-1890;
DA; DA3; DAB; DAC; DAM MST, NOV;
DLB 21, 159, 199; EXPN; LAIT 2; NFS
4; TEA; WLIT 4

Bronte, Emily (Jane) 1818-1848 ... **NCLC 16,
35; PC 8; WLC**
See also AAYA 17; BPFB 1; BRW 5;
BRWC 1; BRWR 1; BYA 3; CDBLB
1832-1890; DA; DA3; DAB; DAC; DAM
MST, NOV, POET; DLB 21, 32, 199;
EXPN; LAIT 1; TEA; WLIT 3

Brontes
See Bronte, Anne; Bronte, Charlotte; Bronte,
Emily (Jane)

Brooke, Frances 1724-1789 .... **LC 6, 48**
See also DLB 39, 99

Brooke, Henry 1703(?)-1783 .... **LC 1**
See also DLB 39

Brooke, Rupert (Chawner)
1887-1915 ..... **PC 24; TCLC 2, 7; WLC**
See also BRWS 3; CA 104; 132; CANR 61;
CDBLB 1914-1945; DA; DAB; DAC;
DAM MST, POET; DLB 19, 216; EXPP;
GLL 2; MTCW 1, 2; PFS 7; TEA

Brooke-Haven, P.
See Wodehouse, P(elham) G(renville)

Brooke-Rose, Christine 1926(?)- ..... **CLC 40,
184**
See also BRWS 4; CA 13-16R; CANR 58,
118; CN 7; DLB 14, 231; EWL 3; SFW 4

Brookner, Anita 1928- .. **CLC 32, 34, 51, 136**
See also BRWS 4; CA 114; 120; CANR 37,
56, 87; CN 7; CPW; DA3; DAB; DAM
POP; DLB 194; DLBY 1987; EWL 3;
MTCW 1, 2; TEA

Brooks, Cleanth 1906-1994 . **CLC 24, 86, 110**
See also CA 17-20R; 145; CANR 33, 35;
CSW; DLB 63; DLBY 1994; EWL 3; INT
CANR-35; MTCW 1, 2

Brooks, George
See Baum, L(yman) Frank

Brooks, Gwendolyn (Elizabeth)
1917-2000 ... **BLC 1; CLC 1, 2, 4, 5, 15,
49, 125; PC 7; WLC**
See also AAYA 20; AFAW 1, 2; AITN 1;
AMWS 3; BW 2, 3; CA 1-4R; 190; CANR
1, 27, 52, 75; CDALB 1941-1968; CLR
27; CP 7; CWP; DA; DA3; DAC; DAM
MST, MULT, POET; DLB 5, 76, 165;
EWL 3; EXPP; MAWW; MTCW 1, 2;
PFS 1, 2, 4, 6; RGAL 4; SATA 6; SATA-
Obit 123; TUS; WP

Brooks, Mel .... **CLC 12**
See Kaminsky, Melvin
See also AAYA 13, 48; DLB 26

Brooks, Peter (Preston) 1938- .... **CLC 34**
See also CA 45-48; CANR 1, 107

Brooks, Van Wyck 1886-1963 .... **CLC 29**
See also AMW; CA 1-4R; CANR 6; DLB
45, 63, 103; TUS

Brophy, Brigid (Antonia)
1929-1995 .... **CLC 6, 11, 29, 105**
See also CA 5-8R; 149; CAAS 4; CANR
25, 53; CBD; CN 7; CWD; DA3; DLB
14, 271; EWL 3; MTCW 1, 2

Brosman, Catharine Savage 1934- ..... **CLC 9**
See also CA 61-64; CANR 21, 46

Brossard, Nicole 1943- .... **CLC 115, 169**
See also CA 122; CAAS 16; CCA 1; CWP;
CWW 2; DLB 53; EWL 3; FW; GLL 2;
RGWL 3

Brother Antoninus
See Everson, William (Oliver)

The Brothers Quay
See Quay, Stephen; Quay, Timothy

Broughton, T(homas) Alan 1936- ..... **CLC 19**
See also CA 45-48; CANR 2, 23, 48, 111

Broumas, Olga 1949- .... **CLC 10, 73**
See also CA 85-88; CANR 20, 69, 110; CP
7; CWP; GLL 2

Broun, Heywood 1888-1939 .... **TCLC 104**
See also DLB 29, 171

Brown, Alan 1950- .... **CLC 99**
See also CA 156

Brown, Charles Brockden
1771-1810 .... **NCLC 22, 74, 122**
See also AMWS 1; CDALB 1640-1865;
DLB 37, 59, 73; FW; HGG; LMFS 1;
RGAL 4; TUS

Brown, Christy 1932-1981 .... **CLC 63**
See also BYA 13; CA 105; 104; CANR 72;
DLB 14

Brown, Claude 1937-2002 ... **BLC 1; CLC 30**
See also AAYA 7; BW 1, 3; CA 73-76; 205;
CANR 81; DAM MULT

Brown, Dee (Alexander)
1908-2002 .... **CLC 18, 47**
See also AAYA 30; CA 13-16R; 212; CAAS
6; CANR 11, 45, 60; CPW; CSW; DA3;
DAM POP; DLBY 1980; LAIT 2; MTCW
1, 2; NCFS 5; SATA 5, 110; SATA-Obit
141; TCWW 2

Brown, George
See Wertmueller, Lina

Brown, George Douglas
1869-1902 .... **TCLC 28**
See Douglas, George
See also CA 162

Brown, George Mackay 1921-1996 ... **CLC 5,
48, 100**
See also BRWS 6; CA 21-24R; 151; CAAS
6; CANR 12, 37, 67; CN 7; CP 7; DLB
14, 27, 139, 271; MTCW 1; RGSF 2;
SATA 35

Brown, (William) Larry 1951- .... **CLC 73**
See also CA 130; 134; CANR 117; CSW;
DLB 234; INT CA-134

Brown, Moses
See Barrett, William (Christopher)

Brown, Rita Mae 1944- .... **CLC 18, 43, 79**
See also BPFB 1; CA 45-48; CANR 2, 11,
35, 62, 95; CN 7; CPW; CSW; DA3;
DAM NOV, POP; FW; INT CANR-11;
MTCW 1, 2; NFS 9; RGAL 4; TUS

Brown, Roderick (Langmere) Haig-
See Haig-Brown, Roderick (Langmere)

Brown, Rosellen 1939- .... **CLC 32, 170**
See also CA 77-80; CAAS 10; CANR 14,
44, 98; CN 7

Brown, Sterling Allen 1901-1989 ...... **BLC 1;
CLC 1, 23, 59; HR 2; PC 55**
See also AFAW 1, 2; BW 1, 3; CA 85-88;
127; CANR 26; DA3; DAM MULT,
POET; DLB 48, 51, 63; MTCW 1, 2;
RGAL 4; WP

Brown, Will
See Ainsworth, William Harrison

Brown, William Hill 1765-1793 .... **LC 93**
See also DLB 37

Brown, William Wells 1815-1884 ...... **BLC 1;
DC 1; NCLC 2, 89**
See also DAM MULT; DLB 3, 50, 183,
248; RGAL 4

Browne, (Clyde) Jackson 1948(?)- ... **CLC 21**
See also CA 120

Browning, Elizabeth Barrett
1806-1861 ... **NCLC 1, 16, 61, 66; PC 6;
WLC**
See also BRW 4; CDBLB 1832-1890; DA;
DA3; DAB; DAC; DAM MST, POET;
DLB 32, 199; EXPP; PAB; PFS 2, 16;
TEA; WLIT 4; WP

Browning, Robert 1812-1889 . **NCLC 19, 79;
PC 2; WLCS**
See also BRW 4; BRWC 2; BRWR 2; CD-
BLB 1832-1890; CLR 97; DA; DA3;
DAB; DAC; DAM MST, POET; DLB 32,
163; EXPP; LATS 1; PAB; PFS 1, 15;
RGEL 2; TEA; WLIT 4; WP; YABC 1

Browning, Tod 1882-1962 .... **CLC 16**
See also CA 141; 117

Brownmiller, Susan 1935- .... **CLC 159**
See also CA 103; CANR 35, 75; DAM
NOV; FW; MTCW 1, 2

Brownson, Orestes Augustus
1803-1876 .... **NCLC 50**
See also DLB 1, 59, 73, 243

Bruccoli, Matthew J(oseph) 1931- ... **CLC 34**
See also CA 9-12R; CANR 7, 87; DLB 103

Bruce, Lenny .... **CLC 21**
See Schneider, Leonard Alfred

Bruchac, Joseph III 1942- .... **NNAL**
See also AAYA 19; CA 33-36R; CANR 13,
47, 75, 94; CLR 46; CWRI 5; DAM
MULT; JRDA; MAICYA 2; MAICYAS 1;
MTCW 1; SATA 42, 89, 131

Bruin, John
See Brutus, Dennis

Brulard, Henri
See Stendhal

Brulls, Christian
See Simenon, Georges (Jacques Christian)

Brunner, John (Kilian Houston)
1934-1995 .... **CLC 8, 10**
See also CA 1-4R; 149; CAAS 8; CANR 2,
37; CPW; DAM POP; DLB 261; MTCW
1, 2; SCFW 2; SFW 4

Bruno, Giordano 1548-1600 .... **LC 27**
See also RGWL 2, 3

Brutus, Dennis 1924- .. **BLC 1; CLC 43; PC
24**
See also AFW; BW 2, 3; CA 49-52; CAAS
14; CANR 2, 27, 42, 81; CDWLB 3; CP
7; DAM MULT, POET; DLB 117, 225;
EWL 3

Bryan, C(ourtlandt) D(ixon) B(arnes)
1936- .... **CLC 29**
See also CA 73-76; CANR 13, 68; DLB
185; INT CANR-13

Bryan, Michael
See Moore, Brian
See also CCA 1

Bryan, William Jennings
1860-1925 .... **TCLC 99**

Bryant, William Cullen 1794-1878 . **NCLC 6,
46; PC 20**
See also AMWS 1; CDALB 1640-1865;
DA; DAB; DAC; DAM MST, POET;
DLB 3, 43, 59, 189, 250; EXPP; PAB;
RGAL 4; TUS

Bryusov, Valery Yakovlevich
1873-1924 .... **TCLC 10**
See also CA 107; 155; EWL 3; SFW 4

Buchan, John 1875-1940 .... **TCLC 41**
See also CA 108; 145; CMW 4; DAB;
DAM POP; DLB 34, 70, 156; HGG;
MSW; MTCW 1; RGEL 2; RHW; YABC
2

Buchanan, George 1506-1582 .... **LC 4**
See also DLB 132

Buchanan, Robert 1841-1901 .... **TCLC 107**
See also CA 179; DLB 18, 35

Buchheim, Lothar-Guenther 1918- .... **CLC 6**
See also CA 85-88

Buchner, (Karl) Georg 1813-1837 . **NCLC 26**
See also CDWLB 2; DLB 133; EW 6;
RGSF 2; RGWL 2, 3; TWA

Buchwald, Art(hur) 1925- .... **CLC 33**
See also AITN 1; CA 5-8R; CANR 21, 67,
107; MTCW 1, 2; SATA 10

Buck, Pearl S(ydenstricker)
1892-1973 .... **CLC 7, 11, 18, 127**
See also AAYA 42; AITN 1; AMWS 2;
BPFB 1; CA 1-4R; 41-44R; CANR 1, 34;
CDALBS; DA; DA3; DAB; DAC; DAM
MST, NOV; DLB 9, 102; EWL 3; LAIT
3; MTCW 1, 2; RGAL 4; RHW; SATA 1,
25; TUS

Buckler, Ernest 1908-1984 .... **CLC 13**
See also CA 11-12; 114; CAP 1; CCA 1;
DAC; DAM MST; DLB 68; SATA 47

Buckley, Christopher (Taylor)
1952- .... **CLC 165**
See also CA 139; CANR 119

Buckley, Vincent (Thomas)
1925-1988 .... **CLC 57**
See also CA 101; DLB 289

Buckley, William F(rank), Jr. 1925- . **CLC 7,
18, 37**
See also AITN 1; BPFB 1; CA 1-4R; CANR
1, 24, 53, 93; CMW 4; CPW; DA3; DAM
POP; DLB 137; DLBY 1980; INT CANR-
24; MTCW 1, 2; TUS

Buechner, (Carl) Frederick 1926- . **CLC 2, 4,
6, 9**
See also AMWS 12; BPFB 1; CA 13-16R;
CANR 11, 39, 64, 114; CN 7; DAM NOV;
DLBY 1980; INT CANR-11; MTCW 1, 2

Buell, John (Edward) 1927- .... **CLC 10**
See also CA 1-4R; CANR 71; DLB 53

Buero Vallejo, Antonio 1916-2000 ... **CLC 15,
46, 139; DC 18**
See also CA 106; 189; CANR 24, 49, 75;
CWW 2; DFS 11; EWL 3; HW 1; MTCW
1, 2

Bufalino, Gesualdo 1920-1996 .... **CLC 74**
See also CWW 2; DLB 196

Bugayev, Boris Nikolayevich
1880-1934 .... **PC 11; TCLC 7**
See Bely, Andrey; Belyi, Andrei
See also CA 104; 165; MTCW 1

Bukowski, Charles 1920-1994 ... **CLC 2, 5, 9,
41, 82, 108; PC 18; SSC 45**
See also CA 17-20R; 144; CANR 40, 62,
105; CPW; DA3; DAM NOV, POET;
DLB 5, 130, 169; EWL 3; MTCW 1, 2

Bulgakov, Mikhail (Afanas'evich)
1891-1940 .... **SSC 18; TCLC 2, 16**
See also BPFB 1; CA 105; 152; DAM
DRAM, NOV; DLB 272; EWL 3; NFS 8;
RGSF 2; RGWL 2, 3; SFW 4; TWA

Bulgya, Alexander Alexandrovich
1901-1956 .... **TCLC 53**
See Fadeev, Aleksandr Aleksandrovich;
Fadeev, Alexandr Alexandrovich; Fadeyev,
Alexander
See also CA 117; 181

Bullins, Ed 1935- ... **BLC 1; CLC 1, 5, 7; DC
6**
See also BW 2, 3; CA 49-52; CAAS 16;
CAD; CANR 24, 46, 73; CD 5; DAM
DRAM, MULT; DLB 7, 38, 249; EWL 3;
MTCW 1, 2; RGAL 4

Bulosan, Carlos 1911-1956 .... **AAL**
See also CA 216; RGAL 4

**Bulwer-Lytton, Edward (George Earle
Lytton)** 1803-1873 .... **NCLC 1, 45**
See also DLB 21; RGEL 2; SFW 4; SUFW
1; TEA

Bunin, Ivan Alexeyevich 1870-1953 ... **SSC 5;
TCLC 6**
See also CA 104; EWL 3; RGSF 2; RGWL
2, 3; TWA

Bunting, Basil 1900-1985 ...... **CLC 10, 39, 47**
See also BRWS 7; CA 53-56; 115; CANR
7; DAM POET; DLB 20; EWL 3; RGEL
2

Bunuel, Luis 1900-1983 ... **CLC 16, 80; HLC
1**
See also CA 101; 110; CANR 32, 77; DAM
MULT; HW 1

Bunyan, John 1628-1688 ..... **LC 4, 69; WLC**
See also BRW 2; BYA 5; CDBLB 1660-
1789; DA; DAB; DAC; DAM MST; DLB
39; RGEL 2; TEA; WCH; WLIT 3

Buravsky, Alexandr .... **CLC 59**

Burckhardt, Jacob (Christoph)
1818-1897 .... **NCLC 49**
See also EW 6

Burford, Eleanor
See Hibbert, Eleanor Alice Burford

Burgess, Anthony . **CLC 1, 2, 4, 5, 8, 10, 13,
15, 22, 40, 62, 81, 94**
See Wilson, John (Anthony) Burgess
See also AAYA 25; AITN 1; BRWS 1; CD-
BLB 1960 to Present; DAB; DLB 14, 194,
261; DLBY 1998; EWL 3; MTCW 1;
RGEL 2; RHW; SFW 4; YAW

Burke, Edmund 1729(?)-1797 .... **LC 7, 36;
WLC**
See also BRW 3; DA; DA3; DAB; DAC;
DAM MST; DLB 104, 252; RGEL 2;
TEA

Burke, Kenneth (Duva) 1897-1993 ... **CLC 2,
24**
See also AMW; CA 5-8R; 143; CANR 39,
74; DLB 45, 63; EWL 3; MTCW 1, 2;
RGAL 4

Burke, Leda
See Garnett, David

Burke, Ralph
See Silverberg, Robert

Burke, Thomas 1886-1945 .... **TCLC 63**
See also CA 113; 155; CMW 4; DLB 197

Burney, Fanny 1752-1840 .... **NCLC 12, 54,
107**
See also BRWS 3; DLB 39; NFS 16; RGEL
2; TEA

Burney, Frances
See Burney, Fanny

Burns, Robert 1759-1796 ... **LC 3, 29, 40; PC
6; WLC**
See also AAYA 51; BRW 3; CDBLB 1789-
1832; DA; DA3; DAB; DAC; DAM MST,
POET; DLB 109; EXPP; PAB; RGEL 2;
TEA; WP

Burns, Tex
See L'Amour, Louis (Dearborn)
See also TCWW 2

Burnshaw, Stanley 1906- .... **CLC 3, 13, 44**
See also CA 9-12R; CP 7; DLB 48; DLBY
1997

Burr, Anne 1937- .... **CLC 6**
See also CA 25-28R

Burroughs, Edgar Rice 1875-1950 . **TCLC 2,
32**
See also AAYA 11; BPFB 1; BYA 4, 9; CA
104; 132; DA3; DAM NOV; DLB 8;
FANT; MTCW 1, 2; RGAL 4; SATA 41;
SCFW 2; SFW 4; TUS; YAW

Burroughs, William S(eward)
1914-1997 .. **CLC 1, 2, 5, 15, 22, 42, 75,
109; TCLC 121; WLC**
See Lee, William; Lee, Willy
See also AITN 2; AMWS 3; BG 2; BPFB
1; CA 9-12R; 160; CANR 20, 52, 104;
CN 7; CPW; DA; DA3; DAB; DAC;
DAM MST, NOV, POP; DLB 2, 8, 16,
152, 237; DLBY 1981, 1997; EWL 3;
HGG; LMFS 2; MTCW 1, 2; RGAL 4;
SFW 4

Burton, Sir Richard F(rancis)
1821-1890 .... **NCLC 42**
See also DLB 55, 166, 184

Burton, Robert 1577-1640 .... **LC 74**
See also DLB 151; RGEL 2

Buruma, Ian 1951- .... **CLC 163**
See also CA 128; CANR 65

Busch, Frederick 1941- ... **CLC 7, 10, 18, 47,
166**
See also CA 33-36R; CAAS 1; CANR 45,
73, 92; CN 7; DLB 6, 218

Bush, Barney (Furman) 1946- .... **NNAL**
See also CA 145

Bush, Ronald 1946- .... **CLC 34**
See also CA 136

Bustos, F(rancisco)
See Borges, Jorge Luis

Bustos Domecq, H(onorio)
See Bioy Casares, Adolfo; Borges, Jorge
Luis

Butler, Octavia E(stelle) 1947- .. **BLCS; CLC
38, 121**
See also AAYA 18, 48; AFAW 2; AMWS
13; BPFB 1; BW 2, 3; CA 73-76; CANR
12, 24, 38, 73; CLR 65; CPW; DA3;
DAM MULT, POP; DLB 33; LATS 1;
MTCW 1, 2; NFS 8; SATA 84; SCFW 2;
SFW 4; SSFS 6; YAW

Butler, Robert Olen, (Jr.) 1945- ...... **CLC 81,
162**
See also AMWS 12; BPFB 1; CA 112;
CANR 66; CSW; DAM POP; DLB 173;
INT CA-112; MTCW 1; SSFS 11

Butler, Samuel 1612-1680 .... **LC 16, 43**
See also DLB 101, 126; RGEL 2

Butler, Samuel 1835-1902 .... **TCLC 1, 33;
WLC**
See also BRWS 2; CA 143; CDBLB 1890-
1914; DA; DA3; DAB; DAC; DAM MST,
NOV; DLB 18, 57, 174; RGEL 2; SFW 4;
TEA

Butler, Walter C.
See Faust, Frederick (Schiller)

Butor, Michel (Marie Francois)
1926- .... **CLC 1, 3, 8, 11, 15, 161**
See also CA 9-12R; CANR 33, 66; CWW
2; DLB 83; EW 13; EWL 3; GFL 1789 to
the Present; MTCW 1, 2

Butts, Mary 1890(?)-1937 .... **TCLC 77**
See also CA 148; DLB 240

Buxton, Ralph
See Silverstein, Alvin; Silverstein, Virginia
B(arbara Opshelor)

Buzo, Alex
See Buzo, Alexander (John)
See also DLB 289

Buzo, Alexander (John) 1944- .... **CLC 61**
See also CA 97-100; CANR 17, 39, 69; CD
5

Buzzati, Dino 1906-1972 .... **CLC 36**
See also CA 160; 33-36R; DLB 177; RGWL
2, 3; SFW 4

Byars, Betsy (Cromer) 1928- .... **CLC 35**
See also AAYA 19; BYA 3; CA 33-36R,
183; CAAE 183; CANR 18, 36, 57, 102;
CLR 1, 16, 72; DLB 52; INT CANR-18;
JRDA; MAICYA 1, 2; MAICYAS 1;
MTCW 1; SAAS 1; SATA 4, 46, 80;
SATA-Essay 108; WYA; YAW

Byatt, A(ntonia) S(usan Drabble)
1936- .... **CLC 19, 65, 136**
See also BPFB 1; BRWC 2; BRWS 4; CA
13-16R; CANR 13, 33, 50, 75, 96; DA3;
DAM NOV, POP; DLB 14, 194; EWL 3;
MTCW 1, 2; RGSF; RHW; TEA

Byrne, David 1952- .... **CLC 26**
See also CA 127

Byrne, John Keyes 1926-
See Leonard, Hugh
See also CA 102; CANR 78; INT CA-102

Byron, George Gordon (Noel)
1788-1824 ..... **NCLC 2, 12, 109; PC 16;**
WLC
See also BRW 4; BRWC 2; CDBLB 1789-
1832; DA; DA3; DAB; DAC; DAM MST,
POET; DLB 96, 110; EXPP; LMFS 1;
PAB; PFS 1, 14; RGEL 2; TEA; WLIT 3;
WP

Byron, Robert 1905-1941 .... **TCLC 67**
See also CA 160; DLB 195

C. 3. 3.
See Wilde, Oscar (Fingal O'Flahertie Wills)

Caballero, Fernan 1796-1877 .... **NCLC 10**

Cabell, Branch
See Cabell, James Branch

Cabell, James Branch 1879-1958 .... **TCLC 6**
See also CA 105; 152; DLB 9, 78; FANT;
MTCW 1; RGAL 4; SUFW 1

Cabeza de Vaca, Alvar Nunez
1490-1557(?) .... **LC 61**

Cable, George Washington
1844-1925 .... **SSC 4; TCLC 4**
See also CA 104; 155; DLB 12, 74; DLBD
13; RGAL 4; TUS

Cabral de Melo Neto, Joao
1920-1999 .... **CLC 76**
See Melo Neto, Joao Cabral de
See also CA 151; DAM MULT; LAW;
LAWS 1

Cabrera Infante, G(uillermo) 1929- . **CLC 5,**
25, 45, 120; HLC 1; SSC 39
See also CA 85-88; CANR 29, 65, 110; CD-
WLB 3; CWW 2; DA3; DAM MULT;
DLB 113; EWL 3; HW 1, 2; LAW; LAWS
1; MTCW 1, 2; RGSF 2; WLIT 1

Cade, Toni
See Bambara, Toni Cade

Cadmus and Harmonia
See Buchan, John

Caedmon fl. 658-680 .... **CMLC 7**
See also DLB 146

Caeiro, Alberto
See Pessoa, Fernando (Antonio Nogueira)

Caesar, Julius .... **CMLC 47**
See Julius Caesar
See also AW 1; RGWL 2, 3

Cage, John (Milton, Jr.) 1912-1992 . **CLC 41**
See also CA 13-16R; 169; CANR 9, 78;
DLB 193; INT CANR-9

Cahan, Abraham 1860-1951 .... **TCLC 71**
See also CA 108; 154; DLB 9, 25, 28;
RGAL 4

Cain, G.
See Cabrera Infante, G(uillermo)

Cain, Guillermo
See Cabrera Infante, G(uillermo)

Cain, James M(allahan) 1892-1977 .. **CLC 3,**
11, 28
See also AITN 1; BPFB 1; CA 17-20R; 73-
76; CANR 8, 34, 61; CMW 4; DLB 226;
EWL 3; MSW; MTCW 1; RGAL 4

Caine, Hall 1853-1931 .... **TCLC 97**
See also RHW

Caine, Mark
See Raphael, Frederic (Michael)

Calasso, Roberto 1941- .... **CLC 81**
See also CA 143; CANR 89

Calderon de la Barca, Pedro
1600-1681 .... **DC 3; HLCS 1; LC 23**
See also EW 2; RGWL 2, 3; TWA

Caldwell, Erskine (Preston)
1903-1987 .... **CLC 1, 8, 14, 50, 60; SSC**
19; TCLC 117
See also AITN 1; AMW; BPFB 1; CA 1-4R;
121; CAAS 1; CANR 2, 33; DA3; DAM
NOV; DLB 9, 86; EWL 3; MTCW 1, 2;
RGAL 4; RGSF 2; TUS

Caldwell, (Janet Miriam) Taylor (Holland)
1900-1985 .... **CLC 2, 28, 39**
See also BPFB 1; CA 5-8R; 116; CANR 5;
DA3; DAM NOV, POP; DLBD 17; RHW

Calhoun, John Caldwell
1782-1850 .... **NCLC 15**
See also DLB 3, 248

Calisher, Hortense 1911- ..... **CLC 2, 4, 8, 38,**
134; SSC 15
See also CA 1-4R; CANR 1, 22, 117; CN
7; DA3; DAM NOV; DLB 2, 218; INT
CANR-22; MTCW 1, 2; RGAL 4; RGSF
2

Callaghan, Morley Edward
1903-1990 ..... **CLC 3, 14, 41, 65; TCLC**
145
See also CA 9-12R; 132; CANR 33, 73;
DAC; DAM MST; DLB 68; EWL 3;
MTCW 1, 2; RGEL 2; RGSF 2; SSFS 19

Callimachus c. 305B.C.-c.
240B.C. .... **CMLC 18**
See also AW 1; DLB 176; RGWL 2, 3

Calvin, Jean
See Calvin, John
See also GFL Beginnings to 1789

Calvin, John 1509-1564 .... **LC 37**
See Calvin, Jean

Calvino, Italo 1923-1985 .... **CLC 5, 8, 11, 22,**
33, 39, 73; SSC 3, 48
See also CA 85-88; 116; CANR 23, 61;
DAM NOV; DLB 196; EW 13; EWL 3;
MTCW 1, 2; RGSF 2; RGWL 2, 3; SFW
4; SSFS 12

Camara Laye
See Laye, Camara
See also EWL 3

Camden, William 1551-1623 .... **LC 77**
See also DLB 172

Cameron, Carey 1952- .... **CLC 59**
See also CA 135

Cameron, Peter 1959- .... **CLC 44**
See also AMWS 12; CA 125; CANR 50,
117; DLB 234; GLL 2

Camoens, Luis Vaz de 1524(?)-1580
See Camoes, Luis de
See also EW 2

Camoes, Luis de 1524(?)-1580 . **HLCS 1; LC**
62; PC 31
See Camoens, Luis Vaz de
See also DLB 287; RGWL 2, 3

Campana, Dino 1885-1932 .... **TCLC 20**
See also CA 117; DLB 114; EWL 3

Campanella, Tommaso 1568-1639 .... **LC 32**
See also RGWL 2, 3

Campbell, John W(ood, Jr.)
1910-1971 .... **CLC 32**
See also CA 21-22; 29-32R; CANR 34;
CAP 2; DLB 8; MTCW 1; SCFW; SFW 4

Campbell, Joseph 1904-1987 .... **CLC 69;**
TCLC 140
See also AAYA 3; BEST 89:2; CA 1-4R;
124; CANR 3, 28, 61, 107; DA3; MTCW
1, 2

Campbell, Maria 1940- .... **CLC 85; NNAL**
See also CA 102; CANR 54; CCA 1; DAC

Campbell, (John) Ramsey 1946- ..... **CLC 42;**
SSC 19
See also AAYA 51; CA 57-60; CANR 7,
102; DLB 261; HGG; INT CANR-7;
SUFW 1, 2

Campbell, (Ignatius) Roy (Dunnachie)
1901-1957 .... **TCLC 5**
See also AFW; CA 104; 155; DLB 20, 225;
EWL 3; MTCW 2; RGEL 2

Campbell, Thomas 1777-1844 .... **NCLC 19**
See also DLB 93, 144; RGEL 2

Campbell, Wilfred .... **TCLC 9**
See Campbell, William

Campbell, William 1858(?)-1918
See Campbell, Wilfred
See also CA 106; DLB 92

Campion, Jane 1954- .... **CLC 95**
See also AAYA 33; CA 138; CANR 87

Campion, Thomas 1567-1620 .... **LC 78**
See also CDBLB Before 1660; DAM POET;
DLB 58, 172; RGEL 2

Camus, Albert 1913-1960 ...... **CLC 1, 2, 4, 9,**
11, 14, 32, 63, 69, 124; DC 2; SSC 9;
WLC
See also AAYA 36; AFW; BPFB 1; CA 89-
92; DA; DA3; DAB; DAC; DAM DRAM,
MST, NOV; DLB 72; EW 13; EWL 3;
EXPN; EXPS; GFL 1789 to the Present;
LATS 1; LMFS 2; MTCW 1, 2; NFS 6,
16; RGSF 2; RGWL 2, 3; SSFS 4; TWA

Canby, Vincent 1924-2000 .... **CLC 13**
See also CA 81-84; 191

Cancale
See Desnos, Robert

Canetti, Elias 1905-1994 .. **CLC 3, 14, 25, 75,**
86
See also CA 21-24R; 146; CANR 23, 61,
79; CDWLB 2; CWW 2; DA3; DLB 85,
124; EW 12; EWL 3; MTCW 1, 2; RGWL
2, 3; TWA

Canfield, Dorothea F.
See Fisher, Dorothy (Frances) Canfield

Canfield, Dorothea Frances
See Fisher, Dorothy (Frances) Canfield

Canfield, Dorothy
See Fisher, Dorothy (Frances) Canfield

Canin, Ethan 1960- .... **CLC 55; SSC 70**
See also CA 131; 135

Cankar, Ivan 1876-1918 .... **TCLC 105**
See also CDWLB 4; DLB 147; EWL 3

Cannon, Curt
See Hunter, Evan

Cao, Lan 1961- .... **CLC 109**
See also CA 165

Cape, Judith
See Page, P(atricia) K(athleen)
See also CCA 1

Capek, Karel 1890-1938 .... **DC 1; SSC 36;**
TCLC 6, 37; WLC
See also CA 104; 140; CDWLB 4; DA;
DA3; DAB; DAC; DAM DRAM, MST,
NOV; DFS 7, 11; DLB 215; EW 10; EWL
3; MTCW 1; RGSF 2; RGWL 2, 3; SCFW
2; SFW 4

Capote, Truman 1924-1984 . **CLC 1, 3, 8, 13,**
19, 34, 38, 58; SSC 2, 47; WLC
See also AMWS 3; BPFB 1; CA 5-8R; 113;
CANR 18, 62; CDALB 1941-1968; CPW;
DA; DA3; DAB; DAC; DAM MST, NOV,
POP; DLB 2, 185, 227; DLBY 1980,
1984; EWL 3; EXPS; GLL 1; LAIT 3;
MTCW 1, 2; NCFS 2; RGAL 4; RGSF 2;
SATA 91; SSFS 2; TUS

Capra, Frank 1897-1991 .... **CLC 16**
See also AAYA 52; CA 61-64; 135

Caputo, Philip 1941- .... **CLC 32**
See also CA 73-76; CANR 40; YAW

Cato the Elder
See Cato, Marcus Porcius
See also DLB 211

Catton, (Charles) Bruce 1899-1978 . **CLC 35**
See also AITN 1; CA 5-8R; 81-84; CANR
7, 74; DLB 17; SATA 2; SATA-Obit 24

Catullus c. 84B.C.-54B.C. .... **CMLC 18**
See also AW 2; CDWLB 1; DLB 211;
RGWL 2, 3

Cauldwell, Frank
See King, Francis (Henry)

Caunitz, William J. 1933-1996 .... **CLC 34**
See also BEST 89:3; CA 125; 130; 152;
CANR 73; INT CA-130

Causley, Charles (Stanley)
1917-2003 .... **CLC 7**
See also CA 9-12R; CANR 5, 35, 94; CLR
30; CWRI 5; DLB 27; MTCW 1; SATA
3, 66

Caute, (John) David 1936- .... **CLC 29**
See also CA 1-4R; CAAS 4; CANR 1, 33,
64, 120; CBD; CD 5; CN 7; DAM NOV;
DLB 14, 231

Cavafy, C(onstantine) P(eter) .... **PC 36;**
TCLC 2, 7
See Kavafis, Konstantinos Petrou
See also CA 148; DA3; DAM POET; EW
8; EWL 3; MTCW 1; PFS 19; RGWL 2,
3; WP

Cavalcanti, Guido c. 1250-c.
1300 .... **CMLC 54**

Cavallo, Evelyn
See Spark, Muriel (Sarah)

Cavanna, Betty .... **CLC 12**
See Harrison, Elizabeth (Allen) Cavanna
See also JRDA; MAICYA 1; SAAS 4;
SATA 1, 30

Cavendish, Margaret Lucas
1623-1673 .... **LC 30**
See also DLB 131, 252, 281; RGEL 2

Caxton, William 1421(?)-1491(?) .... **LC 17**
See also DLB 170

Cayer, D. M.
See Duffy, Maureen

Cayrol, Jean 1911- .... **CLC 11**
See also CA 89-92; DLB 83; EWL 3

Cela (y Trulock), Camilo Jose
See Cela, Camilo Jose
See also CWW 2

Cela, Camilo Jose 1916-2002 .... **CLC 4, 13,**
59, 122; HLC 1
See Cela (y Trulock), Camilo Jose
See also BEST 90:2; CA 21-24R; 206;
CAAS 10; CANR 21, 32, 76; DAM
MULT; DLBY 1989; EW 13; EWL 3; HW
1; MTCW 1, 2; RGSF 2; RGWL 2, 3

Celan, Paul .... **CLC 10, 19, 53, 82; PC 10**
See Antschel, Paul
See also CDWLB 2; DLB 69; EWL 3;
RGWL 2, 3

Celine, Louis-Ferdinand .. **CLC 1, 3, 4, 7, 9,**
15, 47, 124
See Destouches, Louis-Ferdinand
See also DLB 72; EW 11; EWL 3; GFL
1789 to the Present; RGWL 2, 3

Cellini, Benvenuto 1500-1571 .... **LC 7**

Cendrars, Blaise .... **CLC 18, 106**
See Sauser-Hall, Frederic
See also DLB 258; EWL 3; GFL 1789 to
the Present; RGWL 2, 3; WP

Centlivre, Susanna 1669(?)-1723 .... **LC 65**
See also DLB 84; RGEL 2

Cernuda (y Bidon), Luis 1902-1963 . **CLC 54**
See also CA 131; 89-92; DAM POET; DLB
134; EWL 3; GLL 1; HW 1; RGWL 2, 3

Cervantes, Lorna Dee 1954- ..... **HLCS 1; PC**
35
See also CA 131; CANR 80; CWP; DLB
82; EXPP; HW 1; LLW 1

Cervantes (Saavedra), Miguel de
1547-1616 .... **HLCS; LC 6, 23, 93; SSC**
12; WLC
See also BYA 1, 14; DA; DAB; DAC; DAM
MST, NOV; EW 2; LAIT 1; LATS 1;
LMFS 1; NFS 8; RGSF 2; RGWL 2, 3;
TWA

Cesaire, Aime (Fernand) 1913- .... **BLC 1;**
CLC 19, 32, 112; DC 22; PC 25
See also BW 2, 3; CA 65-68; CANR 24,
43, 81; CWW 2; DA3; DAM MULT,
POET; EWL 3; GFL 1789 to the Present;
MTCW 1, 2; WP

Chabon, Michael 1963- ... **CLC 55, 149; SSC**
59
See also AAYA 45; AMWS 11; CA 139;
CANR 57, 96, 127; DLB 278; SATA 145

Chabrol, Claude 1930- .... **CLC 16**
See also CA 110

Chairil Anwar
See Anwar, Chairil
See also EWL 3

Challans, Mary 1905-1983
See Renault, Mary
See also CA 81-84; 111; CANR 74; DA3;
MTCW 2; SATA 23; SATA-Obit 36; TEA

Challis, George
See Faust, Frederick (Schiller)
See also TCWW 2

Chambers, Aidan 1934- .... **CLC 35**
See also AAYA 27; CA 25-28R; CANR 12,
31, 58, 116; JRDA; MAICYA 1, 2; SAAS
12; SATA 1, 69, 108; WYA; YAW

Chambers, James 1948-
See Cliff, Jimmy
See also CA 124

Chambers, Jessie
See Lawrence, D(avid) H(erbert Richards)
See also GLL 1

Chambers, Robert W(illiam)
1865-1933 .... **TCLC 41**
See also CA 165; DLB 202; HGG; SATA
107; SUFW 1

Chambers, (David) Whittaker
1901-1961 .... **TCLC 129**
See also CA 89-92

Chamisso, Adelbert von
1781-1838 .... **NCLC 82**
See also DLB 90; RGWL 2, 3; SUFW 1

Chance, James T.
See Carpenter, John (Howard)

Chance, John T.
See Carpenter, John (Howard)

Chandler, Raymond (Thornton)
1888-1959 .... **SSC 23; TCLC 1, 7**
See also AAYA 25; AMWC 2; AMWS 4;
BPFB 1; CA 104; 129; CANR 60, 107;
CDALB 1929-1941; CMW 4; DA3; DLB
226, 253; DLBD 6; EWL 3; MSW;
MTCW 1, 2; NFS 17; RGAL 4; TUS

Chang, Diana 1934- .... **AAL**
See also CWP; EXPP

Chang, Eileen 1921-1995 .... **AAL; SSC 28**
See Chang Ai-Ling; Zhang Ailing
See also CA 166

Chang, Jung 1952- .... **CLC 71**
See also CA 142

Chang Ai-Ling
See Chang, Eileen
See also EWL 3

Channing, William Ellery
1780-1842 .... **NCLC 17**
See also DLB 1, 59, 235; RGAL 4

Chao, Patricia 1955- .... **CLC 119**
See also CA 163

Chaplin, Charles Spencer
1889-1977 .... **CLC 16**
See Chaplin, Charlie
See also CA 81-84; 73-76

Chaplin, Charlie
See Chaplin, Charles Spencer
See also DLB 44

Chapman, George 1559(?)-1634 . **DC 19; LC**
22
See also BRW 1; DAM DRAM; DLB 62,
121; LMFS 1; RGEL 2

Chapman, Graham 1941-1989 .... **CLC 21**
See Monty Python
See also CA 116; 129; CANR 35, 95

Chapman, John Jay 1862-1933 .... **TCLC 7**
See also CA 104; 191

Chapman, Lee
See Bradley, Marion Zimmer
See also GLL 1

Chapman, Walker
See Silverberg, Robert

Chappell, Fred (Davis) 1936- .... **CLC 40, 78,**
162
See also CA 5-8R, 198; CAAE 198; CAAS
4; CANR 8, 33, 67, 110; CN 7; CP 7;
CSW; DLB 6, 105; HGG

Char, Rene(-Emile) 1907-1988 .... **CLC 9, 11,**
14, 55; PC 56
See also CA 13-16R; 124; CANR 32; DAM
POET; DLB 258; EWL 3; GFL 1789 to
the Present; MTCW 1, 2; RGWL 2, 3

Charby, Jay
See Ellison, Harlan (Jay)

Chardin, Pierre Teilhard de
See Teilhard de Chardin, (Marie Joseph)
Pierre

Chariton fl. 1st cent. (?)- .... **CMLC 49**

Charlemagne 742-814 .... **CMLC 37**

Charles I 1600-1649 .... **LC 13**

Charriere, Isabelle de 1740-1805 .. **NCLC 66**

Chartier, Alain c. 1392-1430 .... **LC 94**
See also DLB 208

Chartier, Emile-Auguste
See Alain

Charyn, Jerome 1937- .... **CLC 5, 8, 18**
See also CA 5-8R; CAAS 1; CANR 7, 61,
101; CMW 4; CN 7; DLBY 1983; MTCW
1

Chase, Adam
See Marlowe, Stephen

Chase, Mary (Coyle) 1907-1981 .... **DC 1**
See also CA 77-80; 105; CAD; CWD; DFS
11; DLB 228; SATA 17; SATA-Obit 29

Chase, Mary Ellen 1887-1973 .... **CLC 2;**
TCLC 124
See also CA 13-16; 41-44R; CAP 1; SATA
10

Chase, Nicholas
See Hyde, Anthony
See also CCA 1

Chateaubriand, Francois Rene de
1768-1848 .... **NCLC 3, 134**
See also DLB 119; EW 5; GFL 1789 to the
Present; RGWL 2, 3; TWA

Chatterje, Sarat Chandra 1876-1936(?)
See Chatterji, Saratchandra
See also CA 109

Chatterji, Bankim Chandra
1838-1894 .... **NCLC 19**

Chatterji, Saratchandra .... **TCLC 13**
See Chatterje, Sarat Chandra
See also CA 186; EWL 3

Chatterton, Thomas 1752-1770 .... **LC 3, 54**
See also DAM POET; DLB 109; RGEL 2

Chatwin, (Charles) Bruce
1940-1989 .... **CLC 28, 57, 59**
See also AAYA 4; BEST 90:1; BRWS 4;
CA 85-88; 127; CPW; DAM POP; DLB
194, 204; EWL 3

Chaucer, Daniel
See Ford, Ford Madox
See also RHW

Chaucer, Geoffrey 1340(?)-1400 .. **LC 17, 56;
  PC 19; WLCS**
    See also BRW 1; BRWC 1; BRWR 2; CD-
    BLB Before 1660; DA; DA3; DAB;
    DAC; DAM MST, POET; DLB 146;
    LAIT 1; PAB; PFS 14; RGEL 2; TEA;
    WLIT 3; WP

Chavez, Denise (Elia) 1948- .... **HLC 1**
    See also CA 131; CANR 56, 81; DAM
    MULT; DLB 122; FW; HW 1, 2; LLW 1;
    MTCW 2

Chaviaras, Strates 1935-
    See Haviaras, Stratis
    See also CA 105

Chayefsky, Paddy .... **CLC 23**
    See Chayefsky, Sidney
    See also CAD; DLB 7, 44; DLBY 1981;
    RGAL 4

Chayefsky, Sidney 1923-1981
    See Chayefsky, Paddy
    See also CA 9-12R; 104; CANR 18; DAM
    DRAM

Chedid, Andree 1920- .... **CLC 47**
    See also CA 145; CANR 95; EWL 3

Cheever, John 1912-1982 ..... **CLC 3, 7, 8, 11,
  15, 25, 64; SSC 1, 38, 57; WLC**
    See also AMWS 1; BPFB 1; CA 5-8R; 106;
    CABS 1; CANR 5, 27, 76; CDALB 1941-
    1968; CPW; DA; DA3; DAB; DAC;
    DAM MST, NOV, POP; DLB 2, 102, 227;
    DLBY 1980, 1982; EWL 3; EXPS; INT
    CANR-5; MTCW 1, 2; RGAL 4; RGSF
    2; SSFS 2, 14; TUS

Cheever, Susan 1943- .... **CLC 18, 48**
    See also CA 103; CANR 27, 51, 92; DLBY
    1982; INT CANR-27

Chekhonte, Antosha
    See Chekhov, Anton (Pavlovich)

Chekhov, Anton (Pavlovich)
    1860-1904 ...... **DC 9; SSC 2, 28, 41, 51;
  TCLC 3, 10, 31, 55, 96; WLC**
    See also BYA 14; CA 104; 124; DA; DA3;
    DAB; DAC; DAM DRAM, MST; DFS 1,
    5, 10, 12; DLB 277; EW 7; EWL 3;
    EXPS; LAIT 3; LATS 1; RGSF 2; RGWL
    2, 3; SATA 90; SSFS 5, 13, 14; TWA

Cheney, Lynne V. 1941- .... **CLC 70**
    See also CA 89-92; CANR 58, 117

Chernyshevsky, Nikolai Gavrilovich
    See Chernyshevsky, Nikolay Gavrilovich
    See also DLB 238

Chernyshevsky, Nikolay Gavrilovich
    1828-1889 .... **NCLC 1**
    See Chernyshevsky, Nikolai Gavrilovich

Cherry, Carolyn Janice 1942-
    See Cherryh, C. J.
    See also CA 65-68; CANR 10

Cherryh, C. J. .... **CLC 35**
    See Cherry, Carolyn Janice
    See also AAYA 24; BPFB 1; DLBY 1980;
    FANT; SATA 93; SCFW 2; SFW 4; YAW

Chesnutt, Charles W(addell)
    1858-1932 .... **BLC 1; SSC 7, 54; TCLC
  5, 39**
    See also AFAW 1, 2; BW 1, 3; CA 106;
    125; CANR 76; DAM MULT; DLB 12,
    50, 78; EWL 3; MTCW 1, 2; RGAL 4;
    RGSF 2; SSFS 11

Chester, Alfred 1929(?)-1971 .... **CLC 49**
    See also CA 196; 33-36R; DLB 130

Chesterton, G(ilbert) K(eith)
    1874-1936 . **PC 28; SSC 1, 46; TCLC 1,
  6, 64**
    See also BRW 6; CA 104; 132; CANR 73;
    CDBLB 1914-1945; CMW 4; DAM NOV,
    POET; DLB 10, 19, 34, 70, 98, 149, 178;
    EWL 3; FANT; MSW; MTCW 1, 2;
    RGEL 2; RGSF 2; SATA 27; SUFW 1

Chiang, Pin-chin 1904-1986
    See Ding Ling
    See also CA 118

Chief Joseph 1840-1904 .... **NNAL**
    See also CA 152; DA3; DAM MULT

Chief Seattle 1786(?)-1866 .... **NNAL**
    See also DA3; DAM MULT

Ch'ien, Chung-shu 1910-1998 .... **CLC 22**
    See Qian Zhongshu
    See also CA 130; CANR 73; MTCW 1, 2

Chikamatsu Monzaemon 1653-1724 ... **LC 66**
    See also RGWL 2, 3

Child, L. Maria
    See Child, Lydia Maria

Child, Lydia Maria 1802-1880 .. **NCLC 6, 73**
    See also DLB 1, 74, 243; RGAL 4; SATA
    67

Child, Mrs.
    See Child, Lydia Maria

Child, Philip 1898-1978 .... **CLC 19, 68**
    See also CA 13-14; CAP 1; DLB 68; RHW;
    SATA 47

Childers, (Robert) Erskine
    1870-1922 .... **TCLC 65**
    See also CA 113; 153; DLB 70

Childress, Alice 1920-1994 . **BLC 1; CLC 12,
  15, 86, 96; DC 4; TCLC 116**
    See also AAYA 8; BW 2, 3; BYA 2; CA 45-
    48; 146; CAD; CANR 3, 27, 50, 74; CLR
    14; CWD; DA3; DAM DRAM, MULT,
    NOV; DFS 2, 8, 14; DLB 7, 38, 249;
    JRDA; LAIT 5; MAICYA 1, 2; MAIC-
    YAS 1; MTCW 1, 2; RGAL 4; SATA 7,
    48, 81; TUS; WYA; YAW

Chin, Frank (Chew, Jr.) 1940- ...... **CLC 135;
  DC 7**
    See also CA 33-36R; CANR 71; CD 5;
    DAM MULT; DLB 206; LAIT 5; RGAL
    4

Chin, Marilyn (Mei Ling) 1955- .... **PC 40**
    See also CA 129; CANR 70, 113; CWP

Chislett, (Margaret) Anne 1943- ...... **CLC 34**
    See also CA 151

Chitty, Thomas Willes 1926- .... **CLC 11**
    See Hinde, Thomas
    See also CA 5-8R; CN 7

Chivers, Thomas Holley
    1809-1858 .... **NCLC 49**
    See also DLB 3, 248; RGAL 4

Choi, Susan 1969- .... **CLC 119**

Chomette, Rene Lucien 1898-1981
    See Clair, Rene
    See also CA 103

Chomsky, (Avram) Noam 1928- ..... **CLC 132**
    See also CA 17-20R; CANR 28, 62, 110;
    DA3; DLB 246; MTCW 1, 2

Chona, Maria 1845(?)-1936 .... **NNAL**
    See also CA 144

Chopin, Kate .... **SSC 8, 68; TCLC 127;
  WLCS**
    See Chopin, Katherine
    See also AAYA 33; AMWR 2; AMWS 1;
    BYA 11, 15; CDALB 1865-1917; DA;
    DAB; DLB 12, 78; EXPN; EXPS; FW;
    LAIT 3; MAWW; NFS 3; RGAL 4; RGSF
    2; SSFS 17; TUS

Chopin, Katherine 1851-1904
    See Chopin, Kate
    See also CA 104; 122; DA3; DAC; DAM
    MST, NOV

Chretien de Troyes c. 12th cent. - . **CMLC 10**
    See also DLB 208; EW 1; RGWL 2, 3;
    TWA

Christie
    See Ichikawa, Kon

Christie, Agatha (Mary Clarissa)
    1890-1976 .. **CLC 1, 6, 8, 12, 39, 48, 110**
    See also AAYA 9; AITN 1, 2; BPFB 1;
    BRWS 2; CA 17-20R; 61-64; CANR 10,
    37, 108; CBD; CDBLB 1914-1945; CMW
    4; CPW; CWD; DA3; DAB; DAC; DAM
    NOV; DFS 2; DLB 13, 77, 245; MSW;
    MTCW 1, 2; NFS 8; RGEL 2; RHW;
    SATA 36; TEA; YAW

Christie, Philippa .... **CLC 21**
    See Pearce, Philippa
    See also BYA 5; CANR 109; CLR 9; DLB
    161; MAICYA 1; SATA 1, 67, 129

Christine de Pizan 1365(?)-1431(?) .... **LC 9**
    See also DLB 208; RGWL 2, 3

Chuang Tzu c. 369B.C.-c.
    286B.C. .... **CMLC 57**

Chubb, Elmer
    See Masters, Edgar Lee

Chulkov, Mikhail Dmitrievich
    1743-1792 .... **LC 2**
    See also DLB 150

Churchill, Caryl 1938- .... **CLC 31, 55, 157;
  DC 5**
    See Churchill, Chick
    See also BRWS 4; CA 102; CANR 22, 46,
    108; CBD; CWD; DFS 12, 16; DLB 13;
    EWL 3; FW; MTCW 1; RGEL 2

Churchill, Charles 1731-1764 .... **LC 3**
    See also DLB 109; RGEL 2

Churchill, Chick 1938-
    See Churchill, Caryl
    See also CD 5

Churchill, Sir Winston (Leonard Spencer)
    1874-1965 .... **TCLC 113**
    See also BRW 6; CA 97-100; CDBLB
    1890-1914; DA3; DLB 100; DLBD 16;
    LAIT 4; MTCW 1, 2

Chute, Carolyn 1947- .... **CLC 39**
    See also CA 123

Ciardi, John (Anthony) 1916-1986 . **CLC 10,
  40, 44, 129**
    See also CA 5-8R; 118; CAAS 2; CANR 5,
    33; CLR 19; CWRI 5; DAM POET; DLB
    5; DLBY 1986; INT CANR-5; MAICYA
    1, 2; MTCW 1, 2; RGAL 4; SAAS 26;
    SATA 1, 65; SATA-Obit 46

Cibber, Colley 1671-1757 .... **LC 66**
    See also DLB 84; RGEL 2

Cicero, Marcus Tullius
    106B.C.-43B.C. .... **CMLC 3**
    See also AW 1; CDWLB 1; DLB 211;
    RGWL 2, 3

Cimino, Michael 1943- .... **CLC 16**
    See also CA 105

Cioran, E(mil) M. 1911-1995 .... **CLC 64**
    See also CA 25-28R; 149; CANR 91; DLB
    220; EWL 3

Cisneros, Sandra 1954- .. **CLC 69, 118; HLC
  1; PC 52; SSC 32**
    See also AAYA 9, 53; AMWS 7; CA 131;
    CANR 64, 118; CWP; DA3; DAM MULT;
    DLB 122, 152; EWL 3; EXPN; FW; HW
    1, 2; LAIT 5; LATS 1; LLW 1; MAICYA
    2; MTCW 2; NFS 2; PFS 19; RGAL 4;
    RGSF 2; SSFS 3, 13; WLIT 1; YAW

Cixous, Helene 1937- .... **CLC 92**
    See also CA 126; CANR 55, 123; CWW 2;
    DLB 83, 242; EWL 3; FW; GLL 2;
    MTCW 1, 2; TWA

Clair, Rene .... **CLC 20**
    See Chomette, Rene Lucien

Clampitt, Amy 1920-1994 .... **CLC 32; PC 19**
    See also AMWS 9; CA 110; 146; CANR
    29, 79; DLB 105

Clancy, Thomas L., Jr. 1947-
    See Clancy, Tom
    See also CA 125; 131; CANR 62, 105;
    DA3; INT CA-131; MTCW 1, 2

Dasgupta, Surendranath
1887-1952 .... **TCLC 81**
See also CA 157

Dashwood, Edmee Elizabeth Monica de la Pasture 1890-1943
See Delafield, E. M.
See also CA 119; 154

da Silva, Antonio Jose
1705-1739 .... **NCLC 114**

Daudet, (Louis Marie) Alphonse
1840-1897 .... **NCLC 1**
See also DLB 123; GFL 1789 to the Present; RGSF 2

d'Aulnoy, Marie-Catherine c.
1650-1705 .... **LC 100**

Daumal, Rene 1908-1944 .... **TCLC 14**
See also CA 114; EWL 3

Davenant, William 1606-1668 .... **LC 13**
See also DLB 58, 126; RGEL 2

Davenport, Guy (Mattison, Jr.)
1927- .... **CLC 6, 14, 38; SSC 16**
See also CA 33-36R; CANR 23, 73; CN 7; CSW; DLB 130

David, Robert
See Nezval, Vitezslav

Davidson, Avram (James) 1923-1993
See Queen, Ellery
See also CA 101; 171; CANR 26; DLB 8; FANT; SFW 4; SUFW 1, 2

Davidson, Donald (Grady)
1893-1968 .... **CLC 2, 13, 19**
See also CA 5-8R; 25-28R; CANR 4, 84; DLB 45

Davidson, Hugh
See Hamilton, Edmond

Davidson, John 1857-1909 .... **TCLC 24**
See also CA 118; 217; DLB 19; RGEL 2

Davidson, Sara 1943- .... **CLC 9**
See also CA 81-84; CANR 44, 68; DLB 185

Davie, Donald (Alfred) 1922-1995 .... **CLC 5, 8, 10, 31; PC 29**
See also BRWS 6; CA 1-4R; 149; CAAS 3; CANR 1, 44; CP 7; DLB 27; MTCW 1; RGEL 2

Davie, Elspeth 1919-1995 .... **SSC 52**
See also CA 120; 126; 150; DLB 139

Davies, Ray(mond Douglas) 1944- ... **CLC 21**
See also CA 116; 146; CANR 92

Davies, Rhys 1901-1978 .... **CLC 23**
See also CA 9-12R; 81-84; CANR 4; DLB 139, 191

Davies, (William) Robertson
1913-1995 .... **CLC 2, 7, 13, 25, 42, 75, 91; WLC**
See Marchbanks, Samuel
See also BEST 89:2; BPFB 1; CA 33-36R; 150; CANR 17, 42, 103; CN 7; CPW; DA; DA3; DAB; DAC; DAM MST, NOV, POP; DLB 68; EWL 3; HGG; INT CANR-17; MTCW 1, 2; RGEL 2; TWA

Davies, Sir John 1569-1626 .... **LC 85**
See also DLB 172

Davies, Walter C.
See Kornbluth, C(yril) M.

Davies, William Henry 1871-1940 ... **TCLC 5**
See also CA 104; 179; DLB 19, 174; EWL 3; RGEL 2

Da Vinci, Leonardo 1452-1519 ..... **LC 12, 57, 60**
See also AAYA 40

Davis, Angela (Yvonne) 1944- .... **CLC 77**
See also BW 2, 3; CA 57-60; CANR 10, 81; CSW; DA3; DAM MULT; FW

Davis, B. Lynch
See Bioy Casares, Adolfo; Borges, Jorge Luis

Davis, Frank Marshall 1905-1987 ...... **BLC 1**
See also BW 2, 3; CA 125; 123; CANR 42, 80; DAM MULT; DLB 51

Davis, Gordon
See Hunt, E(verette) Howard, (Jr.)

Davis, H(arold) L(enoir) 1896-1960 . **CLC 49**
See also ANW; CA 178; 89-92; DLB 9, 206; SATA 114

Davis, Rebecca (Blaine) Harding
1831-1910 .... **SSC 38; TCLC 6**
See also CA 104; 179; DLB 74, 239; FW; NFS 14; RGAL 4; TUS

Davis, Richard Harding
1864-1916 .... **TCLC 24**
See also CA 114; 179; DLB 12, 23, 78, 79, 189; DLBD 13; RGAL 4

Davison, Frank Dalby 1893-1970 ..... **CLC 15**
See also CA 217; 116; DLB 260

Davison, Lawrence H.
See Lawrence, D(avid) H(erbert Richards)

Davison, Peter (Hubert) 1928- .... **CLC 28**
See also CA 9-12R; CAAS 4; CANR 3, 43, 84; CP 7; DLB 5

Davys, Mary 1674-1732 .... **LC 1, 46**
See also DLB 39

Dawson, (Guy) Fielding (Lewis)
1930-2002 .... **CLC 6**
See also CA 85-88; 202; CANR 108; DLB 130; DLBY 2002

Dawson, Peter
See Faust, Frederick (Schiller)
See also TCWW 2, 2

Day, Clarence (Shepard, Jr.)
1874-1935 .... **TCLC 25**
See also CA 108; 199; DLB 11

Day, John 1574(?)-1640(?) .... **LC 70**
See also DLB 62, 170; RGEL 2

Day, Thomas 1748-1789 .... **LC 1**
See also DLB 39; YABC 1

Day Lewis, C(ecil) 1904-1972 . **CLC 1, 6, 10; PC 11**
See Blake, Nicholas
See also BRWS 3; CA 13-16; 33-36R; CANR 34; CAP 1; CWRI 5; DAM POET; DLB 15, 20; EWL 3; MTCW 1, 2; RGEL 2

Dazai Osamu .... **SSC 41; TCLC 11**
See Tsushima, Shuji
See also CA 164; DLB 182; EWL 3; MJW; RGSF 2; RGWL 2, 3; TWA

de Andrade, Carlos Drummond
See Drummond de Andrade, Carlos

de Andrade, Mario 1892-1945
See Andrade, Mario de
See also CA 178; HW 2

Deane, Norman
See Creasey, John

Deane, Seamus (Francis) 1940- ...... **CLC 122**
See also CA 118; CANR 42

de Beauvoir, Simone (Lucie Ernestine Marie Bertrand)
See Beauvoir, Simone (Lucie Ernestine Marie Bertrand) de

de Beer, P.
See Bosman, Herman Charles

de Brissac, Malcolm
See Dickinson, Peter (Malcolm)

de Campos, Alvaro
See Pessoa, Fernando (Antonio Nogueira)

de Chardin, Pierre Teilhard
See Teilhard de Chardin, (Marie Joseph) Pierre

Dee, John 1527-1608 .... **LC 20**
See also DLB 136, 213

Deer, Sandra 1940- .... **CLC 45**
See also CA 186

De Ferrari, Gabriella 1941- .... **CLC 65**
See also CA 146

de Filippo, Eduardo 1900-1984 ... **TCLC 127**
See also CA 132; 114; EWL 3; MTCW 1; RGWL 2, 3

Defoe, Daniel 1660(?)-1731 .. **LC 1, 42; WLC**
See also AAYA 27; BRW 3; BRWR 1; BYA 4; CDBLB 1660-1789; CLR 61; DA; DA3; DAB; DAC; DAM MST, NOV, DLB 39, 95, 101; JRDA; LAIT 1; LMFS 1; MAICYA 1, 2; NFS 9, 13; RGEL 2; SATA 22; TEA; WCH; WLIT 3

de Gourmont, Remy(-Marie-Charles)
See Gourmont, Remy(-Marie-Charles) de

de Gournay, Marie le Jars
1566-1645 .... **LC 98**
See also FW

de Hartog, Jan 1914-2002 .... **CLC 19**
See also CA 1-4R; 210; CANR 1; DFS 12

de Hostos, E. M.
See Hostos (y Bonilla), Eugenio Maria de

de Hostos, Eugenio M.
See Hostos (y Bonilla), Eugenio Maria de

Deighton, Len .... **CLC 4, 7, 22, 46**
See Deighton, Leonard Cyril
See also AAYA 6; BEST 89:2; BPFB 1; CD-BLB 1960 to Present; CMW 4; CN 7; CPW; DLB 87

Deighton, Leonard Cyril 1929-
See Deighton, Len
See also CA 9-12R; CANR 19, 33, 68; DA3; DAM NOV, POP; MTCW 1, 2

Dekker, Thomas 1572(?)-1632 ..... **DC 12; LC 22**
See also CDBLB Before 1660; DAM DRAM; DLB 62, 172; LMFS 1; RGEL 2

de Laclos, Pierre Ambroise Franois
See Laclos, Pierre Ambroise Francois

Delacroix, (Ferdinand-Victor-)Eugene
1798-1863 .... **NCLC 133**
See also EW 5

Delafield, E. M. .... **TCLC 61**
See Dashwood, Edmee Elizabeth Monica de la Pasture
See also DLB 34; RHW

de la Mare, Walter (John)
1873-1956 . **SSC 14; TCLC 4, 53; WLC**
See also CA 163; CDBLB 1914-1945; CLR 23; CWRI 5; DA3; DAB; DAM MST, POET; DLB 19, 153, 162, 255, 284; EWL 3; EXPP; HGG; MAICYA 1, 2; MTCW 1; RGEL 2; RGSF 2; SATA 16; SUFW 1; TEA; WCH

de Lamartine, Alphonse (Marie Louis Prat)
See Lamartine, Alphonse (Marie Louis Prat) de

Delaney, Franey
See O'Hara, John (Henry)

Delaney, Shelagh 1939- .... **CLC 29**
See also CA 17-20R; CANR 30, 67; CBD; CD 5; CDBLB 1960 to Present; CWD; DAM DRAM; DFS 7; DLB 13; MTCW 1

Delany, Martin Robison
1812-1885 .... **NCLC 93**
See also DLB 50; RGAL 4

Delany, Mary (Granville Pendarves)
1700-1788 .... **LC 12**

Delany, Samuel R(ay), Jr. 1942- .... **BLC 1; CLC 8, 14, 38, 141**
See also AAYA 24; AFAW 2; BPFB 1; BW 2, 3; CA 81-84; CANR 27, 43, 115, 116; CN 7; DAM MULT; DLB 8, 33; FANT; MTCW 1, 2; RGAL 4; SATA 92; SCFW; SFW 4; SUFW 2

De la Ramee, Marie Louise (Ouida)
1839-1908
See Ouida
See also CA 204; SATA 20

de la Roche, Mazo 1879-1961 .... **CLC 14**
See also CA 85-88; CANR 30; DLB 68; RGEL 2; RHW; SATA 64

Dumas, Alexandre (fils) 1824-1895 ...... **DC 1; NCLC 9**
See also DLB 192; GFL 1789 to the Present; RGWL 2, 3

Dumas, Claudine
See Malzberg, Barry N(athaniel)

Dumas, Henry L. 1934-1968 .... **CLC 6, 62**
See also BW 1; CA 85-88; DLB 41; RGAL 4

du Maurier, Daphne 1907-1989 .. **CLC 6, 11, 59; SSC 18**
See also AAYA 37; BPFB 1; BRWS 3; CA 5-8R; 128; CANR 6, 55; CMW 4; CPW; DA3; DAB; DAC; DAM MST, POP; DLB 191; HGG; LAIT 3; MSW; MTCW 1, 2; NFS 12; RGEL 2; RGSF 2; RHW; SATA 27; SATA-Obit 60; SSFS 14, 16; TEA

Du Maurier, George 1834-1896 ..... **NCLC 86**
See also DLB 153, 178; RGEL 2

Dunbar, Paul Laurence 1872-1906 ... **BLC 1; PC 5; SSC 8; TCLC 2, 12; WLC**
See also AFAW 1, 2; AMWS 2; BW 1, 3; CA 104; 124; CDALB 1865-1917; DA; DA3; DAC; DAM MST, MULT, POET; DLB 50, 54, 78; EXPP; RGAL 4; SATA 34

Dunbar, William 1460(?)-1520(?) .... **LC 20**
See also BRWS 8; DLB 132, 146; RGEL 2

Dunbar-Nelson, Alice .... **HR 2**
See Nelson, Alice Ruth Moore Dunbar

Duncan, Dora Angela
See Duncan, Isadora

Duncan, Isadora 1877(?)-1927 .... **TCLC 68**
See also CA 118; 149

Duncan, Lois 1934- .... **CLC 26**
See also AAYA 4, 34; BYA 6, 8; CA 1-4R; CANR 2, 23, 36, 111; CLR 29; JRDA; MAICYA 1, 2; MAICYAS 1; SAAS 2; SATA 1, 36, 75, 133, 141; SATA-Essay 141; WYA; YAW

Duncan, Robert (Edward) 1919-1988 .... **CLC 1, 2, 4, 7, 15, 41, 55; PC 2**
See also BG 2; CA 9-12R; 124; CANR 28, 62; DAM POET; DLB 5, 16, 193; EWL 3; MTCW 1, 2; PFS 13; RGAL 4; WP

Duncan, Sara Jeannette 1861-1922 .... **TCLC 60**
See also CA 157; DLB 92

Dunlap, William 1766-1839 .... **NCLC 2**
See also DLB 30, 37, 59; RGAL 4

Dunn, Douglas (Eaglesham) 1942- .... **CLC 6, 40**
See also CA 45-48; CANR 2, 33, 126; CP 7; DLB 40; MTCW 1

Dunn, Katherine (Karen) 1945- .... **CLC 71**
See also CA 33-36R; CANR 72; HGG; MTCW 1

Dunn, Stephen (Elliott) 1939- .... **CLC 36**
See also AMWS 11; CA 33-36R; CANR 12, 48, 53, 105; CP 7; DLB 105

Dunne, Finley Peter 1867-1936 .... **TCLC 28**
See also CA 108; 178; DLB 11, 23; RGAL 4

Dunne, John Gregory 1932-2003 ..... **CLC 28**
See also CA 25-28R; 222; CANR 14, 50; CN 7; DLBY 1980

Dunsany, Lord .... **TCLC 2, 59**
See Dunsany, Edward John Moreton Drax Plunkett
See also DLB 77, 153, 156, 255; FANT; IDTP; RGEL 2; SFW 4; SUFW 1

Dunsany, Edward John Moreton Drax Plunkett 1878-1957
See Dunsany, Lord
See also CA 104; 148; DLB 10; MTCW 1

Duns Scotus, John 1266(?)-1308 ... **CMLC 59**
See also DLB 115

du Perry, Jean
See Simenon, Georges (Jacques Christian)

Durang, Christopher (Ferdinand) 1949- .... **CLC 27, 38**
See also CA 105; CAD; CANR 50, 76; CD 5; MTCW 1

Duras, Marguerite 1914-1996 . **CLC 3, 6, 11, 20, 34, 40, 68, 100; SSC 40**
See Donnadieu, Marguerite
See also BPFB 1; CA 25-28R; 151; CANR 50; CWW 2; DLB 83; EWL 3; GFL 1789 to the Present; IDFW 4; MTCW 1, 2; RGWL 2, 3; TWA

Durban, (Rosa) Pam 1947- .... **CLC 39**
See also CA 123; CANR 98; CSW

Durcan, Paul 1944- .... **CLC 43, 70**
See also CA 134; CANR 123; CP 7; DAM POET; EWL 3

Durfey, Thomas 1653-1723 .... **LC 94**
See also DLB 80; RGEL 2

Durkheim, Emile 1858-1917 .... **TCLC 55**

Durrell, Lawrence (George) 1912-1990 ..... **CLC 1, 4, 6, 8, 13, 27, 41**
See also BPFB 1; BRWS 1; CA 9-12R; 132; CANR 40, 77; CDBLB 1945-1960; DAM NOV; DLB 15, 27, 204; DLBY 1990; EWL 3; MTCW 1, 2; RGEL 2; SFW 4; TEA

Durrenmatt, Friedrich
See Duerrenmatt, Friedrich
See also CDWLB 2; EW 13; EWL 3; RGWL 2, 3

Dutt, Michael Madhusudan 1824-1873 .... **NCLC 118**

Dutt, Toru 1856-1877 .... **NCLC 29**
See also DLB 240

Dwight, Timothy 1752-1817 .... **NCLC 13**
See also DLB 37; RGAL 4

Dworkin, Andrea 1946- .... **CLC 43, 123**
See also CA 77-80; CAAS 21; CANR 16, 39, 76, 96; FW; GLL 1; INT CANR-16; MTCW 1, 2

Dwyer, Deanna
See Koontz, Dean R(ay)

Dwyer, K. R.
See Koontz, Dean R(ay)

Dybek, Stuart 1942- .... **CLC 114; SSC 55**
See also CA 97-100; CANR 39; DLB 130

Dye, Richard
See De Voto, Bernard (Augustine)

Dyer, Geoff 1958- .... **CLC 149**
See also CA 125; CANR 88

Dyer, George 1755-1841 .... **NCLC 129**
See also DLB 93

Dylan, Bob 1941- .... **CLC 3, 4, 6, 12, 77; PC 37**
See also CA 41-44R; CANR 108; CP 7; DLB 16

Dyson, John 1943- .... **CLC 70**
See also CA 144

Dzyubin, Eduard Georgievich 1895-1934
See Bagritsky, Eduard
See also CA 170

E. V. L.
See Lucas, E(dward) V(errall)

Eagleton, Terence (Francis) 1943- .. **CLC 63, 132**
See also CA 57-60; CANR 7, 23, 68, 115; DLB 242; LMFS 2; MTCW 1, 2

Eagleton, Terry
See Eagleton, Terence (Francis)

Early, Jack
See Scoppettone, Sandra
See also GLL 1

East, Michael
See West, Morris L(anglo)

Eastaway, Edward
See Thomas, (Philip) Edward

Eastlake, William (Derry) 1917-1997 .... **CLC 8**
See also CA 5-8R; 158; CAAS 1; CANR 5, 63; CN 7; DLB 6, 206; INT CANR-5; TCWW 2

Eastman, Charles A(lexander) 1858-1939 .... **NNAL; TCLC 55**
See also CA 179; CANR 91; DAM MULT; DLB 175; YABC 1

Eaton, Edith Maude 1865-1914 .... **AAL**
See Far, Sui Sin
See also CA 154; DLB 221; FW

Eaton, (Lillie) Winnifred 1875-1954 .... **AAL**
See also CA 217; DLB 221; RGAL 4

Eberhart, Richard (Ghormley) 1904- .... **CLC 3, 11, 19, 56**
See also AMW; CA 1-4R; CANR 2, 125; CDALB 1941-1968; CP 7; DAM POET; DLB 48; MTCW 1; RGAL 4

Eberstadt, Fernanda 1960- .... **CLC 39**
See also CA 136; CANR 69, 128

Echegaray (y Eizaguirre), Jose (Maria Waldo) 1832-1916 .... **HLCS 1; TCLC 4**
See also CA 104; CANR 32; EWL 3; HW 1; MTCW 1

Echeverria, (Jose) Esteban (Antonino) 1805-1851 .... **NCLC 18**
See also LAW

Echo
See Proust, (Valentin-Louis-George-Eugene) Marcel

Eckert, Allan W. 1931- .... **CLC 17**
See also AAYA 18; BYA 2; CA 13-16R; CANR 14, 45; INT CANR-14; MAICYA 2; MAICYAS 1; SAAS 21; SATA 29, 91; SATA-Brief 27

Eckhart, Meister 1260(?)-1327(?) ... **CMLC 9**
See also DLB 115; LMFS 1

Eckmar, F. R.
See de Hartog, Jan

Eco, Umberto 1932- .... **CLC 28, 60, 142**
See also BEST 90:1; BPFB 1; CA 77-80; CANR 12, 33, 55, 110; CPW; CWW 2; DA3; DAM NOV, POP; DLB 196, 242; EWL 3; MSW; MTCW 1, 2; RGWL 3

Eddison, E(ric) R(ucker) 1882-1945 .... **TCLC 15**
See also CA 109; 156; DLB 255; FANT; SFW 4; SUFW 1

Eddy, Mary (Ann Morse) Baker 1821-1910 .... **TCLC 71**
See also CA 113; 174

Edel, (Joseph) Leon 1907-1997 .. **CLC 29, 34**
See also CA 1-4R; 161; CANR 1, 22, 112; DLB 103; INT CANR-22

Eden, Emily 1797-1869 .... **NCLC 10**

Edgar, David 1948- .... **CLC 42**
See also CA 57-60; CANR 12, 61, 112; CBD; CD 5; DAM DRAM; DFS 15; DLB 13, 233; MTCW 1

Edgerton, Clyde (Carlyle) 1944- ...... **CLC 39**
See also AAYA 17; CA 118; 134; CANR 64, 125; CSW; DLB 278; INT CA-134; YAW

Edgeworth, Maria 1768-1849 .... **NCLC 1, 51**
See also BRWS 3; DLB 116, 159, 163; FW; RGEL 2; SATA 21; TEA; WLIT 3

Edmonds, Paul
See Kuttner, Henry

Edmonds, Walter D(umaux) 1903-1998 .... **CLC 35**
See also BYA 2; CA 5-8R; CANR 2; CWRI 5; DLB 9; LAIT 1; MAICYA 1, 2; RHW; SAAS 4; SATA 1, 27; SATA-Obit 99

Edmondson, Wallace
See Ellison, Harlan (Jay)

Edson, Russell 1935- .... **CLC 13**
See also CA 33-36R; CANR 115; DLB 244; WP

Enchi, Fumiko (Ueda) 1905-1986 ..... **CLC 31**
See Enchi Fumiko
See also CA 129; 121; FW; MJW

Enchi Fumiko
See Enchi, Fumiko (Ueda)
See also DLB 182; EWL 3

Ende, Michael (Andreas Helmuth)
1929-1995 .... **CLC 31**
See also BYA 5; CA 118; 124; 149; CANR
36, 110; CLR 14; DLB 75; MAICYA 1,
2; MAICYAS 1; SATA 61, 130; SATA-
Brief 42; SATA-Obit 86

Endo, Shusaku 1923-1996 ..... **CLC 7, 14, 19,
54, 99; SSC 48**
See Endo Shusaku
See also CA 29-32R; 153; CANR 21, 54;
DA3; DAM NOV; MTCW 1, 2; RGSF 2;
RGWL 2, 3

Endo Shusaku
See Endo, Shusaku
See also DLB 182; EWL 3

Engel, Marian 1933-1985 .... **CLC 36; TCLC
137**
See also CA 25-28R; CANR 12; DLB 53;
FW; INT CANR-12

Engelhardt, Frederick
See Hubbard, L(afayette) Ron(ald)

Engels, Friedrich 1820-1895 .. **NCLC 85, 114**
See also DLB 129; LATS 1

Enright, D(ennis) J(oseph)
1920-2002 .... **CLC 4, 8, 31**
See also CA 1-4R; 211; CANR 1, 42, 83;
CP 7; DLB 27; EWL 3; SATA 25; SATA-
Obit 140

Enzensberger, Hans Magnus
1929- .... **CLC 43; PC 28**
See also CA 116; 119; CANR 103; EWL 3

Ephron, Nora 1941- .... **CLC 17, 31**
See also AAYA 35; AITN 2; CA 65-68;
CANR 12, 39, 83

Epicurus 341B.C.-270B.C. .... **CMLC 21**
See also DLB 176

Epsilon
See Betjeman, John

Epstein, Daniel Mark 1948- .... **CLC 7**
See also CA 49-52; CANR 2, 53, 90

Epstein, Jacob 1956- .... **CLC 19**
See also CA 114

Epstein, Jean 1897-1953 .... **TCLC 92**

Epstein, Joseph 1937- .... **CLC 39**
See also CA 112; 119; CANR 50, 65, 117

Epstein, Leslie 1938- .... **CLC 27**
See also AMWS 12; CA 73-76, 215; CAAE
215; CAAS 12; CANR 23, 69

Equiano, Olaudah 1745(?)-1797 . **BLC 2; LC
16**
See also AFAW 1, 2; CDWLB 3; DAM
MULT; DLB 37, 50; WLIT 2

Erasmus, Desiderius 1469(?)-1536 ..... **LC 16,
93**
See also DLB 136; EW 2; LMFS 1; RGWL
2, 3; TWA

Erdman, Paul E(mil) 1932- .... **CLC 25**
See also AITN 1; CA 61-64; CANR 13, 43,
84

Erdrich, Louise 1954- .... **CLC 39, 54, 120,
176; NNAL; PC 52**
See also AAYA 10, 47; AMWS 4; BEST
89:1; BPFB 1; CA 114; CANR 41, 62,
118; CDALBS; CN 7; CP 7; CPW; CWP;
DA3; DAM MULT, NOV, POP; DLB 152,
175, 206; EWL 3; EXPP; LAIT 5; LATS
1; MTCW 1; NFS 5; PFS 14; RGAL 4;
SATA 94, 141; SSFS 14; TCWW 2

Erenburg, Ilya (Grigoryevich)
See Ehrenburg, Ilya (Grigoryevich)

Erickson, Stephen Michael 1950-
See Erickson, Steve
See also CA 129; SFW 4

Erickson, Steve .... **CLC 64**
See Erickson, Stephen Michael
See also CANR 60, 68; SUFW 2

Erickson, Walter
See Fast, Howard (Melvin)

Ericson, Walter
See Fast, Howard (Melvin)

Eriksson, Buntel
See Bergman, (Ernst) Ingmar

Eriugena, John Scottus c.
810-877 .... **CMLC 65**
See also DLB 115

Ernaux, Annie 1940- .... **CLC 88, 184**
See also CA 147; CANR 93; NCFS 3, 5

Erskine, John 1879-1951 .... **TCLC 84**
See also CA 112; 159; DLB 9, 102; FANT

Eschenbach, Wolfram von
See Wolfram von Eschenbach
See also RGWL 3

Eseki, Bruno
See Mphahlele, Ezekiel

Esenin, Sergei (Alexandrovich)
1895-1925 .... **TCLC 4**
See Yesenin, Sergey
See also CA 104; RGWL 2, 3

Eshleman, Clayton 1935- .... **CLC 7**
See also CA 33-36R, 212; CAAE 212;
CAAS 6; CANR 93; CP 7; DLB 5

Espriella, Don Manuel Alvarez
See Southey, Robert

Espriu, Salvador 1913-1985 .... **CLC 9**
See also CA 154; 115; DLB 134; EWL 3

Espronceda, Jose de 1808-1842 ..... **NCLC 39**

Esquivel, Laura 1951(?)- ... **CLC 141; HLCS
1**
See also AAYA 29; CA 143; CANR 68, 113;
DA3; DNFS 2; LAIT 3; LMFS 2; MTCW
1; NFS 5; WLIT 1

Esse, James
See Stephens, James

Esterbrook, Tom
See Hubbard, L(afayette) Ron(ald)

Estleman, Loren D. 1952- .... **CLC 48**
See also AAYA 27; CA 85-88; CANR 27,
74; CMW 4; CPW; DA3; DAM NOV,
POP; DLB 226; INT CANR-27; MTCW
1, 2

Etherege, Sir George 1636-1692 .... **LC 78**
See also BRW 2; DAM DRAM; DLB 80;
PAB; RGEL 2

Euclid 306B.C.-283B.C. .... **CMLC 25**

Eugenides, Jeffrey 1960(?)- .... **CLC 81**
See also AAYA 51; CA 144; CANR 120

Euripides c. 484B.C.-406B.C. .... **CMLC 23,
51; DC 4; WLCS**
See also AW 1; CDWLB 1; DA; DA3;
DAB; DAC; DAM DRAM, MST; DFS 1,
4, 6; DLB 176; LAIT 1; LMFS 1; RGWL
2, 3

Evan, Evin
See Faust, Frederick (Schiller)

Evans, Caradoc 1878-1945 ... **SSC 43; TCLC
85**
See also DLB 162

Evans, Evan
See Faust, Frederick (Schiller)
See also TCWW 2

Evans, Marian
See Eliot, George

Evans, Mary Ann
See Eliot, George

Evarts, Esther
See Benson, Sally

Everett, Percival
See Everett, Percival L.
See also CSW

Everett, Percival L. 1956- .... **CLC 57**
See Everett, Percival
See also BW 2; CA 129; CANR 94

Everson, R(onald) G(ilmour)
1903-1992 .... **CLC 27**
See also CA 17-20R; DLB 88

Everson, William (Oliver)
1912-1994 .... **CLC 1, 5, 14**
See also BG 2; CA 9-12R; 145; CANR 20;
DLB 5, 16, 212; MTCW 1

Evtushenko, Evgenii Aleksandrovich
See Yevtushenko, Yevgeny (Alexandrovich)
See also RGWL 2, 3

Ewart, Gavin (Buchanan)
1916-1995 .... **CLC 13, 46**
See also BRWS 7; CA 89-92; 150; CANR
17, 46; CP 7; DLB 40; MTCW 1

Ewers, Hanns Heinz 1871-1943 ..... **TCLC 12**
See also CA 109; 149

Ewing, Frederick R.
See Sturgeon, Theodore (Hamilton)

Exley, Frederick (Earl) 1929-1992 .... **CLC 6,
11**
See also AITN 2; BPFB 1; CA 81-84; 138;
CANR 117; DLB 143; DLBY 1981

Eynhardt, Guillermo
See Quiroga, Horacio (Sylvestre)

Ezekiel, Nissim (Moses) 1924-2004 .. **CLC 61**
See also CA 61-64; CP 7; EWL 3

Ezekiel, Tish O'Dowd 1943- .... **CLC 34**
See also CA 129

Fadeev, Aleksandr Aleksandrovich
See Bulgya, Alexander Alexandrovich
See also DLB 272

Fadeev, Alexandr Alexandrovich
See Bulgya, Alexander Alexandrovich
See also EWL 3

Fadeyev, A.
See Bulgya, Alexander Alexandrovich

Fadeyev, Alexander .... **TCLC 53**
See Bulgya, Alexander Alexandrovich

Fagen, Donald 1948- .... **CLC 26**

Fainzilberg, Ilya Arnoldovich 1897-1937
See Ilf, Ilya
See also CA 120; 165

Fair, Ronald L. 1932- .... **CLC 18**
See also BW 1; CA 69-72; CANR 25; DLB
33

Fairbairn, Roger
See Carr, John Dickson

Fairbairns, Zoe (Ann) 1948- .... **CLC 32**
See also CA 103; CANR 21, 85; CN 7

Fairfield, Flora
See Alcott, Louisa May

Fairman, Paul W. 1916-1977
See Queen, Ellery
See also CA 114; SFW 4

Falco, Gian
See Papini, Giovanni

Falconer, James
See Kirkup, James

Falconer, Kenneth
See Kornbluth, C(yril) M.

Falkland, Samuel
See Heijermans, Herman

Fallaci, Oriana 1930- .... **CLC 11, 110**
See also CA 77-80; CANR 15, 58; FW;
MTCW 1

Faludi, Susan 1959- .... **CLC 140**
See also CA 138; CANR 126; FW; MTCW
1; NCFS 3

Faludy, George 1913- .... **CLC 42**
See also CA 21-24R

Faludy, Gyoergy
See Faludy, George

Fanon, Frantz 1925-1961 .... **BLC 2; CLC 74**
See also BW 1; CA 116; 89-92; DAM
MULT; DLB 296; LMFS 2; WLIT 2

Fierstein, Harvey (Forbes) 1954- ..... **CLC 33**
See also CA 123; 129; CAD; CD 5; CPW;
DA3; DAM DRAM, POP; DFS 6; DLB
266; GLL

Figes, Eva 1932- .... **CLC 31**
See also CA 53-56; CANR 4, 44, 83; CN 7;
DLB 14, 271; FW

Filippo, Eduardo de
See de Filippo, Eduardo

Finch, Anne 1661-1720 .... **LC 3; PC 21**
See also BRWS 9; DLB 95

Finch, Robert (Duer Claydon)
1900-1995 .... **CLC 18**
See also CA 57-60; CANR 9, 24, 49; CP 7;
DLB 88

Findley, Timothy (Irving Frederick)
1930-2002 .... **CLC 27, 102**
See also CA 25-28R; 206; CANR 12, 42,
69, 109; CCA 1; CN 7; DAC; DAM MST;
DLB 53; FANT; RHW

Fink, William
See Mencken, H(enry) L(ouis)

Firbank, Louis 1942-
See Reed, Lou
See also CA 117

Firbank, (Arthur Annesley) Ronald
1886-1926 .... **TCLC 1**
See also BRWS 2; CA 104; 177; DLB 36;
EWL 3; RGEL 2

Fish, Stanley
See Fish, Stanley Eugene

Fish, Stanley E.
See Fish, Stanley Eugene

Fish, Stanley Eugene 1938- .... **CLC 142**
See also CA 112; 132; CANR 90; DLB 67

Fisher, Dorothy (Frances) Canfield
1879-1958 .... **TCLC 87**
See also CA 114; 136; CANR 80; CLR 71,;
CWRI 5; DLB 9, 102, 284; MAICYA 1,
2; YABC 1

Fisher, M(ary) F(rances) K(ennedy)
1908-1992 .... **CLC 76, 87**
See also CA 77-80; 138; CANR 44; MTCW
1

Fisher, Roy 1930- .... **CLC 25**
See also CA 81-84; CAAS 10; CANR 16;
CP 7; DLB 40

Fisher, Rudolph 1897-1934 .... **BLC 2; HR 2;**
SSC 25; TCLC 11
See also BW 1, 3; CA 107; 124; CANR 80;
DAM MULT; DLB 51, 102

Fisher, Vardis (Alvero) 1895-1968 .... **CLC 7;**
TCLC 140
See also CA 5-8R; 25-28R; CANR 68; DLB
9, 206; RGAL 4; TCWW 2

Fiske, Tarleton
See Bloch, Robert (Albert)

Fitch, Clarke
See Sinclair, Upton (Beall)

Fitch, John IV
See Cormier, Robert (Edmund)

Fitzgerald, Captain Hugh
See Baum, L(yman) Frank

FitzGerald, Edward 1809-1883 .... **NCLC 9**
See also BRW 4; DLB 32; RGEL 2

Fitzgerald, F(rancis) Scott (Key)
1896-1940 ... **SSC 6, 31; TCLC 1, 6, 14,**
28, 55; WLC
See also AAYA 24; AITN 1; AMW; AMWC
2; AMWR 1; BPFB 1; CA 110; 123;
CDALB 1917-1929; DA; DA3; DAB;
DAC; DAM MST, NOV; DLB 4, 9, 86,
219, 273; DLBD 1, 15, 16; DLBY 1981,
1996; EWL 3; EXPN; EXPS; LAIT 3;
MTCW 1, 2; NFS 2; RGAL 4; RGSF 2;
SSFS 4, 15; TUS

Fitzgerald, Penelope 1916-2000 . **CLC 19, 51,**
61, 143
See also BRWS 5; CA 85-88; 190; CAAS
10; CANR 56, 86; CN 7; DLB 14, 194;
EWL 3; MTCW 2

Fitzgerald, Robert (Stuart)
1910-1985 .... **CLC 39**
See also CA 1-4R; 114; CANR 1; DLBY
1980

FitzGerald, Robert D(avid)
1902-1987 .... **CLC 19**
See also CA 17-20R; DLB 260; RGEL 2

Fitzgerald, Zelda (Sayre)
1900-1948 .... **TCLC 52**
See also AMWS 9; CA 117; 126; DLBY
1984

Flanagan, Thomas (James Bonner)
1923-2002 .... **CLC 25, 52**
See also CA 108; 206; CANR 55; CN 7;
DLBY 1980; INT CA-108; MTCW 1;
RHW

Flaubert, Gustave 1821-1880 .... **NCLC 2, 10,**
19, 62, 66, 135; SSC 11, 60; WLC
See also DA; DA3; DAB; DAC; DAM
MST, NOV; DLB 119; EW 7; EXPS; GFL
1789 to the Present; LAIT 2; LMFS 1;
NFS 14; RGSF 2; RGWL 2, 3; SSFS 6;
TWA

Flavius Josephus
See Josephus, Flavius

Flecker, Herman Elroy
See Flecker, (Herman) James Elroy

Flecker, (Herman) James Elroy
1884-1915 .... **TCLC 43**
See also CA 109; 150; DLB 10, 19; RGEL
2

Fleming, Ian (Lancaster) 1908-1964 . **CLC 3,**
30
See also AAYA 26; BPFB 1; CA 5-8R;
CANR 59; CDBLB 1945-1960; CMW 4;
CPW; DA3; DAM POP; DLB 87, 201;
MSW; MTCW 1, 2; RGEL 2; SATA 9;
TEA; YAW

Fleming, Thomas (James) 1927- ...... **CLC 37**
See also CA 5-8R; CANR 10, 102; INT
CANR-10; SATA 8

Fletcher, John 1579-1625 .... **DC 6; LC 33**
See also BRW 2; CDBLB Before 1660;
DLB 58; RGEL 2; TEA

Fletcher, John Gould 1886-1950 .... **TCLC 35**
See also CA 107; 167; DLB 4, 45; LMFS
2; RGAL 4

Fleur, Paul
See Pohl, Frederik

Floogglebuckle, Al
See Spiegelman, Art

Flora, Fletcher 1914-1969
See Queen, Ellery
See also CA 1-4R; CANR 3, 85

Flying Officer X
See Bates, H(erbert) E(rnest)

Fo, Dario 1926- .... **CLC 32, 109; DC 10**
See also CA 116; 128; CANR 68, 114;
CWW 2; DA3; DAM DRAM; DLBY
1997; EWL 3; MTCW 1, 2

Fogarty, Jonathan Titulescu Esq.
See Farrell, James T(homas)

Follett, Ken(neth Martin) 1949- .... **CLC 18**
See also AAYA 6, 50; BEST 89:4; BPFB 1;
CA 81-84; CANR 13, 33, 54, 102; CMW
4; CPW; DA3; DAM NOV, POP; DLB
87; DLBY 1981; INT CANR-33; MTCW
1

Fontane, Theodor 1819-1898 .... **NCLC 26**
See also CDWLB 2; DLB 129; EW 6;
RGWL 2, 3; TWA

Fontenot, Chester .... **CLC 65**

Fonvizin, Denis Ivanovich
1744(?)-1792 .... **LC 81**
See also DLB 150; RGWL 2, 3

Foote, Horton 1916- .... **CLC 51, 91**
See also CA 73-76; CAD; CANR 34, 51,
110; CD 5; CSW; DA3; DAM DRAM;
DLB 26, 266; EWL 3; INT CANR-34

Foote, Mary Hallock 1847-1938 .. **TCLC 108**
See also DLB 186, 188, 202, 221

Foote, Shelby 1916- .... **CLC 75**
See also AAYA 40; CA 5-8R; CANR 3, 45,
74; CN 7; CPW; CSW; DA3; DAM NOV,
POP; DLB 2, 17; MTCW 2; RHW

Forbes, Cosmo
See Lewton, Val

Forbes, Esther 1891-1967 .... **CLC 12**
See also AAYA 17; BYA 2; CA 13-14; 25-
28R; CAP 1; CLR 27; DLB 22; JRDA;
MAICYA 1, 2; RHW; SATA 2, 100; YAW

Forche, Carolyn (Louise) 1950- .... **CLC 25,**
83, 86; PC 10
See also CA 109; 117; CANR 50, 74; CP 7;
CWP; DA3; DAM POET; DLB 5, 193;
INT CA-117; MTCW 1; PFS 18; RGAL 4

Ford, Elbur
See Hibbert, Eleanor Alice Burford

Ford, Ford Madox 1873-1939 ... **TCLC 1, 15,**
39, 57
See Chaucer, Daniel
See also BRW 6; CA 104; 132; CANR 74;
CDBLB 1914-1945; DA3; DAM NOV;
DLB 34, 98, 162; EWL 3; MTCW 1, 2;
RGEL 2; TEA

Ford, Henry 1863-1947 .... **TCLC 73**
See also CA 115; 148

Ford, Jack
See Ford, John

Ford, John 1586-1639 .... **DC 8; LC 68**
See also BRW 2; CDBLB Before 1660;
DA3; DAM DRAM; DFS 7; DLB 58;
IDTP; RGEL 2

Ford, John 1895-1973 .... **CLC 16**
See also CA 187; 45-48

Ford, Richard 1944- .... **CLC 46, 99**
See also AMWS 5; CA 69-72; CANR 11,
47, 86, 128; CN 7; CSW; DLB 227; EWL
3; MTCW 1; RGAL 4; RGSF 2

Ford, Webster
See Masters, Edgar Lee

Foreman, Richard 1937- .... **CLC 50**
See also CA 65-68; CAD; CANR 32, 63;
CD 5

Forester, C(ecil) S(cott) 1899-1966 ... **CLC 35**
See also CA 73-76; 25-28R; CANR 83;
DLB 191; RGEL 2; RHW; SATA 13

Forez
See Mauriac, Francois (Charles)

Forman, James
See Forman, James D(ouglas)

Forman, James D(ouglas) 1932- .... **CLC 21**
See also AAYA 17; CA 9-12R; CANR 4,
19, 42; JRDA; MAICYA 1, 2; SATA 8,
70; YAW

Forman, Milos 1932- .... **CLC 164**
See also CA 109

Fornes, Maria Irene 1930- .... **CLC 39, 61,**
187; DC 10; HLCS 1
See also CA 25-28R; CAD; CANR 28, 81;
CD 5; CWD; DLB 7; HW 1, 2; INT
CANR-28; LLW 1; MTCW 1; RGAL 4

Forrest, Leon (Richard)
1937-1997 .... **BLCS; CLC 4**
See also AFAW 2; BW 2; CA 89-92; 162;
CAAS 7; CANR 25, 52, 87; CN 7; DLB
33

Frost, Robert (Lee) 1874-1963 .. **CLC 1, 3, 4, 9, 10, 13, 15, 26, 34, 44; PC 1, 39; WLC**
See also AAYA 21; AMW; AMWR 1; CA 89-92; CANR 33; CDALB 1917-1929; CLR 67; DA; DA3; DAB; DAC; DAM MST, POET; DLB 54, 284; DLBD 7; EWL 3; EXPP; MTCW 1, 2; PAB; PFS 1, 2, 3, 4, 5, 6, 7, 10, 13; RGAL 4; SATA 14; TUS; WP; WYA

Froude, James Anthony
1818-1894 .... **NCLC 43**
See also DLB 18, 57, 144

Froy, Herald
See Waterhouse, Keith (Spencer)

Fry, Christopher 1907- .... **CLC 2, 10, 14**
See also BRWS 3; CA 17-20R; CAAS 23; CANR 9, 30, 74; CBD; CD 5; CP 7; DAM DRAM; DLB 13; EWL 3; MTCW 1, 2; RGEL 2; SATA 66; TEA

Frye, (Herman) Northrop
1912-1991 .... **CLC 24, 70**
See also CA 5-8R; 133; CANR 8, 37; DLB 67, 68, 246; EWL 3; MTCW 1, 2; RGAL 4; TWA

Fuchs, Daniel 1909-1993 .... **CLC 8, 22**
See also CA 81-84; 142; CAAS 5; CANR 40; DLB 9, 26, 28; DLBY 1993

Fuchs, Daniel 1934- .... **CLC 34**
See also CA 37-40R; CANR 14, 48

Fuentes, Carlos 1928- .. **CLC 3, 8, 10, 13, 22, 41, 60, 113; HLC 1; SSC 24; WLC**
See also AAYA 4, 45; AITN 2; BPFB 1; CA 69-72; CANR 10, 32, 68, 104; CD-WLB 3; CWW 2; DA; DA3; DAB; DAC; DAM MST, MULT, NOV; DLB 113; DNFS 2; EWL 3; HW 1, 2; LAIT 3; LATS 1; LAW; LAWS 1; LMFS 2; MTCW 1, 2; NFS 8; RGSF 2; RGWL 2, 3; TWA; WLIT 1

Fuentes, Gregorio Lopez y
See Lopez y Fuentes, Gregorio

Fuertes, Gloria 1918-1998 .... **PC 27**
See also CA 178, 180; DLB 108; HW 2; SATA 115

Fugard, (Harold) Athol 1932- . **CLC 5, 9, 14, 25, 40, 80; DC 3**
See also AAYA 17; AFW; CA 85-88; CANR 32, 54, 118; CD 5; DAM DRAM; DFS 3, 6, 10; DLB 225; DNFS 1, 2; EWL 3; LATS 1; MTCW 1; RGEL 2; WLIT 2

Fugard, Sheila 1932- .... **CLC 48**
See also CA 125

Fukuyama, Francis 1952- .... **CLC 131**
See also CA 140; CANR 72, 125

Fuller, Charles (H.), (Jr.) 1939- .... **BLC 2; CLC 25; DC 1**
See also BW 2; CA 108; 112; CAD; CANR 87; CD 5; DAM DRAM, MULT; DFS 8; DLB 38, 266; EWL 3; INT CA-112; MTCW 1

Fuller, Henry Blake 1857-1929 .... **TCLC 103**
See also CA 108; 177; DLB 12; RGAL 4

Fuller, John (Leopold) 1937- .... **CLC 62**
See also CA 21-24R; CANR 9, 44; CP 7; DLB 40

Fuller, Margaret
See Ossoli, Sarah Margaret (Fuller)
See also AMWS 2; DLB 183, 223, 239

Fuller, Roy (Broadbent) 1912-1991 ... **CLC 4, 28**
See also BRWS 7; CA 5-8R; 135; CAAS 10; CANR 53, 83; CWRI 5; DLB 15, 20; EWL 3; RGEL 2; SATA 87

Fuller, Sarah Margaret
See Ossoli, Sarah Margaret (Fuller)

Fuller, Sarah Margaret
See Ossoli, Sarah Margaret (Fuller)
See also DLB 1, 59, 73

Fulton, Alice 1952- .... **CLC 52**
See also CA 116; CANR 57, 88; CP 7; CWP; DLB 193

Furphy, Joseph 1843-1912 .... **TCLC 25**
See Collins, Tom
See also CA 163; DLB 230; EWL 3; RGEL 2

Fuson, Robert H(enderson) 1927- .... **CLC 70**
See also CA 89-92; CANR 103

Fussell, Paul 1924- .... **CLC 74**
See also BEST 90:1; CA 17-20R; CANR 8, 21, 35, 69; INT CANR-21; MTCW 1, 2

Futabatei, Shimei 1864-1909 .... **TCLC 44**
See Futabatei Shimei
See also CA 162; MJW

Futabatei Shimei
See Futabatei, Shimei
See also DLB 180; EWL 3

Futrelle, Jacques 1875-1912 .... **TCLC 19**
See also CA 113; 155; CMW 4

Gaboriau, Emile 1835-1873 .... **NCLC 14**
See also CMW 4; MSW

Gadda, Carlo Emilio 1893-1973 ...... **CLC 11; TCLC 144**
See also CA 89-92; DLB 177; EWL 3

Gaddis, William 1922-1998 ... **CLC 1, 3, 6, 8, 10, 19, 43, 86**
See also AMWS 4; BPFB 1; CA 17-20R; 172; CANR 21, 48; CN 7; DLB 2, 278; EWL 3; MTCW 1, 2; RGAL 4

Gaelique, Moruen le
See Jacob, (Cyprien-)Max

Gage, Walter
See Inge, William (Motter)

Gaines, Ernest J(ames) 1933- .. **BLC 2; CLC 3, 11, 18, 86, 181; SSC 68**
See also AAYA 18; AFAW 1, 2; AITN 1; BPFB 2; BW 2, 3; BYA 6; CA 9-12R; CANR 6, 24, 42, 75, 126; CDALB 1968-1988; CLR 62; CN 7; CSW; DA3; DAM MULT; DLB 2, 33, 152; DLBY 1980; EWL 3; EXPN; LAIT 5; LATS 1; MTCW 1, 2; NFS 5, 7, 16; RGAL 4; RGSF 2; RHW; SATA 86; SSFS 5; YAW

Gaitskill, Mary (Lawrence) 1954- .... **CLC 69**
See also CA 128; CANR 61; DLB 244

Gaius Suetonius Tranquillus c. 70-c. 130
See Suetonius

Galdos, Benito Perez
See Perez Galdos, Benito
See also EW 7

Gale, Zona 1874-1938 .... **TCLC 7**
See also CA 105; 153; CANR 84; DAM DRAM; DFS 17; DLB 9, 78, 228; RGAL 4

Galeano, Eduardo (Hughes) 1940- . **CLC 72; HLCS 1**
See also CA 29-32R; CANR 13, 32, 100; HW 1

Galiano, Juan Valera y Alcala
See Valera y Alcala-Galiano, Juan

Galilei, Galileo 1564-1642 .... **LC 45**

Gallagher, Tess 1943- .... **CLC 18, 63; PC 9**
See also CA 106; CP 7; CWP; DAM POET; DLB 120, 212, 244; PFS 16

Gallant, Mavis 1922- ..... **CLC 7, 18, 38, 172; SSC 5**
See also CA 69-72; CANR 29, 69, 117; CCA 1; CN 7; DAC; DAM MST; DLB 53; EWL 3; MTCW 1, 2; RGEL 2; RGSF 2

Gallant, Roy A(rthur) 1924- .... **CLC 17**
See also CA 5-8R; CANR 4, 29, 54, 117; CLR 30; MAICYA 1, 2; SATA 4, 68, 110

Gallico, Paul (William) 1897-1976 ..... **CLC 2**
See also AITN 1; CA 5-8R; 69-72; CANR 23; DLB 9, 171; FANT; MAICYA 1, 2; SATA 13

Gallo, Max Louis 1932- .... **CLC 95**
See also CA 85-88

Gallois, Lucien
See Desnos, Robert

Gallup, Ralph
See Whitemore, Hugh (John)

Galsworthy, John 1867-1933 .... **SSC 22; TCLC 1, 45; WLC**
See also BRW 6; CA 104; 141; CANR 75; CDBLB 1890-1914; DA; DA3; DAB; DAC; DAM DRAM, MST, NOV; DLB 10, 34, 98, 162; DLBD 16; EWL 3; MTCW 1; RGEL 2; SSFS 3; TEA

Galt, John 1779-1839 .... **NCLC 1, 110**
See also DLB 99, 116, 159; RGEL 2; RGSF 2

Galvin, James 1951- .... **CLC 38**
See also CA 108; CANR 26

Gamboa, Federico 1864-1939 .... **TCLC 36**
See also CA 167; HW 2; LAW

Gandhi, M. K.
See Gandhi, Mohandas Karamchand

Gandhi, Mahatma
See Gandhi, Mohandas Karamchand

Gandhi, Mohandas Karamchand
1869-1948 .... **TCLC 59**
See also CA 121; 132; DA3; DAM MULT; MTCW 1, 2

Gann, Ernest Kellogg 1910-1991 ..... **CLC 23**
See also AITN 1; BPFB 2; CA 1-4R; 136; CANR 1, 83; RHW

Gao Xingjian 1940- .... **CLC 167**
See Xingjian, Gao

Garber, Eric 1943(?)-
See Holleran, Andrew
See also CANR 89

Garcia, Cristina 1958- .... **CLC 76**
See also AMWS 11; CA 141; CANR 73; DLB 292; DNFS 1; EWL 3; HW 2; LLW 1

Garcia Lorca, Federico 1898-1936 ...... **DC 2; HLC 2; PC 3; TCLC 1, 7, 49; WLC**
See Lorca, Federico Garcia
See also AAYA 46; CA 104; 131; CANR 81; DA; DA3; DAB; DAC; DAM DRAM, MST, MULT, POET; DFS 4, 10; DLB 108; EWL 3; HW 1, 2; LATS 1; MTCW 1, 2; TWA

Garcia Marquez, Gabriel (Jose)
1928- .... **CLC 2, 3, 8, 10, 15, 27, 47, 55, 68, 170; HLC 1; SSC 8; WLC**
See also AAYA 3, 33; BEST 89:1, 90:4; BPFB 2; BYA 12, 16; CA 33-36R; CANR 10, 28, 50, 75, 82, 128; CDWLB 3; CPW; DA; DA3; DAB; DAC; DAM MST, MULT, NOV, POP; DLB 113; DNFS 1, 2; EWL 3; EXPN; EXPS; HW 1, 2; LAIT 2; LATS 1; LAW; LAWS 1; LMFS 2; MTCW 1, 2; NCFS 3; NFS 1, 5, 10; RGSF 2; RGWL 2, 3; SSFS 1, 6, 16; TWA; WLIT 1

Garcilaso de la Vega, El Inca
1503-1536 .... **HLCS 1**
See also LAW

Gard, Janice
See Latham, Jean Lee

Gard, Roger Martin du
See Martin du Gard, Roger

Gardam, Jane (Mary) 1928- .... **CLC 43**
See also CA 49-52; CANR 2, 18, 33, 54, 106; CLR 12; DLB 14, 161, 231; MAI-CYA 1, 2; MTCW 1; SAAS 9; SATA 39, 76, 130; SATA-Brief 28; YAW

Gardner, Herb(ert George)
1934-2003 .... **CLC 44**
See also CA 149; 220; CAD; CANR 119; CD 5; DFS 18

Gibson, William 1914- .... **CLC 23**
See also CA 9-12R; CAD 2; CANR 9, 42, 75, 125; CD 5; DA; DAB; DAC; DAM DRAM, MST; DFS 2; DLB 7; LAIT 2; MTCW 2; SATA 66; YAW

Gibson, William (Ford) 1948- ... **CLC 39, 63, 186; SSC 52**
See also AAYA 12; BPFB 2; CA 126; 133; CANR 52, 90, 106; CN 7; CPW; DA3; DAM POP; DLB 251; MTCW 2; SCFW 2; SFW 4

Gide, Andre (Paul Guillaume)
1869-1951 ..... **SSC 13; TCLC 5, 12, 36; WLC**
See also CA 104; 124; DA; DA3; DAB; DAC; DAM MST, NOV; DLB 65; EW 8; EWL 3; GFL 1789 to the Present; MTCW 1, 2; RGSF 2; RGWL 2, 3; TWA

Gifford, Barry (Colby) 1946- .... **CLC 34**
See also CA 65-68; CANR 9, 30, 40, 90

Gilbert, Frank
See De Voto, Bernard (Augustine)

Gilbert, W(illiam) S(chwenck)
1836-1911 .... **TCLC 3**
See also CA 104; 173; DAM DRAM, POET; RGEL 2; SATA 36

Gilbreth, Frank B(unker), Jr.
1911-2001 .... **CLC 17**
See also CA 9-12R; SATA 2

Gilchrist, Ellen (Louise) 1935- .. **CLC 34, 48, 143; SSC 14, 63**
See also BPFB 2; CA 113; 116; CANR 41, 61, 104; CN 7; CPW; CSW; DAM POP; DLB 130; EWL 3; EXPS; MTCW 1, 2; RGAL 4; RGSF 2; SSFS 9

Giles, Molly 1942- .... **CLC 39**
See also CA 126; CANR 98

Gill, Eric 1882-1940 .... **TCLC 85**
See Gill, (Arthur) Eric (Rowton Peter Joseph)

Gill, (Arthur) Eric (Rowton Peter Joseph)
1882-1940
See Gill, Eric
See also CA 120; DLB 98

Gill, Patrick
See Creasey, John

Gillette, Douglas .... **CLC 70**

Gilliam, Terry (Vance) 1940- .... **CLC 21, 141**
See Monty Python
See also AAYA 19; CA 108; 113; CANR 35; INT CA-113

Gillian, Jerry
See Gilliam, Terry (Vance)

Gilliatt, Penelope (Ann Douglass)
1932-1993 .... **CLC 2, 10, 13, 53**
See also AITN 2; CA 13-16R; 141; CANR 49; DLB 14

Gilman, Charlotte (Anna) Perkins (Stetson)
1860-1935 ...... **SSC 13, 62; TCLC 9, 37, 117**
See also AMWS 11; BYA 11; CA 106; 150; DLB 221; EXPS; FW; HGG; LAIT 2; MAWW; MTCW 1; RGAL 4; RGSF 2; SFW 4; SSFS 1, 18

Gilmour, David 1946- .... **CLC 35**

Gilpin, William 1724-1804 .... **NCLC 30**

Gilray, J. D.
See Mencken, H(enry) L(ouis)

Gilroy, Frank D(aniel) 1925- .... **CLC 2**
See also CA 81-84; CAD; CANR 32, 64, 86; CD 5; DFS 17; DLB 7

Gilstrap, John 1957(?)- .... **CLC 99**
See also CA 160; CANR 101

Ginsberg, Allen 1926-1997 .... **CLC 1, 2, 3, 4, 6, 13, 36, 69, 109; PC 4, 47; TCLC 120; WLC**
See also AAYA 33; AITN 1; AMWC 1; AMWS 2; BG 2; CA 1-4R; 157; CANR 2, 41, 63, 95; CDALB 1941-1968; CP 7; DA; DA3; DAB; DAC; DAM MST, POET; DLB 5, 16, 169, 237; EWL 3; GLL 1; LMFS 2; MTCW 1, 2; PAB; PFS 5; RGAL 4; TUS; WP

Ginzburg, Eugenia .... **CLC 59**

Ginzburg, Natalia 1916-1991 .... **CLC 5, 11, 54, 70; SSC 65**
See also CA 85-88; 135; CANR 33; DFS 14; DLB 177; EW 13; EWL 3; MTCW 1, 2; RGWL 2, 3

Giono, Jean 1895-1970 .... **CLC 4, 11; TCLC 124**
See also CA 45-48; 29-32R; CANR 2, 35; DLB 72; EWL 3; GFL 1789 to the Present; MTCW 1; RGWL 2, 3

Giovanni, Nikki 1943- ...... **BLC 2; CLC 2, 4, 19, 64, 117; PC 19; WLCS**
See also AAYA 22; AITN 1; BW 2, 3; CA 29-32R; CAAS 6; CANR 18, 41, 60, 91; CDALBS; CLR 6, 73; CP 7; CSW; CWP; CWRI 5; DA; DA3; DAB; DAC; DAM MST, MULT, POET; DLB 5, 41; EWL 3; EXPP; INT CANR-18; MAICYA 1, 2; MTCW 1, 2; PFS 17; RGAL 4; SATA 24, 107; TUS; YAW

Giovene, Andrea 1904-1998 .... **CLC 7**
See also CA 85-88

Gippius, Zinaida (Nikolaevna) 1869-1945
See Hippius, Zinaida (Nikolaevna)
See also CA 106; 212

Giraudoux, Jean(-Hippolyte)
1882-1944 .... **TCLC 2, 7**
See also CA 104; 196; DAM DRAM; DLB 65; EW 9; EWL 3; GFL 1789 to the Present; RGWL 2, 3; TWA

Gironella, Jose Maria (Pous)
1917-2003 .... **CLC 11**
See also CA 101; 212; EWL 3; RGWL 2, 3

Gissing, George (Robert)
1857-1903 .... **SSC 37; TCLC 3, 24, 47**
See also BRW 5; CA 105; 167; DLB 18, 135, 184; RGEL 2; TEA

Giurlani, Aldo
See Palazzeschi, Aldo

Gladkov, Fedor Vasil'evich
See Gladkov, Fyodor (Vasilyevich)
See also DLB 272

Gladkov, Fyodor (Vasilyevich)
1883-1958 .... **TCLC 27**
See Gladkov, Fedor Vasil'evich
See also CA 170; EWL 3

Glancy, Diane 1941- .... **NNAL**
See also CA 136; CAAS 24; CANR 87; DLB 175

Glanville, Brian (Lester) 1931- .... **CLC 6**
See also CA 5-8R; CAAS 9; CANR 3, 70; CN 7; DLB 15, 139; SATA 42

Glasgow, Ellen (Anderson Gholson)
1873-1945 .... **SSC 34; TCLC 2, 7**
See also AMW; CA 104; 164; DLB 9, 12; MAWW; MTCW 2; RGAL 4; RHW; SSFS 9; TUS

Glaspell, Susan 1882(?)-1948 ..... **DC 10; SSC 41; TCLC 55**
See also AMWS 3; CA 110; 154; DFS 8, 18; DLB 7, 9, 78, 228; MAWW; RGAL 4; SSFS 3; TCWW 2; TUS; YABC 2

Glassco, John 1909-1981 .... **CLC 9**
See also CA 13-16R; 102; CANR 15; DLB 68

Glasscock, Amnesia
See Steinbeck, John (Ernst)

Glasser, Ronald J. 1940(?)- .... **CLC 37**
See also CA 209

Glassman, Joyce
See Johnson, Joyce

Gleick, James (W.) 1954- .... **CLC 147**
See also CA 131; 137; CANR 97; INT CA-137

Glendinning, Victoria 1937- .... **CLC 50**
See also CA 120; 127; CANR 59, 89; DLB 155

Glissant, Edouard (Mathieu)
1928- .... **CLC 10, 68**
See also CA 153; CANR 111; CWW 2; DAM MULT; EWL 3; RGWL 3

Gloag, Julian 1930- .... **CLC 40**
See also AITN 1; CA 65-68; CANR 10, 70; CN 7

Glowacki, Aleksander
See Prus, Boleslaw

Gluck, Louise (Elisabeth) 1943- .. **CLC 7, 22, 44, 81, 160; PC 16**
See also AMWS 5; CA 33-36R; CANR 40, 69, 108; CP 7; CWP; DA3; DAM POET; DLB 5; MTCW 2; PFS 5, 15; RGAL 4

Glyn, Elinor 1864-1943 .... **TCLC 72**
See also DLB 153; RHW

Gobineau, Joseph-Arthur
1816-1882 .... **NCLC 17**
See also DLB 123; GFL 1789 to the Present

Godard, Jean-Luc 1930- .... **CLC 20**
See also CA 93-96

Godden, (Margaret) Rumer
1907-1998 .... **CLC 53**
See also AAYA 6; BPFB 2; BYA 2, 5; CA 5-8R; 172; CANR 4, 27, 36, 55, 80; CLR 20; CN 7; CWRI 5; DLB 161; MAICYA 1, 2; RHW; SAAS 12; SATA 3, 36; SATA-Obit 109; TEA

Godoy Alcayaga, Lucila 1899-1957 .. **HLC 2; PC 32; TCLC 2**
See Mistral, Gabriela
See also BW 2; CA 104; 131; CANR 81; DAM MULT; DNFS 1; HW 1, 2; MTCW 1, 2

Godwin, Gail (Kathleen) 1937- ..... **CLC 5, 8, 22, 31, 69, 125**
See also BPFB 2; CA 29-32R; CANR 15, 43, 69; CN 7; CPW; CSW; DA3; DAM POP; DLB 6, 234; INT CANR-15; MTCW 1, 2

Godwin, William 1756-1836 .. **NCLC 14, 130**
See also CDBLB 1789-1832; CMW 4; DLB 39, 104, 142, 158, 163, 262; HGG; RGEL 2

Goebbels, Josef
See Goebbels, (Paul) Joseph

Goebbels, (Paul) Joseph
1897-1945 .... **TCLC 68**
See also CA 115; 148

Goebbels, Joseph Paul
See Goebbels, (Paul) Joseph

Goethe, Johann Wolfgang von
1749-1832 ... **DC 20; NCLC 4, 22, 34, 90; PC 5; SSC 38; WLC**
See also CDWLB 2; DA; DA3; DAB; DAC; DAM DRAM, MST, POET; DLB 94; EW 5; LATS 1; LMFS 1; RGWL 2, 3; TWA

Gogarty, Oliver St. John
1878-1957 .... **TCLC 15**
See also CA 109; 150; DLB 15, 19; RGEL 2

Gogol, Nikolai (Vasilyevich)
1809-1852 .... **DC 1; NCLC 5, 15, 31; SSC 4, 29, 52; WLC**
See also DA; DAB; DAC; DAM DRAM, MST; DFS 12; DLB 198; EW 6; EXPS; RGSF 2; RGWL 2, 3; SSFS 7; TWA

Goines, Donald 1937(?)-1974 ... **BLC 2; CLC 80**
See also AITN 1; BW 1, 3; CA 124; 114; CANR 82; CMW 4; DA3; DAM MULT, POP; DLB 33

Gold, Herbert 1924- ... **CLC 4, 7, 14, 42, 152**
See also CA 9-12R; CANR 17, 45, 125; CN 7; DLB 2; DLBY 1981

Haggard, H(enry) Rider
1856-1925 .... **TCLC 11**
See also BRWS 3; BYA 4, 5; CA 108; 148; CANR 112; DLB 70, 156, 174, 178; FANT; LMFS 1; MTCW 2; RGEL 2; RHW; SATA 16; SCFW; SFW 4; SUFW 1; WLIT 4

Hagiosy, L.
See Larbaud, Valery (Nicolas)

Hagiwara, Sakutaro 1886-1942 .... **PC 18; TCLC 60**
See Hagiwara Sakutaro
See also CA 154; RGWL 3

Hagiwara Sakutaro
See Hagiwara, Sakutaro
See also EWL 3

Haig, Fenil
See Ford, Ford Madox

Haig-Brown, Roderick (Langmere)
1908-1976 .... **CLC 21**
See also CA 5-8R; CANR 4, 38, 83; CLR 31; CWRI 5; DLB 88; MAICYA 1, 2; SATA 12

Haight, Rip
See Carpenter, John (Howard)

Hailey, Arthur 1920- .... **CLC 5**
See also AITN 2; BEST 90:3; BPFB 2; CA 1-4R; CANR 2, 36, 75; CCA 1; CN 7; CPW; DAM NOV, POP; DLB 88; DLBY 1982; MTCW 1, 2

Hailey, Elizabeth Forsythe 1938- ..... **CLC 40**
See also CA 93-96, 188; CAAE 188; CAAS 1; CANR 15, 48; INT CANR-15

Haines, John (Meade) 1924- .... **CLC 58**
See also AMWS 12; CA 17-20R; CANR 13, 34; CSW; DLB 5, 212

Hakluyt, Richard 1552-1616 .... **LC 31**
See also DLB 136; RGEL 2

Haldeman, Joe (William) 1943- .... **CLC 61**
See Graham, Robert
See also AAYA 38; CA 53-56, 179; CAAE 179; CAAS 25; CANR 6, 70, 72; DLB 8; INT CANR-6; SCFW 2; SFW 4

Hale, Janet Campbell 1947- .... **NNAL**
See also CA 49-52; CANR 45, 75; DAM MULT; DLB 175; MTCW 2

Hale, Sarah Josepha (Buell)
1788-1879 .... **NCLC 75**
See also DLB 1, 42, 73, 243

Halevy, Elie 1870-1937 .... **TCLC 104**

Haley, Alex(ander Murray Palmer)
1921-1992 .... **BLC 2; CLC 8, 12, 76; TCLC 147**
See also AAYA 26; BPFB 2; BW 2, 3; CA 77-80; 136; CANR 61; CDALBS; CPW; CSW; DA; DA3; DAB; DAC; DAM MST, MULT, POP; DLB 38; LAIT 5; MTCW 1, 2; NFS 9

Haliburton, Thomas Chandler
1796-1865 .... **NCLC 15**
See also DLB 11, 99; RGEL 2; RGSF 2

Hall, Donald (Andrew, Jr.) 1928- ...... **CLC 1, 13, 37, 59, 151**
See also CA 5-8R; CAAS 7; CANR 2, 44, 64, 106; CP 7; DAM POET; DLB 5; MTCW 1; RGAL 4; SATA 23, 97

Hall, Frederic Sauser
See Sauser-Hall, Frederic

Hall, James
See Kuttner, Henry

Hall, James Norman 1887-1951 ..... **TCLC 23**
See also CA 123; 173; LAIT 1; RHW 1; SATA 21

Hall, Joseph 1574-1656 .... **LC 91**
See also DLB 121, 151; RGEL 2

Hall, (Marguerite) Radclyffe
1880-1943 .... **TCLC 12**
See also BRWS 6; CA 110; 150; CANR 83; DLB 191; MTCW 2; RGEL 2; RHW

Hall, Rodney 1935- .... **CLC 51**
See also CA 109; CANR 69; CN 7; CP 7; DLB 289

Hallam, Arthur Henry
1811-1833 .... **NCLC 110**
See also DLB 32

Halldor Kiljan Gudjonsson 1902-1998
See Halldor Laxness
See also CA 103; 164; CWW 2

Halldor Laxness .... **CLC 25**
See Halldor Kiljan Gudjonsson
See also DLB 293; EW 12; EWL 3; RGWL 2, 3

Halleck, Fitz-Greene 1790-1867 .... **NCLC 47**
See also DLB 3, 250; RGAL 4

Halliday, Michael
See Creasey, John

Halpern, Daniel 1945- .... **CLC 14**
See also CA 33-36R; CANR 93; CP 7

Hamburger, Michael (Peter Leopold)
1924- .... **CLC 5, 14**
See also CA 5-8R, 196; CAAE 196; CAAS 4; CANR 2, 47; CP 7; DLB 27

Hamill, Pete 1935- .... **CLC 10**
See also CA 25-28R; CANR 18, 71, 127

Hamilton, Alexander
1755(?)-1804 .... **NCLC 49**
See also DLB 37

Hamilton, Clive
See Lewis, C(live) S(taples)

Hamilton, Edmond 1904-1977 .... **CLC 1**
See also CA 1-4R; CANR 3, 84; DLB 8; SATA 118; SFW 4

Hamilton, Eugene (Jacob) Lee
See Lee-Hamilton, Eugene (Jacob)

Hamilton, Franklin
See Silverberg, Robert

Hamilton, Gail
See Corcoran, Barbara (Asenath)

Hamilton, Jane 1957- .... **CLC 179**
See also CA 147; CANR 85, 128

Hamilton, Mollie
See Kaye, M(ary) M(argaret)

Hamilton, (Anthony Walter) Patrick
1904-1962 .... **CLC 51**
See also CA 176; 113; DLB 10, 191

Hamilton, Virginia (Esther)
1936-2002 .... **CLC 26**
See also AAYA 2, 21; BW 2, 3; BYA 1, 2, 8; CA 25-28R; 206; CANR 20, 37, 73, 126; CLR 1, 11, 40; DAM MULT; DLB 33, 52; DLBY 01; INT CANR-20; JRDA; LAIT 5; MAICYA 1, 2; MAICYAS 1; MTCW 1, 2; SATA 4, 56, 79, 123; SATA-Obit 132; WYA; YAW

Hammett, (Samuel) Dashiell
1894-1961 .... **CLC 3, 5, 10, 19, 47; SSC 17**
See also AITN 1; AMWS 4; BPFB 2; CA 81-84; CANR 42; CDALB 1929-1941; CMW 4; DA3; DLB 226, 280; DLBD 6; DLBY 1996; EWL 3; LAIT 3; MSW; MTCW 1, 2; RGAL 4; RGSF 2; TUS

Hammon, Jupiter 1720(?)-1800(?) .... **BLC 2; NCLC 5; PC 16**
See also DAM MULT, POET; DLB 31, 50

Hammond, Keith
See Kuttner, Henry

Hamner, Earl (Henry), Jr. 1923- ...... **CLC 12**
See also AITN 2; CA 73-76; DLB 6

Hampton, Christopher (James)
1946- .... **CLC 4**
See also CA 25-28R; CD 5; DLB 13; MTCW 1

Hamsun, Knut .... **TCLC 2, 14, 49**
See Pedersen, Knut
See also DLB 297; EW 8; EWL 3; RGWL 2, 3

Handke, Peter 1942- .... **CLC 5, 8, 10, 15, 38, 134; DC 17**
See also CA 77-80; CANR 33, 75, 104; CWW 2; DAM DRAM, NOV; DLB 85, 124; EWL 3; MTCW 1, 2; TWA

Handy, W(illiam) C(hristopher)
1873-1958 .... **TCLC 97**
See also BW 3; CA 121; 167

Hanley, James 1901-1985 ..... **CLC 3, 5, 8, 13**
See also CA 73-76; 117; CANR 36; CBD; DLB 191; EWL 3; MTCW 1; RGEL 2

Hannah, Barry 1942- .... **CLC 23, 38, 90**
See also BPFB 2; CA 108; 110; CANR 43, 68, 113; CN 7; CSW; DLB 6, 234; INT CA-110; MTCW 1; RGSF 2

Hannon, Ezra
See Hunter, Evan

Hansberry, Lorraine (Vivian)
1930-1965 ... **BLC 2; CLC 17, 62; DC 2**
See also AAYA 25; AFAW 1, 2; AMWS 4; BW 1, 3; CA 109; 25-28R; CABS 3; CAD; CANR 58; CDALB 1941-1968; CWD; DA; DA3; DAB; DAC; DAM DRAM, MST, MULT; DFS 2; DLB 7, 38; EWL 3; FW; LAIT 4; MTCW 1, 2; RGAL 4; TUS

Hansen, Joseph 1923- .... **CLC 38**
See Brock, Rose; Colton, James
See also BPFB 2; CA 29-32R; CAAS 17; CANR 16, 44, 66, 125; CMW 4; DLB 226; GLL 1; INT CANR-16

Hansen, Martin A(lfred)
1909-1955 .... **TCLC 32**
See also CA 167; DLB 214; EWL 3

Hansen and Philipson eds. .... **CLC 65**

Hanson, Kenneth O(stlin) 1922- .... **CLC 13**
See also CA 53-56; CANR 7

Hardwick, Elizabeth (Bruce) 1916- . **CLC 13**
See also AMWS 3; CA 5-8R; CANR 3, 32, 70, 100; CN 7; CSW; DA3; DAM NOV; DLB 6; MAWW; MTCW 1, 2

Hardy, Thomas 1840-1928 .... **PC 8; SSC 2, 60; TCLC 4, 10, 18, 32, 48, 53, 72, 143; WLC**
See also BRW 6; BRWC 1, 2; BRWR 1; CA 104; 123; CDBLB 1890-1914; DA; DA3; DAB; DAC; DAM MST, NOV, POET; DLB 18, 19, 135, 284; EWL 3; EXPN; EXPP; LAIT 2; MTCW 1, 2; NFS 3, 11, 15; PFS 3, 4, 18; RGEL 2; RGSF 2; TEA; WLIT 4

Hare, David 1947- .... **CLC 29, 58, 136**
See also BRWS 4; CA 97-100; CANR 39, 91; CBD; CD 5; DFS 4, 7, 16; DLB 13; MTCW 1; TEA

Harewood, John
See Van Druten, John (William)

Harford, Henry
See Hudson, W(illiam) H(enry)

Hargrave, Leonie
See Disch, Thomas M(ichael)

Hariri, Al- al-Qasim ibn 'Ali Abu Muhammad al-Basri
See al-Hariri, al-Qasim ibn 'Ali Abu Muhammad al-Basri

Harjo, Joy 1951- ..... **CLC 83; NNAL; PC 27**
See also AMWS 12; CA 114; CANR 35, 67, 91, 129; CP 7; CWP; DAM MULT; DLB 120, 175; EWL 3; MTCW 2; PFS 15; RGAL 4

Harlan, Louis R(udolph) 1922- .... **CLC 34**
See also CA 21-24R; CANR 25, 55, 80

Harling, Robert 1951(?)- .... **CLC 53**
See also CA 147

Harmon, William (Ruth) 1938- .... **CLC 38**
See also CA 33-36R; CANR 14, 32, 35; SATA 65

Harper, F. E. W.
See Harper, Frances Ellen Watkins

Head, Bessie 1937-1986 ...... **BLC 2; CLC 25, 67; SSC 52**
See also AFW; BW 2, 3; CA 29-32R; 119; CANR 25, 82; CDWLB 3; DA3; DAM MULT; DLB 117, 225; EWL 3; EXPS; FW; MTCW 1, 2; RGSF 2; SSFS 5, 13; WLIT 2; WWE 1

Headon, (Nicky) Topper 1956(?)- ..... **CLC 30**

Heaney, Seamus (Justin) 1939- ..... **CLC 5, 7, 14, 25, 37, 74, 91, 171; PC 18; WLCS**
See also BRWR 1; BRWS 2; CA 85-88; CANR 25, 48, 75, 91, 128; CDBLB 1960 to Present; CP 7; DA3; DAB; DAM POET; DLB 40; DLBY 1995; EWL 3; EXPP; MTCW 1, 2; PAB; PFS 2, 5, 8, 17; RGEL 2; TEA; WLIT 4

Hearn, (Patricio) Lafcadio (Tessima Carlos) 1850-1904 .... **TCLC 9**
See also CA 105; 166; DLB 12, 78, 189; HGG; RGAL 4

Hearne, Samuel 1745-1792 .... **LC 95**
See also DLB 99

Hearne, Vicki 1946-2001 .... **CLC 56**
See also CA 139; 201

Hearon, Shelby 1931- .... **CLC 63**
See also AITN 2; AMWS 8; CA 25-28R; CANR 18, 48, 103; CSW

Heat-Moon, William Least .... **CLC 29**
See Trogdon, William (Lewis)
See also AAYA 9

Hebbel, Friedrich 1813-1863 . **DC 21; NCLC 43**
See also CDWLB 2; DAM DRAM; DLB 129; EW 6; RGWL 2, 3

Hebert, Anne 1916-2000 .... **CLC 4, 13, 29**
See also CA 85-88; 187; CANR 69, 126; CCA 1; CWP; CWW 2; DA3; DAC; DAM MST, POET; DLB 68; EWL 3; GFL 1789 to the Present; MTCW 1, 2

Hecht, Anthony (Evan) 1923- ...... **CLC 8, 13, 19**
See also AMWS 10; CA 9-12R; CANR 6, 108; CP 7; DAM POET; DLB 5, 169; EWL 3; PFS 6; WP

Hecht, Ben 1894-1964 ..... **CLC 8; TCLC 101**
See also CA 85-88; DFS 9; DLB 7, 9, 25, 26, 28, 86; FANT; IDFW 3, 4; RGAL 4

Hedayat, Sadeq 1903-1951 .... **TCLC 21**
See also CA 120; EWL 3; RGSF 2

Hegel, Georg Wilhelm Friedrich 1770-1831 .... **NCLC 46**
See also DLB 90; TWA

Heidegger, Martin 1889-1976 .... **CLC 24**
See also CA 81-84; 65-68; CANR 34; DLB 296; MTCW 1, 2

Heidenstam, (Carl Gustaf) Verner von 1859-1940 .... **TCLC 5**
See also CA 104

Heidi Louise
See Erdrich, Louise

Heifner, Jack 1946- .... **CLC 11**
See also CA 105; CANR 47

Heijermans, Herman 1864-1924 .... **TCLC 24**
See also CA 123; EWL 3

Heilbrun, Carolyn G(old) 1926-2003 .... **CLC 25, 173**
See Cross, Amanda
See also CA 45-48; 220; CANR 1, 28, 58, 94; FW

Hein, Christoph 1944- .... **CLC 154**
See also CA 158; CANR 108; CDWLB 2; CWW 2; DLB 124

Heine, Heinrich 1797-1856 .... **NCLC 4, 54; PC 25**
See also CDWLB 2; DLB 90; EW 5; RGWL 2, 3; TWA

Heinemann, Larry (Curtiss) 1944- .. **CLC 50**
See also CA 110; CAAS 21; CANR 31, 81; DLBD 9; INT CANR-31

Heiney, Donald (William) 1921-1993
See Harris, MacDonald
See also CA 1-4R; 142; CANR 3, 58; FANT

Heinlein, Robert A(nson) 1907-1988 . **CLC 1, 3, 8, 14, 26, 55; SSC 55**
See also AAYA 17; BPFB 2; BYA 4, 13; CA 1-4R; 125; CANR 1, 20, 53; CLR 75; CPW; DA3; DAM POP; DLB 8; EXPS; JRDA; LAIT 5; LMFS 2; MAICYA 1, 2; MTCW 1, 2; RGAL 4; SATA 9, 69; SATA-Obit 56; SCFW; SFW 4; SSFS 7; YAW

Helforth, John
See Doolittle, Hilda

Heliodorus fl. 3rd cent. - .... **CMLC 52**

Hellenhofferu, Vojtech Kapristian z
See Hasek, Jaroslav (Matej Frantisek)

Heller, Joseph 1923-1999 . **CLC 1, 3, 5, 8, 11, 36, 63; TCLC 131; WLC**
See also AAYA 24; AITN 1; AMWS 4; BPFB 2; BYA 1; CA 5-8R; 187; CABS 1; CANR 8, 42, 66, 126; CN 7; CPW; DA; DA3; DAB; DAC; DAM MST, NOV, POP; DLB 2, 28, 227; DLBY 1980, 2002; EWL 3; EXPN; INT CANR-8; LAIT 4; MTCW 1, 2; NFS 1; RGAL 4; TUS; YAW

Hellman, Lillian (Florence) 1906-1984 .. **CLC 2, 4, 8, 14, 18, 34, 44, 52; DC 1; TCLC 119**
See also AAYA 47; AITN 1, 2; AMWS 1; CA 13-16R; 112; CAD; CANR 33; CWD; DA3; DAM DRAM; DFS 1, 3, 14; DLB 7, 228; DLBY 1984; EWL 3; FW; LAIT 3; MAWW; MTCW 1, 2; RGAL 4; TUS

Helprin, Mark 1947- .... **CLC 7, 10, 22, 32**
See also CA 81-84; CANR 47, 64, 124; CDALBS; CPW; DA3; DAM NOV, POP; DLBY 1985; FANT; MTCW 1, 2; SUFW 2

Helvetius, Claude-Adrien 1715-1771 .. **LC 26**

Helyar, Jane Penelope Josephine 1933-
See Poole, Josephine
See also CA 21-24R; CANR 10, 26; CWRI 5; SATA 82, 138; SATA-Essay 138

Hemans, Felicia 1793-1835 ...... **NCLC 29, 71**
See also DLB 96; RGEL 2

Hemingway, Ernest (Miller) 1899-1961 .... **CLC 1, 3, 6, 8, 10, 13, 19, 30, 34, 39, 41, 44, 50, 61, 80; SSC 1, 25, 36, 40, 63; TCLC 115; WLC**
See also AAYA 19; AMW; AMWC 1; AMWR 1; BPFB 2; BYA 2, 3, 13, 15; CA 77-80; CANR 34; CDALB 1917-1929; DA; DA3; DAB; DAC; DAM MST, NOV; DLB 4, 9, 102, 210; DLBD 1, 15, 16; DLBY 1981, 1987, 1996, 1998; EWL 3; EXPN; EXPS; LAIT 3, 4; LATS 1; MTCW 1, 2; NFS 1, 5, 6, 14; RGAL 4; RGSF 2; SSFS 17; TUS; WYA

Hempel, Amy 1951- .... **CLC 39**
See also CA 118; 137; CANR 70; DA3; DLB 218; EXPS; MTCW 2; SSFS 2

Henderson, F. C.
See Mencken, H(enry) L(ouis)

Henderson, Sylvia
See Ashton-Warner, Sylvia (Constance)

Henderson, Zenna (Chlarson) 1917-1983 .... **SSC 29**
See also CA 1-4R; 133; CANR 1, 84; DLB 8; SATA 5; SFW 4

Henkin, Joshua .... **CLC 119**
See also CA 161

Henley, Beth .... **CLC 23; DC 6, 14**
See Henley, Elizabeth Becker
See also CABS 3; CAD; CD 5; CSW; CWD; DFS 2; DLBY 1986; FW

Henley, Elizabeth Becker 1952-
See Henley, Beth
See also CA 107; CANR 32, 73; DA3; DAM DRAM, MST; MTCW 1, 2

Henley, William Ernest 1849-1903 .. **TCLC 8**
See also CA 105; DLB 19; RGEL 2

Hennissart, Martha
See Lathen, Emma
See also CA 85-88; CANR 64

Henry VIII 1491-1547 .... **LC 10**
See also DLB 132

Henry, O. ..... **SSC 5, 49; TCLC 1, 19; WLC**
See Porter, William Sydney
See also AAYA 41; AMWS 2; EXPS; RGAL 4; RGSF 2; SSFS 2, 18

Henry, Patrick 1736-1799 .... **LC 25**
See also LAIT 1

Henryson, Robert 1430(?)-1506(?) ...... **LC 20**
See also BRWS 7; DLB 146; RGEL 2

Henschke, Alfred
See Klabund

Henson, Lance 1944- .... **NNAL**
See also CA 146; DLB 175

Hentoff, Nat(han Irving) 1925- .... **CLC 26**
See also AAYA 4, 42; BYA 6; CA 1-4R; CAAS 6; CANR 5, 25, 77, 114; CLR 1, 52; INT CANR-25; JRDA; MAICYA 1, 2; SATA 42, 69, 133; SATA-Brief 27; WYA; YAW

Heppenstall, (John) Rayner 1911-1981 .... **CLC 10**
See also CA 1-4R; 103; CANR 29; EWL 3

Heraclitus c. 540B.C.-c. 450B.C. ... **CMLC 22**
See also DLB 176

Herbert, Frank (Patrick) 1920-1986 .... **CLC 12, 23, 35, 44, 85**
See also AAYA 21; BPFB 2; BYA 4, 14; CA 53-56; 118; CANR 5, 43; CDALBS; CPW; DAM POP; DLB 8; INT CANR-5; LAIT 5; MTCW 1, 2; NFS 17; SATA 9, 37; SATA-Obit 47; SCFW 2; SFW 4; YAW

Herbert, George 1593-1633 ...... **LC 24; PC 4**
See also BRW 2; BRWR 2; CDBLB Before 1660; DAB; DAM POET; DLB 126; EXPP; RGEL 2; TEA; WP

Herbert, Zbigniew 1924-1998 ..... **CLC 9, 43; PC 50**
See also CA 89-92; 169; CANR 36, 74; CD-WLB 4; CWW 2; DAM POET; DLB 232; EWL 3; MTCW 1

Herbst, Josephine (Frey) 1897-1969 .... **CLC 34**
See also CA 5-8R; 25-28R; DLB 9

Herder, Johann Gottfried von 1744-1803 .... **NCLC 8**
See also DLB 97; EW 4; TWA

Heredia, Jose Maria 1803-1839 .... **HLCS 2**
See also LAW

Hergesheimer, Joseph 1880-1954 ... **TCLC 11**
See also CA 109; 194; DLB 102, 9; RGAL 4

Herlihy, James Leo 1927-1993 .... **CLC 6**
See also CA 1-4R; 143; CAD; CANR 2

Herman, William
See Bierce, Ambrose (Gwinett)

Hermogenes fl. c. 175- .... **CMLC 6**

Hernandez, Jose 1834-1886 .... **NCLC 17**
See also LAW; RGWL 2, 3; WLIT 1

Herodotus c. 484B.C.-c. 420B.C. .. **CMLC 17**
See also AW 1; CDWLB 1; DLB 176; RGWL 2, 3; TWA

Herrick, Robert 1591-1674 .... **LC 13; PC 9**
See also BRW 2; BRWC 2; DA; DAB; DAC; DAM MST, POP; DLB 126; EXPP; PFS 13; RGAL 4; RGEL 2; TEA; WP

Herring, Guilles
See Somerville, Edith Oenone

Herriot, James 1916-1995 .... **CLC 12**
  See Wight, James Alfred
  See also AAYA 1; BPFB 2; CA 148; CANR
    40; CLR 80; CPW; DAM POP; LAIT 3;
    MAICYA 2; MAICYAS 1; MTCW 2;
    SATA 86, 135; TEA; YAW

Herris, Violet
  See Hunt, Violet

Herrmann, Dorothy 1941- .... **CLC 44**
  See also CA 107

Herrmann, Taffy
  See Herrmann, Dorothy

Hersey, John (Richard) 1914-1993 .... **CLC 1,
2, 7, 9, 40, 81, 97**
  See also AAYA 29; BPFB 2; CA 17-20R;
    140; CANR 33; CDALBS; CPW; DAM
    POP; DLB 6, 185, 278; MTCW 1, 2;
    SATA 25; SATA-Obit 76; TUS

Herzen, Aleksandr Ivanovich
  1812-1870 .... **NCLC 10, 61**
  See Herzen, Alexander

Herzen, Alexander
  See Herzen, Aleksandr Ivanovich
  See also DLB 277

Herzl, Theodor 1860-1904 .... **TCLC 36**
  See also CA 168

Herzog, Werner 1942- .... **CLC 16**
  See also CA 89-92

Hesiod c. 8th cent. B.C.- .... **CMLC 5**
  See also AW 1; DLB 176; RGWL 2, 3

Hesse, Hermann 1877-1962 ... **CLC 1, 2, 3, 6,
11, 17, 25, 69; SSC 9, 49; TCLC 148;
WLC**
  See also AAYA 43; BPFB 2; CA 17-18;
    CAP 2; CDWLB 2; DA; DA3; DAB;
    DAC; DAM MST, NOV; DLB 66; EW 9;
    EWL 3; EXPN; LAIT 1; MTCW 1, 2;
    NFS 6, 15; RGWL 2, 3; SATA 50; TWA

Hewes, Cady
  See De Voto, Bernard (Augustine)

Heyen, William 1940- .... **CLC 13, 18**
  See also CA 33-36R; 220; CAAE 220;
    CAAS 9; CANR 98; CP 7; DLB 5

Heyerdahl, Thor 1914-2002 .... **CLC 26**
  See also CA 5-8R; 207; CANR 5, 22, 66,
    73; LAIT 4; MTCW 1, 2; SATA 2, 52

Heym, Georg (Theodor Franz Arthur)
  1887-1912 .... **TCLC 9**
  See also CA 106; 181

Heym, Stefan 1913-2001 .... **CLC 41**
  See also CA 9-12R; 203; CANR 4; CWW
    2; DLB 69; EWL 3

Heyse, Paul (Johann Ludwig von)
  1830-1914 .... **TCLC 8**
  See also CA 104; 209; DLB 129

Heyward, (Edwin) DuBose
  1885-1940 .... **HR 2; TCLC 59**
  See also CA 108; 157; DLB 7, 9, 45, 249;
    SATA 21

Heywood, John 1497(?)-1580(?) .... **LC 65**
  See also DLB 136; RGEL 2

Hibbert, Eleanor Alice Burford
  1906-1993 .... **CLC 7**
  See Holt, Victoria
  See also BEST 90:4; CA 17-20R; 140;
    CANR 9, 28, 59; CMW 4; CPW; DAM
    POP; MTCW 2; RHW; SATA 2; SATA-
    Obit 74

Hichens, Robert (Smythe)
  1864-1950 .... **TCLC 64**
  See also CA 162; DLB 153; HGG; RHW;
    SUFW

Higgins, Aidan 1927- .... **SSC 68**
  See also CA 9-12R; CANR 70, 115; CN 7;
    DLB 14

Higgins, George V(incent)
  1939-1999 .... **CLC 4, 7, 10, 18**
  See also BPFB 2; CA 77-80; 186; CAAS 5;
    CANR 17, 51, 89, 96; CMW 4; CN 7;
    DLB 2; DLBY 1981, 1998; INT CANR-
    17; MSW; MTCW 1

Higginson, Thomas Wentworth
  1823-1911 .... **TCLC 36**
  See also CA 162; DLB 1, 64, 243

Higgonet, Margaret ed. .... **CLC 65**

Highet, Helen
  See MacInnes, Helen (Clark)

Highsmith, (Mary) Patricia
  1921-1995 .... **CLC 2, 4, 14, 42, 102**
  See Morgan, Claire
  See also AAYA 48; BRWS 5; CA 1-4R; 147;
    CANR 1, 20, 48, 62, 108; CMW 4; CPW;
    DA3; DAM NOV, POP; MSW; MTCW 1,
    2

Highwater, Jamake (Mamake)
  1942(?)-2001 .... **CLC 12**
  See also AAYA 7; BPFB 2; BYA 4; CA 65-
    68; 199; CAAS 7; CANR 10, 34, 84; CLR
    17; CWRI 5; DLB 52; DLBY 1985;
    JRDA; MAICYA 1, 2; SATA 32, 69;
    SATA-Brief 30

Highway, Tomson 1951- ...... **CLC 92; NNAL**
  See also CA 151; CANR 75; CCA 1; CD 5;
    DAC; DAM MULT; DFS 2; MTCW 2

Hijuelos, Oscar 1951- .... **CLC 65; HLC 1**
  See also AAYA 25; AMWS 8; BEST 90:1;
    CA 123; CANR 50, 75, 125; CPW; DA3;
    DAM MULT, POP; DLB 145; HW 1, 2;
    LLW 1; MTCW 2; NFS 17; RGAL 4;
    WLIT 1

Hikmet, Nazim 1902(?)-1963 .... **CLC 40**
  See also CA 141; 93-96; EWL 3

Hildegard von Bingen 1098-1179 . **CMLC 20**
  See also DLB 148

Hildesheimer, Wolfgang 1916-1991 .. **CLC 49**
  See also CA 101; 135; DLB 69, 124; EWL
    3

Hill, Geoffrey (William) 1932- ...... **CLC 5, 8,
18, 45**
  See also BRWS 5; CA 81-84; CANR 21,
    89; CDBLB 1960 to Present; CP 7; DAM
    POET; DLB 40; EWL 3; MTCW 1; RGEL
    2

Hill, George Roy 1921-2002 .... **CLC 26**
  See also CA 110; 122; 213

Hill, John
  See Koontz, Dean R(ay)

Hill, Susan (Elizabeth) 1942- ...... **CLC 4, 113**
  See also CA 33-36R; CANR 29, 69, 129;
    CN 7; DAB; DAM MST, NOV; DLB 14,
    139; HGG; MTCW 1; RHW

Hillard, Asa G. III .... **CLC 70**

Hillerman, Tony 1925- .... **CLC 62, 170**
  See also AAYA 40; BEST 89:1; BPFB 2;
    CA 29-32R; CANR 21, 42, 65, 97; CMW
    4; CPW; DA3; DAM POP; DLB 206;
    MSW; RGAL 4; SATA 6; TCWW 2; YAW

Hillesum, Etty 1914-1943 .... **TCLC 49**
  See also CA 137

Hilliard, Noel (Harvey) 1929-1996 ... **CLC 15**
  See also CA 9-12R; CANR 7, 69; CN 7

Hillis, Rick 1956- .... **CLC 66**
  See also CA 134

Hilton, James 1900-1954 .... **TCLC 21**
  See also CA 108; 169; DLB 34, 77; FANT;
    SATA 34

Hilton, Walter (?)-1396 .... **CMLC 58**
  See also DLB 146; RGEL 2

Himes, Chester (Bomar) 1909-1984 .. **BLC 2;
CLC 2, 4, 7, 18, 58, 108; TCLC 139**
  See also AFAW 2; BPFB 2; BW 2; CA 25-
    28R; CANR 22, 89; CMW 4; DAM
    MULT; DLB 2, 76, 143, 226; EWL 3;
    MSW; MTCW 1, 2; RGAL 4

Hinde, Thomas .... **CLC 6, 11**
  See Chitty, Thomas Willes
  See also EWL 3

Hine, (William) Daryl 1936- .... **CLC 15**
  See also CA 1-4R; CAAS 15; CANR 1, 20;
    CP 7; DLB 60

Hinkson, Katharine Tynan
  See Tynan, Katharine

Hinojosa(-Smith), Rolando (R.)
  1929- .... **HLC 1**
  See Hinojosa-Smith, Rolando
  See also CA 131; CAAS 16; CANR 62;
    DAM MULT; DLB 82; HW 1, 2; LLW 1;
    MTCW 2; RGAL 4

Hinton, S(usan) E(loise) 1950- .. **CLC 30, 111**
  See also AAYA 2, 33; BPFB 2; BYA 2, 3;
    CA 81-84; CANR 32, 62, 92; CDALBS;
    CLR 3, 23; CPW; DA; DA3; DAC;
    DAM MST, NOV; JRDA; LAIT 5; MAI-
    CYA 1, 2; MTCW 1, 2; NFS 5, 9, 15, 16;
    SATA 19, 58, 115; WYA; YAW

Hippius, Zinaida (Nikolaevna) .... **TCLC 9**
  See Gippius, Zinaida (Nikolaevna)
  See also DLB 295; EWL 3

Hiraoka, Kimitake 1925-1970
  See Mishima, Yukio
  See also CA 97-100; 29-32R; DA3; DAM
    DRAM; GLL 1; MTCW 1, 2

Hirsch, E(ric) D(onald), Jr. 1928- .... **CLC 79**
  See also CA 25-28R; CANR 27, 51; DLB
    67; INT CANR-27; MTCW 1

Hirsch, Edward 1950- .... **CLC 31, 50**
  See also CA 104; CANR 20, 42, 102; CP 7;
    DLB 120

Hitchcock, Alfred (Joseph)
  1899-1980 .... **CLC 16**
  See also AAYA 22; CA 159; 97-100; SATA
    27; SATA-Obit 24

Hitchens, Christopher (Eric)
  1949- .... **CLC 157**
  See also CA 152; CANR 89

Hitler, Adolf 1889-1945 .... **TCLC 53**
  See also CA 117; 147

Hoagland, Edward 1932- .... **CLC 28**
  See also ANW; CA 1-4R; CANR 2, 31, 57,
    107; CN 7; DLB 6; SATA 51; TCWW 2

Hoban, Russell (Conwell) 1925- ... **CLC 7, 25**
  See also BPFB 2; CA 5-8R; CANR 23, 37,
    66, 114; CLR 3, 69; CN 7; CWRI 5; DAM
    NOV; DLB 52; FANT; MAICYA 1, 2;
    MTCW 1, 2; SATA 1, 40, 78, 136; SFW
    4; SUFW 2

Hobbes, Thomas 1588-1679 .... **LC 36**
  See also DLB 151, 252, 281; RGEL 2

Hobbs, Perry
  See Blackmur, R(ichard) P(almer)

Hobson, Laura Z(ametkin)
  1900-1986 .... **CLC 7, 25**
  See Field, Peter
  See also BPFB 2; CA 17-20R; 118; CANR
    55; DLB 28; SATA 52

Hoccleve, Thomas c. 1368-c. 1437 ...... **LC 75**
  See also DLB 146; RGEL 2

Hoch, Edward D(entinger) 1930-
  See Queen, Ellery
  See also CA 29-32R; CANR 11, 27, 51, 97;
    CMW 4; SFW 4

Hochhuth, Rolf 1931- .... **CLC 4, 11, 18**
  See also CA 5-8R; CANR 33, 75; CWW 2;
    DAM DRAM; DLB 124; EWL 3; MTCW
    1, 2

Hochman, Sandra 1936- .... **CLC 3, 8**
  See also CA 5-8R; DLB 5

Hochwaelder, Fritz 1911-1986 .... **CLC 36**
  See Hochwalder, Fritz
  See also CA 29-32R; 120; CANR 42; DAM
    DRAM; MTCW 1; RGWL 3

Hunter, Robert (?)-1734 .... **LC 7**

Hurston, Zora Neale 1891-1960 .... **BLC 2; CLC 7, 30, 61; DC 12; HR 2; SSC 4; TCLC 121, 131; WLCS**
  See also AAYA 15; AFAW 1, 2; AMWS 6; BW 1, 3; BYA 12; CA 85-88; CANR 61; CDALBS; DA; DA3; DAC; DAM MST, MULT, NOV; DFS 6; DLB 51, 86; EWL 3; EXPN; EXPS; FW; LAIT 3; LATS 1; LMFS 2; MAWW; MTCW 1, 2; NFS 3; RGAL 4; RGSF 2; SSFS 1, 6, 11, 19; TUS; YAW

Husserl, E. G.
  See Husserl, Edmund (Gustav Albrecht)

Husserl, Edmund (Gustav Albrecht)
  1859-1938 .... **TCLC 100**
  See also CA 116; 133; DLB 296

Huston, John (Marcellus)
  1906-1987 .... **CLC 20**
  See also CA 73-76; 123; CANR 34; DLB 26

Hustvedt, Siri 1955- .... **CLC 76**
  See also CA 137

Hutten, Ulrich von 1488-1523 .... **LC 16**
  See also DLB 179

Huxley, Aldous (Leonard)
  1894-1963 .... **CLC 1, 3, 4, 5, 8, 11, 18, 35, 79; SSC 39; WLC**
  See also AAYA 11; BPFB 2; BRW 7; CA 85-88; CANR 44, 99; CDBLB 1914-1945; DA; DA3; DAB; DAC; DAM MST, NOV; DLB 36, 100, 162, 195, 255; EWL 3; EXPN; LAIT 5; LMFS 2; MTCW 1, 2; NFS 6; RGEL 2; SATA 63; SCFW 2; SFW 4; TEA; YAW

Huxley, T(homas) H(enry)
  1825-1895 .... **NCLC 67**
  See also DLB 57; TEA

Huysmans, Joris-Karl 1848-1907 ... **TCLC 7, 69**
  See also CA 104; 165; DLB 123; EW 7; GFL 1789 to the Present; LMFS 2; RGWL 2, 3

Hwang, David Henry 1957- .. **CLC 55; DC 4**
  See also CA 127; 132; CAD; CANR 76, 124; CD 5; DA3; DAM DRAM; DFS 11, 18; DLB 212, 228; INT CA-132; MTCW 2; RGAL 4

Hyde, Anthony 1946- .... **CLC 42**
  See Chase, Nicholas
  See also CA 136; CCA 1

Hyde, Margaret O(ldroyd) 1917- ..... **CLC 21**
  See also CA 1-4R; CANR 1, 36; CLR 23; JRDA; MAICYA 1, 2; SAAS 8; SATA 1, 42, 76, 139

Hynes, James 1956(?)- .... **CLC 65**
  See also CA 164; CANR 105

Hypatia c. 370-415 .... **CMLC 35**

Ian, Janis 1951- .... **CLC 21**
  See also CA 105; 187

Ibanez, Vicente Blasco
  See Blasco Ibanez, Vicente

Ibarbourou, Juana de 1895-1979 ..... **HLCS 2**
  See also DLB 290; HW 1; LAW

Ibarguengoitia, Jorge 1928-1983 ..... **CLC 37; TCLC 148**
  See also CA 124; 113; EWL 3; HW 1

Ibn Battuta, Abu Abdalla
  1304-1368(?) .... **CMLC 57**
  See also WLIT 2

Ibn Hazm 994-1064 .... **CMLC 64**

Ibsen, Henrik (Johan) 1828-1906 .... **DC 2; TCLC 2, 8, 16, 37, 52; WLC**
  See also AAYA 46; CA 104; 141; DA; DA3; DAB; DAC; DAM DRAM, MST; DFS 1, 6, 8, 10, 11, 15, 16; EW 7; LAIT 2; LATS 1; RGWL 2, 3

Ibuse, Masuji 1898-1993 .... **CLC 22**
  See Ibuse Masuji
  See also CA 127; 141; MJW; RGWL 3

Ibuse Masuji
  See Ibuse, Masuji
  See also DLB 180; EWL 3

Ichikawa, Kon 1915- .... **CLC 20**
  See also CA 121

Ichiyo, Higuchi 1872-1896 .... **NCLC 49**
  See also MJW

Idle, Eric 1943- .... **CLC 21**
  See Monty Python
  See also CA 116; CANR 35, 91

Ignatow, David 1914-1997 .... **CLC 4, 7, 14, 40; PC 34**
  See also CA 9-12R; 162; CAAS 3; CANR 31, 57, 96; CP 7; DLB 5; EWL 3

Ignotus
  See Strachey, (Giles) Lytton

Ihimaera, Witi (Tame) 1944- .... **CLC 46**
  See also CA 77-80; CN 7; RGSF 2; SATA 148

Ilf, Ilya .... **TCLC 21**
  See Fainzilberg, Ilya Arnoldovich
  See also EWL 3

Illyes, Gyula 1902-1983 .... **PC 16**
  See also CA 114; 109; CDWLB 4; DLB 215; EWL 3; RGWL 2, 3

Imalayen, Fatima-Zohra
  See Djebar, Assia

Immermann, Karl (Lebrecht)
  1796-1840 .... **NCLC 4, 49**
  See also DLB 133

Ince, Thomas H. 1882-1924 .... **TCLC 89**
  See also IDFW 3, 4

Inchbald, Elizabeth 1753-1821 ...... **NCLC 62**
  See also DLB 39, 89; RGEL 2

Inclan, Ramon (Maria) del Valle
  See Valle-Inclan, Ramon (Maria) del

Infante, G(uillermo) Cabrera
  See Cabrera Infante, G(uillermo)

Ingalls, Rachel (Holmes) 1940- .... **CLC 42**
  See also CA 123; 127

Ingamells, Reginald Charles
  See Ingamells, Rex

Ingamells, Rex 1913-1955 .... **TCLC 35**
  See also CA 167; DLB 260

Inge, William (Motter) 1913-1973 ..... **CLC 1, 8, 19**
  See also CA 9-12R; CDALB 1941-1968; DA3; DAM DRAM; DFS 1, 3, 5, 8; DLB 7, 249; EWL 3; MTCW 1, 2; RGAL 4; TUS

Ingelow, Jean 1820-1897 .... **NCLC 39, 107**
  See also DLB 35, 163; FANT; SATA 33

Ingram, Willis J.
  See Harris, Mark

Innaurato, Albert (F.) 1948(?)- ... **CLC 21, 60**
  See also CA 115; 122; CAD; CANR 78; CD 5; INT CA-122

Innes, Michael
  See Stewart, J(ohn) I(nnes) M(ackintosh)
  See also DLB 276; MSW

Innis, Harold Adams 1894-1952 .... **TCLC 77**
  See also CA 181; DLB 88

Insluis, Alanus de
  See Alain de Lille

Iola
  See Wells-Barnett, Ida B(ell)

Ionesco, Eugene 1912-1994 ... **CLC 1, 4, 6, 9, 11, 15, 41, 86; DC 12; WLC**
  See also CA 9-12R; 144; CANR 55; CWW 2; DA; DA3; DAB; DAC; DAM DRAM, MST; DFS 4, 9; EW 13; EWL 3; GFL 1789 to the Present; LMFS 2; MTCW 1, 2; RGWL 2, 3; SATA 7; SATA-Obit 79; TWA

Iqbal, Muhammad 1877-1938 .... **TCLC 28**
  See also CA 215; EWL 3

Ireland, Patrick
  See O'Doherty, Brian

Irenaeus St. 130- .... **CMLC 42**

Irigaray, Luce 1930- .... **CLC 164**
  See also CA 154; CANR 121; FW

Iron, Ralph
  See Schreiner, Olive (Emilie Albertina)

Irving, John (Winslow) 1942- ... **CLC 13, 23, 38, 112, 175**
  See also AAYA 8; AMWS 6; BEST 89:3; BPFB 2; CA 25-28R; CANR 28, 73, 112; CN 7; CPW; DA3; DAM NOV, POP; DLB 6, 278; DLBY 1982; EWL 3; MTCW 1, 2; NFS 12, 14; RGAL 4; TUS

Irving, Washington 1783-1859 . **NCLC 2, 19, 95; SSC 2, 37; WLC**
  See also AMW; CDALB 1640-1865; CLR 97; DA; DA3; DAB; DAC; DAM MST; DLB 3, 11, 30, 59, 73, 74, 183, 186, 250, 254; EXPS; LAIT 1; RGAL 4; RGSF 2; SSFS 1, 8, 16; SUFW 1; TUS; WCH; YABC 2

Irwin, P. K.
  See Page, P(atricia) K(athleen)

Isaacs, Jorge Ricardo 1837-1895 ... **NCLC 70**
  See also LAW

Isaacs, Susan 1943- .... **CLC 32**
  See also BEST 89:1; BPFB 2; CA 89-92; CANR 20, 41, 65, 112; CPW; DA3; DAM POP; INT CANR-20; MTCW 1, 2

Isherwood, Christopher (William Bradshaw)
  1904-1986 .... **CLC 1, 9, 11, 14, 44; SSC 56**
  See also BRW 7; CA 13-16R; 117; CANR 35, 97; DA3; DAM DRAM, NOV; DLB 15, 195; DLBY 1986; EWL 3; IDTP; MTCW 1, 2; RGAL 4; RGEL 2; TUS; WLIT 4

Ishiguro, Kazuo 1954- .. **CLC 27, 56, 59, 110**
  See also BEST 90:2; BPFB 2; BRWS 4; CA 120; CANR 49, 95; CN 7; DA3; DAM NOV; DLB 194; EWL 3; MTCW 1, 2; NFS 13; WLIT 4; WWE 1

Ishikawa, Hakuhin
  See Ishikawa, Takuboku

Ishikawa, Takuboku 1886(?)-1912 ..... **PC 10; TCLC 15**
  See Ishikawa Takuboku
  See also CA 113; 153; DAM POET

Iskander, Fazil (Abdulovich) 1929- .. **CLC 47**
  See also CA 102; EWL 3

Isler, Alan (David) 1934- .... **CLC 91**
  See also CA 156; CANR 105

Ivan IV 1530-1584 .... **LC 17**

Ivanov, Vyacheslav Ivanovich
  1866-1949 .... **TCLC 33**
  See also CA 122; EWL 3

Ivask, Ivar Vidrik 1927-1992 .... **CLC 14**
  See also CA 37-40R; 139; CANR 24

Ives, Morgan
  See Bradley, Marion Zimmer
  See also GLL 1

Izumi Shikibu c. 973-c. 1034 .... **CMLC 33**

J. R. S.
  See Gogarty, Oliver St. John

Jabran, Kahlil
  See Gibran, Kahlil

Jabran, Khalil
  See Gibran, Kahlil

Jackson, Daniel
  See Wingrove, David (John)

Jackson, Helen Hunt 1830-1885 .... **NCLC 90**
  See also DLB 42, 47, 186, 189; RGAL 4

Jackson, Jesse 1908-1983 .... **CLC 12**
  See also BW 1; CA 25-28R; 109; CANR 27; CLR 28; CWRI 5; MAICYA 1, 2; SATA 2, 29; SATA-Obit 48

Keith, Carlos
See Lewton, Val
Keith, Michael
See Hubbard, L(afayette) Ron(ald)
Keller, Gottfried 1819-1890 .... **NCLC 2; SSC 26**
See also CDWLB 2; DLB 129; EW; RGSF 2; RGWL 2, 3
Keller, Nora Okja 1965- .... **CLC 109**
See also CA 187
Kellerman, Jonathan 1949- .... **CLC 44**
See also AAYA 35; BEST 90:1; CA 106; CANR 29, 51; CMW 4; CPW; DA3; DAM POP; INT CANR-29
Kelley, William Melvin 1937- .... **CLC 22**
See also BW 1; CA 77-80; CANR 27, 83; CN 7; DLB 33; EWL 3
Kellogg, Marjorie 1922- .... **CLC 2**
See also CA 81-84
Kellow, Kathleen
See Hibbert, Eleanor Alice Burford
Kelly, M(ilton) T(errence) 1947- ...... **CLC 55**
See also CA 97-100; CAAS 22; CANR 19, 43, 84; CN 7
Kelly, Robert 1935- .... **SSC 50**
See also CA 17-20R; CAAS 19; CANR 47; CP 7; DLB 5, 130, 165
Kelman, James 1946- .... **CLC 58, 86**
See also BRWS 5; CA 148; CANR 85; CN 7; DLB 194; RGSF 2; WLIT 4
Kemal, Yashar 1923- .... **CLC 14, 29**
See also CA 89-92; CANR 44; CWW 2
Kemble, Fanny 1809-1893 .... **NCLC 18**
See also DLB 32
Kemelman, Harry 1908-1996 .... **CLC 2**
See also AITN 1; BPFB 2; CA 9-12R; 155; CANR 6, 71; CMW 4; DLB 28
Kempe, Margery 1373(?)-1440(?) ... **LC 6, 56**
See also DLB 146; RGEL 2
Kempis, Thomas a 1380-1471 .... **LC 11**
Kendall, Henry 1839-1882 .... **NCLC 12**
See also DLB 230
Keneally, Thomas (Michael) 1935- ... **CLC 5, 8, 10, 14, 19, 27, 43, 117**
See also BRWS 4; CA 85-88; CANR 10, 50, 74; CN 7; CPW; DA3; DAM NOV; DLB 289; EWL 3; MTCW 1, 2; NFS 17; RGEL 2; RHW
Kennedy, A(lison) L(ouise) 1965- ... **CLC 188**
See also CA 168, 213; CAAE 213; CANR 108; CD 5; CN 7; DLB 271; RGSF 2
Kennedy, Adrienne (Lita) 1931- .... **BLC 2; CLC 66; DC 5**
See also AFAW 2; BW 2, 3; CA 103; CAAS 20; CABS 3; CANR 26, 53, 82; CD 5; DAM MULT; DFS 9; DLB 38; FW
Kennedy, John Pendleton 1795-1870 .... **NCLC 2**
See also DLB 3, 248, 254; RGAL 4
Kennedy, Joseph Charles 1929-
See Kennedy, X. J.
See also CA 1-4R, 201; CAAE 201; CANR 4, 30, 40; CP 7; CWRI 5; MAICYA 2; MAICYAS 1; SATA 14, 86, 130; SATA-Essay 130
Kennedy, William 1928- ... **CLC 6, 28, 34, 53**
See also AAYA 1; AMWS 7; BPFB 2; CA 85-88; CANR 14, 31, 76; CN 7; DA3; DAM NOV; DLB 143; DLBY 1985; EWL 3; INT CANR-31; MTCW 1, 2; SATA 57
Kennedy, X. J. .... **CLC 8, 42**
See Kennedy, Joseph Charles
See also CAAS 9; CLR 27; DLB 5; SAAS 22
Kenny, Maurice (Francis) 1929- ..... **CLC 87; NNAL**
See also CA 144; CAAS 22; DAM MULT; DLB 175

Kent, Kelvin
See Kuttner, Henry
Kenton, Maxwell
See Southern, Terry
Kenyon, Robert O.
See Kuttner, Henry
Kepler, Johannes 1571-1630 .... **LC 45**
Ker, Jill
See Conway, Jill K(er)
Kerkow, H. C.
See Lewton, Val
Kerouac, Jack 1922-1969 ...... **CLC 1, 2, 3, 5, 14, 29, 61; TCLC 117; WLC**
See Kerouac, Jean-Louis Lebris de
See also AAYA 25; AMWC 1; AMWS 3; BG 3; BPFB 2; CDALB 1941-1968; CPW; DLB 2, 16, 237; DLBD 3; DLBY 1995; EWL 3; GLL 1; LATS 1; LMFS 2; MTCW 2; NFS 8; RGAL 4; TUS; WP
Kerouac, Jean-Louis Lebris de 1922-1969
See Kerouac, Jack
See also AITN 1; CA 5-8R; 25-28R; CANR 26, 54, 95; DA; DA3; DAB; DAC; DAM MST, NOV, POET, POP; MTCW 1, 2
Kerr, (Bridget) Jean (Collins) 1923(?)-2003 .... **CLC 22**
See also CA 5-8R; 212; CANR 7; INT CANR-7
Kerr, M. E. .... **CLC 12, 35**
See Meaker, Marijane (Agnes)
See also AAYA 2, 23; BYA 1, 7, 8; CLR 29; SAAS 1; WYA
Kerr, Robert .... **CLC 55**
Kerrigan, (Thomas) Anthony 1918- .. **CLC 4, 6**
See also CA 49-52; CAAS 11; CANR 4
Kerry, Lois
See Duncan, Lois
Kesey, Ken (Elton) 1935-2001 ... **CLC 1, 3, 6, 11, 46, 64, 184; WLC**
See also AAYA 25; BG 3; BPFB 2; CA 1-4R; 204; CANR 22, 38, 66, 124; CDALB 1968-1988; CN 7; CPW; DA; DA3; DAB; DAC; DAM MST, NOV, POP; DLB 2, 16, 206; EWL 3; EXPN; LAIT 4; MTCW 1, 2; NFS 2; RGAL 4; SATA 66; SATA-Obit 131; TUS; YAW
Kesselring, Joseph (Otto) 1902-1967 .... **CLC 45**
See also CA 150; DAM DRAM, MST
Kessler, Jascha (Frederick) 1929- ...... **CLC 4**
See also CA 17-20R; CANR 8, 48, 111
Kettelkamp, Larry (Dale) 1933- .... **CLC 12**
See also CA 29-32R; CANR 16; SAAS 3; SATA 2
Key, Ellen (Karolina Sofia) 1849-1926 .... **TCLC 65**
See also DLB 259
Keyber, Conny
See Fielding, Henry
Keyes, Daniel 1927- .... **CLC 80**
See also AAYA 23; BYA 11; CA 17-20R, 181; CAAE 181; CANR 10, 26, 54, 74; DA; DA3; DAC; DAM MST, NOV; EXPN; LAIT 4; MTCW 2; NFS 2; SATA 37; SFW 4
Keynes, John Maynard 1883-1946 .... **TCLC 64**
See also CA 114; 162, 163; DLBD 10; MTCW 2
Khanshendel, Chiron
See Rose, Wendy
Khayyam, Omar 1048-1131 ... **CMLC 11; PC 8**
See Omar Khayyam
See also DA3; DAM POET

Kherdian, David 1931- .... **CLC 6, 9**
See also AAYA 42; CA 21-24R, 192; CAAE 192; CAAS 2; CANR 39, 78; CLR 24; JRDA; LAIT 3; MAICYA 1, 2; SATA 16, 74; SATA-Essay 125
Khlebnikov, Velimir .... **TCLC 20**
See Khlebnikov, Viktor Vladimirovich
See also DLB 295; EW 10; EWL 3; RGWL 2, 3
Khlebnikov, Viktor Vladimirovich 1885-1922
See Khlebnikov, Velimir
See also CA 117; 217
Khodasevich, Vladislav (Felitsianovich) 1886-1939 .... **TCLC 15**
See also CA 115; EWL 3
Kielland, Alexander Lange 1849-1906 .... **TCLC 5**
See also CA 104
Kiely, Benedict 1919- ... **CLC 23, 43; SSC 58**
See also CA 1-4R; CANR 2, 84; CN 7; DLB 15
Kienzle, William X(avier) 1928-2001 .... **CLC 25**
See also CA 93-96; 203; CAAS 1; CANR 9, 31, 59, 111; CMW 4; DA3; DAM POP; INT CANR-31; MSW; MTCW 1, 2
Kierkegaard, Soren 1813-1855 ..... **NCLC 34, 78, 125**
See also EW 6; LMFS 2; RGWL 3; TWA
Kieslowski, Krzysztof 1941-1996 .... **CLC 120**
See also CA 147; 151
Killens, John Oliver 1916-1987 .... **CLC 10**
See also BW 2; CA 77-80; 123; CAAS 2; CANR 26; DLB 33; EWL 3
Killigrew, Anne 1660-1685 .... **LC 4, 73**
See also DLB 131
Killigrew, Thomas 1612-1683 .... **LC 57**
See also DLB 58; RGEL 2
Kim
See Simenon, Georges (Jacques Christian)
Kincaid, Jamaica 1949- ...... **BLC 2; CLC 43, 68, 137**
See also AAYA 13; AFAW 2; AMWS 7; BRWS 7; BW 2, 3; CA 125; CANR 47, 59, 95; CDALBS; CDWLB 3; CLR 63; CN 7; DA3; DAM MULT, NOV; DLB 157, 227; DNFS 1; EWL 3; EXPS; FW; LATS 1; LMFS 2; MTCW 2; NCFS 1; NFS 3; SSFS 5, 7; TUS; WWE 1; YAW
King, Francis (Henry) 1923- .... **CLC 8, 53, 145**
See also CA 1-4R; CANR 1, 33, 86; CN 7; DAM NOV; DLB 15, 139; MTCW 1
King, Kennedy
See Brown, George Douglas
King, Martin Luther, Jr. 1929-1968 . **BLC 2; CLC 83; WLCS**
See also BW 2, 3; CA 25-28; CANR 27, 44; CAP 2; DA; DA3; DAB; DAC; DAM MST, MULT; LAIT 5; LATS 1; MTCW 1, 2; SATA 14
King, Stephen (Edwin) 1947- .... **CLC 12, 26, 37, 61, 113; SSC 17, 55**
See also AAYA 1, 17; AMWS 5; BEST 90:1; BPFB 2; CA 61-64; CANR 1, 30, 52, 76, 119; CPW; DA3; DAM NOV, POP; DLB 143; DLBY 1980; HGG; JRDA; LAIT 5; MTCW 1, 2; RGAL 4; SATA 9, 55; SUFW 1, 2; WYAS 1; YAW
King, Steve
See King, Stephen (Edwin)
King, Thomas 1943- .... **CLC 89, 171; NNAL**
See also CA 144; CANR 95; CCA 1; CN 7; DAC; DAM MULT; DLB 175; SATA 96
Kingman, Lee .... **CLC 17**
See Natti, (Mary) Lee
See also CWRI 5; SAAS 3; SATA 1, 67

Korolenko, V. G.
See Korolenko, Vladimir Galaktionovich
Korolenko, Vladimir
See Korolenko, Vladimir Galaktionovich
Korolenko, Vladimir G.
See Korolenko, Vladimir Galaktionovich
Korolenko, Vladimir Galaktionovich
1853-1921 .... **TCLC 22**
See also CA 121; DLB 277
Korzybski, Alfred (Habdank Skarbek)
1879-1950 .... **TCLC 61**
See also CA 123; 160
Kosinski, Jerzy (Nikodem)
1933-1991 .... **CLC 1, 2, 3, 6, 10, 15, 53, 70**
See also AMWS 7; BPFB 2; CA 17-20R; 134; CANR 9, 46; DA3; DAM NOV; DLB 2; DLBY 1982; EWL 3; HGG; MTCW 1, 2; NFS 12; RGAL 4; TUS
Kostelanetz, Richard (Cory) 1940- .. **CLC 28**
See also CA 13-16R; CAAS 8; CANR 38, 77; CN 7; CP 7
Kostrowitzki, Wilhelm Apollinaris de
1880-1918
See Apollinaire, Guillaume
See also CA 104
Kotlowitz, Robert 1924- .... **CLC 4**
See also CA 33-36R; CANR 36
Kotzebue, August (Friedrich Ferdinand) von
1761-1819 .... **NCLC 25**
See also DLB 94
Kotzwinkle, William 1938- ..... **CLC 5, 14, 35**
See also BPFB 2; CA 45-48; CANR 3, 44, 84, 129; CLR 6; DLB 173; FANT; MAICYA 1, 2; SATA 24, 70, 146; SFW 4; SUFW 2; YAW
Kowna, Stancy
See Szymborska, Wislawa
Kozol, Jonathan 1936- .... **CLC 17**
See also AAYA 46; CA 61-64; CANR 16, 45, 96
Kozoll, Michael 1940(?)- .... **CLC 35**
Kramer, Kathryn 19(?)- .... **CLC 34**
Kramer, Larry 1935- .... **CLC 42; DC 8**
See also CA 124; 126; CANR 60; DAM POP; DLB 249; GLL 1
Krasicki, Ignacy 1735-1801 .... **NCLC 8**
Krasinski, Zygmunt 1812-1859 .... **NCLC 4**
See also RGWL 2, 3
Kraus, Karl 1874-1936 .... **TCLC 5**
See also CA 104; 216; DLB 118; EWL 3
Kreve (Mickevicius), Vincas
1882-1954 .... **TCLC 27**
See also CA 170; DLB 220; EWL 3
Kristeva, Julia 1941- .... **CLC 77, 140**
See also CA 154; CANR 99; DLB 242; EWL 3; FW; LMFS 2
Kristofferson, Kris 1936- .... **CLC 26**
See also CA 104
Krizanc, John 1956- .... **CLC 57**
See also CA 187
Krleza, Miroslav 1893-1981 .... **CLC 8, 114**
See also CA 97-100; 105; CANR 50; CD-WLB 4; DLB 147; EW 11; RGWL 2, 3
Kroetsch, Robert 1927- .. **CLC 5, 23, 57, 132**
See also CA 17-20R; CANR 8, 38; CCA 1; CN 7; CP 7; DAC; DAM POET; DLB 53; MTCW 1
Kroetz, Franz
See Kroetz, Franz Xaver
Kroetz, Franz Xaver 1946- .... **CLC 41**
See also CA 130; EWL 3
Kroker, Arthur (W.) 1945- .... **CLC 77**
See also CA 161
Kropotkin, Peter (Aleksieevich)
1842-1921 .... **TCLC 36**
See Kropotkin, Petr Alekseevich
See also CA 119; 219

Kropotkin, Petr Alekseevich
See Kropotkin, Peter (Aleksieevich)
See also DLB 277
Krotkov, Yuri 1917-1981 .... **CLC 19**
See also CA 102
Krumb
See Crumb, R(obert)
Krumgold, Joseph (Quincy)
1908-1980 .... **CLC 12**
See also BYA 1, 2; CA 9-12R; 101; CANR 7; MAICYA 1, 2; SATA 1, 48; SATA-Obit 23; YAW
Krumwitz
See Crumb, R(obert)
Krutch, Joseph Wood 1893-1970 ..... **CLC 24**
See also ANW; CA 1-4R; 25-28R; CANR 4; DLB 63, 206, 275
Krutzch, Gus
See Eliot, T(homas) S(tearns)
Krylov, Ivan Andreevich
1768(?)-1844 .... **NCLC 1**
See also DLB 150
Kubin, Alfred (Leopold Isidor)
1877-1959 .... **TCLC 23**
See also CA 112; 149; CANR 104; DLB 81
Kubrick, Stanley 1928-1999 .... **CLC 16; TCLC 112**
See also AAYA 30; CA 81-84; 177; CANR 33; DLB 26
Kumin, Maxine (Winokur) 1925- ..... **CLC 5, 13, 28, 164; PC 15**
See also AITN 2; AMWS 4; ANW; CA 1-4R; CAAS 8; CANR 1, 21, 69, 115; CP 7; CWP; DA3; DAM POET; DLB 5; EWL 3; EXPP; MTCW 1, 2; PAB; PFS 18; SATA 12
Kundera, Milan 1929- . **CLC 4, 9, 19, 32, 68, 115, 135; SSC 24**
See also AAYA 2; BPFB 2; CA 85-88; CANR 19, 52, 74; CDWLB 4; CWW 2; DA3; DAM NOV; DLB 232; EW 13; EWL 3; MTCW 1, 2; NFS 18; RGSF 2; RGWL 2, 3; SSFS 10
Kunene, Mazisi (Raymond) 1930- ... **CLC 85**
See also BW 1, 3; CA 125; CANR 81; CP 7; DLB 117
Kung, Hans .... **CLC 130**
See Kung, Hans
Kung, Hans 1928-
See Kung, Hans
See also CA 53-56; CANR 66; MTCW 1, 2
Kunikida Doppo 1869(?)-1908
See Doppo, Kunikida
See also DLB 180; EWL 3
Kunitz, Stanley (Jasspon) 1905- .. **CLC 6, 11, 14, 148; PC 19**
See also AMWS 3; CA 41-44R; CANR 26, 57, 98; CP 7; DA3; DLB 48; INT CANR-26; MTCW 1, 2; PFS 11; RGAL 4
Kunze, Reiner 1933- .... **CLC 10**
See also CA 93-96; CWW 2; DLB 75; EWL 3
Kuprin, Aleksander Ivanovich
1870-1938 .... **TCLC 5**
See Kuprin, Aleksandr Ivanovich; Kuprin, Alexandr Ivanovich
See also CA 104; 182
Kuprin, Aleksandr Ivanovich
See Kuprin, Aleksander Ivanovich
See also DLB 295
Kuprin, Alexandr Ivanovich
See Kuprin, Aleksander Ivanovich
See also EWL 3
Kureishi, Hanif 1954(?)- .... **CLC 64, 135**
See also CA 139; CANR 113; CBD; CD 5; CN 7; DLB 194, 245; GLL 2; IDFW 4; WLIT 4; WWE 1

Kurosawa, Akira 1910-1998 ..... **CLC 16, 119**
See also AAYA 11; CA 101; 170; CANR 46; DAM MULT
Kushner, Tony 1957(?)- .... **CLC 81; DC 10**
See also AMWS 9; CA 144; CAD; CANR 74; CD 5; DA3; DAM DRAM; DFS 5; DLB 228; EWL 3; GLL 1; LAIT 5; MTCW 2; RGAL 4
Kuttner, Henry 1915-1958 .... **TCLC 10**
See also CA 107; 157; DLB 8; FANT; SCFW 2; SFW 4
Kutty, Madhavi
See Das, Kamala
Kuzma, Greg 1944- .... **CLC 7**
See also CA 33-36R; CANR 70
Kuzmin, Mikhail (Alekseevich)
1872(?)-1936 .... **TCLC 40**
See also CA 170; DLB 295; EWL 3
Kyd, Thomas 1558-1594 .... **DC 3; LC 22**
See also BRW 1; DAM DRAM; DLB 62; IDTP; LMFS 1; RGEL 2; TEA; WLIT 3
Kyprianos, Iossif
See Samarakis, Antonis
L. S.
See Stephen, Sir Leslie
Labrunie, Gerard
See Nerval, Gerard de
La Bruyere, Jean de 1645-1696 .... **LC 17**
See also DLB 268; EW 3; GFL Beginnings to 1789
Lacan, Jacques (Marie Emile)
1901-1981 .... **CLC 75**
See also CA 121; 104; DLB 296; EWL 3; TWA
Laclos, Pierre Ambroise Francois
1741-1803 .... **NCLC 4, 87**
See also EW 4; GFL Beginnings to 1789; RGWL 2, 3
Lacolere, Francois
See Aragon, Louis
La Colere, Francois
See Aragon, Louis
La Deshabilleuse
See Simenon, Georges (Jacques Christian)
Lady Gregory
See Gregory, Lady Isabella Augusta (Persse)
Lady of Quality, A
See Bagnold, Enid
La Fayette, Marie-(Madelaine Pioche de la Vergne) 1634-1693 .... **LC 2**
See Lafayette, Marie-Madeleine
See also GFL Beginnings to 1789; RGWL 2, 3
Lafayette, Marie-Madeleine
See La Fayette, Marie-(Madelaine Pioche de la Vergne)
See also DLB 268
Lafayette, Rene
See Hubbard, L(afayette) Ron(ald)
La Flesche, Francis 1857(?)-1932 ...... **NNAL**
See also CA 144; CANR 83; DLB 175
La Fontaine, Jean de 1621-1695 .... **LC 50**
See also DLB 268; EW 3; GFL Beginnings to 1789; MAICYA 1, 2; RGWL 2, 3; SATA 18
Laforgue, Jules 1860-1887 . **NCLC 5, 53; PC 14; SSC 20**
See also DLB 217; EW 7; GFL 1789 to the Present; RGWL 2, 3
Layamon
See Layamon
See also DLB 146
Lagerkvist, Paer (Fabian)
1891-1974 ..... **CLC 7, 10, 13, 54; TCLC 144**
See Lagerkvist, Par
See also CA 85-88; 49-52; DA3; DAM DRAM, NOV; MTCW 1, 2; TWA

Lawrence, D(avid) H(erbert Richards)
1885-1930 . **PC 54; SSC 4, 19; TCLC 2,
9, 16, 33, 48, 61, 93; WLC**
See Chambers, Jessie
See also BPFB 2; BRW 7; BRWR 2; CA
104; 121; CDBLB 1914-1945; DA; DA3;
DAB; DAC; DAM MST, NOV, POET;
DLB 10, 19, 36, 98, 162, 195; EWL 3;
EXPP; EXPS; LAIT 2, 3; MTCW 1, 2;
NFS 18; PFS 6; RGEL 2; RGSF 2; SSFS
2, 6; TEA; WLIT 4; WP

Lawrence, T(homas) E(dward)
1888-1935 .... **TCLC 18**
See Dale, Colin
See also BRWS 2; CA 115; 167; DLB 195

Lawrence of Arabia
See Lawrence, T(homas) E(dward)

Lawson, Henry (Archibald Hertzberg)
1867-1922 .... **SSC 18; TCLC 27**
See also CA 120; 181; DLB 230; RGEL 2;
RGSF 2

Lawton, Dennis
See Faust, Frederick (Schiller)

Layamon fl. c. 1200- .... **CMLC 10**
See Layamon
See also RGEL 2

Laye, Camara 1928-1980 ..... **BLC 2; CLC 4,
38**
See Camara Laye
See also AFW; BW 1; CA 85-88; 97-100;
CANR 25; DAM MULT; MTCW 1, 2;
WLIT 2

Layton, Irving (Peter) 1912- .... **CLC 2, 15,
164**
See also CA 1-4R; CANR 2, 33, 43, 66,
129; CP 7; DAC; DAM MST, POET;
DLB 88; EWL 3; MTCW 1, 2; PFS 12;
RGEL 2

Lazarus, Emma 1849-1887 ...... **NCLC 8, 109**

Lazarus, Felix
See Cable, George Washington

Lazarus, Henry
See Slavitt, David R(ytman)

Lea, Joan
See Neufeld, John (Arthur)

Leacock, Stephen (Butler)
1869-1944 .... **SSC 39; TCLC 2**
See also CA 104; 141; CANR 80; DAC;
DAM MST; DLB 92; EWL 3; MTCW 2;
RGEL 2; RGSF 2

Lead, Jane Ward 1623-1704 .... **LC 72**
See also DLB 131

Leapor, Mary 1722-1746 .... **LC 80**
See also DLB 109

Lear, Edward 1812-1888 .... **NCLC 3**
See also AAYA 48; BRW 5; CLR 1, 75;
DLB 32, 163, 166; MAICYA 1, 2; RGEL
2; SATA 18, 100; WCH; WP

Lear, Norman (Milton) 1922- .... **CLC 12**
See also CA 73-76

Leautaud, Paul 1872-1956 .... **TCLC 83**
See also CA 203; DLB 65; GFL 1789 to the
Present

Leavis, F(rank) R(aymond)
1895-1978 .... **CLC 24**
See also BRW 7; CA 21-24R; 77-80; CANR
44; DLB 242; EWL 3; MTCW 1, 2;
RGEL 2

Leavitt, David 1961- .... **CLC 34**
See also CA 116; 122; CANR 50, 62, 101;
CPW; DA3; DAM POP; DLB 130; GLL
1; INT CA-122; MTCW 2

Leblanc, Maurice (Marie Emile)
1864-1941 .... **TCLC 49**
See also CA 110; CMW 4

Lebowitz, Fran(ces Ann) 1951(?)- ... **CLC 11,
36**
See also CA 81-84; CANR 14, 60, 70; INT
CANR-14; MTCW 1

Lebrecht, Peter
See Tieck, (Johann) Ludwig

le Carre, John .... **CLC 3, 5, 9, 15, 28**
See Cornwell, David (John Moore)
See also AAYA 42; BEST 89:4; BPFB 2;
BRWS 2; CDBLB 1960 to Present; CMW
4; CN 7; CPW; DLB 87; EWL 3; MSW;
MTCW 2; RGEL 2; TEA

Le Clezio, J(ean) M(arie) G(ustave)
1940- .... **CLC 31, 155**
See also CA 116; 128; DLB 83; EWL 3;
GFL 1789 to the Present; RGSF 2

Leconte de Lisle, Charles-Marie-Rene
1818-1894 .... **NCLC 29**
See also DLB 217; EW 6; GFL 1789 to the
Present

Le Coq, Monsieur
See Simenon, Georges (Jacques Christian)

Leduc, Violette 1907-1972 .... **CLC 22**
See also CA 13-14; 33-36R; CANR 69;
CAP 1; EWL 3; GFL 1789 to the Present;
GLL 1

Ledwidge, Francis 1887(?)-1917 .... **TCLC 23**
See also CA 123; 203; DLB 20

Lee, Andrea 1953- .... **BLC 2; CLC 36**
See also BW 1, 3; CA 125; CANR 82;
DAM MULT

Lee, Andrew
See Auchincloss, Louis (Stanton)

Lee, Chang-rae 1965- .... **CLC 91**
See also CA 148; CANR 89; LATS 1

Lee, Don L. .... **CLC 2**
See Madhubuti, Haki R.

Lee, George W(ashington)
1894-1976 .... **BLC 2; CLC 52**
See also BW 1; CA 125; CANR 83; DAM
MULT; DLB 51

Lee, (Nelle) Harper 1926- .... **CLC 12, 60;
WLC**
See also AAYA 13; AMWS 8; BPFB 2;
BYA 3; CA 13-16R; CANR 51, 128;
CDALB 1941-1968; CSW; DA; DA3;
DAB; DAC; DAM MST, NOV; DLB 6;
EXPN; LAIT 3; MTCW 1, 2; NFS 2;
SATA 11; WYA; YAW

Lee, Helen Elaine 1959(?)- .... **CLC 86**
See also CA 148

Lee, John .... **CLC 70**

Lee, Julian
See Latham, Jean Lee

Lee, Larry
See Lee, Lawrence

Lee, Laurie 1914-1997 .... **CLC 90**
See also CA 77-80; 158; CANR 33, 73; CP
7; CPW; DAB; DAM POP; DLB 27;
MTCW 1; RGEL 2

Lee, Lawrence 1941-1990 .... **CLC 34**
See also CA 131; CANR 43

Lee, Li-Young 1957- .... **CLC 164; PC 24**
See also CA 153; CANR 118; CP 7; DLB
165; LMFS 2; PFS 11, 15, 17

Lee, Manfred B(ennington)
1905-1971 .... **CLC 11**
See Queen, Ellery
See also CA 1-4R; 29-32R; CANR 2; CMW
4; DLB 137

Lee, Shelton Jackson 1957(?)- .. **BLCS; CLC
105**
See Lee, Spike
See also BW 2, 3; CA 125; CANR 42;
DAM MULT

Lee, Spike
See Lee, Shelton Jackson
See also AAYA 4, 29

Lee, Stan 1922- .... **CLC 17**
See also AAYA 5, 49; CA 108; 111; CANR
129; INT CA-111

Lee, Tanith 1947- .... **CLC 46**
See also AAYA 15; CA 37-40R; CANR 53,
102; DLB 261; FANT; SATA 8, 88, 134;
SFW 4; SUFW 1, 2; YAW

Lee, Vernon .... **SSC 33; TCLC 5**
See Paget, Violet
See also DLB 57, 153, 156, 174, 178; GLL
1; SUFW 1

Lee, William
See Burroughs, William S(eward)
See also GLL 1

Lee, Willy
See Burroughs, William S(eward)
See also GLL 1

Lee-Hamilton, Eugene (Jacob)
1845-1907 .... **TCLC 22**
See also CA 117

Leet, Judith 1935- .... **CLC 11**
See also CA 187

Le Fanu, Joseph Sheridan
1814-1873 .... **NCLC 9, 58; SSC 14**
See also CMW 4; DA3; DAM POP; DLB
21, 70, 159, 178; HGG; RGEL 2; RGSF
2; SUFW 1

Leffland, Ella 1931- .... **CLC 19**
See also CA 29-32R; CANR 35, 78, 82;
DLBY 1984; INT CANR-35; SATA 65

Leger, Alexis
See Leger, (Marie-Rene Auguste) Alexis
Saint-Leger

**Leger, (Marie-Rene Auguste) Alexis
Saint-Leger** 1887-1975 .. **CLC 4, 11, 46;
PC 23**
See Perse, Saint-John; Saint-John Perse
See also CA 13-16R; 61-64; CANR 43;
DAM POET; MTCW 1

Leger, Saintleger
See Leger, (Marie-Rene Auguste) Alexis
Saint-Leger

Le Guin, Ursula K(roeber) 1929- ..... **CLC 8,
13, 22, 45, 71, 136; SSC 12, 69**
See also AAYA 9, 27; AITN 1; BPFB 2;
BYA 5, 8, 11, 14; CA 21-24R; CANR 9,
32, 52, 74; CDALB 1968-1988; CLR 3,
28, 91; CN 7; CPW; DA3; DAB; DAC;
DAM MST, POP; DLB 8, 52, 256, 275;
EXPS; FANT; FW; INT CANR-32;
JRDA; LAIT 5; MAICYA 1, 2; MTCW 1,
2; NFS 6, 9; SATA 4, 52, 99; SCFW; SFW
4; SSFS 2; SUFW 1, 2; WYA; YAW

Lehmann, Rosamond (Nina)
1901-1990 .... **CLC 5**
See also CA 77-80; 131; CANR 8, 73; DLB
15; MTCW 2; RGEL 2; RHW

Leiber, Fritz (Reuter, Jr.)
1910-1992 .... **CLC 25**
See also BPFB 2; CA 45-48; 139; CANR 2,
40, 86; DLB 8; FANT; HGG; MTCW 1,
2; SATA 45; SATA-Obit 73; SCFW 2;
SFW 4; SUFW 1, 2

Leibniz, Gottfried Wilhelm von
1646-1716 .... **LC 35**
See also DLB 168

Leimbach, Martha 1963-
See Leimbach, Marti
See also CA 130

Leimbach, Marti .... **CLC 65**
See Leimbach, Martha

Leino, Eino .... **TCLC 24**
See Lonnbohm, Armas Eino Leopold
See also EWL 3

Leiris, Michel (Julien) 1901-1990 ..... **CLC 61**
See also CA 119; 128; 132; EWL 3; GFL
1789 to the Present

Leithauser, Brad 1953- .... **CLC 27**
See also CA 107; CANR 27, 81; CP 7; DLB
120, 282

le Jars de Gournay, Marie
See de Gournay, Marie le Jars

MacDiarmid, Hugh .... **CLC 2, 4, 11, 19, 63; PC 9**
See Grieve, C(hristopher) M(urray)
See also CDBLB 1945-1960; DLB 20; EWL 3; RGEL 2

MacDonald, Anson
See Heinlein, Robert A(nson)

Macdonald, Cynthia 1928- .... **CLC 13, 19**
See also CA 49-52; CANR 4, 44; DLB 105

MacDonald, George 1824-1905 .... **TCLC 9, 113**
See also BYA 5; CA 106; 137; CANR 80; CLR 67; DLB 18, 163, 178; FANT; MAICYA 1, 2; RGEL 2; SATA 33, 100; SFW 4; SUFW; WCH

Macdonald, John
See Millar, Kenneth

MacDonald, John D(ann)
1916-1986 .... **CLC 3, 27, 44**
See also BPFB 2; CA 1-4R; 121; CANR 1, 19, 60; CMW 4; CPW; DAM NOV, POP; DLB 8; DLBY 1986; MSW; MTCW 1, 2; SFW 4

Macdonald, John Ross
See Millar, Kenneth

Macdonald, Ross ..... **CLC 1, 2, 3, 14, 34, 41**
See Millar, Kenneth
See also AMWS 4; BPFB 2; DLBD 6; MSW; RGAL 4

MacDougal, John
See Blish, James (Benjamin)

MacDougal, John
See Blish, James (Benjamin)

MacDowell, John
See Parks, Tim(othy Harold)

MacEwen, Gwendolyn (Margaret)
1941-1987 .... **CLC 13, 55**
See also CA 9-12R; 124; CANR 7, 22; DLB 53, 251; SATA 50; SATA-Obit 55

Macha, Karel Hynek 1810-1846 .... **NCLC 46**

Machado (y Ruiz), Antonio
1875-1939 .... **TCLC 3**
See also CA 104; 174; DLB 108; EW 9; EWL 3; HW 2; RGWL 2, 3

Machado de Assis, Joaquim Maria
1839-1908 .... **BLC 2; HLCS 2; SSC 24; TCLC 10**
See also CA 107; 153; CANR 91; LAW; RGSF 2; RGWL 2, 3; TWA; WLIT 1

Machaut, Guillaume de c.
1300-1377 .... **CMLC 64**
See also DLB 208

Machen, Arthur .... **SSC 20; TCLC 4**
See Jones, Arthur Llewellyn
See also CA 179; DLB 156, 178; RGEL 2; SUFW 1

Machiavelli, Niccolo 1469-1527 ... **DC 16; LC 8, 36; WLCS**
See also DA; DAB; DAC; DAM MST; EW 2; LAIT 1; LMFS 1; NFS 9; RGWL 2, 3; TWA

MacInnes, Colin 1914-1976 .... **CLC 4, 23**
See also CA 69-72; 65-68; CANR 21; DLB 14; MTCW 1, 2; RGEL 2; RHW

MacInnes, Helen (Clark)
1907-1985 .... **CLC 27, 39**
See also BPFB 2; CA 1-4R; 117; CANR 1, 28, 58; CMW 4; CPW; DAM POP; DLB 87; MSW; MTCW 1, 2; SATA 22; SATA-Obit 44

Mackay, Mary 1855-1924
See Corelli, Marie
See also CA 118; 177; FANT; RHW

Mackenzie, Compton (Edward Montague)
1883-1972 .... **CLC 18; TCLC 116**
See also CA 21-22; 37-40R; CAP 2; DLB 34, 100; RGEL 2

Mackenzie, Henry 1745-1831 .... **NCLC 41**
See also DLB 39; RGEL 2

Mackey, Nathaniel (Ernest) 1947- .... **PC 49**
See also CA 153; CANR 114; CP 7; DLB 169

MacKinnon, Catharine A. 1946- .... **CLC 181**
See also CA 128; 132; CANR 73; FW; MTCW 2

Mackintosh, Elizabeth 1896(?)-1952
See Tey, Josephine
See also CA 110; CMW 4

MacLaren, James
See Grieve, C(hristopher) M(urray)

Mac Laverty, Bernard 1942- .... **CLC 31**
See also CA 116; 118; CANR 43, 88; CN 7; DLB 267; INT CA-118; RGSF 2

MacLean, Alistair (Stuart)
1922(?)-1987 .... **CLC 3, 13, 50, 63**
See also CA 57-60; 121; CANR 28, 61; CMW 4; CPW; DAM POP; DLB 276; MTCW 1; SATA 23; SATA-Obit 50; TCWW 2

Maclean, Norman (Fitzroy)
1902-1990 .... **CLC 78; SSC 13**
See also CA 102; 132; CANR 49; CPW; DAM POP; DLB 206; TCWW 2

MacLeish, Archibald 1892-1982 ... **CLC 3, 8, 14, 68; PC 47**
See also AMW; CA 9-12R; 106; CAD; CANR 33, 63; CDALBS; DAM POET; DFS 15; DLB 4, 7, 45; DLBY 1982; EWL 3; EXPP; MTCW 1, 2; PAB; PFS 5; RGAL 4; TUS

MacLennan, (John) Hugh
1907-1990 .... **CLC 2, 14, 92**
See also CA 5-8R; 142; CANR 33; DAC; DAM MST; DLB 68; EWL 3; MTCW 1, 2; RGEL 2; TWA

MacLeod, Alistair 1936- .... **CLC 56, 165**
See also CA 123; CCA 1; DAC; DAM MST; DLB 60; MTCW 2; RGSF 2

Macleod, Fiona
See Sharp, William
See also RGEL 2; SUFW

MacNeice, (Frederick) Louis
1907-1963 .... **CLC 1, 4, 10, 53**
See also BRW 7; CA 85-88; CANR 61; DAB; DAM POET; DLB 10, 20; EWL 3; MTCW 1, 2; RGEL 2

MacNeill, Dand
See Fraser, George MacDonald

Macpherson, James 1736-1796 .... **LC 29**
See Ossian
See also BRWS 8; DLB 109; RGEL 2

Macpherson, (Jean) Jay 1931- .... **CLC 14**
See also CA 5-8R; CANR 90; CP 7; CWP; DLB 53

Macrobius fl. 430- .... **CMLC 48**

MacShane, Frank 1927-1999 .... **CLC 39**
See also CA 9-12R; 186; CANR 3, 33; DLB 111

Macumber, Mari
See Sandoz, Mari(e Susette)

Madach, Imre 1823-1864 .... **NCLC 19**

Madden, (Jerry) David 1933- .... **CLC 5, 15**
See also CA 1-4R; CAAS 3; CANR 4, 45; CN 7; CSW; DLB 6; MTCW 1

Maddern, Al(an)
See Ellison, Harlan (Jay)

Madhubuti, Haki R. 1942- ... **BLC 2; CLC 6, 73; PC 5**
See Lee, Don L.
See also BW 2, 3; CA 73-76; CANR 24, 51, 73; CP 7; CSW; DAM MULT, POET; DLB 5, 41; DLBD 8; EWL 3; MTCW 2; RGAL 4

Madison, James 1751-1836 .... **NCLC 126**
See also DLB 37

Maepenn, Hugh
See Kuttner, Henry

Maepenn, K. H.
See Kuttner, Henry

Maeterlinck, Maurice 1862-1949 ..... **TCLC 3**
See also CA 104; 136; CANR 80; DAM DRAM; DLB 192; EW 8; EWL 3; GFL 1789 to the Present; LMFS 2; RGWL 2, 3; SATA 66; TWA

Maginn, William 1794-1842 .... **NCLC 8**
See also DLB 110, 159

Mahapatra, Jayanta 1928- .... **CLC 33**
See also CA 73-76; CAAS 9; CANR 15, 33, 66, 87; CP 7; DAM MULT

Mahfouz, Naguib (Abdel Aziz Al-Sabilgi)
1911(?)- .... **CLC 153; SSC 66**
See Mahfuz, Najib (Abdel Aziz al-Sabilgi)
See also AAYA 49; BEST 89:2; CA 128; CANR 55, 101; CWW 2; DA3; DAM NOV; MTCW 1, 2; RGWL 2, 3; SSFS 9

Mahfuz, Najib (Abdel Aziz al-Sabilgi)
.... **CLC 52, 55**
See Mahfouz, Naguib (Abdel Aziz Al-Sabilgi)
See also AFW; DLBY 1988; EWL 3; RGSF 2; WLIT 2

Mahon, Derek 1941- .... **CLC 27**
See also BRWS 6; CA 113; 128; CANR 88; CP 7; DLB 40; EWL 3

Maiakovskii, Vladimir
See Mayakovski, Vladimir (Vladimirovich)
See also IDTP; RGWL 2, 3

Mailer, Norman 1923- ... **CLC 1, 2, 3, 4, 5, 8, 11, 14, 28, 39, 74, 111**
See also AAYA 31; AITN 2; AMW; AMWC 2; AMWR 2; BPFB 2; CA 9-12R; CABS 1; CANR 28, 74, 77; CDALB 1968-1988; CN 7; CPW; DA; DA3; DAB; DAC; DAM MST, NOV, POP; DLB 2, 16, 28, 185, 278; DLBD 3; DLBY 1980, 1983; EWL 3; MTCW 1, 2; NFS 10; RGAL 4; TUS

Maillet, Antonine 1929- .... **CLC 54, 118**
See also CA 115; 120; CANR 46, 74, 77; CCA 1; CWW 2; DAC; DLB 60; INT CA-120; MTCW 2

Mais, Roger 1905-1955 .... **TCLC 8**
See also BW 1, 3; CA 105; 124; CANR 82; CDWLB 3; DLB 125; EWL 3; MTCW 1; RGEL 2

Maistre, Joseph 1753-1821 .... **NCLC 37**
See also GFL 1789 to the Present

Maitland, Frederic William
1850-1906 .... **TCLC 65**

Maitland, Sara (Louise) 1950- .... **CLC 49**
See also CA 69-72; CANR 13, 59; DLB 271; FW

Major, Clarence 1936- ... **BLC 2; CLC 3, 19, 48**
See also AFAW 2; BW 2, 3; CA 21-24R; CAAS 6; CANR 13, 25, 53, 82; CN 7; CP 7; CSW; DAM MULT; DLB 33; EWL 3; MSW

Major, Kevin (Gerald) 1949- .... **CLC 26**
See also AAYA 16; CA 97-100; CANR 21, 38, 112; CLR 11; DAC; DLB 60; INT CANR-21; JRDA; MAICYA 1, 2; MAICYAS 1; SATA 32, 82, 134; WYA; YAW

Maki, James
See Ozu, Yasujiro

Malabaila, Damiano
See Levi, Primo

Malamud, Bernard 1914-1986 .. **CLC 1, 2, 3, 5, 8, 9, 11, 18, 27, 44, 78, 85; SSC 15; TCLC 129; WLC**
See also AAYA 16; AMWS 1; BPFB 2; BYA 15; CA 5-8R; 118; CABS 1; CANR 28, 62, 114; CDALB 1941-1968; CPW; DA; DA3; DAB; DAC; DAM MST, NOV,

McKay, Claude .... **BLC 3; HR 3; PC 2; TCLC 7, 41; WLC**
See McKay, Festus Claudius
See also AFAW 1, 2; AMWS 10; DAB; DLB 4, 45, 51, 117; EWL 3; EXPP; GLL 2; LAIT 3; LMFS 2; PAB; PFS 4; RGAL 4; WP

McKay, Festus Claudius 1889-1948
See McKay, Claude
See also BW 1, 3; CA 104; 124; CANR 73; DA; DAC; DAM MST, MULT, NOV, POET; MTCW 1, 2; TUS

McKuen, Rod 1933- .... **CLC 1, 3**
See also AITN 1; CA 41-44R; CANR 40

McLoughlin, R. B.
See Mencken, H(enry) L(ouis)

McLuhan, (Herbert) Marshall 1911-1980 .... **CLC 37, 83**
See also CA 9-12R; 102; CANR 12, 34, 61; DLB 88; INT CANR-12; MTCW 1, 2

McManus, Declan Patrick Aloysius
See Costello, Elvis

McMillan, Terry (L.) 1951- . **BLCS; CLC 50, 61, 112**
See also AAYA 21; AMWS 13; BPFB 2; BW 2, 3; CA 140; CANR 60, 104; CPW; DA3; DAM MULT, NOV, POP; MTCW 2; RGAL 4; YAW

McMurtry, Larry (Jeff) 1936- .. **CLC 2, 3, 7, 11, 27, 44, 127**
See also AAYA 15; AITN 2; AMWS 5; BEST 89:2; BPFB 2; CA 5-8R; CANR 19, 43, 64, 103; CDALB 1968-1988; CN 7; CPW; CSW; DA3; DAM NOV, POP; DLB 2, 143, 256; DLBY 1980, 1987; EWL 3; MTCW 1, 2; RGAL 4; TCWW 2

McNally, T. M. 1961- .... **CLC 82**

McNally, Terrence 1939- .... **CLC 4, 7, 41, 91**
See also AMWS 13; CA 45-48; CAD; CANR 2, 56, 116; CD 5; DA3; DAM DRAM; DFS 16; DLB 7, 249; EWL 3; GLL 1; MTCW 2

McNamer, Deirdre 1950- .... **CLC 70**

McNeal, Tom .... **CLC 119**

McNeile, Herman Cyril 1888-1937
See Sapper
See also CA 184; CMW 4; DLB 77

McNickle, (William) D'Arcy 1904-1977 .... **CLC 89; NNAL**
See also CA 9-12R; 85-88; CANR 5, 45; DAM MULT; DLB 175, 212; RGAL 4; SATA-Obit 22

McPhee, John (Angus) 1931- .... **CLC 36**
See also AMWS 3; ANW; BEST 90:1; CA 65-68; CANR 20, 46, 64, 69, 121; CPW; DLB 185, 275; MTCW 1, 2; TUS

McPherson, James Alan 1943- . **BLCS; CLC 19, 77**
See also BW 1, 3; CA 25-28R; CAAS 17; CANR 24, 74; CN 7; CSW; DLB 38, 244; EWL 3; MTCW 1, 2; RGAL 4; RGSF 2

McPherson, William (Alexander) 1933- .... **CLC 34**
See also CA 69-72; CANR 28; INT CANR-28

McTaggart, J. McT. Ellis
See McTaggart, John McTaggart Ellis

McTaggart, John McTaggart Ellis 1866-1925 .... **TCLC 105**
See also CA 120; DLB 262

Mead, George Herbert 1863-1931 . **TCLC 89**
See also CA 212; DLB 270

Mead, Margaret 1901-1978 .... **CLC 37**
See also AITN 1; CA 1-4R; 81-84; CANR 4; DA3; FW; MTCW 1, 2; SATA-Obit 20

Meaker, Marijane (Agnes) 1927-
See Kerr, M. E.
See also CA 107; CANR 37, 63; INT CA-107; JRDA; MAICYA 1, 2; MAICYAS 1; MTCW 1; SATA 20, 61, 99; SATA-Essay 111; YAW

Medoff, Mark (Howard) 1940- .... **CLC 6, 23**
See also AITN 1; CA 53-56; CAD; CANR 5; CD 5; DAM DRAM; DFS 4; DLB 7; INT CANR-5

Medvedev, P. N.
See Bakhtin, Mikhail Mikhailovich

Meged, Aharon
See Megged, Aharon

Meged, Aron
See Megged, Aharon

Megged, Aharon 1920- .... **CLC 9**
See also CA 49-52; CAAS 13; CANR 1; EWL 3

Mehta, Gita 1943- .... **CLC 179**
See also DNFS 2

Mehta, Ved (Parkash) 1934- .... **CLC 37**
See also CA 1-4R, 212; CAAE 212; CANR 2, 23, 69; MTCW 1

Melanchthon, Philipp 1497-1560 .... **LC 90**
See also DLB 179

Melanter
See Blackmore, R(ichard) D(oddridge)

Meleager c. 140B.C.-c. 70B.C. ...... **CMLC 53**

Melies, Georges 1861-1938 .... **TCLC 81**

Melikow, Loris
See Hofmannsthal, Hugo von

Melmoth, Sebastian
See Wilde, Oscar (Fingal O'Flahertie Wills)

Melo Neto, Joao Cabral de
See Cabral de Melo Neto, Joao
See also CWW 2; EWL 3

Meltzer, Milton 1915- .... **CLC 26**
See also AAYA 8, 45; BYA 2, 6; CA 13-16R; CANR 38, 92, 107; CLR 13; DLB 61; JRDA; MAICYA 1, 2; SAAS 1; SATA 1, 50, 80, 128; SATA-Essay 124; WYA; YAW

Melville, Herman 1819-1891 ..... **NCLC 3, 12, 29, 45, 49, 91, 93, 123; SSC 1, 17, 46; WLC**
See also AAYA 25; AMW; AMWR 1; CDALB 1640-1865; DA; DA3; DAB; DAC; DAM MST, NOV; DLB 3, 74, 250, 254; EXPN; EXPS; LAIT 1, 2; NFS 7, 9; RGAL 4; RGSF 2; SATA 59; SSFS 3; TUS

Members, Mark
See Powell, Anthony (Dymoke)

Membreno, Alejandro .... **CLC 59**

Menander c. 342B.C.-c. 293B.C. .... **CMLC 9, 51; DC 3**
See also AW 1; CDWLB 1; DAM DRAM; DLB 176; LMFS 1; RGWL 2, 3

Menchu, Rigoberta 1959- .. **CLC 160; HLCS 2**
See also CA 175; DNFS 1; WLIT 1

Mencken, H(enry) L(ouis) 1880-1956 .... **TCLC 13**
See also AMW; CA 105; 125; CDALB 1917-1929; DLB 11, 29, 63, 137, 222; EWL 3; MTCW 1, 2; NCFS 4; RGAL 4; TUS

Mendelsohn, Jane 1965- .... **CLC 99**
See also CA 154; CANR 94

Menton, Francisco de
See Chin, Frank (Chew, Jr.)

Mercer, David 1928-1980 .... **CLC 5**
See also CA 9-12R; 102; CANR 23; CBD; DAM DRAM; DLB 13; MTCW 1; RGEL 2

Merchant, Paul
See Ellison, Harlan (Jay)

Meredith, George 1828-1909 ... **TCLC 17, 43**
See also CA 117; 153; CANR 80; CDBLB 1832-1890; DAM POET; DLB 18, 35, 57, 159; RGEL 2; TEA

Meredith, William (Morris) 1919- .... **CLC 4, 13, 22, 55; PC 28**
See also CA 9-12R; CAAS 14; CANR 6, 40, 129; CP 7; DAM POET; DLB 5

Merezhkovsky, Dmitrii Sergeevich
See Merezhkovsky, Dmitry Sergeyevich
See also DLB 295

Merezhkovsky, Dmitry Sergeevich
See Merezhkovsky, Dmitry Sergeyevich
See also EWL 3

Merezhkovsky, Dmitry Sergeyevich 1865-1941 .... **TCLC 29**
See Merezhkovsky, Dmitrii Sergeevich; Merezhkovsky, Dmitry Sergeevich
See also CA 169

Merimee, Prosper 1803-1870 ... **NCLC 6, 65; SSC 7**
See also DLB 119, 192; EW 6; EXPS; GFL 1789 to the Present; RGSF 2; RGWL 2, 3; SSFS 8; SUFW

Merkin, Daphne 1954- .... **CLC 44**
See also CA 123

Merlin, Arthur
See Blish, James (Benjamin)

Mernissi, Fatima 1940- .... **CLC 171**
See also CA 152; FW

Merrill, James (Ingram) 1926-1995 .. **CLC 2, 3, 6, 8, 13, 18, 34, 91; PC 28**
See also AMWS 3; CA 13-16R; 147; CANR 10, 49, 63, 108; DA3; DAM POET; DLB 5, 165; DLBY 1985; EWL 3; INT CANR-10; MTCW 1, 2; PAB; RGAL 4

Merriman, Alex
See Silverberg, Robert

Merriman, Brian 1747-1805 .... **NCLC 70**

Merritt, E. B.
See Waddington, Miriam

Merton, Thomas (James) 1915-1968 . **CLC 1, 3, 11, 34, 83; PC 10**
See also AMWS 8; CA 5-8R; 25-28R; CANR 22, 53, 111; DA3; DLB 48; DLBY 1981; MTCW 1, 2

Merwin, W(illiam) S(tanley) 1927- ... **CLC 1, 2, 3, 5, 8, 13, 18, 45, 88; PC 45**
See also AMWS 3; CA 13-16R; CANR 15, 51, 112; CP 7; DA3; DAM POET; DLB 5, 169; EWL 3; INT CANR-15; MTCW 1, 2; PAB; PFS 5, 15; RGAL 4

Metcalf, John 1938- .... **CLC 37; SSC 43**
See also CA 113; CN 7; DLB 60; RGSF 2; TWA

Metcalf, Suzanne
See Baum, L(yman) Frank

Mew, Charlotte (Mary) 1870-1928 .. **TCLC 8**
See also CA 105; 189; DLB 19, 135; RGEL 2

Mewshaw, Michael 1943- .... **CLC 9**
See also CA 53-56; CANR 7, 47; DLBY 1980

Meyer, Conrad Ferdinand 1825-1898 .... **NCLC 81**
See also DLB 129; EW; RGWL 2, 3

Meyer, Gustav 1868-1932
See Meyrink, Gustav
See also CA 117; 190

Meyer, June
See Jordan, June (Meyer)

Meyer, Lynn
See Slavitt, David R(ytman)

Meyers, Jeffrey 1939- .... **CLC 39**
See also CA 73-76, 186; CAAE 186; CANR 54, 102; DLB 111

Meynell, Alice (Christina Gertrude Thompson) 1847-1922 .... **TCLC 6**
See also CA 104; 177; DLB 19, 98; RGEL 2

Meyrink, Gustav .... **TCLC 21**
See Meyer, Gustav
See also DLB 81; EWL 3

Michaels, Leonard 1933-2003 ..... **CLC 6, 25; SSC 16**
See also CA 61-64; 216; CANR 21, 62, 119; CN 7; DLB 130; MTCW 1

Michaux, Henri 1899-1984 .... **CLC 8, 19**
See also CA 85-88; 114; DLB 258; EWL 3; GFL 1789 to the Present; RGWL 2, 3

Micheaux, Oscar (Devereaux) 1884-1951 .... **TCLC 76**
See also BW 3; CA 174; DLB 50; TCWW 2

Michelangelo 1475-1564 .... **LC 12**
See also AAYA 43

Michelet, Jules 1798-1874 .... **NCLC 31**
See also EW 5; GFL 1789 to the Present

Michels, Robert 1876-1936 .... **TCLC 88**
See also CA 212

Michener, James A(lbert) 1907(?)-1997 .. **CLC 1, 5, 11, 29, 60, 109**
See also AAYA 27; AITN 1; BEST 90:1; BPFB 2; CA 5-8R; 161; CANR 21, 45, 68; CN 7; CPW; DA3; DAM NOV, POP; DLB 6; MTCW 1, 2; RHW

Mickiewicz, Adam 1798-1855 . **NCLC 3, 101; PC 38**
See also EW 5; RGWL 2, 3

Middleton, (John) Christopher 1926- .... **CLC 13**
See also CA 13-16R; CANR 29, 54, 117; CP 7; DLB 40

Middleton, Richard (Barham) 1882-1911 .... **TCLC 56**
See also CA 187; DLB 156; HGG

Middleton, Stanley 1919- .... **CLC 7, 38**
See also CA 25-28R; CAAS 23; CANR 21, 46, 81; CN 7; DLB 14

Middleton, Thomas 1580-1627 ...... **DC 5; LC 33**
See also BRW 2; DAM DRAM, MST; DFS 18; DLB 58; RGEL 2

Migueis, Jose Rodrigues 1901-1980 . **CLC 10**
See also DLB 287

Mikszath, Kalman 1847-1910 .... **TCLC 31**
See also CA 170

Miles, Jack .... **CLC 100**
See also CA 200

Miles, John Russiano
See Miles, Jack

Miles, Josephine (Louise) 1911-1985 .... **CLC 1, 2, 14, 34, 39**
See also CA 1-4R; 116; CANR 2, 55; DAM POET; DLB 48

Militant
See Sandburg, Carl (August)

Mill, Harriet (Hardy) Taylor 1807-1858 .... **NCLC 102**
See also FW

Mill, John Stuart 1806-1873 .... **NCLC 11, 58**
See also CDBLB 1832-1890; DLB 55, 190, 262; FW 1; RGEL 2; TEA

Millar, Kenneth 1915-1983 .... **CLC 14**
See Macdonald, Ross
See also CA 9-12R; 110; CANR 16, 63, 107; CMW 4; CPW; DA3; DAM POP; DLB 2, 226; DLBD 6; DLBY 1983; MTCW 1, 2

Millay, E. Vincent
See Millay, Edna St. Vincent

Millay, Edna St. Vincent 1892-1950 .... **PC 6; TCLC 4, 49; WLCS**
See Boyd, Nancy
See also AMW; CA 104; 130; CDALB 1917-1929; DA; DA3; DAB; DAC; DAM MST, POET; DLB 45, 249; EWL 3; EXPP; MAWW; MTCW 1, 2; PAB; PFS 3, 17; RGAL 4; TUS; WP

Miller, Arthur 1915- ...... **CLC 1, 2, 6, 10, 15, 26, 47, 78, 179; DC 1; WLC**
See also AAYA 15; AITN 1; AMW; AMWC 1; CA 1-4R; CABS 3; CAD; CANR 2, 30, 54, 76; CD 5; CDALB 1941-1968; DA; DA3; DAB; DAC; DAM DRAM, MST; DFS 1, 3, 8; DLB 7, 266; EWL 3; LAIT 1, 4; LATS 1; MTCW 1, 2; RGAL 4; TUS; WYAS 1

Miller, Henry (Valentine) 1891-1980 .... **CLC 1, 2, 4, 9, 14, 43, 84; WLC**
See also AMW; BPFB 2; CA 9-12R; 97-100; CANR 33, 64; CDALB 1929-1941; DA; DA3; DAB; DAC; DAM MST, NOV; DLB 4, 9; DLBY 1980; EWL 3; MTCW 1, 2; RGAL 4; TUS

Miller, Jason 1939(?)-2001 .... **CLC 2**
See also AITN 1; CA 73-76; 197; CAD; DFS 12; DLB 7

Miller, Sue 1943- .... **CLC 44**
See also AMWS 12; BEST 90:3; CA 139; CANR 59, 91, 128; DA3; DAM POP; DLB 143

Miller, Walter M(ichael, Jr.) 1923-1996 .... **CLC 4, 30**
See also BPFB 2; CA 85-88; CANR 108; DLB 8; SCFW; SFW 4

Millett, Kate 1934- .... **CLC 67**
See also AITN 1; CA 73-76; CANR 32, 53, 76, 110; DA3; DLB 246; FW; GLL 1; MTCW 1, 2

Millhauser, Steven (Lewis) 1943- .... **CLC 21, 54, 109; SSC 57**
See also CA 110; 111; CANR 63, 114; CN 7; DA3; DLB 2; FANT; INT CA-111; MTCW 2

Millin, Sarah Gertrude 1889-1968 ... **CLC 49**
See also CA 102; 93-96; DLB 225; EWL 3

Milne, A(lan) A(lexander) 1882-1956 .... **TCLC 6, 88**
See also BRWS 5; CA 104; 133; CLR 1, 26; CMW 4; CWRI 5; DA3; DAB; DAC; DAM MST; DLB 10, 77, 100, 160; FANT; MAICYA 1, 2; MTCW 1, 2; RGEL 2; SATA 100; WCH; YABC 1

Milner, Ron(ald) 1938- .... **BLC 3; CLC 56**
See also AITN 1; BW 1; CA 73-76; CAD; CANR 24, 81; CD 5; DAM MULT; DLB 38; MTCW 1

Milnes, Richard Monckton 1809-1885 .... **NCLC 61**
See also DLB 32, 184

Milosz, Czeslaw 1911- ...... **CLC 5, 11, 22, 31, 56, 82; PC 8; WLCS**
See also CA 81-84; CANR 23, 51, 91, 126; CDWLB 4; CWW 2; DA3; DAM MST, POET; DLB 215; EW 13; EWL 3; MTCW 1, 2; PFS 16; RGWL 2, 3

Milton, John 1608-1674 ..... **LC 9, 43, 92; PC 19, 29; WLC**
See also BRW 2; BRWR 2; CDBLB 1660-1789; DA; DA3; DAB; DAC; DAM MST, POET; DLB 131, 151, 281; EFS 1; EXPP; LAIT 1; PAB; PFS 3, 17; RGEL 2; TEA; WLIT 3; WP

Min, Anchee 1957- .... **CLC 86**
See also CA 146; CANR 94

Minehaha, Cornelius
See Wedekind, (Benjamin) Frank(lin)

Miner, Valerie 1947- .... **CLC 40**
See also CA 97-100; CANR 59; FW; GLL 2

Minimo, Duca
See D'Annunzio, Gabriele

Minot, Susan 1956- .... **CLC 44, 159**
See also AMWS 6; CA 134; CANR 118; CN 7

Minus, Ed 1938- .... **CLC 39**
See also CA 185

Mirabai 1498(?)-1550(?) .... **PC 48**

Miranda, Javier
See Bioy Casares, Adolfo
See also CWW 2

Mirbeau, Octave 1848-1917 .... **TCLC 55**
See also CA 216; DLB 123, 192; GFL 1789 to the Present

Mirikitani, Janice 1942- .... **AAL**
See also CA 211; RGAL 4

Miro (Ferrer), Gabriel (Francisco Victor) 1879-1930 .... **TCLC 5**
See also CA 104; 185; EWL 3

Misharin, Alexandr .... **CLC 59**

Mishima, Yukio ... **CLC 2, 4, 6, 9, 27; DC 1; SSC 4**
See Hiraoka, Kimitake
See also AAYA 50; BPFB 2; GLL 1; MJW; MTCW 2; RGSF 2; RGWL 2, 3; SSFS 5, 12

Mistral, Frederic 1830-1914 .... **TCLC 51**
See also CA 122; 213; GFL 1789 to the Present

Mistral, Gabriela
See Godoy Alcayaga, Lucila
See also DLB 283; DNFS 1; EWL 3; LAW; RGWL 2, 3; WP

Mistry, Rohinton 1952- .... **CLC 71**
See also CA 141; CANR 86, 114; CCA 1; CN 7; DAC; SSFS 6

Mitchell, Clyde
See Ellison, Harlan (Jay)

Mitchell, Emerson Blackhorse Barney 1945- .... **NNAL**
See also CA 45-48

Mitchell, James Leslie 1901-1935
See Gibbon, Lewis Grassic
See also CA 104; 188; DLB 15

Mitchell, Joni 1943- .... **CLC 12**
See also CA 112; CCA 1

Mitchell, Joseph (Quincy) 1908-1996 .... **CLC 98**
See also CA 77-80; 152; CANR 69; CN 7; CSW; DLB 185; DLBY 1996

Mitchell, Margaret (Munnerlyn) 1900-1949 .... **TCLC 11**
See also AAYA 23; BPFB 2; BYA 1; CA 109; 125; CANR 55, 94; CDALBS; DA3; DAM NOV, POP; DLB 9; LAIT 2; MTCW 1, 2; NFS 9; RGAL 4; RHW; TUS; WYAS 1; YAW

Mitchell, Peggy
See Mitchell, Margaret (Munnerlyn)

Mitchell, S(ilas) Weir 1829-1914 .... **TCLC 36**
See also CA 165; DLB 202; RGAL 4

Mitchell, W(illiam) O(rmond) 1914-1998 .... **CLC 25**
See also CA 77-80; 165; CANR 15, 43; CN 7; DAC; DAM MST; DLB 88

Mitchell, William (Lendrum) 1879-1936 .... **TCLC 81**
See also CA 213

Mitford, Mary Russell 1787-1855 ... **NCLC 4**
See also DLB 110, 116; RGEL 2

Mitford, Nancy 1904-1973 .... **CLC 44**
See also CA 9-12R; DLB 191; RGEL 2

Miyamoto, (Chujo) Yuriko 1899-1951 .... **TCLC 37**
See Miyamoto Yuriko
See also CA 170, 174

Miyamoto Yuriko
See Miyamoto, (Chujo) Yuriko
See also DLB 180

Miyazaki, Kenji 1896-1933 .... **TCLC 76**
See Miyazawa Kenji
See also CA 157; RGWL 3

Miyazawa Kenji
See Miyazawa, Kenji
See also EWL 3

Mizoguchi, Kenji 1898-1956 .... **TCLC 72**
See also CA 167

Mo, Timothy (Peter) 1950(?)- ... **CLC 46, 134**
See also CA 117; CANR 128; CN 7; DLB 194; MTCW 1; WLIT 4; WWE 1

Modarressi, Taghi (M.) 1931-1997 ... **CLC 44**
See also CA 121; 134; INT CA-134

Modiano, Patrick (Jean) 1945- .... **CLC 18**
See also CA 85-88; CANR 17, 40, 115; CWW 2; DLB 83; EWL 3

Mofolo, Thomas (Mokopu)
1875(?)-1948 .... **BLC 3; TCLC 22**
See also AFW; CA 121; 153; CANR 83; DAM MULT; DLB 225; EWL 3; MTCW 2; WLIT 2

Mohr, Nicholasa 1938- .... **CLC 12; HLC 2**
See also AAYA 8, 46; CA 49-52; CANR 1, 32, 64; CLR 22; DAM MULT; DLB 145; HW 1, 2; JRDA; LAIT 5; LLW 1; MAICYA 2; MAICYAS 1; RGAL 4; SAAS 8; SATA 8, 97; SATA-Essay 113; WYA; YAW

Moi, Toril 1953- .... **CLC 172**
See also CA 154; CANR 102; FW

Mojtabai, A(nn) G(race) 1938- ..... **CLC 5, 9, 15, 29**
See also CA 85-88; CANR 88

Moliere 1622-1673 ..... **DC 13; LC 10, 28, 64; WLC**
See also DA; DA3; DAB; DAC; DAM DRAM, MST; DFS 13, 18; DLB 268; EW 3; GFL Beginnings to 1789; LATS 1; RGWL 2, 3; TWA

Molin, Charles
See Mayne, William (James Carter)

Molnar, Ferenc 1878-1952 .... **TCLC 20**
See also CA 109; 153; CANR 83; CDWLB 4; DAM DRAM; DLB 215; EWL 3; RGWL 2, 3

Momaday, N(avarre) Scott 1934- ...... **CLC 2, 19, 85, 95, 160; NNAL; PC 25; WLCS**
See also AAYA 11; AMWS 4; ANW; BPFB 2; BYA 12; CA 25-28R; CANR 14, 34, 68; CDALBS; CN 7; CPW; DA; DA3; DAB; DAC; DAM MST, MULT, NOV, POP; DLB 143, 175, 256; EWL 3; EXPP; INT CANR-14; LAIT 4; LATS 1; MTCW 1, 2; NFS 10; PFS 2, 11; RGAL 4; SATA 48; SATA-Brief 30; WP; YAW

Monette, Paul 1945-1995 .... **CLC 82**
See also AMWS 10; CA 139; 147; CN 7; GLL 1

Monroe, Harriet 1860-1936 .... **TCLC 12**
See also CA 109; 204; DLB 54, 91

Monroe, Lyle
See Heinlein, Robert A(nson)

Montagu, Elizabeth 1720-1800 .... **NCLC 7, 117**
See also FW

Montagu, Mary (Pierrepont) Wortley
1689-1762 .... **LC 9, 57; PC 16**
See also DLB 95, 101; RGEL 2

Montagu, W. H.
See Coleridge, Samuel Taylor

Montague, John (Patrick) 1929- ..... **CLC 13, 46**
See also CA 9-12R; CANR 9, 69, 121; CP 7; DLB 40; EWL 3; MTCW 1; PFS 12; RGEL 2

Montaigne, Michel (Eyquem) de
1533-1592 .... **LC 8; WLC**
See also DA; DAB; DAC; DAM MST; EW 2; GFL Beginnings to 1789; LMFS 1; RGWL 2, 3; TWA

Montale, Eugenio 1896-1981 ... **CLC 7, 9, 18; PC 13**
See also CA 17-20R; 104; CANR 30; DLB 114; EW 11; EWL 3; MTCW 1; RGWL 2, 3; TWA

Montesquieu, Charles-Louis de Secondat
1689-1755 .... **LC 7, 69**
See also EW 3; GFL Beginnings to 1789; TWA

Montessori, Maria 1870-1952 ...... **TCLC 103**
See also CA 115; 147

Montgomery, (Robert) Bruce 1921(?)-1978
See Crispin, Edmund
See also CA 179; 104; CMW 4

Montgomery, L(ucy) M(aud)
1874-1942 .... **TCLC 51, 140**
See also AAYA 12; BYA 1; CA 108; 137; CLR 8, 91; DA3; DAC; DAM MST; DLB 92; DLBD 14; JRDA; MAICYA 1, 2; MTCW 2; RGEL 2; SATA 100; TWA; WCH; WYA; YABC 1

Montgomery, Marion H., Jr. 1925- .... **CLC 7**
See also AITN 1; CA 1-4R; CANR 3, 48; CSW; DLB 6

Montgomery, Max
See Davenport, Guy (Mattison, Jr.)

Montherlant, Henry (Milon) de
1896-1972 .... **CLC 8, 19**
See also CA 85-88; 37-40R; DAM DRAM; DLB 72; EW 11; EWL 3; GFL 1789 to the Present; MTCW 1

Monty Python
See Chapman, Graham; Cleese, John (Marwood); Gilliam, Terry (Vance); Idle, Eric; Jones, Terence Graham Parry; Palin, Michael (Edward)
See also AAYA 7

Moodie, Susanna (Strickland)
1803-1885 .... **NCLC 14, 113**
See also DLB 99

Moody, Hiram (F. III) 1961-
See Moody, Rick
See also CA 138; CANR 64, 112

Moody, Minerva
See Alcott, Louisa May

Moody, Rick .... **CLC 147**
See Moody, Hiram (F. III)

Moody, William Vaughan
1869-1910 .... **TCLC 105**
See also CA 110; 178; DLB 7, 54; RGAL 4

Mooney, Edward 1951-
See Mooney, Ted
See also CA 130

Mooney, Ted .... **CLC 25**
See Mooney, Edward

Moorcock, Michael (John) 1939- ...... **CLC 5, 27, 58**
See Bradbury, Edward P.
See also AAYA 26; CA 45-48; CAAS 5; CANR 2, 17, 38, 64, 122; CN 7; DLB 14, 231, 261; FANT; MTCW 1, 2; SATA 93; SCFW 2; SFW 4; SUFW 1, 2

Moore, Brian 1921-1999 ... **CLC 1, 3, 5, 7, 8, 19, 32, 90**
See Bryan, Michael
See also BRWS 9; CA 1-4R; 174; CANR 1, 25, 42, 63; CCA 1; CN 7; DAB; DAC; DAM MST; DLB 251; EWL 3; FANT; MTCW 1, 2; RGEL 2

Moore, Edward
See Muir, Edwin
See also RGEL 2

Moore, G. E. 1873-1958 .... **TCLC 89**
See also DLB 262

Moore, George Augustus
1852-1933 .... **SSC 19; TCLC 7**
See also BRW 6; CA 104; 177; DLB 10, 18, 57, 135; EWL 3; RGEL 2; RGSF 2

Moore, Lorrie .... **CLC 39, 45, 68**
See Moore, Marie Lorena
See also AMWS 10; DLB 234; SSFS 19

Moore, Marianne (Craig)
1887-1972 .... **CLC 1, 2, 4, 8, 10, 13, 19, 47; PC 4, 49; WLCS**
See also AMW; CA 1-4R; 33-36R; CANR 3, 61; CDALB 1929-1941; DA; DA3; DAB; DAC; DAM MST, POET; DLB 45; DLBD 7; EWL 3; EXPP; MAWW; MTCW 1, 2; PAB; PFS 14, 17; RGAL 4; SATA 20; TUS; WP

Moore, Marie Lorena 1957- .... **CLC 165**
See Moore, Lorrie
See also CA 116; CANR 39, 83; CN 7; DLB 234

Moore, Thomas 1779-1852 .... **NCLC 6, 110**
See also DLB 96, 144; RGEL 2

Moorhouse, Frank 1938- .... **SSC 40**
See also CA 118; CANR 92; CN 7; DLB 289; RGSF 2

Mora, Pat(ricia) 1942- .... **HLC 2**
See also AMWS 13; CA 129; CANR 57, 81, 112; CLR 58; DAM MULT; DLB 209; HW 1, 2; LLW 1; MAICYA 2; SATA 92, 134

Moraga, Cherrie 1952- ...... **CLC 126; DC 22**
See also CA 131; CANR 66; DAM MULT; DLB 82, 249; FW; GLL 1; HW 1, 2; LLW 1

Morand, Paul 1888-1976 .... **CLC 41; SSC 22**
See also CA 184; 69-72; DLB 65; EWL 3

Morante, Elsa 1918-1985 .... **CLC 8, 47**
See also CA 85-88; 117; CANR 35; DLB 177; EWL 3; MTCW 1, 2; RGWL 2, 3

Moravia, Alberto .... **CLC 2, 7, 11, 27, 46; SSC 26**
See Pincherle, Alberto
See also DLB 177; EW 12; EWL 3; MTCW 2; RGSF 2; RGWL 2, 3

More, Hannah 1745-1833 .... **NCLC 27**
See also DLB 107, 109, 116, 158; RGEL 2

More, Henry 1614-1687 .... **LC 9**
See also DLB 126, 252

More, Sir Thomas 1478(?)-1535 .... **LC 10, 32**
See also BRWC 1; BRWS 7; DLB 136, 281; LMFS 1; RGEL 2; TEA

Moreas, Jean .... **TCLC 18**
See Papadiamantopoulos, Johannes
See also GFL 1789 to the Present

Moreton, Andrew Esq.
See Defoe, Daniel

Morgan, Berry 1919-2002 .... **CLC 6**
See also CA 49-52; 208; DLB 6

Morgan, Claire
See Highsmith, (Mary) Patricia
See also GLL 1

Morgan, Edwin (George) 1920- .... **CLC 31**
See also BRWS 9; CA 5-8R; CANR 3, 43, 90; CP 7; DLB 27

Morgan, (George) Frederick
1922-2004 .... **CLC 23**
See also CA 17-20R; CANR 21; CP 7

Morgan, Harriet
See Mencken, H(enry) L(ouis)

Morgan, Jane
See Cooper, James Fenimore

Morgan, Janet 1945- .... **CLC 39**
See also CA 65-68

Morgan, Lady 1776(?)-1859 .... **NCLC 29**
See also DLB 116, 158; RGEL 2

Morgan, Robin (Evonne) 1941- .... **CLC 2**
See also CA 69-72; CANR 29, 68; FW; GLL 2; MTCW 1; SATA 80

Morgan, Scott
See Kuttner, Henry
Morgan, Seth 1949(?)-1990 .... **CLC 65**
See also CA 185; 132
**Morgenstern, Christian (Otto Josef
Wolfgang)** 1871-1914 .... **TCLC 8**
See also CA 105; 191; EWL 3
Morgenstern, S.
See Goldman, William (W.)
Mori, Rintaro
See Mori Ogai
See also CA 110
Moricz, Zsigmond 1879-1942 .... **TCLC 33**
See also CA 165; DLB 215; EWL 3
Morike, Eduard (Friedrich)
1804-1875 .... **NCLC 10**
See also DLB 133; RGWL 2, 3
Mori Ogai 1862-1922 .... **TCLC 14**
See Ogai
See also CA 164; DLB 180; EWL 3; RGWL
3; TWA
Moritz, Karl Philipp 1756-1793 .... **LC 2**
See also DLB 94
Morland, Peter Henry
See Faust, Frederick (Schiller)
Morley, Christopher (Darlington)
1890-1957 .... **TCLC 87**
See also CA 112; DLB 9; RGAL 4
Morren, Theophil
See Hofmannsthal, Hugo von
Morris, Bill 1952- .... **CLC 76**
Morris, Julian
See West, Morris L(anglo)
Morris, Steveland Judkins 1950(?)-
See Wonder, Stevie
See also CA 111
Morris, William 1834-1896 . **NCLC 4; PC 55**
See also BRW 5; CDBLB 1832-1890; DLB
18, 35, 57, 156, 178, 184; FANT; RGEL
2; SFW 4; SUFW
Morris, Wright 1910-1998 .. **CLC 1, 3, 7, 18,
37; TCLC 107**
See also AMW; CA 9-12R; 167; CANR 21,
81; CN 7; DLB 2, 206, 218; DLBY 1981;
EWL 3; MTCW 1, 2; RGAL 4; TCWW 2
Morrison, Arthur 1863-1945 .... **SSC 40;
TCLC 72**
See also CA 120; 157; CMW 4; DLB 70,
135, 197; RGEL 2
Morrison, Chloe Anthony Wofford
See Morrison, Toni
Morrison, James Douglas 1943-1971
See Morrison, Jim
See also CA 73-76; CANR 40
Morrison, Jim .... **CLC 17**
See Morrison, James Douglas
Morrison, Toni 1931- ..... **BLC 3; CLC 4, 10,
22, 55, 81, 87, 173**
See also AAYA 1, 22; AFAW 1, 2; AMWC
1; AMWS 3; BPFB 3; BW 2, 3; CA 29-
32R; CANR 27, 42, 67, 113, 124; CDALB
1968-1988; CN 7; CPW; DA; DA3; DAB;
DAC; DAM MST, MULT, NOV, POP;
DLB 6, 33, 143; DLBY 1981; EWL 3;
EXPN; FW; LAIT 2, 4; LATS 1; LMFS
2; MAWW; MTCW 1, 2; NFS 1, 6, 8, 14;
RGAL 4; RHW; SATA 57, 144; SSFS 5;
TUS; YAW
Morrison, Van 1945- .... **CLC 21**
See also CA 116; 168
Morrissy, Mary 1957- .... **CLC 99**
See also CA 205; DLB 267
Mortimer, John (Clifford) 1923- ..... **CLC 28,
43**
See also CA 13-16R; CANR 21, 69, 109;
CD 5; CDBLB 1960 to Present; CMW 4;
CN 7; CPW; DA3; DAM DRAM, POP;
DLB 13, 245, 271; INT CANR-21; MSW;
MTCW 1, 2; RGEL 2

Mortimer, Penelope (Ruth)
1918-1999 .... **CLC 5**
See also CA 57-60; 187; CANR 45, 88; CN
7
Mortimer, Sir John
See Mortimer, John (Clifford)
Morton, Anthony
See Creasey, John
Morton, Thomas 1579(?)-1647(?) .... **LC 72**
See also DLB 24; RGEL 2
Mosca, Gaetano 1858-1941 .... **TCLC 75**
Moses, Daniel David 1952- .... **NNAL**
See also CA 186
Mosher, Howard Frank 1943- .... **CLC 62**
See also CA 139; CANR 65, 115
Mosley, Nicholas 1923- .... **CLC 43, 70**
See also CA 69-72; CANR 41, 60, 108; CN
7; DLB 14, 207
Mosley, Walter 1952- .... **BLCS; CLC 97, 184**
See also AAYA 17; AMWS 13; BPFB 2;
BW 2; CA 142; CANR 57, 92; CMW 4;
CPW; DA3; DAM MULT, POP; MSW;
MTCW 2
Moss, Howard 1922-1987 . **CLC 7, 14, 45, 50**
See also CA 1-4R; 123; CANR 1, 44; DAM
POET; DLB 5
Mossgiel, Rab
See Burns, Robert
Motion, Andrew (Peter) 1952- .... **CLC 47**
See also BRWS 7; CA 146; CANR 90; CP
7; DLB 40
Motley, Willard (Francis)
1909-1965 .... **CLC 18**
See also BW 1; CA 117; 106; CANR 88;
DLB 76, 143
Motoori, Norinaga 1730-1801 .... **NCLC 45**
Mott, Michael (Charles Alston)
1930- .... **CLC 15, 34**
See also CA 5-8R; CAAS 7; CANR 7, 29
Mountain Wolf Woman 1884-1960 . **CLC 92;
NNAL**
See also CA 144; CANR 90
Moure, Erin 1955- .... **CLC 88**
See also CA 113; CP 7; CWP; DLB 60
Mourning Dove 1885(?)-1936 .... **NNAL**
See also CA 144; CANR 90; DAM MULT;
DLB 175, 221
Mowat, Farley (McGill) 1921- .... **CLC 26**
See also AAYA 1, 50; BYA 2; CA 1-4R;
CANR 4, 24, 42, 68, 108; CLR 20; CPW;
DAC; DAM MST; DLB 68; INT CANR-
24; JRDA; MAICYA 1, 2; MTCW 1, 2;
SATA 3, 55; YAW
Mowatt, Anna Cora 1819-1870 ..... **NCLC 74**
See also RGAL 4
Moyers, Bill 1934- .... **CLC 74**
See also AITN 2; CA 61-64; CANR 31, 52
Mphahlele, Es'kia
See Mphahlele, Ezekiel
See also AFW; CDWLB 3; DLB 125, 225;
RGSF 2; SSFS 11
Mphahlele, Ezekiel 1919- ... **BLC 3; CLC 25,
133**
See Mphahlele, Es'kia
See also BW 2, 3; CA 81-84; CANR 26,
76; CN 7; DA3; DAM MULT; EWL 3;
MTCW 2; SATA 119
Mqhayi, S(amuel) E(dward) K(rune Loliwe)
1875-1945 .... **BLC 3; TCLC 25**
See also CA 153; CANR 87; DAM MULT
Mrozek, Slawomir 1930- .... **CLC 3, 13**
See also CA 13-16R; CAAS 10; CANR 29;
CDWLB 4; CWW 2; DLB 232; EWL 3;
MTCW 1
Mrs. Belloc-Lowndes
See Lowndes, Marie Adelaide (Belloc)
Mrs. Fairstar
See Horne, Richard Henry Hengist

M'Taggart, John M'Taggart Ellis
See McTaggart, John McTaggart Ellis
Mtwa, Percy (?)- .... **CLC 47**
Mueller, Lisel 1924- .... **CLC 13, 51; PC 33**
See also CA 93-96; CP 7; DLB 105; PFS 9,
13
Muggeridge, Malcolm (Thomas)
1903-1990 .... **TCLC 120**
See also AITN 1; CA 101; CANR 33, 63;
MTCW 1, 2
Muhammad 570-632 .... **WLCS**
See also DA; DAB; DAC; DAM MST
Muir, Edwin 1887-1959 . **PC 49; TCLC 2, 87**
See Moore, Edward
See also BRWS 6; CA 104; 193; DLB 20,
100, 191; EWL 3; RGEL 2
Muir, John 1838-1914 .... **TCLC 28**
See also AMWS 9; ANW; CA 165; DLB
186, 275
Mujica Lainez, Manuel 1910-1984 ... **CLC 31**
See Lainez, Manuel Mujica
See also CA 81-84; 112; CANR 32; EWL
3; HW 1
Mukherjee, Bharati 1940- ..... **AAL; CLC 53,
115; SSC 38**
See also AAYA 46; BEST 89:2; CA 107;
CANR 45, 72, 128; CN 7; DAM NOV;
DLB 60, 218; DNFS 1, 2; EWL 3; FW;
MTCW 1, 2; RGAL 4; RGSF 2; SSFS 7;
TUS; WWE 1
Muldoon, Paul 1951- .... **CLC 32, 72, 166**
See also BRWS 4; CA 113; 129; CANR 52,
91; CP 7; DAM POET; DLB 40; INT CA-
129; PFS 7
Mulisch, Harry 1927- .... **CLC 42**
See also CA 9-12R; CANR 6, 26, 56, 110;
EWL 3
Mull, Martin 1943- .... **CLC 17**
See also CA 105
Muller, Wilhelm .... **NCLC 73**
Mulock, Dinah Maria
See Craik, Dinah Maria (Mulock)
See also RGEL 2
Munday, Anthony 1560-1633 .... **LC 87**
See also DLB 62, 172; RGEL 2
Munford, Robert 1737(?)-1783 .... **LC 5**
See also DLB 31
Mungo, Raymond 1946- .... **CLC 72**
See also CA 49-52; CANR 2
Munro, Alice 1931- .... **CLC 6, 10, 19, 50, 95;
SSC 3; WLCS**
See also AITN 2; BPFB 2; CA 33-36R;
CANR 33, 53, 75, 114; CCA 1; CN 7;
DA3; DAC; DAM MST, NOV; DLB 53;
EWL 3; MTCW 1, 2; RGEL 2; RGSF 2;
SATA 29; SSFS 5, 13, 19; WWE 1
Munro, H(ector) H(ugh) 1870-1916 .... **WLC**
See Saki
See also CA 104; 130; CANR 104; CDBLB
1890-1914; DA; DA3; DAB; DAC; DAM
MST, NOV; DLB 34, 162; EXPS; MTCW
1, 2; RGEL 2; SSFS 15
Murakami, Haruki 1949- .... **CLC 150**
See Murakami Haruki
See also CA 165; CANR 102; MJW; RGWL
3; SFW 4
Murakami Haruki
See Murakami, Haruki
See also DLB 182; EWL 3
Murasaki, Lady
See Murasaki Shikibu
Murasaki Shikibu 978(?)-1026(?) ... **CMLC 1**
See also EFS 2; LATS 1; RGWL 2, 3
Murdoch, (Jean) Iris 1919-1999 ... **CLC 1, 2,
3, 4, 6, 8, 11, 15, 22, 31, 51**
See also BRWS 1; CA 13-16R; 179; CANR
8, 43, 68, 103; CDBLB 1960 to Present;
CN 7; CWD; DA3; DAB; DAC; DAM

MST, NOV; DLB 14, 194, 233; EWL 3; INT CANR-8; MTCW 1, 2; NFS 18; RGEL 2; TEA; WLIT 4

Murfree, Mary Noailles 1850-1922 .. **SSC 22; TCLC 135**
See also CA 122; 176; DLB 12, 74; RGAL 4

Murnau, Friedrich Wilhelm
See Plumpe, Friedrich Wilhelm

Murphy, Richard 1927- .... **CLC 41**
See also BRWS 5; CA 29-32R; CP 7; DLB 40; EWL 3

Murphy, Sylvia 1937- .... **CLC 34**
See also CA 121

Murphy, Thomas (Bernard) 1935- ... **CLC 51**
See also CA 101

Murray, Albert L. 1916- .... **CLC 73**
See also BW 2; CA 49-52; CANR 26, 52, 78; CSW; DLB 38

Murray, James Augustus Henry 1837-1915 .... **TCLC 117**

Murray, Judith Sargent 1751-1820 .... **NCLC 63**
See also DLB 37, 200

Murray, Les(lie Allan) 1938- .... **CLC 40**
See also BRWS 7; CA 21-24R; CANR 11, 27, 56, 103; CP 7; DAM POET; DLB 289; DLBY 2001; EWL 3; RGEL 2

Murry, J. Middleton
See Murry, John Middleton

Murry, John Middleton 1889-1957 .... **TCLC 16**
See also CA 118; 217; DLB 149

Musgrave, Susan 1951- .... **CLC 13, 54**
See also CA 69-72; CANR 45, 84; CCA 1; CP 7; CWP

Musil, Robert (Edler von) 1880-1942 .... **SSC 18; TCLC 12, 68**
See also CA 109; CANR 55, 84; CDWLB 2; DLB 81, 124; EW 9; EWL 3; MTCW 2; RGSF 2; RGWL 2, 3

Muske, Carol .... **CLC 90**
See Muske-Dukes, Carol (Anne)

Muske-Dukes, Carol (Anne) 1945-
See Muske, Carol
See also CA 65-68, 203; CAAE 203; CANR 32, 70; CWP

Musset, (Louis Charles) Alfred de 1810-1857 .... **NCLC 7**
See also DLB 192, 217; EW 6; GFL 1789 to the Present; RGWL 2, 3; TWA

Mussolini, Benito (Amilcare Andrea) 1883-1945 .... **TCLC 96**
See also CA 116

Mutanabbi, Al-
See al-Mutanabbi, Ahmad ibn al-Husayn Abu al-Tayyib al-Jufi al-Kindi

My Brother's Brother
See Chekhov, Anton (Pavlovich)

Myers, L(eopold) H(amilton) 1881-1944 .... **TCLC 59**
See also CA 157; DLB 15; EWL 3; RGEL 2

Myers, Walter Dean 1937- .. **BLC 3; CLC 35**
See also AAYA 4, 23; BW 2; BYA 6, 8, 11; CA 33-36R; CANR 20, 42, 67, 108; CLR 4, 16, 35; DAM MULT, NOV; DLB 33; INT CANR-20; JRDA; LAIT 5; MAICYA 1, 2; MAICYAS 1; MTCW 2; SAAS 2; SATA 41, 71, 109; SATA-Brief 27; WYA; YAW

Myers, Walter M.
See Myers, Walter Dean

Myles, Symon
See Follett, Ken(neth Martin)

Nabokov, Vladimir (Vladimirovich) 1899-1977 .... **CLC 1, 2, 3, 6, 8, 11, 15, 23, 44, 46, 64; SSC 11; TCLC 108; WLC**
See also AAYA 45; AMW; AMWC 1; AMWR 1; BPFB 2; CA 5-8R; 69-72; CANR 20, 102; CDALB 1941-1968; DA; DA3; DAB; DAC; DAM MST, NOV; DLB 2, 244, 278; DLBD 3; DLBY 1980, 1991; EWL 3; EXPS; LATS 1; MTCW 1, 2; NCFS 4; NFS 9; RGAL 4; RGSF 2; SSFS 6, 15; TUS

Naevius c. 265B.C.-201B.C. .... **CMLC 37**
See also DLB 211

Nagai, Kafu .... **TCLC 51**
See Nagai, Sokichi
See also DLB 180

Nagai, Sokichi 1879-1959
See Nagai, Kafu
See also CA 117

Nagy, Laszlo 1925-1978 .... **CLC 7**
See also CA 129; 112

Naidu, Sarojini 1879-1949 .... **TCLC 80**
See also EWL 3; RGEL 2

Naipaul, Shiva(dhar Srinivasa) 1945-1985 .... **CLC 32, 39**
See also CA 110; 112; 116; CANR 33; DA3; DAM NOV; DLB 157; DLBY 1985; EWL 3; MTCW 1, 2

Naipaul, V(idiadhar) S(urajprasad) 1932- .... **CLC 4, 7, 9, 13, 18, 37, 105; SSC 38**
See also BPFB 2; BRWS 1; CA 1-4R; CANR 1, 33, 51, 91, 126; CDBLB 1960 to Present; CDWLB 3; CN 7; DA3; DAB; DAC; DAM MST, NOV; DLB 125, 204, 207; DLBY 1985, 2001; EWL 3; LATS 1; MTCW 1, 2; RGEL 2; RGSF 2; TWA; WLIT 4; WWE 1

Nakos, Lilika 1903(?)-1989 .... **CLC 29**

Napoleon
See Yamamoto, Hisaye

Narayan, R(asipuram) K(rishnaswami) 1906-2001 . **CLC 7, 28, 47, 121; SSC 25**
See also BPFB 2; CA 81-84; 196; CANR 33, 61, 112; CN 7; DA3; DAM NOV; DNFS 1; EWL 3; MTCW 1, 2; RGEL 2; RGSF 2; SATA 62; SSFS 5; WWE 1

Nash, (Fredric) Ogden 1902-1971 . **CLC 23; PC 21; TCLC 109**
See also CA 13-14; 29-32R; CANR 34, 61; CAP 1; DAM POET; DLB 11; MAICYA 1, 2; MTCW 1, 2; RGAL 4; SATA 2, 46; WP

Nashe, Thomas 1567-1601(?) .... **LC 41, 89**
See also DLB 167; RGEL 2

Nathan, Daniel
See Dannay, Frederic

Nathan, George Jean 1882-1958 .... **TCLC 18**
See Hatteras, Owen
See also CA 114; 169; DLB 137

Natsume, Kinnosuke
See Natsume, Soseki

Natsume, Soseki 1867-1916 .... **TCLC 2, 10**
See Natsume Soseki; Soseki
See also CA 104; 195; RGWL 2, 3; TWA

Natsume Soseki
See Natsume, Soseki
See also DLB 180; EWL 3

Natti, (Mary) Lee 1919-
See Kingman, Lee
See also CA 5-8R; CANR 2

Navarre, Marguerite de
See de Navarre, Marguerite

Naylor, Gloria 1950- ..... **BLC 3; CLC 28, 52, 156; WLCS**
See also AAYA 6, 39; AFAW 1, 2; AMWS 8; BW 2, 3; CA 107; CANR 27, 51, 74; CN 7; CPW; DA; DA3; DAC; DAM

MST, MULT, NOV, POP; DLB 173; EWL 3; FW; MTCW 1, 2; NFS 4, 7; RGAL 4; TUS

Neff, Debra .... **CLC 59**

Neihardt, John Gneisenau 1881-1973 .... **CLC 32**
See also CA 13-14; CANR 65; CAP 1; DLB 9, 54, 256; LAIT 2

Nekrasov, Nikolai Alekseevich 1821-1878 .... **NCLC 11**
See also DLB 277

Nelligan, Emile 1879-1941 .... **TCLC 14**
See also CA 114; 204; DLB 92; EWL 3

Nelson, Willie 1933- .... **CLC 17**
See also CA 107; CANR 114

Nemerov, Howard (Stanley) 1920-1991 .... **CLC 2, 6, 9, 36; PC 24; TCLC 124**
See also AMW; CA 1-4R; 134; CABS 2; CANR 1, 27, 53; DAM POET; DLB 5, 6; DLBY 1983; EWL 3; INT CANR-27; MTCW 1, 2; PFS 10, 14; RGAL 4

Neruda, Pablo 1904-1973 .. **CLC 1, 2, 5, 7, 9, 28, 62; HLC 2; PC 4; WLC**
See also CA 19-20; 45-48; CAP 2; DA; DA3; DAB; DAC; DAM MST, MULT, POET; DLB 283; DNFS 2; EWL 3; HW 1; LAW; MTCW 1, 2; PFS 11; RGWL 2, 3; TWA; WLIT 1; WP

Nerval, Gerard de 1808-1855 ... **NCLC 1, 67; PC 13; SSC 18**
See also DLB 217; EW 6; GFL 1789 to the Present; RGSF 2; RGWL 2, 3

Nervo, (Jose) Amado (Ruiz de) 1870-1919 .... **HLCS 2; TCLC 11**
See also CA 109; 131; DLB 290; EWL 3; HW 1; LAW

Nesbit, Malcolm
See Chester, Alfred

Nessi, Pio Baroja y
See Baroja (y Nessi), Pio

Nestroy, Johann 1801-1862 .... **NCLC 42**
See also DLB 133; RGWL 2, 3

Netterville, Luke
See O'Grady, Standish (James)

Neufeld, John (Arthur) 1938- .... **CLC 17**
See also AAYA 11; CA 25-28R; CANR 11, 37, 56; CLR 52; MAICYA 1, 2; SAAS 3; SATA 6, 81, 131; SATA-Essay 131; YAW

Neumann, Alfred 1895-1952 .... **TCLC 100**
See also CA 183; DLB 56

Neumann, Ferenc
See Molnar, Ferenc

Neville, Emily Cheney 1919- .... **CLC 12**
See also BYA 2; CA 5-8R; CANR 3, 37, 85; JRDA; MAICYA 1, 2; SAAS 2; SATA 1; YAW

Newbound, Bernard Slade 1930-
See Slade, Bernard
See also CA 81-84; CANR 49; CD 5; DAM DRAM

Newby, P(ercy) H(oward) 1918-1997 .... **CLC 2, 13**
See also CA 5-8R; 161; CANR 32, 67; CN 7; DAM NOV; DLB 15; MTCW 1; RGEL 2

Newcastle
See Cavendish, Margaret Lucas

Newlove, Donald 1928- .... **CLC 6**
See also CA 29-32R; CANR 25

Newlove, John (Herbert) 1938- .... **CLC 14**
See also CA 21-24R; CANR 9, 25; CP 7

Newman, Charles 1938- .... **CLC 2, 8**
See also CA 21-24R; CANR 84; CN 7

Newman, Edwin (Harold) 1919- ...... **CLC 14**
See also AITN 1; CA 69-72; CANR 5

Pancake, Breece D'J .... **CLC 29; SSC 61**
See Pancake, Breece Dexter
See also DLB 130

Panchenko, Nikolai .... **CLC 59**

Pankhurst, Emmeline (Goulden)
1858-1928 .... **TCLC 100**
See also CA 116; FW

Panko, Rudy
See Gogol, Nikolai (Vasilyevich)

Papadiamantis, Alexandros
1851-1911 .... **TCLC 29**
See also CA 168; EWL 3

Papadiamantopoulos, Johannes 1856-1910
See Moreas, Jean
See also CA 117

Papini, Giovanni 1881-1956 .... **TCLC 22**
See also CA 121; 180; DLB 264

Paracelsus 1493-1541 .... **LC 14**
See also DLB 179

Parasol, Peter
See Stevens, Wallace

Pardo Bazan, Emilia 1851-1921 .... **SSC 30**
See also EWL 3; FW; RGSF 2; RGWL 2, 3

Pareto, Vilfredo 1848-1923 .... **TCLC 69**
See also CA 175

Paretsky, Sara 1947- .... **CLC 135**
See also AAYA 30; BEST 90:3; CA 125;
129; CANR 59, 95; CMW 4; CPW; DA3;
DAM POP; INT CA-129; MSW; RGAL 4

Parfenie, Maria
See Codrescu, Andrei

Parini, Jay (Lee) 1948- .... **CLC 54, 133**
See also CA 97-100; CAAS 16; CANR 32,
87

Park, Jordan
See Kornbluth, C(yril) M.; Pohl, Frederik

Park, Robert E(zra) 1864-1944 ..... **TCLC 73**
See also CA 122; 165

Parker, Bert
See Ellison, Harlan (Jay)

Parker, Dorothy (Rothschild)
1893-1967 . **CLC 15, 68; PC 28; SSC 2;
TCLC 143**
See also AMWS 9; CA 19-20; 25-28R; CAP
2; DA3; DAM POET; DLB 11, 45, 86;
EXPP; FW; MAWW; MTCW 1, 2; PFS
18; RGAL 4; RGSF 2; TUS

Parker, Robert B(rown) 1932- .... **CLC 27**
See also AAYA 28; BEST 89:4; BPFB 3;
CA 49-52; CANR 1, 26, 52, 89, 128;
CMW 4; CPW; DAM NOV, POP; INT
CANR-26; MSW; MTCW 1

Parkin, Frank 1940- .... **CLC 43**
See also CA 147

Parkman, Francis, Jr. 1823-1893 .. **NCLC 12**
See also AMWS 2; DLB 1, 30, 183, 186,
235; RGAL 4

Parks, Gordon (Alexander Buchanan)
1912- .... **BLC 3; CLC 1, 16**
See also AAYA 36; AITN 2; BW 2, 3; CA
41-44R; CANR 26, 66; DA3; DAM
MULT; DLB 33; MTCW 2; SATA 8, 108

Parks, Tim(othy Harold) 1954- ...... **CLC 147**
See also CA 126; 131; CANR 77; DLB 231;
INT CA-131

Parmenides c. 515B.C.-c.
450B.C. .... **CMLC 22**
See also DLB 176

Parnell, Thomas 1679-1718 .... **LC 3**
See also DLB 95; RGEL 2

Parr, Catherine c. 1513(?)-1548 .... **LC 86**
See also DLB 136

Parra, Nicanor 1914- ... **CLC 2, 102; HLC 2;
PC 39**
See also CA 85-88; CANR 32; CWW 2;
DAM MULT; DLB 283; EWL 3; HW 1;
LAW; MTCW 1

Parra Sanojo, Ana Teresa de la
1890-1936 .... **HLCS 2**
See de la Parra, (Ana) Teresa (Sonojo)
See also LAW

Parrish, Mary Frances
See Fisher, M(ary) F(rances) K(ennedy)

Parshchikov, Aleksei 1954- .... **CLC 59**
See Parshchikov, Aleksei Maksimovich

Parshchikov, Aleksei Maksimovich
See Parshchikov, Aleksei
See also DLB 285

Parson, Professor
See Coleridge, Samuel Taylor

Parson Lot
See Kingsley, Charles

Parton, Sara Payson Willis
1811-1872 .... **NCLC 86**
See also DLB 43, 74, 239

Partridge, Anthony
See Oppenheim, E(dward) Phillips

Pascal, Blaise 1623-1662 .... **LC 35**
See also DLB 268; EW 3; GFL Beginnings
to 1789; RGWL 2, 3; TWA

Pascoli, Giovanni 1855-1912 .... **TCLC 45**
See also CA 170; EW 7; EWL 3

Pasolini, Pier Paolo 1922-1975 .. **CLC 20, 37,
106; PC 17**
See also CA 93-96; 61-64; CANR 63; DLB
128, 177; EWL 3; MTCW 1; RGWL 2, 3

Pasquini
See Silone, Ignazio

Pastan, Linda (Olenik) 1932- .... **CLC 27**
See also CA 61-64; CANR 18, 40, 61, 113;
CP 7; CSW; CWP; DAM POET; DLB 5;
PFS 8

Pasternak, Boris (Leonidovich)
1890-1960 ...... **CLC 7, 10, 18, 63; PC 6;
SSC 31; WLC**
See also BPFB 3; CA 127; 116; DA; DA3;
DAB; DAC; DAM MST, NOV, POET;
EW 10; MTCW 1, 2; RGSF 2; RGWL 2,
3; TWA; WP

Patchen, Kenneth 1911-1972 .... **CLC 1, 2, 18**
See also BG 3; CA 1-4R; 33-36R; CANR
3, 35; DAM POET; DLB 16, 48; EWL 3;
MTCW 1; RGAL 4

Pater, Walter (Horatio) 1839-1894 . **NCLC 7,
90**
See also BRW 5; CDBLB 1832-1890; DLB
57, 156; RGEL 2; TEA

Paterson, A(ndrew) B(arton)
1864-1941 .... **TCLC 32**
See also CA 155; DLB 230; RGEL 2; SATA
97

Paterson, Banjo
See Paterson, A(ndrew) B(arton)

Paterson, Katherine (Womeldorf)
1932- .... **CLC 12, 30**
See also AAYA 1, 31; BYA 1, 2, 7; CA 21-
24R; CANR 28, 59, 111; CLR 7, 50;
CWRI 5; DLB 52; JRDA; LAIT 4; MAI-
CYA 1, 2; MAICYAS 1; MTCW 1; SATA
13, 53, 92, 133; WYA; YAW

Patmore, Coventry Kersey Dighton
1823-1896 .... **NCLC 9**
See also DLB 35, 98; RGEL 2; TEA

Paton, Alan (Stewart) 1903-1988 ...... **CLC 4,
10, 25, 55, 106; WLC**
See also AAYA 26; AFW; BPFB 3; BRWS
2; BYA 1; CA 13-16; 125; CANR 22;
CAP 1; DA; DA3; DAB; DAC; DAM
MST, NOV; DLB 225; DLBD 17; EWL
3; EXPN; LAIT 4; MTCW 1, 2; NFS 3,
12; RGEL 2; SATA 11; SATA-Obit 56;
TWA; WLIT 2; WWE 1

Paton Walsh, Gillian 1937- .... **CLC 35**
See Paton Walsh, Jill; Walsh, Jill Paton
See also AAYA 11; CANR 38, 83; CLR 2,
65; DLB 161; JRDA; MAICYA 1, 2;
SAAS 3; SATA 4, 72, 109; YAW

Paton Walsh, Jill
See Paton Walsh, Gillian
See also AAYA 47; BYA 1, 8

Patterson, (Horace) Orlando (Lloyd)
1940- .... **BLCS**
See also BW 1; CA 65-68; CANR 27, 84;
CN 7

Patton, George S(mith), Jr.
1885-1945 .... **TCLC 79**
See also CA 189

Paulding, James Kirke 1778-1860 ... **NCLC 2**
See also DLB 3, 59, 74, 250; RGAL 4

Paulin, Thomas Neilson 1949-
See Paulin, Tom
See also CA 123; 128; CANR 98; CP 7

Paulin, Tom .... **CLC 37, 177**
See Paulin, Thomas Neilson
See also DLB 40

Pausanias c. 1st cent. - .... **CMLC 36**

Paustovsky, Konstantin (Georgievich)
1892-1968 .... **CLC 40**
See also CA 93-96; 25-28R; DLB 272;
EWL 3

Pavese, Cesare 1908-1950 .... **PC 13; SSC 19;
TCLC 3**
See also CA 104; 169; DLB 128, 177; EW
12; EWL 3; RGSF 2; RGWL 2, 3; TWA

Pavic, Milorad 1929- .... **CLC 60**
See also CA 136; CDWLB 4; CWW 2; DLB
181; EWL 3; RGWL 3

Pavlov, Ivan Petrovich 1849-1936 . **TCLC 91**
See also CA 118; 180

Pavlova, Karolina Karlovna
1807-1893 .... **NCLC 138**
See also DLB 205

Payne, Alan
See Jakes, John (William)

Paz, Gil
See Lugones, Leopoldo

Paz, Octavio 1914-1998 . **CLC 3, 4, 6, 10, 19,
51, 65, 119; HLC 2; PC 1, 48; WLC**
See also AAYA 50; CA 73-76; 165; CANR
32, 65, 104; CWW 2; DA; DA3; DAB;
DAC; DAM MST, MULT, POET; DLB
290; DLBY 1990, 1998; DNFS 1; EWL
3; HW 1, 2; LAW; LAWS 1; MTCW 1, 2;
PFS 18; RGWL 2, 3; SSFS 13; TWA;
WLIT 1

p'Bitek, Okot 1931-1982 .... **BLC 3; CLC 96;
TCLC 149**
See also AFW; BW 2, 3; CA 124; 107;
CANR 82; DAM MULT; DLB 125; EWL
3; MTCW 1, 2; RGEL 2; WLIT 2

Peacock, Molly 1947- .... **CLC 60**
See also CA 103; CAAS 21; CANR 52, 84;
CP 7; CWP; DLB 120, 282

Peacock, Thomas Love
1785-1866 .... **NCLC 22**
See also BRW 4; DLB 96, 116; RGEL 2;
RGSF 2

Peake, Mervyn 1911-1968 .... **CLC 7, 54**
See also CA 5-8R; 25-28R; CANR 3; DLB
15, 160, 255; FANT; MTCW 1; RGEL 2;
SATA 23; SFW 4

Pearce, Philippa
See Christie, Philippa
See also CA 5-8R; CANR 4, 109; CWRI 5;
FANT; MAICYA 2

Pearl, Eric
See Elman, Richard (Martin)

Pearson, T(homas) R(eid) 1956- .... **CLC 39**
See also CA 120; 130; CANR 97; CSW;
INT CA-130

Pinckney, Darryl 1953- .... **CLC 76**
See also BW 2, 3; CA 143; CANR 79

Pindar 518(?)B.C.-438(?)B.C. .... **CMLC 12;**
PC 19
See also AW 1; CDWLB 1; DLB 176;
RGWL 2

Pineda, Cecile 1942- .... **CLC 39**
See also CA 118; DLB 209

Pinero, Arthur Wing 1855-1934 .... **TCLC 32**
See also CA 110; 153; DAM DRAM; DLB
10; RGEL 2

Pinero, Miguel (Antonio Gomez)
1946-1988 .... **CLC 4, 55**
See also CA 61-64; 125; CAD; CANR 29,
90; DLB 266; HW 1; LLW 1

Pinget, Robert 1919-1997 .... **CLC 7, 13, 37**
See also CA 85-88; 160; CWW 2; DLB 83;
EWL 3; GFL 1789 to the Present

Pink Floyd
See Barrett, (Roger) Syd; Gilmour, David;
Mason, Nick; Waters, Roger; Wright, Rick

Pinkney, Edward 1802-1828 .... **NCLC 31**
See also DLB 248

Pinkwater, Daniel
See Pinkwater, Daniel Manus

Pinkwater, Daniel Manus 1941- .... **CLC 35**
See also AAYA 1, 46; BYA 9; CA 29-32R;
CANR 12, 38, 89; CLR 4; CSW; FANT;
JRDA; MAICYA 1, 2; SAAS 3; SATA 8,
46, 76, 114; SFW 4; YAW

Pinkwater, Manus
See Pinkwater, Daniel Manus

Pinsky, Robert 1940- .... **CLC 9, 19, 38, 94,**
121; PC 27
See also AMWS 6; CA 29-32R; CAAS 4;
CANR 58, 97; CP 7; DA3; DAM POET;
DLBY 1982, 1998; MTCW 2; PFS 18;
RGAL 4

Pinta, Harold
See Pinter, Harold

Pinter, Harold 1930- .. **CLC 1, 3, 6, 9, 11, 15,**
27, 58, 73; DC 15; WLC
See also BRWR 1; BRWS 1; CA 5-8R;
CANR 33, 65, 112; CBD; CD 5; CDBLB
1960 to Present; DA; DA3; DAB; DAC;
DAM DRAM, MST; DFS 3, 5, 7, 14;
DLB 13; EWL 3; IDFW 3, 4; LMFS 2;
MTCW 1, 2; RGEL 2; TEA

Piozzi, Hester Lynch (Thrale)
1741-1821 .... **NCLC 57**
See also DLB 104, 142

Pirandello, Luigi 1867-1936 .. **DC 5; SSC 22;**
TCLC 4, 29; WLC
See also CA 104; 153; CANR 103; DA;
DA3; DAB; DAC; DAM DRAM, MST;
DFS 4, 9; DLB 264; EW 8; EWL 3;
MTCW 2; RGSF 2; RGWL 2, 3

Pirsig, Robert M(aynard) 1928- ... **CLC 4, 6,**
73
See also CA 53-56; CANR 42, 74; CPW 1;
DA3; DAM POP; MTCW 1, 2; SATA 39

Pisarev, Dmitrii Ivanovich
See Pisarev, Dmitry Ivanovich
See also DLB 277

Pisarev, Dmitry Ivanovich
1840-1868 .... **NCLC 25**
See Pisarev, Dmitrii Ivanovich

Pix, Mary (Griffith) 1666-1709 .... **LC 8**
See also DLB 80

Pixerecourt, (Rene Charles) Guilbert de
1773-1844 .... **NCLC 39**
See also DLB 192; GFL 1789 to the Present

Plaatje, Sol(omon) T(shekisho)
1878-1932 .... **BLCS; TCLC 73**
See also BW 2, 3; CA 141; CANR 79; DLB
125, 225

Plaidy, Jean
See Hibbert, Eleanor Alice Burford

Planche, James Robinson
1796-1880 .... **NCLC 42**
See also RGEL 2

Plant, Robert 1948- .... **CLC 12**

Plante, David (Robert) 1940- . **CLC 7, 23, 38**
See also CA 37-40R; CANR 12, 36, 58, 82;
CN 7; DAM NOV; DLBY 1983; INT
CANR-12; MTCW 1

Plath, Sylvia 1932-1963 ..... **CLC 1, 2, 3, 5, 9,**
11, 14, 17, 50, 51, 62, 111; PC 1, 37;
WLC
See also AAYA 13; AMWR 2; AMWS 1;
BPFB 3; CA 19-20; CANR 34, 101; CAP
2; CDALB 1941-1968; DA; DA3; DAB;
DAC; DAM MST, POET; DLB 5, 6, 152;
EWL 3; EXPN; EXPP; FW; LAIT 4;
MAWW; MTCW 1, 2; NFS 1; PAB; PFS
1, 15; RGAL 4; SATA 96; TUS; WP;
YAW

Plato c. 428B.C.-347B.C. ... **CMLC 8; WLCS**
See also AW 1; CDWLB 1; DA; DA3;
DAB; DAC; DAM MST; DLB 176; LAIT
1; LATS 1; RGWL 2, 3

Platonov, Andrei
See Klimentov, Andrei Platonovich

Platonov, Andrei Platonovich
See Klimentov, Andrei Platonovich
See also DLB 272

Platonov, Andrey Platonovich
See Klimentov, Andrei Platonovich
See also EWL 3

Platt, Kin 1911- .... **CLC 26**
See also AAYA 11; CA 17-20R; CANR 11;
JRDA; SAAS 17; SATA 21, 86; WYA

Plautus c. 254B.C.-c. 184B.C. ...... **CMLC 24;**
DC 6
See also AW 1; CDWLB 1; DLB 211;
RGWL 2, 3

Plick et Plock
See Simenon, Georges (Jacques Christian)

Plieksans, Janis
See Rainis, Janis

Plimpton, George (Ames)
1927-2003 .... **CLC 36**
See also AITN 1; CA 21-24R; CANR 32,
70, 103; DLB 185, 241; MTCW 1, 2;
SATA 10

Pliny the Elder c. 23-79 .... **CMLC 23**
See also DLB 211

Pliny the Younger c. 61-c. 112 ...... **CMLC 62**
See also AW 2; DLB 211

Plomer, William Charles Franklin
1903-1973 .... **CLC 4, 8**
See also AFW; CA 21-22; CANR 34; CAP
2; DLB 20, 162, 191, 225; EWL 3;
MTCW 1; RGEL 2; RGSF 2; SATA 24

Plotinus 204-270 .... **CMLC 46**
See also CDWLB 1; DLB 176

Plowman, Piers
See Kavanagh, Patrick (Joseph)

Plum, J.
See Wodehouse, P(elham) G(renville)

Plumly, Stanley (Ross) 1939- .... **CLC 33**
See also CA 108; 110; CANR 97; CP 7;
DLB 5, 193; INT CA-110

Plumpe, Friedrich Wilhelm
1888-1931 .... **TCLC 53**
See also CA 112

Plutarch c. 46-c. 120 .... **CMLC 60**
See also AW 2; CDWLB 1; DLB 176;
RGWL 2, 3; TWA

Po Chu-i 772-846 .... **CMLC 24**

Poe, Edgar Allan 1809-1849 ..... **NCLC 1, 16,**
55, 78, 94, 97, 117; PC 1, 54; SSC 1,
22, 34, 35, 54; WLC
See also AAYA 14; AMW; AMWC 1;
AMWR 2; BPFB 3; BYA 5, 11; CDALB
1640-1865; CMW 4; DA; DA3; DAB;
DAC; DAM MST, POET; DLB 3, 59, 73,

74, 248, 254; EXPP; EXPS; HGG; LAIT
2; LATS 1; LMFS 1; MSW; PAB; PFS 1,
3, 9; RGAL 4; RGSF 2; SATA 23; SCFW
2; SFW 4; SSFS 2, 4, 7, 8, 16; SUFW;
TUS; WP; WYA

Poet of Titchfield Street, The
See Pound, Ezra (Weston Loomis)

Pohl, Frederik 1919- .... **CLC 18; SSC 25**
See also AAYA 24; CA 61-64, 188; CAAE
188; CAAS 1; CANR 11, 37, 81; CN 7;
DLB 8; INT CANR-11; MTCW 1, 2;
SATA 24; SCFW 2; SFW 4

Poirier, Louis 1910-
See Gracq, Julien
See also CA 122; 126; CWW 2

Poitier, Sidney 1927- .... **CLC 26**
See also BW 1; CA 117; CANR 94

Pokagon, Simon 1830-1899 .... **NNAL**
See also DAM MULT

Polanski, Roman 1933- .... **CLC 16, 178**
See also CA 77-80

Poliakoff, Stephen 1952- .... **CLC 38**
See also CA 106; CANR 116; CBD; CD 5;
DLB 13

Police, The
See Copeland, Stewart (Armstrong); Sum-
mers, Andrew James

Polidori, John William 1795-1821 . **NCLC 51**
See also DLB 116; HGG

Pollitt, Katha 1949- .... **CLC 28, 122**
See also CA 120; 122; CANR 66, 108;
MTCW 1, 2

Pollock, (Mary) Sharon 1936- .... **CLC 50**
See also CA 141; CD 5; CWD; DAC; DAM
DRAM, MST; DFS 3; DLB 60; FW

Pollock, Sharon 1936- .... **DC 20**

Polo, Marco 1254-1324 .... **CMLC 15**

Polonsky, Abraham (Lincoln)
1910-1999 .... **CLC 92**
See also CA 104; 187; DLB 26; INT CA-
104

Polybius c. 200B.C.-c. 118B.C. ...... **CMLC 17**
See also AW 1; DLB 176; RGWL 2, 3

Pomerance, Bernard 1940- .... **CLC 13**
See also CA 101; CAD; CANR 49; CD 5;
DAM DRAM; DFS 9; LAIT 2

Ponge, Francis 1899-1988 .... **CLC 6, 18**
See also CA 85-88; 126; CANR 40, 86;
DAM POET; DLBY 2002; EWL 3; GFL
1789 to the Present; RGWL 2, 3

Poniatowska, Elena 1933- . **CLC 140; HLC 2**
See also CA 101; CANR 32, 66, 107; CD-
WLB 3; DAM MULT; DLB 113; EWL 3;
HW 1, 2; LAWS 1; WLIT 1

Pontoppidan, Henrik 1857-1943 .... **TCLC 29**
See also CA 170

Poole, Josephine .... **CLC 17**
See Helyar, Jane Penelope Josephine
See also SAAS 2; SATA 5

Popa, Vasko 1922-1991 .... **CLC 19**
See also CA 112; 148; CDWLB 4; DLB
181; EWL 3; RGWL 2, 3

Pope, Alexander 1688-1744 ...... **LC 3, 58, 60,**
64; PC 26; WLC
See also BRW 3; BRWC 1; BRWR 1; CD-
BLB 1660-1789; DA; DA3; DAB; DAC;
DAM MST, POET; DLB 95, 101, 213;
EXPP; PAB; PFS 12; RGEL 2; WLIT 3;
WP

Popov, Evgenii Anatol'evich
See Popov, Yevgeny
See also DLB 285

Popov, Yevgeny .... **CLC 59**
See Popov, Evgenii Anatol'evich

Poquelin, Jean-Baptiste
See Moliere

Porter, Connie (Rose) 1959(?)- .... **CLC 70**
See also BW 2, 3; CA 142; CANR 90, 109;
SATA 81, 129

Pulitzer, Joseph 1847-1911 .... **TCLC 76**
    See also CA 114; DLB 23
Purchas, Samuel 1577(?)-1626 .... **LC 70**
    See also DLB 151
Purdy, A(lfred) W(ellington)
    1918-2000 .... **CLC 3, 6, 14, 50**
    See also CA 81-84; 189; CAAS 17; CANR
    42, 66; CP 7; DAC; DAM MST, POET;
    DLB 88; PFS 5; RGEL 2
Purdy, James (Amos) 1923- .... **CLC 2, 4, 10,
    28, 52**
    See also AMWS 7; CA 33-36R; CAAS 1;
    CANR 19, 51; CN 7; DLB 2, 218; EWL
    3; INT CANR-19; MTCW 1; RGAL 4
Pure, Simon
    See Swinnerton, Frank Arthur
Pushkin, Aleksandr Sergeevich
    See Pushkin, Alexander (Sergeyevich)
    See also DLB 205
Pushkin, Alexander (Sergeyevich)
    1799-1837 .... **NCLC 3, 27, 83; PC 10;
    SSC 27, 55; WLC**
    See Pushkin, Aleksandr Sergeevich
    See also DA; DA3; DAB; DAC; DAM
    DRAM, MST, POET; EW 5; EXPS; RGSF
    2; RGWL 2, 3; SATA 61; SSFS 9; TWA
P'u Sung-ling 1640-1715 .... **LC 49; SSC 31**
Putnam, Arthur Lee
    See Alger, Horatio, Jr.
Puzo, Mario 1920-1999 .... **CLC 1, 2, 6, 36,
    107**
    See also BPFB 3; CA 65-68; 185; CANR 4,
    42, 65, 99; CN 7; CPW; DA3; DAM
    NOV, POP; DLB 6; MTCW 1, 2; NFS 16;
    RGAL 4
Pygge, Edward
    See Barnes, Julian (Patrick)
Pyle, Ernest Taylor 1900-1945
    See Pyle, Ernie
    See also CA 115; 160
Pyle, Ernie .... **TCLC 75**
    See Pyle, Ernest Taylor
    See also DLB 29; MTCW 2
Pyle, Howard 1853-1911 .... **TCLC 81**
    See also BYA 2, 4; CA 109; 137; CLR 22;
    DLB 42, 188; DLBD 13; LAIT 1; MAI-
    CYA 1, 2; SATA 16, 100; WCH; YAW
Pym, Barbara (Mary Crampton)
    1913-1980 .... **CLC 13, 19, 37, 111**
    See also BPFB 3; BRWS 2; CA 13-14; 97-
    100; CANR 13, 34; CAP 1; DLB 14, 207;
    DLBY 1987; EWL 3; MTCW 1, 2; RGEL
    2; TEA
Pynchon, Thomas (Ruggles, Jr.)
    1937- ...... **CLC 2, 3, 6, 9, 11, 18, 33, 62,
    72, 123; SSC 14; WLC**
    See also AMWS 2; BEST 90:2; BPFB 3;
    CA 17-20R; CANR 22, 46, 73; CN 7;
    CPW 1; DA; DA3; DAB; DAC; DAM
    MST, NOV, POP; DLB 2, 173; EWL 3;
    MTCW 1, 2; RGAL 4; SFW 4; TUS
Pythagoras c. 582B.C.-c. 507B.C. . **CMLC 22**
    See also DLB 176

Q
    See Quiller-Couch, Sir Arthur (Thomas)
Qian, Chongzhu
    See Ch'ien, Chung-shu
Qian Zhongshu
    See Ch'ien, Chung-shu
    See also CWW 2
Qroll
    See Dagerman, Stig (Halvard)
Quarrington, Paul (Lewis) 1953- ..... **CLC 65**
    See also CA 129; CANR 62, 95
Quasimodo, Salvatore 1901-1968 .... **CLC 10;
    PC 47**
    See also CA 13-16; 25-28R; CAP 1; DLB
    114; EW 12; EWL 3; MTCW 1; RGWL
    2, 3

Quatermass, Martin
    See Carpenter, John (Howard)
Quay, Stephen 1947- .... **CLC 95**
    See also CA 189
Quay, Timothy 1947- .... **CLC 95**
    See also CA 189
Queen, Ellery .... **CLC 3, 11**
    See Dannay, Frederic; Davidson, Avram
    (James); Deming, Richard; Fairman, Paul
    W.; Flora, Fletcher; Hoch, Edward
    D(entinger); Kane, Henry; Lee, Manfred
    B(ennington); Marlowe, Stephen; Powell,
    (Oval) Talmage; Sheldon, Walter J(ames);
    Sturgeon, Theodore (Hamilton); Tracy,
    Don(ald Fiske); Vance, John Holbrook
    See also BPFB 3; CMW 4; MSW; RGAL 4
Queen, Ellery, Jr.
    See Dannay, Frederic; Lee, Manfred
    B(ennington)
Queneau, Raymond 1903-1976 ..... **CLC 2, 5,
    10, 42**
    See also CA 77-80; 69-72; CANR 32; DLB
    72, 258; EW 12; EWL 3; GFL 1789 to
    the Present; MTCW 1, 2; RGWL 2, 3
Quevedo, Francisco de 1580-1645 .... **LC 23**
Quiller-Couch, Sir Arthur (Thomas)
    1863-1944 .... **TCLC 53**
    See also CA 118; 166; DLB 135, 153, 190;
    HGG; RGEL 2; SUFW 1
Quin, Ann (Marie) 1936-1973 .... **CLC 6**
    See also CA 9-12R; 45-48; DLB 14, 231
Quincey, Thomas de
    See De Quincey, Thomas
Quinn, Martin
    See Smith, Martin Cruz
Quinn, Peter 1947- .... **CLC 91**
    See also CA 197
Quinn, Simon
    See Smith, Martin Cruz
Quintana, Leroy V. 1944- ...... **HLC 2; PC 36**
    See also CA 131; CANR 65; DAM MULT;
    DLB 82; HW 1, 2
Quiroga, Horacio (Sylvestre)
    1878-1937 .... **HLC 2; TCLC 20**
    See also CA 117; 131; DAM MULT; EWL
    3; HW 1; LAW; MTCW 1; RGSF 2;
    WLIT 1
Quoirez, Francoise 1935- .... **CLC 9**
    See Sagan, Francoise
    See also CA 49-52; CANR 6, 39, 73; CWW
    2; MTCW 1, 2; TWA
Raabe, Wilhelm (Karl) 1831-1910 . **TCLC 45**
    See also CA 167; DLB 129
Rabe, David (William) 1940- .. **CLC 4, 8, 33;
    DC 16**
    See also CA 85-88; CABS 3; CAD; CANR
    59, 129; CD 5; DAM DRAM; DFS 3, 8,
    13; DLB 7, 228; EWL 3
Rabelais, Francois 1494-1553 .... **LC 5, 60;
    WLC**
    See also DA; DAB; DAC; DAM MST; EW
    2; GFL Beginnings to 1789; LMFS 1;
    RGWL 2, 3; TWA
Rabinovitch, Sholem 1859-1916
    See Aleichem, Sholom
    See also CA 104
Rabinyan, Dorit 1972- .... **CLC 119**
    See also CA 170
Rachilde
    See Vallette, Marguerite Eymery; Vallette,
    Marguerite Eymery
    See also EWL 3
Racine, Jean 1639-1699 .... **LC 28**
    See also DA3; DAB; DAM MST; DLB 268;
    EW 3; GFL Beginnings to 1789; LMFS
    1; RGWL 2, 3; TWA

Radcliffe, Ann (Ward) 1764-1823 ... **NCLC 6,
    55, 106**
    See also DLB 39, 178; HGG; LMFS 1;
    RGEL 2; SUFW; WLIT 3
Radclyffe-Hall, Marguerite
    See Hall, (Marguerite) Radclyffe
Radiguet, Raymond 1903-1923 ...... **TCLC 29**
    See also CA 162; DLB 65; EWL 3; GFL
    1789 to the Present; RGWL 2, 3
Radnoti, Miklos 1909-1944 .... **TCLC 16**
    See also CA 118; 212; CDWLB 4; DLB
    215; EWL 3; RGWL 2, 3
Rado, James 1939- .... **CLC 17**
    See also CA 105
Radvanyi, Netty 1900-1983
    See Seghers, Anna
    See also CA 85-88; 110; CANR 82
Rae, Ben
    See Griffiths, Trevor
Raeburn, John (Hay) 1941- .... **CLC 34**
    See also CA 57-60
Ragni, Gerome 1942-1991 .... **CLC 17**
    See also CA 105; 134
Rahv, Philip .... **CLC 24**
    See Greenberg, Ivan
    See also DLB 137
Raimund, Ferdinand Jakob
    1790-1836 .... **NCLC 69**
    See also DLB 90
Raine, Craig (Anthony) 1944- .. **CLC 32, 103**
    See also CA 108; CANR 29, 51, 103; CP 7;
    DLB 40; PFS 7
Raine, Kathleen (Jessie) 1908-2003 .. **CLC 7,
    45**
    See also CA 85-88; 218; CANR 46, 109;
    CP 7; DLB 20; EWL 3; MTCW 1; RGEL
    2
Rainis, Janis 1865-1929 .... **TCLC 29**
    See also CA 170; CDWLB 4; DLB 220;
    EWL 3
Rakosi, Carl .... **CLC 47**
    See Rawley, Callman
    See also CAAS 5; CP 7; DLB 193
Ralegh, Sir Walter
    See Raleigh, Sir Walter
    See also BRW 1; RGEL 2; WP
Raleigh, Richard
    See Lovecraft, H(oward) P(hillips)
Raleigh, Sir Walter 1554(?)-1618 .... **LC 31,
    39; PC 31**
    See Ralegh, Sir Walter
    See also CDBLB Before 1660; DLB 172;
    EXPP; PFS 14; TEA
Rallentando, H. P.
    See Sayers, Dorothy L(eigh)
Ramal, Walter
    See de la Mare, Walter (John)
Ramana Maharshi 1879-1950 .... **TCLC 84**
Ramoacn y Cajal, Santiago
    1852-1934 .... **TCLC 93**
Ramon, Juan
    See Jimenez (Mantecon), Juan Ramon
Ramos, Graciliano 1892-1953 .... **TCLC 32**
    See also CA 167; EWL 3; HW 2; LAW;
    WLIT 1
Rampersad, Arnold 1941- .... **CLC 44**
    See also BW 2, 3; CA 127; 133; CANR 81;
    DLB 111; INT CA-133
Rampling, Anne
    See Rice, Anne
    See also GLL 2
Ramsay, Allan 1686(?)-1758 .... **LC 29**
    See also DLB 95; RGEL 2
Ramsay, Jay
    See Campbell, (John) Ramsey
Ramuz, Charles-Ferdinand
    1878-1947 .... **TCLC 33**
    See also CA 165; EWL 3

Robinson, Marilynne 1944- ...... **CLC 25, 180**
  See also CA 116; CANR 80; CN 7; DLB
  206
Robinson, Smokey .... **CLC 21**
  See Robinson, William, Jr.
Robinson, William, Jr. 1940-
  See Robinson, Smokey
  See also CA 116
Robison, Mary 1949- .... **CLC 42, 98**
  See also CA 113; 116; CANR 87; CN 7;
  DLB 130; INT CA-116; RGSF 2
Rochester
  See Wilmot, John
  See also RGEL 2
Rod, Edouard 1857-1910 .... **TCLC 52**
Roddenberry, Eugene Wesley 1921-1991
  See Roddenberry, Gene
  See also CA 110; 135; CANR 37; SATA 45;
  SATA-Obit 69
Roddenberry, Gene .... **CLC 17**
  See Roddenberry, Eugene Wesley
  See also AAYA 5; SATA-Obit 69
Rodgers, Mary 1931- .... **CLC 12**
  See also BYA 5; CA 49-52; CANR 8, 55,
  90; CLR 20; CWRI 5; INT CANR-8;
  JRDA; MAICYA 1, 2; SATA 8, 130
Rodgers, W(illiam) R(obert)
  1909-1969 .... **CLC 7**
  See also CA 85-88; DLB 20; RGEL 2
Rodman, Eric
  See Silverberg, Robert
Rodman, Howard 1920(?)-1985 .... **CLC 65**
  See also CA 118
Rodman, Maia
  See Wojciechowska, Maia (Teresa)
Rodo, Jose Enrique 1871(?)-1917 .... **HLCS 2**
  See also CA 178; EWL 3; HW 2; LAW
Rodolph, Utto
  See Ouologuem, Yambo
Rodriguez, Claudio 1934-1999 .... **CLC 10**
  See also CA 188; DLB 134
Rodriguez, Richard 1944- .... **CLC 155; HLC**
  2
  See also CA 110; CANR 66, 116; DAM
  MULT; DLB 82, 256; HW 1, 2; LAIT 5;
  LLW 1; NCFS 3; WLIT 1
Roelvaag, O(le) E(dvart) 1876-1931
  See Rolvaag, O(le) E(dvart)
  See also CA 117; 171
Roethke, Theodore (Huebner)
  1908-1963 .... **CLC 1, 3, 8, 11, 19, 46,**
  101; PC 15
  See also AMW; CA 81-84; CABS 2;
  CDALB 1941-1968; DA3; DAM POET;
  DLB 5, 206; EWL 3; EXPP; MTCW 1, 2;
  PAB; PFS 3; RGAL 4; WP
Rogers, Carl R(ansom)
  1902-1987 .... **TCLC 125**
  See also CA 1-4R; 121; CANR 1, 18;
  MTCW 1
Rogers, Samuel 1763-1855 .... **NCLC 69**
  See also DLB 93; RGEL 2
Rogers, Thomas Hunton 1927- .... **CLC 57**
  See also CA 89-92; INT CA-89-92
Rogers, Will(iam Penn Adair)
  1879-1935 .... **NNAL; TCLC 8, 71**
  See also CA 105; 144; DA3; DAM MULT;
  DLB 11; MTCW 2
Rogin, Gilbert 1929- .... **CLC 18**
  See also CA 65-68; CANR 15
Rohan, Koda
  See Koda Shigeyuki
Rohlfs, Anna Katharine Green
  See Green, Anna Katharine
Rohmer, Eric .... **CLC 16**
  See Scherer, Jean-Marie Maurice
Rohmer, Sax .... **TCLC 28**
  See Ward, Arthur Henry Sarsfield
  See also DLB 70; MSW; SUFW

Roiphe, Anne (Richardson) 1935- .. **CLC 3, 9**
  See also CA 89-92; CANR 45, 73; DLBY
  1980; INT CA-89-92
Rojas, Fernando de 1475-1541 ... **HLCS 1, 2;**
  LC 23
  See also DLB 286; RGWL 2, 3
Rojas, Gonzalo 1917- .... **HLCS 2**
  See also CA 178; HW 2; LAWS 1
Roland, Marie-Jeanne 1754-1793 .... **LC 98**
Rolfe, Frederick (William Serafino Austin
  Lewis Mary) 1860-1913 .... **TCLC 12**
  See Al Siddik
  See also CA 107; 210; DLB 34, 156; RGEL
  2
Rolland, Romain 1866-1944 .... **TCLC 23**
  See also CA 118; 197; DLB 65, 284; EWL
  3; GFL 1789 to the Present; RGWL 2, 3
Rolle, Richard c. 1300-c. 1349 ...... **CMLC 21**
  See also DLB 146; LMFS 1; RGEL 2
Rolvaag, O(le) E(dvart) .... **TCLC 17**
  See Roelvaag, O(le) E(dvart)
  See also DLB 9, 212; NFS 5; RGAL 4
Romain Arnaud, Saint
  See Aragon, Louis
Romains, Jules 1885-1972 .... **CLC 7**
  See also CA 85-88; CANR 34; DLB 65;
  EWL 3; GFL 1789 to the Present; MTCW
  1
Romero, Jose Ruben 1890-1952 .... **TCLC 14**
  See also CA 114; 131; EWL 3; HW 1; LAW
Ronsard, Pierre de 1524-1585 . **LC 6, 54; PC**
  11
  See also EW 2; GFL Beginnings to 1789;
  RGWL 2, 3; TWA
Rooke, Leon 1934- .... **CLC 25, 34**
  See also CA 25-28R; CANR 23, 53; CCA
  1; CPW; DAM POP
Roosevelt, Franklin Delano
  1882-1945 .... **TCLC 93**
  See also CA 116; 173; LAIT 3
Roosevelt, Theodore 1858-1919 ..... **TCLC 69**
  See also CA 115; 170; DLB 47, 186, 275
Roper, William 1498-1578 .... **LC 10**
Roquelaure, A. N.
  See Rice, Anne
Rosa, Joao Guimaraes 1908-1967 ... **CLC 23;**
  HLCS 1
  See Guimaraes Rosa, Joao
  See also CA 89-92; DLB 113; EWL 3;
  WLIT 1
Rose, Wendy 1948- . **CLC 85; NNAL; PC 13**
  See also CA 53-56; CANR 5, 51; CWP;
  DAM MULT; DLB 175; PFS 13; RGAL
  4; SATA 12
Rosen, R. D.
  See Rosen, Richard (Dean)
Rosen, Richard (Dean) 1949- .... **CLC 39**
  See also CA 77-80; CANR 62, 120; CMW
  4; INT CANR-30
Rosenberg, Isaac 1890-1918 .... **TCLC 12**
  See also BRW 6; CA 107; 188; DLB 20,
  216; EWL 3; PAB; RGEL 2
Rosenblatt, Joe .... **CLC 15**
  See Rosenblatt, Joseph
Rosenblatt, Joseph 1933-
  See Rosenblatt, Joe
  See also CA 89-92; CP 7; INT CA-89-92
Rosenfeld, Samuel
  See Tzara, Tristan
Rosenstock, Sami
  See Tzara, Tristan
Rosenstock, Samuel
  See Tzara, Tristan
Rosenthal, M(acha) L(ouis)
  1917-1996 .... **CLC 28**
  See also CA 1-4R; 152; CAAS 6; CANR 4,
  51; CP 7; DLB 5; SATA 59
Ross, Barnaby
  See Dannay, Frederic

Ross, Bernard L.
  See Follett, Ken(neth Martin)
Ross, J. H.
  See Lawrence, T(homas) E(dward)
Ross, John Hume
  See Lawrence, T(homas) E(dward)
Ross, Martin 1862-1915
  See Martin, Violet Florence
  See also DLB 135; GLL 2; RGEL 2; RGSF
  2
Ross, (James) Sinclair 1908-1996 ... **CLC 13;**
  SSC 24
  See also CA 73-76; CANR 81; CN 7; DAC;
  DAM MST; DLB 88; RGEL 2; RGSF 2;
  TCWW 2
Rossetti, Christina (Georgina)
  1830-1894 .... **NCLC 2, 50, 66; PC 7;**
  WLC
  See also AAYA 51; BRW 5; BYA 4; DA;
  DA3; DAB; DAC; DAM MST, POET;
  DLB 35, 163, 240; EXPP; LATS 1; MAI-
  CYA 1, 2; PFS 10, 14; RGEL 2; SATA
  20; TEA; WCH
Rossetti, Dante Gabriel 1828-1882 . **NCLC 4,**
  77; PC 44; WLC
  See also AAYA 51; BRW 5; CDBLB 1832-
  1890; DA; DAB; DAC; DAM MST,
  POET; DLB 35; EXPP; RGEL 2; TEA
Rossi, Cristina Peri
  See Peri Rossi, Cristina
Rossi, Jean-Baptiste 1931-2003
  See Japrisot, Sebastien
  See also CA 201; 215
Rossner, Judith (Perelman) 1935- . **CLC 6, 9,**
  29
  See also AITN 2; BEST 90:3; BPFB 3; CA
  17-20R; CANR 18, 51, 73; CN 7; DLB 6;
  INT CANR-18; MTCW 1, 2
Rostand, Edmond (Eugene Alexis)
  1868-1918 .... **DC 10; TCLC 6, 37**
  See also CA 104; 126; DA; DA3; DAB;
  DAC; DAM DRAM, MST; DFS 1; DLB
  192; LAIT 1; MTCW 1; RGWL 2, 3;
  TWA
Roth, Henry 1906-1995 ..... **CLC 2, 6, 11, 104**
  See also AMWS 9; CA 11-12; 149; CANR
  38, 63; CAP 1; CN 7; DA3; DLB 28;
  EWL 3; MTCW 1, 2; RGAL 4
Roth, (Moses) Joseph 1894-1939 ... **TCLC 33**
  See also CA 160; DLB 85; EWL 3; RGWL
  2, 3
Roth, Philip (Milton) 1933- ... **CLC 1, 2, 3, 4,**
  6, 9, 15, 22, 31, 47, 66, 86, 119; SSC
  26; WLC
  See also AMWR 2; AMWS 3; BEST 90:3;
  BPFB 3; CA 1-4R; CANR 1, 22, 36, 55,
  89; CDALB 1968-1988; CN 7; CPW 1;
  DA; DA3; DAB; DAC; DAM MST, NOV,
  POP; DLB 2, 28, 173; DLBY 1982; EWL
  3; MTCW 1, 2; RGAL 4; RGSF 2; SSFS
  12, 18; TUS
Rothenberg, Jerome 1931- .... **CLC 6, 57**
  See also CA 45-48; CANR 1, 106; CP 7;
  DLB 5, 193
Rotter, Pat ed. .... **CLC 65**
Roumain, Jacques (Jean Baptiste)
  1907-1944 .... **BLC 3; TCLC 19**
  See also BW 1; CA 117; 125; DAM MULT;
  EWL 3
Rourke, Constance Mayfield
  1885-1941 .... **TCLC 12**
  See also CA 107; 200; YABC 1
Rousseau, Jean-Baptiste 1671-1741 ...... **LC 9**
Rousseau, Jean-Jacques 1712-1778 .... **LC 14,**
  36; WLC
  See also DA; DA3; DAB; DAC; DAM
  MST; EW 4; GFL Beginnings to 1789;
  LMFS 1; RGWL 2, 3; TWA

Roussel, Raymond 1877-1933 .... **TCLC 20**
    See also CA 117; 201; EWL 3; GFL 1789
    to the Present
Rovit, Earl (Herbert) 1927- .... **CLC 7**
    See also CA 5-8R; CANR 12
Rowe, Elizabeth Singer 1674-1737 ..... **LC 44**
    See also DLB 39, 95
Rowe, Nicholas 1674-1718 .... **LC 8**
    See also DLB 84; RGEL 2
Rowlandson, Mary 1637(?)-1678 .... **LC 66**
    See also DLB 24, 200; RGAL 4
Rowley, Ames Dorrance
    See Lovecraft, H(oward) P(hillips)
Rowley, William 1585(?)-1626 .... **LC 100**
    See also DLB 58; RGEL 2
Rowling, J(oanne) K(athleen)
    1966- .... **CLC 137**
    See also AAYA 34; BYA 11, 13, 14; CA
    173; CANR 128; CLR 66, 80; MAICYA
    2; SATA 109; SUFW 2
Rowson, Susanna Haswell
    1762(?)-1824 .... **NCLC 5, 69**
    See also DLB 37, 200; RGAL 4
Roy, Arundhati 1960(?)- .... **CLC 109**
    See also CA 163; CANR 90, 126; DLBY
    1997; EWL 3; LATS 1; WWE 1
Roy, Gabrielle 1909-1983 .... **CLC 10, 14**
    See also CA 53-56; 110; CANR 5, 61; CCA
    1; DAB; DAC; DAM MST; DLB 68;
    EWL 3; MTCW 1; RGWL 2, 3; SATA 104
Royko, Mike 1932-1997 .... **CLC 109**
    See also CA 89-92; 157; CANR 26, 111;
    CPW
Rozanov, Vasilii Vasil'evich
    See Rozanov, Vassili
    See also DLB 295
Rozanov, Vasily Vasilyevich
    See Rozanov, Vassili
    See also EWL 3
Rozanov, Vassili 1856-1919 .... **TCLC 104**
    See Rozanov, Vasilii Vasil'evich; Rozanov,
    Vasily Vasilyevich
Rozewicz, Tadeusz 1921- ...... **CLC 9, 23, 139**
    See also CA 108; CANR 36, 66; CWW 2;
    DA3; DAM POET; DLB 232; EWL 3;
    MTCW 1, 2; RGWL 3
Ruark, Gibbons 1941- .... **CLC 3**
    See also CA 33-36R; CAAS 23; CANR 14,
    31, 57; DLB 120
Rubens, Bernice (Ruth) 1923- .... **CLC 19, 31**
    See also CA 25-28R; CANR 33, 65, 128;
    CN 7; DLB 14, 207; MTCW 1
Rubin, Harold
    See Robbins, Harold
Rudkin, (James) David 1936- .... **CLC 14**
    See also CA 89-92; CBD; CD 5; DLB 13
Rudnik, Raphael 1933- .... **CLC 7**
    See also CA 29-32R
Ruffian, M.
    See Hasek, Jaroslav (Matej Frantisek)
Ruiz, Jose Martinez .... **CLC 11**
    See Martinez Ruiz, Jose
Ruiz, Juan c. 1283-c. 1350 .... **CMLC 66**
Rukeyser, Muriel 1913-1980 . **CLC 6, 10, 15,
    27; PC 12**
    See also AMWS 6; CA 5-8R; 93-96; CANR
    26, 60; DA3; DAM POET; DLB 48; EWL
    3; FW; GLL 2; MTCW 1, 2; PFS 10;
    RGAL 4; SATA-Obit 22
Rule, Jane (Vance) 1931- .... **CLC 27**
    See also CA 25-28R; CAAS 18; CANR 12,
    87; CN 7; DLB 60; FW
Rulfo, Juan 1918-1986 .. **CLC 8, 80; HLC 2;
    SSC 25**
    See also CA 85-88; 118; CANR 26; CD-
    WLB 3; DAM MULT; DLB 113; EWL 3;
    HW 1, 2; LAW; MTCW 1, 2; RGSF 2;
    RGWL 2, 3; WLIT 1

Rumi, Jalal al-Din 1207-1273 ...... **CMLC 20;
    PC 45**
    See also RGWL 2, 3; WP
Runeberg, Johan 1804-1877 .... **NCLC 41**
Runyon, (Alfred) Damon
    1884(?)-1946 .... **TCLC 10**
    See also CA 107; 165; DLB 11, 86, 171;
    MTCW 2; RGAL 4
Rush, Norman 1933- .... **CLC 44**
    See also CA 121; 126; INT CA-126
Rushdie, (Ahmed) Salman 1947- .... **CLC 23,
    31, 55, 100; WLCS**
    See also BEST 89:3; BPFB 3; BRWS 4;
    CA 108; 111; CANR 33, 56, 108; CN 7;
    CPW 1; DA3; DAB; DAC; DAM MST,
    NOV, POP; DLB 194; EWL 3; FANT;
    INT CA-111; LATS 1; LMFS 2; MTCW
    1, 2; RGEL 2; RGSF 2; TEA; WLIT 4;
    WWE 1
Rushforth, Peter (Scott) 1945- .... **CLC 19**
    See also CA 101
Ruskin, John 1819-1900 .... **TCLC 63**
    See also BRW 5; BYA 5; CA 114; 129; CD-
    BLB 1832-1890; DLB 55, 163, 190;
    RGEL 2; SATA 24; TEA; WCH
Russ, Joanna 1937- .... **CLC 15**
    See also BPFB 3; CA 5-28R; CANR 11,
    31, 65; CN 7; DLB 8; FW; GLL 1;
    MTCW 1; SCFW 2; SFW 4
Russ, Richard Patrick
    See O'Brian, Patrick
Russell, George William 1867-1935
    See A.E.; Baker, Jean H.
    See also BRWS 8; CA 104; 153; CDBLB
    1890-1914; DAM POET; EWL 3; RGEL
    2
Russell, Jeffrey Burton 1934- .... **CLC 70**
    See also CA 25-28R; CANR 11, 28, 52
Russell, (Henry) Ken(neth Alfred)
    1927- .... **CLC 16**
    See also CA 105
Russell, William Martin 1947-
    See Russell, Willy
    See also CA 164; CANR 107
Russell, Willy .... **CLC 60**
    See Russell, William Martin
    See also CBD; CD 5; DLB 233
Russo, Richard 1949- .... **CLC 181**
    See also AMWS 12; CA 127; 133; CANR
    87, 114
Rutherford, Mark .... **TCLC 25**
    See White, William Hale
    See also DLB 18; RGEL 2
Ruyslinck, Ward .... **CLC 14**
    See Belser, Reimond Karel Maria de
Ryan, Cornelius (John) 1920-1974 ..... **CLC 7**
    See also CA 69-72; 53-56; CANR 38
Ryan, Michael 1946- .... **CLC 65**
    See also CA 49-52; CANR 109; DLBY
    1982
Ryan, Tim
    See Dent, Lester
Rybakov, Anatoli (Naumovich)
    1911-1998 .... **CLC 23, 53**
    See also CA 126; 135; 172; SATA 79;
    SATA-Obit 108
Ryder, Jonathan
    See Ludlum, Robert
Ryga, George 1932-1987 .... **CLC 14**
    See also CA 101; 124; CANR 43, 90; CCA
    1; DAC; DAM MST; DLB 60
S. H.
    See Hartmann, Sadakichi
S. S.
    See Sassoon, Siegfried (Lorraine)
Saba, Umberto 1883-1957 .... **TCLC 33**
    See also CA 144; CANR 79; DLB 114;
    EWL 3; RGWL 2, 3

Sabatini, Rafael 1875-1950 .... **TCLC 47**
    See also BPFB 3; CA 162; RHW
Sabato, Ernesto (R.) 1911- .... **CLC 10, 23;
    HLC 2**
    See also CA 97-100; CANR 32, 65; CD-
    WLB 3; DAM MULT; DLB 145; EWL 3;
    HW 1, 2; LAW; MTCW 1, 2
Sa-Carneiro, Mario de 1890-1916 . **TCLC 83**
    See also DLB 287; EWL 3
Sacastru, Martin
    See Bioy Casares, Adolfo
    See also CWW 2
Sacher-Masoch, Leopold von
    1836(?)-1895 .... **NCLC 31**
Sachs, Hans 1494-1576 .... **LC 95**
    See also CDWLB 2; DLB 179; RGWL 2, 3
Sachs, Marilyn (Stickle) 1927- .... **CLC 35**
    See also AAYA 2; BYA 6; CA 17-20R;
    CANR 13, 47; CLR 2; JRDA; MAICYA
    1, 2; SAAS 2; SATA 3, 68; SATA-Essay
    110; WYA; YAW
Sachs, Nelly 1891-1970 .... **CLC 14, 98**
    See also CA 17-18; 25-28R; CANR 87;
    CAP 2; EWL 3; MTCW 2; RGWL 2, 3
Sackler, Howard (Oliver)
    1929-1982 .... **CLC 14**
    See also CA 61-64; 108; CAD; CANR 30;
    DFS 15; DLB 7
Sacks, Oliver (Wolf) 1933- .... **CLC 67**
    See also CA 53-56; CANR 28, 50, 76;
    CPW; DA3; INT CANR-28; MTCW 1, 2
Sackville, Thomas 1536-1608 .... **LC 98**
    See also DAM DRAM; DLB 62, 132;
    RGEL 2
Sadakichi
    See Hartmann, Sadakichi
Sade, Donatien Alphonse Francois
    1740-1814 .... **NCLC 3, 47**
    See also EW 4; GFL Beginnings to 1789;
    RGWL 2, 3
Sade, Marquis de
    See Sade, Donatien Alphonse Francois
Sadoff, Ira 1945- .... **CLC 9**
    See also CA 53-56; CANR 5, 21, 109; DLB
    120
Saetone
    See Camus, Albert
Safire, William 1929- .... **CLC 10**
    See also CA 17-20R; CANR 31, 54, 91
Sagan, Carl (Edward) 1934-1996 .... **CLC 30,
    112**
    See also AAYA 2; CA 25-28R; 155; CANR
    11, 36, 74; CPW; DA3; MTCW 1, 2;
    SATA 58; SATA-Obit 94
Sagan, Francoise .... **CLC 3, 6, 9, 17, 36**
    See Quoirez, Francoise
    See also CWW 2; DLB 83; EWL 3; GFL
    1789 to the Present; MTCW 2
Sahgal, Nayantara (Pandit) 1927- .... **CLC 41**
    See also CA 9-12R; CANR 11, 88; CN 7
Said, Edward W. 1935-2003 .... **CLC 123**
    See also CA 21-24R; 220; CANR 45, 74,
    107; DLB 67; MTCW 2
Saint, H(arry) F. 1941- .... **CLC 50**
    See also CA 127
St. Aubin de Teran, Lisa 1953-
    See Teran, Lisa St. Aubin de
    See also CA 118; 126; CN 7; INT CA-126
Saint Birgitta of Sweden c.
    1303-1373 .... **CMLC 24**
Sainte-Beuve, Charles Augustin
    1804-1869 .... **NCLC 5**
    See also DLB 217; EW 6; GFL 1789 to the
    Present

Silverberg, Robert 1935- .... **CLC 7, 140**
See also AAYA 24; BPFB 3; BYA 7, 9; CA
1-4R, 186; CAAE 186; CAAS 3; CANR
1, 20, 36, 85; CLR 59; CN 7; CPW; DAM
POP; DLB 8; INT CANR-20; MAICYA
1, 2; MTCW 1, 2; SATA 13, 91; SATA-
Essay 104; SCFW 2; SFW 4; SUFW 2

Silverstein, Alvin 1933- .... **CLC 17**
See also CA 49-52; CANR 2; CLR 25;
JRDA; MAICYA 1, 2; SATA 8, 69, 124

Silverstein, Shel(don Allan)
1932-1999 .... **PC 49**
See also AAYA 40; BW 3; CA 107; 179;
CANR 47, 74, 81; CLR 5, 96; CWRI 5;
JRDA; MAICYA 1, 2; MTCW 2; SATA
33, 92; SATA-Brief 27; SATA-Obit 116

Silverstein, Virginia B(arbara Opshelor)
1937- .... **CLC 17**
See also CA 49-52; CANR 2; CLR 25;
JRDA; MAICYA 1, 2; SATA 8, 69, 124

Sim, Georges
See Simenon, Georges (Jacques Christian)

Simak, Clifford D(onald) 1904-1988 . **CLC 1,
55**
See also CA 1-4R; 125; CANR 1, 35; DLB
8; MTCW 1; SATA-Obit 56; SFW 4

Simenon, Georges (Jacques Christian)
1903-1989 .... **CLC 1, 2, 3, 8, 18, 47**
See also BPFB 3; CA 85-88; 129; CANR
35; CMW 4; DA3; DAM POP; DLB 72;
DLBY 1989; EW 12; EWL 3; GFL 1789
to the Present; MSW; MTCW 1, 2; RGWL
2, 3

Simic, Charles 1938- .... **CLC 6, 9, 22, 49, 68,
130**
See also AMWS 8; CA 29-32R; CAAS 4;
CANR 12, 33, 52, 61, 96; CP 7; DA3;
DAM POET; DLB 105; MTCW 2; PFS 7;
RGAL 4; WP

Simmel, Georg 1858-1918 .... **TCLC 64**
See also CA 157; DLB 296

Simmons, Charles (Paul) 1924- .... **CLC 57**
See also CA 89-92; INT CA-89-92

Simmons, Dan 1948- .... **CLC 44**
See also AAYA 16; CA 138; CANR 53, 81,
126; CPW; DAM POP; HGG; SUFW 2

Simmons, James (Stewart Alexander)
1933- .... **CLC 43**
See also CA 105; CAAS 21; CP 7; DLB 40

Simms, William Gilmore
1806-1870 .... **NCLC 3**
See also DLB 3, 30, 59, 73, 248, 254;
RGAL 4

Simon, Carly 1945- .... **CLC 26**
See also CA 105

Simon, Claude (Henri Eugene)
1913-1984 .... **CLC 4, 9, 15, 39**
See also CA 89-92; CANR 33, 117; DAM
NOV; DLB 83; EW 13; EWL 3; GFL
1789 to the Present; MTCW 1

Simon, Myles
See Follett, Ken(neth Martin)

Simon, (Marvin) Neil 1927- ... **CLC 6, 11, 31,
39, 70; DC 14**
See also AAYA 32; AITN 1; AMWS 4; CA
21-24R; CANR 26, 54, 87, 126; CD 5;
DA3; DAM DRAM; DFS 2, 6, 12, 18;
DLB 7, 266; LAIT 4; MTCW 1, 2; RGAL
4; TUS

Simon, Paul (Frederick) 1941(?)- ..... **CLC 17**
See also CA 116; 153

Simonon, Paul 1956(?)- .... **CLC 30**

Simonson, Rick ed. .... **CLC 70**

Simpson, Harriette
See Arnow, Harriette (Louisa) Simpson

Simpson, Louis (Aston Marantz)
1923- .... **CLC 4, 7, 9, 32, 149**
See also AMWS 9; CA 1-4R; CAAS 4;
CANR 1, 61; CP 7; DAM POET; DLB 5;
MTCW 1, 2; PFS 7, 11, 14; RGAL 4

Simpson, Mona (Elizabeth) 1957- ... **CLC 44,
146**
See also CA 122; 135; CANR 68, 103; CN
7; EWL 3

Simpson, N(orman) F(rederick)
1919- .... **CLC 29**
See also CA 13-16R; CBD; DLB 13; RGEL
2

Sinclair, Andrew (Annandale) 1935- . **CLC 2,
14**
See also CA 9-12R; CAAS 5; CANR 14,
38, 91; CN 7; DLB 14; FANT; MTCW 1

Sinclair, Emil
See Hesse, Hermann

Sinclair, Iain 1943- .... **CLC 76**
See also CA 132; CANR 81; CP 7; HGG

Sinclair, Iain MacGregor
See Sinclair, Iain

Sinclair, Irene
See Griffith, D(avid Lewelyn) W(ark)

Sinclair, Mary Amelia St. Clair 1865(?)-1946
See Sinclair, May
See also CA 104; HGG; RHW

Sinclair, May .... **TCLC 3, 11**
See Sinclair, Mary Amelia St. Clair
See also CA 166; DLB 36, 135; EWL 3;
RGEL 2; SUFW

Sinclair, Roy
See Griffith, D(avid Lewelyn) W(ark)

Sinclair, Upton (Beall) 1878-1968 ..... **CLC 1,
11, 15, 63; WLC**
See also AMWS 5; BPFB 3; BYA 2; CA
5-8R; 25-28R; CANR 7; CDALB 1929-
1941; DA; DA3; DAB; DAC; DAM MST,
NOV; DLB 9; EWL 3; INT CANR-7;
LAIT 3; MTCW 1, 2; NFS 6; RGAL 4;
SATA 9; TUS; YAW

Singe, (Edmund) J(ohn) M(illington)
1871-1909 .... **WLC**

Singer, Isaac
See Singer, Isaac Bashevis

Singer, Isaac Bashevis 1904-1991 .. **CLC 1, 3,
6, 9, 11, 15, 23, 38, 69, 111; SSC 3, 53;
WLC**
See also AAYA 32; AITN 1, 2; AMW;
AMWR 2; BPFB 3; BYA 1, 4; CA 1-4R;
134; CANR 1, 39, 106; CDALB 1941-
1968; CLR 1; CWRI 5; DA; DA3; DAB;
DAC; DAM MST, NOV; DLB 6, 28, 52,
278; DLBY 1991; EWL 3; EXPS; HGG;
JRDA; LAIT 3; MAICYA 1, 2; MTCW 1,
2; RGAL 4; RGSF 2; SATA 3, 27; SATA-
Obit 68; SSFS 2, 12, 16; TUS; TWA

Singer, Israel Joshua 1893-1944 ...... **TCLC 33**
See also CA 169; EWL 3

Singh, Khushwant 1915- .... **CLC 11**
See also CA 9-12R; CAAS 9; CANR 6, 84;
CN 7; EWL 3; RGEL 2

Singleton, Ann
See Benedict, Ruth (Fulton)

Singleton, John 1968(?)- .... **CLC 156**
See also AAYA 50; BW 2, 3; CA 138;
CANR 67, 82; DAM MULT

Sinjohn, John
See Galsworthy, John

Sinyavsky, Andrei (Donatevich)
1925-1997 .... **CLC 8**
See Sinyavsky, Andrey Donatovich; Tertz,
Abram
See also CA 85-88; 159

Sinyavsky, Andrey Donatovich
See Sinyavsky, Andrei (Donatevich)
See also EWL 3

Sirin, V.
See Nabokov, Vladimir (Vladimirovich)

Sissman, L(ouis) E(dward)
1928-1976 .... **CLC 9, 18**
See also CA 21-24R; 65-68; CANR 13;
DLB 5

Sisson, C(harles) H(ubert)
1914-2003 .... **CLC 8**
See also CA 1-4R; 220; CAAS 3; CANR 3,
48, 84; CP 7; DLB 27

Sitting Bull 1831(?)-1890 .... **NNAL**
See also DA3; DAM MULT

Sitwell, Dame Edith 1887-1964 ..... **CLC 2, 9,
67; PC 3**
See also BRW 7; CA 9-12R; CANR 35;
CDBLB 1945-1960; DAM POET; DLB
20; EWL 3; MTCW 1, 2; RGEL 2; TEA

Siwaarmill, H. P.
See Sharp, William

Sjoewall, Maj 1935- .... **CLC 7**
See Sjowall, Maj
See also CA 65-68; CANR 73

Sjowall, Maj
See Sjoewall, Maj
See also BPFB 3; CMW 4; MSW

Skelton, John 1460(?)-1529 ..... **LC 71; PC 25**
See also BRW 1; DLB 136; RGEL 2

Skelton, Robin 1925-1997 .... **CLC 13**
See Zuk, Georges
See also AITN 2; CA 5-8R; 160; CAAS 5;
CANR 28, 89; CCA 1; CP 7; DLB 27, 53

Skolimowski, Jerzy 1938- .... **CLC 20**
See also CA 128

Skram, Amalie (Bertha)
1847-1905 .... **TCLC 25**
See also CA 165

Skvorecky, Josef (Vaclav) 1924- ...... **CLC 15,
39, 69, 152**
See also CA 61-64; CAAS 1; CANR 10,
34, 63, 108; CDWLB 4; DA3; DAC;
DAM NOV; DLB 232; EWL 3; MTCW
1, 2

Slade, Bernard .... **CLC 11, 46**
See Newbound, Bernard Slade
See also CAAS 9; CCA 1; DLB 53

Slaughter, Carolyn 1946- .... **CLC 56**
See also CA 85-88; CANR 85; CN 7

Slaughter, Frank G(ill) 1908-2001 ... **CLC 29**
See also AITN 2; CA 5-8R; 197; CANR 5,
85; INT CANR-5; RHW

Slavitt, David R(ytman) 1935- ..... **CLC 5, 14**
See also CA 21-24R; CAAS 3; CANR 41,
83; CP 7; DLB 5, 6

Slesinger, Tess 1905-1945 .... **TCLC 10**
See also CA 107; 199; DLB 102

Slessor, Kenneth 1901-1971 .... **CLC 14**
See also CA 102; 89-92; DLB 260; RGEL
2

Slowacki, Juliusz 1809-1849 .... **NCLC 15**
See also RGWL 3

Smart, Christopher 1722-1771 . **LC 3; PC 13**
See also DAM POET; DLB 109; RGEL 2

Smart, Elizabeth 1913-1986 .... **CLC 54**
See also CA 81-84; 118; DLB 88

Smiley, Jane (Graves) 1949- ...... **CLC 53, 76,
144**
See also AMWS 6; BPFB 3; CA 104;
CANR 30, 50, 74, 96; CN 7; CPW 1;
DA3; DAM POP; DLB 227, 234; EWL 3;
INT CANR-30; SSFS 3

Smith, A(rthur) J(ames) M(arshall)
1902-1980 .... **CLC 15**
See also CA 1-4R; 102; CANR 4; DAC;
DLB 88; RGEL 2

Smith, Adam 1723(?)-1790 .... **LC 36**
See also DLB 104, 252; RGEL 2

Smith, Alexander 1829-1867 .... **NCLC 59**
See also DLB 32, 55

Smith, Anna Deavere 1950- .... **CLC 86**
See also CA 133; CANR 103; CD 5; DFS 2

Smith, Betty (Wehner) 1904-1972 .... **CLC 19**
See also BPFB 3; BYA 3; CA 5-8R; 33-
36R; DLBY 1982; LAIT 3; RGAL 4;
SATA 6

Smith, Charlotte (Turner)
1749-1806 .... **NCLC 23, 115**
See also DLB 39, 109; RGEL 2; TEA

Smith, Clark Ashton 1893-1961 .... **CLC 43**
See also CA 143; CANR 81; FANT; HGG;
MTCW 2; SCFW 2; SFW 4; SUFW

Smith, Dave .... **CLC 22, 42**
See Smith, David (Jeddie)
See also CAAS 7; DLB 5

Smith, David (Jeddie) 1942-
See Smith, Dave
See also CA 49-52; CANR 1, 59, 120; CP
7; CSW; DAM POET

Smith, Florence Margaret 1902-1971
See Smith, Stevie
See also CA 17-18; 29-32R; CANR 35;
CAP 2; DAM POET; MTCW 1, 2; TEA

Smith, Iain Crichton 1928-1998 .... **CLC 64**
See also BRWS 9; CA 21-24R; 171; CN 7;
CP 7; DLB 40, 139; RGSF 2

Smith, John 1580(?)-1631 .... **LC 9**
See also DLB 24, 30; TUS

Smith, Johnston
See Crane, Stephen (Townley)

Smith, Joseph, Jr. 1805-1844 .... **NCLC 53**

Smith, Lee 1944- .... **CLC 25, 73**
See also CA 114; 119; CANR 46, 118;
CSW; DLB 143; DLBY 1983; EWL 3;
INT CA-119; RGAL 4

Smith, Martin
See Smith, Martin Cruz

Smith, Martin Cruz 1942- .. **CLC 25; NNAL**
See also BEST 89:4; BPFB 3; CA 85-88;
CANR 6, 23, 43, 65, 119; CMW 4; CPW;
DAM MULT, POP; HGG; INT CANR-
23; MTCW 2; RGAL 4

Smith, Patti 1946- .... **CLC 12**
See also CA 93-96; CANR 63

Smith, Pauline (Urmson)
1882-1959 .... **TCLC 25**
See also DLB 225; EWL 3

Smith, Rosamond
See Oates, Joyce Carol

Smith, Sheila Kaye
See Kaye-Smith, Sheila

Smith, Stevie .... **CLC 3, 8, 25, 44; PC 12**
See Smith, Florence Margaret
See also BRWS 2; DLB 20; EWL 3; MTCW
2; PAB; PFS 3; RGEL 2

Smith, Wilbur (Addison) 1933- .... **CLC 33**
See also CA 13-16R; CANR 7, 46, 66;
CPW; MTCW 1, 2

Smith, William Jay 1918- .... **CLC 6**
See also AMWS 13; CA 5-8R; CANR 44,
106; CP 7; CSW; CWRI 5; DLB 5; MAI-
CYA 1, 2; SAAS 22; SATA 2, 68

Smith, Woodrow Wilson
See Kuttner, Henry

Smith, Zadie 1976- .... **CLC 158**
See also AAYA 50; CA 193

Smolenskin, Peretz 1842-1885 .... **NCLC 30**

Smollett, Tobias (George) 1721-1771 ... **LC 2,
46**
See also BRW 3; CDBLB 1660-1789; DLB
39, 104; RGEL 2; TEA

Snodgrass, W(illiam) D(e Witt)
1926- .... **CLC 2, 6, 10, 18, 68**
See also AMWS 6; CA 1-4R; CANR 6, 36,
65, 85; CP 7; DAM POET; DLB 5;
MTCW 1, 2; RGAL 4

Snorri Sturluson 1179-1241 .... **CMLC 56**
See also RGWL 2, 3

Snow, C(harles) P(ercy) 1905-1980 ... **CLC 1,
4, 6, 9, 13, 19**
See also BRW 7; CA 5-8R; 101; CANR 28;
CDBLB 1945-1960; DAM NOV; DLB 15,
77; DLBD 17; EWL 3; MTCW 1, 2;
RGEL 2; TEA

Snow, Frances Compton
See Adams, Henry (Brooks)

Snyder, Gary (Sherman) 1930- . **CLC 1, 2, 5,
9, 32, 120; PC 21**
See also AMWS 8; ANW; BG 3; CA 17-
20R; CANR 30, 60, 125; CP 7; DA3;
DAM POET; DLB 5, 16, 165, 212, 237,
275; EWL 3; MTCW 2; PFS 9, 19; RGAL
4; WP

Snyder, Zilpha Keatley 1927- .... **CLC 17**
See also AAYA 15; BYA 1; CA 9-12R;
CANR 38; CLR 31; JRDA; MAICYA 1,
2; SAAS 2; SATA 1, 28, 75, 110; SATA-
Essay 112; YAW

Soares, Bernardo
See Pessoa, Fernando (Antonio Nogueira)

Sobh, A.
See Shamlu, Ahmad

Sobh, Alef
See Shamlu, Ahmad

Sobol, Joshua 1939- .... **CLC 60**
See Sobol, Yehoshua
See also CA 200; CWW 2

Sobol, Yehoshua 1939-
See Sobol, Joshua
See also CWW 2

Socrates 470B.C.-399B.C. .... **CMLC 27**

Soderberg, Hjalmar 1869-1941 ...... **TCLC 39**
See also DLB 259; EWL 3; RGSF 2

Soderbergh, Steven 1963- .... **CLC 154**
See also AAYA 43

Sodergran, Edith (Irene) 1892-1923
See Soedergran, Edith (Irene)
See also CA 202; DLB 259; EW 11; EWL
3; RGWL 2, 3

Soedergran, Edith (Irene)
1892-1923 .... **TCLC 31**
See Sodergran, Edith (Irene)

Softly, Edgar
See Lovecraft, H(oward) P(hillips)

Softly, Edward
See Lovecraft, H(oward) P(hillips)

Sokolov, Alexander V(sevolodovich) 1943-
See Sokolov, Sasha
See also CA 73-76

Sokolov, Raymond 1941- .... **CLC 7**
See also CA 85-88

Sokolov, Sasha .... **CLC 59**
See Sokolov, Alexander V(sevolodovich)
See also CWW 2; DLB 285; EWL 3; RGWL
2, 3

Sokolov, Sasha .... **CLC 59**

Solo, Jay
See Ellison, Harlan (Jay)

Sologub, Fyodor .... **TCLC 9**
See Teternikov, Fyodor Kuzmich
See also EWL 3

Solomons, Ikey Esquir
See Thackeray, William Makepeace

Solomos, Dionysios 1798-1857 .... **NCLC 15**

Solwoska, Mara
See French, Marilyn

Solzhenitsyn, Aleksandr I(sayevich)
1918- .. **CLC 1, 2, 4, 7, 9, 10, 18, 26, 34,
78, 134; SSC 32; WLC**
See Solzhenitsyn, Aleksandr Isaevich
See also AAYA 49; AITN 1; BPFB 3; CA
69-72; CANR 40, 65, 116; DA; DA3;
DAB; DAC; DAM MST, NOV; EW 13;
EXPS; LAIT 4; MTCW 1, 2; NFS 6;
RGSF 2; RGWL 2, 3; SSFS 9; TWA

Solzhenitsyn, Aleksandr Isaevich
See Solzhenitsyn, Aleksandr I(sayevich)
See also EWL 3

Somers, Jane
See Lessing, Doris (May)

Somerville, Edith Oenone
1858-1949 .... **SSC 56; TCLC 51**
See also CA 196; DLB 135; RGEL 2; RGSF
2

Somerville & Ross
See Martin, Violet Florence; Somerville,
Edith Oenone

Sommer, Scott 1951- .... **CLC 25**
See also CA 106

Sondheim, Stephen (Joshua) 1930- . **CLC 30,
39, 147; DC 22**
See also AAYA 11; CA 103; CANR 47, 67,
125; DAM DRAM; LAIT 4

Sone, Monica 1919- .... **AAL**

Song, Cathy 1955- .... **AAL; PC 21**
See also CA 154; CANR 118; CWP; DLB
169; EXPP; FW; PFS 5

Sontag, Susan 1933- .... **CLC 1, 2, 10, 13, 31,
105**
See also AMWS 3; CA 17-20R; CANR 25,
51, 74, 97; CN 7; CPW; DA3; DAM POP;
DLB 2, 67; EWL 3; MAWW; MTCW 1,
2; RGAL 4; RHW; SSFS 10

Sophocles 496(?)B.C.-406(?)B.C. .... **CMLC 2,
47, 51; DC 1; WLCS**
See also AW 1; CDWLB 1; DA; DA3;
DAB; DAC; DAM DRAM, MST; DFS 1,
4, 8; DLB 176; LAIT 1; LATS 1; LMFS
1; RGWL 2, 3; TWA

Sordello 1189-1269 .... **CMLC 15**

Sorel, Georges 1847-1922 .... **TCLC 91**
See also CA 118; 188

Sorel, Julia
See Drexler, Rosalyn

Sorokin, Vladimir .... **CLC 59**
See Sorokin, Vladimir Georgievich

Sorokin, Vladimir Georgievich
See Sorokin, Vladimir
See also DLB 285

Sorrentino, Gilbert 1929- .. **CLC 3, 7, 14, 22,
40**
See also CA 77-80; CANR 14, 33, 115; CN
7; CP 7; DLB 5, 173; DLBY 1980; INT
CANR-14

Soseki
See Natsume, Soseki
See also MJW

Soto, Gary 1952- ... **CLC 32, 80; HLC 2; PC
28**
See also AAYA 10, 37; BYA 11; CA 119;
125; CANR 50, 74, 107; CLR 38; CP 7;
DAM MULT; DLB 82; EWL 3; EXPP;
HW 1, 2; INT CA-125; JRDA; LLW 1;
MAICYA 2; MAICYAS 1; MTCW 2; PFS
7; RGAL 4; SATA 80, 120; WYA; YAW

Soupault, Philippe 1897-1990 .... **CLC 68**
See also CA 116; 147; 131; EWL 3; GFL
1789 to the Present; LMFS 2

Souster, (Holmes) Raymond 1921- .... **CLC 5,
14**
See also CA 13-16R; CAAS 14; CANR 13,
29, 53; CP 7; DA3; DAC; DAM POET;
DLB 88; RGEL 2; SATA 63

Southern, Terry 1924(?)-1995 .... **CLC 7**
See also AMWS 11; BPFB 3; CA 1-4R;
150; CANR 1, 55, 107; CN 7; DLB 2;
IDFW 3, 4

Southerne, Thomas 1660-1746 .... **LC 99**
See also DLB 80; RGEL 2

Southey, Robert 1774-1843 .... **NCLC 8, 97**
See also BRW 4; DLB 93, 107, 142; RGEL
2; SATA 54

Southworth, Emma Dorothy Eliza Nevitte
1819-1899 .... **NCLC 26**
See also DLB 239

Souza, Ernest
See Scott, Evelyn

Thomas, Dylan (Marlais) 1914-1953 .... **PC 2, 52; SSC 3, 44; TCLC 1, 8, 45, 105; WLC**
See also AAYA 45; BRWS 1; CA 104; 120; CANR 65; CDBLB 1945-1960; DA; DA3; DAB; DAC; DAM DRAM, MST, POET; DLB 13, 20, 139; EWL 3; EXPP; LAIT 3; MTCW 1, 2; PAB; PFS 1, 3, 8; RGEL 2; RGSF 2; SATA 60; TEA; WLIT 4; WP

Thomas, (Philip) Edward 1878-1917 . **PC 53; TCLC 10**
See also BRW 6; BRWS 3; CA 106; 153; DAM POET; DLB 19, 98, 156, 216; EWL 3; PAB; RGEL 2

Thomas, Joyce Carol 1938- .... **CLC 35**
See also AAYA 12; BW 2, 3; CA 113; 116; CANR 48, 114; CLR 19; DLB 33; INT CA-116; JRDA; MAICYA 1, 2; MTCW 1, 2; SAAS 7; SATA 40, 78, 123, 137; SATA-Essay 137; WYA; YAW

Thomas, Lewis 1913-1993 .... **CLC 35**
See also ANW; CA 85-88; 143; CANR 38, 60; DLB 275; MTCW 1, 2

Thomas, M. Carey 1857-1935 .... **TCLC 89**
See also FW

Thomas, Paul
See Mann, (Paul) Thomas

Thomas, Piri 1928- .... **CLC 17; HLCS 2**
See also CA 73-76; HW 1; LLW 1

Thomas, R(onald) S(tuart) 1913-2000 .... **CLC 6, 13, 48**
See also CA 89-92; 189; CAAS 4; CANR 30; CDBLB 1960 to Present; CP 7; DAB; DAM POET; DLB 27; EWL 3; MTCW 1; RGEL 2

Thomas, Ross (Elmore) 1926-1995 .. **CLC 39**
See also CA 33-36R; 150; CANR 22, 63; CMW 4

Thompson, Francis (Joseph) 1859-1907 .... **TCLC 4**
See also BRW 5; CA 104; 189; CDBLB 1890-1914; DLB 19; RGEL 2; TEA

Thompson, Francis Clegg
See Mencken, H(enry) L(ouis)

Thompson, Hunter S(tockton) 1937(?)- .... **CLC 9, 17, 40, 104**
See also AAYA 45; BEST 89:1; BPFB 3; CA 17-20R; CANR 23, 46, 74, 77, 111; CPW; CSW; DA3; DAM POP; DLB 185; MTCW 1, 2; TUS

Thompson, James Myers
See Thompson, Jim (Myers)

Thompson, Jim (Myers) 1906-1977(?) .... **CLC 69**
See also BPFB 3; CA 140; CMW 4; CPW; DLB 226; MSW

Thompson, Judith .... **CLC 39**
See also CWD

Thomson, James 1700-1748 .... **LC 16, 29, 40**
See also BRWS 3; DAM POET; DLB 95; RGEL 2

Thomson, James 1834-1882 .... **NCLC 18**
See also DAM POET; DLB 35; RGEL 2

Thoreau, Henry David 1817-1862 .. **NCLC 7, 21, 61, 138; PC 30; WLC**
See also AAYA 42; AMW; ANW; BYA 3; CDALB 1640-1865; DA; DA3; DAB; DAC; DAM MST; DLB 1, 183, 223, 270, 298; LAIT 2; LMFS 1; NCFS 3; RGAL 4; TUS

Thorndike, E. L.
See Thorndike, Edward L(ee)

Thorndike, Edward L(ee) 1874-1949 .... **TCLC 107**
See also CA 121

Thornton, Hall
See Silverberg, Robert

Thorpe, Adam 1956- .... **CLC 176**
See also CA 129; CANR 92; DLB 231

Thubron, Colin (Gerald Dryden) 1939- .... **CLC 163**
See also CA 25-28R; CANR 12, 29, 59, 95; CN 7; DLB 204, 231

Thucydides c. 455B.C.-c. 395B.C. . **CMLC 17**
See also AW 1; DLB 176; RGWL 2, 3

Thumboo, Edwin Nadason 1933- .... **PC 30**
See also CA 194

Thurber, James (Grover) 1894-1961 .. **CLC 5, 11, 25, 125; SSC 1, 47**
See also AMWS 1; BPFB 3; BYA 5; CA 73-76; CANR 17, 39; CDALB 1929-1941; CWRI 5; DA; DA3; DAB; DAC; DAM DRAM, MST, NOV; DLB 4, 11, 22, 102; EWL 3; EXPS; FANT; LAIT 3; MAICYA 1, 2; MTCW 1, 2; RGAL 4; RGSF 2; SATA 13; SSFS 1, 10, 19; SUFW; TUS

Thurman, Wallace (Henry) 1902-1934 .... **BLC 3; HR 3; TCLC 6**
See also BW 1, 3; CA 104; 124; CANR 81; DAM MULT; DLB 51

Tibullus c. 54B.C.-c. 18B.C. .... **CMLC 36**
See also AW 2; DLB 211; RGWL 2, 3

Ticheburn, Cheviot
See Ainsworth, William Harrison

Tieck, (Johann) Ludwig 1773-1853 .... **NCLC 5, 46; SSC 31**
See also CDWLB 2; DLB 90; EW 5; IDTP; RGSF 2; RGWL 2, 3; SUFW

Tiger, Derry
See Ellison, Harlan (Jay)

Tilghman, Christopher 1946- .... **CLC 65**
See also CA 159; CSW; DLB 244

Tillich, Paul (Johannes) 1886-1965 .... **CLC 131**
See also CA 5-8R; 25-28R; CANR 33; MTCW 1, 2

Tillinghast, Richard (Williford) 1940- .... **CLC 29**
See also CA 29-32R; CAAS 23; CANR 26, 51, 96; CP 7; CSW

Timrod, Henry 1828-1867 .... **NCLC 25**
See also DLB 3, 248; RGAL 4

Tindall, Gillian (Elizabeth) 1938- ...... **CLC 7**
See also CA 21-24R; CANR 11, 65, 107; CN 7

Tiptree, James, Jr. .... **CLC 48, 50**
See Sheldon, Alice Hastings Bradley
See also DLB 8; SCFW 2; SFW 4

Tirone Smith, Mary-Ann 1944- .... **CLC 39**
See also CA 118; 136; CANR 113; SATA 143

Tirso de Molina 1580(?)-1648 .... **DC 13; HLCS 2; LC 73**
See also RGWL 2, 3

Titmarsh, Michael Angelo
See Thackeray, William Makepeace

Tocqueville, Alexis (Charles Henri Maurice Clerel Comte) de 1805-1859 .. **NCLC 7, 63**
See also EW 6; GFL 1789 to the Present; TWA

Toer, Pramoedya Ananta 1925- ...... **CLC 186**
See also CA 197; RGWL 3

Toffler, Alvin 1928- .... **CLC 168**
See also CA 13-16R; CANR 15, 46, 67; CPW; DAM POP; MTCW 1, 2

Toibin, Colm
See Toibin, Colm
See also DLB 271

Toibin, Colm 1955- .... **CLC 162**
See Toibin, Colm
See also CA 142; CANR 81

Tolkien, J(ohn) R(onald) R(euel) 1892-1973 .... **CLC 1, 2, 3, 8, 12, 38; TCLC 137; WLC**
See also AAYA 10; AITN 1; BPFB 3; BRWC 2; BRWS 2; CA 17-18; 45-48; CANR 36; CAP 2; CDBLB 1914-1945; CLR 56; CPW 1; CWRI 5; DA; DA3; DAB; DAC; DAM MST, NOV, POP; DLB 15, 160, 255; EFS 2; EWL 3; FANT; JRDA; LAIT 1; LATS 1; LMFS 1; MAICYA 1, 2; MTCW 1, 2; NFS 8; RGEL 2; SATA 2, 32, 100; SATA-Obit 24; SFW 4; SUFW; TEA; WCH; WYA; YAW

Toller, Ernst 1893-1939 .... **TCLC 10**
See also CA 107; 186; DLB 124; EWL 3; RGWL 2, 3

Tolson, M. B.
See Tolson, Melvin B(eaunorus)

Tolson, Melvin B(eaunorus) 1898(?)-1966 .... **BLC 3; CLC 36, 105**
See also AFAW 1, 2; BW 1, 3; CA 124; 89-92; CANR 80; DAM MULT, POET; DLB 48, 76; RGAL 4

Tolstoi, Aleksei Nikolaevich
See Tolstoy, Alexey Nikolaevich

Tolstoi, Lev
See Tolstoy, Leo (Nikolaevich)
See also RGSF 2; RGWL 2, 3

Tolstoy, Aleksei Nikolaevich
See Tolstoy, Alexey Nikolaevich
See also DLB 272

Tolstoy, Alexey Nikolaevich 1882-1945 .... **TCLC 18**
See Tolstoy, Aleksei Nikolaevich
See also CA 107; 158; EWL 3; SFW 4

Tolstoy, Leo (Nikolaevich) 1828-1910 . **SSC 9, 30, 45, 54; TCLC 4, 11, 17, 28, 44, 79; WLC**
See Tolstoi, Lev
See also CA 104; 123; DA; DA3; DAB; DAC; DAM MST, NOV; DLB 238; EFS 2; EW 7; EXPS; IDTP; LAIT 2; LATS 1; LMFS 1; NFS 10; SATA 26; SSFS 5; TWA

Tolstoy, Count Leo
See Tolstoy, Leo (Nikolaevich)

Tomalin, Claire 1933- .... **CLC 166**
See also CA 89-92; CANR 52, 88; DLB 155

Tomasi di Lampedusa, Giuseppe 1896-1957
See Lampedusa, Giuseppe (Tomasi) di
See also CA 111; DLB 177; EWL 3

Tomlin, Lily .... **CLC 17**
See Tomlin, Mary Jean

Tomlin, Mary Jean 1939(?)-
See Tomlin, Lily
See also CA 117

Tomline, F. Latour
See Gilbert, W(illiam) S(chwenck)

Tomlinson, (Alfred) Charles 1927- .... **CLC 2, 4, 6, 13, 45; PC 17**
See also CA 5-8R; CANR 33; CP 7; DAM POET; DLB 40

Tomlinson, H(enry) M(ajor) 1873-1958 .... **TCLC 71**
See also CA 118; 161; DLB 36, 100, 195

Tonna, Charlotte Elizabeth 1790-1846 .... **NCLC 135**
See also DLB 163

Tonson, Jacob fl. 1655(?)-1736 .... **LC 86**
See also DLB 170

Toole, John Kennedy 1937-1969 ..... **CLC 19, 64**
See also BPFB 3; CA 104; DLBY 1981; MTCW 2

Toomer, Eugene
See Toomer, Jean

Toomer, Eugene Pinchback
See Toomer, Jean

Toomer, Jean 1894-1967 .. **BLC 3; CLC 1, 4, 13, 22; HR 3; PC 7; SSC 1, 45; WLCS**
See also AFAW 1, 2; AMWS 3, 9; BW 1; CA 85-88; CDALB 1917-1929; DA3; DAM MULT; DLB 45, 51; EWL 3; EXPP; EXPS; LMFS 1, 2; MTCW 1, 2; NFS 11; RGAL 4; RGSF 2; SSFS 5

Toomer, Nathan Jean
See Toomer, Jean

Toomer, Nathan Pinchback
See Toomer, Jean

Torley, Luke
See Blish, James (Benjamin)

Tornimparte, Alessandra
See Ginzburg, Natalia

Torre, Raoul della
See Mencken, H(enry) L(ouis)

Torrence, Ridgely 1874-1950 .... **TCLC 97**
See also DLB 54, 249

Torrey, E(dwin) Fuller 1937- .... **CLC 34**
See also CA 119; CANR 71

Torsvan, Ben Traven
See Traven, B.

Torsvan, Benno Traven
See Traven, B.

Torsvan, Berick Traven
See Traven, B.

Torsvan, Berwick Traven
See Traven, B.

Torsvan, Bruno Traven
See Traven, B.

Torsvan, Traven
See Traven, B.

Tourneur, Cyril 1575(?)-1626 .... **LC 66**
See also BRW 2; DAM DRAM; DLB 58; RGEL 2

Tournier, Michel (Edouard) 1924- .... **CLC 6, 23, 36, 95**
See also CA 49-52; CANR 3, 36, 74; DLB 83; EWL 3; GFL 1789 to the Present; MTCW 1, 2; SATA 23

Tournimparte, Alessandra
See Ginzburg, Natalia

Towers, Ivar
See Kornbluth, C(yril) M.

Towne, Robert (Burton) 1936(?)- ..... **CLC 87**
See also CA 108; DLB 44; IDFW 3, 4

Townsend, Sue .... **CLC 61**
See Townsend, Susan Lilian
See also AAYA 28; CA 119; 127; CANR 65, 107; CBD; CD 5; CPW; CWD; DAB; DAC; DAM MST; DLB 271; INT CA-127; SATA 55, 93; SATA-Brief 48; YAW

Townsend, Susan Lilian 1946-
See Townsend, Sue

Townshend, Pete
See Townshend, Peter (Dennis Blandford)

Townshend, Peter (Dennis Blandford) 1945- .... **CLC 17, 42**
See also CA 107

Tozzi, Federigo 1883-1920 .... **TCLC 31**
See also CA 160; CANR 110; DLB 264; EWL 3

Tracy, Don(ald Fiske) 1905-1970(?)
See Queen, Ellery
See also CA 1-4R; 176; CANR 2

Trafford, F. G.
See Riddell, Charlotte

Traherne, Thomas 1637(?)-1674 .... **LC 99**
See also BRW 2; DLB 131; PAB; RGEL 2

Traill, Catharine Parr 1802-1899 .. **NCLC 31**
See also DLB 99

Trakl, Georg 1887-1914 .... **PC 20; TCLC 5**
See also CA 104; 165; EW 10; EWL 3; LMFS 2; MTCW 2; RGWL 2, 3

Tranquilli, Secondino
See Silone, Ignazio

Transtroemer, Tomas Gosta
See Transtromer, Tomas (Goesta)

Transtromer, Tomas
See Transtromer, Tomas (Goesta)

Transtromer, Tomas (Goesta) 1931- .... **CLC 52, 65**
See also CA 117; 129; CAAS 17; CANR 115; DAM POET; DLB 257; EWL 3

Transtromer, Tomas Gosta
See Transtromer, Tomas (Goesta)

Traven, B. 1882(?)-1969 .... **CLC 8, 11**
See also CA 19-20; 25-28R; CAP 2; DLB 9, 56; EWL 3; MTCW 1; RGAL 4

Trediakovsky, Vasilii Kirillovich 1703-1769 .... **LC 68**
See also DLB 150

Treitel, Jonathan 1959- .... **CLC 70**
See also CA 210; DLB 267

Trelawny, Edward John 1792-1881 .... **NCLC 85**
See also DLB 110, 116, 144

Tremain, Rose 1943- .... **CLC 42**
See also CA 97-100; CANR 44, 95; CN 7; DLB 14, 271; RGSF 2; RHW

Tremblay, Michel 1942- .... **CLC 29, 102**
See also CA 116; 128; CCA 1; CWW 2; DAC; DAM MST; DLB 60; EWL 3; GLL 1; MTCW 1, 2

Trevanian .... **CLC 29**
See Whitaker, Rod(ney)

Trevor, Glen
See Hilton, James

Trevor, William .. **CLC 7, 9, 14, 25, 71, 116; SSC 21, 58**
See Cox, William Trevor
See also BRWS 4; CBD; CD 5; CN 7; DLB 14, 139; EWL 3; LATS 1; MTCW 2; RGEL 2; RGSF 2; SSFS 10

Trifonov, Iurii (Valentinovich)
See Trifonov, Yuri (Valentinovich)
See also RGWL 2, 3

Trifonov, Yuri (Valentinovich) 1925-1981 .... **CLC 45**
See Trifonov, Iurii (Valentinovich); Trifonov, Yury Valentinovich
See also CA 126; 103; MTCW 1

Trifonov, Yury Valentinovich
See Trifonov, Yuri (Valentinovich)
See also EWL 3

Trilling, Diana (Rubin) 1905-1996 . **CLC 129**
See also CA 5-8R; 154; CANR 10, 46; INT CANR-10; MTCW 1, 2

Trilling, Lionel 1905-1975 .... **CLC 9, 11, 24**
See also AMWS 3; CA 9-12R; 61-64; CANR 10, 105; DLB 28, 63; EWL 3; INT CANR-10; MTCW 1, 2; RGAL 4; TUS

Trimball, W. H.
See Mencken, H(enry) L(ouis)

Tristan
See Gomez de la Serna, Ramon

Tristram
See Housman, A(lfred) E(dward)

Trogdon, William (Lewis) 1939-
See Heat-Moon, William Least
See also CA 115; 119; CANR 47, 89; CPW; INT CA-119

Trollope, Anthony 1815-1882 .... **NCLC 6, 33, 101; SSC 28; WLC**
See also BRW 5; CDBLB 1832-1890; DA; DA3; DAB; DAC; DAM MST, NOV; DLB 21, 57, 159; RGEL 2; RGSF 2; SATA 22

Trollope, Frances 1779-1863 .... **NCLC 30**
See also DLB 21, 166

Trollope, Joanna 1943- .... **CLC 186**
See also CA 101; CANR 58, 95; CPW; DLB 207; RHW

Trotsky, Leon 1879-1940 .... **TCLC 22**
See also CA 118; 167

Trotter (Cockburn), Catharine 1679-1749 .... **LC 8**
See also DLB 84, 252

Trotter, Wilfred 1872-1939 .... **TCLC 97**

Trout, Kilgore
See Farmer, Philip Jose

Trow, George W. S. 1943- .... **CLC 52**
See also CA 126; CANR 91

Troyat, Henri 1911- .... **CLC 23**
See also CA 45-48; CANR 2, 33, 67, 117; GFL 1789 to the Present; MTCW 1

Trudeau, G(arretson) B(eekman) 1948-
See Trudeau, Garry B.
See also CA 81-84; CANR 31; SATA 35

Trudeau, Garry B. .... **CLC 12**
See Trudeau, G(arretson) B(eekman)
See also AAYA 10; AITN 2

Truffaut, Francois 1932-1984 ... **CLC 20, 101**
See also CA 81-84; 113; CANR 34

Trumbo, Dalton 1905-1976 .... **CLC 19**
See also CA 21-24R; 69-72; CANR 10; DLB 26; IDFW 3, 4; YAW

Trumbull, John 1750-1831 .... **NCLC 30**
See also DLB 31; RGAL 4

Trundlett, Helen B.
See Eliot, T(homas) S(tearns)

Truth, Sojourner 1797(?)-1883 ...... **NCLC 94**
See also DLB 239; FW; LAIT 2

Tryon, Thomas 1926-1991 .... **CLC 3, 11**
See also AITN 1; BPFB 3; CA 29-32R; 135; CANR 32, 77; CPW; DA3; DAM POP; HGG; MTCW 1

Tryon, Tom
See Tryon, Thomas

Ts'ao Hsueh-ch'in 1715(?)-1763 .... **LC 1**

Tsushima, Shuji 1909-1948
See Dazai Osamu
See also CA 107

Tsvetaeva (Efron), Marina (Ivanovna) 1892-1941 .... **PC 14; TCLC 7, 35**
See also CA 104; 128; CANR 73; DLB 295; EW 11; MTCW 1, 2; RGWL 2, 3

Tuck, Lily 1938- .... **CLC 70**
See also CA 139; CANR 90

Tu Fu 712-770 .... **PC 9**
See Du Fu
See also DAM MULT; TWA; WP

Tunis, John R(oberts) 1889-1975 ..... **CLC 12**
See also BYA 1; CA 61-64; CANR 62; DLB 22, 171; JRDA; MAICYA 1, 2; SATA 37; SATA-Brief 30; YAW

Tuohy, Frank .... **CLC 37**
See Tuohy, John Francis
See also DLB 14, 139

Tuohy, John Francis 1925-
See Tuohy, Frank
See also CA 5-8R; 178; CANR 3, 47; CN 7

Turco, Lewis (Putnam) 1934- ..... **CLC 11, 63**
See also CA 13-16R; CAAS 22; CANR 24, 51; CP 7; DLBY 1984

Turgenev, Ivan (Sergeevich) 1818-1883 ..... **DC 7; NCLC 21, 37, 122; SSC 7, 57; WLC**
See also DA; DAB; DAC; DAM MST, NOV; DFS 6; DLB 238, 284; EW 6; LATS 1; NFS 16; RGSF 2; RGWL 2, 3; TWA

Turgot, Anne-Robert-Jacques 1727-1781 .... **LC 26**

Turner, Frederick 1943- .... **CLC 48**
See also CA 73-76; CAAS 10; CANR 12, 30, 56; DLB 40, 282

Turton, James
See Crace, Jim

Tutu, Desmond M(pilo) 1931- .. **BLC 3; CLC 80**
See also BW 1, 3; CA 125; CANR 67, 81; DAM MULT

van Itallie, Jean-Claude 1936- .... **CLC 3**
See also CA 45-48; CAAS 2; CAD; CANR 1, 48; CD 5; DLB 7
Van Loot, Cornelius Obenchain
See Roberts, Kenneth (Lewis)
van Ostaijen, Paul 1896-1928 .... **TCLC 33**
See also CA 163
Van Peebles, Melvin 1932- .... **CLC 2, 20**
See also BW 2, 3; CA 85-88; CANR 27, 67, 82; DAM MULT
van Schendel, Arthur(-Francois-Emile)
1874-1946 .... **TCLC 56**
See also EWL 3
Vansittart, Peter 1920- .... **CLC 42**
See also CA 1-4R; CANR 3, 49, 90; CN 7; RHW
Van Vechten, Carl 1880-1964 ... **CLC 33; HR 3**
See also AMWS 2; CA 183; 89-92; DLB 4, 9, 51; RGAL 4
van Vogt, A(lfred) E(lton) 1912-2000 . **CLC 1**
See also BPFB 3; BYA 13, 14; CA 21-24R; 190; CANR 28; DLB 8, 251; SATA 14; SATA-Obit 124; SCFW; SFW 4
Vara, Madeleine
See Jackson, Laura (Riding)
Varda, Agnes 1928- .... **CLC 16**
See also CA 116; 122
Vargas Llosa, (Jorge) Mario (Pedro)
1939- .... **CLC 3, 6, 9, 10, 15, 31, 42, 85, 181; HLC 2**
See Llosa, (Jorge) Mario (Pedro) Vargas
See also BPFB 3; CA 73-76; CANR 18, 32, 42, 67, 116; CDWLB 3; DA; DA3; DAB; DAC; DAM MST, MULT, NOV; DLB 145; DNFS 2; EWL 3; HW 1, 2; LAIT 5; LATS 1; LAW; LAWS 1; MTCW 1, 2; RGWL 2; SSFS 14; TWA; WLIT 1
Varnhagen von Ense, Rahel
1771-1833 .... **NCLC 130**
See also DLB 90
Vasiliu, George
See Bacovia, George
Vasiliu, Gheorghe
See Bacovia, George
See also CA 123; 189
Vassa, Gustavus
See Equiano, Olaudah
Vassilikos, Vassilis 1933- .... **CLC 4, 8**
See also CA 81-84; CANR 75; EWL 3
Vaughan, Henry 1621-1695 .... **LC 27**
See also BRW 2; DLB 131; PAB; RGEL 2
Vaughn, Stephanie .... **CLC 62**
Vazov, Ivan (Minchov) 1850-1921 . **TCLC 25**
See also CA 121; 167; CDWLB 4; DLB 147
Veblen, Thorstein B(unde)
1857-1929 .... **TCLC 31**
See also AMWS 1; CA 115; 165; DLB 246
Vega, Lope de 1562-1635 .... **HLCS 2; LC 23**
See also EW 2; RGWL 2, 3
Vendler, Helen (Hennessy) 1933- ... **CLC 138**
See also CA 41-44R; CANR 25, 72; MTCW 1, 2
Venison, Alfred
See Pound, Ezra (Weston Loomis)
Ventsel, Elena Sergeevna 1907-
See Grekova, I.
See also CA 154
Verdi, Marie de
See Mencken, H(enry) L(ouis)
Verdu, Matilde
See Cela, Camilo Jose
Verga, Giovanni (Carmelo)
1840-1922 .... **SSC 21; TCLC 3**
See also CA 104; 123; CANR 101; EW 7; EWL 3; RGSF 2; RGWL 2, 3

Vergil 70B.C.-19B.C. ... **CMLC 9, 40; PC 12; WLCS**
See Virgil
See also AW 2; DA; DA3; DAB; DAC; DAM MST, POET; EFS 1; LMFS 1
Verhaeren, Emile (Adolphe Gustave)
1855-1916 .... **TCLC 12**
See also CA 109; EWL 3; GFL 1789 to the Present
Verlaine, Paul (Marie) 1844-1896 .. **NCLC 2, 51; PC 2, 32**
See also DAM POET; DLB 217; EW 7; GFL 1789 to the Present; LMFS 2; RGWL 2, 3; TWA
Verne, Jules (Gabriel) 1828-1905 ... **TCLC 6, 52**
See also AAYA 16; BYA 4; CA 110; 131; CLR 88; DA3; DLB 123; GFL 1789 to the Present; JRDA; LAIT 2; LMFS 2; MAICYA 1, 2; RGWL 2, 3; SATA 21; SCFW; SFW 4; TWA; WCH
Verus, Marcus Annius
See Aurelius, Marcus
Very, Jones 1813-1880 .... **NCLC 9**
See also DLB 1, 243; RGAL 4
Vesaas, Tarjei 1897-1970 .... **CLC 48**
See also CA 190; 29-32R; DLB 297; EW 11; EWL 3; RGWL 3
Vialis, Gaston
See Simenon, Georges (Jacques Christian)
Vian, Boris 1920-1959(?) .... **TCLC 9**
See also CA 106; 164; CANR 111; DLB 72; EWL 3; GFL 1789 to the Present; MTCW 2; RGWL 2, 3
Viaud, (Louis Marie) Julien 1850-1923
See Loti, Pierre
See also CA 107
Vicar, Henry
See Felsen, Henry Gregor
Vicente, Gil 1465-c. 1536 .... **LC 99**
See also DLB 287; RGWL 2, 3
Vicker, Angus
See Felsen, Henry Gregor
Vidal, Gore 1925- ...... **CLC 2, 4, 6, 8, 10, 22, 33, 72, 142**
See Box, Edgar
See also AITN 1; AMWS 4; BEST 90:2; BPFB 3; CA 5-8R; CAD; CANR 13, 45, 65, 100; CD 5; CDALBS; CN 7; CPW; DA3; DAM NOV, POP; DFS 2; DLB 6, 152; EWL 3; INT CANR-13; MTCW 1, 2; RGAL 4; RHW; TUS
Viereck, Peter (Robert Edwin)
1916- .... **CLC 4; PC 27**
See also CA 1-4R; CANR 1, 47; CP 7; DLB 5; PFS 9, 14
Vigny, Alfred (Victor) de
1797-1863 .... **NCLC 7, 102; PC 26**
See also DAM POET; DLB 119, 192, 217; EW 5; GFL 1789 to the Present; RGWL 2, 3
Vilakazi, Benedict Wallet
1906-1947 .... **TCLC 37**
See also CA 168
Villa, Jose Garcia 1914-1997 .... **AAL; PC 22**
See also CA 25-28R; CANR 12, 118; EWL 3; EXPP
Villa, Jose Garcia 1914-1997
See Villa, Jose Garcia
Villarreal, Jose Antonio 1924- .... **HLC 2**
See also CA 133; CANR 93; DAM MULT; DLB 82; HW 1; LAIT 4; RGAL 4
Villaurrutia, Xavier 1903-1950 ...... **TCLC 80**
See also CA 192; EWL 3; HW 1; LAW
Villaverde, Cirilo 1812-1894 .... **NCLC 121**
See also LAW

Villehardouin, Geoffroi de
1150(?)-1218(?) .... **CMLC 38**
Villiers de l'Isle Adam, Jean Marie Mathias Philippe Auguste 1838-1889 ... **NCLC 3; SSC 14**
See also DLB 123, 192; GFL 1789 to the Present; RGSF 2
Villon, Francois 1431-1463(?) . **LC 62; PC 13**
See also DLB 208; EW 2; RGWL 2, 3; TWA
Vine, Barbara .... **CLC 50**
See Rendell, Ruth (Barbara)
See also BEST 90:4
Vinge, Joan (Carol) D(ennison)
1948- .... **CLC 30; SSC 24**
See also AAYA 32; BPFB 3; CA 93-96; CANR 72; SATA 36, 113; SFW 4; YAW
Viola, Herman J(oseph) 1938- .... **CLC 70**
See also CA 61-64; CANR 8, 23, 48, 91; SATA 126
Violis, G.
See Simenon, Georges (Jacques Christian)
Viramontes, Helena Maria 1954- .... **HLCS 2**
See also CA 159; DLB 122; HW 2; LLW 1
Virgil
See Vergil
See also CDWLB 1; DLB 211; LAIT 1; RGWL 2, 3; WP
Visconti, Luchino 1906-1976 .... **CLC 16**
See also CA 81-84; 65-68; CANR 39
Vitry, Jacques de
See Jacques de Vitry
Vittorini, Elio 1908-1966 .... **CLC 6, 9, 14**
See also CA 133; 25-28R; DLB 264; EW 12; EWL 3; RGWL 2, 3
Vivekananda, Swami 1863-1902 .... **TCLC 88**
Vizenor, Gerald Robert 1934- .... **CLC 103; NNAL**
See also CA 13-16R, 205; CAAE 205; CAAS 22; CANR 5, 21, 44, 67; DAM MULT; DLB 175, 227; MTCW 2; TCWW 2
Vizinczey, Stephen 1933- .... **CLC 40**
See also CA 128; CCA 1; INT CA-128
Vliet, R(ussell) G(ordon)
1929-1984 .... **CLC 22**
See also CA 37-40R; 112; CANR 18
Vogau, Boris Andreyevich 1894-1938
See Pilnyak, Boris
See also CA 123; 218
Vogel, Paula A(nne) 1951- ... **CLC 76; DC 19**
See also CA 108; CAD; CANR 119; CD 5; CWD; DFS 14; RGAL 4
Voigt, Cynthia 1942- .... **CLC 30**
See also AAYA 3, 30; BYA 1, 3, 6, 7, 8; CA 106; CANR 18, 37, 40, 94; CLR 13, 48; INT CANR-18; JRDA; LAIT 5; MAICYA 1, 2; MAICYAS 1; SATA 48, 79, 116; SATA-Brief 33; WYA; YAW
Voigt, Ellen Bryant 1943- .... **CLC 54**
See also CA 69-72; CANR 11, 29, 55, 115; CP 7; CSW; CWP; DLB 120
Voinovich, Vladimir (Nikolaevich)
1932- .... **CLC 10, 49, 147**
See also CA 81-84; CAAS 12; CANR 33, 67; MTCW 1
Vollmann, William T. 1959- .... **CLC 89**
See also CA 134; CANR 67, 116; CPW; DA3; DAM NOV, POP; MTCW 2
Voloshinov, V. N.
See Bakhtin, Mikhail Mikhailovich
Voltaire 1694-1778 .... **LC 14, 79; SSC 12; WLC**
See also BYA 13; DA; DA3; DAB; DAC; DAM DRAM, MST; EW 4; GFL Beginnings to 1789; LATS 1; LMFS 1; NFS 7; RGWL 2, 3; TWA
von Aschendrof, Baron Ignatz
See Ford, Ford Madox

Ward, Douglas Turner 1930- .... **CLC 19**
See also BW 1; CA 81-84; CAD; CANR 27; CD 5; DLB 7, 38

Ward, E. D.
See Lucas, E(dward) V(errall)

Ward, Mrs. Humphry 1851-1920
See Ward, Mary Augusta
See also RGEL 2

Ward, Mary Augusta 1851-1920 ... **TCLC 55**
See Ward, Mrs. Humphry
See also DLB 18

Ward, Peter
See Faust, Frederick (Schiller)

Warhol, Andy 1928(?)-1987 .... **CLC 20**
See also AAYA 12; BEST 89:4; CA 89-92; 121; CANR 34

Warner, Francis (Robert le Plastrier)
1937- .... **CLC 14**
See also CA 53-56; CANR 11

Warner, Marina 1946- .... **CLC 59**
See also CA 65-68; CANR 21, 55, 118; CN 7; DLB 194

Warner, Rex (Ernest) 1905-1986 ...... **CLC 45**
See also CA 89-92; 119; DLB 15; RGEL 2; RHW

Warner, Susan (Bogert)
1819-1885 .... **NCLC 31**
See also DLB 3, 42, 239, 250, 254

Warner, Sylvia (Constance) Ashton
See Ashton-Warner, Sylvia (Constance)

Warner, Sylvia Townsend
1893-1978 .. **CLC 7, 19; SSC 23; TCLC 131**
See also BRWS 7; CA 61-64; 77-80; CANR 16, 60, 104; DLB 34, 139; EWL 3; FANT; FW; MTCW 1, 2; RGEL 2; RGSF 2; RHW

Warren, Mercy Otis 1728-1814 ..... **NCLC 13**
See also DLB 31, 200; RGAL 4; TUS

Warren, Robert Penn 1905-1989 .. **CLC 1, 4, 6, 8, 10, 13, 18, 39, 53, 59; PC 37; SSC 4, 58; WLC**
See also AITN 1; AMW; AMWC 2; BPFB 3; BYA 1; CA 13-16R; 129; CANR 10, 47; CDALB 1968-1988; DA; DA3; DAB; DAC; DAM MST, NOV, POET; DLB 2, 48, 152; DLBY 1980, 1989; EWL 3; INT CANR-10; MTCW 1, 2; NFS 13; RGAL 4; RGSF 2; RHW; SATA 46; SATA-Obit 63; SSFS 8; TUS

Warrigal, Jack
See Furphy, Joseph

Warshofsky, Isaac
See Singer, Isaac Bashevis

Warton, Joseph 1722-1800 .... **NCLC 118**
See also DLB 104, 109; RGEL 2

Warton, Thomas 1728-1790 .... **LC 15, 82**
See also DAM POET; DLB 104, 109; RGEL 2

Waruk, Kona
See Harris, (Theodore) Wilson

Warung, Price .... **TCLC 45**
See Astley, William
See also DLB 230; RGEL 2

Warwick, Jarvis
See Garner, Hugh
See also CCA 1

Washington, Alex
See Harris, Mark

Washington, Booker T(aliaferro)
1856-1915 .... **BLC 3; TCLC 10**
See also BW 1; CA 114; 125; DA3; DAM MULT; LAIT 2; RGAL 4; SATA 28

Washington, George 1732-1799 .... **LC 25**
See also DLB 31

Wassermann, (Karl) Jakob
1873-1934 .... **TCLC 6**
See also CA 104; 163; DLB 66; EWL 3

Wasserstein, Wendy 1950- ... **CLC 32, 59, 90, 183; DC 4**
See also CA 121; 129; CABS 3; CAD; CANR 53, 75, 128; CD 5; CWD; DA3; DAM DRAM; DFS 5, 17; DLB 228; EWL 3; FW; INT CA-129; MTCW 2; SATA 94

Waterhouse, Keith (Spencer) 1929- . **CLC 47**
See also CA 5-8R; CANR 38, 67, 109; CBD; CN 7; DLB 13, 15; MTCW 1, 2

Waters, Frank (Joseph) 1902-1995 .. **CLC 88**
See also CA 5-8R; 149; CAAS 13; CANR 3, 18, 63, 121; DLB 212; DLBY 1986; RGAL 4; TCWW 2

Waters, Mary C. .... **CLC 70**

Waters, Roger 1944- .... **CLC 35**

Watkins, Frances Ellen
See Harper, Frances Ellen Watkins

Watkins, Gerrold
See Malzberg, Barry N(athaniel)

Watkins, Gloria Jean 1952(?)- .... **CLC 94**
See also BW 2; CA 143; CANR 87, 126; DLB 246; MTCW 2; SATA 115

Watkins, Paul 1964- .... **CLC 55**
See also CA 132; CANR 62, 98

Watkins, Vernon Phillips
1906-1967 .... **CLC 43**
See also CA 9-10; 25-28R; CAP 1; DLB 20; EWL 3; RGEL 2

Watson, Irving S.
See Mencken, H(enry) L(ouis)

Watson, John H.
See Farmer, Philip Jose

Watson, Richard F.
See Silverberg, Robert

Watts, Ephraim
See Horne, Richard Henry Hengist

Watts, Isaac 1674-1748 .... **LC 98**
See also DLB 95; RGEL 2; SATA 52

Waugh, Auberon (Alexander)
1939-2001 .... **CLC 7**
See also CA 45-48; 192; CANR 6, 22, 92; DLB 14, 194

Waugh, Evelyn (Arthur St. John)
1903-1966 .. **CLC 1, 3, 8, 13, 19, 27, 44, 107; SSC 41; WLC**
See also BPFB 3; BRW 7; CA 85-88; 25-28R; CANR 22; CDBLB 1914-1945; DA; DA3; DAB; DAC; DAM MST, NOV, POP; DLB 15, 162, 195; EWL 3; MTCW 1, 2; NFS 13, 17; RGEL 2; RGSF 2; TEA; WLIT 4

Waugh, Harriet 1944- .... **CLC 6**
See also CA 85-88; CANR 22

Ways, C. R.
See Blount, Roy (Alton), Jr.

Waystaff, Simon
See Swift, Jonathan

Webb, Beatrice (Martha Potter)
1858-1943 .... **TCLC 22**
See also CA 117; 162; DLB 190; FW

Webb, Charles (Richard) 1939- .... **CLC 7**
See also CA 25-28R; CANR 114

Webb, James H(enry), Jr. 1946- ...... **CLC 22**
See also CA 81-84

Webb, Mary Gladys (Meredith)
1881-1927 .... **TCLC 24**
See also CA 182; 123; DLB 34; FW

Webb, Mrs. Sidney
See Webb, Beatrice (Martha Potter)

Webb, Phyllis 1927- .... **CLC 18**
See also CA 104; CANR 23; CCA 1; CP 7; CWP; DLB 53

Webb, Sidney (James) 1859-1947 .. **TCLC 22**
See also CA 117; 163; DLB 190

Webber, Andrew Lloyd .... **CLC 21**
See Lloyd Webber, Andrew
See also DFS 7

Weber, Lenora Mattingly
1895-1971 .... **CLC 12**
See also CA 19-20; 29-32R; CAP 1; SATA 2; SATA-Obit 26

Weber, Max 1864-1920 .... **TCLC 69**
See also CA 109; 189; DLB 296

Webster, John 1580(?)-1634(?) ...... **DC 2; LC 33, 84; WLC**
See also BRW 2; CDBLB Before 1660; DA; DAB; DAC; DAM DRAM, MST; DFS 17; DLB 58; IDTP; RGEL 2; WLIT 3

Webster, Noah 1758-1843 .... **NCLC 30**
See also DLB 1, 37, 42, 43, 73, 243

Wedekind, (Benjamin) Frank(lin)
1864-1918 .... **TCLC 7**
See also CA 104; 153; CANR 121, 122; CDWLB 2; DAM DRAM; DLB 118; EW 8; EWL 3; LMFS 2; RGWL 2, 3

Wehr, Demaris .... **CLC 65**

Weidman, Jerome 1913-1998 .... **CLC 7**
See also AITN 2; CA 1-4R; 171; CAD; CANR 1; DLB 28

Weil, Simone (Adolphine)
1909-1943 .... **TCLC 23**
See also CA 117; 159; EW 12; EWL 3; FW; GFL 1789 to the Present; MTCW 2

Weininger, Otto 1880-1903 .... **TCLC 84**

Weinstein, Nathan
See West, Nathanael

Weinstein, Nathan von Wallenstein
See West, Nathanael

Weir, Peter (Lindsay) 1944- .... **CLC 20**
See also CA 113; 123

Weiss, Peter (Ulrich) 1916-1982 .. **CLC 3, 15, 51**
See also CA 45-48; 106; CANR 3; DAM DRAM; DFS 3; DLB 69, 124; EWL 3; RGWL 2, 3

Weiss, Theodore (Russell)
1916-2003 .... **CLC 3, 8, 14**
See also CA 9-12R; 189; 216; CAAE 189; CAAS 2; CANR 46, 94; CP 7; DLB 5

Welch, (Maurice) Denton
1915-1948 .... **TCLC 22**
See also BRWS 8, 9; CA 121; 148; RGEL 2

Welch, James (Phillip) 1940-2003 ..... **CLC 6, 14, 52; NNAL**
See also CA 85-88; 219; CANR 42, 66, 107; CN 7; CP 7; CPW; DAM MULT, POP; DLB 175, 256; LATS 1; RGAL 4; TCWW 2

Weldon, Fay 1931- . **CLC 6, 9, 11, 19, 36, 59, 122**
See also BRWS 4; CA 21-24R; CANR 16, 46, 63, 97; CDBLB 1960 to Present; CN 7; CPW; DAM POP; DLB 14, 194; EWL 3; FW; HGG; INT CANR-16; MTCW 1, 2; RGEL 2; RGSF 2

Wellek, Rene 1903-1995 .... **CLC 28**
See also CA 5-8R; 150; CAAS 7; CANR 8; DLB 63; EWL 3; INT CANR-8

Weller, Michael 1942- .... **CLC 10, 53**
See also CA 85-88; CAD; CD 5

Weller, Paul 1958- .... **CLC 26**

Wellershoff, Dieter 1925- .... **CLC 46**
See also CA 89-92; CANR 16, 37

Welles, (George) Orson 1915-1985 .. **CLC 20, 80**
See also AAYA 40; CA 93-96; 117

Wellman, John McDowell 1945-
See Wellman, Mac
See also CA 166; CD 5

Wellman, Mac .... **CLC 65**
See Wellman, John McDowell; Wellman, John McDowell
See also CAD; RGAL 4

PC Cumulative Nationality Index

Nationality Index

PC-56 Title Index

ISBN 0-7876-7454-0